THE COMPLETE
SURGICAL GUIDE

Other Books Written or Edited by Robert E. Rothenberg

GROUP MEDICINE & HEALTH INSURANCE IN ACTION

UNDERSTANDING SURGERY

THE NEW ILLUSTRATED MEDICAL ENCYCLOPEDIA, 4 volumes

THE NEW AMERICAN MEDICAL DICTIONARY & HEALTH MANUAL

HEALTH IN THE LATER YEARS

REOPERATIVE SURGERY

THE NEW ILLUSTRATED CHILD CARE ENCYCLOPEDIA, 12 volumes

THE DOCTORS' PREMARITAL MEDICAL ADVISER

THE FAST DIET BOOK

THE NEW COMPLETE MEDICAL ENCYCLOPEDIA, 20 volumes

OUR FAMILY HEALTH AND MEDICAL RECORD BOOK

THE COMPLETE SURGICAL GUIDE

THE NEW *UNDERSTANDING SURGERY*

ROBERT E.
ROTHENBERG, M.D., F.A.C.S.

WEATHERVANE BOOKS • NEW YORK

Acknowledgments

The editor wishes to express his deep gratitude to Roberta Hatch, whose assistance in compiling and helping to edit the material in this book was of inestimable value. We are also appreciative of Harry N. Abrams' generosity in permitting us to reproduce some of the line drawings and to adapt some of the text from *The New Complete Medical Encyclopedia for Home Use.*

The author wishes to make special mention of the surgeons who contributed to *Understanding Surgery,* upon which this work has relied so heavily. The help he received from them through their original editorial contributions made the construction of this book a much simpler task. Those to whom the author is particularly grateful are Doctors F. Paul Ansbro, Emanuel H. Feiring, Harry R. Fisher, Milton E. Klinger, Alfred E. Mamelok, Paul S. Metzger, and Richard J. Smith.

To Liboly

Contents

Preface

It is an unfortunate truth that most patients enter hospitals and operating rooms with unnecessary fears and anxieties. A great part of the apprehension stems from a lack of knowledge concerning their illness and the operative procedure that is to be performed upon them. The persistence of these anxieties often interferes greatly with a healthy postoperative reaction and a smooth convalescence.

Fears can be minimized by frank and careful explanation of what lies ahead and by simple, sensible answers to the many questions patients wish to ask. Unfortunately, surgeons are sometimes so busy and so inured to what seems to them a routine procedure that they may•fail to explain details fully or· to dispel unfounded fears adequately. Even when the surgeon does take the time to answer all the questions, the excitement of the moment may cause the patient to overlook many things he will want to know when he regains his composure. Also, on learning of the contemplated operation, his family and friends may bring up many items that were not discussed during the surgical interview.

There is a dearth of reliable, easily understood material from which lay people can learn about surgery and find the answers to perplexing questions. Although this book makes no claim to cover the entire field—for in actuality almost every surgical condition discussed here has been the subject of a complete monograph or book of its own—an attempt has been made to describe the more common surgical diseases and operations. Much of the material has been contributed by patients themselves, who have, by their many queries, pointed the way toward satisfying their surgical curiosity.

Emphasis must be laid upon the fact that the statistics and figures quoted throughout this work are approximations. When it is stated, as an example, that a patient may get out of bed on the second postoperative day or that he may leave the hospital ten days after surgery, it represents merely the practice of the majority of surgeons. It should *not* be concluded, upon reading such information, that a particular surgeon is deviating from good surgical practice if he holds his patient (with a similar condition) in bed several days longer and discharges him from the hospital a few days later.

Methods of surgical practice, as well as techniques of operation, vary markedly and must be altered to suit the needs of the individual case. Good results can be obtained by many surgeons using many different methods. It would be presumptuous to assume that the material contained in this work represents the best or only procedures. Many statements and views are personal, yet an earnest effort has been made to paint a composite picture of standard practice throughout the country.

R. E. R.

INTRODUCTION TO SURGERY

The Safety of Surgery

Every surgical patient wonders, "Will I recover from this operation?" No matter how minor the procedure, a certain amount of natural anxiety exists as to the outcome. It is unfortunate that with the growth of specialization in medicine some of the personal friendship between patient and physician has been lost. Yet the modern surgeon is just as concerned about the patient and his problems as the old-fashioned country doctor used to be. A surgeon is a busy person, sometimes too busy, it seems, to stop and put his arm around his sick charge and tell him that everything is going to be all right. But a surgeon is also a dedicated person, dedicated to the good health and happiness of the people he serves. He will always try to quell anxiety, dispel false fears, and tell the facts about any risks that may be involved. And although something intimate may have been lost over the years, something far more reassuring has been gained: the *safety* of surgery!

The safety of surgery has increased so greatly within the past century that risks today have been reduced to infinitesimal proportions. Exclusive of obstetrical deliveries, it is estimated that there are some 15 to 16 million people operated upon in the United States each year. Improvements in surgical skill and techniques, the liberal use of blood transfusions, advanced methods of anesthesia, the creation of recovery rooms and intensive care units, and the advent of the antibiotic drugs offer tremendous assurance to the preoperative patient that he will survive his operation. Reliable statistics show that 649 out of every 650 people will come through their surgical ordeal alive! The achievement of this safety record by modern medicine is all the more remarkable when one considers the fact that these figures include a large number of people who enter the operating room in desperate condition from accidents or neglected disease.

The huge reduction in operative mortality is not accidental. The great increase in medical knowledge and the vastly improved methods of teaching and training are largely responsible for this happy state of affairs. Great surgeons of the early twentieth century trained pupils who eventually outshone them, and they in turn produce today's surgeons, who, in many instances, excel their predecessors. Truly, each new generation starts where the old one has left off.

Few people realize the extent of training to which an aspiring surgeon is subjected before he is permitted to use his scalpel without supervision. The average surgeon today rarely begins private practice before he is 31 years old. Half his life has been spent in study and preparation. A look into his background would show that he graduated from high school at 17 or 18 years of age, spent four years in premedical college and four more years in medical school. At the age of 25 or 26 years, he began his general internship, which lasted for one year. Then, having been fortunate enough to be chosen from among his colleagues to go on with surgical training, he enters his residency. A surgical residency in the United States in most grade-A hospitals extends for a period of four to five years. At last, at the age of 31, the surgeon is ready to go into private practice. But even at this late stage in his development it is possible that he may not be given the privilege by his hospital to perform major surgery without the supervision of some older surgeon on the staff.

The medical profession has safeguarded the interests of the public even further by providing standards by which surgeons can be qualified and judged. The great American College of Surgeons, founded in 1913, has established a fellowship to which it admits only well-trained surgeons. Its various boards and chapters review the educational background, scientific contributions, ethical standards, and professional abilities of candidates from all over the country. Thus, if a surgeon becomes a Fellow of the American College of Surgeons, the public can safely assume that he is trustworthy.

Within the past 35 years, American Specialty Boards have been established for the purpose of examining physicians in each of the various specialties. These Boards are composed of outstanding men from the particular field, such as eye surgery, brain surgery, general surgery, bone surgery, etc. Each of these Boards meets annually and conducts rigorous written, oral, and clinical examinations for its candidates. Only those doctors who have had the required surgical residencies are permitted to take the examinations. Some Boards require applicants to hold operative clinics, and representatives are sent to observe and to report back on the surgical skill of the candidate. It is not at all unusual for a Specialty Board to fail 30 or 40 percent of the applicants on their first attempt to qualify. It is safe to say that an American Specialty Board diploma in a doctor's office is almost a guarantee of his efficiency.

Surgical security for the public would have little meaning if American hospitals failed to cooperate with the medical profession in its attempts to establish high standards. For instance, if hospitals permitted physicians to perform major surgery whether or not they were qualified, they would be defeating the aims of both the College of Surgeons and the Specialty Boards. Every first-rate hospital in the country seeks the recognition and stamp of approval of the Joint Commission on Accreditation of Hospitals, which is made up of representatives of the American Medical Association, the American College of Surgeons, the American College of Physicians, and the American Hospital Association. In order to obtain this approval, each hospital must meet a set of rigid standards and must agree to permit only ethical and qualified surgeons to be members of its staff. Thus the public is doubly safeguarded against surgery being performed by unqualified men.

As a result of the aforementioned advances and safeguards, death rates from surgery have fallen to almost unbelievable lows. It is rare indeed today to hear of anyone who has died as a result of a gallbladder operation, or the removal of a thyroid or uterus, or from a kidney or bladder operation. And in even the most formidable operations, mortality rates have been lowered to safe levels.

Over the past 30 years, measures have been found to overcome most of the great dangers of surgery, so that today it is unusual for a patient to develop a complication that cannot be controlled. Here is a list of these complications and what has been done about them:

1. Pneumonia: This most feared aftermath of a surgical procedure 30 years ago is now a readily controllable

complication. Antibiotic therapy will usually return the patient to normal within a few days.

2. Embolism: This breaking off and traveling of a blood clot from a lower limb to the lung occurs much less frequently today because of the institution of "early ambulation." Early ambulation means getting the patient out of bed and walking on the first or second postoperative day. This activity keeps the circulation flowing at a more normal rate and tends to prevent blood stagnation, with the possible formation of a blood clot (thrombus). Should a thrombus, or even an embolus, develop, medicine has discovered excellent drugs to prevent the process from spreading. By giving heparin or dicoumarol, mortality rates following embolism have been reduced remarkably. Also, embolism can be prevented from occurring a second time by placing a filter device in the abdominal vena cava.

3. Postoperative shock: This very real complication of surgery formerly resulted in more deaths than any other cause. Today, the surgeons have learned that shock occurs infrequently if the patient has been prepared properly for surgery, is handled carefully during the operation, and is medicated wisely afterward. The most important weapons in the prevention and management of shock have been the development of highly trained shock teams, the liberal use of *blood transfusions,* before, during, or after surgery as the need arises, and the placement of the postoperative patient in a recovery room or intensive care unit where specially trained nurses and physicians are on call 24 hours a day. *Plasma* and plasma-expanding *intravenous fluids,* while not as valuable as whole blood, have also proved helpful in preventing the shock mechanism from taking hold. And finally, the more highly skilled and trained surgeons of

today have learned a great deal better than their predecessors to judge how much surgery a given patient can withstand without developing this serious complication.

4. So common were postoperative *wound infections* in the early, preantiseptic days of surgery that the complication was glorified by calling it "laudable pus." And if the patient died with an extensive, spreading blood infection, some obscure and irrelevant reason was often given for his demise. We now know, of course, that pus is never "laudable," and we try by every means to avoid wound infection. As recently as 1922, approximately 5 per cent of all clean surgical wounds became infected after operation. Today, with improved surgical techniques and the use of antibiotic drugs, this percentage has been reduced greatly. In many large institutions where several thousand operations are performed during the course of the year, it is not unusual to find that not a single patient has died as a result of a complicating wound infection!

5. Postoperative *hemorrhage* and *wound rupture* were so common in the last century that many hospitals assigned surgical interns to watch patients during the night to spot such eventualities at their outset. But today, vastly improved suture materials, better trained surgeons, and the eradication of most wound infections have made these complications exceedingly rare.

In commenting upon the safety of present-day surgery, one cannot stress too strongly the great help given to surgeons by physiologists and chemists. Their discoveries have led to greatly improved methods of preparing the patient for operation. By accurate laboratory tests, they are now able to tell us whether the patient's body mechanism is ready for the surgery to be performed. And by equally ingenious methods, they have discovered ways for the surgeon to bring his patient up to a satisfactory preoperative chemical state. Today a patient deficient in glucose, protein, vitamins, chlorides, potassium, or other essential chemicals can be adequately medicated before surgery is undertaken. These substances are given by mouth or, if necessary, by injection into the veins for a period of days prior to surgical intervention. All medical investigators will agree that these advances in our chemical and physiological knowledge have been of inestimable value in reducing the risks of surgery.

The Need for Surgery

Almost every patient inquires, "Is this operation necessary?" and follows this query with, "And what will happen if I'm not operated upon?" In giving his answers, the surgeon will probably tell the patient that his condition falls into one of the following categories:

1. Emergency surgery: Conditions demanding immediate attention. The patient should be taken directly to the hospital without delay. In this group one would place:

Fractured skull
Gunshot wounds
Stabbings
Extensive burns
Severe lacerations
Large abscesses
Obstruction of urinary bladder
Acute intestinal obstruction
Ruptured ulcer of stomach or duodenum
A clot in a major blood vessel, or an embolism

A penetrating or ruptured aneurysm of a major artery
Major bone fractures
Severe eye injuries
Acute glaucoma
Acute appendicitis
Strangulated hernia
Ruptured ectopic pregnancy
Foreign body in trachea or esophagus (windpipe or foodpipe)
Gangrene of toe, foot, leg

2. Urgent surgery: Conditions requiring prompt attention. The patient should arrange for hospital admission within 24 to 48 hours. In this group one would place:

Kidney or ureteral stones
Cancers of all organs
Mastoid infections
Penetrating or obstructing ulcers of the stomach or duodenum
Bleeding fibroids of uterus
Bleeding hemorrhoids
Twisted ovarian cyst
Acute infection of gallbladder
Sympathetic ophthalmia of the eye

3. Required surgery: Conditions that must be operated upon but do not demand immediate or prompt action. The patient should arrange for hospital admission at some time within a period of a few weeks or months. In this group one would place:

Cataracts of the eye
Spinal fusions
Sinus operations
Corrections of bone deformities
Nonbleeding fibroid tumors of uterus
Simple ovarian cysts
Thyroid operations
Tonsil operations
Prostate conditions without obstruction
Gallbladder inflammation without acute infection
Repair of heart and blood vessel defects
Replacement of arteries

4. Elective surgery: Conditions that should be operated upon, but in all probability, failure to have the surgery performed will *not* result in a catastrophe. In this group one would place:
Simple hemorrhoids
Superficial cysts
Simple hernia without danger of strangulation
Vaginal plastic procedures
Repair of burn scars
Nongrowing fatty or fibrous tumors
Cleft palate and harelip operations
5. Optional surgery: Conditions for which surgery is advisable but not essential. In this group one would place:
Crossed eyes (strabismus)
Cosmetic surgery
Breast plastic operations
Removal of skin blemishes
Operations for unsightly varicose veins
Removal of warts and harmless moles

Having explained the seriousness of the illness, the surgeon then leaves the decision to be operated upon in the hands of the patient. He cannot force his advice to be taken even though he knows well in some instances that extreme measures are necessary to get the patient to do what is best for himself. Occasionally the surgeon encounters a peculiar attitude which seems to imply that his advice stems from a "desire to cut" rather than from a wish to see the patient cured of his ailment. The patient rarely understands that reputable surgeons spend more of their time trying to reduce the number of operations they perform than in attempts to increase their work load. Good surgeons are quick to recommend nonoperative forms of treatment when in doubt as to the effectiveness of surgery. Nothing is more painful to the ethical surgeon than to be confronted repeatedly over the years by one of his poor surgical results!

Patients often want a second opinion before submitting to surgery. If the wish is expressed, it should be granted. Your surgeon, or the family physician who has referred you to the surgeon, will suggest the name of another surgeon who will see you in consultation.

This chapter would be incomplete if it skipped over and ignored the widespread claim that much unnecessary surgery is being performed merely for acquisition of surgical fees. In recent years, magazine articles and newspaper reports have highlighted such practices as fee-splitting and ghost surgery, and there may be some truth to these shocking reports. It is undoubtedly true, however, that most surgery being done today is necessary and the public's faith in the family physician who refers the patient for surgery is justified in the vast majority of cases.

If you are in a strange town and do not know any of the local physicians or if some real doubt exists as to the advisability of engaging the surgeon who has been recommended to you, it might be well to make additional inquiries. There is an official county medical society, a branch of the American Medical Association, in every county in the United States. They are listed in local telephone books. If you call the society, they will furnish you with all the information you will require concerning the man you intend to use. If you have not yet contacted a surgeon, they will give you a list containing the names of some of the reputable men in the area. Ask particularly for his hospital connections and see if he is on the staff of an approved institution. The medical boards and boards of directors in approved hospitals scrutinize carefully the work performed by their own staff members and will not long tolerate surgeons who make a practice of doing unnecessary surgery. A skeptical board in one large institution several years ago made it a custom to review at regular intervals the microscopic reports of all cases in which the appendix had been removed. Normal findings would be noted alongside the name of the operating surgeon, and frequent repetition of such findings would result in the surgeon being brought before the board to explain why he was removing so many normal appendices. All tissues and organs removed during an operation are sent to the laboratory for careful examination. In this manner, the patient is assured that the work done upon him is double-checked by the impartial eye of the microscope. These laboratory findings appear on the medical chart of every case and serve as a permanent record.

There has been quite a bit of publicity given to the phenomenon called ghost surgery. A ghost surgeon is one who operates anonymously, much as a ghost writer performs his function. He is paid, without the patient's knowledge, by the doctor of record, who may not be competent to perform the operation himself. Despite the publicity given to this practice, it is extremely rare and cannot possibly take place if one is operated upon in an approved hospital. Furthermore, ghost surgery is never practiced when a trustworthy family physician recommends the surgeon or when one has exercised normal care in investigating the standing of a surgeon that he has chosen.

Make all your arrangements as to fee *before* you are operated upon. All reputable surgeons will discuss fees with their patients openly and frankly. A fee-split exists when the surgeon, without your knowledge and consent, gives part of his fee to another doctor.

If you follow this advice, you can rest secure in the knowledge that you will not be submitted to unnecessary surgery.

Surgical Costs

Patients should hold a full and frank discussion of the costs of surgery *before* they enter the hospital. Many cordial patient-doctor relationships are severely damaged by misunderstandings concerning fees and allied expenses. Surgeons, family physicians, or their nurses and secretaries are almost always willing to describe the financial obligations associated with the various operations.

In the large majority of instances, medical fees make up a minor part of the total expenses incurred. Because of the high cost of hospital and nursing services, the patient is often embarrassed to find that he has insufficient funds available to pay his surgeon and physician.

The prospective patient must arrange to pay for the following:

1. **Hospital services:** This will cover:
    a) Room and board
    b) Floor (not special) nursing care
    c) Drugs and medications
    d) Treatments such as injections, intravenous solutions, etc.
    e) The use of the operating room and its equipment
    f) The use of the x-ray department
    g) The use of the hospital's laboratory facilities

2. **Special drugs and medications:** Rare or expensive medications or treatments are not covered by the basic hospital bill, and extra charges are the rule.

3. **Special nursing care:** Private

nurses usually work on eight-hour shifts so that three are necessary for around-the-clock coverage. Their services must be paid for separately.

4. Blood transfusions: Blood is given in a great many operative procedures. The blood, and in some hospitals a fee for giving the transfusion, is charged for separately.

5. Anesthesia: Doctor anesthesiologists are now independent of the hospitals in which they work and render their own bills. The giving of anesthesia is no longer considered to be a "hospital service" but rather a "physician service."

6. The physician's fee: There is a great tendency for patients to belittle the importance of the role played by the family physician or the medical consultant in a surgical illness. These are the doctors who make the original diagnosis, who perform the tests to decide if surgery is necessary, and who convince the patient to submit himself to the operative procedure. Then they refer the patient to the surgeon and assume the bulk of the responsibility for selecting the right man to do the job. They look after the general condition of the patient before, during, and after the operation. In many areas in the country, the family physicians assist at the operation itself.

For all of this interest, effort, and work, the medical man is entitled to a substantial fee, and it is sad to report that too many people do not appreciate the worth of their family physicians. All too often patients are overawed by the glamour of surgery and fail to realize that their lives depend just as much on the *decision to operate* as upon the actual operation!

7. The surgeon's fee: This fee should be discussed *before* operation so that the patient can know whether he can

meet his obligations. Most surgeons charge according to the ability of the patient to pay. This custom has developed because the majority of surgeons perform a great many of their operations without charge or for minimal fees. Thus the wealthy patient with the means to pay large fees is indirectly helping to pay the way for the indigent who can afford no fee.

In writing this chapter it had been hoped to record some of the existing costs for the above items. Investigation, however, has shown that costs change so rapidly and vary so widely in different sections of the country that no accurate figures can be set down which would have general application. Suffice it to say that hospital costs have practically quadrupled within the past ten years. This has been largely responsible for the rapid growth of hospital and health insurance plans throughout this country. It is recognized by the public and the medical profession that some system of prepayment or indemnification is necessary to meet these rising costs and to ensure the ability of all to pay for their surgical needs. Those who own insurance policies should examine carefully their provisions to see exactly what benefits will be paid for the surgery they are about to undergo. Surgeons and their secretaries are always willing to assist patients in interpreting the extent of coverage in such policies.

In closing this discussion, it is important to remember that surgeons, given an accurate recital of financial difficulties, will adjust their fees to meet individual situations. And most important of all, they will arrange for free surgical care in the wards of voluntary, city, or county hospitals for those who are unable to pay the going semiprivate rates.

To the Hospital

Before you start for the hospital it is a good idea to check the following items and to be sure to take them along:

1. Your *Blue Cross Hospital Insurance* or other hospital insurance card. If you do not have a card, your hospital will probably ask for payment upon admission.

2. A *checkbook* or sufficient money to make a payment for your hospital stay. (Almost all hospitals today are running at a loss and are supported by philanthropic or public funds. It is essential that they be paid by those who can afford to pay.)

3. Take very little *extra cash* with you. A few dollars for magazines, newspapers, or other small items is all that will be necessary. If additional money is desired, a member of your family can bring it along later.

4. A *timepiece*. However, do *not* take an expensive watch or any costly jewelry with you.

5. Take along a *pen, pencil, stationery,* and *stamps.* You may want to write letters or thank-you notes for those who will remember you during your illness.

6. Most hospitals have *radios* and/or *television* equipment. Inquire about this, and if they have none, you may request permission to bring your own.

7. Take your *toothbrush, toothpaste, comb and brush, shaving kit or cosmetic bag,* and any other personal items needed to make your stay comfortable.

8. Take your own *pajamas or nightgown,* your *slippers and bathrobe.* Modern surgery often means that you will be up and walking soon after your operation.

9. Carry all belongings in as *small* a *case* as possible. Large valises are frowned upon by hospital administrators, as storage space is usually not provided.

10. Take nothing that cannot be replaced. Your hospital room will probably have meager facilities for the safekeeping of cherished personal items.

11. Towels and other linens are supplied by the hospital. However, many patients prefer to bring their own facecloths.

Before and After Surgery

BEFORE

There are certain measures carried out before operation which aid the patient and make the surgeon's task easier. A few of these procedures may occasion some discomfort, but all are important for proper operative preparation:

1. Shaving: It is necessary to shave a much wider area than the incision will occupy in order to ensure surgical sterility. Thus the whole head is shaved for a brain operation, the entire abdomen and pubic area is shaved for an abdominal procedure, and an entire extremity may be shaved for surgery in that area. Shaving is usually carried out the evening before operation by a nurse or orderly.

2. Enema: Since the bowels may not move for several days after an operation, it is customary to give an enema the night before. This is omitted in any case where there is an acute abdominal inflammation, as an enema might stir up or spread the infection.

3. Fasting: Surgery is always best

performed on an empty stomach. Eating and drinking must therefore be forbidden for 10 to 12 hours preoperatively.

4. Sedatives: A good night's sleep before an operation may be difficult to acquire because of necessary preoperative treatments and because of natural anxieties. To offset these factors, adequate doses of sleeping pills are usually prescribed.

5. Narcotics: It is best to have the patient reach the operating room in a calm, semiconscious state. To obtain this goal, injections of narcotics are usually given an hour or two prior to surgery.

6. Stomach tubes: In certain types of abdominal operations, particularly those upon the intestinal tract, it is important to have the stomach and bowels empty and free of fluid and gas. To accomplish this, a plastic or rubber tube is often inserted through the nose into the stomach. Such a tube may be passed the night before surgery or the morning of surgery, and is left in place throughout the operative procedure.

7. Urinary catheter: In certain types of operations, particularly those upon the pelvic organs or bladder, it is desirable that the bladder be empty. To ensure this, a rubber catheter is inserted before the patient leaves for the operating room or upon his arrival there. The catheter is often left to drain throughout the surgical procedure. Another reason for inserting a catheter is to monitor the amount of urine that is excreted during the operative procedure.

8. Blood transfusions: Major surgery is much more serious when performed upon patients who are markedly anemic or who have suffered recent blood loss. Every attempt is therefore made to replenish lost blood and to bring the blood volume back toward normal. This can be successfully accomplished in most cases by giving blood transfusions preoperatively.

9. Intravenous infusions: Surgery is much safer when carried out upon patients with normal blood chemistry. Deficiencies in protein, sugar, chemicals such as potassium, calcium, sodium, chloride, vitamins such as B, C, and K may be dangerous and not conducive to a smooth recovery. Fortunately, all of these substances can be given effectively via the intravenous route. It is customary, therefore, to treat patients deficient in these elements for several days preoperatively.

10. Plasma: The intravenous use of plasma has been largely replaced by the giving of whole blood. However, in rural areas where donor blood is difficult to obtain and where blood banks are not yet established, plasma is used as a substitute for transfusion.

The family should never judge the length or seriousness of an operation by the length of time the patient is in the operating room. It is customary to send for patients some time in advance of the actual time of the operation. Anesthesiologists often make additional preparations that can occupy one-half to one hour. Occasionally the surgeon takes longer than he had expected with the preceding case, thus delaying the time of beginning his next operation. And lastly, in most hospitals the patient is sent from the operating room to a *recovery room,* where special devices and personnel are assembled. The patient will be cared for there by a team who will monitor all vital signs and who will ensure a safe emergence from anesthesia. Patients may spend several hours—or even days—in the recovery room. Or, in exceptionally serious cases, the patient may be sent directly from the recovery room to the intensive care unit.

AFTER

There are wide variations in the postoperative reactions of different people to the same operation. There are those who are extremely sensitive to pain and others who are markedly insensitive. The patient's mental attitude toward his illness also determines to a great extent the kind of postoperative course he will follow. Despite these individual variations, there are certain reactions common to all, and there are specific measures designed to make postoperative convalescence safer and more comfortable:

1. Position in bed: Immediately after surgery, it is customary to have the patient lie flat in bed. Occasional exceptions to this practice are some chest cases in which the patient is placed in a semisitting position, and other cases in which there is a desire to raise the blood pressure by lowering the head and raising the foot of the bed.

After full recovery from the anesthetic, patients are encouraged to change their position frequently and move their legs often. This stimulates circulation, leads to deeper breathing, thus reducing tendencies toward the development of blood clots or postoperative pneumonia.

2. Early ambulation: It has been found that recovery is speeded and complications are minimized by getting the patient out of bed early and getting him to walk about. Many patients can get out of bed the day after the most major type of surgery; others can be ambulatory within two to three days after operation. There are still others, however, who must remain in bed for a week or longer.

3. Fluids and food: Since fluids have been withheld for 10 to 12 hours prior to surgery, most patients are extremely thirsty postoperatively. They may begin to take sips of water or tea within a few hours after operation *providing that they have not undergone a procedure upon their stomach or intestinal tract.* Such patients frequently are forbidden to drink or eat for 48 to 72 hours and then are started on small and frequent feedings of fluids and semisolids. Others will be permitted fluids the same day and a bland diet the day after surgery. A full diet can often be resumed by many patients on the third postoperative day.

4. Stomach tubes: Dilatation of the stomach with air after an abdominal operation is a rather common and distressing complication. To avoid this, a rubber or plastic tube is often passed through the nose into the stomach and allowed to remain there for 12 to 24 hours. Another technique is to pass the tube periodically at 8- to 12-hour intervals, suctioning out the stomach contents and then removing the tube. In a small number of cases it has been found advantageous to create a small opening in the stomach wall (gastrotomy) and to pass a rubber tube through this aperture from an incision on the abdominal wall. Such an opening will close spontaneously within a few days after removal of the tube.

5. Catheterization: Patients frequently find difficulty in urinating for a day or two after surgery. This is especially true when spinal anesthesia has been used or after an operation involving the lower abdomen, genitals, or rectum. Although there are several medications that can be given to stimulate natural voiding, it is sometimes necessary to empty the bladder by passing a catheter into it. This is uncomfortable but does not cause great pain. In older people, catheterization may have to be repeated at regular intervals for several days. When catheterization has to be repeated often, an indwelling (Foley) catheter is usually inserted and allowed to remain in the bladder for a few days. However, the ability to urinate returns spontaneously within about a week's time.

6. Narcotics and sedatives: Pain invariably follows surgery. Fortunately, there are effective drugs that can relieve most postoperative pain. Patients should not hesitate to request medication when the pain is truly severe, but they should realize that recovery will be quicker if they are not too greatly under the influence of narcotics. Drug addiction *does not* occur within the short space of time that a patient is convalescing from the usual acute surgical condition. It takes several weeks for addiction to develop. Recently, effective new nonnarcotic, pain-relieving drugs such as Talwin have been used in some cases instead of potentially addictive narcotics.

Most surgeons will leave orders for a pain-relieving drug to be given every four hours during the first postoperative day, *if necessary*. Thereafter, an occasional dose only may be needed. By the third or fourth day after surgery, most conditions will no longer require narcotics. Sleeping pills, on the other hand, may be given each night throughout the average hospital stay. These medications do not form addictions either.

7. Antibiotic drugs: The use of these medications has worked miracles in saving the lives of surgical patients who otherwise might have died following surgery. Surgeons frequently order regular doses of one or more of these drugs for the first few days after an operation in which infection is anticipated. It is important, always, to inquire about any known allergy that may exist, for if it

does, the surgeon will alter his orders accordingly.

8. Intravenous fluids and medications: Since oral intake of fluids and medicines often must be limited for the first few days after surgery, the intravenous (into the vein) route is utilized. Essential substances such as water, salt, sugar, protein, potassium, calcium, vitamins B, C, and K can all be given into the veins of the arms or legs. It is not unusual for intravenous treatments to be continued for the first four to five days after a serious procedure has been performed.

9. Blood transfusions have saved the lives of innumerable surgical patients who otherwise would have succumbed. The timely use of blood transfusions can prevent and successfully combat surgical shock and can replace the blood lost during the surgical procedure. It should not be concluded, however, that a patient who is given a transfusion must of necessity be desperately sick.

10. Respirators: It has been learned that respiratory difficulties must be overcome quickly during the postoperative period if serious complications are to be avoided. To ensure adequate aeration of the lungs during the first hours and days after surgery, patients who have undergone major surgery are frequently aided by a respirator. This apparatus forces deep breathing and thus encourages aeration and expectoration of mucus that may be obstructing the air passages.

11. Heart medications: People with cardiac conditions who have emerged from surgery may require special medications such as digitalis. This drug will often supply the added support a heart needs during the first stressful days of the postoperative period.

12. Enemas: It is a widespread misconception that to remain healthy, one must have a daily bowel movement.

Failure to evacuate causes considerable concern among people who have just undergone surgery. It is necessary, therefore, to explain that it is not essential to move the bowels for the first few days after operation. The usual time to clean out the lower end of the intestinal tract by prescribing an enema is on the third, fourth, or fifth postoperative day. Frequently a normal bowel movement will occur, thus making an enema unnecessary.

13. Wound dressings: The time for changes of dressings varies greatly, according to the type of procedure that has been done. Clean wounds without drains are left alone until the surgeon is ready to remove the stitches. Draining wounds or infected wounds may require daily changes by the surgeon, intern, or nurse. It is not usually painful to have the dressings of a surgical wound changed, although there are certain specific ones that do produce considerable pain. The surgeon will often prescribe a pain-relieving medication before changing a dressing of the latter type.

14. Removal of sutures and clips: Skin sutures (stitches) are usually removed anywhere from the sixth to the tenth postoperative day, depending upon the location of the wound. Abdominal sutures usually are removed on the seventh or eighth day. Sutures are left in place longer if there is tension upon the wound or if there is any doubt that the wound is healing firmly.

Skin sutures do not dissolve by themselves and must be removed.

Metal clips are sometimes used for the skin instead of silk sutures. Such clips are usually taken out on the fourth, fifth, or sixth day after operation.

It is not very painful to remove sutures or clips. Slight sticking and tugging are usually the only symptoms to accompany this procedure.

There are a number of uncomfortable symptoms common to most postoperative patients, and it might be well to list them and say a word or two about their treatment.

1. Nausea and vomiting occur frequently. They may be due to:

a) Reaction to the anesthetic
b) Reaction to narcotic drugs
c) Dilatation of the stomach
d) Reaction to handling of intra-abdominal organs
e) Taking too much fluid or eating too much too soon after surgery
f) Emotional upset or pain

Nausea and vomiting can often be controlled by passing a tube into the stomach or by withholding all fluids and food by mouth for a 24-hour period. During this time, the patient can be fed intravenously.

2. Gas pains follow most abdominal operations. They will pass within a few days. If the abdomen becomes markedly distended, relief can be obtained by inserting a rubber tube into the rectum or by passing a stomach tube. A rectal tube will aid the passage of gas until such time—usually the third day—as the bowel regains its ability to function normally.

3. Pain in the wound area is universal. This is controlled by the administration of narcotics or sedatives.

4. Dizziness and weakness are an accompaniment of some types of major surgery. These symptoms will disappear within a week or two without treatment.

5. Headache occurs in about 1 of 20 people who have had spinal anesthesia. A large fluid intake plus special medications will usually cause it to subside. These people feel best when lying flat in bed, but they should not hesitate to get up and move about when the headache subsides. Such headaches may not entirely disappear for a week or two after operation.

To the Operating Room

It would, in all probability, be a good thing if surgeons themselves, at one time or another, were placed in the position of being surgical patients. Through such a personal experience they might become more sympathetic toward the apprehension of their patients and might spend more time before surgery in explaining away their fears. To the uninitiated, a ride on a stretcher can be a very frightening ordeal, and the first view of an operating room can be disturbing indeed. Fortunately, patients are first given sedatives and narcotics, which relax them and often produce a happy, somewhat pleasant, semi-intoxicated state. It is not at all uncommon to encounter seriously ill patients who banter and joke with their attendants while en route to their operation. Similarly, it is quite rare, thanks to modern methods of premedication, to see a hysterical preoperative patient.

Most hospitals insist that patients enter the operating room on stretchers no matter how trivial the operative procedure they are about to undergo. This is a sound rule because it ensures the preservation of surgical sterility. Contamination of the operating room might occur if people were permitted to wear their street clothes or walking shoes. The conclusion should not be drawn that the condition is more serious than had been thought, merely because hospital personnel require the patient to disrobe completely and to lie down on a stretcher. Finally, the patient is usually asked to remove all face makeup and nail polish. This will enable the anesthesiologist to note the true color of the skin and will let him know that

the tissues are receiving adequate oxygen.

Surgery, no matter how minor, cannot be performed by the surgeon alone. A well-trained team must be functioning constantly before a patient can receive the benefits of modern techniques. The patient may see only part of the surgical team, but others are performing for him long before and during the actual time of his operation. All those he encounters will be wearing uniforms, caps, and masks so that they spread a minimum amount of bacteria from their clothes or nose and throat.

The **surgical team** is composed of the following personnel:

1. Your own **surgeon,** who will be wearing an operating uniform and cap and mask. He will scrub his hands and arms up to his elbows with antiseptic soap for several minutes before donning his sterile gown and rubber gloves. (You might possibly see the scrub sinks off to the side.)

2. Depending upon the procedure he is about to perform, the operating surgeon may have no assistant or he may have one or two **assistant surgeons.** The patient should not conclude that the presence of one or more assistants implies that he is very seriously ill. Often very minor procedures—because of position or technical peculiarities—require the help of one or more assistant surgeons. Then, too, interns or residents may request permission of the surgeon to "scrub in," for in that way they learn his technique and gain experience by actual participation.

3. The **anesthesiologist,** who will administer the appropriate anesthesia. If the operation is to be performed under local anesthesia, the surgeon himself will usually officiate. While there are still many competent nurse anesthetists practicing today, the trend throughout the country is to have physicians perform the anesthesia. These are well-trained doctors who specialize in their field in the same way as your surgeon specializes in his.

4. The **chief operating room nurse,** whose duties include the overall supervision of the entire operating room staff.

5. The **nurse** in charge of surgical supply. It is her responsibility to see that all instruments, basins, drapes, towels, sponges, sutures, gowns, masks, and gloves are properly sterilized and available for use at all times.

6. The **scrub or suture nurse,** whose duty is to assist at the actual operative procedure. This nurse, who is gowned and gloved exactly like the surgeon, passes the instruments, sutures, sponges, and other necessary materials to the surgeon while he is operating.

7. The **circulating or chase nurse,** who holds herself available at all times to keep the surgeon and scrub nurse supplied or to get additional instruments, sutures, or materials when the current supply is used up. This nurse does not wear a gown or gloves but must handle all sterile material with a sterile instrument.

8. An **orderly** is often on hand to help lift the patient on or off the table and to keep the operating room clean at all times.

9. If heart or major blood vessel surgery is being performed, another full team may be in attendance. This will consist of a **cardiologist** (heart specialist), who will monitor the heart action, pulse beat, respiration, etc., throughout the procedure. He may be accompanied by an assistant cardiologist, who will supervise the monitoring equipment. There will also be a technician, who will supervise and regulate the heart pump machinery.

Although patients occasionally assume an attitude of disinterest toward the equipment in an operating room, most people exhibit considerable curiosity. A detailed description of the surgical paraphernalia might help to dispel some fear. Certainly as one is stretched out flat on his back and placed upon the hard and narrow operating table, the huge overhanging light presents a formidable threat. (Parents often tell their children that they are going to be "x-rayed" or are going to "have their picture taken." This is a mistake, for it fools practically none of them and when they are placed on the table under the lights, they become inordinately frightened when they realize they have been told an untruth.)

Like any workroom constructed solely for utilitarian purposes, the operating room with its gleaming tile and metal looks cold and uninviting. However, its contents are designed so that efficiency and sterility can be maintained at their highest level. The average operating room contains most of the following items:

1. **An operating table:** This is a complex piece of equipment with levers and wheels which can tilt it in any direction, raise or lower the head or torso or extremities to any desired degree. All patients are securely strapped onto the table as a precautionary measure so that sliding or slipping is impossible.

2. **An overhead light:** This is an extraordinary apparatus, costing several thousand dollars, especially designed to throw a strong, penetrating, and shadowless beam over the entire field. There may be one or two standing lights off to the side of the room which can be wheeled into place should additional light be required from a side angle.

3. Near the head of the operating table will be located the **anesthesia machine** with several attached tanks containing oxygen and the various anesthetic gases.

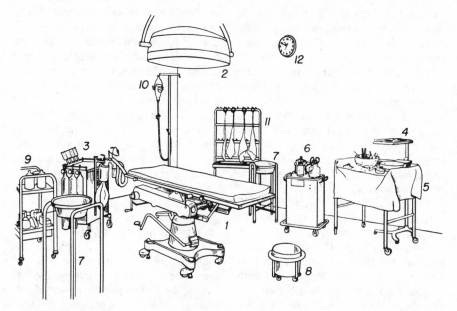

1. Operating table; 2. overhead light; 3. anesthesia machine; 4. Mayo instrument stand; 5. instrument table; 6. suction machine; 7. solution basins; 8. waste bucket; 9. preparation table; 10. intravenous solution and stand; 11. sponge stand; 12. clock.

4. Every operating room has several **Mayo stands,** upon which are placed many of the instruments that will be used to perform the operation. These are simple metal stands constructed so as to support a metal tray which can be slid into place over the operating table after the patient has been cleansed, painted with antiseptic solution, and draped with sterile sheets.

5. The **main instrument table** can be seen off to one side of the room. This table contains all the instruments that could possibly be used in any contingency. It is common practice to have dozens or even hundreds of instruments sterile and ready for use even though the surgeon may never call for them. An operation requiring the use of 10 to 15 clamps will have 75 to 100 ready and waiting if some unforeseen need should arise. The scrub nurse is in constant contact with this table and shuttles back and forth to get additional instruments.

6. One or two **suction machines** are standard equipment. These are used, if necessary, to suck any mucus from the anesthetized throat or to remove fluid material from wounds.

7. Every operating room contains several metal **solution basins** on stands. One will stand behind each surgeon so that he can periodically rinse off his gloves in sterile salt solution. Others contain warm salt solution to moisten towels, drapes, sponge pads; or solution to cleanse the instruments as they are used and discarded by the surgeon.

8. On the floor are **waste buckets,** in which the surgeon throws used sponges or gauze pads.

9. A small **preparation table** containing soap, alcohol, ether, other antiseptics, and gauze pads. From this worktable the circulating nurse or orderly scrubs down the region to be operated upon prior to the application, by the surgeon, of the skin antiseptic.

10. A tall **metal stand** from which intravenous solution flasks or blood transfusion flasks can be suspended.

11. A **sponge stand** from which are hung the used sponges that the surgeon has employed during the operation. Every sponge, as well as every instrument, must be accounted for before the operative wound is closed.

12. A **cardioscope** to monitor the patient's heart action throughout the entire operative procedure.

13. A **clock** on the wall is often present. This tells the entire team how long to scrub, how long instruments must remain in the sterilizer before they are ready for use, and how long the operative procedure has been in progress. All patients should be informed beforehand that the length of the procedure is unimportant and is not a valuable index of the seriousness of the condition. Speed in surgery is not essential, particularly since the advent of improved anesthetic techniques. Patients themselves, if conscious during the operation, should avoid drawing conclusions from noting the passage of time. A minor procedure may take much longer to perform than an extremely serious, lifesaving maneuver. The exceptionally apprehensive patient should, if conscious, converse with his anesthesiologist, who has many excellent and easily applicable methods of alleviating anxiety in any situation.

One added caution to the patient: Surgeons, interns, and nurses often discuss surgical problems within hearing of the patient. This is not good practice. Most often, the conversation relates to some other case and has nothing to do with your condition. Sensitive patients will frequently misinterpret accidentally overheard snatches of conversation, and it may upset them greatly. If you are bothered by such a situation, do not hesitate to have a full and frank discussion with your surgeon as soon as you have recovered from the immediate effects of the anesthesia and operation. And advise him that in the future it would be best if his operating room team refrained from audible discussion which might cause fear among his patients!

There is a natural fear among some people that the surgeon will begin to operate before they are fully anesthetized. Such a fear is completely unfounded! Both the anesthesiologist and the surgeon perform tests—on either waking or sleeping patients—to determine positively that complete anesthesia has been effected.

Before any surgery is begun, the operative field is thoroughly scrubbed with soap and water and antiseptic solutions are applied. The whole body of the patient is then draped with sterile towels and sheets so that only the immediate vicinity of the incision is exposed. This procedure ensures the greatest possible sterility of the operative wound. Should the conscious patient wish to further detach himself from the proceedings, he should ask the anesthesiologist or circulating nurse to cover his eyes with a towel.

Anesthesia

Soon after the patient has made up his mind to submit to surgery, he will ask his surgeon about anesthesia. This is an entirely natural question, for most people are as interested in the elimination of pain during the operation as they are in the removal of the diseased organ.

Although modern anesthesia dates back to 1846, when a Boston dentist first demonstrated ether in an actual surgical case, the science of anesthesia, or as it is called today, *anesthesiology,* is a comparatively recent addition to modern medical specialties. Prior to this past century, surgical anesthesia was obtained by sundry makeshift means such as hypnotism, the use of alcohol in large quantities, or giving huge doses of narcotics to render the patient unconscious. Oliver Wendell Holmes invented the term anesthesia, the literal meaning of which is "lack of sensation." For many years thereafter the art of anesthesia consisted almost exclusively of removing the sensation of pain. Very little thought was given to the general condition of the patient, and his life frequently depended not only on recovery from the surgeon's manipulations but upon surviving the administration of crudely calculated doses of various anesthetic agents such as ether, chloroform, and nitrous oxide. Oxygen requirements, heart action, blood pressure, and pulse were all too often forgotten in the anesthetist's concentration upon putting the patient to sleep and keeping him there. In retrospect, it is strange to contemplate how unimportant surgeons held anesthesia to be and how they permitted inexperienced people such as orderlies, technicians with no medical background, or young medical students to control the fate of their surgical charge. When newer methods such as spinal anesthesia were discovered, the surgeon undertook to apply them himself rather than turn over this highly technical job to a physician specializing in anesthesia. Since the surgeon was primarily concerned with the operation, this was an added burden for him to bear, and he

was frequently unable to detach himself from the operative site to look after the patient's respiration, blood pressure, or other changes that the body undergoes during surgery.

The above-described conditions prevailed in most communities until World War II, at which time the value of the medical anesthetist became so apparent in the case of armed service sick and wounded that the military authorities established the specialist in anesthesia in equal rank with other medical and surgical specialists. This trend became reflected in civilian practice almost immediately as surgeons returned from war and demanded and obtained the services of trained medical anesthesiologists.

Development in the field of anesthesia has been so rapid that it is usually possible to grant the patient his choice as to type of procedure. Most people prefer to sleep during their operation, and this can now be accomplished even when spinal or local anesthesia is the procedure best suited to the particular operation. The actual choice of technique should be left to the anesthesiologist, but combinations of agents can be used so that the surgeon, the patient, and the anesthesiologist himself are all fully satisfied.

PREMEDICATION AND PREANESTHETIC EVALUATION

An important phase of anesthesia is preoperative evaluation and premedication. The anesthesiologist will study the patient's past history and present medical record and will look for possible findings that might influence the choice of anesthetic agent. If the anesthesiologist is not satisfied that the patient will come safely through the anesthesia and surgery, he will, in all probability, recommend the postponement or even cancellation of the procedure. A good surgeon heeds the advice of his anesthesiologist. Having decided upon the technique to be used, he will usually discuss it with his patient and allay any fears that may exist.

The next step is to order medications that will make the patient most receptive to the anesthesia he will receive. These medications will include tablets or injections the night before surgery to ensure a good night's sleep, and narcotics just prior to embarking for the operating room to ensure a relaxed state of mind. Other medications may also be given to dry up bronchial secretions before giving an inhalation anesthesia.

The surgeon can be of assistance in making the anesthesia a smooth procedure by giving advice to his patient before he even enters the hospital. Heavy smokers and drinkers should be ordered to discontinue such practices for several days before operation, since these habits make for anesthetic and postanesthetic complications. Patients should be advised to notify the surgeon should any upper respiratory infection such as a cold or cough develop. These conditions may require postponement of an elective operation, as they often lead to postanesthetic lung complications.

INDUCTION

Too many people carry in their memory the terrifying experience of years ago when a black mask was abruptly clamped over their face and, while they were being held down by nurses and doctors, ether was poured onto the mask. Others recall the pain and shock of a long needle being thrust into their back for a spinal anesthesia. Fortunately, these practices have long faded and modern anesthesia can be a rather pleas-

ant experience. The premedication puts the patient into a happy, drowsy state, or complete sleep can be attained by a simple injection of one of the barbiturates, such as Pentothal, into a small vein in the hand or arm. By such methods of induction, the initial steps of anesthesia are accomplished without the excitement stage which used to linger in the memory long after the pain of the operation had passed. And so it is too with spinal anesthesia. Preliminary medication and the local injection of the skin and muscles of the back with Novocain now make this an almost painless procedure.

TYPES OF ANESTHESIA

1. **General:** This form of anesthesia puts the patient to sleep so that any operation, from head to foot, may be performed. The anesthesia may be light in depth, as for superficial procedures upon the skin, or it may be given to such depths that operations upon the heart, lungs, or abdomen can be carried out. The anesthesiologist always produces a sleep of just sufficient depth to permit safe surgery.

Today the gases used in anesthesia cause no unpleasant effects, as they are not administered until the patient has already been put to sleep with one of the sleep-producing drugs such as Pentothal. And even children, who are not given Pentothal, find the gases tolerable, as they are rendered semiconscious by anesthetic premedications before a mask is applied to the face.

All anesthetic agents for inhalation are used in combination with oxygen. The oxygen content of the air we normally breathe is 21 percent, and *this concentration, or a higher one, must be maintained regardless of the particular gas employed!*

The most widely used agents are the following:

a) *Nitrous oxide.* This gas, formerly referred to as "laughing gas," is one of the oldest and safest and still one of the most widely utilized anesthetic agents. It is almost always used in combination with an intravenous sleep-producing medication such as Pentothal or a newer drug known as Innovar. And since nitrous oxide anesthesia produces little or no muscle relaxation, one of the curare-like muscle-relaxant drugs is also given if a major operative procedure is contemplated.

Another advantage of nitrous oxide is that it can be safely given in combination with other gases such as halothane or ether.

b) *Halothane* (*Fluothane*) is an extensively used inhalation agent which is usually given along with nitrous oxide and oxygen. The advantages of this gas are that it is easy to administer, produces anesthesia with utilization of small quantities, is non-explosive, causes a minimal amount of irritation to the respiratory mucous membranes, and is accompanied by a minimal amount of postoperative nausea or vomiting. Unfortunately, it has been found recently that among sensitive individuals, it is more likely to predispose toward hepatitis (liver inflammation) than other inhalation gases. For this reason, Halothane is now being used less frequently, especially if the patient has suspected impairment of liver function. Also, if a patient requires a second operation within a few weeks or months after an initial one in which Halothane had been used, another anesthetic agent is employed. The reasoning here is that a second administration of Halothane within a short span of time is more conducive to the development of hepatitis.

c) *Cyclopropane.* This gas, the most popular anesthetic agent until the past ten years, is now being used much less frequently. Although it is still considered to be a most effective anesthetic, it has the disadvantage of being highly explosive. Thus everyone in the operating room during a Cyclopropane anesthesia must be wary not to be the source of static electricity. Another disadvantage of Cyclopropane is that it tends to cause heart irregularities.

d) *Ether.* Ether is a chemical liquid which, when exposed to air or oxygen, forms a vapor or gas. It is one of the most reliable and safest of all anesthetic agents, despite the advent of many newer agents. Its disadvantages are that it produces marked postoperative nausea and vomiting in many patients, and also that it can predispose toward explosion if it comes in contact with electricity.

e) *Chloroform.* Although chloroform is a quick and powerful agent, its use has been curtailed greatly because it sometimes exerts a harmful effect upon the heart.

f) *Ethyl chloride and divinyl oxide.* These two drugs have been largely abandoned except when used in children to induce anesthesia.

2. **Intravenous:** This form of anesthesia has become very popular, mainly as an agent to obliterate the excitement stage of anesthesia and to induce sleep. Three drugs—all having rather similar chemical formulas—are most widely used. They are *Pentothal, Evipal,* and *Surital.* After the initial needle injection into the vein of the arm, a solution containing these medications is allowed to drip into the bloodstream at a controlled rate of speed. Sleep is induced

within a matter of minutes or even seconds. These agents have a great usefulness in conjunction with all forms of general, spinal, or even local anesthesia. Frequently, a patient who has been given local or spinal anesthesia will want to go to sleep. In such situations, enough intravenous medication can be given to induce a light, quiet sleep. Such a combination of methods and agents is called *balanced anesthesia* and is being employed in most clinics throughout the country.

Innovar is a drug used to produce a tranquil state and a loss of the sense of pain, but it does not induce a deep level of unconsciousness. The patient can be aroused and can communicate during the period of anesthesia but is unaware of pain. Its use has increased greatly within the past few years when it has been employed in combination with nitrous oxide and muscle-relaxing drugs.

3. Spinal: This method of anesthesia is commonly used for operations within the lower abdominal cavity. By placing a long, thin needle into the spinal canal, an anesthetic agent, such as Novocain, is injected in calculated doses into the spinal fluid. By manipulating the dosage, the site of injection, and the position of the patient on the operating table, the desired level of anesthesia is obtained. A *saddle block* is a form of spinal anesthesia used when the rectum or genital organs are to be operated upon or for the painless delivery of a baby.

Spinal anesthesia completely anesthetizes that portion of the body supplied by the spinal nerves which have been blocked by the anesthetic injected into the spinal canal. Thus the abdomen and lower extremities can be rendered insensitive to pain while the patient remains perfectly conscious and alert.

The fears of complication from spinal anesthesia date back forty years, when amateurs and nonmedical anesthetists officiated. Today spinal anesthesia is one of the safest of all forms when given by properly qualified anesthesiologists. A troublesome complication, which is never permanent yet frequently annoying, is *postspinal headache*. This symptom occurs in about 5 percent of all cases and lasts anywhere from two days to two weeks after surgery.

4. Epidural and caudal: These methods are similar to spinal in that they deaden, for a few hours, the spinal nerves, thus anesthetizing various regions of the body. They differ from spinal anesthesia in that the anesthetic agent is placed *outside* the spinal canal rather than within the canal. Although the completeness of the anesthesia may not be quite as great as in spinal anesthesia, epidural blocks have the advantage of protecting patients against postspinal headaches. Caudal anesthesia has attained considerable vogue lately in obstetrics, where it does much to eliminate labor pains.

5. Regional: Regional anesthesia represents one of the highest developments of the anesthesiologist's art. By means of needles placed in various regions of the body, anesthetic solutions (e.g., Novocain) are injected to "block" or "deaden" temporarily specific nerves supplying particular parts of the body. Thus only the arm, hand, tongue, neck, or side of the face may be anesthetized if the operation is to be limited to these areas. The advantage of this technique is that the heart, lungs, blood pressure, and general condition of the patient are unaffected by the blocking of specific nerves, and many poor-risk patients who could not ordinarily withstand a general or spinal anesthesia can be rendered operable.

6. Topical: This form of anesthesia

consists of spraying or painting an agent such as *cocaine* or *Cyclaine* onto a mucous membrane surface. It is limited almost entirely to eye, nose, and throat procedures. In some instances, it is used merely to induce superficial anesthesia and is followed by injections of Novocain or similar local anesthetics. It is also commonly used to aid the passage of tubes into the trachea (windpipe) or esophagus (food passage). *Endotracheal tubes* are frequently passed to obtain and maintain an unobstructed airway during prolonged and serious operations upon the chest or abdomen.

Before concluding our discussion of types of anesthesia, mention should be made of the valuable aid received from *muscle-relaxant drugs.* These drugs, such as curare (an old Indian poison used on arrowheads) or succinylcholine, when given by injection in proper amounts, produce great relaxation of the muscles of the body. Good muscle relaxation lessens the amount of anesthetic agent, such as ether, nitrous oxide, or halothane, that must be given and aids the surgeon markedly in performing his operative work.

Various areas of the body upon which operative procedures may be performed and the type of anesthesia likely to be employed are as follows:

OPERATION	TYPE OF ANESTHESIA EMPLOYED
Brain	Local or general, with or without intravenous
Eye	Topical, regional nerve block, or general
Bone	For *extremities:* spinal, regional nerve block, or general
	For *spine:* spinal or general
Mouth	Local or regional nerve block
Tonsils	In *children:* general
	In *adults:* local or general
Thyroid	General, through endotracheal tube. Regional or local, only occasionally
Breast	General, for *major surgery*
	Local or general with intravenous, for *minor*
Heart and lungs	General, through endotracheal tube
Abdominal organs	General or spinal, according to the particular case. If the patient prefers to be asleep, intravenous agents are given with the spinal anesthesia
Kidneys, bladder, prostate	Spinal, epidural, or general. General anesthesia when spinal or epidural are contraindicated by general condition of patient
Rectum, anus, and genitalia	Low spinal, caudal, or local; often with intravenous agents. General in some cases
Upper extremity	Regional nerve block, local, or general
Lower extremity	Low spinal, local, regional, or general

QUESTIONS AND ANSWERS

Who should give the anesthesia?

Whenever a doctor-anesthesiologist is available, his services should be used. Nurse-anesthetists, when they are well trained, are competent and can be used with safety in the absence of a physician.

Does it ever happen that the surgeon starts operating before the patient is fully anesthetized?

No!

Do patients ever give away important secrets while talking as they undergo anesthesia?

No. This is a common misconception.

Can a patient choose his own anesthetic?

No. This is the responsibility of the anesthesiologist and the surgeon. However, the patient should definitely state his preference, and if it conforms to the operation to be performed, the surgical team will usually agree to grant the choice.

Do patients have to be awake during spinal or local anesthesia?

No. Intravenous drugs can be given to put the patient to sleep during such anesthesia.

Does the anesthesia ever wear off before the operation is completed?

No. A competent anesthetist always makes sure that the patient stays fully insensitive to pain throughout the entire operation.

How long after the operation does the anesthesia last?

With general anesthesia, the patient usually awakens anywhere from a few minutes to a few hours after the procedure is finished. Local, regional, and spinal anesthesias wear off within one to three hours after operation.

What is done to relieve pain after anesthesia wears off?

Narcotics are given to eliminate much of the pain.

Have advances in anesthesia increased the safety of surgery?

Yes. All physicians and surgeons will agree that the tremendous decrease in operative mortality in the past ten years is almost directly attributable to two great modern advances:

1. The antibiotic drugs
2. Improved anesthetic techniques

Is spinal anesthesia dangerous?

No. Complications of this technique are no less or greater than other techniques.

What about anesthetic explosions?

These are extremely rare accidents, and they do not occur when proper safeguards are taken by the anesthetist. All equipment that might gather static electricity is grounded, and all operating room personnel wear clothing that does not permit static electricity to accumulate. Since the introduction of nonexplosive anesthetic agents, much of the apprehension has disappeared.

What are the complications of anesthesia?

In former years, pneumonia and lung collapse were the commonest complications. Today these complications are extremely rare, and when they do occur, the anesthetist follows a well-prescribed course of treatment which almost invariably leads to prompt cure.

Following spinal anesthesia, headache is the most frequently encountered complication. This, too, can be resolved within a few days by proper treatment or may be avoided entirely if epidural anesthesia is used.

How do modern anesthesiologists prevent complication?

1. By seeing that the patient has, at all times and with any and every type of anesthesia, a proper oxygen intake during the entire operative procedure.

2. By maintaining a proper airway from the outside to the lungs. It is frequently necessary for the anesthetist to pass instruments into the bronchial tubes and suck out mucous secretions.

This helps to prevent postoperative pneumonia or lung collapse.

Does the anesthesiologist look after the general condition of the patient during the operation?

Yes. It is his responsibility to see that heart action, blood pressure, and other vital functions are maintained. He will advise the surgeon if he thinks the patient's condition is precarious. He will treat any evidences of shock by giving shock-preventing medications or by giving blood, plasma, and oxygen.

Can a patient be put to sleep in his room before going to the operating room?

No. This practice was used frequently when certain sleep-producing rectal drugs (Avertin) were given. However, today premedication has largely supplanted this practice since patients can go to the operating room in a drowsy, semiconscious state. This is much wiser, as it affords both the surgeon and the anesthetist a better opportunity to judge, just prior to surgery, the condition of the patient. Furthermore, rectal anesthesias are difficult to control and may interfere with the administration of additional anesthetic agents in the operating room.

How long can one be kept under anesthesia?

When properly administered, anesthesia can be continued for many hours. In certain types of cases, patients are kept under continuous anesthesia for six to eight hours, or longer.

When improperly administered, that is, when sufficient oxygen is not supplied to the patient's brain, even a short anesthesia of five to ten minutes can do permanent damage. Brain cells demand a constant supply of oxygen and they will die if deprived for even a few minutes.

Do patients ever die from an overdose of anesthesia?

Anesthetic deaths are extremely rare today. Modern methods of administration as well as newer techniques in resuscitation render anesthesia extremely safe. Add to this the fact that most anesthesia is now being given by physicians or trained nurse-anesthetists rather than by nonmedical personnel, and the danger is minimal.

What is the special training of a doctor-anesthesiologist?

After the usual internship, the anesthesiologist-in-training must spend two years in a hospital pursuing a regular course of study in anesthesia. He then must spend three years in the practice of anesthesia before he is qualified to take his American Board of Anesthesiology examinations. Passage of these examinations qualifies him as a trained anesthesiologist.

Does the patient have to pay separately for the anesthesia?

Yes. A physician-anesthesiologist is a specialist, just as the surgeon is, and his services are paid for separately. If a nurse-anesthetist, who is an employee of a hospital, gives the anesthesia, this service is sometimes included in the hospital bill.

What is meant by the term preanesthetic evaluation?

It means that the anesthesiologist has made a physical examination of the patient and has decided what type of risk he is. Risks are classified as I, II, III, or IV, according to physical status.

What is the meaning of the term induction of anesthesia?

Induction is the time during which the patient is induced from consciousness to unconsciousness by an anesthetic agent.

What are the agents in use today for inhalation anesthesia?

The commonest agents are:

1. Fluothane or one of the other agents of similar chemical structure.

2. Nitrous oxide. This gas, frequently referred to as laughing gas, is one of the oldest and most utilized agents.

3. Cyclopropane. This gas is now quite widely used, although within the past few years it has been used less frequently.

4. Ethyl ether, or simply, ether. This is a liquid which, at room temperature, forms a vapor, or gas. It is one of the most reliable and safest of all anesthetic agents, and despite the fact that newer chemicals are being widely employed, ether remains one of the most dependable methods.

5. Chloroform. Although chloroform is a quick and powerful agent, its use has been curtailed greatly because it may exert a bad effect upon the heart.

6. Ethyl chloride and vinyl ether. These drugs were used particularly in children to induce anesthesia and were often followed, after sleep had been induced, by ether, which then maintained anesthesia throughout the remainder of the operation. However, these agents are seldom used today.

What is endotracheal anesthesia?

Endotracheal anesthesia is the method in which an inhalation anesthesia is administered by means of a tube that is inserted through the mouth into the trachea (windpipe). Occasionally, the tube is inserted through the nose, down the back of the throat, and into the trachea.

Endotracheal anesthesia permits much better control of the amount of anesthetic agent that is given. By pumping on the anesthesia bag, the anesthesiologist is able to regulate the patient's condition much more readily than without the endotracheal tube.

Most endotracheal tubes are made of rubber and measure from 6 to 12 inches in length. Some of them contain a cuff of rubber which can be inflated so that there is a snug fit when the tube is lodged in the trachea.

Every once in a while, a postoperative patient will complain of soreness of the back of the throat and may cough up small quantities of bloody sputum as a result of the irritation of the endotracheal tube during anesthesia. These symptoms usually subside within a very few days without any permanent damage having been done.

Endotracheal anesthesia is not used for all surgical cases but is reserved for those of long duration and major proportions; those operations done about the face, mouth, or throat; or those in which the patient is lying face down on the operating table. If someone is to undergo a minor operation which will take only 10 to 15 minutes and will not involve entrance into the chest or abdominal cavity, then the placement of the endotracheal tube may be unnecessary.

Are anesthetic agents unpleasant to smell?

No.

Is one type of anesthesia safer than others?

There is no absolute rule about this. It depends upon the type of operation, the surgeon, the patient, and the anesthesiologist. The choice of anesthetic agent should be left to the anesthesiologist.

What does the term premedication mean?

Medications such as narcotics and sedatives are usually given in the patient's room before anesthesia. This puts the patient in a drowsy, comfortable frame of mind so that he is more receptive to the anesthesia.

What are the different levels of anesthesia?
There are four stages:
1. **The stage of analgesia,** in which the patient is conscious, but feels no pain
2. **The state of excitement,** during which the patient may manifest muscular reactions due to delirium
3. **The surgical state,** which is divided into four planes
4. **The stage of respiratory paralysis**

If a patient has once had a poor reaction to anesthesia, does this necessarily mean that he will have a poor reaction to a subsequent anesthesia?
No. An entirely new set of circumstances may be present at the second anesthesia.

How will the anesthesiologist know when the patient is asleep and completely anesthetized?
There are many clinical tests that prove positively that a patient is asleep. The anesthesiologist will test eye reflexes, muscle reflexes, and will note variations in the rate of breathing, heart rate, blood pressure, and other things.

Can anesthesia be safely given to a patient who is dehydrated?
No. Dehydration (inadequate body fluids) is a very serious condition and should be corrected by giving intravenous fluids before surgery or anesthesia is begun.

Is it important that a patient's body be in chemical balance prior to receiving an anesthesia?
Yes. Acidosis or alkalosis are very serious conditions, and severe postanesthetic complications may result unless they are corrected prior to anesthesia.

If there is a choice, should a surgeon postpone an operation when the patient has a cold, sore throat, or other respiratory infection?
Yes, because these conditions may lead to postoperative lung complications.

Is it important for the anesthesiologist to know of any medications or drugs that the patient was taking before coming to the hospital?
Yes. This is essential to know because, upon his learning such information, the anesthesiologist may want to alter his plans for anesthesia.

Is it important for a patient to have an empty stomach before being given an anesthetic?
Yes. Vomiting and aspiration of the vomit into the lungs are a great peril. If an emergency operation must be performed, the patient's stomach should be emptied first with a stomach tube.

Why will one patient awake within a few minutes following a general anesthesia while another may stay asleep for several hours?
Because of differences in age, in metabolic rate, in the anesthetic agent used, and in the duration of the period of anesthesia.

Should the anesthesiologist be informed if the patient has any loose teeth?
Yes, but he, himself, will invariably look. If the teeth are very loose, it may be advisable to pull them prior to anesthesia.

Who supervises the care of the patient immediately after he has emerged from surgery but is still under the influence of the anesthetic?
The anesthesiologist cares for the patient on the way to the recovery room, where specially trained nurses assume

charge until the patient is fully awake. He is then returned to his hospital bed.

What is an anesthetist's airway?

It is a plastic or metal device placed in the mouth while anesthesia is in progress. The airway keeps the tongue and cheeks out of the way and permits the patient to breathe without obstruction.

Is a patient often sent to the recovery room, or to his own room, with an airway in place?

Yes. This is to maintain free passage of air during the awakening period.

What happens to the airway when the patient wakes up?

He spits it out, or else it is removed by the recovery room nurse at her discretion when she thinks it is no longer necessary.

Is it common practice for nurses to use a suction apparatus for removing secretions from the mouth and throat of a patient who is emerging from anesthesia?

Yes. This is done routinely by the anesthesiologist before the patient leaves the operating room, and is done again, as often as necessary, after the patient is in the recovery room.

Does mucus tinged with blood ever come from a patient's mouth as he emerges from anesthesia?

Occasionally this does happen, but it should cause no alarm. Slight scratches of the mucous membranes of the mouth, tongue, or throat often accompany anesthesia.

Is it natural for some patients to vomit when they emerge from anesthesia?

Vomiting is a frequent occurrence following inhalation anesthesia and it should cause no alarm if the patient has regained consciousness. When vomiting takes place while the patient is still unconscious, the nurse in the recovery room will remove the vomit from the mouth and throat with a suction apparatus.

Are a patient's eyes sometimes inflamed and swollen after anesthesia?

Yes. This results from vapors of the anesthetic agent affecting the conjunctiva. After application of castor oil or some other soothing substance, the condition subsides within a day or two.

If a patient vomits or coughs as he emerges from anesthesia, is there danger of breaking open a surgical wound?

No, properly inserted sutures will hold the wound securely.

Is pneumonia a frequent complication following inhalation anesthesia?

No. Years ago, before modern techniques and agents were developed, it was a frequent complication.

Does the anesthesia given to a mother during childbirth ever anesthetize the child who is being delivered?

Yes. Many anesthetic agents are transmitted through the mother to the infant. If the anesthesia is short in duration (10 to 15 minutes), the transmission is not important, but if it is prolonged, transmission can become a major threat to the life of the newborn.

What is done to arouse a newborn who is under the influence of some medication or anesthesia given to his mother during childbirth?

If respirations are seriously impaired, the child should be suctioned out thoroughly, and an endotracheal tube should be placed in the trachea. Oxygen is then carefully administered under a slight positive pressure. Injections of drugs to make the child breathe are seldom useful.

ANESTHESIA IN CHILDREN

Is anesthesia administered to a child the same way as to an adult?

No. Anesthesia administered to a child differs from that given to an adult in many ways, particularly in the apparatus that is used and in the type of anesthesia that is given.

Are special considerations taken when giving a child an anesthetic?

Yes. The type of anesthetic used will depend on many factors. For example, halothane may be indicated for a surgical procedure of short duration where only light anesthesia is required. This anesthetic, however, is inadequate for lengthy operations or where muscle relaxation is necessary. The age of the child is also important in selecting the type of anesthesia. An adolescent can be given intravenous anesthesia to put him to sleep before giving him one of the gases. Intravenous anesthesia, or intramuscular anesthesia with ketamine, is suitable for infants and young children.

The region of the body to be operated upon is also an important factor in the selection of the method of anesthesia and of the agent that will be used. An operation on a hand or foot can sometimes be performed using a local anesthetic with sedation, whereas an abdominal operation will require a general anesthetic.

What is the most frequently used type of anesthesia on infants and children?

Gas-inhalation anesthesia.

What are the various gases employed in giving anesthesia to children?

1. Fluothane
2. Ethyl chloride, rarely
3. Vinyl ether, rarely
4. Ether
5. Nitrous oxide
6. Cyclopropane

At what age can local anesthesia be given to a child?

It can be used at almost any age but is almost always combined with some form of inhalation anesthesia and sedation. A young child cannot be expected to hold still during surgery if only a local anesthetic agent is used.

At what age is spinal anesthesia first given to children?

At the age of 12, or earlier under special conditions.

At what age can intravenous anesthesia first be given to children?

At any age, but it is not employed frequently.

Do newborn children respond well to anesthesia?

A newborn infant is not a very good subject for anesthesia because it takes several days for his respiratory apparatus to become fully operative. Often, the lungs have unexpanded areas that are prone to develop infection if inhalation anesthesia is given at this age.

Does a newborn child always require anesthesia, even for minor surgery?

No. Operations such as circumcision, or the removal of an extra skin tab, can often be done during the first few days of life without any anesthesia whatever.

Can small children tolerate general anesthesia?

Yes.

Prior to undergoing anesthesia, is it important for a child to have his blood tested for a bleeding tendency?

Yes. Such tests are essential.

If it is discovered that a child has a bleeding tendency, what is the course of action?

1. If he is scheduled for an elective operation, such as a tonsillectomy, it

should be postponed until the bleeding tendency has been corrected.

2. If the intended surgery is urgent, a physician who specializes in disorders of the blood should be consulted. The child may require a blood transfusion or special medications before and during the operation, in order to control the bleeding tendency.

Can a child with a very high temperature be safely anesthetized?

No. It is very important to lower body temperature before anesthesia is begun, because high temperature may cause convulsions.

What is the best way to allay anxieties of children who are about to undergo anesthesia?

1. The anesthesiologist should meet the child the day before or the morning of the operation. He should do his best to make friends with the child.

2. The anesthesiologist should inform the child about what is going to take place and let him know that there will not be too much pain or discomfort.

3. The child should be told that he will receive a little jab in the arm that will make him drowsy and sleepy.

4. The child should be told that when he receives the anesthetic he will go to sleep without any discomfort and when he awakes the operation will be over. He should also be assured that his mother will come to see him soon after his operation is over.

5. If the child is actually going to the recovery room, he should be told that he is going to a special room where, along with other children, he will awake from his anesthesia, and that after he awakes he will be brought back to his room, where his mother will be waiting for him.

6. It is essential not to lie to children,

because lying will undoubtedly cause them to react badly when they discover the truth.

At what age are children most likely to be frightened about operations and anesthetics?

Between the ages of 2 and 6 years. It is usually not possible to reason and explain to a child under 3 years of age what is going to happen. It is best to keep the mother as close as possible to the child until the actual onset of anesthesia so that the child has a sense of security. Children over 6 years of age can usually be given a full explanation of what will take place, and naturally the discomfort of anesthesia will be minimized by their understanding.

Is it wise to attempt to fool the child and not tell him that he is going to receive an anesthetic?

No. Children should not be told untruths. On the other hand, too much explanation can also increase fear, as it will reveal the parent's apprehension.

Does the anesthesiologist usually give a child a thorough explanation of what is going to happen?

It is often advisable to explain in detail to a young child just what the doctor is going to do. However, if the child is younger than 6 years, he seldom understands.

ANESTHESIA IN OLDER PEOPLE

Can older people safely undergo surgical anesthesia?

Yes. Anesthesiologists today are well aware of the special problems in operating on older people. If the patient is a good surgical risk, and if the usual techniques of anesthesiology are modified, then anesthesia may be safely administered.

Is there such a thing as being too old to be given an anesthetic?

Not merely because of advanced age. Often, people in their 70s, 80s, or 90s are in remarkably good health and thus can withstand anesthesia without too much risk.

Is it safe to administer local anesthesia to patients past 60?

Yes, unless there is a sensitivity to the drug used as the local anesthetic agent, such as Novocain. Older people are no more sensitive to such drugs than younger people.

Can intravenous anesthetics, such as Pentothal, be given safely to people in their 70s or 80s?

Yes, just prior to general anesthesia. After the patient has gone to sleep, gas anesthesia is substituted. Intravenous sleep-producing sedatives are most valuable for those who may be especially apprehensive about surgery.

Is local anesthesia often used for major surgery on people of advanced age?

There are relatively few indications for local anesthesia in major surgery at any age. However, there are certain patients whose general condition will not permit a general anesthesia. For these few, a form of local or regional anesthesia may be indicated. Operations on a strangulated hernia in poor surgical risks in their 80s are occasionally performed with local anesthesia in combination with Innovar, given intravenously.

Is spinal anesthesia safe for people who are in their later years?

If patients are in good general health, spinal anesthesia is safe at any age. However, if the patient has high blood pressure, hardening of the arteries, or if the operation involves an organ in the upper abdomen (such as the gall-bladder or stomach), it is perhaps best to use a general anesthetic.

What gas (inhalation) anesthesia is best to give to people past 60?

Most older patients can tolerate any of the gases. Special agents are employed only when the patient has an associated condition such as high blood pressure, heart disease, or lung disease.

Can gas anesthesia be given to older people who are known to have bronchitis, emphysema, or some other lung condition?

Yes, but special postoperative precautions are taken to see that accumulating secretions are sucked out of the bronchial tubes at frequent intervals.

Is it safe for older people to receive general anesthesia in a dentist's office?

This is probably not a good idea for anyone, but particularly not for people past 60. Complications of general anesthesia may arise; if they do, it is much better for the patient to be in a hospital, where all necessary facilities to deal with the problem are available.

Do complications arising from anesthesia occur more frequently in older people?

Not in those who are in good health and have not yet shown marked signs of aging. However, complications do occur more often in those who have advanced arteriosclerosis, heart damage, chronic lung conditions, or impairment of kidney or liver function.

What can be done for a very sick older person in order to enable him to receive anesthesia?

1. If the patient is in shock, this condition must be treated by giving blood transfusions, oxygen, and other medications to maintain a satisfactory blood-pressure level.

2. Heart failure or any other form

of heart malfunction must be controlled prior to the anesthesia by digitalis or other drugs.

3. If there is marked anemia, blood must be given prior to anesthesia.

4. If the patient is undernourished, he will require minerals, proteins, and vitamins prior to anesthesia. It may be necessary to give these substances intravenously.

5. If the patient is dehydrated or has acidosis, this condition must be corrected by appropriate intravenous injections.

What special measures should be taken to safeguard older people during anesthesia?

1. It is essential that they receive an adequate supply of oxygen. Brain cells are particularly sensitive to deprivation of oxygen. Since older people may have some hardening of the arteries to the brain, which condition reduces the oxygen supply, it is vital that the amount of oxygen be sufficient during anesthesia.

2. People in their later years are particularly sensitive to narcotics, such as morphine, and to sedatives, such as the barbiturates. In medicating older people before anesthesia, it is therefore important that the dosage of these drugs be carefully calculated. As a rule, people past 60 require only about two thirds of the normal dose of morphine or the barbiturates.

3. Many older people wear dentures; some must be removed before the patient undergoes anesthesia so that they do not become dislodged and block the air passages.

4. Particular care is exercised in choosing the kind of anesthetic agent given to older people. A frank discussion is often held prior to anesthesia to determine the patient's preference and to allay existing fears. In the great majority of instances the anesthetist can vary the method of inducing anesthesia so as to minimize fear.

5. Some men past 60 have enlargement of the prostate gland, which may make urination difficult for the first few days after spinal anesthesia. If the prostatic enlargement is excessive, general rather than spinal anesthesia may be used.

6. Those past 60 have a greater incidence of bronchitis, emphysema, and other pulmonary conditions that make aeration of the lungs somewhat more difficult. For these people, it is sometimes advisable to choose a local or spinal anesthesia, in order to avoid postoperative lung complications.

7. Since the skin on the face may be thinner and more sensitive, the anesthetist will take special care to protect it during inhalation anesthesia.

8. Teeth in older people are often loose. Therefore, when an airway or other instrument is inserted into the mouth during anesthesia, special precautions are taken not to break or loosen teeth further.

9. The covering membrane of the eyes (the conjunctiva) requires special safeguards when a mask is over the face and when anesthetic gases are being used. Excessive irritation may lead to an ulceration of the lining membrane of the eye (the cornea), which takes a great deal longer to heal in a person past 60.

Do older people usually have the same fears about receiving anesthesia as younger people?

There are exceptions, but most older people have a more mature attitude about anesthesia and harbor fewer fears than younger people. They tend to be more relaxed and their reflexes are less violent than those of younger patients. All of this is more conducive to a smooth induction of anesthesia. On the other hand, some older people have an extraordinary fear of death, and this may be evidenced by a strong resistance to anesthesia. A skilled anesthesiologist can do much to allay such fears if he holds a frank discussion with the patient a day or two prior to surgery.

SURGICAL CONDITIONS AND PROCEDURES

Abdominal Injuries

Since the abdominal cavity occupies such a large portion of the torso, it is frequently subjected to injury. The four most common causes of trauma to the abdomen and its contents are:

1. A direct blow
2. A fall
3. Gunshot or stab wounds
4. Blast injuries

A direct blow: Since the abdominal cavity is an enclosed space, a severe blow often produces a sudden increase in intraabdominal pressure, with resultant rupture of one or more organs. As an example, an accident with impact against a steering wheel or other metal part of a car may cause rupture of the liver, the spleen, or a segment of the intestinal tract. When such an incident occurs, the patient may go into shock, evidenced by a weak, rapid pulse, marked perspiration, great apprehension, and a low or absent blood pressure. The diagnosis of an internal injury secondary to a direct blow can usually be made by the history of the injury and by examination of the abdomen. To protect the contained organs from further injury, the abdominal wall usually becomes tense and rigid. The slightest pressure against the abdominal wall will elicit extreme tenderness.

A fall: When someone falls from a height and strikes his abdomen, internal injury is not uncommon. One of the most frequently encountered injuries of this type, especially in children, is rupture of the spleen. Another organ likely to suffer a tear from a fall is the liver.

Gunshot or stab wounds: In this age of violence, gunshot and stab wounds of the abdomen are occurring with increased frequency throughout the world. It is not always possible to tell whether a gunshot or stab wound has completely penetrated the abdominal wall and has injured one of the underlying organs. Often, many hours may pass before symptoms of shock or localized tenderness develop after a gunshot or stab wound. For this reason, it is general practice to operate immediately and to explore almost every abdomen that has been subject to a gunshot or stab wound. There are, of course, some exceptions to this rule, as in cases where it is obvious that the wound is superficial and has not penetrated through all the layers of the abdominal wall.

Blast injuries: People who are in close proximity to an explosion may suffer blast damage to an internal organ even though they bear no outward evidence that an injury has taken place. A nearby explosion may cause a tremendous increase of pressure within the abdominal cavity, causing one of its organs to rupture, or it may produce a tear in blood vessels leading to the intestines. The diagnosis of a blast injury to one of the abdominal organs will become apparent when the patient develops distention, nausea, vomiting, pain, tenderness, and other signs of shock, as described above. When there is a suspicion that a blast injury has occurred, it is essential to open the abdominal cavity surgically and to repair all damaged structures.

QUESTIONS AND ANSWERS

How can one distinguish between an abdominal injury that has caused serious internal damage and one that does not require surgical attention?

Those who have sustained a serious abdominal injury with damage to internal organs will eventually develop signs and symptoms related to that injury. These symptoms will include increasing pain and tenderness over the area of the blow, nausea and vomiting, evidence of shock with rapid pulse, great apprehension, perspiration, a grayish appearance to the skin, and a weak, rapid pulse.

Should an individual who has sustained an abdominal injury be hospitalized?

If there is any suspicion whatever that there may be damage to one of the internal organs, it is essential that the patient be kept under constant observation for at least 24 hours. The best place in which to observe a patient is in a hospital.

How can one tell whether an abdominal injury is subsiding spontaneously or is progressing?

In those cases in which there has been a serious injury to one of the abdominal organs, symptoms will worsen as time passes. Also, x-rays can be most helpful in determining whether an organ has been ruptured. When abdominal bleeding is suspected, a needle can be inserted into the abdominal cavity and an attempt made to withdraw fluid. The presence of bloody fluid within the syringe is evidence that a serious intra-abdominal injury has taken place.

Is it essential to operate upon a patient when the diagnosis of an intraabdominal injury has been made?

Yes. It is important to explore the abdomen to be absolutely certain that no major rupture of organs such as the liver, spleen, or intestines exists. Conservative observation of a patient who has sustained an abdominal injury is more dangerous than surgical intervention.

What can happen if surgery is not performed on someone who has sustained a major abdominal injury?

Bleeding from blood vessels supplying the intestines or bleeding from a rupture of the liver, spleen, or kidneys can prove fatal if it is not controlled. A rupture of a portion of the intestinal tract will, within a very short time, lead to peritonitis unless the damage is repaired surgically.

Do most people who have sustained abdominal injuries recover?

Yes. Those who have suffered a ruptured spleen, a very common injury, can be saved by removing the spleen and by replacing blood loss through transfusions. Those who have sustained a rupture of the liver can be helped by suturing and packing the torn area, thus controlling the hemorrhage. Holes in the stomach, or small or large intestines, can be sutured; and in some instances, irreparably damaged portions of the intestinal tract are excised.

How soon after an abdominal injury should operation be performed?

As soon as it is apparent that there is a need for surgical repair. Such patients can be helped best by prompt surgery so that bleeding within the abdominal cavity is kept at a minimum and leakage from ruptured intestines is minimized.

Is it important to render prompt treatment to the shock that accompanies an abdominal injury?

Yes. This is essential. It is most difficult to attempt to operate upon a patient while he is in shock. To combat it, intravenous infusions and blood transfusions, along with medications to relieve pain, are almost always administered prior to taking the patient to the operating room.

Abdominal Pain

Almost every individual has abdominal pain at some time during the course of each day. He might not interpret the sensation as pain, but in actuality, the urge to evacuate one's bowel or the urge to pass one's urine is accompanied by a sensation of pain. In most instances, the painful sensation is so natural and so expected that the brain does not interpret it as a harmful symptom. Thus, when someone experiences abdominal cramps, he merely evacuates the bowel and thinks nothing of the fact that his urge was triggered by a painful sensation. In the same way, people often disregard the pain that precedes the passage of urine from a full bladder. It is only when pain persists and increases in intensity after evacuation of the bowel or bladder that an individual comes to think of it as being pathological.

Specific illnesses associated with characteristic abdominal pain are as follows:

1. Ulcer: A gnawing pain high in the pit of the abdomen, coming on most often in between meals or awakening the person from sleep. It sometimes bores through the middle toward the back but is usually relieved by eating, taking milk, or an antacid medication.

2. Gallbladder: Sharp, knifelike colicky pain in the upper right portion of the abdomen beneath the rib margin, sometimes radiating to the right side of the back. The pain comes on suddenly, frequently following the ingestion of fried foods, greases, or fats. Gallbladder colic may last for an hour or more and may require an injection of a narcotic to obtain relief.

3. Gastroenteritis ("upset stomach"): The pain starts out high in the pit of the abdomen and is followed by nausea and vomiting. Relief of the pain ordinarily follows vomiting, but is not infrequently followed some time later by cramplike colicky pains over the entire abdomen. These pains usually subside after diarrhea has emptied the lower intestinal tract.

4. Appendicitis: The pain usually begins in the upper midportion of the abdomen and after a few hours gravitates down to the lower right side. It persists and grows steadily worse as the infection of the appendix progresses.

5. Diverticulitis: The pain is located over that portion of the large bowel involved in the inflammatory process, most often the sigmoid colon in the left lower portion of the abdomen. It persists for several days until the inflammation subsides.

6. Intestinal obstruction: Colicky pains throughout the entire abdomen, associated with distention, nausea, vomiting, and inability to move the bowels.

7. Inflammation of the tubes and ovaries: Pain low down in the abdomen, either on one or on both sides, sometimes radiating down the inner aspect of the thigh.

8. Cystitis: Pain directly above the pubic bone in the midline of the lower abdomen, usually accompanied by frequency and pain on urination.

9. Kidney stone colic: Intense pain in the flank, the upper back portion of the abdomen, radiating toward the groin. It may persist from a few minutes to an hour or more and may require an injection of a narcotic for relief. It is

CHARACTERISTIC AREAS OF PAIN FOR ABDOMINAL DISORDERS

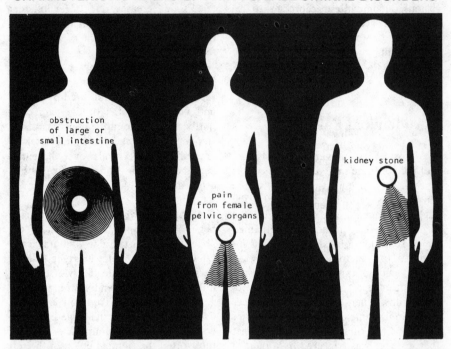

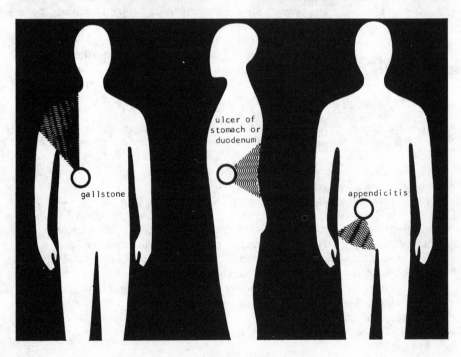

frequently associated with painful urination, sometimes accompanied by the passage of blood.

QUESTIONS AND ANSWERS

How can one distinguish between natural abdominal pain and abdominal pain that is associated with disease or an abnormal condition?

Most normal or physiological pain disappears within a very short period of time. Abdominal pains that last just a few seconds and then spontaneously disappear are most often caused by intense contractions of intestinal muscles. These occur in all people at some time or other and can be safely disregarded. Severe abdominal cramps that disappear after movement of the bowels are also so-called normal pains and require no medical attention. Painful colicky cramps preceding menstruation, or occurring during the first few hours of menstruation, are natural and can usually be tolerated by most women without requiring medical attention.

Any abdominal pain that persists for a period of more than an hour or two without relief by evacuation of the bowel or bladder should be interpreted as due to an abdominal upset or disorder. An exception to this, of course, is the pain associated with the onset of menstruation.

Can abdominal disorders be diagnosed by the specific characteristics of the pain?

Yes, in some cases. For instance, the pain of appendicitis characteristically starts in the upper midabdomen and several hours later is localized in the lower right side of the abdomen. Pain due to gallstones is most frequently located in the upper right side of the abdomen and may radiate to the right shoulder or the right side of the back. Pain accompanying an ulcer of the stomach or duodenum usually is in the upper midportion of the abdomen and often radiates through to the back. Pain due to obstruction of the small or large intestine is usually first felt in the region around the navel and then spreads throughout the rest of the abdomen. The characteristic pain of a stone in the kidney is in the loin with radiation down along the flank toward the groin. Pain arising from the female pelvic organs frequently radiates down the inner aspect of the thigh.

What is meant by radiation of pain?

Some pains start in one area but are directed along the course of nerves to other areas of the body.

Should a person take medications to relieve abdominal pain?

This is permissible only if the condition has been diagnosed previously and a physician has prescribed that certain drugs be taken. Otherwise, it is dangerous for a person to medicate himself for abdominal pain, as this may mask the symptoms of a serious disease.

Should laxatives or enemas be given to relieve abdominal pains?

Not unless specifically prescribed by a physician. A layman is not competent to diagnose the cause of abdominal pain. It is dangerous to medicate without the doctor's specific permission, as a laxative given to someone with acute appendicitis may cause the inflamed appendix to burst. Similarly, an enema given to someone with acute diverticulitis may cause the inflamed area in the bowel to rupture.

How soon after the onset of serious abdominal pain should one contact a physician?

Immediately, if the pain is extreme, as in gallbladder or kidney stone colic.

Less severe pains, if they continue for more than a few hours, demand medical attention.

Are electric pads, hot water bags, or ice bags helpful in relieving severe abdominal pains?

They may afford some temporary relief, but they seldom do much permanent good and often cause great harm from burns. As a rule, they are a poor substitute for a telephone call to one's doctor.

For how long a time can an ice bag or hot water bag be left on the abdomen?

If used, they should be left in place for no more than 20 to 30 minutes at a time. Severe burns can result from their misuse.

Can a parent often diagnose the cause of a child's abdominal pain?

Not always, and in order to be safe, the pediatrician should be telephoned whenever the pain fails to subside within an hour or two.

Is it safe to retire for the night when one is suffering from abdominal pain?

No, though it may be difficult to obtain medical assistance in the middle of the night. A much wiser policy is to contact a physician during the daytime hours.

Will a doctor always give medication to relieve severe abdominal pain?

No. In some cases in which the diagnosis is unclear, he may withhold pain-relieving drugs so as not to mask the symptoms and thus delay a positive diagnosis. As an example, if a doctor were to give morphine to a patient in the initial stages of appendicitis, it might delay his ability to make a precise diagnosis for several hours. During that interval, the inflammatory process within the appendix would progress unabated.

Abortion and Miscarriage

It is not easy to discuss a topic as controversial as abortion without expressing points of view that will find vehement antagonists. Within recent years, there has been a searching reevaluation of long-held beliefs and laws governing abortion. To report accurately on this subject, it should be stated that there is no single American attitude toward abortion, nor are physicians all agreed on the exact indications for surgical termination of a pregnancy.

The doctrine of the Catholic Church holds that once a life has been created within the womb, nothing should destroy it. Therefore, many Catholics feel that there is no situation in which abortion is justified.

Since the January 22, 1973, ruling of the United States Supreme Court, the various states cannot prohibit voluntary abortions during the first three months of pregnancy. The decision is now left to the woman and her doctor! During the remaining six months, states may regulate abortion procedures in ways reasonably related to the mother's health, and, for the final ten weeks of pregnancy, states may prohibit abortion except where physicians find the life of the mother to be endangered. In other words, the law of the land now legalizes and freely permits abortion during the first three months but allows states to make the rules thereafter.

The enormity of the abortion problem and the great need for change should be measured by the fact that the average American woman has one abortion during her lifetime. Another statistic, staggering in its implication, is that there are more than one million abortions performed in this country each year. A great number of them formerly were done illegally. The majority of them are performed upon married rather than unmarried women. Since there are only four million live births in the United States each year, one can calculate that approximately one out of five pregnancies is terminated by abortion.

QUESTIONS AND ANSWERS

Is the term miscarriage synonymous with the term abortion?

Although the meaning of the two words is almost the same, they are not ordinarily used interchangeably. Miscarriage usually refers only to a spontaneous abortion, whereas an abortion can be either spontaneous or induced.

What is the definition of abortion?

It is the expulsion of a human fetus from the uterus during the first six months of pregnancy. Abortion applies to loss of pregnancy at a time when the fetus is unable to maintain life on its own.

At what age is a fetus considered to be living or viable?

When it reaches 26 to 28 weeks of development.

Did the term abortion always imply an illegal procedure?

No. Abortion refers only to the fact that the pregnancy has ended at a time when the fetus has not yet sufficiently developed to be able to maintain life on its own.

How often does miscarriage or abortion occur?

Statistics are not wholly reliable because many abortions and miscarriages are kept secret and are not reported. However, it is estimated that in the United States today, approximately one out of every five pregnancies terminates in miscarriage or induced abortion.

What are the various kinds of abortion?

1. Spontaneous abortion, where no artificial procedures have been employed to bring it on

2. Induced abortion, where medication, instrumentation, or operation have been used to bring about the termination of the pregnancy

Are there various types of spontaneous abortion?

Yes; they are:

1. Threatened abortion
2. Inevitable abortion
3. Incomplete abortion
4. Complete abortion
5. Infected abortion
6. Missed abortion

What are some of the most common causes of spontaneous abortion?

1. Defects in the female egg, the male sperm, the fertilized egg, or the placenta

2. Disease of the uterus, such as an infection or large fibroid tumor

3. Upset in the glandular system of the mother associated with ovarian, thyroid, or pituitary malfunction

4. Constitutional disease in the mother such as diabetes, malnutrition, syphilis, tuberculosis

5. Exposure of the mother to excessive x-ray radiation

6. The taking of poisons or medications which bring on miscarriage

What are some of the symptoms of spontaneous abortion?

1. In the early stages of threatened abortions, staining is the only positive sign. Slight cramps or backache may then develop. This state often continues for days or even weeks.

2. In inevitable abortion, bleeding is

heavier, cramps become regular, severe, and progressive, and the cervix begins to dilate.

3. In incomplete abortion, cramps and bleeding are marked, pieces of tissue are expelled, and the cervix is dilated.

4. In a complete abortion, after increasingly severe cramps and passage of blood clots, a large mass is expelled from the vagina. On examination, it will be found to contain all the products of conception.

What is a threatened abortion?

It is a state during early pregnancy in which there are vaginal staining and abdominal cramps but the cervix remains undilated and the products of conception are not expelled.

What is the treatment for threatened abortion?

1. Bed rest
2. Hormone therapy
3. Administration of large doses of vitamins C and K
4. The giving of sedative drugs

Do all physicians agree that every case of threatened abortion should be treated vigorously in an attempt to save the life of the fetus?

Not all physicians agree that this is the best course of action. Many doctors now believe that abortion takes place much more often in pregnancies in which the developing fetus is abnormal. For this reason they think that it is not good policy always to attempt to save the life of the fetus.

Is the treatment of threatened abortion always successful?

Not always. Many cases will go on to abortion no matter what treatment is carried out.

What is meant by the term inevitable abortion?

It is the state in which bleeding and dilatation of the cervix are so advanced that nothing can be done to prevent expulsion of the fetus from the uterus.

What is the treatment for inevitable abortion?

When it is obvious that an abortion is inevitable, the uterus should be emptied. The evaluation of the inevitability of an abortion is difficult to make, but most gynecologists will give the patient the opportunity to maintain the pregnancy. When it becomes obvious that this is impossible, it is best to empty the uterus completely by performing an operation known as curettage.

What is meant by the term incomplete abortion?

This refers to a condition in which there has been only partial expulsion of the fetus and inner lining of the uterus.

What is the treatment for incomplete abortion?

A curettage should be performed in order to clean out the cavity of the uterus. If a great deal of bleeding has been associated with the miscarriage, blood transfusions may be required.

What is a complete abortion?

It is a state wherein the entire fetal sac and placenta have been fully expelled from the uterus.

What is the treatment for complete abortion?

No surgical treatment is necessary unless severe blood loss has taken place. In that event, blood transfusions should be given. If there is evidence of infection, antibiotics in large doses must be prescribed.

What percentage of abortions require surgical curettage?

Approximately 50 percent of spontaneous abortions are complete and require no operative procedures. If there is any doubt, a curettage should be done to forestall further bleeding or the possible onset of infection.

What is meant by the term missed abortion?

This is a state of pregnancy in which the fetus has died and has been separated from the uterine wall but, instead of being expelled, is retained within the uterine cavity. This constitutes a very trying situation for the patient since the correct treatment is to permit the dead embryo to remain within the uterus for periods up to several weeks. In certain cases, medications are given to bring on the onset of labor. However, the safest course is to wait for the uterus to empty itself spontaneously. This may not occur until many weeks after the fetus has lost its viability (ability to live).

What is habitual abortion?

This is a term applied to repeated abortions in the same patient. The signs, symptoms, and treatment are practically the same for each abortion.

What are believed to be the causes of habitual abortion?

1. Glandular imbalance involving the pituitary, the thyroid, or the ovaries

2. Emotional imbalance of a deep and severe nature

3. Uterine malformation, present since birth

4. Uterine tumors causing the fertilized egg to implant in a poor location

Can habitual abortion ever be helped by medical treatment?

Yes, but it demands thorough investigation into all aspects of the patient's medical and gynecological condition and, following diagnosis, intensive remedial therapy.

What can a woman do to lessen the chances of, or prevent the onset of, miscarriage?

There are several precautionary measures that all women should take when they first learn that they are pregnant. Although it cannot be guaranteed that these measures will prevent miscarriage, they may lessen the chances of such an eventuality. Some of these measures are as follows:

1. Every woman should undergo a thorough physical examination prior to becoming pregnant or upon first learning of her pregnancy. This examination should be performed by a general practitioner or internist. It should include a complete blood count to be sure that the patient is not anemic or does not harbor a systemic infection. It should include a chest examination to make sure that the patient is not suffering from tuberculosis. The examination should evaluate the state of the various endocrine glands, particularly the function of the pituitary, the thyroid, and the ovaries. An examination of the blood should be carried out to make sure that the patient does not have syphilis. If any of the above examinations should reveal an abnormality, immediate treatment should be instituted.

2. Pregnant women should avoid contact with people who have contagious diseases, especially those with respiratory illnesses.

3. Eight hours of sleep should be obtained each night; and during the day, women should avoid overwork. This does not necessarily mean that pregnant women should give up their jobs, but their work should not be so strenuous that it causes exhaustion.

4. A well-rounded diet should be eaten, with particular emphasis on foods that are rich in minerals and iron. It is perhaps best to take supplementary vitamins if one's diet has been limited. Sufficient milk should be drunk so that a calcium deficiency does not develop. Emotional stress and strain should be avoided whenever possible. It has been proved without doubt that people who are in states of high nervous tension have a greater tendency to miscarry.

5. Strenuous intercourse should be avoided during the first two to three months of pregnancy. Intercourse should not take place at that time of each month when the woman would ordinarily menstruate if she were not pregnant.

6. The patient should notify her physician and take to bed should she see any vaginal staining or bleeding, or should she experience lower abdominal pains.

7. The role of many medications and drugs in the causation of miscarriage has not been completely ascertained. It is therefore better for a woman during her early weeks of pregnancy to abstain from taking any medication whatsoever, unless specifically ordered by her physician or obstetrician.

When does abortion require hospitalization?

When the bleeding is profuse or when abdominal cramps become severe and persistent.

What are the greatest dangers associated with abortion?

1. In incomplete abortion bleeding may be so profuse as to threaten life. In such cases prompt transfusion may be lifesaving.

2. Infection following abortion is an uncommon complication, except when the abortion is performed under unsterile conditions. This will require active, strenuous treatment with antibiotic drugs.

3. Rupture of the uterus is a great hazard when an abortion is performed by an untrained individual.

What are the consequences of improper treatment of abortion?

1. Infection may set in and may necessitate the removal of the uterus, tubes, and ovaries.

2. Hemorrhage may occur and can lead to loss of life.

3. Sterility may ensue.

What restrictions are imposed following miscarriage?

1. The patient should restrict activity for one to two weeks.

2. No douches or tub baths should be taken for a period of one month.

3. No sexual intercourse should be engaged in for one month.

Is an abortion carried out by a competent gynecologist in an approved hospital a safe operative procedure?

Yes, it is a very safe procedure. The average patient is able to get out of bed several hours after surgery and can leave the hospital on the next day. Complications of legal abortion are rare, and uneventful recovery almost invariably occurs.

What is the new law governing abortions?

During the first three months of pregnancy, the decision whether or not to have an abortion is a matter to be decided between a woman and her doctor. It is illegal for a state to pass a law prohibiting a woman's right to abortion during this period.

Is sterility likely to be caused by the performance of an abortion?

No.

Are there any pills that can bring on a spontaneous abortion?

No, although there are many drugs on the market which claim to be able to do so. Most of these pills contain a potentially dangerous drug called ergot. Overdose of these drugs may lead to serious, irreversible damage to blood vessels.

Will taking birth control pills for a long time make a woman more susceptible to miscarriage?

No. Statistics have shown that women who have become pregnant after prolonged use of the birth control pills have no greater tendency to miscarry.

Is there any safe method of self-abortion?

No! Attempts to produce abortion upon oneself are associated with a huge incidence of infection, hemorrhage, and fatality.

Should a woman abstain from sexual relations if there is any vaginal staining or bleeding?

Yes. If there is any evidence of a possibility of a miscarriage, sexual relations should be avoided.

Is sexual intercourse conducive to miscarriage?

Some gynecologists feel that sexual relations should not be indulged in during the first few months of pregnancy at the time of the month when the woman would ordinarily have her menstrual period. Except for this time of month, it is safe to have intercourse.

Should a woman stop working if she has vaginal bleeding or staining during the early months of pregnancy?

Yes. Physical inactivity is perhaps best during such times. Bed rest is advised whenever there is the slightest evidence of vaginal bleeding.

Is lower abdominal pain an indication that abortion or miscarriage might be imminent?

In some instances, cramplike abdominal pains may signify that there is a possibility of miscarriage. If these pains persist, the obstetrician should be notified.

What are the various methods of performing abortion?

1. Dilatation and curettage (D & C). This method involves dilating the cervix and scraping out the interior of the uterus with a sharp curette.

2. The suction method. This method employs a suction apparatus which sucks out the products of pregnancy from the interior of the uterus. It is not used for pregnancies that are more than 12 weeks old.

3. Salting-out method. This method is employed for pregnancies that are 12 to 20 weeks old. It involves injection of a salt solution through the cervix into the membranes surrounding the embryo. The reaction will, in most instances, cause the uterus to expel the pregnancy within 48 to 72 hours.

4. Hysterotomy. This is an operative procedure in which the cervix and lower segment of the uterus are incised and the fetus is withdrawn from the uterine cavity. Hysterotomy is reserved for those cases that do not abort following the salting-out procedure and for those pregnancies that are more than 20 weeks old.

What kind of anesthesia is used in performing abortion?

Either a general inhalation anesthesia or a local anesthesia with injection of an anesthetic agent around the cervix is employed.

48

SURGICAL CONDITIONS AND PROCEDURES

Should abortions be done in a doctor's office?

No, because complications such as excessive bleeding or perforation of a uterus require immediate care in a hospital.

Can abortions be safely performed on an outpatient basis?

Yes, provided the facilities of a hospital operating room are available if a complication should arise.

How long a hospital stay is necessary following an abortion?

Patients who are but a few weeks pregnant can usually leave the hospital the same day; those who have undergone the salting-out procedure or hysterotomy will require a four- or five-day hospitalization.

How long does bleeding continue following an abortion?

Active bleeding usually subsides within a day or two; staining may persist for a week or two.

How soon can sexual intercourse be resumed after an abortion?

After the first normal menstrual period has occurred.

How soon after an abortion may one douche?

After the first normal menstrual period has been completed.

Abrasion

An abrasion is a deep scratch or scrape in the skin, in a mucous membrane, or on the membrane covering the eye. Whereas most abrasions will heal spontaneously without leaving any permanent defect, they must receive

proper first aid treatment because of a tendency to become infected.

See also FIRST AID.

QUESTIONS AND ANSWERS

What is the proper first aid treatment for an abrasion?

1. Intensive cleansing of the wound with plain soap and water for five to ten minutes.
2. The removal of any foreign particles such as dirt, cinders, or other material that may have gotten into the wound.
3. The application of a clean dressing. If the abrasion is deep, the patient should be taken to the nearest physician or hospital.

What is the proper first aid treatment for an abrasion of the cornea?

Washing of the eye with warm water, covering it with a patch or bandage, and seeing an eye doctor or going to the emergency room of the nearest hospital.

Should antiseptics such as alcohol, iodine, or other strong substances be poured over an abrasion?

No. It has been found that strong antiseptics do more harm than good. The best insurance against infection is a thorough cleansing for a period of five to ten minutes with ordinary soap and warm running tap water.

Does severe bleeding often take place from an abrasion?

No. Practically all hemorrhage can be controlled by direct pressure over the abrasion with a clean gauze bandage.

What are the special dangers of a deep scrape or abrasion?

If the wound has been incurred out-of-doors, one must guard against tetanus infection. Therefore, it is especially important that all dirt and other foreign material be thoroughly scrubbed out of the scrape or scratch.

What can be done to safeguard the patient against developing tetanus from a deep scrape or an abrasion that has had dirt in it?

1. Adequate cleansing so that all dirt is removed from the wound.

2. Tetanus antitoxin should be given if the patient has not had a previous injection of tetanus toxoid within the past year.

3. Those who have had previous injections of tetanus toxoid should be given a booster shot.

Do deep scrapes and scratches take a long time to heal?

Yes. It is not uncommon for such wounds to take several weeks before they heal completely. Furthermore, for several days after an abrasion has taken place, the skin around it may be red, painful, and swollen.

How can one tell if an abrasion has become infected?

There will be considerable pain, heat, redness, and swelling about the area.

What should be done if an abrasion becomes infected?

Hot wet compresses should be applied and a physician should be seen. In all probability, in order to let out the pus he will remove any scab that has formed. Also, if there is evidence that the infection from an abrasion is spreading to surrounding tissues, he will order hot wet compresses and antibiotic drugs to be given.

Do abrasions often leave permanent scars?

The great majority of them heal without scar formation. However, a deep scratch that has gone down to the very lowest levels of skin may leave a permanent scar.

What can one do to lessen the chances of getting a permanent scar from a deep abrasion?

Prompt treatment, as outlined above, is the best guarantee that permanent scarring will not result.

Abscesses and Infections

Everyone, at one time or another during his life, will develop an infection such as an abscess, boil, pimple, or carbuncle. This is not at all surprising when it is understood that every part of the body is covered by germs at all times. Many of these germs are capable of producing the most serious types of infection. The great wonder is the human body's remarkable ability to resist and control the ever-present bacteria even when the body surface is pierced by a cut or scratch. Despite the body's natural resistance, there are times when the protective mechanism falters and an infection does manage to take hold. Malnutrition, marked anemia, overtiredness, the presence of some generally debilitating disease, or diabetes may cause one to become particularly vulnerable to bacterial invasion. It is at such times that a small pimple may grow into a large boil or carbuncle, or an infection around a fingernail may travel through lymph channels into the general bloodstream.

In the days before the antibiotic drugs, it was not unusual to encounter a simple abscess or superficial infection that would travel to other parts of the body and threaten life. Septicemia, or blood poisoning, frequently became a complication from a seemingly innocent injury such as a blister or a pinprick. Today, septicemia from a superficial abscess or from extension of an arm or leg infection is very rare. It is found only in those patients who have neglected to see a doctor, those who have no access to medical care, or those who happen to have an invading germ that is exceptionally virulent and resistant to antibiotic drugs. Most spreading infections seen today can be controlled readily by proper surgical treatment and by administration of the appropriate antibiotic drugs. It must, however, be emphasized that potent as these drugs are, they do not work in all infections, nor can they be used as a substitute for adequate surgery. The old adage, "When there is pus, let it out," is as true today as it was in former years. However, because of the great effectiveness of antibiotic drugs, surgeons are able in many instances to be much more conservative in their handling of infections. Small incisions can be made in place of large mutilating ones; amputations now are much less frequently required for severe infections; packings and rubber drains can be omitted in some cases where they formerly had been employed. A host of surgical infections that used to require hospitalization can now be successfully treated in the surgeon's office.

Although tremendous progress has been made in the surgical control of abscesses and infections, new problems have arisen since the introduction of the antibiotic drugs. Bacteria, such as the staphylococcus, which were usually not very potent, have, since the antibiotic era, shown a remarkable resistance to many of the antibiotic drugs. Infections, especially in hospitals, can be particularly dangerous because of the virulence of the staphylococcus germ. In full realization of this danger, physi-

cians, nurses, and all hospital employees are careful to avoid transmission of infection from one patient to another.

There are very few conditions in which an individual can help himself as much as in preventing serious infection. The majority of serious complications can be avoided if the patient will follow these simple rules:

1. Every scratch or cut should be cleansed thoroughly with plain soap and water. Soap and water are more efficient in preventing infection than even the most powerful antiseptic, because the latter may burn and damage the already injured tissues.

2. All scratches and cuts should be covered with a clean bandage, and the bandage should be left in place for two to three days.

3. If there is the slightest doubt about whether the scratch or cut is sufficiently serious to require medical attention, a physician should be called on the telephone. He will let the patient know whether it is necessary to have the wound cared for medically.

4. A pimple or boil should never be squeezed. Most of them will dry up and disappear by themselves. If they appear to be enlarging instead of shrinking, then the doctor should be notified. Spreading infection and blood poisoning can follow the squeezing of a pimple or boil. Infections located on the upper lip, nose, and face, are especially dangerous and should be left alone.

5. One should never open his own pimple or boil. If an infection is sufficiently large to require opening, this procedure should be carried out by a physician.

6. Increase in swelling about the infected area or red streaks running from the site of an infection up the arm or

leg is a sign that the infection has spread. A doctor should be seen immediately.

7. Fever and chills are signs that an infection is spreading. The doctor should be seen immediately.

8. If a splinter, or other foreign body, has penetrated the skin's surface, the doctor should be seen. Attempts to rid oneself of the foreign body are frequently followed by infection.

9. The patient should not medicate himself with antibiotic drugs. Inadequate dosages of antibiotics may not control an infection but may cause the germ to become resistant to antibiotic therapy. This is especially true when there is a staphylococcal infection of the skin or tissues beneath the skin.

10. If one must wait a long time between the onset of an infection and the time that a doctor can be seen, the patient should apply warm wet compresses to the area. It is not necessary to add medications to the warm water.

The main principle underlying the treatment of all infections is to keep the process localized to the area of origin. This will be accomplished best by the prompt institutions of the following measures:

1. The infected part or, if necessary, the patient should be placed at complete rest. A patient with an infected hand should not work; someone with an infected foot should not stand or walk.

2. Warm wet dressings should be applied to the infected site. Plain salt solutions or epsom salt solutions should be used. Avoid the application of ointments.

3. Large quantities of water, approximately 10 to 12 glasses a day, should be drunk.

4. Antibiotic drugs should be taken when prescribed by a physician.

5. If the infection has localized and pus has formed, it should be incised by a physician.

QUESTIONS AND ANSWERS

What causes most abscesses or infections?

Various bacteria and occasionally certain parasites. Viruses do not cause pus-forming infections.

Is there any difference between an abscess and a boil?

No. They are the same thing.

When are people particularly susceptible to infection?

When they are overtired, undernourished, anemic, diabetic, or when they are suffering from some general debilitating disease. The first few months after pregnancy is an especially susceptible period.

Do infections or abscesses tend to run in crops?

Yes, because the patient has built up little or no resistance against the germs that have entered the body. On the other hand, if the initial infection is treated adequately with antibiotics and is handled well surgically, the chances for recurrent infection are lessened markedly.

Does a series of boils or abscesses necessarily indicate that there is something wrong with the patient's blood?

Usually not. However, the blood should be examined to rule out the presence of a systemic disease.

Why are infections of the upper lip, nose, and face so dangerous?

Because there is a direct connection through a system of veins between these skin areas and the veins within the skull. Infection of the veins of the brain may occur as a complication of an improperly treated boil or carbuncle of the lip, nose, or face. This is why people are advised never to squeeze a pimple or boil in this region.

What is septicemia?

Blood poisoning, or a condition in which bacteria are living, growing, multiplying, and circulating in the bloodstream. The most serious types of septicemia are those caused by virulent germs such as the staphylococcus, *E. coli,* streptococcus, and others.

Can septicemia ever be cured?

Yes. With the use of antibiotic drugs many patients with septicemia can now be cured. Of course, the original site of infection must be treated by appropriate surgery.

Is it safe for patients to medicate themselves with antibiotics?

No. This is a dangerous procedure. As a matter of fact, inadequate doses of an antibiotic drug may lead to greater resistance on the part of the invading bacteria.

What can be done when a patient develops an allergy or sensitivity to an antibiotic drug?

There are now many excellent antibiotics that can be used to which a patient will not be allergic or sensitive.

How can a physician tell what antibiotic to use in a particular infection?

The proper treatment for most serious infections involves making a culture of the pus that is causing the abscess or carbuncle. The bacteria from the pus are grown and are tested in the laboratory for sensitivity to a large number of antibiotic drugs. An antibiotic to which the bacteria are partic-

ularly sensitive is then prescribed for the patient.

Are there germs that are resistant to all the antibiotics?

Such germs are rarely found. Laboratory tests usually will discover at least one or two antibiotics to which the bacteria are sensitive.

Will it cure an infection to give very large doses of an antibiotic to which the infecting germ is resistant?

Usually not. It is wasteful and will not benefit the patient to give an antibiotic to which a germ is resistant.

Is there a danger in taking an antibiotic that one is known to be sensitive to?

Yes. An antibiotic, such as penicillin, can produce fatal reactions if given to someone who is allergic to it.

Should a patient always tell his doctor about his sensitivity to an antibiotic?

Yes, if he is aware of it. This information is essential for the doctor to have before he prescribes.

Will squeezing or picking a pimple cause more of them to form in the same area?

Yes. This practice is conducive to other infections.

What is the best way to bring an abscess to a head?

By using warm wet compresses. Also, by resting the infected part.

Do abscesses and infections ever subside by themselves?

Yes. With the proper use of warm wet compresses and antibiotic drugs, many will subside without surgery.

Are ointments valuable in bringing an infection to a head?

No.

What is the proper treatment for most abscesses that have localized and come to a head?
They should be opened surgically.

When is a drain inserted into an abscess or infection?
When the infection is deep and the surgeon wishes to keep open a channel for the pus to exit.

Can one go to work while he has an abscess or infection?
Yes, when it is obviously a localized condition and is draining satisfactorily. If the patient's temperature is elevated, or if he must use the part of the body that is involved in the infection, he should stay at home.

Is amputation often necessary to control severe infections?
No. This is not often necessary. However, there are some severe infections, such as spreading gangrene, in which amputation may be necessary to save the life of the individual.

What interferes most with the cure of an infection of an extremity involved in diabetic gangrene?
Diabetic gangrene is often impossible to cure because the circulation of the extremity is poor. Thus, antibiotic drugs that are given do not actually reach the infected area. Moreover, the infected area is unable to recover because of an inadequate supply of blood.

Will the giving of antibiotics help to prevent infection?
Only occasionally, as when they are given to reduce bacteria prior to surgery upon the intestines.

Do antibiotics tend to become less effective when a patient has recurring infection?
Yes, but this situation can often be overcome by changing the antibiotic drug that is used.

Why is the staphylococcus germ so resistant to most antibiotic drugs?
The reason is not known. However, a number of powerful antibiotic drugs are being developed to which the staphylococcus is not resistant. Thus, today, even serious staphylococcal infections can be controlled through the use of these antibiotics.

Can infections caused by the staphylococcus spread from one patient to another?
Yes, especially those infections that occur in hospitals. To safeguard against this eventuality, great precautions must be taken. Hospital patients with staphylococcal infections are isolated, and their dressings are changed by physicians, nurses, and hospital attendants using only the strictest aseptic techniques. Gowns, masks, and gloves should always be worn when dressing a wound infected by staphylococci.

Are many of the common pimples and boils caused by the staphylococcus germ?
Yes. This is one reason why people with crops of pimples or boils find it so difficult to be cured. Also, people with active staphylococcal infections should be excluded from hospital rooms and other hospital areas where they may come in contact with patients who have open wounds.

What is cellulitis?
It is infection of the soft tissues that lie beneath the skin and between the muscles.

What can be done to prevent infections?
1. Periodic physical examinations should be carried out to be sure that one is not suffering from a systemic disease.
2. All cuts should be thoroughly cleansed with soap and water for a

period of five to ten minutes. They should then be covered with a clean bandage.

3. Blackheads, pimples, and boils, even though small, should not be picked or squeezed.

4. Irritating substances should be kept off the skin. Many people are sensitive to deodorants and cosmetics. If one is known to be sensitive to a particular deodorant or cosmetic, it should not be used.

5. If a small infection does develop, the infected part should be placed at rest. One should not work with an infected hand, nor should he walk with an infected foot.

6. Warm wet compresses should be applied to inflamed areas and should be kept in place constantly during the infection.

7. When in doubt about an infection, a doctor should be notified. He will advise on how best to limit the spread of the infection.

Do viruses cause abscesses?

No, although they do invade many organs of the body. However, viral infections are often followed by bacterial invasion. In such instances, abscesses will form.

INFECTIONS IN CHILDREN

Are healthy children able to combat infections as well as adults?

Yes, once they are past the first few months of life. During the first few months, the child may not have developed a sufficient number of antibodies to be able to combat successfully the many bacteria in his environment. The process of developing antibodies takes place rapidly after six months of age, and healthy children may show an even greater resistance to the ordinary bacterial infections than adults.

Do children tend to develop an immunity to the bacteria that flourish in their environment?

Yes, to a great extent. However, such bacteria as the staphylococcus, streptococcus, colon bacillus, and others can cause an infection if they gain access to the child's body through a break in the skin or through one of his apertures.

Can children develop a venereal infection as readily as adults if they are exposed to it?

Yes. There is no natural immunity to the gonococcus or to the spirochete that causes syphilis.

What conditions can affect a child's ability to combat an infection?

1. If a child is undernourished and lacks sufficient body proteins, vitamins, and essential minerals, he will be poorly equipped to combat infections.

2. An anemic child will find it more difficult to mobilize his body resources to combat infection.

3. If there is a disease in one of the major organs, such as the liver, kidneys, or bone marrow, a child will be less able to fight off the invasion of bacteria.

Does the temperature tend to be very high when a child has a bacterial infection?

Yes. Any infection may cause temperatures as high as 105° F to 106° F. in a child. This is not a bad indication, as it demonstrates the child's ability to mobilize his defense mechanisms.

What measures should be taken when a child develops an abscess, a boil, a carbuncle, or a spreading infection beneath the skin (cellulitis)?

1. Whenever a child has a pus-containing infection he should rest in bed.

2. Warm moist compresses containing either ordinary salt solution or epsom salt solution should be applied to the area. Care should be taken not to apply solutions that are so hot that they burn the child.

3. The boil or pimple should never be squeezed.

4. Ointments and powerful antiseptics should never be applied to the infected areas.

5. The parents should never attempt to open the infection themselves by inserting a needle.

6. The child's temperature should be taken regularly, and he should remain in bed as long as there is any elevation in temperature.

7. Hot water bags and electric pads should be avoided. There may a decrease in sensation in the region of the infection, and the child may be burned without realizing it.

8. If the infection does not burst of its own accord within 24 hours, a physician should be consulted.

Will the lymph nodes neighboring a boil, carbuncle, or spreading infection tend to swell and become tender?

Yes. This is the body's way of restraining the bacteria or their toxins from getting into the general bloodstream and spreading the infection.

Does septicemia (blood poisoning) ever affect children?

Yes, but if the original infection is treated vigorously and promptly, septicemia will rarely occur.

What is bacteremia?

Bacteremia is a condition in which bacteria gain access to the bloodstream for a brief period of time. This will cause a marked chill with an abrupt, sudden rise in temperature. If the bacteremia is treated promptly by draining pus from the infection and by giving the appropriate antibiotic drugs, the bacteria will not grow in the bloodstream and cause septicemia.

What is the procedure when the pediatrician suspects the presence of septicemia?

In order to prove this diagnosis, it is necessary to take a sample of blood and grow out a specific germ on a culture medium. This germ is then identified by its growth characteristics and by examination under the microscope. A specific diagnosis is then made.

What is the treatment for septicemia?

After the bacteria have been demonstrated and identified, antibiotic-sensitivity tests are conducted. This means that the germ is grown in media on which samples of the antibiotics have been placed. If the bacteria fail to grow in the area of a particular antibiotic, it means that that antibiotic will be effective in combating the infection. Large doses of the antibiotic will then be prescribed.

Does bacteremia occur very often in children?

Not usually, but occasionally, exceptionally powerful bacteria may pass beyond the localized area of infection, get through the barriers set up by the lymph nodes, and enter the bloodstream.

Can septicemia be cured?

If the diagnosis has been made early and appropriate therapy is instituted promptly, septicemia can usually be controlled.

Is it necessary to give a patient large quantities of fluids when he has an infection?

Yes, because most generalized infections are associated with temperature elevation and profuse sweating. Furthermore, large quantities of fluids tend to dilute the toxins (poisons) produced by the bacteria.

Do viruses ever cause localized boils, abscesses, or carbuncles?

No. A virus rarely causes a pus-forming infection.

Are viral infections more likely to be distributed throughout the entire body?

Yes.

Are antibiotics usually effective in ridding the body of a viral infection?

No. However, they may be given to prevent a secondary invasion of bacteria that would complicate the original viral infection.

Are there any specific medications that can counteract viral infections?

Yes. For example, the measles virus can be prevented from taking hold within the body by vaccinating the child against it. Recently a new drug has been produced that is effective against smallpox, a viral infection. Another new drug is effective against a viral infection of the cornea of the eye.

How successful are the vaccines against viral infections?

Very effective, in certain instances. They are essentially effective in preventing the viral infection, not in curing it.

Do viruses tend to destroy tissue cells in the same manner that bacteria do?

No. The pus-producing bacteria will cause the death of a large number of tissue cells. Viruses will alter the life within the cell, but although they may cause a marked inflammation and interfere with the function of the cell, they are much less likely to kill and destroy the cell completely.

INFECTIONS IN OLDER PEOPLE

Are healthy older people able to combat infections as well as younger people?

Yes. The body's ability to overcome bacterial or viral infections does not diminish greatly if general health is maintained. This is especially true today because of the new antibacterial drugs.

Are aging people more susceptible to the development of infections such as abscesses, boils, and other pus-forming conditions?

Yes. Certain structures, such as the feet, are more likely to become infected because of decreased blood supply, resulting from hardening of the arteries. The entire skin surface, too, becomes more susceptible with age because some of the protective skin oils diminish. Dried-out skin is more readily invaded by bacteria.

What are the general effects of arteriosclerosis on the incidence of infection and in the ability of older people to fight off infections?

Having arteriosclerosis implies that less blood is supplied to the organ or structure invaded by bacteria. With decrease in blood supply, fewer antibodies and white blood cells are carried to the area to combat the infection. Thus, people afflicted with extensive arteriosclerosis are less able to combat infection.

Do diabetes and arteriosclerosis play major roles in making older people more susceptible to infection?

Yes.

Can people over 60 develop immunity to infections to which younger people are not immune?

Yes, to some of the viruses that cause the contagious diseases of childhood. But they develop no added immunity to the streptococci, staphylococci, pneumonia germs, etc.

If an older person is exposed to a venereal infection, can he develop it as readily as a younger individual?

Yes, but, owing to decreased sexual contact, this happens infrequently.

What factors determine the ability of older people to combat an infection?

1. The general state of health. If an individual is undernourished, that is, lacks sufficient body proteins, vitamins, or essential minerals, he will be poorly equipped to combat an infection.

2. The extent of arteriosclerosis is often vitally important in determining ability to withstand infection.

3. The presence or absence of degenerative diseases, such as arthritis, cirrhosis of the liver, or diabetes, will play an important role in determining how well one can fight off infection.

4. Anemia will interfere with the body's ability to overcome an infection.

Are people past 60 more likely than younger people to develop viral infections?

Not necessarily. As a matter of fact, many of the viruses—those causing infantile paralysis, the contagious diseases, and viral pneumonias, for example—most often affect young people. However, there is no natural immunity to viral infections in those who are in their 60s or 70s.

Do people past 60 produce antibodies to combat infections as readily as they did when they were younger?

This essential body function may be somewhat diminished as time passes, but not enough to interfere with ability to combat the usual infections. When there is decreased natural ability to overcome infections, the antibiotic drugs prove most helpful.

Are older people susceptible to development of boils and carbuncles?

Yes. The skin is one of the first structures to show signs of aging. Consequently, skin resistance to such bacteria as staphylococci or streptococci decreases.

What should be done when an older person develops an abscess, carbuncle, or other infection?

1. Such infections should never be self-treated. A physician should be consulted promptly.

a) A pimple, boil, or other pus-containing infection should never be squeezed. This will only spread the infection and may lead to blood poisoning.

b) A needle should never be inserted into a boil or abscess by anyone other than a doctor. This may spread the infection and lead to blood poisoning.

c) Black ointments or other medications should not be applied. They will not affect the pus-bearing area and may do more harm than good.

d) Patients should not medicate themselves, not even with antibiotics.

2. Temperature should be taken regularly whenever there is an infection. If the temperature is high, the patient should stay in bed until the doctor arrives. If a physician is not available, the patient should be taken to the emergency room of the nearest hospital.

3. Warm salt, epsom salts, or boric acid soaks and compresses benefit most infections. Care should be taken not to apply solutions that are too hot, for this might superimpose a burn upon the infection. It is *not* necessary to buy special medications for warm soaks.

4. The infected part should be kept at rest. If a hand or arm is infected, it should not be used. Bed rest is essential if the infection involves the toes or feet.

5. It is best not to use hot water bags, electric pads, and other heating devices on infected areas. This may result in a burn, which will aggravate the infection.

6. If an infection, no matter how

minor, does not disappear within 24 hours, a physician should be consulted.

When an older person has an infection, does the fever usually run as high as it does in younger people?

No. Temperatures as high as 105° F or 106° F are quite rare in older people but are frequent in children and young adults. When high temperature does occur in older people, it usually signifies an overwhelming infection and septicemia (blood poisoning).

Do people over 60 tend to develop infections of the feet?

Yes.

Are kidney infections more frequent in people past 60?

Yes. This is due mainly to two factors:

1. With advanced age there is usually a certain amount of hardening of the arteries that supply the kidneys.

2. There is often obstruction to the free drainage of urine from the kidneys because of enlargement of the prostate gland in men or cystitis in women.

Is pneumonia very common in older people?

Yes. There is increased susceptibility to lung infection as one ages.

Is there a tendency for people past 60 to develop gallbladder infections?

Yes, especially if stones are present. It is estimated that 25 to 30 percent of all women past 60 and approximately 10 to 15 percent of all men have gallstones. The stones often cause obstruction to outflow of bile or interference with circulation of blood to the wall of the bladder. Either of these conditions may result in gallbladder infection.

Is hepatitis (inflammation of the liver) very common in people past 60?

No. It is essentially a disease of younger people. Recently, however, there has been an increase in the number of older people who have suffered from hepatitis. Hepatitis in older people may be due to toxic effects of some poisons rather than to bacterial or viral invasion.

Are bladder infections very common in older people?

Yes. In older women there is often increased laxity in the ligaments and muscles that support the bladder. This condition may prevent the bladder's emptying completely on voiding. As a result, urine stagnates and the bladder becomes infected. In older men, enlargement of the prostate gland often interferes with complete bladder emptying and will result in infection.

Are people past 60 more susceptible to nose, throat, or sinus infections?

No. On the contrary, people past 60 rarely develop acute tonsillitis or streptococcal throat infections. Most sinus infections in older people are chronic and have been present since the middle years.

Are such intestinal infections as colitis, ileitis, and dysentery encountered frequently during the later years?

No. Ileitis and colitis are more common in younger people. Of course, if an older person is exposed to the bacteria or parasites that cause dysentery, he will develop the disease as readily as anyone else.

Does septicemia (blood poisoning) ever affect older people?

Yes. Because older people sometimes have diminished local resistance to infection, deadly bacteria may enter the bloodstream. The possibility of septicemia should be kept in mind when a minor infection is present in an older person.

Is acute rheumatic fever common in people past 60?

No, although older people are more likely than younger ones to develop rheumatoid arthritis and other joint diseases. Acute rheumatic fever, with its high temperature and painful swollen joints, is not very frequent, however. Formerly it was thought that older people *never* developed acute rheumatic fever; recently, investigations have shown that they do occasionally.

Do people in their later years ever develop appendicitis?

Yes.

Are fungal infections common in older people?

Yes, if they are exposed to such infections. However, resistance does tend to increase with the passing of years. This is particularly true for vaginal fungal infections.

Is the treatment of infection usually the same for older people as for others?

Yes, with emphasis on more strenuous methods.

Do older people respond as well as others do to the antibiotic and chemical drugs used in combating infections?

Most of the antibiotic drugs and chemicals are effective in combating infections in older people. However, special care should be taken to make sure that no sensitivity or allergic reaction to these drugs has developed over the years. For example, no older person should be given penicillin without certainty that no allergy exists.

What measures should be taken to prevent infections?

1. Efforts should be directed toward maintenance of good general health. It is essential that a well-rounded diet, with adequate amounts of protein, carbohydrates, vitamins, and minerals, be maintained.

2. Bed rest and prompt treatment of minor infections, such as head colds or other upper-respiratory infections, will often prevent the onset of a more serious infection, such as pneumonia.

3. People should be especially instructed in the need for cleanliness and general care of their skin, since this is often the point of entry for invading bacteria.

4. Surgery is often indicated to prevent an overwhelming infection. For example, someone with a kidney stone should have it operated on in order to avoid major kidney and bladder infections. Similarly, people with gallstones should have their gallbladder removed in order to avoid the possible development of gangrene of the gallbladder or overwhelming infection of the bile ducts and liver.

5. Sedentary people should be encouraged to perform as much physical exercise as can be done safely. Nothing is more conducive to the development of pneumonia or other infections than physical inactivity.

Achalasia

Achalasia is a rather common condition in which there is continued spasm of the lower end of the esophagus at its junction with the stomach. Its exact cause is not known but many investigators feel that it is due to a lack of certain intrinsic nerve fibers within the lower portion of the esophagus. Ordinarily, such nerve fibers would allow the esophageal muscles to relax; but in their absence, the muscles are in a state of more or less permanent spasm. Another group of investigators feel that the condition attacks mainly those who are emotionally unstable and of a highly neurotic temperament. Whatever the cause, people so afflicted suffer greatly from inability to swallow. If the condition persists for many years, the esophagus above the constricted area becomes markedly dilated and collects undigested fluid and food. Continuation of this condition is associated with marked weight loss.

The diagnosis of achalasia can be made from an x-ray taken after the patient swallows barium and by other special tests of esophageal function. Treatment is directed along two main lines:

1. Medical treatment with dilatation of the esophagus by means of tubes that are passed through the mouth. Such dilatation is carried out periodically. If a good result is to be obtained, it usually will take several months before the spasm is relieved. Along with the esophageal dilatation, antispasmodic drugs are given at regular intervals.

2. If the esophageal spasm is chronic and is not greatly benefited following courses of medication and repeated dilatations, then surgery is performed. The chest cavity is opened and the muscle covering the lower end of the esophagus is cut down to, but not including, the mucous membrane. This procedure relieves the symptoms in almost all cases. The operation is relatively simple to perform and is not dangerous even though it involves entering the chest cavity. This procedure is known as the Heller operation. *See also* ESOPHAGUS.

QUESTIONS AND ANSWERS

What causes achalasia?

The cause is not known, but it may be due to lack of certain nerve fibers in the wall of the esophagus.

What are the symptoms of achalasia?

1. Progressive inability to swallow.

2. Regurgitation of undigested food. The food does not taste sour but tastes much as it did when it was first swallowed.

3. Weight loss and malnutrition.

Do all cases of achalasia require surgery?

No. Many people can be helped by repeated dilatations of the esophagus and by the administration of antispasmodic medications. It is estimated that about one in four people will fail to respond to medical management and will require surgery.

What type of surgery is carried out for achalasia?

An incision is made into the chest cavity and the esophagus is mobilized.

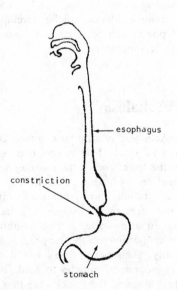

esophagus

constriction

stomach

A marked spasm and constriction of the lower end of the esophagus are characteristic of achalasia.

The muscle fibers of its lower part are severed down to the mucous membrane, thus relieving spasm.

Is the operation dangerous?

No. The majority of patients will recover and will have relief from symptoms.

Achilles Tendon Rupture or Laceration

The Achilles tendon is a powerful structure which attaches the calf muscles to the heelbone. This tendon must be intact in order to maintain a normal gait. Because of its exposed location, directly beneath the skin in back of the heel, the Achilles tendon is subject to frequent injury. Laceration occurs not infrequently during certain sports activities, as in skating or in playing ice hockey. In such instances, the blade of a skate may sever the superficially lying tendon. Spontaneous rupture of the tendon just above its insertion into the heelbone is also a common injury, seen most often during the performance of a physical movement that places extreme stress upon the leg and foot.

When the tendon of Achilles is torn or lacerated, the patient develops severe pain in the back of the leg and ankle, and is unable to walk without holding his foot perfectly rigid. The injury creates a marked limp, and in cases where the tendon is completely severed, the pain may be sufficiently great so as to prevent any weight-bearing or walking.

A torn Achilles tendon should be repaired surgically. This is carried out by making an incision in a longitudinal direction from the back of the heelbone upward for a distance of three to four inches. The severed ends of the tendon are then stitched together and the leg is placed in a plaster cast. When the rupture is located close to the insertion of the tendon in the back of the heelbone, it is sometimes necessary to suture the upper end of the injured tendon directly to the bone. This is accomplished by boring a hole through the bone to make sure that the sutures will not pull out. Several weeks of immobilization are necessary following surgical repair of the Achilles tendon, as the healing process in this area is unusually slow. In addition, there is a tendency for the repair to break down if undue strain is placed upon the tendon before healing is complete. Following cast removal, the patient may walk with a limp for several months thereafter. Complete healing with restoration of normal gait is the usual outcome, but total recovery may be a year-long process.

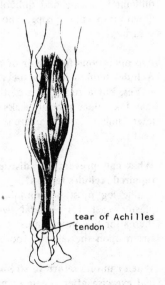

tear of Achilles tendon

QUESTIONS AND ANSWERS

How can one make a diagnosis of a lacerated or ruptured Achilles tendon?

The diagnosis will be obvious upon examining the area above the heel, where the defect in the tendon will be felt readily. Also, typical symptoms are limp and pain on attempting to walk.

Does an injury to the Achilles tendon always lead to complete tear or rupture?

No. There are many instances in which there is only a partial tear. However, because of the importance of this tendon, it is just as necessary to repair a partial laceration or rupture as to repair a complete one. Failure to do so may lead to a permanent limp.

When should surgery be carried out following an injury to the Achilles tendon?

Within a few days after the diagnosis is made. To wait longer may mean that the upper end of the torn tendon will retract upward and will become difficult to locate and difficult to bring down into the proper position for suturing.

Are operations for repair of a ruptured Achilles tendon usually successful?

Yes, but a recurrence of the rupture may take place several weeks or months later unless care is exercised to prevent it.

What can prevent the disruption of a repaired Achilles tendon?

The leg must be immobilized by a plaster cast for several weeks, and thereafter the patient must avoid undue strain upon the leg and foot.

When can one return to strenuous physical exercise after repair of an Achilles tendon?

It usually takes several months to a year before all restrictions can be lifted from a patient who has suffered an injury to this tendon.

What surgical procedure is carried out to repair an Achilles tendon?

The two fragments of the torn tendon are sutured together with a crisscross tendon suture. In cases in which the tear is directly above the heelbone, a hole is bored in the bone, and sutures are placed through this hole into the torn upper portion of the tendon.

Acromioclavicular Joint Separation (Shoulder Separation)

Acromioclavicular joint separation is commonly called "shoulder separation," a condition seen frequently in athletes. The joint is located at the tip, or point, of the shoulder and is composed of the outer end of the collarbone and the upper end of the scapula, or wingbone. When shoulder separation or dislocation is complete, the ligaments connect-

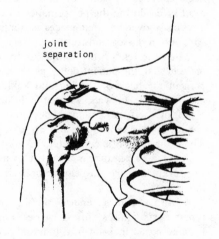

joint
separation

In this diagram, the acromion and the clavicle have been separated by a tear of the ligament that holds them together.

ing the scapula and the collarbone are torn so that the outer end of the collarbone is displaced in an upward and backward direction.

QUESTIONS AND ANSWERS

What is acromioclavicular joint separation?
It is a condition, commonly known as shoulder separation, in which there is a tearing of the ligaments connecting the outer end of the collarbone (clavicle) and the acromial process of the scapula (wingbone).

Will shoulder separation cause interference with the normal function of the shoulder joint?
Yes.

What is the most common cause for shoulder separation?
A fall on the point of the shoulder. This accident occurs most frequently among football players.

Is a shoulder separation a painful injury?
Yes. It causes marked pain upon attempting to move the shoulder joint.

Are all acromioclavicular joint separations complete?
No. A complete dislocation occurs when there is a marked tear with a wide separation between the outer end of the collarbone and the acromial process of the scapula.

What is the characteristic deformity in shoulder separation?
The outer end of the clavicle is displaced in an upward and backward direction, with a marked separation from its normal relation to the acromial process of the wingbone (scapula).

What is the treatment for shoulder separation?
Incomplete dislocations require very little treatment. All that is necessary in such cases is to strap the outer end of the clavicle with adhesive tape placed over a felt pad. A sling is then applied so as to lift the arm and the shoulder. Immobilization is continued for a period of several weeks until the joint is thoroughly stabilized and until all swelling and pain have subsided. Shoulder separations of the complete type usually require surgical intervention, because nonoperative treatment will not effect a cure.

What operation is performed for complete shoulder separation?
Through a skin incision the torn ligaments are exposed and all chips of bone and pieces of cartilage that have been torn away from their normal moorings are removed. The torn ligament is sutured, but this procedure is insufficient to hold the joint firmly in place. It is usually necessary to insert wires through the acromial process of the scapula and down through the outer portion of the clavicle. This will result in the bones healing in a more normal position. The wires can be removed from six to eight weeks after complete healing has taken place.

If the initial surgical treatment described above fails to cure a shoulder separation, is there any other form of treatment available?
Yes. Another operation can be performed, removing about an inch or two of the outer portion of the collarbone. This often leads to a satisfactory result.

What are the chances for full recovery after a shoulder separation?
1. If separation has been incomplete, full recovery takes place almost invariably.

SURGICAL CONDITIONS AND PROCEDURES

2. If a complete separation has been treated adequately by open surgical management, the end result should be a normal or nearly normal shoulder joint.

Can one return to athletic activities after recovery from a shoulder separation?

Yes, but it must be kept in mind that recurrence is a strong possibility, should another fall on the shoulder take place.

Is there any way to prevent acromioclavicular separation?

Yes, by protecting the shoulders with heavy padding.

Adenitis

Adenitis is inflammation of a lymph node, or lymph gland. It is characterized by swelling, pain, tenderness, and sometimes the formation of pus within the node itself.

QUESTIONS AND ANSWERS

What causes adenitis?

Usually it is caused by an infection at some point distant from the lymph node itself. As examples, inflammation of the tonsils or the mucous membrane lining of the throat will lead to adenitis of the lymph nodes in the neck; a severe, spreading infection of a finger may lead to an inflamed lymph node in the armpit; while a severely infected toe or foot may lead to adenitis of a lymph node in the groin.

How does a lymph node become inflamed?

The infection travels from its original site along the lymph channels to the lymph node.

How common is adenitis?

It is exceedingly common following severe localized infection.

How long after an original infection will the lymph nodes become inflamed and enlarged?

This can happen within a period of hours or in a day or two.

What are the usual symptoms and signs of adenitis?

The enlarged node can be felt if it is located in a superficial area such as the elbow region, the knee, the groin, the armpit, or the neck. An inflamed node deep within the abdominal or chest cavity cannot, of course, be felt.

What may happen when an inflammation of a lymph node takes place?

One of several things may occur:

1. The lymph node may contain the infection, overcome it, and the entire process may subside spontaneously.

2. The lymph node may stop the infection from spreading beyond itself, but as a result of this action, the lymph node may become filled with pus and may be destroyed.

3. The infection may be so overwhelming that it passes through the lymph node and goes on to other nodes or into the general bloodstream.

What is the treatment for adenitis?

1. The prime treatment is control of the original site of infection. Thus, if there is an infected finger causing adenitis in the armpit, the infection of the finger must be incised and drained surgically.

2. An inflamed lymph node is often treated successfully by giving antibiotic drugs.

3. To relieve the symptoms of adenitis, warm compresses should be applied to the area of swelling and tenderness. In some instances, cold

compresses may give as much relief as warm compresses.

4. If the adenitis is so extensive that pus develops, it may become necessary to incise and drain the node. Once the pus drains, the infection will subside.

Do most cases of adenitis have to be treated surgically?

No. In the great majority of cases, the adenitis can be controlled if prompt surgical treatment of the primary infection is carried out and antibiotic drugs are given in adequate quantities.

If a lymph node must be incised surgically, will it recover sufficiently to function normally again?

No. Once it has been destroyed by bacteria, it will never function again. Fortunately, the lymph nodes occur in groups, and the loss of one node will not interfere with normal functioning of the others.

Are the lymph nodes ever left swollen as a result of an inflammation?

Yes. However, the nodes will lose their tenderness as time passes.

What can be done to prevent adenitis?

The early treatment of a primary infection such as tonsillitis, streptococcus sore throat, or an infected finger or toe will prevent the spread of the infection to the lymph nodes in the vicinity.

Adenoids

Since the adenoids consist of the same type of glandlike tissue as the tonsils, any discussion of their function and the diseases that affect them should be combined with a discussion of tonsils. Normally, the adenoids are about half the size of the tonsils. They cannot be seen when the patient's mouth is open because they lie on the back wall of the throat above the level of the soft palate. After the twentieth year of life, if they are not chronically infected, adenoids begin to shrink, so that by the time an individual has matured, they rarely are visible, nor do they cause disability.

See also TONSILS AND ADENOIDS.

Adhesions

Adhesions are abnormal fibers or bands that bind various organs or structures to one another. They can occur almost anywhere in the body, but favorite sites are:

1. Joints, where fibrous adhesions may extend from muscle to muscle, or from ligaments to bone or muscle, thus limiting free movement of the joint

2. The chest cavity, in which free expansion of the lungs may be inhibited

3. The abdominal cavity, where adhesions may bind loops of intestine to each other, or may cause loops of intestine to stick to the abdominal wall

QUESTIONS AND ANSWERS

What is an adhesion?

It is a band of abnormal fibrous tissue extending from one internal structure to another.

How common are adhesions?

Adhesions occur very often following inflammation or injury. Adhesions affecting a joint occur almost routinely after a fracture, after a severe injury, or after an inflammatory process such as bursitis. Such adhesions can severely limit motion of a joint. Following a severe case of pneumonia with pus in the chest cavity (empyema), it is not uncommon to find that adhesions form and limit the range of lung expansion and contraction. Adhesions within the abdominal cavity can follow inflammation of any structure, such as the appendix or fallopian tubes. Adhesions are often found during routine surgery. Such adhesions either may cause no symptoms whatever or may be so severe that they obstruct the free passage of food through the intestinal tract. Ad-

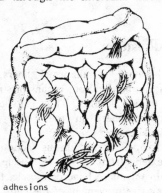

adhesions

Adhesions may cause no symptoms at all or may cause obstruction of the small or large intestine.

hesions affecting a previously inflamed fallopian tube may obstruct the tube so completely as to make pregnancy impossible.

How long do adhesions take to develop?

Most adhesions develop within a few weeks following inflammation, injury, or surgery.

Why is it that some people form adhesions and others do not?

It seems to be an innate tendency of some people and not others. The exact cause of this tendency is not known.

Do most adhesions cause symptoms?

No. The great majority of them produce no symptoms whatever and will undergo stretching as time passes.

When are adhesions most likely to cause symptoms?

When they follow a severe inflammation, a severe injury, or extensive

surgery. For instance, if one has suffered from a very severe bursitis for a long period of time, it is probable that the shoulder will become stiff due to adhesions. Similarly, if one has had an extensive peritonitis with pus in the abdominal cavity, adhesions are much more apt to form than if one has merely had a simple abdominal operation.

What can be done to relieve the symptoms caused by adhesions about a joint?

1. Physical therapy, including heat, exercise, and gentle stretching of the involved joint should be tried.

2. If satisfactory motion about the joint is not obtained from the foregoing measures, injections of procaine (Novocain) and cortisone are sometimes given. This treatment may allow stretching of the adhesive bands with eventual resumption of a complete range of motion.

Is it ever necessary to operate upon a joint because of adhesions?

Yes. Some adhesions are so extensive that they produce a contracture. This is a condition in which a joint is permanently bent out of its normal position because of thick fibrous bands. When such a condition is present it may become necessary to cut the adhesions in order to relieve the contracture.

Is there a tendency for adhesions to form again, once they have been severed?

Yes. For this reason, surgery is never advocated for adhesions unless the symptoms are marked.

Will manipulation of a joint under anesthesia often rupture tight adhesions?

Yes, but in all too many cases new adhesions will form. It must be kept in mind that strenuous manipulation will produce injury and this will be conducive to the formation of new adhesions.

What can be done to relieve symptoms from adhesions within the chest cavity?

If a large area of lung tissue, or an entire lung, is bound down by adhesions, it may be necessary to open the chest cavity surgically and to cut the adhesions with scissors. Following this type of surgery, deep breathing exercises must be carried out for a long time in order to get the lung to resume its usual range of expansion and contraction.

What can be done to relieve symptoms caused by abdominal adhesions?

If intestinal obstruction is caused by an adhesion, immediate surgery is indicated. If extensive adhesions form within the abdominal cavity, it is sometimes necessary to operate for their severance. After completely freeing all structures that have been bound down by the adhesions, the surgeon then attempts to realign these structures so that new adhesions will not develop or, if they do, they will not cause obstruction or interference with intestinal function.

Is a patient who has once developed abdominal adhesions likely to form them a second time?

Yes. For this reason, surgeons are reluctant to operate a second time for abdominal adhesions, if they can possibly avoid it.

Can anything be done to prevent adhesions from forming within the abdominal cavity after surgery?

Yes. The more gently the tissues are handled during an operative procedure, the less likely one is to develop postoperative adhesions. However, despite the most gentle handling of tissues, patients with extensive disease within the abdominal cavity may develop adhesions. Within recent years, several substances have been injected into the abdominal cavity at the conclusion of an operation in an attempt to prevent adhesions. A substance known as hyaluronidase has recently been tried as a deterrent to adhesion formation. Early results from injection of hyaluronidase seem to indicate that it is quite effective.

Will a dietary deficiency cause one to form adhesions more readily?

No. As stated previously, the cause for adhesions is not known. Many healthy people may form a great number of adhesions, while others who are anemic, undernourished, or otherwise debilitated may form few or no adhesions.

The Adrenal Glands

The adrenal glands are triangular-shaped organs located just above each kidney. They measure approximately two inches by one inch in diameter and

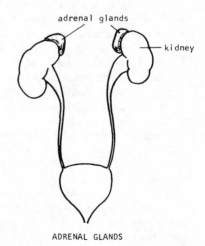

ADRENAL GLANDS

are yellowish in color. These glands have great surgical importance as they are not infrequently the site of tumors. Also, they often function excessively or fail to function sufficiently, thus creating serious diseased states.

The adrenal glands produce hormones which are secreted into the bloodstream and affect many vital bodily functions. Their inner portion (the medulla) produces *adrenalin* and *noradrenalin,* and its outer portion (the cortex) produces *cortisone* and other hormones regulating many aspects of the body's metabolism, including sugar, protein, fat, salt utilization, hair distribution, sex development, etc.

Tumors of the medulla of the adrenal gland cause high blood pressure, often of a special type in that the elevation in pressure comes and goes at various times (paroxysmal hypertension). These tumors are called *pheochromocytomas.*

Overgrowth or tumors of the adrenal cortex may lead to profound disturbances in the body's appearance, with marked changes in vital chemical activities. These changes are included in the disease entity called *Cushing's syndrome.*

In addition to the above-mentioned tumors, primary cancer of the adrenal glands is occasionally encountered, as is cancer that has spread from some other organ to the adrenal gland.

Failure of the adrenal glands to function adequately leads to a condition known as *Addison's disease.* Prior to the advent of cortisone, people with this condition would succumb. Now they can be maintained almost indefinitely by the administration of this substance.

It has been found within recent years that the secretions of the adrenal glands influence the rate of growth and spread of certain types of cancer, principally cancer of the breast. The total surgical removal of both adrenals may prolong life by several months or years in certain cases of breast cancer.

The treatment for any tumor or overgrowth of the adrenal gland which causes marked disturbance in body function is surgical removal. This operative procedure can be performed without undue risk in most patients. An incision over the last rib in the loin, done with the patient lying prone, will give ready access to the adrenal gland. A similar incision on the opposite side will permit approach to the other adrenal. Occasionally the surgeon will decide to approach both adrenals through an incision carried across the upper abdomen with the patient lying in the supine position.

Operative recovery from one-sided (unilateral) or two-sided (bilateral) adrenalectomy is the general rule, although it must be kept in mind that many of these patients are extremely ill and in a state of poor nutrition at the time of surgery.

If an adrenal gland containing a tumor is removed before there has been a spread to surrounding or distant structures, cure can be anticipated. Similarly, adrenal removal for overactivity of function often leads to cure of the clinical condition. Unfortunately, adrenalectomy for cancer of the breast produces only temporary prolongation of life.

QUESTIONS AND ANSWERS

What is the appearance of the adrenal glands and where are they located?

There is one on each side of the body, located just above and adjacent to the kidneys in the upper, back portion of the abdomen. They are small in size (measuring approximately one and one-half to two inches in diameter), yellowish in color, and triangular in shape.

What are the structure and function of the adrenal glands?

The adrenal glands are essential to normal body function because they produce and secrete hormones that are necessary for the maintenance of life. Until the discovery of cortisone, patients suffering severe adrenal failure would invariably die.

Each adrenal gland is divided into a cortex and medulla. The cortex produces hormones that influence the following body functions:

1. The secretion of certain female and male sex hormones.

2. The storage, utilization, and maintenance of body proteins, sugars, and fats.

3. The maintenance of mineral and water balance.

4. The production of chemicals vitally connected with the body's response to stress, strain, and injury.

The medulla produces and secretes adrenalin and noradrenalin (these substances are also known as epinephrine and norepinephrine). These hormones, after secretion into the bloodstream, have the following effects:

1. They reduce muscle fatigue, thereby permitting sustained physical exertion.

2. They stimulate the heart by increasing the force of its contractions.

3. They increase the rate of blood clotting.

4. They increase the concentration of sugar in the blood, thereby making more sugar available to the body tissues.

What hormones are secreted by the adrenal cortex?

1. Steroids, which include cortisone-like hormones.

2. Aldosterone, a hormone that en-ables the body to retain adequate quantities of sodium. An individual could not live without aldosterone because his body would not retain the essential mineral sodium.

3. Androgens, hormones that promote growth and are also responsible for the retention of such vital substances as nitrogen, phosphorus, and potassium. The androgen hormones bring about the development of sex characteristics, particularly in the male.

4. Estrogens, hormones that are similar to those secreted by the ovaries and are necessary for growth and also for the development of secondary sex characteristics in the female.

Are the medulla and cortex of the adrenal glands actually two separate organs with different functions?

Yes.

What is the overall effect of the secretion of adrenalin?

It prepares the body for action in response to danger or stress. It is the secretion that prepares the body for "fight or flight."

What happens if the adrenal glands fail to function properly or if they are removed surgically?

The adrenal glands are essential to the continuation of life. Their failure to function or their total removal will lead to weight loss, debility, and eventually to death, unless adrenal hormones are supplied through medication.

What disease is most likely to ensue if the cortex of the adrenal glands fails to function?

Addison's disease results. This is a condition in which there is a chronic deficiency of the adrenal cortex with resulting debility, weight loss, and eventually, if untreated, death.

70
SURGICAL CONDITIONS AND PROCEDURES

Is Addison's disease common?
No. It occurs in only one person out of 100,000.

What are the symptoms of Addison's disease?
Loss of appetite, nausea, vomiting, emotional instability, and discoloration of the skin and mucous membranes.

Does untreated Addison's disease always end fatally?
Yes.

What is the present treatment for Addison's disease?
It is treated by giving adrenal cortical hormones. These hormones consist of substances allied to cortisone.

Can an individual live normally with Addison's disease?
Yes, if he continues to take a sufficient quantity of adrenal hormones.

Are there other diseases involving the cortex of the adrenal glands?
Yes. Cushing's disease may occur. This condition is associated with excess production of the hormone of the adrenal cortex.

What are the symptoms and signs of Cushing's disease?
1. A flattened and rounded (moon) face
2. Redistribution of fat to the upper torso, neck, and shoulders, giving the patient a buffalolike appearance
3. The appearance of purplish streaks in the skin of the abdomen, thighs, and arms
4. Markedly elevated blood pressure
5. Increased amounts of sugar in the blood

Is Cushing's disease common?
No. It is quite rare.

Is there any cause of Cushing's disease other than overactivity of the adrenal cortex?
Yes, in certain cases, it is due to a tumor within the gland, or to the malfunctioning of the pituitary gland in the base of the brain.

What is the treatment for Cushing's disease?
1. X-ray treatment of the pituitary gland has been found to decrease the activity of the adrenal cortex and thus to rid the body of the symptoms of the disease. It is well known that pituitary secretions stimulate the adrenal cortex to secrete.
2. Surgical removal of part of the adrenal gland or removal of a tumor present within the gland often leads to cure.

Will the patient eventually succumb if Cushing's disease goes untreated?
Yes, in the great majority of cases.

Is the medulla of the adrenal gland ever involved in a disease process?
Yes. A tumor known as a pheochromocytoma sometimes forms within the medulla of the gland.

What effect does a tumor of the medulla have upon the body?
This tumor will cause elevated blood pressure, attacks of anxiety, palpitations, overactive metabolism, and increased blood sugar.

What is the treatment for pheochromocytoma?
The tumor can be cured by surgical removal. To accomplish this an incision is made in the flank over the region of the adrenal gland.

Does recovery from this type of tumor usually take place after surgery?
Yes.

Do the adrenal glands ever develop cancer or other tumors?

Yes, but rarely. Recently, a condition called Conn's syndrome has been discovered. It is supposedly caused by tiny tumors of the adrenal glands. These affect production by the adrenals of a specialized hormone concerned with the regulation of body minerals and fluids. Patients with so-called Conn's syndrome may display a variety of symptoms. One of the most common is high blood pressure. It has been claimed by authorities in this field that these tumors may be more common than hitherto believed and may be present in approximately 10 percent of all people who are presently classified as hypertensives. In addition to high blood pressure, people with Conn's syndrome sometimes display generalized weakness, periodic paralysis, excessive thirst, excessive urination, and intermittent headaches. They may also show a diabetic tendency.

The diagnosis of Conn's syndrome is quite complex and specialized. Its presence may be suspected from the aforementioned signs and symptoms, but the exact diagnosis can be made only at a few specialized research institutions. In the future, it is anticipated that the diagnosis of Conn's syndrome will be more routine and that surgery for the removal of these tumors will become a significant factor in the cure of those with high blood pressure.

Does an individual ever develop an acute insufficiency of the adrenal glands?

Acute insufficiency of the hormones of the adrenal cortex may result from injury or from hemorrhage into the gland due to an overwhelming infection. If someone is so affected, he will go into shock. Unless large doses of cortisone are given immediately, death may ensue within a short time.

What is aldosteronism?

This is a condition resulting from oversecretion of the hormone aldosterone. It is characterized by great muscular weakness, excess output of urine, tetany with convulsions, and marked elevation of blood pressure. When it occurs in children, it can result in premature adolescence.

Does the adrenal gland ever develop cysts?

Yes, but this is a very rare condition.

How can a cyst of the adrenal gland be diagnosed?

By an x-ray technique known as arteriography, in which a dye is injected into the gland's arteries through the aorta.

Can one distinguish between a cyst and a tumor of the adrenal gland?

Yes, by performing an arteriogram. This is important to do because cysts of the adrenal are benign, whereas many tumors of the gland are malignant.

What is the treatment for a cyst of the adrenal gland?

If it grows to a large size, it should be removed surgically.

What is the adrenogenital syndrome?

It is a congenital (present since birth) condition caused by oversecretion of the adrenal hormone androgen. In the female this may lead to pseudohermaphroditism with development of male sex characteristics and a male appearance of the female genitals. In the male, the adrenogenital syndrome may cause premature sexual development. Some of these male children may be fully formed genitally when they are only a few years of age.

Treatment with cortisone frequently induces normal sexual maturation.

What is feminization?

It is a condition occurring in children who have a tumor in the cortex of the gland. This results in the excess production of the hormone estrogen. In the female child this will cause premature sexual development.

Can a patient lead a normal life with one adrenal gland?

Yes, if the remaining gland is normal.

Is adrenal function usually maintained at normal levels in aging individuals?

Yes, but only to a degree. Some investigators believe that the aging process itself is accelerated or brought on by a decrease in adrenal function, particularly in the cortex of the gland. This contention has not been proved, although there is great similarity between the generalized weakness and slowing of metabolism that is seen in some older people and that seen in young people afflicted with disease within the adrenal glands.

Do the adrenal glands ever become overactive in older people?

It is thought that in women who have passed the menopause, the cortex of the adrenals takes over and secretes hormones similar to some of the ovarian hormones. It is also believed that a like process takes place in the aging male; the adrenal cortex secretes a hormone akin to the male sex hormone. If these theories are correct, it would mean that there may be increased activity of the adrenals during the later years of life.

What are some of the symptoms that might develop in aging people whose adrenal glands show inadequate function?

1. In the female, there may be flushes, inability to contract and relax the blood vessels properly, and a state of general lassitude and weakness.

2. In the male, there may be fatigue, loss of muscle tone, and, occasionally, loss of calcium in the bones.

3. In both sexes, inadequate function of the adrenal cortex may lead to faulty mineral metabolism and arthritis.

Can special precautions be taken during the younger years to preserve adrenal gland function later in life?

Yes. More and more investigators feel that excessive strain throughout the middle years will eventually take its toll upon adrenal function. The adrenals are the organs that respond to stress, anxiety, and strain. The draining effect on these glands throughout a long, stressful life may lead to premature loss of the ability to secrete the necessary amount of vital hormones. For this reason, young people should try to avoid unnecessary stress and should seek a way of life that will minimize undue strain and anxiety.

Are the adrenal glands ever removed surgically to slow down the spread of cancer?

Yes. It has been found in some cases of cancer of the breast that removal of both adrenal glands will inhibit the spread of the cancer. This form of treatment is extremely drastic, and is only advocated when the breast cancer has already spread widely throughout the body. This operation is known as adrenalectomy.

How effective is removal of the adrenal glands in cases of disseminated cancer?

It may result in prolongation of life for a few months or, at best, a year or two.

After removal of the adrenal glands for cancer, how is life maintained?

By giving cortisone to replace that ordinarily produced by the adrenals.

Also, great care is taken to regulate the amount of salt and potassium included in the diet. These substances must be measured precisely throughout the rest of the patient's life so that their metabolism can be maintained within normal limits.

ADRENALECTOMY

The treatment for any overgrowth or tumor of the adrenal glands which causes marked disturbance in the body function is surgical removal. Such an operative procedure is called adrenalectomy. It can be performed without grave risk in most patients. An incision over the 10th, 11th, or 12th rib in the loin, performed while the patient lies prone, will give ready access to the adrenal glands. Occasionally, the surgeon will decide to approach the adrenal glands through an incision carried across the upper abdomen with the patient lying in a supine position. Operative recovery from removal of one or both adrenal glands is the general rule, although it must be kept in mind that many of these patients are extremely ill at the time of surgery and the risk is therefore somewhat greater than average.

QUESTIONS AND ANSWERS

For what conditions is surgical removal of the adrenal glands advisable?
1. When a tumor is present in the gland
2. When there is marked overactivity of glandular secretion
3. When there is a cyst within the gland
4. In certain cases of cancer of the breast when the cancer has spread throughout the body

Can a patient survive without both adrenal glands?
Only if he receives regular, substantial doses of cortisone to replace the glandular secretion.

Will it be necessary for someone who has had both adrenal glands removed to take regular doses of cortisone for the rest of his life?
Yes.

Is it possible to cure a patient who has a malignant tumor of an adrenal gland?
Yes, if the operation is performed at a time before the tumor has spread beyond the confines of the gland.

How long after the removal of one or both adrenal glands does it take for the wound to heal?
Ten to fourteen days.

How long after removal of an adrenal gland will there be improvement in the general condition of the patient?
Within a few days.

How soon after removal of both adrenal glands must cortisone treatment be started?
Immediately.

Alcohol

Surgery upon people who habitually imbibe large quantities of alcohol is often more complicated than surgery upon nondrinkers. Heavy drinkers usually are more difficult to anesthetize, and during anesthesia they tend to secrete a great deal of mucus. As a consequence, the lungs may not be as completely aerated as the anesthesiologist might wish. It is also thought that the chronic alcoholic requires a much greater quantity of the anesthetic agent to attain the necessary level of anesthesia.

Postoperative lung complications such as bronchitis and pneumonia are also encountered more frequently among alcoholics and heavy drinkers. Because of this fact, it is extremely important that the heavy drinker be encouraged to breathe deeply and to ambulate actively following surgery. It is also essential that he be made to expectorate and bring up phlegm that might collect in his respiratory tract during the first few postoperative days.

Confirmed alcoholics may require alcohol during the immediate postoperative period. Unless this is given, these patients may develop marked withdrawal symptoms or delirium tremens.

QUESTIONS AND ANSWERS

Are alcoholics and heavy drinkers greater surgical risks than those who are not chronic users of alcohol?

Yes. This does not mean to say, however, that one cannot carry out successful surgery upon this group of people. It does mean that they must be watched more closely for surgical complications.

Should a heavy drinker be encouraged to discontinue drinking prior to an elective operative procedure?

Yes. Those who are to undergo elective major surgery should be instructed to cut down or cut out the drinking of alcohol for at least a week prior to the date that surgery will be performed. This will minimize the chances of difficulty during anesthesia and postoperative complications such as bronchitis, pneumonia, or lung collapse.

Do alcoholics usually require larger doses of anesthesia in order to produce adequate sleep and abolition of pain sensations?

Yes. Adequate anesthesia can be obtained in these patients, but larger doses of the anesthetic agent may be required.

What can the anesthesiologist do to minimize the complications of anesthesia in an alcoholic?

He will take special care to medicate the patient to decrease his bronchial secretions. Also, during the operation, he will take extra care to suck out as much of the mucous secretions as possible.

What other postoperative complications must be guarded against in the alcoholic?

Since the chronic alcoholic may suffer from liver damage, it is particularly important to see to it that liver function is maintained following major surgery. This is accomplished by supplying large quantities of glucose (sugar) and protein throughout the postoperative period.

What types of surgery are most likely to induce postoperative liver damage?

Operations upon the liver itself, the gallbladder, or the bile ducts. In addition, all major surgery, especially procedures of several hours' duration, places a strain upon the liver.

●
Is it necessary to withhold surgery from a patient who is a chronic alcoholic?

No, but special precautions must be taken, and it must be stated clearly to the patient or his family that the risks of surgery are greater than if the patient were not addicted to alcohol.

Amniocentesis

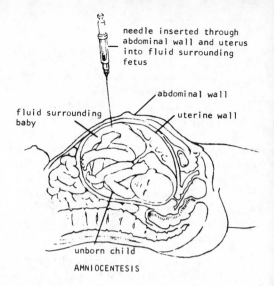

needle inserted through abdominal wall and uterus into fluid surrounding fetus

abdominal wall

uterine wall

fluid surrounding baby

unborn child

AMNIOCENTESIS

Amniocentesis is a procedure in which a long thin needle is inserted through the abdominal wall into a pregnant uterus. The needle is so placed that it strikes the fluid surrounding the fetus rather than the fetus itself.

The purpose of amniocentesis is to withdraw and examine a sample of the amniotic fluid in which the unborn infant bathes. It has been discovered that by examining cells within the amniotic fluid it is possible to determine the sex of the unborn child. If these cells, under microscopic examination, show chromatin bodies, then the unborn child is a female. If no chromatin bodies are seen, the unborn child is a male.

It is also possible in some cases to examine cells obtained through amniocentesis and determine chromosome deformities in the unborn child. Thus, a diagnosis of mongolism or some other inherited defect may be spotted before the child has fully developed.

QUESTIONS AND ANSWERS

How does amniocentesis help to study conditions of the unborn child?

Analysis of the fluid withdrawn through the needle, usually no more than an ounce, will often tell a great deal about the child's chemical metabolism, his blood, and his chances of being born normal.

At how early a stage in embryo development can amniocentesis be performed?

Some investigators have performed it as early as the beginning of the sixth month of pregnancy.

What can fetologists now tell from examining the fluid that surrounds the baby?

It can be clinically analyzed and a great many things can be told about it. Since a child urinates into the amniotic fluid, the urine can be tested for the presence of sugar or abnormal amounts of protein. From this analysis, it is possible to determine whether or not the child has cystic disease or diabetes. Other analyses undoubtedly will reveal other abnormalities that the unborn child might suffer.

Is amniocentesis a dangerous procedure?

No. Although it is a relatively new method of investigation, some scientists in the field have already performed this procedure upon some 6,000 or 7,000 unborn babies. One doctor reported only 3 complications from 5,000 examinations.

Is it likely that the procedure will be still further refined until it will be completely safe?

Yes, but we have not yet reached the stage where it is recommended to all pregnant women.

Can the sex of the unborn child be predicted with amniocentesis?

Yes. The amniotic fluid withdrawn through the needle contains thousands of superficial cells of the unborn child which are sloughed off into the fluid. These are skin cells and cells of the lining of the mouth and the respiratory tract. These cells are then placed under a high-power microscope, and the chromosomes within these cells can be studied for determination of sex.

Is amniocentesis recommended in order to determine the sex of the child?

No. Tapping the womb for this information is considered too extreme a procedure for the information that is obtained. However, the day may come when the procedure may be refined to such a state that it will be safe for all women to subject themselves to it.

Can amniocentesis reveal anything about whether the unborn child will be normal or abnormal?

Yes. In many instances it is possible, by studying the cells within the amniotic fluid, to determine whether or not the unborn child will be a normal healthy child.

How can examination of the cells in the amniotic fluid help to determine whether or not an unborn child has some deformity or inherited condition?

1. If an unborn child's family is known to have members with hemophilia (bleeders), it is extremely important to know whether the fetus is male or female, because only males develop hemophilia. If it is discovered that the unborn child is a female, the mother can be assured that hemophilia is no problem.

2. Cell examination may reveal that there is an extra chromosome in the unborn child's cells. This may indicate that the child will have mongolism.

3. Cell examination may reveal chromosome abnormalities associated with grossly deformed and defective fetuses. Many of these fetuses are stillborn.

Should a family in which there are known cases of hemophilia consider the possibility of amniocentesis?

Yes. A pregnant woman with knowledge that there is hemophilia in her family would be very concerned if she had a male child. By examining the chromosomes within the cells, the fetologist may be able to assure her that a female will be born.

What can a woman do if she is told that a male child will be born?

A woman from a family with hemophilia would have to decide whether or not to terminate the pregnancy if she is carrying a male fetus. Today, an abortion because of this situation may be permitted in the United States, and it is practiced in certain other countries throughout the world.

Amputations

Very little comfort can be offered the patient who faces amputation except that the procedure may be a means of saving his life or may be an escape from repeated, fruitless attempts to rehabilitate a useless extremity. Fortunately, recent surgical advances have resulted in improved techniques in reconstructive measures, so that many seemingly nonfunctional limbs can be restituted. All surgeons are loath to perform destructive surgery, and whenever there is any possible way of preserving an arm or leg, they will do so.

During World War II and the Korean War, great progress was made in the physical and psychological rehabilitation of amputees. They lived together in hospitals and taught one another methods of getting along and ways of effectively using artificial limbs. As a result, a much healthier attitude developed toward amputation. People, child and adult alike, nowadays are determined not to permit the loss of an extremity, or part of an extremity, to interfere too greatly with normal living. And the vast majority, aided by remarkably improved artificial limbs, do live active, productive lives even when there has been the loss of more than one extremity.

The major indications for amputation are as follows:

1. Disturbances in circulation: The arms and legs are supplied with long arteries which maintain relatively few connections with smaller vessels. Thus, when a main artery in the leg or arm becomes clotted or damaged beyond repair, gangrene may set in unless prompt surgical methods are instituted to restore the blood supply. As mentioned in the discussion of blood vessel surgery, one of the truly great advances of recent years is the successful employment of arterial grafts. Many a doomed limb with threatened gangrene has been saved either by a bypass arterial graft or by vascular surgical attack directly upon a clotted or sclerotic artery.

The commonest site of disturbance in circulation is in the leg, and it comes on as a result of arteriosclerosis (hardening of the arteries). Of course, this condition is seen most often in older people, but it does occur secondary to arterial disease and diabetes in younger age groups. Untreated arteriosclerosis, with closing off of the main vessels in the thigh or leg, frequently terminates in gangrene and will necessitate amputation of the leg below or above the knee in order to save life. Gangrene is often seen as a complication of an in-

fection in the foot in an elderly individual who also suffers from arteriosclerosis. And there are other diseases of the arteries and veins, such as thromboangiitis obliterans (Buerger's disease) and Raynaud's disease, which can cause obstruction of the blood vessels with resultant gangrene.

2. Tumors: Malignant tumors, usually cancer of the bone or malignant growths of the muscle or connective tissue, are an indication for amputation. To save life, the diagnosis must be made early in the course of the disease before spread to distant organs has occurred.

Unfortunately, malignant bone tumors are afflictions of youth and cause many tragic deaths. Parents must be enlightened so that they understand the urgency of giving permission to amputate in order to save life!

Luckily, these cancers do not constitute a very commonly seen disease.

3. Infection: Severe, spreading hand infections and rapidly extending foot infections were formerly indications for amputation. *Today it is rarely necessary to amputate for infection.* Wide incision and drainage of the infected area, even if it involves laying open an entire extremity, and the administration of large doses of antibiotic drugs bring the great majority of infections under control.

However, when the infection has caused irreparable gangrene, amputation must be done. Also, when an infection such as tetanus or gas gangrene has set in and jeopardizes the patient's life, an amputation may be indicated.

4. Injury (trauma): The mechanical age and "the age of violence" have created a tremendous increase in the number of serious injuries to extremities. Wherever possible, the surgeon will try to preserve tissue, and in recent years many incredible operations have been performed in which totally severed members have been resutured to the body. Despite these wonderful achievements, it is still necessary to amputate fingers, toes, hands, and legs that have been traumatized beyond repair. Interestingly enough, soft-part injury is often a more decisive factor than injury to bone or blood vessel in determining whether amputation is necessary. An arm or leg in which there is irreversible damage to skin, subcutaneous tissue, tendons, and muscle may require amputation despite the presence of a reparable bone injury.

5. **Deformities:** There are occasional situations in which an extreme deformity is an indication for amputation. Birth deformities such as extra fingers or toes, or even an extra arm or leg, should be amputated. Occasionally one encounters a hand or foot that is so undeveloped and deformed at birth that it should be amputated and replaced by a useful artificial appliance.

Acquired deformities secondary to crippling injuries or infections are sometimes treated best by amputation if surgical repair is impossible. A knee bent upon itself in such a way that it cannot be straightened may interfere greatly with locomotion. In such a case, an amputation above the knee, with a good artificial leg, may permit near normal walking. A leg hopelessly damaged by paralysis, or one that is so short that it cannot touch the ground or bear weight, should often be amputated and replaced by an artificial limb. A finger stiffened permanently by an injury or bent upon itself in a contracture may interfere greatly with hand function. Amputation of such a digit will permit the patient the full use of the other fingers.

The site for any amputation must be carefully evaluated before operation. The guiding principle underlying all amputations is to select a site that will permit good healing of the stump. This means that the circulation must be adequate at the level selected.

In the lower extremity, *weight-bearing* is a prime consideration, and a site should be chosen to effect the best application of an artificial leg. *It is often wiser to amputate above the knee rather than below even when some of the extremity below the knee can be saved!* This is because artificial limbs usually function better with a thigh amputation than with a leg amputation.

In the upper extremity, the important consideration is *motion and function.* The aim in this area is, therefore, to preserve all the tissue possible.

Amputations of the lower extremity are carried out under spinal anesthesia whenever possible. In an extremely sick patient, the leg can be amputated under refrigeration. This is a technique in which the leg is packed in ice for several hours until it becomes insensitive to pain.

Operative recovery from a major amputation is the general rule, although there is considerable danger in performing these procedures on elderly people who are highly toxic as a result of infection and gangrene. These patients must be supported with blood transfusions and given large doses of the antibiotic drugs.

The technique in most amputation operations is to cut across the skin, muscles, and connective tissues, tie off all the blood vessels, saw through the bone, and sew the skin flaps together. In cases where infection is widespread, the skin may not be stitched together at the time of the primary amputation. A secondary revision of the stump is then performed at a later date.

Clean amputation stumps usually heal within two weeks, and an artificial limb can be applied, in many cases, immediately after surgery.

After surgery, it is important to encourage the patient to move the stump frequently. This is to prevent a contraction or deformity of the joint directly above the site of amputation. The patient is gotten out of bed as soon as possible.

Pain in the amputation stump is sometimes caused by a sensitive scar, infection in or under the skin, bone spurs, or an irritation of the cut nerves. A peculiar phenomenon is sometimes encountered in which the patient feels pain in the amputated limb. This is called "phantom pain" and may be characterized by pain felt down in the toes of an amputated leg. Phantom pain is supposedly caused by irritation of the cut nerve in the stump. It will usually disappear by itself within a few months.

Artificial limbs (prostheses) are now made so cleverly and function so efficiently that it is difficulty in many cases to know that the patient is an amputee. People who cannot afford expensive appliances can often be helped by welfare agencies, to which they may be referred by their surgeon. Instructions in the use of artificial arms and legs can be obtained in almost every community, and amputees can benefit greatly by frequent discussions of mutual problems with fellow amputees.

QUESTIONS AND ANSWERS

What are the commonest conditions requiring amputation?
1. Gangrene secondary to hardening of the arteries and diabetes
2. Widespread infection which has

destroyed the extremity and threatens life
3. Malignant tumors
4. Injury which has caused irreparable damage
5. Crippling deformities that prevent use of an artificial appliance or interfere with function of the extremity

What is the rationale underlying the amputation of deformed parts?
Certain birth deformities and acquired deformities limit the use of the extremity more by their presence than if they were amputated. A good artificial appliance can be much more useful than a useless, deformed part.

What are the diseases that most often create poor circulation in the limbs?
1. Arteriosclerosis
2. Diabetes
3. Thromboangiitis obliterans (Buerger's disease)
4. Raynaud's disease

Can an arm or leg with damaged blood supply ever be saved?
Yes, by inserting a blood vessel graft or by reaming out the narrowed passageway of a blocked artery. (*See* BLOOD VESSELS.)

Are foot amputations very common?
No. Most foot conditions can be controlled without amputation. However, toe amputations for gangrene are quite common.

Is amputation often performed for infection?
No. Most infections can be controlled with surgical incision and drainage plus the use of the antibiotics and specified antitoxins. However, certain cases of gas gangrene or tetanus may require amputation.

Is amputation of the leg a serious procedure?

Yes, particularly in those patients who are elderly and who are toxic from a gangrenous infection.

How long can one wait with a gangrenous or badly infected limb before amputation?

Amputation must be performed when signs indicate that the life of the patient is endangered by the gangrene.

How long does it take to perform:

Leg amputation?	20 to 40 minutes
Toe amputation?	10 to 20 minutes
Arm amputation?	20 to 40 minutes
Finger amputation?	10 to 20 minutes

What is the principle governing amputations of the fingers, hand, or arm?

To preserve as much tissue as possible and amputate only in those cases where no possible hope remains for saving the part.

How does the surgeon determine the level at which to amputate?

1. Circulation must be adequate at the amputation site. The poorer the circulation, the higher the level of amputation.

2. As much of the extremity as possible is saved.

3. A site is chosen which will permit the best usage of an artificial appliance.

Why is it sometimes better to amputate above the knee when the upper leg appears to be normal?

An artificial leg can often function better if the amputation is made above, rather than below, the knee. Also, the circulation of the leg may be deficient without its being apparent preoperatively.

Is the skin of the stump of an amputated limb always closed tightly at operation?

No. When infection is anticipated because of the extent of the gangrene, or when the circulation of the region is doubtful, the stump may be drained or even left open and not sutured.

If the amputation stump has not been covered with skin, what secondary operation is done?

Reamputation or revision of the stump with skin closure.

Are leg amputation stumps drained?

Only if the limb was markedly infected or gangrenous.

How soon after amputations can the patient get out of bed?

One to two days. The more active the patient the quicker he will recover.

Are the antibiotic drugs given postoperatively?

Yes. They will help to control wound infection.

What special care is necessary for amputation stumps?

1. They must be bandaged and kept clean.

2. If the skin has not been closed over the stump, traction (pulling) must be made on the skin so that it does not shrink and draw up from the end of the stump.

How long a hospital stay is necessary for:

Leg amputation?	10 to 14 days
Toe amputation?	1 week
Arm amputation?	10 to 14 days
Finger amputation?	1 to 2 days

How long does it take an amputated leg stump to heal?

About ten days to two weeks, unless circulation at the stump level is inadequate.

How soon after amputation can an artificial leg be worn?

If healing without infection takes place within two weeks, a leg may be fitted shortly thereafter. In some cases, a temporary artificial limb is applied at the time of amputation.

How long does it take to learn to use an artificial leg?
Two to four weeks.

Can a patient learn to walk if he has had both legs amputated?
Yes, but with greater difficulty than when one leg is lost.

Are artificial arms very satisfactory?
Yes, they can be used most effectively after prolonged practice.

Can an artificial hand be made to look and function like a real hand?
The most effective artificial hands are constructed of metal, and no attempt is made to preserve the appearance of a human hand. However, nonuseful artificial hands can be made to resemble normal hands.

What is "phantom pain"?
A pain felt in the amputated extremity.

Is it ever necessary to reamputate a limb?
Yes. Certain amputations (guillotine) are done as lifesaving measures without regard to the future usefulness of the limb. In some of these cases, reamputation is indicated so that a satisfactory artificial limb may be fitted.

What can be done if an amputation stump becomes chronically ulcerated and does not heal?
Reamputation at a higher level where the circulation is better may be required.

Is there any regrowth of a part once it is amputated?
No.

Aneurysm

An aneurysm is a thinning and weakness of the wall of an artery. The defect causes a bulge on the vessel's surface much like a blister on an automobile tire. Rupture of the artery at the site of the aneurysm is not uncommon.

QUESTIONS AND ANSWERS

What is an aneurysm?
An aneurysm is a weakness in the wall of an artery, resulting in a bulge in its surface. It can be compared to a blister on an automobile tire. There is also a thinning of the wall, which predisposes to rupture of the artery.

What causes an aneurysm?
1. The most frequent cause of aneurysm is arteriosclerosis. The normal elastic lining of the arterial wall is replaced by fibrous tissue, which lacks the power of contraction and expansion that normal tissue has. With the continued pressure of the blood coursing through it, this weakened area in the arterial wall tends to thin out, stretch, and bulge.
2. Decades ago, when many patients with syphilis went for years without treatment, there were many instances of syphilitic aneurysm of the large vessels, especially the aorta. Today, syphilis is a rare cause of aneurysm.
3. Aneurysms are occasionally produced by injury to an artery, as from a gunshot or stab wound.

What are common sites for aneurysms?
In the arteries supplying the brain, in the thoracic (chest) and abdominal

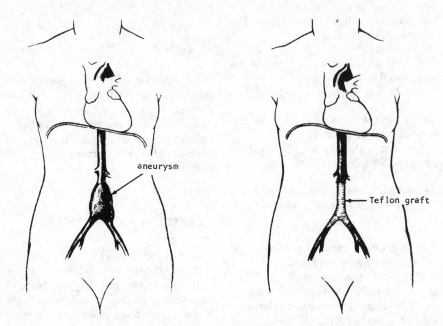

aneurysm

Teflon graft

An aneurysm of the aorta (left) may rupture and cause death. The affected segment should be replaced by a Teflon or Dacron graft.

aorta, or wherever an artery has been injured.

Is there any way to prevent an aneurysm from forming?

Up to the present time, no method has been found for avoiding this phenomenon. When methods of delaying the arteriosclerotic process are discovered, aneurysms will probably be much less common.

What is the treatment for an aneurysm of a major artery?

If a patient has an aneurysm of an artery within the skull and it has been diagnosed prior to rupture, surgery for its correction may be possible. Although considerable brain damage may result from this type of surgery, it must be remembered that a ruptured aneurysm within the skull usually is fatal. If the aneurysm is within the abdominal

aorta, the affected segment of the aorta can be removed surgically and a Dacron or Teflon graft can be sutured in its place. Such operations can now be carried out successfully in the great majority of cases. If the aneurysm is in an artery of the arm or leg, the involved segment can be removed and an arterial graft sutured in its place.

Do aneurysms tend to rupture soon after they form?

No. Many people live for several years with unruptured aneurysms. However, the danger of rupture, with fatal hemorrhage, always exists.

What are the dangers of an aneurysm?

The wall of the vessel in the area of the aneurysm is thinned out, weakened, and subject to rupture. This frequently takes place unless the aneurysm is surgically removed. Rupture may lead to death from hemorrhage within a few minutes or hours.

Do children ever develop aneurysms?
Yes. Aneurysms sometimes appear as a birth deformity within one of the blood vessels of the brain.

How can one tell if a child has an aneurysm of the brain?
Headache, convulsions, paralysis, and loss of sensation in the extremities may develop as the aneurysm grows in size. Often, the initial manifestations occur after the aneurysm has leaked and bled, in which event severe headache, vomiting, stiff neck, and loss of consciousness may begin abruptly without warning.

Will x-rays help in making a diagnosis of an aneurysm?
Yes. A procedure known as arteriography is performed. This means that a fluid, opaque to x-rays, is injected into an artery which is in the neck and leads to the brain. A skull x-ray is then taken which will visualize the blood vessels within the brain. Abnormal configurations of the vessels can be demonstrated readily through this technique.

Is surgery for aneurysm successful?
Yes. Advances in blood vessel surgery have made the cure of aneurysm possible in the great majority of cases. Aneurysms of the aorta, located in the chest cavity, are more difficult to correct than those located in the abdomen. Despite this fact, an increasing number of chest cavity aneurysms have been successfully treated by surgery.

Can surgery help a patient with an aneurysm of a blood vessel in the brain?
None of the surgical techniques now available are wholly satisfactory, but since the outlook is so grave, surgical treatment must be undertaken whenever feasible. The risks are great, but they are even greater if surgery is not performed.

What are the chances for recovery following surgery for an aneurysm of the brain?
Brain surgeons report that they can save approximately four out of five of those upon whom they operate before the aneurysm ruptures. Of those who survive, about 20 percent suffer permanent disability of some type.

Angiography

Angiography is the study of blood vessels by a specialized technique in which contrast-producing material is injected into blood vessels prior to taking x-rays. By this method it is possible to diagnose abnormalities of blood vessels in the brain, the heart, or any other part of the entire circulatory system.

QUESTIONS AND ANSWERS

What is angiography?
It is an x-ray technique for the study of blood vessels. It is carried out by taking x-rays after the injection of a contrast-producing medium into the circulation.

What are some of the conditions that can be diagnosed through angiography?
1. Brain cysts
2. Aneurysms or other abnormalities of the arteries of the brain
3. Brain tumors
4. Brain blood clots or hemorrhage
5. Heart abnormalities
6. Defects in the blood vessels of the heart
7. Constriction of various arteries

8. Aneurysms of various arteries

9. Arteriosclerosis of an artery

10. False connections between arteries and veins (arteriovenous fistulas)

11. Abnormalities of the blood vessels of the kidneys, intestines, and other organs

What is angiocardiography?

It is a specialized x-ray technique whereby the chambers of the heart can be outlined after injection of a contrast-producing medium. Abnormalities in the blood vessels of the heart can also be seen on angiocardiography.

What is angioradiography?

It is another term meaning x-ray of blood vessels.

What is an arteriogram?

It is an x-ray of an artery after the injection of a contrast-producing medium.

What is a lymphangiogram?

It is a technique for x-raying lymph channels after the injection of a contrast-producing material.

over to the appropriate authorities to be tested for rabies.

QUESTIONS AND ANSWERS

What is the first aid treatment for animal bites?

1. The wound should be scrubbed thoroughly for five to ten minutes with mild soap and warm water.

2. A sterile gauze bandage or, if this is not available, a clean handkerchief should be applied to the area that has been bitten.

3. If bleeding is severe, apply direct pressure.

4. Iodine, alcohol, and other antiseptics should not be poured over the wound.

5. Every attempt should be made to apprehend the biting animal. It should then be turned over to the appropriate authorities and tested to make sure that it is not rabid.

6. The patient should be taken to a doctor, who will in all probability give him a booster shot of tetanus toxoid and possibly some antibiotics.

Animal Bites

A bite inflicted by a domesticated pet or any other animal can be serious because of the extent of the laceration and the danger of infection. Some bites tear the flesh deeply and may cause severe bleeding. All bites present the possibility of infection, and rabies may develop if the biting animal is rabid. First aid measures must be instituted immediately, and the bite should be treated by a physician as soon as possible if the skin is punctured. Every attempt should be made to catch the biting animal, and it should be turned

Ankle

See BONE CONDITIONS; FRACTURES.

Antibiotics

The discovery of the various antibiotics has been one of the most remarkable medical advances of this century. They have minimized the dangers of surgery to such a degree that heretofore formidable operations can now be carried out with every expectation of success. The sterilization of the intestinal tract preoperatively has enabled surgeons to remove large diseased segments of both small and large intestines without the great fear of peritonitis which existed previously. The postoperative use of antibiotics in infected surgical cases has also enhanced enormously the chances of healing and recovery. The mortality rate from ruptured appendicitis or from a ruptured gallbladder, as in many other conditions, has plummeted as a result of the judicious use of antibiotics. Wound infection, a common occurrence in the preantibiotic era, has also been reduced markedly by the wise usage of antibiotic drugs.

Despite the great advantages of the antibiotics, surgeons are keenly aware of the fact that their use must not be accompanied by any letdown in the scrupulous antisepsis which is part and parcel of every operative procedure. The antibiotics are not cure-alls, and wound infections and postoperative infections still do occur no matter how large a dose of antibiotics is prescribed. Moreover, antibiotics can be used injudiciously, thus stimulating infections rather than inhibiting them. This is particularly true when an antibiotic is only effective in inhibiting the growth of certain bacteria but is ineffective against others. In such cases, the unaffected bacteria may grow at an extremely rapid rate and may become more virulent. Thus, in recent years, one notes that the staphylococcus, inhibited in the past by bacteria that grew alongside it, frequently exerts an overwhelming effect upon the body's resistance when it survives the administration of an ineffective antibiotic drug.

Antibiotic drugs are composed of extracts of living organisms, such as molds, which have the ability to destroy bacteria. Due to intensive medical and pharmaceutical research, dozens of excellent antibiotic drugs are now available to fight infection.

Taking an antibiotic without knowledge of its proper use can result in increasing the resistance of bacteria to the drug. This will ultimately cause a decrease in the body's response to antibiotic medication. As an example, antibiotics should not be taken for ordinary simple infections that will clear up by themselves.

It is essential that antibiotics be ordered only by a physician, and they should never be taken without his supervision. Some of the antibiotics have toxic effects and may injure the blood-forming organs, the liver, the kidneys, and other vital structures.

QUESTIONS AND ANSWERS

Is it safe for people to prescribe antibiotics for themselves?

No. Antibiotics are powerful drugs and may sometimes be highly toxic to vital organs such as the liver and kidneys. Self-medication may therefore be extremely dangerous. In addition, one can develop resistance to certain antibiotics if they are used too often. Thus, their administration for a mild infection may make them ineffective when they are really needed in a serious illness.

Can people who are not allergic to a particular antibiotic develop an allergy at a later date?

Yes. Many people do *not* display sensitivity to a drug the first time it is given but will develop an untoward reaction when it is given on a subsequent occasion. This is another reason why it is unwise to give antibiotics unless they are absolutely necessary to overcome an infection.

If a person is allergic to one antibiotic drug does this necessarily mean that he will be allergic to others?

No. It is not at all unusual to encounter people who are allergic to penicillin but who are not allergic to other antibiotic medications.

Are antibiotics given prophylactically to patients who are about to undergo surgery?

In certain types of cases, such as those involving intestinal surgery, antibiotics are given preoperatively in order to decrease the number of bacteria within the intestinal tract. However, antibiotics are usually not given preoperatively, but are used following surgery when infection may complicate the postoperative recovery.

Is it possible to obviate surgery for infection by giving antibiotics in large doses?

In some cases this is possible. On the other hand, most infections requiring surgery will have to be operated upon despite the administration of antibiotics. The old dictum, "When there is pus, let it out," still holds true today.

Can the judicious use of antibiotics ever turn extensive surgery into less extensive surgery?

Yes. In many instances, infections such as those involving a hand or foot can be sufficiently controlled by antibiotics so that a much smaller incision and a much less extensive operative procedure is necessary to produce a cure.

Can intraabdominal infections, such as appendicitis or acute gallbladder disease, ever be treated successfully by antibiotics alone?

In some instances, the infection can be controlled so that surgery can be delayed. However, the ultimate cure of acute appendicitis or gallbladder disease will usually require surgical removal of these diseased organs.

Can kidney infections be controlled through antibiotics?

In most instances, yes.

What is meant by an antibiotic sensitivity test?

It is a laboratory procedure carried out to determine which antibiotic medication will be most effective in treating a particular infection. The bacteria causing the infection are grown in a culture medium containing various antibiotic drugs. The bacteria will grow in those areas on the culture medium where there is an ineffective antibiotic, but the bacteria will not grow on the medium in the vicinity of an antibiotic that is effective against those particular bacteria. As a result, the physician can learn which antibiotic medication will be most effective in treating a particular germ.

Should an antibiotic sensitivity test be carried out prior to administering an antibiotic drug?

Yes. This will save a great deal of time and will benefit the patient greatly. It is useless to give even large doses of an antibiotic to which the bacteria are not sensitive. As an example, a staphylococcus germ causing a wound infection may be totally resistant to the administration of penicillin but may be controlled readily by the use of another antibiotic such as Keflin. In this case, the administration of penicillin would be valueless and would delay the ultimate cure of the infection.

Do children respond as well to antibiotics as do adults?

Yes. In many instances their response is better, as they have not yet developed resistance to the use of these drugs.

Do older people respond as well to antibiotics as younger people do?

Usually they do, but some antibiotics, such as penicillin, may cause an allergic reaction if they have been given on several occasions previously. Fortunately, if the patient fails to respond to one antibiotic, another usually can be found to which he will respond favorably.

Anticoagulants

Anticoagulants are chemicals that inhibit the blood clotting mechanism. These medications do not prevent clotting completely but slow down the process so that unwanted clotting will not occur. Clotting of blood within the veins of the legs or pelvis is one of the chief causes of embolism, and the phenomenon can often be prevented by the use of anticoagulant drugs such as Heparin or Coumadin.

During and following most heart or blood vessel surgery, it is essential to administer anticoagulants. The proper use of these medications in such cases will allow transplanted vessels, arterial grafts, vein grafts, or a transplanted heart to function without the fear that blood will clot and thus destroy the effectiveness of the operation.

The use of anticoagulant drugs is also advocated for patients who have phlebitis (inflammation of veins) and in those patients who have a known tendency toward the formation of blood clots. While a patient is on anticoagulant drugs, his blood is tested periodically to determine the level of blood clotting. This test is known as a prothrombin time, and will show rather accurately the necessary dosage of anticoagulant to be given. Too much anticoagulant medication may cause unwanted bleeding, and it is therefore important to regulate dosages carefully.

As a result of judicious use of anticoagulant drugs, the incidence of pulmonary embolism following surgery has been reduced markedly.

QUESTIONS AND ANSWERS

What is an anticoagulant medication?

It is one given in order to delay, suppress, or prevent blood coagulation (clotting). The two most widely used medications for this purpose are heparin and Coumadin.

For what conditions are anticoagulant medications given?

1. In coronary thrombosis. The idea behind anticoagulant medication in this condition is that extension of the blood clot within the coronary artery will be prevented by making the blood less susceptible to coagulation.

2. In thrombophlebitis. Here too the idea is to prevent extension or breaking off of a piece of a blood clot that has formed within a vein. It has been found that in thrombophlebitis, anticoagulant medications will often prevent an embolus. (An embolus is a piece of clotted blood that has broken away from the site at which it formed and has traveled to a distant part of the body.)

Is there a tendency for people who are being given anticoagulant medications to bleed excessively?

Yes. It is necessary to keep a careful check on the clotting and bleeding time of the blood of all patients who are on this type of therapy. It is especially important to watch patients who have very high blood pressure or advanced hardening of the arteries. These individuals may have a tendency to suffer stroke, including hemorrhage in the brain.

What is done when a patient has abnormal bleeding while on anticoagulant therapy?

Usually, the blood can be made to clot normally within a very short time by the administration of large doses of vitamin K.

Do some people who are on anticoagulants tend to bleed from the rectum?

Yes. A great number of people have hemorrhoids, and there is a tendency for these people to bleed when they are being given anticoagulants.

Is there a tendency for women to bleed excessively during menstruation when they are being given anticoagulants?

Yes.

Do some people bleed from the kidney or bladder while being given anticoagulants?

Yes.

Do some people who are on anticoagulant medications bleed from their gums?

Yes.

Can an accurate check on anticoagulant therapy be obtained?

Yes, by taking repeated blood tests. The test most often performed for this purpose is called a "prothrombin time." If this test shows that too much of the anticoagulant medication has been employed, the medication will be discontinued or its effect will be modified by giving an effective dose of vitamin K.

How effective is anticoagulant therapy in the treatment of coronary thrombosis?

Some internists believe that it greatly decreases the chances for extension of the clot within the coronary artery dur-

ing the acute episode, but the evidence is not conclusive. Thus, anticoagulant therapy may aid recovery.

How effective is anticoagulant therapy in the treatment of thrombophlebitis?

Most physicians agree that anticoagulants will decrease markedly the number of patients who will develop an embolus.

For how long are anticoagulants prescribed in cases of coronary thrombosis or thrombophlebitis?

In order to be most effective, they must be given for several weeks.

Antisepsis

Antisepsis is the prevention of infection by the destruction or inhibition of the growth of bacteria. An antiseptic is any substance that will prevent the development of infection or inhibiting the growth of bacteria or by destroying them.

QUESTIONS AND ANSWERS

What is antisepsis?

Antisepsis is any method of preventing infection. It is sometimes carried out by the use of antiseptic solutions or substances. The antiseptic process can be aided by the sterilization of anything used in treating a patient. Therefore, antisepsis is best maintained by boiling or otherwise heating utensils, instruments, and other things that might come into contact with a patient. It must be understood that it is not quite possible to live in a world that is free from bacteria and that total antisepsis is not possible under ordinary circumstances.

How is antisepsis carried out surgically?

In order to keep bacteria at an absolute minimum in an operating room, everyone who has contact with the patient on the operating table must scrub his hands and arms with antiseptic soap for a period of at least ten minutes. The surgeon, his assistants, and the operating nurses then don sterile rubber gloves, clothing, footwear, and gauze masks. The part of the patient's body that is the site of the operation is then thoroughly scrubbed with soap and water, and is painted several times with an antiseptic solution. The entire area to be operated upon is then draped in sterile towels and sheets, and the remainder of the patient's body is covered with sterile drapes. Throughout the entire operation, no one not thoroughly scrubbed and gowned is permitted to come into contact with anyone on the operating team.

Surgical antisepsis is also maintained by keeping the traffic in the operating room to a minimum and by not permitting anyone to attend an operation who has the slightest infection that might be communicated to the patient. Even in an operating room, however, it is not always possible to obtain total antisepsis.

Do patients always get an infection if there is a failure of antiseptic techniques?

No. Fortunately, one's body has a natural ability to ward off infection. Unless bacteria enter a surgical wound in large numbers, the body may be able to overcome them and thus prevent infection.

Do scrubbing the skin and the application of antiseptic solutions completely sterilize skin surfaces?

No. It is believed that some bacteria continue to live in the deeper layers of the skin, especially along the sweat glands and in hair follicles. These bacteria may be stunned by the antiseptic soaps and solutions and thus may be made temporarily harmless. When this happens they are unable to invade the open incision, and infection will not result.

Will the pouring of strong antiseptics into an open wound help to prevent infection?

No. Strong antiseptic solutions should never be poured into open wounds because this kills tissue cells. When dead tissue is present, it is much easier for bacteria to gain a foothold.

What is the best procedure for preventing infection of an open wound?

1. The wound area should be placed under a tap of water in order to wash out any dirt particles.

2. The wound should be thoroughly scrubbed for a period of five to ten minutes with a mild soap and warm running water.

3. A sterile bandage should be placed over the wound.

4. The patient should be taken to a doctor's office where professional treatment can be given.

Antitoxins

An antitoxin is a substance produced by the body in order to neutralize the toxins (poisons) produced by bacteria. Antitoxins are produced naturally by the body, often resulting from the individual's once having had a specific infection. Thus, if a patient has had diphtheria, his body will produce antitoxins that will afford him immunity to a subsequent attack of the disease.

90

90

SURGICAL CONDITIONS AND PROCEDURESSURGICAL CONDITIONS AND PROCEDURES

QUESTIONS AND ANSWERS

Can antitoxins be produced artificially?
Yes. Laboratory animals are used to manufacture antitoxins. This is done by giving toxins in small doses to the animal and allowing time for its blood to develop antitoxins. The animal's blood is then withdrawn and the serum is separated, purified, and chemically prepared so that it can be injected into a human being.

What are some of the surgical diseases that can be treated by antitoxins?
There are several diseases that can be treated by antitoxins, but their use today is rather limited because of newer methods of treatment. However, tetanus responds to treatment with an antitoxin.

Are antitoxins necessary if a patient has already been immunized?
No. They are rarely needed if one has received immunization. However, if the immunization is no longer effective, he may require injections of an antitoxin.

Must care be exercised in injecting antitoxins?
Yes, especially if the patient is allergic. An allergic person often may have marked sensitivity to the horse serum in which the antitoxin has been developed. It is very dangerous to give such a patient the antitoxin without first testing him for horse serum sensitivity. If he is found to be sensitive, he must be desensitized by giving him very tiny doses of the antitoxin at carefully spaced intervals.

How can a patient be tested for sensitivity to horse serum?
By injecting a small quantity of the serum into his skin and noting the reaction within 10 to 15 minutes. If a large red welt forms at the injection site,

it can be concluded that the patient is sensitive to the horse serum. Another method is to place one drop of the serum into the patient's eye. If the membrane of the eye becomes inflamed, it can be assumed that the patient is sensitive to the horse serum.

Can nonallergic people also have reactions to antitoxin?
Yes. Some may develop serum sickness following the administration of antitoxin. Serum sickness occurs usually in about four to five days after the antitoxin is given. It is characterized by fever, painful swelling in the joints, and enlargement of the lymph nodes. The condition usually subsides in a few days without doing any great harm.

Anuria

One of the most dread complications of surgery is kidney failure. This is associated with anuria, a condition in which there is little or no output of urine. It is well known that anuria is incompatible with life, and those patients who fail to get rid of their wastes through the urine will eventually succumb to uremic poisoning.

Anuria is a rare complication of surgery but is more likely to occur following very extensive and serious operations such as an operation upon the heart, lungs, or a major abdominal organ. It is also more apt to be encountered among those patients who suffer from chronic kidney damage with poor kidney reserve.

QUESTIONS AND ANSWERS

What conditions are most likely to bring on anuria with kidney failure?
Any operative procedure that is followed by shock. Surgical shock, with

its accompanying low blood pressure, is often associated with an inability of the kidneys to manufacture and excrete urine.

Are there any other conditions that might lead to anuria?

Yes. Postoperative dehydration can result in kidney failure with inability to maintain adequate urinary output.

What is the best way to safeguard against postoperative anuria?

The patient must receive adequate intake of fluids and electrolytes (sodium, chloride, and potassium), and postoperative shock must be combated by the administration of proper amounts of blood or plasma.

How can one tell whether anuria is approaching?

The urinary output of every patient who has undergone surgery is carefully watched and computed. Postoperative patients normally manufacture and excrete 1 cc of urine per minute. This amounts to approximately one and a half quarts of fluid during each 24-hour period.

How does one measure urinary output in a postoperative patient?

All seriously sick postoperative patients must have intake of fluid and output of fluid calculated carefully. This is accomplished by inserting a catheter into the bladder and measuring all the urine that is excreted.

Is anuria a frequent complication of surgery?

Fortunately, it is a rare complication.

Will the use of an artificial kidney (hemodialysis) help to tide over the surgical patient with anuria?

Yes. Death from lack of urinary output is due to accumulation of waste materials within the bloodstream.

Uremic poisoning sets in and eventually leads to death. By dialysis, or the use of the artificial kidney, it is possible to clear the bloodstream of these poisons and thus prevent uremia from ensuing.

Will the use of the artificial kidney always cure uremia?

No. It is essential that the kidneys begin to function again in order for the patient to recover. This may involve the giving of large quantities of fluids, blood, and essential chemicals such as sodium, chloride, and potassium.

Are there any medications that can prevent anuria?

When it is noticed that the urinary output is lower than normal, sometimes the use of a chemical known as mannitol is indicated. However, the underlying cause for the lowered urinary output must be combated.

Is anuria known by any other names?

Yes. It is also called acute kidney failure, acute renal failure, acute tubular necrosis, and lower-nephron nephrosis.

What are some of the conditions that may predispose a person to anuria?

1. Rapid hemorrhage
2. A sudden drop of blood pressure when on the operating table
3. Extensive burns
4. Septicemia, a condition in which bacteria circulate and grow in the bloodstream
5. Crushing injury
6. Destruction of blood cells as a result of a mismatched blood transfusion
7. Interruption of circulation that takes place during operations upon the heart or great blood vessels
8. Certain conditions of pregnancy in which there is massive hemorrhage, or in which there is toxemia or infection

9. Certain poisons, such as mercury and carbon tetrachloride

10. Massive doses of x-ray radiation

Does anuria ever take place as a result of surgical shock or sudden injury?

Yes, both of these conditions are common causes of anuria. It is believed that during these conditions there is intense constriction of the blood vessels in the kidney. As a consequence, the tubular cells of the kidney receive little or no blood and are thereby damaged. With the tubular cells damaged, urine is not excreted.

Does anuria ever come on slowly?

It can either be abrupt, as when it follows shock, or it can come on slowly over a period of days as a result of damage to the kidney from poisons.

What are the symptoms of anuria?

The most important symptom is the lack of urinary output. A certain amount of blood is often found in the urine, if any is being excreted. Most patients who are suffering from anuria will develop heart failure and may also have congestion of the lungs. In about one of four patients, the blood pressure rises. If the anuria continues for any length of time, infection usually sets in and the patient may be overwhelmed by septicemia. Finally, if the anuria is complete, the patient develops all of the symptoms of uremia, with a typical urine smell to the breath, muscle twitching, and eventually coma that ends in death.

Is it possible to reverse the trend of anuria?

Yes. Anuria can sometimes be overcome if the underlying cause for the disease is brought under control. If shock is the cause, it must be treated rapidly by giving intravenous fluids and blood transfusions. Infection must be treated with large doses of antibiotics.

In some cases, in order to rid the body of the poisons that are causing the anuria, it may be necessary to employ an artificial kidney.

Is it common for patients who have had anuria to begin suddenly to void large quantities of urine?

Yes. This is known as the diuretic phase of the condition and does not necessarily mean that the kidney has fully recovered from its damage. It is necessary, during this phase, to replace the salt that is lost from the body and to give as much fluid as is necessary to maintain hydration.

How dangerous is anuria?

It is estimated that more than half of the people who are anuric for 24 hours will die no matter what treatment is begun. The results will depend to a large measure upon the associated illness or condition that has produced the kidney failure.

If someone recovers from anuria, is he likely to have some permanent kidney damage?

Yes, if the destruction of the tubular cells has been extensive. Such people may develop high blood pressure, which remains permanent, and may eventually, years later, develop uremia.

Is there any way to prevent anuria?

To a certain extent, one can take measures to prevent it. First, a seriously ill patient should never be permitted to become dehydrated. To prevent this it is necessary to give large quantities of water, salt, and sugar. If the patient has lost a large amount of blood or fluid during a prolonged operative procedure, this must be replaced promptly. Failure to do this may lead to anuria. Also, dehydration contributes to the production of shock. If a patient has been exposed to infection and septicemia is feared, massive doses of antibiotics must be given. If poisons have been allowed to gain access to the kidneys, early dialysis with an artificial kidney may be a lifesaving procedure. And finally, constriction of blood vessels in the kidney may be combated by giving cortisone or some similar drug.

Anus

See RECTUM AND ANUS.

Aorta

The aorta is the largest artery in the body. It begins at the exit of the left ventricle of the heart, and its branches carry blood to all parts of the body. That portion of the aorta which is in the chest has branches to the lungs, the heart itself, and the head and neck. The aorta then descends into the abdomen where its branches supply all of the structures beneath the diaphragm. In the lower abdomen, it divides into two blood vessels which supply the pelvic organs and the lower extremities.

See also HEART.

QUESTIONS AND ANSWERS

What is the aorta?

It is the largest artery in the entire body, extending from the heart and arching through the upper chest and then down through an opening in the diaphragm to the abdomen.

Are children ever born with abnormalities of the aorta?

Yes. One of the most frequently encountered birth deformities of this structure is called coarctation. This is a segmented narrowing, or constriction, of the aorta within the chest. As a consequence of this abnormality, high blood pressure and other signs of heart malfunction may develop.

What can be done about coarctation of the aorta?

Modern blood vessel surgery can correct the deformity by cutting out the narrowed portion of the aorta and stitching the normal portion above to the normal portion below. If the area of narrowing is too long to permit this procedure, then a Dacron or Teflon arterial graft is inserted after excision of the narrowed portion.

Can coarctation be cured by surgery?

In the great majority of cases a cure results. Of course, it must be realized that surgery of this type is very serious. Nevertheless, since most of those with coarctation will eventually die if they do not have surgical correction of the defect, it is advisable to go through with the operation.

What is the most common condition affecting the aorta during adulthood?

The most common condition is an aneurysm, a weakening and bulging of the wall of an artery. When this occurs, there is a likelihood that the aneurysm will rupture and cause sudden death. To forestall this, the aneurysm should be removed surgically and replaced by an arterial graft.

What causes aneurysms of the aorta?

1. Arteriosclerosis occurring in advanced age.

2. Syphilis. This cause has become much less common in recent years since syphilitic aneurysms are almost always the result of untreated syphilis, and prompt treatment of syphilis is fairly common today. With the early and thorough treatment of syphilis by anti-

biotic medications, aneurysms will rarely develop.

Can an aneurysm of the aorta in the chest be cured?

Yes, but it is difficult to do so. The removal of an aneurysm in the chest is fraught with much greater danger than when the aneurysm is located in the abdomen.

Is it ever possible to save a patient who has ruptured an aneurysm of the aorta?

Yes, if there has not been great loss of blood before the patient can be taken to the operating room. If the patient survives long enough to reach the operating room, surgery can remove the aneurysm. An immediate placement of an aortic graft, to take the place of the defect in the vessel, may then be made.

How can one tell if an aortic aneurysm ruptures?

When this takes place, it is accompanied by severe pain in the chest or abdomen. Blood escapes between the layers of the wall of the aorta or out into surrounding tissues. Massive hemorrhage, ending in death within a few minutes, may occur.

What other condition affecting the aorta is frequently encountered?

Arteriosclerosis, or hardening of the aorta. This may be so extensive that the blood flow through this vessel is diminished to a mere trickle.

Can one survive if there is marked arteriosclerosis of his abdominal aorta with stoppage of blood flow?

Advancing arteriosclerosis takes place over a period of years during which collateral circulation through the smaller arteries develops and supplies the organs normally nourished by blood from the aorta. Of course, the organs do suffer from reduced blood supply when the main aortic flow is impaired.

Can surgery help arteriosclerosis of the aorta?

Yes, if it involves the abdominal portion of the vessel. In some cases, the aorta is replaced by a Dacron or Teflon graft; in other cases, the vessel is opened and the arteriosclerotic plaques are cored out. This latter operative procedure is known as an endarterectomy.

How helpful is an endarterectomy in overcoming arteriosclerosis?

Arteriosclerosis is accompanied by the collection of calcium plaques on the inner surface of the aorta. As these plaques pile up, they obstruct the flow of blood. Their removal through endarterectomy may reestablish a near-normal blood flow.

Is endarterectomy of the aorta a dangerous procedure?

It is a major operation, but the patient will almost always recover from it. Blood vessel surgery today has attained a high degree of safety.

After the inner lining of the aorta has been cored, how is blood flow reestablished?

After coring the inner lining, the blood vessel is stitched with special arterial sutures. The temporary clamps, which have been placed above and below the vessel during the operation, are released and blood flow is reestablished.

How does a physician discover the presence of disease within the aorta?

An aortogram is made by an x-ray technique that lights up the inner lining of the aorta, thus revealing abnormalities such as aneurysm, coarctation, or any marked arteriosclerosis. An opaque substance is injected into the aorta prior to taking the aortogram.

How is the opaque material injected into the aorta when making an aortogram?

There is more than one way:

1. If the physician desires to visualize the aorta in the chest, a small catheter (hollow plastic tube) is fed through a vein in the arm or neck until it reaches the heart. The opaque material is then injected through the catheter into the heart, and as opaque material is expelled by the heart's contractions, it will light up and outline the aorta.

2. If the physician desires to visualize the abdominal aorta, he does so either by injecting a needle through the muscles of the back directly into the aorta, or by inserting a plastic catheter into the femoral artery in the groin and pushing it up into the abdominal aorta. After the catheter is in place, the contrast-producing material is injected. It will light up and outline the abdominal aorta and its branches.

Apoplexy

See BLOOD VESSELS; NEUROSURGERY.

Appendicitis

The appendix is the wormlike structure projecting down from the cecum, the first portion of the large intestine, which is located in the right lower part of the abdomen. The appendix serves no function and is believed to be a vestige of man's primitive past. Normally, it is as thick as a lead pencil, and it varies in length from about one and a half to eight inches. When inflamed, infected, filled with pus, or gangrenous due to impairment of its blood supply, it may be enlarged eight to ten times its normal size.

The appendix moves about a great deal within the abdominal cavity and may assume several different positions. Because of this movement, the appendix, when inflamed, may cause symptoms that resemble diseases of other abdominal organs such as the ovaries, the fallopian tubes, the urinary bladder, the kidneys, the gallbladder, the liver, the stomach, or the large bowel.

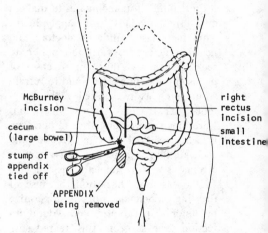

McBurney incision

cecum (large bowel)

stump of appendix tied off

APPENDIX being removed

right rectus incision

small intestine

Acute appendicitis occurs in both sexes, slightly more often in males than in females, at any age from a few months to 90 or more years. It is found most frequently in young adults. Its onset is usually abrupt, with generalized cramps throughout the entire abdomen, nausea, vomiting, and a slight rise in body temperature. Then, within 6 to 18 hours, the pain localizes in the right lower part of the abdomen. The patient is usually constipated and has little or no appetite. Examination will reveal tenderness and spasm of the abdominal muscles in the right lower part of the abdomen. A blood count, almost always performed to confirm the diagnosis, usually will show an increase in the white blood cells.

It must be mentioned, however, that only about 85 percent of all cases follow the typical pattern and sequence of events just described. In the remainder of the cases, some of the most characteristic symptoms, such as generalized cramplike pain, muscle spasm, or nausea and vomiting, may be absent, or the pain may be located on the left side of the abdomen or even in the upper portion of the abdominal cavity. Thus the physician or surgeon may find it quite difficult in such cases to make a conclusive diagnosis of appendicitis. This fact has stimulated doctors and health officials to warn the public to seek medical assistance in all cases of persistent abdominal pain and to refrain from giving laxatives to relieve the symptoms. Years ago, when operations were much more dangerous to perform, it was essential that a precise and accurate diagnosis be made. To operate erroneously for appendicitis in the 1920s was more hazardous because of the high incidence of postoperative pneumonia, peritonitis, and wound infection. The surgeon truly feared subjecting his patient to these risks unless it was absolutely necessary. *While surgeons are just as precise and accurate today in arriving at the correct diagnosis, they hesitate less in their decision to operate when the diagnosis is in doubt. This attitude has developed because it has been proved statistically that it is more dangerous not to operate in a doubtful case than to perform an exploratory procedure.* The penalty the patient pays for a missed diagnosis is peritonitis and possible death. The penalty he pays for having been operated upon in the presence of a normal appendix is little more than the economic loss occasioned by the opera-

tion plus the mild postoperative discomfort which he suffers for a few days.

The universal teaching in all medical circles therefore is *When in doubt, operate.*

There are other types of appendicitis, which have been variously labeled chronic appendicitis, recurrent appendicitis, mechanical appendicitis. These are characterized by occasional episodes of pain in the right lower portion of the abdomen, loss of appetite, nausea, constipation, on and off over a period of several months or years. Such conditions can be caused by partial obstruction of the lining of the appendix or by a marked kink in the appendix or by adhesions which press upon the appendix or that portion of the large intestine from which it originates. Although there is a sizable group of surgeons who doubt the existence of these types of appendicitis, all medical men have witnessed many instances where removal of the organ has resulted in complete freedom from further symptoms.

The treatment for appendicitis is immediate appendectomy (removal of the appendix). This can be the simplest of all major surgical procedures, or it can be one of the most difficult and taxing. A master surgeon may remove an appendix in seven to eight minutes or it may require two or more hours. Adhesions, abscess formation, location of the appendix in a remote position, all serve to prolong the operating time in certain cases. When the patient has had appendicitis for several days, it is not unusual to find the appendix inextricably bound down to adjacent loops of small intestine or intimately adherent to an abscess wall. In these cases, it is often wiser to merely drain off the pus and not risk the spread of the infection by attempting to remove the appendix. Luckily, this set of circumstances occurs in but one or two cases in a hundred. When it does happen, the patient is told to return in two to three months for the removal of the appendix during a quiescent period when all infection has subsided.

Appendectomy is performed either through an oblique muscle-splitting incision two to five inches long (the McBurney incision) in the right lower quadrant of the abdomen, or through a longitudinal incision of similar length. The appendix is delivered into the wound, its base is securely tied off, and the organ is cut across with a knife and removed. The abdominal wall is closed tightly in layers, except in a very small number of cases where the appendix has burst and peritonitis (pus in the abdominal cavity) has resulted. In these cases, the surgeon may insert one or more rubber tubes into the abdominal cavity in order to drain off pus. With the advent of the antibiotic drugs, drainage is necessary only rarely. Today peritonitis can be controlled remarkably well with surgical drainage plus the administration of antibiotics. Indeed, death following appendicitis is seldom seen except in those patients who have sought care too late in the course of the disease. Before the sulfa and antibiotic drugs, mortality rates for appendicitis ranged from 2.5 to 5 percent in the United States. Today the mortality rate has dropped to considerably less than 1 percent, and would practically disappear if people would call a physician when a pain in the abdomen continues for more than a few hours.

QUESTIONS AND ANSWERS

Is appendicitis caused by swallowing pits or other foreign bodies?
No.

Why must appendicitis be operated upon?
Because it rarely subsides by itself, if left alone, and in a large number of cases the appendix goes on to burst.

How long after the onset of appendicitis can an appendix burst?
Usually not until the condition has existed for one to three days.

What happens if the appendix bursts?
It spreads pus throughout the abdominal cavity, leading to peritonitis and death in approximately 25 percent of the untreated cases.

Do icebags help an attack of appendicitis to subside without operation?
No. However, a certain number of cases will undergo spontaneous subsidence.

If an attack of appendicitis subsides without surgery, does it tend to recur?
Yes. Any subsequent attack may be followed by rupture and peritonitis.

Does appendicitis ever develop without the patient's knowledge?
Yes. Every once in a while a patient has so little sensitivity to pain that he doesn't experience many of the usual symptoms. He may walk around with appendicitis, or even an abscess of the appendix, for many days before he feels sick enough to consult his physician.

Can appendicitis be cured medically?
In a small percentage of cases, huge doses of antibiotic drugs will halt the progress of an infection in the appendix. This is, however, a risky form of treatment and is followed by a much greater incidence of complication and failure than surgical removal of the organ.

How soon after the diagnosis is made should an operation be performed?
In an acute case, the patient should go to the hospital immediately and be

operated upon within several hours. In the recurrent or mechanical or chronic cases, surgery can be performed at the patient's convenience.

Is the white blood cell count always increased in attacks of appendicitis?
Not always. Usually the count rises from the normal of 6,000 to 8,000 white blood cells per cubic millimeter of blood to 10,000, 12,000, or even up to 20,000. However, a normal count does *not* rule out appendicitis.

Are there any other conditions involving the appendix besides ordinary infection?
Yes. In about 1 to 2 percent of those cases operated upon, a tumor of the appendix is found. These are called argentaffin tumors or carcinoids. They resemble a cancer microscopically but are less malignant in behavior.

Is appendectomy a serious operation?
Not usually. If the appendix has already ruptured and peritonitis has set in, it is a serious operation.

Are results from appendectomy usually good?
Yes; results are almost uniformly good.

How long a hospital stay is necessary?
1. For the average uncomplicated case, approximately one week.
2. For the ruptured appendix with or without peritonitis, the length of stay is prolonged to two to four weeks.

Are special preoperative preparations necessary?
No.

What type of anesthesia is used?
Either spinal or inhalation anesthesia can be used.

How long does it take to perform an appendectomy?
Anywhere from a few minutes to one to two hours, depending on the diseased state of the organ.

How long is the incision and where is it made?
Two to four or five inches in length. The incision is made in the right lower quadrant of the abdomen.

Is the incision painful after operation?
Only for the first two to three days.

How soon after surgery can the patient get out of bed?
In the uncomplicated case, the day following surgery. When peritonitis or other complications ensue, the patient may be forced to remain in bed for several days or even weeks.

Are blood transfusions usually given for appendicitis?
No. There is practically no blood loss in this condition.

Are any special postoperative routines followed?
In the uncomplicated case, no unusual postoperative treatments are given. Where peritonitis has set in, special measures, such as stomach tubes, intravenous medications, and antibiotics, are given. To rest the intestinal tract, nothing by mouth is ordered for the first day or two after operation.

Are special nurses necessary?
Only in the very sick cases, such as those associated with peritonitis or medical complications.

How long does it take an appendix wound to heal?
Approximately one week if it is not drained or infected. If it is infected or

drained, it may take several weeks to heal.

Is it common for an appendix wound to become infected?

Yes, because an infected organ has been removed through the wound.

Is it common for an appendix wound to collect serum?

Yes. A light pinkish-red fluid sometimes collects in the wound several days after the operation. This is drained off by the surgeon simply by inserting a clamp, and occasions the patient practically no discomfort.

Is an appendix scar disfiguring?

Not unless the wound has been drained or infected. Some scars of appendix operations are barely visible a year or so after operation.

Is convalescent care necessary?

Not in the great majority of cases. Usually only in those who have recovered from a severe peritonitis infection.

How soon can one return to work?

1. After the uncomplicated case: two to three weeks.

2. After peritonitis: six weeks to three months.

Does one have to follow a special diet after appendectomy?

No. Normal diet should be resumed as soon as the acute postoperative period has passed.

If constipated after appendectomy, can a laxative be taken?

It is best not to take a laxative until two to three weeks after recovery from appendectomy. However, an enema can be administered within a few days after surgery.

How soon can one bathe or shower after operation?

As soon as the wound is healed; usually within one week to ten days: If the wound is draining, sponge baths should be taken.

Is the appendix ever left in place during surgery?

Yes, in very seriously sick patients where generalized peritonitis exists and where the appendix is in an inaccessible position.

Should a patient whose appendix has been left in place return for its removal?

Yes. In six to ten weeks after hospital discharge.

Do appendix operations result in abdominal pain from adhesions?

No. Occasionally slight pain is felt in the operative region due to distention of the bowel with gas. This has no significance.

How soon after appendectomy can one do the following:

Take an automobile ride?	3 weeks
Drive a car?	4 weeks
Return to physical labor?	4 to 6 weeks
Do ordinary housework?	3 to 4 weeks
Lift heavy objects	6 to 8 weeks
Engage in ordinary athletic games?	6 to 8 weeks
Return to sexual relations?	3 to 4 weeks
Go dancing?	4 weeks

What is believed to cause appendicitis?

The exact cause is not known, but most surgeons agree that obstruction of the passageway in the appendix is a primary condition. Such an obstruction may result from inflammation caused by bacteria that reach the appendix through the bloodstream. The process may be mechanical, being initiated by a kink in the appendix or by a small hard concretion of feces blocking its passageway. Also, a fibrous growth that narrows the passageway of the structure may cause appendicitis. The appendix is easily obstructed because it has a small opening and no exit. In an occasional case, it is believed that infestation of the appendix by worms may initiate an inflammation.

Is the incidence of appendicitis on the decline?

Yes. In the United States appendicitis has decreased by approximately 50 percent within the past 20 years. The exact cause of this is not known.

Do people past 60 often develop appendicitis?

Yes, but it is much less common than in children and young adults.

Are the symptoms and signs of appendicitis different in older people?

In many instances it is much more difficult for the surgeon to make the diagnosis, because the symptoms are less marked. There may be a smaller temperature rise, less abdominal pain and tenderness, and a smaller rise in the white blood cell count, especially in those who are in their 70s or 80s.

Is there a greater tendency for an inflamed appendix to rupture or become gangrenous in aged people?

Yes. Arteriosclerosis of the blood vessels supplying the appendix may contribute to a rapid spread of inflammation, with early rupture or gangrene.

Can patients over 60 withstand an appendectomy as well as younger people?

Yes, if their heart, kidneys, and other vital organs are in satisfactory condition. The removal of the appendix is not a dangerous operation, particularly with modern anesthesia and operative techniques.

Is inhalation anesthesia preferred for older people undergoing an appendectomy?

Usually, yes.

Do people past 60 require special care after appendectomy?

Yes. They must be encouraged to resume physical activity immediately in order to restore circulation, which has a tendency to become sluggish following an operation. Also, they should be made to sit up in bed and to get out of bed as soon as possible in order to keep their lungs aerated and to decrease the chances of lung complications.

What conditions may be confused with appendicitis?

1. Gastroenteritis, or an upset stomach. A major distinction between this condition and appendicitis is the fact that diarrhea accompanies gastroenteritis whereas constipation is usually associated with appendicitis. Also, gastroenteritis tends to cause generalized abdominal pains without localizing in the right lower quadrant of the abdomen and without muscle spasm. Finally, gastroenteritis will usually subside within 24 to 48 hours, whereas the symptoms of true appendicitis will continue.

2. Mesenteric adenitis, a condition in which the lymph nodes that drain the small intestine are inflamed and the peritoneal lining of the abdominal cavity is irritated. This condition may cause many of the symptoms of appendicitis, and operations are sometimes performed on children with mesenteric adenitis because it is impossible to distinguish one condition from the other. In most instances, mesenteric adenitis will have been preceded by an upper respiratory infection, and the abdominal symptoms and signs of this condition are milder than those of an acute infection of the appendix.

3. An infection of the urinary tract. Such an infection may mimic appendicitis. For this reason, it is absolutely essential that a complete urinalysis be performed before diagnosis of and surgery for appendicitis.

4. Pneumonia. In young children, pneumonia in the right lower lobe of the lung may simulate appendicitis. An x-ray examination of the child's chest will usually clarify the diagnosis.

5. Meckel's diverticulitis. This is a condition that may mimic appendicitis. It is an inflammation of an outpouching of the small intestine in the right lower portion of the abdomen. The distinction between inflammation of this structure and appendicitis is the fact that there is usually blood in the stool with Meckel's diverticulitis but not with appendicitis.

6. A ruptured cyst of the right ovary. This condition may sometimes be confused with appendicitis. This takes place almost exclusively in adolescent girls who have already begun to menstruate. This condition can usually be distinguished from appendicitis because the symptoms almost invariably develop at a time in between a girl's menstrual periods, when the egg ruptures from the ovary.

7. An inflammation of the fallopian tube (salpingitis), with or without an inflammation of the ovary.

Are antibiotics alone effective in treating appendicitis?

Intensive doses of antibiotics can bring about a subsidence of certain mild cases of appendicitis. However, this is not considered to be good practice, because appendicitis has a tendency to recur. This type of treatment should be reserved for patients who are too sick from other causes to undergo surgery.

Is there any way to prevent appendicitis?

No.

Arterial Transplants

It has been found that shaped Dacron or Teflon grafts are much better than arteries themselves to replace damaged arteries. There is less tendency for clotting to take place within the transplant when an artificial substance such as Teflon or Dacron is used. Another reason that the plastic substances are better than transplanted blood vessels is that the rejection phenomenon does not take place. Today, these substances are widely utilized to replace segments of clotted or arteriosclerotic blood vessels such as the aorta in the abdomen and the major arteries in the pelvis, thighs, and legs.

See also BLOOD VESSELS.

Arteriography

Arteriography is an x-ray technique used for visualization of arteries. It is carried out by injecting an opaque substance, which produces contrast, directly into the arterial system. With this technique, it is possible to see the outlines of practically any artery in the body.

QUESTIONS AND ANSWERS

How is an arteriogram of the arteries in the neck and head performed?

By injecting an opaque substance directly into the carotid artery in the neck.

Can one visualize the arteries supplying the kidneys?

Yes, by inserting a catheter into the femoral artery in the groin and feeding it upward until it reaches the renal artery going to the kidney. An opaque substance is then injected through the catheter, and x-rays are taken.

Can one visualize the aorta with arteriography?

Yes, either by inserting a catheter through the femoral artery and feeding it up toward the aorta or by inserting a needle through the back directly into the aorta in the abdominal region. The aorta is then visualized by injecting an opaque material.

Can the arteries of the lower extremities be seen by means of arteriography?

Yes. By injection of an opaque material either through the aorta or through the femoral artery in the groin.

What types of abnormalities can be seen by arteriography?

1. Aneurysms
2. Birth deformities of the arteries
3. Arteriosclerosis
4. Thrombosis of an artery
5. Narrowing of an artery
6. Arteriovenous fistulas, false connections between an artery and a vein
7. Leakage from an artery, such as from a ruptured vessel in the brain, liver, kidney, stomach, intestines, etc.

Does blood vessel surgery often rely upon the results of arteriography?

Yes. Vascular (blood vessel) surgeons usually will not operate until they have a satisfactory set of arteriograms of the involved area. These will enable them to plan the surgery in advance.

Arteriosclerosis

See BLOOD VESSELS.

Arthritis

There are three major types of arthritis that can be helped surgically.

1. **Rheumatoid arthritis:** This type comes on during early adult life and is associated with swelling and deformity of the hands and elbows. It is encountered more often in women than in men. Its exact cause is unknown.

2. **Osteoarthritis** is a degenerative process seen mostly in people who are entering the later years. It is characterized mainly by joint deformity of the fingertips, the spine, the hips and lower extremities. There is relatively little joint swelling, but marked pain, limitation of motion (especially on arising in the morning), and evidence of calcium deposit around the joints as seen on x-rays.

3. **Infectious arthritis** is an inflammation of a joint secondary to bacterial invasion. Usually the process is limited to a single joint and is typified by redness, heat, and painful swelling of the involved joint. This type of arthritis can occur at any age.

Surgery for advanced rheumatoid arthritis of the hand is discussed elsewhere in this book. Suffice it to say that operative intervention is indicated when deformity and joint-and-tendon immobility interfere with adequate hand function.

Surgery for osteoarthritis can afford considerable relief in several different bodily areas. Often, when osteoarthritis involves the vertebrae of the spine and neck, irregular bony deposits will press upon nerves leaving the spine and will cause severe shooting pains (neuralgia) along the course of these nerves. Spinal fusion in such cases will frequently bring about relief by eliminating the motion and pressure upon the nerves.

In some cases of major joint osteoarthritis, the cartilage lining the joint tears, becomes flaky, and its edges will become heaped up and irregular. The joint may become extremely painful and motion will be limited. In certain cases of this type, great relief from pain may be obtained by fusing the joint. When this is done in a hip, a knee, or an ankle, the patient may walk with a limp, but often this is small price to pay for relief of pain and a strong, stable limb.

There are cases of osteoarthritis in which fusion is not necessary but a less radical procedure can produce fairly good results. Here, the surgeon smooths out and molds irregular joint surfaces and removes the diseased, thickened joint lining. After such surgery, an active course of physical therapy is required to keep the joint moving freely.

Perhaps one of the most dramatic advances in the orthopedic treatment of arthritis is *joint replacement with a metal appliance*. In properly selected cases, artificial metal joints can restore normal motion and stability to the limb. The hip, knee, shoulder, elbow, and finger all lend themselves to this type of surgery under appropriate circumstances. It must be kept in mind, however, that a joint is merely a fulcrum about which a limb moves, and if it lacks healthy surrounding muscles, tendons, and ligaments to supply power and direction, an artificial joint will be of little value.

There are other newly designed operations to aid the patient with a severely affected joint. In properly chosen cases, a strip of polyethylene plastic, a sheet of fibrous tissue grafted from the thigh, a specially designed metal cup, etc., can be placed between arthritic joint surfaces to act as a buffer and provide a smooth pivot about which the bones can glide.

Infectious bacterial arthritis can be controlled in many instances by administration of the appropriate antibiotic drug. However, when frank pus is present, it may be necessary to make an incision directly into the joint and evacuate the abscess.

QUESTIONS AND ANSWERS

What are the most common types of arthritis that lend themselves to surgical treatment?
1. Rheumatoid arthritis
2. Osteoarthritis
3. Infectious arthritis

What procedures are done for rheumatoid arthritis?
When a hand has become severely crippled by this disease, reconstructive hand surgery may be of great benefit. Swollen tissues can be removed, rough joint surfaces can be smoothed and molded, tendons can be freed of adhesions and given new sheaths, etc.

What are some of the operations that will help one with osteoarthritis?
1. Spinal fusion for severe osteoarthritis of the spine
2. Removal of painful bony growths about osteoarthritic joints
3. Joint fusion, especially about the hip, knee, or ankle
4. Removal of thickened, inflamed joint linings and molding of joint surfaces
5. In selected cases, replacement of severely damaged joints with artificial metal appliances

When is it necessary to operate for infectious arthritis?
When the infection fails to subside after antibiotic treatment and when a joint contains frank pus.

What is the difference between arthritis and bursitis?
Bursitis is an inflammation of the tissues around a joint. It involves soft tissues and not the bone. Arthritis is a disease of the entire joint, including its lining, the bones, and their covering.

Will cortisone or cortisonelike drugs cure arthritis?
No. They may bring about temporary relief in cases of rheumatoid arthritis, but when the medication is discontinued, symptoms usually reappear. Moreover, the steroid (cortisone and the like) drugs have little effect in cases of osteoarthritis and may be dangerous when given for infectious arthritis.

Arthroplasty

Arthroplasty is the term used to describe the plastic reconstruction or surgical replacement of a joint. It is a procedure performed most often when a joint is markedly restricted in its motion or is so painful that the patient is unable to bear weight upon it. Those joints most frequently subjected to arthroplasty are the hip joint, the shoulder joint, and the elbow joint. In arthroplasty, metals are used to replace the bones. The metal most often used is vitallium, which is a composite of cobalt, chromium, carbon, molybdenum, and manganese. Occasionally, SMO steel, an alloy, is used instead of the vitallium.

QUESTIONS AND ANSWERS

For what conditions is arthroplasty most frequently performed?
1. In any condition accompanied by permanent, painful restriction of joint motion

2. When a joint has been irrevocably destroyed by a severe fracture with failure of normal healing processes
3. When the bones making up a joint have been hopelessly destroyed by chronic arthritis or some other degenerative disease process
4. When it is necessary to remove a joint, or part of a joint, because of a bone tumor

What are some of the joints that can be replaced through arthroplasty?
The hip joint, the elbow joint, the shoulder joint, finger joints.

What metals are used to replace the bones?
The artificial joints (prosthetic devices) are composed of metals known as vitallium or SMO steel. Vitallium is a composite of several metals, including cobalt, chromium, carbon, molybdenum, manganese, etc. SMO steel is an alloy of stainless steel and molybdenum.

How successful is arthroplasty?
As this is a relatively new operative procedure, one must expect a certain number of failures. However, it is safe to state that great relief from pain and improvement in motion follow most of these operations. Of course, they must be performed only by specialists who have had wide experience in the field.

What is the most frequent cause for failure of an arthroplasty?
Postoperative infection. Should this take place and not be controlled, it may be necessary to remove the metal device.

If one arthroplasty procedure fails, is it possible to reoperate at a later date?
Yes, but results are likely to be less satisfactory. It is essential that all infection be cleared up before reinserting a metal device.

Is hip replacement a safe operation?

Yes. It not only has proven to be safe but has become the accepted procedure in cases of irreparable destruction of the head of the thighbone.

Is the hip socket ever replaced at the same time as the head of the thighbone?

Yes. It is essential that the metal head of the thighbone (femur) glide smoothly on the hip socket. To accomplish this, the bony socket is reamed out and a metal cup is inserted which will fit the new metal head of the femur.

Can both hip joints be replaced if they have been severely damaged by fracture or arthritis?

Yes. This operative procedure is being done regularly in many large orthopedic centers throughout the country.

Does rejection often set in when a metal hip arthroplasty has been carried out?

No. The body seems to accept the metal without attempting to reject it.

Can people walk again after hip arthroplasty?

Yes. Some may have a little limp but this will tend to disappear after the passage of several months' time.

Will arthroplasty relieve the pain of arthritis?

Yes. This is one of the main reasons for advocating its performance.

Can older people be subjected to hip replacement?

Yes. Many in their 70s and 80s have successfully undergone this operation.

Artificial Kidney

An artificial kidney is an apparatus especially designed to remove from the blood toxic substances that have accumulated because of renal (kidney) failure. The two poisons that accumulate in greatest quantity when the kidneys fail are urea and potassium. The artificial kidney is hooked up to the circulatory system of the patient so that blood flows through the apparatus. As the blood travels through, urea, potassium, and other toxic substances are removed.

QUESTIONS AND ANSWERS

What is the name given to the use of the artificial kidney?

It is called dialysis, or hemodialysis. A patient attached to an artificial kidney is said to undergo dialysis.

What is the composition of an artificial kidney?

It is a cellophane tube surrounded by a chamber containing fluids that approximate the composition of normal body fluids. The patient's blood is pumped through the tubing where poisons diffuse through the cellophane into the surrounding bath. The purified blood then flows back into the patient.

In what conditions will an artificial kidney prove helpful?

1. Chronic kidney deficiency with inability to eliminate urea, potassium, or other toxic substances

2. In an overwhelming infection, extensive burns, or acute kidney failure following surgical shock

3. In cases of poisoning by barbiturates, salicylates, bromides, arsenic, lead, mercury, and other chemicals

What substances can be removed from the blood with the artificial kidney?

1. Potassium
2. Urea

3. Poisons such as barbiturates, salicylates, and the heavy metals

Is an artificial kidney the same thing as a kidney transplant?

No.

Is dialysis helpful if there is an acute kidney shutdown, with failure of excretion of urine?

Yes. However, should the patient be unable to overcome the cause of the kidney failure, dialysis will not result in a cure.

Have lives ever been saved with the artificial kidney when patients have taken an overdose of poison?

Yes. Many people who reach the hospital in coma due to an overdose of a barbiturate or some other poison have been saved through use of the artificial kidney.

Can any doctor perform dialysis with an artificial kidney?

No. It requires a highly trained, experienced group of physicians working together as a team. Also, the paramedical personnel of the hospital must be fully aware of the complications of dialysis. It is therefore recommended that the procedure be carried out only in an institution which is fully familiar with the apparatus.

Is the repeated use of an artificial kidney helpful in tiding over a patient with destroyed kidneys until an organ for transplantation has been found?

Yes. Throughout the country, there are hundreds of people with destroyed kidneys who are kept alive for months by dialysis treatments two to three times a week. Then, when a donor kidney is available, they undergo kidney transplantation.

How long is a patient kept on an artificial kidney?

The treatment usually lasts five to six hours and is carried out two to three times a week. This is sufficient to keep the blood reasonably free from dangerous levels of poisonous accumulations.

Can a patient be taught to use an artificial kidney at home?

Yes, but he will need the cooperation of a member of his family. Approximately 2,000 to 3,000 people in this country are now utilizing artificial kidneys on a full or partial home basis.

Is it possible to sustain life with the artificial kidney when no kidney function exists?

Yes. There are a few dozen people with no kidneys at all, or kidneys totally destroyed by disease, who are being kept alive for weeks or months in the hope that a donor kidney will become available as a transplant.

Artificial Limbs

See AMPUTATIONS; RECONSTRUCTIVE ORTHOPEDIC SURGERY.

Atrial Defects

See HEART.

Back

Four-footed animals and man are both swayback. Somewhere along the line of evolution, *Homo sapiens* developed into a two-footed (biped) animal and his forefeet—or hands—were freed for more useful pursuits. But his back has paid the penalty ever since, as it was forced to develop four curves in order to maintain proper balance in

the upright posture! The resultant spinal column is subject to intense stresses and strains, being greatest at the waist, where the movable portion of the spine ends.
See also SPINE.

QUESTIONS AND ANSWERS

LOWER BACK PAIN

What are some of the common causes of lower back pain?
1. Injury from lifting heavy objects, for example, or from a fall with twisting of the back
2. Arthritis of the spine
3. Hernia of an intervertebral disk (slipped disk) or degeneration of the disks

What is the difference between lumbago, sacroiliac sprain, and slipped disk?
Lumbago is pain caused by a severe and prolonged spasm of the muscles in the lower back region, secondary to an injury or to any of the other causes of lower back pain. It is now thought that sacroiliac sprain is a nonexistent condition and that the symptoms are, in reality, caused by a slipped disk.

What takes place when a slipped disk occurs?
Some of the cartilage that normally forms a cushion between the various vertebral bodies is dislocated and slips from its normal position into one in which it is subject to pressure each time a person moves. This creates great pain.

Are there certain types of people who are more prone to lower back pain?
Yes, those who are born with weakness or abnormalities in the structure of the vertebrae in the lumbar or sacral regions or who have poorly developed back musculature.

How can one tell beforehand whether his back is susceptible to sprain or to a slipped disk?
Usually this is not possible to forecast. In some instances x-rays will demonstrate malformations which should warn an individual against strenuous physical labors.

What is sciatica (sciatic neuritis)?
Sciatic neuritis is associated with pain along the course of the nerve, that is, pain starting in the lower back and descending to the buttock, back of the thigh, calf, and on to the foot.

If a patient has once had an attack of lower back pain, does this predispose him toward a chronic or recurring condition?
Yes.

Will wearing a back brace, a strongly constructed corset, or other orthopedic appliance prevent one from developing pain in the lower back?
Yes, insofar as a good support will tend to prevent sudden twisting movements of the spine and will remind the patient that he must be careful to avoid excessive physical strain.

What are the symptoms that distinguish the various conditions causing lower back pain, such as lumbago, sciatic neuritis, or slipped disk?
Lumbago is accompanied by muscle tenderness and pain either in the center of the back or on one side. (It is not a term descriptive of a disease but merely represents a symptom.) Sciatic neuritis and slipped disk often produce the same set of symptoms, described above.

What is the usual medical treatment for chronic lower back pain?
1. Sleeping on a firm mattress with a board between the mattress and the bedspring
2. Taking salicylates or other pain-

relieving medications at regular intervals

3. Application of superficial and deep heat treatments

4. Prescribed exercises to relieve spasm and strengthen the back musculature

5. Avoidance of sudden movements and excessive physical strain.

Is there any satisfactory surgical treatment for chronic lower back pain?

If the pain is due to a birth deformity of the spine, a spinal-fusion operation will often eliminate the pain, by stiffening and thus limiting painful movements of the vertebrae. If the pain is caused by a slipped disk, surgical removal of the dislocated disk will often bring about a cure.

Can emotional imbalance cause chronic lower back pain?

Yes, but before it is decided that the symptoms are emotional in origin, it is essential to rule out all organic causes.

Do thin people have a greater tendency than fat people to develop chronic conditions of the lower back?

No.

Should people with chronic lower back pain perform heavy physical duties?

No.

What motions are most likely to produce recurrences of lower back pain or sprain?

1. Sudden forward bending

2. Sudden rotation of the trunk

3. Unbraced lifting of heavy objects

Do infections, such as infected teeth, tonsils, or sinuses, play an important role in the causation of chronic conditions involving the lower back?

No. This was held to be true years ago, but today it is generally accepted that there is little correlation between infections and conditions involving the muscles and bones of the lower back.

How effective are physiotherapy treatments, such as diathermy, whirlpool baths, or muscle exercises, in relieving or treating chronic conditions of the lower back?

If used judiciously, these treatments are very helpful in relieving painful conditions of the lower back.

How can one tell when to discard back supports or other orthopedic appliances?

If pain and discomfort have ceased for approximately six months, gradual discontinuance of such appliances is permissible. At first, they should be discarded for short periods of time, until finally, after several weeks of freedom from symptoms, they can be abandoned completely.

Do x-rays always reveal the presence or absence of conditions of the lower back?

No. It is necessary, under certain circumstances, to perform highly specialized x-ray studies to uncover evidence of lower back disease. And even when special studies are conducted, the

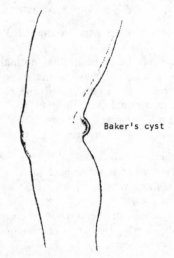

Baker's cyst

x-rays may not reveal the nature of the particular ailment.

Should those with chronic backache take cortisone or similar medications?
Although these medications may alleviate symptoms, they do not bring about a cure. Moreover, if these drugs are taken over a long period of time, unfavorable side effects may develop. Certainly, cortisone should never be taken unless it has been prescribed by a doctor.

Baker's Cyst

A Baker's cyst is a fluid-filled sac of varying size in the back of the knee. Occasionally these cysts may so enlarge that they appear at the inner side of the knee as well.

QUESTIONS AND ANSWERS

Are Baker's cysts most common among cooks and bakers?
No. They are called Baker's cysts because they were first described by an English surgeon named Baker.

Are Baker's cysts connected with the knee joint itself?
They are most often connected with the inside of the knee joint, although a valvelike fold of tissue often serves to separate the fluid of the cyst from the joint.

Are all masses in the back of the knee Baker's cysts?
No. Blood vessel enlargements (aneurysms) and tumors may also occur in the back of the knee.

What is the treatment for a Baker's cyst?
Surgical removal.

Is removal of a Baker's cyst a serious operation?
No. Recovery is usually complete, and there is no interference with the function of the knee following surgery.

Baldness

Within recent years some plastic surgeons and dermatologists have utilized hair transplants to hide baldness. In this procedure, carried out under great magnification, the surgeon or dermatologist removes a hair and its follicle from the fringes of the scalp and transplants it into a bald area on the top of the head. In order for it to succeed, the implant must "take" in much the same way as any other graft must survive in its new location. As one can surmise, it is a long and tedious process to transplant a sufficient number of hairs so as to cover a significant area of baldness. The operation must be done in several sessions extending over a period of weeks or months.

QUESTIONS AND ANSWERS

Is surgery for baldness successful?
It is too early to state, as the procedure is only in an experimental stage. Some people have claimed satisfactory results, especially when the bald area is not too large.

Will all hairs that are transplanted survive?
No. A considerable number of transplanted hairs will die.

Can surgery for baldness be carried out all at one sitting?
No. It is a tedious job in which a limited number of hairs can be trans-

planted at any one time. It is therefore necessary for people who wish this kind of surgery to have repeated procedures.

Are all plastic surgeons or dermatologists equipped to perform baldness surgery?

No. There is a very small number of surgeons or dermatologists who perform this type of work.

Can hair from distant parts of the body be transplanted to the scalp?

It is mechanically possible, but the hair would look unnatural if transplanted from another part of the body.

Can full-thickness segments of skin with hair be transplanted from one part of the body to another?

Yes, but there is a tendency for hairs so transplanted to die, thus leaving a bald spot.

Bandaging

Every adult should learn the rudiments of bandaging. There are several excellent first aid manuals from which one can learn, so that if an emergency arises, and bandaging is needed, one can be of assistance.

An important fact to keep in mind is never to apply a bandage so tightly that it interferes with circulation. It is much better to apply a bandage too loosely than too tightly.

See also FIRST AID.

Bartholin Glands and Cysts

The Bartholin glands are located in the lower part of the major lips surrounding the opening of the vagina.

Their function is to secrete mucus into the region of the vaginal entrance. The purpose of these secretions is to lubricate the area during intercourse. Mucus exits from the glands through narrow ducts, and it is not at all uncommon for one or both of these ducts to become blocked by inflammation or infection. As a consequence, the gland enlarges and forms a cyst or abscess. A noninfected cyst of a Bartholin gland may cause no symptoms and may remain small, attaining a size no larger than a pea. On the other hand, some cysts grow to the size of a lemon and cause great pain. The majority of cysts eventually do become infected and will require surgery.

There are three main surgical procedures performed to cure cysts or infections of the Bartholin glands:

1. The cyst or abscess may be needled and the fluid or pus within it withdrawn. (This procedure can be carried out in a gynecologist's office.)

2. A Bartholin cystectomy may be performed with complete excision of the entire gland. This procedure is not used very often today. It has been

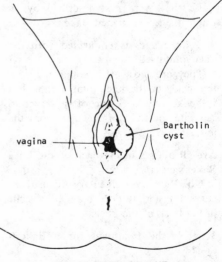

CYST OF BARTHOLIN GLAND

replaced by a lesser operation that produces equally good results.

3. The procedure in common use today is called marsupialization. This operation consists of opening the cyst or abscess, evacuating its contents, and stitching the edges of the gland to the skin of the labia.

This operation has been found to be as effective as total removal of the gland, and it entails much less dissection and less discomfort to the patient.

QUESTIONS AND ANSWERS

What are the symptoms of a Bartholin cyst?

There may be no symptoms, if the cyst is small, or there may be pain when walking and during intercourse.

What is a Bartholin abscess?

It is an infected cyst.

What are the symptoms of a Bartholin abscess?

Pain and tenderness in the area, along with fever and a discharge of pus if the abscess should break.

Do Bartholin cysts always have to be removed?

Not necessarily. Very often the small ones which cause no symptoms are left alone. They should, however, be examined periodically by the gynecologist.

Does one have to go to the hospital for an operation upon a Bartholin cyst or abscess?

Yes, unless the gynecologist merely aspirates the cyst or abscess in his office.

What is the surgical treatment of a Bartholin abscess?

Incision and drainage under general anesthesia. Often, infected cysts recur and require further surgery. Complete excision or marsupialization (sewing the edges of the cyst to the skin and leaving it open) are then performed. This type of treatment is best carried out after the acute infection has subsided.

Where is the incision made when operating upon a Bartholin gland?

Just inside the vaginal lips, directly over the cyst.

How long a hospital stay is necessary for an operation upon a Bartholin cyst or abscess?

The patient usually can leave the hospital on the third day after surgery.

What kind of anesthesia is given for an operation upon a Bartholin cyst or abscess?

General inhalation anesthesia.

How long after an operation upon a Bartholin gland can intercourse be resumed?

When complete healing has taken place. This is usually a matter of four to five weeks.

Basal Cell Cancer

A basal cell cancer is a skin tumor that forms on exposed areas of the body. More than 90 percent of cases involve the head or neck. They usually consist of roundish small areas that begin as pea-sized lesions but may grow to the size of a dime or nickel. Basal cell cancers are also called epitheliomas or rodent ulcers. The latter name is given to this type of cancer because it has a tendency to ulcerate and to form scabs.

Diagnosis of a basal cell cancer can usually be made by knowledge of the history of the lesion. The characteristic history is that of a sore which does not heal over a period of several weeks or months. Some of these lesions can be diagnosed by noting a pearl-colored, raised border around the circumference of the tumor.

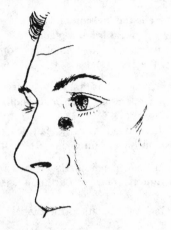

A basal cell cancer of the skin is frequently found on the side of the nose. It is usually curable by surgery or x-ray treatment.

QUESTIONS AND ANSWERS

Can a basal cell cancer of the skin be cured?

Yes. Cure can be brought about in 100 percent of cases unless the patient has not sought treatment until the tumor has spread extensively to surrounding tissues.

Do basal cell cancers often spread to distant parts of the body?

No. They are a locally destructive tumor but they rarely threaten life.

What is the treatment for basal cell cancer?

There are three main types of treatment:

1. X-ray radiation
2. Electrocoagulation with an electric needle

3. Complete excision of the tumor and surrounding normal skin and underlying tissue

For what cases is each type of treatment indicated?

1. X-ray radiation is usually reserved for small basal cell cancers located in areas where it is technically easier to use x-rays than to excise the lesion surgically.

2. Electrocoagulation is usually reserved for small, early basal cell tumors.

3. Excision is carried out for the larger, invading basal cell lesions. In these instances, it is good practice to replace the excised tissue with a free skin graft.

Is there much disfigurement following treatment of a basal cell cancer?

No. Even large tumors leave very little disfigurement because grafts, usually taken from skin behind the ear, blend well into the skin of the nose or face. It will, of course, take several months or years before the line marking the site of the graft disappears.

Benign Tumors

All tumors are classified as benign or malignant. This is a rather sharp delineation and perhaps is not as accurate as it might be, for some tumors are benign but so potentially malignant that they constitute a danger to life. Other tumors classified as malignant grow so slowly and show so little tendency to spread and endanger life that they should probably be classified as benign. In medical parlance, a benign tumor is one that remains localized at its point of origin, shows little or no tendency to spread to distant parts of the body, and seldom endangers life. On microscopic examination of a benign tumor, the pathologist will note that the cells vary very little from normal and show no atypical characteristics. The evidence of benignity or of malignancy is confined to the characteristics of the individual tumor cells and relates to their adherence to or deviation from normal. Thus, a benign tumor cell will have a relatively normal nucleus, whereas a malignant cell will have mitotic figures within the nucleus and will show an abnormal tendency to divide and grow rapidly. In addition to the configuration of the individual cells, a benign tumor is characterized by lack of invasiveness. This means that the tumor stays within bounds, is rather well circumscribed, and does not appear to break out into surrounding tissues. On the other hand, a cancer, or malignant tumor, breaks through the normal tissue boundaries and invades surrounding tissues indiscriminately.

QUESTIONS AND ANSWERS

What are some of the common benign tumors?

Almost all organs and tissues can be the site of a benign tumor. Benign fatcell tumors are called lipomas. Benign tumors of connective tissue are called fibromas. Benign glandular tumors are called adenomas. Benign skin tumors take many forms, including keratosis, skin polyps, moles, and the common wart. Benign tumors within the skull and involving the covering of the brain are known as meningiomas. Benign tumors of the vocal cords are known as laryngeal polyps.

Are there any organs or structures in the body that are free from the possibility of benign tumor formation?

No. Every organ or tissue in the body is capable of undergoing tumor formation, either benign or malignant.

Will the removal of a benign tumor stimulate the formation of a cancer?

No. It is a common misconception that the removal of a benign tumor may stimulate recurrence and a cancerous change. This superstition is completely unfounded.

Can a pathologist always tell whether a tumor is benign or malignant?

No. There are a certain number of tumors that defy classification. Such tumors and sufficient surrounding tissue should be removed, and the patient should be observed periodically over several years to make sure that recurrence does not take place. At the slightest sign of recurrence of a tumor of this type, reoperation is indicated.

Can a benign tumor ever be dangerous?

Yes, on occasion. Every once in a while, a benign tumor will grow to such size that by pressure upon other organs it will endanger their health and life. As an example, some fibroid tumors of the uterus have grown to such size that they have caused obstruction of the intestines; some lipomas (fatty tumors) have grown to such size that they have interfered with the function of other organs.

Do benign tumors ever turn into malignant ones?

Yes, but the great majority of malignant tumors are thought to arise as cancers from their very earliest stages of development. Despite this fact, there is a sizable group of benign tumors that will become malignant if they are not removed.

How can one tell when a benign tumor is undergoing change and becoming malignant?

There are several indications, the most important ones being:

1. Any skin growth that becomes ulcerated, bleeds, and forms a sore that does not heal over a period of several weeks should be suspected of undergoing malignant changes.

2. Any mole that changes color and starts to grow in size should be suspected of becoming malignant.

3. Any tumor anywhere in the body that abruptly undergoes an increase in size should become suspect.

4. Any benign tumor that has been quiescent for a long period of time and then suddenly starts to bleed should be suspected of possible malignant change.

Is it safer to ignore a benign tumor or to have it removed?

It is far safer to have every benign tumor removed surgically, because no physician can ever be positive that it will not one day undergo malignant degeneration. Even the most benign lipoma, mole, fibrous tumor, or adenoma can turn into a malignant, spreading growth.

Biliary Colic

Biliary colic is the term used for the severe, sudden, excruciating pain in the right upper part of the abdomen that accompanies the obstruction of the gallbladder or bile ducts by a stone. The pain is caused by the intense contractions of the gallbladder, or its bile ducts, in an attempt to pass the bile beyond the obstructing stone. The characteristic pain is extremely intense and usually radiates from the right upper part of the abdomen through to the back or to the right shoulder region. The pain can stop as quickly as it begins if the stone is passed through the duct or if it drops back into the gallbladder or duct. Biliary colic tends to be recurrent until the stone is either passed into the intestinal tract or removed surgically.

See also GALLBLADDER.

Biliary Obstruction

Obstruction to the flow of bile from the liver or gallbladder through its ducts into the intestines is almost invariably associated with jaundice. This results in yellow discoloration of the whites of the eyes and the skin, a lightening of the stool with eventual development of a clay color, and a deepening of the yellow color of the urine. If obstruction to the flow of bile is not relieved, the patient will develop liver damage. This may exist for several weeks before its signs become evident.

Biliary obstruction is most commonly caused by:

1. A stone in the common bile duct leading from the liver to the intestines.

2. A tumor of the head of the pancreas which surrounds the exit of the bile duct into the duodenum, the first portion of the small intestine.

3. A tumor of the bile ducts themselves.

4. An inflammation with a plug of mucus causing sufficient swelling of the terminal end of the common bile ducts so that bile cannot get through. This is seen in certain types of hepatitis.

5. A tumor within the liver in the region of the bile ducts, pressing upon the ducts, and causing obstruction to the outflow of bile.

6. Advanced cirrhosis of the liver with compression of the bile ducts as they enter from the liver.

See also GALLBLADDER; JAUNDICE.

Biopsy

A biopsy is the removal of tissues from the body so that they may be examined both grossly and under a microscope. Whenever the exact diagnosis of a localized or generalized lesion is desired and cannot be made without examining the tissues directly, a biopsy is performed.

QUESTIONS AND ANSWERS

Who usually performs a biopsy?

Most biopsies are performed by a surgeon or physician specially trained to do the procedures. Biopsies are sometimes taken in the physician's office, at other times in the operating room of a hospital. Once the tissues are removed, they are examined by a pathologist.

For what conditions are tissues most frequently taken for biopsy?

1. For tumors, to distinguish between a benign or malignant condition. The tumor may be located anywhere in the body, including the skin, tissues directly beneath the skin, the breast, or any other tissue within the skull, chest cavity, or abdomen.

2. Blood diseases in which an exact diagnosis of the abnormality is necessary. In this instance, a biopsy is taken from the bone marrow by inserting a needle into the hipbone or breastbone. A bone marrow study is then carried out by the hematologist or pathologist.

3. Biopsies of lymph nodes (glands) are extremely common in order to make a diagnosis of a tumor, leukemia, Hodgkin's disease, lymphosarcoma, or other gland conditions.

4. Liver biopsies are sometimes performed by inserting a needle through the right side of the chest directly into the liver and sucking out a few cells. This may enable one to learn whether there is a tumor within the liver or whether there is inflammation or disease of the liver.

5. Splenic biopsies are sometimes taken in blood diseases. This will reveal the exact kind of blood condition from which the patient is suffering.

6. Skin biopsies are often taken by dermatologists to determine the exact nature of a dermatitis or other kind of skin lesion.

Does the surgeon try to take out all of the diseased tissue or just a piece of it when he performs a biopsy?

If it is feasible to remove all of the lesion, he will do so. For example, if there is just one enlarged lymph node, the surgeon generally will remove the entire node and send it to the laboratory. On the other hand, if an entire organ such as the liver or spleen is suspected of being diseased, then only a small piece of tissue will be removed for biopsy purposes.

Is a large specimen required in order to perform a satisfactory microscopic examination?

Usually not.

How soon after tissues have been removed will the pathologist be able to give a final diagnosis?

This can sometimes be given almost immediately. In other instances, it may take several days before the pathologist will be able to render a definite diagnosis.

What is a frozen section?

The term frozen section refers to the fact that the tissue is quick-frozen in order to make it suitable for immediate microscopic examination. The tissue is taken from the patient while he is on the operating table and is submitted immediately to the pathologist, who usually has the frozen-section apparatus close to the operating room. In this way, the operating surgeon will find out quickly what he is dealing with and will be able to direct his operation accordingly.

Are frozen-section biopsies always accurate?

No. There are certain types of tissues that do not lend themselves to immediate microscopic diagnosis. However, recent advances in the methods of taking frozen sections have made them almost as accurate as the more time-consuming methods of preparing tissues in a laboratory.

What is the special value of a frozen-section biopsy?

It will give an immediate answer, in most instances, to whether the tissue submitted for examination is benign or malignant. This is often the most decisive factor in determining what type of operation a surgeon will perform.

Can a diagnosis of cancer of the lung be made through biopsy?

In some cases, yes. This will entail the passage of a metal tube from the mouth down the throat and into the windpipe. The procedure is known as bronchoscopy. The bronchoscopist will often be able to see a lesion obstructing a bronchial tube in the tumor area. He will then be able to take a piece of the tumor and remove it for microscopic examination.

What is a scalenus node biopsy?

This is a procedure in which an incision is made at the base of the neck, and lymph nodes that lie above the dome of the lungs are removed and sent to the laboratory for examination. If these nodes show cancer, removal of the lung will in all probability be of little help to the patient. If, on the other hand, the biopsy is negative, the surgeon will proceed to operate for removal of the lung tumor.

What is meant by a needle biopsy?

This is a test whereby a needle is placed into a diseased area, and cells or contents are withdrawn and examined by the pathologist.

Are needle biopsies always as accurate as ordinary biopsies?

No, because the amount of tissue that can be obtained from needle withdrawal is sometimes so small that it makes interpretation difficult.

What is an incisional biopsy?

It is cutting into a diseased area with a scalpel and removing a portion of it. This fragment is subjected to gross and microscopic examination by the pathologist.

What is an excisional biopsy?

It is the removal of the entire diseased area, which is then submitted to the pathologist for diagnosis.

Birth Deformities of the Extremities

The presence at birth of a skeletal or muscular deformity is a sad occurrence which casts a shadow over an otherwise happy event. Fortunately, congenital deformities of this type are relatively rare, and modern treatment has progressed to a point where great benefit can be obtained when they are encountered. Of the 30 to 40 different orthopedic abnormalities seen at birth, many have a strong heredity factor. Actually, it is known that birth deformities are found ten times more often in children where there is a family history of a similar kind of condition. Clubfoot, congenital dislocation of the hip, and supernumerary digits (extra fingers or toes) are among the most common of these malformations.

Other deformities, such as the absence of a part of an arm or leg, are seen very rarely and are attributed to a failure of normal development of the embryo. Still another group of deformities, of which torticollis (wryneck) is perhaps the most common, is thought to arise from an injury to the developing embryo.

Conservative, or nonoperative, treatment will succeed in the great majority of instances in correcting or alleviating the symptoms of these deformities. To achieve good results, treatment must be begun immediately after birth and must continue, without interruption, until maximum improvement or cure has been obtained. Surgery is reserved for the small number of cases in which the nonoperative form of treatment has failed.

Congenital clubfoot is a deformity in which the foot is foreshortened, flexed on the ankle, and turned inward. It is often seen in conjunction with other deformities elsewhere in the body. It occurs more often in boys.

The conservative treatment of clubfoot consists of placing the foot in the correct position and maintaining it there with a plaster cast. The cast is changed frequently, and at the time of the change, the foot is manipulated so that eventually it will be maintained in an overcorrected position. Treatment should be begun immediately after birth.

If the nonoperative treatment should fail to bring the desired results, surgical intervention is in order. A *plantar stripping* procedure may be performed on a child between the ages of 1½ to 3 years. This operation, done under general anesthesia, calls for an incision about two inches long on the inner aspect of the foot. The fibrous tissues beneath the skin in the sole of the foot are stripped away from the bones so as to permit the foot to assume a more normal position. To further this end, one of the important tendons (the posterior tibial) is partially severed and lengthened. The skin is then closed and a plaster cast applied in the corrected position.

A second operation is frequently performed at a later age to lengthen the heel cord (Achilles tendon) and thus permit the heel to touch the ground. This is done through a small skin incision on the inner aspect of the heel.

Still other operations are advocated in older children or adults who have had inadequate early treatment. Some of these procedures are extremely complicated and involve removal of portions of the bones of the foot and fusion of certain of the joints. Highly satisfactory results can be obtained from many of these operations, although it is often necessary to sacrifice mobility (the ability to move) in favor of stability and good position.

The important point to make in regard to treating clubfoot is that each surgical procedure must be followed by intensive nonoperative treatment. Failure to do this will lead to recurrence of the deformity.

See also CLUBFOOT.

Congenital dislocation of the hip is a serious malformation seen about seven times more often in females than in males. It may occur in one or both hips but is much more common in the left hip. Its cause is unknown but heredity undoubtedly plays a strong role.

Specifically, the condition is one in

which the head of the femur (thigh-bone) fails to stay in its socket. Instead, it rides up high on the ilium (a bone of the pelvis). The condition is often not diagnosed until the child attempts to walk, at which time a limp is noted if the deformity is one-sided and a waddle is present if the dislocation involves both hips.

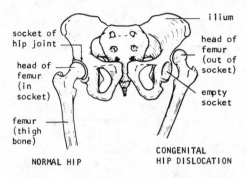

socket of hip joint

head of femur (in socket)

femur (thigh bone)

NORMAL HIP

ilium

head of femur (out of socket)

empty socket

CONGENITAL HIP DISLOCATION

Conservative, nonoperative treatment can cure the majority of these unfortunate children, but to obtain the best results, it must be started during the first year of life. Treatment consists of traction (pulling) on the leg in order to bring down the head of the femur into its socket. Once this has been accomplished—and it sometimes takes several weeks of steady pulling—the position must be maintained by plaster fixation. The plaster must be worn anywhere from 6 to 18 months in order to prevent the head of the femur from slipping out again.

When the foregoing line of attack fails, an operation must be performed. An incision is made on the front of the thigh over the pelvic bone. Tight and deforming muscles are lengthened, and the head of the thighbone is levered into the hip joint after the socket has been cleared of soft tissue. The natural socket (acetabulum) is occasionally deepened by turning down a flap of

bone from the wing of the ilium. This maneuver will form a shelf to hold the head of the femur in place. It may also be necessary to divide the thighbone and reposition it so that when it heals, the hip is snugly directed into the joint socket. The wound is closed and a plaster cast extending from the toes to the chest is applied.

There are other operations to correct congenital dislocation of the hip. All are effective when performed by competent orthopedists on properly selected patients. Although this surgery is of major proportions, recovery is the general rule and results are usually most satisfactory.

Congenital wryneck (torticollis) is a condition in which the child is born with his head twisted to one side. It is due to a contracture (shortening) of one of the largest muscles in the neck, the sternocleidomastoid. If the condition is left uncorrected, the head, face, and spine may become asymmetrical.

Conservative methods in early infancy are tried first, with gentle stretching of the neck, massage, and braces. However, when this approach fails—as it often does—operation is resorted to. The surgical procedure, a simple one, consists of making an incision in the lower neck and cutting the sternocleidomastoid muscle loose from its attachment to the collarbone. The child's head is then rotated to a slightly overcor-

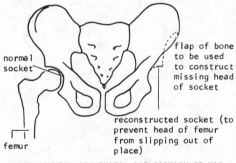

normal socket

femur

flap of bone to be used to construct missing head of socket

reconstructed socket (to prevent head of femur from slipping out of place)

OPERATION FOR CONGENITAL DISLOCATION OF HIP

rected position and is fixed in that manner in plaster for several weeks. The surgery is not dangerous and the end results are rewarding.

QUESTIONS AND ANSWERS

Are birth deformities more common in families that have a history of such deformities?

Yes. Unfortunately, many of these deformities tend to be inherited through the genes. If the parents have one child with a limb abnormality, the incidence of a second child being born with a deformity is many times greater than in the general population.

What are the most frequently encountered deformities of the extremities?

1. An extra finger or toe
2. Webbed fingers or toes
3. Absent fingers or toes
4. Clubhand
5. Phocomelia (absence of a portion of the arm or leg)
6. Annular bands
7. Absence of an entire arm or leg
8. Congenital wryneck (torticollis)
9. Congenital dislocation of the hip
10. Congenital clubfoot
11. Congenital coxa vara
12. Congenital discoid meniscus
13. Congenital pseudarthrosis of the tibia (shinbone)
14. Osteogenesis imperfecta

Are deformities of the fingers or toes inherited?

Yes. They are seen in greater numbers in families having a history of previous members who were deformed. Fortunately, many deformities of fingers or toes can be repaired shortly after birth.

What is the treatment for a sixth finger or toe (supernumerary digit) that is located next to the little finger or little toe?

It should be removed. This is a simple operative procedure and can often be performed before the newborn leaves the hospital.

What is the treatment for an extra thumb?

Before surgery is performed, it must be determined which thumb has the better bone support and better tendon structure. Quite often, the smaller thumb functions better than the larger one. If this is found to be the case, the smaller thumb should be saved and the larger one amputated. If a decision is made to save the larger thumb even though it has inadequate tendon supply, then the tendons from the smaller thumb must be transferred to the larger thumb.

What is the treatment for a child born with fingers missing?

If the thumb is absent, surgery is performed to rotate the index finger into the thumb's position. The finger is shortened, brought farther up on the hand, and transferred along with its tendons and nerves. This is called a pollicization. The new "thumb" results in a hand that both functions and appears more normal.

If fingers are absent from the center of the hand (middle or ring fingers), hand surgeons can bring the adjacent fingers together and close the palm for better function and appearance.

Is a pollicization operation dangerous?

No. It is a highly delicate operation done only by specialists in hand surgery, but it is not dangerous to the patient and can usually be performed in one stage.

Is webbing of the fingers and toes a common birth abnormality?

Yes.

Can surgery be performed to correct webbed fingers?

Yes. Surgery is usually recommended between the ages of 2 and 4 years. Release of the web consists of transferring portions of skin to the base of the newly formed cleft and covering the sides of the fingers with either rotated skin or skin grafts.

Are the bones also involved in webbed fingers?

Frequently the bones are also fused together. Surgery can separate these fused bones, but the procedure is more extensive than releasing a simple syndactyly (webbing of the skin only).

Is it necessary to correct webbed toes?

No. The toes can function quite satisfactorily when webbed.

What is a clubhand?

It is a birth deformity characterized by the partial or complete absence of one of the bones of the forearm. Usually it is the radius (the forearm bone on the thumb side) that is affected.

What is the appearance of a clubhand?

The hand forms a 90-degree angle with the forearm and frequently cannot be replaced in normal alignment. Most often the entire limb is shortened, the forearm is curved, and there are abnormalities of the hand consisting of a small or absent thumb and stiffness of the fingers.

How is a clubhand treated?

Casts or splints may be applied to prevent the deviation of the hand from becoming too severe. When the hand cannot be realigned at the end of the forearm, surgery should be performed.

What type of surgery is done for a clubhand?

The soft tissues on the concave (thumb) side of the forearm must first be released. This includes dividing or lengthening tight tendons and providing more skin by appropriate skin transfers. Usually at a second procedure, the hand is realigned at the end of the forearm and held there either by bone graft, by wrist fusion, or by fashioning a socket in the wrist bones for the forearm.

Is surgery usually successful for a clubhand?

Yes. There is usually great improvement in both the function and appearance of the hand.

What is phocomelia?

Phocomelia is a birth abnormality in which a portion of the forearm, arm, leg, or thigh is absent; and parts of the limb farther away from the body (the hand or foot) are normal. Thus the hand may attach directly to the shoulder, or the leg may attach directly to the pelvis.

Can an expectant mother do anything to prevent having her child born with phocomelia?

To a certain extent, yes. She should avoid taking any drugs or medications without the advice of her obstetrician. She should not take "samples," home remedies, or medications used by friends or other members of the family. She should inform any doctor she visits that she is pregnant so that he may be appropriately guided in his prescription of drugs and x-rays.

Can phocomelia be treated successfully by surgery?

Usually not. It has been found, however, that even very short or deformed limbs can often be used to help fit or move an artificial limb and should not be removed without careful study. Even a few fingers attached directly to the shoulder have been sucessful in working an artificial arm.

Is absence of an entire arm or leg a common deformity?
No. Fortunately it is an exceedingly rare deformity.

What is wryneck (torticollis)?
It is a twisted neck found at birth.

What causes wryneck?
Wryneck may be due to a tightening and scarring of one of the large neck muscles (the sternocleidomastoid muscle). This is thought to be caused by abnormal position of the fetus before birth. Occasionally, wryneck may be due to abnormality of the bones of the neck (Klippel-Feil syndrome) or the shoulder (Sprengel's deformity).

Do children tend to outgrow wryneck?
No.

What is the nonoperative treatment of wryneck?
Gentle and persistent stretching of the tight muscles. The child should be encouraged to turn his head toward the tightened side. The crib should be placed so that the window or his favorite toy is toward the side of involvement. Casts are frequently used to straighten the neck.

What is the surgical treatment of wryneck?
The tightened and scarred muscle is removed. It is cut both above the collarbone and below the mastoid bone of the ear.

Is surgery for wryneck dangerous?
No.

Are the results of wryneck surgery usually satisfactory?
Yes.

What is congenital dislocation of the hip?
It is a congenital deformity of the pelvis and hip that makes the thigh (hip) tend to ride up out of its socket.

Is congenital dislocation of the hip more common in boys or in girls?
It is seven times more frequent in girls than in boys.

What is a dysplastic or subluxated hip?
A dysplastic hip is one in which the hip socket is shallow but no dislocation has taken place. A subluxated hip is one that is shifted out of its normal position but still maintains contact with the joint.

Are children frequently born with the hip completely dislocated?
No. Most frequently they are born with a dysplastic hip that gradually subluxates and then dislocates as the child begins to stand and walk.

Does a birth injury cause congenital dislocation of the hip?
No. This is one of the very few types of dislocation that have nothing to do with injury.

How can a dysplastic or congenitally dislocated hip be recognized?
The skin folds on the backs of the thighs and buttocks are not symmetrical, the affected leg cannot be brought out as far as the normal limb, the limb appears shortened, and the groin fold is deepened. If the diagnosis is not made early, the condition may first be noted when the child begins to walk and limps or waddles.

How is a dysplastic or dislocated hip treated?

If the condition is noted early, placing a double diaper or pillow diaper on the child will frequently bring the hips in the proper position to deepen the hip socket and prevent dislocation. At times, casts or braces may be employed to perform the same function. If the condition is noted after dislocation has occurred, a traction device (or use of a cast) must be applied. By traction, the hip is gradually brought adjacent to the hip socket. At this point the legs are brought outward so that the hip faces deeply within the socket.

Is surgery ever necessary for congenital dislocation of the hip?

Yes. If the hip cannot be brought within the socket by traction and casting, surgery is necessary. One of several operative procedures may be performed. The hip socket may be cleared of fat and capsule and scar tissue, and the thighbone placed within it; the thighbone (femur) may be cut through (osteotomized) and the hip rotated so that the head of the femur faces the socket while the foot faces forward; the socket may be deepened; a ledge of bone may be placed above the socket to prevent the hip from dislocating; or the entire pelvis may be rotated so as to deepen the socket.

What factors determine the operation necessary for congenital dislocation of the hip?

The age of the patient, the degree of dislocation, the amount of twist that has formed in the thighbone, and the depth of the hip socket.

Is a cast worn after surgery for congenital dislocation of the hip?

Yes.

What will happen if a congenital dislocation of the hip is not treated?

A limp and ultimate arthritis of the hip joint are virtually inevitable.

What are the results of treatment for congenital dislocation of the hip?

If the treatment is early, the results are excellent. If it is later, the results are usually good.

What is congenital clubfoot?

Congenital clubfoot is a deformity of the foot noted at birth. The heel cord is tight and the foot is turned in with the sole facing inward and upward.

Is clubfoot common?

Yes. It occurs once in every 1,000 births and is twice as common in males as females.

What causes clubfoot?

Faulty development of the embryonic foot due to local abnormalities of muscle and bone.

How is clubfoot treated?

The foot is placed in a plaster cast that holds the bones in an "overcorrected" position. With each change of cast, the foot is again manipulated so as to gradually stretch tight ligaments and muscles. Not all of the deformities of the clubfoot are corrected in any one cast change.

What are Dennis-Brown bars?

Dennis-Brown bars are metal bars to which an infant's shoes are attached. The bars may be bent and the shoes rotated to any desired position. Many orthopedists and pediatricians prefer the use of Dennis-Brown bars to casts in the treatment of clubfoot.

How soon should treatment of clubfoot be begun?

Within the first few days after birth.

Does corrected clubfoot recur?

Yes. It very frequently recurs, and so the child's feet must be examined periodically during the first five or six years of life.

Is surgery ever necessary in the treatment of clubfoot?

Yes. If the clubfoot has not been corrected in the first year or year and a half, surgery is indicated.

What are the surgical procedures that may be performed for clubfoot?

Tight ligaments and muscles may be released from the concave side of the foot; bones may be fused or compressed on the convex side of the foot; tendons may be transferred; or tendons may be lengthened.

Are operations for clubfoot dangerous?

No.

Are the results of surgery for clubfoot satisfactory?

Yes. Satisfactory results are obtained in most instances.

Is it necessary to continue exercising and manipulating the foot even after surgery has corrected the clubfoot deformity?

Yes. Even after surgery there is a marked tendency for clubfoot to recur. This tendency may be overcome by continued manipulation, massage, exercises, and special shoes.

Are operations for the relief of muscle and bone deformities serious?

Yes. They are highly technical procedures that must be planned carefully before they are begun. Many conditions require multiple operations extending over a period of several years before the optimum results can be obtained.

Will children outgrow clubfoot and similar deformities if they are left untreated?

No.

Does the position the fetus has in its mother's womb ever cause any bone abnormalities at birth?

Yes. The fetal position may have some effect upon wryneck, congenital dislocation of the hip, and clubfoot deformities.

Are children often born with overlapping fifth toes?

Yes. This seems to be a familial tendency.

How are overlapping toes corrected?

This deformity can be corrected rather readily through surgery and is worth performing if the overlap is marked.

Why should surgery be performed for overlapping toes?

Children are often embarrassed when other children tease them about their overlapping toes. Furthermore, as the child grows older, the deformity tends to worsen rather than improve. Also, painful corns and calluses may develop over the overlapping toe.

Are children ever born with one arm or one leg much shorter than the other?

Yes.

What can be done about deformities involving a short arm or leg?

An artificial limb may be used if the difference between the short limb and the normal limb is great.

What is congenital coxa vara?

It is a deformity of the thighbone (femur). The angle between the upper end of the femur and the shaft of the femur is decreased from the normal.

What are the symptoms of congenital coxa vara?

The involved leg is often shortened. There is a painless limp and limited motion at the hip. The child may walk with a waddling gait if both hips are affected.

How is coxa vara treated?

Surgery must be performed to reconstitute the normal alignment of the deformed portion of the thighbone.

What is congenital discoid meniscus?

It is an abnormal disk-shaped cartilage formed at the outer half of the knee joint.

What causes congenital discoid meniscus?

Discoid meniscus was originally thought to represent a normal embryonic structure that failed to disappear after birth. More recently, it has been found that the discoid meniscus may result from the normal ring of cartilage (meniscus) of the knee being pulled in and out of the joint by abnormal ligaments. Thus the disk portion of the meniscus may really represent scar tissue.

What are the symptoms of discoid meniscus?

Intermittent pain, with clicking and locking of the knee in young children.

What is the treatment of discoid meniscus?

It should be removed surgically.

Will a knee be normal if the discoid meniscus is removed?

Yes.

What is congenital pseudarthrosis of the tibia?

Pseudarthrosis of the tibia is an abnormality of the shinbone (tibia), usually occurring at or shortly after birth, eventually causing a fracture of the tibia.

What causes congenital pseudarthrosis of the tibia?

The cause is unknown. Many physicians feel it is the result of nerve tumors that develop within the bone substance of the tibia.

What is the treatment for congenital pseudarthrosis of the tibia?

Bone grafts are the treatment. Grafts must often be done in several stages. Postoperatively, a cast or brace must be worn for several years.

What is osteogenesis imperfecta?

Osteogenesis imperfecta is a defect in the formation of the bone-forming cells. It is accompanied by relaxation of joints, weak musculature, and frequently definite blueness in the whites of the eyes. The thin, fragile bones are subject to numerous fractures. In severe cases, an embryo with osteogenesis imperfecta may suffer so many fractures while it is developing that it is a stillborn.

Is there any satisfactory treatment for children with osteogenesis imperfecta?

Nothing can be done to improve the quality of the bones. However, children with this affliction should avoid any contact sports and be guarded particularly against falls or other injuries. Bones that have become deformed because of frequent fractures within their shafts can be realigned and straightened by surgery.

Birth Deformities of the Female Genital Organs

Unfortunately, birth deformities of the external and internal female organs are encountered from time to time. Some of these defects can be remedied through surgery while others do not lend themselves to surgical correction. Those that can be helped through operative intervention are the following:

Imperforate hymen: This is a condition in which the maidenhead, covering the vaginal opening, contains no perforations. Often the diagnosis is not made until the child reaches puberty. Then it is discovered that menstruation is unaccompanied by the passage of blood from the vagina, and retention of the blood within the vaginal canal causes severe discomfort.

Imperforate hymen is readily corrected by a simple incision under light general anesthesia.

Enlarged clitoris: Some infants, for unknown reasons, are born with an abnormally large clitoris. Many years ago, when midwives performed large numbers of deliveries, these females were occasionally erroneously labeled as males and were brought up as males by their parents. Today, of course, this mistake is not made.

If the clitoral enlargement is the sole defect, it can be corrected readily by excision of the structure. This will not interfere with normal sex life or sensations in later years and is extremely important to carry out while the infant is still young and unaware.

Fusion of the labia majora: Every once in a while a female is born with the major lips of the vulva fused in the midline. If this deformity is associated with clitoral enlargement, it may have the outward appearance of the male genitals. However, on close examination the attending obstetrician and pediatrician will have no trouble in making the correct diagnosis.

If fusion of the lips is the only defect, it can be corrected surgically by incising and separating them in the midline. If clitoral enlargement is also present, it is treated by excision.

Absence of the vagina: This is a rare congenital defect and is, in some cases, accompanied by other deformities of the female genital system. Correction through surgery is delayed until physical maturity is attained during the late teen years. Then a careful evaluation must be made to see if other defects are also present.

There are several methods of constructing a vagina. Perhaps the most widely used method consists of creating a space between the rectum and bladder and lining this space with a skin graft taken from the patient's thigh.

If the uterus, tubes, and ovaries are normal, it is possible that pregnancy will take place after plastic reconstruction of the vagina. Interestingly enough, sexual sensations are reported to approach normal in those who have undergone this operation.

Septate vagina: Rarely, complete fusion of the two sides which go to form the vagina does not take place. In such cases there may be a septum (partition) running down the center of the vagina which will interfere with sexual relations. The defect can be remedied easily by severing the septum and stitching the mucous membrane together so that normal anatomy is established.

Septate or bicornuate uterus: There are varying degrees of uterine deformity, from the existence of two separate cervices and uteri to a partial septum occurring in the midportion of a fused uterus. Lack of complete fusion in development can result in a heart-shaped uterus (bicornuate) containing one cervix but two compartments to the body of the organ.

Many of these deformities cause no trouble during menstruation and con-

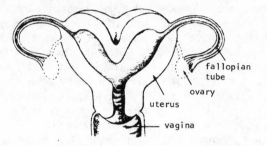

A bicornuate uterus, a common birth deformity of the uterus, is shown here.

ception. In some instances, however, there is interference with ability to become pregnant or there is a history of repeated miscarriage. If these complications arise, the deformity can be corrected by surgical plastic procedures carried out through an abdominal incision.

Pseudohermaphroditism: This is a condition in which the external genitals appear to be of one sex but the gonads (ovaries or testicles) are of another sex. Whenever this unhappy situation is encountered, and fortunately it is rare, the attending physician must pursue a detailed investigation to determine the predominant sex. In order to discover this, an abdominal operation may be necessary to examine the gonads and to take a biopsy of them to determine microscopically whether they resemble the ovary or the testicle.

In many of these cases, the genital structures are so underdeveloped that the gonads cannot be easily located or recognized. In most instances, unless the structures are predominantly male and the gonads prove to be rather well-developed testicles, it is best to treat the infant as a female. Experience has shown that it is much easier for these children to live as girls than as boys. Furthermore, reconstructive surgery favors the female sex as it is easier to plastically reshape the tissues into those of a female. And finally, the newly constructed tissues are more likely to function adequately in adult life if the female configuration is established.

QUESTIONS AND ANSWERS

Are congenital deformities of the female genitals common?

No. They are quite rare.

What are the more frequently seen birth defects of the female genitals?

1. Nonperforated hymen
2. Enlargement of the clitoris
3. Fusion of the lips of the vulva
4. Absence of the vagina
5. Septate (partitioned) vagina
6. Septate or bicornuate uterus
7. Pseudohermaphroditism

Are these defects correctable?

Yes. Most lend themselves to surgical plastic procedures which will reestablish normal or near normal anatomical relations.

Do congenital defects of the female genitals always lead to abnormal outward appearance of the individual?

To the contrary. The child will look and act as a female provided the ovaries are present.

Can a child with defects of the genitals have normal sex feelings and marital relations upon attaining maturity?

Yes, in most instances.

Can pregnancy take place in a female born with defects of the genital tract?

Yes, in some cases, provided the uterus, tubes, and ovaries are normal.

Can proper determination of sex be made despite deformities of the external genitals?

Yes. A trained physician can make the correct diagnosis as to sex and will be able to outline the proper type of corrective surgery. If doubt as to sex still exists after external inspection, abdominal surgery and biopsy of the gonads (ovaries or testicles) is performed.

Birthmarks

See SKIN AND SUBCUTANEOUS TISSUES.

Bites

See FIRST AID; INSECT BITES AND STINGS.

Black Eye

A black eye is a hemorrhage under the skin of the eyelids and surrounding tissues, caused by the rupture of small blood vessels. It usually results from a direct blow but may also occur from a contusion or laceration above the eyes, with seepage of blood down to the tissues beneath the skin surrounding the eyes.

See also EYES.

QUESTIONS AND ANSWERS

What is the first aid treatment for a black eye?

Cold, wet compresses should be applied directly over the injured area.

Is it ever advisable to apply warm compresses rather than cold?

After 24 hours, warm compresses may be of more value because they may hasten absorption of the blood clot.

Should one apply raw meat or herbs to a blackened eye?

No. These practices go back to early folklore. Any benefit that can be derived from these substances can be obtained better from cold, wet compresses.

When should medical aid be sought for a black eye?

In all cases, because the local swelling of the lids may hide an underlying injury to the surface of the eye or to the eyeball itself. It is therefore much safer for the eye to be examined by a physician, even though one suspects that there is no underlying damage.

Does a severe black eye ever endanger sight?

No, unless the eyeball itself has also been injured by the blow that caused the black eye.

Can one tell whether the eyeball itself has been injured when the lids are swollen from a black eye?

Usually not. It is also better not to disturb the eye by attempting to force open the swollen lids. This procedure is better performed by the eye doctor who has special skill and instruments for this purpose.

Will permanent discoloration result when a black eye subsides?

Only in very rare instances. In such cases, there may be some hemoglobin deposited beneath the skin, which may leave a slightly dark discoloration.

Bladder

See URINARY BLADDER.

Bleeding

A great many people are unduly alarmed by the sight of blood and they tend to interpret bleeding as being much more serious than it usually is. This fear of bleeding often dates back to the fears and frights of early childhood.

It is important to remain calm when someone shows evidence of internal or external bleeding. In the great majority of instances, the bleeding will control itself. People rarely bleed to death unless a major blood vessel has been severed.

As mentioned in the first aid section of this book, most bleeding from the body's surface can be controlled by direct pressure with a clean handkerchief or piece of gauze. It is seldom necessary to apply a tourniquet, and this should be done only if direct pressure over a wound fails to stop the bleeding.

It should be kept in mind that the average male adult has approximately six quarts of blood within his body and that the loss of even one or two quarts will not cause death; the same holds true for the female, who has approximately one pint to one quart less blood in her body.

Bleeding from any source should be an indication to call one's physician. In most instances, the bleeding will prove to be of minor significance, but there are also a great many major disorders that first evidence themselves by bleeding. Listed here are areas from which blood may originate:

1. Bleeding beneath the conjunctiva of the eyes. When this occurs spontaneously in an older person it may signify elevated blood pressure with the rupture of a small blood vessel. So-called bloodshot eyes may indicate merely an inflammation with dilatation rather than rupture of a blood vessel.

2. Bleeding from the ears is seen frequently following head injury. It often is evidence of a fracture of the base of the skull. In other cases, where there has been no injury, bleeding from the ear may be indicative of an ear infection.

3. Bleeding from the nose is usually due to an eroded blood vessel in the septum of the nose but may also be a sign of high blood pressure or some other major disorder.

4. Bleeding from the gums is extremely common and can originate from any one of many conditions. Pyorrhea, tartar between the teeth and gums, and a pulled tooth are obvious reasons for bleeding from the gums. People who have vitamin deficiencies often bleed from the gums, as do those who suffer from blood diseases such as hemophilia.

5. Violent coughing can cause bleeding from the throat, larynx, or bronchial tubes. However, in all patients who have coughed up blood, a medical search should be conducted to rule out the possibilities of tuberculosis or lung tumor.

6. The vomiting of blood may be secondary to an upset stomach with violent heaving, or it may be due to

gastritis (an inflammation of the stomach), to a stomach tumor, or to an ulcer of the stomach or duodenum. The latter is perhaps the most frequent cause of the vomiting of blood.

7. The passage of blood in the stool may appear as a jet-black, tarry stool if the site of origin of the blood is in the stomach, duodenum, or small intestine. The passage of bright-red blood in stools may be from hemorrhoids, from a rectal fissure or fistula, or from higher up in the large bowel. A bowel tumor, ulcerative colitis, or diverticulitis is a frequent cause of rectal bleeding which demands thorough investigation.

8. Bleeding from the nipple of the breast is often suggestive of a breast tumor and should demand an immediate medical consultation.

9. Bleeding from the vagina, other than that from ordinary menstruation, should always be followed by a pelvic examination. There are dozens of conditions that might cause unexpected vaginal bleeding. Some are relatively minor, such as bleeding after intercourse or bleeding due to an inflammation of the cervix. Other causes may be due to upset in hormone activity. However, in every instance, tumor within the uterus must be considered as a possible cause.

10. Bleeding from the penis or from the urethra of the female invariably indicates a disorder arising within the urinary tract. It may be due to a simple infection of the bladder or kidneys, or it may indicate the presence of stones or tumor. In any event, thorough urological study should be carried out.

See also FIRST AID.

Blood Banks

It is impossible to calculate the great number of lives that have been saved as a result of the establishment of blood banks. The blood is stored in a refrigerated state ready for immediate use whenever needed in an emergency.

A unit of blood is 500 cc, or about one pint. A blood bank in a small hospital may have approximately 12 to 15 units on hand, whereas larger institutions may store as many as 100 units at a time.

Sodium citrate is added to the blood to keep it from clotting. Some of the blood is kept in glass bottles, while other units are stored in plastic bags. It has been found that blood platelets, so important for blood clotting, are quickly destroyed when the blood is stored in glass bottles, but they tend to survive for much longer periods when the blood is kept in a plastic bag.

See also BLOOD TRANSFUSIONS.

QUESTIONS AND ANSWERS

Who supplies the blood that hospitals have in blood banks?

Some hospitals draw their blood directly from volunteer donors; others purchase their blood from large voluntary or commercial blood centers.

Is it common practice for relatives of a patient to donate their blood to the blood bank?

Yes. This practice has been growing rapidly throughout the country and is a most important source for blood.

Must a relative of a patient have the same blood type in order to donate blood to the bank?

No. The relative's blood may be used for some other patient who may require it later.

Do blood banks try to store every type of blood?

Yes, but this is not always possible, as certain rare types may be quickly used up when a patient requires several transfusions.

What does a blood bank do when it runs out of a particular type of blood?

It may borrow from a bank in another hospital, or it may purchase some from a blood center.

How long can one store blood for transfusion?

In a refrigerated state, it is possible to store blood for 35 to 40 days and still use it. However, many hospitals discard blood after it has been in storage for 25 to 30 days.

How can one ensure that the stored blood does not contain bacteria or viruses?

Blood is always collected from donors under the most sterile conditions. However, it is not possible to ensure freedom from virus contamination. It is, on the other hand, completely possible to make certain that no bacteria get into the bank blood.

Does hepatitis ever result from receiving bank blood?

Yes. It is not the banking of the blood itself that causes the hepatitis but the existence of a virus within the blood of the donor. Even if the blood were transferred directly from a donor who harbored the virus of hepatitis, the virus would be transmitted to the recipient.

What are "packed cells"?

This is blood that contains only the cellular elements and is devoid of most of the plasma. This type of blood is transfused to patients when the blood volume is adequate and it is desired mainly to supply needed red and white blood cells.

Is a small sample of donor blood saved after the transfusion has been given?

Yes. This is important to do, should the patient develop a transfusion reaction. It then becomes possible to use this tiny sample of retained donor blood and to test it again with the patient's blood.

Must a patient be cross-matched for each and every transfusion?

Yes. This is essential. Although the patient and the donor may have the same blood types, their subgroups may be different and the bloods may be incompatible.

Does an individual's blood type ever change?

It is exceedingly rare for blood type to change, but some of the subgroups in patients with a condition known as hemolytic anemia may undergo change.

Blood Chemistry

The preparation of a patient for surgery and his postoperative care are tasks that require a thorough knowledge of body chemistry. No book on surgery would be complete without noting the importance of the various chemical actions and reactions that take place within the body in response to the trauma of a surgical procedure. It is essential, therefore, that every effort be made preoperatively to see that the chemical balance, respiratory balance, and liver and kidney functions are well maintained. A good state of hydration must be carefully preserved and an adequate intake of chemicals, calories, proteins, and vitamins must be provided for every patient who is about to undergo a surgical operation.

Chemical balance may go awry unless the patient receives ample supplies of oxygen and has an adequate number of red blood cells to supply his tissues during and after a major operation. It is also essential to maintain adequate levels of vitamins B, C, and K in order to promote sound wound healing and adequate blood coagulation after surgery.

On admission to the hospital, every patient undergoes blood chemical analysis. If deficiencies exist, needed chemicals are supplied either by mouth or by intramuscular or intravenous injection. Surgeons will not undertake major surgical procedures if patients are deficient in essential chemicals such as sodium, chloride, potassium, phosphorus. After surgery, when patients are often unable to take nourishment by mouth, these chemicals are supplied by intravenous injection. In addition, essential vitamins are injected intravenously or intramuscularly. Respiratory balance is also maintained by administration of oxygen through nasal catheters or by use of a respirator. Patients must be encouraged to breathe deeply and to expel mucus from their bronchial tubes. If they require assistance, inhalation therapists will suck out mucus collections and will teach the patient how to aid himself.

It is safe to state that many of the remarkable improvements in surgical results within recent years have been due to the maintenance of chemical balance during the preoperative, operative, and postoperative periods.

The following data show the major chemical elements in blood, give the normal quantities, and state abnormal conditions that may result from alterations in chemical balance.

Blood Transfusions

A blood transfusion is a safe and effective method of treating a problem

CHEMICAL ELEMENTS IN THE BLOOD

SUBSTANCE	NORMAL CHILD	NORMAL ADULT	ABNORMAL
Sodium	133 to 134 milliequivalents per liter	137 to 143 milliequivalents per liter	Decreased amounts may occur from excess vomiting or loss of body fluids, thus endangering normal body processes.
Potassium	3.6 to 5.0 milliequivalents per liter	4 to 5 milliequivalents per liter	Marked alterations occur in many disease states and may disturb heart function. Potassium quantities must be in balance with sodium quantities.
Calcium	9.6 to 10.8 milligrams per 100 cc	9 to 11 milligrams per 100 cc	Increased amounts may indicate overactivity of, or a tumor of, the parathyroid glands. Decreased amounts occur in tetany and certain bone diseases.
Chlorides	96 to 108 milliequivalents	585 to 620 milligrams per 100 cc	Decreased amounts usually result from loss of salt from the body. Excessive loss is incompatible with normal body function.

SURGICAL CONDITIONS AND PROCEDURES

SUBSTANCE	NORMAL CHILD	NORMAL ADULT	ABNORMAL
Phosphorus	3.0 to 4.5 milli-equivalents	3 to 4.5 milligrams per 100 cc	Variations in amounts may indicate functional disorder of the parathyroid glands or bone disease.
Carbon-dioxide combining power	24 to 32 milli-equivalents	55 to 75 volumes percent	Decrease indicates acidosis; increase indicates alkalosis.
Glucose (sugar)	70 to 110 milligrams per 100 cc	80 to 120 milligrams per 100 cc	Increased amounts may indicate presence of diabetes mellitus. Decreased amounts are present in hyperinsulinism.
Cholesterol	Infants: 80 to 125 milligrams per 100 cc Children: 170 to 250 milligrams per 100 cc	130 to 240 milligrams per 100 cc	Increased amounts may indicate a tendency toward premature hardening of the arteries. Increased amounts are also seen in some pregnant women and in disorders of the thyroid gland.
Bilirubin	0.2 to 0.8 milligrams per 100 cc (may be 1 or more milligrams in newborns)	0.1 to 0.25 milligrams per 100 cc	Increased quantities may indicate jaundice, obstruction to normal flow of bile from the liver, or liver disease.
Phosphatase	3 to 13 Bodansky units	1.5 to 4 units per 100 cc	Increased quantities indicate obstruction to flow of bile from the liver or jaundice.
Total protein (serum)	6.0 to 8.0 grams per 100 cc	6.5 to 8.2 grams per 100 cc	Decreased amounts are seen in debilitated states and in chronic illness.
Serum albumin and globulin	4.5 to 5.5 grams of serum albumin per 100 cc; 1.7 to 3.0 grams of globulin per 100 cc	1.5 to 2.5 grams per 100 cc 2.5 to 3.0 grams per 100 cc	A reversal of the ratio so that there is more globulin than serum albumin indicates poor protein metabolism.
Fibrinogen	0.2 to 0.4 grams per 100 cc	0.2 to 0.6 grams per 100 cc	Decreased amounts indicate a bleeding tendency.
Nonprotein nitrogen (whole blood)	25 to 40 milligrams per 100 cc	25 to 45 milligrams per 100 cc	Increased amounts may indicate kidney or genitourinary disorder.
Urea nitrogen (whole blood)	7 to 15 milligrams per 100 cc	12 to 15 milligrams per 100 cc	Increased amounts may indicate kidney disease (nephritis, etc.).
Creatinine (whole blood)	0.5 to 2 milligrams per 100 cc	1 to 2.5 milligrams per 100 cc	Increased amounts may indicate inability of kidneys to excrete urine (as in obstruction due to markedly enlarged prostate gland).
Uric acid	2.5 to 3.5 milligrams per 100 cc	2 to 4.5 milligrams per 100 cc	Increased amounts may indicate presence of gout.
Icterus index	4 to 6 units	4 to 6 units	Increased reading indicates presence of jaundice.

that might otherwise result in serious illness or death. Patients are only transfused when it is essential to do so, and it is seldom recommended merely to give the patient a boost.
See also BLOOD BANKS.

QUESTIONS AND ANSWERS

Should blood transfusions be given under the direct supervision of a physician?
Yes, most emphatically. A transfusion means taking blood from a healthy individual and injecting it into a patient. This is a serious procedure and is sometimes associated with complications demanding expert knowledge.

Who should perform the blood grouping (typing) preparatory to the giving of a blood transfusion?
A well-qualified laboratory employing expert technicians should always be used to type the patient's blood. Accidents occur if correct typing and cross-matching are not performed.

What are the various blood types?
In actuality, the proper term is *blood group*, not blood type. However, most laymen do use the expression blood type.
The various groupings are A, B, O, and AB.

Should people know their blood groups (types) so that if an accident should occur they can be transfused more quickly?
Yes. It is wise to know one's own blood group. The blood must always be reexamined prior to transfusion. The blood to be given must always be matched with the recipient's blood before transfusion.

When given under proper supervision, are blood transfusions safe?
Yes.

What are some of the complications of blood transfusions?
1. **Chills and fever.** This is a common complication.
2. **Allergic reactions, such as hives and asthma.** When this occurs, the transfusion is usually stopped.
3. **Jaundice.** This may occur as long as three to four months after the transfusion has been given.
4. **Shock,** from giving the wrong type of blood or contaminated blood. This is an extremely rare event.

Is it important to transfuse blood of the same group and subgroup?
Yes. It has been discovered that even though people may be of the same blood type they may have varying subgroups. In such cases, the bloods of the two people may not be compatible.

How can one tell that the blood of the donor and the blood of the recipient are incompatible?
By taking a small sample of the donor's blood and mixing it with the recipient's blood. This is a laboratory procedure that can be performed within a few minutes. When blood of incompatible types is mixed, the blood cells agglutinate, or clump. If the two are compatible, the red blood cells do not clump.

Can children safely be given blood transfusions?
Yes. They have reactions no more frequently than adults.

Is it important to transfuse blood with the same Rh factor?
Yes. Rh-positive blood should be transfused to Rh-positive recipients, and Rh-negative blood should be transfused to Rh-negative recipients.

Can very old people tolerate blood transfusions?
Yes. They respond in much the same manner as people who are younger.

134

SURGICAL CONDITIONS AND PROCEDURES

Are there special benefits from transfusing blood from a relative to a recipient?

No. Blood from donors is just as satisfactory as from a member of a patient's family.

Is bank blood as good as fresh blood?

No. Whenever possible, fresh blood is preferable. However, it is seldom possible to get a sufficient quantity of fresh blood when several units are required.

What is a unit of blood for transfusion?

Commonly, a unit is 500 cc, or approximately one pint.

Why is fresh blood better than bank blood?

Bank blood tends to lose some of its most beneficial components when it is stored. These components include platelets, fibrinogen, and oxygen. Also, bank blood tends to have an increased quantity of potassium, and may contain other chemicals that may cause untoward reactions in the recipient.

When does a physician decide to use fresh rather than bank blood?

When it is most desirable to obtain those components that are lacking in bank blood. If the main object of the transfusion is to increase the number of red blood cells, then bank blood is as adequate as fresh blood.

Should all healthy people have their blood group (type) determined?

Yes. This is a wise procedure although it is not absolutely necessary since every patient must be typed and matched each time he receives blood from a donor. If a patient's blood type is rare, however, it is extremely helpful for him to know his type, so that if a transfusion is required, a search for a suitable donor may begin without delay.

Are there satisfactory methods for combating reactions to transfusions?

Yes. Most reactions can be mitigated by proper medical treatment.

What is meant by an exchange transfusion?

This is a special type of blood transfusion usually performed on newborns who have a blood condition known as erythroblastosis. It attempts to exchange all or most of the infant's blood for new blood and thus get rid of the blood causing the disease. This must be performed only by an expert in the field.

What is meant by an intrauterine transfusion?

Within recent years it has been found possible to transfuse the fetus while it is still in its mother's womb. This is done in cases where erythroblastosis (Rh-factor disease) is suspected. By an ingenious procedure performed under fluoroscopic x-ray, a needle is inserted through the mother's abdominal wall, through the wall of her uterus, and into the embryo. Blood is transfused directly to the embryo in this manner, thus protecting the child against the development of erythroblastosis.

When are blood transfusions usually indicated?

1. When there has been a sudden acute loss of blood due to hemorrhage or injury.

2. When the bone marrow is not functioning properly in producing blood cells. This occurs in debilitating diseases or diseases associated with profound anemia. Transfusions will temporarily improve the patient's condition.

3. When marked blood loss is anticipated from an impending surgical procedure.

When are blood transfusions withheld?

When the physicians in attendance

believe that the patient's own natural mechanisms will be able to overcome the blood deficiency or loss. It is much better to permit the bone marrow to restore blood than to give blood artificially by transfusion.

Can the various forms of anemia be treated successfully by giving blood transfusions?

Transfusions only temporarily correct a blood deficiency and do not relieve the underlying cause of an anemia. The one exception to this is when anemia has been caused solely by hemorrhage.

Should a specialist supervise the giving of blood transfusions?

Yes, if one is available. Specialists known as pathologists number among their duties matching of the blood, obtaining the proper type of blood, and its administration. It must be remembered that there are possible complications following blood transfusions, and these demand the expert knowledge of a pathologist.

Are accidents of matching and cross-matching frequent?

No, they are extremely rare. Every well-qualified laboratory has expert technologists and uses double-checking methods to protect patients against mismatched blood.

Do people ever have bad reactions to transfusions even when the proper type of blood has been given?

Yes. Some people may have allergic responses, and others may react with high fever or chills. Complications due to the presence of a virus in the transfused blood may lead to jaundice from hepatitis several weeks after the transfusion has been given.

Will allergic people tend to have more severe reactions to transfusions than nonallergic people?

Yes. In these patients, transfusions may bring on an episode of hives or asthma.

Are there medications that can be given to control allergic reactions to transfusions?

Yes. The antihistaminic drugs will control most allergic reactions within a short period of time.

What complications can occur from giving incorrectly matched blood?

There may be chills, fever, kidney-function failure, hepatitis, or even death from shock.

Do blood transfusions often cause lasting harmful effects?

No. Such reactions are exceedingly rare.

Do patients recover from hepatitis secondary to blood transfusions?

Yes, the great majority recover, although it may take several weeks before they feel themselves again.

Are there substances that can be given as a substitute for blood?

In emergencies, when blood is not readily available, stored plasma can be given to replace lost blood. Also, when the patient has hemorrhaged and there is need to combat shock, substances that expand the circulating blood volume are sometimes helpful in maintaining the patient until real blood can be obtained. One of these substances is known as dextran.

Is it ever necessary to give blood to a newborn?

Yes, especially the exchange type of transfusion given when the child has Rh-factor disease. In hemorrhagic disease of the newborn, transfusions may also be necessary.

Blood Vessels

This section is devoted to a discussion of the many remarkable advances in surgery of the blood vessels (vascular surgery) and will deal in greater detail with operations upon the arteries than upon the veins. The problems of varicose veins and of cirrhosis of the liver are considered elsewhere in this book.

One of the inexorable penalties of aging is hardening of the arteries. The process takes place eventually in all people if they live long enough, but the rate at which it occurs varies greatly from one person to another. There are also great variations within an individual's body so that it is not at all unusual to find one set of vessels to be deeply involved in arteriosclerosis while others escape the process almost completely. Before the advent of modern vascular surgery, these changes could not be overcome to any great extent, and patients were forced to lead a restricted, an invalided, or a shortened life as a consequence of their disease. Today the development of arterial grafts, arterial reconstruction, and the elaboration of an operation known as *endarterectomy* have revolutionized the medical attitude toward arteriosclerosis and, indeed, have brought about many changes in society's thoughts on the aging process.

In the early days of blood vessel grafting, it was found that the use of materials such as *animal arteries* or arteries from other humans led to ultimate failure. The recipient would reject such grafts (homografts) as foreign bodies; and within a few days to a few

weeks, clotting, graft degeneration, and hemorrhage at the graft site would result. All too often death would ensue before reoperation could be undertaken.

Within the past few years, surgeons have employed replacement grafts made of woven or knitted Teflon or Dacron, which are inert when placed within the body and are not rejected as foreign bodies. This material is cut to the appropriate diameter, length, and shape of the artery to be replaced. Most of these grafts are immersed in a receptacle containing a quantity of the patient's own blood so that the minute spaces between the weave or knit will become filled with blood clot. This maneuver reduces leakage after the blood flow is reestablished. The passageway of the grafts is kept clear, and after the diseased portion of artery has been excised (removed), the graft is cut to fit and is stitched in its place.

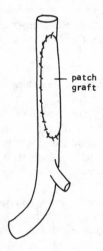

patch graft

Although the preceding description of the technique of arterial replacement might make it appear that this type of operation is extremely simple, this is not the actual fact. However, it is good to report that in many clinics throughout the country arterial replacement surgery is being carried out every day in a routine fashion with successful outcome in well over 95 percent of cases. Endarterectomy is an operation in which the diseased artery is opened and its lining—containing calcium plaques which narrow the passageway —is scraped out. The vessel is then sutured, leaving a clean inner lining and a wider passageway. As healing takes place, a new lining (endothelium) forms and often remains free of new arteriosclerotic patches for several years. The decision as to whether arterial replacement or endarterectomy should be the procedure of choice depends largely upon the anatomical location of the diseased blood vessel. If it is located where replacement with a graft would be technically too difficult, then endarterectomy might be the better procedure to perform.

Endarterectomy is occasionally done in conjunction with *arterial reconstruction*. This may involve the insertion of a Dacron or Teflon patch to widen the passageway in a portion of a diseased artery.

Vascular surgery has also proved of inestimable value in several other conditions that had previously been considered beyond help. Arteries are sometimes clogged by an embolus (clot of blood) which has originated from the wall of a damaged heart. These clots tend to lodge in arteries supplying the brain, in the aorta (the large artery leaving the heart and traveling down to the chest and abdomen) at its bifurcation (division) in the lower abdomen, in the iliac arteries in the pelvis, in the femoral arteries in the thighs, and in the popliteal arteries in the bend of the knees. Prompt surgery within a few hours after the embolus has occurred can save many of these patients. The clogged artery is opened and the blood

clot is removed. Blood flow is reestablished after suturing the opened artery. This procedure has come to be known as *embolectomy*.

A not uncommon complication of major surgery in the chest or abdomen is the formation of blood clots in the veins of the legs, thighs, or pelvis. In an occasional case where this takes place, a piece of the clot breaks off and travels through the veins and right side of the heart, finally to lodge in the lungs. (This is called a pulmonary embolus.) If the clot is big and a major vessel of the lung is clogged, sudden death may ensue. Fortunately, in most cases a small clot forms, but even though the patient does not die, serious complications will arise. The patient may go into shock, with rapid breathing and a poor pulse. Heroic measures will then be necessary to save him. When a patient suffers more than one nonfatal embolus of this type, serious consideration should be given to *tying off the inferior vena cava*. This will mean opening the lower abdomen and passing a ligature (stitch) around this large vein which carries the blood from the lower extremities and pelvis to the heart and lungs. Many lives have been rescued by this operative maneuver.

It should be understood that arterial surgery is not advocated in every patient who has arteriosclerosis, nor is ligation of the vena cava advised in everyone who has suffered an embolus from a clot in a vein of the leg or pelvis. On the other hand, when the passageway of an important artery has become so blocked that the life of an organ or limb is threatened, then arterial surgery is indicated. Similarly, repeated embolus to the lungs is an indication to tie off the vena cava to prevent a fatal subsequent embolus.

Replacement grafts are used for aneurysms of the aorta in the chest and

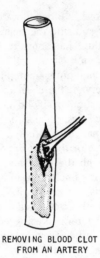

REMOVING BLOOD CLOT
FROM AN ARTERY

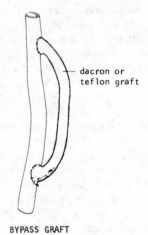

dacron or
teflon graft

BYPASS GRAFT

tion of the aorta with a Teflon or Dacron replacement graft is advisable.

Bypass grafts are utilized frequently to restore circulation to the legs. It has been found that the arteriosclerotic process often closes down the femoral

abdomen and for aneurysms or blockage of the femoral artery in the thigh and the popliteal artery in the knee region. An aneurysm is an abnormal dilatation and weakness in the wall of an artery. The most frequent site for such an abnormality is the abdominal aorta. As time passes, aneurysms tend to grow in size, until eventually they rupture. When this happens, fatal hemorrhage is the usual outcome. In order to avoid this catastrophe, preventive excision of the aneurysm-bearing por-

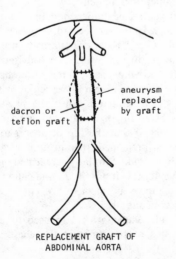

dacron or
teflon graft

aneurysm
replaced
by graft

REPLACEMENT GRAFT OF
ABDOMINAL AORTA

arteries in the thighs and the popliteal arteries in the knee region but spares the vessels in the lower leg. When this situation obtains, a Teflon or Dacron graft is attached to the normal or near-normal iliac artery in the pelvis—above the level of the clogged femoral artery —and is carried down through the thigh and is sutured to the normal or near-normal artery in the leg. This operative maneuver has already saved thousands of limbs from gangrene and eventual amputation. Some surgeons prefer to use a vein graft, taken from the patient's own body, when it is necessary to use a bypass graft that will traverse the knee joint. It has been found that vein grafts are more pliable and will conform better to the bending action of the knee than a Dacron or Teflon graft.

Endarterectomy is indicated for isolated areas of narrowing due to calcified arteriosclerotic patches in the lining of such arteries as the carotid artery in the neck, the abdominal aorta in the abdomen, and the iliac arteries in the pelvis. If too long a segment of the aorta and iliac arteries is involved, graft replacement may be the preferred procedure. In some cases, a combination of endarterectomy *and* the placement of a patch graft will afford the best improvement of the passageway.

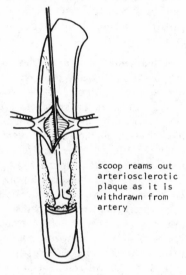

scoop reams out arteriosclerotic plaque as it is withdrawn from artery

ENDARTERECTOMY

As vascular surgeons become more adept at arterial reconstructive techniques, they are approaching many problems that were considered heretofore to be insoluble. Thus one notes that many patients with high blood pressure caused by arteriosclerotic narrowing of the artery to the kidney (the renal artery) can be cured by endarterectomy of this vessel and the placement of a patch graft. Others, who have suffered cerebral thrombosis (a stroke) as a result of arteriosclerosis of the carotid artery in the neck, have been similarly benefited by the same procedure. And more recently, vital arteries supplying blood to the intestines have been subjected to the endarterec-

tomy and patch graft techniques with successful results in some cases.

In conclusion, it is safe to conjecture that in the not too distant future, new knowledge will enable vascular surgeons to prolong life for an ever-increasing number of people who are afflicted with impaired blood supply to the brain, the heart, the liver, the limbs, and other vital structures.

QUESTIONS AND ANSWERS

Do all the arteries in the body undergo arteriosclerosis at the same time?

No. There is great variation within the same body as to the rate at which changes take place. It is not uncommon for an individual to have marked hardening of some vessels while others escape the process almost completely.

Can anything be done surgically to help arteriosclerosis?

Yes. Modern advances in vascular surgery have made it possible to improve many conditions in which the arteries are diseased.

What are some of the operations that can be done for diseased arteries?

1. Arteries that have undergone thrombosis (clotting), or have extensive hardening, or have developed an aneurysm (an outpouching and weakness in their wall) can often be replaced by a graft.

2. Some arteries with narrowed and thickened linings due to arteriosclerosis can be scraped out (endarterectomy) so that the passageway becomes broader and permits increased blood flow.

3. Certain arteries that are narrowed can be brought back to normal or near-normal diameter by the application of an arterial patch.

4. Arteries whose passageways have become obstructed can sometimes be bypassed by the application of a by-pass graft. Such a graft is attached above and below the clogged artery, thus reestablishing blood flow parallel to the diseased vessel.

What materials are used for arterial grafts?

It has been found that the plastic materials Teflon and Dacron make the best grafts. Formerly, arteries from animals or from other humans were used, but they proved not to be as satisfactory as Teflon and Dacron. Occasionally a vein from the patient's own body is taken and is used as a graft.

Are operations in which arterial grafts are inserted often successful?

Yes. Advances in arterial surgery have developed to such a degree that well over 90 percent of the grafts work efficiently.

What are some of the areas in which arterial grafts are found to be most helpful?

1. In certain cases of cerebral thrombosis (stroke), an arterial graft, often of the patch type, is inserted into the carotid artery in the neck, thus widening its diameter and resulting in increased blood flow to the brain.

2. When the aorta, the large artery leading from the heart, develops an aneurysm (a weakening and blistering of its wall), the diseased segment can be replaced by an arterial graft. This is a most successful grafting procedure when the abdominal aorta is involved, and has already proved to be lifesaving in thousands of cases.

3. When the arteries of the legs have become so arteriosclerotic that there is danger of gangrene developing, a bypass arterial graft extending from the iliac artery in the pelvis to the femoral artery in the lower thigh will sometimes save the limb.

4. Severe arteriosclerosis of the renal artery to the kidney is a frequent cause of high blood pressure. A patch or a full arterial graft replacing a diseased renal artery may restore kidney function and result in the restoration of normal or near-normal blood pressure levels.

5. In accidents in which arteries have been severed or badly injured, grafts may be successfully employed. This is particularly helpful in injuries to the arms or legs.

Can hardening of the arteries in the legs be helped by any procedure other than arterial grafting?

Yes. An operation known as *lumbar sympathectomy* sometimes causes the blood vessels in the legs to dilate and carry more blood. This may reduce the pain seen so often among those with arteriosclerosis of the vessels in the legs. Unfortunately, sympathectomy fails to help a great many of these patients, and even if it does prove helpful for one leg, surgeons often hesitate to recommend its employment on both sides for male patients, as it will result in impotence.

For what conditions is endarterectomy most helpful?

In cases in which the lowermost portion of the abdominal aorta and the iliac vessels in the pelvis are arteriosclerotic. In such cases, the aorta and the iliac vessels are opened and the lining is scraped out, with removal of the calcium plaques. The vessels are then closed and blood flow is reestablished.

What is meant by the term "arterial reconstruction"?

This may involve endarterectomy and the application of a patch graft.

Can vascular surgery aid people who have suffered an embolus?

Yes. Patients with damaged heart valves tend to collect blood clots upon them. Frequently a piece of blood clot will break loose and get into the general circulation. The clot may lodge in an artery in the brain, causing a stroke; it may lodge at the division of the aorta in the lower abdomen, thus cutting off blood supply to the legs; or it may go down into the thigh or knee to obstruct blood supply to the lower leg. When these emboli occur, immediate operation is sometimes lifesaving. The clogged artery can be opened and the clot removed, thus restoring blood flow. This procedure, known as embolectomy, to be effective must be carried out within a few hours after the embolus occurs.

Is vascular surgery ever helpful when a patient develops a pulmonary embolus from a clot in the legs or in the pelvis?

Yes, in some cases. If there are recurrent emboli, it is advisable to tie off the inferior vena cava. This is the large vein in the abdomen which returns blood from the lower limbs to the heart. It is ligated through an incision in the abdomen. As a consequence of this procedure, clots will be prevented from reaching the lungs.

Are operations upon major arteries, such as the carotid artery in the neck, the aorta in the chest or abdomen, and upon the arteries of the lower legs, serious?

Yes, but it should be kept in mind that the conditions for which they are performed are also serious. In most instances, failure to have surgery will mean that the patient will eventually succumb. On the other hand, many of these patients are being salvaged through vascular surgery.

How successful is surgery for coronary artery disease?

Many operations have been tried to improve circulation to the heart muscle

when a coronary artery has been thrombosed or when its passageway has been narrowed by arteriosclerosis. An operation that has claimed considerable success is the transplantation of the terminal end of the internal mammary artery from its normal position beneath the breastbone to the heart muscle wall. This brings new blood supply which makes up for the inadequate supply due to the diseased coronary artery. Another operation, accompanied by some success, is gas endarterectomy of the coronary artery. In this procedure, the arteriosclerotic lining of the vessel is loosened from its attachments by gas which is blown into it. The lining is then picked out, leaving a widened passageway.

The most popular procedure today is the so-called coronary bypass operation. This involves taking a segment from the saphenous vein in the thigh and transplanting it so that it bypasses the obstructed portion of the coronary artery. One end of the vein is sutured to the aorta and the other end is implanted into the coronary artery within the heart muscle at a point beyond the obstruction. Large amounts of blood thereby reach the heart muscle by "going around" the damaged portion of the coronary artery. Early reports of this procedure show marked improvement in heart circulation and gratifying relief of the anginal pains which are so characteristic of this condition. In some clinics, reports indicate that approximately 85 percent of those who undergo the "bypass" operation are benefited. As a result, this operation has practically supplanted other operations devised to improve circulation to the heart muscle. Indications are that in the not too distant future, the coronary bypass operation will be performed in this country on some 25,000 people each year.

How soon after surgery upon the arteries can one get out of bed and return to normal activity?

This will vary greatly, depending upon which artery has been operated upon. In most instances, the patient will be able to get out of bed within a few days and will be able to leave the hospital within two to three weeks. The outcome of arterial surgery is usually known within 24 to 48 hours after its performance. If the operation is a success, blood flow will be reestablished immediately and will be maintained continuously. If the surgery is not successful, this, too, will become apparent within a short period of time, as blood flow will cease with a few hours to a day or two.

If an arterial graft is unsuccessful, can the operation be done over again with any hope of success?

Yes. There are many cases on record where an initial graft has failed to restore blood supply but reoperation has been followed by a successful result.

Blue Baby

This condition gets its name from the blue appearance of the skin of these newborn children. The dusky tinge results from a combination of heart and blood vessel abnormalities associated with oxygen-poor blood circulating throughout the body. Prior to the introduction of cardiac surgery most of these children died before they reached adolescence. Today, there are several operations which transpose and reimplant some great blood vessels of the heart so that blood is diverted and flows back into the lungs for reoxygenation before it is circulated generally through-

out the body. By these ingenious operations, relief from shortness of breath and the bluish discoloration of the skin is obtained in most of these infants, and their life expectancy is prolonged greatly.

Operations for this condition, also called the tetralogy of Fallot, are serious and delicate and are not without a considerable surgical mortality. However, surgery offers the only hope for these cardiac cripples who otherwise would be destined to a short, unhappy existence. The operation is performed while the infant is connected to a cardiopulmonary pump.

See also HEART.

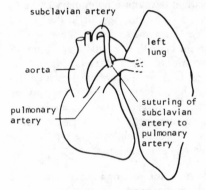

OPERATION FOR "BLUE BABY"

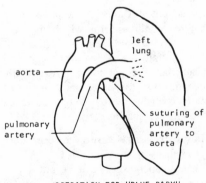

OPERATION FOR "BLUE BABY"

QUESTIONS AND ANSWERS

What is the tetralogy of Fallot?

In an infant with this condition, the skin and mucous membranes appear blue (cyanotic) because his blood is receiving inadequate amounts of oxygen. For this reason, a child with the tetralogy of Fallot is called a blue baby. The condition is caused by a combination of four heart and blood vessel abnormalities.

Should children who have a tetralogy of Fallot be subjected to surgery?

Yes. Most of these children will die within a few years unless they are treated surgically.

What operations are performed to correct the defects in the tetralogy of Fallot?

There are several brilliantly conceived operations to transpose and reimplant some of the great blood vessels of the heart so that blood is diverted and made to flow back into the lungs for reoxygenation before it is circulated generally throughout the body. In one operation, the large subclavian artery branching off the aorta is cut across and implanted into the pulmonary artery, which goes to the lungs. In another operation, the pulmonary artery is sutured directly to the aorta.

At what age is a child with the tetralogy of Fallot operated on?

This depends on the child's ability to survive without surgery. If life cannot be maintained in an infant, then immediate surgery is mandatory. The fewer the symptoms from the condition, the longer one can wait.

Will these children be relieved of their symptoms following surgery?

Yes, the relief is remarkable. The bluish color disappears, the shortness of breath disappears, and life expectancy is prolonged.

Must a child be placed on a cardiopulmonary pump while an operation for the tetralogy of Fallot is being performed?

Yes.

How successful are operations for cure of the tetralogy of Fallot?

In a hospital where there is a well-trained cardiac surgical team, recovery can be expected in more than 90 percent of cases.

Boils

See ABSCESSES AND INFECTIONS.

Bone Conditions

Man is endowed with an excellent skeletal structure that is sturdy enough to withstand tremendous pressures throughout many decades. It is quite remarkable, when one considers the fact that the evolution of man was from a four-footed animal to a biped, that the bones and joints are so relatively free from disease. Of course, some people have birth deformities of the joints, and these unfortunate people do have a great deal of difficulty in locomotion; also there are children who are afflicted by bone disease and who suffer greatly throughout their lives.

The appearance of every adult depends greatly upon his skeletal development and growth as a child. For this reason, and also because many diseases or conditions are correctable when treated early, it is important that parents seek medical advice promptly when a child shows symptoms of joint or bone trouble.

The bony structure has great capacity to heal after injury, but the healing process in bones takes a good deal longer than it does for most soft tissues. In this highly mechanized civilization the incidence of fracture and damage to bones and joints has increased greatly, but fortunately orthopedic remedial measures have kept pace. The increased safety of orthopedic surgery has permitted a great number of procedures to be performed to obtain quicker, more anatomical, and better functional results when bones or joints are traumatized.

BONE INFECTIONS

See OSTEOMYELITIS.

BONE CYSTS

What is a bone cyst?

It is a defect in the bone that appears hollow on an x-ray film.

What are some of the more important causes of cyst formation?

1. **Unicameral bone cyst,** a type of benign "tumor" of bone.

2. **Neurofibromatosis,** a diffuse syndrome of small nerve tumors, some of which may occur in bone.

3. **Adamantinoma of the tibia,** a dangerous tumor of the shinbone that occurs in older adolescents and young adults.

4. **Infections.** Certain types of bone infection (echinococcosis) may cause cyst formation in bone.

What is the treatment for a bone cyst?

If the bone cyst borders on the epiphysis (growth plate), it will continue to grow in size and is called an active bone cyst. When it does not border on the epiphysis, it is an inactive cyst and will not grow in size. An active bone cyst should be scraped and filled with bone chips. An inactive bone cyst may be treated the same way if it is large. If it is small, no treatment is usually needed.

Does a bone cyst ever become malignant?

Rarely, yes. An osteochondroma (nonmalignant bone tumor) of the pelvis may sometimes turn malignant.

BONE TUMORS

What are the more common forms of bone tumors?

1. **Osteochondroma** is a benign knobby protuberance near a joint of the limbs.

2. **Enchondroma** is a benign, painless swelling in the middle of a limb bone. It may become malignant when multiple and in the larger bones of the limbs. (Rarely malignant in the fingers.)

3. **Nonossifying fibroma** is a benign, small, painless bump near a joint, usually found incidentally in x-rays for injury.

4. **Fibrous dysplasia** is a benign enlargement of several bones on only one side of the body and usually appears in girls. Often it is associated with early puberty and "beauty marks" over the skin.

5. **Ewing's sarcoma** is very malignant and causes pain, swelling, and tenderness. Usually it affects one of the bones of the lower limbs or pelvis.

6. **Osteogenic sarcoma** is malignant and causes pain and swelling. Usually it affects the long bone of a lower limb (thighbone).

Where are bone tumors most frequently seen?

They are seen most often in the bones about the knee joint but occur almost anywhere in the body.

Do injuries often result in bone tumors?

No, although frequently an injury may call the child's or parent's attention to a tumor that was previously unrecognized.

What are the usual symptoms of a bone tumor?

Pain and local swelling.

Will an x-ray show the presence of a bone tumor?

Yes.

Do children ever develop malignant bone tumors?

Yes, unfortunately. Osteogenic sarcoma is the most common malignant tumor of bone in children.

How can one distinguish between a benign and a malignant bone tumor?

The various types of tumors have characteristic appearances on x-ray examination. A bone biopsy is often necessary to verify the clinical and x-ray diagnosis.

What should be done for the ordinary nonmalignant bone tumor?

Often a bone tumor is curetted (scraped) clean of the tumor tissue to prevent its enlargement. If a cavity is formed by the curetting of a bone, a bone graft is usually placed in the cavity in order to strengthen the bone and prevent fracture.

If a benign bone tumor is of a kind that is likely to become malignant in the future, such as osteochondroma of the pelvis, or if it interferes with function or causes pain, or if there is any uncertainty about the nature of the tumor tissue, it is best removed.

Are operations for the removal of benign bone tumors very serious or dangerous?

No.

Is cobalt or x-ray treatment ever given along with surgery in the treatment of a bone tumor?

Yes. Malignant tumors are frequently treated with cobalt radiation or x-rays before or after surgery in order to prevent the spread of the tumor cells or to kill tumor cells that may have become implanted near the tumor site. The treatment of benign tumors with x-rays or cobalt radiation is rarely, if ever, indicated.

Do benign bone tumors tend to become malignant?

Most do not.

At what ages are children most likely to develop malignant tumors of the bone?

Between the ages of 10 and 16 years.

What is the treatment for a malignant bone tumor?

Malignant bone tumors will cause death unless an amputation high above the tumor is performed. Although this is a radical procedure, it is often the only way to save a life.

Can patients be cured of malignant bone tumors?

Yes, patients with malignant bone tumors often can be cured if treatment is begun early.

GIANT CELL TUMORS

What is a giant cell tumor?

A giant cell tumor is a benign tumor usually affecting the end of a bone just adjacent to the joint surface.

146
SURGICAL CONDITIONS AND PROCEDURES

At what age are giant cell tumors usually seen?
In people between 20 and 40 years of age.

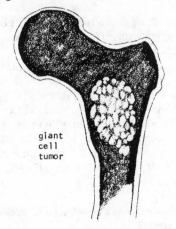

giant
cell
tumor

Do giant cell tumors ever become malignant?
Yes, occasionally.

FIBROUS DYSPLASIA

What is fibrous dysplasia?
Fibrous dysplasia is a rare disorder of bone where bony tissue is replaced by a combination of fibrous and cartilaginous tissue. It usually affects only one side of the body.

How can one make a diagnosis of fibrous dysplasia?
There is deformity of limb and face due to abnormal growth of the bones. Frequently the bone deformities are accompanied by early puberty, blotches of increased skin pigmentation, and early skeletal maturation.

Is fibrous dysplasia inherited?
No.

Is there any treatment for fibrous dysplasia?
Surgical removal of a localized bone tumor may prove helpful.

Will a child tend to outgrow fibrous dysplasia?
After growth has ceased, the deformities do not progress.

SEGMENTAL RESECTION
OF BONE

What is segmental bone resection?
It is the surgical removal of a portion of a bone, leaving the other tissues, such as muscles, nerves, and blood vessels, in place.

What is used to replace the bone that has been removed?
1. A piece of bone taken from some other part of the body.
2. A metal device, shaped like the bone that has been excised. The metal substance most widely employed for this purpose is vitallium.

What are some common indications for segmental bone resection?
1. Loss of function of the patient's own bony structures, as occurs in advanced arthritis or other deforming diseases of the head of the femur (hipbone).
2. Nonmalignant bone tumors or cysts that have caused extensive bone destruction.
3. Bone infection (osteomyelitis) that has resulted in marked bone destruction.
4. Malignant bone tumors, particularly those that tend to be limited and will not recur when once removed.

How successful is segmental bone resection with reconstruction by a bone graft or insertion of a metal replacement device?
Results are constantly improving, and in many instances, the patient can regain normal or near-normal use of his limb. Of course, the results are best when a bone resection has been carried out for a noncancerous condition.

Bowel Obstruction

See INTESTINES.

Brain Surgery

See HEAD INJURIES; NEUROSURGERY.

Brain Tumors

See NEUROSURGERY.

Branchial Cysts

During its early development in the mother's womb, the embryo has gill slits like those seen on fish. These structures usually have disappeared by the time the child is born. In an occasional case, however, remnants of these gill slits, called branchial cysts, remain, and cyst formation occurs.

See also THYROGLOSSAL DUCT CYST.

QUESTIONS AND ANSWERS

What are branchial cysts?

Branchial cysts are remnants of grooves that are incompletely absorbed as the embryo develops. In other words, they represent a congenital birth deformity.

Where are branchial cysts located?

In the neck or in front of the ear.

Congenital deformity of the ear. The opening of a branchial cyst is depicted.

How is the diagnosis of a branchial cyst made?

An unusual opening may be seen on the side of the face, behind the ear, or along the side of the neck. This branchial cyst periodically opens to discharge a small amount of fluid.

Is there a tendency for the opening of a branchial cyst to become sealed off and for fluid to collect behind it?

Yes, and this will manifest itself by enlargement and the formation of a thickened mass.

Should branchial cysts be removed surgically?

Yes. The operation is not dangerous, but requires a meticulous dissection of all tissues so that the cyst does not recur.

Do branchial cysts always appear during childhood?

No. Occasionally, they are not evident until early adult life, when an unusual opening is seen on the side of the face or behind the ear, or along the lateral aspect of the neck as far down as the collarbone.

Should branchial cysts be removed when they are noted in adults?

Yes, because every once in a while they may undergo malignant degeneration if left alone.

Are operations for the removal of branchial cysts dangerous?

No. They may be complicated, however, by the fact that some cysts have long tracts leading from them, and these must be traced all the way to their openings. The opening may be far up in the back of the throat.

Is there a tendency for branchial cysts to recur, once they have been removed?

If incompletely removed, they may recur and will require a second operation.

Breasts

It is no great cause for wonder that the female breast is involved in so many abnormal conditions during the life of a woman. First of all, in today's highly civilized society, the breast rarely fulfills its function. The majority of modern women either do not nurse at all or perhaps nurse but one child for a period of a few weeks. It is well known that organs that are not fully utilized get into trouble more often than those that are constantly put to the use that nature intended for them. Secondly, the breast is repeatedly subjected to fluctuations in its structure and function by the various cycles through which women pass. Adolescence, the menstrual cycle, pregnancy, nursing, and menopause (change of life) all affect the breast's anatomy and physiology. Thirdly, it is one of the last organs in the body to mature, and this development takes place during the trying period of adolescence rather

than in the comfortable confines of a mother's womb. And lastly, the breast is in an exposed and unprotected position where it is all too often subjected to direct injury.

Surgery upon the breast divides into two main categories: that for malignant conditions and that for nonmalignant diseases. Often it is difficult for the examining surgeon to determine positively whether the lesion he is examining is malignant or nonmalignant. For this reason, the following rule is now followed by most surgeons throughout the world: *Every localized lump should be removed from every breast.*

Like all general rules, this one has its exceptions. The commonest exception is a condition known as chronic cystic mastitis. This entity has also been called Schimmelbusch's disease, shoddy breasts, or lumpy breasts, and is characterized by many small, poorly outlined lumps which occur throughout both breasts. These lumps often appear and disappear periodically and are strongly influenced by the woman's menstrual cycle or state of hormone balance. Physicians can best tell about this condition by examining women before and after their periods since these masses tend to get larger (and somewhat painful) just before the period and to get smaller or even to disappear when menstruation has ceased. In most instances, this disease is treated by rectifying the glandular imbalance which is thought to be the cause. On occasion, however, surgery will be recommended for the purpose of clinching the diagnosis positively by examining the removed tissue under the microscope. (*See also* SCHIMMELBUSCH'S DISEASE.)

Noncancerous conditions are called benign or nonmalignant. These constitute the majority of breast lumps which women develop. Present-day education and propaganda, unfortunately, have led people to believe that most lumps are cancerous. This unhappy circumstance not only has resulted in excessive hysteria but also has produced a skepticism among patients who are told that their condition is a minor one. The following are benign breast lesions:

1. Cysts: These occur most often in women between 35 and 45 years of age.

2. Adenoma or fibroadenoma or cystadenoma: These firm, ovoid, solid, nonpainful growths are seen most often in young women between the ages of 18 and 35. They vary in size from that of a small bean to that of an orange.

3. Papilloma and intraductal papilloma: This lesion consists of a warty growth inside a duct of the breast and is usually first discovered because of yellowish, greenish, or bloody discharge from the nipple.

4. Galactocele (milk cyst): This condition should really be classified as a cyst. It is caused by the blockage of a milk duct and is seen in women who have recently borne children.

5. Fat necrosis and hematoma: These two conditions arise from injuries to the breast caused by a direct blow. Because of the firmness of these lesions, they are occasionally diagnosed incorrectly as cancer.

6. Breast abscess: Such infections are often found in nursing mothers, although the breast is no more susceptible to the development of an inflammation than any other part of the body.

It must be remembered that the male breast, that peculiar mistake of nature, is also subject to disease. Two benign conditions occur quite often:

1. Adolescent nodule: This is a firm, round swelling under the nipple of boys beween the ages of 11 and 17 years. It requires no surgery and will usually disappear spontaneously within a few months.

2. Gynecomastia: This word means "female breast" and refers to a condition seen in some men in which one or both breasts are enlarged. When it occurs in young men it usually affects both breasts and is the cause for considerable embarrassment. When seen in men in their 50s or 60s, it more often involves one breast and creates anxiety because of the fear that the enlargement is due to cancer. Although the origin of gynecomastia is not known, it is a fact that men with this condition are almost always normal in every other respect, including their sexual development. In the very rare instance, gynecomastia can be caused by a tumor of the testicle or liver disease. Also, men who are receiving *female* sex hormone injections for the treatment of a cancer of the prostate gland will develop gynecomastia.

Although treatment for gynecomastia is not essential, surgery is often recommended in order to allay fear of cancer or the attendant embarrassment that the condition so often produces. In an older man it is of particular importance to remove the gland to be certain that cancer is not present. Surgery will consist of removing all the breast tissue which lies beneath and adjacent to the nipple. The nipple need not be removed in performing this operation. The operation, carried out under general anesthesia, is an extremely simple one and the patient is confined to the hospital for no more than two to three days.

Cancer of the breast takes more lives unnecessarily than any other form of malignancy, for if diagnosed sufficiently early, most breast cancer is curable through surgery. It is safe to say that if we altered the now-popular dictum "See your dentist twice a year" to "See your doctor twice a year," and if we made sure that he examined and x-rayed the breasts, the great majority of breast cancers would be discovered in their very early and curable stages.

Since no surgeon is smart enough to be 100 percent accurate in diagnosing various breast conditions, the following method of safeguarding the patient has been almost universally adopted:

1. All patients should enter the hospital for the removal of the lump. The lump is removed and examined right at the operating table by both the surgeon and the pathologist. The latter will make a microscopic examination of the tissue within a matter of five minutes.

2. If the lump proves to be benign (noncancerous), the wound is closed and the patient is returned to her room. A rush microscopic section is then made so that complete and final confirmation of the nature of the lesion may be given within 24 to 48 hours. If the lump is doubtful in appearance, a frozen section is made right then and there while the patient is still on the operating table. The specimen is then examined microscopically by the pathologist. If he is then *certain* that the condition is cancerous, the surgeon proceeds to remove the entire breast and the glands draining the area (radical mastectomy).

3. If, after examining the frozen section, there is the slightest doubt in the pathologist's mind, the surgeon will not remove the breast but will close the wound and await the results of a more leisurely and thorough microscopic examination of the tissue in the hospital. After this study has been completed, usually two to three days, a radical operation will be performed, or if the lesion has proved to be benign, the patient will be sent home.

Cancer of the male breast, which occurs 100 times less frequently than female breast cancer, is treated in the same manner as just described.

See also MASTECTOMY.

QUESTIONS AND ANSWERS

Must a breast with a lump be operated upon?

Yes. It is necessary to remove the lump in order to examine it thoroughly under a microscope. The one exception is the large cyst which the surgeon may aspirate and have the fluid removed subjected to microscopic examination.

What breast conditions do not require surgery?

Breasts with chronic cystic mastitis, the so-called lumpy breasts.

It is not essential to operate upon the adolescent nodules seen in boys or upon the enlarged breasts (gynecomastia) seen in men.

Can a surgeon tell, before operation, whether a lump is cancerous?

In the great majority of cases the surgeon *can* make a correct diagnosis. However, this is not good enough! One hundred percent accuracy must be the goal. Only after the lump is removed and a section carefully examined under a microscope—and only then—can a diagnosis be made with complete certainty.

How can x-raying a breast help to make a diagnosis?

A technique known as mammography may reveal a tumor long before it can be felt by the examining physician.

What kind of operation will be performed?

Simple removal of the lump through an incision about two inches long is usually the first procedure performed. If the cyst or tumor proves to be benign (not cancerous), that is all the surgery that will be required.

If the tumor is found to be cancerous, the entire breast is removed.

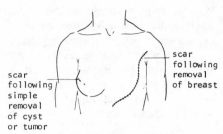

scar
following
simple
removal
of cyst
or tumor

scar
following
removal
of breast

INCISIONS FOR BREAST OPERATIONS

Is the operation disfiguring?

Simple removal of a lump leaves a small scar which will become hardly visible within a few months.

The total removal of the breast does leave a large scar extending from the shoulder diagonally down to the upper abdomen. However, there is no external disfigurement, because today women can purchase brassieres which will hide completely the fact that a breast has been removed.

Is it wise to seek another opinion before subjecting oneself to surgery?

Of course. A patient should see as many physicians as are required to convince herself of the proper course of action. However, almost all surgeons are in agreement that lumps must be removed from breasts.

When should a biopsy be taken?

The term *biopsy* means that a piece of a tumor is removed for microscopic examination. Since it is technically just as simple to remove the entire tumor mass, this form of treatment has replaced the biopsy in most medical centers.

How long a hospital stay is necessary?

If a simple excision of a cyst or tumor is performed, the patient may be released within one to three days.

If a breast excision has been performed, the patient usually remains in the hospital for seven to ten days.

How long does the operation take?

Simple lump excision requires about 15 to 25 minutes; mastectomy requires anywhere from 1½ to 4 hours, depending upon the rapidity of the surgeon's technique. Some excellent surgeons prefer to work slowly.

If cancer is found, should the surgeon tell the patient?

Although there is a difference of opinion on this point, most surgeons tell the patient the truth. This practice has grown markedly in recent years, as the cure rate for cancer has steadily increased.

Is it a dangerous operation?

No. Neither the simple excision of a cyst or tumor nor the removal of an entire breast is a dangerous procedure. Mortality from the operation is exceedingly rare and must be classified as accidental.

What are the chances for a complete cure if it proves to be cancer?

Approximately four out of five women with cancer of the breast can be saved if it is discovered before the tumor has spread beyond the gland. The percentage would be even higher were it not for the fact that so many patients seek advice so late in the course of their disease. The mortality among men with cancer of the breast is somewhat greater than among women.

What will happen if an operation is not performed?

If the patient does not follow the surgeon's advice, she is taking a great risk. If the condition is benign, it may grow to such large proportions that it will cause disfigurement and destruction of surrounding breast tissue. Or a benign lesion might eventually turn into a malignant one. If a cancer is not operated upon, it will eventually lead to the patient's death.

Should x-ray, cobalt, hormone, or chemical treatments be used instead of surgery for breast cancer?

No, but these are extremely valuable tools when used in conjunction with surgery. The exception is the far advanced, neglected case of cancer in which surgery would be of no benefit.

How soon must the operation be done?

As soon as any lump is discovered, arrangements should be made for its removal; that is, within a period of two to three weeks at the most.

Is any special preparation necessary before undertaking this type of surgery?

No. Even the most radical breast operations can be tolerated well by the average patient.

What kind of anesthesia will be used?

General anesthesia with inhalation of nitrous oxide, halothane, cyclopropane or ether is the method of choice. However, for very small and superficial benign cysts or tumors, some surgeons prefer to use local anesthesia with procaine or some similar agent.

Are special nurses necessary?

After a radical operation, special nurses are helpful for the first two to three days.

Does a lump in one breast predispose toward the formation of a lump in the other breast?

Yes. A person who has had a lump in one breast is slightly more prone toward developing a similar condition either in the same or in the other breast. It is essential, therefore, that women have their breasts examined at least once a year!

Will the surgeon always be able to tell whether the growth is cancerous while the patient is on the operating table?

No. Even frozen-section examinations are not 100 percent accurate. It is occasionally necessary to wait two to three days for final report from the pathology department.

Do breast tumors arise as a result of an injury or blow?

No.

Is x-ray treatment necessary after operation?

The medical profession is divided in its opinion on this subject. However, it is safe to say that certain types of cases are definitely benefited by a course of postoperative x-ray treatments.

Is the operation painful?

Simple tumor removal produces very little postoperative pain.

Pain in the wound area and pain in the shoulder and arm on the involved side are common symptoms after a radical breast operation. This pain may last for four to seven days before subsiding. Swelling of the entire arm is sometimes encountered. This distressing complication may persist for several months after surgery.

How soon after surgery will the patient get out of bed?

Simple tumor removal does not actually require any bed sojourn. Patients who have undergone breast removal should get out of bed the day following operation. They should be encouraged to use their arm, even though painful, and especially to raise the arm over the head.

Will plastic surgery be necessary after the radical operation?

Usually skin edges can be brought together without too much difficulty. If the surgeon has removed a great deal of skin, it is occasionally necessary to graft skin to close over the raw area.

There is no truly satisfactory plastic operation which will replace a removed breast, although plastic repair has been attempted.

Does a benign lump, if not removed, turn into a cancer?

Perhaps occasionally, but many pathologists believe that benign tumors seldom become cancerous. The main reason for advocating their removal is that one can never be positive it is actually benign until one has removed it.

Should a patient allow herself to become pregnant after a breast operation?

After the removal of a simple non-malignant tumor, it is perfectly permissible.

It is inadvisable to have children after a breast has been removed because of cancer. Pregnancy tends to stimulate growth of all breast tissue.

Can a woman who has had a benign breast tumor removed be permitted to nurse a baby?

Yes. The existence of a benign breast tumor has no bearing upon nursing.

Should change of life be induced among younger women after breast removal for cancer?

This is practiced by some surgeons if there is concern that the tumor may have spread beyond the breast area. It is accomplished by removing the ovaries.

How long does it take to convalesce from a breast operation?

After a simple operation, recovery is immediate and complete. Following a radical operation, it takes four to six weeks to make a complete recovery. The arm on the involved side may re-

quire special physiotherapy, in certain instances, for several months post-operatively.

Will recovery be complete?

Yes. People whose breasts have been removed should return to completely normal lives, unless, of course, they happen to fall into that unfortunate category wherein the cancer has not been completely removed. It is natural for women who have undergone breast removal to be psychologically depressed. The best way to combat this is for them to return as soon as possible to their normal way of life.

Does an operation upon the breast affect sex life?

No. Normal sex relations can be resumed at any time after the wound has healed.

How long does it take the wound to heal?

The wound of a simple operation heals in seven to nine days. Unless it has been impossible to close the original wound, wounds of radical operations are usually healed by the end of the third postoperative week.

When, after operation, can one bathe?

As soon as the wound is healed. Following a simple tumor removal, usually within a week. After total breast removal, it may take three to four weeks before one can bathe.

Are tumors of the breast inherited or do they tend to run in families?

There is no actual proof that benign tumors or cancers of the breast are inherited or tend to run in families.

How often should a patient be rechecked after operation?

About once every six months.

Is it permissible to undergo breast surgery during a menstrual period?

Yes.

PLASTIC OPERATIONS UPON THE BREAST

Most women place great importance upon the size and shape of their breasts. Young and old alike display exceptional interest in this part of their anatomy and are quick to discuss with their family doctor or surgeon any concern they may have over deviations from normal. Women with markedly enlarged (hypertrophied) and hanging (pendulous) breasts are unhappy people who resort to all sorts of devices to hide their condition. Fortunately, plastic surgery has devised competent ways of reshaping breasts and more and more women are submitting to these operations.

It should be emphasized that breast plastic operations are advocated only for those who have marked breast deformity. These are major operative procedures and should not be performed indiscriminately upon whimsical women who wish to correct minor sagging or reduce slight enlargement. Furthermore, it should be recognized that a good result will depend upon the selection of a skilled plastic surgeon who has had wide experience in the field.

The indications for plastic operations upon the breasts are as follows:

1. **Marked enlargement:** Such breasts are heavy and exert a constant, painful pull on the shoulders with cutting of the brassiere straps into the skin.

2. **Marked sagging:** Such breasts may hang six to eight inches below their normal position. Also, the skin underneath these breasts is difficult to care for and frequently becomes irritated.

3. **Marked underdevelopment of the breasts or marked disparity in the size of the two breasts.**

4. **Marked psychological disturbance:** Many young women attribute their inability to get married to their deformed breasts. Because of self-consciousness, they abstain from participation in many social activities, refuse to wear bathing suits and evening gowns.

There are several surgical procedures for the correction of enlarged and pendulous breasts. Each has its advocates, and each is a good operation when performed carefully and expertly. Plastic operations upon the breast must be performed in the hospital under general anesthesia. Whenever possible, both breasts are operated upon at the same time. The procedures often take 1½ to 2½ hours for each breast. It is important, therefore, that the patient be in excellent general health before undertaking this type of surgery.

The essential principle underlying these procedures is to preserve the blood supply to the nipple and the blood supply of the skin flaps. In performing these operations, the nipple is encircled with an incision but is left attached to the underlying breast tissue. Skin flaps are elevated from the underlying breast tissue by undermining the skin in an outward direction from the nipple. The excess breast tissue is then cut off. The remaining breast, with nipple attached, is then brought up to a higher location and the nipple is brought through a snug-fitting hole which is fashioned in the upper skin flap. The excess skin from the lower part of the breast is then cut away and all skin edges are neatly sutured.

The wounds are drained to permit the exit of serum which usually forms. The drains are removed in two to three days

STEPS IN PLASTIC
OPERATION FOR
ENLARGED, HANGING
BREAST

155

BREASTS

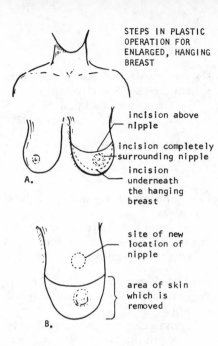

A.
incision above nipple
incision completely surrounding nipple
incision underneath the hanging breast

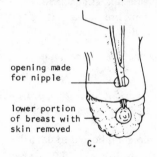

B.
site of new location of nipple
area of skin which is removed

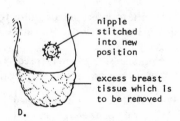

clamp grasping nipple to pull it, and its attached breast, to new position

opening made for nipple
lower portion of breast with skin removed

C.

nipple stitched into new position
excess breast tissue which is to be removed

D.

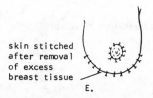

skin stitched after removal of excess breast tissue

E.

but the stitches are permitted to remain in place for 10 to 12 days. The patient can get out of bed on the first or second postoperative day and may leave the hospital, with stitches still in place, anywhere from the fifth to the eighth day after operation.

The most frequently encountered complication of breastplasty in former years was postoperative infection. Such infection would destroy the cosmetic result and leave the patient with areas which would drain pus for months afterward. Fortunately, the proper use of antibiotic drugs has minimized this danger. Today excellent results are being obtained in the overwhelming majority of cases.

Within recent years, plastic sacs containing an inert fluid have been devised for the purpose of enlarging the appearance of the breast. These sacs are made in a convex, round shape to conform to the size of the breast. An incision is made below each breast and a pouch is fashioned by the surgeon beneath the breast tissue on the chest wall. After all bleeding has been controlled, the plastic sac is slipped into this pouch, thus elevating the overlying breast tissue and giving the appearance of enlargement. The skin incision is then sutured.

It must be kept in mind that this operative procedure should be performed only by expert plastic surgeons under the most rigid aseptic conditions. Although the operation is simple to carry out, not all patients will accept such a large foreign body and their tissues will fail to encapsulate it. In such cases, a draining sinus will develop and the sac will have to be removed. A second attempt can be made several months later if all inflammation has subsided, but the chances are that a similar rejection of the inserted sac will take place.

When is it best to undergo breastplasty?

Young unmarried women with a marked deformity and a marked psychological disturbance occasioned by the breasts may be operated upon. However, more satisfactory results will follow if surgery is done after women are finished having children.

Are plastic operations ever performed to make breasts larger?

Yes. Plastic sacs containing an inert fluid have been inserted beneath the breasts to give the appearance of enlargement.

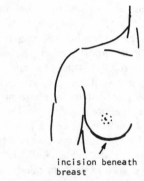

incision beneath breast

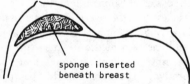

sponge inserted beneath breast

PLASTIC SURGERY TO ENLARGE APPEARANCE OF BREASTS

Are there cases where only one breast is enlarged?

Yes, but this is not very common.

Are operations done to cure inverted nipples?

Not usually.

Do plastic operations interfere with sensations in the breast?

No.

Do the breasts swell during menstrual periods after these operations?

The breasts will react postoperatively the same as they did before operation.

Is pregnancy permissible after a breastplasty?

Yes.

Can a woman nurse a child after these operations?

Yes, in those cases in which the nipple has been left attached to its underlying breast tissue.

Are breasts ever removed solely because they are hypertrophied (markedly enlarged)?

Yes. In older women with markedly enlarged breasts, simple removal may be advisable instead of a complicated plastic operation.

Are breast plastic operations serious?

Yes. However, breastplasty is not a dangerous operation.

Are breast plastic operations painful?

No.

What are the various operative procedures for enlarged and pendulous breasts?

These are too complicated to describe in detail. See diagrams which sketch one of the many operative procedures.

Is it safe to inject silicone directly into the breasts in order to make them larger?

No. The silicone may predispose to tumor formation within the breast.

What kind of anesthesia is used?

General anesthesia.

Are special nurses necessary?

No.

Are blood transfusions necessary?

No.

What are the possible complications of breastplasty?
1. **Postoperative infection.** This is guarded against by scrupulous antiseptic surgical technique and by giving large doses of antibiotic drugs.
2. **Asymmetry with the nipples** at different levels.
3. If the plastic operation is to make the breasts appear larger, **the plastic sacs may be rejected** and will cause a discharge from the wound. The sponges will then have to be removed.

How soon after surgery can one get out of bed?
One to two days.

How long a hospital stay is necessary after breastplasty?
Five to eight days.

Are special postoperative measures necessary?
No.

Should special brassieres be worn after breast plastic operations?
No, but a snug-fitting brassiere should be purchased and worn steadily for several weeks.

How long do these wounds take to heal?
Ten to fourteen days.

Are the scars of breast operations very noticeable?
No. Incisions about the nipple disappear almost completely, and incisions beneath the breast usually fade to a barely distinguishable thin white line.

Are scars of these operations visible in bathing suits or evening gowns?
No.

How successful are these procedures?
In the hands of expert plastic surgeons, results are excellent.

If the results of these plastic operations are unsatisfactory, can the procedure be done over again?
Yes, but reoperation is more difficult than the original operation, and the results are not as satisfactory.

Are the results of breastplasty usually permanent?
Yes, although normal aging tends to cause all breasts to lose their youthful contours.

Do the breasts tend to regrow after having been reduced in size?
Not usually, unless the patient becomes very stout.

Do the breasts tend to sag again after being elevated?
Not for many years, unless there is marked weight gain.

How soon after surgery can one do the following?

Bathe	10 to 14 days
Housework	3 to 4 weeks
Resume physical exercise	4 to 5 weeks
Resume sexual relations	4 weeks

BREASTS IN OLDER WOMEN

When do a woman's breasts start to show signs of aging?
At about the time of menopause (change of life). The changes consist mainly of loss of the breast gland tissue and its replacement by fibrous tissue. Since the ovaries are no longer actively secreting hormones, breast tissue undergoes a certain amount of atrophy (degeneration). There is also a loss in fat tissue of the breast.

Do the contour and appearance of the breasts in women past menopause change?
Yes. Breasts tend to become flatter and to sag. This is caused by degen-

eration of gland and fat tissue and their replacement by fibrous tissue. In addition, the ligaments that hold up the breasts on the chest wall become lax.

Is there any way to prevent breasts from sagging and becoming flabby as one grows older?

To a limited extent. If a woman takes the following measures during her 20s and 30s, her breasts will have a better chance of retaining a more youthful appearance:

1. Avoid getting too stout. Overweight will cause the skin of the breasts to stretch. When weight is lost, the skin becomes streaked and has less elasticity.

2. Avoid undernourishment. This will cause the fat tissue to disappear and will weaken the tissues that hold the breasts in their proper position.

3. Special care of the breasts should be taken during pregnancy and during the nursing period. The obstetrician's instructions should be followed carefully. The contour of the breasts is often unnecessarily altered by failure to take proper care of them at this time.

4. A well-fitted, uplift brassiere should always be worn. Creams, hormone ointments, and other such preparations are of doubtful value. Certainly, hormone ointments should be used only on a doctor's prescription. Breast pumps and the so-called exercisers are valueless.

Can plastic surgery on the breasts be successfully performed on women past 60?

Yes. With the longer life-span and the increased desire of older women to retain their youthful appearance, plastic surgery on the breasts is being performed increasingly. Although vanity usually stimulates a woman's decision to undergo this operation, there are frequently medical advantages. Older women with heavy pendulous breasts receive great relief through plastic surgery.

How often should women past 60 have their breasts examined?

Twice each year. If this practice is adhered to, tumors can be discovered during the early stage. (Four out of five cancers of the breast can be cured if they are discovered before they have spread to surrounding lymph nodes.)

Should older women rely solely on self-examination of the breasts?

No! This is very unwise if it is substituted for examination by a physician.

What is the significance of a lump in the breast of a woman who has passed the menopause?

Unfortunately, the majority of lumps that develop in the breasts of women past menopause are malignant. However, there are benign tumors, such as fatty tumors and areas of fat necrosis (degeneration), which develop after menopause. In addition, older women who lose a great deal of weight may discover in the breast a deep lump that has gone unnoticed for many years. Such lumps are almost always benign.

What is the significance of a discharge of blood or another substance from the nipple in a woman past 60?

This usually indicates that there is a tumor within the ducts of the breast. In many such cases, the lump cannot be felt. Secretion from the nipple occasionally takes place when a patient has been having intensive hormone treatment. This is, however, uncommon.

What causes painful breasts in women past 60?

They occur in women who are markedly obese and whose breasts are pendulous. They also occur in older women who are receiving large doses of female sex hormones. Another cause is an inflammation within the breast (mastitis), occasionally appearing as a complication of a virus infection that has traveled throughout the body. Finally, pain in the breasts may sometimes be brought on by improperly fitting brassieres.

Is cancer of the breast usually associated with pain?

No. Most malignant breast tumors are painless.

What is the significance of a chronic ulcer or sore on the nipple?

This often indicates the presence of a malignant tumor in the breast. The appearance of such an ulcer should stimulate a woman to seek medical advice promptly.

Can a blow or injury to the breast cause cancer to develop?

No. Many women relate the onset of a breast tumor to a blow or injury they received. The explanation is as follows: A woman is unaware that she has a lump until she receives a blow on the breast. The pain occasioned by the blow causes her to examine the breast and to discover a lump that has been there for some time.

Is acute inflammation of the breast common in women past 60?

No. It is rare.

Are malignant diseases of the breast more common in women past 60 than in younger women?

No. Statistics show that cancer of the breast occurs more often in women between the ages of 45 and 60 than in those over 60. However, there is too great an incidence of this disease in women of all ages.

Is cancer of the breast in older women curable?

Yes. As a matter of fact, malignant tumors tend to grow more slowly in older women, thus giving them a better chance for cure than many younger women. Of course, they must seek medical care early in the course of the disease.

Is it safe for women past 60 to undergo extensive surgery for the removal of a breast cancer?

Yes. Even the most radical breast-removal operation can be tolerated by older women, provided they are in a satisfactory state of general health. Only when someone is debilitated or has severe heart, liver, or kidney disease will extensive surgery be risky.

What is the significance of enlargement of the breasts in older women who are receiving hormone therapy?

Large doses of female hormone may cause a senile breast to become active again. The glands will respond to the influence of the hormone and the breasts will increase in size. When the hormones are discontinued, the breasts return to their quiescent state.

Can older women tolerate x-ray or cobalt treatments for breast cancer?

Yes.

BREASTS IN OLDER MEN

Does the male breast ever become enlarged in men past 60?

Yes. For some reason, the tissue in the male breast (which is essentially the same tissue as in the female) often enlarges and may become tender to the touch. This condition is known as adenomatous disease of the breast or gynecomastia.

What can be done about enlargement of the breasts in stout men?

Obviously, the best advice for them is to lose weight. However, despite weight loss, some men do have large, pendulous breasts, which cause them considerable embarrassment. They can undergo surgery for the removal of excess breast tissue if they so desire.

Is diffuse enlargement of one or both male breasts usually a sign of malignancy?

No. Male breast cancer, a rare disease, is usually characterized by an irregular, firm lump in one segment of the breast beneath the nipple.

Is enlargement of the male breast in older men usually associated with loss in virility?

No. Enlargement of the male breast is no indication whatever of degree of virility.

Will the taking of medications ever cause enlargement or gynecomastia of the male breast?

Yes, and such enlargement will subside when the medication is discontinued.

What is the significance of an isolated lump in the male breast?

It may be caused by an inflammation or by a tumor. Whatever the cause, surgery should always be performed so that the tissue can be subjected to microscopic examination.

What is the treatment for adenomatous disease of the male breast?

Because it is not always possible by external examination to distinguish between this benign condition and a malignant growth, surgery is often recommended. This may consist of removal of the nipple and underlying breast tissue in order to obtain sufficient material for microscopic analysis.

Are operations on the male breast dangerous?

Even radical surgery for cancer can be tolerated if the patient is in satisfactory health.

Does the nipple always have to be removed when the underlying breast tissue is excised?

No. If the operation is for adenomatous disease and not for cancer, the nipple can often be left in place.

How common is cancer of the male breast?

It is nowhere near as common as in females. When it does occur, it often affects men who are in their 60s and 70s.

What is the treatment for cancer of the male breast?

It differs very little from the surgery for cancer of the female breast. The entire breast, underlying muscles of the chest wall, and lymph nodes in the armpit are removed.

BREASTS IN CHILDREN AND ADOLESCENTS

Are children ever born with swollen breasts?

Yes, the nipples and breasts of newborn males and females are sometimes considerably swollen.

What causes the swelling of a newborn's breasts?

In most instances, the breasts contain milk.

Why do both male and female newborns sometimes have milk ooze from their nipples?

The unborn child is affected by the hormones circulating in the mother's blood. The same hormones that stimulate the mother's breasts to secrete milk can affect the unborn child so that his or her glands secrete milk.

Should a newborn who is secreting milk be treated?

No treatment is necessary, although

the nipples should be sponged with a mild cleaning solution. After a few days the influence of the mother's hormones will disappear and the breasts will dry up.

Should the milk ever be squeezed out of the breasts of a newborn?
This is not necessary and can cause irritation and injury to these delicate glands.

Do newborns who secrete milk ever develop a cyst within their breasts?
Yes, this does occasionally happen. If one of the ducts in the breast becomes clogged, the milk within it may form a small cyst.

What can be done for these cysts?
They should be watched. If the cysts do not become infected, they will probably be absorbed and disappear spontaneously within a short time.

Do newborns who secrete milk ever develop abscesses of the breast?
Yes, this occurs every once in a while and is probably caused by the secondary infection of a clogged milk duct.

What is the treatment for a breast abscess in a newborn child?
The abscess should be incised and drained. This can be done as an office procedure without anesthesia.

Will a breast abscess in a newborn girl cause a deformity of her breast when she matures?
No. As the child grows older the scar of the incision that is made to drain the breast abscess will become practically invisible.

Should a lump be removed from the breast of a female child who has not yet reached puberty?
This is perhaps best not done, because what might be interpreted as a tumor may be only an enlargement of the en-tire glandular structure. If this tissue is removed, the child will not develop a normal breast as she matures. This can be psychologically disturbing.

How can a physician distinguish between a true tumor of the breast and precocious enlargement of the gland?
A needle biopsy will tell whether there is any abnormal tumor tissue. If the report of a needle biopsy is negative, then the enlargement should be left alone. It is only when a needle biopsy shows tissues indicative of malignancy that surgery to remove the tumor should be undertaken.

Do adolescent girls (15 or 16 years of age) ever develop breast tumors?
Yes, occasionally an adolescent may develop what is known as a fibroadenoma. This is a benign (nonmalignant) tumor.

What is the treatment for a fibroadenoma of the breast?
Simple excision through a small opening is all that is necessary.

Why should a fibroadenoma be treated?
Because such tumors have a tendency to enlarge and because one cannot always be positive that the tumor is just a simple fibroadenoma unless it is removed and examined microscopically.

Is the operation for removal of a fibroadenoma serious?
No. It is a simple operative procedure performed under a light general anesthesia and requires but a day or two of hospitalization.

Do fibroadenomas tend to recur?
Not at the site from which one has been removed. Occasionally a girl will develop another tumor in another location.

Is a fibroadenoma an indication of a glandular upset?

Usually not. The cause of these tumors is completely unknown, but they usually do not accompany disturbances in menstruation or other gland functions.

Will the removal of a fibroadenoma from an adolescent girl's breast prevent her from breast-feeding when she has children?

No.

Will a fibroadenoma ever turn into a cancer if it is not removed?

No. The current medical opinion is that this type of tumor practically never develops into a cancer.

Can an injury such as a severe direct blow cause an adolescent girl to develop a breast tumor?

No. It is a common misconception that breast tumors result from injuries. If, however, a breast is severely bruised, hemorrhage can take place. This may form a blood clot that will liquefy and may need to be evacuated surgically.

GYNECOMASTIA

What is gynecomastia?

Gynecomastia is unusual enlargement of the breasts of a male child, adolescent, or adult.

Is gynecomastia necessarily an abnormal condition?

No. In some adolescent boys it is a variant of normal development. It is thought to be caused by the secretion of a substance similar to the female sex hormone by the testicles during puberty.

Is there a tendency for gynecomastia to be inherited?

Yes. It will often be found that the father had the same condition.

Is gynecomastia ever associated with liver disease?

Yes, but not frequently.

Is gynecomastia ever associated with other gland disorders?

Yes. Infrequently, a tumor of the testicle or of the adrenal gland is present. However, in such cases it will be obvious that the primary disease is not in the breast area.

What happens to the enlarged breasts of adolescent boys?

The secretion of the substance similar to the female sex hormone usually ceases as the testicles mature, and the breasts do not enlarge further. As the child matures and grows bigger, the breasts appear smaller.

Is gynecomastia painful?

No.

Is surgical removal of enlarged breasts ever indicated?

Some boys have very large breasts that cause great embarrassment. It is not at all infrequent that they will ask that something be done about the condition. In these cases, surgery may be indicated if the breasts remain oversized.

What surgery can be performed for gynecomastia?

The breast tissue is removed although the nipple is left behind. A transverse incision is made above the nipple for a distance of about two inches. The nipple is reflected downward and the underlying breast tissue is removed in one piece. The nipple is then sutured back to the skin and held firmly against the chest wall with a compression bandage. Some surgeons perform the same procedure through an incision made below the nipple.

Are operations for gynecomastia successful?

Yes, invariably. All that will remain

is a linear scar above or below each nipple.

What is meant by pseudogynecomastia?
Pseudogynecomastia is a prominent deposit of fat beneath the nipple. It is seen in some boys who are too fat.

Should any local treatment be given for pseudogynecomastia?
No. However, these children should be encouraged to lose weight.

What is an adolescent nodule?
This a form of gynecomastia in which there is a small, firm, round, tender swelling just beneath the nipple.

Who tends to get adolescent nodules of the breast?
They are usually noted in boys who are somewhat preadolescent, between 11 and 14 years old. Occasionally an adolescent nodule is seen in a girl 10 or 11 years old.

Adolescent nodules require no treatment and will disappear spontaneously in a few months to a year. It is important to assure the mother that these lumps are not tumors but represent a precursor of adolescence.

ENLARGEMENT OF THE BREASTS

Is enlargement (hypertrophy) of the breasts ever seen in little girls?
Yes. This is an unusual condition but it is occasionally seen in children during their first three years of life. In some cases there may be enlargement of one breast only.

Is enlargement of the breasts of a young girl always a sign of precocious puberty or tumor formation?
No. More often it is just a benign abnormality unassociated with any other demonstrable disease.

Is it important to examine these young girls to make sure they do not have precocious puberty due to a tumor in the ovary, pineal gland, or adrenal gland?
Yes.

What happens to abnormally large breasts in a child less than nine years old?
In many instances, the enlargement subsides as the child grows older. In other cases, it continues until real puberty takes place.

SUPERNUMERARY NIPPLES

Are supernumerary nipples a common congenital abnormality?
Yes, this is not an infrequent finding. Some children are born with an extra nipple in the same vertical line as the normal nipple but down in the lower part of the chest or upper abdomen, either on one side or both sides. Other children may be born with two to six extra nipples located at various levels on the abdominal wall along the nipple line.

Do boys as well as girls ever have extra nipples?
Yes, just as frequently.

Are these extra nipples support for the thesis that man has evolved from some lower form of animal life?
Yes.

Do extra nipples tend to bulge as a girl reaches puberty and her breasts start to enlarge?
Usually not. There is almost no gland tissue beneath the extra nipples.

What should be done about extra nipples?
For cosmetic reasons, they are best excised in a girl, especially if they are located in an area that may be exposed.

Is the removal of an extra nipple a serious operation?

No. It is a simple procedure that can be performed under light general anesthesia when the child is young, or under local anesthesia in an older child.

What kind of scars result from the removal of extra nipples?

Insignificant transverse linear scars.

Which is more noticeable, the extra nipple or the scar left after its excision?

The extra nipple is much more noticeable than the thin-lined scar that follows its removal.

Bronchiectasis

Bronchiectasis is an infectious process of unknown cause in which there is widening and destruction of portions of of the bronchial tubes that branch into the lungs. When there is loss of elasticity in the walls of a bronchus, there is stagnation of secretions. Infection then sets in and leads to recurrent attacks of pneumonia or lung abscess. People with bronchiectasis have a foul odor to their breath, spit up large

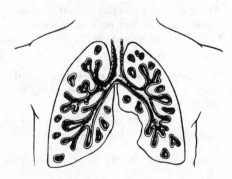

A cutaway drawing of the lungs shows the abnormal widening of the bronchial tubes that is typical of bronchiectasis.

quantities of infected mucus, and sometimes cough up blood. Because of the tendency of this disease to be localized to one portion of the lungs, usually the lowermost portion, the best treatment is removal of these sections of the lung through surgery. Great improvement will follow removal of the involved lobe of the lung.

See also LUNGS.

QUESTIONS AND ANSWERS

How can a diagnosis of bronchiectasis be made?

By performing a bronchography. This is a procedure in which a liquid mixture is allowed to run down into the bronchial tubes so as to outline and fill them with an opaque substance. On x-ray, an excellent outline of the large and small bronchial tubes will be demonstrated. If bronchiectasis is present, it will be seen on the x-ray film.

Does bronchiectasis frequently affect young people?

No. It is found mostly in older people who have had long-standing bronchitis or have had severe episodes of pneumonia.

Are there various forms of bronchiectasis?

Yes. There is a rare form, congenital bronchiectasis, that exists from birth. The most common type is acquired bronchiectasis.

What are the symptoms and complications of bronchiectasis?

Chronic, long-standing cough, usually with profuse expectoration, asthma, thinning of the air sacs of the lungs (emphysema), hemorrhage from the bronchial tubes, lung abscess formation, or pneumonia.

Can bronchiectasis be diagnosed by an ordinary x-ray of the chest?

Not definitely. It may be necessary to pass a tube into the bronchial tubes (bronchoscopy) or to perform a bronchography in order to clinch the diagnosis.

What are the principles of treatment for bronchiectasis?

1. Maintenance of adequate drainage of the mucous secretions from the bronchial tubes. To accomplish this, the secretions must be loosened, and certain expectorant medications are given toward that end.

2. The giving of antibiotic drugs to control the infection.

3. The use of inhalations of various drugs which may dilate the bronchial tubes.

4. Postural drainage (coughing in various positions with the upper part of the body dependent or hanging down over a bed or table) may be very helpful in ridding the bronchial tubes of pus and mucus. This type of exercise should be done several times a day.

Is surgery ever indicated for bronchiectasis?

Yes, if the bronchiectasis is localized, that is, if there is widening in a small area of the lungs. In such an event, that portion of the lung can be removed successfully by surgery. Also, severe hemorrhage from bronchiectasis is an indication to remove that area of the lung.

Is surgery for bronchiectasis dangerous?

Today, operations for the removal of part or all of the lung (lobectomy or pneumonectomy) can be carried out safely by chest surgeons.

What are the chances of recovery following surgery for bronchiectasis?

Well over 95 percent will recover and be cured, provided all of the diseased portions of the lung are removed. The amount of lung tissue that can be removed safely can be determined by properly performed pulmonary function tests.

How long a period of hospitalization is necessary?

The usual period of hospitalization after removal of a lobe of a lung is two to three weeks.

Can a patient breathe normally after having a lobe of a lung removed?

Yes. If only one lobe has been removed he can lead a completely normal life without shortness of breath or other respiratory symptoms.

How can bronchiectasis be prevented?

1. Nothing can be done to prevent congenital bronchiectasis inasmuch as a child is born with the defect.

2. Early diagnosis and prompt treatment of pneumonia, especially in infancy and childhood.

3. One of the main underlying causes for all bronchiectasis is chronic bronchitis. Therefore, it is extremely important that a child or adult receive prompt and thorough treatment for any chronic cough or bronchial tube infection. This will usually involve the giving of large doses of antibiotics.

4. It may be necessary for people who are subject to repeated, severe attacks of bronchitis to move to a warm, dry climate, if they happen to live in an area where there are extremely cold temperatures.

5. Cigarette smoking causes chronic irritation of the bronchial tubes and predisposes toward bronchiectasis. Anyone with a tendency toward recurrent bronchitis, or anyone who has a chronic cough because of smoking, should give up the habit, or face the danger of eventual bronchiectasis.

6. Those with asthmatic bronchitis should receive ongoing care from an

allergist in an attempt to discover and eradicate the irritating factor. Certainly, as asthmatic should not smoke cigarettes, as this will predispose toward bronchiectasis.

Bronchoscopy and Bronchography

Bronchoscopy is a procedure in which a rigid metal tube, called a bronchoscope, is inserted into the throat, past the vocal cords, into the windpipe (trachea), and down into the bronchial tubes.

Bronchography is a procedure in which a liquid mixture is allowed to run down into the bronchial tubes so as to fill them with an opaque substance. On x-ray, excellent outlines of the large and small bronchial tubes will be seen.

See also LUNGS.

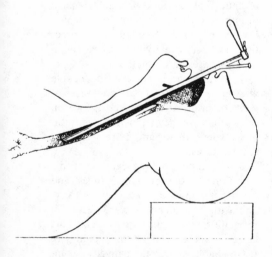

Local anesthesia reduces a patient's pain before the bronchoscope is inserted into diagnostic position.

QUESTIONS AND ANSWERS

What is the main value of bronchoscopy?

It is of great value in lung conditions in which x-ray and sputum examinations do not give a definite diagnosis. Bronchoscopy may show the site of origin of bleeding; it may reveal foreign bodies that have been aspirated into the lungs; it may show a tumor in the bronchus, or the location of a cancer of the lung. It will also show the point of blockage of a bronchus.

Another value of bronchoscopy is that secretions can be sucked up from deep down in a bronchial tube, and these secretions can be submitted for microscopic examination. On examination of this material, cancer cells can be detected, if a cancer exists in a lung or bronchial tube.

What is the main value of bronchography?

In outlining the large and small bronchial tubes, it is possible to see whether they are deformed or dilated. A diagnosis of bronchiectasis can be made on bronchography, as can a diagnosis of obstruction of a bronchial tube.

Can bronchial tube obstruction be relieved through bronchoscopy?

Yes. Since suction can be carried out through a bronchoscope, it is possible to remove pus, mucus, or foreign bodies that wholly or partially block the passageways.

Can pieces of tissue from a bronchus or lung be removed through a bronchoscope?

Yes. This material is used for biopsy purposes and is extremely important in making an exact diagnosis of existing disease. A diagnosis of cancer of the lung is frequently made on bronchoscopy.

Is it possible to stop bleeding through bronchoscopy?

Yes, occasionally, an area of bleeding or ulceration can be cauterized through a bronchoscope, thus effecting a cure.

Can atelectasis (lung collapse) be helped through bronchoscopy?

Yes. Most atelectasis is caused by mucus plugging a bronchus. Through passage of a bronchoscope, an obstructing mucous plug can be sucked out, thus allowing the lung to reexpand.

Can postoperative pneumonia be prevented through bronchoscopy?

Often, a postoperative pneumonia originates from atelectasis and plugging of the bronchial tubes. If bronchoscopy is carried out promptly within the first few hours and the plug of mucus is removed, pneumonia may be prevented.

Can the life of a newborn child ever be saved through bronchoscopy?

Yes, on occasion. If there is fluid obstructing the respiratory passages in a newborn, prompt bronchoscopy may save the child's life. After insertion of the bronchoscope, the fluid secretions are sucked out and oxygen is pumped into the infant's lungs. This is sometimes a lifesaving procedure.

Is bronchoscopy helpful in making a diagnosis of bronchiectasis?

Yes.

Is bronchoscopy a painful procedure?

It is very uncomfortable, but the throat and respiratory passages are anesthetized by local anesthetic agents, thus reducing the pain.

Is general anesthesia given in order to perform bronchoscopy?

It is used occasionally. The giving of inhalation anesthesia may alter the appearance of the respiratory passages so that the desired information might not

be obtained as readily as when the patient is not anesthetized. However, marked sedation can be given before the procedure is undertaken, and this will reduce the amount of discomfort.

How long does it take to perform a bronchoscopy?

The average bronchoscopy rarely lasts more than one-half hour.

What type of physicians are trained to perform bronchoscopy?

The procedure is usually performed either by a chest surgeon or by an otolaryngologist.

Does a patient have to be hospitalized to undergo bronchoscopy?

Most bronchoscopies are done in the hospital, but when one is performed mainly for diagnostic purposes the patient may go home shortly after the procedure is completed.

Bruises

A bruise, or contusion, results from hemorrhage into the skin or into the subcutaneous or muscle tissues. This type of bleeding stops by itself and rarely requires treatment. The swelling and bluish-black discoloration often attain huge size and are out of all proportion to the seriousness of the injury.

In a small number of cases the hemorrhage forms a fluid or semifluid collection beneath the skin or in between the muscles. This condition is called a hematoma. Most hematomas absorb over a period of several days to several weeks, but a certain number of them will require further treatment. In such cases the blood remains liquid or forms soft clots which fail to absorb. The surgeon will insert a large needle and attempt to suck out the retained blood into an attached syringe. If this is not possible because of clot formation, a small incision is made into the hematoma and the clot is evacuated.

QUESTIONS AND ANSWERS

Is a bruise the same thing as a contusion?
Yes.

What happens when tissues are bruised?
There is rupture of tiny capillaries and small blood vessels, with outpouring of serum and blood into the tissues.

Do some people tend to bruise more easily than others?
Yes. For some unknown reason, some individuals seem to have more fragile capillaries and small blood vessels than others. They will show black-and-blue marks on much lighter impact than those with sturdier capillaries and blood vessels.

Do women tend to bruise more readily than men?
Yes.

What is the best treatment for a superficial bruise of the skin, subcutaneous tissues, or underlying muscles?
Cold applications in the form of ice or wet compresses should be placed in contact with the bruised area. This will tend to cut down the amount of serum and blood that seeps out into the tissues, and will reduce swelling.

How long should cold applications be left in place?
No more than 20 to 30 minutes at a time. It must be kept in mind that the constant contact of ice or very cold compresses may produce more tissue damage than the bruise itself has caused.

Do bone bruises tend to last for a long time?
Yes. A severe bruise of a bone is frequently associated with a small hemorrhage beneath the periosteum, the thin membrane covering the bone's surface. Some bone bruises may last for many weeks or months before the pain and swelling in the area subside.

Do bruises ever require surgical treatment?
Yes. Sometimes there is so much bleeding into the tissues that the body does not absorb all of the hemorrhage. In this event, liquid blood accumulates and may have to be removed by a needle or incised surgically. Such a collection of blood in the tissues is known as a hematoma.

Should an individual seek medical advice if he or she bruises without apparent injury?
Yes. This may be indicative of a blood disorder such as purpura, or deficiency of blood platelets.

Can spontaneous bruising be caused by taking certain medications?
Yes. People who are sensitive to certain drugs such as aspirin or some of the antibiotic medications may accumulate collections of blood beneath the skin due to the toxic effects of these drugs on the capillaries. The capillaries become more permeable or may rupture as a result of sensitivity to certain medications or drugs.

Should an individual who has spontaneous appearance of bruises undergo a complete blood count?
Yes.

Buerger's Disease

Buerger's disease, or thromboangiitis obliterans, is an inflammation of the arteries and veins, and the adjacent nerves, in the extremities. The inflammatory process sometimes involves blood vessels within the abdominal cavity, the chest, and the brain, but this frequently cannot be proved.

The exact cause of Buerger's disease is unknown, but it is thought to be a process quite different from that of arteriosclerosis. It affects younger individuals, usually men in their 20s, 30s, and 40s, rather than older people.

The one factor that stands out in the causation of Buerger's disease is smoking.

QUESTIONS AND ANSWERS

Does Buerger's disease ever affect the blood vessels of the heart, brain, kidneys, or intestines?

Yes, but it is extremely difficult to confirm such a diagnosis.

What is the medical treatment for Buerger's disease?

1. *Smoking is absolutely forbidden.* Many patients will show immediate and remarkable improvement within a few weeks after they stop smoking.

2. Physiotherapy may be carried out to improve the blood supply to the extremities.

3. Medications to relax blood vessel spasm often prove helpful.

4. Nerve blocks (involving the blocking with Novocain of those nerves that cause blood vessels to contract) have proved to be helpful in certain cases.

What causes Buerger's disease?

The exact cause is unknown, but it is interesting to note that most of these patients are heavy tobacco smokers. In a certain small percentage of cases, it is thought that the eating of large quantities of rye bread may be associated with the onset of this condition.

What are the symptoms of Buerger's disease?

The symptoms are caused by inflammation of the blood vessels, which will eventually lead to occlusion. At first, the patient may experience coldness or an aching pain in one of his limbs. Next, he may have severe pain along the course of the blood vessels. Eventually there may be the consequences of the inadequate blood supply, with ulceration or areas of gangrene in the skin of the involved extremity. Finally, a toe or even an entire extremity may become gangrenous.

Is this disease more common among Jewish people?

It was once thought that this disease was predominant among Jewish people, but recent statistics have proved that its distribution is widespread and not limited to any one group.

Is surgery ever beneficial in the treatment of Buerger's disease?

Yes. In certain isolated cases, a lumbar sympathectomy in the lower back has helped by severing those nerves that stimulate blood vessel contraction.

Is lumbar sympathectomy a dangerous operative procedure?

No. Recovery will occur in practically all cases.

How is lumbar sympathectomy performed?

Through incisions made in the loins.

What is the outlook for a patient with Buerger's disease?

This disease tends to be chronic and lasts many years. If it has not progressed too far, and if the patient gives up smoking and carries out other measures listed above, he may avoid the most serious complication, gangrene of an extremity.

Is Buerger's disease found in women?

Yes, but it is much more commonly encountered in men.

Are patients with Buerger's disease more comfortable in warm climates?

Yes. Because of reduced circulation associated with the condition, people will feel much less pain in a warm, rather than a cold, atmosphere.

Does elevating a limb affected with Buerger's disease help to relieve the pain?

No. One of the characteristic signs of Buerger's disease is that it becomes worse when the extremity is kept in an elevated position.

Will applications of heat help a limb with Buerger's disease?

No, although the administration of medications that dilate the blood vessels will relieve symptoms in some cases.

Will the symptoms of Buerger's disease tend to subside if a heavy smoker gives up tobacco?

Yes, in many instances, especially if the patient has not had the disease for a very long time.

Bunions

A bunion is an inflammation and swelling of the bursa of the great toe with thickening of the subcutaneous tissues and skin overlying the bursa. It is often associated with a deformity of the toe which is forced inward toward the other toes.

See also CORNS; FEET.

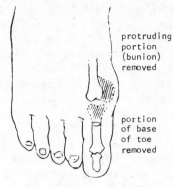

protruding portion (bunion) removed

portion of base of toe removed

POSTOPERATIVE APPEARANCE

QUESTIONS AND ANSWERS

What is a bunion?

An inflammation of the bursa in the region of the base of the big toe, associated with an enlargement of the head of the first metatarsal bone.

What causes bunions?

1. A malformation of the bony structure in the bone leading to the base of the big toe (metatarsal).

2. The wearing of too narrow a shoe and too high a heel.

What is the treatment for bunions?

1. Wearing wider shoes and lower heels.

2. Surgical correction of the bony deformity with removal of portions of the metatarsal head and bone at the base of the big toe.

How successful is the treatment for bunions?

Surgery is successful in curing bunions in almost all cases.

Do bunions tend to recur once they have been satisfactorily treated?

Not if adequate surgery has been carried out.

Burns

A burn can be a trivial matter demanding no treatment, or it can cause death within a matter of a few hours. Generally speaking, burns do not cause fatalities if they involve less than one third of the body's surface. Extensive second and third degree burns involving more than one third of the body's surface present great danger to life.

First degree burns are characterized by redness of the skin and rarely cause injury to any but the most superficial cells of the skin. *Second degree burns* damage all but the deepest layers of the skin and recovery may take many weeks or even months. *Third degree burns* extend through all the layers of the skin and may involve the tissues beneath the skin. Skin subjected to a third degree burn does not heal, and the surface thus involved will have to fill in from growth inward of the healthy skin surrounding the area. In recent years, it has become common practice not to wait for this slow process to take place. Instead, skin from other parts of the patient's body is grafted to the damaged area.

Emergency treatment of burns should be along the following lines:

1. Run cold water over the burned area steadily for 10 minutes.

2. Apply a dry, sterile bandage to the burned area. If such a bandage is not available, cover the region with a clean handkerchief or towel.

3. Do *not* apply butter, oil, or any ointment.

4. If the area involved is extensive, keep the patient warm and transport him to the nearest hospital as soon as possible.

Innumerable medications have been applied to burned areas, but most surgeons now agree that simple Vaseline gauze dressings are as effective as any of the more elaborate medications. Nature takes its own steady course in bringing about healing of the burned tissues, and antiseptic or antibiotic ointments applied locally offer little additional aid. Treatment now consists of the following:

1. Combating the shock which often accompanies severe burns. (Blood or plasma transfusions and sedatives may be necessary.)

2. Gentle cleansing of the burned areas with soap and water.

3. Cutting away loose pieces of dead skin (debridement).

4. Application of Vaseline gauze dressings covered by large compression bandages. These firm bandages help to prevent leakage and loss of serum from the burned areas. These dressings may be left in place for one to two weeks provided the general condition of the patient remains good and it is evident that no infection of the burned areas has set in.

5. Large doses of antibiotic drugs given by mouth or by injection. They will help to prevent infection of the burned areas, a frequent complication in the days before the introduction of these medications.

6. Grafting of healthy skin to areas where third degree burns have completely destroyed the skin.

Before concluding the discussion on treatment of burns, mention should be made of another method of treatment which has recently been advised. This is called the exposure treatment. It consists of leaving the burned areas completely uncovered and open to the air. Its advocates state that crusts form naturally within a day or two and that healing under these crusts proceeds rapidly.

See also FIRST AID; SUNBURN.

QUESTIONS AND ANSWERS

What are the various types of burns?

1. **First degree:** Involving only the most superficial layers of skin.

2. **Second degree:** Involving all the layers of skin except the deepest layer.

3. **Third degree:** Extending through *all* the layers of skin and sometimes involving the subcutaneous tissues.

Should butter, oil, or ointments be applied to burned areas?

Not by first-aiders!

How often will the surgeon change the dressing on a burn?

As infrequently as possible. Perhaps no more often than every two weeks provided that the burn is not infected. Too frequent changing will interfere with healing.

Infected burn wounds may require daily dressing changes.

Are all burns caused by excessive heat?

No. There are many other types of burns, such as those caused by chemicals, alkalis, or strong acids. Also, some burns are caused by electricity or radiations such as x-rays and radioactive substances.

What is the proper first aid treatment for burns?

1. **First degree burns** involve only the superficial layers of the skin and seldom require a physician's care. When they first occur, the burned area should be placed under running cold tap water for 10 minutes. If the burn is extensive, the patient should lie in a tub of cold water with the faucet running. After this, the areas can be covered with plain Vaseline gauze dressings, or any other mild and soothing ointment.

2. **Second degree burns** go through all but the deepest layer of skin. The average layman can make the diagnosis readily by comparing normal skin to the burned areas, where the top layers are obviously missing. There is a serum ooze from the surface and blister formation. When this type of burn is first incurred, the following measures should be instituted:

a. Burned areas should be placed under cold running water for 10 to 15 minutes.

b. After the water treatment, dirt or adherent clothing should be gently washed off with cotton or toilet tissue and a mild soap.

c. Large amounts of fluids should be taken by mouth.

d. Clean gauze pads, or a clean handkerchief, should be used to cover the burned areas. Ointments should *not* be applied to this type of burn.

e. Blisters should *not* be opened.

f. A physician's care should be sought as soon as possible. Until then, a pain-relieving medicine may be given.

3. **Third degree** burns extend through all layers of skin and may involve underlying tissues. First aid should consist of the same treatment as for second degree burns. These people may be more likely to display shock, and treatment for this complication must be prompt.

4. **Respiratory tract burns.** It has been learned recently that many burn deaths are due not to skin involvement but to damage suffered by the membranes of the nose, throat, bronchial tubes, and lungs from inhaling extremely hot air at the time of the accident. These tissues will become swollen and will secrete large amounts of fluid, mucus, and serum which may cause interference with breathing. First aid cannot be of much assistance here, but on isolated occasions, when breathing

has stopped but a heartbeat continues, a *tracheotomy may be lifesaving.* (*See* TRACHEOTOMY.)

5. Chemical burns and radiation exposure. The patient should be immediately immersed in cold running water for at least 20 minutes. The exposed areas should be washed over and over again, using plain water only. Sterile or clean dressings should be applied and the patient transported to the nearest physician or hospital.

6. Eye burns. The patient should lie down and the first-aider should flush out the eyes thoroughly for at least 10 minutes with plain cold water. Medical care should be sought at once after this treatment has been given.

What should be done about the shock that accompanies burn?

A diagnosis of shock can be made from the following symptoms and signs:

1. The patient is usually conscious or semiconscious, with great apprehension and fear noticeable.

2. There is great thirst.

3. The pupils of the eyes are dilated.

4. The skin is moist, cold, and clammy, with a grayish tint.

5. The pulse is very rapid and weak.

6. Breathing is shallow and rapid.

Patients in shock should receive the following first aid treatment:

1. They should be made to lie down flat with the legs placed at a higher level than the head.

2. All tight clothing should be loosened.

3. If active external bleeding is noted, take appropriate action. (*See* BLEEDING; FIRST AID.)

4. Cover with blankets but do not overheat. If room is warm and patient does not complain of cold, do not add coverings.

5. Obviously fractured or dislocated bones should be splinted unless immediate medical help is available. (*See* FRACTURES.)

6. Do *not* give coffee, alcohol, tea, or anything else by mouth unless it can be determined with absolute certainty that there is no injury to any of the abdominal organs. If this can be ascertained, it is permissible to give warm water and an available pain-relieving medicine.

7. Patients should be transported in a flat position to a hospital as soon as possible.

What is the major aim of surgery in the treatment of burns?

1. To overcome shock

2. To prevent overwhelming infection and septicemia from the absorption of bacteria from burned surfaces

3. To maintain respiratory balance, thus preventing alkalosis or acidosis

4. To maintain chemical balance and prevent the loss of large quantities of protein and chemicals through oozing from the burned surfaces

5. To promote healing of all burned areas

What surgical procedures may be carried out in cases of severe third degree burns?

Attempts are made to cover the burned areas with split-thickness skin grafts taken from unburned portions of the body or even from a donor. This will prevent inordinate loss of essential body fluids through oozing.

Does skin grafted to a freshly burned area always take?

No, but it may survive long enough to tide the patient over the first few critical days.

Should most extensive third degree burns ultimately be grafted with skin taken from another part of the body?

Yes. Grafting will prevent much

scarring and will reduce the incidence of contractures which often take place when burned skin is permitted to heal by itself, without grafting.

Are older people more likely than younger people to get burned?

Yes, because many older people are slower in reacting to situations in which there is danger of burns. Kitchen accidents, burns from cigarettes, electrical burns, etc., may result because of a slowing down of protective mechanisms. In addition, decreased sensitivity of nerve endings in older people—in the fingertips, for example—may result in failure of the individual to be warned that he is being burned.

Are burns more serious to older people?

Yes, because the older the patient the more likely it is that the burn will produce shock, an upset chemical balance, or an overwhelming infection.

How can burns and fire injuries be prevented?

1. Every home should have a readily accessible fire extinguisher, and it should be checked regularly.

2. People who smoke should never leave a lighted cigarette, cigar, or pipe untended. This is particularly important if children are in the vicinity, as they may drop burning tobacco into an area that might ignite.

3. Matches and cigarette lighters should be kept out of reach of infants and young children.

4. Fireplaces should be screened. People should never go to sleep while a fire is still burning in a fireplace.

5. A kerosene or other type of auxiliary heater should never be left untended, nor should people go to sleep while the heater is lighted.

6. Handles on cooking utensils should be turned away from the front of the stove.

7. A frayed electric cord should be discarded. Any electrical equipment should be discarded if its cord is defective.

8. Overexposure to sunlight can cause severe burns of the skin or the membrane covering the eyes. It is especially important to see that small children are not overexposed. They should come in from the sun whenever their skin begins to show a red tint.

9. Smoking in bed is dangerous. It causes a tremendous number of deaths from burns each year.

10. People who are under the influence of alcohol should be watched closely when they smoke. They may drift into sleep and permit a lighted cigarette or cigar to slip from their hands.

Bursitis

Bursitis is an inflammation of a bursa, a small fluid-filled sac located between muscles and joints, or between ligaments and bone. There are many

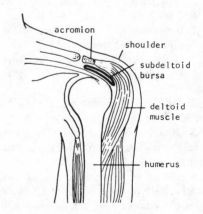

The subdeltoid bursa, located in the shoulder, is one of the sites most frequently involved in bursitis.

bursas throughout the body and they serve to permit ligaments, muscles, and parts of joints to move freely and with a minimum of friction. The bursal sacs are lined with cells which secrete a small amount of fluid. When a bursa becomes inflamed, the affected joint becomes painful and its movement is markedly limited.

QUESTIONS AND ANSWERS

What is bursitis?

It is an inflammation in which the fluid in the bursa is increased, or it is an inflammation of the lining of the bursa. In many cases, liquid calcium is present in the bursal fluid. Few conditions cause more excruciating pain than acute bursitis.

What causes bursitis?

It is most commonly caused by an injury or sudden sprain. Bacterial infections, and even tuberculosis, have been known to cause bursitis.

Where are the most common sites for bursitis?

1. The shoulder region, as in subdeltoid and subacromial bursitis
2. The elbow region
3. The hip region
4. The knee region
5. The region near the big toe (bunions are actually inflammations of the bursa)

Do people past 60 often develop bursitis?

Yes.

What are the signs and symptoms of bursitis?

Pain and extreme tenderness about the involved bursa and inability to move the joint without excruciating pain. The symptoms are, for some reason, much worse at night. X-rays will often reveal a calcium deposit in the inflamed bursa.

What brings on bursitis?

The most common cause is injury from a twist, a fall, or a strain in the region of the joint. Also, infections elsewhere in the body (teeth and sinus, for example) are thought to trigger this painful condition.

What are the types of bursitis?

1. **Acute bursitis.** This comes on within a few hours or a day or two, and is associated with severe pain and tenderness.
2. **Chronic bursitis.** This may represent the remnants of an acute bursitis that has not completely subsided, or it may be an independent condition not preceded by an acute condition. In the chronic form of this condition there is a nagging, aching pain in the region of the bursa, with stiffening of the underlying joint. Frequently, chronic bursitis, if untreated, may lead to permanent limitation of motion of the involved joint.

What is the treatment for bursitis?

There are several methods of treatment, depending on whether the bursitis is acute or chronic and on the severity of the condition.

1. The best treatment for the severe case is to inject the inflamed bursa with a mixture of procaine (Novocain) and a cortisonelike medication. The bursa is washed out with this solution and any liquid calcium is removed through the needle. Often, a dramatic cure will take place within a day or two. If initial treatment does not relieve the condition, it should be repeated every third or fourth day.
2. Chronic cases are also treated by the injection method, but it may take several weeks to months to obtain relief. The stiffness about the involved joint is

often due to muscle spasm, which will be relieved by the injections.

3. X-ray treatments have helped many cases of bursitis, but it is perhaps best to reserve this form of treatment for cases that fail to respond to injections.

4. In stubborn cases, it is occasionally necessary to operate and remove the diseased bursa. This is not a serious operation, even for those who are in their later years.

Does bursitis ever recur?

Yes, if there is another injury to the bursal region.

How effective is the treatment for bursitis?

In over 90 percent of cases, the aspiration of the bursa and the injection of hydrocortisone will bring about relief of the acute phase of the disease.

If medical or injection treatment of bursitis fails, will surgery cure bursitis?

Yes.

How serious is the operation for removal of a bursa?

It is considered to be a minor operative procedure with minimum risks.

How long can bursitis last?

If the acute phase subsides but calcium deposits and stiffness within the area persist, bursitis can become chronic and may last for months or years.

Is there a tendency for bursitis to recur in some people?

Yes, particularly among people in occupations in which trauma (injury) to the region tends to recur, as among orchestra conductors, painters, and housemaids.

What can be done to prevent recurrent bursitis?

If it is likely that the bursa will be subject to repeated injury, it is best to remove the bursa surgically.

Can an extremity or joint function normally after removal of a bursa?

Yes. Even though bursas are helpful in expediting the movements of muscles and tendons over bony prominences, they are not essential to normal function.

Cancer

The best treatment for cancer and other malignant conditions is *prevention,* not surgery! It is admitted by all who deal with this disease that surgical removal of a fully developed cancer is, in reality, *late* treatment, even though it is often followed by complete cure. The ultimate goal toward which all are working is the recognition of malignant tendencies that can be reversed before a tumor actually develops. A partial achievement of this goal, and one that can be attained through improved education, is the diagnosis of tumors when they are still so early in their development that they are localized and have not spread to distant tissues. In such situations, early surgical excision is curative in the vast majority of cases.

Toward achieving earlier detection, new diagnostic tests have been evolved and Cancer Detection Centers have been established in most sizable communities throughout the country to carry out these tests.

The term "cancer in situ" has come into common usage to describe those lesions which are so young that they have not yet spread into the structure of the organ harboring them. Thus, cancer in situ involving the cervix of the uterus can be discovered merely by swabbing the surface of the cervix with a cotton applicator. (This is known as the Papanicolaou test.) Early malignant change limited to the superficial areas of a polyp within the rectum can be diagnosed merely by snipping off the polyp and submitting it for microscopic examination. Early cancer of the breast can frequently be diagnosed before a lump can be felt merely by x-raying the organ and noting characteristic changes on the film. (This is known as mammography.) Early cancer of a bronchial tube of the lung can sometimes be detected by careful microscopic examination of sputum, and early stomach cancer can occasionally be diagnosed by examining stomach washings after the passage of an abrasive balloon. And so it goes, with many other new methods of early diagnosis too numerous to mention here.

Perhaps the greatest deterrent to the discovery of the cause of cancer is the fact that cancer is not one, but 40 or 50 allied diseases. Leukemia is as dissimilar to bowel cancer as a sprained ankle is to a fractured arm. Thus the causative factor of one type of cancer may have little or nothing to do with that which causes another type of lesion. As an example, medical investigators are sure that constant and repeated contact with coal tar products can culminate in certain skin cancers among petroleum workers, but they are equally certain that these substances have nothing to do with the formation of a brain or bowel tumor in other people. The existence of so many variations in the appearance, activity, and life cycle of different types of cancer makes it exceedingly difficult to postulate one underlying cause for all forms of the disease.

There is considerable satisfaction in the knowledge that surgery, despite its shortcomings in this area, today offers the cancer patient hopes he never had a mere few decades ago. It should not be forgotten that the great majority of cancers are curable if they are discovered and treated vigorously during their early stages of growth. Valuable adjuncts to treatment in the form of chemicals, hormones, radioisotopes, and radiation agents, such as radium, x-rays, and cobalt, have increased the already high cure rates obtained through modern surgical methods. (*See* CHEMOTHERAPY IN CANCER.)

By far the greatest help in curing cancer is yet to come, and will not come until people are willing to look this disease squarely in the eye, talk about it openly, and fight it by seeking medical advice as soon as they develop a suspicious symptom. In order to do this intelligently, it is necessary to be aware of some of the signs that a tumor might present:

1. Brain: Repeated severe headache; sudden episodes of vomiting not preceded by nausea; blurred vision, double vision, or loss of vision; sudden loss of hearing in one ear; loss of sense of balance; onset of paralysis or numbness or sensation in an arm, leg, or side of face; convulsions or fits; personality changes coming on within a short period of time.

2. Mouth: Any sore or ulcer of the lips, cheeks, gums, or tongue which fails to heal within a few weeks; whitish plaques which appear on the tongue, gums, or inside of the cheeks; bleeding from the mouth on repeated occasions.

3. Throat: Hoarseness that persists more than three to four weeks; a lump in the neck, under the chin, or at the angle of the jaw; repeated coughing of blood or hemorrhage of unexplained origin.

4. Sinuses: Repeated bloody discharge from the nose; swelling of the face.

5. Breasts: A lump or change in size of the breast; a lump in the armpit; a change in the shape of the nipple; a sore, ulcer, or persistent irritation of the nipple; repeated yellow, green, brown, or bloody discharge from the nipple, a change in the texture of the skin of the breast.

6. Esophagus: Difficulty in swallowing; a sense of fullness beneath the breastbone; repeated regurgitation of undigested food.

7. Lungs: Chronic cough which continues despite medications to clear it up; chronic cough unassociated with a respiratory infection; pain in one side of the chest, usually nagging and not severe; coughing up of blood; weight loss and anemia.

8. Stomach: Rather abrupt onset of indigestion after eating; loss of appetite; vomiting of material that has the appearance of coffee grounds; tar-colored stools; weight loss and lack of energy.

9. Gallbladder and bile ducts: Pain in the upper abdomen; indigestion; loss of appetite; jaundice (yellow color to skin) with or without abdominal pain.

10. Large bowel: A change in usual bowel habits; persistent change in appearance of stool; blood-streaked or bloody stool; dark red stools; increasing constipation; abdominal cramps and distention; repeated vomiting; progressive anemia; a lump in the abdomen (a late sign).

11. Cervix or uterus: Bleeding from the vagina in women past the menopause (change of life); irregular bleeding in women who have not reached the menopause; unusual discharge from the vagina; bleeding after intercourse; a mass developing in the lower abdomen (a late sign).

12. Genitourinary tract: Blood in the urine; pain or swelling in the flank or in the lower abdomen, worse on void-ing; increased frequency of urination; inability to urinate; painless swelling of a testicle.

13. Lymph nodes: Any painless lump or lumps in the neck, armpit, or groin; lack of energy; loss of appetite; weight loss; anemia.

14. Skin: Any change in size or color of a mole or wart; any sore on the skin anywhere on the body that fails to heal within three to four weeks; the development of any new blemish, sore, wart, or mole, especially if it is an area subject to repeated irritation.

15. Subcutaneous tissues: Any lump that appears anywhere beneath the skin, whether painful or not.

Obviously, not everyone who develops one of the preceding signs or symptoms will be found to harbor a tumor. However, the physical examination that the symptom has stimulated will undoubtedly redound to the patient's benefit. Then, too, if an early growth is uncovered, surgical removal will have its best chance of producing a complete cure.

According to recent statistics of the American Cancer Society, there are approximately 383,700 cases of cancer in the United States each year, of which 180,435, or 47 percent, are cured. And it is safe to conjecture that these figures will improve rapidly as we perform earlier diagnoses, more expert surgery, and more efficient methods of treatment with old and new anticancer drugs, hormones, and radiation techniques.

There are several prevalent misconceptions which influence many people to refuse indicated surgery for cancer. One of these is the belief that operative intervention will stimulate a tumor to grow and spread. Whereas this idea might have had some kernel of truth 30 to 40 years ago, when surgeons

FIVE-YEAR SURVIVAL RATE FOR CANCER AT VARIOUS SITES

(Localized Disease Only)

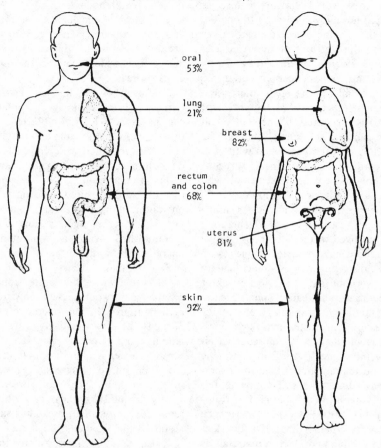

oral
53%

lung
21%

breast
82%

rectum
and colon
68%

uterus
81%

skin
92%

The chances of recovering from cancer are much greater than is commonly believed. The percentages shown here will increase as research brings about more knowledge of the disease and more effective treatment.

sometimes performed skimpy excisions of tumors and left behind malignant cells in the vicinity of the primary growth, it is not valid today. Modern surgical techniques for cancer obliteration include wide removal of the primary tumor, its surrounding tissue, and the lymph channels and lymph nodes that drain the tumor area. Such operations *do not* cause a cancer to grow or spread! On the contrary, they afford the patient his greatest chances for cure.

Another misbelief, and one that has caused countless thousands of premature and unnecessary deaths over the years, is the thought that once cancer is present, nothing can be done about it.

Stupidly, some people say that if they ever found out that they had a malignancy, they would destroy themselves or would not allow a surgeon to operate upon them. One need only to refer again to the statistics of the American Cancer Society to see that 90 to 95 percent of all skin cancer is cured, 75 percent of all cancers of the uterus and 61 percent of cancers of the cervix of the uterus are cured, 58 percent of all breast cancers are cured, etc., in the United States each year. And with each new cure that is obtained, surgeons learn how to help the next person who develops a similar condition.

Cancer surgery as a rule is much more extensive than it was a generation ago. Improved methods of preoperative preparation have enabled surgeons to excise diseased tissues much more widely without fear of surgical shock or an operating table catastrophe. Greater understanding of respiratory physiology has resulted in vastly improved anesthetic techniques. As a consequence, it is rare indeed to hear of an anesthetic death no matter how radical the operative procedure. The availability of unlimited quantities of blood for transfusion has cut down greatly on the dangers from hemorrhage. The development of Teflon and Dacron materials as arterial grafts has permitted surgeons to excise cancer-invaded blood vessels which formerly precluded complete removal of a spreading tumor. And lastly, and perhaps most important, surgical research has produced a whole new set of operative methods for the removal of organs that were hitherto unapproachable.

It might be informative to mention just a few of the recent technical accomplishments in the field of radical cancer surgery:

1. Most cancers of the thyroid gland in the neck can now be removed completely and a radical dissection of the neck can be done to clear the area of invaded lymph nodes.

2. Cancer of the larynx, the tongue, and the salivary glands can now be excised along with adjacent structures and glands which may be the site of cancer spread.

3. Cancer of the middle and lower portions of the esophagus (foodpipe) can be removed with replacement of this structure by an isolated segment of large bowel which will conduct food down to a new opening in the stomach.

4. An entire lung, or a portion thereof, can be excised for cancer. This operation, judged to be so dangerous just a few years ago, is now readily accomplished with a minimum of operative risk and mortality.

5. For many years it has been feasible to remove the entire stomach, or the major portion thereof, for a malignant growth. This operative procedure is now a relatively safe one, although ultimate cure rates from this type of cancer remain disappointing.

6. The entire pancreas, if involved in a cancer that has not spread too widely to other organs, can now be removed surgically, as can similar lesions of the bile ducts.

7. Cancer of the liver, isolated to one or the other of its two lobes, can now be excised successfully. Also, if cancer invasion of the liver from a distant organ is limited to one area, it can often be removed.

8. Malignant tumors of any portion of the large bowel can be surgically excised provided that there has not been a general spread throughout the abdominal cavity. When the growth is located in the right side of the bowel, the entire right colon and the lymph nodes that drain this portion of the large intestine are excised. When the transverse portion of the bowel is the seat of cancer, it and its dependent lymph nodes are removed. Similarly, the entire left colon can be removed, along with the associated lymph nodes, when cancer invades that area.

9. In former years, whenever a malignancy was found to invade one of the major abdominal blood vessels, such as the aorta, mesenteric or renal arteries, the operative procedure was limited to local removal of the primary tumor. Today there are numerous occasions when a localized involvement of a major artery can be overcome by excision of the cancerous vessel, followed by the insertion of a plastic arterial graft.

10. Some kidney cancers which were heretofore considered to be inoperable because of blood vessel extension are now amenable to removal plus blood vessel grafting.

11. The so-called super-radical breast removal has developed to a state wherein the cure rate has been increased considerably. In this operation, not only are the breast, underlying tissues, muscles, and lymph nodes in the armpit removed, but the *internal mammary glands* beneath the breastbone and ribs are dissected out.

12. Cancer of the cervix and uterus which had spread to surrounding structures used to be considered unsuited for surgical treatment. Today radical pelvic operations, known as *exenteration procedures,* have salvaged many of these unfortunate women. Some of these operations include removal of the rectum, the urinary bladder, the vagina, cervix, uterus, tubes, ovaries, and all the lymph nodes and soft connective tissues in the pelvis. An artificial opening is fashioned for the outlet of stool on the abdominal wall, and the tubes (ureters) leading from the kidneys are implanted into an isolated segment of small intestine which is brought up to the abdominal wall. (See discussion of ileal bladder operation, p. 856.)

13. Malignant tumors of the bones of the lower extremity are extremely dangerous and carry an extraordinary high mortality rate. Radical amputation procedures with removal of the entire extremity and a portion of the pelvis (hemipelvectomy) have been rewarded by cure in cases that were formerly fatal in all instances.

14. Cancerous moles (melanomas) and other malignancies of the skin and subcutaneous tissues are frequently treated by wide removal and extensive dissection of all lymph channels and lymph nodes draining the area. Thus, if the tumor originated in the thigh or leg, the groin and abdominal cavity on the involved side are carefully dissected until all lymph nodes that might be involved are excised. In a similar fashion, all nodes in the armpit are removed if the tumor originated on the upper extremity or back.

These operations are usually accompanied by skin grafts to cover over the defects left by the wide local excision of the primary growth.

Before leaving this subject, it should be stated again that the surgical treatment of cancer is not the ultimate answer. Although in most cases it offers the best opportunity for cure thus far available, a day will come when this scourge of mankind will be eliminated or successfully overcome through medical means. New discoveries in the field of medical genetics, new concepts of the role of the virus, new understanding of cell chemistry and physiology, will indubitably unlock the door to cancer control.

QUESTIONS AND ANSWERS

What is cancer?

It is disorderly wild growth of tissue

cells. If the process continues unchecked, the normal structure and function of an organ are destroyed. Cancer cells may be likened to weeds in a well-kept garden which get out of control and outgrow and kill the flowers. Eventually, if the weeds are not eradicated, the entire garden will be destroyed.

Are there any organs that are exempt from cancer?

No. Any organ may be affected by cancer or a cancerlike growth.

How prevalent is cancer today?

It is estimated that *one in eight people* will lose his life as a result of cancer.

Is cancer on the increase?

Yes. The reasons for this are threefold:

1. People are living longer today and cancer is more prevalent in the seventh, eighth, and ninth decades of life.

2. Cancer is being diagnosed more often as better medical diagnostic tools have been discovered and people seek medical care more frequently.

3. There is an actual increase in the disease for all age groups.

Do benign tumors turn into malignant ones?

Some do; some don't. Unfortunately, it is not always possible to know which tumor will remain harmless and which one will undergo malignant changes. Therefore it is wise to have *all* tumors removed when they first make their presence known.

What age groups are more prone to develop cancer?

The later ages, after 60. However, it must be clearly understood that no age group is immune. Cancer among infants and children is encountered all too often.

Is cancer on the increase among children?

No, but improved methods of cancer diagnosis may make it appear so.

Are there any age groups that are less likely to develop cancer?

Young children, adolescents, and young adults, though they possess no immunity, develop cancer less often than older people.

Is there a tendency for cancer to occur more often in men than in women?

No. The incidence is approximately the same. However, certain types of cancer show up more often in one sex. For instance, lung cancer is more prevalent among men; breast cancer among women.

Is there a special type of person who is most likely to develop cancer?

No, but some investigators feel that stout people are somewhat more susceptible than thin people.

Is there a type of person who has less chance of developing cancer?

No. However, the person who submits to thorough health examinations at regular intervals is better protected, since the presence of cancer may be detected at an earlier and more curable stage in its development.

Is cancer inherited?

No. But most physicians agree that a *tendency* toward cancer may be inherited. For this reason, those who have a family history of many cases of cancer should be especially certain to undergo regular health checkups.

Should the history of cancer in a family cause one to hesitate to marry into that family?

No. There are practically no families in which some history of cancer cannot be found.

Are certain races more likely or less likely to develop cancer?

No race is known to have any special immunity toward all forms of cancer.

Are there certain ethnic groups that are more likely or less likely to develop cancer?

No, but certain peoples have habits peculiar to their own way of life which may predispose them to the more frequent development of certain types of cancer. Thus, in cultures where people smoke heavily there may be a greater incidence of lung cancer than exists among peoples who use no tobacco.

Does climate or the place in which one lives have any influence on the incidence of cancer?

Cancer exists throughout the world.

What causes cancer?

Cancer is not one, but many, diseases. The cause of certain cancers, such as cancer of the skin of the hands among those who work unprotected with petroleum products, is well known. Other cancers are thought to arise from other chronic irritants, such as tobacco. Some cancers are attributed to nests of primitive cells present since birth, which never matured, and which suddenly, in later life, undergo stimulation and grow wild. Also, some investigators now believe viruses are the cause of certain cancers.

Is cancer contagious?

It is not thought to be, although some investigators think that cancers are associated with virus invasion.

Does smoking play a role in the development of cancer?

Two or three types of cancer have been attributed to smoking. For many years, the medical profession has indicted pipe smoking as a strong contributory factor in the development of lip and tongue cancer. Within recent years, most physicians agree that there is a very close relationship between heavy cigarette smoking over a period of years and the development of lung cancer.

Are lip and tongue cancer caused by smoking now as much as they used to be?

No. Modern pipes filter out much of the hot smoke and tar, which are thought to be the cancer-stimulating factors.

Should those who have been smoking for 30 or 40 years stop smoking in order to avoid the possible development of lung cancer?

Unfortunately, if they have been smoking for that long, most of the damage has already been done. Therefore, if people in their later years want to continue to smoke, perhaps it would be unwise to force them to stop. On the other hand, young cigarette smokers would be wise to study the statistics previously given and then come to their own decision.

Does drinking of alcoholic beverages have anything to do with cancer development?

No.

Is there much variation in the virulence of cancer?

Yes. Some cancers are extremely slow-growing and will never destroy the host; others (like certain of the blood conditions, such as acute leukemia) may destroy the host within a few weeks.

Is cancer caused by a blow or other physical injury?

Practically never. This is a very common misconception.

What actually takes place when an organ undergoes cancerous degeneration?

The cancer cells outgrow the normal cells within the organ. They often use up most of the available nourishment and oxygen meant for the normal tissues, thus causing the normal tissues to starve and die.

Does cancer behave in the same manner in all people?

No. It has a tendency to progress more rapidly in children, adolescents, and young adults, whereas it grows and spreads more slowly in people who are old.

How does cancer spread?

1. By direct extension to neighboring organs and tissues
2. By traveling along the lymph channels and to lymph nodes
3. By entering the bloodstream and traveling to distant parts of the body

(*See also* METASTASIS.)

What causes cancer to spread from one part of the body to another?

Cancer cells break loose from their site of origin and get into the lymph channels or blood vessels.

Is there any way to prevent the spread of cancer from one part of the body to another?

Yes. By removal of the primary tumor when it is in an early stage of development.

Is cancer in older people always a progressive disease?

No. In a small number of instances, the cancer grows so slowly that it almost appears to be stationary. The patient lives out his normal life-span, succumbing to some totally unrelated condition. Although this occasionally occurs, no one should omit active treat-ment, for the great majority of malignant growths, unfortunately, do end fatally if they are untreated.

Do most tumors tend to grow more rapidly and to spread more quickly in younger people?

Yes.

Is it true that the number of people with cancer is greater today than it was years ago?

Yes. This can be explained partially by the fact that more people today are living into their 70s and 80s. Since there are more cancers in this age group, the incidence of cancer for the total population is increasing. Despite this consideration, statistics do show an actual increase in *all* age groups. Moreover, better diagnostic methods have uncovered cancers that, years ago, would have gone undiagnosed.

Is there any way to prevent cancer?

The best method is to have a complete physical examination once or twice a year. Also, report any unusual symptoms to your doctor at any time between regular examinations. The finding of a lump anywhere in the body or occurrence of unexpected bleeding from any orifice in the body, while not necessarily indicative of cancer, should nevertheless stimulate a visit to your doctor.

What precautions can people take in their middle years to diminish their chances of getting cancer in the later years?

1. Stay thin or get thin! It has been demonstrated statistically that there are more cases of cancer in fat people than in thin ones.
2. Stop smoking!
3. Have all benign (noncancerous) growths removed. Tumors of the skin, breasts, mouth, throat, intestinal tract,

rectum, thyroid, urinary tract, or genital organs can, if neglected, undergo changes to cancer. Their removal when the patient is still in the middle years is usually a simple, safe operation.

4. Have a thorough, complete physical examination performed at least once a year.

5. Report bleeding or discharge from any orifice as soon as it is noted.

6. Avoid handling irritating substances without adequate protection. Certain petroleum and tar products and radioactive chemicals have been shown definitely to induce cancer if they are in day-to-day contact with the skin over a period of years. If one's occupation requires that he handle such substances, he should take every possible precaution.

What are some of the early warning symptoms of cancer?

SKIN

1. Change in color, repeated bleeding, or growth of a mole or wart

2. Any skin sore that fails to heal after three to four weeks, especially if it is on the nose, face, or an area that is exposed to repeated irritation

BREAST

1. Any change in the size of the breast

2. Bloody, yellow, or green discharge from the nipple

3. Any lump in the breast, usually painless

4. Any dimpling or change in the texture of the skin of the breast

5. Any persistent irritation, scaling, or ulcer of the nipple

LUNGS

1. Pain in the chest

2. Chronic cough

3. Spitting up of blood, or hemorrhage

4. Unexplained weight loss

5. Unexplained pallor or anemia

MOUTH, PHARYNX, AND LARYNX

1. Hoarseness that lasts more than a few weeks

2. Ulcerations, whitish plaques, sores, lumps—anywhere on the lips, tongue, cheeks, throat, and so on—that fail to disappear within two or three weeks

3. Repeated bleeding from the tongue, cheeks, or throat

STOMACH

1. Loss of appetite for more than two weeks

2. Indigestion, especially after eating, if it persists for more than two to three weeks

3. Bloody or coffee-ground vomit

4. Tar-black stool from someone *not* taking iron-containing pills

5. Weight loss, weakness, and lethargy (often late symptoms)

COLON AND RECTUM

1. Change in ordinary bowel habits

2. Change in appearance, size, and consistency of stool

3. Bleeding on moving bowels

4. Dark red blood in stools; tarry stools

5. Increasing difficulty in moving bowels

6. Distention of abdomen

7. Abdominal cramps, often colicky

8. Episodes of vomiting, sometimes of fecal material

9. Unexplained anemia

KIDNEYS, BLADDER, OR PROSTATE

1. Blood in the urine

2. Burning on urination

3. Increased frequency of urination

4. Inability to urinate

UTERUS AND CERVIX

1. Vaginal bleeding in women past the menopause

2. Unusual vaginal bleeding, especially when the menstrual period is not expected

3. Unusual vaginal discharge

4. Vaginal bleeding after intercourse

5. In younger women, any excessive bleeding during menstruation

How can one tell if he has a hidden cancer?

Cancer often does not cause symptoms until it has existed for quite some time. This is another reason an annual or semiannual checkup is advisable.

Are cancer detection examinations helpful in discovering premalignant growths and early cancer?

Definitely yes. However, such examinations must be done *every year* or whenever a warning symptom develops. All too many people have one cancer detection examination and then neglect themselves for years thereafter. Also, a cancer detection examination is not a substitute for the regular annual general physical checkup.

Are there any disadvantages in a cancer detection examination?

Not in the examination itself, but in the reaction of some people who, on learning that they are free of cancer, proceed to neglect themselves thereafter. At some later time, if they do develop symptoms of cancer, they recall only the clean bill of health they once received and, instead of seeking immediate advice, do not visit their doctors until it is too late.

Are there any satisfactory blood tests to determine if one has cancer?

Not at present, but indications are that such tests will soon be a reality.

Will cancer always show on x-ray examination?

No.

Does cancer ever disappear by itself without treatment?

There are a few authenticated cases on record of a known cancer that has disappeared by itself and not returned.

Will cancer always end fatally if not treated?

No. There are cases, by far the minority, where the cancer grows so slowly that the patient lives out his normal life-span and dies of an unrelated condition. This is particularly true among old people.

How can one tell if a cancer has already spread from its organ of origin?

A wide surgical removal of the primary tumor with surrounding normal tissue will often reveal, under microscopic examination, whether the cancer has already spread; that is, microscopic examination may spot cancer cells that have broken loose and become lodged in adjacent tissues.

Do cancer patients show weight loss early in the course of their disease?

No, unless the tumor is in the gastrointestinal tract, where it interferes with eating or food absorption.

Do cancer patients usually show anemia early in the course of their disease?

No, unless marked bleeding has been associated with the tumor.

Do cancer patients often show loss of appetite early in the course of their disease?

No, unless the tumor is in the stomach or esophagus.

Is it likely that a time will come when there will be one cure for all cancer?

This is doubtful, since cancer is so many different diseases. Even now, we have cures for some forms of cancer.

Should a patient be told if he has a cancer?

People have a right to know what is wrong with them *when they want to know*. If the patient would rather not know, then he should *not* be informed.

Is there a tendency for cancer to recur after it has been removed?

Yes, but periodic examinations may spot such a recurrence at a stage when it can be controlled or eradicated.

Does diet have anything to do with the recurrence of cancer?

No.

It a patient has recovered from a cancer, can he return to a normal life?

This depends upon the location of the cancer and the form of treatment that was administered. The great majority of those who have recovered from cancer *do* return to normal or near-normal activity.

Is there a tendency for a patient who has had one cancer to develop another elsewhere in the body?

Yes, but this situation can be handled satisfactorily by frequent, thorough medical surveys.

Can pregnancy have a harmful effect upon a woman who has recovered from a cancer?

Yes. It may sometimes reactivate the growth of tumors in certain organs which are influenced by the hormones of the body.

Why is it that surgery is advocated for some patients with cancer, and x-ray treatment is advocated for other patients with cancer?

Both surgery and x-ray are valuable forms of treatment, but certain cancers respond better to one type than to the other. A combination of both often gives the patient the best chance for recovery.

SURGICAL TREATMENT OF CANCER

Does surgery ever cause cancer to spread?

Not unless the surgery has failed to remove the entire primary growth. In most cases of adequate cancer surgery, the opposite effect is obtained.

What is the major difference between cancer surgery and surgery for other conditions?

Cancer surgery is usually more radical. It involves not only the excision of the diseased organ but removal of the connective tissues, lymph channels, and lymph nodes that drain the cancerous site. In this manner, the surgery attempts to get rid of cancer cells that may have already strayed from their original site.

Should a patient with a malignancy go to a special "cancer surgeon"?

Only in special instances. All qualified surgeons are trained to do cancer surgery. On the other hand, there are a limited number of surgeons who specialize in rare types of cancer surgery, such as the removal of part of the liver, the so-called exenteration procedures, etc. The family physician will know to whom the cancer patient should be referred.

Should a patient with a malignancy go to a special "cancer hospital" for treatment?

Here, too, the decision should be made by the family physician. Accredited hospitals are well equipped to perform almost all types of surgery, with the possible exception of some new procedure that has not had time to become known by the majority of surgeons in the community.

Can a surgeon tell whether a tumor is benign or malignant when he removes it?

In most instances, yes. However, there are some that he will not be able to distinguish merely by looking and feeling. This is why all suspicious growths are submitted for microscopic examination.

How accurate are frozen-section biopsies?

They will differentiate between a cancerous and noncancerous growth in almost all instances. Whenever there is the slightest doubt as to its accuracy, the pathologist will withhold a diagnosis until the regular microscopic sections are studied several days later.

How long does it take to get a frozen-section biopsy report?

Just 15 to 20 minutes. These tests are performed while the patient is on the operating table. The surgeon will not proceed until the report is relayed to him from the pathologist.

How long does it usually take for regular microscopic reports to be made by the average pathology department?

Anywhere from three to seven days.

How reliable are microscopic reports of tissue examinations?

They are extremely reliable and can be accepted in practically every case. Whenever there is the slightest doubt in a pathologist's mind as to the malignancy of a specimen, he will send it on to one or more of his colleagues for their opinion. A final answer in such cases may not be forthcoming for a period of weeks.

Should all types of cancer be treated surgically?

No, although the best chance of cure in most cases is through early surgical removal of the growth. Certain types of malignancies are best treated with anticancer drugs, radiation treatment, hormones, or a combination of these.

How can one tell whether surgery has resulted in a permanent cure?

The soundest evidence is by noting the passage of time. Relatively few cancers recur after a lapse of five to ten years.

Can people recover from a malignancy even if it has spread to adjacent structures at the time of surgery?

Yes. This is the main reason why surgeons will dissect out tissues adjacent to a malignant growth. Often they are successful in removing all the cancer cells that have spread from the region of the original growth.

Do cancer patients usually react more severely to surgery than those who are operated upon for other conditions?

Yes, in many instances, because the surgery itself is likely to be more extensive. Moreover, some patients neglect treatment until the cancer has caused excessive weight loss, anemia, and upset in nutritional states.

If a cancer recurs, can it be removed again?

Yes. There are many people whose tumor was not removed completely at the first operation who, after a second procedure with wide excision of the diseased tissues, will make a permanent recovery.

Does the size of a tumor always denote its degree of malignancy?

No. Some very large tumors may be perfectly benign while some microscopic tumors may be highly malignant.

Why is it that surgeons are sometimes unable to remove a cancer completely?

Because it has already spread too

widely or has spread to organs that cannot be surgically excised.

Can the surgeon always be certain, after he has operated, that he has totally removed the entire growth?

In most instances, yes, but not always. A small nest of cancer cells which would be visible only through a high-powered microscope will, of course, be indiscernible to the operating surgeon.

How has modern surgery minimized the chances of recurrent cancer?

By more extensive removal of tissues surrounding the primary growth. In almost every area of the body it has become possible, through new and improved techniques, to excise lymph nodes, connective tissues, and neighboring organs which may be invaded by cancer cells.

Is it advisable for a patient who has recovered from the removal of a malignant growth to have regular follow-up examinations?

It is essential. No matter how long the interval of elapsed time since surgery, all such patients should continue to undergo periodic examinations. It should be kept in mind that recurrences can frequently be overcome through additional surgery.

What is meant by the term "second look" operation?

This is a term applied mainly to cases of malignancy within the abdomen. A "second look" operation is one performed upon a patient who has no evidence of recurrence of disease. Its purpose is to explore the abdominal cavity some six months to a year after the original operation in order to discover if there has been a silent, nonsymptom-producing spread of the cancer.

Are "second look" operations performed very often by most surgeons?

No. The great majority of surgeons prefer not to reoperate unless the patient shows some indication that there might be recurrence of disease.

According to American Cancer Society statistics, what percentage of cancers in the United States are cured each year?

Approximately 47 percent. This figure is much lower than it should be; it includes those people who received little or ineffectual treatment because they sought medical care long after their symptoms began and the cancer had spread.

According to American Cancer Society statistics, what is the percentage of "potential cures" that could be obtained in this country if people presented themselves for treatment early during the course of their disease when symptoms first appeared?

Approximately 63 to 64 percent.

What advances in the treatment of cancer can be foreseen at this time?

Most physicians feel that the future treatment of cancer will be chemical rather than surgical.

NONSURGICAL ANTICANCER TREATMENT

What measures are used to treat cancer without surgery?

There are several methods:

1. X-ray treatment, cobalt treatment, radium treatment, and the application of radioactive substances such as iodine, phosphorus, gold, and others.

2. The use of hormone injections and tablets. It has been found that cancer of the breast is sometimes inhibited by the giving of large doses of male or female sex hormone; the growth of a cancer of the prostate is inhibited by the administration of large doses of female hormone.

3. The administration of certain

chemical drugs that are found to be effective in killing cancer cells. (*See* CHEMOTHERAPY IN CANCER.)

Has much progress been made in the application of x-ray and radioactive substances in treating cancer?

Yes. Every year new radioactive substances are being produced and new techniques for their use have been found. All have some inhibitory effect on the growth and spread of malignant tissue. Unfortunately, it is admitted that this method of treatment will not be the final answer to overcoming cancer.

Is it likely that an ultimate cure for cancer will originate through the use of hormones?

Most investigators agree that this approach to the treatment of cancer will not lead to a final cure. Most cancers are uninfluenced by the administration of hormones.

What appears to be the future of chemotherapy (treatment with chemicals)?

New drugs are constantly being discovered that have greater and greater limiting effects upon the spread and growth of cancer. Some of these drugs are so effective that they can cause a cancer to disappear temporarily. It is expected that within the next decade or two more effective chemicals will be found in the treatment of cancer, but few investigators feel that the final solution to the cancer problem will be in the field of chemotherapy.

Can cancer ever be "cured" by the use of x-rays or radioactive substances, hormones, or chemicals?

The right word here is not *cured* but rather *destroyed*. There is no doubt that radioactive substances can completely and permanently destroy some cancers. Also, it has been found that in a small

number of cases, chemicals appear to permanently destroy and inhibit the growth of malignant cells.

Are there any recent statistics on the effectiveness of chemicals in the treatment of cancer or allied diseases?

Yes, the American Cancer Society recently issued an article in which it stated that certain types of malignant tissue can be temporarily inhibited or even permanently destroyed through chemotherapy. Listed among the statistics are the following:

1. Eighty to ninety percent of children with acute leukemia can be benefited and their lives prolonged through chemotherapy.

2. Seventy percent of those children with kidney tumors can be definitely benefited and their lives prolonged through the use of chemical agents.

3. Seventy percent of men with cancer of the prostate can look toward benefit from the use of chemotherapy.

4. Thirty to forty percent of women with cancer of the breast can be benefited and their lives prolonged through the administration of chemical drugs.

5. Fifty to eighty percent of those with chronic leukemia can be helped through chemotherapy.

6. Eighty to ninety percent of people with Hodgkin's disease can be benefited greatly by a course of chemotherapeutic agents.

7. Thirty to forty percent of those with cancer of the testicles can receive benefit from chemotherapy.

8. Thirty to forty percent of women with cancer of the ovaries can be helped through chemotherapy.

Startling as it may seem, there is a very small percentage of cases in which it is thought that cancer can be "cured" through the use of chemical agents. Thus, it is thought that approximately two percent of children with acute leukemia can be "cured," two percent of children with malignant kidney tumors can be "cured," and three and one-half percent of children with a certain type of nerve tumor called neuroblastoma can be "cured."

Are the radioactive substances, hormones, and chemical agents often used in conjunction with surgical treatment for cancer?

Yes. With few exceptions, these methods of treatment are combined with surgery. Of course, there are certain conditions, such as leukemia, lymphosarcoma, and Hodgkin's disease, that do not lend themselves to surgical treatment.

If radiation therapy, chemotherapy, and hormone therapy are only of temporary benefit, why should cancer patients be subjected to them?

First of all, improvements in these forms of treatment are taking place every day, and one day it may be possible that more permanent results will follow their use. Second and more important, there is the possibility that these people can be kept alive long enough to be available when a true cure for their disease is discovered.

Carbuncles

A carbuncle is a pustular infection, usually larger and more extensive than an abscess, that comes to a head in several areas rather than in one area. Most carbuncles appear in the skin and tissues beneath the skin, but others may develop within organs such as the liver or kidney. Whereas many people suffer-

ing from an ordinary boil do not develop fever or systemic reactions, it is not uncommon for those afflicted with a carbuncle to develop high fever and malaise.

See also ABSCESSES AND INFECTIONS.

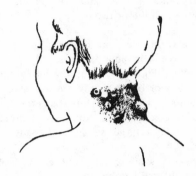

The back of the neck is a favorite site of carbuncles because of its relatively poor blood supply and the fact that it is frequently subject to irritation.

QUESTIONS AND ANSWERS

What is the difference between a carbuncle and a boil?

A carbuncle is much more extensive, is usually associated with generalized symptoms, and comes to a head in several different areas rather than in one area.

Where are carbuncles most likely to develop?

A carbuncle is most likely to develop in an area where it is more difficult for the pus to gain exit. As an example, the skin of the back of the neck has such thick fibrous tissue beneath it that pus from an abscess may have great difficulty in coming to a head in one spot. As a consequence, the infection extends out sideways in various directions and may find several exits.

Are carbuncles treated in the same way as any other infection?

Yes, but it is often necessary to incise them much more widely in order to get adequate drainage of the pus. Furthermore, in many cases, those afflicted with carbuncles will require bed rest, large fluid intake, and the administration of antibiotic drugs.

Is a carbuncle more likely to appear in an area with poor blood supply?

Yes. Those areas of the body that have poor blood supply are less able to combat infections. Thus, bacteria may gain greater hold and may spread, involving a larger segment of tissue.

Do the same germs that cause boils usually cause carbuncles?

Yes. It is not so much a matter of the type of bacterial invasion but the extent to which it involves the tissues that differentiates between a boil and a carbuncle.

What are some of the favorite sites for carbuncles?

1. The back of the neck
2. The buttocks
3. The nose

Does the surgical incision of a carbuncle differ from that of an ordinary boil?

Yes. Most carbuncles are so extensive that they require wide incisions often taking the shape of a cross. As carbuncles are frequently associated with gangrenous destruction of tissues, this tissue is usually excised through the incision.

Is hospitalization often necessary in treating a carbuncle?

Yes. Many people with carbuncles are extremely ill and will require hospitalization for several days.

Are people with diabetes more susceptible to the development of carbuncles?

Yes. The inability of the diabetic individual to combat infection is well known, and, as a consequence, he is prone to the development of carbuncles.

Are older people more susceptible to carbuncles than children and young adults?

Yes. Older people tend to have poorer circulation and blood supply. Thus, their tissues are more susceptible to infection and extension of infection with eventual carbuncle formation.

What can be done to prevent the formation of carbuncles?

1. Patients with diabetes should make sure that their diabetes is under control. A diabetic who is well controlled is not especially prone to the development of carbuncles.

2. Anyone with a boil that seems to be enlarging and not coming to a head should seek prompt surgical advice. The incision and drainage of a boil may prevent the development of a carbuncle.

3. No boil should ever be squeezed. This may lead to extension of the infection to adjoining tissues, with the formation of a carbuncle.

4. Those with large boils should go to bed, drink large quantities of fluids, and apply warm compresses. If the boil does not come to a head within a day or two, a physician should be notified.

5. Scrupulous cleanliness of the skin is important in decreasing the incidence of infection. It is especially important that older people and diabetics observe good bodily hygiene.

6. Nose picking should be avoided, as the pulling of hairs or picking of the nose makes one more likely to develop a nasal infection with resultant carbuncle formation.

7. Underwear and shirts should be

changed frequently and kept clean. Scraping and chafing of tight or soiled linen can decrease the resistance of skin to bacterial invasion.

Carcinoid Tumors

Carcinoid tumors are those that arise from certain cells (argentaffin) lining the intestinal tract. They are usually small, but may grow to large size when they spread to other organs. The typical carcinoid is firm in consistency and yellow in color. When such a tumor is examined under the microscope it has many of the appearances of a true cancer but can be distinguished because of its characteristic cell structure and staining properties. Eighty to ninety percent of carcinoid tumors are located in the region of the appendix and beginning of the large bowel. They may also be found in the gallbladder or bile duct, and occasionally they may arise from a tumor within an ovary or testicle.

Although carcinoid tumors do sometimes spread to other organs, the course of the disease is quite unlike that of cancer. People with carcinoid tumors have been known to live a long time although there has been a spread of the tumors throughout their bodies.

Most carcinoid tumors that have enlarged and spread to other organs produce a substance known as serotonin. This serotonin usually arises from the carcinoid tumors that have spread to the liver or other organs, and produce symptoms such as periods of flushing which starts in the face and neck and may extend down onto the body, rapid heartbeat with palpitations, abdominal pain, diarrhea, and often wheezing. It is thought that flushing of the skin takes place when there is an increased amount of serotonin secreted into the bloodstream by the carcinoid tumor.

See also CANCER.

QUESTIONS AND ANSWERS

What is a carcinoid tumor?

It is a tumor that has many of the qualities and appearances of cancer but runs a benign rather than a malignant course.

What are the most frequent sites of origin of a carcinoid tumor?

The appendix, the terminal portion of the small bowel, the large bowel and abdominal organs to which the carcinoid may spread.

How can one make the diagnosis of a carcinoid tumor?

Unless the tumor has spread to many other organs, the diagnosis is frequently difficult to make and may be an accidental finding on operation. When the carcinoid has spread to the liver and other abdominal tissues a particular set of symptoms, known as the carcinoid syndrome, may develop.

What are the symptoms of the carcinoid syndrome?

1. Flushing of the skin, with feelings of great heat

2. Palpitation of the heart

3. Feelings of weakness

4. Abdominal cramps with diarrhea

How common are carcinoid tumors of the appendix?

It is estimated that of every 100 appendices removed, one will harbor a carcinoid tumor.

Do carcinoids of the appendix frequently spread to other organs?

No. They usually remain localized. It is the carcinoid that originates in the small intestines, large intestines, or elsewhere that is most likely to spread to other organs within the abdomen.

Are carcinoids ever associated with ulcers of the stomach or duodenum?

Yes. In some patients the first indication that a carcinoid is present will be hemorrhage from a duodenal ulcer. Upon operation a tumor will be found at the site of the bleeding.

Why is it that cancers tend to kill as they spread while carcinoid tumors are compatible with long life, even though they spread to other organs?

The answer to this question is not known. We can only point out that a carcinoid is not in actuality a malignant tumor.

Do all carcinoids spread to other tissues?

No. Conversely, approximately 80 to 85 percent of all carcinoid tumors remain localized and do not spread (metastasize).

Does a carcinoid syndrome always develop in patients who have carcinoids that have spread to other organs?

No. It is only when a large amount of the liver tissue is involved by a spread of the tumor that a carcinoid syndrome develops.

Are there any clinical tests to establish the diagnosis of carcinoid tumors?

Yes, when they spread to other organs a special analysis of the urine will show an increased level of a urinary component known as 5-HIAA.

What is the treatment for a carcinoid tumor?

It should be removed surgically. Even when it has spread throughout the abdomen, as much of the carcinoid should be removed as possible. The more bulk of the tumor that is re-

moved, the greater are the chances of eliminating the symptoms of the carcinoid syndrome.

How long can a patient live who has a carcinoid tumor that has spread throughout the abdomen?

Some may live indefinitely and may never succumb to the effects of this tumor; others will die within a few years.

Is there any way to prevent the development of a carcinoid tumor?

No. Unfortunately, they arise spontaneously without foreknowledge or symptoms.

Will the giving of chemicals or x-ray radiation help in the treatment of carcinoid tumors?

No. Unlike cancer, the carcinoid is insensitive to radiation or to chemotherapy.

Carcinoma

See CANCER.

Cardiac Arrest

Cardiac arrest in surgery is stoppage of the heartbeat during the course of anesthesia or operation. Though there may be several reasons for unexpected cardiac arrest during the course of surgery, the most common cause is thought to be insufficient oxygen supply. Cardiac arrest can occur during a minor operative procedure as well as during a major operation, although it is more frequently encountered during the latter.

Today, heart action is monitored during a major operative procedure by hooking up the patient to a cardioscope. This permits the anesthesiologist to note the heart action at all times and allows countermeasures to be taken should the heartbeat become irregular or show signs of weakening.

It is essential that immediate steps be instituted to overcome cardiac arrest. When such action is taken within the first minute after the arrest occurs, a large percentage of cases can be saved. However, when cardiac arrest persists for more than a minute or two, the outcome is usually tragic.

QUESTIONS AND ANSWERS

What causes cardiac arrest?

The heart may stop beating suddenly from one of a great number of causes. However, the term cardiac arrest has assumed a rather specific meaning and usually is used when referring to unexpected heart stoppage during the course of a surgical operation or unexpected stoppage due to an acute heart attack.

What causes cardiac arrest during surgery?

The exact cause of this rare condition is not known, but most anesthesiologists and surgeons think that the catastrophe is triggered by deprivation of oxygen in the tissues, by blood loss, by excessive manipulation of tissue, or by overdosage of anesthetic agents or preanesthetic agents. Another cause may be a heart attack which the patient suffers due to the emotional strain of surgery.

How common is cardiac arrest during surgery?

Fortunately, it is exceedingly rare, and occurs only once in every several thousand operative procedures.

Does cardiac arrest only occur during the course of a very serious operation or when the patient is extremely ill?

Not necessarily. Cases of cardiac arrest have been known to occur during minor operative procedures on healthy young patients. It is true, though, that most cardiac arrests do take place when the general health of the surgical patient is poor and when the operative procedure is lengthy and serious.

What procedure is carried out when cardiac arrest is noted during the course of an operation?

If it takes place during a chest operation, the heart is taken in the hand and massaged so that approximately 60 beats per minute are maintained. If the arrest occurs while operating on the abdomen or some other part of the body, closed cardiac massage is carried out immediately.

How soon should cardiac massage be carried out after cardiac arrest has been diagnosed?

It must be done *immediately!* Unless active cardiac massage, along with mouth-to-mouth artificial respiration, is carried out within seconds or, at the most, within one minute after the heart has stopped, it is usually impossible to save the patient.

Can first-aiders carry out cardiac massage?

Yes. It has been found that the closed method of cardiac massage is as effective as the open method, and anyone can learn to do it.

How is closed cardiac massage performed?

1. The patient is placed flat on his back on a hard surface. If he is lying on a bed when cardiac arrest occurs, he should be placed upon the floor.

2. The first-aider should kneel and straddle the patient.

SURGICAL CONDITIONS AND PROCEDURES

3. The first-aider then places the heel of the palm of his right hand on the patient's breastbone.

4. The left hand is placed over the right hand, and a rhythmic pushing down and relaxation on the breastbone is carried out. The breastbone is depressed anywhere from one to two inches and then released.

5. This pressure and relaxation of pressure should be repeated every one to two seconds for at least 10 to 15 minutes, or until the heartbeat and breathing are resumed.

6. If someone else is available, he should render mouth-to-mouth artificial respiration at the same time as the heart is being massaged.

7. If no one else is available, the person doing the resuscitation must do both mouth-to-mouth ventilation and cardiac massage, intermittently. Massage without mouth-to-mouth breathing is useless!

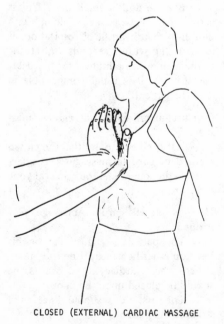

CLOSED (EXTERNAL) CARDIAC MASSAGE

How can one tell if cardiac massage is necessary?

In almost all instances, when cardiac arrest takes place, breathing also stops. The first-aider will note that the patient is not breathing and has no pulse, and when he puts his ear to the patient's chest, no heartbeat will be heard.

Can closed cardiac massage be carried out on the street?

It can be carried out anywhere. The main thing to remember is that unless the procedure is instituted immediately after the heart has stopped, it will be to no avail.

Can closed cardiac massage help someone whose heart has stopped secondary to electrocution?

Yes. However, everyone must be cautioned not to touch anybody who is still in contact with electricity. If the afflicted one is free and clear of electric current, cardiac massage, along with mouth-to-mouth artificial respiration, may save him.

Is cardiac massage often successful in cases of cardiac arrest?

Not usually. It is estimated that only 10 to 20 percent of patients who suffer cardiac arrest can be saved. In most instances, the underlying cause for the cardiac arrest is of such a serious nature that recovery is not possible.

Should mouth-to-mouth breathing always accompany closed cardiac massage?

Yes. This is difficult to do when the first-aider is alone with the patient. In this event, the pressure and relaxation on the chest wall should be carried out approximately 10 to 15 times and then it should be interrupted for mouth-to-mouth breathing one or two times. In other words, the first-aider must switch his position from that of straddling the patient to the usual position when rendering mouth-to-mouth breathing.

What other measures are taken to get the heart to beat again?

1. The anesthetic agent is discontinued and pure oxygen is pumped into the lungs by the anesthesiologist so that the patient receives the equivalent of 20 to 30 deep breaths per minute.

2. If there has been a great deal of blood loss, blood is transfused into the patient.

3. If the patient is dehydrated, intravenous fluids are run into the veins rapidly to restore fluid volume.

4. In some instances, adrenalin is injected directly into the heart chamber to stimulate the heart to begin to beat again.

5. If the cardiac arrest occurs during the course of a heart operation and the patient has been taken off the heart-lung pump, he is replaced on the pump and circulation is maintained artificially by this means.

6. In some cases, the heart is stimulated with an electric current in order to restore its action.

How long should cardiac massage be continued in a case of cardiac arrest?

It should be maintained until a normal rhythm is reestablished. One of the first signs of recovery is an occasional spontaneous heartbeat. This will be noted on viewing the cardioscope. It is a mistake to discontinue cardiac massage before a good heartbeat has been fully reestablished.

Cardiac Catheterization

Cardiac catheterization is a method of studying the chambers of the heart by introducing an opaque polyethylene tube into a vein in the arm and pushing the tube until it enters the heart itself. This procedure is performed to determine if there is valve damage or a birth deformity of the heart.

QUESTIONS AND ANSWERS

How is cardiac catheterization performed?

This will depend upon whether or not the catheter (a long polyethylene tube) is to be passed into the right atrium (auricle) or the left atrium.

If the right side of the heart is to be catheterized, the catheter is inserted, under absolutely sterile conditions, into a vein in the arm or neck and is pushed along through the vein until it reaches the right atrium.

If the left side of the heart is to be catheterized, the catheter is inserted, again under sterile conditions, into an artery in the patient's arm or thigh and is pushed along until it reaches the left ventricle. In some instances, it may enter the left atrium.

How can the physician follow the exact position of the catheter?

All cardiac catheterization is carried out under fluoroscopy so that the position of the tube is known at all times and its progress can be traced accurately.

Is cardiac catheterization a dangerous procedure?

No, but it is a serious procedure. It must be carried out in a hospital, and if the patient is a young child, it may be necessary to anesthetize him first.

When is cardiac catheterization recommended for a child?

When it is obvious that there is some defect that may require surgical correction. It is not generally used to make a diagnosis of a heart condition that the pediatrician feels can be corrected with medications.

How accurate is cardiac catheterization in determining the exact nature of a heart deformity?

The nature of the vast majority of deformities in the atria and ventricles and in the septa that separate them can be determined with great accuracy.

What additional information can be gained from cardiac catheterization?

1. The pressure of the blood as it passes through the various heart chambers can be measured.

2. Samples of blood can be taken and analyzed for their oxygen content.

3. Contrast media (dyes) can be injected through the catheter so that the shape of the heart chambers and the direction of blood flow will show up on x-ray film.

What is a contrast medium?

A contrast medium is a substance, usually containing iodine, that is injected into the bloodstream. On x-ray film the contrast medium will show up as a dense shadow. Thus the heart chambers and the great blood vessels coming to or going from the heart can be outlined and their defects can be observed.

What are some of the deformities that can be diagnosed by cardiac catheterization?

1. Defects in the septum separating the left and right atria.

2. Defects in the septum separating the left and right ventricles.

3. Stenosis (constriction) of the pulmonic artery.

4. Abnormalities of the great blood vessels that enter or leave the heart. The most familiar of these abnormalities is the tetralogy of Fallot, which is the so-called blue baby condition.

5. Coarctation (narrowing) of the aorta.

6. Defects in valve function.

7. Patent ductus arteriosus (a condition in which an embryonic blood vessel connecting the lung artery and the aorta fails to close before birth).

Are both the left and the right sides of the heart ever catheterized simultaneously?

Yes. In such cases, one catheter will be fed through the veins into the right side of the heart while the other catheter will be fed through the arteries into the left side of the heart. By this method of catheterization and by the expert interpretation of the results, it may be possible to learn about all four chambers and about all the blood vessels of the heart at one time.

Carotid Arteriosclerosis

The carotid arteries lie on either side of the neck and supply blood to the head. Within recent years, it has been shown that certain cases of stroke (cerebral thrombosis) are due to blockage of the carotid arteries in the neck. In such cases, it is sometimes possible to relieve the symptoms of the stroke by operating upon these blood vessels.

QUESTIONS AND ANSWERS

Are operations upon the carotid artery often successful?

Yes, if it has been determined before surgery that the stroke is secondary to narrowing or clotting of the carotid artery.

What operation is performed upon the carotid artery to relieve the symptoms of a stroke?

A procedure known as endarterectomy with the insertion of a patch graft is carried out. This involves an incision into the carotid artery and the scraping out of its thickened lining. Any blood clot that has taken place in the vessel is also removed. The passageway is made broader, and permits increased blood flow by this procedure. After the blood vessel has been scraped out and any blood clot and ateriosclerotic material removed, a patch graft is placed over the incision, thus further enlarging the vessel's passageway.

What material is used for the patch graft on the carotid artery?
Either Teflon or Dacron.

How can a diagnosis of carotid artery disease be made?
By the performance of a special x-ray test known as arteriography.

Carotid Body Tumors

There is a rather rare tumor, some 500 having been reported in medical literature, arising from the carotid body. This is a nerve structure located in the notch between the internal and external carotid arteries in the neck. These large arteries supply the brain and the rest of the head with blood.

The carotid body has a certain amount of control over the rate and depth of breathing, and it supposedly can produce an increase in blood pressure by causing arteries to contract. Most tumors (chemodectomas) of the carotid body are diagnosed because of the presence of a lump in the neck located at the division of the carotid artery into an internal and external branch.

Most carotid tumors are benign, but some do undergo cancerous degeneration.

The treatment for a carotid body tumor is surgical removal through an incision in the neck. Most tumors can be removed without endangering the important structures in the vicinity of the growth. However, occasionally, a tumor can be only partially removed. In these latter instances, recovery ensues despite the fact that a portion of the growth has been left behind.

Carpal Tunnel Syndrome

One of the major nerves (the median) to the hand passes through the wrist in a tight compartment called the carpal tunnel. Through this tunnel, which is bounded by the rigid bones and ligaments, pass the nerves, the tendons, and their sheaths. Within the confines of this small space the median nerve may become compressed if there is any swelling of the contents within the compartment. Arthritic disease, injury, and hemorrhage all may cause swelling with a sensation of pins and needles in the fingertips. The little finger is not affected. Numbness of the fingers and gradual swelling and weakness of the hand eventually ensue if the condition persists. Surgical cure is rapid and dramatic when the carpal tunnel is opened and the ligament overlying the nerve is severed.
See also HAND.

QUESTIONS AND ANSWERS

What is the carpal tunnel syndrome?
It is pain along with numbness and tingling in the fingers of the hand due to compression of the median nerve by the carpal ligament in the wrist.

Is the carpal tunnel syndrome a frequent occurrence?

Yes, especially in those with rheumatoid arthritis or in those who have suffered an injury or hemorrhage in the wrist. It is also seen quite often among stenographers and those who use their hands for strenuous manual labor.

Is the surgery for carpal tunnel syndrome serious?

No. It is a very simple operation and is rarely, if ever, complicated.

Is it ever necessary to operate upon the nerve to relieve the symptoms of the carpal tunnel syndrome?

No. All that is necessary is to cut the constricting carpal ligament. This will allow sufficient room for the nerve and tendons within the wrist, and symptoms will subside within a period of a few days to a few weeks.

Can permanent damage to the median nerve result if a tight ligament is not severed?

Yes. There have been cases on record where permanent nerve damage has been done, resulting in loss of sensation and function of the middle three fingers of the hand.

Where are operations for carpal tunnel syndrome carried out?

In a hospital, under general anesthesia. A stay of only two to three days is required.

Cataract

Although cataracts were recognized and written about in Biblical times, it was not until the middle of the seventeenth century that the true nature of this affliction was recognized. About this time, it was generally accepted that cataract was caused by a clouding or opacity within the lens.

The lens is a transparent, colorless body, biconvex in shape, located in the eyeball just behind the pupil. It is similar to the lens of a camera and performs the same function. In the adult it measures about one-fifth inch in thickness and about one-third inch in diameter. The lens is enclosed in a transparent capsule and is held in place by several fine ligaments called zonules. The function of the lens is to focus light rays so that they may form a perfect image on the *retina*. The retina is similar to the film in the back of a camera and performs the same function as this film. Clouding or opacity of the lens within its structure prevents rays of light from entering the eyeball and results in blurring of vision, much in the same manner as a cloudy lens in a camera would result in a blurred picture.

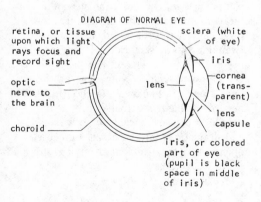

DIAGRAM OF NORMAL EYE

retina, or tissue upon which light rays focus and record sight

optic nerve to the brain

choroid

sclera (white of eye)

iris

cornea (transparent)

lens

lens capsule

iris, or colored part of eye (pupil is black space in middle of iris)

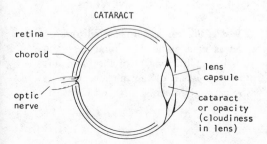

CATARACT

retina

choroid

optic nerve

lens capsule

cataract or opacity (cloudiness in lens)

Cataracts are extremely common, and best estimates are that one of every 20 people, sooner or later, will develop this condition. Cataracts have a tendency to occur in both eyes, but in 10 percent of cases the involvement affects but one eye. They are classified as follows:

1. **Congenital or senile:** According to the time of life when they first appear.

2. **Liquid, soft, or hard:** According to their consistency.

3. **Nuclear, cortical, or capsular:** According to the exact location of the cataract in the lens.

4. **Traumatic:** Cataracts secondary to injury of the eye or the lens itself.

5. **Stationary or progressive:** According to the rate of development. They may become stationary during any of the stages of development.

6. **Partial or complete:** According to the extent of the opacity or cloudiness. The term "ripe" has been used to describe a *complete* cataract. Cataracts present the following symptoms:

a) *Blurring of vision:* This depends upon the location of the clouding of the lens. The farther back in the lens clouding occurs, the sooner will blurring of vision occur. The greater the distribution of the clouding, the more marked is the blurring of vision. Blurring is least when the clouding is in the outer margin of the lens. The most significant characteristic of the blur is that it cannot be eliminated by the use of eyeglasses. As the cataract grows, blurring increases until the time is reached when the patient may be able to see only light.

b) *Rainbow colors and halos:* Certain types of cataract present this aberration of vision which is usually associated with glaucoma but which can also be caused by a central type of cataract.

c) *Double vision:* This is an occasional symptom but is not always characteristic of cataract.

d) *Nearsightedness:* An increase of nearsightedness, or a decrease of farsightedness, may develop in certain types of cataracts known as *nuclear cataracts.* If the patient is in his advanced years and is normally farsighted, he may reach a stage where he believes his sight is improving and he may discard his eyeglasses. This peculiar phenomenon is called "second sight."

When the patient presents himself for an examination, the ophthalmologist will shine an ordinary light into his eyes. The cataract formation will usually become apparent instantly as a gray or white opacity (cloudiness) on a black background. On examining the eye further with an ophthalmoscope (an instrument that permits the physician to look directly into the eyeball and as far back as the retina), the cataract appears as a black opacity on a red background.

In former days, it was necessary to wait until the cataract was "ripe" or "mature" before performing surgery. This sometimes took many years, during which period the patient had very little vision in the eye. Now, with improved surgical techniques, a cataract can be removed while it is immature, thus doing away with a long waiting period of blindness.

There is no satisfactory medical treatment for cataract. Periodically, medical "cures" involving drops, "fish lens" injections, and other methods are given publicity. It is true that extensive research is being done to cast further light on the degenerative metabolic processes that cause cataract. While such work may eventually shed light on the prevention and medical dissolution of lens opacities, none of this research has provided an answer as yet. To date, surgical treatment, which means removal of the opaque lens, is the only satisfactory approach.

Surgical removal of a cataract is indicated when vision is sufficiently reduced to interfere with one's occupation or usual activities. A thorough general physical survey, including a medical and dental checkup, is necessary before surgery is undertaken. The chest must be clear, as coughing, either during or after surgery, may have a very unfavorable effect upon the outcome of the operation. Bad teeth may act as a focus of infection and contribute toward a postoperative eye infection. The urine must be examined for the presence of sugar, as diabetes during surgery and during the postoperative period may increase the incidence of complications and decrease the body's ability to ward off infection.

Cataract operations are performed in the hospital, and until recently most of them have been performed under local anesthesia. With the great recent improvements in the methods of administering general anesthesia, many eye surgeons now prefer it to local anesthesia.

Within the past decade, there have been several important advances in cataract surgery. One of the principal advances is the use of improved needles and suture material. These sutures can now be placed with greater facility and in greater numbers, thereby making for a more secure operative wound. Other improvements are the use of finer instruments and better magnification of the operative field. These allow for greater accuracy and skill on the part of the surgeon, and as a consequence, there is a greater percentage of successful results. One further dramatic advance in the last few years has been the introduction of a liquid enzyme called chymotrypsin. When this chemical is injected into the eye, the attachments of the lens are chemically destroyed, without affecting the rest of the eye. This facilitates the removal of the lens in many patients in whom extraction would ordinarily have been much more difficult. This enzyme has proved particularly useful in younger patients who require cataract or lens extraction. The latest addition to improved cataract surgery has been the use of an applicator to the lens which freezes it and thereby facilitates its removal without breaking the capsule.

There are three methods of cataract removal:

1. Needling: This procedure is usually reserved for children. It consists of opening the capsule of the lens with several small cuts, using a small needle knife. Fluid (aqueous) of the eyeball then enters the lens and dissolves the cataract.

2. Linear extraction: In this method the eyeball is opened with an incision at the point where the white of the eye (sclera) meets the colored portion of the eye. The lens capsule is then exposed and opened. The cataract is flushed out with salt solution (saline).

3. Extraction: This is the procedure usually done in people over 35 years of age and as most cataracts develop in this group, it is by far the most common operative procedure performed.

A flap of conjunctiva (the membrane covering the white of the eye) is dissected down to the edge of the cornea. An incision (cut) is made at the upper border of the cornea at the limbus. The iris (the muscle responsible for contraction and dilatation of the pupil and for the color of one's eyes) is then grasped with a forceps and a small piece is removed. The removal of this piece of iris is called an *iridectomy*. Following this, three to five fine sutures of silk or catgut are placed through the cornea and the sclera. These are used to close the wound after the lens has been removed. The entire lens is then grasped with a forceps (or with a suction apparatus called an erysiphake) and is slowly teased out of the eyeball. The corneoscleral sutures, previously placed, are then closed, tied, and cut. The flap of conjunctiva is stitched in place with a fine suture material.

The patient is confined to bed for two days after the operation. The operated eye is dressed daily and is kept bandaged for one week. In most instances, the unoperated eye is permitted to remain exposed throughout the entire postoperative period.

While the patient should lie quietly in bed for the first two days after surgery in order to reduce the chances of hemorrhage and rupture of the wound, it is no longer necessary to immobilize the head. Fortunately, complications such as hemorrhage, wound rupture, and infection are now rare. The operative wound heals with fair security in approximately ten days, and complete healing takes place in five to six weeks.

The results of cataract operations are excellent in over 90 percent of cases. The patients are permitted to use their eyes within four weeks after surgery. Sight is restored in these people when they wear eyeglasses. The eyeglasses are so ground that they are curved to take over the function that the natural lens formerly performed. While vision obtained with these glasses may at first appear to be strange, the patient adjusts to it after a few weeks and can function normally.

When both eyes are affected by cataract, the standard practice has been not to operate upon both eyes during the one hospital admission. While this still remains the rule in most cases, improved methods have made it permissible to depart from this practice under special circumstances. An interval of six weeks to six months is usually advised between operations.

In cases where only one eye has been affected by cataract and the other eye is normal, until recently it has not been possible to use both eyes together with the help of eyeglasses. However, the advent of *contact lenses* has changed this situation. With these lenses, not only may a patient with a cataract operation on one eye use both of his eyes together, but these lenses, in addition, can give the patient more natural vision than ordinary cataract lenses.

Within the past few years, experiments with a plastic lens, which is surgically inserted into the eyeball to replace the patient's clouded lens, have been in progress and have proved successful in many instances. While this procedure is still in the experimental stage, it may someday become the standard operating procedure for cataract.

QUESTIONS AND ANSWERS

What is a cataract?
A clouding or opacity of the lens.

What causes cataracts?
The cause of most cataracts is unknown. Cataracts represent a degenerative, aging tissue process and are often associated with diabetes, injury, deficiency of the parathyroid gland in the neck, or overexposure to ultraviolet rays. X-rays or atomic radiation may also cause cataract formation. A few have been caused by taking a weight reducing drug called dinitrophenol. Recently a drug called MER-29, used to reduce blood cholesterol, was shown to cause cataracts. (Neither of these drugs is being marketed today.)

How does cataract interfere with vision?

It stops rays of light from entering the eyeball.

Does overuse of the eye ever cause cataracts?

No.

Are cataracts inherited?

Not necessarily, but they may run in families.

How can one prevent cataracts from forming?

Usually cataracts cannot be prevented from forming.

Can they be cured medically?

No.

Do cataracts get well by themselves?

No.

What is the outlook for a child born with cataracts?

If cataracts are in both eyes, the child should be operated on at one year of age. The outlook is favorable if the back of the eye is healthy. The use of corneal lenses has improved the outlook even further. However, it must be stated that unfavorable results are not uncommon in cases of congenital cataract.

What is the outlook for an adolescent with cataracts?

Good. This is especially so since the advent of the new enzyme chymotrypsin.

How long do cataracts take to become ripe?

Usually one to two years, but this varies considerably. Some types never become ripe. Others achieve a certain amount of maturity and never progress beyond that.

Must a cataract be ripe before it is operated upon?

No. This is no longer necessary because of better surgical techniques.

When should a cataract be removed?

When the cataract progresses to the point where it interferes with the patient's ability to work or live happily.

What can happen if the operation is advised and the patient refuses?

The cataract may become overripe. If it does, the eye can become inflamed and damaged beyond repair. Eventually the eyeball may have to be removed.

How many people have a cataract in one eye only and never develop one in the other eye?

About 10 percent.

Should a cataract always be removed from one eye when the other eye has no cataract?

Not always. Sometimes this presents a difficulty, since the postoperative wearing of glasses will be too uncomfortable. The difference in the strength of the lens required to give good vision will be so great that the patient will be unable to wear the glasses. Also, the dazzling of light in the operated eye may become very annoying. However, if the cataract in the one eye is ripe, it should be removed. Then, if the patient can tolerate a corneal lens in his operated eye, the difficulties are minimized. It should be noted that a patient who has had a cataract removed can readily tolerate a contact lens.

When should a unilateral cataract (on one side only) be removed?

When it shows signs of becoming ripe or overripe. If not removed, it may cause a severe inflammation with ultimate loss of the eye and permanent blindness.

How long an interval should exist between cataract operation on both eyes?

From four weeks to six months, as a rule. If one-eyed vision interferes with work, the period between operations should be decreased.

Are there any special preoperative measures that one should take before cataract operation?
Yes. A general medical and dental checkup is necessary. Diabetes must be controlled before operation. Sources of infection, such as bad teeth, must be cleared up.

What is done in a cataract operation?
The cloudy (opaque) lens is removed from the eyeball, leaving an optically clear area through which the patient can see.

Is this operation dangerous?
No.

Is the operation painful?
No.

What kind of anesthesia is used?
Local or general anesthesia.

Where is the incision made?
At the border of the white part of the eye (sclera) and the colored part of the eye. The incision is placed on the eyeball so that it lies under the upper lid.

How long does it take to perform the operation for cataract removal?
About 45 minutes.

How long must the patient stay in bed?
Two days.

Are private nurses necessary?
Yes, in a general hospital. Not necessarily, in a hospital especially devoted to eye surgery. If the patient has only one eye, private nurses should be employed.

How long must the patient stay in the hospital?
About one week.

Is the postoperative period painful?
Generally, no.

What postoperative directions should be followed?
The usual postoperative directions are medicated eyedrops to hasten healing and lessen chances of infection; protection of the eye with a metal shield attached to the forehead and cheek, especially during sleeping; the patient is not permitted to stoop or lift heavy objects for several weeks.

Are special postoperative diets necessary?
No, unless the patient is a diabetic. Foods requiring strenuous chewing are usually omitted from the diet for one to two weeks.

How successful are cataract operations?
Excellent vision (with glasses) is restored in more than 90 percent of cases. In most cases in which the results are poor, it is due to a defect in the retina rather than a defect in the cataract operation.

Do cataracts recur once they have been removed?
Yes. They recur in about 10 percent of cases. Most of these patients can be reoperated upon and cured.

What are the most frequently encountered complications of cataract surgery?
1. Hemorrhage into the eye
2. Rupture of the wound
3. Postoperative wound infection

Have these complications been reduced by improved methods?
Yes. Hemorrhages are rare indeed because of improved methods of suturing the wound. The antibiotic drugs have decreased the incidence of infection to a very large extent.

Does hemorrhage after cataract operation lead to loss of vision?

Usually not. Small hemorrhages will disappear without any ill effect. A large hemorrhage may lead to loss of vision. Fortunately, this is a rare complication.

Does a postoperative infection ever lead to loss of vision?

Yes, if the infection is deep and severe. A mild postoperative infection will not affect vision.

Is the eye deformed by cataract removal?

No.

Is there any visible scar from cataract removal?

No.

Must one be careful not to strain the eyes after a cataract operation?

Yes.

Can contact lenses be worn instead of eyeglasses after cataract removal?

Yes, especially when one eye has been operated upon and there is no cataract in the other eye.

How soon after operation is one permitted to use his eye for the following:

Ordinary activity around the house?	4 weeks
Reading?	4 weeks
All work and usual activities?	8 weeks

Can one drink an alcoholic beverage after cataract operations?

Not for six weeks after surgery has been performed.

How soon after surgery can one

Bathe?	4 weeks
Take an automobile ride?	4 weeks

Drive a car?	6 weeks
Resume light work?	6 weeks
Resume heavy work?	6 weeks
Resume sexual relations?	6 weeks

Cecostomy

Cecostomy is the creation of an artificial opening into the cecum through surgery. The cecum is the first portion of the large intestine located in the right lower part of the abdomen. This operation is sometimes performed to relieve obstruction of the large bowel. When carried out, it is usually a preliminary procedure done in order to relieve acute obstruction, prior to a definitive operation to remove the underlying cause of the intestinal disorder.

After an opening has been made into the cecum, a large rubber tube is usually placed into the opening and the abdomen is closed. Gas and liquid feces are then permitted to escape through the tube into a drainage bottle at the side of the bed.

See also INTESTINES.

Cellulitis

Cellulitis is an infection of the loose fat and connective tissues that lie beneath the skin and between muscle planes. The same germs, such as the streptococcus, the staphylococcus, and others, that cause the average abscess or carbuncle can cause cellulitis. A characteristic of this type of infection is that it spreads over a wide area, because there are few barriers to prevent its spread in the loose connective tissues.

QUESTIONS AND ANSWERS

Can a localized infection, such as a pimple or boil, lead to cellulitis?

Yes, if the infection is not drained or if it is squeezed so that bacteria get into the surrounding connective tissues.

What are the symptoms of cellulitis?

The involved area becomes swollen, painful, hot, and red. If a large area of tissue, such as an arm or a leg, is involved, the patient will run a high fever and will show other signs of a toxic reaction.

What is the treatment for cellulitis?

1. A patient with cellulitis should go to bed and remain there until temperature is normal for at least two days.
2. The involved part should be kept at complete rest.
3. Hot, wet applications should be placed around the involved area.
4. Antibiotic drugs should be prescribed to limit the spread of the infection.
5. If pus has formed, the inflamed area will have to be opened surgically.

Does cellulitis ever lead to a bloodstream infection?

Occasionally, if it is not treated adequately or if the invading bacteria happen to be present in large numbers and are virulent in nature.

Is it ever necessary to hospitalize an individual with cellulitis?

Yes, especially if surgical drainage of the infected area is required.

Is erysipelas a form of cellulitis?

Yes. It is a particularly toxic infection involving the skin and tissues beneath the skin. A streptococcus germ is usually the cause of this type of cellulitis.

In what part of the body can cellulitis occur?

It can occur anywhere in the body, including the face, the scalp, the neck, the torso, and the arms or legs.

Is cellulitis more apt to affect people with lowered resistance?

Yes. Those in good health have a greater capacity to limit the spread of localized infection.

Cerebral Palsy

Although there are many possible causes of cerebral palsy, heredity does not play an important role. Because one child has the condition, parents need not fear that future children will be so afflicted. A great number of children with cerebral palsy are not severely crippled, and with new surgical procedures to relieve spastic muscles and with improved methods of training, many of these children will be enabled to lead productive, happy lives.

QUESTIONS AND ANSWERS

What is cerebral palsy?

Cerebral palsy is not a single disease, but a group of neurological disorders that affect children and begin at birth. These children have difficulty in walking and have many involuntary movements of the muscles of the face and limbs. Speech in children with cerebral palsy is often affected and becomes blurred and difficult to understand.

In most cases there is no mental deficiency, but in some cases there may be severe mental deficiency.

Is this condition known by any other name?

Yes. Little's disease, congenital diplegia, and infantile hemiplegia are all names for cerebral palsy.

How common is cerebral palsy in children?

It is estimated that 25,000 annually are born with it and about 1 out of every 200 children admitted to children's hospitals has this condition.

Is cerebral palsy always present at birth, or can it develop later on in life?

The term applies specifically to a condition that is present at or before the birth of the child.

What may cause cerebral palsy?

1. A difficult labor, an excessively prolonged labor, or lack of oxygen to the unborn child during labor
2. An actual brain injury during the process of delivery
3. A disorder in the type of brain cells that are inherited by the child
4. An illness of the mother during the first three months of her pregnancy
5. Brain cysts with which the child is born
6. Neurological degeneration occurring while the child is still unborn

Is cerebral palsy hereditary?

No. It is congenital—in other words, the child is born with it—but it is not inherited.

If a parent has one child who has cerebral palsy, what are the chances that any future children will have the condition?

No greater than for the general population.

Does cerebral palsy tend to run in families?

No.

How is cerebral palsy diagnosed?

By noting symptoms and signs, such as spasticity, purposeless (athetoid)

movements of the arms, legs, and face, and difficulty in walking or using the hands. There is frequently a history of injury during childbirth, and sometimes x-rays of the brain will reveal characteristic defects.

Is there more than one type of cerebral palsy?

Yes. The various types include:

1. **Spastic type,** the most common type. The arms are held close to the chest, the elbows are bent, the wrists are flexed, and the palms are turned downward. The thighs are held tightly against each other, the knees are turned inward, and the child tends to walk on his toes because of tight heel cords.

2. **Rigid type.** All muscles of the limbs are firm, rigid, and virtually unyielding. Attempts to move the joints have been likened to bending a lead pipe.

3. **Tremorous type.** There is uncontrollable shaking while awake, particularly of the upper limbs.

4. **Athetoid type.** There is uncontrollable writhing of the limbs and of the muscles of the face.

5. **Flaccid type.** There is virtual paralysis of the muscles of the limbs, almost like the lifeless paralysis of muscles after poliomyelitis. Very rare.

6. **Ataxic type.** Unsteadiness of gait. A child with this disease tends to walk with his legs wide apart.

What is the outstanding characteristic of the muscular disorder in cerebral palsy?

There are stiffness and spasticity, resulting in awkward, jerky, stiff-limbed motions, and sometimes there is a degree of paralysis of the affected limb.

Are children with cerebral palsy usually normal mentally?

Sometimes there are mental changes,

but many such children are perfectly normal mentally.

How can the pediatrician distinguish cerebral palsy from other conditions?
The presence of spastic paralysis, significant limb postures and atrophies, and the history of the birth usually help the pediatrician diagnose cerebral palsy.

Can a definite diagnosis of cerebral palsy be made by x-ray examination?
Only if the palsy is due to porencephaly and special x-ray examinations are taken. (Porencephaly involves the presence of cysts within the brain substances. Most children with cerebral palsy do *not* have brain cysts.)

What is the treatment for cerebral palsy?
The treatment must be twofold: orthopedic corrective braces and devices, along with surgical procedures to relieve spastic muscles and tendons; and psychiatric treatment to maintain good mental and emotional health. Appropriate family care and schooling are important.

Is surgery ever helpful in treating cerebral palsy?
Yes. In specially selected cases it can be quite helpful.

In what types of cerebral palsy is surgery most often helpful?
Surgery is most successful in the spastic types of palsy. It is least successful in the athetoid type and is of practically no value in the rigid type.

Is surgery in cerebral palsy patients often successful?
Yes. However, parents should not expect surgery to render a spastic child's limb normal in appearance or in function. The purpose of surgery is to improve, not to cure, the condition. Surgery in indicated cases may shorten or even eliminate the years needed for physical therapy. It may allow for more comfortable fitting of braces, and may sometimes eliminate the need for braces altogether. Surgery is only one part of the total treatment of the child with cerebral palsy.

Can surgery improve the intelligence of a mentally retarded child with cerebral palsy?
No. But with proper speech training and with improvement in the function of limbs following surgery, the intelligence of a child may appear to improve, because he is more able to express himself.

What type of orthopedic measures can help in alleviating some of the abnormal conditions that accompany cerebral palsy?
Muscles and tendons can be transferred to new positions, certain nerves can be divided to relieve muscle spasm, and ligament muscles can be severed to permit relaxation of a spastic limb. In addition to these surgical maneuvers, braces and orthopedic appliances are found to be most useful.

Cervical Rib

A cervical rib is an extra rib extending from the vertebra in the neck just above the uppermost normal rib. A cervical rib is a birth deformity sometimes causing no symptoms whatever, but at other times resulting in marked pain in the neck and down along the arm to the wrist and hand. The symptoms caused by a cervical rib are due to compression of some of the nerves that pass from the spinal column in the neck down into the arm.

QUESTIONS AND ANSWERS

Is cervical rib a common birth deformity?

Yes. It is a rather frequent anomaly of the skeletal structure.

Does a cervical rib always cause symptoms?

No. In many instances it is only discovered accidentally upon x-raying the neck and upper chest of an individual. In the majority of people who have a cervical rib, there are no symptoms whatever.

What is the treatment for someone with cervical rib and marked pain down the arm?

The treatment consists either of surgical removal of the exra rib or of the cutting of fibrous tissue that leads from the rib to the muscles of the lower neck. It has been found that the cutting of this tissue is often sufficient to relieve any pressure upon the nerves going to the arm. In occasional cases, when the rib is especially large and the symptoms are particularly severe, the cervical rib is removed.

Does relief of symptoms usually follow removal of a cervical rib?

Yes. The operation for this condition is successful in almost all cases.

Cervix

The cervix, or neck of the womb, is that portion of the uterus which appears in the vagina. It is a small, firm, muscular organ with a canal through its center (the cervical canal), extending from the vagina to the interior of the body of the uterus. The cervix is the only portion of the uterus that can actually be seen during the course of an office pelvic examination.

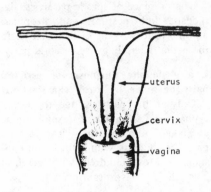

The cervix of the uterus protrudes into the vagina.

QUESTIONS AND ANSWERS

How is the cervix examined?

A special instrument known as a speculum is inserted into the vagina.

What is the function of the cervix?

1. It guards the cavity of the uterus from invasion by bacteria or other foreign particles.

2. It allows for the passage of sperm into the cavity of the uterus.

3. It protects the developing embryo during pregnancy.

4. It opens during labor to allow for the passage of the baby.

5. It permits the escape of menstrual blood.

What is cervicitis?

It is an inflammation of the cervix.

What are the various types of cervicitis?

1. **Erosion of the cervix:** a raw, reddened area appearing at the opening of the cervical canal in the vagina. This may be primary, appearing in young girls who have a developmental disorder

causing an absence of the normal membrane covering of the cervix. Erosions may be secondary, developing as a consequence of injury received during labor, or as a result of operative disturbance, such as after curettage.

2. Cystic cervicitis: a condition in which small cysts develop on an inflamed cervix during the healing process. As the surface of the cervix heals, some of its glands are sealed over and form cysts.

3. Hypertrophic cervicitis: a condition in which there is a large overgrowth of the entire substance of the cervical body. It is often associated with cyst formation and erosion.

4. Chronic cervicitis: recurrence of any of the above.

What are the causes of cervicitis?
1. Bacteria, fungi, or parasites
2. Injury secondary to delivery or surgery
3. A congenital deficiency in the normal covering layer of the cervix

What are the symptoms of cervicitis?
1. The most pronounced symptom is vaginal discharge (leukorrhea). The appearance of the discharge may vary from a colorless mucus to a whitish or yellowish discharge.
2. Vaginal bleeding after sexual intercourse.
3. In severe cases, menstrual bleeding may be heavier than normal or may be preceded or followed by staining for a day or two.

Does cervicitis ever interfere with the ability to become pregnant?
Occasionally. In such cases it is necessary to clear up the cervicitis before pregnancy can take place.

What is the treatment for cervicitis?
1. If an infection is present, it must be eradicated by appropriate medication.

2. Douching helps to keep local infection under control; an acid douche may prevent the recurrence of an infection caused by a fungus or parasite.
3. Simple erosion of a cervix can be treated by cauterizing with silver nitrate applications, by electrocauterization, or by cryosurgery.
4. Extensive erosions or cyst formation requires more active and forceful treatment with electrocauterization.
5. Chronic hypertrophy of the cervix may be treated by cauterization, but the more pronounced cases may require hospitalization for amputation of the cervix.

How is electrocauterization of the cervix performed?
It is an office procedure in which incisions are burned into the cervix by means of an electrically heated, metal-tipped instrument. The burning incisions, of which many are made, cause the eroded or infected tissue to die and fall away from the underlying healthy cervical tissue. In time, the healthy tissue is able to grow again and to cover the entire cervix.

Is cauterization of the cervix a painful procedure?
No. It is accompanied by relatively little discomfort. There may be a feeling of warmth in the vagina and some cramps may follow, but it does not produce any disability.

How long does cauterization take to perform?
In the hands of a competent gynecologist, only a few minutes.

What is the patient to expect after cauterization of the cervix?
In most instances, there will be an increased vaginal discharge for a week to ten days. This may be heavy, foul-smelling, and grayish in color. After

seven or eight days, vaginal bleeding may ensue. This is due to the sloughing of the infected tissue.

What precautions should be taken after cauterization of the cervix?

The patient should abstain from intercourse and douches for 12 to 14 days.

Is it necessary to take douches at any time following cauterization?

Sometimes. After the slough has been expelled, in about 12 to 14 days, daily douches with warm water and an acid solution may be taken to prevent reinfection. These douches should be continued for approximately three weeks except during the menstrual period.

How long does it take for healing to be complete after cauterization?

Approximately six weeks.

Are medications inserted into the vagina following cauterization?

Some gynecologists recommend the daily insertion of antibiotic vaginal suppositories to prevent reinfection.

Is there a tendency for cervicitis or cervical erosion to recur?

Yes. If it recurs, treatment should be started again. It is not unusual for a slight recurrence to take place, but this will respond if treated promptly.

Does the gynecologist examine for cancer in all cases in which there is an abnormality of the cervix?

Yes. A competent gynecologist will be able to decide what type of condition requires further investigation. He will take a cancer smear and do a biopsy of the suspicious area.

What is a cancer smear (Papanicolaou smear)?

It is a method of collecting surface cells from the vagina and cervix and examining them, with special staining techniques, to see if they are malignant.

Should all women have a cervical cancer smear?

All women past the age of 20 should have a routine vaginal smear taken every year. Also, a smear should be taken at any time when a lesion is suspected.

Is it painful to take a cancer smear?

Absolutely not. The entire procedure takes no more than a few seconds and is performed merely by swabbing the surface of the cervix and the vagina.

What is a cervical polyp?

It is a small benign tumor arising from the cervix. It usually has a thin stalk and assumes the size and shape of a pea, cherry, or grape.

What causes cervical polyps to grow?

The cause is unknown. They can occur in both young and old women.

What are the symptoms of cervical polyps?

Vaginal discharge, staining between periods, pre- and post-menstrual staining, and cramps. One, or all, of these symptoms may appear, or there may be no symptoms whatever.

What is the treatment for cervical polyps?

They should be removed in the office of the gynecologist, or, under certain circumstances, in the hospital. This is considered a minor operative procedure and is accompanied by little discomfort.

Do polyps tend to recur?

Once a polyp has been removed it will not grow. However, women who have developed one polyp do have a tendency to form others. These, too, should be removed.

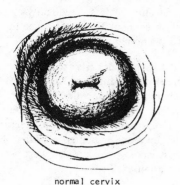

normal cervix

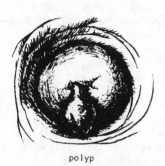

polyp

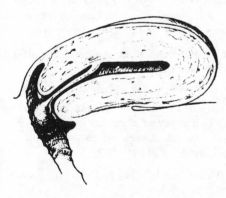

At top is a normal cervix. Center shows a polyp protruding from the cervix. In the side view, at the bottom, the cervical polyp is shown protruding into the vagina.

Are the polyps of the cervix ever malignant?
Rarely.

Do polyps interfere with pregnancy?
Usually not.

What is hypertrophy of the cervix?
An overgrowth or elongation of the cervix occurring with or without inflammation. In many cases it is associated with prolapse of the uterus, cystocele, or rectocele.

What causes hypertrophy of the cervix?
The cause is unknown.

What are the symptoms of hypertrophy of the cervix?
If it is associated with cystocele, rectocele, or prolapse of the uterus, the symptoms are urinary or rectal. If it exists alone, the symptoms may consist of pressure in the vagina or the presence of a mass protruding through the vaginal opening.

Does hypertrophy of the cervix interfere with marital relations?
Yes. The presence of a mass filling the vagina may make intercourse almost impossible. Pain during intercourse may be the result of displacement of the enlarged cervix.

What is the treatment for hypertrophy of the cervix?
When associated with prolapse, cystocele, or rectocele, the cervix is removed as part of the vaginal plastic operation. When the hypertrophy of the cervix exists alone, it is amputated surgically.

Where is the incision made for amputation of the cervix?
Entirely within the vaginal canal.

Is amputation of the cervix a major operation?
No. It is considered a relatively minor operation and is accompanied by very little risk or postoperative discomfort.

How long a hospital stay is necessary for amputation of the cervix?

Approximately five to six days.

What postoperative precautions are necessary after amputation of the cervix?

It takes approximately three to four weeks to complete convalescence. Marital relations and douching are not permitted for approximately six weeks.

Will amputation of the cervix interfere with subsequent pregnancy?

Pregnancy *can* take place after amputation of the cervix, but delivery will probably be performed by cesarean section. When the cervix has been amputated, it is often difficult for the neck of the womb to dilate sufficiently to allow for the passage of the baby. Also, there is danger of rupture of this lower segment during labor.

Does hypertrophy of the cervix ever lead to cancer?

No.

Is cancer of the cervix a common condition?

Yes, it accounts for 25 percent of all cancer found in women.

What causes cancer of the cervix?

The exact cause is unknown. There are many theories, but none of them has been fully substantiated.

At what age is cancer of the cervix usually encountered?

It can occur at any age, but is seen most often in women between 30 and 50 years of age.

Does cancer of the cervix tend to run in families?

No.

Do Jewish women seem to have a certain type of immunity to cancer of the cervix?

It is true that cancer of the cervix is found much less frequently among Jewish women. The exact cause for this odd phenomenon is not known.

Is it wise to seek early treatment for any abnormal condition of the cervix in an attempt to prevent cancer?

Definitely, yes. Many competent gynecologists feel that erosion, laceration, inflammation, or benign growths of the cervix may predispose toward cancer formation.

Can cancer of the cervix be prevented?

Not only is cancer prevention actually possible, but a *late* cancer can be avoided through early treatment. Thus, periodic vaginal examinations will uncover many cancers in their early curable stages.

What are the early symptoms of cancer of the cervix?

Very early cancer may cause no symptoms whatever. This is one of the main reasons for periodic vaginal examinations. Later on, there may be vaginal discharge, bleeding after intercourse, bleeding after douching, or unexplained bleeding between periods.

Can early cancer of the cervix be detected by a cancer smear?

Yes.

What is the value of the cancer smear?

It can reveal cancer cells at a *very early stage* of their development, thus allowing for extremely early treatment.

What is noninvasive cancer of the cervix?

This is a condition, also called *in situ* cancer of the cervix, in which the cancer is limited to the most superficial layer of cells and there is no spread to the deeper tissues. This term is used to distinguish it from *invasive* cancer, in which the spread has extended beyond the superficial layers of cells into the deeper tissues, including the lymph channels and the bloodstream.

How accurate is the cancer smear in diagnosing cancer?
A positive cancer smear is accurate in about 97 percent of cases.

Does a positive cancer smear constitute sufficient investigation of a cancer of the cervix?
No. Whenever a cancer smear is positive, a biopsy and/or curettage should be taken to make the diagnosis and location absolutely certain. A positive smear may indicate cancer of the uterine body as well as cancer of the cervix.

What is a biopsy?
A biopsy means the removal of a small piece of tissue for diagnosis. It can be done in the office with a special instrument and is virtually painless. Occasionally, a larger biopsy has to be performed. This has to be done in the hospital under anesthesia.

What is the treatment for cancer of the cervix?
This will depend entirely upon the stage of development of the cancer at the time it is discovered. There are three ways of treating this disease:
1. By use of radium and x-ray
2. By wide surgical removal of the cervix, uterus, tubes, ovaries, and all the lymph channels draining the area
3. By a combination of radium, x-ray, and surgery

Who will determine what form of treatment should be administered?
The gynecologist will know which form of treatment to institute after the invasiveness and extent of the cancer have been determined.

What are the chances of recovery from cancer of the cervix?
Early cancer of the cervix can be cured in almost all cases—by either radium, x-ray, surgery, or a combination of these forms of treatment.

As the extensiveness of the disease increases and the operative procedures become more involved, recovery rates are lower. In the most extensive cases, the mortality rate is high and the rate of cure is extremely low.

Is it painful to insert radium into the vagina?
No. This procedure is carried out in the hospital, under anesthesia.

Does radium remain inside the body permanently?
No. The radium is usually applied in capsules, and after a sufficient number of radioactive rays have been transmitted, the capsule is removed.

How long does radium usually remain within the genital tract?
Anywhere from 72 to 144 hours, according to the specific dosage indicated.

How long a hospital stay is necessary when radium is inserted?
Anywhere from one to seven days.

Is the application of radium followed by postoperative discomfort?
Yes, because an extensive packing is inserted into the vagina when radium is being used. This discomfort is controlled by use of sedatives.

Is x-ray treatment often given along with radium treatment?
Yes. This is given in the weeks before and/or after radium implantation, in order to reach parts not reached by the radium.

Are there any postoperative symptoms following radium implantation?
Yes. Disturbance in bowel function and burning and frequency of urination

are quite often complications of radium treatment of the cervix.

Does cancer ever recur after radium treatment for cancer of the cervix?
Yes. Some cancers are resistant to radium or inaccessible to it. Recurrence will depend upon the stage of the disease at the time radium and x-ray treatment were given.

Can a patient return to normal living after radium treatment for cancer of the cervix?
Yes, in the majority of instances.

Can a patient become pregnant after radium treatment for cancer of the cervix?
Because ovarian function will have been destroyed by the radium treatment, pregnancy will not take place. Menstruation will also cease as a result of radium therapy.

What type of surgery is performed for cancer of the cervix?
1. Hysterectomy for *in situ* or early *invasive* cancer
2. Exenteration for extensive and advanced cancer

What is meant by an exenteration operation for cancer of the cervix?
This is an extremely complicated operative procedure in which the entire uterus, cervix, vagina, tubes, ovaries, lymph nodes, bladder, and/or rectum are removed for extensive cancer. Artificial openings are made for the passage of urine and stool.

Can cancer of the cervix be cured by such radical surgery?
Only the occasional case. It must be remembered that this type of surgery is carried out only on those who have extensive or recurrent cancer and who would have died without surgery.

Is this operation dangerous?
Yes.

What is the future outlook for those afflicted with cancer of the cervix?
Earlier detection can lead to a substantially higher cure rate in years to come. The advent of the cancer smear now permits the diagnosis to be made at earlier stages in the development of the disease. The earlier the cancer is detected and the earlier the treatment is started, the better are the patient's chances.

Cesarean Section

Cesarean section is the term used to describe the delivery of a baby through an incision in the lower abdominal wall and through the lower portion of the uterus. The derivation of the term "cesarean section" is not completely clear, but the popular belief that Julius Caesar was delivered in this manner is not true.

Approximately 5 percent of all deliveries in this country are performed by this method. Although this type of delivery is extremely safe when done by qualified obstetricians in approved hospitals, nevertheless it is performed only when there are definite reasons for not permitting delivery through the vagina. The personal desire of the patient or her husband for a cesarean delivery does *not* constitute a valid medical indication.

A cesarean operation is performed through a low abdominal incision approximately six inches long. It is most commonly made longitudinally, and less frequently transversely. Spinal anesthesia is most commonly used, but general anesthesia may be chosen in some cases, especially when hemorrhage has occurred prior to delivery. After the abdominal cavity has been entered, an incision is made through the wall of the uterus, and the obstetrician inserts his hand and delivers the head of the baby. After the child has been withdrawn completely, the umbilical cord is ligated and cut, and the placenta (afterbirth) is manually removed. The incision in the wall of the uterus is sutured tightly, and the abdominal wall is closed in the same manner as a surgical wound made for any other operation. The patient is usually out of bed on the following day, and leaves the hospital about ten days later.

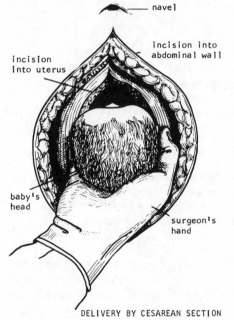

DELIVERY BY CESAREAN SECTION

It is felt that once a patient has been delivered in this fashion, future pregnancies should be handled by repeat cesarean section operations. The reason for this is that the wall of the operated uterus may be weakened and may rupture during the violent contractions of a subsequent labor. Thus the usual prac-

tice is to schedule a repeat cesarean delivery about a week before the expected onset of labor. In some cases the obstetrician may decide to wait until the very onset of labor before operating. In common specific instances, delivery through the vaginal route may be permitted even though previous deliveries have been performed by cesarean section.

Repeat cesarean sections are often performed through the same site after excising the old scar.

The question of how many cesarean section deliveries a woman may have is always of great interest. Although there are isolated cases on record with as many as ten cesarean deliveries, in general patients are advised that additional pregnancy is inadvisable after three or four such deliveries. For this reason, if moral and religious beliefs are not violated, the obstetrician may agree to perform sterilization at the time of the cesarean section operation. This procedure is never performed without a specific signed request by the patient and her husband.

QUESTIONS AND ANSWERS

What is a cesarean section?
Delivery of a baby via an incision in the lower abdomen and an incision in the uterus.

What are the indications for cesarean section?
1. **Disproportion,** where the baby's head is too large or the mother's bony pelvis is too small to allow delivery from below
2. **Prolonged or ineffective labor** which fails to respond to the usual methods of stimulation and where normal vaginal delivery seems improbable in a reasonable time

3. Placenta praevia, when the afterbirth (placenta) lies in front of or below the baby's head. This is fraught with danger to mother and baby because of the danger of hemorrhage

4. Abruptio placenta, when the placenta separates from the uterus before the delivery of the baby has taken place and where bleeding is too brisk to permit waiting for delivery from below

5. Abnormal presentation, such as one in which the baby is coming down with an arm or a shoulder first and delivery from below is almost impossible without great danger

6. Prolapsed cord, where the umbilical cord comes out through the vagina before delivery and delivery is not thought to be imminent

7. Breech presentation in first pregnancies, where the obstetrician fears some disproportion between the baby's head and the pelvis

8. Elderly women having their first baby, where some other abnormality exists

9. Repeated previous stillbirths from unknown causes, where previous babies have died within the last few weeks of pregnancy or after the onset of labor

10. Preeclampsia or eclampsia, where elevated blood pressure and other symptoms, with or without the onset of convulsions, make delivery urgent as a lifesaving measure

11. Previous surgery, such as:

a) Previous cesarean section

b) Removal of fibroid tumors from the uterus

c) Previous plastic operations upon the vagina, where delivery from below may lead to rupture of the cervix or vaginal structures

12. Diabetes, where extremely large babies make delivery from below improbable

13. A fibroid of the uterus or an ovarian cyst or other tumor which obstructs the pelvis and will prevent a normal passage of the baby through the birth canal

14. Fetal distress (other than that resulting from praevias and abruptios

Are all of the preceding indications for cesarean section absolute?

No. It must be understood that there are many variable factors which will help the obstetrician to make his decision.

When will the obstetrician know whether a cesarean section will be necessary?

This varies considerably. He may know on his first examination of the patient during the early days of pregnancy, or he may not know until after labor has been in progress for several hours.

Are there various types of cesarean section?

Yes. There are many different technical procedures, but all types involve an abdominal incision, with the removal of the baby through an incision into the wall of the uterus.

What types of anesthesia are used for cesarean section?

1. General anesthesia
2. Spinal or epidural block
3. Caudal
4. Local Novocain anesthesia

The type of anesthesia will be determined by the mother's condition and the preference of both the obstetrician and the anesthetist.

Where is the incision made for cesarean section?

In the lower abdomen, either a longitudinal incision in the midline or a transverse incision across the pubis.

How is the baby delivered in cesarean section?

After the abdominal wall has been

opened and the wall of the uterus has been incised, the surgeon's hand is inserted into the uterus and the baby is gently lifted out. The cord is tied off in the usual manner, and the surgeon again inserts his hand and separates the afterbirth from the uterine wall. The incision in the uterus is then sutured with two layers of stitches, and the abdomen is closed tightly.

Is the infant's life endangered by a cesarean delivery?

On the contrary, often the best chance of obtaining a live baby is by performing this operation.

How long does it take to perform a cesarean section?

Anywhere from 45 to 60 minutes.

How many cesarean sections is it safe for a woman to have?

Usually three or four. However, if the patient desires to have more children because of religious beliefs or other reasons, she may be allowed to have as many cesarean sections as she wishes.

How often are babies delivered by this method?

Approximately 5 of every 100 deliveries in this country are performed by cesarean section.

Can a patient have a cesarean section upon request?

No. There are definite reasons involving the safety of the mother and baby in every case requiring this procedure.

Is cesarean section a safe operation?

Yes. It is very safe.

Can a patient who has once had a cesarean section ever be delivered from below in subsequent pregnancies?

Yes. However, such a patient must be watched very closely from the very onset of labor, and the operating room must be alerted at all times to perform an emergency cesarean section should a complication arise.

Is it true that most people who have had one cesarean section will be delivered by the same method in future pregnancies?

As a general rule, this is true.

Is cesarean section a painful operation?

Not particularly.

When does the patient get out of bed after cesarean section?

The day following surgery.

Are special nurses necessary?

They are not essential but are helpful for the first few days.

How long after cesarean section will vaginal bleeding continue?

For two to three weeks, followed by the usual discharge that ensues after a pregnancy.

Does cesarean section interfere with subsequent menstruation?

No.

How long after cesarean section will the first menstrual period appear?

In about six weeks.

Can a baby be breast-fed after cesarean section?

Yes.

How long after a cesarean section can one safely become pregnant again?

Having had a cesarean section delivery plays no part in this decision. The physician will advise the patient as he would after a vaginal delivery.

Does a cesarean section delivery make it more difficult to become pregnant again?

No.

When is a sterilization procedure performed in conjunction with a cesarean section delivery?

Only when the patient and her husband have requested the procedure in writing.

Why should a woman have future cesarean deliveries following the first one?

Because of the fear that a future labor might cause rupture of the uterus.

How long a hospital stay is necessary after cesarean section?

About eight to ten days.

Does cesarean section interfere with future pregnancies?

Not unless sterilization has been carried out at the time that the cesarean section was performed.

How soon after cesarean section can one do the following?

Bathe:	4 weeks
Douche:	6 weeks
Drive an automobile:	5–6 weeks
Resume sexual relations:	6–8 weeks
Resume all activities:	8–10 weeks

Chalazion

Chalazion stems from infection of a sebaceous gland of the eyelids in which the secretions of the gland become blocked and cannot gain exit. The result is a balloonlike effect, the "balloon" in this case being filled with secretions and pus rather than air. The presence of a chalazion is noted by the appearance of a firm pealike knot in the eyelid. Often the infection starts as an inflammation of the entire eyelid and later localizes to one area. As there are 30 to 40 sebaceous glands in each eyelid, chalazions are sometimes multiple.

Small cysts frequently clear up with the use of hot, wet compresses and antiseptic ointments, as used with sties. Larger cysts usually require surgical removal under local anesthesia. Procaine or a similar local anesthetic agent is injected under the skin of the eyelid covering the affected gland. A special clamp is then placed on the lid so that it may be everted (turned inside out). The gland is then painlessly removed from the underside of the lid. No stitches are necessary and an eye patch is worn for approximately 12 to 14 hours. Complete healing takes place within a week to 10 days.

See also EYES.

A chalazion is a cyst of an eyelid. It often requires surgical removal under local anesthesia.

Chemotherapy in Cancer

There is an ever-increasing number of chemicals and drugs that have been found effective in slowing down the growth of cancers and allied conditions. Although these chemicals rarely can produce complete and permanent destruction of the malignancy, they frequently are successful in prolonging life. It is generally understood that many patients are subjected to surgery at a time when the cancer has already spread from its original site to distant parts of the body. In such instances, the surgical removal of the local offending malignancy cannot produce a permanent cure. When evidence of a distant growth of a malignancy is noted, the surgeon often calls upon the chemotherapist for aid.

QUESTIONS AND ANSWERS

Is chemotherapy helpful in many different kinds of cancer or allied conditions?
Yes. By a trial and error method of experimentation, many different chemicals have been found that react against many different types of malignancy. Some are highly effective against one form of cancer but are totally ineffective against another.

Are there physicians who specialize in the chemical treatment of cancer and other malignant diseases?
Yes. Most large institutions have such a staff member.

Is chemotherapy ever used in the treatment of cancer in conjunction with other forms of treatment?
Yes. Frequently, chemotherapy is used along with x-ray radiation or with hormone therapy.

What are some of the conditions that can be aided by the use of chemotherapy?
Almost any type of malignant condition can be helped to a certain extent by chemotherapy.

In what areas of malignancy have chemicals proved to be most effective?
In the treatment of some of the blood malignancies such as leukemia and Hodgkin's disease. Also, in the treatment of certain malignancies of the testicles and tumors of the kidney in infants and children.

What types of malignancy are most likely to respond to chemical treatment?
Those malignancies that are composed of rapidly growing, undifferentiated tissues are the most likely to respond favorably. As an example, a highly undifferentiated tumor of the testicles may respond very favorably to chemotherapy, as may a malignant tumor of the kidney (Wilms' tumor) in infants.

For how long a period can life be prolonged by the use of chemical agents in cancer?
There are some cases that have been kept alive for many years by the continued use of chemotherapy. In less fortunate patients, life may be prolonged for only a short few months.

Are there dangers to the use of chemotherapy in cancer?
Yes. In some patients, the chemical agents destroy huge numbers of white blood cells and thus hamper the body's natural defense mechanisms.

Do patients ever die sooner because of the use of chemotherapy?
In a small percentage of cases, this does take place. As mentioned, in certain patients the use of the chemical agents will destroy the body's defense mechanisms to such an extent that the patient will succumb to an overwhelming infection.

Is chemotherapy often used after a tumor has been removed surgically?
No. If the surgeon thinks that he has completely removed the malignancy, chemotherapy is not advocated.

At what stage in the life cycle of a cancer is chemotherapy recommended?
1. When it is obvious that the cancer has spread beyond its local site of origin
2. When there is a generalized malignancy, as in tumors of the blood or lymph nodes
3. In cases in which there is a recurrence of the tumor following surgery

that there is a marked psychosomatic aspect to the disease. The unfortunate victims of chronic ulcerative colitis seem to be highly neurotic and sensitive people. None of the sulfa or antibiotic drugs has been successful in curing the condition. There is a tendency for the disease to flare up and subside periodically, but complete cure, without surgery, takes place in less than half the cases. Another 25 percent of the patients will live on as intestinal

Cholecystectomy

See GALLBLADDER.

Cholecystitis and Cholelithiasis

See GALLBLADDER.

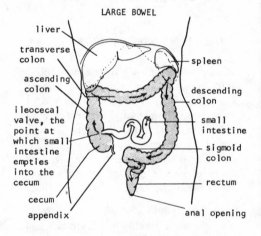

Chronic Ulcerative Colitis

Chronic ulcerative colitis is one of the most serious inflammations of the large intestine and is found most often in men and women in their third and fourth decades of life. The disease extends over a period of years and is characterized by innumerable ulcerations which may involve but one segment or may be found throughout the entire length of the colon. Patients with this serious illness have fever, lose weight, develop anemia, and have frequent, bloody, watery bowel movements. The specific bacteria causing the infection have not been determined. Although ulcerative colitis is believed to be essentially a bacterial infection, it is, nevertheless, common knowledge

cripples, never fully recovering but never quite sick enough to require surgical intervention. To save the lives and cure the remaining 25 percent of these patients, surgery is essential.

In the acute phases of the disease, surgery may consist of taking a loop of small intestine (the ileum) out onto the abdominal wall and opening it. This procedure is called *ileostomy*. Intestinal contents then drain out before reaching the diseased large bowel, thus permitting the inflamed and ulcerated areas to rest and heal. If permanent healing does take place, no further surgery is required, and in some 10 percent of all cases it is permissible to reestablish continuity and close the ileostomy opening. In the majority of cases, unfortunately, total healing of the ulcers does not take place, and the artificial opening must remain out on the abdominal wall permanently. If the ulcerative process continues and the symptoms of diarrhea and rectal bleeding persist despite the ileostomy, then a *colectomy* must be performed. This entails the surgical removal of the entire large bowel. Such an operation is sometimes performed in two stages, but in the majority of cases, a one-stage total removal of the large bowel is carried out. Although these operations appear to be formidable, they carry with them a recovery rate well over 90 percent. It must be remembered, too, that these operations are undertaken as lifesaving measures in patients who, unoperated, would die of their disease. Another factor that has stimulated surgeons to remove the entire diseased bowel is the realization that cancer develops much more frequently in bowel involved in ulcerative colitis than in normal bowel.

Patients can learn to live fairly normal, happy lives with a permanent opening (ileostomy) on their abdominal wall. The small bowel takes over most of the large bowel's functions after a few months' time. People become adjusted to their ileostomy and learn how to care for it so that it causes relatively little discomfort. They wear an airtight, specially designed bag over the opening to abolish odors and guard against unexpected leakage.

Until such time as a medical cure can be found, surgery must be the treatment of choice in approximately 25 percent of all cases of ulcerative colitis.

QUESTIONS AND ANSWERS

What causes ulcerative colitis?

The cause is not definitely known, but many investigators feel that the disease is bacterial in its origin. Emotionally disturbed people in their 20s or 30s are more prone to develop this condition than emotionally stable and older individuals.

What are the symptoms of this condition?

Ulcerative colitis often has its onset in early youth or adulthood, with continuing diarrhea, abdominal cramps, and the appearance of blood and mucus in the stools. There may be as many as 15 to 20 or even 30 movements a day. If this keeps up, the patient becomes markedly dehydrated and develops high fever and a prolonged anemia.

What is the usual course of ulcerative colitis?

The condition may continue for several weeks and then subside, only to appear again at a later date within the next few months or years.

How is the diagnosis of ulcerative colitis made?

1. By noting the characteristic symptoms
2. By examining the large bowel through the sigmoidoscope and noting the characteristic x-ray findings

What is the treatment for ulcerative colitis?

1. In mild cases, medical management is advisable. This will include a bland diet, antibiotic drugs, and the prescribing of cortisone or a similar medication. The majority of early cases will subside under this regimen.

2. In advanced or recurrent cases, surgery is often necessary. This may require the removal of the entire large bowel. When this procedure is carried out, the small bowel (ileum) is brought out onto the abdomen in the form of a permanent ileostomy.

What are the chances for recovery from a severe case of ulcerative colitis?

The chances are excellent, provided surgery is performed at an appropriate time on those patients who do not respond to medical treatment after a thorough trial.

When the entire large bowel has been removed, will the patient always have an ileostomy opening on his abdomen?

Yes, but the great majority of patients learn to manage their ileostomy effectively.

Is it ever possible to save the rectum when operating upon a case of ulcerative colitis?

In a small number of cases of ulcerative colitis, the rectum is not involved in the disease process and can be preserved. In some cases, although there are unfortunately not very many, the small bowel (ileum) can be stitched directly to the rectum at the time of the initial surgical procedure. In other cases, an ileostomy is performed at the initial procedure and the patient is permitted to make an operative recovery. Then, some months or years later, if it is discovered that the rectum is completely free of the disease process, the ileostomy can be taken down and the ileum can then be stitched to the rectum. It must be emphasized that this procedure cannot be performed on the great majority of those who must undergo surgery for ulcerative colitis.

Will the patient with an ileostomy be able to lead a full life?

Yes. There are literally thousands of people with permanent ileostomies who go to business and perform all the functions that normal people perform.

Is psychotherapy helpful in treating ulcerative colitis?

Yes, but only when the patient is seen early in the course of the disease.

Is there any way to prevent colitis?

No, but if prompt and early treatment is carried out, a great deal can be done to prevent the disease from getting worse.

What may happen if surgery is not performed upon a patient with severe chronic ulcerative colitis?

1. Eventually, death may ensue from an acute attack that involves fever, dehydration, and uncontrollable diarrhea.

2. Cancer of the bowel will develop in a large percentage of those patients who have an active ulcerative colitis for more than ten years.

What is granulomatous colitis?

It is a form of chronic inflammation of the large bowel associated with ulcerations and also with the formation of granulation tissue.

Is granulomatous colitis different from ulcerative colitis?

The two conditions are quite similar but there is a tendency for the granulomatous colitis to spread up from the large bowel into the small intestines.

Is the treatment for granulomatous colitis the same as that for ulcerative colitis?

In most instances, yes. However, some people with granulomatous colitis have a tendency for their conditions to subside more frequently than those who have advanced ulcerative colitis.

Is there a tendency for abscesses about the anus to form in people who have ulcerative or granulomatous colitis?

Yes. These infections will often require surgical drainage.

Is there a tendency for people with ulcerative or granulomatous colitis to form fistulas?

Yes. False tunnels between the rectum and the vagina in the female, or the rectum and the skin of the buttock in the male, are very frequent complications.

What is the treatment for a child with ulcerative colitis?

Every attempt should be made to bring the condition under control. Medical treatment must be carried out on a broad scale and must include the cooperation of the pediatrician, a psychiatrist, an allergist, and a specialist in diarrheal diseases. Attempts to reduce the number of bacteria in the intestinal tract are made by giving the child certain sulfa and antibiotic drugs. Nonirritating diets must be prescribed in order to reduce the number of diarrheal stools. Extensive tests must be conducted to make certain that the colitis is not precipitated by a food allergy. Medications are given to slow down the peristalsis (active movements of the intestine) in the hope that the number of stools will be reduced. Any child who has chronic diarrhea will have a tendency to become dehydrated and depleted of minerals and vitamins. Fluids, minerals, and vitamins must therefore be given to many of these children, sometimes by injection. If the ulcerative colitis is progressive and the child's life is endangered, it may be necessary to tide him over an acute attack by giving him cortisone or similar steroid medications.

Children who fail to respond to adequate, prolonged medical management will require surgery. This will entail the removal of the diseased portion of the large bowel and the creation of an ileostomy.

Do most children recover from ulcerative colitis?

Yes, but total recovery is very difficult to achieve and may eventually involve surgery with removal of all the ulcerated bowel.

What percentage of children will recover from ulcerative colitis without surgery?

Approximately 80 percent. The other 20 percent will die if surgery is not performed.

Circumcision

Circumcision is the surgical removal of the foreskin from the head of the penis. This operation permits easy cleaning with daily removal of the collection of smegma, a cheeselike secretion, naturally found in the groove just behind the head of the penis. It is extremely rare for a man circumcised in infancy to develop cancer of the penis. In addition, women married to men circumcised at birth develop cancer of the cervix of the uterus less often. This is attributed to the fact that smegma is not deposited in the vaginal canal during marital relations.

See also PENIS.

QUESTIONS AND ANSWERS

When is the best time to perform circumcision?

The operation is most conveniently performed at birth. This ensures a good local hygienic environment from the beginning of life. At this time the baby has no recall and there is no psychological trauma. If the child is less than one month old, no anesthesia is required when performing this operation. It is usually done in the hospital.

If the baby is premature and very small, circumcision is best delayed for a few months.

Are there any complications of circumcision?

At all ages, bleeding-time and clot-

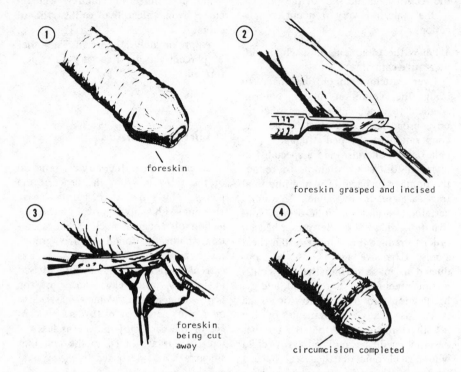

① foreskin

② foreskin grasped and incised

③ foreskin being cut away

④ circumcision completed

These diagrams show one method of performing circumcision. Most male infants born today are circumcised because it is a safeguard against the development of cancer of the penis. Furthermore, a circumcised penis is much easier to keep clean than is one that has not been circumcised.

ting-time tests should be performed first, since circumcision is often associated with oozing of blood. If there is an unusual tendency to bleed, there may be considerable postoperative hemorrhage, which may be difficult to control. Other than this, there are few complications.

Parents should be cautioned against ritualistic circumcision performed by unskilled hands. Infection may cause permanent damage to the organ.

How long does it take for a circumcision wound to heal?

Several days to two weeks.

How long a hospital stay is necessary when an older child is circumcised?

From one to three days.

What is the home care for a child who has been circumcised?

He may leave the hospital a day or two after circumcision with the raw area covered by a protective dressing. The dressing will prevent contact with a soiled diaper and will protect the sensitive tip of the penis from irritation or possible infection.

If the dressing falls off, it should be replaced daily for the first few days.

A soothing ointment, such as boric

acid ointment or sterile Vaseline, should be applied to the tip of the penis when the dressing is off.

If there is oozing of blood, the parent should not become alarmed but should merely apply a clean dressing and pressure with her fingers to the oozing area.

Will circumcision overcome the habit of masturbation in an older child?

In the great majority of children, circumcision has no effect. Masturbation is rarely the result of inflammation or irritation of the foreskin.

Is anesthesia necessary when performing circumcision on infants?

No.

Is anesthesia necessary when circumcising older children or adults?

Yes.

Are there any harmful effects from circumsion?

No.

Why is circumcision recommended universally?

Because it is almost certain insurance against the development of cancer of the penis, since this condition rarely occurs in circumcised males. It is also recommended because it is more hygienic and permits easier cleansing of the penis.

Is it true that women who are married to circumcised men are less likely to get cancer of the cervix of the uterus?

Some investigators hold the theory, which seems to be borne out by recent statistics, that some of the material in an uncircumcised penis may act as an irritant when in contact with the cervix of certain women and that, therefore, women married to circumcised men are less likely to develop cancer of the cervix.

When is the proper time to circumcise a newborn child?

Before he leaves the hospital, between the fifth and eighth days.

Should the child's blood be tested prior to performing circumcision?

Yes. It is essential to determine that no blood clotting abnormality exists prior to performing circumcision. If such a condition is present, circumcision should not be performed, as it may be followed by severe hemorrhage.

How long after a circumcision has been performed on an adult can sexual relations be resumed?

It is common for the head of the penis to be swollen and tender for several weeks after circumcision in an adult. For this reason, it may take a month or more before sexual relations can be resumed.

Does circumcision alter the sex sensations?

No. It affects neither desire nor potency.

Does cancer occur in a circumcised penis?

No. This is one of the reasons why the procedure is now universally advocated.

Cirrhosis of the Liver

Cirrhosis of the liver is a chronic condition in which there is degeneration of the active liver cells and replacement by inert fibrous tissue cells. The liver tissue becomes scarred, and as a consequence of this process, impairment of liver function to a slight or greater degree sets in.

See also LIVER.

QUESTIONS AND ANSWERS

What causes cirrhosis of the liver?

1. Any disease process that involves the liver may eventually lead to cirrhosis, that is, destruction of liver cells and replacement by scar tissue.

2. The association between excess drinking of alcoholic beverages and the occurrence of cirrhosis is well known. It is thought that the liver damage results from the combined effect of the toxic action of the alcohol upon the liver and the poor nutritional intake usually associated with those who drink to excess.

3. Cirrhosis is sometimes secondary to an inherited birth defect, such as in Wilson's disease (hepatolenticular degeneration) or galactosemia.

4. In children, cirrhosis sometimes develops secondary to chronic inflammatory conditions of the liver; the cirrhosis in these instances represents the end result of a chronic inflammation.

5. Prolonged obstruction of the outflow of bile from the liver into the intestinal tract will result in a type of cirrhosis called biliary cirrhosis.

6. Cirrhosis is sometimes secondary to chronic congestion of the liver associated with heart disease and impaired circulation.

7. Repeated episodes of hepatitis (liver infection) from whatever cause, such as malaria, syphilis, or infectious or viral hepatitis, may ultimately lead to cirrhosis.

8. Cirrhosis is sometimes seen as an associated condition of cystic fibrosis.

9. A certain number of cases of cirrhosis are of unknown origin.

Do most people who drink large quantities of alcohol develop cirrhosis?

No. It is mainly those who drink and do not eat normally who are most apt to develop the disease. Failure to eat while taking large quantities of alcohol deprives the liver of necessary sugar, protein, and mineral substances that are necessary for it to function normally.

What are the symptoms of cirrhosis?

These vary with the degree of liver destruction and liver reserve. Many cases go undetected and without symptoms for years. As liver function deteriorates, it may be accompanied by loss of appetite, nausea, vomiting, and weight loss. There may be abdominal discomfort, fullness in the upper abdomen, and indigestion. When the disease progresses, there may be listlessness and weakness, with loss of energy. When extensive liver destruction has taken place, the legs and abdomen may become swollen with fluid (dropsy), jaundice may come on, and the patient's mental state may become confused and disoriented. The final outcome may be coma and death.

Is cirrhosis always fatal?

No. If it is detected at an early stage, and if proper treatment is carried out, a patient with cirrhosis may live his normal span of years.

How is cirrhosis of the liver diagnosed?

By studying the patient's history and by physical examination, as well as by certain laboratory tests performed upon the blood, urine, and stool.

How is cirrhosis of the liver treated?

First, it is important to remove any toxic influences, such as infection, obstruction to the outflow of bile, or liver poisons that the patient may be taking. Next, there must be a satisfactory dietary intake, with the proper amounts of minerals and vitamins. Finally, if obstruction to the liver is marked, it may be necessary to perform an operation known as a portacaval shunt. This will shunt some of the blood from the portal vein to the inferior vena cava, thus relieving some of the liver obstruction.

Is cirrhosis ever complicated by hemorrhage?

Yes. Varicose veins within the esophagus will frequently bleed in cases of advanced cirrhosis. This is caused by these veins becoming swollen because they carry blood that ordinarily would have gone through the liver had it not been involved in cirrhosis.

Is the liver always enlarged in cirrhosis?

No. During the later stages it may become shrunken and smaller than normal.

Is the spleen often enlarged in cirrhosis of the liver?

Yes.

Can surgery help people with cirrhosis of the liver?

Yes. Many of these patients can be helped through surgery. Because cirrhosis prevents much of the blood from coursing through the liver, operations have been devised which shunt the blood around the liver and thus aid circulation. The two most common operations of this type are:

1. Portacaval shunt, in which the portal vein is stitched to the vena cava. This permits much of the blood to pass directly into the general circulation instead of being held up by a cirrhotic liver.

2. A splenorenal shunt, in which the vein from the spleen is stitched to the left kidney vein. This also allows much of the blood that would ordinarily have gone to the liver to be shunted directly into the general circulation.

Are operations for cirrhosis of the liver serious?

Yes, but many excellent results have been obtained through the performance of these procedures.

What are the chances for improving cirrhosis through these operations?

More than half the patients are benefited by the shunt operations. Since the vena cava and the renal vein do not enter the liver, much of the load upon the cirrhotic organ is relieved.

Are the chances of hemorrhage decreased through performance of shunt procedures?

Yes. A successful shunt operation in most instances will prevent fatal hemorrhage from developing.

Are special preoperative measures necessary before operating for cirrhosis?

Yes. It is wise to see that the patient has a large sugar and protein intake. This is carried out by feeding sugar and protein by mouth and by intravenous injections. The liver is protected and best prepared for surgery by limiting the quantity of fat intake and by seeing that large quantities of sugar, vitamins, and protein are given.

CIRRHOSIS IN CHILDREN

How common is cirrhosis of the liver in children?

It is rare in the United States and Europe. It is seen more often in the Far East and Near East and in tropical areas in the Western Hemisphere.

What are some of the signs and symptoms of cirrhosis of the liver in children?

The most prominent sign is an enlarged liver that feels firm to the touch. Other manifestations occur when liver function fails and bleeding tendencies accompanied by a lesser or greater amount of jaundice develop.

Cirrhosis of the liver is a chronic disease that is drawn out over a period of years; the loss of liver function is gradual. Periods of mild fever are not uncommon, and there are many abnormalities in the child's blood chemistry. Secondary anemia generally develops, along with bleeding from the intestinal tract or from varicose veins that develop in the esophagus. Eventually, serious cases of cirrhosis will cause symptoms of brain damage and impairment of kidney function. Coma and death may follow.

What is the treatment for cirrhosis of the liver in children?

1. If the cirrhosis is caused by a mechanical obstruction to the outflow of bile as a result of a birth deformity or pressure on the bile duct, these should be treated surgically. A short-circuiting operation in which the gallbladder is connected directly with the intestinal tract can greatly benefit a child who has an undeveloped or malfunctioning common bile duct.

2. If the cirrhosis is secondary to repeated liver infections caused by bacteria or parasites, the condition can be alleviated by the administration of either antibiotic or antiparasitic drugs.

3. If the cirrhosis is secondary to heart failure with chronic congestion of the liver, it can often be remedied by heart surgery for the correction of the cardiac defects.

4. In certain obscure types of cirrhosis, cortisone or allied drugs have proved beneficial.

5. If the cirrhosis has obstructed the flow of blood from the veins that go to the liver, a short-circuiting operation known as a portacaval shunt may be attempted. In this operation, venous blood that ordinarily would circulate through the liver is shunted so that it passes directly into the large vena cava and then into the heart. This will spare

the liver additional work and may lead to improvement of the cirrhosis. The liver will continue to receive arterial blood through the hepatic artery.

6. Almost all children who have cirrhosis of the liver have vitamin, mineral, and other nutritional deficiencies. In addition, they eventually develop anemia. To combat these symptoms, they must be given large doses of vitamins and minerals, and from time to time they may require blood transfusions.

7. To overcome the bleeding tendencies, the child should receive large doses of vitamin K and repeated transfusions of fresh blood.

8. A child with cirrhosis must be particularly safeguarded against fresh infections, and therefore he should be immunized against all diseases for which immunization is known. If the child is exposed to a disease for which there is no vaccine, he should receive prophylactic gamma-globulin injections.

Claudication

Claudication, also known as intermittent claudication, is characterized by pain and tenderness of the muscles of the legs upon walking or exercise. The pain may be cramplike and so severe that it prevents the patient from walking. The pain is usually relieved within a minute or two by rest. Claudication is thought to be due to a spasm, along with arteriosclerosis, of the arteries supplying the muscles of the legs. When insufficient blood reaches the muscles, they tend to go into spasm and cause great pain. With rest, the arteries relax and more blood goes to the muscles, thus relieving the intense, acute pain. The more severe the impairment of circulation, the less exercise is required to produce the pain that is characteristic of claudication, and the more slowly does the pain disappear when resting. *See also* ARTERIOSCLEROSIS; BLOOD VESSELS; BUERGER'S DISEASE.

QUESTIONS AND ANSWERS

How can one make a diagnosis of intermittent claudication?
1. The symptoms are so characteristic that the diagnosis is obvious. Anyone who has severe cramplike pains in the calf of the legs on exercise or walking, in most instances, is suffering from claudication.
2. Examination of the pulses of the arteries of the feet shows they are usually diminished in those who suffer from intermittent claudication.
3. There may be abnormal bluish discoloration of the skin, particularly when the feet are in a pendent position.
4. Those who suffer from intermittent claudication may have unusually cold feet, even in moderate climates.

What group of people is most likely to develop claudication?
1. Those who are in their later years, namely, the seventh, eighth, and ninth decades of life.
2. Males are more commonly affected than females.
3. Those with diabetes tend to have a greater incidence of arteriosclerosis in the vessels of their legs, and thus are more apt to suffer from claudication.
4. Those who smoke large quantities of tobacco are more likely to develop claudication than those who abstain.

What is the treatment for claudication?
1. In mild cases, drugs such as Arlidin can be given to relax arterial spasm.
2. Those who smoke, and especially cigarettes, should be made to give up the habit, and this will often improve circulation and lessen the incidence of arterial spasm.
3. Those subject to claudication should be advised to wear warm shoes, warm woolen stockings, and long underwear. This will keep the lower extremities from getting cold and thus reduce the chances of arterial spasm with consequent claudication.
4. Those subject to episodes of claudication should walk slowly, with frequent periods of rest.
5. If x-rays show marked hardening of the arteries in the legs, surgery should be considered.

What surgery can be performed to relieve claudication secondary to arteriosclerosis within the vessels of the legs?
Bypass grafts are utilized frequently to restore circulation to the legs. It has been found that the arteriosclerotic process often closes down the main arteries in the thighs and the popliteal arteries in the knee region, but spares the vessels in the lower leg. When this situation obtains, a graft (made of Teflon or Dacron) can be attached onto the normal or near-normal iliac artery in the pelvis and can be carried down through the thigh to the normal or near-normal artery in the leg. This surgical procedure can vastly increase the blood supply to the leg and thus eliminate the symptoms of claudication. Some surgeons prefer to use a vein graft, taken from the patient's own body, when it is necessary to use a bypass graft that will traverse the knee joint. It has been found that vein grafts are more pliable and will conform better to the bending action of the knee than a Teflon or Dacron graft.

Are there any other surgical procedures that can relieve claudication?
Yes. An operation known as lumbar-sympathectomy sometimes causes the

vessels in the legs to dilate and carry more blood. This may reduce the episodes of pain seen so often among those with arteriosclerosis of the arteries in the legs. Unfortunately, this operation does not help all patients.

Does gangrene ever occur as a complication of claudication?

People with claudication usually have a certain degree of arteriosclerosis of the blood vessels. When this process becomes sufficiently advanced, blood supply may dwindle to such a degree that gangrene will set in.

Does claudication ever occur in young people?

Yes, if they suffer from a condition known as Buerger's disease.

Is claudication ever relieved by cessation of smoking?

Yes. Occasionally, a patient with mild claudication and only minor signs of arteriosclerosis will be freed from all symptoms if he stops smoking.

Is it safe for a patient with claudication to resume walking after his pain has subsided?

Yes, but it must be realized that the pain will probably recur after the resumption of walking or exercise.

Is there any way to prevent claudication?

1. People with a family history of early arteriosclerosis should be sure to follow a low-cholesterol diet throughout their middle and later years.

2. It has been well established that the smoking of tobacco induces arterial spasm. For this reason, those who have a tendency toward arteriosclerosis or an arterial spasm should abandon smoking.

3. Obesity places extra demands upon the circulatory system. Therefore, those with a tendency toward arteriosclerosis or claudication should avoid overweight.

Cleft Palate

Cleft palate is a birth deformity in which the roof of the mouth fails to fuse. As a result, the mouth and nasal cavities are not separated from each other. It is seen once in every thousand births. Its cause is unknown, although there is a tendency for this malformation to run in families.

A cleft palate is a great handicap, as it interferes with normal feeding, permits food and fluid to get into the nose and nasal cavity, and makes normal speech impossible.

The best time to operate upon children with cleft palate is somewhere between the ages of 1½ to 2½ years. The operation is a difficult one and demands the ministrations of an expert in the field. Although operative recovery takes place in almost all patients, there is a sizable number of instances in which the operation fails to close the palate. Second and third operations are frequently necessary.

The techniques of suturing the roof of the mouth are quite complex, but all involve the stitching together of sturdy flaps. The suturing must be done without too much stretching of the flaps or they will pull away from one another instead of fusing.

These operations are performed under general anesthesia. Feedings may be begun several hours after surgery. Antibiotic drugs are given to promote healing.

It is not sufficient merely to restore normal anatomy to cure this condition. Speech training is essential, as these children have a tendency to faulty speech even after the palate has been satisfactorily repaired.

See also LIPS, MOUTH, AND TONGUE.

QUESTIONS AND ANSWERS

What is cleft palate?

A birth abnormality with failure of the two sides of the roof of the mouth to fuse in the midline.

How common is cleft palate?

About 1 in 1,000 births.

What is the best age at which to operate upon cleft palate?

Between 1½ to 2½ years.

What operative procedure is performed to cure cleft palate?

The tissues of the palate on each side of the cleft are undercut, mobilized, and stitched together in the midline.

Are operations for cleft palate serious?

Yes.

How successful are cleft palate operations?

Good results are obtained in the majority of uncomplicated cases, although it may be necessary to perform two or even three procedures to obtain the best results.

If the original operation for repair of cleft palate fails, can it be done over again?

Yes, but it must be emphasized that these are complicated operations which require the services of the most expert surgeons.

Does cleft palate tend to run in families?

Yes. Marriage between two people who both have a family history of cleft palate is inadvisable; their children are more likely to inherit this deformity. If they do marry, they should seriously consider adopting children rather than having natural ones.

Does cleft palate often appear along with harelip?

Yes, they are frequently seen together.

What precautions must be taken during the first year and a half to two years of the child's life before operating on a cleft palate?

Every attempt must be made to prevent infection and the breathing of food or fluid into the windpipe and lungs. These children have difficulty in swallowing, and it is perhaps best to feed them in an upright position. Soft nipples with enlarged openings or special cleft-palate nipples should be used on bottles. It may also be advisable for the mother to insert a plastic, denturelike covering on the roof of the mouth during feeding times to prevent food from going up into the nasal cavity.

Is it necessary to feed some infants with cleft palate through stomach tubes?

If the cleft is very marked and it is difficult to nourish the newborn adequately, it may be necessary to put a tube into the stomach for occasional major feedings.

What is the aim of surgery for cleft palate?

To resuture the roof of the mouth so that the two sides of the cleft heal together solidly, thus establishing normal anatomy.

Should a child have a special nurse after an operation for cleft palate?

This is very important, as the child must receive expert specialized care in order to ensure that the palate heals satisfactorily.

What special care is given after surgery for cleft palate?

Feedings are often given with a medicine dropper or through a stomach tube placed through the nose. Fluid diet is maintained for approximately three weeks after the operation. If the child has a habit of putting things into his mouth, it may be necessary to restrain his hands until the suture line in the roof of the mouth has completely healed.

Will a child automatically learn to speak normally after the cure of cleft palate?

Not necessarily. If, after surgery, there is adequate length and flexibility of the soft palate, normal speech is practically assured. With inadequate soft palate formation, speech therapy will be necessary to compensate for the anatomical defect. Many children will require a certain amount of speech therapy.

How effective is speech therapy in these cases?

Most children will have greatly improved speech, although not all will be able to speak completely normally.

Is it often necessary to insert a denture-like speech appliance in the roof of the mouth of a child with cleft palate?

Yes. Whether or not this is necessary should be decided by an expert speech therapist.

Are there speech therapists who specialize in the treatment of children with cleft palate?

Yes. The local medical society should be contacted for the names of such therapists.

If several operations have failed to close a cleft palate completely, can a child wear an artificial palate?

Yes, but it must be understood that this palate is rigid and will not have the flexibility that is necessary for normal speech.

What are some of the complications of untreated cleft palate?

Frequent infections of the ears are seen. This is thought to be caused by the regurgitation of foods and fluids into the eustachian tubes of the middle ear. More important, an untreated cleft palate will lead to deformities of the arch of the roof of the mouth and to teeth deformities that will eventually require extensive dental treatment. Speech defects that may never be overcome can develop in children who go too many years without correction of a cleft palate.

Are there agencies that assist parents with the very expensive costs of curing cleft palate and improving speech?

Yes. Most states have speech-correction commissions and funds set aside for just this purpose. A whole group of people are necessary to bring about the cure of cleft palate. This group may include a child psychiatrist, a social worker, a speech therapist, a public health nurse, a dentist, a nose and throat specialist, a pediatrician, and a plastic surgeon.

Is there any way to prevent cleft palate?

No, since it is an inherited birth deformity.

Clubfoot

Congenital clubfoot is a deformity in which the foot is foreshortened, is flexed on the ankle, and turned inward. It is often seen in conjunction with other deformities elsewhere in the body. It occurs more often in boys.

The conservative treatment of clubfoot consists of placing the foot in the correct position and maintaining it there with a plaster cast. The cast is changed frequently, and at the time of the change, the foot is manipulated so that eventually it will be maintained in the corrected position. Treatment should be begun immediately after birth.

If the nonoperative treatment should

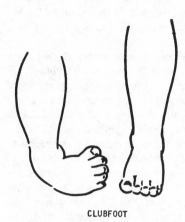

CLUBFOOT

factory results can be obtained from many of these operations although it is often necessary to sacrifice mobility (the ability to move) in favor of stability and good position.

The important point to make in regard to treating clubfoot is that each surgical procedure must be followed by intensive nonoperative treatment. Failure to do this will lead to recurrence of the deformity.

See also BIRTH DEFORMITIES OF THE EXTREMITIES.

fail to bring the desired results, surgical intervention is in order. A plantar stripping procedure may be performed on a child between the ages of one and one-half and three years. This operation, done under general anesthesia, calls for an incision about two inches long on the inner aspect of the foot. The fibrous tissues beneath the skin in the sole of the foot are stripped away from the bones so as to permit the foot to assume a more normal position. To further this end, one of the important tendons (the posterior tibial) is partially severed and lengthened. The skin is then closed and a plaster cast applied in the corrected position.

A second operation is frequently performed at a later age to lengthen the heel cord (Achilles tendon) and thus permit the heel to touch the ground. This is done through a small skin incision on the inner aspect of the heel.

Still other operations are advocated in older children or adults who have had inadequate early treatment. Some of these procedures are extremely complicated and involve removal of portions of the bones of the foot and fusion of certain of the joints. Highly satis-

QUESTIONS AND ANSWERS

Do congenital deformities such as clubfoot always have to be operated upon?

No. Nonoperative orthopedic treatment, when persistently used, will often cure the condition.

What is the medical management for clubfoot?

Manipulation and placement of the foot and leg in a plaster cast in an over-corrected position will often lead to correction of this deformity. It is necessary to change the cast often, and casts may have to be worn for several months or even a year or more.

Will children tend to outgrow clubfoot without treatment?

No.

Does clubfoot usually affect one or both feet?

Usually, it affects only one foot.

What operations are performed for clubfoot?

1. Stripping away fibrous tissue in the sole of the foot

2. Tendon-lengthening procedures

3. Joint fusions to fix the foot in a useful position

Are operations for clubfoot dangerous?

No, but some of them are major procedures that should be performed only by experts in the field of orthopedic surgery.

Are special postoperative measures necessary after operations for clubfoot?

Yes. Continued orthopedic treatment, such as application of casts, braces, special shoes, massage, manipulation, and special baths, is essential to obtain the best results.

Is it ever necessary to perform more than one operation to correct clubfoot?

Yes. In a certain number of cases, total correction does not follow an initial operative procedure. In these instances reoperation is often most rewarding.

Is clubfoot common?

Yes. It occurs once in every 1,000 births, and is twice as common in males as in females.

What causes clubfoot?

Faulty development of the embryonic foot due to local abnormalities of muscle and bones.

What are Dennis-Brown bars?

Dennis-Brown bars are metal bars to which an infant's shoes are attached. The bars may be bent and the shoes rotated to any desired position. Many orthopedists and pediatricians prefer the use of Dennis-Brown bars to plaster casts in the treatment of clubfoot.

How soon should the treatment of clubfoot begin?

Within the first few days after birth.

Is clubfoot thought to be an inherited abnormality?

Yes.

If parents have one child with clubfoot, does this mean that subsequent children will also have the same condition?

Usually not. Most inherited conditions such as clubfoot are recessive characteristics, and the chance of other children being affected is very small.

Should two people marry if there is a history in both families of clubfoot?

They may marry, but they should carefully consider whether they want to have natural children, and the advice of medical experts should be obtained. Most inherited conditions are recessive and will affect only a few scattered members in a family tree. However, if a particular defect such as clubfoot exists in both families, the defect may assume dominant patterns and the chances of its appearance in offspring will be great. In such cases, it might be wiser for a couple to adopt children rather than have their own.

Cobalt

Cobalt is a metallic element. It is a part of living tissues. In the human body, deficiency of cobalt leads to anemia; an excess of dietary cobalt may lead to the opposite of anemia, a condition known as polycythemia. The main value of cobalt within the human body is as a component of vitamin B_{12}.

Radioactive cobalt is now being used extensively in radiation therapy. It has supplanted conventional x-ray therapy in most clinics throughout the world. It has been found that the radiations emanating from radioactive cobalt have greater penetrating power and cause less damage to skin and superficial tissues and bone. For this reason, most large institutions are equipped today with cobalt therapy machines as well as ordinary x-ray and radium therapy apparatus.

QUESTIONS AND ANSWERS

Does the use of radioactive cobalt have the same effect as x-ray therapy treatment?
Yes. In both instances ionizing radiation is delivered to the tissues.

Is radioactive cobalt treatment painful?
No, nor is treatment with any of the other radiation substances.

Do people develop radiation sickness from the use of radioactive cobalt?
Yes. The reactions are very similar to those that follow extensive treatment with conventional radiation therapy machines. However, in the treatment of certain tumors, fewer untoward symptoms follow the use of cobalt radiation.

Can greater doses of radiation sometimes be given by using cobalt therapy?
Yes, inasmuch as there is less skin damage from cobalt therapy than from the conventional x-ray radiation. This permits the radiologist to give larger roentgen-unit doses.

What is cobalt-60?
Cobalt-60 is chemical cobalt that has been made radioactive in an atomic pile. It gives off gamma rays similar to those from radium, which it has widely replaced in radiation therapy.

What actually takes place when cobalt radiation affects tissue cells?
There is a disturbance of the chemical activity within the cell, making it unable to function normally. This is a desired effect when radiation is applied to tumor or other abnormal cells. As a consequence of the cobalt radiation, actual destruction of these cells may take place.

For what conditions is cobalt treatment most often recommended?
Following surgery in which a malignant tumor has been removed. In such cases, cobalt may be given to prevent regrowth of tumor cells that may have been left behind. It frequently destroys those cells that are beyond the reach of the surgeon's scalpel.

Cobalt may be especially beneficial after surgical removal of a brain tumor, lung tumor, kidney tumor, or breast tumor.

Do normal tissues become affected by the use of cobalt radiation?
Yes, but fortunately, they are less sensitive to the effects of the rays. Accordingly, normal tissues may recover while tumor tissues will die.

What are some of the advantages of cobalt radiation over x-rays?
1. Cobalt is less likely to cause skin burns.
2. Cobalt can penetrate into the body tissues better than conventional x-rays.
3. Cobalt has less tendency to produce radiation sickness.

Coccyx

The coccyx is a small bone at the very end of the spinal column. It is formed by the union of four tiny, rudimentary vertebrae. Because of its location at the very end of the spine, the coccyx is subject to injury resulting from falls in a sitting position. The usual history of such injury is that the area of the coccyx struck a protruding object, such as the edge of a step.

Injuries to the coccyx are extremely painful, although they are not serious. The three most common injuries are contusion, dislocation, and fracture.
See also BACK; SPINE.

QUESTIONS AND ANSWERS

What are the main symptoms of injury to the coccyx?

Pain in the area is a common symptom, whether it takes the form of a contusion, dislocation, or fracture. The pain is worst on sitting.

How can the extent of an injury to the coccyx be diagnosed?

By two methods:

1. By taking an x-ray of the coccyx. This will reveal whether it is dislocated or fractured.

2. The insertion of an examining finger into the rectum will usually reveal whether or not there has been dislocation of the coccyx.

What is the treatment for a severe bruise or contusion of the coccyx?

1. Lying in a hot tub of water will often tend to relieve pain.

2. The administration of pain-relieving analgesic medications such as aspirin will often tend to relieve distress.

3. The patient should sit on a soft cushion or rubber ring until the pain subsides.

What is the treatment for a dislocation of the coccyx?

The dislocation can usually be relieved by the physician through insertion of a finger into the rectum and gentle pressure to replace the coccyx into a normal position. If the patient remains inactive for a few days and avoids reinjury, the coccyx will usually maintain its normal position. In these cases, as in cases of severe contusion, hot baths, analgesic drugs, and avoidance of sitting on hard surfaces will help to relieve pain.

What is the treatment for a fractured coccyx?

The fracture is usually associated with a dislocation displacement. Treatment will consist of repositing the coccyx in normal position. Then, treatment is the same as that for dislocation or contusion. It may be necessary in some cases to advise the patient to wear a firm girdle or belt when walking.

Does pain after injury to the coccyx often last for several weeks?

Yes. In certain instances, whether the underlying injury is mere contusion or whether it is dislocation or fracture, the pain is so severe for such a prolonged period of time that surgical removal of the coccyx is indicated.

Is removal of the coccyx a serious operation?

No. It is a very simple procedure, often carried out under low spinal anesthesia. Recovery takes place within a few days, and the patient's wound heals within a week to ten days.

Does removal of the coccyx always relieve the pain in the area?

No. In certain cases, removal of the coccyx will not relieve the pain.

What is coccydynia?

It is pain in the region of the coccyx, not necessarily associated with a history of injury.

What causes coccydynia?

The cause is not known, but is seen quite often among neurotic women.

What is the treatment for coccydynia?

Some cases can be relieved by local injections of an anesthetic agent such as Novocain. In other cases, where the pain is persistent and severe, removal of the coccyx may be indicated. It is important before carrying out this procedure to determine that the coccyx is the cause of the pain. As mentioned previously, some people will continue to have pain in the area even after the coccyx has been surgically removed.

Colectomy

See INTESTINES.

Colitis

See CHRONIC ULCERATIVE COLITIS.

Colostomy

A colostomy is an operation in which the large bowel is brought onto the abdominal wall and opened. This is frequently performed to relieve large bowel obstructions or is done as a preliminary surgical maneuver prior to the removal of a segment of diseased bowel.
See also INTESTINES.

QUESTIONS AND ANSWERS

What is an "artificial opening" of the bowel?
A loop of intestine is brought outside of the body into the abdomen. A hole is made in the bowel and the stool is permitted to come out through such an opening rather than through the rectum.

What type of anesthesia is used?
General anesthesia; and in an occasional case, spinal anesthesia.

How long do these operations take to perform?
A preliminary colostomy can be performed in one-half to one hour. More extensive operations involving bowel removal may take two to four hours.

Are the wounds very unsightly or painful?
No.

Are blood transfusions needed?
Yes, in some cases.

Where is the incision made for the artificial opening (colostomy)?
Directly over the loop of bowel which is to be brought out onto the abdominal wall.

What special postoperative measures are taken?
1. No fluid or food is given by mouth for the first few days. This permits the intestine to remain in a state of complete rest.
2. Decompression of distended bowel through stomach tubes is continued.
3. Large doses of antibiotic drugs are given to prevent peritonitis.
4. Fluids and minerals are replenished by intravenous feedings.

Is the immediate postoperative period uncomfortable?
Yes. For four to five days.

Are special nurses required postoperatively?
Yes, when the patient can afford them.

How soon after surgery can one get out of bed?
Most of the seriously ill patients and those with colostomy remain in bed for several days after surgery. When obstruction has been relieved merely by snipping an adhesion, the patient can get up the day following surgery.

How soon after surgery can one resume:

Bathing?	When the wound has completely healed
Normal eating?	In 10 days to 2 weeks
Work, social	If *no colostomy*, in

life, and 3 or 4 weeks. *If* **sexual relations?** *a colostomy has been done,* within 3 or 4 months, providing that all the necessary operations have been completed.

Is convalescent care necessary?

Yes, for several weeks, except in the simple cases in which obstruction has been completely cured at the first operation.

How does one prevent leakage from a colostomy opening?

A well-fitting colostomy bag is worn which prevents leakage of stool, fluid, or gases; or the colostomy is irrigated regularly and the contents of the bowel are evacuated.

Can one live normally after part of the large intestine has been removed?

Yes. Patients who have permanent colostomies learn to live normal and productive lives.

Concussion

Concussion of the brain is a term applied when a brief period of unconsciousness follows a head injury. Some concussions are accompanied by little hemorrhages within the brain or the tissues surrounding the brain, whereas other concussions have no such associated injury. Surgical treatment for the average concussion is not required, since in uncomplicated cases, spontaneous recovery is the rule. The patient should, however, be observed for the development of symptoms such as increasing drowsiness and weakness of the limbs. These symptoms might indicate bleeding within the skull.

QUESTIONS AND ANSWERS

What is cerebral concussion?

It is a head injury accompanied by a short period of unconsciousness. It is often followed by headaches and dizzy feelings for some period of time. Concussion is usually not disabling, though often it is associated with moderate emotional disturbance, anxiety, and worry.

What is the outlook for cerebral concussion?

Ultimate recovery almost invariably takes place. However, some patients tend to have recurring headache or dizziness at varying intervals for an indeterminate period, occasionally for many months. Emotional disturbance is often present and tends to increase and prolong the symptoms. Older patients are more apt to have prolonged symptoms from a cerebral concussion than are younger ones.

Does cerebral concussion affect the mind?

No.

Is cerebral concussion likely to cause serious trouble at a later date?

The great majority make a complete recovery. There are, however, a small number of people who, as a result of a head injury, develop a blood clot around the brain. This is known as a subdural hematoma. It evidences itself many weeks or months later by progressive symptoms which will require neurosurgery for removal of the blood clot. Therefore, it is wise for people who have had even minor head injuries to receive periodic physical examinations by a neurologist as long as any symptoms persist.

What is the postconcussion syndrome or the posttraumatic state?

It is a group of symptoms that often

follow cerebral concussion and include headache and dizziness. There may also be excessive fatigue and lack of energy, a feeling of pressure on the head, and inability to carry on sustained work. Emotional factors are also encountered, with worry and depression being seen quite often.

What is the treatment of the postconcussion syndrome?

Psychotherapy is most important. It must be sustained, prolonged, persistent, and frequent. Suitable work that falls within the tolerance of the patient and with due recognition and assessment of his disability is important.

Are the headaches and dizziness following concussion ever permanent?

No. Sooner or later, these symptoms will subside.

Should x-rays be taken even if a patient has lost consciousness only momentarily?

Yes. It is not possible to make the distinction between concussion and skull fracture merely on physical examination. For this reason, following a concussion it is important to x-ray the skull to find out if there has been a fracture.

What is the proper first aid treatment for a concussion of the brain?

1. The patient, upon regaining consciousness, should be made to lie quietly.

2. The patient should be transported on a stretcher to a hospital.

Are there any ways to prevent concussion?

Yes. People should wear protective helmets whenever they are engaged in any activity that might result in a blow upon the head. This is essential for those who ride motorcycles and for people who work in construction jobs where objects may fall from heights. Also, those who engage in athletic events that might result in severe blows around the head should never engage in them without wearing a protective helmet.

Contusions

A contusion results from a hemorrhage into the skin or into the subcutaneous or muscle tissues. This type of bleeding stops by itself and seldom requires treatment. The swelling and bluish-black discoloration often attain a huge size out of all proportion to the seriousness of the injury.

In a small number of cases, the hemorrhage forms a fluid or semifluid collection beneath the skin or in between the muscles. This condition is called a hematoma. Most hematomas are absorbed after a period of several days to several weeks, but a certain number of them will require additional treatment. In such cases the blood remains liquid or forms soft clots that fail to be absorbed. The surgeon will insert a large needle and attempt to suck out the retained blood into an attached syringe. If this is not possible because of clot formation, a small incision is made into the hematoma and the clot is evacuated.

QUESTIONS AND ANSWERS

Is a bruise the same thing as a contusion?

Yes, they are essentially the same.

What is the best first aid treatment for a contusion?

The application of ice or a cold wet compress sometimes will lessen the amount of bleeding into the skin or the tissues beneath the skin. One must be cautioned that ice should not be permitted to remain constantly in contact with the skin as it may cause a burn. For this reason, ice should be applied for only 30 minutes at a time, with an interval of another 30 minutes before reapplication.

How long should cold applications be used following a contusion?

Intermittent applications of ice or cold should be continued for no longer than six to eight hours. After this period of time has elapsed, full benefit will have been received from this method of treatment.

Will tight bandaging prevent a contusion from bleeding?

Yes, but it is important not to cut off the circulation to the area. This type of treatment is best carried out by a physician.

Does the bluish discoloration secondary to a contusion always disappear?

Yes, but in certain instances where there has been bleeding into the skin a slight amount of residual discoloration may persist.

How long does it take the average discoloration to be absorbed?

The discoloration secondary to a mild contusion may disappear within five to seven days; that associated with severe contusion may not disappear entirely for several weeks.

Is it common for the bluish discoloration to appear around the foot when the site of injury is higher up along the leg?

Yes. Blood seeps down through the tissue planes and may appear beneath the skin of the foot even when the site of the injury is in the calf or ankle region. This discoloration will disappear usually within a week's time.

The Cornea

The cornea is a clear, thin, transparent membrane in the front part of the eyeball. It serves the same function as the crystal of a watch. It is circular in shape, a little more than a quarter of an inch in diameter and covers the iris, or colored portion of the eye. The center of the iris contains a round opening called the *pupil*. This area appears black, and it is through here that light rays pass. The size of the pupil changes according to the amount of light to which it is exposed. When the pupil is exposed to a great deal of light, the iris muscle contracts and the pupil becomes smaller. Conversely, when the pupil is exposed to less light, the iris muscle relaxes and the pupil becomes larger. When the pupil is dilated, more light enters the eye, thus permitting better vision in a dark environment.

The margin of the cornea where it joins the sclera, or the white of the eye, is known as the *limbus*. The limbus is an important landmark, as it is the site where surgical incisions are made for many eye operations.

There are three common surgical conditions that affect the cornea:

1. Foreign bodies
2. Lacerations (cuts)
3. Scars (opacities)

1. Foreign bodies gain access to the eye despite the protection afforded by eyelashes and eyelids. When they become embedded in the cornea, they cause pain, tearing, and redness. *All foreign bodies must be removed from the cornea* or they will eventually cause serious eye disturbance and interference with vision. Ashes, dust, and dirt are frequently washed away by the tears, but in certain instances are not. Solid particles such as steel, coal, iron, and simple cinders may adhere to the cornea and must be removed by a physician.

Before removing a corneal foreign body, the eye should be anesthetized with eyedrops. The superficial particles can often be washed out by means of simple irrigation or may be wiped off with a sterile piece of cotton on an applicator. Some foreign bodies are so deeply embedded that the general physician may not wish to attempt their removal. These patients are referred to an ophthalmologist, who will use a sharp instrument, known as a spud, to remove the particle. Such a procedure leaves a small open wound which, if not treated properly, may lead to an infection and ulceration that can become chronic. The ulcer may heal but scar formation and interference with vision may be the final outcome.

2. **Lacerations** of the cornea are serious and constitute emergencies, which should be treated by an ophthalmologist immediately. Such wounds must be treated and closed tightly with sutures under local or general anesthesia. The edges of the laceration are brought together with fine black silk sutures. In recent years, these sutures and the needles used to insert them have been so greatly improved that the chances of a permanent scar and loss of vision have been reduced remarkably. After suturing, an antiseptic solution is placed in the eye and a secure bandage is applied. The wound, depending upon its extent, will take from one to three weeks to heal. When healed, the sutures are removed.

Failure to treat corneal lacerations adequately may lead to infection, scar formation, and loss of vision or even the loss of the eye!

3. **Scars of the cornea** may be due to injury, inflammation, ulceration, or congenital deformities of the structure, such as conical cornea or keratoconus. If the scar is of recent origin and is not very extensive, it may clear up with the use of eyedrops containing cortisone and an antiseptic agent. Such medications must be administered with great care, as overuse may lead to other corneal infections, such as herpes, or to temporary glaucoma. It should be noted that extensive scarring of the cornea may cause blindness.

If the remainder of the eye is healthy, blindness caused by corneal scarring may be helped by *corneal transplants* or grafts. It must be emphasized, however, that of the 500,000 or more blind in this country, only about 20,000 are suitable patients for corneal transplant. This is because the cornea is the only part of the eye related to vision that can be successfully replaced, whereas blindness is most often caused by disease in other parts of the eye.

In order to obtain normal corneal tissue for transplantation operations, *eye banks* have been set up in most areas of the United States. These are nonprofit, charitable organizations which obtain donor eyes from people who will them upon their death. They store the eyes and supply them to surgeons, without charge, for use in appropriate cases. There are always more patients in need of this type of surgery than there are donor eyes available.

The operative procedure entails removing a circular area of the scarred, opaque cornea from the eye of the living patient and stitching a circular piece of clear, healthy cornea of the same size from the donor eye in its place. The operation can be performed under local or general anesthesia and is successful in the majority of cases. The degree of success frequently depends on the original condition that has caused the scar to form. Although great disappointment is felt, no actual harm is done the patient if the graft should fail to remain clear, since transplantation procedures are performed only upon those eyes that have no useful vision. Postoperative care consists of keeping the patient quietly in bed for two to three days. The operated eye is bandaged for 10 to 14 days, after which time vision is permitted.

QUESTIONS AND ANSWERS

Can most blind people be helped by corneal transplant operations?

No. Most people cannot be helped because the underlying cause of blindness lies elsewhere in the eyeball. One out of 25 can be helped.

Who can benefit from these operations?

Only those whose source of blindness is a scarred cornea. The rest of the eye must be normal.

Can a whole eye be transplanted?

No. Only the cornea.

Where can one obtain a corneal transplant?

From an eye bank. Ask your doctor about it.

Does it cost much money to obtain a donor eye from an eye bank?

No. These are charitable organizations and make no charges.

What happens if the transplant fails?

Unless certain very rare complications set in, no harm has been done, since the eye did not have useful vision beforehand.

Is the other eye affected if the transplant operation fails?

No.

How successful are corneal transplants?

The majority are successful but the underlying cause of the corneal scarring often determines the chances of success.

If the operation is successful, does it change the color or alter the appearance of the eye?

No. The operated eye will look the same as a normal eye.

Is the grafted cornea more likely to develop disease than the patient's own cornea?

No.

Is the operation dangerous?

No.

Is the operation painful?

No.

What kind of anesthesia is used?

Local or general.

How long must the patient stay in bed after surgery?

Two to three days.

Are private nurses necessary?

No.

How long a hospital stay is necessary for a transplant operation?

Generally two to three weeks.

Are eyeglasses necessary after corneal transplant operations?

Not always. This will have to be determined after the operation.

How soon after operation can one:

Bathe?	2 to 4 weeks
Drive a car?	6 to 8 weeks
Read?	4 to 5 weeks
Resume work?	8 to 10 weeks, depending on nature of work
Resume sexual relations?	7 to 8 weeks

How can one donate his eyes (after death) to an eye bank?

He must inform his next of kin of his intention to make such a donation. When death occurs, the next of kin must notify the local eye bank, the ophthalmologist, or the County Medical Society, requesting that the eyes be removed immediately. It is important that the undertaker be informed so that he does not embalm the body before the eyes have been removed.

Corns

Corns are thickened layers of skin on the foot, usually the toes, composed of excessive amounts of swollen skin cells. *See also* BUNIONS; FEET.

QUESTIONS AND ANSWERS

What causes most corns?

1. Birth deformities of the toes, such as overlapping toes
2. Deformity of the metatarsal arch of the foot
3. Abnormal pressure between bony prominences and shoes, or between adjacent toes
4. Wearing shoes that are too narrow
5. Improper gait

What are the various forms of corns?

1. Soft corns form between the toes. They are soft because the thickened skin layers are softened by constant perspiration.
2. Hard corns form on top or on the sides of toes or elsewhere on the foot.

What is the treatment for corns?

1. Well-fitting shoes should be bought. This is especially important for women whose vanity often dictates that they purchase shoes too small for them. Also, as a child grows, he must have frequent changes of shoes so that there is not undue pressure on the foot.
2. If the individual has flat feet or any other type of foot defect, such as a weak metatarsal arch, the defect must be corrected or a corn will not disappear.
3. If the corn persists, medications containing salicylic acid may be applied directly to the corn, or a corn plaster or corn pad can be applied. It is always best to consult an orthopedic surgeon or a licensed podiatrist when a corn fails to disappear after treatment for a reasonable length of time.

How effective are the corn remedies so widely advertised?

Since they do not attack the underlying causes, they can only serve as temporary relief.

Will paring a corn (cutting off the top layers) cure most corns?

No. The underlying cause of the corn must be overcome. Mere cutting or paring a corn will not cure it.

Should older people be particularly careful about cutting corns themselves?

Yes. In older people, there is a diminished blood supply to the feet and toes, and they are therefore much more susceptible to infections than young people. Because of this, corns in older people should be treated by a physician or licensed podiatrist only. Self-treatment can lead to dangerous infection.

Should people with diabetes be especially careful about cutting corns?

Yes, since they are more susceptible to infection than those without this illness. They, in particular, should have their corns tended professionally.

How can corns be prevented?

By wearing shoes that fit correctly, by

removal of abnormal bony prominences, by correcting abnormal alignment of the foot or toes (often by surgery), or by placing felt or rubber pads behind an area of abnormal pressure on the sole of the foot.

Coronary Artery Disease

See HEART.

Craniotomy

See NEUROSURGERY.

Crossed Eyes (Strabismus)

Strabismus (crossed eyes) may involve one or both eyes which may turn inward to the nose, outward, or occasionally upward. It may be present constantly or only occasionally and it may be present at birth or appear any time up to age 5.

When crossed eyes are noted at birth or within the first 6 months, the crossing may be only of a temporary nature. If the crossing is constant, it is due either to abnormal attachments of the muscles that move the eyeball or to an abnormality in the brain that causes paralysis of one or more of the muscles of the eyeball or an incoordination of the muscles. Small hemorrhages in the brain as a result of birth injury may have a similar effect.

When crossing of the eyes comes on during the first year or two of life, it is usually due to a weakness of the fusion center in the brain. The brain center, when functioning properly, coordinates the movements of the eyes so that they work together as a team. Each eye forms its own image and these two images must be fused together as one in order to achieve normal vision. The description of all the mechanisms involved in the causation of crossed eyes would be far too complex for the average layman to understand. However, it may prove informative to list some of the factors that are at work in causing this condition.

1. A weak fusion center in the brain will fail to coordinate eye muscle movements.

2. A weak or paralyzed eye muscle. Each eye has six muscles which permit it to move smoothly in any direction. When one or more do not function, the eye will turn or become crossed. The muscle opposite the weak one may then become overactive.

3. Farsightedness. Most infants are born farsighted, so that the image tends to focus behind the eye. In an attempt to get the image to focus directly on the retina (the seeing part of the back of the eyeball similar to the film of a camera), there is a tendency for the eyes to converge or turn in. A normally functioning fusion center will not permit this to happen. If, however, the fusion center is weak, this phenomenon will take place.

4. Nearsightedness. Relatively few infants are born nearsighted. Nearsightedness, or myopia, means that the image focuses in front of the retina. When these children attempt to correct their defect, they discover that accommodating and converging (turning in) makes the vision worse. They therefore do not accommodate or converge and the eye-

ball tends to swing in an outward direction. (In very unusual cases, lack of fusion can result in the eyeball turning inward rather than in an outward direction.) A normally functioning fusion center will not permit this to happen. If, however, the center is weak, these phenomena will occur.

The most serious complication of strabismus is that the vision tends to become progressively worse in the crossed eye. Because the image does not fall properly upon the retina, the first result is double vision. This is very annoying and nature overcomes it by suppressing the image within the crossed eye. If this continues over a period of years, the vision in such an eye never develops the way it should and even the wearing of eyeglasses will not help the situation. This condition is known technically as amblyopia ex anopsia. To combat this, the child is made to wear a patch over the good eye. This procedure will force the crossed eye to focus better and thus maintain its vision. When the child cannot be made to wear a patch, eyedrops that blur the good eye are sometimes substituted. This is used in very young patients whose active cooperation cannot be obtained.

In cases of farsightedness, special eyeglasses are prescribed. In addition to benefiting vision, the glasses will tend to overcome the excess convergence. Special eye exercises (orthoptics) can be given to reinforce the above measures. Eyeglasses can be given to children as young as 2 years of age and eye exercises may be started at 5 years or even younger, depending upon the child. Formerly, when a child reached 6 years of age with untreated poor vision and crossed eyes, it was almost impossible to improve his vision.

It should be emphasized that it is very important to have a child with crossed eyes examined and treated *early*, preferably before age 3. As soon as a parent notices crossing of an infant's eye, a consultation with an ophthalmologist should be sought. Reliance upon the hope that the child will outgrow the condition is foolhardy and may cause irreparable harm.

Treatment for crossed eyes differs widely from patient to patient and will depend largely upon the type and cause of crossing. Strabismus (also known as squint) due solely to farsightedness can be corrected partially or completely by wearing eyeglasses. In recent years, certain eyedrops which constrict the pupil have been successfully substituted for eyeglasses and have worked particularly well in children who reject the use of eyeglasses or who break them repeatedly. These drops, of course, must be given only under the supervision of an ophthalmologist. Strabismus due partly to farsightedness and partly to weakness of the eye muscles will be helped only partially by eyeglasses or drops. Strabismus associated with nearsightedness, on the other hand, is not benefited very much by the wearing of glasses. In these cases, eyeglasses are prescribed more to correct the defect in vision than to correct the crossing of the eyes. Patients in whom the eyes are almost straightened by wearing eyeglasses or taking drops can often be cured completely if the glasses or eyedrops are continued without interruption. This often takes place even without eye exercises. It should be pointed out that when eyes are badly crossed even while wearing glasses, exercises will be of little benefit and surgery will be necessary to bring about a cure.

Treatment for crossed eyes, including surgery, can be carried out as early as six months of age. As a matter of fact, the earlier treatment is started, the better the chance for a good final result, for the sooner the patient will start to develop better seeing habits. *See also* EYES.

QUESTIONS AND ANSWERS

What causes crossed eyes?
1. Weakness of the fusion center in the brain which coordinates eye movements.
2. Brain hemorrhage during birth which causes partial muscle paralysis.
3. Eye muscles which are attached to the eyeball in abnormal positions.
4. Farsightedness plus a weak fusion center in the brain.
5. Nearsightedness plus a weak fusion center in the brain.
6. A weakness of one or more of the muscles that move the eye. These muscles are attached to the outer surface of the eyeball.
7. An overaction of one or more of the muscles that move the eye.
8. An abnormality of one or more of the nerves that supply the muscles that move the eye.
9. A cancer or birth defect.
10. In rare instances, a disturbance in the part of the brain that supplies the nerves to the eye muscles.

Is it natural for the eyes of a newborn to coordinate poorly during the first few weeks of life?
Yes. It takes four to six months before the muscles of one eye begin to coordinate with those of the other eye. During this time it is not unusual for the parents to think that their child has crossed eyes.

How can one distinguish the newborn's normal lack of eye coordination from crossed eyes?
With true crossed eyes (strabismus), one eye usually remains crossed constantly. This is not the situation in normal lack of eye coordination.

Do children born with apparently normal eyes ever develop crossed eyes as they grow up?
Yes, occasionally, at ages 3 to 6 years due to excessive farsightedness.

Is squint the same thing as crossed eyes (strabismus)?
Yes.

What is meant by comitant squint?
In comitant squint, the degree of crossed eyes is the same no matter in what direction the child looks.

What is noncomitant squint?
In noncomitant squint, the degree or amount of turning of the eyes differs depending on the direction the child looks. In certain directions there may be no turn or squint, while in other directions it may be very pronounced.

What is a cast in an eye?
This is a nonmedical term that usually refers to the turning out of one eye.

How does a cast differ from crossed eyes?
It does not. It simply refers to one type of crossing, that is, an outward turn of one eye.

Should an eye specialist be consulted if a child's eyes turn in or turn out after two or three months of life?
Yes. The sooner a complete eye examination is carried out, the better, especially to determine whether there is a disease in the eye.

Does a newborn ever outgrow crossed eyes without any treatment?
Yes, if the crossing is due to incoordination. However, if crossed eyes persist beyond 6 months of age, the chances are that the child has true strabismus.

At what age can crossed eyes be definitely diagnosed?

An ophthalmologist may be able to suspect the condition at any time from birth onward, and by the time the child is 6 months old, the condition can be determined with certainty.

Can overstimulation of the child cause the eyes to coordinate poorly?

Not unless the child has poor coordination to start with.

Can a parent do anything to make the child's eyes coordinate better?

No.

Do children with crossed eyes always have double vision?

No. Many children suppress the image in the crossed eye and therefore do not see double.

Is there a tendency for crossed eyes to run in families?

Yes. It is not unusual to find parents and children who have crossed eyes.

Does a child usually become aware of the fact that he has crossed eyes before he reaches school age?

Yes. For this reason it is very important to treat the condition before the child starts school so that he will not lose vision in the defective eye, and will not suffer from the teasing of his classmates because of his appearance.

Do children with crossed eyes find learning to read difficult?

Yes. Approximately one out of four children with crossed eyes is found to be very slow in achieving the average level of reading.

Can a child with crossed eyes who has a high IQ still have difficulty learning to read?

Yes.

Is it easier to cure a child whose eye turns in than one whose eye turns out?

Yes, generally it is easier. However, both conditions present problems that may be difficult to overcome.

Is it always necessary to operate on a child with crossed eyes?

No.

Do children ever recover spontaneously from crossed eyes?

Few children who have true crossed eyes will recover without treatment.

What percentage of children will recover with nonsurgical treatment of crossed eyes?

Approximately half the cases.

What is the medical (nonsurgical) treatment of crossed eyes?

1. The wearing of appropriate eyeglasses

2. The regular instillation into the eyes of special eyedrops

3. The covering of one eye (patching) to overcome suppression of vision

4. The practice of eye exercises (orthoptics)

When does the eye specialist cover an eye in the treatment of strabismus?

When the turning eye is not being used.

How effective in maintaining vision is the covering of first one eye and then the other eye?

Patching is very effective before the age of 6 years. After equal vision is obtained in the two eyes, alternate patching is necessary to maintain the vision in both eyes.

At what age is it possible to treat crossed eyes with patching?

At any age. In infants between 6 months and a year old, eyedrops to blur the vision in one eye may be used instead of covering the eye with a patch.

This blurring of vision will force the infant to use, rather than suppress, the other eye.

At what age can a child be given eyeglasses to help correct crossed eyes?

The earliest is when the child is about 18 months old. If the eyes cross constantly before this time, however, surgery is probably indicated.

Does wearing eyeglasses usually straighten crossed eyes completely?

It may in some cases, but it does not usually do so.

How long must eyeglasses be worn to be effective in the treatment of crossed eyes?

In cases of excessive farsightedness, for many years. In others, for 4 to 6 years.

Are crossed eyes merely unsightly or do they impair vision?

They impair vision.

SURGICAL TREATMENT

To straighten crossed eyes, surgery is directed toward strengthening the weak, underacting muscles and weakening the strong, overacting muscles which govern the movements of the eye. These extraocular muscles, six in number, are attached at various sites around the eyeball and all are easily approachable surgically.

A muscle is strengthened by cutting off a piece (approximately one-fourth inch) nearest its attachment to the eyeball and restitching it to the same site. Thus the muscle is strengthened by being shortened.

A muscle is weakened by detaching it from its usual attachment and restitching it farther back (approximately one-fourth inch) on the eyeball. Thus the muscle is weakened by producing a slack in it.

Operations for strabismus are safe procedures. Since the muscles are on the outside of the eyeball, the latter does not have to be opened, and consequently there is virtually no danger of damaging the eye or vision. Only the conjunctiva, the membrane covering the eye, need be opened to reach the muscles. This structure can be closed readily without scarring. Strabismus operations are performed under general anesthesia in children and under either local or general anesthesia in adults. Before proceeding with surgery, the ophthalmologist studies the patient carefully and decides which of the six extraocular muscles are too weak, which are normal, and which are overacting. He will thereby have a fairly good plan of action and will know whether it will be necessary to alter one, two, or all of the muscles. Depending upon the severity of the condition and upon his operative findings, he may operate on one eye only or he may elect to operate upon both eyes at the same time.

The results of surgery are good in the great majority of cases. The degree of success will depend upon which muscles are involved and the extent of involvement. In the majority of cases, one operation will succeed in straightening the eye but many cases require two, and some even three, operations. The fact that more than one operation is needed does not necessarily mean that the outlook is worse than if only one operative procedure is required.

The length of hospital stay in strabismus surgery is usually no more than three to four days, assuming that the patient is admitted one day prior to surgery. There is little postoperative pain, and both eyes need be covered for only one day. After surgery, eye ointments and cold compresses are employed for about two weeks. The patient can usually resume most of his activities within three to four weeks.

At what age should a child be operated on to correct crossed eyes?
When he is as young as possible. The child can be subjected to surgery as early as 6 months of age. The younger he is when operated on, the easier it will be for him to develop normal eye coordination.

Is the degree of crossed eyes important as a guide to surgical treatment?
Yes. The worse the crossing, the more important it is that corrective surgery be performed early.

Are operations on crossed eyes dangerous?
No.

What anesthesia is used when operating on a child with crossed eyes?
General ether anesthesia is used.

Where are the incisions made to correct crossed eyes?
In the conjunctiva, the transparent membrane covering the white of the eyes. The eyeball itself is not opened in an operation to correct crossed eyes.

How long does an operation for crossed eyes take?
Approximately one hour for the uncomplicated case.

What operative procedures are done to correct crossed eyes?
1. A weak eye muscle is strengthened by shortening it. This is accomplished by removing a segment of the muscle involved and stitching the two cut ends together.
2. An overacting muscle is weakened by lengthening it. This is accomplished by separating it from its attachment to the eyeball and implanting it farther back on the eye, thus weakening its pulling action.

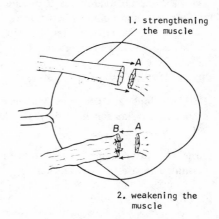

1. strengthening the muscle

2. weakening the muscle

Is it common for both eyes to be crossed?
Yes. In these cases, both eyes must be operated on, and the operation may take longer than one hour.

Does an operation for crossed eyes involve entering the eyeball itself?
No.

Are operations for crossed eyes very painful to children?
No.

Are there any scars visible after an operation for crossed eyes?
Scars are minimal since the incisions are made along the side of the eyeball, underneath the eyelids.

What are the complications of surgery for crossed eyes?
Complications are not frequent, but when they do occur they take the following forms:
1. There may be an occasional overcorrection. The operative procedure may convert an eye that turns in into one that turns out.
2. In an occasional case, a cyst may

form in the line of the incision in the conjunctiva.

If the results of an operation for crossed eyes are not satisfactory, is it possible to reoperate and obtain a better result?

Yes. This is done very often. In many instances, the second operative procedure will correct the remaining turning of the eye.

For how long are the eyes bandaged after an operation for crossed eyes?

One day.

How soon after surgery can a child be permitted to use his eyes normally?

In three to four days the child's eyes will function normally.

How long a hospital stay is necessary after surgery for crossed eyes?

Three to four days.

What limitations should be placed upon the physical activities of a child who has undergone an operation for crossed eyes?

Active sports, swimming, and bicycling should be prohibited for a few weeks. Reading and looking at television are allowable as soon as the child returns home from the hospital.

How soon after the operation can one know that the results are permanent?

It will take a period of six months after the operation before one can judge the results of surgery for strabismus.

Is there a danger of straining an eye that has recently been operated on for strabismus?

No.

What percentage of operations to correct crossed eyes are successful?

On the average, about 80 to 85 percent of results are good. The percentage

is higher for children who have simple, uncomplicated strabismus; it is lower for those who have marked defects and involvement of both eyes.

When a crossed eye has reduced vision, is vision ever restored by correcting the crossing?

Yes, if the child is operated on before he reaches 5 years of age. Restoration of vision is also expedited by placing a patch over the uncrossed eye for several weeks before and after the corrective surgery. This will help to restore vision to the crossed eye. It should be emphasized that the earlier surgery is performed for strabismus and the earlier patching is carried out, the better will be the outcome.

Do children ever see double after an operation for crossed eyes?

Yes, but not very often. When double vision does occur, it usually disappears within a short time.

Cryosurgery

Cryosurgery is the use of cold as a means of destroying diseased tissues. The so-called cold scalpel is an electrode which delivers such intense cold to an area that it not only freezes tissues but destroys them permanently. As the electrode is small, it can pinpoint accurately the area to be affected, leaving surrounding tissues unharmed.

QUESTIONS AND ANSWERS

How is cryosurgery used in the treatment of Parkinson's disease?

A specially designed electrode is inserted through the nose into the base of the brain until it reaches the nerve cells of the brain that are responsible for the palsy. When the precise area has been contacted, the electrode is made cold and the nerve cells (ganglions) are destroyed through freezing. In most cases, these procedures, when performed by those specially trained in the field, are successful in stopping much of the palsy.

Has palsy (Parkinson's disease) been helped greatly through cryosurgery?

Yes. Thousands of people, who formerly suffered from the shaking of palsy, have been helped tremendously through the use of cryosurgical techniques.

Can cancer be operated upon through the use of cryosurgery?

It has been shown that some cancers can be destroyed by the use of cold. However, techniques have not yet been refined to a point where cryosurgery can be used as a common form of cancer treatment. Initial results in the treatment of certain bone tumors, especially those in the legs, by cryosurgical techniques have been most encouraging.

Can the pituitary gland in the base of the skull be destroyed through cryosurgery?

Yes. This procedure is done in patients who have a tumor of the pituitary and also in some cases of advanced cancer of the breast. It has been shown that destruction of the pituitary gland in some cases will slow down growth of a breast cancer.

Cryptorchidism

See TESTICLES.

Curettage

Curettage is a general term applied to an operative procedure in which the interior of a body cavity is scraped out with an instrument known as a curette. Such scraping may be carried out for the removal of a tumor or other abnormal tissues or to obtain material for diagnostic purposes.

The most frequent use of the term curettage applies to dilating the cervix of the uterus and scraping out the uterine cavity. It is therefore discussed more fully under the heading Dilatation and Curettage.

In dentistry, curettage is used for the removal of a cyst or inflammatory tissue in the crypt left by a tooth. It also is sometimes used to remove tooth fragments and other debris from a tooth socket.

In general surgery, tracts such as fistulas or chronic inflammatory areas are sometimes curetted in order to remove the offending tissue.

See also DILATATION AND CURETTAGE.

Curvature of the Spine

A side-to-side curvature of the spine, known as scoliosis, leads to an S-shaped or C-shaped spinal column. This causes a marked distortion of the back. Kyphosis is a sharp backward prominence of the spine, usually located at the lower part of the chest and noted soon after birth or when a child reaches walking age.

See also SCOLIOSIS; SPINE.

Cushing's Syndrome

Cushing's syndrome, or Cushing's disease, is a condition affecting the cortex of the adrenal gland, and is associated with an excessive production of cortical hormone.

See also ADRENAL GLANDS.

QUESTIONS AND ANSWERS

What are the characteristics of Cushing's disease?
1. Redistribution of fat to the upper torso, neck, and shoulders, giving the patient a "buffalo" appearance
2. A fattened and rounded "moon" face
3. Peculiar purplish streaks in the skin of the abdomen, thighs, and arms
4. The development of male body characteristics in a female
5. Elevated blood pressure
6. Elevated blood sugar content

What hormone of the adrenal cortex is secreted in excess amounts in this condition?
Hydrocortisone.

Is Cushing's disease a common disease?
No.

What causes Cushing's disease?
In certain cases, a tumor of the adrenal cortex is the cause. In other cases, overactivity of normal adrenal cortex function.

Can Cushing's disease be treated successfully?
Yes.

What is the treatment for Cushing's disease?
1. X-ray treatment of the pituitary gland in the skull. This will cut down its stimulation of the adrenal gland, resulting in lessened adrenal secretion.
2. Surgical removal of part of the adrenal gland or removal of any tumor that may be found within the gland substance.

What will happen if Cushing's disease goes untreated?
The patient will succumb to it.

Why is it that x-ray treatment of the pituitary gland will help to arrest Cushing's syndrome?
Because the adrenal glands are directly under the control of the pituitary gland in the brain. Limiting the amount of hormone secretion by the pituitary will often result in lessened secretions by the adrenal glands.

Is an operation upon the adrenal glands for Cushing's syndrome serious?
Yes. It is a major procedure, but when carried out by specialists in the field, recovery is the general rule.

Is it ever necessary to give cortisone to those who have had most of their adrenal gland removed?
Yes. It is not an accurate operation and it is sometimes possible that more adrenal tissue is removed than one would have liked. In these cases, insufficiency of the adrenal gland may develop and it may be necessary, therefore, to support the patient with injections or pills of cortisone.

Do children ever develop Cushing's syndrome?
Yes.

Cuts

Most cuts and lacerations seem much more serious than they actually are. People are sometimes frightened by the amount of bleeding, but most superficial bleeding will stop spontaneously after a little while. If one judges the seriousness of the injury by the amount of blood seen, he will usually overestimate the damage that has been done. It is only when a major blood vessel is severed that bleeding is dangerous. Scalp wounds are particularly frightening, as they bleed very actively at the start. However, almost all scalp wounds will stop bleeding by themselves when gentle pressure is applied.

Here are some first aid hints for treating cuts and lacerations:

1. The wounded area should be cleansed with soap and large quantities of warm water. Moist cotton can be used to wipe dirt from the wound.

2. Strong antiseptics such as iodine, alcohol, or commercial products should not be poured onto a cut or laceration. These will burn the already damaged tissues and will delay healing.

3. Simple pressure applied directly over the laceration with the palm of the hand or the fingers is usually sufficient to control most hemorrhage. The pressure must be maintained for several minutes in order to stop the bleeding. If such pressure does not stop the bleeding, the wound will usually require stitching.

4. If the bleeding continues and the injury is located on an arm or leg, a tourniquet may be placed *above* the area of the laceration. It is important that a tourniquet *never* be left in place for more than 15 minutes at a time without releasing it. Permanent damage to the tissues beyond the area of the tourniquet can occur if there is an extended obstruction to circulation. If the bleeding appears to have diminished or stopped after the tourniquet is released, it should not be reapplied.

5. A clean gauze dressing or, if this is not available, a clean handkerchief should be placed over the wound until medical care can be obtained.

6. Whenever in doubt, a person with a laceration should be taken to a physician's office or to the nearest hospital. Most lacerations will heal quickly if they are cleaned and sutured by a physician.

7. If an artery has been damaged, one will be able to note an intermittent spurting of blood that corresponds to the pulse beat. This is almost always an indication that suturing will be required.

8. If the injured person is unable to move one of his fingers or toes, a tendon may have been severed. This will require the expert attention of a surgeon.

9. If a finger or toe beyond the area of laceration is numb, a nerve may have been severed.

10. Lacerations in the neck should be firmly pressed with the fingers until the injured person can be brought to the nearest physician. No attempt should be made to stop bleeding in the neck region by the application of a tourniquet.

11. Neither bandages nor tourniquets should be applied so tightly that tissues beyond the tourniquet turn blue or numb.

See also FIRST AID.

QUESTIONS AND ANSWERS

How often should bandages be changed?

If there is no discharge through the bandage and no swelling or redness about it, it can be left in place for several days.

How should a tourniquet be applied?

A clean handkerchief should be placed around the limb, just above the laceration. A knot should be tied and tightened by placing a pen or pencil (or even a stick of wood) in the knot and then twisting the knot until bleeding stops. Tourniquets must be released every few minutes in order to allow some circulation. If the bleeding has stopped when the tourniquet is released, the tourniquet should not be reapplied.

Cystic Hygroma

Cystic hygroma is a rare, nonmalignant cystic tumor of the neck found in infants and young children. It is often difficult to remove the entire growth surgically, and it is sometimes necessary to reoperate if the cyst recurs. This tumor seldom becomes malignant, its worst aspect being its unsightly appearance.

QUESTIONS AND ANSWERS

What causes cystic hygroma?

It is probably a development deformity of the lymph channels as they emerge from the jugular veins in the neck.

At what age is a child most likely to develop a cystic hygroma?

It is usually seen by the time he is a year or two old.

Are any symptoms or signs attributable to a cystic hygroma?

None other than the appearance of the mass in the neck.

How is the diagnosis of a cystic hygroma made?

There is a soft, flabby swelling visible in the neck, usually out to one side. The borders of the tumor are not well defined, and the tumor does not appear to have a firm capsule around it.

What is the treatment for cystic hygroma?

Complete surgical removal of the tumor is indicated. This may be a very difficult task technically, because of the many ramifications of the hygroma.

If it causes no symptoms, why must a cystic hygroma be removed?

Because it has a tendency to enlarge and may extend toward important structures in the throat and anterior part of the neck. Furthermore, it will become unsightly.

At what age can children be operated on for the removal of a cystic hygroma?

The sooner they are operated on, the better, as these tumors have a tendency to grow, and the larger they are, the more difficult it is to remove them in their entirety.

Is it always possible to remove a cystic hygroma in its entirety?

No. In many cases, portions of the hygroma are left behind and the cyst may grow back.

What is the treatment for a recurrent cystic hygroma?

Either another attempt may be made to remove the remaining portions surgically or x-ray treatments may be given.

Is an operation for cystic hygroma serious?

No, because the dissection is carried out almost completely beneath the skin. However, the surgeon must be careful not to damage any of the nerves in the vicinity of the hygroma.

Cystocele and Rectocele

A cystocele is a protrusion, or hernia, of the urinary bladder wall down into the vagina. It may vary in degree from a mild bulge into the vagina to a maximum descent in which almost the entire bladder protrudes through the vaginal opening. A cystocele is thought to be produced by a relaxation, weakening, or degeneration of a ligament that normally holds the bladder in its proper position.

A rectocele is a protrusion, or hernia, of the rectal wall up into the vagina. Again, the degree of herniation varies markedly from case to case. A rectocele may be due to a tear following the delivery of a child, or it may be due to relaxation, weakening, or degeneration of the muscles and fibrous tissues that normally hold the rectum in its proper position.

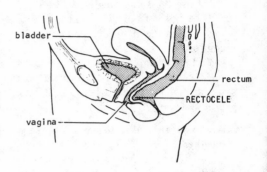

QUESTIONS AND ANSWERS

How often do cystoceles and rectoceles occur?

They are very common conditions. The incidence is greater in women who have borne many children. Also, women past 40 years of age are likely to develop these conditions as their supporting ligaments begin to stretch and weaken.

Do women who have never given birth develop a cystocele or rectocele in their later years?

Yes, as a result of a weakening of their muscles and ligaments in the area.

What are the usual symptoms of a cystocele?

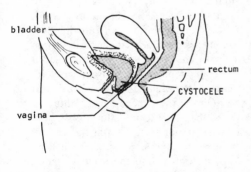

1. A small cystocele may produce no symptoms.

2. Protrusion of the bladder into the vaginal canal and an uncomfortable feeling in the area.

3. Frequency of urination.

4. Leaking urine upon coughing, sneezing, or laughing.

5. The sensation after voiding that the bladder is not completely emptied.

6. Symptoms of cystitis brought on by an infection of the urine.

How is a diagnosis of cystocele made?
By a simple pelvic examination.

What are the symptoms of a rectocele?
1. A bulge from the rectal area into the vagina, with accompanying discomfort.
2. Increasing constipation, with a feeling that the stool is just at the exit but cannot be expelled because of lack of muscle power.

Are cystocele and rectocele usually seen together?
Yes. Since these conditions have a similar origin, one usually finds both of them present.

Are cystocele and rectocele often associated with prolapse of the uterus (fallen womb)?
Yes.

What is the treatment for cystocele and rectocele?
Mild cases may be controlled by the use of a pessary, an appliance inserted into the vagina to maintain normal position of the bladder and uterus. Special exercises for the muscles surrounding the vagina may be helpful. More advanced cases are treated surgically.
Surgery consists of repairing and shortening the ligaments and surrounding fibrous tissues that hold the bladder and rectum in their proper positions.

Are operations for the repair of cystocele and rectocele dangerous?
No. They can be safely performed on healthy women of any age.

Is the repair of a cystocele and rectocele a form of vaginal "plastic surgery"?
Yes, that is, it is a procedure for taking up the slack in stretched or degenerated ligaments.

How long is one incapacitated by such an operation?
Today, with modern surgical methods and techniques, patients usually get out of bed the day after surgery and leave the hospital within five to ten days.

Is it possible for an older woman to have marital relations following surgical repair of a cystocele or rectocele?
Yes.

If cystocele, rectocele, and prolapse of the uterus are present at the same time, will all three conditions be repaired during one operation?
Yes.

Can anything be done to prevent the development of cystocele, rectocele, or prolapse of the uterus?
No, but if they are present during the younger years, it is a good idea to have them repaired at that time.

To avoid surgery, can a pessary be worn instead?
Most cases of advanced cystocele, rectocele, or prolapse of the uterus cannot be held in place satisfactorily by the use of a pessary. (It is somewhat similar to a man's wearing a truss to hold in a hernia, in that it may work for a short time, but not indefinitely.)
If a pessary does satisfactorily retain a cystocele, rectocele, or prolapse, it must be removed, cleansed, and reinserted at regular intervals. This must be done by the gynecologist. Failure to do so may lead to infection, ulceration, or even tumor formation in the vagina. In some instances, pessaries have been known to grow into the vaginal tissues, requiring surgery to remove them.

What are the chances of recurrence after surgery for cystocele and rectocele?
After competent surgery, the chances of recurrence are less than 10 percent.

Are there any visible scars following vaginal plastic operations?

No.

What type of anesthesia is used for these procedures?

Either spinal or general anesthesia.

How long do these operations take to perform?

A complete vaginal plastic operation may take anywhere from one to two hours.

Are operations upon the vagina very painful?

No.

Are any special postoperative precautions necessary?

Yes. A catheter may be placed in the bladder for a few days in order to aid restoration of bladder function.

How soon after vaginal operations are patients permitted to get out of bed?

Usually the day following surgery.

What is the effect of vaginal plastic operations upon the bladder and rectum?

Occasionally, for the first week or two there may be difficulty in urinating. Also, in operations for rectocele there may be difficulty in moving one's bowels for a similar period. These complications are temporary and will subside spontaneously.

Do stitches have to be removed after these operations?

No. The stitches are absorbable and do not have to be removed.

Is it common to bleed after operations upon the vagina?

Yes. Slight staining may continue on and off for several weeks.

Do vaginal plastic operations interfere with sexual relations?

No. When the tissues have healed, intercourse can be resumed. This usually takes six to eight weeks.

Is the term "plastic repair" the same as the term "repair of cystocele and rectocele"?

Yes.

Can women have babies after surgery for a cystocele or rectocele?

Yes, but delivery may have to be performed by cesarean section, as surgery may have interfered with the ability of the tissues to stretch and dilate sufficiently. Also, vaginal delivery might bring on a recurrence of the cystocele or rectocele.

Cystoscopy

A cystoscopic examination is one in which the interior of the bladder is viewed directly through a tubular metal instrument known as a cystoscope. Cystoscopes are equipped with lights and lenses which permit excellent visualization of the inside of the bladder. In addition, the outlet of the ureters from the kidneys may be studied through this instrument, as may the size and configuration of the prostate gland.

See also KIDNEYS AND URETERS; PROSTATE GLAND; URINARY BLADDER.

QUESTIONS AND ANSWERS

Is a cystoscopic examination painful?

In the female, it is virtually painless. In the male, there is some discomfort, but this can be minimized by using local anesthetic agents. In children, cystoscopy is performed under general anesthesia.

What are the aftereffects of cystoscopy?

Some temporary urinary discomfort

and possibly some blood in the urine. There also may be a rise in temperature for a day or two.

Is it necessary to be hospitalized for a cystoscopic examination?

Usually not. Most cystoscopic examinations can be done in the urologist's office. When catheters are to be placed through the cystoscope into the ureters and up toward the kidneys, hospitalization is often advised. When such catheters are to be left in place for a few days, hospitalization is mandatory.

Is it less painful to cystoscope a female than a male?

Yes, because the urethra is much shorter in the female.

Can infants and children be cystoscoped?

Yes, through specially devised miniature pediatric cystoscopes. There are instruments small enough to conduct examinations even in newborns.

Is anesthesia necessary before an infant or child can be cystoscoped?

In many infants, satisfactory cystoscopy may be conducted under simple sedation, adjusting the amount of sedation to the age of the child. It also is possible to examine some young children under local anesthesia that will decrease the sensitivity of the urethra. However, when the age of understanding is reached (6 to 9 years), there is often psychological harm if the child is conscious when the area is inspected, and it is preferable in these cases to give general anesthesia.

Cystotomy

A cystotomy is an operative procedure in which a surgical opening is made into the bladder. It is usually car-

ried out to relieve urinary obstruction caused by an enlarged prostate or is performed in order to remove a bladder stone or tumor.

See also PROSTATE GLAND; URINARY BLADDER.

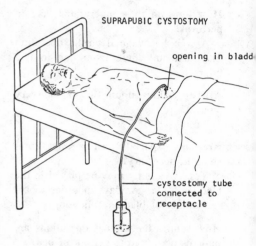

SUPRAPUBIC CYSTOSTOMY

opening in bladd

cystostomy tube connected to receptacle

QUESTIONS AND ANSWERS

Is a cystotomy often performed as the first-stage procedure in the removal of the prostate gland?

Yes. In some patients, because of their poor general health or poor kidney function, infection, or associated diseases, it is too risky to remove the prostate gland at one time. In these cases, a preliminary cystotomy is performed to obtain free urinary drainage. When cystotomy is performed for this reason, it is called a first-stage prostate operation.

Where is an incision made in the performance of a cystotomy?

A linear incision is usually made on the abdomen just above the pubic bone.

After performance of a cystotomy, where does the urine drain?

Through a tube onto the abdominal wall. This tube is then attached to a receptacle which can be allowed to hang at the patient's bedside or can be strapped to his leg.

Is the prostate gland usually removed through the cystotomy opening?

Yes.

After removal of the prostate gland, is urine permitted to drain through the cystotomy opening onto the anterior abdominal wall?

Yes.

Is it necessary to close a cystotomy opening in order to restore normal channels of urination?

No. Within two to three weeks after removal of a prostate gland, urine will flow again through normal channels and the opening on the anterior abdominal wall will close spontaneously.

Will a cystotomy wound heal spontaneously after removal of a bladder stone or tumor?

Yes. However, if the tumor of the bladder is malignant, an operation for the removal of the entire structure will probably be carried out. After that, urine will no longer drain through normal channels, but will be shunted into the intestines or bowels.

Cysts

A cyst is a sac containing a liquid or semisolid material. Practically every tissue and organ of the body can be subject to cyst formation.

As cysts grow, the sac becomes disproportionately large compared to the exit. As a consequence, in many instances, the exit leading out of the cyst becomes blocked. When this occurs, the liquid or semisolid material within the cyst causes the cyst to grow greatly in size.

Cysts that grow to a large size may interfere with function of adjacent organs or of the organ in which the cyst is developing. This may require surgical drainage or removal of the cyst and its surrounding wall.

In the superficial tissues, such as the skin, one often notes cysts forming on the sebaceous glands. When these are on the scalp, they are known as wens. Cysts of this type often become infected and will require surgical incision and drainage, or removal.

Cysts can sometimes be multiple and can destroy the function of an organ. One of the prime examples of this type of cyst is the polycystic kidney in which the kidney is the site for hundreds of cysts that have formed. These cysts will ultimately interfere with kidney function.

Cysts can also form within the brain, the lungs, the thyroid gland, the breast, the liver, pancreas, spleen, and ovaries. When they attain large size, they frequently will require surgical removal.

For details on specific types of cysts, see articles on the above-mentioned organs.

Cytology

Cytology is that branch of science which deals in the study of cells, their structure, origin, and function. Those who specialize in this field are known as cytologists. Tremendous progress has been made recently in the field of cytology with the development of high-powered microscopes that can magnify a cell so that the nucleus of the cell and its chromosomes can be seen. Thus, many inherited diseases and chromosomal defects can now be diagnosed through the science of cytology. Similarly, cytologists have been able to make diagnoses of cancer merely by taking smears of individual cells from body cavities and body secretions.

QUESTIONS AND ANSWERS

Can certain inherited defects be diagnosed merely through examination of cells?

Yes. This, in most instances, has now become a commonplace procedure and is carried out in all accredited hospitals. Various types of blood cells, or cells scraped from the mucous membrane on the inside of the mouth, can be specially prepared and examined under high-powered microscopes. By analysis of the chromosomes found in the nuclei, many inherited diseases or abnormalities can now be spotted.

How are cytological studies helpful in diagnosing cancer or allied diseases?

1. By taking a swab of the cervix of the uterus and by examining this material under the microscope, diagnosis of incipient cancer of the female genitals can often be diagnosed. This is known as the Papanicolaou or Pap test. Every female over 21 should have such a test performed each year.

2. Cells taken from washings of the stomach can be examined to determine the presence or absence of cancer.

3. Superficial cells can be scraped off sores or ulcers and can be subjected to cytological tests.

4. Urine specimens can be centrifuged and the sediment can be examined for the presence of malignant cells from higher up in the urinary tract.

5. Cells removed by tapping a cyst of the breast or cells obtained from a nipple discharge can reveal the presence of a malignancy.

6. Cells obtained by puncturing the breastbone and sucking up tissue through a syringe will often reveal the presence of a blood disease such as leukemia. This procedure is termed a bone marrow study.

7. A biopsy of the liver or spleen can be obtained through insertion of a needle into these organs and withdrawing some cells into a syringe.

Does one require special training to become a cytologist?

Yes. It is a specialty like any other in medicine and requires intense and prolonged study to attain proficiency.

Can Pap tests be done with ordinary microscopes?

Yes, but those who examine smears must be specially trained so that they can pass judgment upon the submitted specimens.

Can cells for cytological examination also be obtained by needle aspiration?

Yes. Where a tumor is deep-seated and cannot be approached by swabbing, it is perfectly feasible to insert a needle and to suck out a few cells for examination.

Are cytological specimens the same as biopsy material?

In actuality, the cells obtained for cytological inspection do constitute biopsy. The difference is that only a small number of cells are usually obtained when cytological methods are used. The ordinary biopsy material contains a larger quantity of tissue. In both instances, a pathologist must examine the material under the microscope and be in a position to make an accurate diagnosis.

Deafness

Deafness is loss of hearing. It may be partial or complete, congenital or acquired, static or progressive. Deafness, in addition to being caused by inherited defects in the hearing apparatus, may be caused by any interference with the reception or transmission of sound waves along the ear canal through the middle ear to the inner ear and then along the acoustic nerve to the brain.

Until recently, deaf people were limited, in their quest for improved hearing, to the use of mechanical aids or lip reading. Then, with the advent of the Lempert fenestration operation, many were helped to improved hearing. Today the fenestration procedure has been superseded by newer methods which offer a much greater incidence of successful results and a much lower rate of recurrence of deafness.

It must be understood that only those people who have defects due to conduction deafness can be aided by surgery. Those whose hearing loss is caused by inadequacy of the acoustic nerve (the nerve of hearing), unfortunately, cannot be benefited.

To understand the various operative procedures for deafness, it is first necessary to outline how normal hearing takes place:

Sound waves enter the external ear canal and strike the eardrum, causing it to vibrate. Directly on the inner aspect of the drum are three tiny bones—the malleus, incus, and stapes. The drum vibrations are transmitted to these bones which, in turn, vibrate and transmit the impulses to the inner ear. This is accomplished by the stapes, part of which extends through an opening in the bone overlying the inner ear. The inner ear is filled with a fluid surrounded by a membrane. When the stapes vibrates, the impulses are conveyed through the fluid to special nerve endings. The impulses then travel up from the nerve endings to the acoustic nerve, which carries them to the brain, where they are recorded as hearing.

In conduction deafness, the stapes is rigid and fixed (ankylosed), and therefore is unable to transmit the sound waves through the opening in the bone to the fluid of the inner ear.

The operation now being performed most often is the so-called stapes operation (stapedectomy). This procedure is done under local anesthesia, and since the structures are so small, magnification is employed by use of a specially designed microscopic device. An incision is made adjacent to the eardrum and the drum is elevated, exposing the middle ear with its three small bones. The stapes, which is fixed in position instead of being mobile, is then removed. This will uncover an opening into the inner ear. This opening is covered with a graft composed of a portion of a vein, or fat tissue, or some other material. A small plastic tube or piece of stainless steel wire is attached to the graft and is then connected to the two remaining ear bones (the malleus and incus). After this has been accomplished, the eardrum is put back in its normal position.

According to most ear surgeons, there are several distinct advantages of the stapes operation over the original fenestration procedure. First, a higher percentage of patients will regain hearing, and second, fewer patients will develop any recurrence of deafness in the ensuing years. With the stapes procedure, a shorter period of hospitalization is necessary and convalescence is more rapid. Lastly, the stapes operation does away with the need to explore and remove mastoid bone cells, thus reducing the hazards of the operation.

In certain cases of deafness caused by infection and perforation (hole) of the eardrum, an operation known as tympanoplasty has proved to be effective. This procedure is beneficial only after all evidences of bacterial infection have been cleared up. Tympanoplasty may take one of several forms, but all aim toward repair of the perforation in the drum and reestablishment of its ability to vibrate and transmit sound waves. This is sometimes accomplished by inserting a graft to cover the perforation. *See also* EARS; MASTOIDECTOMY.

QUESTIONS AND ANSWERS

When there is deafness of one ear, will the other ear become involved too?

Deafness may occasionally be limited to one ear when it is secondary to an infection, but this is not the general rule. In most cases of otosclerosis, when one ear is involved, the other ear will show a loss of hearing sooner or later.

Do both ears tend to go deaf at the same time?

Not necessarily. There may be a wide interval, or there may be no impairment of hearing in the other ear if one ear is affected.

What kinds of deafness are encountered?
1. Congenital deafness
2. Central deafness due to involvement of the brain
3. Perceptive deafness due to involvement of the internal ear or acoustic nerve
4. Conduction deafness due to involvement of the middle ear or auditory canal

What is congenital deafness?

This is a type with which one is born and is based upon the abnormal development or lack of development of the nerve of hearing.

What causes congenital deafness?

It is thought that many cases occurring in newborns are caused by diseases which the mothers had during the first few weeks of their pregnancies. Toxins from certain diseases, such as German measles, are transmitted to the young embryo and cause maldevelopment of the hearing apparatus.

What are some of the causes of inner ear deafness?
1. Diseases such as mumps, influenza, scarlet fever, and malaria
2. Drugs such as quinine, salicylates, and streptomycin
3. Occupations such as boilermaking, piloting an airplane, and others
4. Fractures through the temporal bone of the skull which traverses the ear mechanism
5. Allergic reactions involving the labyrinth
6. Hemorrhage into the inner ear
7. Tumors of the nerve of hearing (the acoustic nerve)

How can deafness caused by a defect in the inner ear be distinguished from deafness caused by trouble in the middle ear?

Middle ear deafness does not involve disease of the transmission mechanism. Thus, if a vibrating tuning fork is held against the mastoid bone behind the ear, the vibrating sound is intensified, as it can be transmitted through the undamaged inner ear. If the deafness is a result of disturbance in the inner ear or in the acoustic nerve, the tuning fork vibrations will not be heard.

What causes middle ear (conduction) deafness?
1. Impacted wax
2. A foreign body in the external ear canal
3. A discharge in the canal
4. Narrowing of the canal due to inflammation of the skin of the canal
5. Tumors of the external auditory canal
6. Perforated eardrum
7. Inflammation of the middle ear

8. Tumor of the middle ear
9. Lack of mobility of the stapes bone in the middle ear
10. A blocked eustachian tube
11. A degenerative disease known as otosclerosis

What is the incidence of conduction deafness?

It is estimated that about five out of every hundred people have deafness caused by disturbance in their conduction apparatus. Fortunately, only one of these five people has impairment to such degree that it requires medical attention.

Are hearing aids effective?

Yes. There are wonderful new hearing aids being manufactured, and constant improvements are being made all the time. However, aids are not effective in all types of hearing loss.

Is surgery helpful in the treatment of deafness?

Yes, in certain types of deafness. If the deafness is caused by the presence of fluid in the middle ear, an incision in the eardrum which permits the fluid to escape will often be followed by a complete return of hearing.

In cases in which the deafness is secondary to rigidity of the stapes bone in the middle ear, surgery may bring about excellent relief.

What is otosclerosis?

Otosclerosis is a disease of the middle ear.

What are the harmful results of otosclerosis?

Otosclerosis is the most common cause of deafness, usually of the conduction type.

What are the symptoms of otosclerosis?

Deafness is the outstanding symptom, but occasionally it causes noises in the ears. There are no abnormal ear findings on examination.

Does otosclerosis always cause deafness?

No.

What is the treatment for otosclerosis?

The operation performed most often now is known as stapedectomy. This operation is carried out under local anesthesia utilizing magnification instruments because of the small size of the parts being operated upon. A small incision is made adjacent to the eardrum and the drum is elevated, exposing the middle ear with its three small bones. One of these small bones, the stapes, is then removed, thus uncovering an opening into the inner ear. This opening is covered with a small graft, usually a piece of vein or a plastic material. A small plastic tube or piece of stainless steel wire is attached to the graft and is then connected to the two remaining small bones of the ear (the incus and the malleus). When this portion of the operation has been completed, the eardrum is returned to its normal position.

Is the fenestration operation performed frequently for deafness?

Not any more. It has been found that the stapes operation results in a much higher percentage of cure, and furthermore, recurrence of deafness is much less likely to take place after this procedure than following the fenestration operation.

For what conditions is the stapes operation most effective?

Those cases of deafness caused by rigidity of the stapes bone of the middle ear and those caused by otosclerosis. In order for the stapes operation to be successful, the acoustic nerve (the nerve of hearing) must function normally and the eardrum must be normal.

Can the stapes operation be performed at any age?

Yes. This is not a major operation in the sense that it is dangerous or cannot be carried out at any age.

Does hearing ever worsen after a stapes operation?

This occurs only in extremely rare instances.

Is the stapes operation followed by very much pain?

No.

Are there any scars visible following the stapes operation?

No, inasmuch as the incision is made within the ear canal.

If the patient is deaf in both ears, is the stapes operation usually carried out simultaneously in both ears?

No. The usual practice is to perform them several weeks or months apart.

How long following a deafness operation can the patient get out of bed?

In a day or two.

Are there many complications following stapes surgery?

No. Those that do occur will usually disappear within a few weeks' time.

What may be some of the complications following stapedectomy?

1. Failure to obtain improvement in hearing
2. Noises in the ear
3. Dizziness and headache

Are the benefits following surgery permanent?

Yes, in the great majority of cases.

What percentage of patients who undergo deafness operations are benefited?

With recent improvement in techniques, approximately 85 to 90 percent of patients will have improved hearing.

If the initial operation for deafness has failed, is it possible to reoperate and obtain a better result?

Yes. There have been many successes with secondary operations for deafness where the first operations have failed to obtain good results.

How long after the surgery has been performed will the patient know whether hearing will return?

If there is going to be a good result, it occurs almost immediately.

How long a hospital stay is necessary after stapes surgery?

Usually no more than two to three days.

When can a patient return to his usual work?

Within approximately two weeks.

Is the fenestration operation ever carried out following failure of a stapes operation?

In isolated instances where the stapes operation has failed to obtain a good result, a satisfactory result may follow a fenestration procedure.

How does the mobilization of the stapes operation differ from stapedectomy?

In a mobilization operation the stapes bone is not removed, but is merely manipulated so as to free it from its adhesions or restrictions. It has been found that the adhesions may re-form after surgery, and therefore removal of the stapes bone with a substitute graft has been found to be a more satisfactory operation.

What is tympanoplasty?

This is an operation performed to restore hearing by repairing the damage to, or by replacement of, the eardrum. The medical term for the eardrum is the tympanic membrane.

How does the surgeon perform a tympanoplasty?

He may merely mobilize the edges of the hole in the drum and stitch them together; or more commonly, if the drum is extensively damaged, he will replace it entirely with a vein graft. This type of surgery is usually performed using magnification because of the small size of the structure in the area.

Is tympanoplasty a successful operative procedure?

Yes, providing the underlying small bones of hearing and the inner ear are essentially normal. It will do little good to repair a damaged eardrum if the underlying bones are diseased or restricted by adhesions.

Debridement

Debridement is a term used in surgery denoting a specific method of treating a wound. Debridement consists of removing all of the dead tissue surrounding the wound. This procedure is carried out very frequently in war injuries when, due to shrapnel or bullet wounds, skin, subcutaneous tissue, and muscle tissue are devitalized. To leave such dead tissue in a wound would court infection and possible gangrene.

After debridement of wounds, a clean surface should remain, and all of the tissue left behind should be viable (capable of living). Debrided wounds are often left open to heal, rather than closed at the time of debridement. This technique is followed in order to avoid the suturing of a wound that may subsequently become infected. Debridement can also be carried out, in some instances, by chemical means. There are substances, such as Ilase, which through enzyme action will chemically dissolve dead tissue.

Desmoid Tumors

A desmoid tumor is a relatively rare type of growth seen most often in women who have borne children. A desmoid is composed of firm connective tissue which develops within muscles, especially within the abdominal muscles. The masses can grow to quite a large size and sometimes become as big as a grapefruit.

The exact origin of desmoid tumors is unknown, but some investigators feel that they develop secondary to tearing and hemorrhage within muscle fibers. On microscopic examination the tumors are found to be composed of actively growing fibrous connective-tissue cells.

Desmoid tumors spread to adjoining tissues but are not malignant and do not metastasize to other parts of the body.

The treatment for desmoid tumor is surgical excision. This is sometimes quite difficult, as it is necessary to remove a great deal of muscle tissue along with the tumor. When it involves the abdominal wall, its removal sometimes leaves the area without adequate muscle and fibrous support. Although the tumor does not spread to distant parts of the body, there is a tendency for it to recur locally. It is therefore necessary to excise very widely along with surrounding normal tissue.

Detachment of the Retina

The retina is continuous with the optic nerve which originates in the brain. It lines the interior of the back two-thirds of the eyeball. It is the light-receptive layer and may be compared to photographic film in that it is equipped to receive light impulses. The retina is transparent and is of purple-red color. When light enters the eye and strikes the retina, the purple-red color is bleached. It is the bleaching that causes an impulse to travel along the optic nerve (the main nerve of the eye) to the visual area in the brain, where the impulse is transformed and translated by the brain into sight.

Just outside the retina is the choroid layer, to which it is attached and from which it receives its blood supply and nourishment. Detachment of the retina results from a tear or hole in the retina so that it becomes separated from the underlying choroid. The detached portion then flaps loosely within the fluid of the eyeball in much the same manner as a piece of wallpaper would if it separated from its wall. Naturally, this phenomenon interferes with proper nourishment and function of the retina and will therefore interfere with sight. Detachment of the retina is caused by any of the following:

1. **Injury.** A blow to the head or directly to the eye may cause a tear in the retina with ensuing hemorrhage in the choroid layer and interior of the eye. Such a concussion may result in separation of the overlying retina.

2. **Retina degeneration.** This occurs in extreme nearsightedness (high myopia) and in some patients with marked hardening of the arteries of the retina.

3. **Tumor of the choroid.** A growth within the choroid layer will shove the retina away and cause a detachment. This type is known as a solid detachment.

The symptoms of detachment of the retina come on suddenly and without pain. The patient notices a dark veil before one eye. Generally this is at first located toward the periphery (the outside) of the field of vision, but day by day it tends to spread toward the center. Sometimes there is merely a diffuse fog which prevents distinct sight. If the detachment is in the periphery of the field of vision and is extending slowly, several weeks may pass before central vision is interfered with. Conversely, when the detachment has taken place near the macula (the most sensitive part of the retina), marked reduction in sight may ensue almost immediately. Other symptoms that often occur are distortion of the shape of objects, blurring of vision, flashes of light, and spots before the eyes.

The diagnosis of retinal detachment can usually be made readily by use of the ophthalmoscope, an instrument that permits one to look through the pupil directly into the interior of the eye. Before this examination, the ophthalmologist will instill eyedrops to dilate the pupil and thereby obtain a wide opening into which he can peer. The detachment will evidence itself by changes in the appearance and color of the retina, by changes in the appearance of the choroid blood vessels, and by actually seeing the tear or tears in the retina. If the detachment has been caused by a tumor growing in the choroid, a characteristic picture will be evident which will distinguish it from other causes of detachment. *This is extremely important, as a tumor may necessitate removal of the entire eye to save the patient's life!*

Until about forty years ago, there was virtually no treatment for this condition and blindness was the usual outcome. Today surgical treatment saves the sight in more than 75 percent of cases of retinal detachment.

Early surgery is very important! The patient must be hospitalized. A much better view of the area of detachment is obtained after a rest period, and the eye surgeon can therefore plan more efficiently exactly where to attack the detachment.

The surgery of retinal detachment has advanced greatly during the past 15 years. Prior to that time, it consisted of applying an electric needle (diathermy coagulation) to the outer surface of the eyeball (sclera) over the area of the retinal tear and detached retina. The effect was to set up an inflammatory reaction between the separated retina and its underlying choroid. As the inflammation subsided over a period of several weeks, connective tissue formed and sealed off the tear or hole. Following this, the fluid which accumulated between the retina and the choroid was drained and the retina would settle back into place. Within recent years, freezing (cryosurgery) has been used effectively in certain cases and has been found to cause less tissue destruction than diathermy.

While the diathermy coagulation technique, as just described, is still used in certain simple cases of retinal detachment, it has been replaced by newer methods of treatment. The general principle underlying the new procedures is to reduce the size of the eyeball, thus eliminating excess stretching of the retina. With a smaller area to cover, the retina is under less tension or stretch. Once this is accomplished, diathermy and fluid drainage are performed.

To decrease the size of the eyeball, thin segments of the sclera are cut out and the edges are stitched together. Other techniques employ artificial implants to turn the sclera in, thus diminishing the size of the eyeball. While diathermy coagulation shrinks the eye to a certain extent when it is applied, the buckling and shortening procedures accomplish it to a much greater extent.

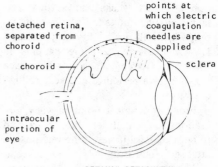

RETINAL DETACHMENT

In these operations, the conjunctiva (the lining membrane over the white portion of the eye) is dissected away from the sclera (white of the eye). In certain cases one or more of the extraocular muscles are temporarily detached from the eyeball in order to gain access to more remote areas of the globe. These muscles are sewn back prior to completing the operation.

Each patient with retinal detachment requires individual preoperative study in order to localize the tears and form a plan of surgical attack. Following surgery, eyes are bandaged for three to four days, after which time the unoperated eye can be exposed. The operated eye may be exposed in ten days to two weeks. If a buckling procedure has been performed, the patient may get out of bed within a week to ten days after surgery; if diathermy coagulation has been the method of treatment, he must remain in bed for three to six weeks. Moreover, pinhole spectacles are necessary after diathermy coagulation but are usually not required if one of the buckling operations has been carried out.

If the retina becomes reattached in six weeks, the chances are excellent that the result will be permanent. If inspec-

270

tion after six weeks shows that reattachment has not taken place, reoperation will in all probability be necessary. However, there are some patients in whom improvement will take place slowly over a period of one year following surgery.

From a technical point of view, operations for retinal detachment are said to be successful if the retina remains reattached. Unfortunately, retinal reattachment is not always accompanied by a restoration of useful vision. Failure of vision to return may be due to injury by diathermy of the vital central area of the eye where acute vision is located. Such injury is sometimes unavoidable if the detachment involves this portion of the retina.

A recent advance in surgery for this condition is the use of the light photocoagulator or the laser light, which can be so controlled as to be focused exactly upon the retinal tear. The effect of the light is to set up an inflammation much in the same manner as diathermy coagulation. Successful use of this method of treatment has been reported from many clinics. With the laser light procedure, the patient can enter the hospital, receive the treatment, and go home the same or the next day. The laser can also be used as an adjunct to other forms of treatment should a retinal tear develop after surgery or when a small tear has been missed in the original operation. The laser has been of especial value in sealing off small tears that would have eventually become large retinal detachments requiring extensive surgery.

Good results in retinal detachment surgery depend upon several factors:

1. **Duration.** The sooner the patient is operated upon, the better the expected result.

2. **Location.** Detachments farther away from central vision give better results than those located near the center of the eye.

3. **Size.** Small detachments give better results than the very large ones.

4. **General state of the retina.** The less the degree of retinal degeneration, the better the postoperative outlook. Generally, the younger the patient, the less the retinal degeneration.

See also EYES; LASER SURGERY.

QUESTIONS AND ANSWERS

What is the retina?
A continuation of the optic nerve which lines the interior of the eyeball. It is the structure that receives the light rays and transmits the impulses to the brain, where they are transformed into sight.

What is retinal detachment?
A separation of the retina from its underlying choroid layer.

What harm does it do?
It interferes with vision by blocking nourishment and oxygen supply to the retina. As it progresses, it may cause blindness.

What causes detachment?
1. Retinal degeneration with associated disease of the fluid (vitreous humor) internal to the retina
2. Injury
3. Retinal degeneration secondary to extreme nearsightedness or arteriosclerosis
4. Tumor of the choroid
5. Inflammations within the eye

Is retinal detachment inherited?
Only in a few instances.

Is it caused by overuse of the eyes or chronic eyestrain?
No.

Can it be cured by medication?
No.

What are the symptoms of detached retina?
1. Sudden, painless appearance of a dark veil before the eye
2. Diffuse fog before the eye, preventing distinct light perception
3. Distortion of the shape of objects before the eyes
4. Flashes of light and spots before the eyes
5. Progressive loss of vision extending over a period of weeks

Does this condition usually affect both eyes?
No. It usually affects one eye only but can affect the second eye eventually.

How is the diagnosis made?
By actual visualization of the detachment by the ophthalmologist when he looks into the eye with an ophthalmoscope.

Can the eye surgeon distinguish between a detached retina secondary to a tumor and one produced by other causes?
Generally, yes.

Must the detached retina always be treated surgically?
Yes.

What if surgery is refused?
1. Untreated detachment will terminate in loss of vision in the eye. The eye will frequently degenerate and may have to be removed because of pain resulting from the degeneration.
2. If a detachment is secondary to a malignant tumor, death will result from spread of the tumor to other parts of the body.

What operations are performed for retinal detachment?
1. Diathermy coagulation (electric needle application) to the sclera overlying the area of the detachment
2. Buckling and other shortening procedures of the eye combined with diathermy coagulation
3. Light coagulation with the laser
4. Freezing (cryosurgery) of the sclera over the area of detachment
5. Removal of the eye (enucleation) in those cases of detached retina caused by malignant tumors

How successful are operations for a malignant choroid tumor?
Following eye removal, approximately 50 percent of all patients will survive for 15 years or more.

How successful is electric diathermy coagulation in operations for detached retina?
About 80 percent of cases are cured by coagulation. The percentage of successes climbs even higher when buckling or shortening procedures are used. With the use of laser light coagulation, approximately 90 percent of tears or holes in the retina can be sealed off.

What percentage of cases of detached retina are due to tumors of the choroid?
About 1 percent.

What anesthesia is used in operating upon retinal detachment?
Local or general anesthesia.

How long after electric coagulation must one stay in bed?
Three to six weeks.

How long after buckling or shortening operative procedures must one stay in bed?
One week to ten days.

How long after light coagulation by the laser must one stay in bed?
One does not have to stay in bed at all after light coagulation.

Are special nurses necessary in retinal detachment surgery?

No.

Must glasses be worn after surgery?

Generally, yes. This will depend largely upon whether glasses were worn prior to surgery.

Are electric coagulation or buckling operations serious?

Yes, as far as vision is concerned. As far as danger to life is concerned, no.

How often is it necessary to reoperate because of failure of the initial operation?

In almost 50 percent of cases when simple electric coagulation has been employed. The need to reoperate has decreased considerably since the introduction of the buckling and other eye-shortening procedures.

How does electric coagulation bring about a cure?

It produces an inflammatory reaction between the detached retina and its underlying choroid layer. As the inflammation subsides over a period of weeks, adhesions are formed and they drag the retina back toward the choroid. The ultimate result of this process is the formation of solid connective tissue which binds the retina and the edges of the tears to the choroid. It might be noted here that when buckling or other eye-shortening procedures are used, diathermy is also used in order to produce an inflammatory reaction.

Does retinal detachment often recur?

Yes, in about 25 percent of cases.

How does one prevent recurrence?

By avoiding injury to the head. The patient should also abstain from strenuous physical exertion such as lifting heavy objects.

Do the size and location of the detachment influence the chances of cure?

Yes. The larger the area of detachment and the nearer it is to the central vision, the more difficult it is to cure.

How soon after diagnosis should an operation be performed?

As soon as possible. Within a period of days.

Is special preoperative preparation necessary?

Remaining flat on the back in bed for two to three days prior to surgery may, in some patients, cause the retina to settle down temporarily and thus improve the chances of accurate coagulation treatment.

How long a hospital stay is necessary?

Two weeks with diathermy coagulation. Seven days with diathermy plus buckling or shortening procedures.

How long does it take to perform diathermy coagulation?

About one hour. Diathermy plus a buckling or shortening procedure may take anywhere from two to four hours.

Is there much pain in the eye after the operation?

No.

Do the eye muscles have to be cut to reach the area to be coagulated or buckled?

Yes, this is often necessary.

Does cutting the muscles cause crossed eyes?

No. The muscle or muscles are stitched back to the sclera before completing the operation, and they will function normally again in almost all instances.

Are special postoperative measures necessary?

The antibiotic drugs are often given

postoperatively to promote good healing without infection.

Are there any visible scars from the ordinary detachment operation?

No.

Is convalescent care required?

Yes, for a period of approximately six weeks after surgery.

Why must a patient remain inactive for so long after the operation?

Because the main purpose of the operation is to get the retina to adhere to the underlying choroid. Movement of the patient, or even excess motion of the eyes, may interfere with this taking place. Inactivity is more essential in diathermy surgery and less necessary in buckling and other shortening procedures which are combined with diathermy.

Does operation ever cause the detachment to become worse?

Very rarely.

How often should one return to the ophthalmologist for a periodic examination following retinal detachment surgery?

Every four to six months.

How soon after electric coagulation can one do the following?

Bathe	3 weeks
Ride in a car	3 to 6 weeks
Drive a car	6 weeks
Perform all duties	8 to 12 weeks
Resume sexual relations	4 to 6 weeks

Deviated Septum

A deviated septum is a deflection or crookedness in the wall that separates the two portions of the nose. It is often accompanied by inability to breathe through one or both nostrils.

Deviated septum and other deformities of the nasal septum are developmental in origin in the great majority of cases. If the septal deformity interferes with proper nasal respiration or obstructs the openings into the sinuses, it should be corrected surgically.

Corrective operations, called submucous resection, are performed in the hospital with local anesthesia. An incision is made just inside one nostril through its lining membrane and septal cartilage but not through the lining membrane of the other nostril. The lining membrane is then elevated from both sides of the septum, and any spurs, or deflected portions of cartilage or bone, are removed. Vaseline gauze packing is then inserted into the nasal cavities to keep the lining membrane against the lining membrane of the opposite side and to control bleeding. These operations are highly successful in almost all cases. Hospitalization need only be for two to four days, and recovery is prompt. Poor results are encountered mainly in those cases where surgery was not actually indicated.

See also NOSE AND SINUSES.

QUESTIONS AND ANSWERS

What is a deviated nasal septum?

The nasal septum is the partition in the nose that divides it into two chambers. It is composed of cartilage and bone. When this partition is crooked and not in the midline, it is called a deviated or deflected septum.

What causes a septum to become deviated?

Many cases are due to faulty development. However, injuries to the nose,

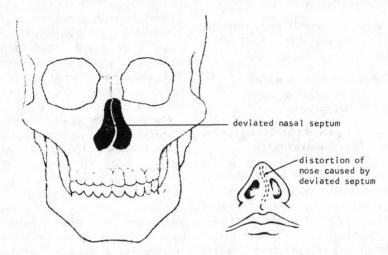

deviated nasal septum

distortion of
nose caused by
deviated septum

Deviated septum is a common condition affecting the nose. It may occur as a result of injury or it may be present from birth. A markedly deviated septum interferes with normal breathing and should be corrected surgically.

such as dislocation or fracture, can cause the formation of this defect.

Does the presence of a deviated septum cause symptoms?

Usually not. Many people have markedly deflected septums without nasal blockage. When there are symptoms, they take the form of blockage of the free and easy passage of air through one or both nostrils, headaches, or both.

How can a deviated septum that causes nasal blockage be corrected?

This is corrected by performing an operation known as submucous resection of the nasal septum.

Is a submucous resection a dangerous operation?

No. The operation is performed through an intranasal incision. The membranes on either side of the bony and cartilaginous septum are elevated, and spurs, ridges, and deformed sections of the bone and cartilage are cut

away. The operation is performed under local anesthesia.

At what age should submucous resection be carried out?

As this is an elective operation, it should not be done until the nasal bones have developed full growth, usually when the patient is about 17 years of age or older.

How successful are operations for deviated septum?

In well-selected cases, the results are exceptionally good.

Are there any complications to this operation?

Very rarely, there may be bleeding when the nasal packing is taken out. This can be readily controlled by the surgeon.

How soon after an operation for a deviated septum can one return to work?

Usually within 10 to 14 days.

How long a period of hospitalization is necessary?

Two to four days.

Is an operation for deviated septum very painful?

No.

How soon after submucous resection can one breathe normally again?

Within five to ten days.

Is there a visible scar following operation for deviated septum?

No.

Is a submucous resection operation ever performed at the same time as a plastic operation to improve the appearance of the nose?

Yes. The two procedures are often combined and done at the same time.

Are the results of a plastic operation upon the nose affected by the presence of a deviated septum?

No. However, when a plastic surgeon notes the presence of a deviated septum, he may repair it at the same time.

Diaphragmatic and Hiatus Hernias

Diaphragmatic and hiatus hernias are extremely common defects which take place most frequently alongside the point where the esophagus (foodpipe) passes through the diaphragm from the chest into the abdomen. Some diaphragmatic hernias result from lack of development of the diaphragm or from rupture of the diaphragm due to an injury. These hernias are characterized by abdominal organs, such as a portion of the stomach, small intestines, or large bowel, entering the defect and lodging in the chest cavity.

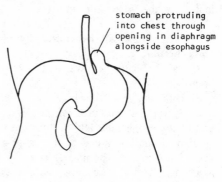

DIAPHRAGMATIC (HIATAL) HERNIA

stomach protruding into chest through opening in diaphragm alongside esophagus

QUESTIONS AND ANSWERS

What is a hiatus hernia?

This is a form of diaphragmatic hernia in which a portion of the stomach protrudes into the chest cavity through the aperture created by the esophagus (foodpipe) as it leads into the abdominal cavity.

How is the diagnosis of a hiatus hernia made?

By taking x-rays of a patient after he has swallowed barium.

Is a hiatus hernia a common type of hernia?

It is exceptionally common, and occurs in a sizable number of people who are in their 40s, 50s, and older.

Is hiatus hernia more common in people past 60 years of age?

Yes. It is estimated that almost 10 percent of all people over 70 develop a small hiatus hernia.

Are symptoms always present when someone has a hiatus hernia?

No. As a matter of fact, relatively few people with a hiatus hernia have symptoms, and the diagnosis is made

SURGICAL CONDITIONS AND PROCEDURES

frequently on a routine x-ray examination of the upper intestinal tract.

What symptoms can be caused by a hiatus hernia?
1. Pain beneath the lower end of the breastbone.
2. Difficulty in swallowing.
3. Symptoms of an ulcer of the lower end of the esophagus. This is due to irritation of the lower end of the esophagus following the hernia. It is often associated with a burning sensation, belching, and acid eructation.
4. Bleeding from the lower end of the esophagus or stomach.

Must everyone with hiatus hernia be operated upon?
No. The great majority of these cases have no symptoms and therefore will not require surgery.

When is surgery for hiatus hernia indicated?
1. When there is severe and repeated hemorrhage from the stomach or esophagus
2. When nutrition is interfered with by obstruction of the passage of food
3. When pain is unbearable and is repeated over a prolonged period
4. When a portion of the stomach becomes caught in the hernial sac and is not released

Is there a tendency for hiatus hernia to recur once it has been operated upon?
Only in about 10 percent of cases.

What is the treatment of hiatus hernia in people over 60?
About one out of four who have this type of hernia have no symptoms at all. No treatment is necessary for them. Another 25 percent have very mild symptoms that require little or no treatment.

Still another 25 percent have symptoms that are like those of a stomach ulcer or an inflammation of the gallbladder. A few people have symptoms that are like those of angina pectoris (pain in the heart region). The treatment of all the above should consist of:
1. Eating only small quantities of food at one time
2. Walking or standing for about half an hour after each meal
3. Sleeping propped up on pillows
4. Eating a diet free of greasy, fried, highly seasoned foods
5. Taking milk and antacids if symptoms similar to those of an ulcer are present
6. Reducing, if the patient is overweight
The last 25 percent have symptoms severe enough to make surgery advisable. These people may develop an ulcer of the lower end of the esophagus or the upper end of the stomach at the point of herniation. Such ulcers may be accompanied by severe pain and may hemorrhage dangerously. Others may develop chronic irritation (esophagitis) causing narrowing of the esophagus and obstruction to the passage of food.

Is recovery the general rule after surgery for hiatus hernia?
Yes.

When is an abdominal incision indicated in operating upon a hiatus hernia?
When the surgeon suspects that along with the hiatus hernia there is associated abdominal disease. It is not at all uncommon for an ulcer of the duodenum to be present along with hiatus hernia.

Is it more dangerous to operate through an incision in the chest?
No, but an incision into the chest

cavity is a more extensive operation than an abdominal incision. It should be noted that it is easier technically for a surgeon to repair a hernia of the diaphragm through the chest than through the abdomen.

How is the diagnosis of a diaphragmatic hernia made in a child?

From the time of birth, the child may appear to be short of breath and thus may have a bluish discoloration of his skin. Along with this, there may be regurgitation and vomiting at feedings. On listening to the chest, the pediatrician may hear the gurgling sounds usually associated with the movement of fluids within the stomach or intestinal tract. The diagnosis is usually confirmed by taking an x-ray and noting the presence of the stomach, small bowel, or large bowel within the chest cavity.

What is the treatment for a diaphragmatic hernia found at birth?

Immediate surgery is necessary to prevent the child from dying. An upper abdominal incision is made, and the rent or defect in the diaphragm is closed with sutures. If a large number of bowel loops or abdominal organs were protruding into the chest cavity, the abdominal cavity may prove to be too small to contain them after the rent in the diaphragm has been closed. When such a situation exists, the skin and subcutaneous tissues are closed over the intestines, but no attempt is made to close the muscular layers of the abdominal wall. This will produce an incisional hernia, which can be repaired when the child is several months older.

What are the chances for recovery following an operation on a newborn for a diaphragmatic hernia?

If the newborn has been operated on early and if expert surgical care has been rendered, more than 90 percent of these children should recover.

What can be done if one portion of the diaphragm failed to develop, causing abdominal organs to be pushed up into the chest cavity?

In these cases, although there may not be any muscle tissue in the diaphragm, there is, most often, a thin fibrous membrane. Here, an artificial diaphragm can be created by using a plastic material instead of the normal diaphragm. This material (Marlex or Mercelline) is sutured over the thin membrane separating the chest from the abdominal cavity. As time progresses, this will become a thick membrane and will keep the abdominal organs down in the abdominal cavity.

What is the treatment for a hole in the diaphragm due to an injury?

Surgical repair should be carried out. This is done through an incision in the chest or the abdominal cavity. In these cases, the organs that have extended up into the chest are reposited in the abdomen, and the hole in the diaphragm is sutured tightly.

What causes a diaphragmatic hernia that is not of the hiatus type?

A diaphragmatic hernia is usually caused by a birth defect in the formation of the large muscle known as the diaphragm. This defect will permit some of the abdominal contents to protrude up into the chest. The most common organs to be found in the chest are the stomach, the small intestine, the large intestines, and the spleen. When the diaphragmatic hernia is located on the right side of the body, part of the liver may protrude into the chest cavity.

Is inflammation of the esophagus (esophagitis) often associated with hiatus hernia?

Yes. Also, as a result of prolonged

inflammation of the esophagus, an ulcer may develop. This is caused by acid juices from the stomach regurgitating into the esophagus.

Will a person with hiatus hernia develop symptoms from an inflammation or ulcer of the esophagus?

Yes. Burning, difficulty in swallowing, and indigestion may result.

Is surgery for repair of a hiatus hernia indicated when a patient hemorrhages severely?

If a patient has more than one marked hemorrhage associated with hiatus hernia, it is an indication for surgery to be performed. Some of these hemorrhages, especially in older people, can endanger life.

Is surgical repair of a hiatus hernia indicated when the patient develops an esophageal ulcer?

Yes. This is one of the prime indications for surgical intervention.

Should an obese person lose weight prior to being operated upon for a hiatus hernia?

Yes, if it is at all possible. The recurrence rate following surgery is vastly greater among fat people than among those of normal weight.

Is there any way to prevent a hiatus hernia?

No.

Is there any way to prevent a diaphragmatic hernia?

No, except insofar as certain diaphragmatic hernias result from violent and strenuous physical activity. A sudden strain while lifting a heavy object from the ground level is a cause for diaphragmatic strain and possible rupture. Such activity should be performed only by those who are in proper physical condition for strenuous labor.

Can a diaphragmatic hernia or hiatus hernia be repaired a second time if it has recurred?

Yes, and the chances of the second recurrence are great unless the patient is thin and in good physical condition.

Is hiatus hernia often seen in association with an ulcer of the duodenum?

Yes, for some unknown reason this combination of conditions is often encountered. It is one of the main reasons why the abdominal surgical approach to the repair of a hiatus hernia is indicated. When a hiatus hernia is repaired through an incision in the chest cavity, it is not possible to treat the ulcer surgically.

What is an "upside-down stomach"?

It is a lay term for a diaphragmatic hernia in which the stomach is in the chest cavity. Since the stomach usually rotates in an upward direction when it protrudes into the chest cavity, it assumes an "upside-down" position.

Diet

The state of nutrition plays an important role in surgery. Poorly nourished tissues heal slowly after surgery; and where malnutrition is marked, failure to heal may result. It is vital that a patient who is to undergo elective surgery be in a satisfactory state of nutrition and that his body contain normal quantities of essential vitamins and minerals. For this reason, blood tests are taken preoperatively to note the adequacy of protein, sugar, and chemical substances. It is especially dangerous to operate upon a patient with inadequate blood proteins or low quantities of vitamins B, C, and K. Similarly, one should not perform elective surgery upon a patient with deficient sodium, chloride, potassium, or other minerals.

Unfortunately, some patients must be operated upon immediately because of the acute nature of their disease. If they are out of nutritional balance at the time, immediate steps must be taken to reestablish normal levels. This is carried out preoperatively by the administration of blood transfusions, plasma, or the intravenous infusion of proteins, sugar, and chemicals such as chloride, sodium, and potassium. Various vitamins may also be given. It is often necessary to give these substances rapidly and in large quantities over a period of a few days in order to ready the patient for his surgical procedure.

Since patients may not be able to resume normal diet soon after major surgery, essential nutriments are given by intravenous feedings of sugar, vitamins, and minerals. Then, as recovery takes place, patients resume the oral intake of essential nutriments.

Although surgeons frequently rely upon artificial means of establishing normal nutrition, it is always better, if possible, to feed the preoperative and postoperative patient by natural means. Therefore, intravenous feedings and medications are limited to those who cannot eat or drink naturally.

QUESTIONS AND ANSWERS

Are nourishing substances such as sugar, protein, and essential vitamins and minerals always given to patients intravenously?

No. Whenever patients are able to take nourishment by mouth, it is preferred. Artificial intravenous medications and feedings are restricted to those who cannot take nourishment by mouth.

How soon after a major operative procedure are people permitted to eat and drink?

This will depend upon the part of the body that has been operated upon. If the operation involves the gastrointestinal tract, feedings may be withheld for three, four, or even more days. However, if the chest has been operated upon, or if the operation is unrelated to the digestive tract, patients may be given fluids to drink within several hours after surgery, and they may be permitted to eat the following day.

Should overweight people try to lose weight prior to undergoing elective surgery?

Yes. Obese patients take anesthesia less well than those of normal weight. Moreover, wounds heal more slowly in those who are obese.

Is it essential that people have an adequate vitamin intake prior to surgery?

Yes. Wound healing is particularly slow among those who may have a vitamin B or C deficiency. Also, people who lack vitamin K are more apt to develop bleeding tendencies postoperatively.

Should undernourished people attempt to attain normal weight before undergoing elective surgery?

Yes. Wound healing is markedly retarded by malnutrition.

Dilatation and Curettage

Dilatation and curettage is an operative procedure performed upon the cavity of the uterus through the vagina.

It consists of scraping out the lining of the uterus after dilatation of the cervix. Special instruments are used to dilate the cervix; uterine dilators and special instruments known as curettes are used to scrape out the uterine cavity.

It is necessary to dilate the cervix in order for the curetting instrument to be inserted, and for this reason, the procedure is usually known by the abbreviation "D and C." Curettage is done in a hospital under light general anesthesia. A hospital stay of one to two days is all that is necessary. There are no, or minimal, aftereffects apart from slight vaginal bleeding for a few days.

Dilatation of the cervix alone without curettage may be indicated in certain cases in which the cervical canal is narrowed to a point of causing severe discomfort during menstrual periods. This condition is almost entirely limited to women who have borne no children, as the process of childbearing results in permanent widening of the canal's passageway. Simple cervical dilatation can sometimes be performed in the gynecologist's office or, more usually, in a hospital under general anesthesia. Results of this procedure are uniformly good in patients in whom the menstrual pain was due primarily to the narrowed cervical canal.

Curettage, or scraping out of the uterine cavity, is performed for a variety of reasons:

1. Diagnostic purposes: To get a specimen of the lining of the uterus (endometrium) and subject it to microscopic examination in order:

a) To tell if a growth is developing within the body of the uterus.

b) To diagnose the cause for upset in the regular menstrual cycle.

c) To discover the cause for inability to become pregnant.

d) To spot the origin of excessive menstrual bleeding.

e) To establish the cause for failure to menstruate.

2. Therapeutic purposes, or as a method of treatment:

a. Miscarriage: When a woman has miscarried during the first few months of pregnancy, the products of conception and the overgrown lining of the uterine cavity may not have been completely expelled. It is then necessary to scrape and clean out the cavity of the uterus.

b. In certain tumors of the body of the uterus, radium is utilized by placing it for a number of hours within the uterine cavity. Prior to doing this, the lining is usually scraped out.

c. Endometrial hyperplasia or endometrial polyps. Curettage is done in these benign conditions characterized by overgrowth of the lining of the uterine cavity.

QUESTIONS AND ANSWERS

What is a curettage?

This is an operation performed upon the cavity of the uterus through the vagina. It consists of scraping out the lining membrane of the uterus. Special instruments are used to dilate the cervix and to scrape out the uterine cavity.

Why is curettage performed?

1. For diagnostic purposes.

2. For therapeutic purposes.

3. A curettage is often diagnostic and therapeutic at the same time, as in cases of hyperplasia or polyps of the uterus.

When is a diagnostic curettage performed?

1. In cases of unexplained uterine bleeding.

2. In cases in which a polyp of the uterine cavity is suspected.

3. In cases in which a cancer of the body of the uterus is suspected.

4. In cases in which tuberculosis of the lining of the uterus is suspected.

When is a therapeutic curettage performed?

1. When a disorder, such as a polyp, of the lining membrane of the uterus has already been diagnosed, curettage may result in a cure.

2. When an overgrowth of the lining membrane of the uterus (endometrial hyperplasia) has been diagnosed, a curettage will often bring about a cure.

3. Following a miscarriage, when parts of the fetus or placenta remain behind. Curettage in such instances will clean out the cavity and thus restore normalcy.

How long a hospital stay is necessary following curettage?

Approximately one to two days.

Are there any visible incisions following curettage?

No. It is done completely through the vagina.

How soon after the curettage can one return to work?

Within one week.

What restrictions must be followed after curettage?

Douching and intercourse must not be performed for two to four weeks.

What is another name for curettage?

It is commonly called a "D and C" operation. This stands for dilatation and curettage.

Is D and C a painful operation?

No. It is performed under general anesthesia in the hospital.

Is D and C a dangerous operation?

No. When performed in a hospital by a competent gynecologist, it is perfectly safe.

Can normal pregnancy take place after a curettage?

Yes. A curettage performed by a competent gynecologist in a hospital will not interfere with subsequent pregnancies.

Can endometrial polyps be removed through curettage?

Yes. Also, whenever they protrude through the cervix into the vagina, they can be removed by clamping or crushing with an instrument inserted through the vagina.

Is it necessary to perform a dilatation and curettage in order to take a biopsy of the lining of the uterus?

No. The taking of a biopsy is an office procedure and is performed simply by the insertion of a special instrument through the vagina and cervix into the uterine cavity. A very tiny piece of tissue is all that must be removed in order to ensure a satisfactory microscopic examination.

Is a curettage always necessary following a miscarriage?

No. If all the tissue has been expelled and bleeding is minimal, it may not be necessary. However, many gynecologists feel it is best for the procedure to be done after every miscarriage in order to be certain that the uterine cavity is cleaned of all debris.

Dislocations

See ACROMIOCLAVICULAR JOINT SEPARATION; FRACTURES; JOINTS.

Diverticulosis and Diverticulitis

Diverticulosis is a condition in which there are weaknesses in the muscular wall of the bowel which permit pouches of mucous membrane to sag through. Diverticula are found most frequently in the sigmoid colon, although they may be found anywhere throughout the entire length of the large bowel. It is estimated that 5 to 10 percent of all people have diverticula but that symptoms are encountered only when they become inflamed or when fecal matter becomes stuck in them. Inflammation of these outpouchings is termed diverticulitis.

Diverticulitis produces abdominal pain over the site of the diverticula (usually in the left lower part of the abdomen) and is accompanied by fever and abdominal tenderness. A soft, low-residue, bland diet, bed rest, and antibiotics are instituted for this ailment. Surgery is reserved for the severe cases in which an abscess has formed or the bowel has ruptured or has become obstructed. In such cases, the abdomen is opened and the pus is drained. Occasionally a colostomy will be performed to relieve obstruction.

Fortunately, the majority of patients with diverticulitis will recover without surgery. However, if there are repeated attacks it is advisable to operate and remove the involved portion of bowel. *See also* INTESTINES.

QUESTIONS AND ANSWERS

What is a diverticulum of the large intestine?

It is a protrusion of a small portion of the mucous membrane that lines the

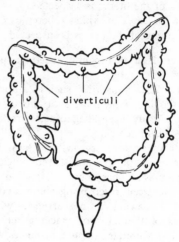

CONGENITAL DIVERTICULOSIS
OF LARGE BOWEL

diverticuli

large bowel through the muscle wall of the bowel. The outpouching, or protrusion, gives the appearance of a pea or grape. Diverticula are analogous to blisters on an automobile tire.

What is diverticulosis?

It is a condition in which there are many diverticula protruding from the wall of the large bowel.

What causes diverticula to form in older people?

They are thought to be caused by a progressive weakness in the musculature of the bowel, aggravated by chronic constipation.

How frequent is diverticulosis in people in their later years?

It is estimated that approximately 10 percent of all people in their late 60s or 70s will develop some diverticula of the large intestine.

Does diverticulosis always produce symptoms?

No. The great majority of people with diverticulosis have no symptoms, and the diagnosis is made incidentally during the course of a routine x-ray examination of the lower intestinal tract.

What is diverticulitis?

It is an inflammation of a diverticulum.

What are the symptoms of diverticulitis?

Since the left portion of the colon is most frequently involved, there is usually pain in the lower left part of the abdomen. When pressure is applied to this area, there are pain and spasm of the abdominal muscles. The patient may also have temperature, constipation, nausea, and vomiting. In some cases, there is bleeding from the rectum. Occasionally, an inflamed diverticulum will rupture, causing peritonitis or the formation of an abscess within the abdominal cavity.

What causes a diverticulum to become inflamed?

Usually, inflammation is caused by the accumulation of hard stool in the diverticulum.

Is diverticulitis very common in older people?

Is is estimated that approximately one in ten of those who have diverticulosis will at some time or other develop diverticulitis.

Do most cases of diverticulitis subside spontaneously or do they require surgery?

Most cases subside with medical treatment over a period of a week or two.

What medical advice should be followed by those who have diverticulosis?

1. They should make every attempt to have regular bowel movements. Lubricants or laxatives should be taken when necessary.

2. Food containing large amounts of roughage, highly seasoned foods, and large quantities of alcoholic beverages should be avoided.

3. If abdominal pain develops, the doctor should be consulted.

Do people with diverticulosis ever hemorrhage from a diverticulum?

Yes, once in a while. This is not a common occurrence, however.

How can one distinguish between diverticulitis and a tumor of the large bowel?

A barium enema x-ray will make the distinction in the great majority of cases. Also, some tumors of the area can be seen directly through a sigmoidoscope.

What is the treatment for diverticulitis?

If a diverticulum is mildly inflamed, or if several of them are mildly inflamed, the patient is taken off food by mouth and is fed intravenously. Antibiotics are given to control the infection. As the inflammation subsides, usually after hospitalization, the patient recovers spontaneously. If, on the other hand, an abscess has formed, or if the inflammation does not subside, surgery becomes necessary.

What surgery is recommended for diverticulitis that does not respond to medical treatment?

1. If the patient is in satisfactory general health, the inflamed segment of bowel is removed and the bowel's continuity is reestablished.

2. If peritonitis has resulted from the diverticulitis, it is necessary to drain the abdominal cavity and to perform a temporary colostomy (opening of the bowel onto the abdominal wall) rather than to attempt removal of the bowel segment in the presence of severe infection.

3. When a drainage procedure and colostomy have been performed, it is necessary to wait several weeks for the peritonitis to subside. Then the patient

is brought back to the hospital for removal of the diseased segment of bowel.

4. Several weeks after the second operation, the patient is again operated on to close the colostomy, thus reestablishing the normal continuity of the bowel.

Is recovery usual after surgery for diverticulitis?

Yes. In a great majority of cases, the patient makes complete recovery from this type of surgery, although three major operations over a period of several weeks or months may be required.

Does diverticulitis lead to cancer?

No, although sometimes both are present simultaneously.

Does diverticulitis ever recur after surgery?

Yes, unless the diseased loops of bowel have been removed.

What are the chances for recovery and cure after operation?

Well over 95 percent.

Are special hospital preparations required before operation?

Yes. Delayed operation is preferable to permit the antibiotic drugs to take effect and to allow the acute inflammation to subside.

Feedings and medications are given through the veins instead of by mouth. The intestinal tract is kept empty and deflated with stomach and intestinal tubes.

How long a hospital stay is necessary?

Usually two to three weeks.

What type of anesthesia is used?

General anesthesia and, in some cases, spinal anesthesia.

Where is the usual site of incision?

In the left lower part of the abdomen.

How long do these operations take to perform?

Simple surgical drainage, one half to three quarters of an hour. Drainage plus a colostomy, about one hour. Bowel removal, two to four hours.

Are blood transfusions necessary?

Only in those patients upon whom removal of the diseased bowel is to be carried out.

Are special nurses advisable after operation?

Yes, if the patient can afford them. Three to four days is usually long enough.

Does one have to follow a special diet after surgery?

Yes, a bland diet, low in roughage. The patient should avoid spices and alcoholic beverages.

How often should one be rechecked after surgery?

If the bowel has not been removed, checkups should be done every few months.

Is length of life affected by diverticulosis?

No. The presence of diverticulosis has no effect upon length of life.

Dumping Syndrome

The set of symptoms known as the dumping syndrome includes flushing of the skin, profuse sweating, palpitation of the heart, and occasional nausea or diarrhea, occurring anywhere from 15 minutes to an hour after eating a meal. The syndrome is seen in those who have undergone surgery upon the stomach, usually with removal of part of the stomach, for an ulcer of the duodenum, an ulcer of the stomach, or a stomach tumor.

The dumping syndrome was much more common when the operation of choice for ulcer was extensive removal of the stomach. Today, this procedure is not often done for ulcer, and has been largely replaced by vagotomy with the removal of only forty to fifty percent of the stomach.

The incidence of the dumping syndrome following stomach removal is variously reported as ranging from 4 to 15 percent of those operated upon. It has been noted that the more neurotic the patient, the more likely is he to develop the symptoms attributed to the dumping syndrome.

There have been several theories to explain the cause for the dumping syndrome. Perhaps the one held most widely is that the symptoms result from the sudden thrust of undigested food from the small stump of remaining stomach directly into the intestinal tract. It is thought that this may result in the outpouring of large amounts of insulin with consequent hypoglycemia (too little sugar in the blood). Thus, the symptoms attributed to the dumping syndrome are in reality similar to insulin shock where an excess of insulin burns up a great amount of blood sugar in a very short period of time.

The treatment of the dumping syndrome is not specific and must be a trial and error procedure. Most patients who have these symptoms will tend to lose them after the passage of several months or a year or two from the time of operation. They should be urged not to eat too large a meal at any one time and to eat slowly and chew thoroughly. Also, they should be advised to drink fluids at times other than when they are eating the major part of their solids. Lastly, the symptoms of the dumping syndrome seem to be much less if the patient will lie down for a half to three quarters of an hour after eating. Because the dumping syndrome is thought to be associated with an outpouring of insulin, many physicians feel that the patient should eat a low-carbohydrate diet.

There have been several rather intricate operations performed to relieve the dumping syndrome but these have not proved to be uniformly successful. Moreover, they are serious operations and should not be embarked upon unless the symptoms are so severe that they make life intolerable for the patient.

See also STOMACH AND DUODENUM.

Duodenal Ulcer

See STOMACH AND DUODENUM.

Dupuytren's Contracture

Dupuytren's contracture is a thickening, tightening, and contraction of the tissue fibers that lie beneath the skin of the palm. It affects men much more often than women and occurs most frequently during the middle years of life. Over a period of months or years, the fibrous tissue of the palm thickens and forms cords which extend to the fingers and pull them down into the palm. The little and ring fingers are most frequently affected, but the middle finger is also involved at times. The thumb and index fingers are practically never afflicted by this type of contracture.

Although injury has long been suspected as the cause for this crippling condition, it has never been proved, and many investigators think that the condition is inherited.

This type of contracture does not involve tendons or nerves, and the surgical removal of the overgrown fibrous tissues will not jeopardize motion or sensation in the hand. If surgery is done early, the contracted tissue can be removed with relative ease. Later the skin and joints of the hand may become so tightened that grafts and skin rotation procedures may have to be undertaken.

QUESTIONS AND ANSWERS

What operative procedure is carried out for Dupuytren's contracture?

An incision is made on the palm of the hand and all of the overgrown fibrous tissue is excised. Care is taken not to injure the ligaments that lie beneath the superficial layer of the palm.

Are operations for Dupuytren's contracture dangerous?

No, but they are sometimes long, tedious procedures that may take an hour or two before all of the excess fibrous tissue can be dissected out and removed.

Are the results of operations for Dupuytren's contracture usually good?

Yes. Every once in a while there may be a recurrence, but even if this does take place, reoperation will effect a cure.

Can full use of the hand be regained after operation for Dupuytren's contracture?

In most instances, yes. There are some cases, though, where the finger has been bent down for so long a time that there is a contracture of the ligaments above the finger joints. It may be necessary, in these cases, to do further

procedures to mobilize the joint capsules and to operate to regain normal joint function of the digit.

Is it ever necessary to use a skin graft when operating for Dupuytren's contracture?

Yes. If the condition has gone on for many years, the skin is sometimes so overgrown by fibrous tissue that in such cases a segment of skin may have to be removed and be replaced by a skin graft from some other part of the body.

Is it ever necessary to cut away tendons when operating for Dupuytren's contracture?

No. The condition involves the fibrous tissue that lies superficial to the tendons, and the tendons themselves are not involved.

What will happen if Dupuytren's contracture goes untreated?

Some cases progress so far that the finger is bent down completely onto the palm of the hand. In some of these cases, the contracture will cause such constriction of the joints that the finger will become a useless digit.

Ears

PLASTIC SURGERY OF THE EARS

Some unfortunate children are born with deformities of the ears. The most common ones are as follows:

1. Protruding or folded ears
2. Lop ears
3. Deformities of the external ear
4. Deformities of the external ear canal

The shape of the ears tends to be an

inherited characteristic, so that one often sees several members of one family who have protruding ears, lop ears, or other deformities.

There is no need for anyone to suffer continued embarrassment and self-consciousness because of protruding or folded ears. These deformities can be corrected readily by simple, effective operations which cause very little pain or discomfort.

Some children are born with protruding or folded ears. They are not caused, as some parents think, by the infant lying upon the ears when they are in a folded position. Although protruding or folded ears are usually present on both sides, occasionally there is involvement of one side only.

Ears normally are set at about a 25-degree angle from the skull. They may protrude, due to cartilage deformities, to such an extent that they form a right angle to the side of the head. Another variation is the so-called lop ear, in which the ear is bent upon itself.

The best age at which to perform corrective surgery is about 13 to 14 years, when the ear has attained almost maximum growth and when the procedure can be carried out under local Novocain anesthesia. However, it is psychologically wiser to operate before the child reaches school age, and is subjected to the ridicule of his classmates. In this event, general anesthesia will be used.

The operative procedure for protruding ears consists of removing an elliptical section of skin and cartilage from the angle which is formed between the ear and the skull. This is done through an incision in back of the ear. As only the skin on the back of the ear is removed, the skin overlying the cartilage on the outer surface of the ear will appear excessive and wrinkled after completion of this operation. Over a

period of a few months this effect will disappear.

The operation for a folded or lop ear is quite similar except that the elliptical removal of skin and cartilage takes place farther out on the back surface of the ear.

The edges of cartilage surrounding the removed section are sutured together, and the skin wound is restitched with silk sutures. A firm dressing is applied to maintain the new position, and the ear is bandaged snugly to the side of the head. These dressings are left in place for about ten days until solid healing has occurred. They are then taken off and the sutures are removed.

Considerable swelling may follow these operations but assurance should be given that it will disappear within a few weeks or months. Complications of these procedures are seen only rarely and consist of:

1. **Hemorrhage beneath the skin,** which may result in deforming blood clots.

2. **Postoperative wound infection:** If this occurs, it will be corrected by giving appropriate doses of antibiotic drugs.

The cosmetic result of these operations is excellent and in those exceedingly rare instances in which the end result is not too satisfactory, a second operation can bring about correction. *See also* DEAFNESS; MASTOIDECTOMY.

QUESTIONS AND ANSWERS

Will an infant develop deformed ears because he lies upon them when they are in a folded position?

No. This is a common misconception.

Are folded and lop ears seen on one side only?

Yes, but there are many more cases in which both ears are misshapen.

Is hearing disturbed by deformities of the external ear?

No.

Will plastic surgery upon the external ear influence hearing?

No.

Can large ears be made smaller?

Yes, through plastic surgery.

Is plastic surgery upon the ears difficult?

No. The only difficult case is when the external ear is totally or partially lacking. In such an instance, very complicated skin grafting is required to create a new external ear.

At what age should a child be operated upon for correction of deformed ears?

When the child is old enough to cooperate and not disturb his bandages. This means usually just before school age, between the ages of 4 and 6. Some surgeons advocate not operating upon these children until they reach the age of 13 or 14.

What operative procedure is carried out for protruding or lop ears?

An elliptical skin incision is made behind the ear and an elliptical section of skin and cartilage is removed. The skin edges are then sutured one to the other, which brings the ear back into normal position and appearance. A firm dressing is applied so that the ear will remain in its new position, the head is snugly bandaged, and the bandages are left in place for about ten days, until solid healing has taken place.

Is there any swelling of the ear following these operations?

Yes, but this will disappear within a few days to several weeks.

Are the cosmetic results of these operations good?

Yes. In the great majority of cases they are excellent.

What anesthesia is used for operations of this type?

For children, general anesthesia. For adults, local anesthesia.

Are the scars of these operations visible?

No, as the incisions are behind the ears in the folds of the skin lines.

How long a period of hospitalization is necessary?

From two to five days.

If the results are not perfectly satisfactory, can these operations be done over again?

Yes. Reoperation may correct residual deformities.

Will strapping a child's folded and protruding ears cure them?

No, because the underlying birth deformity in the cartilage cannot be cured by the application of a bandage.

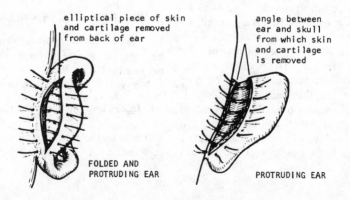

elliptical piece of skin
and cartilage removed
from back of ear

FOLDED AND
PROTRUDING EAR

angle between
ear and skull
from which skin
and cartilage
is removed

PROTRUDING EAR

CONGENITAL DEFORMITIES OF THE EAR

What are some other birth deformities of the ears besides protruding and lop ears?

1. Absence of the external ear canal. This is usually accompanied by maldevelopment of the middle ear, although the inner ear, which controls the sense of balance, is usually intact.

2. Absence of the external ear. In these cases, if there is a normally developed external ear canal, middle ear, and inner ear, hearing is not greatly interfered with.

3. Minor deformities of the external ear such as absent parts or extra tabs of tissue. Can usually be corrected through plastic surgery.

4. A branchial cyst remnant in front of the ear. This represents failure of one of the gill slits to close during life of the embryo. It will be diagnosed by a small opening usually in front of the ear. This may require surgery when the child has matured somewhat.

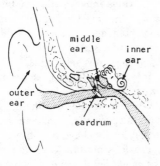

Sound waves received by the external ear are transmitted through the ear canal and the middle ear to nerves in the inner ear, which send impulses to the brain.

How common are these congenital deformities of the ear?

Absence of the external ear canal occurs in approximately one in two thousand cases of ear disease. Absence of the whole external ear is quite rare, but one does see partial deformities in the formation of the external ear. Both of these deformities are more likely to occur on one side than on both sides.

Can surgery be helpful for congenital deformities of the ear?

To construct an external ear canal in these cases is usually not of great value, since hearing cannot be restored. This is due to the fact that the eardrum and the middle ear are usually underdeveloped. There are extensive plastic operations for the construction of a new external ear; these operations may be worthwhile psychologically, but the ultimate results are not too acceptable from a cosmetic point of view.

RUPTURED EARDRUM

What is a ruptured eardrum?

An eardrum with a hole in it, usually as a result of a middle ear infection.

Will a ruptured eardrum cause diminished hearing?

Yes, if the perforation remains permanently.

Do holes in eardrums tend to close spontaneously?

Yes. Sometimes they do not, but there are methods of treatment that will result in closure in many cases.

If a child has a ruptured eardrum, how old must he be before an operation can be performed?

About 4 to 5 years old. This is when social problems with swimming and other activities can arise. In children younger than 4 there may be technical difficulties with the operation.

Are there any operations to repair a ruptured eardrum?

Yes. Operations known as myringoplasty or tympanoplasty can effect a satisfactory closure.

Should someone with a chronically ruptured eardrum go swimming?

Yes, but he should wear a bathing cap or use earplugs. Furthermore, he should be instructed not to dive or swim underwater. Despite precautions, water may get through perforated drums, and, because of possible infection, it might be advisable to prohibit swimming completely in some cases.

Is there any nonsurgical way to repair a ruptured eardrum?

If there is no continuing infection in the middle ear and no discharge through the hole in the drum, it is often possible to close the hole by cauterizing. The margins of the perforation are touched with trichloroacetic acid, and a patch is placed over the perforation. This may have to be done several times before the hole closes completely. If infection persists, the perforation will not heal by itself.

PIERCED EARS

Is it safe to have ear lobes pierced?

Yes, but it should be done by a surgeon, as infection can sometimes result.

Is the piercing of ears painful?

No. Ear lobes are quite insensitive to pain, and the piercing hurts little more than an injection for vaccination.

What should be done if the ear lobes become infected after being pierced?

Warm, wet compresses should be applied to the ear lobes, and the doctor will probably prescribe antibiotic drugs.

At what age can ears be pierced?

At any age, but it is wisest to do it when an individual is very young, before she begins to play in dirt. It can also be done when the child is an adolescent.

Do the holes tend to close down?

Yes. To ensure that the holes in the ear lobes remain open, earrings must be worn most of the time.

Should all those who wear earrings remove them during physical activity?

Yes; the lobe can be injured if the earring catches on something.

Ectopic Pregnancy

An ectopic (tubal) pregnancy occurs when a fertilized egg is trapped in a fallopian tube instead of passing through the tube into the uterus. When this happens, the embryo grows in this abnormal location and distends the tube. Within a few weeks, the patient will develop lower abdominal pain and slight vaginal staining.

See also FALLOPIAN TUBES.

QUESTIONS AND ANSWERS

What causes ectopic (tubal) pregnancy?

1. **Previous inflammation of the tube** is by far the most common cause of ectopic pregnancy. Approximately 25 percent of all cases occur in women who have had previous salpingitis.

2. **Infection following abortion,** or following the delivery of a child.

3. **Ovarian or uterine tumors** which have produced mechanical compression, distortion, or blockage of a tube.

4. **Previous peritonitis** (inflammation of the abdominal cavity) which has created adhesions of a tube and has distorted its channel.

5. **A birth deformity of the tube.**

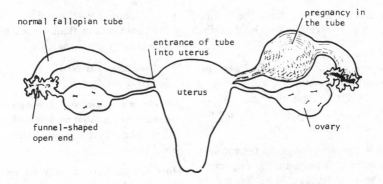

normal fallopian tube

entrance of tube into uterus

uterus

funnel-shaped open end

pregnancy in the tube

ovary

6. Unknown causes in women who are otherwise perfectly normal.

How often does an ectopic pregnancy occur?

In approximately 1 out of every 300 to 400 pregnancies.

How soon after the egg is fertilized can an ectopic pregnancy occur?

Immediately after its fertilization.

How soon after an ectopic pregnancy occurs can a diagnosis be made?

Usually within four to six weeks.

What are the symptoms of an ectopic pregnancy?

In the early stages of an unruptured ectopic pregnancy, the patient usually misses a menstrual period but does have slight vaginal staining. Some pain develops in the lower abdomen, particularly after intercourse. All of the signs seen during early pregnancy, including morning sickness, breast enlargement, etc., may be present. When an ectopic pregnancy ruptures, the aforementioned symptoms may be followed by severe shock, fainting, marked pallor, abdominal pain, pain in the shoulder region, and pressure in the rectum.

Does a tubal pregnancy ever last nine months and result in the normal birth of a child?

No.

What causes the symptoms when an ectopic pregnancy ruptures?

There is actual rupture of the tube accompanied by great loss of blood into the abdominal cavity.

What is meant by the term "tubal abortion"?

This is a situation in which the fertilized egg or young embryo is expelled from the end of the tube into the abdominal cavity. In many of these cases the symptoms are not as severe as in a ruptured ectopic pregnancy, for the tube itself does not rupture and there is much less blood loss and shock.

Is the pregnancy test always positive in ectopic pregnancy?

No. There are many cases in which the pregnancy test will be negative. This will depend upon whether the pregnancy is still viable (alive).

How does the gynecologist make the diagnosis of ectopic pregnancy?

By noting the appearance of the symptoms previously described, associated with the presence of a pelvic mass in the region of the fallopian tube. A positive pregnancy test will also help to establish a diagnosis.

In suspected cases, a needle may be inserted into the pelvic cavity through the vagina to note the presence of blood within the pelvic cavity. Or an instru-

SURGICAL CONDITIONS AND PROCEDURES

ment can be inserted from the vagina into the pelvic cavity to visualize the tubes.

Is there any known method of preventing ectopic pregnancy?

No, except to treat all disease within the pelvis prior to permitting the patient to become pregnant.

What is the best method of treatment when an ectopic pregnancy is suspected?

If the diagnosis cannot be determined positively, the safest procedure is to operate and examine the tubes under direct vision. Although this involves an abdominal operation, it is much safer to follow this procedure than to permit a patient to progress to a stage where the tube will rupture.

What is the treatment for ectopic pregnancy?

1. When a definite diagnosis has been made, the patient should be operated upon immediately and the tube removed.

2. Blood transfusions should be given rapidly if there has been marked blood loss.

3. Suspected cases should be watched carefully and advised to call the physician should there be any change in their condition.

Are the ovaries removed when operating for ectopic pregnancy?

No, unless they are diseased.

What is the greatest danger in ectopic pregnancy?

Hemorrhage.

What are the chances of recovery following ectopic pregnancy?

When modern facilities are available and prompt surgery is performed, practically all cases recover. A mortality of 4 percent still occurs, unfortunately, but this is due largely to the fact that many cases do not receive early surgery.

Is the operation itself a serious one?

No more serious than the removal of a tube for any other reason.

What anesthesia is used?

General anesthesia.

Are blood transfusions necessary during operation for a tubal pregnancy?

Yes, when there has been rupture with blood loss.

How long a hospital stay is necessary after an ectopic pregnancy?

Five to ten days.

What treatments are given prior to operating upon a patient with a ruptured ectopic pregnancy?

Transfusions are given to get the patient out of shock and thus permit surgery.

Are there any special postoperative treatments necessary after an ectopic pregnancy?

No.

Is it possible for someone to have a normal pregnancy after an ectopic pregnancy?

Yes. The removal of one tube or ovary does not prevent a subsequent pregnancy, nor does it necessarily mean that another ectopic pregnancy will occur.

Is a woman who has had one tubal pregnancy likely to develop one on the other side?

Not necessarily. However, she is somewhat more prone to do so than someone who his never had an ectopic pregnancy.

How soon after operation for an ectopic pregnancy can one become pregnant again?

It is wise to wait at least six months.

How soon after an ectopic pregnancy will menstrual periods return?

Usually in six to eight weeks.

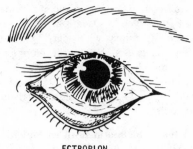

ECTROPION

Ectropion and Entropion

Ectropion is a condition in which the margin of the upper or lower eyelid turns out. It can be caused by scarring or by the loss of elasticity of the tissues, as occurs during the later years of life. When the lower eyelid is involved, involuntary tearing often constitutes a most annoying symptom. In this condition, too, surgery can produce a good result in the great majority of instances. By a plastic operative procedure, a portion of the inside of the eyelid is removed so as to cause the lid to turn inward.

Entropion is a condition in which the margin of the upper or the lower eyelid turns in, causing the eyelashes to rub against and irritate the eyeball. It develops as a result of injury or scarring consequent to an old inflammation. Should secondary infection be superimposed, scarring of the cornea with subsequent loss of vision may ensue. It is therefore important to correct the condition surgically during the early stages of its development. The operation to correct entropion is a simple plastic procedure carried out under local anesthesia. A portion of the inside of the eyelid is cut away in such a manner as to cause the lid to bend outward. The operation

leaves no visible scar and the results are excellent in most cases.

QUESTIONS AND ANSWERS

What is the most common cause of ectropion?

With advancing age, there is a loss of elastic tissue within the eyelid, allowing it to fall away from the eyeball. Other cases are caused by scarring secondary to inflammation or injury.

What are the symptoms of ectropion?

Since the eyelid, usually the lower one, has fallen away from the eyeball, tears run out onto the cheeks rather than into the tear duct.

Who is most likely to develop ectropion?

Older people whose elastic tissue of the eyelid is replaced with fibrous tissue.

What is the treatment for ectropion?

A simple operation, performed under local anesthesia, in which a portion of the inside of the eyelid is removed so as to cause the lid to turn inward.

What is entropion?

It is a condition in which the margin of the upper or lower eyelid turns in, causing eyelashes to rub against and irritate the eyeball.

What causes entropion?

It usually develops as a result of scar-

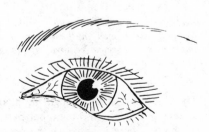

ENTROPION

ring consequent to an old inflammation of the eyelid. Occasionally it results from an injury with scarring. Another type is caused by overdevelopment of the muscle that closes the eyelids. This is the result of excessive squeezing of lids, particularly in older, high-strung people.

What is the treatment of entropion?

It is corrected by an operation, performed under local anesthesia, in which a portion of the inside of the eyelid is cut away in such a manner as to cause the lid to bend outward. The procedure is successful in almost all cases.

In addition to surgery, the eyelashes are plucked to make sure that they do not rub against the eyeball.

Is it important to operate to repair an eyelid with entropion?

Yes, because the continued rubbing of the eyelashes against the eyeball will lead to permanent scarring and loss of vision.

Embolus and Embolism

An embolus is a piece of clotted blood that has become detached from the lining of the heart or a vein or artery.

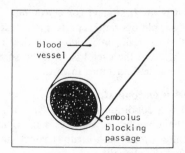

Cross section of a blood vessel showing its passageway blocked by an embolus (clotted blood).

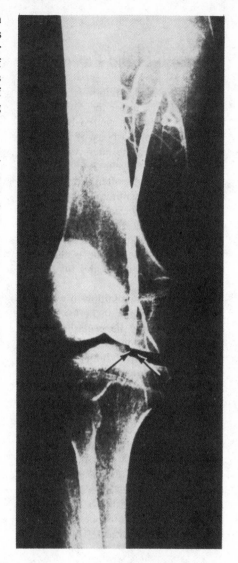

An arteriogram clearly indicates that an embolus has lodged in the artery at the knee. Prompt surgical removal of the embolus will save the limb.

The embolus travels through the bloodstream and lodges in some other part of the body, where it obstructs the normal blood flow.

QUESTIONS AND ANSWERS

What is an embolism?

It is a condition caused by obstruction of the blood flow by an embolus.

What are the symptoms of embolism?

1. If a major vessel is blocked, sudden death (within seconds) may result. This occurs most often in pulmonary embolism.

2. If death does not follow the blockage of a major vessel, shock may ensue. The patient will become cold, clammy, and perspire freely; heart action will weaken; pulse will become rapid; and blood pressure will go down.

3. If the embolus has lodged in the brain, a stroke will result.

4. If the embolus has lodged in the lungs, the result will be shock, severe chest pain, difficulty in breathing, and spitting of blood.

5. If the embolus lodges in the aorta at the site where that vessel divides to send arteries to each leg, then pain, coldness, and loss of pulsations will be noted in both legs. This type of embolus is often associated with shock.

6. If the embolus lodges in an artery in the thigh or leg, that limb will become cold and blue and will lose its pulsations.

Do older people display a greater tendency to develop embolism than younger people?

Yes, because impaired heart function, seen so often in older people, permits blood clots to form in the chambers of the heart. Also, blood circulation in the veins in the legs and pelvis tends to become sluggish, thus permitting blood to clot in the veins. When either of these conditions prevails, the chances are great that a piece of this clotted blood will break away and travel to some distant part of the body.

In what sites are emboli most likely to originate, and where are they most likely to lodge?

Many originate from the left atrium (auricle) or from the valves of the left side of the heart as a secondary condition to impaired heart function or rheumatic heart disease. When emboli from this site break away, they may lodge in the arteries of the legs or in a vessel in the brain. Gangrene of one or both legs or a stroke may be a consequence. If the embolus should go to a kidney or some other organ, the function of that organ will be seriously impaired.

If the embolus originates from a vein in the leg or pelvis (as sometimes occurs as a postoperative complication), it usually travels to the lungs and causes a pulmonary embolism.

Can surgery help when an embolus has lodged in one of the main arteries in the thigh or leg?

Immediate surgery is necessary to save the limb. An operation is performed in which the obstructed artery is opened and the embolus is removed (embolectomy). If this procedure is carried out within a few hours after the embolization has taken place, circulation may be restored and the life of the limb preserved.

Can surgery help when an embolus has traveled to the brain?

It is often difficult to locate the exact site at which the embolus has lodged when it affects one of the small arteries in the brain. For this reason, it is seldom feasible to operate for the removal of an embolus to the brain.

Can surgery help when a pulmonary (lung) embolus has occurred?

Usually not, although there are a few cases on record in which immediate surgery has saved the patient's life.

Are there methods of preventing an embolism?

Yes.

1. Medications to improve heart regularity and function will decrease the chances of blood clots forming in it.

2. In cases of rheumatic heart disease where infected blood clots may lodge on the valves (subacute endocarditis), huge doses of antibiotic and anticoagulant drugs may block an embolus from breaking away.

3. Older people with large varicose veins in their legs should have them tied off or stripped, especially if they are to undergo future abdominal surgery.

4. Following surgery, patients should be made to move around in bed, to exercise their legs, and to get out of bed as soon as possible. This will help to prevent clots from forming in the veins of the legs and pelvis.

5. Anticoagulant drugs should be given those who appear to be in danger of getting blood clots. Such medications keep the blood more fluid, thus reducing the possibility of clot formation. This type of treatment is frequently carried out both before and after surgery.

6. If embolism has already occurred, treatment with anticoagulant drugs may prevent the extension of the clot and may help to preserve fluidity of blood that is on the point of clotting. (Anticoagulant therapy must be carried out only under the constant supervision of a specialist, as severe hemorrhage may result unless the treatment is carefully regulated.)

What are some of the anticoagulant drugs, and how do they work in cases of embolism?

The two main drugs are heparin and dicoumarol. They work by prolonging clotting time of the blood, thus reducing its tendency to clot.

Does spontaneous recovery ever take place after a patient has sustained a pulmonary embolus, cerebral embolus, or embolus to a major artery at other sites?

Yes. However, unless the underlying cause of the embolus is eliminated, the chances of recurrent, eventually fatal emboli are great.

What is the outlook for recovery in pulmonary embolism?

The outlook is good in the majority of cases. Formerly, about 85 percent of those affected had nonfatal embolism, while about 15 percent of cases were fatal. Since the introduction of the anticoagulant drugs, only a small percentage of cases end fatally.

How important is bed rest after pulmonary embolism?

It is very important indeed. Once a clot has formed, the patient must be kept at complete rest so that no further clot formation takes place and so that the chances of a piece of the clot breaking off are minimized.

Can the extent of a pulmonary embolus be seen on an x-ray?

Yes. It will usually show up as a haze on the lung dome.

Empyema

Empyema is a condition in which pus forms in the space between the lung and the chest wall (the pleural cavity). It was encountered often in bygone days as a complication of pneumonia. Today, it is a relatively rare condition, since pneumonia is controlled so effectively with antibiotics. However, when a case of pneumonia has been neglected or has been treated inadequately, empyema may develop. An incision into the chest cavity with drainage of the pus is the treatment of choice and will result in a cure in the great majority of cases.

QUESTIONS AND ANSWERS

Is empyema seen very often today?

No, except in outlying districts where people might develop pneumonia and go untreated because medical care is unavailable. Such individuals may develop empyema as a complication of pneumonia.

How can one tell that a patient with pneumonia is developing empyema?

The patient appears to be recovering from pneumonia and his temperature is on its way down to normal when suddenly and abruptly there are increased temperature and pain in the chest, and the patient appears to be having a relapse. Examination will reveal increased dullness and flatness over the involved side of the chest, and characteristic sounds can be heard with a stethoscope. X-rays of the lungs will reveal a fluid collection in the pleural cavity. If a needle is inserted into the pleural cavity, pus can be withdrawn.

What is the treatment for empyema secondary to pneumonia?

The antibiotics are effective in curing a large number of these cases. However, it is first necessary to tap the chest with a needle and to culture the germs that are withdrawn. Antibiotic-sensitivity tests will then be carried out to determine which drug will be most effective.

Is it ever necessary to operate upon people who have empyema?

Yes. If there is a large amount of pus, antibiotics can rarely cause it all to be absorbed. In these cases, it may be necessary to perform a thoracotomy. In this operation, an incision is made into the chest cavity over the empyema abscess, and the pus is drained out.

Will most people recover from operations for empyema?

Yes. The patient may be hospitalized for two weeks or more, but recovery is the general rule.

Does empyema ever occur secondary to a tuberculous infection?

Yes. It often occurs when the original tuberculous lesion has not been treated adequately.

Is it ever necessary to operate upon a patient who has empyema secondary to tuberculosis?

Yes. Drainage may be necessary if a large amount of pus has accumulated.

Are children more prone to develop empyema than adults?

Yes. This is because they have a somewhat greater susceptibility to pneumonia than do adults.

See also LUNGS.

Endometriosis

Endometriosis is a condition in which cells normally lining the interior of the uterus are found growing on the surface of other abdominal organs, such as the fallopian tubes, ovaries, ligaments, intestines, and lining of the abdominal cavity. Characteristically, this peculiar disorder will produce lower abdominal pain beginning a week to ten days prior to menstruation, increasing in intensity as menstruation approaches, and subsiding about the second or third day of the period. When endometriosis involves an ovary, it may form a cyst. If these cysts grow larger than two inches in diameter, then surgical removal of the ovary is indicated. If women over 40 years of age are affected, then removal of the uterus, both tubes, and ovaries will produce a cure.

Endometriosis in young women without cyst formation can be helped considerably by giving appropriate doses of various sex hormones.

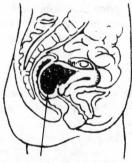

area of endometriosis

In endometriosis, cells that normally line the interior of the uterus grow outside the uterus on the surface of the intestinal wall or rectum.

QUESTIONS AND ANSWERS

What is endometriosis?

The growth of cells which normally lie in the uterus on the surface of other structures such as the outside of the uterus, the fallopian tubes, the ovaries, the intestines or bowel, and others.

What causes endometriosis?

The exact cause is unknown. One theory is that the lining cells of the uterus are expelled through the fallopian tubes by a reverse peristaltic action in the tubes during menstrual periods.

Does endometriosis ever cause ectopic (tubal) pregnancy?

There are many gynecologists who believe that endometriosis is sometimes associated with ectopic pregnancy when tissue that normally lines the uterine cavity grows in the fallopian tubes and attracts the fertilized egg, causing it to implant there.

Does endometriosis ever cause a blocked fallopian tube and thus prevent pregnancy from taking place?

Yes. If the cells grow to very large dimensions, they may completely block the passageway through the narrow tube and thus prevent pregnancy from taking place.

Does endometriosis ever cause painful and difficult menstruation (dysmenorrhea)?

It is one of the greatest causes of painful menstruation.

Is removal of the uterus (hysterectomy) ever indicated because of endometriosis?

Occasionally, because of extremely severe menstrual pain that is unrelieved by hormone treatment, hysterectomy is advised. Such an operation is only carried out when medical treatment for the endometriosis has proven unsatisfactory over a number of years and when the patient is positive that she does not wish to become pregnant.

How do endometrial cells exist in abnormal positions?

They implant upon the surface of other structures and grow as small nests of cells. They vary in size from that of a pinhead to the size of an orange. They often form cysts which contain a chocolate-appearing fluid that represents old, bloody menstrual-like material.

What abnormal conditions are produced by these endometrial implants?

They may cause firm adhesions between the tubes and the ovaries or the bladder, the bowel, or the uterus. They may form cysts. These cysts may twist or rupture, causing acute abdominal pain and distress.

Do these endometrial implants function like normal uterine cells?

Yes. They become distended and engorged with blood as each menstrual period approaches, and they bleed when menstruation takes place.

What are some of the symptoms of endometriosis?

1. It may cause no symptoms whatever and be discovered accidentally in surgery for another condition.

2. There may be marked pain before and during the menstrual period.

3. There may be marked pain on urination, defecation, or during intercourse.

4. Menstrual bleeding may be markedly increased.

5. Inability to become pregnant is a reflection of extensive endometriosis.

What is the treatment for endometriosis?

1. Treatment is usually medical and will include the administration of male sex hormones or enough female sex hormones to temporarily stop menstrual periods. However, this type of treatment cannot be pursued indefinitely without harmful results.

2. In persistent cases of endometriosis with marked symptoms, hysterectomy may have to be performed. This is reserved for women past the childbearing age or for those whose symptoms are so severe that they demand treatment.

3. In young women in the childbearing age, pregnancy causes temporary relief, since the cyclic influence which causes the symptoms of endometriosis is interrupted.

Does endometriosis lead to cancer?

No.

What can happen if endometriosis is permitted to go untreated?

The symptoms may become progressive and debilitating. If the endo-metriosis involves the bowel or intestinal tract, obstruction of the bowel may take place. In certain cases, endometrial cysts will grow so large that they will create pressure on other organs and will demand surgery. Endometrial cysts sometimes twist or rupture, thus requiring immediate surgical intervention.

Does endometriosis ever affect the ovary?

In about one out of eight cases of endometriosis, the condition is found in the ovary. It is almost always associated with endometrial implants elsewhere within the abdominal cavity.

Endotoxin Shock

Endotoxins are poisons produced by bacteria and liberated by them when the bacterial cell is destroyed. Such endotoxins may gain access to the bloodstream and produce the generalized reaction of shock.

The most common bacteria to cause endotoxin shock are the so-called gram-negative bacilli. Such organisms are frequently present within the body, and when they take hold and grow without control, they liberate huge quantities of toxin, or poison. Endotoxin shock is seen occasionally after surgical operations of major proportions, or after an overwhelming infection, especially in the urinary tract.

See also SHOCK.

QUESTIONS AND ANSWERS

Is endotoxin shock known by any other name?

It is sometimes referred to as gram-negative sepsis.

What are the symptoms and signs of endotoxin shock?

1. The patient is usually conscious or

semiconscious, and shows great apprehension and fear.

2. There is great thirst.

3. The pupils of the eyes are dilated.

4. The skin is moist, cold, and clammy and has a grayish tint.

5. The pulse is weak and very rapid.

6. Breathing is shallow and rapid.

7. There may be intermittent periods of chills followed by high temperatures to 104° F or above.

8. Blood cultures will show the presence of gram-negative organisms in many instances.

What is the treatment for endotoxin shock?

Treatment must be directed toward the eradication of the infection. This may involve the giving of massive doses of various antibiotic medications to which the bacteria are sensitive. The general condition of the patient is usually grave in endotoxin shock, and it is therefore necessary to support him with adequate amounts of intravenous fluid and minerals and to give steroids such as cortisone.

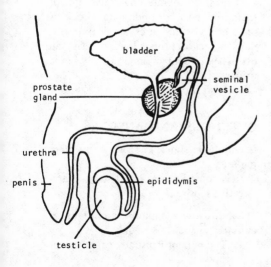

What is the outcome of endotoxin shock?

Many patients will respond to treatment and can be saved, but there is a sizable mortality even when prompt and vigorous treatment has been carried out.

Entropion

See ECTROPION AND ENTROPION.

Epididymitis

Epididymitis is an inflammation of the epididymis, which is a structure immediately adjacent to, and connected with, the testicle. The epididymis is made up of many little tubules, which contain the sperm that have been produced in the testicular gland. In the epididymis the sperm undergo further maturing. They are then propelled into the seminal duct and are widespread.

QUESTIONS AND ANSWERS

Are infections of the epididymis common?

In years gone by, when gonorrheal infection was so poorly controlled, many infections of this structure were seen. Today, however, antibiotic therapy has reduced the incidence of infection within the epididymis.

What are some of the causes other than gonorrhea for infections of the epididymis?

It is sometimes encountered after an operation upon the prostate gland or it may follow a cystoscopic examination. It frequently follows vigorous prostatic massage which forces infected material from the prostate down the connecting duct to the epididymis.

How can one prevent infections of the epididymis?

In operations, the best way to prevent it is to tie off and cut the vas deferens (the tube connecting the epididymis with the seminal vesicles) before carrying out surgery upon the prostate. In medical conditions, such as prostatitis, massage should be carried out very gently, and the patient should void after treatment.

What are the harmful effects of epididymitis?

In addition to being a very painful condition, with swelling, fever, and extreme tenderness of the testicle, epididymitis is often followed by sterility if it involves both sides.

What is the treatment for acute epididymitis?

Treatment consists of bed rest, liberal fluid intake, the application of ice to the affected side, and the administration of antibiotics.

How long does the acute phase of epididymitis last?

About five to seven days, but the swelling may not subside for several weeks.

Is surgery ever necessary for epididymitis?

Yes, when an abscess has formed. This will require drainage.

Does acute epididymitis ever become chronic?

Yes. There are cases in which the infection subsides only partially and flares up from time to time.

What is the treatment for chronic or recurring epididymitis?

The surgical removal of the epididymis.

Is epididymitis ever caused by tuberculosis?

Yes, occasionally.

What are the symptoms and signs of an infection of the epididymis?

Pain and scrotal swelling are the most prominent symptoms. The enlarged, sensitive epididymis can be felt in the posterior (back) and inferior (lower) portion of the scrotal sac. It may become large enough to fill the greater part of the pouch. Pain is relieved by elevating the scrotum and by giving pain-relieving medications. Most often there is a slight elevation in temperature.

Do children ever get infections of the epididymis?

Yes, but rarely. Epididymitis in children is rarely caused by gonorrhea or tuberculosis, as it is in adults. A complication of epididymitis is the development of a hydrocele.

Epispadias

See HYPOSPADIAS AND EPISPADIAS.

Esophagus
(The Foodpipe)

The esophagus, or foodpipe, is a long hollow muscular tube extending from the back of the throat down to the stomach. Its sole purpose is to act as a conduit for food and liquid.

Some 25 years ago, before the development of modern chest surgery, it was extremely rare for people to recover from serious disorders of the esophagus. Today, however, the esophagus can be approached surgically and operated upon with safety. And although surgical conditions of this structure are not among the most frequently encountered, those that do occur are serious and often threaten life.

1. **Birth deformities** of the esophagus are relatively rare conditions. Usually they consist of an abnormal opening or connection between the esophagus and trachea (foodpipe and windpipe), or an interruption in the continuity of the esophagus as it descends toward the stomach. Frequently, when an opening into the trachea is present, the child swallows and some of the milk goes into the lungs, or if there is lack of continuity between the foodpipe and the stomach, he vomits everything he swallows.

These children become critically ill within the first few days of life and the outlook is poor. Pneumonia, from milk entering the lungs, often develops and this greatly increases the surgical risk. Nevertheless, modern surgical and anesthetic techniques have developed to such a state that a considerable number of these patients can be saved.

The operation is performed under general anesthesia, the chest cavity is opened and the connection between the esophagus and trachea is taken down. The openings are then tightly closed, thus reestablishing normal anatomy. If the esophagus has an undeveloped segment with normal structure above and below it, the abnormal portion is removed and the esophagus is reunited. In some cases, the defect is so extensive that this is not possible. When this type of deformity is encountered, the diaphragm is opened and the stomach is pulled up into the chest. An artificial connection is then made between the lowermost portion of normal esophagus, above the obstruction, and the stomach.

2. **Inflammation of the esophagus** (esophagitis) is usually not a surgical

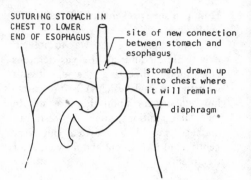

SUTURING STOMACH IN CHEST TO LOWER END OF ESOPHAGUS

site of new connection between stomach and esophagus

stomach drawn up into chest where it will remain

diaphragm

condition but is often found in association with a diaphragmatic (hiatal) hernia. These hernias permit a small portion of the stomach to protrude up into the chest cavity through the opening in the diaphragm through which the esophagus passes. In these cases, acid juices from the stomach may regurgitate into the esophagus, producing marked irritation and inflammation. Burning, difficulty in swallowing, and indigestion may result.

The cure of this form of esophageal inflammation lies in the surgical repair of the hernia. (*See* DIAPHRAGMATIC AND HIATUS HERNIAS.) This is a safe effective procedure.

3. **Injuries to the esophagus** were seen much more frequently years ago when lye and other disinfectants were common household items. For some inexplicable reason, children would swallow the lye and burn a portion of their esophagus. If they recovered from the accident, obstruction and scarring of the esophagus took place. It was then necessary to perform a *gastrostomy*. This meant a permanent opening of the stomach on the abdominal wall through which the child would be fed for the rest of its life.

If the scarred and obstructed segment is not too extensive, it is now possible to open the chest cavity, remove the injured portion (*esophagectomy*), and reunite the normal esophagus above and below. If the damaged area is extensive, as is usually the case, it is excised. The stomach is then brought up into the chest and sutured to the normal esophagus above, in the same manner as shown in the preceding illustration.

4. Diverticula of the esophagus: These are outpouchings of the mucous membrane lining of the esophagus through its own muscle wall. A saclike deformity is thus created. (See illustration.) The commonest location is in the neck, but

esophagus. Such obstruction will require surgical correction.

The operation consists of a direct approach over the area of the diverticulum in the neck or the chest. A careful dissection of the sac is carried out. In most instances, the diverticulum will be removed and its opening into the esophagus tied off. If this is technically too hazardous or difficult, then the sac is inverted so that its entrance will lie at a level below the sac. This maneuver will prevent food or liquid from collecting within it. (See illustration.)

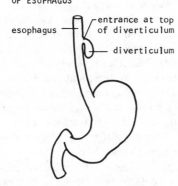

DIVERTICULUM
OF ESOPHAGUS

esophagus — entrance at top of diverticulum

— diverticulum

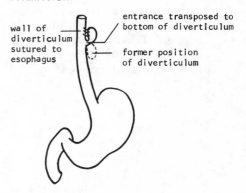

INVERSION OF
DIVERTICULUM

wall of diverticulum sutured to esophagus

entrance transposed to bottom of diverticulum

former position of diverticulum

they also are seen quite frequently in the middle or lower portions of the esophagus. They may attain two to three inches in diameter with an aperture from the esophagus of one to two inches. When they attain this size, and because they tend to have their sac portion at a lower level than the opening into the esophagus, food and liquid tend to collect and stagnate within them. Diagnosis of these diverticula becomes apparent when some of the food or liquid is regurgitated into the mouth in its original, undigested form. X-rays with barium will clearly demonstrate their presence. As they grow and large quantities of food are contained within them, they exert more and more pressure upon the

These operations are now carried out with safety, and although they are regarded as major procedures, recovery takes place in practically all cases.

5. Esophageal spasm or achalasia is a common condition of unknown origin in which there is continued spasm of the lower end of the esophagus at its junction with the stomach. Theories have been propounded that the lower end of the esophagus becomes spastic and constricted because it lacks certain nerve fibers which permit it to relax and dilate. Another group of investigators feel that the condition attacks mainly those who are emotionally unstable and of a highly neurotic temperament. Whatever its

304

SURGICAL CONDITIONS AND PROCEDURES

cause, people so afflicted suffer greatly from progressive inability to swallow. The esophagus above the constricted area becomes markedly dilated and collects food and fluid. During a period when the spasm is particularly aggravated and prolonged, these people may lose weight and literally starve.

Diagnosis of achalasia can be made on x-ray with a barium swallow.

Treatment is directed along two lines:

a) The majority of these patients can be effectively treated by repeated courses of esophageal dilatation with tubes passed through the mouth.

b) If the esophageal spasm is chronic and is not permanently benefited from thorough courses of medication and dilatation, then surgery is performed. The chest cavity is opened and the muscle wall of the lower end of the esophagus is cut down to, but

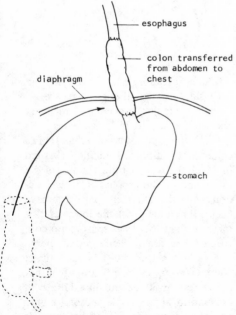

COLONIC INTERPOSITION FOR ESOPHAGECTOMY

not including, the mucous membrane. This will effectively relieve the symptoms in almost all cases. The operation is relatively simple to perform and is usually followed by recovery, unless some unforeseen complication arises.

6. Most tumors of the esophagus are malignant. Estimates show that about 1 percent of all cancer deaths are due to cancer of the esophagus. This disease effects men more often than women and occurs most frequently between the ages of 50 and 70 years. Because of their origin in the lining membrane, tumorous obstructions to swallowing come on early and malnourishment and weight loss are characteristic findings.

As with all cancer, the treatment is early and extensive surgical removal. This procedure, *esophagectomy*, is being practiced more widely throughout the country as technical abilities improve. It is necessary to remove a wide segment of esophagus, and therefore the stomach or an isolated segment of the large bowel is brought up into the chest and sutured to the lower end of the remaining esophagus. If bowel has been used to replace the esophagus, its lower end is connected with the upper portion of the stomach to restore the food passageway. Within recent years, it has become possible to remove almost the entire chest portion of the esophagus and to replace the defect thus produced with a plastic tube. (See illustration.)

Although a large number of these cases reach the operating table late in the course of the disease, more and more patients are being helped by radical surgical removal of the tumor.

QUESTIONS AND ANSWERS

Are birth deformities of the esophagus seen very often?

Fortunately, such birth deformities

are seen only rarely. When a birth deformity does occur, it usually takes one of the following forms:

1. In about 90 percent of cases, the lower end of the esophagus has failed to develop and there is a false connection (fistula) between the lower end of the esophagus and the trachea (windpipe). This deformity, known as a tracheoesophageal fistula (TEF) with atresia of the esophagus, is a very serious one and is often associated with deformities elsewhere in the body.

2. There may be atresia (failure of development) of the esophagus without a false connection betweeen it and the trachea. This type of deformity is seen much less frequently.

3. The esophagus may be complete and extend from the back of the throat down to the stomach, but there is, along its course, a fistula (false connection) between it and the trachea.

4. A band, web, or membrane may extend across the passageway of the esophagus, but the organ is normal in all other respects.

5. There may be a constriction of a portion of the esophagus.

What might cause one to suspect the presence of a deformity of the esophagus in a newborn?

The repeated regurgitation of milk that has not been soured or curdled by the action of the stomach juices.

Can children with these birth deformities survive without treatment?

No. These children will die unless corrective operative procedures are carried out promptly.

How is the diagnosis of an esophageal deformity made?

If a false connection exists between the foodpipe and windpipe, the child will choke and turn blue every time he attempts to feed. This happens because milk gets into the trachea from the esophagus. If there is atresia (lack of development) of the lower end of the esophagus or an obstructing membrane, the child will regurgitate undigested formula and it will be obvious that no milk is reaching his stomach. Constrictions of the esophagus or webs may cause only partial obstruction and the child may regurgitate some of his feedings but not all of them.

Can x-rays help to make the diagnosis of esophageal deformities?

Yes. If the child is given a small amount of barium or other contrast medium (hypaque) to swallow and then is x-rayed, the deformities will become apparent.

What operations are performed to relieve deformities of the esophagus?

1. If a tracheoesophageal fistula exists, the chest cavity must be opened by a surgeon, the connection must be detached, and each organ must be repaired separately.

2. If the lower end of the esophagus is undeveloped, the stomach is drawn up into the chest through the diaphragm and is stitched to the part of the esophagus that is normal.

3. A congenital web or membrane can usually be severed or dilated by the passage of an instrument known as an esophagoscope. If the obstruction cannot be relieved in this manner, then the chest cavity is opened, the esophagus is exposed and incised, and the obstruction is removed surgically.

4. Quite often, strictures of the esophagus can be relieved completely by dilating them with special dilators passed through the mouth. If this does not relieve the condition, it will be necessary to open the chest cavity and repair the defect directly.

Is it always possible to operate upon a child who has a fistula connecting his esophagus and trachea?

No, because many of these children have other deformities that make them extremely poor operative risks. In other cases, if the diagnosis is not made early enough, milk may get into the child's lungs and produce pneumonia, which also increases the surgical risk in this type of operation.

What are the chances of recovery following operations for tracheoesophageal fistula or esophageal atresia?

The mortality rate in these cases is very high, and the chances of recovery are no more than two out of three. However, until very recently all of these children died.

Are strictures (constriction) of the esophagus very common?

No. This is a rather rare deformity. The diagnosis is made when the child vomits undigested food particles on frequent occasions and x-rays reveal the exact nature of the stricture.

Do children recover from operations to correct a stricture of the esophagus?

Yes, the great majority will recover, provided they are otherwise healthy.

Are burns of the esophagus very common?

No. Some twenty or thirty years ago, lye burns of the esophagus were seen quite frequently, and these could destroy the entire lining of the esophagus. Today, happily, this is an extremely rare accident, as parents are alert to the dangers of children swallowing substances that might cause a burn and keep such substances away from children.

Can one burn his esophagus by drinking liquids that are too hot?

Yes, but this does not happen very often unless one takes a tremendous gulp of a hot liquid. In most instances, the minute the hot liquid enters his mouth, one will spit it out. A hot liquid is more likely to burn one's mouth than the esophagus.

What is the treatment for a burn of the esophagus?

The patient should be urged to take fluids as soon as possible. If nourishment cannot be taken by the fifth or sixth day after the accident, it is necessary to perform an abdominal operation known as a gastrostomy. This is a procedure in which the front wall of the stomach is brought out onto the abdomen and a hole is made in it. The patient is fed artificially through a tube that is sutured into this opening in the stomach. When the passageway through the esophagus heals sufficiently and remains open, the gastrostomy opening on the abdominal wall is unhooked and closed.

How can a physician tell that a person has burned his esophagus?

In most of these cases, the physician will be able to see burns on the inside of the mouth, and these will be a valuable clue. In addition, it is usually obvious what substance caused the burn.

Is it possible to dilate an esophagus that is constricted as a result of a burn scar?

Yes. The patient is made to swallow a string, and the lower end of the string is recovered through the gastrostomy opening. The upper end of the string is taped with adhesive tape to the patient's face. A specially designed metal dilator is tied to the upper end of the string and drawn down through the esophagus by pulling on the lower end of the string, which has been drawn out through the gastrostomy opening on the abdominal wall. This maneuver is repeated many times until the constriction is dilated and no longer obstructs the free passage of fluids and food.

How soon after a burn of the esophagus can dilatations be carried out?

Between three and four weeks after the accident.

Do people with burns of the esophagus ever respond to surgery?

If the burned area is localized and there is normal esophagus above it, it is sometimes practical to remove the burned area. In this type of case, the stomach is brought up through the diaphragm and the upper portion of the stomach is stitched to the lower normal end of the esophagus, thus reestablishing a passageway from the throat into the stomach.

Does the swallowing of lye cause a severe inflammation of the mucous membrane lining the esophagus?

Yes. The injury is actually a burn.

Will the inflammation or burn of the esophagus sometimes lead to the development of pneumonia?

Yes. An inflammation of the lungs is commonly associated with an inflammation of the esophagus.

What causes varicose veins of the esophagus?

The condition is seen almost exclusively in those people who have severe cirrhosis of the liver. Since blood cannot get from the intestinal tract through the cirrhotic liver, it bypasses the liver and travels along the veins of the esophagus. This vastly increased blood volume causes the veins of the esophagus to dilate and become varicosed.

What harm can come from varicosities of the esophagus?

Eventually, when the veins become too distended and dilated, they may rupture and cause an extremely severe hemorrhage. Hemorrhage from the rupture of such varicosities is often the immediate cause of death in patients with cirrhosis of the liver.

Can anything be done to relieve varicose veins of the esophagus?

Yes. An operation known as a portacaval shunt is sometimes performed. This means suturing the large portal vein in the abdomen directly to the vena cava, thus bypassing the flow of blood from the liver and from the varicose veins.

An operation known as a splenorenal shunt is sometimes performed. In this procedure, the large vein from the spleen is sutured to the main kidney vein on the left side. This too will shunt the blood away from the liver and away from the varicose veins of the esophagus.

Do people ever swallow foreign bodies that get stuck in the esophagus?

Yes, this happens quite frequently, especially in childhood.

What types of foreign bodies may get lodged in the esophagus?

Open safety pins; straight pins, needles, and nails; coins, such as a quarter or half-dollar; large buttons; and any other object whose diameter is larger than the width of the lower end of the esophagus.

How can a parent tell that a child has a foreign body stuck in his esophagus?

The child will usually cry and complain of pain in his lower chest. If he is too young to describe the pain, his parents may see that he is trying to vomit or swallow and is able to do neither. The child may breathe a little more rapidly than normal, but breathing is not severely affected.

What should the parent do if he suspects that a child has swallowed a foreign body?

If it is known that the object has a sharp point, no attempt should be made to get the child to vomit it up. This may cause damage to the lining of the esophagus.

If it is known that the swallowed object is round and has no sharp edges, the child may be turned upside down and rapped sharply on the back. If this fails to bring up the object, a finger should be placed down the back of the child's throat to cause vomiting. If this fails, the child should be taken to the pediatrician or the nearest hospital, where x-rays will be taken to locate the exact position of the foreign body.

How can foreign bodies be removed from the esophagus?

These procedures demand the expert attention of a physician specially trained in the use of an instrument known as an esophagoscope. An esophagoscope is a rigid, hollow metal tube that is passed through the mouth, down the throat, and into the esophagus. Because the tube is lighted, the physician will be able to see the passageway of the esophagus as it descends downward through the chest toward the stomach. With a long instrument placed through the esophagoscope, the physician can often grasp and withdraw the foreign body.

Is the removal of a foreign body from the esophagus a serious procedure?

Yes, as the esophagus is a delicate membranous tube and is easily injured.

Is it ever necessary to operate upon a person to remove a foreign body from the esophagus?

Every once in a while, a sharp-pointed foreign body will perforate the esophagus and lie partially within the passageway and partially outside. In such cases it is wiser to operate than to attempt to remove the object through an esophagoscope and thus chance tearing and severely damaging the esophagus.

What operation is performed to accomplish this type of removal?

The chest cavity must be entered through a long incision between the eighth and ninth ribs on the left side of the chest. The esophagus is then exposed and opened, and the foreign body is removed. After removal of the foreign body, the esophagus is sutured and the chest cavity is closed.

Is this a serious operative procedure?

Yes, just as serious as any other chest operation. However, recovery is the rule in almost all instances.

What is chalasia?

Chalasia is an abnormality of the muscle sphincter between the lower end of the esophagus and the beginning of the stomach. The child vomits and fails to gain weight during the first few weeks of life.

How is chalasia distinguished from pyloric stenosis?

The main distinguishing features are that in chalasia, no bile is present in the vomitus and no mass (lump) is felt in the upper abdomen, whereas both these findings are present in pyloric stenosis.

What is the cause of chalasia?

The cause is not known, but some physicians feel that it is associated with a small hiatus hernia (diaphragmatic hernia).

Is chalasia a very common condition in children?

No. The incidence of chalasia appears to have increased recently, but this is thought to be due to better diagnostic methods.

What is the treatment for chalasia?

Most children will respond to medical management and will require no surgery. The treatment will consist of thickening the baby's formula by the addition of a cereal, such as farina, and maintaining the infant in a sitting-up position for an hour following each feeding.

How long does chalasia last?

It may be troublesome throughout the first year or two of a child's life, but most children will recover from it and be able to hold their feeding after this time.

What are esophageal diverticula?

Outpouchings of mucous membrane through the muscle wall of the esophagus. They form sacs which collect food and liquid.

Are these diverticula common?

Yes.

How do esophageal diverticula harm people?

1. There is repeated regurgitation of food into the mouth.
2. They press upon the esophagus and cause obstruction.
3. They cause repeated lung infections.

Do all diverticula have to be removed surgically?

No. The small ones and those that produce no symptoms can be left alone.

What operative procedures are carried out for diverticula?

1. They are removed completely and tied off at their base.
2. Less often, the diverticulum is lifted up and stitched to the wall of the esophagus so that its opening lies at the bottom of the sac. This will prevent food and liquid collection.

Are these operations dangerous procedures?

No, but they are major procedures. Recovery takes place almost invariably.

Where are the incisions made for operations upon esophageal diverticula?

Over the region of the diverticulum, either in the neck or in the chest.

What is achalasia?

Chronic spasm of the lower end of the esophagus.

What causes achalasia?

The cause is unknown but may be due to lack of certain nerve fibers in the esophageal wall.

What are the symptoms of achalasia?

1. Progressive inability to swallow
2. Regurgitation of food
3. Malnutrition and weight loss

Do all cases of achalasia require surgery?

No. The majority can be helped by periodic dilatation of the esophagus.

Is dilatation of the esophagus dangerous or painful?

It is not dangerous or painful but is a rather uncomfortable procedure.

Which cases of achalasia are operated upon?

Those that fail to respond to dilatations; about one of four.

What operative procedure is carried out?

The muscle fibers in the area of spasm are cut.

Is the operation dangerous?

No.

Do the majority of operated cases get relief from spasm?

Yes.

How common is cancer of the esophagus?

About 1 percent of all cancer.

Who is most likely to develop cancer of the esophagus?

Men over 50 years of age.

What are the symptoms?

1. Progressive difficulty in swallowing
2. Weight loss
3. X-ray findings showing a characteristic deformity

Does surgery offer hope of a cure for this type of cancer?

Yes. More and more cases are being cured by wide removal of the esophagus.

Is the cure rate high for cancer of the esophagus?

No, because too many cases first reach the surgeon at a time when the tumor has already spread beyond the esophagus.

Are most operations upon the esophagus serious?

Yes, but mortality rates with improved techniques have been reduced to truly safe levels.

How long a hospital stay is necessary after a major operation upon the esophagus?

Usually two to four weeks.

Where are the incisions made for esophageal operations?

In between the ribs on the side of the chest. They are approximately ten inches inches long.

What anesthesia is used?

General anesthesia through a tube placed in the trachea.

Are blood transfusions necessary?

Yes.

Are special nurses necessary?

Yes.

How soon after esophageal surgery can one get out of bed?

In one to three days.

Is the chest drained after esophageal operations?

Yes. A rubber tube is placed in the chest cavity for a few days after surgery.

How is a patient fed after an esophageal operation?

1. By intravenous fluids containing sugar, protein, and vitamins
2. By a rubber tube passed through the esophagus into the stomach

How soon after surgery can liquid and food be taken by mouth?

Usually within three to five days.

Are oxygen tents used after esophageal operations?

1. Yes, as in all operations performed through the chest
2. Not if the esophagus has been approached through a neck incision

Exophthalmic Goiter

Exophthalmic goiter is a disease caused by overactivity of the thyroid gland with production of huge quantities of the thyroid hormone. It is characterized by marked prominence of the eyeballs which give a popeyed appearance. In this condition there is a smooth, uniform enlargement of the thyroid gland in the neck accompanied by the following symptoms: tremor of the fingers; marked weight loss, despite an increased appetite; extremely rapid heartbeat; and marked nervousness, with fits of irritability and crying. Prior to the introduction of chemotherapeutic agents, surgical removal of the bulk of the thyroid gland was the preferred treatment. Today, most cases of exophthalmic goiter can be brought under control by giving antithyroid drugs or radioactive iodine.

Exophthalmic goiter is also known as Basedow's disease or Graves' disease.

See also GOITER; THYROID GLAND.

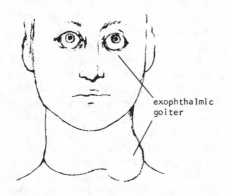

exophthalmic
goiter

QUESTIONS AND ANSWERS

Are there any toxic effects from the overproduction of thyroid hormone?

Yes. If this condition continues too long, severe damage can be caused to the heart muscle. The liver and other vital organs can also be adversely affected by the increased body metabolism evoked by overactivity of the thyroid gland.

Who is most likely to develop exophthalmic goiter?

It can be seen in all age groups, but is most common in young adult females.

What is the treatment for exophthalmic goiter?

1. The antithyroid drugs such as thiouracil are given.

2. In selected cases, radioactive iodine is given.

3. In the occasional case that does not respond to the above medications, surgical removal of 90 percent of the thyroid gland is indicated.

Will the majority of cases of exophthalmic goiter respond to the antithyroid drugs or radioactive iodine?

Yes.

Does the bulging of the eyes recede after the overactivity of the thyroid gland has been controlled?

Not always. If the bulging of the eyes has continued for a long period of time, they will not recede, even though the overactivity of the gland has been relieved.

Is any surgery possible for the bulging of the eyes?

Some surgical procedures have been tried but most of them have been unsuccessful. This is one of the reasons it is so important to seek medical attention early, when overactivity of the thyroid gland is noted and is associated with a bulging of the eyes.

If surgery must be carried out for exophthalmic goiter, does recurrence ever take place?

Only in about 1 out of 20 cases. In such instances, radioactive iodine is usually effective in bringing it under control.

Eyes

The specialty of eye surgery is practiced by physicians known as ophthalmologists or oculists. Because of the exquisite sensitivity of the eyes and the great dependence of all people upon their function, inordinate fear usually develops whenever it is discovered that an eye operation must be performed. Moreover, the public is poorly informed on the manner in which eye surgery is carried out. As an example, it is not at all unusual for patients to inquire whether the eye "is removed from its socket" when it is operated upon. Of course, this is not true. Similarly, patients often express the fear that they might be able to see the operation as it proceeds under local anesthesia. This, too, is untrue.

Fortunately, with expanded education on health matters, more and more people are learning that eye surgery is safe to perform and that wonderful advances have enabled the eye surgeon to obtain remarkably good results in the great majority of cases. In the ensuing section, many of the operative procedures performed upon the eyes will be described.

See also CATARACT; CORNEA; CROSSED EYES; DETACHMENT OF THE RETINA; ECTROPION AND ENTROPION; GLAUCOMA; NEARSIGHTEDNESS; PTERYGIUM.

THE EYELIDS

The eyelids function to protect the eyes from dust, irritating vapors, foreign bodies, external injury, and excessive light. In addition, they assist in keeping the eyes moist and lubricated by circulating the tears. The latter, in themselves, wash away dust as well.

The following are common surgical conditions of the lids:

Sties (hordeolum)
Cysts (chalazion)
Trichiasis
Entropion
Ectropion
Tumors
Injuries (lacerations, bruises, burns)
Paralysis (Bell's palsy)

1. Sties (hordeolum) are infections of the base of the eyelash and are commonly associated with whitish pus under the skin, coming on after a day or two of initial redness and tenderness. Sties often subside spontaneously with the use of hot, wet compresses and oint-ments containing an antiseptic or antibiotic substance. "Yellow oxide of mercury" used to be a favorite medication in this condition but it has been replaced by more modern and effective ointments. If medical measures fail to cause a sty to abate, a small incision is made to let out the pus. Cure follows rapidly when this is done.

Sties occur more commonly in children, as they have the habit of rubbing their eyes with dirty fingers. In those people who have frequent recurrence of sties, the general health, the vitamin intake, and the state of the blood should be investigated.

2. Cysts (chalazion) result from infection of a sebaceous gland of the eyelids in which the secretions of the gland become blocked and cannot gain exit. The result is a balloonlike effect, the "balloon" in this case being filled with secretions and pus rather than air. The presence of a chalazion is noted by the appearance of a firm pealike knot in the eyelid. Often the infection starts as an inflammation of the entire eyelid and later localizes to one area. As there are 30 to 40 sebaceous glands in each eyelid, chalazions are sometimes multiple.

Small cysts frequently clear up with the use of hot, wet compresses and antiseptic ointments, as used with sties. Larger cysts usually require surgical removal under local anesthesia. Procaine, or a similar local anesthetic agent, is injected under the skin of the eyelid covering the affected gland. A special clamp is then placed on the lid so that it may be everted (turned inside out). The gland is then painlessly removed from the underside of the lid. No stitches are necessary and an eye patch is worn for approximately 12 to 14 hours. Complete healing takes place within a week to 10 days.

3. Trichiasis is a condition in which the eyelashes turn in and rub against the eyeball. To cure the condition, the offending lashes must be plucked. In order to avoid infection, this should be done only by the ophthalmologist. Should the lashes grow back, they can be destroyed by an electric needle. This procedure is carried out under local anesthesia and causes little reaction.

4. Entropion is a condition in which the margin of the upper or the lower eyelid turns in, causing the eyelashes to rub against and irritate the eyeball. It develops as a result of injury or scarring consequent to an old inflammation. Should secondary infection be superimposed, scarring of the cornea with subsequent loss of vision may ensue. It is therefore important to correct the condition surgically during the early stages of its development. The operation to correct entropion is a simple plastic procedure carried out under local anesthesia. A portion of the inside of the eyelid is cut away in such a manner as to cause the lid to bend outward. The operation leaves no visible scar, and the results are excellent in most cases.

5. Ectropion is a condition in which the margin of the upper or lower eyelid turns out. It can be caused by scarring or by the loss of elasticity of the tissues, as occurs during the later years of life. When the lower eyelid is involved, involuntary tearing often constitutes a most annoying symptom. In this condition, too, surgery can produce a good result in the great majority of instances. By a plastic operative procedure, a portion of the inside of the eyelid is removed so as to cause the lid to turn inward.

6. Tumors of the eyelids are common. The majority are benign, but as it is not always possible to distinguish the benign from the malignant upon simple inspection, it is wisest to remove all tumors affecting this structure. Since most of these tumors involve only the skin, they can (including the malignant growths) be removed successfully with every expectation of cure. This is done under local anesthesia and in most instances, the wound will heal without leaving a disfiguring scar. Even when it is necessary to remove a major portion of the eyelid for a cancerous growth, plastic surgical procedures can be instituted to restore normal or near-normal appearance.

7. Injuries: One of the most common injuries to the lids is "black eye," which clears by itself without complication. It is most important, however, in extensive injury to the eyelids to make sure that there is no accompanying injury to the eyeball or fracture of the bones of the orbit. Burns of the lids must be treated promptly to avoid scarring and disfigurement that would make subsequent surgery necessary. Extensive cuts and lacerations of the lids are best sutured by ophthalmologists, who are more familiar with their anatomy and function than the general physician or surgeon.

8. Paralysis (Bell's palsy) is a condition in which an eyelid cannot be closed tightly because the nerve supplying the lid has beeen injured or is the seat of an inflammation. The condition may be permanent or temporary, depending upon its underlying cause. If the paralysis is due to nerve inflammation (as in facial paralysis), it will in most instances clear spontaneously within a few weeks' to a few months' time. On the other hand, if the nerve to the eyelid has been cut during an operation upon the mastoid or during the course of removing a tumor of the parotid (salivary) gland in the angle of the jaw, then the paralysis will be permanent.

Inability to close the eye is a serious condition, as the eyeball cannot be properly protected against dust, dirt, and excessive light. The eyeball becomes dry as the winking action, which helps tears to constantly wash the eyeball, is lost. This will lead to infection and ulceration of the delicate surface of the eye. People who have a temporary paralysis resulting from nerve inflammation should protect the eye by wearing airtight goggles and by washing out the eye frequently with special solutions. It is sometimes necessary for those who have lid paralysis secondary to a severed nerve to undergo an operation in which the upper lid is stitched to the lower lid. This will protect the surface of the eyeball until such time as an operation can be performed to repair the damaged nerve.

EYE REMOVAL (Enucleation)

The loss of sight is one of life's greatest tragedies. Many people feel that loss of sight is a worse penalty than death. This is evidenced by the fact that people frequently will resist advice to have an eye removed even when it is pointed out to them that withholding consent may endanger life. Patients not uncommonly hold on to the hope of saving vision long after the surgeon has informed them that sight is irretrievably lost.

Removal of an eye is indicated in the following conditions:

1. Severe injury: When sight has been lost and there is no possible chance of regaining it. These eyes have usually been subjected to extensive hemorrhage and are very painful. They rarely heal and even if healing does take place, the eye is blind, misshapen, and ugly. The ophthalmologist will know within three to six weeks after injury whether recovery can possibly ensue.

2. Malignant tumors: The commonest malignancy is a sarcoma of the choroid. This is seen in both children and adults and when apprehended, should be followed by early removal of the eye. Failure to do so will lead to spread of the growth to other parts of the body and eventual fatality. On the other hand, prompt removal (enucleation) of the eye can lead to complete cure in the majority of cases.

3. Sympathetic ophthalmia: This is a strange condition which affects the *healthy* eye after an injury to the other eye. It usually has its onset within three to four weeks after injury but may be delayed for as long as a year after the accident. The cause of sympathetic ophthalmia is unknown. One school of thought believes that it is an allergic phenomenon, and another group thinks that the inflammation travels from the injured eye to the uninjured eye along the lymph channels in the optic nerve. Whatever its cause, this condition is most serious, as it may result in loss of vision in both eyes.

When an injured eye heals promptly without pain or redness, the patient may feel secure that sympathetic ophthalmia will not occur. However, if pain and redness do develop and healing does not take place promptly, the eye surgeon is faced with the problem of deciding whether the eye should be removed. The problem is especially difficult if the injured eye still retains some vision. While repeated examinations with a special instrument called a slit lamp are helpful in determining the status of the uninjured eye, once sympathetic ophthalmia has developed, removal of the injured eye will no longer impede the progress of the inflammation. For this reason, it is always safest to remove an irreparably injured *blind eye* and not wait for signs of sympathetic ophthalmia to appear in the good eye. It should be noted, however, that the use of the steroid medications such as cortisone and ACTH has saved many eyes affected with sympathetic ophthalmia.

4. Blind eyes, from whatever cause, are more prone to develop *tumors* within them than sighted eyes. For this reason, many eye surgeons recommend their removal as a routine procedure. This trend has not developed greatly because people always harbor the dream that one day, by some miracle of surgery or faith, they will see again.

In the past, many patients refused eye removal because of the poor cosmetic result. This reason is no longer valid, as artificial eyes have been perfected to the point where they are almost indistinguishable from real eyes. Refinements of operative techniques have resulted in people with artificial eyes being able to move them almost as well as natural eyes.

The operation for eye removal (enucleation) is performed under general anesthesia in children and under local or general anesthesia in adults. There is little pain associated with this type of operation. The surgical maneuvers are quite simple and involve the cutting of the conjunctiva (the membrane that covers the eyeball and lines the eyelids), the muscles attached to the outer coat (sclera) of the eyeball, and the optic nerve in the rear of the eyeball. A gold or glass ball, to which the cut muscles can be stitched, is placed and secured into the eye socket and the conjunctiva is sutured over it. In recent years, specially designed implants have been developed which are inserted into the eye socket. These will facilitate the motion of the artificial eye which is later to be placed in the socket over the sewn conjunctiva.

After eye removal, bandages are applied and the patient is kept in bed for approximately two days. Hospital discharge usually takes place some six to seven days after surgery.

An artificial eye can be inserted in the orbit within a month after surgery. It is removed at night, at which time it is cleansed.

QUESTIONS AND ANSWERS

What are the indications that an eye should be removed?
1. Severe injury with permanent loss of sight
2. Malignant tumor within the eye
3. Danger of involvement of the uninjured eye (sympathetic ophthalmia)

Can the eye surgeon make a diagnosis early enough in the course of sympathetic ophthalmia to save the good eye?
Yes.

How long should one wait before making a decision whether to permit eye removal?
As long as the eye surgeon thinks it is permissible! The wait should be no longer than two weeks.

What happens if the operation is refused by the patient who is developing sympathetic ophthalmia in the good eye?
Loss of sight in both eyes may result.

In sympathetic ophthalmia, does removal of the injured eye prevent inflammation in the other eye?
Yes, if the injured eye is removed early enough, i.e., before a deep inflammation starts in the uninjured eye. If the injured eye is removed late, the inflammation in the other eye may go on to blindness. Reports indicate that ACTH, cortisone, or its derivatives may be of great help in halting the progress of this condition.

Can a whole eye be transplanted from one person to another?
No.

How common are malignant tumors of the eye?

Fortunately, this is a rare condition.

What are the chances of a permanent cure after eye removal for a malignant tumor?

Good, if the eye is removed before the growth has spread to other organs.

Is eye removal a painful operation?

No.

Is eye removal a dangerous procedure?

No.

What anesthesia is used?

In children, general anesthesia; local or general anesthesia in adults.

How long does enucleation (eye removal) take to perform?

Approximately 30 to 60 minutes.

Is there much pain during the postoperative period?

No.

Are special nurses necessary?

No.

How long after operation must one stay in bed?

Two days.

How long a hospital stay is necessary?

Six to seven days.

Does a patch have to be worn over the eye that has been removed?

Only for the first few weeks; i.e., until an artificial eye can be worn.

How soon after the operation can an artificial eye be obtained?

In approximately two to three weeks. The first artificial eye may be temporary. Once the socket has settled down to a definite shape, a permanent eye can be made.

How old must children be before they learn to take care of artificial eyes by themselves?

Nine to ten years of age.

Can artificial eyes be made to execute motions in unison with the good eye?

Yes.

Do artificial eyes tend to fall out of their sockets?

No.

Do artificial eyes ever crack or break when an injury in the area is sustained?

Plastic eyes are shatterproof and unbreakable. Glass eyes may break but this almost always occurs when they are dropped on a hard surface. Injury to the eye region practically never causes shattering of a glass eye. If it did occur, damage would not be serious or difficult to repair.

What happens to the artificial eye when one cries or tears?

It will also tear.

How often should an artificial eye be removed?

It is best to take the artificial eye out when going to bed at night. The eye socket and the artificial eye should then be cleansed thoroughly. This will decrease the amount of secretion from the eye.

Is it difficult to remove or replace an artificial eye?

No, it takes a few seconds to learn how to do it and just a few seconds to perform.

Does it hurt to insert or take out an artificial eye?

No.

How long does it take a socket to heal after eye removal?

Two to three weeks.

Are the eyelids normal after eye removal?
Yes.

Do patients with one eye have to wear glasses for the sake of the other eye?
No.

Can vision be normal with one eye?
Yes, except for difficulty in judging distance.

Can one judge distance with only one eye?
Yes, if the eye was removed during childhood. When an eye has been removed in adult life, ability to judge distance may or may not develop.

Is it a strain on the remaining eye to be used without the help of the other eye?
No. In some respects, the remaining eye is relieved of a strain in that it no longer has to coordinate vision with the removed eye.

Is there a visible scar after eye removal?
No.

How soon can one do the following after eye removal:
Bath or shower? 2 to 3 weeks
Do ordinary
  housework? 2 weeks
Resume sexual
  relations? 2 to 3 weeks
Resume light
  physical work? 2 weeks
Resume heavy
  physical work? 4 to 6 weeks
Ride in an auto-
  mobile? 1 to 2 weeks
Drive a car? Whenever the patient has relearned to judge distance

TUMORS OF THE EYE

How common are tumors within the eyeball?
They are rare.

What are the usual types of tumors within the eyeball?
1. Malignant melanomas that arise in the middle, or pigmented, layer of the eye
2. Retinoblastomas

What age groups are most prone to develop these tumors?
A retinoblastoma usually occurs in children under the age of 5. It occurs in one eye in most cases, but sometimes occurs in both eyes. The malignant melanoma of the choroid usually occurs in adults between the ages of 40 and 60 and involves one eye only.

What causes tumors of the eye?
The cause is unknown.

What are some of the symptoms of an eye tumor?
1. Blurred vision in one eye
2. Lightning flashes shooting across the field of vision of one eye
3. Patchy loss of vision, possibly shifting in position, in one eye
4. Blindness developing in an eye that previously had good vision

How can a diagnosis of an eye tumor be made?
The ophthalmologist will look into the interior of the eye with various instruments and will be able to make his diagnosis by the characteristic appearance of these tumors. The diagnosis is not difficult to make.

What are the symptoms of retinoblastoma in children?
If the child is very young, he may not complain at all. The parent, however, may notice a peculiar yellow color in the pupil. Older children may complain of blurring of vision. In adults, there may be blurring of vision. However, some patients may have no symptoms, and the condition is recognized only on routine examination by the eye specialist.

What is the treatment for retinoblastoma when only one eye is involved?

The eyeball should be removed as soon as possible. If both eyes are involved, the eye with the larger tumor is usually removed and the tumor in the other eye is treated with x-ray and radium.

What will happen if the operation is not performed?

The condition will spread to other parts of the body and cause death.

What are the chances of recovery in adults?

The chances for recovery are good.

What are the chances for recovery when children have eye tumors?

Eye tumors in children are very serious. However, latest reports are encouraging, and more and more children are being saved.

What tumors can affect children's eyes?

1. Retinoblastoma, a malignant tumor of the retina in the back of the eye

2. Melanoma, a malignant tumor of the choroid membrane, which lies behind the retina

At what ages are children most likely to develop eye tumors?

Retinoblastomas usually occur before a child is 5 years old; melanomas are seen in much older children.

What is treatment for melanoma of the eye?

Prompt removal of the eye.

What are the chances of saving the life of a child who has melanoma of the eye?

If the eye is removed promptly, as many as four out of ten such children can be saved.

Do eye tumors ever affect both eyes?

This rarely happens in melanoma, but it happens quite often in retinoblastoma.

Is there any way to prevent the formation of eye tumors?

No.

Face and Neck Plastic Operations

Plastic operations upon the face and neck have increased in popularity within recent years. The so-called face-lift operation of many years ago was done mainly upon those in the theatrical professions, but today more and more of the general public are taking advantage of the great advances that have been made in this field of plastic surgery.

QUESTIONS AND ANSWERS

Are plastic operations upon the face and neck successful?

Yes, in the great majority of cases. It must be understood, however, that as one advances in age, the wrinkles are bound to reappear. In other words, the benefits from this type of surgery are mainly seen during the first three to five years after the procedure has been carried out.

What defects can be corrected through facial plastic operations?

1. Wrinkles of the face and forehead can be reduced to a great extent.

2. Laxity of the skin of the eyelids can be eradicated, along with "crow's feet," lateral to the eyelids.

3. Excess skin and wrinkles of the neck can be greatly reduced through plastic surgery.

4. Wrinkles about the mouth can be eradicated to a considerable extent.

What technique is used during the course of plastic surgery upon the face?

The skin is undermined through incisions made along the hairlines of the forehead, in front of the ears, and along the back of the neck. After the skin is thoroughly undermined, excess skin is removed and the remaining skin is re-sutured in a taut position. Also, excess skin of the eyelids is removed through crescent-shaped incisions on the upper and lower lids.

Are plastic operations upon the face and neck safe to perform?

Yes. Of course, it is important that the general health of the patient be satisfactory before undertaking surgery so that there will be good wound healing. A patient with a chronic, debilitating disease may not heal satisfactorily.

Should patients undergo a thorough physical and psychological examination prior to facialplasty?

Yes. Such examinations are essential. Firstly, it is absolutely necessary that the general health of the patient is good before undergoing facialplasty. Secondly, the patient must be psychologically attuned to undergo this type of surgery. There are many patients who are emotionally unsuited for plastic surgery and they should not undergo it.

Are psychiatric consultations sometimes advisable prior to doing facialplasty?

Yes. A psychiatrist will often be able to determine whether a particular individual is emotionally well equipped or poorly equipped for this type of experience.

Are operations upon the face and neck always done at one sitting?

No. In some instances the surgeon may do only the neck and chin at one sitting and may leave the eyes and rest of the face for a second operation.

What determines whether the surgeon does the entire operation at one time or does it in stages?

The extent of the reparative work that is to be done, the general condition of the patient, and other technical considerations which only the surgeon can determine preoperatively.

How long does it usually take to perform a complete facial plastic operation?

Anywhere from two to five hours.

Are facial plastic operations usually done under local anesthesia?

Yes. It is infrequent that general anesthesia will be used during plastic surgery although there is no contraindication to its use.

Is a plastic operation upon the face and neck a very painful procedure?

Not particularly. The skin is thoroughly anesthetized with a local anesthetic agent.

Is there a great deal of blood loss during the performance of a facial plastic operation?

No. Blood transfusions are not required in these cases.

How long a hospital stay is necessary for a facial plastic operation?

Usually three to five days. The general recovery of the patient takes place quickly, but there is a good deal of postoperative swelling which will require bed rest for several days.

Is there much disfigurement of the face and neck following plastic surgery?

Yes. There is a great deal of swelling, and there may be a bruised appearance for quite some time following this type of surgery. In most instances, full recovery from the plastic operation does not take place for several weeks.

What are the expectations of good results from facial plastic surgery?

Well over 90 percent of people will obtain a good result.

Are the results permanent?

Not usually. As one ages, especially those who are in their 60s and 70s, wrinkles will reappear.

Can a second plastic operation be done upon the face and neck when wrinkles and other evidences of aging recur?

Yes. Secondary operations are not infrequent in this type of condition. Secondary results may be even better than the results of the first operation.

Are appearances ever made worse by plastic surgery?

This occurs rarely in those patients who have developed a postoperative infection. It should be mentioned that some people cannot become accustomed to their new appearance and they interpret it as being less attractive than their preoperative appearance. Naturally, one's appearance is a subjective determination, and there may be patient dissatisfaction even when the surgeon believes that he has obtained a good cosmetic result.

Fallopian Tubes

The fallopian tubes, or oviducts, are a pair of tubular structures located on each side of the upper portion of the uterus. Each tube is about four inches long, and its narrow passageway connects at the inner end with the internal cavity of the uterus. (See illustration.) The outer end communicates with the abdominal cavity near the ovary.

The function of the fallopian tubes is to receive the mature egg into its funnel-shaped opening, to allow the male sperm cells to travel up it from the uterus, and to provide a channel for the egg (whether fertilized or not) to pass down to the uterus. If the egg has been fertilized, it implants within the wall of the uterus. This migration down the tube usually takes about seven days.

In general, it is presumed that an egg from the right ovary will enter the right fallopian tube and that one from the left ovary will enter the left tube. However, normal pregnancy can take place when a fallopian tube on one side and the ovary on the opposite side have been removed.

Operations upon the fallopian tube or tubes are performed through a low abdominal incision, either longitudinal or transverse, under spinal or general anesthesia. The main reasons for surgery are:

1. Ectopic (tubal) pregnancy.

2. Inflammation or abscess of a tube or tubes (salpingitis).

3. Plastic surgery upon a closed or twisted fallopian tube in order to promote the chances of pregnancy.

4. Prevention of pregnancy by tying and cutting both fallopian tubes (sterilization)

5. At times, as discussed in the sections on the uterus and ovary, the fallopian tubes are removed as part of a larger operation.

1. Ectopic (tubal) pregnancy: If the fertilized egg should fail to reach the uterine cavity and develop normally at that site, an ectopic (abnormally located) pregnancy results. An ectopic (tubal) pregnancy occurs when the fertilized egg is trapped in the fallopian tube during its journey down to the uterine cavity. When this happens, the embryo grows in this abnormal location and distends the tube. Within a few weeks the patient will develop lower abdominal pain and slight vaginal staining. It is estimated that one out of every 300 to 400 pregnancies is an ectopic pregnancy.

The most frequent causes of a tubal pregnancy are:

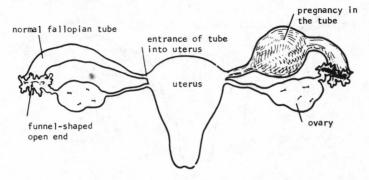

normal fallopian tube

entrance of tube into uterus

pregnancy in the tube

uterus

funnel-shaped open end

ovary

a) Previous inflammation of the tube, causing distortion or adhesions. This accounts for about 25 percent of cases.

b) Endometriosis (*see* ENDO-METRIOSIS), with tissue normally lining the uterine cavity growing into the fallopian tube and attracting the fertilized egg to implant.

c) Congenital (from birth) deformity in the structure of the tube, preventing free passage of the fertilized egg.

d) External adhesions or kinks in the tube from previous peritonitis (as from a ruptured appendix, etc.).

e) Previous surgery performed upon the fallopian tube resulting in a partially obstructed passageway.

f) At times a tubal pregnancy will occur without any of the above conditions being present. The patient may have had previous normal pregnancies, and may have future normal pregnancies, with the one remaining fallopian tube.

Symptoms of a tubal pregnancy are varied. Usually, however, there is a missed menstrual period with general symptoms of pregnancy (breast enlargement, morning sickness, etc.). There may be pain on one side of the lower abdomen, which increases in severity. The diagnosis of an unruptured tubal pregnancy is always considered by the gynecologist when examining a woman of childbearing age who has lower abdominal pain, menstrual irregularity, and a tender mass in the region of the tube. Pregnancy tests *cannot* be depended upon as an aid in diagnosing this condition. In rare instances, there may be a normal pregnancy in the uterus and a twin pregnancy in one of the fallopian tubes. If early symptoms are absent or not recognized, rupture of the tube may take place (usually between the third and sixth week of the pregnancy) with subsequent intra-abdominal hemorrhage. This represents a serious surgical emergency, as pain is intense, and the patient often faints and goes into shock due to the extensive internal bleeding. Immediate blood transfusion and surgery are necessary in order to save her life. In almost all cases, unless the patient fails to receive treatment within a few hours, surgical recovery will be possible. The involved tube is removed through an incision in the lower abdomen. Rarely, a small pregnancy may be removed and the tube left behind. This is done only if it is felt that the involved tube will not be the seat of another tubal pregnancy.

The patient may be out of bed within a day or two after operation and can usually be discharged from the hospital in eight to ten days.

2. Inflammation of the fallopian

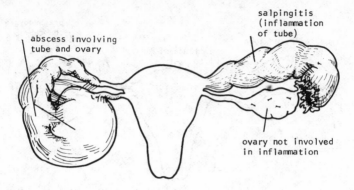

tubes (salpingitis): Infection of the internal female organs can often be treated nonsurgically with appropriate antibiotics. In certain cases, despite intensive antibiotic medication, an abscess will form involving the tube and adjacent ovary. If such an abscess becomes large and painful, surgery must be performed. In younger women who desire future pregnancies, every attempt is made to conserve as much normal tissue as possible. Unfortunately, when a frank abscess once develops, it is usually necessary to take out the tube and often the involved ovary. If both tubes are severely infected, sterility is almost always the inevitable outcome.

3. Plastic (corrective) surgery upon the fallopian tubes: When complete blockage of both fallopian tubes exists, the patient cannot become pregnant. If the blockage is of a minor nature, it is sometimes possible to overcome it merely by "blowing out the tubes" by passing a small amount of carbon dioxide gas through them. This is known as the Rubin insufflation procedure. It is not very painful and can be performed in the gynecologist's office.

With marked blockage and tube closure, the only hope for relief is through surgery. However, the most recent statistics on the results of plastic operations upon the tubes are not too encouraging. Only about 10 to 20 per-

cent of women so treated become pregnant subsequently.

Such surgery should be performed only by those gynecologists specially trained in the field of tubal plastic surgery. The actual operations are carried out through a low, midline abdominal incision under spinal or general anesthesia and are safe insofar as operative recovery is concerned. In certain procedures a cuff is made at the ends of the tube in order to open them and in an attempt to keep them open. Recent procedures employ the use of plastic tubes to replace most of the involved, closed tube.

It must be mentioned that all other causes of sterility should be ruled out before embarking upon plastic tubal surgery, and particular emphasis should be placed upon the fact that approximately 40 percent of all cases of sterility are due to deficiency in the male rather than the female.

4. Ligation of the tubes (sterilization): The prevention of conception by surgical interruption of the fallopian tubes is a simple procedure carried out through a low, midline abdominal incision. Recovery is prompt, and barring accident or unforeseen complication, the operation carries with it no risk. The tubes may be crushed with heavy clamps, or a portion may be cut out, or they may be tied off with heavy sutures, or both tubes may be removed in their entirety. Any of these techniques is adequate to prevent pregnancy from ever occurring.

The indications for sterilization, however, must be strictly adhered to. Legal indications for sterilization are often specifically prescribed by the laws of the community, and they vary from state to state and from country to country. The medical indications for sterilization usually apply to those patients who are too ill to be able to carry a baby through to full-term delivery and whose lives would be endangered by such a pregnancy. These patients include those with severe heart disease, severe kidney disease, marked mental illness, advanced tuberculosis, cancer, etc. Sterilization is often performed following the second or third cesarean delivery.

This subject should not be left without stating that the patient and her husband always have the right to make their own decision concerning sterilization. If religious beliefs convince them not to have sterilization performed despite the appreciation of the medical status, it is inadvisable to urge such a procedure too strongly. Those who are persuaded against their will to act in contradiction to their firmly established religious beliefs may suffer great emotional conflict and harm.

5. **Under the following circumstances normal fallopian tubes are removed:**

a) When the uterus is removed, the tubes no longer serve any useful function and therefore are excised.

b) Occasionally, in removing a diseased ovary, the blood supply to the tube becomes impaired, thus indicating its removal.

c) In older women past the age of childbearing, any operation upon the uterus or ovaries will include tube removal.

See also ECTOPIC PREGNANCY; TUBO-PLASTY.

QUESTIONS AND ANSWERS

What is an ectopic (tubal) pregnancy?
One occurring in a fallopian tube rather than in its normal location in the uterus.

How often does a tubal pregnancy occur?
About one in every 300 to 400 pregnancies.

How long can a tubal pregnancy grow before causing symptoms?
From three to six weeks.

Does a tubal pregnancy ever last nine months and result in the normal birth of a child?
No.

Must tubal pregnancies always be operated upon?
Yes.

What are the symptoms of an ectopic pregnancy?
They vary considerably but usually consist of irregularity of the menstrual flow with slight vaginal spotting, lower abdominal pain, and other signs of early pregnancy. If the tube ruptures, bleeding occurs and is followed by faintness and shock.

Is operation for an ectopic pregnancy an emergency procedure?
Yes.

Should an operation be performed if a tubal pregnancy is strongly suspected, even if not definitely diagnosed?
Yes. In such cases it is much more dangerous not to operate than to operate.

What may happen if a ruptured ectopic pregnancy is not operated upon?
The patient may bleed to death.

Is operation for ectopic pregnancy dangerous?

No, but it is serious if the patient has bled and is in shock. In these cases, transfusions must be given and the bleeding tube must be removed promptly.

Is a woman who has had one tubal pregnancy likely to develop one on the other side?

Not necessarily. However, she is somewhat more prone to do so than someone who has never had an ectopic pregnancy.

Are blood transfusions necessary during operation for a tubal pregnancy?

Yes, when there has been rupture with blood loss.

Does inflammation of the fallopian tubes always cause sterility?

Not in mild cases treated early and vigorously with antibiotics.

Can sterility caused by closed tubes ever be corrected?

Yes. If the closure is of a minor nature, it can often be cured by the Rubin insufflation procedure. If the tubes are closed secondary to previous infection, plastic surgery can remedy the condition in about 10 percent of cases.

What surgical procedures can be performed to sterilize a woman?

1. The fallopian tubes can be tied, cut, or removed.
2. A hysterectomy (removal of the uterus) can be performed.
3. The ovaries can be removed.

Can a woman, once sterilized, ever have further surgery to make her fertile again?

No. And this is the reason why great thought should be given prior to performing sterilization.

What is salpingitis?

Inflammation of a fallopian tube.

Does salpingitis usually involve both tubes?

Yes, and the same infection often spreads to involve the ovaries.

When is surgery necessary in cases of salpingitis?

When there is marked abdominal discomfort of a continuous or repeated nature, when abscess formation is apparent, and when nonsurgical treatment with antibiotics has failed to clear up the infection.

What incisions are made for operations upon the fallopian tubes?

Small lower abdominal incisions, either longitudinal or transverse in direction.

What kind of anesthesia is used for operations upon the fallopian tubes?

1. General anesthesia for bleeding tubal pregnancy
2. General or spinal anesthesia for all other operations upon the tubes

How long after an operation can the patient get out of bed?

Usually the day following surgery.

How long is the average hospital stay after surgery upon the fallopian tubes?

Seven to ten days.

Is it worthwhile to save the uterus when operating for abscesses of both tubes and both ovaries?

No. If both tubes and both ovaries must be removed, then the uterus will serve no useful function and should be removed.

Will surgery upon the fallopian tubes affect menstrual periods?

No.

Will operations upon the fallopian tubes affect sexual activity?

No.

Does removal of the fallopian tubes cause menopause (change of life)?

No. Menopause symptoms result only from removal of both ovaries.

After operation on the fallopian tubes when can one:

Bathe?	2 weeks
Resume household duties?	4 weeks
Drive a car?	4 weeks
Resume marital relations?	4 weeks

Fatty Tumors

See LIPOMAS; SKIN AND SUBCUTANEOUS TISSUES.

Feet

1. Calluses, corns, and bunions are never the theme of charity fund-raising drives or television appeals, yet they cause millions of people severe suffering. For those who have benefited little from endless years of corn plasters, cotton wadding, and repeated paring, surgery can offer excellent relief.

The mechanism of corn, callus, and bunion formation usually involves abnormal pressure from ill-fitting shoes or improper support for the walking and working foot. It should be known that skin and underlying tissue react to abnormal pressure by becoming inflamed and thickened. Thus corns and calluses may develop. Moreover, tight shoes are often responsible for pushing the large toes out of alignment, thus leading to pressure of the metatarsal

bone upon its overlying fatty tissues and skin. These tissues swell, redden, become tender, and form into a bunion.

Calluses and corns occur most often over toe joints that are bent and stiff due to improper shoes or to abnormally tense, tight muscles and tendons. If the stiff toe joints are straightened surgically and the tight tendons and muscles are released and loosened, the calluses and corns usually disappear. Naturally, these operative procedures must be followed by the wearing of sensible, well-fitting shoes.

When a bunion grows to a large size and the underlying bony deformity is marked, surgery should be performed. The protruding portion of the bone is removed, and the joint between the foot and big toe is remodeled. Tense, tight ligaments are lengthened and normal anatomy is reconstructed. In some cases, the metatarsal bone in the foot just behind the big toe is fused to the toe bone or is shifted in position so as to narrow the foot.

2. "Morton's toe": This is a painful condition of the sole of the foot adjacent to the third and fourth toes. The pain is thought to be due to irritation and thickening of the nerve that supplies the skin of these toes. Cure can be effected by making an incision on the sole of the foot, dissecting out and cutting this nerve. Although sensation to the involved toes may be disturbed, it does not interfere with function of the foot.

3. Bone spur: The ligament that maintains the arch of the foot extends from the forefoot (just behind the toes) to the heel. If, due to weak foot tendons or repeated strain or poor foot mechanics, this ligament is unduly stretched, it may become inflamed at its attachment to the heelbone (os calcis). Along with the inflammation and thickening of the ligament, a spur of bone develops. Relief of symptoms may be obtained by giving injections of Novocain and cortisone and by the wearing of better-fitting shoes. At times, this form of therapy does not bring relief and it is necessary to perform surgery. At operation, the inflamed, thickened ligament is severed and the bony spur is excised. Cure of symptoms is the usual outcome of this procedure. *See also* BUNIONS; CORNS.

QUESTIONS AND ANSWERS

What are corns and calluses?

Thickenings of the skin about the toes and feet.

What causes calluses and corns?

1. Abnormal pressure from poorly fitting, tight shoes

2. Abnormally tense, tight foot muscles and tendons which result in bent, stiff toe joints

What is a bunion?

A swelling, thickening, and inflammation of the skin and tissues beneath the skin at the base of the big toe.

What causes bunions?

Malalignment of the bone just behind the big toe, with deformity of the joint at the base of the toe. Improper shoes may produce the malalignment.

Are bunions inherited?

No, except that the particular type of foot might be inherited, thus predisposing someone to bunion formation.

Is surgery indicated for corns or calluses?

Yes, if they do not disappear spontaneously after wearing properly fitting shoes and if they are thought to be due to stiff toe joints.

What operation is done for corns and calluses?

The stiff joints are straightened and the tense, tight tendons and muscles are released. If the underlying bone is abnormal, this too must be corrected.

Should bunions be operated upon?

Yes, if they are large and cause marked foot deformity.

What operation is done for bunions?

The joint at the base of the big toe is straightened by removing a portion of the metatarsal bone and by releasing and transferring certain ligaments and tendons.

Are operations for calluses, corns, and bunions usually successful?

Yes.

Is it necessary to place the foot in a cast after a bunion operation?

Yes, usually.

Can surgery help those who have a painful heel associated with an inflamed, thickened ligament and a bone spur?

Yes, by cutting the inflamed, thickened ligament and removing the spur on the heelbone (calcaneus).

How can bunions be prevented?

By wearing shoes of the correct size and shape. Narrow-toed shoes are particularly to be avoided.

How can corns be prevented?

By wearing shoes that fit correctly, by the removal of abnormal bony prominences, by correcting abnormal alignment of the foot or toes (often by surgery), or by placing felt or rubber pads behind an area of abnormal pressure on the sole of the foot.

What is the treatment for corns?

Medications containing salicylic acid may be applied directly to the corn, or a corn plaster or corn pad can be applied. It is always best to consult an orthopedic surgeon when a corn fails to disappear after being treated for a reasonable length of time.

CONGENITAL VERTICAL TALUS

What is congenital vertical talus?

Congenital vertical talus is a congenital (birth) abnormality of the foot in which the anklebone (the talus) dislocates into the arch of the foot.

How is it diagnosed?

There is a hard, bony mass in the arch of the foot. The mass is tender to pressure when examined.

How is congenital vertical talus treated?

The talus (anklebone) is surgically elevated so that it is no longer located in the arch of the foot. It is held in this new position by fusing the bones or by transferring ligaments.

FLATFOOT

What is flatfoot (pes planus)?

Flatfoot, or pes planus, is a depression of the longitudinal arch of the foot, sometimes associated with a turning outward of the heel.

How common is flatfoot?

It is one of the most common structural deformities seen in human beings.

What are the causes of flatfoot?

1. Weakness of the ligaments and muscles of the arch

2. Paralysis of some of the leg muscles, as after polio

3. Spasm of muscles on the outer side of the leg (peroneal spastic flatfoot)

4. Congenital vertical talus

5. Hypermobile flatfoot (splayfoot)

6. Faulty development of bony structures

7. Failure to have adequate orthopedic treatment for potential foot weaknesses during childhood

Do the feet of newborns normally look flat?

Yes. This is due to baby fat filling out the arch of the foot.

How can it be determined that an individual actually has flatfoot rather than feet that just give the appearance of being flat?

The true flatfoot not only will appear flat but will also tend to turn outward. The heel cord will describe a gentle arch to the outer side of the foot.

Will wearing improper shoes cause one to develop flat feet?

No, but it will aggravate the tendency if it exists.

How can people avoid developing flatfoot?

Often, proper exercises can be helpful in strengthening the small muscles of the foot and stretching a tight heel cord.

Does an individual with flatfoot always have pain?

No. The condition is sometimes completely painless.

Where are the pains usually located in flatfoot?

1. Along the sole of the foot

2. Up the back of the legs

3. In the heels

What treatment is usually given for flatfoot?

1. A series of exercises

2. Well-fitted shoes

3. Arch supports prescribed by an orthopedist

What are the advantages of wearing arch supports?

In small children, it is possible that prolonged wearing of arch supports may influence the subsequent development of the longitudinal arch. In adults, arch supports serve only to relieve symptoms.

Are leather arch supports helpful in treating flatfoot?

Yes.

Is it helpful to place a wedge on the inner side of the heel in cases of flatfoot?

Yes.

Is it necessary to treat someone with flatfoot who has no symptoms?

Often he will require no treatment.

Should flatfooted people without symptoms wear arch supports or corrective shoes?

It is not necessary in such cases.

What exercises should one do to help improve flatfoot?

1. With bare feet, he should try to pick up marbles from a carpeted floor and place them in a deep bowl.

2. He should stand several inches away from a wall and gently push back and forth from the wall while keeping soles and heels flat on the floor.

Should physical activities be limited because of flatfoot?

No.

What causes peroneal spastic flatfoot?

This condition is due to pain in the joints between the small bones of the rear part of the foot. This pain is most often due to an abnormal bony block uniting two of the bones and throwing abnormal stress on the other joints of the foot. This is called a tarsal coalition or tarsal bridge or bar. (The tarsals are the small bones at the back of the foot.)

Peroneal spastic flatfoot may also be due to arthritis of the tarsal joints, to infection, or to trauma (injury).

How is peroneal spastic flatfoot diagnosed?

The foot is held rigid with the sole facing outward. Any attempt to turn the sole inward causes pain. If the peroneal spastic flatfoot is due to a tarsal bridge, this can be diagnosed on x-ray examination.

What is the treatment for peroneal spastic flatfoot?

The application of plaster casts, manipulation, and sometimes surgery.

Why do some children walk with their toes turned out?

This is usually due to flatfoot or tight heel cords. It is known as splayfoot.

What should be done to correct splayfoot?

Special shoes should be worn with a metal arch support attached to a metal flange on the outer side of the foot.

HAMMERTOE

What is hammertoe?

A deformity in which the toe is bent upon itself and is mallet-shaped.

What causes hammertoe?

1. Birth deformity
2. The wearing of improper shoes

What is the treatment for hammertoe?

Surgical correction of the deformed toe, as well as the adjacent toes, which may also be somewhat deformed.

Is surgery effective in curing hammertoe?

Yes.

HEELS

What causes painful heels?
1. Excessive prominence of the back of the heelbone (os calcis).
2. Inflammation about the heel cord.
3. Bursitis about the heel cord. (Bursitis is an inflammation of a tissue sac lying between a bone and its overlying muscles, tendons, or ligaments.)

Do children often get pain in their heels?
Yes, especially between the ages of 6 and 10 years.

Can pain in the heels be relieved by wearing special shoes?
In many instances, yes.

What changes in the shoes are advised for those who have painful heels?
1. If the pain is due to a prominent heelbone (os calcis), then a highbacked shoe with the stiff heel counter removed would be advised.
2. If the painful heel is due to tendonitis (inflammation of a tendon) of the heel cord, an elevated heel may give relief.

What causes a bone spur of the heel?
If there are weak foot tendons or repeated strain, the ligament that maintains the arch of the foot is unduly stretched. It may then become inflamed at its attachment to the heelbone, and along with the inflammation, a spur of bone develops.

How can the pain of a bone spur be relieved?
By giving injections of Novocain and cortisone and by the wearing of wellfitting shoes.

Is it ever necessary to operate for a bone spur?
Yes, occasionally. At operation, the inflamed, thickened ligament is severed and the bone spur is excised.

MORTON'S TOE

What is Morton's toe?
It is a painful condition of the sole of the foot adjacent to the third and fourth toes.

What causes Morton's toe?
The pain is thought to be due to irritation and thickening of the nerve that supplies the skin of the toes that are afflicted.

What is the treatment for this condition?
Cure can be effected by making an incision on the sole of the foot, dissecting out and cutting the affected nerve. Although sensation to the involved toes may be disturbed, the operation does not interfere with the function of the foot.

Must all patients with Morton's toe undergo surgery?
No. Those who suffer only mildly from the condition can often be relieved greatly by wearing a wider shoe.

PES CAVUS

What is pes cavus?
Pes cavus is an excessively high arched foot, the opposite of flatfoot.

Is pes cavus common?
Yes.

What are the symptoms of this condition?
It is usually not noticed before the age of 7 years. The child will develop calluses under the balls of his feet. The characteristic appearance of the foot with the high arch, toes pushed backward over the top of the foot, and prominence of the heel is more striking than are the symptoms of the deformity.

What is the treatment for pes cavus?

1. The tight fibers (plantar fascia) on the sole of the foot are stretched (by someone else, not the patient himself).

2. Special shoes, with a bar across the base of the foot just in front of the toes are often helpful.

3. If the deformity continues, surgery may be required.

PIGEON TOES

What causes pigeon toes?

1. Abnormal bony development of the feet

2. Turning in of the bones of the leg

3. Abnormality of the hip

What is the significance of pigeon toes?

If pigeon toes are due to deformity of the hip, it is essential that the hip deformity be corrected.

Do corrective shoes help people who have pigeon toes?

Yes.

What kind of shoes should be worn for pigeon toes?

Shoes with an arch support and a medial heel wedge or sometimes a lateral sole wedge.

PLANTAR WARTS

What is a plantar wart?

A painful callused area on the sole of the foot.

What causes plantar warts?

Infection, plus a deformed arch formation, plus the wearing of shoes that do not fit properly.

What is the treatment for plantar warts?

Removal by one or more of the following means

1. Surgical excision

2. Electric cauterization

3. Burning with caustic medications

4. X-ray therapy

BIRTH DEFORMITIES OF THE FOOT

See BIRTH DEFORMITIES OF THE EXTREMITIES; CLUBFOOT.

Felon

A felon, or whitlow, is an infection of the finger pad at the tip of the finger. It is a rather treacherous type of infection because it is most difficult for pus to gain exit from the closed-end space, and it is therefore drained down to the bone of the tip of the finger. When the bone becomes involved in infection, osteomyelitis results and the bone may be partially or totally destroyed. This complication of felon will lead to marked deformity of the fingertip.

QUESTIONS AND ANSWERS

What causes most felons?

A prick from an unclean pin or needle. A scratch or a sharp blow can also cause a felon.

What are the symptoms of a felon?

Within a period of two to three days after having been injured, the tip of the finger becomes red, hot, tense, and very painful.

Will hot wet soaks cause most felons to subside spontaneously?

If applied soon after the finger has been injured, these dressings may help. Unfortunately, once pus has formed in the closed space of the finger pad, it will require surgical drainage.

Can medical treatment with antibiotics cure most felons?
Occasionally, it will cause one to subside completely, but more usually, surgical drainage will be necessary.

How can one tell whether finger deformity will result from a felon?
X-rays will show the presence or absence of bone involvement. If the tip of the bone is not involved and the felon has been drained adequately, in all probability finger deformity will not result.

Does it take long for a felon to heal?
Yes. Some felons may require several weeks before they are completely healed. Although they often will leave a sizable scar on the finger pad, this will tend to disappear over a period of months or years.

Is hospitalization necessary for a felon?
In most instances, these infections are better drained in the hospital either under a light general anesthesia or under regional block anesthesia.

How can felons be prevented?
1. People should exercise extreme care when diapering a child to be certain that they are not stuck with a pin.
2. If one is accidentally stuck by a pin or needle, he should consult his physician and inquire as to the need for preventive antibiotic therapy.
3. No infection should be squeezed out or self-treated. Inadequate self-treatment may lead to an extensive infection of the finger and underlying bone.
4. Thick, protective gloves should be worn when there is a possibility of handling material that contains spicules of glass or sharp wires or needles.

Female Genital Organs

See BARTHOLIN GLANDS AND CYSTS; BIRTH DEFORMITIES OF THE FEMALE GENITAL ORGANS; CERVIX; CESAREAN SECTION; CYSTOCELE AND RECTOCELE; DILATATION AND CURETTAGE; ECTOPIC PREGNANCY; ENDOMETRIOSIS; FALLOPIAN TUBES; HYMENOTOMY; HYSTERECTOMY; LEUKOPLAKIA; OVARIES; TUBOPLASTY; UTERUS; VAGINA; VULVECTOMY.

Fetological Surgery

Fetological surgery is surgery upon the fetus, the unborn child. Although this type of surgery is feasible, to date there have been but few operative procedures performed upon the fetus while it is in its mother's womb. Those cases that have been reported are instances in which the mother's abdominal wall has been opened, an incision has been made into the pregnant uterus, and a leg of the fetus has been withdrawn into the surgical wound. A needle is then inserted into the blood vessels of the unborn child's thigh, and an exchange transfusion is carried out, thus controlling erythroblastosis (Rh-factor disease). This operation has been restricted to those few instances in which it was thought inadvisable to await the child's birth for fear that a stillborn might result.

It is conceivable that a time will come when many birth defects will be diagnosed while the child is still within its mother's uterus. If it is then determined that a defect is surgically correctable, it may be advisable to operate upon the fetus before the defect has fully developed. As an example, one day it may be possible to diagnose clubfoot upon an unborn child. In such a case, it might be feasible to correct such a deformity before the child is born, thus obviating a great deal of pain and hardship for the infant during the first year of life. Other defects too, possibly including heart and blood vessel abnormalities, might one day be amenable to correction prior to birth.

QUESTIONS AND ANSWERS

Can a limb of an unborn infant be withdrawn from its mother's uterus, operated upon and reposited, with a prospect for correction of a congenital disease?

Yes. This has been carried out several times, especially in cases of Rh-factor disease. Of course, the child's entire body is not withdrawn from the uterus. The subsequent delivery of the mother is carried out by cesarean section when the fetus has approached or reached full term.

Are there increased dangers of a stillbirth when a fetus is operated upon?

No. In the few cases reported, the fetuses have continued to develop normally until delivery.

Have fetuses with Rh-factor disease actually been saved by exchange transfusions carried out through fetological surgery?

Yes. There are quite a number of such cases on record.

Have fetologists discovered many new things about unborn children?

Yes. Formerly, it was thought that the fetus had no life of its own within the womb and just floated there, inert and totally unconscious. More recently, by fine testing, it has been discovered that the unborn child is quite alert and reacts quite vigorously to events surrounding him.

What has been discovered about unborn children through tests?

1. It has been found that when the mother gets into positions very uncomfortable for the fetus, it reacts by kicking and forcing her to move into a position which it finds more comfortable.

2. It has been discovered that loud noises are transmitted through the fluid surrounding the unborn child and that it sometimes becomes very disturbed by these noises. The action is noted by a rapid rise in pulse rate.

3. It has been found that the fetus's body chemistry reacts to the comfort or discomfort of its surroundings, and to the health or disease of its mother.

4. It has been found that the fetus has pain sensitivity and that it will try to wriggle away when a painful stimulus approaches the surface of its body.

Is it considered dangerous to x-ray the mother in order to note characteristics of the fetus?

To x-ray the mother during the first few weeks or months of pregnancy is considered to be an unwise procedure, as the x-rays may possibly cause birth deformities. One or two x-rays of the mother during the last few weeks of the pregnancy are not considered to be too dangerous, but obstetricians dislike recommending the procedure because all is not yet known about the ultimate effect of x-rays upon the child. Consequently, x-ray examination of the pregnant woman has fallen into relative disuse.

How can the fetologist study the unborn child?

Most of the studies are conducted by inserting a thin, hollow needle through the abdominal wall of the mother, and then on through the wall of the uterus into the fluid surrounding the unborn baby. This procedure is known as amniocentesis.

Is it conceivable that the day will come when an unborn child will be able to be removed completely from the mother's womb except for the attachment of the umbilical cord?

Yes. These experiments have already been performed successfully upon animals. It is entirely possible that at some future date it will be feasible to remove a fetus, perform surgery to correct a life-threatening defect, and then replace the fetus in its mother's womb. The womb and abdominal wall will then be sewn closed.

Fibroids

See UTERUS.

Fibromas

A fibroma is a benign (noncancerous) fibrous tumor arising from connective tissues. It may occur anywhere on the surface of the body, beneath the skin, or in various internal organs. A favorite site for fibromas is an arm or a leg.

QUESTIONS AND ANSWERS

How can one diagnose the presence of a fibroma?

If it is in the superficial tissues, there will be a firm, hard, rounded lump. This lump may be pea-sized or may grow very large, reaching the size of a grapefruit.

Do fibromas cause symptoms?

In some cases, there is pain in the area, particularly when the fibroma is in a place that is subject to body pressure. Thus, if a fibroma is located about the waist, or on the sole of a foot, or on an elbow, it may become painful. Also, in occasional cases, the fibroma grows in close proximity to a nerve and causes painful pressure upon it.

What is the treatment for fibromas?

If they show growth or if they cause pain, they should be removed by surgical excision. Fibromas are often resistant to x-ray treatment.

Do fibromas ever become malignant?

This seldom happens, but in rare instances, a fibroma may turn into a malignant fibrosarcoma.

Is there a tendency for fibromas to recur once they have been surgically removed?

No.

Do fibromas ever occur in the skin?

Yes. Dermatofibromas are exceedingly common.

First Aid

THE ROLE OF THE FIRST-AIDER

At one time or another, everyone is called upon to render first aid in an emergency. Unless he has taken courses in the subject, there is usually considerable concern as to what should be done. Some are fearful that they will harm rather than help the victim; others, though well-meaning, through overly energetic maneuvers may actually complicate the situation.

Experience has shown that in the great majority of emergencies, it is better for the uninformed laymen to do too little than too much! This dictum is particularly applicable in urban and suburban areas where expert medical help is never more than minutes away.

The following are some good general rules to observe before giving first aid:

1. If expert medical aid is in the immediate vicinity, it is far better to leave the scene of the emergency to fetch help than to attempt to play the role of a professional.

2. If the emergency takes place in an urban area, remember that police and firemen are well trained in first aid and can do more to help than an untrained or partially trained first-aider.

3. If the emergency takes place in a rural area, remember that there are usually police road patrols available. Ask the first passerby to summon them.

4. Ask the whereabouts of the nearest hospital, and if it is nearby, dispatch someone to notify them that help is needed.

5. In every community, telephone operators know how to obtain help in the quickest way. Tell them of the problem and let them follow it up with the proper agencies.

6. Never forget that great physical damage can result from unnecessarily moving the victim of an accident. Of course, if he is pinned under a heavy object or cannot breathe, every attempt should be made to free him. However, it is always better to move the offending object away from the injured person than to attempt to tug and pull the individual out from his confined position.

7. Remember that the safest position for an injured person is to lie flat on the floor or ground with his chin up and the collar, tie, and belt loosened. Do not lift up a patient to a sitting, semisitting, or standing position. Do not give him a cigarette, water, whiskey, or anything else to drink, even if he asks for it.

8. It is a good idea to carry a first aid manual in the glove compartment of the car. It should be consulted whenever the opportunity presents itself to help someone in need.

9. Many people who are prone to fainting spells, seizures, diabetic shock, or convulsions carry specific instructions in their clothing, wallet, or handbag. If an individual is found unconscious, search his or her apparel for this information.

HEMORRHAGE (FROM OPEN WOUNDS)

Most bleeding from open cuts and wounds looks much worse than it actually is, and unless there is a sizable artery severed, it will usually stop by itself. It is therefore important for the first-aider not to panic when he sees a great deal of blood! In a methodical way he should take the steps outlined below:

1. Scalp wounds and head injuries: The first thing to determine is whether the injury has caused any damage within the skull. If the patient has not lost consciousness, this is an indication that perhaps the injury is limited to the scalp. If there is no bleeding from the ear, the nose, or the mouth, it is also a sign that there may not have been a fracture or severe concussion. Look at the patient's pupils, and if they appear equal, this too is a good sign. Most important, talk to the patient and note whether his mind is clear and he is well oriented.

Loss of consciousness, unequal pupil size, bleeding from the nose, ears, or mouth are frequent indications that the skull and brain may have been injured. Such an individual should not be moved until medical help arrives. He should lie flat on his back, and his chin should not be permitted to fall forward on his chest.

The scalp laceration, whether accompanied by more serious injury or not, should be treated by applying a sterile gauze pad and tight bandage. If such a pack or bandage is not available, a clean handkerchief or a sanitary napkin should be used. Another handkerchief or scarf, or a sleeve of a shirt, can be used as a makeshift bandage.

Steady manual pressure for at least ten minutes should be applied directly over the wound after the dressing and bandage are in place. This will stop most of the bleeding from scalp wounds.

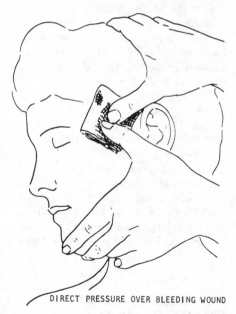
DIRECT PRESSURE OVER BLEEDING WOUND

Do not pour antiseptics into an open cut or wound. If medical help will not be available within a period of a few hours, the wound should be cleansed with mild soap and plenty of water.

2. Face wounds: Rarely does a wound of the face bleed so severely that the general condition of the patient is endangered. If a pumping blood vessel is seen, a sterile gauze pad, a sanitary napkin, or a clean handkerchief should be applied directly over the area and steady, firm pressure with the fingers should be applied. The patient can often do this for himself.

Cleansing should be with a mild soap and cool water. No antiseptics or ointments should be used.

3. Neck wounds: Most lacerations of the neck are superficial and will not involve the major arteries (the carotids). However, the large jugular vein and its branches lie directly beneath the skin, and they are often severed, resulting in fatal hemorrhage if untreated.

Bleeding from the neck should be given first aid by the application of a gauze pad or other makeshift dressing, and steady manual pressure directly over the wound. Lives have sometimes been saved by maintaining this hand pressure until the victim can be transported to a hospital.

No bandage should be placed around the neck, as it may cause interference with breathing.

4. Wounds in the arms or legs: First the patient should lie down. Then the first-aider should apply a gauze pad or other makeshift dressing. The extremity should be bandaged snugly but not so tightly as to constrict circulation. If bleeding continues, steady finger and hand pressure should be applied directly over the bandage for five to ten minutes. If bleeding still continues, a *tourniquet* should be applied just above the wound site.

An opened handkerchief, a scarf, a leather or cloth belt, a sleeve of a shirt, can all be used to make a tourniquet.

Tourniquets can be tightened by inserting a stick or long pencil into the knot of the encircling bandage and then turning it sufficiently to stop bleeding. A tourniquet applied too loosely will increase bleeding!

Tourniquets must be loosened at least once every 15 minutes or they may cause severe permanent damage to circulation. If, after loosening a tourniquet, bleeding is only mild or stops altogether, do not reapply the tourniquet. Apply it again for a 15-minute period only if hemorrhage is brisk and continuous.

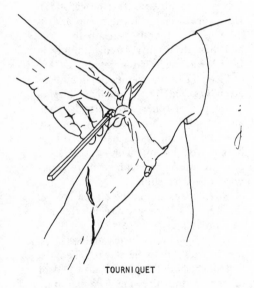

TOURNIQUET

5. Chest wounds: The first-aider can tell almost immediately if a wound has penetrated into the pleural (chest) cavity, as there will be a sucking and blowing of air as the patient breathes. Chest wounds should be covered immediately to stop the sucking and blowing action. Handkerchiefs, scarfs, or any other available material should be applied and tightly sealed with adhesive tape if it is available.

The patient should be placed in a sitting or semisitting position and transported in that manner to the nearest hospital.

Stab or bullet wounds of the chest will usually cause death within a very short time if they have pierced the main chambers of the heart or the large blood vessels. However, many chest wounds pierce only the lungs, and bleeding from this organ does not tend to cause immediate death. Moreover, there are a considerable number of patients with heart wounds who can be saved if they are taken immediately to the hospital!

6. Abdominal wounds: It is rarely possible for a first-aider to know whether an abdominal wound is superficial or has penetrated into the abdominal cavity. For this reason, every such laceration, stab, or gunshot wound should be taken very seriously, and the patient should be taken as soon as possible to the nearest hospital.

Bleeding from the abdominal wall should be covered with a gauze pad or makeshift dressing, and an encircling bandage should be applied if adhesive tape is not available.

The patient should lie flat and *nothing should be given to him by mouth.* This is very important, as there may be perforation of the stomach or intestines.

If the abdominal wound is severe and intestines are spilling out from the abdominal cavity, a handkerchief or shirt should be spread to contain them. Many patients of this type can be saved if they receive prompt surgical treatment.

HEMORRHAGE (FROM WITHIN THE BODY)

1. Nosebleed: Over 90 percent of nosebleeds originate at the anterior part of the nose from the septum (the central partition between the nostrils).

They can in most instances be controlled by packing cotton tightly into the nostril and applying steady, firm finger pressure to the side of the nose. The patient should be placed in a sitting position with the head tilted slightly forward. Pressure should be maintained for at least 10 to 15 minutes. If these measures fail to stop the bleeding, it usually indicates that the hemorrhage originated from the posterior (back) part of the nose. These cases should be hospitalized so that a posterior nasal packing can be inserted.

The many old devices, such as placing a cold key or wet rag on the back of the neck, have been discarded as valueless.

DIRECT PRESSURE FOR NOSEBLEED

2. Bleeding from the mouth: This type of bleeding can be diagnosed by the fact that it is bright red in color and is not clotted or mixed with sputum which has been coughed up. Blood coming down from the back of the nose is usually darker in color and may contain some clot.

Tongue biting, often secondary to an epileptic seizure or to a sudden head injury, will cause mouth bleeding. Such lacerations usually do not cause dangerous hemorrhage. However, if the patient is unconscious, *it is very important to turn his head to one side* so that the blood will run out of the mouth rather than down the throat. Choking and suffocation can result from a minor tongue laceration in an unconscious patient unless this simple first aid measure is followed.

Bleeding from the gums or cheeks can be seen readily on inspection. First aid treatment should consist of mouth washings every four hours with a flat spoonful of table salt dissolved in a glass of warm water.

3. Bleeding from the ear: This usually accompanies a head injury with fracture of the skull. No local first aid need be given but the patient should, of course, be treated immediately for his head injury. No attempts should be made to clean out the ear canal or stop the bleeding. If a piece of sterile cotton is available, it can be tucked lightly into the ear canal.

4. Bleeding from the lung: Severe lung hemorrhage may be associated with tuberculosis, lung abscess, or tumor. Most often the blood is coughed up and is seen to be frothy and mixed with sputum.

An initial hemorrhage from a lung is rarely extensive, but the patient is often overwhelmed with apprehension. First aid consists of transporting the patient in a flat or semirecumbent position to a hospital. Before doing this, it is best to contact the family physician for specific instructions.

Occasionally people will bring up small amounts of blood with a severe coughing spell. This may be merely from rupturing a small capillary in a bronchial tube and has no serious implication. Nevertheless, the physician should be notified so that he can rule out lung disease.

5. Bleeding from the esophagus: This occurs from rupture of a varicose vein secondary to cirrhosis of the liver. First aid will involve immediate transportation to a hospital. Bleeding from the esophagus may be abrupt and copious. There may be no associated vomiting.

6. Bleeding from the stomach and upper intestines: Hemorrhage from the stomach or duodenum is most often due to an ulcer. The blood is vomited, and appears either bright red if the hemorrhage is very active or dark brown (coffee-grounds color) if it has remained in the stomach long enough for the acid to have acted upon it.

Do not give the patient anything to drink. Cover him with warm blankets if he is cold. Do not permit him to sit up or stand. The pulse should be taken and recorded. If it becomes more rapid over a period of one-half to one hour, it indicates that bleeding is continuing. If the patient breaks out into a sweat, feels weak and faint, and the pulse goes beyond 100 beats per minute, it indicates that a state of hemorrhagic shock is imminent.

As soon as a patient vomits blood the family physician should be notified. In all probability, he will advise hospitalization by ambulance.

7. Bleeding from the rectum: This type of bleeding may be associated with many conditions. When it is bright red, it usually signifies that the origin is near to the rectum or the lower bowel. When it is dark red, it may originate higher up in the large bowel. When it is jet black,

it usually means that it has come down from the stomach or duodenum.

Rectal bleeding is serious but rarely requires immediate first aid measures. The physician should be notified, and the patient should await his instructions.

8. Vaginal bleeding: Severe bleeding from the vagina may ensue from menstruation, from glandular imbalance, from a miscarriage, or may be due to fibroids of the uterus. The patient should be put to bed, an ice bag placed over the lower abdomen, and the physician called. No attempt should be made to stop the bleeding by placing anything in the vagina.

9. Urinary bleeding: Hemorrhage from a kidney, ureter, or bladder is evidenced on urination. Seldom is this type of bleeding sufficiently copious to require first aid. However, medical consultation should be sought without delay.

10. Bleeding into the tissues beneath the skin: Bruises with hemorrhage into the subcutaneous tissues are common injuries suffered by almost everyone at one time or another. The average bruise requires no first aid treatment. However, if pain and swelling appear to be extensive and progressive, firm pressure over the area should be applied for 15 to 20 minutes. In some cases, this may cause the bleeding to stop. Ice bags may be applied to the area but should not be left in place for more than one-half hour at a time, as they may produce a localized frostbite effect.

A collection of blood beneath the skin is called a hematoma. Although most of these collections will absorb over a period of a week or two, some grow to such size that they will require aspiration with a needle or surgical incision and drainage.

11. Abdominal internal hemorrhage: Bleeding into the abdominal cavity may result from rupture of a major blood vessel such as the aorta, from rupture of an ectopic pregnancy, or from injury to an organ such as the spleen or liver. Whatever the cause, it is a most serious condition requiring emergency hospitalization.

Symptoms of abdominal hemorrhage will be those of shock (see below). The patient should lie flat in bed or have the foot of the bed elevated four to six inches. Blankets should be applied to keep the patient warm. Nothing should be given by mouth. The family physician should be summoned immediately but if he is unavailable, an ambulance should be called to take the patient to the hospital.

SHOCK

The most common cause of shock is hemorrhage, either internally or from an exposed wound. This serious condition can also be produced by overwhelming blood poisoning (septicemia, with bacteria circulating in the bloodstream), by absorption of toxins (poisons) into the bloodstream, by extremely painful injuries even if not accompanied by great blood loss, by extensive burns, by chemical agents and electrical agents, and by extreme nervous and mental disturbance.

A diagnosis of shock can be made from the following symptoms and signs:

1. The patient is usually conscious or semiconscious, with great apprehension and fear noticeable.

2. There is great thirst.

3. The pupils are dilated.

4. The skin is moist, cold, and clammy, with a grayish tint.

5. The pulse is very rapid and weak.

6. Breathing is shallow and rapid.

Patients in shock should receive the following first aid treatment:

1. They should be made to lie down flat with the legs placed at a higher level than the head.

2. All tight clothing should be loosened.

3. If active external bleeding is noted, take appropriate action (*see* HEMORRHAGE).

4. Cover with blankets but do not overheat. If room is warm and patient does not complain of cold, do not add coverings.

5. Obviously fractured or dislocated bones should be splinted (*see* FRACTURES) unless immediate help is available.

6. Do *not* give coffee, alcohol, tea, or anything else by mouth unless it can be determined with absolute certainty that there is no injury to any of the abdominal organs. If this can be ascertained, it is permissible to give warm water and an available pain-relieving medicine.

7. Patients should be transported in a flat position to a hospital as soon as possible.

BURNS

If a burn victim is in shock, the shock should be treated first (*see* SHOCK).

1. First degree burns involve only the superficial layers of the skin and seldom require a physician's care. When they first occur, the burned area should be placed under running cold tap water for 10 minutes. If the burn is extensive, the patient should lie in a tub of cold water with the faucet running. After this, the areas can be covered with plain Vaseline gauze dressings or any other mild soothing ointment.

2. Second degree burns go through all but the deepest layer of skin. The average layman can make the diagnosis readily by comparing normal skin to the burned areas, where the top layers are obviously missing. There is a serum ooze from the surface and blister formation. When this type of burn is first incurred, the following measures should be instituted:

a) Burned areas should be placed under cold running water for 10 to 15 minutes.

b) After the water treatment, dirt or adherent clothing should be gently washed off with cotton or toilet tissue and a mild soap.

c) Large amounts of fluids should be taken by mouth.

d) Clean gauze pads, or a clean handkerchief, should be used to cover the burned areas. Ointments should *not* be applied to this type of burn.

e) Blisters should *not* be opened.

f) A physician's care should be sought as soon as possible. Until then, a pain-relieving medicine may be given.

3. Third and fourth degree burns extend through all layers of skin and may involve underlying tissues. First aid should consist of the same treatment as for second degree burns. These people may be more likely to display shock, and treatment for this complication must be prompt.

4. Respiratory tract burns: It has been discovered recently that many burn deaths are due not to skin involvement but to damage suffered by the membranes of the nose, throat, bronchial tubes, and lungs from inhaling extremely hot air at the time of the accident. These tissues will become swollen and will secrete large amounts of fluid, mucus, and serum which may cause interference with breathing. First aid cannot be of much assistance here, but on isolated occasions, when breathing has stopped but a heartbeat con-

tinues, a *tracheotomy may be lifesaving* (*see* TRACHEOTOMY).

5. Chemical burns and radiation exposure: These people should be immediately immersed in cold running water for at least 20 minutes. The exposed areas should be washed down over and over again, using plain water only. Sterile or clean dressings should be applied and the patient transported to the nearest physician or hospital.

6. Eye burns: The patient should lie down and the first-aider should flush out the eyes thoroughly for a period of at least 10 minutes with plain cold water. Medical care should be sought at once after this treatment has been given.

FROSTBITE AND EXPOSURE

The patient should be wrapped in blankets and taken to a warm room. *Sudden overheating is not good!* The room should be at approximately 70°F and slow thawing should be permitted to take place. If a tub is available, the patient should be immersed in lukewarm (not hot) water for 20 minutes. Following this, the body should be dried gently, making sure not to rub vigorously over possibly frostbitten parts such as the tip of the nose, the ears, the fingers, or toes. Any area that appears dark blue and seems to have lost its circulation should be covered by a dry, clean dressing.

If a frozen victim appears to be having trouble in breathing, mouth-to-mouth artificial respiration should be started and continued until respirations approach normal.

Frostbitten and exposed patients should be given food and warm liquids. *Do not:*

1. Rub frostbitten part. Let it thaw out by itself.

2. Start moving frostbitten parts in

an attempt to improve circulation. They will regain motion naturally if irreparable freezing has not occurred.

3. Apply *hot* water to frozen part.

4. Give alcohol to patient to drink or apply it to frozen parts.

BITES

1. Human or animal bites:

a) The wound should be washed thoroughly for 5 to 10 minutes with soap and water.

b) Do *not* apply any antiseptic to an open wound.

c) If bleeding is severe, apply direct pressure (*see* HEMORRHAGE).

d) Seek medical care no matter how trivial the bite may appear to be. The physician may deem it advisable to give tetanus antitoxin, rabies inoculations, or antibiotics.

e) Report all animal bites to the local board of health or police.

2. Insect bites: There are still many disease-carrying insects in this world, and as people travel more, they are increasingly exposed. To overcome this danger, prophylactic vaccination and immunization should be obtained before going to a strange part of the world. The average bee, wasp, hornet, mosquito, fly, scorpion, or spider sting should receive the following first aid:

a) If a stinger is visible, it should be plucked out gently.

b) If marked swelling in the area of the bite comes on quickly, a tourniquet should be applied in order to slow absorption. The tourniquet should be loosened for 5 minutes every 15 minutes.

c) Antihistamine tablets should accompany all travelers and should be given if there is marked local swelling or evidences of a generalized allergic reaction.

d) People known to be allergic or especially sensitive to bee or wasp stings should have a previously prepared, ready-to-give injection of epinephrine (adrenalin) handy. (Physicians should make these available beforehand to such patients.)

e) To relieve local itching, a paste made of baking soda or diluted household ammonia may be applied locally.

f) If a child tends to scratch the bitten area, restrain his arms until the itch subsides.

g) Scorpion bites about the face or neck of a child, and black widow spider bites should be treated more or less as snake bites. The patient should remain quiet and should be transported to the nearest physician or hospital.

FEMALE BLACK WIDOW SPIDER

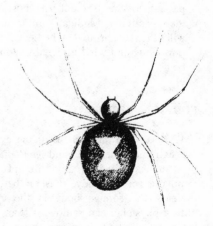

3. Snake bites:

a) Never assume that the bite has been caused by a nonpoisonous snake! Treat them all as if they are dangerous.

b) A tourniquet should be immediately applied above the site of the bite. Loosen at 15-minute intervals.

c) A knife should be used to make crossed incisions over the two fang marks. These incisions should go straight through the skin, and each should be between ¼ and ½ inch long.

d) The bite should be sucked out thoroughly. Poisonous venom does no harm when taken into the mouth, even if it is accidentally swallowed. Repeat the sucking out of the wound 12 times at 5-minute intervals.

e) Patient should lie down and remain absolutely quiet until he can be transported to a hospital.

f) Immerse bitten part in cold water.

g) If possible, find and kill the snake. It should be taken with the patient to the hospital for positive identification. Medical authorities will then determine whether it is poisonous and what antivenin should be given.

FOREIGN BODIES

1. Eyes: The membranes of the eyes are extremely delicate, and *gentleness* must be exercised in any attempt to remove a foreign body. It is far better to leave the foreign body in the eye until a physician can remove it than to use rough methods in trying to remove it yourself.

a) Foreign bodies should not be permitted to remain in the eye overnight. Go to the nearest hospital emergency room if your doctor is not available.

b) Do not rub the eyelids. This will *not* dislodge the particle and may cause it to go deeper into the tissues.

c) Blink the eyelids rapidly. This may stimulate the tears to flow and it may be washed out by itself.

d) If the particle feels like it is in the lower lid, draw it down and let a few drops of warm water run over the area. If it is beneath the upper lid, bend it up and run water over it.

e) If washing out the eye fails to dislodge the particle, expose the affected lid again, look in a mirror in a good light, take the moistened edge of a clean handkerchief, and wipe the particle away. If this fails, let it stay where it is until a doctor can treat it.

f) If a foreign body is seen to be over the pupil or iris (colored portion) of the eye, do *not* try to remove it yourself.

g) After removing a foreign body, place two or three drops of mineral oil or castor oil in the eye. This will tend to soothe any irritation. Again, do *not* rub the eyelids.

2. Nose: Children occasionally stick foreign bodies in their noses, and once in a great while, an insect may enter the nasal passage of a child or adult. Tickling the opposite nostril or having the patient sniff pepper will usually induce sneezing. This will dislodge many foreign bodies. If it does not, see a physician.

3. Ears: The ear canal ends with the eardrum and no significant damage can result from a foreign body getting into this passage. Although it is a frightening sensation, insects will cause no harm in an ear canal. Have the patient lie down, turn his head to one side, and pour in some mineral oil, castor oil, or even some ordinary olive oil. This will usually float out the invader. If it does not, see a physician. Do *not* poke anything into the ear canal, as this may do real harm to the drum.

4. Splinters, glass, dirt, and other foreign bodies beneath the skin should only be removed by first-aiders when a portion of them protrudes from the skin. If such is the case, grab the protruding portion of the foreign body gently and pull it out slowly and steadily. Then wash the area with soap and water and apply a clean dressing.

Do *not* try to remove a splinter or other foreign body which lies completely beneath skin level. When done by an amateur, this may cause it to go deeper or may produce a spreading infection.

Scratches, abrasions, and cuts with dirt in them should be scrubbed with soap and water.

5. Swallowed or aspirated foreign bodies: Most patients who swallow a foreign body require no first aid, as the foreign body will pass directly into the stomach. If there is difficulty in talking or breathing, it indicates that the foreign body may have passed into the larynx or trachea (windpipe). Such patients require immediate first aid:

a) An index finger should be placed into the mouth and should be swept around the base of the tongue and throat. This will often dislodge a foreign body or cause a cough reflex that will bring it up.

b) The patient should take in a deep breath very slowly and then should cough violently.

c) Patients should be turned upside down, urged to cough, and struck sharply on the back of the chest.

d) A tracheotomy should be done only as a lifesaving measure if the patient obviously cannot breathe (*see* TRACHEOTOMY).

e) If obstruction to breathing is only partial, transport patient to nearest hospital in a sitting position.

It is amazing that most swallowed foreign bodies will pass through the entire intestinal tract without difficulty. Marbles, nickels, pennies, dimes, buttons, nails, and even pins may cause no trouble. Those who have swallowed such objects should be x-rayed repeatedly by the physician to note the progress of the object. The stools should be carefully examined each day to note the passage of the foreign body.

Open safety pins, quarter or half-dollar pieces, and other large objects occasionally require surgery for their removal.

A normal diet should be taken by those who have swallowed foreign bodies, and laxatives should not be given.

6. Rectum or vagina: Foreign bodies that cannot be retrieved from these areas by the individual herself can be removed easily by a physician. There is no cause for alarm as no harm will result except in the rare instance.

An enema tip or a thermometer, even if broken, can be extracted without difficulty, although it may be necessary to give a light general anesthesia to relax the rectal muscles.

The vagina is a blind passageway and a diaphragm, internal sanitary protection, cotton, etc., can always be removed without difficulty. A squatting position is the best one to use in an attempt to remove a vaginal foreign body. If it cannot be done by the patient herself, it is permissible to let the material remain in overnight.

ELECTRIC SHOCK

Here are the essential Dos and Don'ts:

1. *Never touch* anyone who is still in contact with an electric current until it is ascertained *positively* that the electricity has been disconnected. Electrocution may be the penalty.

2. To disconnect the victim as quickly as possible from the electric contact, do the following:

a) Turn off the switch, or pull out the electric plug going to the contact.

b) Take a dry wooden stick or board and shove the wire away from the victim, or push the victim away from the contact.

c) If necessary, take an ax with a wooden handle to chop the wire making the contact.

d) Do not move or touch the patient unless your body and hands are dry and you are standing on dry ground.

3. If victim is not breathing, start immediate mouth-to-mouth breathing and continue it as long as there is a heartbeat (*see* ARTIFICIAL RESPIRATION).

4. If there is no heartbeat, start immediate cardiac massage and mouth-to-mouth breathing. Continue at least 15 to 20 minutes before abandoning the effort.

5. If breathing and heartbeat have been restored, then:

a) Cover with warm blanket or coat.

b) Cover any burned area with sterile dressing or clean handkerchief (*see* BURNS).

c) Do not move victim but seek medical aid to transport patient to hospital.

FRACTURES, DISLOCATIONS, AND SPRAINS

Here are some general principles governing first aid to those with a possible fracture, dislocation, or severe sprain:

1. If professional help can be obtained within a short time, then *do not move* the patient or the injured limb.

2. *Do not* allow weight-bearing of any kind.

3. *Don't* attempt to straighten out a broken limb unless you are far from help and know that you will be responsible for transporting the injured.

4. If a compound fracture has taken place and a piece of bone protrudes through broken skin, do *not* attempt to shove it back. Cover wound with dressing.

5. If there is a pain-relieving medicine at hand, give a large dose to allay pain.

6. Cover the patient if he is cold.

7. If no professional aid will be immediately available, *splint* the fractured, dislocated, or sprained limb. (See instructions for splints below.)

8. Remember that splints can be improvised from twigs, pieces of wood, a cane or umbrella, several pieces of cardboard held together, etc. Bandages to hold them in place can be fashioned from handkerchiefs, scarfs, shirts, etc.

9. Neck or back injuries require especially careful handling. Have patient lie flat on his back with head pointing straight up. Hold head between hands so that neck does not bend forward or to either side. Transport in straight position on a blanket, automobile seat, or other flat object.

Here are the best ways to splint injured parts:

1. **Neck:** Place board beneath the head extending down the spine to the waist. Bandage around the forehead and beneath the arms.

2. **Back:** Place patient on flat board. Bandage should encircle patient beneath the arms and around the hips.

3. **Collarbone:** Place one board across the back at shoulder level, and another board perpendicularly down the

back, thus forming a T. Bandage over and under the armpits to hold the cross-board in place. Bandage around waist to keep the upright board in place.

4. Fingers or hand: Stuff an unopened roll of bandage, rolled stockings, or socks into the palm of the hand and secure in place with the hand in fist position.

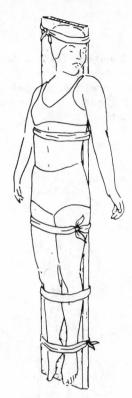

SPLINT FOR BROKEN BACK

SPLINT FOR BROKEN FINGER

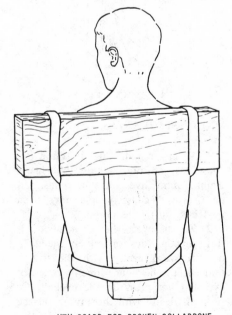

"T" BOARD FOR BROKEN COLLARBONE

IMMOBILIZATION FOR BROKEN HAND

5. Upper arm: Bend securely to side of body by encircling bandage. Do not bend elbow.

6. Lower arm or wrist: Place splint under forearm to elbow. Bend elbow to right angle. Place arm in sling.

7. Thigh or leg: The best splint is the uninjured leg. Place board beneath entire extent of injured thigh and leg and tie to the uninjured extremity. The leg should be out straight.

BANDAGE-IMMOBILIZATION FOR INJURED SHOULDER

SPLINT FOR BROKEN LEG

SPLINT AND SLING FOR BROKEN FOREARM

UNCONSCIOUSNESS

1. When an individual is found unconscious, do not assume that he is drunk. Many lives have been lost unnecessarily because people have been neglected on this assumption.

2. To discover whether someone is truly unconscious or merely sleeping, press upward firmly with the thumb underneath the bone directly over the eye. Do not press on the eyeball. Or press in firmly with the thumb on the

tissues directly behind the earlobes. If the patient is unconscious, there will be no reaction. If he is drunk, semiconscious, or in a deep sleep, he will grimace from the pain.

3. Search the patient's clothing for information on whether he is an epileptic, diabetic, cardiac patient, etc. You may find specific information how to aid him.

4. Loosen tight collars, ties, belts, etc., to facilitate breathing.

5. Take pulse at wrist or put ear to chest to note heartbeat. (*See* CARDIAC MASSAGE.)

6. If difficulty in breathing is apparent, give artificial respiration. (*See* ARTIFICIAL RESPIRATION.)

7. Elevate chin to aid breathing.

8. Note if there is bleeding from the ear, mouth, or nose. Also note if there is an obvious head wound or bruise. (*See* HEAD INJURIES.)

9. Cover victim with blanket or coat if he is cold.

10. If active convulsion is taking place, place a folded handkerchief between the teeth to prevent tongue-biting. Be careful *not* to insert your own fingers or you may be bitten severely.

11. Do *not* try to arouse patient by sitting him up or throwing water in his face.

12. Give nothing to drink by mouth.

13. Call ambulance by telephoning police.

14. If patient regains consciousness, as in fainting or epileptic seizures, reassure him, keep him quiet, and do not permit him to stand up for at least 15 minutes after recovery.

There are three first aid measures with which all should be familiar. These are *Artificial Respiration, Cardiac Massage,* and *Tracheotomy.*

ARTIFICIAL RESPIRATION

Although there are several effective ways of performing this maneuver, *mouth-to-mouth* breathing is now advocated as the quickest, simplest, and most effective procedure. It should be applied in all conditions in which breathing has stopped, including suffocation, drowning, gas poisoning, heart attacks, strokes, etc.

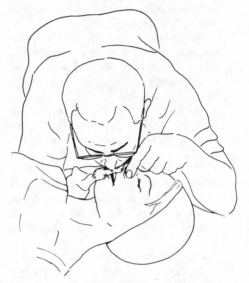

ARTIFICIAL RESPIRATION BY
MOUTH TO MOUTH BREATHING

1. Place patient out flat on his back with chin up and head tilted backward.

2. Loosen all tight clothing.

3. With fingers, pinch the patient's nostrils closed.

4. Place your mouth squarely against the patient's mouth and blow as hard as you can. (It is permissible to place a thin, opened handkerchief between your lips and the patient's, although this may decrease the effectiveness of the procedure to some degree.)

5. Take your mouth away to permit the exit of the air you have blown in.

6. Repeat this maneuver every five to six seconds.

7. Continue as long as there is a heartbeat.

8. If heartbeat stops, carry out cardiac massage (see below), interrupting the heart massage every six seconds to do mouth-to-mouth breathing.

9. If someone is available to assist, then the mouth-to-mouth breathing and the cardiac massage should be conducted simultaneously.

10. Switch tasks periodically when fatigued. Remember that resuscitation may take hours to succeed and should *never* be discontinued as long as the heart keeps beating.

11. Listen for heartbeat by placing your ear against patient's chest. Take pulse at the wrist, in the neck, or at the temple.

12. If there is mucus in the mouth or throat, turn patient on his side and lower the head to permit it to run out of the corner of the mouth. Wipe out sticky mucus with a tissue or handkerchief.

13. If there is water in the lungs secondary to submersion, tilt patient into upside down position and maintain it as long as water runs out.

14. Tracheotomy should be performed only as a last resort when it is obvious patient is *choking.*

15. After patient is revived, do not move him for at least one-half hour. Keep warm and give nothing by mouth.

CARDIAC MASSAGE

Closed cardiac massage has proved to be practically as effective as open cardiac massage. The open method is best applied in hospitals and in operating rooms when heart stoppage (cardiac arrest) is encountered.

To carry out closed cardiac massage:

1. Place patient flat on back on hard surface. If in bed, place on the floor.

2. Kneel and straddle patient.

3. Put heel of your right hand on patient's breastbone.

4. Place left hand on top of your right hand and push down so that breastbone is depressed for one to two inches.

5. Release.

6. Repeat pressure and release every second for a minimum of ten minutes, or until heartbeat is restored.

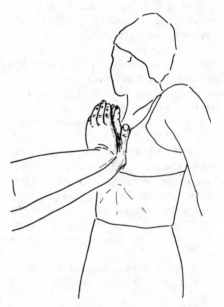

CLOSED (EXTERNAL) CARDIAC MASSAGE

7. If breathing has also stopped, interrupt the cardiac massage every six or seven seconds in order to bend over and carry out vigorous mouth-to-mouth breathing.

8. If assistance is available, mouth-to-mouth breathing should be conducted simultaneously with cardiac massage.

9. If an occasional spontaneous pulse

beat or heartbeat is noted, continue massage until a rhythm is reestablished.

10. Do not move patient after recovery until an ambulance arrives.

TRACHEOTOMY

This emergency measure has saved numerous lives when obstruction is at the level of the larynx (voice box) in the neck. Common conditions causing such an obstruction are *choking from foreign bodies;* inflammatory conditions of the larynx due to *laryngitis, croup, and diphtheria; burns* of the larynx from inhalation of steam or vapors; *spasm* of the larynx from drowning or aspiration of liquid materials; *severe infections of the floor of the mouth or neck* which create pressure on the trachea or larynx; *wounds or injuries* of the larynx or nearby neck structures, etc.

Tracheotomy should be done only as a last resort when breathing is impossible and it is obvious that the patient is choking to death.

As a lifesaving measure, a penknife or other sharp instrument is inserted into the neck and directly into the trachea (windpipe). To do this:

1. Place patient flat on back.

2. Lift up chin as far as it will go.

3. Feel the Adam's apple.

4. Slide fingers down to area just below Adam's apple where you will feel the rings of the trachea (windpipe).

5. Select space between first and second ring to plunge the knife.

6. Make sure knife is inserted as near as possible to the middle of the neck.

7. When air gushes in and out of hole, you will know the knife is in the windpipe.

8. Twist the knife so as to hold open the hole in the trachea.

9. Keep knife in place and trans-

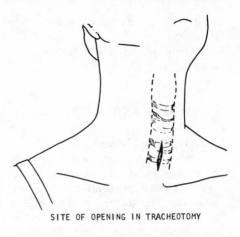

SITE OF OPENING IN TRACHEOTOMY

port patient as soon as possible to nearest hospital.

10. If opening should close, enlarge it in a vertical direction upward and downward.

11. Do not delay the procedure in order to sterilize the knife blade or to put an antiseptic on the neck.

12. Tracheotomy will be of no value unless there is a heartbeat.

Fissure in Ano

A fissure in ano is a slitlike ulcer or crack in the lining of the anal skin causing pain whenever there is an attempt to move the bowels. It usually starts as a superficial scratch but fails to heal because of the repeated contractions and stretchings of the anal orifice. If this process continues for any length of time, the fissure gets deeper and its walls become inflamed and thickened. At this stage, it will require surgical removal, with cutting of the underlying circular sphincter muscle. By severing this sphincter muscle, the anus is put to rest temporarily, the spasmodic contractions are interrupted, and the whole area heals in solidly.

See also HEMORRHOIDS; RECTUM AND ANUS.

QUESTIONS AND ANSWERS

What is a fissure in ano?

It is a small crack in the mucous membrane lining of the anal outlet, usually caused by constipation or by scratching due to the irritation of the anus. The cracked surface becomes infected and an ulcer forms. The ulcer tends to remain, as it is kept open by the stretching at bowel evacuation.

How common is fissure in ano?

It is a very common rectal condition.

What are the symptoms of fissure in ano?

There is pain on attempting to move the bowels. Also, a drop or two of red blood found on the toilet paper after the individual has cleaned his anus. On inspection, a physician will be able to see the actual ulceration in the mucous membrane at the anal outlet.

Is constipation very common with fissure in ano?

Yes, because bowel evacuation is avoided due to the marked pain that results.

What is the treatment for fissure in ano?

Medical treatment may result in healing in many cases if carried out early. The patient takes lubricants, such as mineral oil, and inserts medicated suppositories into the rectal canal. Those patients who fail to respond to medical management must be operated upon.

Does fissure in ano usually heal following medical management?

Yes. It will often heal spontaneously if stool softeners are given and if local irritation is eliminated.

Do fissures in ano ever recur?

Yes, if the bowel habits of the individual are not regular and there is repeated constipation.

What operation is performed when a fissure in ano is not cured through medical management?

A simple operation is done, in which the ulcerated fissure is removed and the superficial fibers of the underlying sphincter ani muscle are severed. As these severed muscles and mucous membrane heal, the anal canal will be widened and will permit the ready passage of stool.

How long does it take for a fissure to heal following surgery?

It may require several weeks for complete healing to take place.

Is bowel function usually normal following an operation for fissure in ano?

Yes. Healing takes place within a few weeks and bowel function returns to normal.

What can happen if a fissure is neglected?

Chronic constipation may develop, and also, the patient may develop hemorrhoids.

Do children ever develop fissure in ano?

Yes. It is seen in those youngsters who have bad bowel habits and who become constipated. The treatment is the same in children as in adults.

Do older people ever develop fissure in ano?

Yes, because constipation is seen very often among the aged. The treatment for older people is the same as that for younger ones.

FISTULA AND FISSURE IN ANO

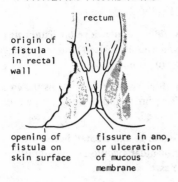

origin of
fistula
in rectal
wall

rectum

opening of
fistula on
skin surface

fissure in ano,
or ulceration
of mucous
membrane

Fistula in Ano

A fistula in ano may be described as an abnormal communication between the lining membrane of the rectum or anus and the skin surface near the anal opening. They are so common that they constitute about one fourth of all conditions originating in and about the rectum or anus. Fistulas are almost always the end result of a previous infection which started in the rectal or anal wall and tunneled its way out to the skin surface. The patient typically gives a history of having had a painful "boil" or abscess alongside the rectum which opened and discharged pus for several days. The abscess opening would then heal and discharge alternately over a period of weeks or months. Because of this tendency, it is important that surgeons warn their patients of possible future fistula formation whenever they treat a boil or abscess near the rectum. Often an interval of several months may elapse between the original infection and the establishment of a fistulous tract. In untreated, advanced cases, it is not at all uncommon to find multiple openings on the skin and a tunnel that extends in many directions for a dis-

tance of two to four inches from its origin.

Every patient with a true fistula in ano should be operated upon because these communications, once established, practically never heal spontaneously. To leave them untreated is to invite further abscess formation and extension of the tract. Occasionally a fistula in ano will surround the entire anal circumference and will have to be treated surgically in several stages. The function of the anal sphincter may be jeopardized as the sphincter muscle must be cut in order to lay open the tract.

The proper surgical treatment is to follow the tract carefully with a probe all along its course and to lay it wide open. The edges are trimmed and the whole tunnel, now unroofed, is excised and the wound is permitted to heal in from the bottom. Care is always exercised to sever the sphincter muscle in a proper manner so that no loss of control of anal function results. When the entire tract has been removed, the wound heals in about one to four months.

See also RECTUM AND ANUS.

QUESTIONS AND ANSWERS

How common is fistula in ano?

Fistulas comprise approximately one fourth of all conditions about the anus or rectum.

What causes fistulas?

They represent the end result of an infection that has originated in the rectal or anal wall and which has tunneled its way out to the skin surface.

Are fistulas ever caused by tuberculosis?

A very small percentage of fistulas are associated with tuberculosis of the lungs. However, today this is an extremely rare occurrence.

What are the symptoms of fistula in ano?

The patient usually gives a history of a painful boil or abscess alongside the rectum which opened and discharged pus at some time previously. The abscess closed and opened alternately over a period of several weeks or months, leaving a small discharge but causing relatively little pain.

What happens if a fistula in ano is not treated?

The fistulous tract tends to spread and tunnel about the rectum and may reach the surface at several points alongside the rectum or anus. Also, the sphincter muscle controlling the outlet may be damaged by an untreated fistula.

What is the treatment for fistula?

All fistulas that fail to heal over a period of several weeks should be operated upon.

What kind of operation is performed?

The fistulous tract is removed or laid open widely. This usually includes cutting the sphincter muscle, as in the operation for a fissure in ano.

Are the hospital procedures and the preoperative and postoperative measures for fistula in ano similar to those for fissure in ano and hemorrhoids?

Yes.

What are the chances for cure of a fistula after surgery?

Excellent. Only rarely will a fistula recur. Occasionally, a large extensive chronic fistula will recur and reoperation will become necessary in order to effect a permanent cure.

Does bowel function return to normal after a fistula operation?

Yes, within a few weeks.

How long do fistulas take to heal?

This is a more extensive operation than a fissure operation and the tissues may take from one to four months to heal fully.

Do older people develop fistula in ano?

Occasionally. It is much more common in young adults.

Do children ever develop fistula in ano?

Yes, but it is not very frequently encountered.

Is fistula in ano treated in the same manner in older people as in younger ones?

Yes.

What percentage of people who have an abscess alongside the anal opening develop fistulas?

Approximately 50 percent.

Foreign Bodies

See FIRST AID.

Fractures

A fracture is any break in the continuity of a bone. Fractures are classified as:

1. **Simple (closed) fractures,** when the skin overlying the bone has remained intact

2. **Compound (open) fractures,** when the skin in the vicinity of the break has been lacerated, torn, or punctured

3. **Comminuted fractures,** when a bone has been broken in two or more places

These terms do not necessarily connote the severity of a fracture. A so-called simple fracture may be broken so badly that it may require much more intensive and prolonged care than a compound fracture.

In order to heal, a fracture must first be set, or in medical terms, reduced. This will involve bringing the various fractured fragments into good anatomical alignment and holding them in that position so that the healing process may progress normally. In many cases, the periosteum (a thick tissue covering most bones) will remain untorn and will hold the fractured ends in place. When this situation prevails, the surgeon will not be required to reduce or set the fracture. However, in a sizable number of cases, muscles surrounding the broken bone will pull the fragments out of position so that they become angulated, slide past one another, twist, or telescope. In such instances, it will be necessary to set the bone fragments back into their normal position.

Many fractures can be set under local or general anesthesia by stretching the muscles sufficiently to permit the bone ends to come together in good position. They are then held in place by one of several methods of immobilization.

Some fractures cannot be reduced without surgical intervention. The bone ends may be too shattered to permit simple restoration and maintenance of normal anatomical positions. In other fractures, muscle, fibrous tissue, or fat may lodge between the bone ends, thus preventing reestablishment of normal position. And in still other cases, it may be quite impossible to guide isolated bone fragments back into their normal position without surgical intervention.

In performing open surgery upon a fracture, an incision is made over the fracture site, the bone fragments are manually replaced into their proper posi-

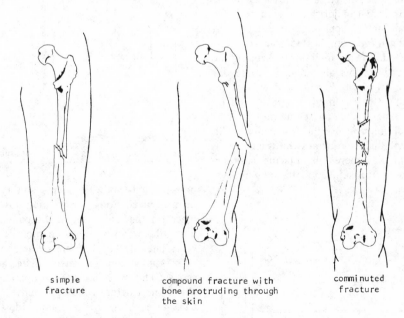

simple
fracture

compound fracture with
bone protruding through
the skin

comminuted
fracture

The femur, or thighbone, like any other bone, is subject to three basic types of fracture. They are: a simple fracture, in which there is no break in the skin; a compound fracture, in which the skin is torn or punctured; and a comminuted fracture, in which a bone has been broken in two or more places.

tions and are held there by some means of internal fixation. To carry out this procedure, some form of anesthesia is essential.

The reduced fracture must be held in proper position until nature has had a chance to promote solid bone healing. With some impacted (telescoped) fractures, and with fractures through bones that are well clothed with a strong surrounding shield of ligaments and muscle (as in certain breaks about the leg and shoulder), immobilization may not be necessary. Unfortunately, in most cases the ends of the broken bone would slip out of place and heal improperly or not at all unless some form of immobilization were applied.

There are a great many methods of maintaining the fractured bones in good position throughout the period necessary for healing. The commonest of these is to apply a plaster cast. This is adequate for the great majority of fractures which are not too difficult to reduce. However, in the more complicated fractures, one of the following methods of keeping the bones in proper alignment is employed:

1. Traction: Weights and pulleys are attached to the injured area to line up the bones and to overcome muscle pulls which might cause the fragments to slip out of line. Sometimes the traction can be applied merely by placing adhesive tape on the skin and attaching pulleys

and weights to it. In other cases, it is necessary to drill a steel pin through a bone beyond the fracture site and to apply the pulleys and weights to such a pin. This is called skeletal traction.

2. Application of metal screws is often performed after setting the fracture at open operation. Such screws are most useful in oblique fractures as they

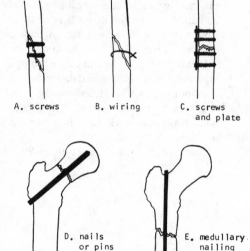

A. screws   B. wiring   C. screws and plate

D. nails or pins   E. medullary nailing

F. bone graft

pass through both fragments and hold them in place. Some screws may stay in place for the remainder of the patient's life. Others can be removed months or years later if they become bothersome.

3. Application of metal plate and screws: This method is used at operation where the fracture is straight across, or transverse. A plate is laid alongside the set fracture extending above and below the fracture site. It is held there by placing metal screws through it into the fragments. It, too, may be removed

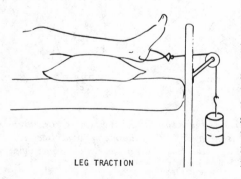

LEG TRACTION

months or years later or, if it creates no symptoms, may be permitted to remain indefinitely.

4. Wiring is done at operation by encircling the broken bone. This technique is occasionally sufficient to keep the fragments in good alignment but is not used very widely today.

5. Nails or pins: This method employs steel nails or pins which are hammered through the marrow of the bone and engage both fragments, thus keeping them in line. The fractures of the neck of the femur at the hip are most often treated in this manner.

6. Medullary nailing: This technique employs a long steel rod which is hammered into the marrow of long bones and engages both fragments. This is used to treat fractures of the shaft of the long bones: thigh, leg, arm, and forearm.

7. Bone grafts are sometimes used to make fractures heal more rapidly. The graft, taken from some other part of the patient's body, such as a hip or leg, is molded into the fracture site. Or a sliding bone graft may be shifted from a portion of the fractured bone. When small chips of spongy bone are used as a graft, their cells survive the transfer and soon begin to form new bone at the fracture site. If large blocks of bone are grafted, they serve to stabilize the fracture but do not actively participate in forming new bone (callus).

A recent advance in orthopedic surgery has been the establishment of bone banks. These banks obtain unneeded bone from patients and process it so as to render it sterile and available at some future date. Such "bank bone" is particularly valuable when large amounts are required to fill in gaps in the region of fractures. It must be mentioned that bank bone is not nearly as effective in stimulating bone growth as bone taken from the patient's own body. Moreover, bank bone frequently produces inflammatory tissue reactions as the fracture is healing.

The trend toward operative treatment of fractures has increased greatly within recent years because more satisfactory reductions can be obtained under direct, open manipulation on an operating table and because infection can now be minimized by the administration of proper dosages of the many antibiotic drugs. Some patients with fractures which formerly required many months of hospitalization and bed care can now be up and around within a period of weeks. Better techniques of immobilization and reduction in the number of bone infections have markedly decreased the incidence of nonhealing fractures.

Union is defined as the healing of a fracture, and bones are said to heal with normal union, delayed union, or, if they fail to heal at all, nonunion.

If set properly and if no infection has occurred, most fractured bones will heal by normal union within a few weeks' time. However, there are breaks in certain bones that are accompanied by interference with the blood supply, and these fractures are subject to delayed healing. As an example, fractures of the lower third of the leg involving the tibia (shinbone) are notorious for their slow healing for this reason. In other instances, despite the best of orthopedic management, union fails to take place. This circumstance is found in about 30 percent of all fractures involving the neck of the femur in the hip region, and in some cases where the long bones such as the tibia (shinbone) or ulna (forearm bone) are broken.

The commonest causes of delayed union and nonunion are:

1. Improper immobilization

2. Interference with blood supply to the bone as a result of the fracture

3. Loss of bone substance so that the broken ends do not meet

4. Extensive injury to the soft parts—muscles, ligaments, blood vessels, lymph channels—surrounding the fracture

5. Infection at the fracture site

6. Excessive traction

7. Soft tissue (such as muscle or fibrous tissue) which gets in between the ends of the broken bones and prevents them from knitting together

In the great majority of cases, the orthopedist can overcome nonunion. He can reset a poorly reduced fracture; he can help to overcome infection by draining off pus and by administering large doses of antibiotic drugs; he can build up the general health of his patient by giving proper medications. On the other hand, when the blood supply has been badly damaged and where extensive soft part injury has accompanied the fracture, he can only wait for nature to take its course in bringing about repair.

Surgery can be most helpful in cases where x-ray examination shows no tendency toward healing or where there is evidence of loss of bone between the ends of the fractured bones. In such cases, operation is performed. The ends of the fractured bone are "freshened" (the scar tissue between the bone ends is removed and healthy bone is exposed), and a bone graft is inserted connecting the fragments. The bone graft is usually obtained from the patient himself (autogenous graft), from the wing of the ilium (above the hip region), or may be taken from the fractured bone itself by sliding down a piece of one of the fragments (sliding graft). Occasionally bone is obtained from a bone bank and consists of bone from another human (homogenous graft). It may be derived from the rib of a patient who has undergone a chest operation or from a patient who has just died and who is undergoing a postmortem examination or from someone who has just lost an extremity. Naturally, these segments of bone must be obtained under the most sterile conditions, and they must be specially treated and stored.

Results of fracture treatment are divided into anatomical and functional. The aim, of course, is to obtain a perfect anatomical *and* a perfect functional result. If this is not possible, the patient and surgeon will be most satisfied if function can be restored.

When bone heals, new bone (callus) is laid down between the fragments. As healing takes place, a small amount of contraction ensues and this may lead to slight shortening of the bone. In most instances this is limited to but a fraction of an inch and is of no consequence.

Of great importance is the occasional patient who obtains a perfect anatomical result but function fails to return to normal. This unhappy situation may be caused by failure of healing of the injured muscles and ligaments which surround the broken bone. Intensive physiotherapy with massage, exercises, whirlpool baths, heat treatments, etc., is necessary for these people. Rehabilitation techniques have been perfected in recent years so that marked improvement can be obtained in the great majority of patients who have sustained crippling fractures.

In the final consideration of end results, a word must be said about the desire of the patient to get well. Nowhere else in the field of surgery is this so important a factor! An uncooperative patient may have the finest apparent cure of his fracture but if he lacks the will to get better, he may regain practically no use of his injured part. The patient must use the healing part in spite of pain—if instructed to do so—and he must keep in mind that the longer a muscle, joint, or bone is unused, the greater will be its difficulty in regaining proper function!

See also BONE CONDITIONS; JOINTS; SPINE.

QUESTIONS AND ANSWERS

What is a fracture?

It is any break in the continuity of a bone, no matter how slight or great. A fracture and a break are exactly the same thing.

Is first aid treatment for fractures very important?

It is essential. Improperly handled fractures may convert a minor injury into a serious one: the fractured ends of the bones may be jarred out of alignment, may puncture through the skin, may lacerate adjacent nerves, or, in some severe injuries, may cause paralysis, shock, or infection if good first aid treatment is not given.

What are some of the best first aid treatments for a fracture?

1. If the fracture involves the neck region, it is essential that the head be supported and not allowed to move in any direction.

2. If the back is involved, a board should be placed under the back and the patient should remain in a rigid, straight, supine position.

3. If the thigh or leg is fractured, it should bear no weight. The leg should be splinted in a straight position between two pillows or padded boards.

4. If the arm is fractured, it should be placed in a sling and bound snugly to the body for support.

Is it wise to apply a tourniquet if there is bleeding associated with a fracture?

No, absolutely not. A tourniquet is a most dangerous first aid measure. Improperly applied tourniquets have caused more damage by gangrene, paralysis, and *increased* bleeding than is generally realized. Firm pressure should be placed over a bleeding wound and the limb should be immobilized.

What are the various types of fractures?

1. Simple (closed) fracture, whenever there is no break in the skin overlying a bone.

2. Compound (open) fracture, whenever there is a laceration or a puncture wound of the skin in the vicinity of a broken bone.

3. Comminuted fracture, whenever the bone is broken in two or more places. Comminuted fractures may be simple or compound depending upon whether or not the skin over the fracture is broken.

Are compound and comminuted fractures usually more serious than simple fractures?

Yes, but not in all cases. A bone may have minor breaks in two places that are less severe than one major break. In such an instance, a noncomminuted fracture might be more serious than a comminuted fracture. Similarly, a compound fracture in which the contamination is slight may be less serious than a comminuted or simple fracture in which the bones are very severely damaged and are markedly displaced.

What other classifications of fractures are there?

1. Transverse fracture: the fracture extends straight across a bone.

2. Spiral fracture: there is a spiral or twisting type of fracture along a bone.

3. Oblique fracture: one in which the break occurs at an angle through the bone.

4. Incomplete (greenstick) fracture: a fracture which does not extend all the way through a bone.

What are the basic underlying principles in treating all fractures?

1. First, it is important to see that the general condition of the patient is taken care of. In other words, if a patient is in shock or has other serious injuries in addition to the fracture, he must be treated before attention is concentrated upon the broken bone.

2. Line up the broken parts of the bone so that they will heal in their normal position. This is called setting a fracture or reduction of a fracture.

3. Make sure that the fragments of the bone stay in good position until solid healing has taken place. This is called immobilization of the bone.

What is a pathological fracture?

A fracture through diseased bone.

What are the signs and symptoms of a fractured bone?

Pain, swelling, and false motion in the region of the fracture.

Does one always hear a crack when a bone breaks?

No.

Should fractures be set immediately after they occur?

Yes, as soon as feasible. However, in many instances, the setting of a fracture is purposely delayed for several hours or several days if surgical shock is present or if there is a great deal of swelling surrounding the fracture. In such cases, shock, infection, and soft tissue injuries may be treated before reducing the fracture.

Where should fractures be set?

Minor fractures may be set in the surgeon's office; major fractures of the longer bones must be set in the hospital, where facilities are usually more adequate.

What are some of the methods generally used in setting fractures?

1. Closed reduction; the bones are brought into proper position by external manipulation of the fragments, without resorting to surgery.

2. Open reduction; surgery is performed and the site of the fracture is exposed. The surgeon then gets the bones back into normal position by manually straightening them and bringing the ends together.

How does the treatment for compound fractures differ from that for simple fractures?

1. Before attention is given to setting a compound fracture, the wound of the fracture must be thoroughly cleansed, foreign bodies and any dead tissues must be removed, and bleeding must be controlled.

2. If shock is associated with a compound fracture, it must be treated by giving the patient intravenous solutions, plasma or blood.

3. In treating a compound fracture, booster shots of tetanus toxoid should be given along with antibiotics to control any possible infection.

4. Only after these measures have been carried out is attention directed toward bringing the broken bones of a compound fracture into alignment.

How is the pain controlled when a fracture is set?

One of various types of anesthesia may be given:

1. Local anesthesia. Novocain or some similar medication injected into the fracture site renders it numb.

2. Inhalation anesthesia. General anesthesia should not be given on a full stomach; there is too much danger of vomiting, which may lead to respiratory problems.

3. Intravenous anesthesia. There are

several drugs which can produce sleep and obliterate pain when administered intravenously.

Do orthopedists ever delay the setting of a fracture for a day or two because there is so much swelling and inflammation in the injured area?

Yes.

How are fractured bone ends held in place while they heal?

1. Plaster cast. A crinoline bandage covered with plaster of paris (a cast) is placed around the injured limb. The cast may be lined with cotton, felt, or stockinette (a stockinglike cotton bandage). In order to hold the fractured fragments securely, a cast usually extends past the joint on each side of the fractured bone. The cast for a fractured forearm will thus immobilize the elbow and wrist. The cast for a fractured femur (thighbone) will immobilize the knee and the foot and will extend to include the trunk. A cast that includes a limb and a portion of the trunk is called a spica cast. Frequently, excellent immobilization of a fracture may be obtained by the use of a plaster splint or half a cast.

2. Traction. By gently and constantly pulling upon the end of a fractured bone, the soft tissues clothing the fracture site (the muscles and periosteum, or bone covering) will hold the fractured ends in proper alignment. Traction may be applied through bandages taped to the skin (skin traction), through a metal pin inserted through bone (skeletal traction), or through the weight of a cast applied to the limb (hanging cast).

3. By themselves. Some fractures, such as certain fractures of the shoulder blade and of the fibula (one of the two bones of the leg), are adequately held in position by the muscles and ligaments

that surround them and need no further immobilization.

4. By surgery.

How can surgery immobilize a fractured bone?

There are many metals that cause virtually no reaction when placed in bone. The orthopedic surgeon has at his disposal metal screws, pins, nails, and wires that can be placed across a fracture site to maintain the reduced position of the fragments. A metal plate (rectangular strip of metal screwed to the outside of a bone) may also be used. Some of these devices are placed on the inside of the bone, some on the outside, and some through the entire width of the bone.

Occasionally a bone graft may be inserted across the fracture site to help immobilize a fracture.

Where does the bone come from that is used in bone grafts?

1. The bone may be taken from another part of the patient's body, such as below the elbow, the shin, or the pelvis. This is called an autogenous bone graft and causes no inflammation. It is the only type of graft that has living cells capable of forming bone.

2. Bone may also come from a bone bank. This bone may either come from other humans (homogenous bone graft) or from animals (heterogenous bone graft). In either case, the bone is specially treated to make it sterile and to remove as much of the irritating protein substances as possible.

Of what metals are the pins and screws used for fracture surgery made?

Some are stainless steel. Others are alloys usually of steel, or cobalt, molybdenum, and nickel.

Is a cast necessary if surgery has been performed on a fracture?

Usually, yes. Metal appliances may

bend or break if subjected to the great stresses of normal activity. A limb must therefore be protected from these stresses by a plaster cast even after a screw or pin has been inserted.

Is it painful to apply a cast?
No. It is no more uncomfortable than applying a bandage.

When a fracture has been reduced, will a patient be in pain after he awakens from the anesthesia?
Little pain persists after the fracture is set and the cast is properly applied. Fracture pain will usually disappear within a few hours after immobilization.

Why is a very large cast often applied to a patient who has a relatively minor fracture?
It is usually essential that the joint above and the joint below the area of fracture be encased in a cast in order to obtain adequate immobilization.

Does the orthopedist often trim the cast after it has been applied?
Yes. Particularly if there is any swelling, a cast may be trimmed or even split open within the first few hours after or the day after it has been applied.

What is a spica?
A spica is a cast that extends onto the trunk from the arm or leg. These casts are often applied for fractures around the shoulder or thigh.

Will there be pain in the bone during the days after a plaster cast has been applied?
Usually not. Any pain under a cast, particularly if not directly over the region of the fractures, may represent undue pressure. It should be reported to the physician.

Are casts ever changed and reapplied during the course of healing?
Yes, very often. As soft tissue swelling subsides, the cast may lose its snug fit. To correct this, a new cast is applied.

Does it hurt to remove a cast?
No.

Does a cast give off any heat?
Within the first hour or two after a cast is applied, the combination of the plaster granules with the water used in the application causes heat to form. This will cause the limb to feel warm as the cast dries.

How long does it take a cast to dry?
A cast becomes stiff in five to ten minutes, but most casts applied to the leg or arm do not become completely dry for one day. Some body casts may remain moist for several days.

Can anything be done to hasten the drying of a cast?
Yes. Exposing the cast to air and sunshine will hasten drying.

How does the orthopedist determine the length of time that a cast must be worn?
Experience has shown that various fractures heal at different rates of speed. The fracture site can be x-rayed, either through the cast or with the cast off, and the progress of the healing can be determined.

What is a cast saw?
A cast saw is an electrical instrument frequently used to remove a plaster cast. The cast saw does not rotate like a carpenter's saw, but oscillates (rocks back and forth) so as to avoid injuring the skin below the cast.

What kind of cast or splint is usually applied for the following fractures?
Neck: Body cast with headpiece
Collarbone (clavicle): Figure-of-eight bandage
Shoulder blade (scapula): Sling
Ribs: Taping

Humerus: Cast from upper arm to wrist and hand

Forearm (radius): Cast from upper arm to hand

Forearm (ulna): Cast from upper arm to hand

Elbow: Cast from upper arm to hand

Wrist: Cast from below elbow to hand

Hand: Cast from below elbow to hand

Fingers: Cast from above wrist to fingertip

Upper spine: Body cast with headpiece

Lower spine: Body cast

Pelvis: Bed sling

Hip: Usually none (treated by surgery)

Thigh (femur): Cast from foot to pelvis

Knee: Cast from ankle to upper thigh

Leg (tibia): Cast from upper thigh to foot

Leg (fibula): Bandage

Ankle: Cast (with walking heel) from knee to toes

Foot: Cast (often with walking heel) from knee to toes

Toes: Bandage of toes to each other

Is it ever possible to walk while wearing a cast on the leg?

Yes. In certain simple fractures of the leg, walking upon the cast is permissible. This is accomplished by applying a rubber heel on the sole of the cast.

Is it necessary to exercise the muscles and tendons while the patient is in a cast?

Yes. The orthopedist will prescribe the necessary exercises.

Can a patient allow a cast to get wet?

No. It should be kept dry for the entire length of time that it is worn.

What should be done if a cast accidentally becomes wet?

If only the outside of it is wet, the cast should be exposed to air and sunshine. A patient should never be permitted to walk on a wet leg cast. If the entire cast has become soft and wet, the physician should be notified so that he can replace it with a new one.

Is there any way to prevent a cast from becoming very dirty?

It is more important to keep it from getting wet. A wet cast collects dirt and soon becomes soft and frayed. An individual with a leg cast or body cast should take only sponge baths. An individual with a cast extending only on the forearm and hand may take a tub bath if there is a rubber mat on the floor of the tub and a hand railing at the side of the tub. The cast should be protected with a plastic bag while the person is in the tub.

An oversized woolen or cotton stocking may be placed over the footpiece of a leg cast to protect it from being soiled and to keep dirt from getting under the plaster.

Both leg and arm casts may be protected from dirt by covering them with four-inch or six-inch stockinette, which can be obtained from drugstores or surgical-supply houses.

What can one do when there is itching beneath a cast?

It is usually best to inform the doctor about it. Severe itching may mean that the cast has become too loose and is irritating the skin or that the patient has dropped some object into the cast. In either case, the cast may have to be removed.

What should be done if the cast breaks?

If a leg cast breaks, the patient should be taken off his feet immediately, and the injured leg should be propped between two pillows. If an arm cast breaks, the arm should be placed in a sling. In any event, the physician should be notified.

Is a bone completely healed when the cast is removed?

Not always. Sometimes there is enough bone scar (callus) to permit the cast to be removed. This does not necessarily mean the fracture is completely healed.

Is it normal to have swelling after a cast is removed?

Yes. This may persist for several months.

Is it natural for an arm or leg to look withered after it has been taken out of a cast?

Yes. This is because the muscles and tendons have been inactive during the time the patient was in a cast. In almost all instances, unless there has been nerve damage, the muscles will regain their tone and strength and the limb will return to normal.

Why does the skin appear scaly or hairy after a cast is removed?

Normal daily wear and tear of the skin of the limbs rubs off dead skin cells and hair fragments. When the skin of a limb is protected for several weeks by a plaster cast, these dead cells accumulate and give the limb the scaly and hairy look. This abnormal appearance will last only a week or two.

What does the term "knitting" mean?

It is a nonmedical term meaning healing of a fracture.

What is the meaning of the term "union of a fracture"?

It is the healing of a fracture by the formation of bony scar.

What causes delayed healing or nonunion of fractures?

1. Inadequate or delayed reduction (setting) of the fracture
2. Improper immobilization of the fracture after it has been reduced
3. Interruption of the blood supply to the bone as a result of the original fracture injury
4. Loss of bone substance caused by an extensive fracture
5. Infection of the soft tissues and the fractured bone fragments
6. Too much traction placed upon the ends of a fracture
7. Severe damage to the muscles, ligaments, blood vessels, and lymph channels in the vicinity of the fracture
8. The presence of muscle or other soft tissue between the fractured fragments
9. Discontinuing immobilization too soon

What is the treatment for a nonunited fracture?

A poorly set fracture can be reset. Proper immobilization can be obtained by applying a new cast or by applying traction. Loss of bony substance can be corrected by the use of a bone graft. Infection can usually be controlled by draining away pus, cutting away dead tissue, and giving adequate doses of antibiotic drugs. Excessive traction can be released. If the blood supply at the fracture site has been damaged and major soft-tissue injury has taken place, a bone graft may be required.

Does the state of the general health of the patient often influence the rate at which fractures heal?

Yes. The patient in poor general health may not heal his bony fracture as well as a healthy person.

Do fractures with many fragments (comminuted) heal with more difficulty than simple fractures?
Yes, sometimes.

How often is it necessary to x-ray a fracture?
1. Immediately before it is set
2. Immediately after it is set
3. Approximately seven to ten days after it is set
4. Approximately every few weeks, if it is a slow-healing fracture
5. After the cast has been removed

Is it dangerous or harmful to x-ray a fracture?
No, because only small doses of radiation are usually necessary. If repeated x-rays are taken about the abdomen, lead shields may be used to protect the testicles or ovaries from the x-ray radiation.

Is it usually necessary to give a patient extra vitamins and large quantities of milk in order to hasten the healing of a fracture?
No, unless the patient is debilitated by other illnesses. A normal person on a normal diet will get enough minerals and vitamins to heal a fractured bone.

Can arthritis come from a fracture?
Yes. If the fracture extends within a joint, that joint may develop arthritis.

Do patients need physiotherapy after a fracture has healed?
Yes, in many instances.

Is a bone with a healed fracture as strong as it was previously?
Yes.

Is a bone once fractured more likely to become fractured again?
No.

Do people feel pain at a fracture site in rainy weather?
Yes, sometimes for several months thereafter.

Are arms or legs ever shorter after a fracture is healed?
Yes, occasionally. This usually does not interfere with good function.

Are the limbs ever permanently deformed following fracture?
1. A few fractures may result in nonunion or death of one of the fragments due to poor blood supply. This may lead to deformity of the limb.
2. Occasionally a fracture line may pass through the growth plate of a bone, causing unequal growth at the two sides of the bone with consequent deformity.

By what standards do orthopedists judge the results of the treatment of a fracture?
1. Anatomical result
2. Functional result

What is the difference between the anatomical and the functional result?
The bones may be set in perfect alignment and this will thereby constitute a fine anatomical result. Yet, in a certain number of these cases, the function of the extremity may be poor. Conversely, the bones may not be in strict anatomical alignment but the extremity may be restored to completely normal function. This, then, will be a good functional result even though it is a poor anatomical result.

Which is more important, a good functional result or a good anatomical result?
Obviously, a good functional result is more important.

FRACTURES IN CHILDREN

Do fractures in children heal just as quickly as those in adults?

Yes. In most instances, they heal even more quickly, because a child has better circulation and his tissues recover from injury more easily.

Does shortening of a child's arm or leg occur following a fracture?

Very rarely. Fractures are more likely to cause increased growth than shortening of a limb. In rare instances, if the fracture line runs just adjacent to the growth plate (epiphysis) of a bone, the ultimate length of the limb may be decreased. If the fracture is in the middle of a long bone, however, there is no chance of interference with growth, since the epiphyses are toward the ends of the bone.

Is it essential for good healing that a fracture be set properly?

Yes. Proper reduction of fractures is important. However, in children, certain degrees of displacement or angulation of fractured fragments will correct themselves with growth of the bones. Such displacement or angulation may thus be far preferable to risking infection and nonunion of the fracture by operating to secure perfect alignment.

Is it always best to get perfect end-to-end alignment of the fractured ends of a bone?

Surprisingly, no. In young children, bones will frequently overgrow as much as one inch after a fracture. Many orthopedists thus prefer to have the fractured ends of a bone of the lower limb reduced side-to-side, so that the final result will be a limb of normal length.

Are metal screws, nails, wires, pins, and rods used as often in children as they are in adults?

No. Children's bones heal so easily that surgery is rarely required in children's fractures.

Do children tend to outgrow a deformity caused by a fracture?

Yes. Children have tremendous ability to overcome such deformities. Parents should not worry about a lump in the vicinity of a healed fracture. This is due to the callus that has formed in the area, and it will disappear as the bone lengthens and the child grows older.

What special instructions should be given to a child who is about to have a cast changed?

He must be told that the cast remover —usually an electric, motor-driven instrument—makes lots of noise but cannot hurt him. If this is thoroughly explained to the child before cast removal, some of his fears will be allayed.

Is it always necessary to anesthetize a child when replacing a cast?

Not if the child is old enough to cooperate voluntarily.

At what age can a child be taught to use crutches?

At the age of 3 or 4 years.

Should a child who has had a fracture but is otherwise normal be limited in his physical activities?

After the fracture has healed there need be no restrictions.

How can one tell if a newborn infant has suffered a fracture as the result of a birth injury?

When one of the long bones of the arms or legs is broken, the newborn

CHART I

FRACTURES OF THE SHOULDER REGION AND ARM

BONE FRACTURED	METHOD OF TREATMENT	LENGTH OF HOSPITAL STAY	PERIOD OF IMMOBILIZATION	TIME UNTIL FULL RECOVERY
SHOULDER BLADE	a) Sling	None	2–4 weeks	4–6 weeks
(scapula)	b) Cast	2–3 days	6–8 weeks	8–10 weeks
COLLARBONE	a) Figure-of-eight bandage	None	4–6 weeks	6–8 weeks
(clavicle)	b) Traction	3–4 weeks	4–6 weeks	6–8 weeks
	c) Cast	3–4 days	4–6 weeks	6–10 weeks
ARM BONE	d) Operation	5–7 days	3–4 weeks	4–6 weeks
(humerus)				
1. Neck of humerus	a) Sling	None	3–4 weeks	8–12 weeks
	b) Velpeau bandage (body and arm)	None	3–4 weeks	8–12 weeks
	c) Traction and cast	3–5 weeks	4–6 weeks	10–12 weeks
	d) Spica cast (body and arm)	3–5 days	4–6 weeks	10–12 weeks
	e) Operation	5–7 days	4–6 weeks	10–12 weeks
2. Shaft of humerus	a) Hanging cast	None or 2–3 days	4–6 weeks	10–12 weeks
	b) Spica cast (body and arm)	2–5 days	6–8 weeks	10–12 weeks
	c) Traction and cast	3–4 weeks	6–8 weeks	10–12 weeks
	d) Operation	5–7 days	6–10 weeks	10–14 weeks
3. Elbow region	a) Plaster cast	2–4 days	4–6 weeks	10–12 weeks
	b) Traction and cast	3–4 weeks	4–6 weeks	10–12 weeks
	c) Operation	5–7 days	4–8 weeks	12–16 weeks
4. Epiphyseal separation (at the growth line)	a) Cast	0–3 days	3–4 weeks	8–10 weeks
	b) Operation	5–7 days	3–6 weeks	10–12 weeks
FOREARM BONES				
1. Radius				
a) Head or radius	a) Sling	None	10 days	10–12 weeks
	b) Plaster splint	None	10 days	10–12 weeks
	c) Operation	5–8 days	10 days	10–12 weeks
b) Shaft of radius	a) Cast	0–3 days	6–8 weeks	12–16 weeks
	b) Operation	5–7 days	6–10 weeks	12–16 weeks
c) Near wrist	a) Cast	0–3 days	4–6 weeks	10–12 weeks
	b) Operation	5–7 days	6–8 weeks	10–12 weeks
2. Ulna				
a) Olecranon (elbow)	a) Cast	0–3 days	4–6 weeks	10–12 weeks
	b) Operation	5–7 days	3–5 weeks	10–12 weeks
b) Shaft of ulna	a) Cast	0–3 days	6–10 weeks	12–16 weeks
	b) Operation	5–7 days	8–10 weeks	12–18 weeks
c) Distal end (near wrist)	a) Cast	0–2 days	4–6 weeks	8–10 weeks
	b) Operation (rare)	3–5 days	10 days	4–6 weeks
3. Radius and ulna combined	a) Cast	0–5 days	6–10 weeks	12–16 weeks
	b) Operation	5–7 days	6–10 weeks	12–18 weeks
4. Distal end radius and ulna at wrist	a) Cast	0–5 days	4–6 weeks	10–12 weeks
	b) Operation	5–7 days	4–8 weeks	10–14 weeks
WRIST BONE				
1. Scaphoid	Cast	None	10–14 weeks	14–20 weeks
2. Other wrist bones	Cast	None	4–6 weeks	6–10 weeks
HAND				
1. Metacarpals	a) Cast or splint	None	2–3 weeks	4–6 weeks
	b) Traction and cast	0–3 days	2–3 weeks	5–7 weeks
	c) Operation	3–5 days	2–3 weeks	5–7 weeks
2. Phalanges (fingers)	a) Splint	None	2–3 weeks	4–6 weeks
	b) Traction	0–2 days	2–3 weeks	6–8 weeks
	c) Operation	3–5 days	2–3 weeks	6–8 weeks

child will not move the extremity. In addition, the limb is often warm and swollen.

FRACTURES IN OLDER PEOPLE

Are people over 60 more likely to suffer fractures than younger people?
Yes. Not only are their bones more brittle, but also their reactions to impending injury are slower.

Are older people more likely to go into shock when there is a fracture?
Yes. For this reason, it is essential to give first aid quickly and to get the patient to the nearest doctor or hospital as soon as possible.

Do broken bones heal more slowly in people over 60?
Yes, because there is usually less calcium in their bones. In addition, the muscles and tendons surrounding the broken bone have less recuperative power.

What extra measures should be taken to promote healing of fractures in older people?
1. If the patient has a vitamin or mineral deficiency, tablets or injections should be given to supplement the usual intake of these chemicals.
2. Calcium tablets may be given if a blood analysis shows the amount of this chemical to be low.

What are the usual lengths of time for recovery from fractures in older people?

Hipbone	1 year
Wrist bone	3 months
Skull fracture	2 months
Spine fracture	6 months
Ankle fracture	6 months
Pelvic fracture	4 months

Is it usual for older people to require exercises, baths, heat therapy, and other forms of treatment after the fracture has healed?
Yes. They will usually require extensive physical therapy and rehabilitation.

Frostbite

Frostbite is a burn caused by exposure to excessive cold.
See also FIRST AID.

QUESTIONS AND ANSWERS

What is the major complication of frostbite?
If it is severe and lasts for several hours, the frostbitten tissue may become gangrenous. Consequent loss of fingers or toes is not unusual in older people.

What is the first aid treatment for frostbite?
1. The person with frostbite should be warmed gradually, not placed immediately in a hot room.
2. If pain is severe, codeine or aspirin should be given.
3. Warm liquids and hot foods should be given.
4. All wet or frozen clothing should be removed, and the patient should be wrapped in warm blankets.
5. The frostbitten areas should be permitted to warm spontaneously in a room heated to about 72° F.
6. A sterile dressing should be placed over the frostbitten areas, but no antiseptics should be applied.
7. As soon as circulation returns, the part should be gently exercised.

CHART II

FRACTURES OF THE PELVIC REGION AND LEG

BONE FRACTURED	METHOD OF TREATMENT	LENGTH OF HOSPITAL STAY*	PERIOD OF IMMOBILI-ZATION*	TIME UNTIL FULL RECOVERY*
PELVIS	a) Bed rest	4–6 weeks	4–8 weeks	10–12 weeks
	b) Operation	3–6 weeks	4–8 weeks	10–12 weeks
THIGHBONE (femur)				
1. Neck (near hip)	Operation	3–5 weeks	6–12 months	12 or more months
2. Intertrochanteric	a) Traction	6–10 weeks	3–6 months	6–9 months
area (near hip)	b) Operation	2–4 weeks	3–6 months	6–9 months
	c) Cast	6–10 weeks	3–6 months	6–12 months
	d) Hip replacement	3–4 weeks	None	6–10 months
3. Shaft of thighbone	a) Cast and brace	6–12 weeks	6–9 months	10–12 months
	b) Traction and cast or brace	6–12 weeks	6–9 months	10–12 months
	c) Operation			
	without cast	10–21 days	4–6 weeks	12 months
	with cast	6–12 weeks	6–9 months	12 months
4. Supracondylar area	a) Cast	3–4 months	3–4 months	6–10 months
(near knee)	b) Traction and cast or brace	6–10 weeks	4–6 months	8–10 months
	c) Operation and cast or brace	3 weeks to 4 months	3–4 months	6–8 months
KNEECAP (patella)	a) Cast	0–5 days	4–6 weeks	10–16 weeks
	b) Operation	5–10 days	2–5 weeks	10–16 weeks
LEG				
1. Shinbone (tibia)				
a) Condyle (upper end)	a) Cast	0–7 days	10–12 weeks	6–9 months
	b) Operation	5–10 days	10–12 weeks	6–9 months
b) Midshaft	a) Cast	0–10 days	3–5 months	6–9 months
	b) Traction and cast or brace	6–10 weeks	3–5 months	6–9 months
	c) Operation and cast	10–20 days	3–5 months	6–9 months
c) Distal third	a) Cast	0–7 days	3–9 months	9–20 months
(lower third)	b) Operation and cast	5–12 days	3–9 months	9–20 months
	c) Traction and cast or brace	6–10 weeks	3–9 months	9–20 months
2. Fibula	a) Bandage	None	2–4 weeks	6 weeks
	b) Cast	None	2–4 weeks	6 weeks
ANKLE				
1. Medial malleolus	a) Cast	0–3 days	6–8 weeks	9–12 weeks
(tibia)	b) Operation	5–10 days	6–12 weeks	10–16 weeks
2. Lateral malleolus (fibula)	Cast	0–3 days	6–8 weeks	9–12 weeks
3. Bi- or tri-malleolar	a) Cast	0–5 days	6–12 weeks	12–16 weeks
(tibia and fibula)	b) Operation	5–10 days	6–12 weeks	12–16 weeks
FOOT				
1. Tarsals				
a) Os calcis (heel bone)	a) Cast	0–10 days	12–16 weeks	5–6 months
	b) Operation	7–14 days	12–16 weeks	5–6 months
b) Others (foot bones)	Cast	0–5 days	5–8 weeks	8–12 weeks
2. Metatarsals	a) Cast with or without traction	0–5 days	5–6 weeks	8–10 weeks
	b) Operation	5–10 days	5–6 weeks	8–10 weeks
3. Phalanges (Toes)	Bandage or cast	None usually	2–3 weeks	4–6 weeks

* Note: These estimates are for simple, noncompound fractures.

What parts of the body are most frequently frostbitten?

The ears, the tip of the nose, the fingers, and the toes. These are areas where the entire blood supply is directly beneath the skin, and they are therefore more subject to injury from cold than are other areas of the body protected by large amounts of fat beneath the skin's surface.

Should frostbitten areas be massaged in order to restore circulation?

No! This can do much harm and no good.

Is it good practice to rub snow into a frostbitten area?

No!

Can one tell immediately whether or not permanent damage has been done by frostbite?

No. Gangrene may set in several days after the exposure. Conversely, tissue that looks as if it might become gangrenous may recover after a few days.

How much warmth should be applied to a frostbitten part?

Ordinary room temperature is all that is necessary.

Should antiseptics be applied to frozen areas?

No, they may cause further burn.

Are any medications helpful in aiding a frostbitten part to regain normal circulation?

Yes, but they must be prescribed by a physician.

Can frostbite be prevented?

Yes, by avoiding prolonged exposure to cold. Parents should be particularly careful to see that children do not stay out too long in the cold, as children are especially prone to frostbite. The tip of the nose, the ears, and the fingers and toes are favorite sites for frostbite and should be protected as much as possible. Heavy woolen socks, warm gloves, and earmuffs should be worn whenever it is necessary to stay out in the cold.

Funnel Chest

Funnel chest (pectus excavatum) is an indentation of the chest in the region of the breastbone (sternum). In the past it was usually caused by vitamin-D deficiency and rickets. Today it is seen mainly in children with a birth deformity of the chest. Occasionally it results from a congenitally short tendon of the diaphragm.

QUESTIONS AND ANSWERS

Will funnel chest ever interfere with breathing?

Yes. Some cases have "paradoxical respiration." In this situation the chest wall pulls inward when the child inhales and expands when he exhales. This is opposite to the normal motions of the chest wall. With severe deformities, the indented or funnel chest may displace the lungs and heart, further interfering with respiration.

What is the treatment for funnel chest?

If the condition is mild and does not interfere with the function of the lungs or heart, it can be ignored. However, if there is a marked deformity, surgery may have to be performed in order to improve respiratory and cardiac function.

Is surgery successful in relieving severe funnel chest?

Yes, in a great majority of cases.

Will a child with funnel chest naturally tend to outgrow it?

No. Once the deformity has developed, it will not disappear as the child matures.

Must a child's physical activity be limited if he has funnel chest?

Not unless there is interference with breathing.

Should funnel chest be operated upon to improve the cosmetic appearance of an individual?

No. The operation for correction of funnel chest is a major procedure and is not recommended merely to improve the appearance of the chest.

Can funnel chest be prevented?

Those cases that are due to a lack of vitamin D can certainly be prevented by making sure that children have sufficient vitamin D in their diet. There is no known method of preventing funnel chest that is a congenital deformity.

Furuncles and Furunculosis

A furuncle is a pimple, boil, or small abscess. Most furuncles are caused by staphylococcal infections of the skin, although other bacteria are also capable of causing this type of infection. Furunculosis is a condition in which crops of boils appear on various parts of the body over a prolonged period of time. This condition is most often caused by a staphylococcus germ to which the patient has developed insufficient antibodies.

See also ABSCESSES AND INFECTIONS.

QUESTIONS AND ANSWERS

What is the treatment for a furuncle?

Most furuncles will heal spontaneously *if left alone*. Furuncles should *not* be squeezed, as this tends to spread the infection. If a furuncle is particularly painful, warm compresses should be applied frequently. Those that contain large amounts of pus should be opened surgically.

Do most furuncles open by themselves?

Some will open and drain spontaneously; others will absorb and scab over.

When should one seek surgical attention for a furuncle?

When it is extremely painful or when it enlarges and is obviously developing a "head" which will require lancing.

Is furunculosis a common condition?

It is not infrequently seen, particularly among adolescents and young adults. For some reason or other, some people are not able to build up their own defense mechanism against a particular strain of staphylococcus. As a result, they develop crops of boils which come and go over a period of weeks or months.

Do most people who suffer from furunculosis have diabetes?

No. Although the blood should be tested to be sure that diabetes is not present, the great majority of people who have furunculosis are not diabetics.

What is the treatment for furunculosis?

1. Those boils that contain a large amount of pus should be opened surgically.

2. The general health of the patient should be safeguarded, and the patient should be urged to observe good hygiene. Some people with furunculosis do not wash or bathe sufficiently, thus increasing the likelihood of developing more abscesses.

3. The general nutrition of the patient must be adequate. If there is a vitamin lack, this should be combated by taking supplementary vitamins.

4. Certain antibiotics are particularly effective against staphylococcal infections. These antibiotics should be taken over a prolonged period of time, under the guidance of a physician.

5. In those cases that do not respond to the foregoing measures, a vaccine may be made from pus taken from one of the abscesses. This vaccine, given in repeated doses, may cause the condition to subside.

Does furunculosis ever continue indefinitely?

No. Even though it may last several weeks or months, eventually it will subside spontaneously.

Is it ever advisable to squeeze a furuncle?

No. This is a bad practice, especially if the infection is located on the face.

Does furunculosis ever attack people who observe good body hygiene?

Yes.

Gallbladder and Gallstones

A search of ancient medical literature will reveal a knowledge of gallbladder disease, especially gallstones, as far back as the days of the Talmud. Although not mentioned with great frequency in early writings, as the centuries have unfolded one can find an increasing number of references on this subject. It is safe to conjecture that as man's diet became more complicated and as he began to eat richer foods, grew fatter, and indulged in less physical exercise, his gallbladder functioned less efficiently and conse-

quently became more prone to the formation of gallstones. Today, with overeating and emphasis on heavy, greasy foods the gustatory custom rather than the exception, it is no wonder that disorders of this organ have become one of the commonest of all ailments.

The gallbladder is a pear-shaped sac lying adjacent to and partially attached to the underside of the liver in the right upper part of the abdomen. It is located just beneath the arch of the ribs and connects, through a system of ducts or tubes, both with the liver and with the first portion of the small intestine (duodenum). (See illustration.)

The function of this organ is to receive the bile produced and secreted by the liver and to concentrate and store it. When a meal is eaten, especially one with a high fat content, the gallbladder contracts. This contraction forces the concentrated bile out into the ducts which lead into the intestine. The intestine will receive a supply of dilute bile directly from the liver and a supply of concentrated bile from the gallbladder. This bile is essential for the digestion of fats and fatlike substances. (*See also* BILIARY OBSTRUCTION.)

The gallbladder is notorious for its habit of manufacturing gallstones. So prevalent is this unfortunate peculiarity that it is estimated that approximately 25 percent of all women and 10 percent of all men will develop gallstones at some time or other before they reach 60 years of age.

Two main causes for the formation of stones have been rather generally accepted, although there are several other theories backed by interesting evidence. The two most popular beliefs are:

1. That an upset in the patient's chemistry—specifically, failure of fat and cholesterol metabolism—causes stones to crystallize and precipitate out from the fluid bile

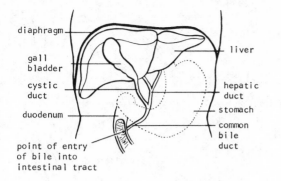

diaphragm

gall bladder

cystic duct

duodenum

liver

hepatic duct

stomach

common bile duct

point of entry of bile into intestinal tract

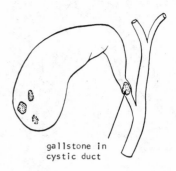

gallstone in cystic duct

2. That stones are the aftermath of previous infection which may have occurred many years before. As one physician stated, "Gallstones are the tombstones of infection."

Gallbladder disease is seen about three times more often in women than in men and produces symptoms usually between the ages of 35 and 55 years. Pregnancy, since it is often complicated by an imbalance in fat and cholesterol metabolism, may be responsible for this greater frequency in women. Acute infections of this structure, however, whether stones are present or not, are almost as frequently encountered in men. An old medical aphorism still aptly describes the kind of person most likely to develop gallbladder disease: "Fair, fat, and forty." However, it should be remembered that thin people are not immune to this type of infection and also, it should be mentioned, that occasionally one discovers gallbladder disease in children.

The mere existence of stones does not mean that surgery *must* be performed immediately, but the wisest course is to undergo surgery before complications develop. Although there are many people in this world who, despite a gallbladder filled with stones, never develop symptoms, nevertheless, the majority of people so afflicted will sooner or later

turn up with one or more of the following symptoms:

1. Indigestion after eating fried, fatty, or greasy foods

2. Indigestion after eating such vegetables as turnips, cabbage, sprouts, radishes, pickles, etc.

3. Indigestion after eating certain raw fruits and fruit skins

4. Nausea, heartburn, bloating, and flatulence (distention due to gas)

5. Attacks of pain—sometimes taking the form of excruciating knifelike, colicky spasmodic pain—in the upper right part of the abdomen and often shooting to the back or right shoulder region

A diagnosis of gallbladder disease can be made readily by x-rays. Pills containing a dye are given by mouth, or the dye is injected into a vein in the arm, which will cause the gallbladder and (in some cases) the bile ducts to become visible when x-rayed. If there are stones blocking the duct of the gallbladder, the dye will not reach the cavity of the organ and it will not be visible on the x-ray film. In other cases, the stones will appear as negative shadows in an otherwise visualized gallbladder or ducts. Failure of the gallbladder to visualize after the dye is given is proof that disease is present.

The severe pain seen so often in gall-

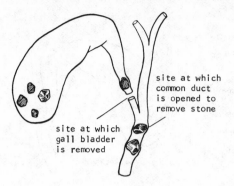

site at which
common duct
is opened to
remove stone

site at which
gall bladder
is removed

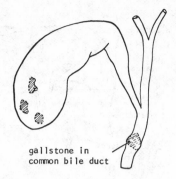

gallstone in
common bile duct

bladder disease is the result of one of the stones getting caught in the small cystic duct which leads away from the gall-bladder. (See illustration.) This duct normally has the diameter of an ordinary lead pencil. Under the stimulation of food, the bladder contracts powerfully and forces a stone into this duct (tube), which usually has a smaller diameter than that of the stone. An acute episode of this kind can have any of three endings: the stone can drop back into the gallbladder and the attack subsides; the stone can remain stuck in this small duct, thus producing an acute infection which will require more or less immediate surgery for the removal of the organ; or the stone can pass through this duct into the common duct. Once in the common bile duct, the stone either will pass through into the intestine or may get caught just at the exit of the duct into the intestine. Should this latter situation take place, the entire flow of bile is obstructed and the patient develops jaundice. Jaundice (with yellow discoloration of the skin) is a serious complication demanding urgent surgery. In these cases, not only must the stone-bearing gallbladder be removed but the common duct must be opened and the obstructing stone (or stones) picked out.

A gall bladder may contain but a solitary stone, a few stones or may harbor several hundred. They vary in size from that of a millet seed or pea to that of a hen's egg. There is no correlation between the number and size of the stones and the symptoms they produce. Sometimes a single small stone will cause more trouble than a huge one or a sackful of jagged ones.

QUESTIONS AND ANSWERS

Where is the gallbladder, and what is its function?

The gallbladder is a pear-shaped sac attached to the underside of the liver, beneath the ribs, in the right upper part of the abdomen. Its function is to receive bile, produced and secreted by the liver, and to store and concentrate it for use when needed in the processes of digestion.

For what types of food is bile particularly necessary in digestion?

Bile is essential for the digestion of fats and fatlike substances.

How does bile reach the intestinal tract?

Through a system of ducts or tubes. The cystic duct leads from the gallbladder into the common bile duct. The common bile duct is the result of the joining of the two hepatic ducts which originate in the liver. Bile from the liver and the gallbladder travels down the common bile duct and enters into the intestine at the ampulla of Vater in the second portion of the duodenum.

If the liver produces and secrets bile, what is the special function of the gallbladder?

To store and concentrate bile so that an additional supply can be secreted into the intestine when it is needed after the eating of a meal.

Are disorders of the gallbladder and bile ducts very common?

It is generally agreed that disease of the gallbladder and malfunction of the sphincter at the end of the common duct constitute the most ordinary cause of indigestion.

What foods often disagree with the individual who has a gallbladder disorder?

Any fried and greasy foods, French fried potatoes, heavy sauces, gravies, chicken or turkey skins, eggs fried in lard, turnips, cabbage, cauliflower, radishes, sprouts, and certain raw fruits.

What causes gallbladder disease?

1. Infection, with bacteria. This may result in an acute or chronic inflammation in the same manner that infection involves the appendix, tonsils, or any other organ.

2. A functional disturbance in which the gallbladder fails to empty when it is called upon to secrete bile.

3. A chemical disturbance causing stones to precipitate out from the bile. These stones may create an obstruction to the passage of bile along the ducts and into the intestinal tract.

Are gallstones always caused by an upset in chemistry within the gallbladder?

No. Gallstones may result from a chemical disturbance, or they may form as a result of infection within the gallbladder.

How prevalent are gallstones?

It is estimated that approximately one out of four women and one out of eight men will develop gallstones at some time or other before they reach 60 years of age.

Is there a special type of person who is most likely to develop gallbladder disease?

Yes. It is thought that the heavy-set type of person who eats a large amount of fats and greases is most likely to develop gallbladder disease. However, the condition is seen in all ages and in all types of people.

Does gallbladder disease tend to be inherited or run in families?

No. However, obesity, a predisposing factor, does tend to be a familial characteristic.

Does childbearing predispose one to the formation of gallstones?

Yes. Pregnancy produces a disturbance in fat and cholesterol metabolism. This is often followed by stone formation within a few months after the pregnancy has terminated.

Does gallbladder disease often take place during pregnancy?

Not very frequently. (It is seen most commonly in women who have had one or two children.)

What takes place when the gallbladder becomes acutely inflamed?

The blood supply to the wall of the gallbladder may be interfered with and the gallbladder may become filled with pus or its walls may undergo gangrenous changes as the result of inadequate circulation.

What causes most acute inflammation of the gallbladder?

A stone blocking the cystic duct.

What takes place when there is a chronic inflammation of the gallbladder?

Stones, resulting either from previous inflammation and infection or from an upset in chemistry within the gallbladder, will be associated with a thickening and chronic inflammation of the gallbladder wall. This will lead to poor filling and emptying or even to nonfunctioning of the gallbladder.

What takes place when there is a functional disorder of the gallbladder or bile ducts?

This condition is characterized by failure of the gallbladder to empty and secrete bile when it is called upon to do so. Or there may be spasm at the outlet of the common bile duct which interferes with the free passage of bile into the intestinal tract. The patient has indigestion, heartburn, and an inability to digest fatty foods, greases, and certain raw fruits and vegetables.

Are functional disorders of the gallbladder usually accompanied by the formation of gallstones?

Not necessarily.

At what age does gallbladder disease first develop?

In the 30s and 40s, although it is occasionally seen in younger people.

Is there any way to prevent gallbladder disease or the symptoms of a poorly functioning gallbladder?

Moderation in one's diet, with the eating of small quantities of fats, fried foods, and greases, will cut down on the demands made upon the gallbladder and may lessen the chances of symptoms due to inadequate function.

How can one tell if he has gallbladder disease?

1. Acute gallbladder disease (acute cholecystitis) is at all times accompanied by an elevation in temperature, nausea, and vomiting, along with pain and tenderness in the right upper portion of the abdomen beneath the ribs. An x-ray of the gallbladder may reveal a nonfunctioning organ or may demonstrate the presence of stones. A blood count may show the presence of an acute inflammation.

2. Chronic disease of the gallbladder (chronic cholecystitis), when accompanied by stones, may cause excruciating attacks of colicky pain in the right upper portion of the abdomen. This is usually due to a stone being stuck in the cystic duct or bile duct. The pain often radiates to the right shoulder or through to the back. There are nausea, vomiting, and tenderness in the abdomen, which may cease abruptly within a half-hour or so if the stone drops back into the gallbladder or passes through the obstructed duct. X-ray studies in chronic gallbladder disease usually show a nonfunctioning gallbladder and sometimes demonstrate the presence of gallstones.

3. Functional disturbances of the gallbladder evidence themselves by chronic indigestion; inability to digest fats, greases, and certain raw fruits and vegetables; and heartburn. X-ray studies in these cases may show poor filling and poor emptying of the gallbladder.

Is there a test that will make a positive diagnosis of gallbladder disease?

Yes, an x-ray test called a cholecystogram. This is done by giving the patient a specific dye in the form of pills. Some hours later, x-rays of the gallbladder are taken, and if the gallbladder is normal, the dye will fill up and outline the organ. The x-ray will also show emptying after the ingestion of a fatty meal. Sometimes, instead of giving the dye by mouth, it is injected into the veins prior to taking the x-rays.

What is the significance of a gallbladder not showing on x-ray film?

This means that the gallbladder is not functioning. Often, if the gallbladder fails to visualize with the dye, a second and larger dose of dye is given. Should the gallbladder not show with a double dose of dye, this is clear-cut evidence that the gallbladder is diseased.

Do gallstones always show on x-ray examination?

No. In some cases there may be many stones present and still they will not show on x-ray.

Can x-rays show stones in the bile ducts?

Yes. A relatively new diagnostic process called intravenous cholangiography will demonstrate stones in the bile ducts. This is performed by injecting the dye directly into a vein of the patient's arm and taking x-rays immediately thereafter.

Is this type of test dangerous?

No.

How does a physician decide whether to advise medical or surgical treatment for gallbladder disease?

The functional disorders of the gallbladder, when not accompanied by stone formation, are best treated medically. All other disturbances of the gallbladder are best treated surgically.

Is the medical management for functional disorders of the gallbladder very helpful?

Yes, when the patient cooperates by adhering closely to a sensible diet and when the patient takes medications as needed.

Does a patient with gallstones always have to be operated upon?

Not in all instances. There are many people who have stones in their gallbladder that produce no symptoms. However, if gallstones cause any symptoms whatever, it is safer to operate than not to operate. In particular, young people and diabetics should be operated upon if they have gallstones.

What is the medical management for gallbladder disease?

1. The avoidance of those foods that can produce indigestion, such as fats, greases, sauces, stuffings, and certain raw vegetables and raw fruits

2. The eating of a bland, well-rounded diet, with no large meals

3. The use of certain medications to relieve spasm of the bile ducts and to reduce excess acidity in the stomach

When is a gallbladder operation absolutely necessary?

1. When an acute inflammation is present. This can be diagnosed by elevated temperature, pain and tenderness in the vicinity of the gallbladder, an elevated white blood cell count, and x-ray evidence of a diseased organ.

2. When the patient is having recurrent attacks of severe, colicky pain due to the presence of gallstones.

3. When, in the presence of positive proof of gallbladder malfunction, the patient is suffering from chronic indigestion, nausea, flatulence, and pain in the right upper part of the abdomen.

4. When jaundice, caused by an obstructing stone, is present.

What will happen if an operation is not performed?

1. If jaundice persists because of a gallstone, the patient may eventually die from the toxic effects of the bile obstruction.

2. If an acute inflammation of the gallbladder progresses, gangrene of the organ may result. Or the infected gallbladder may rupture. Either of these

eventualities can cause death-dealing peritonitis unless immediate surgery is performed.

3. Recurrent attacks of gallstone colic can lead to a stone being passed into the common bile duct, where it may cause complete bile obstruction and jaundice.

4. Cancer of the gallbladder develops in approximately 1 to 2 percent of those patients who have chronic gallbladder inflammation with stones.

Why does the presence of jaundice complicate the disease?

Because jaundice indicates a blockage of the flow of bile from the liver into the intestine. Such a blockage, if not relieved, may lead to death from a toxic condition known as cholemia.

Is jaundice always caused by a gallstone?

No. There are many nonsurgical causes of jaundice. However, by a combination of chemical tests, one can determine rather accurately whether the jaundice is caused by stone blockage or by some medical condition not requiring surgery.

How long does the jaundice take to disappear after operation?

Several weeks. However, the patient knows within a day or two that the jaundice is subsiding because the urine becomes lighter in color and the stool resumes its normal color.

How can one tell whether jaundice is caused by an obstructing gallstone or some other cause?

There are many tests that help to provide a conclusive diagnosis as to whether the jaundice is obstructive or inflammatory in nature. A thorough history and physical examination, x-ray examinations, and several blood chemical tests will usually reveal the correct diagnosis.

Do stones predispose toward the formation of cancer in the gallbladder?

Yes. Approximately 1 to 2 percent of those who have stones in the gallbladder will eventually develop a cancer. This is an important reason for advocating surgery upon gallbladders containing stones, regardless of the presence or absence of symptoms.

Is removal of a gallbladder (cholecystectomy) a dangerous operative procedure?

No. It is no more dangerous than the removal of an appendix.

Can't medication cure gallbladder disease without resorting to an operation?

No. All one can hope for is temporary relief from an acute attack. No known drug will cure gallbladder disease. Much active research is in progress directed toward the prevention of gallstone formation but, to date, these experiments have been unsuccessful.

Is there any way to dissolve gallstones?

No. For generations, charlatans have claimed that they could dissolve stones, but there is absolutely no method known at this time by which this may be accomplished.

Does surgery always relieve the symptoms caused by a functional disorder when the gallbladder is known to be free of stones?

Although a certain percentage of these patients are benefited by gallbladder removal (cholecystectomy), others are not.

When operating upon the gallbladder does the surgeon remove the entire organ or just the stones?

In almost all cases, the gallbladder is removed. However, there are occasional cases where the organ is so acutely inflamed and the patient so sick that the surgeon may decide merely to remove the stones and place a drain into the gallbladder. This procedure takes less time to perform and carries with it less risk.

Are the bile ducts removed when operating upon the gallbladder?

No. There must be a free passage of bile from the liver into the intestines. The bile ducts are therefore left in place.

How does the surgeon remove stones from the bile duct?

He makes a small incision into the duct, picks out the stone or stones with a specially designed instrument, and then drains the duct with a rubber tube (T-tube). This tube is removed anywhere from a few days to a few weeks later, depending upon the subsequent tests and x-ray findings.

Are operations upon the gallbladder considered major operations?

Yes, but not dangerous operations.

How long does it take to remove a gallbladder?

Approximately three-quarters to one hour. However, some surgeons will perform this procedure in a half hour. Complicated cases may require longer periods of time.

How does one prepare for the operation?

Very little preoperative preparation is required for the patient with a chronic condition. Limitation of fatty foods and the eating of large quantities of sugar and protein is a good way to prepare for this operation.

Patients with acute infections frequently need considerable hospital preparation with intravenous medications, antibiotics, vitamin therapy, and occasionally blood transfusions.

What kind of anesthesia will be used?

Most surgeons use inhalation anesthesia with gas, oxygen, and ether, or other inhalant anesthetics.

How long will it take for the wound to heal?

Since these wounds are drained, they usually take 12 to 14 days to heal solidly.

How long must one remain in the hospital?

In uncomplicated cases, the average hospital stay is from 9 to 14 days. Most surgeons get their patients out of bed the day following surgery.

Are special nurses necessary?

Not actually necessary, but the average patient is comforted by such care for the first two to three postoperative days.

Is it common practice to remove the appendix while operating primarily for a gallbladder condition?

Yes, providing the gallbladder is not acutely inflamed. This practice is prophylactic and prevents a future attack of appendicitis.

What are the special preoperative measures used in these cases?

1. The passage of a tube through the nose to make sure that the stomach is empty at the time of surgery

2. The giving of intravenous medications before operation in the form of fluids, glucose, certain vitamins, particularly vitamin K in the presence of jaundice to protect against possible postoperative hemorrhage

3. The giving of antibiotics to the patient who has an acutely inflamed gallbladder or an inflammation of the bile ducts

Are blood transfusions necessary in gallbladder operations?

Not usually; only in the most seriously sick and complicated cases.

Where are the incisions made for gallbladder disease?

Either a longitudinal incision in the right upper portion of the abdomen or an oblique incision beneath the rib cage on the right side is carried out for a distance of five to seven inches.

Are drains usually placed in gallbladder wounds?

Yes. One or two rubber drains will be inserted following surgery. These will stay in place anywhere from six to ten days.

Are gallbladder operations especially painful?

No. There may be some pain on deep breathing or coughing for a few days after surgery, but the operative wound is not exceptionally painful.

How soon after surgery can the patient get out of bed?

For the ordinary case, on the first or second postoperative day.

What special postoperative measures are carried out?

1. In the ordinary operation for a chronically inflamed gallbladder with stones, there are few special postoperative orders. The patient may eat the day after surgery, but fats, greases, raw fruits and vegetables should not be included. Antibiotics may be given if there is fear of infection. A stomach tube is sometimes passed through the nose and kept there for the first day in order to avoid discomfort from distention.

2. The patient operated upon for an acute gallbladder inflammation or for jaundice will probably receive intravenous solutions, drainage of the stomach through a tube inserted through the nose, medications with vitamin K to counteract jaundice, and large doses of

antibiotics for a few days. Occasionally, blood transfusions are also given.

How soon after a gallbladder operation can one do the following?

Bathe	In about 2 weeks
Walk outdoors	2 weeks
Climb stairs	2 weeks
Do housework	5 to 6 weeks
Drive a car	6 weeks
Resume sexual relations	4 to 5 weeks
Return to work	5 to 6 weeks
Resume all physical activities	6 weeks

Is posthospital convalescent care necessary?

No.

Is it common for indigestion to persist for several weeks after removal of the gallbladder?

Yes.

Is it necessary to follow dietary precautions after gallbladder removal?

Yes. The patient should stay on the same kind of diet he followed before surgery, that is, a bland low-fat diet.

Should a woman whose gallbladder has been removed allow herself to become pregnant?

Yes, if she so desires.

What are the aftereffects of gallbladder surgery?

Patients whose gallbladders are removed return, with very few exceptions, to completely normal lives. It is wise, however, to watch one's diet for some time after surgery, as there is a tendency to gain weight.

What are the chances of recovery from a gallbladder operation?

The mortality rate from gallbladder surgery is less than 1 percent. A fatality occurs mainly in the very complicated case or in people who have neglected to seek treatment early.

What organ takes over the function of the gallbladder after its removal?

The bile ducts take over the duties of the gallbladder. This may take three to four months before it works smoothly, and during this interval the patient may suffer from mild indigestion or pains caused by spasm of the common bile duct.

Do symptoms of gallbladder disease ever persist or recur after surgery?

Yes. Approximately 10 percent of patients who have been operated upon for gallbladder disease will continue to have symptoms after surgery. These symptoms are thought to be caused by spasms of the lower end of the common bile duct (biliary dyskinesia).

What are the chances of recurrence or continuation of symptoms after operation?

Minor symptoms may persist in some 5 to 10 percent of patients whose gallbladders have been removed. These symptoms are thought to be caused by spasm of the lower end of the common bile duct. However, they are rarely severe or disabling. Most postoperative symptoms can be adequately relieved by antispasmodic medication.

Do patients ever form stones again after they have once been removed?

If the gallbladder has been removed, they cannot re-form stones in the gallbladder. However, a very small percentage of patients may re-form stones in the common bile duct or in the stump of the cystic duct which has been left behind.

What treatment is carried out when patients re-form stones in the common bile duct?

Reoperation is necessary. This is a serious procedure but the great majority of people will recover.

Is there any way to prevent stones from re-forming?

Not really, except that one should guard against infection and follow a sane, sensible, bland low-fat diet.

How often should one return for a checkup after a gallbladder operation?

About six months after surgery and then again a year after surgery.

Does gallbladder removal affect length of life?

Yes, the chances for leading a long and healthy life are greater after the removal of a diseased gallbladder.

Ganglions

Ganglions are thin-walled cysts of tendons or joints. They are filled with a colorless, jellylike substance. They are seen most frequently on the back of the wrists in children and young adults. Many of them cause no symptoms and disappear by themselves over a period of months. But others grow quite large (one or two inches in diameter) and cause great pain on motion of the wrist. Occasionally these cysts are found on the fingers or about the ankle joint.

Ganglionic cysts must be removed in the hospital under local or general anesthesia. Those that originate from the wrist joint may be exceedingly difficult to remove in their entirety and, as a consequence, have a tendency to recur. It must also be mentioned that ganglions tend to be multiple, and a new one may form in the same region where one has already been removed.

The hand usually swells greatly after the surgical removal of these cysts, and it is often impossible to return to work for several days.

Treatment of recurrent ganglionic cysts by injection with an irritating solution has been advocated by some surgeons. This is a procedure not without risk if the cyst connects with a joint, as it may cause an irritation of the joint lining and consequent interference with free motion.

Some surgeons have treated ganglions successfully by needling them, withdrawing the jellylike contents of the cyst, and injecting cortisone. The old custom of smashing them with a book is mentioned only to be condemned.

QUESTIONS AND ANSWERS

Are ganglions very common?

Yes. They are seen very often in children and young adults. They may also occur, although less frequently, among older people.

What are the accepted methods of treatment for a ganglion?

1. Surgical removal, under either local or general anesthesia, in a hospital. This is carried out when the ganglion grows to large size or is painful.

2. Needling of the ganglion, with the injection of a sclerosing solution. (This procedure is not carried out very often today.)

3. Needling of the ganglion, removal of its contents, and injection of cortisone.

How often do ganglions recur once they have been removed surgically?

It has been estimated that about 10 percent of them will recur and will require further treatment.

Is it wise to break a ganglion by hitting the wrist with a book or other object?

No. This is a poor form of treatment and is often followed by recurrence.

Are ganglions painful?

Yes. They sometimes are very painful, especially among those who work with their hands.

Is there a great deal of swelling of the hand following surgical removal of a ganglion?

Yes. It may remain this way for several days. People should be advised beforehand that they will be unable to carry out their usual work duties for approximately one week after surgical removal of this type of cyst.

Gangrene

The term gangrene denotes death of tissue, usually involving a rather wide area of the body. Most gangrene is associated with loss of blood supply to an area, invasion by secondary bacteria, and subsequent putrefaction. There are a great number of types of gangrene; some of the most frequently encountered are:

1. **Arteriosclerotic gangrene.** This type is secondary to hardening of the arteries and is seen most often in the feet and legs.

2. **Cutaneous gangrene.** This is a form of localized pustular gangrene of the skin seen in young children, and is caused by a severe staphylococcal infection.

3. **Diabetic gangrene.** This occurs in people who have diabetes, and is usually associated both with hardening of the arteries to the legs and with secondary bacterial invasion of the feet and legs.

4. **Dry gangrene.** This type occurs without bacterial invasion, and is often associated with loss of arterial blood supply to a part of the body. The tissues dry up and become shriveled.

5. Embolic gangrene. This is a type that follows the blocking of an artery by an embolus.

6. Frostbite gangrene. This type is due to the shutting off of arterial blood supply due to cold. The areas of frostbite gangrene are usually small and are limited to fingers, toes, tip of the nose, ears, cheeks, and other parts of the body that usually are exposed.

7. Gas gangrene. This most serious type is due to death of tissues secondary to an injury, usually involving the tissues beneath the skin and muscles. The gangrene is associated with a particular group of bacteria, the clostridia.

8. Oral gangrene. This is associated with a gangrenous ulceration of the mouth. It is also known as noma.

9. Pressure gangrene. This type is due to pressure of hard substances against one area of the body. The most common type is the bed sore, or decubitus ulcer, seen in old, debilitated, chronically sick individuals.

10. Progressive gangrene. This is a type in which the gangrene extends from one area to another, as from a toe to a foot or from a foot to a leg.

11. Raynaud's gangrene. This is gangrene of the skin of the fingers, secondary to arterial spasm.

12. Thrombotic gangrene. This type is secondary to thrombosis and closure of the passageway through an artery.

13. Traumatic gangrene. That which is caused as a result of an accident.

14. Trophic gangrene. This type of gangrene is due to degeneration of the nerve supply to a part.

QUESTIONS AND ANSWERS

Are any types of gangrene preventable?

Yes. Many types of gangrene are preventable. As examples, diabetic gangrene can be avoided by scrupulous attention to hygiene of the toes and feet in diabetics and by controlling the diabetes with insulin or other antidiabetic drugs; gas gangrene can be avoided by immediate surgical attention to an open wound and removal of all dead tissue from such a wound; arteriosclerotic gangrene may be prevented by inserting arterial grafts to improve circulation to the limbs.

What is the treatment for gangrene?

Once a segment of tissue or an organ of the body has died as a result of gangrene, it must be removed surgically. This applies to gangrene of the intestines secondary to the shutting off of blood supply to the intestinal wall; it also applies to a leg in which gangrene has already set in. Within recent years, treatment of gas gangrene has been improved greatly through the use of the hyperbaric chamber.

Is it possible to limit the spread of a gangrenous process once it has set in?

Yes, by vigorous and energetic treatment of the cause of the gangrene. Thus, gangrene of a toe in a diabetic may be limited to the toe by regulation of the diabetes and by treatment to improve the circulation to the lower limb. Control of infection associated with gangrene through the use of antibiotic medications also will limit the spread of the process.

Gastrectomy

Gastrectomy is a surgical procedure in which a part or all of the stomach is removed because of disease. Subtotal gastrectomy, often carried out to cure an ulcer of the stomach or duodenum, usually consists of the removal of that portion which contains the acid-secreting glands. The operation is also performed in an extended form upon patients who have a malignant tumor of the stomach. A total gastrectomy is reserved for those patients who have a cancer involving the upper portion of the stomach near the esophagus.

When subtotal gastrectomy is performed, the small intestine is brought up and is attached to the stump of the stomach; when total gastrectomy is performed the small intestine is sutured to the lower end of the esophagus (food-pipe).

See also STOMACH AND DUODENUM.

Gastric Ulcer

See STOMACH AND DUODENUM.

Genitourinary System

Along with the nervous system, gastrointestinal system, circulatory system, and respiratory system, the genitourinary system is one of the five major body systems. The structures that make up the genitourinary system are as follows:

In males and females:
1. The left and right kidneys.
2. The left and right ureters, which lead from the kidneys to the urinary bladder.
3. The urinary bladder.
4. The urethra, which leads from the bladder to the outside.

In males only:
1. The prostate gland, which surrounds the outlet of the bladder.
2. The seminal vesicles, which lie above the prostate gland and to the side

of the ejaculatory ducts which deliver the sperm. The vesicles secrete fluid which contributes to the ejaculate.
3. The left and right testicles, with coverings and blood supply.
4. The left and right vas deferens, which lead from the testicles to the prostatic portion of the urethra, uniting with the duct of the seminal vesicles to form the ejaculatory duct.

In females only:
1. The uterus.
2. The fallopian tubes.
3. The left and right ovaries.

Throughout one's life, the genitourinary system can function smoothly or it may be the site of innumerable diseases including birth deformities, infections, or tumor formation.

See also specific organs.

QUESTIONS AND ANSWERS

BIRTH DEFORMITIES OF THE GENITOURINARY SYSTEM

Are any parts of the genitourinary tract ever deformed at birth?

Birth deformities are thought to be more common in the genitourinary tract than in any other system of the body. Ten percent of all newborns have some deformity in this system, and 35 to 40 percent of all body deformities are urogenital deformities.

Are birth deformities encountered in which there is lack of bladder function?

Yes. Major bladder disturbances are noted when a child is born with spinal cord defects, because bladder function is controlled by nerves originating in the spinal cord. Disturbance in nerve supply and function may cause the bladder to be unable to contract and empty itself properly. This is known as an atonic or neurogenic bladder. Along with the inability of the bladder to contract, there is often a spasm of the muscles controlling the outlet of the organ and an inability to relax them.

What is the treatment for a bladder that is unable to contract with sufficient force to empty itself?

Surgical procedures have been devised to increase the size of the outlet so that the weak bladder muscles will meet with less resistance when they contract. Also, spinal cord defects may be treatable by neurosurgery.

What are some of the more common birth deformities of the genitourinary tract?

1. Absent kidneys. This is a rare deformity. The child with this condition will die within a few days.

2. Incomplete kidney formation, with absence of certain essential elements or failure of the various elements to unite one with the other. This deformity also usually causes death.

3. Polycystic kidneys, which have many large cystic masses that prevent adequate function. Children with this condition may survive but have kidney difficulties in adulthood.

4. Congenital constriction of the kidney outlet (pelvis). Such a malformation will cause slowed and inadequate flow of urine from the kidney to the bladder.

5. Abnormally placed blood vessels, located near the kidney outlet, that cause partial blockage of the urine as it exits and passes down toward the bladder.

6. Horseshoe kidney, a not uncommon birth deformity. In this condition, the two kidneys are fused and lie across the back of the abdomen. In normal anatomy, there is a separate organ on each side. In most such children, kidney function is normal.

7. Ectopic kidney. In this deformity, one kidney or both kidneys are not in the usual anatomical position. A not uncommon deviation is for one kidney to be located lower down in the abdomen, sometimes in the pelvic region.

8. Duplications of the kidneys or ureters. The ureter is the tube leading from the kidney to the bladder. Sometimes there may be a double kidney on one side and a normal single kidney on the opposite side of the abdomen. In other instances there may be a single kidney on each side but a double ureter leading to the bladder.

9. Exstrophy of the bladder, a deformity in which there has been failure of the anterior wall to develop fully. In these children, the bladder lies on the abdominal wall with its interior visible, and urine pours out over the abdomen.

10. Congenital constriction of the bladder outlet, a rather common condition, as is narrowing of a portion of the urethra (the tube leading from the bladder to the outside).

11. Hypospadias and epispadias are seen quite often in newborn males. In these deformities the urethra fails to extend the entire length of the penis but terminates short of the tip.

12. Undescended testicle is perhaps the most common of all birth malformations of the genital tract.

13. Pseudohermaphroditism, a rare but extremely serious birth deformity in which the external genitals do not clearly resemble a particular sex. Thus a child may be born with an enlarged clitoris that resembles a penis or may have a divided scrotum containing no testicles that resembles the lips of the female vulva. In many of these cases it is not easy to determine on first inspection whether the child is male or female, and further investigation will be necessary to make an accurate determination.

14. Congenital hydrocele. Some male

infants are born with a collection of fluid surrounding the testicle. This will cause a considerable swelling of one side of the scrotal sac. If the hydrocele has resulted from undue pressure in a breech delivery as the child passed through the birth canal, it will absorb within a few days. Some hydroceles, however, will persist for several months or may not disappear at all. These can be considered true birth deformities and will require surgical correction.

INFECTIONS OF THE URINARY TRACT

What are some of the outstanding symptoms of infections of the urinary tract?

1. High fever and chills, with the fever mounting as high as 104° F to 105° F.

2. If pyelitis (perhaps the most common infection) or pyelonephritis is present, there will be pain on the involved side in the region of the affected kidney and loin.

3. With cystitis, there will be marked frequency of urination and pain over the lower portion of the abdomen in the region of the bladder.

4. The urine will be cloudy in color and, on microscopic examination, will be found to contain pus cells, red blood cells, and bacteria.

5. There may be pain and burning on urination, especially with cystitis.

What causes infection of the urinary tract in infants?

Urinary infection in children under two years (the diaper age) is frequently produced by spread through the bloodstream from infection in the intestinal tract or in the respiratory system. Ascending infection from the urethra may also produce urinary tract infections,

especially in females. The bacteria responsible for the urinary tract infections are commonly those found in the intestinal tract or in the respiratory system.

Is it common for children who have kidney or bladder infections to vomit and have diarrhea?

Yes, these are common symptoms of kidney infections in children, and the vomiting and diarrhea may be so severe that they may overshadow symptoms of the urinary tract itself. Diarrhea secondary to a urinary tract infection may cause dehydration with upset in the chemical balance of acids and alkalis in the body fluids.

Are infections of the urinary tract more common in females?

Yes. The urethral canal leading from the bladder to the exterior is relatively short in females and contains no curves or narrowed zones. This anatomical construction may make it easier for germs to find their way into the bladder and produce cystitis.

What are the most common types of infections of the urinary tract?

1. Urethritis, an inflammation of the tube leading from the bladder to the exterior. Urethritis often occurs secondary to an inflammation about the vagina.

2. Cystitis, an inflammation of the urinary bladder. Cystitis may follow urethritis and may lead to pyelitis or pyelonephritis.

3. Pyelitis and pyelonephritis, infections of the outlet of the kidney and of the kidney substance itself. These inflammations may follow cystitis, an inflammation of the urinary bladder.

How long does it take an infection of the urinary tract to develop?

This will depend on the virulence

(strength) of the organism introduced and the degree of susceptibility or intactness of the organ involved. Symptoms can develop within 24 to 48 hours after bacteria gain access to the bladder or kidneys.

What drugs are most widely used for treating infections of the urinary tract?

Although all of the drugs listed here are effective with a variety of organisms, some may give better results with specific germs than others. Sensitivity tests may be performed before a specific antibiotic or other antibacterial medication is prescribed.

1. Sulfonamide drugs, such as gantrisin and its derivatives
2. Nalidixic acid
3. Oxytetracycline
4. Chloramphenicol
5. Kanamycin sulfate
6. Nitrofurantoin
7. Methenamine mandelate
8. Gentamycin
9. Ampicillin
10. Colimycin

Are special diets necessary for those who have infections of the urinary tract?

Usually not. The patient should be encouraged to drink large quantities of fluids, assuming that kidney function is intact and that there is no interference with the formation of urine. Highly seasoned foods are to be avoided.

What is the general treatment for infections of the urinary tract?

1. The patient should be given large quantities of fluids to drink. This will tend to flush out the kidneys and the bladder and to dilute the infected urine.
2. If the fever is very high, alcohol sponging and fever-reducing drugs such as aspirin will make the patient more comfortable.

3. Suitable antibacterial medication should be given.
4. After the acute phase of the illness has subsided, the urinary tract should be examined to determine any abnormalities. This will involve special x-rays, cystoscopic examination, and other special tests.

How serious are infections of the urinary tract?

The seriousness of an infection of the urinary tract depends to a considerable extent on the type of bacteria present. Some are very difficult to eradicate. Of greater importance is the presence or absence of urinary tract obstruction and the primary condition that initiated the infection. Relief of urinary obstruction is of paramount importance. Once the urine flows freely, many infections will clear without assistance of antibacterial agents.

Do infections of the urinary tract ever follow acute tonsillitis or a respiratory disease?

Yes. Certain cases of nephritis, pyelitis, and pyelonephritis come on after an acute infection of the tonsils or after a respiratory infection such as a severe cold, grippe, bronchitis, or pneumonia.

Are infections of the urinary tract contagious?

No, unless the gonorrhea germ is the causative bacteria. In these cases, contagion is a factor and isolation is necessary. Other forms of urinary infections are not contagious.

Is hospitalization necessary for infections of the urinary tract?

Only if the patient is running a very high temperature and the infection is not brought readily under control by the administration of the appropriate antibiotic or chemical drug.

Do convulsions ever occur in small children with infections of the urinary tract?

Yes. No treatment is necessary for the convulsions, as these will cease when the urinary infection subsides.

Are there any injections, immunizations, or vaccinations that can prevent recurrence of infections of the urinary tract?

No.

Will the taking of vitamins or iron help to protect an individual against infections of the urinary tract?

No.

Will infections of the kidney, ureters, or bladder affect future childbearing in a female?

Not unless there has been widespread, serious damage to kidney function. Such girls may be instructed not to chance pregnancy when they reach maturity.

How often should a urine specimen be examined when a person has an infection of the urinary tract?

Daily.

How does one determine the best antibiotic to use in a urinary infection?

A urine specimen is collected under sterile conditions so that it will not pick up germs from the outside environment. This specimen is cultured and the specific germ in the urine causing the infection is grown. Various antibiotic drugs are then spread near growths of colonies of these bacteria. The area where there is least growth or no growth indicates that the drug in the area is effective against the germ. This is known as an antibiotic sensitivity test.

Should the urine be examined regularly after an individual has fully recovered?

Yes. It is wise to have a specimen taken every month for at least one year after recovery from a serious urinary infection.

Can surgery be helpful in curing structural deformities that lead to urinary tract infections?

If there is a stricture of the outlet of the kidney causing repeated infections, this can be corrected through a plastic operation upon the outlet. Also, abnormal blood vessels that may cause an interference with the outflow of urine from the kidneys to the bladder can usually be treated surgically. Bladder malformations and defects of the urethra are also sometimes the cause of repeated infections, and these can often be treated surgically.

Do female children ever develop an inflammation of the urethra that is not gonorrheal in origin?

Yes. This is a very common type of infection and is usually the result of poor hygiene. Also, some young girls have a habit of sticking things into the urethra and vagina. These articles may cause an infection.

How can one distinguish an infection due to gonorrhea from one caused by other germs?

By culturing the pus in the area and by examining it under a microscope. If the infection has been caused by gonococcal bacteria, these bacteria will be visible under the microscope.

Do infants and children ever develop the same diseases of the genitourinary tract as adults?

Yes, but their reaction to these conditions is sometimes considerably more severe than in adults. Children become dehydrated more quickly and show greater evidence of toxemia (poisoning).

How is it determined that a kidney is so badly infected that it must be removed?

Under no circumstances should a kidney be removed until it has been demonstrated that there is another kidney present on the opposite side that is capable of sustaining life. Such determination is made by kidney function tests and by x-rays. An infected kidney should be removed when it has poor or no function and when it causes severe symptoms that are not relieved by surgery or medical management. It should also be removed when the infection is apt to spread to other parts of the body, including the normal kidney on the opposite side.

What sulfa drugs are most widely used for treating infections of the urinary tract?

Sulfa drugs are favored for overall use on a long-term basis for urinary tract infections. There are many good preparations, among which are sulfisoxazole, sulfadiazine, and sulfamethizole.

When pus is found in a female's urine, does this always indicate an infection of the urinary tract?

No. In certain of these cases the source of the pus is a vaginal infection, especially if the urine is taken from a voided specimen, not from a catheterized specimen. In the female, a specimen of urine for examination should be obtained by passing a catheter into the bladder after cleansing the vaginal area. A voided specimen picks up contaminated elements from the vaginal secretions.

Is there a tendency for infections of the urinary tract to recur?

To a certain degree, yes. It is therefore important that an individual who has once had a urinary tract infection be given large quantities of fluids to drink at all times and that he be watched very carefully to avoid conditions that might trigger another infection.

In chronic recurrences it is well to obtain bacterial culture studies in order to find the specific organism responsible for the trouble. Then, with the use of sensitivity tests, the specific antibacterial agent that may yield efficient results is administered. A common cause for recurrent urinary tract infections is the presence of an obstruction that interferes with the free flow of urine. X-ray studies are very useful in localizing areas of obstruction. The relief, by surgery if necessary, of an obstruction is essential to the cure of a chronic or recurrent infection.

What are some of the possible complications of a serious infection of the urinary tract?

Repeated pyelitis or pyelonephritis may cause permanent kidney damage that will affect the individual for the rest of his life. Prolonged kidney infections lead to contracted kidneys, with changes similiar to those in chronic glomerulonephritis. The outlook for such people is bleak, because of their inability to eliminate waste products. If the nephritis and toxemia are progressive, high blood pressure and enlargement of the heart will surely ensue.

Can one tell by looking at the urine that an infection is subsiding?

When the urine becomes crystal clear, one can be fairly certain that the infection has been brought under control. This can be done by placing some of the urine in a test tube and holding it up to a light. Of course, further urine analysis and a urine culture are necessary to be positive that the infection has cleared. If it has, the urine will no longer contain albumin, red blood cells, pus cells, or bacteria.

Geriatric Surgery

See SURGERY IN THE AGED.

Glaucoma

The front of the eyeball is filled with a watery fluid known as *aqueous humor,* which circulates through the eye much like blood circulates throughout the body. Under normal circumstances, this fluid is maintained at a constant pressure. In glaucoma, there is an increase in this pressure which, if unchecked, will endanger sight. The increased pressure compresses the blood vessels at the back of the eye which supply the optic nerve. When this nerve receives inadequate nourishment, its fibers die and loss of vision results.

Glaucoma, in one form or another, affects approximately 2 percent of all people over 40 years of age. Unfortunately, many people may not be aware that they have glaucoma until a good deal of vision has been lost.

Occasionally glaucoma is seen at birth or in childhood. Farsighted individuals are more prone to develop glaucoma than those with normal vision or nearsightedness. However, those without refractive errors can also develop glaucoma. At first, the presence of glaucoma may be detected only in one eye, but it must be considered to be a condition that will eventually involve both eyes.

The *tension* of the eye is called intraocular pressure and is maintained by the secretion of aqueous humor. This fluid normally escapes at the angle of the eyeball through a special exit (the canal of Schlemm) at a rate equal to the rate of its secretion. If the rate at which the secretion is produced exceeds that at which it drains from the eyeball, an increase in tension of intraocular pressure results.

The tension of the eyeball is measured with a *tonometer.* This instrument records pressure when it is placed directly upon the anesthetized cornea. Any tension registering above 20 millimeters of mercury on the tonometer is considered to be elevated.

Glaucoma may be classified as *acute* or *chronic.*

QUESTIONS AND ANSWERS

What is glaucoma?
A disease in which the tension or pressure within the eyeball is increased. This may lead to irreparable damage to the optic nerve and blindness.

What causes glaucoma?
In open angle simple glaucoma, aging causes closure of pores through which fluid is removed from the eye. In closed angle simple glaucoma, there is a defect within the eye which causes blockage of the flow of fluids.

Is it a serious disease?
Yes.

Is glaucoma inherited?
It may well be, as there are some families who seem to be particularly affected.

Can improper use of the eye lead to glaucoma?
No.

Does glaucoma affect one or both eyes?
Usually both eyes are affected. However, if only one eye is affected, the chances are that the other eye will eventually be involved.

What precautions should be taken to prevent glaucoma from affecting the good eye?

Eyedrops (pilocarpine or eserine) should be taken to keep the pupil contracted.

How often does glaucoma affect the uninvolved eye?

In acute glaucoma, it may never affect the uninvolved eye. In chronic glaucoma, it may involve the opposite eye in more than 50 percent of cases.

Who is most prone to develop glaucoma?

Farsighted people over 40 years of age, especially those who are exceptionally emotional.

What are the various types of glaucoma?

Acute and chronic.

What are the symptoms and signs of acute glaucoma?

Acute glaucoma has a warning stage characterized by blurring of vision, rainbow halos around lights, pain in the eye, pain in the head near the eye, and slight redness of the eye. Examination shows sluggish reactions of the pupil and an increased tension. These symptoms may last until the high blood pressure is controlled with medications or surgery. Rarely, the symptoms disappear spontaneously. Mild attacks, of which the patient may not be aware, may occur on and off until the patient abruptly goes into the severe stage of the disease. With each mild attack, some damage is done to the outflow channels of aqueous humor. When the tension reaches a high level, the following symptoms appear:

1. Marked reduction in vision
2. Severe pain in the eye and head
3. Nausea and vomiting

4. Swollen eyelid and marked redness of the eye
5. Hazy cornea, dilated pupil, and a greenish reflex on shining a light into the eye
6. A tension ranging from 50 to 80, or more

What are the symptoms and signs of chronic glaucoma?

Chronic glaucoma usually develops gradually and in many instances the patient is unaware of its presence until the condition is well advanced. Slight blurring of vision might be the first clue that something is wrong, or the diagnosis may be made during a routine eye examination. Such an examination may reveal one or more of the following signs:

1. Changes in the appearance of the main (optic) nerve of the eye, as seen on inspection with an ophthalmoscope
2. Reduction in the field of vision
3. Increased intraocular tension

What is the medical treatment for glaucoma?

The most disastrous consequence of glaucoma, whether acute or chronic, is that the increased tension is transmitted to the blood vessels nourishing the main (optic) nerve of the eye. This occurs gradually in a chronic case and in a few days, or even hours, in an acute case. To avoid damage to the optic nerve and blindness, intensive treatment must be instituted immediately upon discovery of glaucoma. In the acute case, a trial period of medical treatment for 12 to 24 hours may be attempted. This consists of:

1. Eyedrops (pilocarpine) or similarly acting drugs which constrict the pupil and thus open and widen the escape angle of the eye so that more fluid can drain. If this treatment is effective, it will lower intraocular tension.

2. The immediate use of certain drugs, given by mouth or by injection, which will cause a decrease in the production of aqueous humor. Treatment with these drugs is known as osmotherapy, and constitutes a significant advance in the medical management of acute glaucoma.

3. If intraocular tension is not reduced by the preceding measures within 24 hours, immediate surgery to save the sight must be performed. If the tension is brought down, eventual surgery is nevertheless indicated in order to prevent the recurrence of an acute attack. The results of glaucoma surgery are invariably better if it can be performed electively after the pressure of the eye has been reduced. Fortunately, since the advent of osmotherapy, the pressure can be brought down before such surgery in most patients.

What surgical procedure is carried out for acute glaucoma?

Iridectomy. This is an operation in which a piece of the iris (the colored portion of the eye) is removed. This widens the escape angle of the eye and permits fluid to drain out at a more normal rate. Furthermore, iridectomy prevents recurrence of acute attacks.

What surgical procedure is carried out for chronic glaucoma?

Various filtration operations in which a new channel for escape of fluid is established. The fluid is made to exit from the eyeball and drain under the conjunctiva (the membrane covering the white part of the eye).

Is it essential to operate for glaucoma?

1. Yes, in acute glaucoma, unless the pressure is lowered to normal, or below normal, within 24 hours by medical treatment. Even if this is accomplished, surgery is essential to prevent recurrence of the acute attack.

2. If the vision is still intact, surgery is advisable in chronic glaucoma only when pressure cannot be reduced by medication.

What will happen if surgery is refused?

Blindness is the end result of uncontrolled glaucoma in a large proportion of cases.

Are glaucoma operations painful?

No.

Are the operations serious?

Yes, as far as vision is concerned.

Are both eyes operated upon at the same time?

No. If both eyes are affected and need surgery, usually two to seven days are permitted to elapse before the second eye is operated on.

How long after the operation must one remain in bed?

One to two days.

Are private nurses necessary?

No.

How long a hospital stay is necessary?

Four to five days (for each eye).

What special postoperative measures are necessary?

1. Special eyedrops are given to reduce reaction.

2. Heavy work must be avoided for three to four weeks.

How successful are the operations for glaucoma?

For acute glaucoma, very successful. For chronic glaucoma, moderately successful, depending on how long the disease has existed. Surgery in late glaucoma is often not successful.

In what percentage of cases is vision restored after operations for glaucoma?

In acute glaucoma, approximately 95

percent. This will depend largely upon how long the pressure has been allowed to remain at high levels. In chronic glaucoma, it will depend largely upon the length of time the condition has existed prior to surgery.

Can the eye be used as much as desired after an operation for glaucoma?
Yes.

Is it necessary to remove stitches after these operations?
Sometimes, but it is not painful to do so.

What scars are visible after an eye operation for glaucoma?
None.

How long does it take for the wound to heal?
Two to three weeks.

Do the operations disturb the appearance of the eye?
There will be a change in the appearance of the iris above the pupil, but this is covered by the upper eyelid and will therefore not be very noticeable.

Must eyedrops be used after surgery?
Sometimes. Very often, no drops will be needed.

Must glasses be worn after glaucoma operations?
Not unless they were worn previously.

Can sunlight hurt the eyes in this condition?
No.

Is it necessary to return for periodic examinations after an attack of glaucoma?
Yes. The physician will pay particular attention to the health of the uninvolved eye.

Glomus Tumors

A glomus tumor is a tiny growth, usually pea-sized or smaller, composed of connecting arterioles and venules, and containing a very rich supply of nerves. (Arterioles are tiny arteries; venules are tiny veins.) A favorite site for the location of a glomus tumor is beneath a fingernail or toenail, on the pads of the fingers or toes, or on the upper or lower extremities just beneath the skin. A characteristic of a glomus tumor is that it is extremely tender to the touch. This is thought to be due to the rich nerve supply to the growth.

Because of their location beneath the skin or beneath the nail bed, glomus tumors cannot be seen, but they can be localized by their great sensitivity and pain on pressure.

The treatment for a glomus tumor is surgical removal. If it happens to be located beneath a nail, the nail will have to be removed first.

QUESTIONS AND ANSWERS

How common are glomus tumors?
They are a rather uncommon type of tumor, but should be considered whenever anyone complains of marked pain beneath a fingernail and a slight bluish discoloration is noted. Also, they should be kept in mind whenever there is an extremely tender, localized, pea-sized nodule beneath the skin of an extremity.

Do glomus tumors ever become malignant?
No.

Does pain from a glomus tumor ever run up an arm or a leg?
Yes. The radiation of pain from these tumors is often very extensive.

Do these tumors tend to recur once they are removed?

No.

Goiter

A goiter is an enlargement of the thyroid gland. It may involve the entire gland or only part of it; it may be associated with overactivity of thyroid secretions, or it may be present with normal thyroid activity or with an underactive gland. Goiters are classified according to their extent, and also according to their association or lack of association with abnormal thyroid function. Thus, goiters are called diffuse when they involve both lobes of the gland in uniform fashion. They are called nodular when there is an irregular enlargement of a part of the thyroid gland, with other areas appearing normal.

These are the main classifications of goiter according to type:

1. **Colloid goiter.** This is a smooth enlargement of the entire thyroid gland, not associated with overactivity of function. It is seen often in geographic areas where there is an iodine deficiency in drinking water. Colloid goiters often affect adolescent children and young adults.

2. **Nodular nontoxic goiter.** This is an irregular enlargement of the thyroid gland, not associated with excess secretion of thyroid hormone. Nodular goiters can be noted as single nontoxic goiters or multiple nodular nontoxic goiters.

3. **Toxic goiter.** This is an enlargement of the thyroid gland associated with overactivity of function and excess secretion of the thyroid hormone. It is associated with increased basal metabolic rate.

A toxic goiter can be either diffuse toxic goiter (Graves' disease) or a nodular toxic goiter. Graves' disease is also known as an exophthalmic goiter and Basedow's disease.

See also EXOPHTHALMIC GOITER; THYROID GLAND.

Grafts

See SKIN AND SUBCUTANEOUS TISSUES; ORGAN AND TISSUE TRANSPLANTS.

Granulomatous Colitis

Granulomatous colitis is a form of chronic inflammation of the large bowel associated with ulcerations and with the formation of granulation tissue. It is very similar to ulcerative colitis but there is a tendency for the granulomatous type to spread up from the large bowel into the small intestines. People afflicted by granulomatous colitis are somewhat less likely to develop cancer than those with chronic ulcerative colitis, but they do form fistulas and abscesses about the rectum, and have the same tendency for the ulcerations to become chronic. There is a slightly greater chance for someone with granulomatous colitis to have spontaneous subsidence of his condition than one who has ulcerative colitis. However, a great number of people with this condition will require surgical removal of the ulcerated portion of the bowel.

See also CHRONIC ULCERATIVE COLITIS.

Gynecomastia

See BREASTS.

Hair Transplants

See BALDNESS.

Hand

The hand is a superb organ of sensation and motion. It is a finely tooled machine powered by an intricate network of muscles and tendons. Techniques of hand repair and reconstruction have developed into a special field of surgical study.

CONGENITAL (BIRTH) DEFECTS OF THE HANDS

The thalidomide tragedy of the early 1960s brought to the public attention the problem of deformed hands and arms, and pointed out the fact that such abnormalities are not always inherited. They may be the result of an infection (German measles), a drug (thalidomide), or excessive irradiation (x-ray) occurring during the first two months of pregnancy. It is unlikely that injuries, diet, emotional disturbance, or fright during pregnancy have anything to do with their development, despite the long-standing existence of these contentions.

1. An **extra finger** (supernumerary digit) is the most frequent congenital abnormality of the hand. When it is attached by a tiny strand of skin, it can be removed shortly after birth. However, a *double thumb* must be carefully examined before surgery. One of the two thumbs may have better tendon, the other better bone support. Frequently it is the smaller digit that functions best and should be saved.

2. **Missing fingers:** Occasionally a child may be born with one or more of the fingers absent. Recent surgical advances have afforded the trained hand surgeon many ways to replace a missing thumb. He may rotate, transpose, and shorten the index finger so that it will work and look like a normal thumb. In one operation, the skin, tendons, muscles, nerves, and blood vessels are carefully shifted with the finger so that sensation and motion are retained. A thumb may also be replaced by fixing a segment of bone from the hip or collarbone onto the side of the hand, and covering it with a padded skin graft. This maintains the five-digit hand but the new thumb will have no joint and will therefore serve only as a post against which the other fingers act. The transfer of toes to replace missing fingers or thumbs has also been attempted, with occasional success. This procedure requires many operative stages and awkward hand-to-foot plaster cast immobilization. The resulting "fingers" and "thumb" are short and usually have poor sensation.

3. **Club hand:** Birth deformity caused by the partial or complete absence of one of the two bones of the forearm is known as club hand. Most frequently the thumb side of the forearm is affected. Without its proper support, the hand is pulled into the defect left by the missing bone (radius). As the tendons and skin shorten, it becomes increasingly more difficult to replace the hand into its proper position. The

thumb may be absent, the forearm bowed.

Casts or splints may straighten the club hand, but a substitute must be made for the missing bone. A slot may be fashioned in the wrist bones and the hand wedged into place. The missing radius may be substituted by a bone graft from the leg or hip. If there is difficulty in bringing the deviated hand into position, the skin and tendons may be lengthened (soft tissue release) before performing bone surgery. Although the operated club hand remains somewhat short and stiff, its improved appearance and function justify surgical attempts at correction.

4. Phocomelia: As an embryo develops, its cells form the upper arm first, then the forearm, and finally the hand. Thus, if a drug or x-ray were to stunt the limb's growth before it had completed its development, the hand or forearm would attach directly to the shoulder without the upper arm intervening. This has been called phocomelia, or "seal limb," because of its appearance. (It is this deformity that occurred most often when embryos were exposed to thalidomide.) Although surgery has provided no answer in the treatment of phocomelia, ingenious artificial limbs have been made for these children; many of them function amazingly well.

5. Webbed fingers (syndactyly) is a rather common deformity of the hand. The webbing may consist merely of an enlarged skin fold between adjacent fingers. However, in severe cases, the bones, tendons, and skin of two or three fingers may all be joined together.

Webbed fingers can be separated surgically. A skin graft is usually placed along the sides of the separated fingers. If a web acts to restrain the growth of a finger, it may bow and deviate toward its rather shorter partner. Webbing

should be corrected by the age of 18 months to 2 years if it is extensive. The correction of simple incomplete webbing may be postponed until the child is 3 to 4 years of age.

6. Annular bands are deep skin grooves which occasionally encircle the wrist, hand or fingers. They may extend deeply to bone. In the wrist and the palm, annular bands can be removed surgically by rotating triangles of adjacent skin and fatty tissue into the grooves. This is known as a Z-plasty operation. When bands of this type are located in the fingers or thumb, a Z-plasty operation might improve their appearance.

INJURIES TO THE HAND

There is a peculiar tendency for people to consider an injury to a finger as a minor accident. Nothing could be further from the truth! A carpenter with a numb fingertip becomes a clumsy craftsman; a stiff finger marks the end of a concert pianist's career; the professional ballplayer is benched when he fractures a small bone in his hand. Repair of severed tendons or nerves and the adequate treatment of bone fracture in the hand is a major task requiring special surgical training and skill.

1. Fractures. There are eight small bones at the base of the hand (the carpals) which are subject to fracture. The scaphoid, or "boat-shaped," carpal bone is at the base of the thumb and frequently is broken in a fall onto the outstretched hand. It has a poor blood supply and heals slowly. If healing is unduly delayed, the surgeon may elect to place a small core of bone across the fracture site in an attempt to speed its healing. At times, a portion of this bone must be removed or the wrist must be fused surgically if the fracture fails to heal and continues to cause pain.

Fractures of the bones of the fingers and thumb usually do not require surgery unless the fragments cannot be maintained in alignment with plaster splints or traction. If this becomes necessary, surgical correction of malalignment will utilize the insertion of small steel pins. Most important is the avoidance of a stiff joint through excessive immobilization.

2. Injured tendons: Without gliding tendons to carry out flexion and extension, fingers become stiff and powerless. In certain regions of the palm and fingers, the tendons are so intimately related to one another and so firmly held against the bone that the most trivial injury may lead to firm fibrous adhesions. These areas are known to the hand surgeon as "no-man's-land." Tendons injured here must not be sewn together. The wounds must be closed and a tendon graft inserted some weeks later. The cut tendon and its covering are completely removed from the finger. A tendon graft is taken from an expendable wrist or foot tendon. After being threaded through the finger, one end is joined to the fingertip and the other to the cut tendon in the palm. This is a most delicate operation requiring the greatest cooperation between the patient and his surgeon, if motion and strength are to be restored.

3. A cut nerve in the hand or wrist may be sutured immediately after the injury or, if proper facilities are unavailable at the time, several weeks later. When a nerve is sutured, sensation and muscle power do not return at once. Tiny nerve fibers must find their way across the suture line and then down narrow tubes of special cells until they reach the skin and muscles. At best, nerve fibers grow about one or two inches a month. It may take up to six

months before sensation returns to a fingertip after its nerve has been repaired at the wrist. If fine sensation is needed in a critical area of the hand, such as a fingertip, a segment of normal skin with its nerve and blood supply intact can be transferred from a less essential region (such as the back of the hand or side of the ring finger). Immediate delicate sensation is thereby restored.

The small muscles of the hand usually do not recover their function completely after their nerves have been cut. If there is subsequent deformity or weakness, normal tendons can be transferred to replace the motion of their paralyzed neighbors.

4. Dupuytren's contracture (*See* DUPUYTREN'S CONTRACTURE.)

5. Trigger finger: This is a condition in which a finger will, on occasion, snap and lock when bent. There are usually pain and a pea-size lump at the base of the finger which represents a thickening of the tendon. As the tendon is pulled through the ligaments of the finger, it is trapped first on one side, then on the other, causing the locking, the snapping, and the pain.

Trigger fingers sometimes respond to injections of cortisone beneath the ligaments, but more commonly the condition is not cured until the tight finger bands are surgically released.

6. Carpal tunnel syndrome: One of the major nerves to the hand passes through the wrist in a tight compartment called the carpal tunnel. Through this tunnel, which is bounded by rigid bones and ligaments, pass the median nerve, and nine tendons and their sheaths. It is therefore not surprising that the nerve may become compressed if there is any swelling of the contents within this compartment. Rheumatoid disease, injury, hemorrhage, all may cause swelling, with a sensation of pins and needles in the fingertips. The little finger is unaffected. Numbness of the fingers and gradual swelling and weakness of the hand eventually ensue if the condition persists. Surgical cure is rapid and dramatic when the carpal tunnel is opened and the ligament overlying the nerve is divided.

7. Arthritis: In rheumatoid arthritis of the hand, inflammation of the joints and the sheath of the tendons causes widespread deformities. Tendons may rupture or become displaced, allowing the fingers to drift into bizarre positions. The small muscles of the hand become inflamed and tighten, adding to the stiffness of already swollen joints. Bones may be dislocated, nerves become compressed. The ravages of the rheumatoid hand pose severe problems to the hand surgeon who contemplates reconstruction. In recent years this challenge has been met successfully. Swollen tissues can be replaced, joints molded and bones relocated. Early surgical intervention of this kind can restore the delicate balance of the hand before it becomes so deformed that repair is impossible.

QUESTIONS AND ANSWERS

Are all birth deformities of the hand inherited?

No. Some are inherited; some result from infections in the mother during the early months of pregnancy; most are from unknown causes.

What are the chances of a second child having the same birth defects as the first child?

If a parent has the same defect as the first child, the chances are that a second child will have the same deformity. If no relative has the same defect as the first child, the chances are small that the second child will be so affected.

Will vitamins prevent the birth of deformed children?

No.

Can an absent thumb be replaced?

A missing thumb can be replaced by appropriate grafts and tissue transfers.

If a normal muscle is used to replace a paralyzed one, won't another part of the hand then become paralyzed?

No. There are many extra muscles and tendons in the hand. They can be transferred safely with no loss of power.

Can numbness in the hand come from disease in the neck?

Yes. The nerves of the hand take origin from the spinal cord in the neck. Certain types of injury and arthritis of the neck can cause pressures on these nerves, with consequent numbness in the hand.

Is hand surgery dangerous?

No. Most hand surgery is delicate to perform but presents no danger to the patient.

Are locked fingers the result of arthritis?

Very rarely. They are usually caused by a tight ligament over the finger tendons.

Is it best to exercise a sprained wrist?

Many so-called sprained wrists are in actuality fractures of a small bone in the hand. Fractured bones must be put to rest with a plaster cast.

Does it hurt to take out pins used in hand surgery?

No. They are easily removed under local anesthesia.

What can be done for rheumatism of the hand?

Many surgical procedures can be done to improve the function and the appearance of the arthritic hand.

Will an arthritic hand become stiffer after surgery?

No. Tight muscles and joints are usually relaxed by surgical releasing procedures.

Will arthritis elsewhere in the body become worse after surgery on an arthritic hand?

No.

Can medication cure arthritis of the hand?

In early cases, medication and injections often halt the progress of the disease. Later, however, medical treatment cannot correct deformities.

What is Dupuytren's contracture?

A tightening and thickening of the fibers between the skin and the tendons of the palm of the hand, which cause the fingers to be pulled into flexion.

Can this be corrected by surgery?

Yes.

Will surgery for Dupuytren's contracture paralyze the hand?

No. Neither the nerves nor the tendons are cut in surgery to correct this condition.

What is a claw hand?

It is a hand that has become deformed because of muscle paralysis.

Can it be corrected surgically?

Yes.

Can cut tendons and nerves to the hand be repaired at once?

If the wound is clean and treatment is rendered within the first few hours, nerves can usually be repaired immediately. Tendons cut within the fingers and in some areas of the palm usually cannot be repaired at the time of the accident; they must be repaired by a tendon graft several weeks later.

Why can't all tendon injuries to the hand be repaired immediately?

If a tendon cut in a finger is repaired at once, it is almost certain to scar down to the surrounding tissues and not function well. It is best merely to close the wound and operate again six weeks later. In the second operation, a tendon graft is inserted into the finger and the cut tendons are removed.

Is a finger completely numb if its nerve has been cut?

No. Since there are two major nerves to each finger, some sensation may remain when only one nerve has been severed.

If a child is very young, how can one tell if a nerve has been cut?

1. The infant will not pull his hand away if the injured finger is irritated with a pin.

2. The injured finger will be dry to the touch. This is because the sweat glands of the finger are supplied by the skin nerves and are paralyzed as soon as the nerve has been divided.

Is the repair of a hand nerve a dangerous operative procedure?

No. In children, the results of surgery are usually very good, and the operation itself is not dangerous.

What is a ring injury?

A ring injury is usually caused when a finger ring gets caught on something. The skin of the finger is torn toward the fingertip. Often a segment of skin will be ripped by the ring and turned inside out like a glove.

Are ring injuries serious?

Yes. They frequently result in loss of the finger.

How are ring injuries treated?

The laceration is carefully repaired after thoroughly cleansing the open wound. A snug compression bandage is applied and the arm is placed in an elevated position to promote drainage of serum and blood from the veins.

If a child with a cut hand is able to move all of his fingers, does this mean that no tendons have been cut?

No. The knuckle joints are moved by short muscles of the hand, not by the long tendons. Only the middle and tip joints of the fingers are moved by the long tendons. If the finger is held straight at these joints and can only bend at the knuckles, then the tendons to the finger have been cut.

Is tendon grafting to the fingers a dangerous operation?

No, but it is a highly delicate operation, and it requires complete cooperation between the patient and hand surgeon.

Is surgery ever necessary for crushed or fractured fingers?

Yes. If the injury has caused rotation or severe angulation of a finger and the deformity cannot be corrected by manipulation or traction, then surgery may be necessary to align the fracture fragments.

How should a burned hand be treated?

If the hand is scalded, it should immediately be placed in cold water to prevent excessive swelling. If the burn involves only the outer layers of the skin, thin Vaseline dressings may be applied. Deeper burns require hospitalization and treatment with antibiotics and skin grafts.

What can be done for fingers deformed by tight scars from burns?

The scars can be removed and replaced by skin grafts or by rotating flaps of adjacent skin to cover the scarred area.

What is Z-plasty?

Z-plasty is a procedure in which contraction from a scar (as on a finger) is released by making a Z-shaped incision and transferring the two portions of the Z to provide greater skin length in the line of the scar.

What is a hand surgeon?

A hand surgeon is an orthopedic surgeon, plastic surgeon, or general surgeon who has further specialized in the treatment and diagnosis of injuries and deformities of the hands.

What can be done for a hand partially paralyzed because of a nerve injury, polio, or cerebral palsy?

Joints can be stabilized by fusion, contracted tendons can be released, and paralyzed muscles can be replaced by tendon transfer.

What is Volkmann's contracture of the hand?

Volkmann's contracture of the hand is a scarring of the flexor muscles of the forearm or hand that causes the tendons to tighten and the fingers to clamp down firmly in the palm. Often the nerves to the hand are also involved, causing paralysis and pain.

What causes Volkmann's contracture?

It usually follows swelling of the forearm after injuries in the elbow region.

Can Volkmann's contracture be prevented?

Yes, usually. After fractures about the forearm or elbow, any swelling of the fingers or pain in the hand occurring after the cast has been applied should immediately be reported to the doctor. The cast must not be allowed to remain too tight, even for a few hours.

What is a trigger finger?

A trigger finger is a finger that cannot extend or flex without a painful snap. It happens when a finger or thumb flexor tendon is caught under a fibrous pulley at the base of the digit.

Is trigger finger or trigger thumb common in children?

Yes, particularly trigger thumb when the tip joint is held in the bent position. This condition is sometimes noted in a newborn child.

How is trigger thumb treated?

The tight ligament pulley is released surgically. Recovery from the deformity is immediate, and thereafter the finger can move normally.

If a normal muscle is used to replace a paralyzed one, won't another part of the hand then become paralyzed?

No. There are many extra muscles and tendons in the hand. They can be transferred safely with no loss of power.

Hardening of the Arteries

See BLOOD VESSELS.

Hashimoto's Disease

Hashimoto's disease is a name given to a chronic inflammation of the thyroid gland associated with a rubbery hardness and swelling of both lobes of the gland. Usually, there is neither overactivity nor underactivity of secretion of thyroid hormone in this condition, but once in a while, there may be a variation from normal.

Hashimoto's disease is thought to be a form of thyroiditis and is characterized by slight to moderate pain on pressure over the gland with an occasional elevation in temperature. The condition can also exist without any tenderness or rise in temperature.

Some investigators feel that Hashi-

moto's disease predisposes to eventual cancer within the gland.

Since the entire gland is involved in the inflammatory process, surgical removal is not advocated. In some cases, the enlargement of the gland in this condition compresses the trachea (windpipe), and this may require surgical decompression. To accomplish this, that portion of the thyroid which overlies the trachea is removed, but the remainder of each lobe is not disturbed. If the diagnosis of the disease is made prior to surgery, treatment will consist of the giving of steroids such as cortisone rather than surgery. Eventually, the inflammation will burn itself out and may lead to destruction of the thyroid's ability to produce sufficient hormone. In these cases, thyroid tablets will be administered.

See also THYROID GLAND.

Head Injuries

Head injuries are extremely common, varying in degree from the relatively minor cut scalp to the serious bruising of the brain associated with profound loss of consciousness. Fortunately, the skull offers excellent protection to the underlying brain, so that many blows to the head injure only the relatively unimportant superficial tissues. Those of a more severe nature may fracture the skull and cause damage to the brain, which may be bruised (contusion) or even torn (laceration).

See also NEUROSURGERY.

QUESTIONS AND ANSWERS

HEAD INJURIES IN CHILDREN

Do infants and children frequently sustain head injuries?

Yes. Practically every child injures

his head at one time or another, and many children injure their heads repeatedly.

Are head injuries very serious in children?

As in adults, head injuries vary considerably in the degree of severity. Considering the frequency with which children hurt themselves, it is obvious that the great majority of head injuries are relatively minor.

Should a physician be consulted whenever a child has a head injury?

Yes, especially in the younger age group, since it may be difficult to distinguish between an insignificant injury and a serious injury. This is particularly advisable if the child has been rendered unconscious by an injury. It is also advisable to call a physician if the child bleeds from the ears or nose.

How can one distinguish between a minor head injury and a serious one?

Loss of consciousness, persistent or increasing drowsiness, vomiting, bleeding from the scalp or from the ears, nose, or mouth, severe headache, widening of one pupil, and weakness of a limb are indications of a serious or potentially serious injury. If the injury is minor, the child may cry and wish to be left alone, but soon responds in his usual manner.

Does brain damage accompany most of the head injuries that infants and children get?

No. The skull offers excellent protection to the underlying brain, so that many blows cause damage only to the relatively unimportant superficial tissues. More severe blows may result in fracture of the skull, with varying degrees of injury to the brain.

Is there usually a great deal of superficial bleeding following a head injury?

Only if there is an associated lacera-tion of the scalp, in which case the bleeding may be profuse. Head injuries may be accompanied by bleeding from the nose, mouth, or ears.

Why is there profuse bleeding following a scalp laceration?

Because the scalp has a rich blood supply. Such bleeding is readily controlled by pressure applied over a dressing. In itself the bleeding is usually not significant and will stop spontaneously after continued pressure for 10 to 15 minutes.

Does a bump on the head following a fall indicate serious damage to the skull?

The bump merely indicates that bleeding has occurred beneath the scalp. In itself, the bump is of little significance. The presence or absence of other symptoms and signs determines how serious the injury is.

What are the most common head injuries?

Injuries to the superficial structures (scalp) occur most frequently. Bleeding may take place beneath the scalp, leading to the formation of a soft, tender lump (hematoma), or the scalp may be lacerated. Of the various types of head injury affecting the brain, concussion (momentary loss of consciousness) is the most common.

What is the treatment for a hematoma of the scalp?

No special treatment is necessary. The application of a cold compress may alleviate discomfort and limit the extent of the hematoma.

Should children who sustain head injuries with large hematomas have their skulls x-rayed to rule out a fracture?

Yes. It is always safer to obtain positive evidence that there is no fracture.

Is x-raying the skull harmful to the child?

No.

Should lacerations of the scalp be repaired surgically?

Yes, after the surrounding hair has been shaved, the scalp has been adequately cleansed with soap and water and an antiseptic solution, and the wound itself has been thoroughly irrigated. Before this is done, however, one must be certain that an underlying skull fracture has not been overlooked.

Is it painful to repair the wound in a child's scalp with stitches?

No, it is not particularly painful to close the wound with a few stitches. If the child cannot tolerate the procedure without anesthesia, a small amount of Novocain can be injected into the skin surrounding the laceration.

Will the surgeon inspect the wound carefully to make sure that there is no injury to deep tissues before he stitches it?

Yes, and if any doubt remains, he will have an x-ray of the skull taken.

How can the surgeon tell that the injury is more serious than a simple scalp laceration?

Other signs and symptoms usually occur if the injury is serious. Loss of consciousness, even for a brief period, indicates that the injury has affected the brain. Persistent headache, drowsiness, and vomiting indicate a more serious injury. A fracture will be revealed by x-rays of the skull.

Is it natural for a child to vomit after a severe head blow?

This is a very common reaction. The child may also seem somewhat apathetic and prefer to be left alone.

What should be done when a baby falls on his head?

1. If the crying lasts no more than a few minutes, if the baby's color remains unchanged, and if he does not vomit, there has probably been no damage to the brain and he may resume normal activities as soon as he wishes.

2. If a more severe blow has been sustained and there is vomiting, loss of appetite, headache, drowsiness, or actual loss of consciousness, a doctor should be consulted.

Should a child who falls asleep following a severe blow to the head be awakened at regular intervals?

Yes, to make sure that he is merely asleep and not lapsing into a coma.

What is the significance of unconsciousness in a child who has had a recent head injury?

Prolonged unconsciousness from the moment of injury indicates a severe degree of trauma. Coma occurring after consciousness has been regained usually signifies increased intracranial pressure due to hemorrhage and must be dealt with as a surgical emergency. A child who appears dazed initially but becomes increasingly stuporous must also be suspected of intracranial hemorrhage and treated accordingly.

Heart

Despite its great importance in the maintenance of life, it is recognized that the heart is merely a muscular pump whose sole job is to propel blood throughout the body. Its location in the chest can be approached surgically without difficulty, and its tissues, when handled by a competent cardiac surgeon, will withstand manipulation and the insertion of sutures and graft materials. Nevertheless, less than 25 years ago, there was great hesitancy on the part of surgeons to operate upon this structure. The fear of sudden cardiac stoppage (arrest) and of fatal hemorrhage acted as deterrents to those who might otherwise have attempted to correct heart defects.

The remarkable advances in cardiac surgery within the past two decades constitute one of the most thrilling chapters in medical history. Today surgeons can help cardiac patients as readily as they can aid sufferers from surgical conditions elsewhere in the body. Most of the mechanical obstacles to the surgical approach to the inside of the heart have already been overcome and the remaining ones appear slated for early solution. Techniques have been devised, and have been developed to function satisfactorily, to permit the heart to be operated upon openly while empty of blood. Various pump apparatuses have been created to act as an artificial heart and lungs during the time required for the operation to be performed. This permits more accurate operative maneuvers to be carried out and eliminates much of the fear of hemorrhage which would accompany surgery upon a working heart filled with blood. Indeed, in some cases, the heart can be purposely stopped (artificial cardiac arrest) for a few minutes in order to permit more accurate surgical repair of defects in its muscle structure. When the repair is completed, the heart is started again and the pump is discontinued. (See illustration.)

Even at this early stage of its development, surgery upon the heart has already rehabilitated many thousands who were formerly relegated to a life of invalidism or early death. It is difficult to discuss in detail all of the various heart conditions which may respond to surgical treatment, but an attempt will be made to deal with most of them briefly.

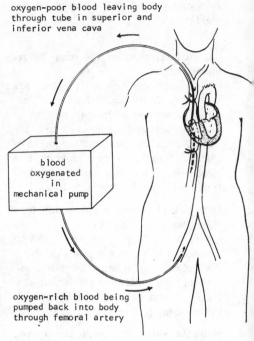

oxygen-poor blood leaving body through tube in superior and inferior vena cava

blood oxygenated in mechanical pump

oxygen-rich blood being pumped back into body through femoral artery

THE ACTION OF THE MECHANICAL HEART

HEART CONDITIONS PRESENT SINCE BIRTH (CONGENITAL DISEASES)

1. Patent ductus arteriosus: During the life of the embryo, a blood vessel communication exists between the aorta (the main artery leading off from the heart) and the pulmonary artery (the artery carrying blood to the lungs for oxygen). Such a communication is essential while the child is developing in order to shunt blood away from the lungs of the embryo and into the aorta. (Naturally, the lungs of the embryo do not breathe while the child floats in the fluid within the mother's womb.) After birth, however, the newborn's lungs expand and function. The communication (the ductus arteriosus) is no longer necessary, and in most infants

PATENT DUCTUS
ARTERIOSUS

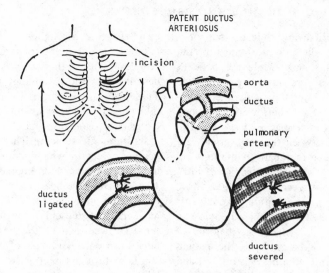

incision

aorta

ductus

pulmonary
artery

ductus
ligated

ductus
severed

it closes off within the first few months of life.

For some unknown reason, the communication occasionally persists and alters the normal exchange of blood between the heart and the lungs. These children are underdeveloped, short of breath, become especially susceptible to bacterial infections, and sooner or later develop heart failure (failing heart function). Operation upon these infants is indicated early and is successful in practically every case. General anesthesia is administered and the left chest is opened. The patent (open) ductus is isolated, tied off, and severed. If no other deformity coexists, cure is complete. (See illustration.)

2. Septal defects: Defects in the walls (septa) which normally divide the heart into four chambers are fairly common. They cause difficulty because they permit blood which has not yet received its oxygen supply from the lungs to be mixed with blood which has just received its supply and is about to be circulated throughout the body. The distant tissues thereby are fed by blood that is deficient in oxygen.

Some septal defects are very small and cause no symptoms, while others are large and severely disabling. The latter, especially if they appear likely to produce chronic invalidism or to terminate life at an early age, should be corrected surgically. The operative proce-

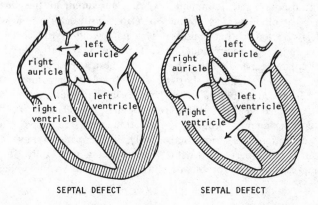

SEPTAL DEFECT

SEPTAL DEFECT

dure is carried out while the patient is attached to the pump-oxygenator and, in many instances, while the patient's body temperature has been reduced so as to slow circulation and other metabolic processes. (The lowering of body temperature is termed *hypothermia.*)

Defects between the two auricles are usually easier to repair than those between the two ventricles (see illustration). However, techniques have been so improved within recent years that a successful surgical outcome can be anticipated in the great majority of both types of cases. With the patient "on the pump," the heart is opened and the defect is sutured (stitched). If the defect is so large that suturing will not readily bring the edges together, a patch of Teflon or Dacron is placed over the hole and stitched into place. During the performance of some of these operations the heart is purposely stopped for a few minutes in order to facilitate the technical maneuvers of suturing.

3. "Blue baby" (tetralogy of Fallot): This condition gets its name from the blue appearance of these newborn infants. The blue color results from the fact that a combination of heart and blood vessel abnormalities (usually four are present) permits blood, poor in oxygen, to circulate throughout the body. By a brilliantly conceived operation which transposes and reimplants some of the great blood vessels of the heart, blood is diverted so that it flows back into the lungs for reoxygenation before it is circulated generally throughout the body. Immediate relief of shortness of breath and the bluish color (cyanosis) is obtained in these patients and their life expectancy is prolonged.

While this operation is a serious and delicate one, it is being performed with ever-increasing safety and success by heart surgeons throughout the country. It offers the only hope for these cardiac cripples who otherwise would be destined to a short, unhappy existence. These operations are performed with the patient hooked up to a pump-oxygenator. (*See also* BLUE BABY.)

4. Pulmonic stenosis: This is a congenital defect in which there is either an underdeveloped pulmonary artery (leading from the heart to the lungs), a constricted pulmonary valve opening, or an abnormal muscular barrier within the right ventricle of the heart which cuts down on the amount of blood that can flow through the artery to the lungs. Within recent years, operations have been devised whereby an incision is made, while the patient is on the pump, into the pulmonary artery and the pulmonic valve is inspected under direct vision. If the valve is found to be constricted, it must be cut and dilated so as to permit more blood to flow through it. If the pulmonary artery is found to be narrowed, it will have to be widened, using a plastic procedure and a patch graft.

Children with marked pulmonary stenosis are invalids with extreme shortness of breath, inability to lead any kind of active life, and are scheduled for an early demise unless operated upon. The operative procedures are successful in the great majority of cases.

5. Coarctation of the aorta: This is a serious birth deformity in which there is a narrowing of the aorta (the main artery leaving the left side of the heart) in the chest. It produces symptoms such as high blood pressure, absence of pulses in the lower extremities, and development of collateral or auxiliary circulation over the upper part of the body. These patients have an average life expectancy of only 35 years and usually die with apoplexy, heart failure,

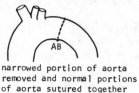
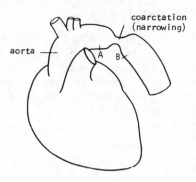

coarctation
(narrowing)

aorta

A B

COARCTATION OF AORTA

narrowed portion of aorta
removed and normal portions
of aorta sutured together

AB

graft of blood vessel
inserted in place of
narrowed aorta

bacterial infections, or rupture of the aorta.

Surgical treatment of these cases consists of removing the narrowed area of aorta and restitching the aorta above and below (see illustration). If the narrowed area is too long to permit the ends above and below to be brought together, then a graft composed of Teflon or Dacron mesh is utilized. Satisfactory results ensue from this operation in well over 85 percent of cases.

ACQUIRED HEART CONDITIONS

1. Rheumatic heart disease: It is estimated that 1 percent of the population of our country develops rheumatic fever, and of these, the majority will develop disease of the heart valves. An inflammation of the edges of the valve sets in and causes thickening, scarring, calcification, and deformity. As a result, the valve opening becomes narrowed and rigid. The normal elasticity of the valve is lost and blood flows through with difficulty (stenosis of the valve). In other cases, the valves fail to close tightly after the blood has been expelled, allowing for a backflow or regurgitation (insufficiency of the valve).

Constrictions of the two main valves on the left side of the heart are called

mitral stenosis and *aortic stenosis*. Ingenious operations have been devised which have brought about tremendous improvement in these patients:

a) In the early days of heart surgery, *mitral stenosis* was treated exclusively by *closed mitral commissurotomy*. This was a technique in which the surgeon's finger was inserted through the auricle and onto the mitral valve. (See illustration.) Blood loss was prevented by placing a purse-string set of sutures about the auricle where the finger was inserted. The adhesions about the diseased

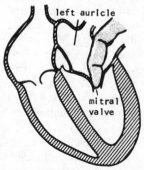

left auricle

mitral
valve

CLOSED MITRAL COMMISSUROTOMY
FOR MITRAL STENOSIS

valve were separated blindly by the finger, and scar tissue was torn and the valve dilated until it reached a normal diameter. In some cases where the scar tissue was too thick to manipulate with the finger, a specially constructed "finger-knife" was attached, thus enabling the surgeon to sever adhesions and scar tissue. While results of these procedures were relatively good, it was discovered that the closed method was followed by a sizable percentage of recurrences of stenosis (narrowing) of the valve. In other cases, especially those in which the finger-knife was used, too large an opening was created and the patient suffered from *mitral insufficiency* rather than *mitral stenosis.*

As a result of these so-called late failures, the majority of patients with mitral stenosis are now being operated upon with the "open heart" technique. This means that they are placed on the pump, the heart is opened and the mitral valve visualized directly. Its defects are repaired and the heart is closed. Within recent years it has been found that some mitral valves are so damaged that even repair under direct vision will not result in an efficiently functioning valve. In such cases an artificial ball valve is stitched into place between the auricle and ventricle. (See illustration.) Prior to this maneuver, it is necessary to cut away the diseased valve tissue. Operations upon the mitral valve are best performed while the heart continues to beat so that valvular function can be evaluated.

b) Until recently, most surgery for *mitral insufficiency* had failed to gain fruitful results. Attempts to reduce the size of the mitral valve with sutures or the insertion of Teflon cloth or felt were unsuccessful in most instances. Today, however, better results can be obtained through open heart surgery performed while

the patient is on the pump. Artificial valves are proving so satisfactory that it is safe to conjecture that more and more people with mitral insufficiency will be treated in this manner rather than by valve repair.

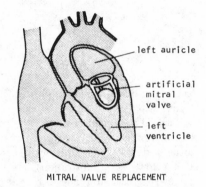

MITRAL VALVE REPLACEMENT

c) *Tricuspid valve stenosis* (the valve between the right auricle and the right ventricle) is usually associated with mitral stenosis, and if diagnosed, should be repaired at the same time. It is best accomplished under vision through an incision which splits the breastbone (sternum). Initial treatment should consist of cutting the adhesions and scars so as to enlarge the opening.

d) *Aortic stenosis,* or constriction of the valve leading out of the heart into the great blood vessel known as the aorta, can be helped surgically. A midline chest incision is made which splits the breastbone (sternum). The aorta is opened after the patient is placed on the pump (cardiopulmonary bypass) and the body temperature is lowered (hypothermia). Diseased aortic valve tissue is removed and artificial valve leaflets are fashioned out of Dacron and are stitched into place. These artificial leaflets are tailored so that they appear as reproductions of the normal aortic valve structure.

Older techniques, such as introducing a specially devised instrument to forceably dilate and separate adhesions about the valve, have been largely abandoned.

e) Aortic insufficiency: Several different operations have been employed for this condition. The patient is subjected to the same incision as for aortic stenosis, is placed on the pump, and is given hypothermia. In some cases, the valve is made narrower by specially placed sutures or by removing one of the cusps of the valve. In other cases, an artificial ball valve is inserted to replace the diseased valve.

2. Coronary artery disease: The coronary artery is the artery of the heart which supplies blood to the heart muscle wall. *Closure (occlusion or thrombosis) of the coronary artery, or one of its branches, is the commonest cause of death today.* The disease affects men more than women and is most prevalent during the prime of life—40 years and older. During recent years, this dread disease has been noticed among younger and younger age groups so that men in their teens or twenties are by no means exempt.

The disease is characterized by arteriosclerosis of the coronary artery in some people, while in others the vessel appears normal except for the clot contained within it. Sudden severe pain in the chest which radiates to the left shoulder and down the arm is typical. If a large thrombosis (clot in the coronary artery) has resulted, there may be sudden death. If the patient survives the initial attack, he will run a slight temperature for a few days, and be weak and short of breath. The pain in the chest may persist for several days.

Electrocardiographic tracings will reveal heart muscle damage.

Surgical treatment for coronary artery disease has recently undergone great transition. Some years ago, attempts were made to improve the circulation to heart muscle by instilling talcum powder into the sac surrounding the heart. The maneuver has been completely discarded and new operations have been devised to accomplish improved blood supply for the wall of this vital structure. These procedures are as follows:

a) Transplantation of the internal mammary artery (which runs longitudinally beneath the breastbone), so that its end is buried directly in the heart muscle, has improved circulation in many cases. Those who have done this operation claim good results in a large majority. However, the so-called *bypass operation,* described below, has now replaced this procedure in almost all surgical clinics throughout the country.

b) Direct endarterectomy of the coronary artery has been performed in a considerable number of cases with successful results. The technique involves opening the coronary artery and removing its arteriosclerotic inner lining. This is accomplished by detaching the inner lining from the rest of the arterial wall either by blowing it out with a strong burst of carbon dioxide gas or by reaming it out with a metal curette. The main application of endarterectomy is in those patients who have an isolated patch or two of arteriosclerosis within the coronary arteries. It is not very effective in those patients who have widespread arteriosclerosis involving the smaller branches of the arterial system. Moreover, mortality figures are high for this operative procedure.

c) The operation most in favor today has been named the *coronary bypass operation*. This procedure involves dissecting out a portion of the large saphenous vein in the thigh and utilizing it as a free graft from the aorta to a portion of the coronary

artery that is beyond the point of arteriosclerosis, obstruction, or thrombosis. The newly placed graft carries large quantities of blood from the aorta above the arteriosclerotic coronary artery to a healthy portion of the coronary artery within the heart muscle wall. Although the technique of performing this bypass is quite delicate, results have been highly satisfactory in over 80 percent of patients. Also, the procedure has a relatively low mortality when performed upon properly selected patients. If it is discovered that these grafts remain open over a period of years, it is safe to predict that this operation will replace all others that have been so far devised to improve coronary circulation.

3. Diseases of the pericardium: The pericardium is a membrane which completely encircles the heart and the origins of the great blood vessels, forming a sac (pericardial sac). The heart glides smoothly under this membrane as it fills and empties. Infections of the pericardial sac occur occasionally and produce fluid or pus which create increasing pressure upon the heart. If the fluid or pus accumulate in too great amounts, it will interfere with the normal filling and emptying mechanism of the heart and may terminate in heart failure.

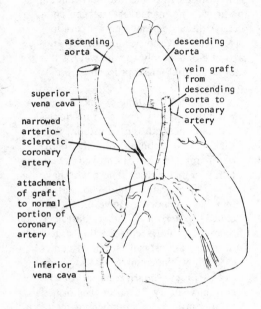

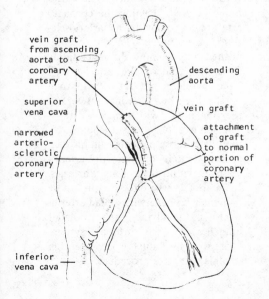

Surgical treatment consists of draining out this infected material. The operative procedure is simple; a small incision is made in the chest wall and, under local or general anesthesia, the sac is opened and drained. Large doses of the antibiotic drugs are given to control the growth of the invading bacteria.

Occasionally, because of repeated infections, there are marked thickening and calcification of the pericardium. In other instances, it may become adherent to the heart and cause compression.

This is termed chronic constrictive pericarditis and demands surgical removal of the adherent pericardium.

QUESTIONS AND ANSWERS

What is spontaneous cardiac arrest?
Involuntary heart stoppage.

Can cardiac arrest be treated successfully?
Yes. By rhythmic heart massage, about 20 to 30 percent of cases can be saved. If the chest is open, manual massage is done. If the chest is closed, closed cardiac massage is instituted.

Will a time ever come in surgery when most heart conditions can be operated upon?
Yes.

What is "heart failure"?
The inability of the heart to circulate the blood in its normal fashion. This leads to damming up of the blood in the tissues.

What is rheumatic heart disease?
A deformity of the valves of the heart due to the scarring and adhesions of a rheumatic fever infection.

Can damaged, deformed valves be cured medically?
No.

Does rheumatic heart disease ever cause heart failure?
Yes.

What is the difference between mitral stenosis and mitral insufficiency?
Mitral stenosis is a tight, narrowed valve on the left side of the heart between the auricle and the ventricle.
Mitral insufficiency is a valve that does not close completely after heart contraction, thus permitting blood that has already been pumped into the ventricle to flow back (regurgitate) into the auricle.

Is the surgical treatment of mitral stenosis satisfactory?
Yes.

Is the surgical treatment of mitral insufficiency satisfactory?
Yes.

Does mitral valve stenosis ever recur after once being corrected?
Yes, occasionally.

Is it possible to help patients who have narrowing (stenosis) of both the mitral and aortic valves?
Yes.

What is aortic stenosis?
A narrowing and deformity of the valve between the left ventricle and the aorta.

What is aortic insufficiency?
Incomplete closure of the aortic valve which permits blood that has already been pumped into the aorta to flow back (regurgitate) into the heart.

Is the surgical treatment of aortic stenosis satisfactory?
Yes.

Is the surgical treatment of aortic insufficiency satisfactory?
Yes.

Are operations for valve conditions dangerous?
Moderately, but no more than an operation of similar magnitude elsewhere in the body.

Will the rate of cure increase as more surgeons perform these operations and improve their operative techniques?
Yes.

Do all patients with valve disease of the heart have to be operated upon?

No. Only those whose activity is limited and who find life difficult to live happily.

Can these patients, if successfully operated, return to normal living?

Their life is made more comfortable. However, some restrictions on activity must often be continued.

Is their life expectancy improved by operation?

Yes.

Is the blue color (cyanosis) altered after a successful heart operation?

Yes, the blue color usually disappears.

Are operations upon the pericardium (the sac surrounding the heart) dangerous?

Not usually.

Should patients who have had coronary closure (thrombosis) be advised to have subsequent surgical treatment?

Not usually. Surgery for this condition must await elaboration of improved surgical procedures.

Does the future of coronary disease appear to be surgical?

Present studies would indicate that the underlying cause of coronary disease may be metabolic. Preventive medical measures will probably be the treatment of the future, but new surgical techniques may be found which will alleviate suffering from this disease.

Do people with stab wounds or gunshot wounds of the heart usually survive?

No.

Do heart wounds always have to be operated upon?

No; not if the blood leakage stops spontaneously.

What procedure is carried out for heart wounds?

Exposure and suturing of the wound.

What anesthesia is used for heart operations?

General anesthesia administered through a tube placed in the trachea (windpipe).

What is the site of the incision for heart operations?

An incision is made between the ribs overlying either the front or the side of the heart in some cases. In others, a midline chest incision is made and the breastbone is split.

Are blood transfusions given during heart surgery?

In most cases.

Are special nurses necessary after heart operations?

Yes. They are essential!

How long a hospital stay is required after heart operations?

Ten days to three weeks.

Do heart operations affect one's breathing?

Yes. By improving the oxygen supply to the circulating blood and by correcting defects in the heart structure, breathing is greatly improved. Shortness of breath often is completely alleviated by a successful heart operation.

After heart operations should one do strenuous physical exercise?

No.

Are operations upon the heart dangerous?

Refinements in the techniques have reduced the dangers of heart surgery remarkably, so that it is fast approaching the degree of safety obtained in some of the other major fields of surgical endeavor.

Can all people with heart disease be operated upon?

No. Only certain types of heart conditions lend themselves to surgical help.

Is it difficult to approach the heart surgically?

No. Incisions into the chest cavity make the heart readily available to the surgeon.

Have methods been devised which permit bypassing of the heart during surgery?

Yes, there are heart pumps which can take the place of the heart during the time that it is undergoing surgery. This permits the surgeon to open the heart and operate upon it under direct vision and in a bloodless field.

What is meant by "hypothermia" in heart surgery?

This means lowering the body temperature so that heart action is slowed down markedly and body requirements for blood and oxygen are reduced.

When will physicians recommend heart surgery?

1. When it is felt that the ultimate chances for survival are greater with surgery than without surgery.

2. When a person is leading an invalided, useless life, and desires the chance for more normal living through heart surgery.

3. When a reasonable chance for cure or improvement exists through heart surgery and when the patient or his family fully understand the risks involved.

What is meant by open heart surgery?

Open heart surgery means opening one or more of the chambers of the heart in order to repair damage within. There are several methods of performing open heart surgery.

How long does it take to perform open heart operations?

About three to six hours. A great deal of this time is spent in the preparation of the patient for actual heart surgery. Two or three hours may be occupied in preparing the cardiopulmonary pump and in inserting the catheters into the proper arteries and veins in order to bypass the heart. Opening the chest, exposing the heart, and readying it for surgery will also take time. The time spent in actually repairing the cardiac defect or replacing one or more valves varies from a few minutes to three, or even more, hours.

Does the heart ever stop beating while it is being handled by a surgeon?

This is a rare occurrence. Contrary to common belief, the heart is a rather sturdy organ and can be handled surgically almost as well as any other organ in the body. Furthermore, if it should stop beating during an operation, it can be compressed by the surgeon's hands and drugs can be given, which will, in most instances, cause it to resume beating.

Is it ever necessary to stop the heart during an operation?

Yes. Frequently the heart is stopped (artificial cardiac arrest) in order to enable the surgeon to repair a defect while the heart muscle is at rest and not contracting. This is done by giving certain drugs in sufficient quantities to stop the heartbeat. After the defect is repaired, the heart is stimulated with other drugs to resume beating.

Do heart conditions tend to recur once they have been benefited by heart surgery?

No. The majority of successful results in heart surgery are of a permanent nature.

Can those who have undergone successful heart operations return to a completely normal life?

Yes, in many instances. Sometimes, however, it is necessary for them to restrict their physical activity even though the operation may have been extremely successful.

Is it ever possible to reoperate upon a patient who has had a poor result from heart surgery?

Yes. Many of those who underwent mitral valve surgery for rheumatic fever in the early days of this type of treatment have developed recurrences of their disease. These patients can now be successfully reoperated on, and a damaged valve can be repaired under direct vision with the heart open, or the valve can be replaced with an artificial valve.

SURGERY FOR CONGENITAL HEART DEFECTS

How common is congenital heart disease?

About 25,000 children are born each year in the United States with congenital heart defects. Most of these defects can be corrected surgically.

What congenital heart defects can be corrected surgically?

1. Patent ductus arteriosus
2. Defects in the septa (walls) of the heart
3. Pulmonic stenosis
4. Coarctation of the aorta
5. Tetralogy of Fallot ("blue baby")

Do children ever outgrow congenital defects?

Rarely. A patent ductus may close within the first year of life, however.

How is a diagnosis of a congenital heart defect made?

By listening to the heart and noting characteristic murmurs and changes in the size and shape of the heart. Also by passing a catheter through a vein in the arm into the heart chambers and then taking x-rays. This technique is known as *cardiac angiography,* and has developed to such an accurate state that precise diagnoses of heart defects can be made in most cases.

Can congenital heart defects be cured with medications?

No.

Do most patients operated upon for congenital heart defects survive the operation and benefit from it?

Yes.

Do these defects interfere with normal living?

Yes. The majority of congenital cardiac defects lead to limitation of activity. Some cases are completely disabled.

Is a patient's life expectancy prolonged if he is successfully operated upon for a congenital heart defect?

Yes.

Do congenital defects recur once they are corrected?

Usually not.

What is a patent ductus arteriosus?

During the child's life in the embryo, a communication exists between the aorta (the main artery leading off from the heart) and the pulmonary artery (the artery carrying blood to the lungs for oxygen). Such a communication is necessary during fetal life to shunt blood away from the lungs of the embryo and into the aorta. After the child is born, however, his lungs begin to expand and function, and this blood vessel communication is no longer necessary. In most infants, it closes off within the first few weeks or months of life. For some unknown reason, the communication continues to exist in some infants and alters the normal exchange of blood between the heart and lungs.

Do children with a patent ductus arteriosus have symptoms as a result of their defect?

Yes. They are frequently physically underdeveloped, are markedly short of breath, and are particularly susceptible to bacterial infections. Sooner or later, they will develop heart failure.

Should surgery always be performed on a child who has a patent ductus arteriosus?

Yes, and the results of tying off and severing the open artery are successful in practically every case.

Are defects in the septa (walls) that normally divide the heart into four chambers very common?

Yes. This is a common congenital defect, and it causes difficulty because it permits blood that has not yet been oxygenated by the lungs to mix with oxygenated blood. Thus, blood that is insufficiently oxygenated will be permitted to circulate throughout the body.

Do all septal defects cause symptoms?

No. Some defects are so very small that they cause no symptoms and will require no treatment.

What symptoms can be caused by septal defects?

The larger defects may produce chronic invalidism to such an extent that the child will not be able to live for more than a very few years unless the defect is corrected by surgery. However, it is generally better to correct septal defects before symptoms develop; otherwise irreversible damage to the lungs may result.

Is it necessary to place a child on a cardiopulmonary pump while repairing septal defects?

Yes, and often hypothermia is used at the same time in order to lower heartbeat rate and the rate of blood flow.

Are defects between the two atria (atrial septal defect) easier to repair than those between the two ventricles (ventricular septal defect)?

Yes, but advances in cardiac surgical techniques have been so great that successful outcomes can be expected in both types of cases.

How are septal defects repaired?

With the child on the cardiopulmonary pump, the heart is opened and the defect is stitched (sutured). If the defect is so large that suturing will not readily bring the edges together, a patch of Dacron or Teflon is used to cover the hole, and this is stitched into place. During the performance of some of these operations, the heart is purposely stopped for a few minutes in order to facilitate the technical maneuvers of suturing. Some of these maneuvers would be very difficult for the surgeon to perform while the heart is beating.

How successful are operations to repair septal defects?

A successful outcome can be expected in the great majority of cases. Recently, it has been found that such children may have several defects in the septa, and this will, of course, complicate the repair and increase the chances of an unsatisfactory result.

Should all children who have septal defects undergo operations?

No. Children should undergo this type of surgery only if they cannot live because of their defect. Some children in this category are undernourished and underdeveloped and lead the lives of invalids. Other children, although without sickness, will become ill and die before maturity unless heart surgery is performed to correct the septal defect.

What is pulmonic stenosis?

Pulmonic stenosis is a congenital defect in which there is either an underdeveloped pulmonary artery leading from the heart to the lungs, a constricted pulmonary valve opening where the blood goes from the heart into the pulmonary artery, or an abnormal muscular barrier within the right ventricle of the heart that cuts down on the amount of blood that can flow through the artery to the lungs.

What are the symptoms of pulmonic stenosis?

Many children with this condition have extreme shortness of breath and cannot lead any kind of physical life. Most will die at a very early age if not treated surgically.

Is there any way to overcome pulmonic stenosis?

Yes. Operations have been devised whereby an incision is made into the pulmonary artery and the pulmonic valve is exposed to view. If the valve is found to be constricted, it is cut and dilated so that more blood can flow through it. If the pulmonary artery is found to be narrowed, it is widened by using a plastic procedure and a patch graft.

Must the child be on the cardiopulmonary pump when an operation for pulmonic stenosis is performed?

Yes.

How successful are operations for the relief of pulmonic stenosis?

The great majority of children are benefited immeasurably.

What is coarctation of the aorta?

Coarctation of the aorta is a serious congenital deformity in which there is narrowing of the aorta, the main artery leaving the left side of the heart and going to supply blood to the tissues throughout the body.

What are the symptoms of coarctation of the aorta?

The child will have no pulses in his lower extremities and very high blood pressure. He will develop large collateral circulation over the upper part of his body.

Can a child grow to maturity if he has coarctation of the aorta?

Yes, but his life expectancy will be not more than 35 years. It is therefore wise to operate during childhood for the correction of this defect.

What operation is performed to correct coarctation of the aorta?

The narrowed area of aorta is removed, and the normal aorta above and below it is stitched together. If the narrowed section is too long to permit the two ends above and below to be brought together, then a blood vessel graft composed of Dacron or Teflon mesh is used.

How successful are operations to relieve coarctation of the aorta?

The results are satisfactory in approximately 85 to 90 percent of cases.

What is the tetralogy of Fallot?

In an infant with this condition, the skin and mucous membranes appear blue (cyanotic) because his blood is receiving inadequate amounts of oxygen. For this reason, a child with the tetralogy of Fallot is called a blue baby. The condition is caused by a combination of four heart and blood vessel abnormalities.

Should children who have tetralogy of Fallot be subjected to surgery?

Yes, for most of these children will die within a few years unless they are treated surgically.

What operations are performed to correct the defects in the tetralogy of Fallot?

There are several operations carried out in the treatment of this condition. Most children with tetralogy of Fallot can obtain relief through open heart surgery with correction of pulmonary artery obstruction and closure of the septal defect. Palliative (helpful but not curative) operations include transposing and reimplanting some of the large blood vessels of the heart so that blood is diverted and made to flow back into the lungs for reoxygenation before it is circulated generally throughout the body.

Will these children be relieved of their symptoms following surgery?

Yes, the relief is remarkable. The bluish color disappears, the shortness of breath disappears, and life expectancy is prolonged.

At what age is a child with the tetralogy of Fallot operated on?

This depends on the child's ability to survive without surgery. If life cannot be maintained in an infant, then immediate surgery is mandatory. The fewer the symptoms from the condition, the longer one can wait.

Must a child be placed on a cardiopulmonary pump while an operation for the tetralogy of Fallot is being performed?

Yes, when an open heart surgical procedure is performed.

How successful are operations for cure of the tetralogy of Fallot?

In a hospital where there is a well-trained cardiac surgical team, recovery can be expected in more than 90 percent of cases.

Is it possible to treat a birth deformity of the heart with medications?

No. Since there are structural defects, they will not respond to drugs or medications.

Can a child outgrow a congenital heart defect?

No, except that in certain instances a patent ductus arteriosus closes spontaneously within the child's first year of life. Also, if the abnormal opening between the two ventricles of the heart is small, there may be "functional closure" as the child grows older and the opening becomes relatively smaller. With the natural enlargement of the heart that takes place as a child grows, there may no longer be mixing of the blood from the two sides of the heart. Thus, although the septal defect persists, the child has no symptoms.

Are there some congenital deformities of the heart that cannot be corrected surgically?

Yes. There are many deformities, such as the absence of an atrium, the absence of the septum separating the two ventricles, or multiple malformations of the major blood vessels, that cannot be corrected. Children with such conditions usually die before they reach maturity.

SURGERY FOR ACQUIRED HEART CONDITIONS

What acquired heart conditions can be helped through heart surgery?

1. Rheumatic heart disease, a condition in which there is constriction or other deformity of the heart valves secondary to rheumatic fever

2. Coronary artery disease

3. Pericarditis, an inflammatory condition of the sheath (pericardium) which surrounds the heart

4. Stab wounds or gunshot wounds

How common is rheumatic heart disease?

It is estimated that one percent of the population will develop rheumatic fever, and the majority of these will have some permanent damage to their heart valves.

What is the specific type of damage caused to the heart valves?

There will be scarring, thickening, and deformity as a result of the rheumatic infection. The valve most frequently involved is the mitral valve, which separates the left atrium from the left ventricle.

How is the mitral valve damaged?

There may be either a constriction (narrowing) of the valve, known as mitral stenosis, or a laxity of the valve so that it does not close properly, known as mitral insufficiency.

What operations are performed to correct defects in the mitral valve?

In the early days of heart surgery, mitral stenosis was treated exclusively by a procedure known as closed mitral commissurotomy (valvuloplasty). This is a technique in which the surgeon's finger is inserted through the left atrium and on to the mitral valve. Blood loss is prevented by placing a set of sutures about the atrium at the site where the finger is inserted. The mitral valve is then separated by the inserted finger, scar tissue is torn, and the valve is opened until it reaches a more nearly normal diameter. In cases where the scar tissue is found to be too thick to be manipulated with the finger, the surgeon uses a specially designed finger-knife that enables him to sever ad-

hesions and scar tissue. The results of this operation are successful in the great majority of cases. However, within the past 10 to 15 years it has been discovered that a small percentage of patients develop recurrent defects in the valve after such surgery. As the valve heals following the valvuloplasty, some patients develop mitral stenosis (narrowing of the aperture) while others develop mitral insufficiency (too wide an aperture).

Consequently, the operation is now performed with the open heart technique. The patient is placed on a cardiopulmonary pump, the heart is opened, and the valve can be repaired under direct vision.

Does the tricuspid valve, which separates the right atrium from the right ventricle, ever become involved in the rheumatic process?

Yes, and if damage is found to be present, it can be corrected when the mitral valve is repaired.

Are any other valves of the heart ever damaged by rheumatic fever?

The aortic valve, separating the left ventricle from the large artery known as the aorta, also may become involved in either aortic stenosis or aortic insufficiency.

What percentage of patients operated upon for rheumatic heart disease survive the operation?

This will depend upon the exact nature of the disease and the operation that is performed. Approximately 97 to 98 percent of those patients with mitral stenosis and 85 to 90 percent of those requiring valve replacement will survive.

What percentage are benefited?

Nearly all those who survive.

Is it ever necessary to replace a damaged heart valve with an artificial valve?

There are remarkable new devices that have been developed to replace the mitral and aortic valves. These procedures are performed much more often on adults who have had valvular disease than on children. A child's heart will grow along with the rest of his body, and an artificial valve may be too small to function properly as the heart grows larger and places a strain on the graft.

What operations are performed upon those with coronary artery disease?

Several operations have been devised. The most popular ones today involve using a patient's leg vein to bypass coronary artery obstruction or the transplanting of the internal mammary artery from beneath the breastbone into the heart muscle.

An older procedure in which talcum powder was instilled into the sac surrounding the heart has been discarded. This procedure was called poudrage.

Are there any other operations for coronary artery disease?

Yes, although they are still in the experimental stage. Some surgeons have cored out the narrow channel of the coronary artery in the attempt to restitute its passageway. These operations are very serious and often must be carried out while the patient is on the heart pump. This procedure is known as coronary endarterectomy.

Are the results of surgery for coronary artery disease satisfactory?

There is a growing number of patients who can be benefited substantially by the various operations described above for coronary artery disease. However, many of those who have had coronary thrombosis will not, at the present time, lend themselves to surgical treatment.

What is the pericardium?

The pericardium is the membrane that completely encircles the heart and the origin of the large blood vessels. This membrane forms a sac known as the pericardial sac. The heart slides smoothly under this membrane as it fills and empties.

What diseases of the pericardium can occur?

People occasionally develop a condition known as pericarditis, in which fluid or pus forms in the pericardial sac.

What is the treatment for pericarditis?

If the fluid or pus accumulation is too great, it will interfere with the normal filling and emptying of the heart and may result in heart failure. It is therefore necessary to tap the pericardial sac and drain out the fluid or pus. If this can be accomplished merely by needle puncture and aspiration, open heart surgery is not necessary.

What operation is performed if pericardial fluid or pus cannot be drained by needle aspiration?

A simple operation in which a small incision is made in the chest wall and the pericardial sac is exposed. An opening is then made into the sac and the fluid or pus is drained.

Is it ever necessary to remove some of the pericardium?

Yes. As a result of infection, adhesions may form between the pericardium and the outer heart-muscle wall. This can interfere greatly with normal heart function. In such circumstances it is necessary to open the chest widely and to excise large portions of the pericardium so that normal heart function may be restored.

Are operations for pericarditis in children very common?

No. Most of these operations are performed on adults when the pericardium restricts the heart. However, when it is necessary to perform the operation on a child with this condition, it is almost always successful.

Are the following necessary before operations on the heart are performed?

Blood transfusions? Yes, when there is marked anemia.

Antibiotic medications? Not in most cases.

Intravenous medications? Yes, as the patient will not eat for a number of hours before surgery.

Stomach tubes? No.

Bladder catheters? Yes, in order to measure output of urine.

Vitamin injections? No.

Special diets? No.

Other special preparations? Yes, including various blood tests and x-rays.

Are the following necessary after operations on the heart?

Private duty nurses? Yes, for several days.

Antibiotic medications? Yes, to protect the patient from infection.

Intravenous infusions? Yes.

Blood transfusions? Yes, if there has been marked blood loss during surgery.

Stomach tubes? Occasionally.

Special postoperative measures? Yes.

Postoperative vitamins? Yes.

Convalescent posthospital care? Yes, in many cases.

HEART TRANSPLANTATION

The entire world has been thrilled by the recent heart transplant operations in which a normal heart has been taken from someone who has just died and has been transplanted into the chest of a patient who was about to die from an incurable heart condition. Most of the recipients of heart transplants have had organs that have been so damaged by disease, and have had so little functioning heart muscle left, that they could have survived only for a few days or weeks at most.

The surgeons who have attempted

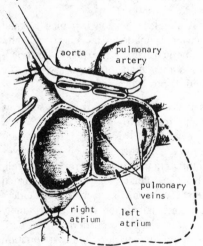
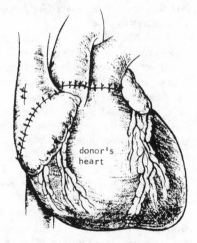

In the drawing of a heart transplant (left), the major part of a diseased heart, shown by the dotted lines, has been cut away. The upper chambers of the heart and the main vein and arteries are left. As shown in the drawing (right), they are all sutured to the new, or donor's, heart, to which blood circulation and function are restored.

the first heart transplants are known to everyone. The difficulties that have attended the first two hundred or so heart transplants are mainly those involving the rejection phenomenon, or overwhelming infection involving the lungs or bloodstream, and are not primarily the difficulties that accompany the technical maneuvers of the surgery. It is a completely feasible technical operation, and the world may look forward to a day when heart transplantation will be a rather routine procedure, not calling for the type of publicity that now accompanies it. Suffice it to say, heart transplantation will have limited use because there will always be a short supply of donor hearts and there will always be a limited number of people who will be willing to and need to take the risk of such surgery.

Is it possible to transplant a heart from one individual to another with an expectancy of success?

Yes. Within the next few years, many of the complications of this type of surgery may be overcome. When that time arrives, heart transplantations will be done in much larger numbers and with a much greater expectancy of success. At present, the indications for, and the likelihood of, success in this type of operation are limited. Heart transplantation must be classified as a highly experimental procedure, generally failing because of rejection.

Hemangiomas

A hemangioma is a benign tumor composed of dilated blood vessels. They are seen very often in the skin, but they may also appear in internal organs such as the liver, the lungs, and the kidneys.

Hemangiomas of the skin may appear at any time from birth to old age. They are recognized as red spots on the skin and vary in size from that of a pinhead to that of a five-cent piece. If they are located in an area that is subject to repeated irritation, such as the skin of the face in men or on the fingers, they may bleed.

Most hemangiomas are harmless and do not grow, bleed, or become malignant. If they are unsightly, as on the tip of the nose or on the face or lips, they should be destroyed with an electric needle or by freezing with carbon-dioxide snow. Larger ones must be removed surgically under anesthesia in a hospital.

QUESTIONS AND ANSWERS

Are hemangiomas very common?

They are one of the most common tumors. They are seen as small, red, blister-type spots on the surface of the skin.

What is the treatment for hemangiomas of the skin?

Unless they are unsightly or appear in an area where they may be irritated, they are usually left alone. If they are subject to repeated injury and bleed frequently, they should be destroyed.

Is there a tendency for people to grow hemangiomas as they age?

Yes. These tumors seem to increase in number as one reaches the later years of life.

What is the best treatment for hemangiomas?

Small skin hemangiomas can be destroyed with an electric needle or can be destroyed through freezing either with carbon-dioxide snow or through newer cryosurgical techniques. Large ones, such as those that appear in internal organs, if they have a tendency to bleed or to interfere with function, may have to be removed through wide surgical excision.

What is the treatment for hemangioma of the liver?

Unless it is very large or unless there is danger that it will bleed, it may be left alone. On the other hand, if it grows to very great size or bleeds, a portion of the liver may have to be removed along with the hemangioma. This is a most serious operative procedure.

Will hemangiomas of the lung ever cause hemorrhage?

Yes. When this takes place, either the hemangioma itself must be removed or the lobe of the lung harboring the tumor must be excised.

Is x-ray therapy ever indicated in the treatment of hemangioma?

Yes. Certain of these tumors can be destroyed by this means, but if the tissue is on the skin's surface, a considerable scar may result following the x-ray radiation.

Do hemangiomas ever become malignant?

Yes, but this is a rare occurrence. When they do, they form a tumor known as a hemangioendothelioma.

Are children often born with hemangiomas?

Yes, a great many children are born with hemangiomas.

Where do hemangiomas usually appear in children?

On the brow, the scalp, the nape of the neck, the face, the torso, or the extremities.

Do hemangiomas ever close off and form hard, round, marblelike lumps in the skin?

Yes. These are known as sclerosing hemangiomas. They may remain that way indefinitely. Sometimes they are painful, especially when located in a spot where pressure is brought to bear. In such cases, the hemangioma should be removed surgically.

What does a cavernous hemangioma look like?

It is a raised, red, soft tumor found on the skin. Most of these hemangiomas are quite large.

What is the treatment for a large cavernous hemangioma?

These are true tumors involving fairly large blood vessels. Their removal is an extremely serious operative procedure, and when they occur about the head, surgery must be performed by a neurosurgeon.

Why is it necessary for a neurosurgeon to operate on cavernous hemangiomas located in the head?

Because some of the blood vessels extend within the tissues overlying the brain.

Is it usually necessary to operate on a patient with a cavernous hemangioma located in the head area?

Yes, because sooner or later a severe hemorrhage may ensue. Also, if the tumor presses on the brain it may eventually cause brain damage.

The neurosurgeon should consult with the physician, and together they will determine the best time to carry out the operation.

Are cavernous hemangiomas involving blood vessels covering the brain curable?

Most of them can be successfully removed without any permanent ill effects. However, occasionally the tumor is so extensive that only partial removal is feasible. In other instances, several operations are necessary to relieve the condition.

Hematomas

A hematoma results from hemorrhage into the skin or the tissues beneath the skin, or into the substance of an organ or tissue. The blood is usually clotted or semiclotted.

Most collections of blood secondary to internal bleeding will be absorbed into the body. Occasionally, when a hematoma is not absorbed, the blood remains liquid and will require removal either by needle-and-syringe withdrawal or by a surgical incision into the hematoma.

See also BRUISES; FIRST AID; SUBDURAL HEMATOMA.

QUESTIONS AND ANSWERS

Is a cauliflower ear a hematoma?

Yes. It is due to bleeding between the skin of the ear and the underlying cartilage. The cartilage is unable to absorb the collection of blood, and it therefore organizes and becomes scar tissue. This leads ultimately to a deformity of the ear.

What should be done for hematoma of the ear?

In order to safeguard the patient from developing a cauliflower ear, the hematoma must be evacuated either by needle withdrawal or by making an incision into the area.

Are hematomas beneath the skin of the skull very common?

Yes. The scalp is supplied richly with blood vessels and the underlying bone is unable to absorb any hemorrhage in the area. As a result, hematomas are likely to form.

Hemorrhage

See BLEEDING; FIRST AID.

Hemorrhoids

It has been estimated that nearly one third of all adults at one time or another suffer from hemorrhoids or some other local disease of the anus or rectum. In addition to hemorrhoids, this area is commonly the site for fissures (ulcers of the mucous membrane), fistulas (abnormal tracts or tunnels extending from the wall of lower rectum out to the skin), and polyps (nonmalignant growths of the rectal and anal mucous membrane).

Fortunately, rectal conditions are not always so severe and so persistent as to require surgery. Often patients can be relieved of their discomfort by judicious medical management.

Hemorrhoids are composed of varicose dilatations of those veins that drain the rectal and anal regions. Many investigators feel that these veins break down and become incompetent because of the extraordinary strain placed upon them by modern living habits. Irregularity of bowel evacuation, prolonged sojourns upon the toilet, and chronic constipation are contributors toward their formation. Certain people seem to inherit weakness of these blood vessels so that even minor strain may cause varicosities to form. Others are engaged in occupations which entail

NORMAL ANATOMY

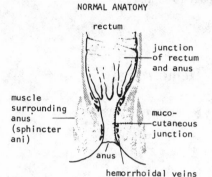

strenuous muscular activity and this seems to make them more prone to develop hemorrhoids. Pregnancy, because of the pressure of the baby's head in the pelvis, predisposes to hemorrhoid formation. And lastly, one cannot omit mention of the psychological aspects of rectal and anal disease, for it has been observed by all physicians that emotionally unstable or neurotic people have an extremely high incidence of trouble in this region.

The mere existence of hemorrhoids does not indicate the need for surgery in every case. However, many of these weakened blood vessels become involved in an inflammatory process or infection which originates from the lining of the rectum, and this may ultimately require operative treatment. Also, the repeated contraction and expansion of the anus during bowel evacuation and the recurrent passage of stool over the hemorrhoidal area often produce marked irritation with accompanying ulceration and hemorrhage. Or infection of the walls of the rectal veins may result in a phlebitis, with painful clot formation (thrombosed hemorrhoids). When hemorrhoids become inflamed or clotted, they enlarge and tend to be pushed out

INTERNAL AND EXTERNAL
HEMORRHOIDS

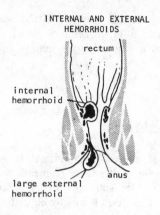

of the anus during defecation and to appear externally as firm, extremely painful lumps. Any one of the preceding situations, such as repeated hemorrhage, severe infection, or thrombosis, is an indication for surgical removal of the hemorrhoids.

Hemorrhoids are classified as *internal* or *external*, but in most instances, both types are present. Those that originate from the rectal wall above the sphincter muscle are termed *internal*, whereas those that arise below this area in the region of the anal canal are termed *external*. The importance of this distinction is that in certain cases, the internal type can be treated by the injection method instead of surgery. On the other hand, external hemorrhoids do not lend themselves to injection treatment.

Surgery for hemorrhoids involves the dissection of the veins from their surrounding structures with special care not to injure the underlying sphincter muscle. The hemorrhoids are tied off close to their origin and are removed. The entire operative procedure is extremely simple to perform and is not at all dangerous. It does, however, take a good deal of experience to learn just how much tissue to remove and how much to leave behind. Too enthusiastic removal of tissue may lead occasionally to a constriction of the outlet which can prove bothersome postoperatively. Too scant a procedure may permit the veins left behind to form new hemorrhoids.

QUESTIONS AND ANSWERS

What are hemorrhoids?

They are varicose dilatations of the veins which drain the rectum and anus.

What causes hemorrhoids?

It is felt that these veins break down and their valves become incompetent because of the strain placed upon them by irregular living habits. Chronic constipation, irregularity of bowel evacuation, and prolonged sojourns on the toilet are thought to be conducive toward hemorrhoid formation. Pregnancy, because of the pressure of the baby's head in the pelvis, also leads toward hemorrhoid formation.

How common are hemorrhoids?

This is the most common condition in the anal region and affects almost 30 percent of the population at one time or another.

How can one tell if he has hemorrhoids?

There are one or more swellings or bulges about the anus, which become more pronounced on bowel evacuation. There is also a sense of fullness in the anal region, more pronounced on bowel evacuation. Hemorrhoids are frequently painful and may be accompanied by considerable rectal bleeding.

Is there any way to prevent getting hemorrhoids?

Yes, to a certain extent. Regular bowel evacuation, the eating of a good diet with sufficient roughage, and the avoidance of straining at stool will diminish the chances of getting hemorrhoids.

How can a positive diagnosis of hemorrhoids be made?

Your physician will be able to tell by a rectal examination whether hemorrhoids are present.

What are the various forms of treatment for hemorrhoids?

1. Medical treatment, which includes the taking of lubricants to ensure a regular stool and the use of medicated suppositories inserted into the rectum

2. The injection treatment, if the hemorrhoids are of the internal type

3. Surgical removal of the hemorrhoids

Do all types of hemorrhoids respond to the injection treatment?

No. Only the internal type can sometimes be successfully treated by this method.

What can happen if hemorrhoids are not treated?

1. They may bleed severely and cause a marked anemia with all of its serious consequences.

2. The hemorrhoids may become thrombosed (clotted), producing extreme pain in the region.

3. The hemorrhoids may prolapse (drop out of the rectum and not go back in again).

4. Hemorrhoids may become strangulated and gangrenous.

5. Hemorrhoids may become ulcerated and infected.

Does neglect of hemorrhoids ever lead to the formation of cancer of the rectum?

No, but the abrupt development of hemorrhoids is occasionally secondary to the development of a tumor in the large bowel.

What determines whether or not surgery is recommended for hemorrhoids?

Those cases that do not respond to

adequate medical management must be operated upon.

Will the surgeon perform other tests before performing a hemorrhoidectomy?

Yes. The surgeon will perform a sigmoidoscopy to make sure there is no disease high up in the rectum above the hemorrhoids.

Can sigmoidoscopy reveal the presence of a cancer in the rectum or lower bowel?

Yes. That is the main value of performing this examination.

How and where is the sigmoidoscopy performed?

It is done in the surgeon's office by the passage of a sigmoidoscope into the rectal canal. A sigmoidoscope is an instrument about ten inches long which allows direct visualization of the entire rectum and the lower portion of the large bowel (the sigmoid).

Is sigmoidoscopy a painful examination?

No. Only slight discomfort accompanies sigmoidoscopy.

Is hemorrhoidectomy a serious operation?

No. The risks are negligible.

Are hemorrhoids sometimes an indication that other disease exists in the lower intestinal tract?

Yes. That is the reason sigmoidoscopy and x-rays are advocated before the decision is made to remove the hemorrhoids.

Is hospitalization necessary when hemorrhoids are to be removed?

Yes. The hospital stay will last anywhere from four to seven days.

What are the chances for full cure following the removal of hemorrhoids?

Well over 95 percent.

Is there a tendency for hemorrhoids to recur?

Yes, but the number of such instances is small.

Is hemorrhoidectomy followed by much pain?

Yes, for the first week or two after the operation.

What is done when the hemorrhoids are removed?

The varicosed veins are dissected out from the surrounding tissues and are ligated and cut away.

What anesthesia is used?

Usually a low spinal or caudal anesthesia, although a local anesthesia or a general anesthesia may be given.

How long does it take to perform a hemorrhoid operation?

About 15 to 20 minutes.

Are any special preoperative measures necessary before hemorrhoidectomy?

No, except to see that the bowel is empty before operation.

What special diet is necessary after hemorrhoidectomy?

The avoidance of highly seasoned foods and alcoholic beverages.

How soon after a hemorrhoid operation will bowel function return to normal?

It may take several weeks before bowel function returns completely to normal.

What special postoperative measures are usually advised?

A lubricant, such as mineral oil, is taken twice a day, and the patient is told to sit in a tub of warm water two or three times a day. Frequent postoperative visits to the surgeon will be necessary.

Is it common to have bleeding at the stool following a hemorrhoid operation?

Yes. This may continue for a few days to a few weeks after operation.

Should one return for regular checkups after a hemorrhoid operation?

Yes, about every six months.

Do hemorrhoids ever occur in children?

Yes, but only rarely. When they do, most hemorrhoids will subside unless they are associated with an underlying disease. Stool softeners and lubricants should be given to ease the passage of stool.

Are older people likely to develop hemorrhoids?

Yes. Constipation and straining to evacuate the bowels predispose older people toward formation of hemorrhoids.

What is meant by the term prolapsed hemorrhoids?

Prolapsed hemorrhoids, which originate in the rectal canal, are hemorrhoids that are forced out during evacuation. In many cases the sphincter muscle of the anus contracts after the bowels have been evacuated, and the hemorrhoids are left on the outside.

What can older people do to prevent hemorrhoids?

1. Attempts to move the bowels should be made at the same time each morning. Right after breakfast is the most desirable time.

2. No more than 15 minutes should be spent in attempting to have a movement. Excessive straining predisposes toward hemorrhoids.

3. If there is constipation, fresh fruits, raw vegetables, and any bran products should be eaten regularly, and a lubricant such as mineral oil should be taken daily.

4. If attempts to move the bowels fail, a small enema should be taken.

Do hemorrhoids ever lead to the development of cancer?

It is thought that they do not.

What measures should be taken to avoid recurrence of hemorrhoids?

1. Keep bowel movements regular by using lubricants and eating a proper diet.

2. Avoid straining at the stool or sitting too long on the toilet.

3. Avoid excessive use of alcoholic beverages or highly seasoned foods.

Are hemorrhoids ever an indication that something else is wrong with the intestinal tract?

Yes. A tumor higher up in the large bowel may cause hemorrhoids to appear.

Is removal of hemorrhoids a serious operation for older people?

Not unless their general condition is extremely poor. Even then, measures can be taken so that they can safely undergo hemorrhoidectomy.

Are hemorrhoids in older people likely to recur after surgical treatment?

No. However, if they happen to be associated with a bowel tumor that has not been removed, recurrence is quite possible.

Hepatectomy

See LIVER; ORGAN AND TISSUE TRANSPLANTS.

Hernia (Rupture)

The human body is composed of several distinct compartments: the head, neck, chest, abdomen, and limbs. All of these regions are connected by large blood vessels and other vital structures which course through from one section to another. It is remarkable that, in an anatomical mechanism as complicated as ours, so few developmental defects occur. However, our bodies are not perfect and we are heir to a considerable number of imperfections which either are present at birth or develop during our lifetime.

For reasons unknown, a rather sizable number of children are born with hernias. In these children, there has been a failure of complete development at certain exit or entrance points in their body compartments. Thus hernias are most frequently noted in the groin, where large vessels pass from the abdomen into the thigh, or in the region where the genital cord has left the abdominal cavity. Similarly, ruptures are often noted in newborns at the site of the umbilical cord or in the diaphragm close to the region where the esophagus (food-pipe) leaves the chest and enters the abdomen.

Acquired hernias develop later in life at the same sites as the congenital (present from birth) hernias. In this age of push buttons and mechanical devices which spare physical effort, one notes a steadily increasing deterioration in the muscular development of man. Thus strain and stress in the regions that are the potential sites for hernia formation more often produce damaging tears in the tissues. It is not strange, therefore, that the less physically active office worker or businessman of today is not as well equipped to withstand these muscular strains as was his harder working great-grandfather of days gone by.

A hernia exists wherever a defect permits a structure to leave its normal confines and to extend into a region where it does not belong. Some hernias, or ruptures, are small and incomplete and permit merely the lining of a body cavity to poke through the defect. Others are large and allow extensive protrusion of important internal structures such as small intestine or large bowel.

The abdominal cavity, the largest in the body, contains many weak points in its wall. A tear at any one of these sites may be followed by the emergence of some intraabdominal tissue, thus producing a hernia. Sudden and marked increases in intraabdominal pressure, as from lifting a heavy weight or straining forcefully, may precipitate such a tear in the lining of this cavity. Thus intestine or other normally intraabdominal structures may enter the space created by the tear and appear under the skin as a definite and visible bulge. Marked gains in weight, the growth of a large tumor, pregnancy, chronic straining at stool, or a persistently heavy cough are other conditions that cause increased intraabdominal pressure and thus may lead to a tear in the lining with subsequent protrusion of abdominal contents.

TYPES OF HERNIA

1. Inguinal hernia: This is the commonest type and occurs in the groin. It is more frequently encountered in men because of the more strenuous nature of their work. Occasionally inguinal hernias are present in both groins and this is then termed a bilateral inguinal hernia. Inguinal hernias are classified as *direct* or *indirect,* the latter following the course of the inguinal canal, the former protruding more directly through tears in the abdominal wall musculature nearer to the midline of the body. (See illustrations.) Inguinal hernias are of the "sliding" variety when part of the protruding sac is made up of bowel wall.

DIRECT INGUINAL HERNIA

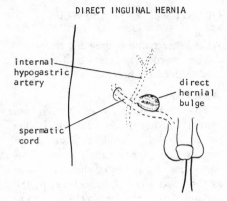

internal hypogastric artery

direct hernial bulge

spermatic cord

takes place in the region of the navel and is most frequently seen in newborns or in women following pregnancy. In children, a large percentage of these heal spontaneously before the second birthday. However, if this does not occur, surgery should be performed. (See illustration.)

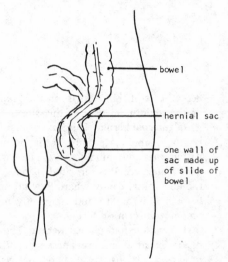

bowel

hernial sac

one wall of sac made up of slide of bowel

SLIDING HERNIA INVOLVING SIGMOID COLON

INDIRECT INGUINAL HERNIA

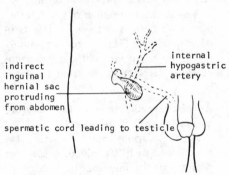

indirect inguinal hernial sac protruding from abdomen

internal hypogastric artery

spermatic cord leading to testicle

These hernias are considerably more difficult to cure by surgery. (See illustration.)

2. Femoral hernia: This type is located just below the groin, and here the sac extends along the large femoral blood vessels which supply the thigh. This hernia is seen more often in women.

3. Ventral hernia: A hernia of this type is usually found in the lower midline of the abdomen and frequently results from the separation of the abdominal wall musculature which follows pregnancy.

4. Umbilical hernia: This rupture

5. Incisional hernia: This hernia takes place through an old operative scar and is caused by poor wound healing.

6. Epigastric hernia: This variety is located in the upper midline of the abdomen and is thought to be due to a

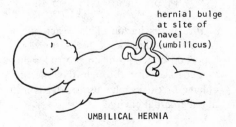

hernial bulge at site of navel (umbilicus)

UMBILICAL HERNIA

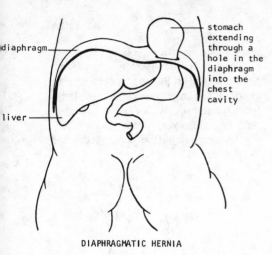

diaphragm

stomach extending through a hole in the diaphragm into the chest cavity

liver

DIAPHRAGMATIC HERNIA

defect, existing since birth, in the lining of the abdominal wall at this site.

7. Internal hernia: This kind of hernia is not visible externally as it occurs within the abdominal cavity when organs enter crevices or subdivisions of the abdominal cavity where they do not belong. It is a rare and frequently unrecognized form of hernia.

8. Lumbar and gluteal hernia: These occur because of weaknesses in the posterior portions of the abdominal wall and appear as bulges at various sites in the back or buttocks. They are the least common of all ruptures.

9. Diaphragmatic hernia: This type has been diagnosed more often in recent years because of better x-ray techniques. It occurs when any abdominal organ, such as stomach, intestine, or bowel, protrudes through a weakness or rent in the diaphragm and enters the chest cavity. One form has been publicized as the "upside-down stomach." (*See also* DIAPHRAGMATIC AND HIATUS HERNIAS.)

10. Hiatus hernia: This is actually a form of diaphragmatic hernia in which a portion of the stomach protrudes into the chest cavity through the aperture created by the esophagus as it leads into the abdominal cavity.

QUESTIONS AND ANSWERS

What other name is used for hernia?

The word "rupture" is frequently used to denote a hernia.

What causes hernia?

The great majority of hernias are caused by defects or weakness in the muscular and connective tissue structures which separate the various compartments or cavities of the body, such as the chest from the abdomen, or the abdomen from the limbs. Other hernias result from an injury that tears the muscular or connective tissue barriers at various exit points of the body compartments.

Are many hernias present at birth?

Yes. A sizable number of children are born with hernias because of defects in development. These are commonly noted in the region of the navel (umbilical hernia) or in the groin (inguinal hernia).

At what specific areas in the body are hernias most likely to occur?

At the various points where large structures, such as blood vessels or portions of the intestinal tract, leave or enter the various body cavities. At these sites there are loose tissues which, when placed under great strain, may separate and tear.

What types of strain or injury are most likely to lead to a rupture?

1. Lifting of heavy objects

2. Sudden twists, pulls, or muscle strains

3. Marked gains in weight which cause an increase in intraabdominal pressure

4. The growth of a large abdominal tumor which displaces the organs

5. Pregnancy, with its accompanying increase in intraabdominal pressure

6. Chronic constipation, with its associated straining at stool

7. Repeated attacks of coughing, which create sudden increases in intraabdominal pressure

How common is hernia?

It is one of the most common of all conditions requiring surgery.

Are men more prone than women to develop hernia?

Yes, if it is the type that results from physical strain and effort, such as hernia in the groin (inguinal hernia). Women are more likely to get hernias of the umbilical region (navel) as a result of pregnancy.

Do hernias tend to run in families or to be inherited?

No, but the kind of muscular development that one possesses does tend to be inherited.

When is medical, rather than surgical, management advocated in the treatment of hernia?

1. If a hernia has recurred two or more times after surgery and the patient's tissue structures appear to be poor, it is probably best not to attempt surgical repair a third or fourth time, as it will be met with failure in a large percentage of cases.

2. People who are markedly overweight should not be operated upon until they reduce, as repairs in these people are notoriously unsuccessful.

3. People with serious medical conditions, such as active tuberculosis or serious heart disease, are probably best treated without surgery.

4. People with small hernias who are in their seventh or eighth decade of life are perhaps best treated medically unless the hernia causes severe symptoms.

What is the medical treatment for hernia?

The wearing of a support or truss to hold the hernial contents within the abdominal cavity.

As a general rule, should trusses be worn for prolonged periods of time before surgery is carried out?

No. Trusses tend to weaken the structures with which they are in constant contact. Therefore, they should not be worn for more than a few weeks prior to surgery.

Why isn't the wearing of a truss rather than surgery advised in all hernias?

Because trusses do not cure hernias. They merely hold the hernial contents in place. As people get older and hernias enlarge, trusses work less satisfactorily.

Are any dangers involved in neglecting to operate upon hernias?

Definitely, yes. The chance of strangulation of bowel is always present, and such a situation is dangerous to life.

Is the injection treatment satisfactory in the treatment of hernias?

No. This method has been abandoned as dangerous and ineffectual.

Do hernias tend to disappear by themselves?

No. The only hernias that ever disappear by themselves are the small hernias of the navel seen in newborns, and an occasional small inguinal hernia in a newborn.

How effective is surgery in the treatment of hernia?

The vast majority of hernias can be repaired successfully by restoring and reinforcing the torn structures, replacing the extruded structures into their normal anatomical location, and removing the outpouching of abdominal tissue (peritoneum) which makes up the hernial sac.

When is the best time to operate upon hernias?

Hernia operations are usually elective procedures, and the time for their repair can be chosen by the patient to suit his convenience. It must be remembered, however, that most hernias tend to enlarge; the larger the hernia, the more difficult it is to repair and the greater the chance of subsequent recurrence.

Are hernia operations dangerous?

No. They are rarely followed by complications, except when the operation has been carried out for strangulation. In such cases, gangrenous bowel or intestine may be encountered, and this will entail extensive serious surgery for removal of the gangrenous portions.

When is a hernia operation an emergency procedure?

When the hernia strangulates, a condition in which an organ, such as the intestine or bowel, is caught in the hernial sac and its blood supply is interfered with. Under such circumstances, the patient must be operated upon immediately! Failure to do so will lead to gangrene of the strangulated hernial contents and possible death from peritonitis.

Will surgeons delay operations in elective cases if the patient is overweight?

Yes. If the patient is too stout, the repair of the hernia is similar to an attempt at stuffing too much clothing into a small valise. If such a valise does close, the great pressure from within is likely to pop it open.

What procedure is carried out when gangrenous intestine or bowel is found in a hernia?

The gangrenous portions of bowel are removed. This is a most serious and complicated operation, with numerous dangers. The mortality rate in these cases has been lowered remarkably by improved surgical techniques and the use of antibiotic drugs, but the procedure still constitutes one of the most formidable in abdominal surgery.

Are hernia operations particularly painful?

No, except for pain in the operative region for a few days after the surgery has been performed.

Are operations for diaphragmatic hernia particularly dangerous?

No, but these are more extensive procedures than those for hernias in the abdominal region.

How are diaphragmatic hernias repaired?

In most instances, an incision is made in the chest along the ribs, the chest cavity is opened, and the defect or rent in the diaphragm is sutured after the misplaced organs have been replaced into the abdominal cavity. Another effective approach to this type of repair is through an abdominal incision.

Is repair of a diaphragmatic hernia usually successful?

Yes, in the great majority of cases.

How long do hernia operations take to perform?

The simple inguinal hernias can be repaired in one half to three quarters of an hour. The more extensive hernias, such as the diaphragmatic or the incarcerated ones in which the herniated organs are firmly attached to the sac wall, may take several hours to repair.

What kind of anesthesia is used?

For hernias below the level of the navel, spinal anesthesia is most often employed. Diaphragmatic hernias and hernias in the upper abdomen are often operated upon under general inhalation anesthesia.

How long a hospital stay is necessary after surgery?

Six to 7 days for the ordinary hernia; 10 to 12 days for the more complicated types.

How soon after operation can the patient get out of bed?

With the almost universal employment of early ambulation, most patients get out of bed the day following surgery.

Can coughing or sneezing cause a recurrence of the hernia?

No, despite the fact that patients often feel as though they have ripped open all of their stitches when they cough.

What are the chances of recurrence following surgery?

More than 90 percent of hernias are cured permanently after surgery. Most recurrences are seen in elderly people or in those who have particularly fragile muscle and connective tissues.

How long does it take for the average hernia wound to heal?

Seven to ten days.

What precautions should be taken to prevent hernia recurrence?

1. The patient should not permit himself to gain a large amount of weight.
2. Pushing, pulling, or lifting heavy objects (those over 40 to 50 pounds) should be avoided whenever possible.
3. All strenuous exercise should be avoided for a period of four to six months.

If hernias do recur, what procedure is indicated?

About four out of five recurrent hernias can be cured by reoperation.

Is it common for patients to have slight pain, numbness, or tingling in the wound or along the scrotum for several weeks or months after hernia operations?

Yes. This happens occasionally but will disappear spontaneously.

Are grafts ever inserted in repairing recurrent hernias?

Yes. Plastic meshes (Marlex or Mersilene) or metal meshes of tantalum often prove extremely helpful in supporting a weak abdominal wall. Their use has led to cure in innumerable cases of recurrent hernia.

Should patients who have been operated upon for hernia wear trusses or abdominal supports?

No. Surgical repair is sufficient protection.

Is sex life affected by the repair of an inguinal hernia?

No. The testicles and the other genital structures are not interfered with when hernia repair is carried out.

Will operating on both sides increase the risk of surgery?

No.

Can normal physical activity ever be resumed by someone who has undergone a hernia repair?

Most certainly, yes.

Can a woman permit herself to become pregnant after a hernia operation?

Yes, within a few months after surgical recovery.

How soon after a hernia operation can one do the following:

Bathe?	3–5 days
Walk outdoors?	3–10 days
Climb stairs?	7–10 days
Do housework?	2–3 weeks
Drive a car?	2–3 weeks

Resume sexual relations?	4 weeks
Return to work?	6–8 weeks
All physical activities?	3–6 months

How often should one return for a checkup following a hernia operation?

Approximately every six months, for a period of two years.

HERNIA IN CHILDREN

What are the different types of hernia most frequently encountered in children?

1. Inguinal hernia (in the groin)

2. Umbilical hernia (hernia of the navel)

3. Epigastric hernia (in the midline in the upper abdomen)

4. Diaphragmatic hernia (a defect in the diaphragm separating the abdominal cavity from the chest cavity)

5. Femoral hernia (just below the groin in the thigh)

6. Omphalocele (a large hernia in the region of the navel)

Are children ever born with hernias?

Yes. Almost all hernias in children are present at birth, although a hernia may not become evident until the child is several months old.

Is the presence of a hernia evidence that the child is generally weak or poorly developed?

No. Hernias can appear in completely healthy children who have well-developed musculature.

Can constipation with straining at stool, a chronic cough or whooping cough, or an excessive physical strain cause a hernia in a child?

No. A hernia may first become apparent after such a strain, but in actuality the hernial sac has been present since the child's birth. Strain may bring out the hernia, but it does not really cause it.

Is a hernia often associated with an undescended testicle or hydrocele?

Yes. The three conditions often occur together.

When an undescended testicle, hydrocele, and hernia occur together, should they all be remedied at the same time?

Yes.

Should parents restrict the physical activities of a child who has once been operated on for a hernia?

No. In almost all instances, repair of a hernia is permanent and the tissues in the area of repair will be just as strong as they are in children who have never had a hernia. It is therefore completely unnecessary for parents to restrict the activity of a child because he has once had a hernia.

Is there a tendency for inguinal hernias to occur on both sides?

Yes. It has been estimated that even when it is possible to diagnose only the hernia on one side in a child, in two out of three cases the child also has a small hernia on the other side.

Does a child ever have symptoms with an inguinal hernia?

Yes. If a loop of bowel gets into the hernial sac, the child may become irritable, refuse his feedings, and may fuss considerably. If the loop of bowel gets caught in the hernial sac and cannot get out, a condition known as incarceration is said to exist. This will give the child more pain and may cause him to vomit his feedings. If the circulation to the incarcerated loop of bowel is cut off, the child becomes very ill and a strangulation is said to exist.

Children with strangulated hernias will vomit repeatedly and become markedly dehydrated, and if it is left untreated for several hours the strangulated loop will undergo gangrene.

How often does incarceration of an inguinal hernia occur in children?
In approximately 10 to 15 percent of cases.

What is the treatment for an inguinal hernia in infants and children?
All inguinal hernias should be repaired surgically. There was a time when surgeons would recommend waiting until the child was a year old or older. Today, surgery is recommended when the child reaches three to four months of age. Of course, if the hernia becomes incarcerated or if it is thought that it is becoming strangulated, surgery is performed immediately no matter what the infant's age.

Is there a tendency for an inguinal hernia to recur after it has once been repaired?
Not in children.

Should a child with a hernia wear a truss?
No. Surgery is so simple and so effective that a truss is no longer recommended for a hernia in a child.

Should a hernia be repaired in a premature infant who has once incarcerated the hernia?
As soon as the infant weighs six to seven pounds, it is safe to operate. This is true even though many surgeons prefer to wait until the child has established himself better and has reached three months of age.

Can a child return to full physical activity after the repair of a hernia?
Yes. After the postoperative period has passed, a child can return to full activity without fear of recurrence.

Is it necessary for a child to wear an abdominal support or a truss after an inguinal hernia has been repaired?
No.

Does a hernia operation on a male child affect his testicles?
No.

What causes an umbilical hernia?
An imperfect closure or weakness of the umbilical ring at the site where the umbilical cord emerged from the abdomen.

If a newborn's navel protrudes, does this mean that he has an umbilical hernia?
Yes, but the defect may be so slight that it cannot be considered a hernia that requires surgical treatment.

Does an umbilical hernia cause any symptoms?
Usually not. However, if a loop of intestine or a portion of the omentum (the fatty apron covering the intestines) becomes incarcerated in the hernial sac, it may result in pain, nausea, and vomiting.

Is it necessary to operate on all umbilical hernias?
No. The great majority of them will become smaller and the umbilical ring will close by the time the child reaches one to two years of age. It is only the larger defects that measure more than half an inch to one inch in diameter that will require surgical repair. The operation is a simple, safe procedure.

Is strapping an umbilical hernia helpful in getting it to heal?
Many pediatricians feel that strapping the umbilical region with adhesive tape will aid the closure of the umbilical ring. However, most surgeons feel that this does not help much if at all, and that if the ring is going to close it will do so spontaneously.

How does a surgeon determine which umbilical hernias should be repaired and which should be treated medically?

Umbilical hernias that measure between two thirds of an inch and one inch in diameter will probably not close spontaneously and will eventually have to be repaired surgically.

Is the navel deformed after the repair of an umbilical hernia?

Yes. It may appear that there is a great deal of excess tissue in the area, but eventually this will shrink and the normal appearance of the navel will be restored. This may take several weeks or months.

How is an epigastric hernia diagnosed in a child?

There will be a bulge at the site of the hernia. On examining the area with his finger, the pediatrician will feel a defect in the tissues.

Must all epigastric hernias be corrected surgically?

Yes. They have a tendency to grow larger as the child grows older, and since the operation is simple and not dangerous, surgery is recommended in almost all instances when the defect is larger than the tip of one finger.

How common are epigastric hernias in children?

They are less frequently encountered than some other types of hernia.

What causes a diaphragmatic hernia?

A diaphragmatic hernia is usually caused by a birth defect in the formation of the large muscle known as the diaphragm. This defect will permit some of the abdominal contents to protrude up into the chest. The most common organs to be found in the chest are the stomach, the small intestine, the large intestine, and the spleen. When the diaphragmatic hernia occurs on the right side of the body, portions of the liver may protrude into the chest cavity.

How is the diagnosis of a diaphragmatic hernia made in a child?

From the time of birth, the child will appear to be short of breath and may display a bluish discoloration of his skin. Along with this, there may be regurgitation and vomiting at feedings. On listening to the chest, the pediatrician may hear the gurgling sounds usually associated with the movement of fluids within the stomach or intestinal tract. The diagnosis is usually confirmed by taking an x-ray and noting the presence of the stomach, small bowel, or large bowel within the chest cavity.

What is the treatment for a diaphragmatic hernia found at birth?

Immediate surgery is necessary to prevent the child from dying. An upper abdominal incision is made and the rent or defect in the diaphragm is closed with sutures. If a large number of bowel loops or abdominal organs were protruding into the chest cavity, the abdominal cavity may prove to be too small to contain them after the rent in the diaphragm has been closed. When such a situation exists, the skin and subcutaneous tissues are closed over the intestines, but no attempt is made to seal the muscular layers of the abdominal wall. This will produce an incisional hernia, which can be repaired when the child is several months older.

What is an "upside-down stomach"?

"Upside-down stomach" is the nonmedical term given to a diaphragmatic hernia in which the stomach, or a portion of it, has protruded into the chest cavity.

How large is an omphalocele?

It may be very small, no more than

an inch or two in diameter, or it may be so large that it contains most of the abdominal organs, including the small and large intestines, the spleen, and the liver.

Must an omphalocele always be repaired?

Yes. A child cannot live unless the omphalocele is repaired, as it will rupture within a short period of time and the intestines and other abdominal organs will spill out.

How soon after birth is an omphalocele repaired?

A child with an omphalocele should be taken from the delivery room directly to the operating room for surgery.

What operative procedure is carried out for an omphalocele?

If it is a very small defect, the omphalocele sac is opened and its contents are placed back into the abdominal cavity. The abdomen is then closed. The peritoneum, the muscles, and the fascial wall are sutured in separate layers. Unfortunately, in most omphaloceles there is a very large defect in the abdominal wall and it is not possible to put all the organs into the abdominal cavity and to make a satisfactory abdominal-wall repair. Furthermore, the abdominal cavity often is not large enough to accommodate all the organs that have been occupying the omphalocele. For this reason, it is often advisable merely to raise up skin flaps on the abdominal wall surrounding the omphalocele and to bring the skin together over the abdominal contents. The effect of this is to transform the omphalocele into a large abdominal hernia. Then, when the child has grown for several months and his abdominal cavity has enlarged, a second operation is performed in which the various structures of the abdominal wall are closed in layers.

HERNIA IN OLDER PEOPLE

Are people past 60 more likely to develop hernias than young people?

They are more likely to get hernias of the acquired type, but less likely to get those of the congenital variety. The latter kind is due to a weakness that is present from birth, but a hernia may not appear clinically until the individual is several years old or until he strains himself severely.

What are common causes of hernia in older people?

Increase in pressure in the abdominal cavity as a result of marked gain in weight, as a result of severe straining to evacuate the bowels (secondary to chronic constipation), or as a complication of a tumor mass growing in the abdominal cavity. In addition, the muscle and fibrous tissues in older people are weakened and less able to prevent structures within the abdominal cavity from emerging through openings in the abdominal wall. Severe spasms of coughing or sneezing resulting in a sudden increase of pressure in the abdominal cavity may also produce a hernia.

Is the sudden development of a hernia in an older person sometimes an indication of some more important disease?

Yes. There may be a tumor in the intestinal tract or a growth in some other organ in the abdominal cavity. It also may be associated with enlargement of the prostate gland.

A tumor in the large bowel may necessitate inordinate straining while evacuating the bowels. This repeated straining may lead to the development of a rupture. Similarly, an enlargement of the prostate may cause excessive straining while urinating.

Should all hernias in older people be operated on?

The great majority of people in their

70s and 80s who have small hernias will not require surgery or any other form of treatment.

Is it safe to operate on older people for a hernia?

Yes. Almost all hernia operations are well tolerated by older people, even when their general health may not be very robust. Repair of a diaphragmatic hernia is the most serious operation, but even it can be performed safely in the great majority of cases. Inguinal (groin), femoral, umbilical, and incisional hernias are usually minor operations, unless strangulation has taken place.

When should surgery be recommended for people over 60 who have hernias?

1. When a structure, such as a segment of intestine, protrudes through the hernia opening and does not readily return to its normal position. This condition is known as incarceration. The doctor should be called immediately.

2. When strangulation of a hernia takes place: when a loop of intestine or large bowel has protruded through the hernia opening and its circulation has been cut off. If surgery is not carried out within a few hours, gangrene of the intestine or bowel will set in and the patient's life will be in danger.

3. When the hernia has become progressively larger, permitting more and more abdominal contents to pass into the sac.

4. When severe pain is a persistent symptom.

5. When a truss or abdominal support cannot hold the hernia in place. In such patients the intestines push through the hernia opening despite the support.

When should surgery not be performed on older people with hernias?

1. When they are in their late 70s, 80s, or 90s and experience no symptoms.

2. When they are in their late 70s and 80s and a truss holds the hernia in place without causing undue discomfort.

3. When a debilitating condition or organic disease makes the patient a poor operative risk.

Are hernias more likely to recur in older people?

Yes, particularly when the general health is poor.

Can people in their 80s or 90s tolerate surgery for strangulated hernia?

It is remarkable how many people of very advanced age successfully survive this type of surgery. Of course, if too much time has elapsed since onset of strangulation, the outlook for recovery is poor.

What anesthesia is preferred for older people who must undergo surgery for a hernia?

In all probability a general anesthesia will be given. Spinal anesthesia is reserved for healthier, younger individuals in their 60s. Occasionally, a very old patient is operated on under local anesthesia.

Should recurrent hernia in older people be repaired by reoperation?

Repair of recurrent hernias in older people is followed by less rewarding results than in younger people. However, if there is incarceration or if there is danger of strangulation, then reoperation must be undertaken.

Should older people be kept inactive after the repair of a hernia?

No. It has been proved that patients who lie quietly in bed too long after surgery do not heal as well as those who are out of bed and active. Early ambulation seems to stimulate healing and to lessen the incidence of postoperative complications, such as pneumonia and thrombosis of blood vessels.

Is it necessary for older people who have been operated on for hernia to take special postoperative precautions?

Yes. For several months following surgery, they should avoid lifting heavy objects or doing strenuous physical work. It is also advisable that they lose weight if they are obese.

Should a healthy person past 60 severely restrict his physical activity merely because there is a greater tendency to develop a hernia?

No. If one is healthy and is accustomed to taking physical exercise, he may continue to do so. Normal physical exercise will not cause a hernia. It is sudden, abrupt strain, rapid gain in weight, or the development of an expanding tumor in the abdominal cavity that predisposes one to hernia formation.

Herniated Intervertebral Disk

The intervertebral disks are made up of solid, gel-like, elastic tissue contained within a rim of fibrous tissue. They act as shock absorbers to the spinal column. A fall, strain, or just the natural wear and tear that accompany the stress of maintaining the erect posture may cause a protrusion of the disk center (nucleus pulposus) through its encircling rim. The herniation of the disk usually takes place posteriorly (backward), as this is the area where the fibrous rim is weakest. Severe back pain ensues, and if the bulging part of the disk presses upon a nerve exiting from the spine, the pain will travel along the nerve's pathway down the leg. This condition is known as *sciatica,* or sciatic neuritis. If the fibrous rim of the disk ruptures com-

pletely, the nucleus may extrude so far as to create sufficient nerve pressure to cause weakness, loss of reflexes, numbness, or complete loss of sensation in certain areas of the foot and leg, and wasting of leg muscles in addition to excruciating pain.

It should be emphasized that not all back pain or sciatica is caused by a ruptured disk. Spinal cord tumors, deformities of the joints of the vertebrae, severe arthritis of the spine, and other conditions may also give rise to back pain with radiation down the legs.

Occasionally the neck vertebrae are affected by slipped disks and cause great pain in the shoulders, neck, and head.

The diagnosis of a slipped disk is made conclusively by the use of myelogram x-rays. This is a test performed in the hospital in which an opaque substance is injected into the spinal canal and x-ray films are taken. A positive myelogram is one in which an obstruction deformity is noted on the x-ray film corresponding to the level of the suspected herniated disk.

The taking of a myelogram is a safe, practically painless procedure with no significant ill effects.

Most patients with herniated disks recover after prolonged bed rest. Traction (stretching) of the lower limb on the affected side and the wearing of a back brace help to hasten recovery. Despite these measures, full recovery in a severe case may take several months.

In approximately 10 to 20 percent of cases of severe herniation, symptoms do not subside on a regime of bed rest and traction. Such patients should then be operated upon for the removal of the disk. The operation is carried out under either spinal or general anesthesia through a four- or five-inch incision in the back over the region of the herniated disk. In most instances, it is possible to remove the disk without cutting out any part of the bone of the vertebra. However, in some instances, it is necessary to chip away nonvital portions of one or two vertebrae, thus performing a *laminectomy.*

If the patient is a young man who is engaged in heavy manual labor, the surgeon may feel that some instability of the spine may follow the operation and he will therefore elect to do a *spinal fusion* after removing the disk. As there are some 33 separate vertebrae, fusing two or three will not result in any noticeable loss of back motion. Following spinal fusion, the patient is placed in a body cast which must be worn for several weeks. He will then wear a back brace for several more weeks or months. The average spinal fusion requires anywhere from three to six months to heal completely. Fortunately, the patient can be up and about in his cast and will not be forced to remain in the hospital for more than ten days to two weeks.

Operations for herniated disk, whether or not they are accompanied by lami-

nectomy or spinal fusion, are safe procedures which carry no intrinsic dangers. The patient can usually get out of bed by the third to fifth postoperative day, and within a month after surgery he can resume sedentary work. Those who have not undergone spinal fusion, and therefore will not be in a plaster cast, make a somewhat quicker recovery but they should nevertheless take precautions not to return to strenuous work.

See also SPINE.

QUESTIONS AND ANSWERS

What is a slipped disk?

A slipped disk is a displacement backward of the disk from the space between the bones of the spine.

How does it happen?

It occurs because of the weakening of the fibrous ring holding the disk in place.

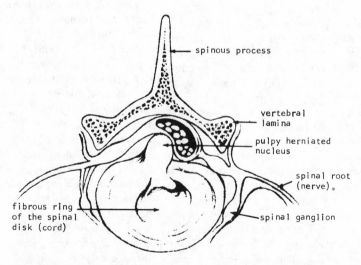

spinous process

vertebral lamina

pulpy herniated nucleus

spinal root (nerve)

spinal ganglion

fibrous ring of the spinal disk (cord)

To remove a herniated disk, the lamina of the vertebra is chiseled away and the protruding disk, or piece of cartilage, is removed.

Is a slipped disk painful?
Yes.

To whom does it happen?
Active adults ranging from the ages usually of 30 to 50 years.

How can one be sure he has a slipped disk?
Only by adequate and careful orthopedic, neurological, and x-ray examination.

Is a myelogram x-ray dangerous?
No.

Do people ever get well by themselves from a slipped disk?
Yes.

Do slipped disks develop in more than one part of the spine?
Yes, occasionally.

Do slipped disks tend to recur?
Not if the slipped disk has been removed. About 30 percent of those treated conservatively may recur, however.

If operation is not necessary and traction is performed, is it painful?
No, merely uncomfortable.

How long must one remain in traction?
If traction is successful, seven to ten days.

What percent of patients with a slipped disk need surgery?
Most surgeons feel that those suffering repeated attacks of pain from a slipped disk should be operated upon. This probably means about 10 to 20 percent of those afflicted.

What happens if surgery is not performed in indicated cases?
Progressive nerve involvement and occasional paralysis in the leg.

Does the bone always have to be removed when operating upon a slipped disk?
With newer methods of positioning the patient, bone need not always be removed.

What is a laminectomy?
The removal of a small portion of bone of the spine in order to reach and remove a disk.

Is a laminectomy a serious operation?
Yes, but it is not a dangerous one.

Is the spine weakened by a laminectomy?
No.

Are special preoperative measures necessary before hospitalization?
No.

What kind of anesthesia is used?
General anesthesia.

What is done during a laminectomy?
A portion of the lamina is removed, the nerve root and disk are exposed, and the disk is removed.

Must a spinal fusion be done along with a laminectomy?
In most cases, no.

Are blood transfusions necessary?
No.

Are special postoperative procedures required?
No.

Are special nurses necessary?
They are very helpful for the first 48 to 72 hours.

How soon after operation can the patient get out of bed?
About three to five days after the operation.

How long a hospital stay is necessary?
About ten to fourteen days.

Is convalescent care necessary?

Not usually, but advisable if it can be obtained.

Are the patients ever worse after surgery has been performed?

No.

What are the results of operations for slipped disk?

About 80 percent are cured.

If the muscles have become weak and thin as a result of a slipped disk, do these muscles regain their normal size and strength?

No. There is partial recovery only.

Where is the operative scar in an operation for a slipped disk?

About a four- to six-inch scar directly over the vertebra involved.

Is the scar painful?

No.

Is the scar ugly?

No.

How long does it take the wound to heal?

About two to three weeks.

How soon after surgery can one:

Bathe?	2 to 3 weeks
Drive a car?	4 to 6 weeks
Return to work?	2 to 3 weeks
Resume normal social activity?	About 6 weeks
Resume strenuous physical activity?	This is unwise at any time!
Resume sexual relations?	About 2 months

What kind of surgeon performs an operation for a herniated disk?

Either a neurosurgeon or an orthopedic surgeon. In some hospitals, both types of surgeons will act as a team in operating upon a slipped disk.

Hiatus Hernia

See DIAPHRAGMATIC AND HIATUS HERNIAS.

Hip

The hip joint is composed of the ball-shaped head of the thighbone (femur) and a socket-shaped concavity composed of the pelvic bones. The main brunt of the weight of the head, chest, and abdomen is carried by the hipbone, and it is therefore no cause for wonder that it is subject to so many diseases.

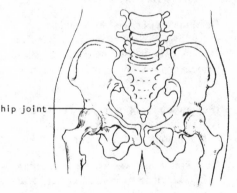

hip joint

Some of the disorders of the hip that demand the most attention are:

1. Congenital dislocation of the hip
2. Infantile coxa vara
3. Acquired coxa vara
4. Coxa valga
5. Slipped epiphysis of the hip
6. Perthes' disease
7. Arthritis of the hip
8. Fracture of the hip

See also ARTHRITIS; BONE CONDITIONS; FRACTURES; JOINTS.

CONGENITAL DISLOCATION OF THE HIP

Congenital dislocation of the hip is a serious malformation seen about seven times more often in females than in males. It may occur in one or both hips but is much more common in the left hip. Its cause is unknown but heredity undoubtedly plays a strong role.

Specifically, the condition is one in which the head of the femur (thighbone) fails to stay in its socket. Instead, it rides up high on the ilium (a bone of the pelvis). The condition is often not diagnosed until the child attempts to walk, at which time a limp is noted if the deformity is one-sided and a waddle is present if the dislocation involves both hips.

Conservative, or nonoperative treatment can cure the majority of these unfortunate children, but to obtain the best results, it must be started during the first year of life. Treatment consists of traction (pulling) on the leg in order to bring down the head of the femur into its socket. Once this has been accomplished—and it sometimes takes several weeks of steady pulling—the position must be maintained by plaster fixation. The plaster must be worn anywhere from 6 to 18 months in order to prevent the head of the femur from slipping out again.

When the foregoing line of attack fails, an operation must be performed. An incision is made on the front of the thigh over the pelvic bone. Tight and deforming muscles are lengthened, and the head of the thighbone is levered into the hip joint after the socket has been cleared of soft tissue. The natural socket (acetabulum) is occasionally deepened by turning down a flap of bone from the wing of the ilium. This maneuver will form a shelf to hold the head of the femur in place. It may also be necessary to divide the thighbone and reposition it so that when it heals, the hip is snugly directed into the joint socket. The wound is closed and a plaster cast extending from the toes to the chest is applied.

There are other operations to correct congenital dislocation of the hip. All are effective when performed by competent orthopedists on properly selected patients. Although this surgery is of major proportions, recovery is the general rule and results are usually most satisfactory.

QUESTIONS AND ANSWERS

Is congenital dislocation of the hip more common in boys or in girls?

It is seven times more frequent in girls than in boys.

What is a dysplastic or subluxated hip?

A dysplastic hip is one in which the hip socket is shallow but no dislocation has taken place. A subluxated hip is one that is shifted out of its normal position but still maintains contact with the joint.

Are children frequently born with the hip completely dislocated?

No. Most frequently they are born with a dysplastic hip that gradually subluxates and then dislocates as the child begins to stand and walk.

Does a birth injury cause congenital dislocation of the hip?

No. This is one of the very few types of dislocation that has nothing to do with injury.

How can a dysplastic or congenitally dislocated hip be recognized?

The skin folds on the backs of the thighs and buttocks are not symmetrical, the affected leg cannot be brought out as far as the normal limb, the limb appears shortened, and the groin fold is deepened. If the diagnosis is not made early, the condition may first be noted when the child begins to walk and limps or waddles.

How is a dysplastic or dislocated hip treated?

If the condition is noted early, placing a double diaper or pillow diaper on the child will frequently bring the hips into proper position to deepen the hip socket and prevent dislocation. At times, casts or braces may be employed to perform the same function. If the condition is noted after dislocation has occurred, a traction device (usually a cast) must be applied. By traction, the hip is gradually brought adjacent to the hip socket. At this point the legs are brought outward so that the hip faces deeply within the socket.

Is surgery ever necessary for congenital dislocation of the hip?

Yes. If the hip cannot be brought within the socket by traction and casting, surgery is necessary. One of several operative procedures may be performed. The hip socket may be cleared of fat and capsule and scar tissue, and the thighbone placed within it; the thighbone (femur) may be cut through (osteotomized) and the hip rotated so that the head of the femur faces the socket while the foot faces forward; the socket may be deepened; a ledge of bone may be placed above the socket to prevent the hip from dislocating; or the entire pelvis may be rotated in order to deepen the socket. The method chosen depends on several factors.

What factors determine the operation necessary for congenital dislocation of the hip?

The age of the patient, the degree of dislocation, the amount of twist that

has formed in the thighbone, and the depth of the hip socket.

Is a cast worn after surgery for congenital dislocation of the hip?

Yes.

What will happen if a congenital dislocation of the hip is not treated?

A limp and ultimate arthritis of the hip joint are virtually inevitable.

What are the results of treatment for congenital dislocation of the hip?

If the treatment is early, the results are excellent. If it is later, the results are usually good.

INFANTILE COXA VARA

Congenital coxa vara is a deformity of the thighbone (femur) wherein the angle between the upper end of the bone and the shaft of the bone is decreased from normal. The region is known as the femoral neck and there is usually an angle of 135° between the head of the femur and its shaft. Coxa vara may be mild or marked; in some cases the angle is less than a right angle. Such a deformity will restrict abduction of the leg and will be accompanied by a limp.

What are the symptoms of congenital coxa vara?

The involved leg is often shortened. There is a painless limp and limited motion at the hip. The child may walk with a waddling gait if both hips are affected.

How is coxa vara treated?

Surgery must be performed to reconstitute the normal alignment of the deformed portion of the thighbone.

ACQUIRED COXA VARA

Acquired coxa vara comes mainly from slipping of the epiphysis of the head of the femur. The epiphysis is the growth line of the bone and it sometimes becomes dislocated, causing the position of the head of the femur to be out of line with the shaft. In effect, the child develops an angulation that is more acute than the normal 135° between the head and the shaft of the thighbone.

What is acquired coxa vara?

It is a deformity in the angulation between the head and the shaft of the thighbone resulting from a slipping of the epiphysis.

What is the treatment for acquired coxa vara?

Surgery is necessary. The neck of the femur bone is cut across and reset at the proper 135° angle.

COXA VALGA

This deformity is the opposite of coxa vara. In other words, the shaft-neck angle is increased and may present almost a straight line instead of the normal angulation. The most frequent causes of coxa valga in a child are poliomyelitis, spastic paralysis with spasm of muscles that pull the thighbone, and a persistent tilting of the pelvis.

What is the treatment for coxa valga?

Marked coxa valga must be treated surgically with a section of the bone being removed from the femur, and by breaking the bone and setting is so as to create a decreased angulation between the neck and the shaft of the bone.

Are results satisfactory after operation for coxa valga?

In most instances, yes. It must be understood that these operations should be performed by an expert orthopedist who has had a great deal of experience in this field.

SLIPPED EPIPHYSIS OF THE HIP

A slipped epiphysis is a displacement of the growth plate of a long bone and the end of the bone beyond it. It is most common at the hip. In this location, it is called a slipped femoral epiphysis.

When is a child most likely to develop a slipped femoral epiphysis?

At the time of most rapid adolescent growth. In boys, this is between the ages of 14 and 16; in girls it is between the ages of 10 and 14.

Is slipped epiphysis more common in boys or girls?

Eighty-five percent of the patients are boys.

What are the chances of the other hip becoming abnormal if there is a slipped femoral epiphysis on one side?

In 25 to 40 percent of the cases, the disease ultimately involves both sides.

What causes a slipped epiphysis?

Most frequently the condition is caused by the gradual sliding force of the weight of the child upon the growth plate. At times, a fall or twisting injury may cause the epiphysis to slip.

What type of boy or girl is most apt to develop a slipped epiphysis?

A tall, heavy child.

How is a slipped femoral epiphysis diagnosed?

It may be suspected when the child complains of discomfort in the groin after activity. There may be some stiffness at the hip and a limp. Later, there is tenderness around the hip. The thigh is drawn to the midline and the foot is rotated outward. There is pain on attempts to bring the thigh outward or to rotate the foot inward.

The diagnosis is confirmed by characteristic x-ray findings.

What is the treatment for a slipped epiphysis?

The child must stay off his feet. He should be taken to the hospital, where the hip should be operated on.

Will a slipped epiphysis lead to a shortening of the leg?

Yes, if the condition is severe. The shortening is partly due to the drawing inward of the thigh and partly due to the slip itself.

What surgery is done for a slipped femoral epiphysis?

If the slip is only mild, metal pins are placed across the epiphysis to prevent further slip. If the slip is more severe, a wedge of bone is removed from the femur to restore the normal configuration of the upper portion of the bone where it forms the hip. In some cases, a protruding edge of bone is removed from the end of the femur to allow normal motion.

PERTHES' DISEASE

Perthes' disease is a condition in which a deficient blood supply to the head of the femur (hip) causes death to the cells of the hip. Its technical name is osteochondritis deformans juvenilis.

How common is Perthes' disease in children?

It is a fairly common cause of persistent hip pain in children.

Who usually develops Perthes' disease?

Boys between the ages of 4 and 10 years.

What causes Perthes' disease?

The cause is unknown. It is *not* due to infection or injury.

What are the signs and symptoms of Perthes' disease?

A limp is the earliest sign. Later there may be a mild, ill-defined pain, which may seem to come from the knee as well as the hip. There is usually stiffness of the hip. The condition can be diagnosed by x-rays.

What is the treatment for Perthes' disease in children?

The child must be kept off his feet, and the involved hip must bear no weight until the hip has been restored to its normal appearance on x-ray examination.

How serious is Perthes' disease?

If allowed to go untreated, it will result in collapse of the hip and ultimate severe arthritis of the hip joint.

What is meant by "restoring the hip" in Perthes' disease?

In Perthes' disease, death of the bone cells in the hip causes the cells to crumble. They are gradually replaced by blood vessels and scar tissue. If no weight is borne by the hip, new cells will replace the old cells and the hip once again will be strong and of normal shape.

How long does it take for the hip to be restored in Perthes' disease?

Often, three to five years.

Can a child with Perthes' disease use a brace or crutches in order to keep the involved hip from bearing weight?

Usually not. No child can be trusted to use the brace or crutches at all times. He must be under constant supervision. This is best done in a hospital or by keeping the child in bed at home.

Won't a child suffer severe psychological damage by being kept at bed rest for several years?

He may, but advice from a psychiatrist should be obtained. The children usually do very well once the disease is cured and they are again up and about.

Several years of bed rest is far more preferable to the other alternative: a permanently deformed hip.

ARTHRITIS OF THE HIP

Since the hip bears so much weight throughout all of life, it is not unexpected that it is frequently the site of arthritis. Although rheumatoid arthritis does affect this joint, one encounters degenerative arthritis more frequently. This is a condition seen in advanced age.

Is arthritis of the hip joint a very common condition?

Yes. It is seen with increasing frequency in older people.

Is arthritis of the hip very painful?

Yes. It is also very debilitating and interferes greatly with walking.

Will rest in bed for prolonged periods of time help arthritis of the hip joint?

It may relieve the pain, but it will do nothing to bring about a cure.

Are there any special treatments for arthritis of the hip joint?

Yes. Advanced degenerative arthritis of the joint may so interfere with walking that the patient becomes an invalid. In these cases, operative replacement of the head and neck of the femur with a metal structure designed to conform to the normal anatomical structures is often advocated. Remarkable cures of arthritis of the hip have been obtained with these metal replacements.

FRACTURE OF THE HIP

Fracture of the hip is one of the most common injuries to people over 60 years of age.

Are fractures of the hip serious?

Yes. First of all, they may be fol-lowed by numerous complications such as embolism or pneumonia. Secondly, they often lead to permanent deformity, with resultant limitation of walking.

Is it ever necessary to perform an open operation for a fracture of the hip?

Yes. In many instances the hip joint is opened, the bones are placed in correct position, and are held there with metal nails or plates.

Are hip fractures treated by long periods of bed rest and immobilization in a cast?

No. A metal pin is hammered through the neck of the fractured bone to hold it in place and the patient gets out of bed in a day or two. Casts are no longer applied for fractured hips.

How long may it take the average hip fracture to heal?

Particularly in older people, the length of time may be very great. However, the average length of time for total healing of a hip fracture is anywhere from 8 to 12 months.

Do most people recover completely from hip fracture?

Yes, but many of them will always have a limp.

Is pulmonary embolism a frequent complication of hip fracture?

For reasons unknown, a pulmonary embolus is a not infrequent complication of hip fracture, especially in older people. For this reason, it is important that their circulation be maintained and that they not lie inactive in bed because of their fracture.

Hip Replacement

Hip replacement, or arthroplasty, is an operative procedure performed to relieve "incurable" conditions involving the hip joint. It is carried out when the head of the femur (thighbone) has been irreparably destroyed by a fracture and in cases in which the hip joint has been destroyed by arthritis or some other degenerative disease.

The operation requires removal of the head, neck, and part of the shaft of the thighbone and restitution of the smooth concave contours of the hip socket. The head, neck, and part of the shaft of the femur is then replaced by a metal device composed of Vitallium or SMO steel. Vitallium consists of several metals such as cobalt, chromium, carbon, molybdenum, and manganese. SMO steel is an alloy of stainless steel and molybdenum. In cases in which the bony hip socket has also been badly damaged, an artificial metal socket is inserted.

QUESTIONS AND ANSWERS

For what conditions is hip replacement most frequently done?

1. In a case of severe hip fracture with failure of the fractured fragments to heal, or where healing has taken place but has been followed by a chronically painful, or stiff, joint

2. In markedly advanced cases of osteoarthritis of the joint

3. In degenerative conditions, such as Perthes' disease

What age group is most likely to require hip replacement?

People who are in their later years, especially those in the 60s or 70s.

Is hip replacement a serious operation?

Yes, but it is one that usually does not endanger life. It is being performed with increasing frequency in recent years with ever better results.

Is hip replacement advocated for patients with bone tumors?

Usually not, because most bone tumors in people of advanced age are malignant and thus will require high amputation rather than bone replacement.

How is hip replacement carried out?

An incision is made on the outer aspect of the involved hip and upper thigh. The incision is carried down to expose the joint. The diseased portion of the head and neck and part of the shaft of the femur (thighbone) are removed and the joint socket is smoothed out or replaced. The metal, artificial hip, whose outline conforms to the bony outline of the femur, is then placed in the socket and the hollow bottom end of the device is placed over the shaft of the thighbone as a sleeve. Muscles are then resutured over the graft and the skin is closed over the muscles.

For how long a period is the patient hospitalized after hip replacement?

For approximately 10 to 14 days.

How soon after the operation is the patient permitted to get out of bed?

Within a day or two. He is also permitted to do a certain amount of walking with the help of a crutch, cane, or walker. Weight-bearing is begun several days after hip replacement.

How successful is hip replacement?

It is successful in the majority of cases. In almost all instances there is relief from pain and improvement in motion.

What is the most frequent cause of failure after hip replacement?

Postoperative infection. Should this take place and not be controlled, it may be necessary to remove the artificial hip.

If one hip replacement operation fails, is it possible to reoperate at a later date?

Yes, but results may not be as satisfactory. It is essential that all infection be cleared up before reinserting another artificial hip.

Will a patient walk with a limp after hip replacement?

Some people may limp, but others can walk without any limp whatever.

What is the recuperative period following hip replacement?

There may be pain and difficulty on walking for several weeks or months after this operation. The rate of recovery may be closely related to the general condition of the patient.

Is there a tendency for the body to reject the metal hip device?

No. Vitallium and SMO steel are inert and they seldom evoke a rejection response by the body.

Is it possible to replace both hips when they are irreparably damaged by disease?

Yes. Some surgeons will do both sides during one operation; others will permit an interval of several days or weeks to elapse between replacement operations.

Hirschsprung's Disease

Hirschsprung's disease, or megacolon, is a condition of the large bowel present from birth. It is seen more often in males than in females and represents about 1 in every 10,000 hospital admissions. It is characterized by obstinate constipation and tremendous distention of the colon. When untreated, this unhappy disease lasts throughout life and keeps the patient in a state of perpetual concern and discomfort. X-rays of the intestinal tract show huge enlargement of the large bowel with an area of constriction somewhere in the descending colon or near the region where the sigmoid colon joins the rectum. Latest investigations have shown that the underlying cause for this condition is the absence of certain nerve fibers in the wall of the constricted portion of the bowel. These nerves are necessary to permit the contracted bowel to dilate normally. The constantly constricted area causes the bowel above to dilate and become overgrown in its attempts to force the stool beyond the narrowed portion. Within recent years, complete cures have been obtained for this previously incurable ailment. Total recovery can be obtained by removing the segment of narrowed bowel and stitching together the normal bowel above and below. This operation, although of major and serious proportions, is now a safe procedure and is followed by cure in well over 95 percent of the cases.

QUESTIONS AND ANSWERS

Is there a tendency for Hirschsprung's disease to run in families?

Yes, although it has never been proved that it is a truly inherited condition.

What causes Hirschsprung's disease?

It is caused by a developmental deformity in which certain nerve cells (parasympathetic ganglion cells) are missing from various portions of the bowel. The most commonly affected region is the portion of the bowel just above the rectum. These nerves are essential for making the bowel dilate and relax. If they are missing, the bowel will be held in a state of perpetual spasm. In attempts to propel the feces forward, the bowel above the spastic constriction enlarges, and because it is difficult to get the gas and feces beyond this contracted area, the bowel dilates tremendously.

How can the diagnosis of Hirschsprung's disease be made?

By characteristic findings on x-ray examination after the lower bowel has been outlined with barium. Also, by snipping out a small piece of tissue from the constricted portion of bowel and examining it for the presence of the normal ganglionic nerve cells. If these cells are absent, the patient has Hirschsprung's disease.

Are there varying degrees of severity of Hirschsprung's disease?

Yes. In some cases, the area of constricted bowel is very limited and the constriction is not too great. The free passage of feces will be restricted to a certain extent, but the child will be able to adjust to this. In severe cases, the child may go a week or longer without an evacuation, and the bowel above the constricted area may be four or five times its normal size.

Do children tend to outgrow Hirschsprung's disease?

No. Since the disease is an anatomical deformity caused by the absence of certain nerve cells, spontaneous recovery will not take place. However, a child with a mild case may be able to go through life without too much discomfort, although he will have an enlarged, dilated bowel and difficult bowel movements.

What is the treatment for Hirschsprung's disease?

1. Mild cases can be treated medically. This will include the giving of lubricants, such as mineral oil, the administration of stool softeners, and the repeated administration of enemas. The enema should contain three to four ounces of mineral or olive oil and salt water. As it is often necessary to flush out the lower bowel repeatedly, tap water should not be used, as large quantities of tap water can sometimes lead to collapse and shock.

2. Severe cases should be treated surgically by removing the constricted portion of large bowel.

Is surgical treatment for Hirschsprung's disease effective?

Yes. Cure will result in the vast majority of cases.

Do all cases have to be operated upon?

No. A small percentage of cases will get well over a period of years through medical management.

What usually happens if surgery is not performed?

The child continues with abdominal distention and constipation. The bowel must be emptied by enemas at regular intervals. Eventually these children become miserable, never develop fully, are undernourished, and may develop heart trouble.

Is surgery for this condition serious?

Yes, but cure can now be offered to the great majority of these children.

Does the condition ever recur after surgery?

Only in a very small percentage of cases. When it does, an additional removal of constricted bowel may result in permanent cure.

When is the best time to perform surgery for this condition?

As soon as the nourishment and general condition of the child have been brought up to the maximum state of improvement.

Approximately how long a hospital stay is necessary?

Three to four weeks.

Are special preparations necessary before operating?

Yes:

1. The bowel should be emptied as completely as possible with repeated enemas and irrigations.

2. A fluid or low-residue diet is given.

3. Antibiotic drugs are given to prevent peritonitis from developing after surgery.

4. Transfusions are given to combat the anemia.

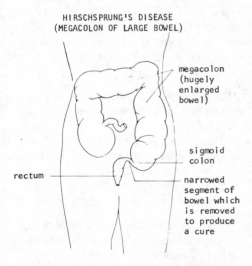

HIRSCHSPRUNG'S DISEASE
(MEGACOLON OF LARGE BOWEL)

megacolon (hugely enlarged bowel)

sigmoid colon

rectum

narrowed segment of bowel which is removed to produce a cure

What operative procedure is performed for Hirschsprung's disease?

Since there is usually a constricted area in the lower portion of the sigmoid colon and upper portion of the rectum, this segment of bowel is removed.

The child must enter the hospital several days before surgery in order to be prepared properly for it. Preparation will involve daily enemas and colonic irrigations to rid the bowel of retained stool and the administration of antibiotic drugs and chemical agents such as neomycin or kanamycin to sterilize the bowel. The child's blood chemistry is evaluated carefully and chemical deficiencies are replaced through intravenous infusions. If the child is anemic, blood transfusions may be given before the operation.

The operation is performed through a large incision in the left lower portion of the abdomen. The entire constricted area of sigmoid bowel and rectum is removed, and the normal bowel above it is sutured down to the rectum within a short distance from the anal outlet. This operation is called a colectomy.

How long does it take to perform a colectomy?

From two to five hours.

Is it necessary to perform a colostomy with an opening of the intestine onto the abdominal wall for Hirschsprung's disease?

No, because it is possible to stitch the normal bowel above the excised constriction to the normal rectum below, thus retaining intestinal continuity and function.

What is the expectation for recovery from a colectomy?

Although the operation is serious, more than 95 percent of children who undergo it recover and have spectacularly good relief of their symptoms.

On how young a child can this operation be performed safely?

It can be performed on a child who is just 2 or 3 years old, provided that his general condition and nutritional state are good.

How long a hospital stay is necessary after colectomy for Hirschsprung's disease?

Three to four weeks.

How soon after a colectomy will the bowels start to function normally?

It may be several weeks before they begin to function normally.

Are the following necessary before operations for Hirschsprung's disease?

Blood transfusions: Yes, if the child is anemic

Antibiotic medications: Yes

Intravenous medications: Yes

Stomach tubes: Yes

Bladder catheters: Yes

Vitamin injections: Yes

Special diets: Yes, a low-residue diet is given

Other special preparations: Yes, the bowel must be thoroughly cleared of feces and sterilized before surgery

Are the following necessary after operations for Hirschsprung's disease?

Private duty nurses: Yes, for several days

Antibiotic medications: Yes, usually

Intravenous infusions: Yes, for several days, as the child will not be fed by mouth

Blood transfusions: Yes, usually

Stomach tubes: Yes

Special postoperative measures: Yes, as the need arises

Postoperative vitamins and tonics: Yes

Convalescent posthospital care: Yes, unless there are adequate facilities for the child at home

How soon after an operation for this disease can a child do the following?

Get out of bed:	1–3 days
Leave the hospital:	3–4 weeks
Climb stairs:	4–5 weeks
Bathe or shower:	2–3 weeks
Go outdoors:	4–5 weeks
Return to school:	2–3 months
Play games:	3–4 months

Will an operation for Hirschsprung's disease interfere with the child's development?

On the contrary, these children usually have a tremendous spurt in their growth after a successful operation of this type.

Does the operation interfere with the future ability to bear children?

No.

Is a large, dilated colon (megacolon) ever present without a constricted portion of the bowel?

Yes. This condition is thought to occur in some children who are severely constipated due to psychological difficulties. This is not true Hirschsprung's disease because there is no anatomical abnormality of the nerve cells in the bowel wall.

Will children with megacolon that is psychological in origin respond well to surgery?

No. In fact, they may be harmed by surgery. Unless the constricted portion of the bowel is located by x-ray examination, it is best not to perform surgery for this type of megacolon.

What should be done for a child who has megacolon but shows no constricted area of bowel?

He should receive psychiatric treatment. The constipation, of course, must be treated with stool softeners and frequent enemas.

Horseshoe Kidney

A horseshoe kidney is a common name for a birth deformity in which the right and left kidneys are fused at corresponding poles. Thus, the two kidneys, almost always fused at their upper poles, form one structure having the general shape of a horseshoe.

See also KIDNEYS AND URETERS.

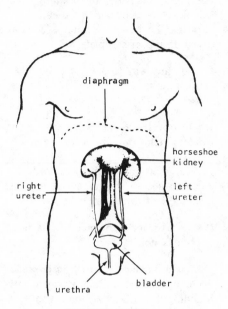

HORSESHOE KIDNEY

A horseshoe kidney is one in which the two kidneys are joined together. This is a not uncommon birth deformity of the genitourinary tract.

QUESTIONS AND ANSWERS

Is a horseshoe kidney a common birth deformity?

Yes, it is seen quite frequently.

Is horseshoe kidney in actuality two distinct organs?

Yes. Although the substance of the two kidneys is fused, each side continues to function as an individual unit, with its own nephrons, collecting tubules, and its own ureters leading down, one on either side of the midline, to the bladder.

What is the special significance of a horseshoe kidney?

If, in later life, kidney disease develops, it is essential to determine from which side of the fused kidney the disease originates, since only that part should be removed.

Is kidney function usually normal in an individual with horseshoe kidney?

Yes.

In later life, does a condition ever develop where one side of the horseshoe kidney is diseased while the other remains healthy?

Yes. This occurs quite often. It should be kept in mind that the two sides of the horseshoe function independently.

Hydrocele

There are two types of hydrocele, namely, congenital hydrocele and acquired hydrocele. The congenital type occurs in some male infants who are born with a collection of fluid surrounding the testicles. Some of the congenital types are the result of undue pressure in breech delivery, in which event the fluid will probably be absorbed within a few days after birth. Other congenital hydroceles will persist for several months or may not disappear at all. These can be considered to be true birth deformities and will require surgical correction. Acquired hydroceles occur mainly in adults.

See also GENITOURINARY SYSTEM; TESTICLES.

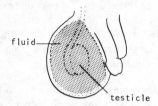

The fluid surrounding the testicle is evacuated when the hydrocele sac is removed surgically.

QUESTIONS AND ANSWERS

What is a hydrocele?

A hydrocele is an excessive accumulation of the fluid secretion contained in a thin-walled sac overlying the testicle and, at times, structures at a higher level within the scrotum. The size varies usually from that of a small hen's egg to that of a large orange. In long-neglected cases the cystic mass becomes very large, causes discomfort, and may obscure the penis.

Is the testicle normally surrounded by a small amount of fluid?

Yes. This fluid helps to protect the testicle from injury. It is normally present in such small amounts that no swelling is seen.

Is there a tendency for more fluid to surround the testicles of a newborn?

Yes, but this usually absorbs during the first few weeks of life. It is when it fails to absorb after a period of three or four months that a true hydrocele is said to exist.

What causes hydrocele in a newborn or young child?

Hydrocele may be due to faulty drainage of fluid formed from the lining of the sac overlying the testicle. As the infant grows, the lymphatic draining channels develop and drain more efficiently, reducing the hydrocele, and eventually it will disappear completely.

Is there any way to prevent a hydrocele from forming?

No.

Do hydroceles in newborns and young children tend to disappear spontaneously?

A large proportion of them do. If one does not absorb within several months, it should be treated surgically.

Does a hydrocele endanger the testicle?

Usually not.

How is a diagnosis of hydrocele made?

On examination, fluid is noted surrounding the testicle. A bright light held behind the scrotum will illuminate it as the light passes through the fluid. To confirm the diagnosis, the physician can put a needle into the scrotum and withdraw some of the fluid from the hydrocele sac.

Is hydrocele ever confused with a hernia?

Yes. This not always a simple distinction to make, because both conditions cause a swelling of the scrotum.

Is there a satisfactory nonsurgical treatment for hydrocele?

In occasional cases good results can be obtained merely by withdrawing the fluid surrounding the testicle with a needle. If the fluid does not form again, the hydrocele is cured. Surgical treatment, however, is simple and almost always successful.

Is it wise to tap the fluid from a hydrocele and have a urologist inject a chemical substance into the scrotum to prevent recurrence?

This is not a very wise procedure in a child. In certain adult cases of hydrocele, replacement of the fluid with a sclerosing solution sometimes produces a cure. However, in a child, it is best not to inject such substances, as they may interfere with the normal growth of the testicle. In some cases the hydrocele sac is a continuation of a communication into the abdomen, and the injected fluid may travel to the abdomen and produce peritonitis.

What is the surgical treatment for hydrocele?

A small incision is made through the wall of the scrotum to the hydrocele. The wall of the hydrocele is then opened and the fluid is drained out. The major portion of the wall is cut away. The small remaining borders are then sutured to the adjacent tissue.

Is there a tendency for hydroceles to recur once they have been removed surgically?

No.

Does a hydrocele ever become strangulated, or does bowel ever get into it?

No, because it is a small, completely circumscribed cystic mass that usually has no connection with the abdominal cavity.

Does a female child ever develop a hydrocele?

Yes. There is a condition in the female known as hydrocele of the canal of Nuck. This is often associated with a hernia.

What is the treatment for a hydrocele of the canal of Nuck in a female child?

If the hydrocele is absorbed during the first few months of life, no treatment is necessary. However, if the hydrocele persists or enlarges, an operation is performed and the entire hydrocele is removed. During the course of this operation, which is conducted through an incision in the groin, the tissues are inspected to note the presence or absence of an inguinal hernia. If there is a hernia, it is repaired at the same time.

Hydrocephalus

Hydrocephalus is a relatively common disorder of infants in which the head enlarges abnormally because of an excessive amount of cerebrospinal fluid within the brain. An interference with its circulation and absorption is responsible for the accumulation of a large quantity of fluid. The size of the head may reach enormous proportions. Various surgical procedures have been devised in an attempt to deal with this condition but the results, though encouraging, are not invariably satisfactory. An operation may be performed either for the purpose of reducing the formation of fluid or in order to shunt the fluid so as to facilitate its absorption or elimination from the body. Currently it is the practice in many clinics to divert the excess fluid from the brain into the heart.

See also NEUROSURGERY.

QUESTIONS AND ANSWERS

What causes hydrocephalus?

Injury during birth, congenital malformations, and infections (meningitis) in early life are the usual causes.

Is hydrocephalus a common disorder in infants?

Yes, it is fairly common.

What are the signs and symptoms of hydrocephalus?

The head enlarges out of proportion to the rest of the body and may reach enormous size. In addition, the fontanels (soft spots) are widened and may bulge, and the eyes often appear to be depressed downward.

Are there any operations that successfully treat hydrocephalus?

Many operations have been devised for the treatment of this condition, but unfortunately none has proved uniformly successful. In recent years most of these operations have involved the use of plastic tubes to shunt the cerebrospinal fluid into other body cavities from which it can be absorbed. The operation currently favored is one in which the cerebrospinal fluid is diverted into the heart.

Can hydrocephalus cause permanent brain damage?

Yes, if untreated, the pressure of the fluid on the brain will eventually destroy sufficient brain cells so as to cause mental retardation and other physical disabilities.

Is hydrocephalus ever self-limited?

Yes. In approximately 25 percent of cases, spontaneous arrest occurs. About a third of such cases exhibit normal intelligence.

Hymenotomy

The hymen (maidenhead) is a membrane which, at birth, covers the entrance to the vagina. It varies greatly in thickness and size of its opening in various individuals and may even be absent from birth. It frequently ruptures spontaneously during childhood or

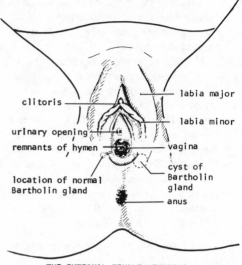

THE EXTERNAL FEMALE GENITALS

early adulthood as a result of physical exercise. The use of Tampax or other internal sanitary napkins will also tend to enlarge or destroy it. The normal hymen during childhood and adolescence has several small perforations within it through which vaginal secretions and menstrual fluid can gain ready exit. However, in rare instances, the hymen is a complete structure without any openings whatsoever. In such cases a young female may have all the symptoms of menstruation, including the pains and the feeling of discharge, but there will be no bleeding from the vaginal orifice. When this occurs, a surgical opening must be made in the hymen with a scalpel. The procedure is usually a very simple one, carried out in the hospital under light general anesthesia.

Under most circumstances, the hymen is ruptured more or less completely during initial sexual intercourse. This experience may be accompanied by no pain or bleeding at all, or may be associated with considerable pain and bleeding. During the premarital examination which most young women have, it will be easy for their physicians to foretell the degree of difficulty that might ensue from initial intercourse. If a very rigid hymen is found to exist, the gynecologist will suggest either dilatation of the opening with an instrument or the performance of a *surgical hymenotomy*. A surgical hymenotomy is performed under general anesthesia in the hospital and consists of making an incision into the structure and controlling the bleeding with a few catgut sutures. Whenever doubt exists as to the possibility of marital difficulties in this regard, it is wisest to have a surgical hymenotomy performed.

QUESTIONS AND ANSWERS

What is an imperforate hymen?

It is a condition in which the maidenhead covering the vaginal opening contains no perforations. This may not be obvious at birth, but becomes apparent when the child reaches puberty. At that time, she will have all the symptoms of menstruation but there will be no accompanying passage of blood from the vaginal canal. The blood collects within the vagina, a condition called hematocolpos.

Are females usually born with an imperforate hymen?

No. An opening is present in a great majority of female newborns.

If a girl's hymen is broken, does this mean she is not a virgin?

No. Many activities other than sexual intercourse may cause a rupture of the hymen.

Are girls ever born with a ruptured, wide-open hymen?

Yes, but this is not very common.

Is it common for the hymen to be ruptured during a girl's first ten years of life?

No.

Does the hymen always bleed when it is ruptured?

No.

Can physical activities such as bicycle or horseback riding cause a girl's hymen to rupture?

Yes.

Is it ever necessary to repair a ruptured hymen in a child?

No.

What is hematocolpos?

Hematocolpos is a condition in which the maidenhead (hymen) completely blocks the vaginal canal. Menstrual blood cannot get out and is dammed back into the vagina.

Will a nonperforated hymen cause amenorrhea?

No. It is not actually failure to menstruate but failure of the menstrual fluids to gain exit from the vagina that results.

How is the diagnosis of hematocolpos made?

The patient has symptoms of menstruation without flowing. Low abdominal discomfort usually occurs, and the physician can feel the mass of collected blood in the vagina by rectal examination.

What is the treatment for hematocolpos?

Incision of the hymen, performed under general anesthesia in a hospital. An overnight stay is all that will be necessary.

What is hymenotomy?

Surgical incision of an extremely rigid or nonperforated hymen.

When should a hymenotomy be performed upon a child?

1. When the hymen is completely intact and prevents the outflow of menstrual fluid

2. When it is essential that the gynecologist do a thorough pelvic examination

3. When there is vaginal bleeding in a child too young to menstruate

4. When a tumor of the cervix, uterus, or ovaries is suspected and a preliminary curettage (scraping) is to be carried out

How can a gynecologist examine a young girl when her hymen is not perforated?

In most instances, he can perform a satisfactory pelvic examination by inserting a finger into the rectum. Exceptions to this method are stated in the answer to the preceding question.

When is it necessary to operate upon the hymen?

1. For an imperforate hymen

2. At the time of marriage, when a thickened or rigid hymenal ring makes sexual intercourse difficult or impossible

Is hymenotomy always necessary when intercourse is difficult?

No. Most cases of painful intercourse are due to vaginal spasm. This spasm is brought about by tension and fear of sexual relations. By proper advice and instruction, newly married women can overcome many of their fears, thus controlling the spasm.

Is difficulty in breaking the hymen a common occurrence?

No. It is relatively rare.

How soon after hymenotomy can sexual relations be attempted?

About three to four weeks.

Is a hymenotomy always necessary if initial sexual relations prove to be difficult or painful?

No. Very often fear and anxiety can cause spasm of the muscles surrounding the vaginal opening. These reactions can frequently be overcome through proper medical advice and education.

Should a husband use strong force to initiate marital relations?

No. A patient and understanding approach will do more than force in accomplishing necessary relaxation. Such an attitude will also help to prevent emotional and physical distress.

How long is the hospital stay for hymenotomy?

One or two days.

Is stretching of the hymen often a substitute for hymenotomy?

Yes. It is frequently possible to stretch the hymen sufficiently to permit intercourse. This procedure may have to be repeated several times in a gynecologist's office.

Hyperalimentation

Hyperalimentation is a technique employed in the treatment of patients who are markedly undernourished and who must undergo major surgery. It is also used postoperatively for some patients who cannot be fed through the gastrointestinal tract for protracted periods of time. Hyperalimentation has been found helpful in cases where nutrition is difficult to maintain because of substances lost through a fistula of the intestines.

Hyperalimentation involves the giving of huge quantities of calories, minerals, and vitamins directly into the bloodstream by placing a cannula into the subclavian vein in the neck. After its insertion, the cannula (a hollow plastic tube) is attached to bottles of intravenous solutions containing amino acids, glucose, and various essential vitamins and minerals.

QUESTIONS AND ANSWERS

In what diseases is hyperalimentation often used?

In far advanced cancer associated with marked debilitation, in chronic infections where it has been impossible to maintain proper nutritional levels, and in cases where there has been a loss of ingested food and fluids through a fistulous tract. Patients with a fistula of the intestinal tract tend to heal poorly because they cannot maintain adequate nutrition. Hyperalimentation helps these people to attain this state and thus to promote the healing of the fistula.

For how long a period of time can one maintain hyperalimentation?

It can be continued for several weeks, but maximum benefit from hyperalimentation will usually be obtained within the first three or four weeks of the treatment.

Will hyperalimentation tend to promote better wound healing in those who are undernourished?

Yes.

Hyperbaric Chamber

The hyperbaric chamber is a recent addition to the weapons medicine has created in its fight against disease. The chamber, a large air-sealed room, contains gases which are under pressures that are greater than atmospheric pressure. At sea level, the atmospheric pressure is designated as 1 atmosphere; increased pressures are designated as greater than 1. When oxygen is inhaled at pressures that are increased over the normal atmospheric pressure, greater quantities of oxygen pass through the lung cells into the bloodstream. This supersaturation with oxygen of the whole body, including the blood plasma, the red blood cells, the fluid between the cells, and the tissue cells themselves, has proved to be of great value in the treatment of certain medical and surgical conditions.

There is a growing list of disorders in which the hyperbaric chamber has been shown to benefit the patient. Some of these are:

1. Patients with gangrene caused by anaerobic bacteria, including gas gangrene and gangrene caused by tetanus, are benefited because the bacteria can live only in an oxygen-free atmosphere. When in a hyperbaric chamber, receiving oxygen under pressure, the body becomes so saturated with the oxygen that the bacteria die.

2. In certain cases of gangrene where there is badly impaired circulation in the limbs, the hyperbaric chamber has been found helpful in limiting the extent of the gangrenous process. The increased oxygen supply to the limbs through blood vessels narrowed by the disease makes possible the survival of tissue that would otherwise have died from lack of oxygen.

3. Patients with severe ulcerations of the legs or with bedsores have been stimulated to rapid healing by treatment in the hyperbaric chamber.

4. Patients who are suffering from the bends (caisson disease) have been helped immeasurably by hyperbaric chamber treatment. In these cases, the bubbles of gas that have gotten into the tissues are forced back into circulation by treatment under the increased pressure of the hyperbaric chamber.

5. Carbon monoxide poisoning. In this condition, carbon monoxide, instead of oxygen, combines with the hemoglobin in the red blood cells. In the hyperbaric chamber, oxygen under pressure combines with the hemoglobin, and therefore reaches the tissues.

6. In cases of massive coronary thrombosis, with obstruction of circulation to a segment of heart muscle, treatment in the hyperbaric chamber seems to have benefited patients considerably. By receiving oxygen under pressure, less heart muscle is destroyed by the blood clot in the coronary artery.

7. In certain cases of cerebral edema and coma, it has been found that treatment in a hyperbaric chamber causes a reduction of the swelling of the brain.

8. Surgery has been carried out in certain instances in the hyperbaric chamber for heart and blood vessel disorders. It has been found that the supersaturation of the blood with oxygen during these procedures helps the tissues greatly to survive. This is especially important because there may be temporary depletion of oxygen supply to the brain during certain heart and blood vessel operations carried out under normal atmospheric conditions.

9. Hyaline membrane disease (respiratory distress syndrome) is occasionally helped dramatically by placing the newborn child in the hyperbaric chamber.

10. Asphyxia of the newborn.

11. In combination with x-ray treatments for malignant tumors.

See also EMBOLUS AND EMBOLISM.

QUESTIONS AND ANSWERS

How successful is treatment of the above conditions with hyperbaric oxygenation?

In most instances, the patients have been helped tremendously through this new method.

How much of an increase above atmospheric pressure is there in the hyperbaric chamber?

In most instances, the pressure is doubled. In other words, the pressure is 2 atmospheres.

Is the oxygenation carried by the blood plasma as well as that carried by the red blood cells increased when a patient is in the hyperbaric chamber?

Yes. There is a greater amount of oxygen physically in solution in the plasma when one is in the hyperbaric chamber.

Is the increased pressure always limited to 2 atmospheres in cases of gas gangrene?

No. There are some clinics in which oxygen at 3 atmospheres pressure has been used, especially in the treatment of severe infections of gas gangrene.

How high must the atmospheric pressure go in order to treat a case of bends?

In these cases, the pressure in the hyperbaric chamber is raised as much as seven times normal atmospheric pressure.

How greatly can the amount of oxygen in the blood plasma be increased while in the hyperbaric chamber?

It is estimated that by doubling the pressure of inhaled oxygen, the amount of oxygen in the plasma is increased by 16 times.

Is treatment in the hyperbaric chamber helpful to a person who has had an embolus in a blood vessel of a limb?

Yes. It enables the tissues that would ordinarily die rather quickly after lodgment of the embolus to survive until surgery for removal of the embolus can be carried out. The chamber has helped many people who would have required amputation had they not been placed under pressure oxygenation.

Is the hyperbaric chamber helpful to patients who suffer from gas gangrene or tetanus infections?
Yes. There are many types of bacteria, called anaerobes, that cannot survive in the presence of oxygen. Thus, they die when the patient is in the highly oxygenated atmosphere of the chamber. Gas gangrene and tetanus infections fall into this category.

Is placement in the hyperbaric chamber ever helpful in the treatment of cancer?
Recent investigations have shown that while a patient is in a hyperbaric chamber, the effects of some of the anticancer drugs are enhanced. This work is in its experimental stage, so that no absolute conclusions can be drawn at this time.

Is the hyperbaric chamber helpful in the treatment of malignant tumors by x-ray?
It has been thought for some time that lack of oxygen in cancer cells reduces their sensitivity to x-ray radiation. With the increased oxygen saturation obtained in the hyperbaric chamber, these same cancer cells become markedly sensitive to radiation and can then be destroyed more readily.

Is hyperbaric chamber therapy helpful to people who have suffered a stroke due to thrombosis?
Early reports indicate that it can help such people by reducing the edema of the brain and increasing the oxygen supply to damaged brain tissue.

How long can a patient remain in the hyperbaric chamber?
The maximum time appears to be approximately three days. However, most patients are treated by intermit-tent sessions of several hours each in the chamber.

Can any harm result from staying too long in the hyperbaric chamber?
Yes. It is thought that lung damage may follow if a patient is left in the hyperbaric chamber for a period beyond his tolerance. The calculation of the exact time that a patient can tolerate oxygen under pressure must be made by the specialist who supervises the hyperbaric treatments.

Must a patient be decompressed when he emerges from the hyperbaric chamber?
Yes, in much the same way as a diver is decompressed when he emerges from a dive.

Hyperparathyroidism

See PARATHYROID GLANDS.

Hypertension

See BLOOD VESSELS.

Hyperthyroidism

See THYROID GLAND.

Hypoparathyroidism

See PARATHYROID GLANDS.

Hypophysectomy

Hypophysectomy is a term used to describe the surgical removal of the pituitary gland, which lies in the base of the skull. Although the operation is a delicate one and is often complicated by considerable hemorrhage, it can now be carried out without too much risk by trained neurosurgeons. The problem of hypophysectomy has always been a considerable challenge to the neurosurgeon because of the difficulties of removing the entire substance of the gland. As a result, other techniques for destruction of the pituitary gland have been developed. These include x-ray radiation of the gland; the placement of radioactive yttrium seeds within the substance of the pituitary gland; the use of electrocoagulation to destroy the gland substance; and finally, the use of cryosurgical techniques with the employment of the "cold scalpel" to destroy the gland.

See also PITUITARY GLAND.

QUESTIONS AND ANSWERS

What are some of the main indications for hypophysectomy?

There are a good number of indications for removal of the pituitary gland. Among the most common are:

1. Pituitary tumor.

2. Gigantism or acromegaly resulting from marked overactivity of pituitary hormone secretion or due to an actual pituitary tumor.

3. Cushing's syndrome associated with overactivity of the pituitary secretion or with an actual pituitary tumor.

4. In cases of cancer that has spread all over the body, especially breast cancer, it has been found that destruction of the pituitary gland sometimes causes the cancer to recede. It has been found that hypophysectomy in this type of case may prolong life for several months or up to two or three years.

How common are pituitary tumors?

They constitute about 10 percent of all brain tumors.

How does one decide whether to perform a surgical hypophysectomy or to use other means to destroy the gland?

In most cases, attempts are made to destroy the pituitary gland with x-rays, the implantation of radioactive seeds, or the application of cryosurgery. If these attempts fail, then surgical hypophysectomy is indicated.

Is hypophysectomy a dangerous operation?

It is serious but in the hands of a competent neurosurgeon, it is not dangerous. Recovery is the general rule.

Hypoproteinemia

Hypoproteinemia is a term applied to a condition in which there is an abnormally small amount of protein in the plasma of the blood. There are numerous situations in which there can be too little circulating protein in the blood. Some of those most frequently encountered are:

1. Starvation with inadequate intake of protein.

2. Deficient diets in which carbohydrate and fat are ingested but protein is eaten in inadequate quantities.

3. Malabsorption diseases in which an adequate quantity of protein is ingested but is not absorbed through the intestines. In this category, there are a great number of conditions.

4. Upset in metabolism in which sufficient protein is ingested and absorbed, but is not synthesized properly by the liver and other metabolic organs.

5. Conditions in which there is an abnormal loss of protein, as in extensive burns with loss of huge quantities of plasma.

QUESTIONS AND ANSWERS

Is hypoproteinemia a serious deterrent to those who must undergo major surgery?

Yes. People with too little blood protein are poor surgical risks, and postoperative wound healing will be impaired if the hypoproteinemia is severe.

Is it common practice to postpone elective surgery upon people with hypoproteinemia?

Yes, because wound healing will be markedly impaired in these people. Also, they are much more prone to develop postoperative infection and wound disruption.

How does one diagnose hypoproteinemia?

All patients are subjected to blood chemical analysis prior to surgery. This analysis will reveal immediately whether they have adequate supplies of protein in their circulating blood.

What is the treatment for hypoproteinemia in surgical patients?

First of all, elective operations are usually postponed until protein levels approach or reach normal. In order to help bring this about, a high caloric diet rich in protein is advised. If, because of the nature of the illness, the patient is unable to take large amounts of food by mouth, proteins can be given intravenously.

How does one restore protein levels by intravenous injection?

Repeated blood transfusions, infusions of blood plasma, or solutions containing amino acids are given in large quantities. In some cases, hyperalimentation is instituted.

What are some specific dangers of operating upon a patient with severe hypoproteinemia?

1. A suture line along the bowel may leak, thus leading to peritonitis or to the formation of a fistula.

2. The surgical wound may not heal properly, eventuating in wound rupture.

3. Those with hypoproteinemia are prone to postoperative complications such as pneumonia, kidney infections, or overwhelming bloodstream infection.

Will hyperalimentation, the giving of repeated blood transfusions, or the infusion of amino acids always remedy hypoproteinemia?

No. In some patients, especially those who have had a long-standing chronic illness, it is not possible to restore normal levels preoperatively. These patients often can, however, be maintained at a satisfactory level of protein metabolism by carrying out hyperalimentation postoperatively as well as preoperatively.

Hypospadias and Epispadias

Hypospadias is a birth deformity in which the urethra (the tube leading from the urinary bladder through the penis) falls short of its normal point of termination at the tip of the penis. It is present, to a greater or lesser degree, in approximately one of every 200 male births. In this condition, the urethra may end anywhere along the undersurface from the base of the shaft to the base of the head of the organ.

Minor degrees of hypospadias require no treatment, particularly if the child can void standing up and if the penis is not sharply bent when it is erect. Should these symptoms be present, the defect should be repaired.

The operation is a delicate plastic one, best performed before school age.

It is often done in stages, with the first procedure concentrating upon straightening the penis by cutting away constricting bands of fibrous tissue on its undersurface. The second stage, done about a year later, consists of reconstructing the urethral canal so that it terminates at or near the end of the penis. There are quite a few techniques to accomplish this, but all make use of

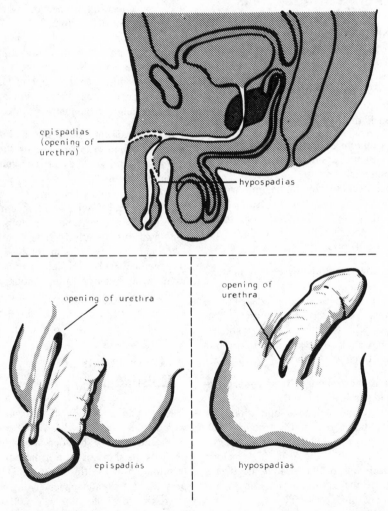

Epispadias and hypospadias are birth deformities of the urethra. These abnormalities can be eliminated by plastic surgery on the penis.

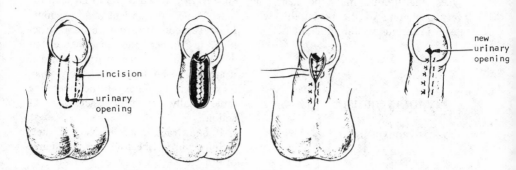

Plastic surgery to correct hypospadias starts with an incision on the underside of the penis (above left) from a point below the urinary opening to the tip of the penis. A tube is rolled from the skin (above center) leading from the urethra to the tip of the penis. The tube is finally sutured as is the incision (above right). The drawing at the right shows the operation completed.

the skin on the undersurface so that it is rolled into a tubular structure. During the healing process, urine is drained either onto the abdomen via a cystostomy or through the perineum by a tube. When the new urethral canal has healed, normal voiding is resumed and the artificial openings close promptly.

None of the various operations for hypospadias give 100 percent satisfactory results. However, reoperation with closure of any leaks that may develop along the line of reconstruction will, in the end, bring about a cure in the overwhelming majority of cases.

Epispadias is a deformity similar to hypospadias except that the urethral opening is on the *upper* surface of the shaft. It is less common but equally important and demands similar reconstructive surgery. An extreme degree of epispadias is one in which the entire urethra is open, the abdominal wall and pubic bones are deficient, and the bladder lies open and bare. This is known as exstrophy of the bladder. This condition requires transplantation of the ureters to the intestinal tract, removal of the bladder, and closure of the abdominal wall and upper surface of the penis.

See also PENIS; URETHRA.

QUESTIONS AND ANSWERS

Will a child grow up to have a normal sex life even if he has had hypospadias or epispadias in infancy?

Yes. If this condition has been corrected, the sperm will be ejaculated in a normal manner from the tip of the penis. These defects have nothing to do with potency or with the formation of live sperm cells by the testicles.

How successful are operations for the cure of hypospadias and epispadias?

Good results are obtained in about 90 percent of the cases. If the first operation is not successful, it is often possible to get a good result by reoperating.

Are there varying degrees of these deformities?

Yes. In certain cases the urethra ends right near the tip of the penis and no symptoms result. In the more severe types, the urethra may end near the very beginning of the penis; this will result in serious voiding difficulties.

Hypothyroidism

See THYROID GLAND.

Hysterectomy

Hysterectomy, in its strict sense, is the term that refers only to the surgical removal of the uterus. It does not refer to removal of ovaries or fallopian tubes, which, in some situations, are removed at the same time. The operation is most often performed through a lower abdominal incision of some four to six inches in length. Some surgeons prefer a longitudinal incision while others prefer to gain abdominal entry through a transverse incision placed just above the pubic hairline.

If the lowermost portion of the uterus (the cervix) is left behind, the operation is called subtotal or supracervical hysterectomy. Today the vast majority of hysterectomies include removal of the cervix (total hysterectomy) in order to eliminate the possibility of its developing a malignancy at some future time.

In some cases, the uterus is removed through the vagina (vaginal hysterectomy). This procedure is not technically feasible or advisable if the uterus is greatly enlarged by tumor or if it is not freely movable because of scars or adhesions.

In operating upon the uterus, a decision must be made whether to leave the ovaries in place or to remove one or both of them. Inflamed or cystic tubes

and ovaries should be removed with the uterus unless the patient is very young. Many surgeons will remove these structures in women past menopause but will leave at least one ovary in place if it appears to be normal and the woman is younger. Findings at the operating table usually dictate the exact course of action.

If one ovary is left in place, hysterectomy will not be followed by change of life.

Hysterectomy, whether or not it is accompanied by removal of the ovaries and tubes, and whether it is performed through an abdominal incision or through the vagina, usually requires a hospital stay of between five to ten days. It is performed in about one and one-half to two hours under spinal or general anesthesia.

See also CERVIX; UTERUS.

QUESTIONS AND ANSWERS

For what reasons is hysterectomy performed?

1. Fibroid tumors: This is by far the most common indication for hysterectomy. However, it must be kept in mind that the mere presence of fibroid tumors without symptoms does not warrant surgery. Intermittent, persistent, or uncontrollable uterine bleeding, severe abdominal pain, a rapidly enlarging mass, a tumor larger than a grapefruit, and continued interference with urine and bowel function are the most frequently encountered indications for hysterectomy.

Fibroids are sometimes the cause of sterility or repeated miscarriages. By x-ray studies of the uterine cavity and tubes (hysterogram), the possible role that fibroids play in these conditions can be determined.

All patients with fibroids ask whether

the tumors will turn into cancer. *Authorities now agree that this takes place very rarely.*

2. Excessive uterine bleeding: There are several causes of persistent uterine bleeding not associated with fibroid tumors which, when not controlled by simpler surgery such as curettage, may require hysterectomy. These conditions include severe menopausal bleeding due to hormonal disturbance and an entity known as adenomyosis. The latter condition is characterized by an increase in the total bleeding surface area of the uterine lining due to an abnormal infolding of this lining into the wall of the uterus.

3. Precancerous conditions: Removal of the lining of the uterus by curettage and microscopic examination may reveal a premalignant (precancerous) appearance. In such cases, hysterectomy with removal of the ovaries and tubes is definitely indicated. Many patients have been spared the formation of true cancer by hysterectomy performed upon them because the pathologist has spotted the presence of premalignant cells. It is one of the most cogent reasons for diagnostic curettage in cases of uterine bleeding during the later menstrual years.

4. Cancer of the uterus: Cancer of the cervix and cancer of the body of the uterus are two separate and distinct diseases. Cancer of the cervix, as mentioned above, if in its early stages, may be treated by an extensive operation called a *radical* hysterectomy. In other cases, cervical cancer is treated by radium and x-ray, or by both radiation and surgery.

Routine cancer detection smears (Papanicolaou smears) are essential for the early detection of cervical cancer and should be done on all adult females each year.

Cancer of the body of the uterus is more commonly found in older women and may give rise to abnormal bleeding in the immediate premenopausal and menopausal years, or it may precipitate sudden uterine bleeding many years after the menopause. Cancer of the body of the uterus is treated by total hysterectomy (often preceded by a short period of radium insertion), with removal of both ovaries and tubes.

As with all cancers, the earlier the detection, the better the chances for complete cure. A very high percentage of patients who are treated for early malignancies of the cervix or body of the uterus are completely cured.

5. Postdelivery hysterectomy: On rare occasions it is necessary to remove the uterus following childbirth. This is done because of life-endangering hemorrhage secondary to a large tear in the uterus or to diseased conditions of the afterbirth. Hysterectomy is also performed occasionally upon a woman who has had several previous cesarean section operations and in whom it is found to be impossible or dangerous to repair the uterus properly.

Can fibroid tumors be removed without removing the uterus?

Yes. This is called a myomectomy. It is carried out only when it is thought that the fibroid tumors are interfering with the patient's becoming pregnant or are causing miscarriages.

What is an abdominal hysterectomy?

Removal of the uterus through a low abdominal incision.

What is a vaginal hysterectomy?

Removal of the uterus through the vagina.

What is a radical hysterectomy?

It is a procedure carried out for cancer of the cervix or uterus. It involves removing all of the pelvic organs along with their surrounding lymph nodes and lymph channels.

Is recovery the general rule after radical hysterectomy?

Yes. Although this is a very extensive operation, the mortality rate for it is very low when performed by an expert in gynecology.

Are the ovaries always removed when a hysterectomy is done?

No. This depends upon the age of the patient, the condition of the ovaries, and the primary reason for doing the hysterectomy. If a malignancy is present, both ovaries are removed.

Can a patient have menstrual periods after hysterectomy?

No.

Does this mean hysterectomy brings on menopause?

Not necessarily. Menopause is caused by decrease or cessation of ovarian function, not by removal of the uterus. Thus, if one or both ovaries are left in place, menopause will not be precipitated despite the fact that menstruation will cease.

Does hysterectomy affect sexual urges or sexual activity?

No. Even if both ovaries are removed, no change in the patient's sexual urges will be produced. In actuality, many patients state that sexual relations are improved after hysterectomy. Discussion with the gynecologist prior to surgery will do much to banish unfounded beliefs and superstitions regarding this subject.

Is hysterectomy a dangerous operation?
No.

How long does it take to perform hysterectomy?

Approximately one to two hours.

What type of anesthesia is used?

Spinal or general anesthesia.

How long is the hospital stay following hysterectomy?

Usually, from five to ten days.

When is the patient allowed out of bed?

Most patients are out of bed the day after surgery.

When can one shower after hysterectomy?

As soon as the wound has healed solidly. Usually within two weeks.

When can one bathe after hysterectomy?

Four weeks.

How soon after hysterectomy may one do the following?

Resume sexual relations:	6 weeks
Do housework:	4–6 weeks
Return to light work:	6 weeks
Resume all activities:	10 weeks

Are there any aftereffects on bowel or urinary function?

It may be difficult to urinate for a few days postoperatively, and for this reason a catheter (rubber tube) is often inserted into the bladder. Also, the bowels will not resume their normal function for the first few days. However, there are no permanent aftereffects on urinary or bowel function.

Ileitis

Ileitis, or, as it is also known, regional ileitis or regional enteritis, is a nonspecific inflammation of that part of the small intestine called the ileum. This disease occurs mainly in young men and women and is characterized by ulceration, abscess formation, and perforations and adhesions of the various loops of intestine to one another. When ileitis progresses, surgery must be performed. One of two operative procedures is usually carried out: either a short-circuiting operation of the diseased loops of bowel so that no food flows along the inflamed area, or removal of the diseased loops of intestine, with implantation of healthy small intestine into the large intestine.

See also INTESTINES.

REGIONAL ILEITIS

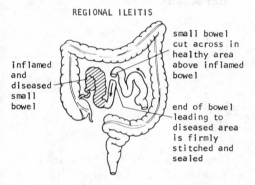

inflamed and diseased small bowel

small bowel cut across in healthy area above inflamed bowel

end of bowel leading to diseased area is firmly stitched and sealed

QUESTIONS AND ANSWERS

What causes ileitis?

Although it is thought that it is caused by a germ, the specific germ producing the inflammation has not been discovered.

Is ileitis usually an acute infection?

It may have an acute onset, but it does tend to become a chronic disease lasting over a period of months or years.

What are the signs and symptoms of this disease?

It may have its onset with acute attacks of lower or midabdominal cramps, several loose stools per day, loss in appetite, and a mild fever. The condition often subsides after a few days but recurs at intervals over a period of weeks. Eventually, the inflammation of the small bowel may cause obstruction

to the passage of stool. There will then be marked abdominal distention, nausea, vomiting, and inability to move the bowels.

Is regional ileitis a common condition?

Yes. It is most often seen in people in their 30s and 40s.

How is the diagnosis of regional ileitis made?

It is usually established by characteristic x-ray findings.

What is the course of this disease?

1. In the mild form, an attack may last just a few days and disappear, never to return again.

2. In the more severe form, there are repeated attacks of fever, abdominal cramps, and loose stools. Eventually, there may be abscess formation within the bowel and small intestinal obstruction.

What is the treatment for regional ileitis?

1. In the milder cases, bed rest, a bland diet excluding spices and alcohol, and the administration of antibiotic drugs. Emphasis is laid upon avoidance of excessive work and emotional strain. Some of the steroid (cortisone) drugs have been found to give remarkable relief in acute cases.

2. When the disease is far advanced, surgical treatment is necessary. This may involve removing the inflamed portion of the small bowel and joining normal bowel above it to the transverse colon (ileotransverse colostomy). In certain cases, the inflamed bowel is not removed, but the normal small intestine above the inflammation is joined to the large bowel, thus bypassing the inflamed bowel. The inflammation subsides in the great majority of cases, because the fecal stream does not course over the inflamed intestine.

Can ileitis be cured by surgery?

Yes. There is a high percentage of cure following surgery. Moreover, if a first attempt to eradicate the disease fails, a second operation will frequently be rewarded by cure.

Is an ileostomy or colostomy (an opening of the small intestine or the large bowel through the abdominal wall) necessary in cases of ileitis?

No. The continuity of the intestinal tract is restored when performing surgery for ileitis.

What is the outlook for recovery in a patient with regional ileitis?

Excellent.

Is there any way to prevent regional ileitis?

Unfortunately, since the cause of this condition is not known, recommendations to avoid it cannot be given.

Is there a type of individual who is more prone to develop regional ileitis?

It is thought that the overworked, fatigued, highly strung individual is more likely to develop this condition. However, well-adjusted people also may develop regional ileitis.

Can one lead a normal life after part of the small bowel has been removed or bypassed?

Yes. There are some 20 feet of small intestine, and less than half its length is necessary for the maintenance of normal intestinal function.

Does regional ileitis, once subsided, have a tendency to recur?

Yes, in a small number of cases.

Does regional ileitis tend to run in families or to be inherited?

No.

Should a special diet be followed after an episode of regional ileitis?

Yes. A bland diet should be followed for a period of months or even years.

Do older people get ileitis as frequently as younger people?

No.

Ileostomy

See CHRONIC ULCERATIVE COLITIS; INTESTINES.

Ileus

Ileus is a term denoting obstruction or paralysis of the small intestine. It is accompanied by severe pains of a colicky nature in the abdomen, abdominal distention, vomiting, and eventually dehydration and a rise in temperature. To overcome ileus, the cause for the obstruction or paralysis must be found and eliminated.

There are several types of ileus; the most frequently encountered are:

1. Adynamic ileus. This is also known as paralysis of the small intestine. It is seen sometimes following a surgical operation upon one of the abdominal organs.

2. Dynamic ileus. This type is secondary to an obstruction of the small intestine.

3. Mechanical ileus. This is seen when an adhesion obstructs the small bowel or when the small bowel is twisted.

4. Meconium ileus. This is the type of intestinal obstruction seen in newborn children and is caused by a thick mass of fecal contents with which the child is born.

See also INTESTINES.

Infection

See ABSCESSES AND INFECTIONS.

Infertility

See STERILITY AND FERTILITY; TUBO-PLASTY.

Ingrown Toenail

Ingrown toenail can be a most troublesome condition, especially since it has a tendency to recur. It involves the big toe much more often than any other toe. In adolescents, a common cause for ingrown toenail is the wearing of poorly fitting, tight shoes and cutting the toenail deeply at the corners.

To avoid ingrown toenail, people should cut their big toenails straight across and should not cut them deeper at the corners.

See also FEET.

QUESTIONS AND ANSWERS

What is an ingrown toenail?

An ingrown toenail is a condition in which the sharp point at the front of the nail grows into the groove in the skin alongside the nail.

Which nail is most frequently involved?

The nail on the big toe.

Do ingrown toenails often affect the other toes?

No, this is quite rare.

At what age are people most likely to get ingrown toenails?

During puberty, when the spurt in growth is particularly rapid.

What causes ingrown toenails?

Some result when the nail is cut too short along the side so that the nail grows into the groove instead of coming up onto the skin surface. In other instances, an ingrown toenail may be caused by shoes that are too small. Children grow very rapidly during puberty and need frequent changes in shoes. There are some other cases in which the cause of the condition cannot be determined.

How should one cut his toenails in order to avoid getting an ingrown toenail?

Toenails should be cut straight across so that the sides of the nail can emerge from the lateral groove in the skin adjacent to the nail.

Do ingrown toenails become infected very often?

Yes. The sharp point of the nail that grows down into the skin groove will almost invariably cause a painful infection.

What is the treatment for an infected ingrown toenail?

1. If there is a marked infection with swelling and redness of the tip of the toe, the patient should soak the toe several times a day in hot water containing either salt or epsom salts.

2. To cure an ingrown toenail, the sharp ingrown portion of nail must be lifted out from its position in the skin groove.

3. After the infection has subsided completely, it may be necessary to perform an operation on the toe to eliminate the possibility of a recurrence.

Should people ever try to lift out an ingrown toenail themselves?

No. This may spread the infection and aggravate the injury.

Can an operation for an ingrown toenail be performed in the surgeon's office?

Yes, but in many instances it is better to put the patient in the hospital for a day and give him a light general anesthesia. In an office, where only a local anesthesia can be given, many people will resist the injection of a local anesthetic agent.

What operative procedure is performed for ingrown toenails?

There are several different procedures, some more radical than others. One of the most common is to split the nail completely from its tip down through the nailbed and to take out the portion that is adjacent to the skin groove. Then the side groove in the skin is completely eliminated, so that when the nail grows in, it will stay above the surface of the skin.

Some surgeons prefer to remove the entire toenail and to cut out both side skin grooves. Without these side skin grooves, it is difficult for a nail to become ingrown.

Is it common for there to be a good deal of bleeding following an operation on an ingrown toenail?

Yes, but this will stop spontaneously after a little while.

How long after an operation on an ingrown toenail can a patient get out of bed?

As soon as the anesthesia has worn off.

Can a person wear ordinary shoes immediately after an operation for an ingrown toenail?

No. He must wear a shoe that has the area for the big toe cut out.

How soon after an operation for an ingrown toenail can a person resume all physical activities?

Perhaps two to three weeks after surgery. The toe is quite sensitive after this operation, and injury to it may cause bleeding and severe pain.

Does the new nail that grows in after an operation for an ingrown toenail sometimes show deformities?

Yes. The accompanying infection of the ingrown toenail, plus the operative procedure for its removal, may result in a permanently deformed toenail.

Is there a tendency for ingrown toenails to recur no matter what operative procedure is performed?

Yes. In approximately one out of five cases, the ingrown toenail will recur.

Is there any way of preventing the recurrence of ingrown toenails?

Yes. Some sterile cotton should be placed underneath the side of the nail as it grows out. This will force the nail to grow out rather than deeply into the skin groove.

Insect Bites and Stings

Everyone, sooner or later, is bitten or stung by some type of insect. Most insect bites are harmless and cause relatively little discomfort. However, if someone is allergic to the sting of an insect, it can be a very serious reaction requiring immediate treatment. Those who are markedly allergic have been known to succumb from the sting of an insect to which they have a marked allergy.

There are innumerable types of insects throughout the world that bite or sting humans, but in this country, stings and bites are seen most often from mosquitoes, sandflies, wasps, hornets, bees, yellow jackets, chiggers, fleas, spiders, and scorpions.

QUESTIONS AND ANSWERS

What can people do to avoid being stung by an insect?

The likelihood of stings can be lessened by taking certain simple precautions:

1. Any sort of food will attract these insects. Outdoor cooking or eating, feeding pets out-of-doors, garbage cans left uncovered, the dribble from a child's popsicle or candy—all will attract insects. Keeping food covered until the moment of disposal, meticulous cleaning about the garbage area, repeated spraying of outdoor recreational areas and garbage cans with insecticides will tend to keep insects away.

2. Gardening should be done cautiously.

3. Since perfumes, hair sprays, hair tonic, suntan lotion, and many other cosmetics attract insects, these substances should not be used. Flowing garments in which insects might become caught, bright colors, flowery prints, and black should be avoided. Light colors, such as white, green, tan and khaki, are thought neither to attract nor to antagonize bees.

4. Shoes should be worn at all times when outdoors except on a hard, sandy beach.

5. Plain common sense will prevent many a sting. Calm, quiet behavior without sudden movements or flailing of arms, avoidance of situations known to attract insects, and keeping a sharp lookout usually will prevent trouble.

What precautions can insect-sensitive people take?

When outdoors, they should always keep with them a kit containing epinephrine (adrenalin) for injection, some antihistamine tablets, and a tourniquet. On being stung, these drugs should be used immediately and a physician should be seen.

Is the skin eruption surrounding an insect's sting or bite an allergic phenomenon?

Yes.

Is it ever necessary to hospitalize an allergic individual who has been bitten by an insect?

Yes, especially if there is no emergency medical kit at hand or if a physician is not available.

Are people ever allergic to the stings of bees, hornets, wasps, or yellow jackets?

Yes.

Can people who are sensitive to insect stings be treated prophylactically?

Yes. They should first be tested with extracts from the insects and then hyposensitized with the appropriate injection material.

Should such hyposensitization be carried out for a person who has other allergic tendencies?

No, not unless he has a known sensitivity to the sting of an insect.

Why do some people seem to be more attractive to insects than others?

It is not the person but his surroundings that will attract insects. A person who is near uncovered garbage cans or where people are cooking or eating food outdoors is apt to be stung. Similarly, if the person uses large amounts of perfume, hair sprays or tonics, suntan lotion, or cosmetics, all of which attract insects, he is apt to be stung.

Once a person becomes allergic to the bite of an insect, will this allergy continue?

Yes, and unfortunately the severity of the allergic response will increase with each future sting.

If someone is allergic to the bite of one insect, will this make him allergic to the stings of other insects as well?

Usually if a person is sensitive to bee stings he may be sensitive also to the stings of hornets, wasps, and yellow jackets. If he is sensitive to this group of insects, he does not necessarily have to be sensitive to the bites or stings of other insects.

Can an insect sting ever be fatal?

Yes. Highly allergic people have been known to die after being stung by a bee, hornet, wasp, or yellow jacket. Fortunately, this is an extremely rare occurrence.

Are bites and stings dangerous from such insects as fleas, sandflies or mosquitoes, wasps, hornets, bees, or chiggers?

Bites or stings from these insects are usually not serious.

What is the first aid treatment for insect stings and bites?

1. If a stinger (bee, wasp, etc.) has been left in place, pluck it out. Do so gently, in order to avoid breaking the stinger.

2. If a great deal of swelling is present, this indicates a marked sensitivity to the bite poison. In such cases, place a tourniquet above the bite area so that the poison will be more slowly absorbed.

3. If the bite is caused by an insect that burrows under the skin, such as a chigger, or by one that attaches itself to the skin, such as a tick, wash the area thoroughly with soap and water. A drop or two or turpentine may dislodge a tick or kill a chigger. Cover with Vaseline so that the insect cannot breathe.

4. Antiallergic (antihistamine) medications may be prescribed by your physician to reduce the swelling and itching.

5. Do *not* scratch a bite area, as that may lead to greater absorption of the poison or to infection.

What is the first aid treatment for a black widow spider bite?

1. It should be treated just like a snake bite, by making a crossed incision over the bite and sucking out the poison.

2. A tourniquet should be applied above the bite just tight enough to cut off the return circulation. The pulse should still be obtainable.

3. Medical consultation should be sought quickly, as there are counteracting medications to the bite of a black widow spider.

4. Physical exertion should be avoided as much as possible.

What should be done for the bite of other spiders, poisonous centipedes, scorpions, or tarantulas?

These should be treated similarly to a black widow spider bite.

Are the bites or stings of centipedes, scorpions, or tarantulas very serious?

Usually not. The only time a bite or a sting from these insects endangers life is when it happens to a young infant or when the bite is on the face or neck. However, bites or stings from these insects may produce severe temporary symptoms and great discomfort.

Intensive Care Unit

The intensive care unit (ICU) is a special facility set up by most hospitals today in order to care for the desperately and critically sick. It has equipment to treat any possible emergency and is staffed by specially trained nurses and physicians.

QUESTIONS AND ANSWERS

What is an intensive care unit?

It is a highly organized section of a hospital, with anywhere from 4 to 12 beds, depending upon the size of the hospital. The unit, known as an ICU, is equipped with every known device for the emergency care, as well as continuing care, of critically ill patients.

What equipment is usually contained in the ICU?

Oxygen and other gases, intravenous fluids and medications for every kind of emergency, blood and transfusion equipment, special instruments for any emergency surgical procedures such as tracheotomy or for the control of hemorrhage, rubber and plastic tubes for passage into the trachea to establish an adequate airway, equipment for cardiac resuscitation, electrocardiographs that monitor heart action on a 24-hour basis, a cardiac pacemaker to keep a failing heart beating, and other such devices.

How is an ICU staffed?

Perhaps more important than the equipment in the ICU is the nursing and medical personnel who staff it. All ICU personnel are specially trained to meet the various emergencies that might arise. Nurses in the ICU know how to give intravenous medications; how to support a failing heart; how to give cardiac massage and artificial respiration; how to handle severe hemorrhage and respiratory obstruction.

The intern and resident staff assigned to supervise the ICU are also given special instructions on how to treat critical situations that demand immediate lifesaving attention.

Do all hospitals have intensive care units?

Practically every accredited hospital has now established this type of facility.

Has the ICU resulted in the saving of many lives?

It is estimated that many thousands of lives that would otherwise have been lost have been saved by admission of patients to ICUs. Hospitals are now reporting that the salvage rate of patients with acute coronary thrombosis has more than doubled since the institution of intensive care units.

Do some hospitals have special ICUs devoted exclusively to the care of patients who have suffered heart attacks?

Yes. These are called coronary intensive care units.

How long is a patient kept in an ICU?

Until the critical stage of his illness has passed. This may be a matter of only a few hours, or may be for a period of several weeks.

Intermittent Claudication

Intermittent claudication is a condition in which there is severe, cramplike pain in the muscles of the legs on walking or exercise. The pain is relieved within a minute or two on complete rest. Claudication is seen in association with with hardening of the arteries of the legs.

See also CLAUDICATION.

Intestinal Obstruction

Obstruction of the small intestine is often brought on by the mechanical block created by adhesions from a former operation. Such adhesions, caused by previous inflammation within the abdominal cavity, consist of strands of tissue that press upon loops of the small bowel and twist and obstruct them. An obstructed segment of small intestine will not permit passage of food and will lead to marked distention, vomiting, dehydration, and eventually a dangerously toxic state. Failure to relieve the obstruction may also result in rupture of the distended bowel, with subsequent peritonitis and death. People who have undergone operations upon the appendix or the uterus, fallopian tubes, and ovaries are most prone to develop adhesions which cause obstructions of the small intestine. Although such an occurrence may take place in only one of several hundred abdominal operations, nevertheless it presents a serious problem when it does take place. Small bowel obstructions of this type may come on anytime from a few days to many years after an operation.

Acute large intestinal obstruction is one of the commonest and most serious of all surgical conditions within the abdomen. In the broad sense, any interference with the progressive advance of the intestinal contents through the large bowel constitutes obstruction. This in-terference is caused, in many instances, by a tumor within the bowel which has grown to sufficient size to block the passage of stool or gas. Less often, a tumor growing outside the bowel will compress it sufficiently to produce obstruction. The second most frequent cause of obstruction is the formation of adhesions in the abdominal cavity which twist and distort the bowel so as to shut off the progress of the stool. Also, in occasional cases, diverticulitis or a foreign body within the bowel may cause obstruction.

The symptoms of obstruction are colicky abdominal pains, inability to pass gas or move the bowels, vomiting, and progressive distention of the abdomen. As the obstruction continues, the patient vomits more and more of his intestinal contents until eventually he may vomit fecal-like material. If this situation remains untreated, a gravely toxic condition develops which will result in death within a few days. The higher the site of obstruction within the abdomen, the more acute are the symptoms. Obstruction in the descending colon, the sigmoid colon, or near the rectum is usually longer in developing and symptoms come on more slowly than obstruction on the right side of the bowel.

Treatment is directed toward immediate relief of the obstruction before the patient is overwhelmed by the absorption of poisons from the stagnant intestinal contents or before the bowel bursts from overdistention. This sequence of events can take place within a day or two if surgery is not performed promptly.

The object of surgery in acute cases is to relieve the obstruction whether or not the underlying cause is removed. Frequently a loop of distended bowel above the point of obstruction is brought out onto the abdominal wall and opened without any attempt at the time to discover the disease process causing the obstruction. This procedure is called a colostomy and is done in such cases as a lifesaving measure.

If the obstruction is on the right side of the large bowel, a cecostomy is performed.

If the obstruction is on the left side of the large bowel, a transverse colostomy is usually performed.

If, at operation, an adhesion is discovered as the provoking cause of the obstruction, such an adhesion is cut and a colostomy may not have to be performed.

It is rarely safe to remove a tumor during a time when the bowel is overdistended and acutely obstructed. If such a procedure is attempted, death may result from peritonitis due to leakage about the line of sutures in the greatly distended bowel.

The safest approach is to make a vent in the distended bowel (colostomy) and to allow the distention and inflammatory reactions to subside. Then, several days to several weeks later, when the patient has been thoroughly studied by x-rays, an operation can be undertaken to remove the underlying cause of the obstruction. The colostomy is then closed at a third operation performed several weeks thereafter. When the offending cause of the obstruction has been removed, closure of the colostomy is a safe and simple procedure.

See also INTESTINES.

QUESTIONS AND ANSWERS

Does obstruction of the small intestine only follow a previous operation?

It often does, but other conditions can produce it, too. A tumor sometimes ob-structs the bowel. Infection within the abdominal cavity usually causes adhesions to develop and these may eventually produce obstruction. Small intestine within a hernia sometimes becomes obstructed, and a large gallstone occasionally will cause obstruction. Occasionally, torsion twisting may produce obstruction.

What are the commonest causes of obstruction of the small intestine?

1. Bands of adhesions
2. A loop of bowel getting caught in a hernial sac

Is there any way to prevent the formation of adhesions?

No. However, the more gently tissues are handled during surgery, the fewer adhesions will form. Despite careful operative technique, there is an unfortunate group of people who have an extraordinary tendency toward the formation of adhesions.

Is an operation for intestinal obstruction serious?

Yes. However, most people recover rather quickly except when peritonitis has developed or when the obstruction has been present for several days prior to surgery.

Does intestinal obstruction ever recur after surgery?

Occasionally, if new adhesions form and they create pressure upon the bowel. This happens, fortunately, in a very small percentage of cases.

Does small bowel obstruction ever get better without surgery?

Only when the obstruction is partial.

How is partial obstruction treated medically?

By passage of a rubber tube through the nose or mouth into the stomach and small intestine. The fluid and gaseous distention is then relieved by suction through the tube. Frequently, by collapsing the bowel in this manner, the pressure from the adhesion is released.

How long should one wait with intestinal obstruction before going to the hospital?

Intestinal obstruction is a serious condition demanding immediate hospitalization. The decision whether surgery is required will usually be made within 24 hours after hospital admission.

What will happen if an operation is not performed?

1. If the underlying condition is complete intestinal obstruction, death will occur within a few days.

2. If the intestine has ruptured or been perforated, death from peritonitis will take place within a few days.

3. If the underlying disease is a malignant tumor, death will occur in several months.

4. If the disorder is a benign cyst or tumor, symptoms may continue without change for many months or years until a time is reached when the growths will produce intestinal obstruction or severe hemorrhage. Occasionally the benign tumors will turn into cancerous growths.

5. Although some cases of regional ileitis do respond to medical management alone, most will terminate in perforation, abscess formation, and an obstruction if not operated upon.

6. Today, typhoid fever and tuberculosis of the intestinal tract are treated medically unless perforation develops.

What are the commonest causes of large bowel obstruction?

1. A tumor growing within the bowel

2. A tumor growing outside the bowel but creating pressure upon the passageway

3. Diverticulitis

4. A twist of the large bowel (volvulus)

5. Telescoping of the small bowel into the large bowel in children (intussusception)

6. Adhesions creating pressure on the bowel

What are the symptoms of intestinal obstruction?

1. Colicky abdominal pains

2. Distention of the abdomen

3. Increasing constipation

4. Progressive vomiting

5. Complete inability to move the bowels or pass gas

Is obstruction always complete?

No. Partial obstruction usually comes on first. This is evidenced by increasing constipation. Obstruction is complete when neither gas nor stool can be passed.

What will happen if the obstruction is not relieved?

The abdomen will become greatly distended; vomiting becomes progressive until finally fecal-like material may be regurgitated. Chemical balance is upset from loss of intestinal juices and death may ensue from these changes. Or the distended bowel above the point of obstruction may rupture, and a rapidly fatal peritonitis may set in.

Is large bowel obstruction ever relieved without surgery?

Yes, if it has been produced by a kink, such as in volvulus, or by telescoping of the bowel, or if pressure upon the bowel is released spontaneously. This occurs infrequently, however.

Does large bowel obstruction come back after it is once relieved?

No. Once relieved, it practically never recurs.

What operations are done for large bowel obstruction?

1. A direct attack on the cause of

obstruction. This would entail cutting an adhesion or relieving a kink or removing a tumor. This form of surgery is usually reserved for the early cases or for those in which the obstruction is not complete.

2. An indirect approach with the relief of obstruction by making an artificial opening (colostomy) in the distended bowel above the point of obstruction. Then, at a later date, when the patient's general condition has improved, a second operation is performed to remove the underlying cause of the obstruction. Often, a third operation is necessary, weeks or months later, to close the artificial opening performed at the first operation.

Intestines

THE SMALL INTESTINE

The small intestine is approximately 20 feet long and is composed of that portion of the intestinal tract which extends from the exit of the stomach to the entrance to the large bowel. There are *three portions:* the first 8 to 10 inches beyond the stomach, called the *duodenum;* the second portion, approximately 8 feet long, termed the *jejunum;* and the last 11 feet, named the *ileum.* It is within these coils of intestine that most of the digestion and absorption of food take place.

The duodenum is the most frequent site for ulcer formation. Its anatomy and surgery are so intimately associated with the stomach that it has been discussed in the section STOMACH AND DUODENUM.

The jejunum and ileum, usually referred to as the small bowel, are remarkably free from disease. In the days before water purification and milk pasteurization, typhoid fever and tuber-culosis were common infections in this part of the intestinal tract, but today these diseases are seldom encountered. Although fat or muscle tumors and benign cysts do arise in the small intestine, they are not seen very often. But more important is the startling fact that malignant growths such as cancer and sarcoma, for some unknown reason, only rarely attack this area of the body.

The following are conditions of the small intestine requiring surgery:

1. **Regional ileitis,** a nonspecific inflammation of the small intestine, occurs quite frequently, mainly in young men and women. This disease is characterized by ulceration, abscess formation, and small perforations and adhesions of the various loops of ileum to one another. When this condition progresses, surgery must be performed. One of two procedures will be carried out; either a short-circuiting operation of the diseased loops of bowel so that no food flows along the inflamed area, or removal of the diseased loops, with implantation of healthy small intestine into the large intestine. (*See also* ILEITIS.)

2. **Intestinal obstruction:** A great number of the operations which are being done upon the small intestine are necessitated by this rather common disturbance. It is most often brought on by the mechanical block created by adhesions from a former operation. Such adhesions, caused by previous inflammation within the abdominal cavity, consist of strands of tissue which press upon loops of small bowel and may twist and obstruct them. An obstructed segment of bowel will not permit passage of food and will lead to marked distention, vomiting, dehydration, and eventually to a dangerously toxic state. Failure to relieve the obstruction may also result in rupture of the distended bowel, with subsequent peritonitis and death.

People who have undergone operations upon the appendix or the uterus, tubes, and ovaries are most prone toward the development of the adhesions which cause obstruction. Whereas such an occurrence may take place in only one of several hundred abdominal operations, nevertheless it presents a serious problem to the surgeon. This condition is treacherous in that it may come on anywhere from a few days to many years after an operation.

3. Strangulation of the small bowel is often seen when a loop becomes caught in the sac of a hernia (rupture). This condition is quite common and demands immediate surgery, as strangulation of the bowel will terminate in gangrene and rupture if not relieved within a matter of hours.

4. A perforation in the small bowel will lead to spillage of intestinal contents into the general abdominal cavity with the development of the severest kind of peritonitis. The same bacteria that aid so greatly in the digestion of food while inside the intestine, upon entrance into the abdominal cavity will become markedly toxic and will cause an overwhelming infection and death if not combated promptly. Gunshot or stab wounds or automobile accidents in which sharp objects have been driven into the abdomen must be submitted to immediate operation. On rare occasions, a swallowed fishbone or needle may cause a perforation in the small bowel, and this, too, will require surgical intervention.

Operative procedures performed for the various conditions of the small bowel consist of either bypassing the involved area or removing it, and in lesser conditions, simple repair with sutures. Surgeons do not hesitate to remove irreparably diseased loops of small intestine. Less than half the total length of the small bowel is necessary for the

continuation of normal digestive processes. It is usually not too complicated a surgical maneuver to remove the involved intestine and to stitch together the loops above and below the diseased area.

Surgical procedures for the correction of conditions of the small intestine are as follows:

1. Advanced inflammation of the small intestine (*regional ileitis, tuberculosis of intestine, etc.*): When it is certain that the infection will not subside with medical management, one of two operations is performed:

a) Removal of all the diseased loops of small bowel, with implantation of a healthy loop of small intestine above the inflamed area into the large bowel in the region of the transverse colon.

b) Nonremoval of the diseased loops, but short-circuiting them by taking a healthy loop above the area and implanting it into the large bowel in the region of the transverse colon. This operation is called an *ileotransverse colostomy*. (See illustration.)

By short-circuiting the diseased region so that no food flows through it, cure of the infection is obtained in the vast majority of cases.

2. For benign or malignant cysts or tumors: Removal of the involved loops with end-to-end or side-to-side suturing

ILEO TRANSVERSE COLOSTOMY

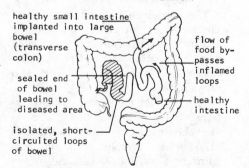

healthy small intestine implanted into large bowel (transverse colon)

sealed end of bowel leading to diseased area

isolated, short-circuited loops of bowel

flow of food by-passes inflamed loops

healthy intestine

(anastomosis) of normal intestine. (See illustration.)

3. For intestinal obstruction due to adhesions: When obstruction without damage to the circulation of the bowel occurs, the mere cutting of the adhesions will be sufficient to obtain a cure.

When circulation to a segment of bowel has been damaged beyond repair, it is necessary to remove it. The operating surgeon will often relieve the obstruction and pressure on the circulation and then watch the involved loop for several minutes, or as long as one-half hour, to give it a chance to return to normal.

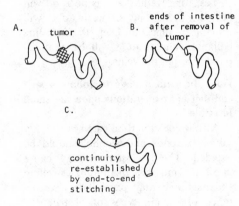

A. tumor

B. ends of intestine after removal of tumor

C. continuity re-established by end-to-end stitching

4. For strangulated bowel: When prolonged strangulation by an adhesion or by the bowel being caught in a hernial sac has produced irreversible circulatory changes or gangrene of the wall, such a segment must be removed. The healthy segments of bowel above and below the area are then sutured (anastomosed) to one another.

5. For perforation of small intestine: When a hole exists in the bowel, no matter whether it originates from the perforation of an ulcer or from a gunshot or stab wound or any other cause, it must be repaired immediately. Failure to do so will result in peritonitis and probable death. Tears in the small bowel are repaired by simple stitching. Care must be taken in sewing up holes not to narrow the diameter of the bowel or obstruction may ensue. All surgeons, particularly those who have done war surgery, are aware of the need for a meticulous search for holes in the small bowel. A tiny entrance wound on the skin of the abdomen may be the only external evidence of injury, and yet eight to ten perforations in the small bowel may be found on surgical exploration of the abdominal cavity.

What is regional ileitis?

A serious infection of the small bowel. Its origin is unknown and the specific germ that causes it has not been discovered. It tends to become a chronic disease and will eventually lead to ulceration, abscess formation, and perforation of the small bowel.

Are cures obtained in regional ileitis?

Yes. There is a high percentage of cure following surgery. Furthermore, should a first attempt to eradicate the disease fail, a second operation, with removal of the diseased bowel, will frequently be followed by cure.

Approximately how long a hospital stay is necessary for the following surgery:

Intestinal perforations? 2 to 6 weeks

Intestinal obstruction? 10 days to 4 weeks

Strangulation with intestinal removal? 10 days to 4 weeks

Benign cysts, benign or malignant tumors? 10 days to 3 weeks

Regional ileitis? Indefinite; anywhere from 2 weeks to 3 months

What will happen if operation is not performed?

1. If the underlying condition is *complete intestinal obstruction,* death will occur within a few days.

2. If the intestine has *ruptured* or

been *perforated,* death from peritonitis will take place within a few days.

3. If the underlying disease is a *malignant* tumor, death will occur in several months.

4. If the disorder is a *benign* cyst or tumor, symptoms may continue without change for many months or years until a time is reached when the growths will produce intestinal obstruction or severe hemorrhage. Occasionally the benign tumors will turn into cancerous growths.

5. Although some cases of *regional ileitis* do respond to medical management alone, most will terminate in perforation, abscess formation, and obstruction if not operated upon.

6. Today *typhoid fever* and *tuberculosis of the intestinal tract* are treated medically *unless* perforation develops.

Are special hospital preparations necessary before operating upon the small intestine?

Yes. Every attempt should be made to deflate distended bowel before surgery. This is done by the passage of stomach tubes. Every attempt must be made to reestablish chemical balance by the giving of fluids and other substances intravenously.

What type of anesthesia is advised in operations upon the small intestine?

Most often, spinal. Less often, general.

How long do these operations take to perform?

Anywhere from one to three hours, depending upon the findings within the abdomen.

Can cures be obtained in operations for malignant tumors of the small intestine?

Yes, provided that the cases are diagnosed at an early stage.

Are blood transfusions necessary?

In many of the small intestinal disturbances requiring surgery, blood will benefit the patient greatly.

Where is the usual site of incision?

Usually just to the left or right of the navel, extending for a distance of two to three inches above and below this structure.

Are special nurses necessary after operations of this type?

Whenever the patient can afford it, special nurses should be employed for two to four days after surgery.

Is the postoperative period uncomfortable?

Yes, for several days, as no food will be permitted. The stomach tube will remain in place to keep the intestine collapsed and feeding will be administered through the veins.

Does the patient have to follow a special diet after operations upon the small intestine?

A full diet should be eaten but highly seasoned foods and alcohol should be avoided. These substances may cause intestinal mucous membrane swelling (edema) and may precipitate a recurrence of certain types of obstruction. Spicy foods and alcohol are also poor fare for regional ileitis or other intestinal disorders.

How soon after surgery can the patient get out of bed?

If the patient has been very sick, the surgeon may want to keep him in bed for several days. If distention has subsided and normal bowel function has returned, the patient may be permitted to get out of bed on the first postoperative day.

How soon after operation can one bathe?

As soon as the wound is healed.

How long do the wounds take to heal?

Approximately two weeks.

Is convalescent care necessary?

If the patient has suffered from regional ileitis, or peritonitis, or has had several loops of bowel removed, then convalescent care for two to three weeks will probably be required and will certainly be most beneficial.

Can one live normally after part of the small intestine has been removed?

Yes. Less than half the 20 feet is necessary for normal living.

How often after surgery should one be rechecked by his physician?

About once every four months.

How soon after successful surgery can the patient return to work?

In approximately six to ten weeks, depending upon the severity of the operation.

THE LARGE INTESTINE

People spend more time in trying to regulate their bowels and are more concerned about the variations in function of this part of their body than perhaps any other. Peculiarly, emotional upsets, periods of physical and mental strain, and nervous tensions seem to influence intestinal function markedly. Many people attribute their well-being or unhappiness to the particular state of their bowel function and feel that they are slaves to its caprices. There is some justification to these attitudes, since diseases of the large intestine are so widespread and are almost always accompanied by change in bowel habit. It is safe to surmise that many serious illnesses could be avoided, and many lives saved, if people sought medical help when first they noticed rectal bleeding or an upset in their usual bowel function. However, all too often people ignore these significant symptoms until

the underlying disease has reached an advanced state.

The large intestine, also called the *colon* or *large bowel,* is composed of the final five to seven feet of the intestinal tract. It originates in the right lower part of the abdomen at the cecum, where the small intestine terminates. The large intestine courses up the right side of the abdomen for about 1 to 1½ feet in a part called the *ascending colon.* At this point (the hepatic flexure), close to the liver under the ribs, it makes a turn to the left and crosses to the left upper portion of the abdomen. This segment is 2 to 2½ feet long and is named the *transverse colon.* At a point near the spleen (the splenic flexure), under the ribs on the left side, it turns and courses down the left side of the abdomen to the pelvis. This portion is called the *descending colon* and is approximately 2 to 2½ feet long. An S-shaped loop of the descending colon is found just before it forms the rectum. This S-shaped segment is called the *sigmoid colon.* The rectum is about 8 to 10 inches long and is located within the pelvis behind the urinary bladder. Its final two inches comprise the *anal region.*

The large bowel not only is subject to many inflammatory conditions but is one of the commonest regions in which cancer develops. It is also afflicted with certain deformities, present since birth, which cause great difficulty later in life. Its extremely thin walls and solid stool contents make it particularly vulnerable to ulceration and rupture. Many of these conditions respond well to surgery, and it is fortunate indeed that people can live comfortably even after large segments of the bowel have been removed. Diseases of the appendix and rectum have been discussed in other sections and will therefore be omitted here.

INFLAMMATORY DISEASES
OF THE LARGE BOWEL

1. Chronic ulcerative colitis is a very serious inflammatory disease of the large bowel, sometimes involving the small bowel. It is accompanied by bouts of fever, bloody diarrhea, weakness, and a characteristic set of generalized symptoms, including joint aches and pains, and sometimes by infections or inflammations around the anus. (*See also* CHRONIC ULCERATIVE COLITIS.)

2. Amebic and bacillary dysentery are infections of the large intestine caused by specific bacteria. Although these infestations tend to be chronic, most patients can now be cured by giving intensive treatment with some of the newly discovered drugs. Surgery is required in these conditions only as an emergency measure when an ulcer ruptures through the wall of the bowel or when intestinal obstruction results from the scar tissue of healing ulcerations. Luckily, these complications are quite rare.

3. Tuberculosis and syphilis of the colon were encountered rather frequently 30 to 40 years ago. Since improved milk pasteurization, tuberculous colitis has become a medical rarity in this country; and with intensive treatment for early syphilis now the rule, invasion of the large intestine with this germ is exceedingly uncommon. When these conditions do occur, surgery is required only in the rare instance when rupture of an ulceration takes place or when obstruction of the bowel due to scarring sets in.

4. Lymphopathia venereum is a chronic infection of the rectum and anal regions which often leads to abscess formation, chronic discharge of pus, and ultimate constriction and obstruction of the lower bowel or anal region. Many cases can now be cured

through medication, but on occasion complete healing will take place only when the bowel is put at complete rest by short-circuiting the flow of stool. An artificial opening of the large bowel (colostomy) above the diseased region is therefore performed in such cases. The colostomy is closed months later when the infection has been cured by medical management.

What is ulcerative colitis?

It is a chronic infection of the large bowel caused by bacteria. It is characterized by bloody stools, diarrhea, fever, weight loss, anemia, and great weakness. It tends to affect young people in their 20s, 30s, and 40s. It may involve only the rectum and lower bowel, or the ulcerative process may extend throughout the entire length of the large bowel, and in rare instances may spread to the small intestine.

What causes ulcerative colitis?

In all probability a specific germ, but its exact recognition still escapes the medical profession. It seems to affect people of exceptionally nervous temperaments.

Does ulcerative colitis always require surgery?

No. Somewhere between 50 to 70 percent of sufferers can be carried along on medical treatment alone.

What kind of operations are performed for this condition?

1. An ileostomy, or artificial opening of the small intestine upon the abdominal wall, is usually done as a preliminary procedure.

2. Total removal of the large bowel (complete colectomy) is carried out in those patients who are not cured by simple ileostomy.

3. In a small number of cases, the terminal 4 or 5 inches of rectum is preserved and is sutured to the ileum. This procedure can be done only when the rectum is free of the ulcerative process. Of course, all diseased large bowel is removed before hooking up the ileum to the rectum.

Are these operations serious?

Yes, but operative recovery takes place in more than 95 percent when only ileostomy is necessary and in more than 90 percent of those upon whom ileostomy plus total large bowel removal must be performed.

What happens if advice to be operated is not followed?

In the 25 percent of cases where surgical treatment is essential, death from overwhelming toxemia will result if surgery is not performed.

How does the surgeon decide whether to leave in the diseased bowel or remove it?

If the ulcerated area involves most of the large bowel, has been in existence for several years, and has failed to respond to energetic medical treatment, the surgeon will probably decide to remove it. Otherwise, the patient may be given the chance to heal the ulcers and an ileostomy only will be done.

What are the chances of cure from surgery?

Excellent, unless surgery has been done too late in the course of the illness. More than 90 percent of those upon whom either ileostomy alone or ileostomy plus bowel removal has been carried out will return to normal activity.

Does ulcerative colitis, if untreated, ever turn into cancer?

Yes. The large bowel afflicted over a period of years with ulcerative colitis is much more likely to develop cancer than the normal bowel.

What is an ileostomy?

An artificial opening of the small intestine on the abdominal wall.

What takes the place of the large bowel if it is removed?

The small intestine, after a period of several months, satisfactorily takes over all the functions of the large bowel.

How long after operation does the artificial opening begin to function?

With improved methods of ileostomy, intestinal function is resumed within a matter of hours after surgery.

How soon can a patient get out of bed after surgery?

Within one to three days if the general condition is satisfactory.

Are special nurses required postoperatively?

Yes, when the patient can afford them.

Are special postoperative measures necessary?

Yes:

1. The patient will receive nothing by mouth for a few days and will receive nourishment and vitamins through intravenous injections.

2. A rubber tube will be inserted into the stomach through the nose in order to keep the abdomen from becoming distended with gas.

3. Antibiotic drugs are usually given to combat postoperative infection.

4. Blood may be given to support the heart and blood pressure.

How long does it take to learn to control an ileostomy?

Several weeks. Most patients develop their own special techniques and learn to control them with ease.

Are the stools through an ileostomy liquid or solid?

For the first several weeks or months

they are liquid. Thereafter the stool becomes semisolid.

Does bleeding take place from the ileostomy opening?

Yes. From time to time slight bleeding or oozing of pink serum issues from the ileostomy opening. This is not serious and usually disappears after the mucous membrane of the opening becomes accustomed to its new anatomical position on the abdominal wall.

Can the ileostomy be closed and the intestinal tract be reestablished?

Yes, but only in a small percentage of the cases. Complete and total healing of the ulcerated large bowel must be proved beyond doubt before the ileostomy is closed and the bowel passageway reestablished.

Are special preparations necessary before operation?

Yes:

1. A low-residue diet is taken for several days preoperatively.

2. High vitamin intake is administered in the form of pills or injections.

3. Blood transfusions are given if marked anemia is present.

4. Large doses of sulfa and antibiotic drugs are given to sterilize the bowel contents before surgery.

What type of anesthesia is used?

Either spinal or general, depending on the general condition of the patient at the time of operation.

Are blood transfusions necessary?

Yes, usually.

Where is the incision made for ileostomy?

In the right lower portion of the abdomen.

Where is the incision made for bowel removal?

Longitudinally, near the midline of the abdomen.

How long does it take to perform an ileostomy?

Approximately three-quarters to one hour.

What is the average hospital stay after ileostomy?

If the patient is in the acute phase of ulcerative colitis and is running high temperatures, a hospital stay of several weeks may be required.

If the ileostomy has been done during a quiet interval period, then a stay of 10 to 14 days is all that may be necessary.

Is postoperative convalescent care necessary?

In acute cases, such care is essential for several weeks or months. No convalescent care is needed for those operated upon during a quiet interval period.

What care of the ileostomy is necessary?

1. It should be sponged off regularly with plain warm soap and water.

2. The skin about the opening should be kept clean.

3. A good-fitting ileostomy bag should be obtained.

4. Certain bulk-forming medications are sometimes taken if the stool is too liquid.

When can one bathe?

As soon as the abdominal wound has healed. In those not acutely ill, within two weeks.

Does it matter if the ileostomy opening gets wet?

No!

Can patients eat everything after ileostomy?

Yes, but highly seasoned and spicy foods should be avoided. Alcohol should also be avoided, except in small amounts.

Can the patient return to work with an ileostomy?

Yes.

Can a patient live a normal life with an ileostomy?

Yes. However, he must spend several weeks learning to care for it. An airtight bag over the opening is used to effectively seal off leakage and odors.

Does an ileostomy interfere with one's sexual life?

No. After learning control, an artificial opening will in no way interfere with one's sexual life.

Is length of life affected by ulcerative colitis?

If cure has been obtained through surgery or by medical means, these people will live as long as unaffected people.

MECHANICAL CONDITIONS OF THE LARGE BOWEL

1. *See* INTESTINAL OBSTRUCTION.

2. **Foreign bodies:** It is astonishing to see some of the bizarre foreign bodies that people take into their mouths and swallow. Adults, as well as children, swallow fish bones, chicken bones, pins, needles, screws, coins, paper clips, toothpicks, and many other odd indigestibles. Some are taken accidentally by normal people, while others are swallowed by psychotics or perverts. By some peculiar miracle, most of these objects pass harmlessly through and out the entire length of the intestinal tract. Occasionally a pin or nail or fish bone will get stuck in the wall of the bowel and will puncture it. When this occurs, a leakage of stool will take place into the abdominal cavity and peritonitis will develop. Such an eventuality will demand immediate operation, with removal of the foreign body, closure of the hole in the bowel wall, and drainage of the abdominal cavity. In former years, perforation by a foreign body carried with it an extremely high mortality. Today, thanks to the antibiotic drugs and improved surgical techniques, death in these conditions is the exception and not the rule.

3. **Volvulus or torsion** is a condition in which the bowel twists on itself, shuts off its own blood supply, and causes intestinal obstruction. It occurs most frequently in the sigmoid colon and is seen mostly in middle- or old-aged people. (See illustration.) The sigmoid colon

VOLVULUS OF LARGE BOWEL

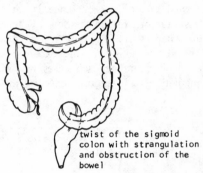

twist of the sigmoid colon with strangulation and obstruction of the bowel

is particularly movable and is suspended by long attachments (the mesentery) which permit it to twist and become entangled.

Volvulus is a dangerous condition because it leads very often to a complete shutting off of blood supply to the bowel and consequent gangrene. Immediate surgery is necessary. The bowel is untwisted and removal of a segment is carried out if gangrene has developed. If the circulation returns satisfactorily, no bowel removal is necessary, as the mere untwisting will cure the condition. Fortunately, volvulus practically never recurs after surgery. The mortality in these cases is high because the diagnosis is usually made late, when gangrene has already set in.

4. Intussusception is a condition in which the small intestine (ileum) telescopes into the large intestine (cecum and ascending colon) in the right lower part of the abdomen. (See illustration.) Such a situation produces obstruction of the bowel. It is seen almost exclusively in children under 3 years of age.

When intussusception occurs, the child suffers colicky pains, vomiting, the passage of blood and mucus by rectum, and a lump can be felt in the abdomen at the site of the telescoping. As soon as the diagnosis is made, operation is performed. By gentle pulling, the small intestine can be taken out of its abnormal position. Recurrence is rare unless a tumor exists in the bowel at the point where the telescoping has taken place. Recovery is the rule except in long-standing undiagnosed cases where strangulation and gangrene have set in.

INTUSSUSCEPTION OF
SMALL BOWEL

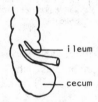

ileum

cecum

ABNORMALITIES OF THE LARGE BOWEL PRESENT SINCE BIRTH

There are several types of abnormalities (congenital anomalies) of the large intestine with which people are born. The most frequently encountered conditions of this type are (1) diverticulosis, (2) multiple polyposis, and (3) megacolon or Hirschsprung's disease.

1. Diverticulosis is a condition in which there are weaknesses in the muscular wall of the bowel which permit pouches of mucous membrane to pout through. Diverticula are found most frequently in the sigmoid colon, although they may be found anywhere throughout the entire length of the large bowel. It is estimated that 5 to 10 percent of all people have diverticula but that symptoms are encountered only when they become inflamed or when fecal matter becomes stuck in them. Inflammation of these outpouchings is termed *diverticulitis*.

Diverticulitis produces abdominal pain over the site of the diverticula (usually in the left lower part of the abdomen) and is accompanied by fever and abdominal tenderness. A soft, low-residue, bland diet, bed rest, and antibiotics are instituted for this ailment. Surgery is reserved for the severe cases in which an abscess has formed or the bowel has ruptured or has become obstructed. In such cases, the abdomen is opened and the pus is drained. Occasionally a colostomy will be performed to relieve obstruction.

Fortunately, the majority of patients with diverticulitis recover without surgery. However, if there are repeated attacks it is advisable to operate and remove the involved portion of bowel.

What is diverticulosis?

A condition in which there are pouches of mucous membrane which poke out through the muscle wall of the large bowel.

What is diverticulitis and what is the difference between this condition and diverticulosis?

Diverticulitis means an inflammation of one or more of these pouches or protrusions. Almost 10 percent of all people have such pouches (diverticula). Their mere existence, without inflammation, is called diverticulosis.

What causes:

1. Diverticulosis? A deformity of the bowel with which people are born, or which develops in later life for some unknown reason.

2. Diverticulitis? Inflammation of one or more of the pouches is usually caused by stagnant food getting caught in a diverticulum and eventually producing an infection.

What is the medical treatment for diverticulitis and diverticulosis?

1. Foods low in roughage and devoid of irritating spices.

2. Bed rest.

3. Antibiotic drugs.

4. In severe cases, intravenous feedings are given and the intestine is decompressed with rubber tubes passed through the nose.

Does surgery always have to be performed for these conditions?

Diverticulosis is not treated surgically unless there is repeated, uncontrollable hemorrhage. Diverticulitis requires surgery only when complications set in.

What will happen if surgery is refused when recommended?

Surgery is required in diverticulitis when one or more of the inflamed pouches threatens to rupture or does rupture. When this happens, abscess formation or peritonitis results. This will need surgical drainage.

What operations are performed?

If the inflamed pouches rupture and have produced peritonitis, drainage of the pus through an abdominal incision is performed. An accompanying colostomy is often performed to place the inflamed bowel at complete rest.

If the diverticulitis recurs, the diseased loop of bowel may be removed and the normal bowel above and below

sutured together to reestablish the normal passageway.

Are operations for diverticulitis serious?

Yes, but recovery takes place in almost all cases.

How soon can one get up after surgery?

Usually within one to three days.

When can one:

Bathe? When the wound has healed completely

Return to social and sexual life? Within 6 weeks

Return to work? Within 2 to 3 months

How long does it take the wound to heal?

If the wound has been drained, it may take three to six weeks to heal. An undrained wound usually heals in two weeks.

Is convalescent care necessary?

Not in most cases.

2. Multiple polyposis is an uncommon disease which tends to run in families. The entire colon, including the rectum, is studded with wartlike growths called polyps or adenomas, which vary in size and shape from a pinhead to a plum. The condition rarely causes symptoms until adulthood, when blood and mucus are passed in the stool and rapid loss in weight and anemia occur. An examination of the rectum and lower sigmoid immediately reveals the nature of the disease to the surgeon. The majority of those afflicted with this condition eventually develop cancer in one or more of the polyps. Cure can be obtained only by removal of the entire large bowel. A permanent ileostomy (artificial opening) must be performed following bowel removal. Local removal of polyps is valueless in this condition, as literally hundreds of growths are present. As surgical techniques have improved, more and more of these people are being saved. They learn to live productive and comfortable lives despite the existence of the bowel opening on the abdominal wall.

In an occasional case, the rectum contains only a few polyps. If this situation obtains, it may be possible to burn out the polyps locally, to preserve the rectum, and to stitch the small intestine directly to the rectum.

3. Megacolon, or Hirschsprung's disease is a condition of the large bowel present from birth. It is seen more often in males than in females and represents about 1 in every 10,000 hospital admissions. It is characterized by obstinate constipation and tremendous distention of the colon. When untreated, this unhappy disease lasts throughout life and keeps the patient in a state of perpetual concern and discomfort. X-rays of the intestinal tract show huge enlargement of the large bowel with an area of constriction somewhere in the descending colon or near the region where the sigmoid colon joins the rectum. Latest investigations have shown that the underlying cause for this condition is the absence of certain nerve fibers in the wall of the constricted portion of the bowel. These nerves are necessary to permit the contracted bowel to dilate normally. The constantly constricted areas causes the bowel above to dilate and become overgrown in its attempts to force the stool beyond the narrowed portion. Within recent years, complete cures have been obtained for this previously incurable ailment. Total recovery can be obtained by removing the segment of narrowed bowel and stitching together the normal bowel above and below. This operation, although of major and serious proportions, is now a safe procedure and is followed by cure in well over 95 percent of the cases.

What is megacolon or Hirschsprung's disease?

It is a condition, present since birth, in which the large bowel is tremendously enlarged and distended. A contracted segment, usually only a few inches long, is usually found in the sigmoid part of the left colon and this is thought to cause the enlargement above.

What causes it?

It is thought that the constricted portion of bowel has certain nerves missing, thus preventing normal relaxation and dilatation.

Can it be cured?

Yes.

Do all cases have to be operated upon?

No. A small percentage of cases will get well over a period of years with medical management.

What happens if surgery is not performed?

The child continues with abdominal distention and constipation. The bowel must be emptied by enemas at regular intervals. Eventually these children become miserable, never develop fully, are undernourished, and may develop heart trouble.

What operation is performed for this condition?

The constricted loop of bowel is removed (colectomy), and the bowel above and below the constriction is sutured together.

Is surgery for this condition serious?

Yes, but cure can now be offered to the great majority of these children.

Does the condition ever recur after surgery?

Only in a very small percentage of cases. When it does, an additional removal of constricted bowel may result in permanent cure.

When is the best time to perform surgery in this condition?

As soon as the nourishment and general condition of the child have been brought up to the maximum state of improvement.

Approximately how long a hospital stay is necessary?

Three to four weeks.

Are special preparations necessary before operating?

Yes:

1. The bowel should be emptied as completely as possible with repeated enemas and irrigations.

2. A fluid or low-residue diet is given.

3. Antibiotic drugs are given to prevent peritonitis from developing after surgery.

4. Transfusions are given to combat the anemia.

Where is the usual site for incision?

The left lower portion of the abdomen.

How long does the operation take to perform?

Bowel removal in these cases takes anywhere from two to five hours.

Are blood transfusions necessary?

Yes, these are usually given both before and during the operative procedure.

Are special nurses necessary after operation?

Yes, for several days.

What special postoperative measures are carried out?

1. Nothing by mouth.

2. The intestinal tract is kept deflated for two to four days with stomach tubes.

3. Feedings and medications are given intravenously.

4. Antibiotic drugs are given.

Is the postoperative period uncomfortable?

Yes, for four to five days.

Does a special diet have to be followed postoperatively?

Only for the first week or two after surgery.

How soon after surgery can the patient get out of bed?

In one to three days.

How soon after surgery should the bowels start to function normally?

This may take four or five days to several weeks.

How soon can one:

Bathe? When the wound has completely healed; usually 2 weeks

Go back to school? When bowel function has returned to normal

Return to all activities? In 2 to 3 months

Is convalescent care necessary?

Only in those children who have been seriously run-down before operation.

Does the operation interfere with normal development?

No. As a matter of fact, these children usually spurt tremendously in their development after a successful operation for this condition.

Does the operation interfere with the future ability to bear children?

No.

How often should the patient be rechecked after surgery?

Twice a year.

Is length of life affected by this surgery?

No.

TUMORS OF THE COLON

There are two main types of tumors which grow in the large intestine; the benign growth, such as *adenomas* or *polyps,* and the malignant growths, such as *cancer.*

Adenomas or single polyps of the large bowel are very common, occurring in some 10 to 15 percent of all adults. These growths are not to be confused with multiple polyposis, where there are literally hundreds of growths extending throughout the whole length of the colon. More often than not, these adenomas cause few symptoms during the early period of their existence. They are found most often on routine intestinal x-ray examination. *As some of these growths have a tendency to degenerate into cancer if left alone, their early removal is essential!* Painless rectal bleeding is the most frequent indication of the presence of a polyp. When they grow to large size, they may obstruct the bowel and produce the typical symptoms associated with obstruction.

Polyps or adenomas of the colon occur in people of all ages. Cure, through surgical removal, can be obtained without great operative risk. When the polyp is within eight inches of the anal opening, it can be removed through the rectum. A sigmoidoscope is passed through the anus and the polyp is burned or snared off through this instrument. When the polyp is higher than eight inches from the anal opening, it must be removed through an abdominal incision. The colon in the region of the polyp is opened and the polyp is removed at its base. The bowel is then closed and healing takes place within a week to ten days. Careful examination of the growth is necessary at the time of operation to make sure that malignant changes have not set in. If cancer is found within the substance of the polyp, that segment of the bowel is removed.

One of the commonest locations for *cancer* is in the large intestine. Luckily, most of these tumors produce symptoms early in the course of their growth and treatment can be started at a time when cure is still possible. Cancer of the bowel is found more often in men than in women and usually occurs in people in their 40s, 50s, and 60s. Although a definite estimate of percentages cannot be made, it is believed that a considerable number of these cancers originate in benign tumors (adenomas or polyps) which have lain dormant for years.

Cancer of the right side of the large bowel is accompanied by marked anemia, loss of weight and strength, and the finding of a lump on abdominal examination. X-rays of the colon will show an irregular deformity. These symptoms take place slowly over a period of several weeks or months.

Cancers of the transverse colon, descending colon, and sigmoid usually are discovered at an earlier stage in their development because of the acute nature of the symptoms they produce. Repeated passage of blood from the rectum, change in bowel habits with increasing constipation, and ultimately intestinal obstruction, with its characteristic colicky pains, distention, and vomiting, ensue. Occasionally the bowel will rupture due to the extension of the tumor through the wall and the distention that takes place over the obstructing tumor. The marked anemia, weakness, and weight loss seen in cancer of the right half of the colon are usually absent in cancer of the left side.

The proper treatment for cancer of the colon is prompt surgical removal of the affected portion. This must be done in stages if marked obstruction has taken place, but otherwise the entire procedure may be effected at one time.

When acute obstruction exists, a colostomy is first performed. This is executed by bringing up a loop of bowel onto the abdominal wall, opening it, and permitting its contents to drain out. Then, several days or weeks later, a second operation is performed for the removal of the diseased bowel. The bowel opening on the abdominal wall can be closed at a third operation, several weeks or months thereafter, provided that the bowel continuity had been reestablished at the time of the removal of the cancer.

Preparations for colon surgery should be carried out for several days prior to operation. A low-residue diet and cleansing enemas are usually advised. The patient is also given sulfa and antibiotic drugs in order to sterilize the intestinal contents. As a result, surgery can now be performed without too great a fear of postoperative peritonitis. The extremely high operative mortality seen 30 years ago has been reduced so greatly that colon surgery today is accomplished with safety and the promise of surgical recovery in well over 95 percent of cases. Furthermore, the relatively sterile state of the bowel has made it possible to reduce the number of operations that must be performed. Surgeons can now remove the cancer-bearing portion of the bowel and sew together the ends above and below without the fear, prevalent previously, that the suture line might break down because of bacterial infection. Formerly it was necessary to bring the diseased loops of bowel out onto the abdominal wall in one procedure, to remove them at another operation several days later, and then to perform surgery a third time several weeks or months later to close the open ends above and below the removed segment.

The greatest concern of people who must undergo large bowel surgery is the possibility that a *colostomy* will be performed. They are depressed by the thought of living with a bowel opening on their abdominal wall. They are revolted by the possibility of soilage and spillage, and they are disgusted by the possibility that unpleasant odors will emanate from such an opening. Advances in recent years can relieve most of these anxieties. First, the number of patients who will require a colostomy has been reduced greatly by the newer techniques which permit one-stage operations. These operations involve the *immediate reestablishment* and union of the bowel above and below the diseased loop. Secondly, improved postoperative methods have cut down considerably the interval of time necessary between the temporary colostomy and its ultimate closure at a second-stage operation. Thirdly, and most important of all, better techniques and methods in caring for permanent colostomies permit patients to lead normal and productive lives. Systems of irrigating a colostomy have led, in the great majority of instances, to a state where the bowel need be cleansed just once daily and will remain clean and free of offensive odor until the next day.

OPERATIONS UPON THE COLON

The simplest way to explain the various operations upon the large bowel would be with the aid of diagrams:

With a tumor located in any portion of the shaded region of the illustration, the entire right half of the colon—including the appendix and the last six to eight inches of small intestine—is removed. The small intestine is divided at point A and the portion not removed with the colon is implanted into the transverse colon at point B. This operation, called right hemicolectomy, is usually performed in one stage and does not require a colostomy. When completed, the flow of stool is continuous and the patient lives a completely normal life. Operative recovery usually takes about two to four weeks.

TUMORS OF THE CECUM, ASCENDING COLON, AND HEPATIC FLEXURE OF TRANSVERSE COLON

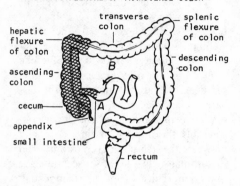

With the tumor in the transverse colon, the involved area is widely removed and the ends of normal bowel are sutured to one another. No colostomy is performed unless marked intestinal ob-

struction was present prior to operation. Points A and B are sutured together after the shaded area is removed.

In this type of case, too, the involved area is widely removed and the normal ends are sutured together at points A and B. Colostomy is only performed in these cases as a preliminary measure if obstruction is encountered before operation.

TUMOR OF THE TRANSVERSE COLON

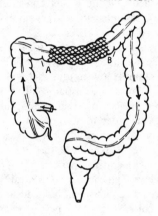

TUMOR OF THE SPLENIC FLEXURE

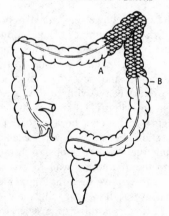

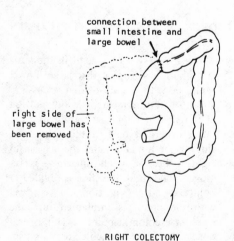

RIGHT COLECTOMY

Tumors found anywhere along the shaded area shown on the descending colon are treated by wide removal and suturing of normal bowel above and below. Every attempt is made in all of these operations to remove as much bowel as possible above and below the growth in order to make sure that it is eradicated completely. A preliminary colostomy is done in these cases only if obstruction is present.

TUMOR OF THE LOWER SIGMOID COLON AND RECTUM

When the growth is in the region of the lower sigmoid colon and rectum— anywhere from the anal opening to six inches upward—the best chances for a permanent cure are obtained by removing the entire anus, rectum, and sigmoid colon. The descending colon is then brought out onto the abdominal wall in the form of a *permanent colostomy*. This operation is called an *abdomino-perineal resection*.

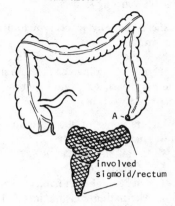

TUMOR OF THE LOWER SIGMOID COLON AND RECTUM

A

involved sigmoid/rectum

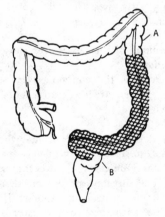

TUMOR OF THE DESCENDING COLON AND SIGMOID COLON

A

B

The shaded area made up of sigmoid, rectum, and anus is removed and the descending colon, at point A, is brought out to the abdominal wall as a permanent colostomy. The anal region heals in slowly over a period of several weeks. Operative recovery from this procedure takes two to four weeks and there is a lengthy convalescent period of two to four months.

It should be stressed that great progress has been made in colon surgery for both benign and malignant tumors. If a malignancy has not spread, permanent cure can now be obtained in the great majority of cases! The number of failures could be reduced tremendously if the public would only go for periodic health checkups, including a rectal examination, and would submit to examination of the lower bowel with special instruments and x-rays.

What causes tumors of the large bowel?

The true cause of tumor formation is unknown. However, harmless benign tumors, if neglected, may turn into cancer.

How can one distinguish between a harmless tumor and a cancer of the bowel?

The positive way is to submit the tumor to microscopic examination. This is done for all bowel tumors.

How does one know if he has a tumor?

Rectal bleeding and a change in one's

normal bowel habits are the two most reliable warning signals.

Is there any way to prevent tumor formation?

No. However, by periodic health checkups, including rectal examination, one may learn of a tumor before it has become dangerous.

What are some of the symptoms of a bowel tumor?

1. Rectal bleeding.
2. Jet-black stools.
3. Change in bowel habits.
4. Alternating constipation and diarrhea.
5. Colicky abdominal pains.
6. Late symptoms may be anemia, weakness, loss of weight and appetite.

Is surgery in these conditions necessary?

Yes. Every bowel tumor should be removed.

Are operations for tumors serious?

They may be very minor or very serious. Polyps near the rectum can often be removed through the rectum, without anesthesia, in a surgeon's office.

Do hemorrhoids (piles) ever turn into cancer?

No.

How long can one wait before undergoing surgery for tumors of the bowel?

As soon as the diagnosis is made, arrangements should be made for surgery.

What will happen if surgery is refused?

A benign tumor (adenoma or polyp) may develop into a cancer. An established cancer will eventually spread and lead to death if not removed.

What kind of operations are performed for tumors of the bowel?

1. For benign adenomas or polyps, simple removal of the tumor at its base. The bowel segment is rarely removed.

2. Wherever possible, the malignant tumor (cancer), along with a generous portion of bowel above and below, is removed and the ends of normal bowel are sutured one to the other. If the passageway cannot be reestablished, then an artificial opening (colostomy) is made on the abdominal wall. In any event, the surgeon always attempts to remove the entire tumor regardless of his or the patient's desire to avoid an artificial opening.

What are the chances of recovery and cure for these conditions?

All benign tumors are curable. Operative recovery from surgery in cancer of the bowel is well over 90 percent. Somewhat more than half of colon cancer cases can now be permanently cured through effective surgery.

Do growths ever recur?

If a growth has been widely removed at a time before it has spread to neighboring structures, it will not recur. Otherwise, recurrence may take place.

Do tumors of the bowel ever cause obstruction?

Yes. It is the commonest cause of large bowel (colon) obstruction in adults.

How does the surgeon decide whether or not to make an artificial opening (colostomy) in cases of bowel tumors?

1. The surgeon's prime consideration is to remove the entire tumor! If this can be accomplished and still leave sufficient normal bowel above and below the tumor, he will reestablish the passageway.

2. In cases where marked intestinal obstruction has been caused by the tumor, the surgeon will probably perform a *temporary colostomy* to relieve the obstruction.

Are all colostomies permanent?

No.

How does the surgeon decide whether or not to close a colostomy?

If he can reestablish the normal passageway, he will do so. The colostomy will then be closed at a separate operation several weeks or months later.

How long a hospital stay is necessary in these conditions?

It will vary according to the procedure. Patients who have had simple polyps removed through the rectum may go home in a day or two, if they have been hospitalized. People who have had a benign tumor removed through the abdomen may go home in 10 to 14 days, when the wound has healed. Many of the extensive operations are done in several stages and this may require two or three hospitalizations, each one of several weeks' duration.

What special preoperative preparations are necessary?

1. Preoperative sterilization of the bowel by intensive medication with sulfa and antibiotic drugs for two to four days before operation

2. Low-residue or liquid diet for several days

3. If obstructed, decompression through the passage of stomach and intestinal tubes

4. Vitamin, mineral, and glucose feedings by vein

5. Blood transfusions if patient is anemic

What type of anesthesia is used?

General, occasionally spinal.

What is the usual site of incision?

Over the site of the tumor. Usually a longitudinal abdominal incision five to eight inches long.

How long do these operations take to perform?

Simple colostomy? ½ to 1 hour

Bowel removal? From 2 to 5 hours, depending upon the procedure

Removal of tumor through the abdomen? 1 to 2 hours

Are blood transfusions necessary?

Yes, for the more serious procedures involving bowel removal.

Are special nurses necessary after operation?

Yes, except for the minor procedures.

Is the postoperative period uncomfortable?

Yes, for four to five days following the major operations.

What special postoperative treatments are given?

1. Nothing by mouth for two to four days

2. Intravenous feedings of glucose, proteins, vitamins, and minerals

3. Stomach and intestinal tubes to deflate the intestinal tract

4. Antibiotic drugs to prevent peritonitis

5. Blood transfusions when necessary

How soon after surgery do the bowels resume functioning?

A colostomy may take four to five days before beginning to function.

After the bowel above and below a tumor has been sutured together, it usually remains inactive for several days. Bowel function returns in four to seven days postoperatively.

Are special diets necessary after surgery?

Only for the first few weeks. Thereafter, normal diet may be resumed.

How soon after surgery can the patient get out of bed?

Within one to three days unless he is

exceptionally sick as the result of obstruction or an unusually severe operation.

How soon after surgery can one:

Bathe? When the wound has completely healed

Resume normal social life and sexual relations? Within 2 months after the final operation

Return to work? Within 2 to 3 months after the final operation

Is postoperative convalescent care advisable?

Yes.

Can one live a full and active life after removal of part or even all of the large bowel?

Yes.

How often after surgery should one return for a checkup?

Every six months.

Is special care necessary for a colostomy?

Yes, and this can be learned over a period of several weeks without great difficulty.

Is length of life affected by tumors of the bowel?

Not if the tumor—even if it was a cancer—has been widely removed at a time before it had spread to other organs!

Can one learn to live comfortably and actively even though there is a permanent colostomy?

Yes. Tens of thousands of people today live full and happy lives after they have mastered the technique of emptying their bowels through the artificial opening each morning. Many go 24 to 48 hours without the need to pay further attention to the colostomy.

Intracranial Hemorrhage

Intracranial hemorrhage is any hemorrhage that takes place within the skull. It can be secondary to injury or may be caused by the rupture of a blood vessel of the brain.

See also NEUROSURGERY.

Intubation

The term intubation usually refers to endotracheal intubation. This is an anesthetic procedure in which a tube is passed through the mouth, or occasionally through the nose, into the windpipe in order to maintain an airway during anesthesia. Intubation is usually performed after the patient has already been rendered unconscious by the administration of an anesthetic agent.

See also ANESTHESIA.

Intussusception

Intussusception is a condition in which the small intestine (ileum) telescopes into the large intestine (cecum and ascending colon) in the right lower part of the abdomen. Such a situation produces obstruction of the bowel. It is seen almost exclusively in children under 3 years of age.

When intussusception occurs, the child suffers colicky pains, vomiting, the passage of blood and mucus by rectum, and a lump can be felt in the abdomen at the site of the telescoping. As soon as the diagnosis is made, operation is performed. By gentle pulling, the small intestine can be taken out of its abnormal position. Recurrence is rare unless a tumor exists in the bowel at the point where the telescoping has taken place. Recovery is the rule except in longstanding undiagnosed cases in which strangulation and gangrene have set in.

See also INTESTINES; MECKEL'S DIVERTICULUM; PYLORIC STENOSIS.

QUESTIONS AND ANSWERS

What is the apex of an intussusception?

The apex of an intussusception is the leading point where the small intestine telescopes into the large intestine.

What causes intussusception?

The cause is not always apparent. Some of the predisposing conditions are:

1. A band of tissue from the peritoneum (the lining of the abdominal cavity) in the area, which seems to fix the small intestine in an abnormal position

2. A Meckel's diverticulum

3. A polyp in the small intestine

4. A tumor in the small intestine

Does intussusception tend to run in families?

No.

Do children who have intussusception usually show other birth deformities?

No. It occurs most often in otherwise healthy children.

What are some of the signs and symptoms of intussusception?

The child will develop colicky pains over his entire abdomen, will vomit, and will pass blood and mucus through the rectum. Examination by the pediatrician will reveal a lump at the site of the telescoping, usually in the right lower portion of the abdomen or in between the right lower and right upper parts of the abdomen.

How can the pain of intussusception be distinguished from the pain caused by ordinary colic?

In the case of intussusception, the pains come and go every 15 to 20 minutes, and they have no relationship to the child's feedings. As the condition progresses, approximately four out of five children will have gross blood in their stool, and upon examination the pediatrician will be able to feel a mass in the abdomen. The mass is quite characteristic to touch and will usually establish the diagnosis of intussusception without much doubt.

Can x-rays help in making the diagnosis of intussusception?

Yes. A barium mixture is injected through the child's rectum into his colon and is observed under a fluoroscope. There is a characteristic filling defect seen at the site where the small bowel has telescoped into the large bowel. It will also be evident that there is an obstruction at this point.

How can one distinguish between intussusception and other conditions?

This is not always easy. Intussusception is distinguished from a Meckel's diverticulum by the fact that a mass can be felt in the abdomen. It is distinguished from appendicitis because of the appearance of blood in the stool. It is distinguished from pyloric stenosis by the fact that children with intussusception are considerably older than those who have pyloric stenosis; in addition, in cases of pyloric stenosis there is no blood in the stool.

What is the treatment for intussusception?

1. Some doctors advocate nonoperative treatment, in which fluid is injected under steadily increasing pressure into the large bowel through the rectum. A certain amount of barium is mixed with the fluid so that the results can be observed directly by fluoroscoping the child. Some proponents of this method of treatment state that it will cure the majority of children with intussusception and that the telescoped portion of small intestine will return to its normal anatomical location. All are agreed that this method is dangerous if the intussusception has been present for more than 24 hours, because there is too great a chance that the bowel will be ruptured by the increased pressure. Also, all are agreed that if this method does not produce a prompt reduction of the intussusception, surgery is indicated.

2. Many surgeons feel that the safest procedure is to operate on these children and manually pull out the telescoped or intussuscepted portion of small bowel from the large bowel. If a band of peritoneum is found to be causing the intussusception, this adhesive band is severed. If a Meckel's diverticulum is discovered to be the origin of the intussusception, it is excised. If the small intestine is found to contain a polyp or tumor, the growth must be removed before the operation is concluded. After the intussusception has been corrected and the underlying cause has been eradicated, the abdomen is closed in layers.

Is it always possible to relieve the intussusception manually?

If the surgeon pulls on the small intestine, it will come out with ease in the great majority of cases. However, if the intussusception has been present for more than 24 hours, this portion of the bowel may have become gangrenous, and in these cases it will be necessary to remove the intestinal segment.

Where is the incision made when operating for intussusception?

In the right lower portion of the abdomen.

Is an operation for intussusception very serious?

It is not serious if it is carried out within the first 24 hours. In such cases practically all children recover. However, difficulties are encountered if the condition has existed for 24 hours or more, because peritonitis or gangrene of the telescoped portion of the bowel may have developed.

Is there a tendency for intussusception to recur once it has been corrected?

No. Recurrences are rare and practically never occur if the underlying cause of the intussusception was removed at the original operation. On the other hand, if a polyp or any other condition that caused the original intussusception was left behind at the original operation, it may cause the condition to recur at some time in the future.

Are there any permanent aftereffects of intussusception?

No. Normal bowel continuity will be restored and the intestines will function normally.

Are the following necessary before operations for intussusception?

Blood transfusions? No, unless the child has had the condition for several days.

Antibiotic medications? No, unless the child has had the condition for several days.

Intravenous medications? Yes.

Stomach tubes? Yes.

Bladder catheters? No.

Vitamin injections? No.

Special diets? No.

Other special preparations? No,

unless the child is markedly dehydrated from vomiting.

Are the following necessary after operations for intussusception?

Private duty nurses? Yes, for a day or two.

Antibiotic medications? Yes, if a portion of the bowel has been removed.

Intravenous infusions? Yes, for two to three days.

Blood transfusions? No.

Stomach tubes? Yes, for two to three days.

Special postoperative measures? No, unless a portion of the bowel has been removed.

Postoperative vitamins and tonics? No.

Convalescent posthospital care? No.

Will a child have to be on a special diet after recovering from intussusception? No.

How soon after an operation for intussusception can a child:

Get out of bed? One day, unless part of the bowel has been removed.

Leave the hospital? In uncomplicated cases, one week.

Walk up and down stairs? 7 to 10 days.

Go outdoors? 10 to 14 days.

Return to school? 4 to 5 weeks.

Play games? 6 to 8 weeks.

Resume all normal physical activities? 2 to 3 months.

Jaundice

Jaundice, yellow discoloration of the skin and eyes due to bile pigments in the blood, is a symptom rather than a disease. Normally, bile pigments arise from the breakdown of hemoglobin in the red blood cells when these cells are destroyed. The life of the ordinary blood cell is no longer than 60 to 90 days. When the hemoglobin is liberated following the breakdown of a red blood cell, it is excreted by the liver. If, for any reason, the liver is unable to excrete the bile pigment or if new pigment is produced at a faster rate than the liver can excrete it, there will be an accumulation of the bile pigment in the serum of the blood. This will result in the yellowish discoloration of the skin and the whites of the eyes. In fact, all of the tissues and organs of the body become somewhat stained yellow by the accumulation of the bile pigment.

QUESTIONS AND ANSWERS

What are the main causes of jaundice?

1. It may be caused by an obstruction to the flow of bile from the liver into the intestinal tract.

2. It may be caused by disease within the substance of the liver itself.

3. It may be caused by the destruction of an excess number of red blood cells by the spleen and other organs. The destruction of these cells may take place at such a rapid rate that the liver is unable to excrete the bile pigments in adequate quantities.

What is the name of the bile pigment that causes jaundice?

Bilirubin.

Is it usually possible to see jaundice under an artificial light?

No. In order to make the diagnosis from clinical observation, it is necessary to view the patient in daylight.

How can a diagnosis of jaundice be made accurately?

By testing the blood for bile pigment. The normal amount of bilirubin in the blood is 0.5 to 1.2 mg per 100 cc of blood. When the bilirubin level rises to

2 to 3 mg per 100 cc of blood, jaundice is indicated.

What is an icterus index test?

It is one to determine the quantity of bile pigments circulating in the blood. In jaundice, the icterus index is elevated.

What is obstructive jaundice?

It is that type in which there is an obstruction to the flow of bile through the bile ducts into the small intestine. Obstructive jaundice can be either partial or complete. When partial, although the patient may appear to be discolored yellow, the stools may retain their normal brown color and the urine may not be very dark in color. When obstructive jaundice is complete, the urine becomes a very dark yellow-orange color and the stool, because of the lack of bile pigment, becomes clay-colored.

What are some of the common causes of the obstructive type of jaundice?

1. Stones in the bile ducts
2. Cancer of the head of the pancreas, obstructing the outlet of the bile duct into the intestines
3. A tumor of the bile duct
4. Inflammation of the bile duct, especially in the region where it empties into the intestinal tract

What are some of the common causes of jaundice secondary to diseases in the liver?

1. Infectious hepatitis secondary to a virus infection
2. Cirrhosis of the liver
3. Homologous serum jaundice that is secondary to a blood transfusion
4. Toxic hepatitis, secondary to poisoning by a drug or poison
5. Infection of the liver, with abscess formation, secondary either to a germ or a parasite, such as that found in amoebic dysentery

6. Blood diseases, with inability of the liver to secrete bile
7. Cancer of the liver

What is hemolytic jaundice?

It is that caused by the destruction of red blood cells and hemoglobin.

What is homologous serum jaundice?

It is a condition that follows the administration of a blood transfusion or vaccine made from human serum that is contaminated with a certain virus.

Do abscesses of the liver ever cause jaundice?

Yes, if they are large enough to press upon major bile ducts and obstruct the outflow of bile through them.

What is acute yellow atrophy of the liver?

It is a very serious condition, often terminating fatally, in which there is widespread degeneration and death of liver tissue. Acute yellow atrophy is most often caused by a poison that has been taken into the body.

Is jaundice seen in acute yellow atrophy?

Yes.

Does jaundice often affect those over 60?

Yes. It is frequently encountered in older people.

What types of jaundice are most likely to affect older people?

They have no immunity to any type, although jaundice precipitated by virus infections and/or associated with blood diseases is more common in younger age groups.

Can a physician diagnose which of many causative agents has produced the jaundice?

Yes. Laboratory tests, as well as x-rays, will aid him in making a precise diagnosis.

What is the treatment of jaundice?

This depends on the cause of the jaundice. If the cause lies outside of the liver (obstructive jaundice), such as a stone blocking the bile duct or a tumor of the bile duct or of the head of the pancreas, then surgery will be necessary to relieve the obstruction. If the jaundice is caused by cirrhosis of the liver, surgery to shunt the blood from the portal vein should be considered. If the jaundice is the result of a blood disease or disease in the liver substance, then medical management of the disease must be undertaken.

Can there be a full recovery from an attack of jaundice?

Yes, if the underlying cause has been eradicated. However, when jaundice persists for several weeks it often results in permanent damage to the liver.

What regimen should people follow who have recovered from jaundice?

1. They must not overwork or subject themselves to physical strain for six months to a year.

2. They should avoid all fatty, greasy, or fried foods for at least one year.

3. They should eat large amounts of protein and sugar for at least one year.

4. They should not drink alcoholic beverages.

5. They should take no medications or drugs without the explicit approval of their physician.

6. They should take supplemental vitamins.

7. They should be checked by a doctor each month for a year after an attack of jaundice.

Is surgery necessary when jaundice is due to a gallstone obstructing the bile ducts?

Yes. Gallstones cannot be dissolved and most of them do not pass spontaneously.

What will happen if an operation is not performed to relieve obstructive jaundice due to gallstones?

1. If jaundice persists because of a gallstone, the patient may eventually die from the toxic effects of the bile obstruction.

2. If an acute inflammation of the gallbladder progresses because of a stone obstructing its duct, gangrene may set in. Or the infected gallbladder may rupture. Either of these eventualities can cause peritonitis with possible death.

3. Cancer of the gallbladder develops in approximately 1 to 2 percent of those patients who have had stones in their gallbladder for several years.

Does jaundice complicate gallbladder disease?

Yes. Jaundice indicates a blockage of the flow of bile from the liver into the intestines. Such a blockage, if not relieved, may lead to death from a condition known as cholemia.

How long does jaundice take to disappear after obstruction has been relieved?

The blood tests may show a return to normal bilirubin quantities within a period of a few days. Also, the urine may lighten in color and the stool resume its normal brown hue within a few days. However, the patient's skin and whites of his eyes may remain yellow for a few weeks before all of the pigment is absorbed.

What is catarrhal jaundice?

It is another name for infectious hepatitis.

What is congenital hemolytic jaundice?

It is another name for hemolytic anemia. This condition is an inherited one in which red blood cells are destroyed much more rapidly than normal. Also, the red cells are thought to be much more fragile than normal. In hemolytic jaundice, one also finds an enlarged spleen.

What is hematogenous jaundice?

It is the type due to excess destruction of red blood cells by a toxin or chemical poison.

What is hepatocellular jaundice?

It is that type resulting from injury or inflammation, or failure of function, of liver cells.

What is regurgitational jaundice?

It is that type due to obstruction of bile with reabsorption of bile pigments into the bloodstream.

JAUNDICE IN CHILDREN

What is the significance of jaundice in the newborn?

Jaundice in a newborn child may have very little clinical significance, as in so-called physiological jaundice, or it may be caused by a very serious condition.

What is physiological jaundice?

Physiological jaundice appears during the third or fourth day of a child's life and merely represents an inability of the young liver to excrete adequate amounts of bile pigments. It clears spontaneously within a few days as the liver develops normal function.

Is physiological jaundice called by any other name?

It is also known as icterus neonatorum.

What are some of the more serious conditions that can cause jaundice in a newborn?

1. Erythroblastosis (Rh-factor disease)

2. Blood poisoning (septicemia) that is caused by an overwhelming infection
3. Hemolytic anemia
4. A birth deformity with incomplete development of the bile ducts or an abnormality in the formation of the liver itself
5. Hepatitis
6. Congenital syphilis
7. Many rare conditions, such as galactosemia and toxoplasmosis

What are some of the causes of obstructive jaundice in children?

1. Birth deformities of the bile ducts with failure of complete development. In some instances, the common bile duct that leads from the liver to the intestinal tract is not formed. This will result in complete obstruction of the flow of bile and deep jaundice.
2. An acquired obstruction of the bile duct secondary to a tumor or cyst that is growing on the outside but is compressing the duct and thus obstructing it.
3. An obstruction of the small channels within the liver if these are swollen secondary to an infection of the liver cells. This is seen in hepatitis and is known as hepatocellular obstruction.
4. Cirrhosis in older children. This is a process in which there is replacement of the liver cells by fibrous tissue, with obstruction to the outflow of bile through the bile channels.
5. Rarely, gallstones in the common bile duct.

What are some of the clinical manifestations of obstructive jaundice?

A yellow discoloration of the whites of the eye, the skin, and the mucous membranes is soon apparent. The urine is dark, and when shaken, the foam is yellow-tinged. Because bile is not flowing into the intestinal tract, the stool is clay-colored rather than the normal yellowish brown. There may be severe itching of the skin caused by the accumulation of bile pigments. Blood tests will show a characteristic elevation of the quantity of bilirubin circulating in the blood. If the jaundice continues unabated there is a tendency to bleed and the patient may develop bleeding from his gums or intestinal tract.

What is atresia of the bile ducts?

Atresia of the bile ducts is a birth deformity in which the bile ducts have not formed normally. It is associated with an obstructive type of jaundice.

What is Gilbert's disease?

Gilbert's disease is a hereditary condition, the sole manifestion of which is jaundice. The jaundice is usually very slight and the child may live a completely normal life, except that he will have a tendency to tire easily. Children with this rare condition (also known as familial nonhemolytic jaundice) lead normal lives and have normal life-spans.

What is familial nonhemolytic jaundice with kernicterus?

This is a rare type of congenital disease in which there is severe jaundice resulting in involvement of the brain and liver. This condition is sometimes seen in several members of the same family. The child often has a very poor outlook because of the severity of the jaundice and the extensive nervous system involvement. The child may die during early infancy unless repeated exchange transfusions are performed to clear the blood of the accumulated bile pigments.

Jejunal Ulcer

A jejunal ulcer is seen in a small percentage of patients who have previously undergone an operation for ulcer of the duodenum. In the performance of this operation it is not uncommon for the surgeon to link the stomach, or the stump of the stomach, if a gastrectomy has been performed, to the jejunum. The jejunum is the first portion of the small intestines immediately beyond the duodenum.

In approximately 2 to 3 percent of those patients who have undergone gastrectomy and also in approximately 7 to 8 percent of those who have merely had the short-circuiting gastrojejunostomy, an ulcer will develop at the site of the suture line. This is known as a jejunal ulcer or a gastrojejunal ulcer.

See also STOMACH AND DUODENUM.

QUESTIONS AND ANSWERS

What causes a jejunal ulcer?

In the great majority of cases, it follows ulcer surgery and appears at the line where the stomach or stump of the stomach has been stitched to the jejunum. It is believed by most surgeons that jejunal ulcers result from inadequate removal of acid-bearing stomach tissue or inadequate vagotomy, an operation that severs the vagus nerve which controls the secretion of acid in the stomach. As a consequence, the jejunum is constantly bathed in acid juices which ultimately results in ulceration.

What is the treatment for a jejunal ulcer?

1. Attempts are at first made to get the ulcer to heal with medications. In these cases, antacids are given along with drugs to decrease the amount of acid secreted by the stomach cells. Such medications as Pro Banthine are given.

2. If the above medical management fails, as it often does, reoperation is necessary.

What reoperations are performed to cure a jejunal ulcer?

If an adequate vagotomy has not been performed at the first operation, this is completed at the second one. An adequate vagotomy will usually result in the spontaneous healing of a jejunal ulcer.

If an adequate vagotomy has already been performed at the first operation, but the stomach has not been removed, the surgeon may then take down the linkage of the stomach to the jejunum and perform what is known as a high gastrectomy. This will involve removal of approximately 75 percent of the stomach with suturing of the stump of the stomach to the jejunum.

Can most jejunal ulcers be cured by re-operation?

Yes, although the surgery necessary to bring about a cure is often extensive.

If the amount of acid that the stomach secretes is reduced markedly, is it likely for a jejunal ulcer to form?

No, because, in most instances, it arises from too much acid being secreted by the stomach or stump of the stomach.

Joints

A joint is a part of the body where two or more bones are joined, usually so that there can be movement between them. There are a good number of different types of joints in the body, the most common types are:

1. The ball-and-socket joint. This is found in the hip and shoulder.

2. A compound joint. This is one formed of three or more bones, such as the wrist joint.

3. Immovable joint. This type is one in which the two bones are joined so solidly that there is no movement between them. Such joints are seen between the vertebrae of the sacrum.

4. Movable joint. This type includes the elbow, knee, hip, shoulder, wrist, and the joints of the fingers and toes.

5. Phalangeal joint. This is a joint between the various bones of the toes or fingers.

6. Uniaxial joint. This is one in which movement is in one axis only, such as the knee joint.

See also ACROMIOCLAVICULAR JOINT SEPARATION; ARTHRITIS; BACK; BONE CONDITIONS; BURSITIS; FEET; FRACTURES; HAND; HERNIATED INTERVERTEBRAL DISK; HIP; KNEE; SCOLIOSIS; SPINE.

QUESTIONS AND ANSWERS

What is a Charcot's joint?

It is enlargement of a joint with arthritis. This is due to syphilis of the spinal cord (tabes dorsalis).

What is a flail joint?

One with abnormal mobility, especially one involving overextension.

What is a joint mouse?

It is a loose piece of cartilage or other substance within the cavity of a joint.

What is a joint fusion?

A surgical procedure performed for the purpose of joining (fusing) bones that make up a joint. This operation is sometimes carried out to improve stability in an otherwise poorly functioning joint. The procedure is also known as arthrodesis.

Is it natural for some children and adolescents to have aches and pains in their joints?

Yes. These are popularly known as growing pains. In actuality, they are probably the result of forgotten strains and stresses that the child has experienced during strenuous physical activity, and do not represent any growth phenomenon.

It is natural for the cartilages that line joints to thin out as the person advances in age?

Yes. This will result in stiffness and pain in the joint. The process of aging also is accompanied by the secretion of less lubricating fluid from the joint surfaces.

Is it natural for joints to limber up and gain more mobility as they are used during the course of a day?

Yes. This is especially the case with older people who may have the beginning of arthritic processes in their joints. Motion and exercise will cause more fluid to be secreted from joint surfaces, thus lubricating and making the joint more functional.

Do joints tend to become stiff from disuse?

Yes. Regular exercise is essential for normal joint function.

Is it common for some women to have joint aches and pains around the time of menopause?

Yes. This may not be a true arthritis, but a condition known as arthralgia.

Is it true that some people can predict damp or rainy weather by pains in their joints?

For some odd reason, this is true in some cases. Certain older people, particularly, are able to do this. The pain is usually in a joint that is or has previously been the site of an arthritic process.

What is arthralgia?

It is pain in a joint, possibly associated with some limitation of mobility. It differs from arthritis in that there are no permanent cartilaginous, bony, or soft tissue changes.

How can a physician distinguish between arthralgia and arthritis?

In most cases of arthritis, the changes can be seen on x-ray examination. A patient with arthralgia may have perfectly normal-appearing joints on x-ray.

ARTHROPLASTY

What is arthroplasty?

It is the term used to describe the plastic reconstruction or surgical replacement of a joint.

For what conditions is arthroplasty most frequently performed?

1. In any condition accompanied by permanent, painful restriction of joint motion
2. When a joint has been irrevocably destroyed by a severe fracture with failure of normal healing processes
3. When the bones making up a joint have been hopelessly destroyed by chronic arthritis or some other degenerative disease process
4. When it is necessary to remove a joint, or part of a joint, because of a bone tumor

What are some of the joints that can be replaced through arthroplasty?

1. The hip joint
2. The elbow joint
3. The shoulder joint
4. Finger joints

What metals are used to replace the bones?

The artificial joints (prosthetic devices) are composed of metals known as Vitallium or SMO steel. Vitallium consists of several metals such as cobalt, chromium, carbon, molybdenum, and manganese. SMO steel is an alloy of stainless steel and molybdenum.

How successful is arthroplasty?

As this is a relatively new operative procedure, one must expect a certain number of failures. However, it is safe to state that great relief from pain and improvement in motion follow most of these operations. Of course, they must be performed only by specialists who have had wide experience in the field.

What is the most frequent cause for failure of an arthroplasty?

Postoperative infection. Should this take place and not be controlled, it may be necessary to remove the metal device.

If one arthroplasty procedure fails, is it possible to reoperate at a later date?

Yes, but results are likely to be less satisfactory. It is essential that all infection be cleared up before reinserting a metal device.

Keloid

A keloid is an overgrown scar which, on microscopic examination, shows a tremendous number of fibrous connective tissue cells. It also contains a large amount of intercellular material known as collagen.

Keloids occur often after a deep abrasion (scratch), after a burn, or after a laceration or a surgical incision. They are particularly prevalent among Negroes, but white people are not immune to keloids.

See also SKIN.

QUESTIONS AND ANSWERS

What is a keloid?

It is a peculiar type of reaction of the skin to an abrasion, laceration, burn, or surgical wound in which there is excessive scar formation. Instead of a flat, thin, white line of healing, there are marked thickening, elevation, redness, and itching of the healed scar.

What causes keloids?

The cause is unknown. Some people have an inherent tendency to form keloids after receiving a cut or surgical incision. This tendency is especially prevalent among Negroes.

How is the diagnosis of a keloid made?

The diagnosis is made merely by looking at a scar. It will be found to be exceptionally hard, thick, and raised above the skin surface. The patient may complain of burning and itching in the area.

What is the treatment for keloids?

1. Some physicians recommend giving x-ray therapy or cobalt treatments without surgery. This method has not been found to be very effective.

2. Recently, some investigators have found that keloids can be diminished in size by giving repeated injections of cortisone into and beneath the keloid. These must be repeated every few days for several months. Although some investigators have noted a satisfactory reduction in the size of a keloid with this method, most agree that it is not the best form of treatment.

3. If the keloid is more than one year old, it should be treated by surgical excision followed by immediate x-ray therapy. The x-ray treatments should be given on the day of surgery and for a day or two thereafter. This method of treatment seems to obtain the best results.

Are results of treatment less satisfactory if the keloid has existed for a long time?

They are supposed to be, especially if the keloid is several years old.

If the keloid is excised, what are the chances of another developing?

A keloid very frequently recurs after

excision. The recurring keloid is usually larger. The combination of surgery and x-ray therapy is successful in more than 50 percent of the cases in which it is performed.

How can a doctor know whether a patient will develop a new keloid after an old one has been excised?

There is no way of knowing.

When is it advisable to remove a keloid surgically?

When it is on an exposed part of the body and is exceptionally disfiguring. The keloid should be removed one or two years after it first appears.

Does a patient who has once developed a keloid in an operative scar have greater chances of developing another one if he needs to be operated upon again?

The tendency seems to persist throughout life. For this reason, it is perhaps wise to give a prophylactic x-ray treatment on the scar immediately following a second surgical procedure. This may prevent a keloid from forming.

Do keloids ever turn into malignant skin conditions?

No. Although they may grow to tremendous size, they are never cancerous.

When a keloid recurs, is it likely to be bigger than when it was first excised?

Yes. Keloids have the peculiarity of growing larger if the first removal is unsuccessful.

Kidneys and Ureters

The kidney is a bean-shaped, brownred gland covered over by a glistening, thin capsule. Normally it measures about four inches in length, two inches in width, and approximately one and a half inches in thickness. There are two kidneys, one on each side of the posterior (back) portion of the abdomen, located rather high in the loin (see diagram) behind the organs lying within the abdominal cavity.

The kidneys are glandular structures which secrete urine. They filter from the blood waste products which go to form urine and return to the circulating blood those substances that are necessary for normal chemical balance. This process takes place in the solid part of the organ and is one of the most complicated chemical reactions to occur within the human body. When the kidneys are too severely damaged by disease to function properly, uremia or kidney failure may result.

The central portions of the kidney are hollow and receive the liquid urine. The urine leaves the kidneys and passes down a long tubular structure (the ureter) which connects with the bladder. This ureter is in actuality a duct with a thin-walled, funnel-shaped beginning portion called the renal pelvis. The pelvis of the ureter lies partly within and partly outside the substance of the kidney.

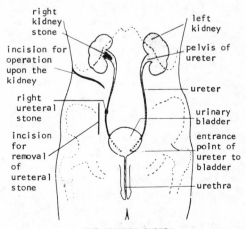

THE URINARY SYSTEM

The ureters are about 10 to 12 inches long and lie beneath the abdominal cavity. On either side of the midline, lying on top of thick muscles, the ureters course downward and enter the bladder through separate openings (the ureteral orifices) situated about two inches from one another.

There are four principal conditions affecting the kidneys which require surgery, and each of these will be considered in turn.

See also GENITOURINARY SYSTEM; NEPHRECTOMY.

KIDNEY STONES

The exact causes of kidney stone formation are not known, but several predisposing factors are recognized as playing dominant roles:

1. Disorders of calcium metabolism (with or without disease of the parathyroid glands in the neck).

2. Disorders of protein metabolism.

3. Vitamin deficiencies.

4. Tendencies toward gout, with disorders of uric acid metabolism.

5. Obstruction at the outlet of the kidney resulting in interference with drainage of urine from the kidney.

6. Urinary infections.

7. Drugs: Certain medications used to promote greater excretion of urine may also increase the output of uric acid, which may crystallize and form stones.

Although the exact mechanism producing the deposit of a stone is not clearly understood, it is known that chemicals precipitate out of the urine to form the various types of stone. Once the stone has formed, several events may take place:

1. The stone may remain in the kidney and produce no symptoms, its discovery being accidental in the course of examination for some unrelated condition.

2. The stone may remain in the kidney and cause repeated episodes of pain; it may result in infection, which will be apparent on examination of the urine; it may cause urinary bleeding.

3. The stone may remain in the kidney and grow in size to such an extent that it will cause progressive deterioration of the health of the kidney. In long-neglected cases, the entire function of the organ may be destroyed. In some cases the stone grows to several inches in diameter and may form a cast (known as a staghorn or coral stone) which completely fills the kidney.

4. The stone may leave the kidney and travel into the kidney tube (ureter) leading to the bladder. When this occurs, exquisite and excruciating pain (colic) may ensue.

The decision as to the necessity of surgically removing a kidney stone will depend upon:

1. **The general health of the patient:** The surgeon must evaluate the patient's ability to withstand the major operation. He must also decide how much damage to general health is being created by the stone's presence. Most patients take this type of surgery without serious reactions.

2. **The health of the other kidney:** Surgeons must always think in terms of both kidneys. People cannot live without at least one functioning kidney. It is dangerous to operate upon or remove a kidney containing a stone unless it has been determined that the other kidney has sufficiently good function to sustain life.

3. **The extent of damage to kidney function:** Removal of a kidney stone often restores a damaged kidney to near normal function. A completely func-

tionless kidney containing a stone should be removed in its entirety.

4. The likelihood of its passing through the urinary system by itself: Small stones which may be able to squeeze down the narrow kidney tube (the ureter is only about one fifth to one quarter of an inch in diameter in some of its narrow portions) and into the bladder can be treated with a policy of watchful waiting.

5. The intensity and frequency of the pain (colic) attributable to the stone: Frequently patients who suffer many attacks of colic will beg the surgeon to operate in order to relieve them.

6. The severity of the infection accompanying the stone: Severe infection is an indication for early surgery. Failure to operate may constitute a threat to the life of the kidney or even the life of the patient.

Operation is usually carried out under general anesthesia with an eight- to ten-inch-long incision starting in the loin on the affected side and extending around the side toward the front of the body. The level of this incision is just below the last rib and above the hipbone. The incision is carried through the fat tissues beneath the skin and through the muscles of the loin. The kidney is exposed and the stone is removed either through a cut made directly through the substance of the kidney (a nephrotomy) or by opening the kidney outlet (renal pelvis) over the stone (pyelotomy). These incisions into the kidney are closed after stone removal, and rubber drains are inserted and are permitted to emerge through the skin wound for a period of about a week. Only when the kidney shows extensive damage or infection is it necessary to remove the whole organ rather than the stone. This procedure is called a *nephrectomy*.

Recovery takes place in 98 percent of these cases, the patient being permitted to get out of bed on or about the second or third postoperative day and to leave the hospital in 10 to 14 days.

URETER STONES

Stones practically never form in the ureter but it is the commonest site for them to become lodged after passing down from the kidney proper. As a matter of fact, most operations upon the ureters are for the purpose of removing stones that have become stuck in its narrow passageway. When this happens, extreme colicky pain develops in the back and abdomen along the course of the ureter. If the stone is large it may completely block the ureter, and continuation of the obstruction will inevitably result in infection of the stagnant urine. Fortunately, the majority of these stones are small, and 80 to 90 percent of them pass spontaneously or with the help of manipulation carried out by catheters (long plastic tubes) passed through a cystoscope (an instrument that permits the urological surgeon to look directly into the bladder and to insert the catheters).

Stones in the ureter can usually be demonstrated by special x-ray examination, and studies of such films will give a clue as to whether spontaneous expulsion is possible. However, in about 10 to 20 percent of the cases, the stone gets stuck within the passageway of the ureter and does not pass on down into the bladder. These patients must be submitted to operation. An abdominal incision about four to five inches long is made over the region of the stone, and the ureter is exposed. A small nick is made in the ureter and the stone is removed. The procedure is performed in most hospitals under spinal or general anesthesia, is a perfectly safe maneuver, and leads to recovery within a week or ten days.

Most stones that are small enough to pass down the ureter into the bladder will also pass out of the bladder through its outlet (the urethra).

TUMORS AND CYSTS OF THE KIDNEY AND URETER

Tumors of the kidney can be divided into malignant growths (cancer) and the benign or innocent cysts. They may be found in both males and females of any age but tend to be discovered more often during the advanced years of life. There is one exception to this finding and that is the Wilms' tumor, a cancerous growth within the kidney seen in young children. Unless removed at a very early stage in its development, this tumor will result in loss of life within a year or two.

Kidney tumors produce three main signs which should act as warnings:

1. Pain in the loin over the kidney area

2. Blood in the urine

3. The feeling of a lump or mass in the kidney region

Cysts may be present as a solitary sac enclosed by a membrane and containing watery fluid or they may be multiple in number and involve both kidneys. Their size varies from that of a small grape to that of a grapefruit. They are usually harmless, but since it is often difficult on examination, and on obtaining a history of symptoms, to distinguish them from tumors, surgery is recommended. At operation, it becomes obvious immediately that they are benign.

Polycystic kidneys is a condition present from birth which evidences itself in adult life. It is a condition in which both kidneys are enlarged to several times normal by innumerable small and large cysts. Surgical treatment for this deformity is the performance of a kidney transplant.

Tumors of the ureter are very uncommon and tend to be found in people past 50 years of age. They manifest their presence by bloody urine, pain in the flank, and eventual obstruction to the flow of urine to the bladder. The diagnosis is made only after special x-ray examination.

The surgical treatment of tumors of the kidney and ureter is total removal of these structures.

The surgical treatment of cyst of the kidney is simple removal of the cyst.

Fortunately, people can live perfectly normal lives with one healthy kidney!

Kidney removal (nephrectomy) is considered a major procedure but recovery follows in well over 95 percent of the cases. It is usually performed, with the patient lying on his side, through an incision extending from the loin around onto the abdomen. The level is just below the last rib and above the hipbone. General anesthesia is preferred. In carrying out this operation, the entire kidney and renal pelvis and ureter on the affected side are removed after tying off the large blood vessels that supply and drain the organ. Unless the tumor has spread to surrounding blood vessels or other organs, most patients can expect a cure. Certainly here is one instance where early attention to symptoms, such as blood in the urine, can be rewarded by cure of a malignant growth!

Tumors of the ureter must almost always be accompanied by kidney removal on the same side, as a kidney without a channel for the drainage of its urine to the bladder is a useless organ.

OBSTRUCTION AT THE KIDNEY OUTLET
(Ureteropelvic Obstruction)

During the course of development of the kidney and its associated structures, certain abnormalities in anatomy may take place at or near the outlet, which prevent easy and free exit of the urine from the kidney.

The commonest are (1) strictures (narrowing), (2) bands of adhesions, and (3) misplaced blood vessels.

Such obstruction leads to a building up of pressure within the kidney pelvis and transmission of this pressure to the kidney substance, with eventual deterioration of function and degeneration of the organ. The condition is diagnosed by special x-ray studies which will reveal the obstruction.

Surgical intervention is required to remove the source of the obstruction, and this can be effected without appreciable danger in the great majority of cases. If, however, extensive damage has already been caused, removal of the kidney (nephrectomy) is necessary.

DIVERSION OF THE URINE FROM THE BLADDER

It sometimes becomes necessary to divert and interrupt the normal flow of urine into the bladder. This serious maneuver is carried out in an attempt to cure the following illnesses:

1. *Cancer of the bladder*
2. *Chronic, incurable bladder infections,* such as tuberculosis
3. When abnormal openings, *fistulas,* exist between the bladder and one of its neighboring organs, such as the uterus, vagina, or bowel
4. Certain birth deformities of the spinal cord which cause paralysis of the urinary bladder

For these unfortunate patients the urologist will perform one of three operative maneuvers:

1. Diversion of the urine directly from the kidney to the skin by means of a drainage tube inserted into the kidney. This is called a *nephrostomy.* (See diagram.)
2. Diversion of the urine by attaching the ureters to the skin. This is called a *cutaneous ureterostomy.* (See diagram.)

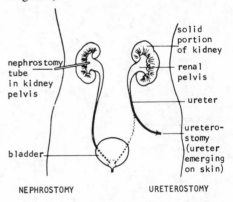

NEPHROSTOMY   URETEROSTOMY

3. Diversion of the urine by implanting the ureters into the lower large bowel. This is called a *uretero-colostomy.* (See diagram.)

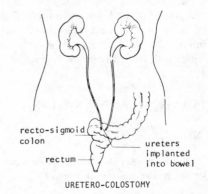

URETERO-COLOSTOMY

4. Diversion of the urine by implanting the ureters into an isolated loop of ileum (small intestine). This is called

an *ileal loop bladder*. After implantation of the ureters into this short segment of small intestine, one end of the intestine is stitched to the abdominal wall. Urine will then flow continuously out of this opening into a specially designed receptacle. (See diagram.)

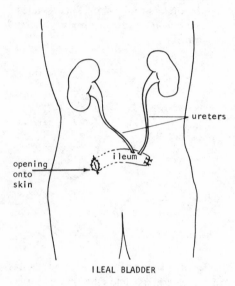

opening
onto
skin

ureters

ileum

ILEAL BLADDER

In all but the third instance, the patient must wear a specially designed receptacle to catch the continuous flow of urine. When the ureters have been implanted into the large bowel, urine is henceforth passed from the rectum.

QUESTIONS AND ANSWERS

KIDNEY AND URETER STONES

Is there a way to crush or dissolve stones in the kidney or ureter?
No.

When is stone removal an emergency procedure?
1. When the stone blocks the kidney

outlet and infected urine becomes trapped in the kidney
2. When the stone completely blocks the ureter

Are operations for kidney or ureter stones dangerous?
No. Recovery is expected in practically all cases. The main exception is in people who have marked kidney damage *on both sides.*

What preliminary steps are taken in the hospital?
Often, when kidney or ureter blockage exists, the urologist will pass a catheter (tube) beyond the obstruction in order to permit drainage of the infected urine. This may be allowed to drain for a few days before undertaking surgery.

Are special preparations necessary before operations for stone?
1. Large amounts of fluids should be taken.
2. If infection accompanies stone formation, large doses of antibiotic drugs should be given.

Are special tests done before operation?
Yes:
1. Accurate x-ray films must be taken just prior to surgery to make sure of the exact location of the stone or stones. Occasionally a stone will move, and unless recent x-rays have been taken, it may be difficult to locate during surgery.
2. Complete blood counts and blood chemistry determinations are taken to denote the general state of health and the extent of kidney damage, if any.

Does the surgeon usually know in advance whether he will be forced to remove the kidney or part of it?
Yes. X-rays will give him fairly accurate information.

Is it ever necessary to remove the kidney or part of the kidney along with the stone?

Yes. Occasionally kidney damage is so widespread that the whole organ must be removed. In other instances, only a portion of the kidney is removed (heminephrectomy) in order to prevent stone recurrence.

What kind of anesthetic is used?

General anesthesia is used for removal of stones in the kidney and upper ureter. Spinal is sometimes used for removal of stones in the mid and lower ureter.

How long do operations for stone removal take to perform?

Approximately one to two and a half hours.

Where is the incision made?

1. For kidney stones, an eight- to ten-inch incision is made obliquely from the flank onto the abdomen at a level below the rib cage and above the hipbone.

2. A four- to five-inch incision is made obliquely in the flank if the stone is in the upper ureter, or a four- to five-inch incision running longitudinally on the abdomen if the stone is lodged in the lower ureter.

Are blood transfusions necessary?

Not as a routine. In extensive cases of kidney stones where technical difficulties are anticipated, they will be necessary.

Are drainage tubes inserted after operation?

Yes:

1. After kidney stone operations where infection has been present, rubber drains are inserted and permitted to remain in place for a week or two.

2. After ureter stone operations, a drain is sometimes inserted for a week to ten days.

Does urine drain onto the skin when drains are inserted?

It may for some time after the drain is removed. The normal flow reestablishes itself spontaneously within a short period of time.

Is there much postoperative pain in these operations?

Moderate, but no more than for any major procedure.

Are special nurses advisable?

Yes, for two to four days.

When can the patient get out of bed?

Within two to three days after surgery.

What special postoperative measures are carried out?

1. For a day or two, intravenous fluids are given to maintain a good fluid intake.

2. One or more of the antibiotic drugs are often given to prevent or control infection.

Are the wounds painful?

Moderately. For several months after surgery the patient may feel tingling and peculiar "pins and needles" sensation in the wound, due to the fact that small nerves have been cut in making the incision.

How long a hospital stay is necessary if no complications develop?

Kidney stone   10 days to 2 weeks
Ureter stone   8 to 10 days

Is convalescent care necessary?

After kidney stone, it may be helpful but is not necessary. After ureter stone, none is needed.

Is follow-up medical care important?

Yes. The patient should return to the urologist regularly for wound inspection, urine examination, and tests for kidney function. X-ray studies of the ureter are especially important postoperatively to make sure that no narrowing has taken place as a result of the operation.

Is pregnancy permissible after these operations?

Yes, if there has been complete recovery. A year's interval should elapse before becoming pregnant.

Does stone formation recur?

In approximately 15 to 25 percent of all cases.

What can be done to help prevent stone recurrence?

1. Large fluid intake. About eight to ten glasses of water daily.

2. Special diets, depending on the composition of the stone.

3. Certain medications, depending on the composition of the stone, such as acidifying or alkalinizing preparations.

4. Removal of one or more parathyroid glands in the neck, if a tumor or overactivity of one of these structures has been shown to be the cause of the stone formation.

Will the removal of a tumor of a parathyroid gland prevent the formation of new stones?

Yes, in most instances.

How often must the dressing be changed after hospital discharge?

Daily. This can be done by the patient or a member of the family.

How soon after operation can one:

Bathe?	As soon as the wound is healed; 2 to 3 weeks
Drive a car?	About 4 to 6 weeks
Resume light work?	About 6 to 8 weeks
Resume usual activities?	About 6 to 8 weeks

Are operations sometimes complicated by postoperative renal failure, kidney shutdown, anuria, and other kidney malfunctions?

Yes. These are some of the most serious complications of major surgery.

How can one guard against the development of renal shutdown after surgery?

The internist and the surgeon must discover before surgery whether or not the body chemistries are adequate to withstand the contemplated surgery. This is determined by examining the blood and urine and by performing other tests to determine the adequacy of vital organs, such as the liver, heart, and kidneys. If the operation is not absolutely essential, it should not be carried out if the patient shows marked impairment of kidney function.

Is failure of liver function often associated with kidney failure?

Yes, especially after a major operation. This is called hepatorenal failure or the hepatorenal syndrome.

If impairment of liver and kidney function has been discovered preoperatively, is there any way to improve it so that surgery can be performed safely?

To a limited extent. The liver should be supported by feeding large quantities of sugar and by withholding fats from the diet. The kidneys should be supported by attempts to bring the various blood chemicals into more normal balance. This is a complicated procedure and should be supervised by the internist. Of course, people with advanced kidney damage cannot be helped greatly, but sufficient temporary improvement may be obtained to permit essential surgery.

If kidney failure or kidney shutdown does take place after surgery, what can be done about it?

1. Measures will be taken to maintain

in the patient as normal a balance of electrolytes (chemicals such as sodium, chloride, and potassium) as possible.

2. Fluid intake and output will be carefully watched, and attempts will be made to bring them into proper balance.

3. If poisons, such as urea nitrogen, accumulate in large quantities in the blood, the artificial kidney may be used.

4. If kidney failure is associated with blood loss, blood transfusions will be given.

DIVERSION OF THE URINE FROM THE BLADDER

What conditions require diversion of the urine from the bladder?

1. Some types of cancer of the bladder.

2. Incurable chronic bladder infections which have caused the bladder to become shrunken and useless.

3. Abnormal openings between the bladder and vagina or bowel which do not lend themselves to direct correction.

4. Certain birth deformities of the nervous system which are associated with paralysis of the bladder.

What procedures are done to divert the urinary stream?

1. Permanent nephrostomy: This means a permanent connection between the kidney and the skin.

2. Cutaneous ureterostomy: This means a permanent connection between the ureter and the skin.

3. Uretero-colostomy: This means a permanent implantation of the ureter into the lower bowel.

4. Ileal loop bladder or uretero-ileostomy. This involves the utilization of a segment of small intestine to act as a conduit for the urine.

Are these operations serious?

Yes, but modern techniques have resulted in a very high degree of success.

How long do these operations take to perform?

Nephrostomy	1½ to 2 hours
Ureterostomy	1½ to 2 hours
Uretero-colostomy	2½ to 3 hours
Uretero-ileostomy	
(ileal loop bladder)	3 to 4 hours

Are both sides usually operated upon at the same time?

An attempt is always made to do both sides at the same time. However, this is not always possible because of the poor general health of the patient.

Is the bladder removed at the same time as the ureters are detached?

Only if the general condition of the patient will permit it. Otherwise the ureters are taken care of, either by bringing them to the skin surface or by transplanting them at the first operation, and the bladder removal is carried out at a future time.

Where do the tubes emerge after a nephrostomy?

From the side of the body below the ribs.

What provision is made for collecting the urine that drains to the skin?

Special receptacles are attached to the skin openings and connect by tubes to bags strapped to the leg.

Are special measures necessary after nephrostomy and ureterostomy?

Yes.

1. Drugs must be taken to forestall urinary infection.

2. The tubes must be irrigated at regular intervals.

3. The tubes must be changed at regular intervals.

Where do the tubes emerge after a ureterostomy?

Near the front of the abdomen at about the level of the navel.

Can the flow of urine be voluntarily controlled after nephrostomy or ureterostomy?

No. There is a steady, uncontrolled flow.

What provision is made for collecting the urine from ureterostomy openings?

Catheters (tubes) are inserted into the skin openings and are attached to receptacles strapped to the leg.

Where does the urine flow after an ileal loop bladder is performed?

Into a special plastic receptacle which is cemented around the opening on the abdominal wall.

Does any stool pass with the urine when an ileal loop bladder operation has been performed?

No. The small intestinal (ileal) loop is completely isolated from the rest of the intestinal tract.

How is the urine passed after ureterocolostomy (implantation of the ureters into the bowel)?

For the first few days a tube will be placed in the rectum to drain off the urine as it is excreted. Later the rectal tube is removed and the urine is voided spontaneously at intervals. At first these intervals are short, but they increase as time progresses and the rectum accommodates itself to the presence of liquid contents. Eventually these patients can hold their urine for several hours.

Will there be involuntary loss of urine after the colon transplant operation?

Ordinarily not, since the rectal sphincter muscle will control the expulsion of the liquid contents in the same way as it does solid contents.

Does stool (feces) back up and go into the implanted ureters?

No. The flow is always in the opposite direction.

How long is the convalescent period after ureteral transplant operations?

Two to three months.

Are special postoperative procedures necessary after these operations?

Yes:

1. Drugs to minimize urinary infection must be taken.

2. Periodic x-ray and blood chemistry studies must be undertaken to determine the state of general health and kidney function.

What can be done, following a transplant operation, if it is found that kidney function is deteriorating?

The ureters must then be taken out of the intestine or bowel and brought to the skin, thus performing a permanent cutaneous ureterostomy, or the kidneys must be drained directly to the skin (permanent nephrostomy).

What are the chances of a successful result with a ureteral transplant operation?

About 70 to 80 percent.

Which ureteral transplantation operation is more successful?

It has been found that kidney and liver damage is more likely to take place after transplanting the ureters into the large bowel. For this reason, the ileal loop bladder operation is now used more frequently.

KIDNEY TUMORS AND CYSTS

What symptoms and signs do kidney tumors produce?

1. Blood in the urine

2. Pain in the loin over the kidney region

3. The presence of a mass or lump in the kidney area

4. Unexplained fever, sweats, malaise, and weight loss

What is the treatment for a kidney tumor?

Prompt removal of the entire kidney. Preliminary x-ray therapy and postoperative x-ray treatments are also advised in certain types of kidney tumor.

Is the removal of a kidney a serious operation?

Yes, but if the opposite kidney is normal, the removal of one kidney will not adversely affect life.

Is kidney removal (nephrectomy) a dangerous operation?

No. Recovery, with an uncomplicated postoperative course, is the usual outcome.

How long is the patient in the hospital after an operation for removal of a kidney?

Ten to twelve days.

What are some of the common forms of cystic disease of the kidney?

1. Congenital polycystic kidneys. This is a condition with which a person is born and is characterized by numerous large and small cysts, usually of both kidneys. Kidney function is impaired in this type of disease as the individual grows older. This condition occurs in families.

2. Solitary cyst of the kidney. This type usually does not impair kidney function.

What are the symptoms of solitary cyst of the kidney?

Usually, there are no symptoms. Occasionally, there may be pain and blood in the urine.

What are the symptoms in polycystic kidney disease?

As the patient grows into adulthood there may be pain in the kidney area, blood in the urine, infection, and elevated blood pressure.

What is the treatment for polycystic kidneys?

There is no effective treatment for the cysts themselves. When complications arise, such as infection, stone formation, or excessive pain, these are treated by ordinary measures. With the advent of kidney transplants, it is now possible to help some of these unfortunate patients.

What is the treatment for a solitary cyst of the kidney?

The cyst itself is removed, leaving the remainder of the kidney in place. Once in a great while, a solitary cyst can be treated by withdrawing the fluid and injecting a solution which induces the cyst to close itself off. This is not, however, the most common method of handling solitary cysts.

Are tumors of the ureter very common?

No. They are extremely rare.

What forms do tumors of the ureter usually take?

The great majority of them are malignant.

What are the symptoms of tumors of the ureter?

Blood in the urine, obstruction to the passage of urine into the bladder, and eventual infection.

How is the diagnosis of a tumor of the ureter made?

By x-ray studies of the urinary tract and by noting obstruction on attempted passage of a catheter up the ureter.

What is the treatment for a tumor of the ureter?

Removal of the ureter along with its kidney and a portion of the bladder surrounding the entrance of the ureter.

What is a ureterocele?

A cystic formation at the bladder end of the ureter due to an abnormal opening of the ureter into the bladder. There is also a weakness in the wall of the ureter in its lowermost portion, probably the result of a birth deformity.

What are the symptoms of a ureterocele?

There may be no symptoms at all and the condition may be discovered accidentally during the course of a routine investigation for some other condition in the urinary tract. Ureteroceles can, however, be the cause of a chronic infection in the bladder and kidney, and also, by blocking the outflow of urine, damage the ureters and kidneys.

What is the treatment for a ureterocele?

If it is a small one, it can be treated successfully by enlarging the opening of the ureter into the bladder. Some ureteroceles may be treated through a cystoscope, either by burning off a portion of the cyst or by shaving off a portion of it. If the ureterocele is large, it may be necessary to operate and remove it through an opening made in the bladder.

Are operations for ureterocele successful?

Yes.

Are these operations dangerous?

No.

ABSCESS OF THE KIDNEY

Does abscess of the kidneys occur very often?

No. It is relatively rare. Males are three times more likely than females to have the condition. It is usually the right kidney that is affected.

What causes kidney abscesses?

The usual cause is a spread through the bloodstream of a *Staphylococcus aureus* organism that may have had its origin from an infection in the skin, possibly a boil or an infected laceration. There may be a period of several weeks or months between the original infection and the ultimate appearance of the kidney abscess.

What are the symptoms and signs of a kidney abscess?

1. There is often a history of preceding infection, such as an attack of acute tonsillitis, a severe upper respiratory infection, or a boil or infected laceration of the skin.

2. The patient will have tenderness on pressure over the kidney area and a swelling may be felt in the region.

3. There will usually be chills or chilly sensations and a fever that fluctuates from near normal to 103° F or 104° F daily.

4. Blood examination will show a markedly increased white cell count.

5. X-rays may reveal an irregular enlargement of the kidney.

6. In most cases the urine will not show pus, as the abscess is usually located away from the pelvis of the kidney, where the urine collects.

How serious is an abscess of the kidney?

It is a serious infection, but it can be cured by the judicious use of antibiotic drugs and by surgical drainage of the abscess. If the abscess is not drained, it may break through the capsule surrounding the kidney and out into the tissues in the area. Such an abscess may spread up toward the chest cavity and down toward the pelvic region. This condition is very serious, but fortunately it takes place only rarely with modern methods of treatment.

What is the treatment for a kidney abscess?

In the early stages, when the inflammation has not proceeded to pus formation, bed rest and antibiotics may be sufficient treatment. However, the diagnosis is not usually made at this early stage of the disease. Generally, by the time a definite diagnosis is made, surgical drainage of the abscess is the only proper method of treatment.

Rapid healing with complete restoration of the normal kidney function is the general rule in these cases.

How does an abscess of a kidney differ from a carbuncle of a kidney?

An abscess is a well-confined mass of softened, liquefied inflammatory tissue that comes to a single head. A carbuncle may have several pockets of softened, liquefied inflammatory tissue that never coalesces to form one head.

The treatment for an abscess is simple incision and drainage, and there is a great expectancy of a cure. Since satisfactory drainage of a carbuncle is difficult because of the many pockets of pus, it may be wiser to remove the kidney, providing the opposite kidney is normal. This may not be necessary in all cases of carbuncle of the kidney; in some cases the carbuncle is small enough so that all the pockets can be adequately drained without removing the organ.

KIDNEY INJURIES

What are the common causes for kidney injuries?

1. Automobile accidents
2. Athletic events, such as football or boxing
3. A fall from a height with a direct blow to the kidney area

How can one tell if he has a kidney injury?

1. By noting pain and tenderness in the kidney region
2. By noting blood in the urine

What is the treatment for kidney injuries?

For the minor injuries which make up the great majority, bed rest is the main form of treatment. If the bleeding is alarming and the x-ray shows a badly damaged kidney, surgery may become necessary for removal of the organ, or drainage of the blood and urine that have escaped from the injured kidney.

Can a damaged kidney ever be restored surgically?

Yes. If the damage has not been too extensive, the kidney may be sutured instead of being removed.

Is it often necessary to operate for a kidney injury?

The great majority will get well without surgery.

How can one tell whether surgery is necessary?

By noting whether the urine clears and whether there is evidence of restored kidney function. If blood continues to appear in the urine and kidney function fails to return, or if the patient's general condition deteriorates and there is swelling in the loin, surgery is indicated. Pyelograms and angiograms are also useful in diagnosis of the extent of injury.

Do children often injure the kidneys?

This is not very common. When it occurs, it is usually the result of a severe blunt blow to the loin or side caused by falling from a height or by an automobile accident. If the child has a congenitally deformed kidney, such as a polycystic type, mild blows may cause serious injury.

What is the outlook for someone who has sustained a severe kidney injury?

Fortunately, it is extremely rare for both kidneys to be simultaneously damaged in one accident. If one kidney is functioning normally and the damaged kidney appears capable of salvage, it is left in place. Healing will usually take place in time, and satisfactory function of the kidney will return. It is essential that the patient's blood pressure be followed carefully. There is occasional elevation of blood pressure when the blood supply to a kidney has been damaged irreparably. Should this happen, it may become necessary to remove the injured kidney, provided the opposite organ is functional.

TRANSPLANTATION OF KIDNEYS

Can kidneys be successfully transplanted from one individual to another?

Yes. The technical procedure is perfectly feasible. However, difficulties following transplantation of a kidney often ensue when the rejection reaction sets in, and this may occur anywhere from a few weeks to a year or two after the operation has been performed.

What causes a kidney to die after it has been successfully transplanted?

A phenomenon known as the rejection reaction takes place. All people have antibodies whose duty it is to protect against invading foreign bodies. Tissue cells from other animals or humans are judged by the host to be foreign bodies, and the normal protective mechanisms of the host are mobilized to destroy them. Thus a transplanted kidney will be attacked by the white blood cells of the host and the grafted organ may die.

When is kidney transplantation indicated?

It is performed only as a lifesaving measure in a patient who would otherwise die due to kidney failure. In this category, one would place conditions such as uremia, polycystic kidneys, chronic inflammation of the kidney due to multiple stones or overwhelming infection, or a malignant tumor of a kidney in a patient who has only one kidney.

What kidney transplants are most likely to succeed?

It has been found that permanent survival of a grafted kidney is most likely to take place when the organ is transplanted from one identical twin to another.

Can kidneys from animals be successfully transplanted to humans?

In recent years it has been discovered that kidneys from chimpanzees, or even dogs, may survive within a human body for quite some time. However, their survival rate is not good.

Can anything be done to overcome the rejection reaction?

Yes. There are many measures that can be taken to tide the host over the period when the rejection reaction is at its height. Various drugs, such as Imuran, antilymphocyte serum, corticoids, and x-ray radiation to the site of the transplant can be given. This may slow down or entirely stop the host from producing the antibodies which will kill the transplant.

How successful are kidney transplants?

In certain clinics throughout the world where this work is done in large numbers, it has been found that kidney transplantation can be carried out successfully in more than half of those people upon whom it has been attempted. There are now several thousand cases on record where a transplanted kidney has lived for as long as five years.

What can be done if the transplanted kidney fails to survive?

The patient can be reoperated and a new kidney from another donor can be inserted.

Is it ever indicated to transplant the kidney from its normal position in the upper back to the pelvic region?

Yes. In instances where the ureter, the tube leading from the kidney to the bladder, is the site of a malignant tumor or where the ureter has been destroyed by injury or disease, it has been found possible to salvage the kidney by lifting it from its normal position and transplanting it in the same manner as one would transplant a kidney from another individual.

Are operations for kidney transplantation serious?

Of course they are. It must be realized that these procedures are only carried out on those who would otherwise succumb to kidney failure. A kidney is never transplanted to an individual who has at least one functioning kidney.

BIRTH DEFORMITIES OF THE KIDNEYS AND URETERS

What are some of the more common birth deformities of the kidneys and ureters?

1. **Absent kidneys.** This is a rare deformity. The child with this condition will die within a few days.

2. **Incomplete kidney formation,** with absence of certain essential elements or failure of the various elements to unite one with the other. This deformity also usually causes death.

3. **Polycystic kidneys,** which have many large cystic masses that prevent adequate function. Children with this condition usually survive but have kidney difficulties in adulthood.

4. **Congenital constriction of the kidney outlet (pelvis).** Such a malformation will cause slowed and inadequate flow of urine from the kidney to the bladder.

5. **Abnormally placed blood vessels,** located near the kidney outlet, that cause partial blockage of the urine as it exits and passes down toward the bladder.

6. **Horseshoe kidney,** a not uncommon birth deformity. In this condition, the two kidneys are fused and lie across the back of the abdomen. In normal anatomy, there is a separate organ on each side. In most such children, kidney function is normal.

7. **Ectopic kidney.** In this deformity one kidney or both kidneys are not in the usual anatomical position. A not uncommon deviation is for one kidney to be located lower down in the abdomen, even in the pelvic region.

8. **Duplications of the kidneys or ureters.** The ureter is the tube leading from the kidney to the bladder. Sometimes there may be a double kidney on one side and a normal single kidney on the opposite side of the abdomen. In other instances there may be a single kidney on each side but a double ureter leading to the bladder.

Are children ever born with only one (solitary) kidney?

Yes, although congenital absence of a kidney is rare. It occurs less than once in 500 births. The total size of a solitary kidney frequently equals that of two normal kidneys, and the total function approximates the output of two normal kidneys.

Are the kidneys always located in the upper back portion of the abdomen?

No. Occasionally, one or both kidneys are located much farther down in the pelvic area. As the child grows older, this may be confused with an abdominal tumor. Whenever a child is suspected of having a lower abdominal tumor, x-rays should be taken in order to rule out the presence of a pelvic kidney.

Are there ever more than two kidneys in a newborn child?

Yes. The rather common deformity that produces a double kidney on one side is due to a splitting of the ureter, as in a fork of a road, as it develops in the young embryo. When the split ureter enters the primitive cell masses that will go to form kidney substance, it stimulates the formation of two separate and distinct organs, although the substance of the kidneys remains fused. It is possible to have a double kidney on each side of the spinal column.

Are the two kidneys ever found on the same side of the body?

Yes, occasionally. This occurs in a condition called crossed renal ectopia, where the two masses that develop into the kidneys become fused and lie together on one side. The ureter leading from the ectopic kidney (the one that is out of normal position) crosses over the spine to enter the bladder on the opposite side.

Is it important for the examining pediatrician to feel the kidneys of a newborn?

Yes, because occasionally a misplaced kidney, a polycystic kidney, or one containing a large cyst or tumor can be felt at birth.

In general, what is the treatment for birth deformities of the kidneys and ureters?

The treatment depends upon the particular structure in which the defect occurs and upon the possible interference with function. The methods of treating the most frequently encountered deformities are as follows:

1. Absent kidneys. There is currently no treatment for a child born with no kidneys. Even the transplantation of a kidney from another child would prove inadequate, because nearly always other necessary structures, such as the ureters and the bladder, are also missing.

2. Incomplete formation of kidneys. These defects also rarely lend themselves to any type of treatment or surgical correction. Most children with such conditions have accompanying defects and cannot live.

3. Polycystic kidneys. In most of these cases there is sufficient kidney function to permit the child to grow and develop. The real trouble comes when they reach adulthood and their kidney function fails to sustain them and they develop kidney infections. Many of these patients will benefit from the graft of a normal kidney from another individual.

4. Congenital constriction of the kidney outlet. If the interference with free drainage of urine is marked, these children should undergo surgery. Good results with relief of the obstruction can be obtained by plastic repair of the kidney outlet and removal of the narrowing.

5. Abnormally placed blood vessels constricting the kidney outlet should be corrected surgically. This can be accomplished without danger to the child, and the results are almost always completely satisfactory. It is important that these procedures be performed at the right time, before the continued obstruction has caused permanent kidney damage.

6. Horseshoe kidneys require no surgery, as most of them function normally. However, if the child develops kidney stones or some other condition requiring surgery, it is essential that the kidney not be removed. The inadvertent removal of a horseshoe kidney would leave the child without any functioning kidney tissue.

7. Ectopic kidney. Many malpositioned kidneys function normally and require no treatment. Others may be small in size and function poorly. However, they rarely require surgical removal. Every once in a while, an ectopic kidney will be mistaken for an abdominal tumor and it will be surgically removed.

8. Double kidneys on one or both sides and double ureters on one or both sides rarely require treatment. There are numerous tests to determine which of the kidneys is functional, and this is important to know before operating for disease within one of them. In many cases, all three, or all four, function and contribute well to the body economy.

9. Exstrophy of the bladder usually demands early surgery, or the child will develop serious urinary infection and will die.

10. Congenital constriction of the bladder outlet or narrowing of a portion of the urethra can be corrected by dilatation with specially devised instruments. Cases that do not respond to this form of manipulative treatment can be treated surgically.

11. Hypospadias and epispadias can be corrected by plastic repair, using a tubelike graft of skin from the shaft of the penis as a substitute urethra. These operations may require several stages before a final good result is obtained.

12. Undescended testicles can be repaired surgically with good results in those cases in which the testicle has emerged from the abdominal cavity and is lodged in the inguinal canal.

13. Pseudohermaphroditism and all other deformities of the external genitals require intensive study before definitive treatment is begun. If the defects are obvious and reparable (which is unusual), they should be corrected as soon as possible. However, it is sometimes extremely difficult to determine the true sex, and in these cases, an exploratory abdominal operation is necessary. After opening the abdominal cavity, a piece of the tissue that re-

sembles either the ovaries or testicles is removed and is examined microscopically. This reveals whether the tissue is ovarian or testicular and whether the cells will be able to mature sufficiently to function. Whenever the true sex is doubtful it is always better to aim to conform to the female rather than the male sex. This is wise because the female genitals can be molded when the child gets older so as to conform to the female configuration. It is impossible for a surgeon to construct a functioning penis and testicles. Thus it may be wise to remove any primitive, potentially nonfunctioning testicular tissue found within the abdomen and to excise a rudimentary or poorly developed penis. If ovarian tissue has been found on abdominal examination, then an enlarged clitoris resembling a penis should be excised. At a later date the structure resembling the scrotal sac can be surgically treated so as to construct vulval lips. A vagina can be constructed when the child reaches early adulthood.

14. Hydroceles. A hydrocele present at birth should be observed over a period of several months without treatment. If after the child has reached one year of age the hydrocele persists, it should be surgically excised. There is often an accompanying hernia, which can be repaired at the same time.

HIGH BLOOD PRESSURE AND KIDNEY DISEASE

What is the relationship between high blood pressure and kidney disease?

Long-standing high blood pressure over a period of years may eventually cause kidney disease due to disturbance in the circulation of the kidney. Conversely, severe kidney disorders often lead to high blood pressure.

It has been found within recent years that arteriosclerosis of the renal artery, the main artery to the kidney, also can cause high blood pressure.

Is it ever possible to cure high blood pressure by surgery upon the blood vessels to the kidney?

Yes. It can now be determined accurately by special x-ray techniques whether the major artery to the kidney is narrowed. If this condition is found to be present, plastic surgery upon the renal blood vessel can often be carried out successfully. If the narrowing is due to arteriosclerosis, the inner lining of the artery is reamed out or a patch graft made of Teflon or Dacron is applied. This will increase the blood supply to the kidney, in many instances eliminating the cause for the high blood pressure.

Knee

THE DERANGED KNEE (TORN CARTILAGE)

The knee is one of the most frequently injured joints in the body. This is not an unexpected finding since the knee joint is almost constantly in use, bears a great share of the body weight, yet is able to move in only one plane or direction. In other words, the range of motion of the knee cannot conform too well to the many twists and turns the average person makes. Athletes and people who work with the knees slightly bent and who perform tasks requiring body rotation are most prone to develop knee injuries.

The knee joint is composed of the smooth surfaces of the thighbone (the femur) and the major leg bone (the tibia). The kneecap (patella) rides freely in front of the joint and serves to make the thigh muscles more efficient.

Within the joint, lying upon the inner and outer edges of the tibia (leg bone) and attached to the capsule, are two half-moon-shaped structures known as the semilunar cartilages or menisci. (See diagram.) These are semihard, gristle-like, smooth substances which minimize the friction in the joint and act as shock absorbers. In the usual injury, the knee is twisted in a slightly bent position, and either the inner or outer cartilage is torn away from its underlying attachment (capsule). The cartilage can also be torn when it is twisted while in a squatting position.

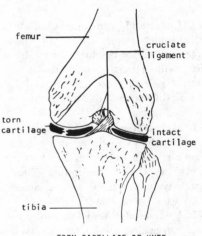

TORN CARTILAGE OF KNEE

This injury gives rise to the following symptoms:

1. Pain in the knee

2. "Locking," or inability to straighten the knee, in about 60 percent of the cases

3. Swelling of the joint which comes on within three to four hours after the accident

4. Inability to bear weight on the leg

5. A feeling of weakness and instability in the joint

These symptoms may continue for a week or more, after which time the swelling and pain subside and the leg can again be straightened. However, there is a tendency for the knee to "give way" or bend suddenly without warning. A feeling of weakness in the joint persists. This condition arises because the edge of the torn cartilage travels about in the joint and interferes with stable muscle control and smooth flexion and extension.

Although it is most unusual for both semilunar cartilages to be torn at the same time, the knee is so weakened by the injury that the other cartilage is much more susceptible to tear should another injury ensue.

TREATMENT

Since most (95 percent) torn cartilages will not heal spontaneously, patients who have persistent pain and weakness about the joint should undergo surgery. If, on the other hand, it is the first injury and the damage does not appear to be severe, the leg may be placed in a plaster cast for two to three weeks. Operation may be postponed indefinitely if symptoms subside after the cast is removed.

The operation for a torn cartilage is performed under low spinal or general anesthesia through a three- to four-inch incision made in a longitudinal direction on either the inner or outer aspect of the kneecap. The joint is opened and the torn cartilage can be located easily. It is freed from its attachments and removed with a knife or scissors. The joint is then closed tightly, the skin sutured, and an elastic compression bandage is bound around the joint. For two to three days after operation, the leg is kept in an elevated position to relieve swelling. While still in bed, the patient is taught special exercises to maintain the function of the muscles controlling the knee joint. These exercises are continued after the patient is up and about. This is essential, for otherwise there might be considerable weakness, which would become evident when the patient attempted to resume normal activity.

Recovery takes place in practically all cases. Within several weeks after surgery, full use of the joint returns, although some mild weakness in the area may remain for three to four months.

QUESTIONS AND ANSWERS

What is the function of the semilunar cartilages in the knee joint?
They serve as shock absorbers and also as stabilizers of the joint.

What happens when a person gets a torn knee cartilage?
One of the gristlelike cartilages at the margin of the tibia (the main leg bone) is torn away from its attachments.

Can the diagnosis of a torn cartilage be made on x-ray examination?
No. Cartilage is not visible on x-ray and therefore the examination is negative.

What symptoms accompany this injury?
1. Severe pain in the knee region.
2. In over half the cases, a locked knee occurs, with inability to straighten the leg.
3. Swelling of the joint.
4. Tenderness on pressure over the region of the torn cartilage.
5. Inability to walk or stand on the knee.

What is the usual mechanism of a torn cartilage?
Severe twisting strain on a partially bent knee.

Do torn cartilages heal by themselves?
Rarely.

How soon after surgery may walking be attempted?
About 12 to 15 days.

Is convalescent care necessary?
No.

What are the results of this procedure?
Excellent.

Is a knee support worn after surgery?
Yes, occasionally an elastic support is worn until the muscles are restored to normal power.

Is a cast worn after surgery?
No.

Is the knee ever worse after operation?
No.

Does the operation result in a stiff knee?
No, unless the patient neglects to do the prescribed exercises.

Does complete return to normal function follow surgery?
Yes, but prolonged treatment and special exercises for several months may be necessary to attain this end.

What are the special exercises?
Bending and straightening the knee, usually against resistance in order to strengthen the knee muscles.

Is the scar disfiguring?
No.

How long does the operation take to perform?
Thirty to 45 minutes.

What procedure is carried out?
The joint is opened, the torn cartilage is grasped with a forceps and cut away in its entirety.

Are both semilunar cartilages (the inner and outer) removed at operation?
No. Only the torn one is removed.

Is it a painful operation?
Only for the first day or two after surgery.

Does the knee joint swell after operation?
Yes, in some cases.

Are special nurses necessary?
No.

How soon after surgery can one get out of bed?
Three to five days.

Is it necessary to use crutches?
Yes, for a week or so after getting out of bed.

How long a hospital stay is required?
Seven to ten days.

Do all torn cartilages have to be operated upon?
No. Some of them will subside with rest and placement in a cast for several weeks.

Which patients should be subjected to surgery?
Those in whom there is no relief from pain and swelling after rest or the application of a cast. Also, those who have repeated injuries or in whom the knee buckles under or locks on frequent occasions.

Does the cartilage ever grow back after removal?
Only a small rim may re-form around the edges of the joint's surface.

Can the knee function normally without the cartilage?
Yes.

What will happen if surgery is refused in the severe case?
The knee will remain weak, painful, and unstable. Arthritis will eventually result.

Is the operation for a torn cartilage dangerous?
No.

Are special preoperative measures necessary?
No.

What anesthesia is used?
Usually spinal, occasionally general.

What kind of incision is made?
A three- to four-inch longitudinal incision on either the inner or outer aspect of the knee adjacent to the kneecap.

How long does it take the wound to heal?
Ten to 12 days.

How soon after operation can one:
Bathe?	12 to 14 days
Drive a car?	3 to 4 weeks
Resume light work?	3 to 4 weeks
Resume heavy work?	6 to 8 weeks
Resume athletics?	3 to 6 months
Dance?	6 weeks

Lacerations

See CUTS; FIRST AID.

Laminectomy

Laminectomy is an operative procedure in which one or more laminae, a series of bony plates which cover the spinal cord, are removed. Each vertebra has two laminae which slope toward each other, creating a long archway in which the nerves of the spinal cords are safely lodged.

See also HERNIATED INTERVERTEBRAL DISK; NEUROSURGERY.

QUESTIONS AND ANSWERS

For what purposes are laminae excised?
Whenever a surgeon wishes to gain access to the spinal cord he must first remove the laminae in order to expose the underlying cord structures. This procedure is carried out most often when a spinal cord tumor is present.

Must more than one lamina be removed when operating for a spinal cord tumor?
Yes. To get adequate exposure for removal of such a tumor, it is sometimes necessary to remove several laminae.

Is a laminectomy ever performed for a slipped disk?
Yes. In some cases, in order to better visualize and remove the slipped disk, it is necessary to perform a laminectomy. In other cases, the disk can be removed without the performance of a laminectomy.

How is a laminectomy performed?
The patient is placed on his abdomen and an incision is made in the midline or just to one side of the midline of the back over the vertebrae. The incision is carried down through the soft tissues and muscles until the bony plate of the vertebra is exposed. When the lamina is thoroughly exposed it is chipped away with a bone-chipping instrument.

Is a laminectomy a dangerous operative procedure?
No. The technique of the procedure is not complicated but the underlying condition for which the laminectomy is performed may be a serious one. Thus, if the laminectomy is performed in order to remove a spinal cord tumor, it may involve the excision of several laminae and a very delicate operation upon the cord structures.

Is recovery the general rule following laminectomy?

Yes. The actual removal of the lamina, as stated, is not dangerous and recovery takes place in almost all instances. However, if the underlying diseased cord structures cannot be removed or restored, the outcome of the operation may not be successful.

Is the spine permanently weakened by laminectomy?

No. There is adequate support even after the removal of several laminae.

Large Intestine

See INTESTINES.

The Larynx

The larynx is a semirigid framework of cartilages held together by ligaments and moved on one another by attached muscles. It is lined with mucous membrane which is continuous with the throat above and the trachea (windpipe) below. The larynx forms the prominence in the neck commonly known as the "Adam's apple."

The chief functions of the larynx are as follows:

1. Speech is created by air coursing through its passageway while the vocal cords vary their position so as to narrow or widen the aperture.

2. Breathing: Air is permitted to enter the trachea below by action of laryngeal muscles, which keep the vocal cords apart.

3. The larynx has a valvular action which closes the entrance to the trachea

to food or any foreign particle. This same action prevents the escape of air from the lungs when it is found necessary "to hold one's breath."

There are three main categories of disease which involve the larynx and demand surgical treatment:

1. Obstruction of the larynx: Laryngeal obstruction is a serious threat as it may close down the passage of air into the lungs and cause suffocation. The commonest causes are:

a) Abscess formation.

b) Perichondritis (an inflammation of the lining of the laryngeal cartilage).

c) Severe croup (a specific kind of acute laryngitis seen in young children).

d) Acute inflammatory processes involving surrounding structures (Ludwig's angina, from an infection in the floor of the mouth).

e) Injuries or wounds of the larynx or nearby neck structures.

f) Foreign bodies which get stuck in the larynx. (This may happen with children who swallow coins.)

g) Burns of the larynx from drinking scalding liquids or inhaling live steam.

h) Inhalation of severely irritating vapors.

Laryngeal obstruction usually has a sudden onset and rapid progress. One notes difficulty in breathing, pallor, and restlessness, with blueness of the mucous membranes coming on from incomplete intake of oxygen.

Treatment must be immediate. If the cause of the obstruction, such as a foreign body, can be relieved mechanically, no time should be lost. The patient is taken to a hospital, where an expert laryngoscopist passes an instrument down the throat and extracts the foreign body. If the cause of obstruction is an irritating vapor, the patient should be immediately removed from it and given oxygen.

However, when the obstruction threatens life and the underlying cause—as enumerated above—cannot be instantly relieved, then a *tracheotomy* is performed.

If necessary as a lifesaving measure, tracheotomy can be performed without anesthesia or sterility. In an emergency, to prevent total asphyxiation, a knife is inserted into the neck over the trachea in the midline and the trachea is opened. (See diagram.) This will allow air to reach the lungs from a point below the obstruction.

When time permits, a tracheotomy is performed in the hospital under local anesthesia. The head is extended so that the neck is on the stretch. An incision about two inches long is made in the midline from a point below the Adam's apple downward. The trachea is exposed and three cartilages are severed. A tracheotomy tube (cannula) is inserted and is kept in place by a tape which is tied around the neck. It is important that all blood vessels be carefully ligated during this procedure to prevent blood from seeping into the opening in the trachea and getting down into the lungs.

Postoperative care of a tracheotomy is of great importance. Suction must be used frequently. Special nurses should be employed until the patient is out of danger.

Response to tracheotomy is dramatic, with immediate relief of the symptoms of the obstruction. Of course, if the underlying cause is a laryngeal abscess, laryngeal perichondritis, an acute inflammation, a wound, or a burn, then the condition must be attended to promptly. Abscesses must be opened, wounds must be repaired, and inflammations must be brought under control with appropriate doses of the various antibiotic drugs. Thanks to these new medications, most infections of the larynx will respond rapidly.

2. Paralysis of the larynx: Paralysis of one vocal cord will cause hoarseness and voice change but does not endanger

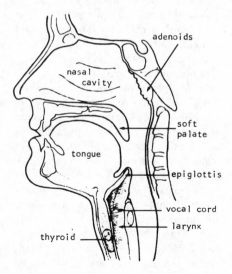

Larynx, side view.

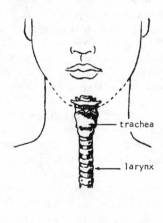

Larynx, front view.

life. However, when both vocal cords become paralyzed they relax toward the midline and interfere markedly with the ability to breathe air into the lungs. The ability to breathe out is not affected.

The causes of paralysis of the vocal cords are:

a) Bulbar poliomyelitis (infantile paralysis affecting the base of the brain).

b) Injury to the nerves supplying the larynx during the surgical removal of the thyroid gland. (This is an extremely rare occurrence.)

c) Cancer of neighboring structures, such as the esophagus, thyroid, or glands in the chest, which extends and involves the nerves to the larynx.

Surgical treatment for paralysis of both vocal cords consists of a preliminary tracheotomy to ensure an adequate passageway. An operation is undertaken subsequently which will fix one of the cords in an open position, thus allowing a free air channel. Repair of severed nerves is notoriously unsatisfactory. Also, little can be done to help the patient with a cancer that has invaded the nerves to the larynx.

3. Tumors of the larynx: Tumors of the larynx are exceptionally common. They give a clue to their presence in that they cause *hoarseness* in almost every case. *Anyone who is hoarse for more than a few weeks should see a nose and throat surgeon for examination of his larynx.*

The great majority of laryngeal tumors are benign (noncancerous). They consist of growths arising from the mucous membrane lining of the larynx and vocal cords. (See illustration.) As mentioned, hoarseness is the main symptom, but difficulty in breathing may develop if the tumor becomes large enough to obstruct the passageway. Less common complaints are cough,

blood-tinged sputum, pain, and difficulty in swallowing.

The treatment of all benign tumors is their surgical removal. This is accomplished either in the hospital or in the surgeon's office under local anesthesia with a spray. The procedure is usually simple and painless, and the results are excellent. The patient should be warned, however, that certain of the benign papillomas (wartlike growths) have a tendency to recur and that further surgery may be necessary.

TUMOR OF LEFT VOCAL CORD

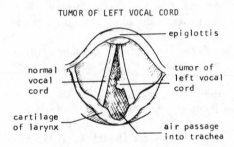

People who have undergone surgery upon their vocal cords should be advised not to use their voice for several weeks. Failure to abide by this advice may lead to delayed healing of the vocal cords and permanent damage to the speaking voice!

Cancer of the larynx is a relatively common disease seen mainly in men over 50 years of age. Although the cause is unknown, excessive use of tobacco, constant abuse of the voice, and the habit of drinking exceptionally hot liquids seem to appear in the majority of histories taken from patients with cancer of the larynx.

As hoarseness is an early symptom, many of these cases can be seen when still in a curable state. *It is estimated that 85 percent of these tumors can be cured* and leave the patient with a fairly good speaking voice and a natural air passage if they are diagnosed before they have spread to surrounding tissues.

The diagnosis is made by careful examination of the larynx through a laryngoscope and by snipping off a piece of tissue (biopsy) and sending it to the laboratory for microscopic examination. Treatment is never begun until an exact determination of the nature of the growth has been obtained.

Treatment of cancer of the larynx consists of surgery or x-ray irradiation, or a combination of both. The surgery may be limited to the partial removal of the larynx when the cancer is small and has involved only one vocal cord, or it may include removal of the entire larynx (total laryngectomy). These are major operative procedures, performed under either local or general anesthesia.

A *partial laryngectomy* is performed through a longitudinal incision in the midline of the neck extending above and below the larynx. The cartilages are split in the midline and the larynx is entered. The entire cancerous area involving the one side is removed with a wide portion of the surrounding tissue. Bleeding is controlled with an electric coagulating current. The cartilages are reunited in the midline and the skin is sutured with silk. A tracheotomy is usually done as a preliminary step to this operation to ensure an adequate air passage. The tracheotomy tube may be removed at the conclusion of the operation or may be removed several days later.

Recovery is usually uneventful, with the patient able to get out of bed in a day or two and leave the hospital in a week to ten days.

Total laryngectomy is a much more extensive operation, performed under general anesthesia, through a similar but longer incision in the neck. The trachea is cut across below the larynx and is stitched to the skin. A tracheotomy tube is inserted and this, in turn, is connected to the anesthesia apparatus. The entire larynx is then removed, separating it from all its attachments and closing it off from the throat. The muscles and skin are then closed, but the opening of the trachea onto the skin of the neck is permanent.

Operative recovery takes place in well over 95 percent of these patients, and eventual cure will depend on whether the cancer was totally excised.

Although these people must breathe through an opening in their neck for the rest of their lives, it is remarkable how many of them develop useful voices without a larynx.

Recent advances in x-ray irradiation give promise to sufferers from certain forms of laryngeal cancer. Indeed, for certain growths, x-ray treatment may be more efficacious than surgery. This determination must be made after careful evaluation of each case by the surgeon.

See also TRACHEOTOMY.

QUESTIONS AND ANSWERS
What is tracheotomy?

An opening through the neck into the windpipe.

What condition is a tracheotomy performed for?

1. To save life from suffocation when the larynx is obstructed

2. As a preliminary procedure prior to removal of the larynx

What are the symptoms of obstruction of the larynx?

1. Difficulty in breathing in

2. Pallor and restlessness

3. Blue color to lips

4. Rapid pulse and respiration

What first aid should be given someone who is choking from a foreign body in the larynx or trachea?

1. Often, a finger inserted into the

back of the throat will retrieve a foreign body.

2. If the patient is a child, turn him upside down.

3. Encourage coughing.

4. Transport patient in a sitting position to the nearest hospital.

When should an emergency tracheotomy be done?

When it is apparent that the patient will suffocate within a few minutes unless something is done.

Is tracheotomy a dangerous operation?

No.

Where is the incision made for a tracheotomy?

In the lower midline of the neck below the Adam's apple.

Are special nurses necessary after tracheotomy?

Yes, for at least two days, to suck secretions out of the tracheotomy opening and to teach the patient how to care for himself.

Can one take care of a tracheotomy oneself?

Yes.

What determines when a tracheotomy tube can be removed?

When the patient can breathe comfortably with the tracheotomy tube plugged, it is an indication that it is safe to remove it.

Will the hole of a tracheotomy heal by itself?

Yes, if normal breathing through the nose is resumed after removal of the tracheotomy tube.

Can one eat normally after a tracheotomy has been performed?

Yes.

What is the significance of hoarseness?

Prolonged hoarseness indicates disease of one or both of the vocal cords. Hoarseness which does not clear up within a week should be an indication to see your physician.

Are infections of the larynx serious?

Many of them can be.

Do all infections of the larynx have to be operated upon?

No. The antibiotic drugs bring the great majority under control. It is only when marked obstruction of the larynx results from the infection that surgery becomes necessary.

Should all tumors of the larynx be operated upon?

Yes.

How is a tumor of the larynx or vocal cords seen?

By either direct or indirect laryngoscopy. *Indirect laryngoscopy* means looking at the larynx with the aid of a mirror placed in the throat. *Direct laryngoscopy* means the passage of a specially devised instrument directly down into the larynx.

How is the diagnosis of a laryngeal tumor established?

By removing a piece of tumor tissue (biopsy) and sending it to the laboratory for microscopic examination.

What operative procedure is done for benign (nonmalignant) tumors of the larynx?

The tumor is removed through the mouth. No external incision is necessary.

Does the speaking voice return after infections of the larynx or after the removal of a benign tumor of the larynx?

Yes. However, it is advisable not to talk for a few weeks after these conditions have been treated.

What can cause paralysis of the larynx?
1. Infantile paralysis (poliomyelitis)
2. Injury secondary to a thyroid operation
3. Spread of a cancer from some nearby organ to the larynx

Is laryngeal paralysis serious?
Yes. The nerves rarely recover normal function.

What operative procedure is done to help those with paralysis of the larynx?
A permanent tracheotomy is performed.

What is a laryngectomy?
Removal of the larynx.

Is a permanent tracheotomy performed when the larynx is completely removed?
Yes.

Are operations for removal of the larynx serious?
Yes, but operative mortality has been reduced to 1 to 2 percent.

What anesthesia is used for laryngectomy (removal of the larynx)?
Usually general; occasionally local.

Where is the incision made for laryngectomy?
In the midline of the neck.

Is the scar ugly?
No.

Are blood transfusions necessary after laryngectomy?
Yes.

Are special nurses necessary after laryngectomy?
Yes.

How long a hospital stay is necessary after laryngeal removal?
About 10 to 14 days.

Can one speak after partial removal of the larynx?
Yes, but the quality of the voice is altered.

Can one speak after total removal of the larynx?
Yes, but the voice is sometimes difficult to understand unless the listener concentrates intently.

Is convalescent care advisable after laryngectomy?
Yes.

Laser Surgery

The laser is a device that produces an extremely concentrated beam of light which emits so much heat that it can destroy any substance known to man; it is many thousands of times more intense than the most powerful light beam hitherto known. The beam can be narrowed and aimed so accurately, and the heat can be delivered in so short a time, that it will destroy only diseased tissue, leaving the surrounding healthy tissue unaffected.

QUESTIONS AND ANSWERS

What are some of the special features of the laser?
The laser beam is so powerful and emits so much heat that it can destroy any substance known to man. This includes the toughest metal and stone.

Of what benefit is the laser in surgery?
It has been found possible to harness the laser so that it can be pinpointed exactly upon a small area of body tissue that one might wish to destroy. Thus, the laser has been used to destroy tumor

cells. It can be directed to such a small area and can be made to deliver its concentrated heat energy in so small a fraction of a second that it will destroy only diseased tissue and will leave surrounding tissues unharmed.

Has the laser been used successfully in the treatment of detachment of the retina of the eye?

Yes. By concentrating the beam to the point where the retina has become detached from its underlying membrane, it has been found possible to burn and coagulate the area, thus causing the retina to retract and become reattached.

Is there an advantage to using the laser rather than the scalpel in surgery?

Although the laser has not yet had wide application in surgery, its intense heat is known to cause coagulation of blood vessels. Thus, as it cuts, it controls bleeding. One day, the laser may greatly modify surgical techniques which now involve the clamping and tying off of severed blood vessels.

Is the laser dangerous?

Improperly used, it can be extremely dangerous. However, refinements in its use are taking place very rapidly, and the day is not far off when surgeons will learn how to employ it with a high degree of safety.

Is it possible that the laser will extend the range of surgery?

Yes. Through its use, it may be possible to destroy tissues which have been, up to now, unapproachable. As we know, there are certain areas within the body that cannot be attacked surgically because attempts to gain access to them would cause uncontrollable hemorrhage. Through the use of the laser, it is conceivable that hemorrhage will be so well controlled that all body areas will lend themselves to surgical approach.

Leukoplakia

The word leukoplakia means white plate. Leukoplakia manifests itself as a disease in which there are thickened white patches of epithelium on the mucous membranes. The most common places for leukoplakia to appear are the mouth, the gums, the inner lining of the cheeks, the palate, the tongue, and the mucous membranes of the female genitals. Leukoplakia occasionally occurs in the back of the throat or on the vocal cords of the larynx. The patches are usually elevated, roughened or barklike.

See also LIPS, MOUTH, AND TONGUE; VULVECTOMY.

QUESTIONS AND ANSWERS

Is leukoplakia of the tongue known by any other name?

It is frequently known as smoker's tongue.

What age group is most likely to develop leukoplakia?

It is most often seen in middle-aged people or those who are in later years.

Is leukoplakia of the mouth seen more often in men than in women?

Yes. However, since smoking has become so fashionable among women, the incidence of the condition is on the rise in that sex.

What is the significance of leukoplakia?

It is of great significance because it supposedly can be a forerunner of cancer. This is one of the definite instances in medicine where a noncancerous condition (such as leukoplakia) can lead to malignant degeneration.

What are the symptoms of leukoplakia?

Often, there are none at all, and the condition may be noticed accidentally by the patient himself or by the dentist or physician. Occasionally, there are burning, tingling, and cracking in a leukoplakic plaque.

What is the treatment for leukoplakia?

1. Stop smoking.

2. Remove all possible sources of local irritation, such as poorly fitting dentures or roughened skin edges.

3. Removal of the leukoplakic patch either by an electric needle or by surgical excision of the area.

What causes leukoplakia of the mouth?

Although the precise causes are not known, it is thought that tobacco smoking and poorly fitting dentures are the most important contributing factors. Chewing tobacco and snuff, used extensively some years ago, were also thought to cause leukoplakia.

Does leukoplakia usually develop into cancer?

In the great majority of cases, it does not. However, measures must be taken to check it, or cancer may result. It is considered to be a precancerous condition.

What measures should be taken to prevent leukoplakia of the mouth from developing into cancer?

1. Smoking should be discontinued.

2. Chewing tobacco and snuff should not be used.

3. Drinking of alcoholic beverages should be stopped, except for an occasional drink.

4. All possible sources of local irritation, such as rough edges of teeth, infected decayed teeth, and badly fitting artificial teeth, should be remedied.

5. General health should be checked regularly to make certain that there is no underlying vitamin deficiency or disease such as syphilis.

6. Patches of leukoplakia that seem to be growing or developing into ulcerations should be removed. This can be done either by burning the plaques away with an electric needle or by surgical excision.

Should people with leukoplakia of the mouth visit a doctor frequently?

Yes, it is wise to visit the doctor every three to four months so that he may note whether any changes have taken place in the appearance of the patches of leukoplakia.

Must leukoplakia of the mouth always be treated actively?

No. In the great majority of cases, the process is so slow that active treatment is not necessary. Most cases can be held stationary by taking the precautions listed above.

When does it become necessary to treat leukoplakia actively?

When it ulcerates or shows marked growth.

What measures can be taken to prevent leukoplakia of the female genitals from becoming cancerous?

The patches of leukoplakia should be removed surgically if they start to grow or become ulcerated.

Do all cases of leukoplakia of the female genitals have to be treated actively?

Not unless areas of ulceration appear or the spread of the disease is extensive.

What is leukoplakia of the vulva?

It is a disease of the skin of the vulva characterized by an overgrowth of cells and a tendency toward the formation of cancer. The areas of leukoplakia look grayish-white and develop a parchment-like appearance.

What causes leukoplakia of the vulva?

The exact cause is unknown, but it is supposedly related to a decrease in the secretion of ovarian hormone which takes place after menopause.

Who is most likely to develop leukoplakia?

Women who have passed the menopause.

Is leukoplakia of the vulva a common condition?

No. It is relatively infrequent.

What are the symptoms of leukoplakia of the vulva?

Itching is the most striking feature of this condition. Scratching will often lead to secondary infection from surface bacteria and may lead to inflammation, swelling, pain, redness, and even bleeding from the vicinity.

Does leukoplakia ever develop into cancer of the vulva?

Yes. It is estimated that about 25 percent of the cases of cancer of the vulva originated from leukoplakia. However, this does not mean that all women with leukoplakia will develop cancer.

How long does it usually take for leukoplakia to develop into cancer?

This is a very slow process which takes place over a period of years. There is, therefore, plenty of time to eradicate the lesions before they undergo malignant changes.

What is the treatment for leukoplakia of the vulva?

1. If infection is present, antibiotic drugs should be given locally and orally.

2. If itching is severe, anesthetic ointments should be applied.

3. Ovarian hormones should be given to forestall the progress of the disease.

4. Because of its precancerous nature, surgical removal of the involved tissues is often carried out.

Does leukoplakia ever clear up by itself?

Temporary relief often results from medical management, but surgery is the only real cure for this condition.

Is hospitalization necessary for removal of areas of leukoplakia?

The great majority of these cases can be treated adequately in the surgeon's office by use of an electric needle. However, when patches must be removed from the throat or from the larynx, hospitalization is advised.

Can successful treatment of leukoplakia avoid the development of cancer?

Yes. People with leukoplakia should be kept under constant supervision so that the progress of the disease can be noted.

Lipomas

Lipomas are tumors composed of fat tissue and are perhaps the most common tumors in the entire body. Most of them lie directly beneath the skin, but others may appear between muscles or under the mucous membrane lining of the intestinal tract, or occasionally in the tissues beneath the lining of the abdominal cavity. The cause of lipomas is not known but they are seen somewhat more frequently in stout people. They vary in size from that of a pea to that of a football, or larger. On examination, lipomas feel soft and are usually freely movable under the skin and do not appear to be firmly attached to surrounding structures. Most lipomas are painless and cause no symptoms, but occasionally a lipoma is very painful due to a nerve passing through its substance.

There is a disease known as lipodystrophy in which fat metabolism is disturbed. In this condition, a patient may develop few or many areas of painful lipomas.

QUESTIONS AND ANSWERS

Are lipomas usually benign?

A great majority of them are benign, but once in a while, a lipoma will undergo rapid growth and will turn into a malignant liposarcoma.

How can one tell whether a lipoma has become malignant?

It will show rapid growth and will change its consistency to touch, becoming harder.

Should lipomas be removed?

If they remain stationary in size, most of them can be left alone. However, the great majority do show signs of growth over a period of time, and it is therefore best that they be removed.

How is a lipoma removed?

It can usually be removed under local anesthesia in a hospital. An incision is made in the skin, and the fatty tumor is dissected out. If a large defect remains in the area where the tumor was located, a rubber drain is inserted. Otherwise the skin is sutured tightly. Large lipomas are removed under general anesthesia.

Where is the removal of a lipoma usually carried out?

In the hospital, and unless the tumor is a particularly large one, a one- or two-day stay is all that is required.

Do lipomas affect people of all ages?

Yes, but they are seen less often in childhood or among those who are in their later years.

What causes lipomas?

The cause is unknown.

Do lipomas tend to recur once they have been removed?

No. However, it must be kept in mind that an individual who forms one lipoma has a tendency to form others. Thus, another lipoma may form near where the original one was excised.

What is Dercum's disease?

It is a disease in which there are areas of painful fatty tumors in the tissues beneath the skin. It is also known as adiposis dolorosa.

Is there any way to prevent recurrence of lipomas?

If one is very obese, he should reduce. It is well known that lipomas are seen more often in overweight people.

Lips, Mouth, and Tongue

Through the medium of modern advertising, people have been made particularly conscious of the importance of oral hygiene. With this awareness, they have paid much more attention to the care of their teeth and the condition of their gums and tongue. As a consequence, there has been a definite lowering in the incidence of diseases within the mouth.

From the medical point of view it is quite remarkable that so few infections of the lips, gums, mouth, and tongue occur, for indeed these structures are always surrounded and covered by disease-producing bacteria. The healthiest mouths contain streptococci, staphylococci, and pneumonia germs, and it is only because of the great powers of resistance with which nature has endowed these tissues that infections take hold so infrequently.

THE LIPS

The lips are made up of highly sensitive skin and mucous membrane. Because of their exposed position, it is only natural that they should be injured frequently or often involved in a disease process. Perhaps the commonest surgical conditions of the lips are the following:

1. Lacerations and bruises: It is extremely important that cuts about the lips be stitched accurately. This is particularly necessary when the laceration extends beyond the mucous membrane onto the skin. Failure to obtain good approximation of skin edges may lead to an ugly scar formation and alteration of the appearance of a patient's entire face. Whenever possible, the services of an accomplished surgeon should be engaged, as he will know better how to do the repair with a minimal amount of deformity.

The lips swell greatly even with slight injury. This occurs because the tissues within them are spongy and elastic and permit the collection of large amounts of blood and serum. Surgery is not necessary for bruises. The swelling will subside spontaneously over a period of a few days. Cold applications immediately after an injury may help to prevent some of the swelling.

2. Infections: Pimples, boils, abscesses, and carbuncles about the lips are extremely common, especially among adolescents and young adults. *They should NEVER be squeezed or opened by the patient.* Boils and carbuncles of the upper lip are especially dangerous because the drainage from that area leads directly into a pool of veins at the base of the brain. Infection traveling along this route may cause a *cavernous sinus thrombosis* (a clot of these veins within the skull). Fortunately, today the prompt administration of large doses of appropriate antibiotic drugs can forestall such an outcome.

The treatment of the vast majority of infections about the lips is to leave them alone to subside by themselves. Larger boils or carbuncles are opened surgically only when they have fully localized, and then only a small nick will be made to permit the exit of pus. The smaller the incision the better, as scar formation will be less conspicuous.

3. Tumors of the lip: Benign, noncancerous tumors of the mucous membranes of the lips are quite common and usually take the form of *warty growths* or of benign blood vessel tumors (hemangiomas). They can be cured in almost all instances by one of the following methods of treatment:

a) Excising them with an elliptical incision with a knife and then carefully stitching the cut edges together

b) Burning them away with an electric needle

c) Freezing them with carbon dioxide snow

d) Treating them with x-ray or radium

Cancer of the lip comprises about 30 percent of all malignant growths about the oral cavity. It afflicts men 20 times more often than women and usually begins in the sixth or seventh decade of life. The lower lip is involved in 95 percent of cases. Chapping, overexposure to sunburn, smoking, and biting are thought to be factors in the development of lip cancer.

Treatment of cancer of the lip is very satisfactory, and cure can be obtained in the majority of cases through wide surgical removal. Happily, spread of the growth to the glands of the neck takes place late in the course of the disease. Since the tumor is so easily recognized by its exposed location, treatment can usually be started before any spread has occurred. The operation, performed under general anesthesia, involves a V-shaped removal of the tumor-bearing section of the lip. It is astounding to note how the lip will stretch and return to near-normal appearance even after excising half its length. Cures can sometimes be obtained in cases where the cancer has already spread to the neck. These patients must undergo a thorough dissection of the neck with the removal of all the glands. This procedure requires a long incision from below the ear to the collarbone and entails several hours of meticulous dissection; nevertheless, the results are excellent and cure is obtained frequently.

Certain types of lip cancer can be treated effectively without surgery by judicious employment of radium and x-rays. The decision as to the applicability of this approach must be left up to the surgeon and to the pathologist who has examined a piece of the tumor which has been removed.

4. Harelip, or cleft lip, is a developmental deformity with failure of union of the upper lip. This condition, as well as cleft palate (which is often seen in association with harelip), occurs in approximately one of every thousand births. The cause is unknown, but there is a tendency for this malformation to run in families.

Operation for correction of this condition should be carried out as soon as possible, preferably within the first few weeks of life. This can be done if the child is feeding properly, but if feedings are not being taken well, it is advisable to postpone surgery for several weeks or months. One cannot stress too strongly the advantages to the parents and to any existing brothers and sisters of bringing home a normal baby from the hospital.

The purpose of the operation is to restore the lip to its normal anatomy and to maintain it there so that normal growth and development will follow. There are many techniques to accomplish this, but it would be beyond the scope of this book to describe them in detail. Suffice it to say that the ununited portions of the deformed lip must be taken down and stitched together with extreme care and accuracy so that healing in the normal position will result. A surgeon well trained in the art of plastic surgery should be engaged for this task. (See illustration.)

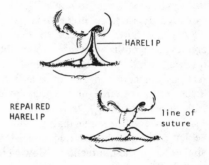

HARELIP

REPAIRED HARELIP

line of suture

The operation is performed under light general anesthesia and feedings are resumed within several hours after the child has returned from the operating room. Recovery is prompt and sutures are removed within five to eight days postoperatively. Barring postoperative infection or some unforeseen complication, cosmetic results from harelip operations are usually excellent.

Should the end result of the procedure be poor, secondary operations can be performed at a later date. These procedures require expert planning and the outcome will be directly proportional to the skill of the surgeon.

THE MOUTH

1. Lacerations are seen in children when they ram sticks or other sharp objects into their mouths. Other lacerations occur from biting the cheek or from an external blow which forces teeth through the membrane.

Small lacerations can be left to heal by themselves, care being taken to observe good oral hygiene with frequent mouth rinsings. Large lacerations should be accurately sutured under local anesthesia if possible, or general anesthesia in small children.

2. **Surgical infections** within the mouth usually originate from infected or abscessed teeth. Some of these can be very serious, and *Ludwig's angina* can actually threaten life by extension of swelling down the neck so that it creates dangerous pressure upon the trachea (windpipe). Other dental infections are common and may lead to involvement of the underlying bone with development of *osteomyelitis.*

The general principle that pus must be let out through a surgical incision applies to all these infections. However, treatment has become much more conservative since the advent of the antibiotic drugs. We no longer fear a fatal outcome from these infections although they still demand expert care. People with osteomyelitis of the jaw, Ludwig's infection of the floor of the mouth, or spreading neck infections from an infected tooth must be hospitalized. Early incision and drainage with the insertion of rubber drains into the abscess cavity must be carried out. Recovery may take a week to ten days.

3. **The uvula** is the backward extension of the soft palate, or roof of the mouth. When it is very long, it may cause a tickling sensation in the throat and a feeling that something is stuck in that vicinity. This condition is treated by *uvulectomy,* an operation done under local anesthesia, in which the excess portion is clamped and cut off with a scissors.

4. **Tumors of the mucous membrane** of the mouth or of the palate are not very common, although *leukoplakia,* a potentially cancerous condition, is seen often. This condition is characterized by an overgrowth of the membrane cells and is thought to be caused by the constant irritation of jagged, defective teeth or from the sharp edges of poorly fitting dentures or from tobacco. If untreated, chronic ulcers or cancer may develop in these mouths! Treatment consists of correcting the dental defect and burning away patches of leukoplakia with an electric needle or excising them surgically.

Cancer of the membranes of the mouth must be treated with wide surgical removal and/or x-ray and radium. Cure can be obtained in most instances where early treatment has been instituted.

The *torus palatinus* is a bony growth in the midline of the hard palate. These tumors occasionally become quite large—an inch in diameter—and necessitate surgical removal. This is done, under local anesthesia, by incising the mucous membrane and chiseling away the growth. Recovery is prompt and uneventful.

5. **Cleft palate** is a birth deformity in which the roof of the mouth fails to fuse fully. As a result, the mouth and nasal cavities are not separated from each other. It is seen once in every thousand births. Its cause is unknown, although there is a tendency for this malformation to run in families.

A cleft palate is a great handicap, as it interferes with normal feeding, permits food and fluid to get into the nose and nasal cavity, and makes normal speech impossible.

The best time to operate upon children with cleft palate is somewhere between the ages of 1½ to 2½ years. The operation is a difficult one and demands

CLEFT PALATE

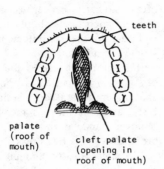

palate
(roof of
mouth)   cleft palate
(opening in
roof of mouth)

END RESULT OF CLEFT
PALATE OPERATION

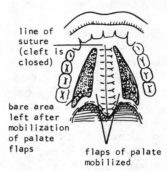

line of
suture
(cleft is
closed)

bare area
left after
mobilization
of palate
flaps

flaps of palate
mobilized

the ministrations of an expert in the field Although operative recovery takes place in almost all patients, there are a sizable number of instances in which the operation fails to close the palate. Second and third operations are frequently necessary.

The techniques of suturing the roof of the mouth are quite complex but all involve the stitching together of sturdy flaps. (See illustration.) The suturing must be done without too much stretching of the flaps or they will pull away from one another instead of fusing.

These operations are performed under general anesthesia. Feedings may be begun several hours after surgery. Antibiotic drugs are given to promote healing.

It is not sufficient merely to restore normal anatomy to cure this condition. Speech training is essential, as these children have a tendency to faulty speech even after the palate has been satisfactorily repaired.

THE TONGUE

The tongue is a thick, strong, extremely mobile and gifted muscle, covered in its mouth portion by a skin-like mucous membrane containing taste buds. The tongue originates in the throat, and when the jaws are closed, it completely fills the mouth.

1. Lacerations of the tongue are extremely common. Because of its muscular composition, bleeding stops by itself rather readily following the average laceration. For this reason it is unnecessary to suture the smaller lacerations.

Large cuts should be accurately sutured. Healing takes place rapidly.

2. Surgical infections, such as abscesses or carbuncles, are practically never seen in the tongue. (Nonsurgical infections such as syphilis or tuberculosis are occasionally encountered but are not germane to the subject of this book.) The tongue has exceptional ability to resist surgical infection because of its extremely rich blood supply.

3. Birth deformities of the tongue are not very common. The two most frequently encountered are:

a) A shortened frenulum: The frenulum is a fold of tissue which runs from the middle of the undersurface of the tongue to the floor of the mouth. When it is very short, it prevents free motion of the tongue and results in the condition known as *tongue-tie.* It can be corrected easily, at birth, by cutting it with a scissors.

The same procedure is carried out under local anesthesia if it is discovered for the first time at a later age.

b) *A geographic tongue:* One in which there are many deep crevices on the surface of the tongue running haphazardly in different directions. There is no treatment for this condition, and indeed none is necessary. The deformity is noticeable only to the patient himself or is seen upon examination by a doctor or nurse. It has no medical significance.

4. Leukoplakia of the tongue is a serious condition requiring early and prolonged treatment. It starts with deep red plaques or patches which slowly turn a bluish white. These areas represent an overgrowth of the cells. They may occupy only a fraction of an inch, or they may involve the major portion of the tongue's surface. A sense of irritation and discomfort may be produced by these plaques, or they may be symptomless. *The great danger of leukoplakia is that, if untreated, some of the areas may become cancerous.*

Leukoplakia is thought to be caused by any one of the following:

  a) Tobacco smoking

  b) Alcohol

  c) Sharp-edged or diseased teeth

  d) Faulty-fitting and sharp-edged dentures

The treatment of leukoplakia consists of eradicating the above irritants and treating the local areas by *electrodesiccation* or surgical removal.

If electrodesiccation is done, under local anesthesia, the patches are systematically removed. To accomplish this, the patient may require many treatments and he should be kept under observation periodically for a number of years. Leukoplakia has a tendency to recur, and recurrent areas must be retreated. The appearance of an ulcer or hard growth in one of these patches often indicates cancerous change. A piece of such tissue should be removed and sent to the laboratory for microscopic examination.

If surgical excision is the treatment of choice, the patient is hospitalized, and under general anesthesia the diseased areas of mucous membrane are removed and normal membrane is brought over the raw areas.

5. Cancer of the tongue comprises about 20 percent of all tumors within the oral cavity. It is mainly a disease of middle or old age, and approximately 85 percent of all cases occur in men. Tobacco, rotten and sharp-edged teeth, poorly fitting artificial dentures, and leukoplakia are considered the predisposing causes of this form of cancer. Years ago, when pipes contained no filters, the sharp bite of tobacco and hot smoke were thought to be causative factors. Indeed, tongue cancer was called "pipe smoker's cancer."

The cancer usually appears as a painless, thickened, ulcerated area along the margin of the tongue. As it enlarges, it may become inflamed and tender and may bleed slightly from time to time.

Treatment of cancer of the tongue consists of surgical removal when this is possible. Cancers located on the side of the tongue can be successfully treated by removing half the tongue (hemiglossectomy). Cancers of the tip of the tongue, or in the middle of the forward portion of the tongue, must be treated by surgical removal of the front two thirds of the tongue. Cancers of the base of the tongue are almost impossible to cure surgically, and radium and x-ray treatments are employed instead.

If the cancer is operated upon before spread to the neck has taken place, more than half the cases can be cured.

If there has already been a spread, then an extensive dissection of the neck is carried out in an attempt to eradicate the disease.

A carefully calculated combination of surgery and radiation treatment will bring the highest cure rate in this disease.

It is remarkable that large portions of the tongue can be removed without permanently damaging the ability to chew or swallow. With training, many of these patients learn to talk again even when more than half the tongue has been removed.

QUESTIONS AND ANSWERS

THE LIPS

Are operations upon the lips serious?
No, but all repairs must be done accurately to avoid ugly scars.

What kind of anesthesia is used?
In children, general anesthesia. In adults, local anesthesia.

What is done for severe bruises of the lip?
They are left alone to get well by themselves.

Is hospitalization necessary for lip infections?
Usually not, but if there is high temperature and evidence of spread, then hospital admission is advisable.

What is the correct treatment for lip infections?
1. Warm, wet dressings
2. Large doses of antibiotic drugs
3. Surgical drainage, only when the infection has come to a head

Are infections about the lips dangerous?
Yes, because the infection can travel into the brain.

What is the treatment for benign tumors of the lip?
1. Removal with an elliptical incision and stitching
2. Removal with an electric needle
3. Removal by freezing with carbon dioxide snow
4. Removal with x-ray or radium treatments

Are benign tumors of the lip seen very frequently?
Yes. They take the form of warty growths or blood vessel tumors (hemangiomas).

Can all benign tumors be cured?
Yes.

Do they ever turn into cancer?
Some of the warty growths may have such a tendency and therefore should be removed.

Is cancer of the lip common?
It constitutes approximately 30 percent of all malignant growths about the oral cavity.

Can one prevent cancer of the lip from occurring?
To a certain extent; by avoiding irritants such as excessive sunburn, excessive chapping, excessive lip biting, smoking a pipe without an effective filter.

Which lip is most affected by cancer?
The lower lip is affected in 95 percent of all cases.

Will treatment for cancer of the lip bring about a cure?
Yes, in those cases where extensive spread to the neck has not yet taken place.

What is the treatment for cancer of the lip?
Wide V-shaped removal of a wedge

of the lip containing the cancer. Also, wide neck dissection if there has been spread to the glands in the neck.

What anesthesia is used when operating upon cancer of the lip?
General.

How long a hospital stay is necessary after surgery for cancer of the lip?
Six to nine days.

Are special nurses advisable after major operations upon the lip?
Yes, if an extensive neck dissection has also been performed.

Are the scars very disfiguring after partial removal of the lip?
No. It is amazing how the lip will regain almost normal appearance after large sections of it have been removed.

What is harelip?
A failure of the two sides of the upper lip to join or fuse.

What causes harelip?
Incomplete fusion during the development of the embryo.

What is the proper treatment for harelip?
Operative repair by a competent surgeon.

When should harelip be operated upon?
If possible, within the first month of life.

Is it wise to do the harelip operation before the newborn leaves the hospital?
Yes. This will not only aid the infant but save much embarrassment to the parents.

Are harelip operations dangerous?
No.

How soon after harelip operations can feedings be resumed?
Within a few hours.

How long does it take for a harelip wound to heal?
Six to nine days.

Are the scars of harelip operations permanent?
Yes, but they tend to fade over the years so that they become hardly noticeable.

Are the results of harelip operations good?
Yes, when performed by an expert in the field.

What can be done if the harelip operation fails to get a good cosmetic result?
It can be done over again, usually with good results.

THE MOUTH

What are the usual causes of lacerations of the mouth?
1. Sticks which children fall upon or accidentally jam in the mouth
2. Biting of the cheek by one's own teeth

Must all mouth lacerations or infections be operated upon?
No. Most lacerations will heal spontaneously, and most mouth infections can be cleared up with medications and antibiotic drugs.

What is the uvula?
The soft downward projection of the back of the roof of the mouth.

Does the uvula cause symptoms when it is enlarged?
Yes. It causes a tickling sensation in the throat and a hacking cough.

Is hospitalization necessary for uvula operations?
No.

What operation is performed for an enlarged uvula?
Under local anesthesia in the sur-

geon's office, the excess portion is clamped and snipped off with a scissors.

Are tumors of the lining of the mouth common?

No, except leukoplakia, which must be considered as a forerunner of cancer.

What is cleft palate?

A birth abnormality with failure of the two sides of the roof of the mouth to fuse in the midline.

How common is cleft palate?

About 1 in 1,000 births.

What is the best age at which to operate upon cleft palate?

Between 1½ to 2½ years.

What operative procedure is performed to cure cleft palate?

The tissues of the palate on each side of the cleft are undercut, mobilized, and stitched together in the midline. (See illustration on page 541.)

Are operations for cleft palate serious?

Yes.

How successful are cleft palate operations?

Good results are obtained in the majority of uncomplicated cases, although it may be necessary to perform two or even three procedures to obtain the best results.

If the original operation for repair of cleft palate fails, can it be done over again?

Yes, but it must be emphasized that these are complicated operations which require the services of the most expert surgeons.

Does speech automatically return to normal after repair of a cleft palate?

No. Speech training is necessary for prolonged periods of time afterward.

THE TONGUE

What general diseases of the body are most frequently reflected in changes of the appearance of the tongue?

Deficiency diseases, such as certain types of anemia (pernicious anemia). Also, generalized skin conditions will give a characteristic appearance to the tongue.

What condition of the body is most closely reflected in the appearance of the tongue?

The state of hydration or dehydration. The tongue appears dry and coated whenever the patient lacks the proper amount of fluids within his body.

Is the tongue responsible for the sense of taste?

Yes. There are taste buds located throughout the surface of the tongue. These are largely responsible for sensing sour, sweet, salt, and bitter tastes.

Is it natural for people to lose their sense of taste when they have a cold?

Yes. Much of taste depends upon the sense of smell. When a nasal mucous membrane is inflamed by a cold or allergy, the sense of smell is impaired. This, in turn, will diminish the acuteness of the sense of taste.

Is it natural for people to lose their sense of taste as they grow older?

Not if they are healthy and have no vitamin deficiency or generalized disease.

What is glossitis?

It is an inflammation of the tongue.

Is the tongue often involved in an infection or inflammation or true abscess formation?

No. The tongue is peculiarly immune to the formation of abscesses. This may possibly be attributed to its very rich blood supply.

What is the treatment for inflammations of the tongue?

Since glossitis is usually a sign or a symptom of some disease elsewhere, the treatment will depend upon the causative factor. Whenever a local irritant is causing a change in the tongue, this must be eliminated.

Do people often bite their tongues?

Yes. This commonly happens when they are trying to eat too quickly, or when they talk while eating.

What is the treatment for a bitten or lacerated tongue?

Most lacerations of the tongue are so minor that they need no suturing. Bleeding will stop by itself, and the individual should wash out his mouth frequently. The person with a lacerated tongue should go on a liquid or soft diet for two or three days, until the laceration heals.

What should be done for a severe laceration of the tongue that continues to bleed?

The patient must be taken to a surgeon, who will suture the laceration.

Does a person ever bite his tongue during a convulsion?

This is one of the most frequent causes of injury to the tongue. It can be prevented by placing a handkerchief between the teeth to hold the jaws open during a convulsion. Great caution should be exercised in doing this, because a person who is having convulsions may inadvertently bite someone's finger. To avoid this, the jaws should always be pried open from the side, not from the front, and fingers should never be placed between the teeth of a person during a convulsion.

Can a person ever swallow his tongue?

Not in the literal sense. However, when a person is unconscious or is having a convulsion, the tongue may drop backward and thus shut off the airway to the trachea (windpipe) and lungs.

Are children ever born with deformities of the tongue?

Yes. There are three major types of deformities. These are:

1. Geographic tongue, a tongue that has deep crevices and ridges throughout its length. The condition has no significance, and although it may be unpleasant to look at, it creates no symptoms, nor does it cause the child any pain or discomfort.

2. Forked tongue, a rather rare deformity in which the tip of the tongue has not completely fused. If this deformity is marked, it can be easily corrected with plastic surgery. A wedge is cut out between the fork and the two sides of the tongue are sutured together. Recovery from these operations is rapid.

3. A shortened frenulum. The frenulum is a fold of tissue which runs from the middle of the undersurface of the tongue to the floor of the mouth. When it is very short, it prevents free motion of the tongue and results in the condition known as tongue-tie. It can be corrected easily, at birth, by cutting it with a scissors. The same procedure is carried out under local anesthesia if it is discovered for the first time at a later age.

Will a shortened frenulum interfere with the mobility of the tongue?

Yes. It sometimes prevents the child from extending the tongue completely or from raising it up to the roof of his mouth.

Can a shortened frenulum ever lead to speech defects?

Yes, occasionally.

At what age can tongue-tie be recognized?

If the frenulum is shortened and the

tongue is tied down to the floor of the mouth, it is easily recognizable at birth, when the mouth of the newborn is examined routinely.

What is the treatment for tongue-tie?
The frenulum should be cut with scissors or a knife immediately after birth.

If the frenulum is not cut when the child is born, can it be done at a later date?
Yes. It is a minor operative procedure and can be done under a light anesthesia.

When should this operation be performed?
During the first few weeks or months of an infant's life. It may also be done at the time of tonsillectomy.

Is the tongue often the site of tumor formation?
Yes.

What are the common tumors of the tongue?
1. Leukoplakia. This is really not a true tumor but is a forerunner of tumor formation.
2. Blood vessel tumors (hemangioma).
3. Wartlike tumors (papillomas).
4. Gland cell tumors (adenomas).
5. Connective tissue tumors (fibromas).
6. Cysts of the tongue occasionally caused by failure of the thyroid gland to develop fully (thyroglossal cysts).
7. Cancer of the tongue.

What is leukoplakia of the tongue?
An overgrowth of the skinlike cells of the tongue.

What causes leukoplakia?
Jagged, sharp-edged teeth, poorly fitting dentures, the drinking of excess alcohol over a period of years, and to-bacco smoking are thought to be important factors in causing leukoplakia.

What is the surgical treatment for leukoplakia?
Burning away the patches with an electric needle or surgically removing the diseased areas.

Does leukoplakia, once treated, tend to recur?
Yes.

What is done for recurrent leukoplakia?
It must be treated again.

Does leukoplakia ever turn into cancer?
Yes, if untreated.

How can one tell when leukoplakia is turning into cancer?
An ulcer, or cracking, or peeling develops in a leukoplakic area and the surrounding region becomes firm and hard.

Is cancer of the tongue common?
It constitutes about 20 percent of all malignant growth about the oral cavity.

What causes cancer of the tongue?
The exact cause is not known but irritant factors such as jagged, sharp-edged teeth, ill-fitting dentures, and pipe smoking are thought to play an important part.

Is cancer of the tongue curable if surgery is performed?
Yes, if it is operated upon before it has spread.

Is tongue removal a serious operation?
Yes.

Are operations upon the tongue painful?
Yes.

What anesthesia is used for operations upon the tongue?
General anesthesia with a tube placed into the trachea.

What operative procedures are carried out for cancer of the tongue?

1. Removal of half the tongue if the cancer is located along the side of the tongue

2. Removal of the front half or two thirds of the tongue if the cancer is located near the tip

3. X-ray and radium treatment if the cancer is back toward the base of the tongue

Are blood transfusions necessary for tongue operations?

Very often there is a considerable blood loss and transfusions are necessary.

Are special nurses necessary for major tongue operations?

Yes, for several days.

Is radium or x-ray treatment ever given in conjunction with, or instead of, surgery for tongue cancer?

Yes, when it is impossible to remove the entire cancer and when there has been spread to the glands in the neck.

Is convalescent care indicated after extensive operative procedures upon the tongue?

Yes.

How does one eat after partial tongue removal?

For the first few days, fluids can be given through a tube placed into the nose and extending into the stomach. Thereafter, the patient will be able to eat by himself.

Can people talk after partial tongue removal?

Yes, they can train themselves to speak again even after removal of large portions of the tongue.

Is any external scar visible after tongue operations?

Not within the mouth. However, there are extensive operations for removal of part of the tongue, part of the jawbone, and the glands in the neck, which do leave a large and disfiguring scar. These procedures are done for tumors of the tongue which have extended into the glands of the neck.

Liver

The liver is a large glandular organ, irregularly shaped, and of reddish-brown color. It resembles exactly the very familiar appearance of beef liver and is of similar consistency. Most of the upper abdominal cavity beneath the diaphragm and ribs is occupied by the liver. It stretches across the upper abdomen for approximately eight inches, extends for six to seven in a vertical direction and measures five to six inches from front to back. The right portion, or lobe, is about three times larger than the left lobe. The liver manufactures and secretes bile, some of which is stored in the attached gallbladder.

In addition to being the largest organ, the liver serves more functions than any other structure. It receives the digested food elements through veins called the *portal system*. This system originates in the walls of the intestinal tract and merges into the large portal vein, which enters the liver in its midportion. After many complicated chemical changes within the liver cells, the basic food elements are dispatched into the general circulation for distribution and use by the tissues of the body. (See diagram.)

The following are the most important functions of the liver:

1. The storage of sugar and the regulation of the amount of sugar that circulates in the blood

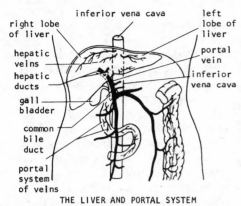

right lobe of liver

hepatic veins

hepatic ducts

gall bladder

common bile duct

portal system of veins

inferior vena cava

left lobe of liver

portal vein

inferior vena cava

THE LIVER AND PORTAL SYSTEM

2. The production and storage of body proteins, the regulation of circulating proteins, and the control of the many by-products of protein metabolism

3. The storage and utilization of fats

4. The breaking down of toxic and harmful substances that may be circulating in the blood; this function is called "detoxification"

5. The manufacture of bile and bile salts, which are secreted through the bile ducts into the intestines and which aid in the digestion of fats and other food substances

6. The manufacture of prothrombin, a chemical essential to normal blood clotting

Until recently, operative surgery upon the liver has been rather strictly limited. The liver is composed of soft and spongy tissue which bleeds readily and does not hold together by placement of ordinary sutures. Surgeons have hesitated, therefore, to attempt removal of tumors or cysts from this organ. However, new operative techniques have been devised which permit the removal of either the right or left lobe of this organ with a considerable degree of safety.

The liver may be operated upon for the following conditions:

1. Injuries: Gunshot wounds, stab wounds, rupture of the liver from a fall, or automobile accidents are common occurrences. There is usually evidence of internal bleeding and shock, indicating the need for surgical attack. In such cases, the liver is sutured, the hole is packed with one of the newer substances that control bleeding (Gelfoam, Oxycel, or Surgicel), and the abdominal cavity is drained.

Since the liver has a tendency to stop bleeding spontaneously, recovery occurs in most of these cases. The trouble is that too many people have other injuries along with the liver injury, and these allied conditions often prove fatal.

2. Abscesses: Liver abscesses, and abscesses above or below the liver (subdiaphragmatic or subhepatic), were once rather frequent complications of abdominal surgery. Pus from an infected appendix or gallbladder, or pus from peritonitis, would spread into the liver or collect above or below it. When this happened, it was necessary to open the abdomen and drain off the pus. This was a dangerous procedure and carried with it a high mortality.

We are indeed fortunate that antibiotic drugs control most of these infections and, by being given early in the course of an illness, prevent the formation of liver abscesses or collections of pus above or below the liver.

In the rare instance where surgery *is* required, these same drugs ensure recovery in the great majority of cases.

Amebic liver abscesses are caused by the parasite of amebic dysentery. This condition is still prevalent in tropical countries throughout the world. There are new drugs that have proved very effective in curing these infections, but occasional cases still require an abdominal operation with incision and drainage of the abscess cavity.

3. Cysts and tumors: There are several types of cysts that involve the liver.

The echinococcus cyst is caused by a parasite that infests dogs. When this gets into the human body it usually lodges in the liver and forms a huge cystic mass which may grow to the size of a grapefruit. The cyst should be removed surgically.

Blood cysts or tumors (hemangiomas) and lymph cysts or tumors (lymphangiomas) are seen occasionally. They can be diagnosed when they cause a swelling of the liver which can be felt by the examining physician, but more often they are encountered accidentally during an operation for an unrelated condition. Since they do not become malignant and because they would be most difficult to remove, surgeons usually prefer to leave them alone.

The liver appears to be the commonest site for the deposit of cancer cells which have spread from other organs. Cancer anywhere in the abdominal cavity, if not removed, will eventually invade the liver, as will malignant tissue from the breast, the prostate, and other organs. When this has occurred, surgery is of no avail! Once in a great while, however, a single isolated spread (metastasis) will be found, and this may lend itself to surgical removal.

So common is the spread of cancer to this region that surgeons invariably examine the liver before attempting an extensive removal of the organ primarily affected. If liver cancer is detected, the surgeon may abandon, as useless, his attempts to remove the primary growth.

Primary cancer of the liver is fatal in most cases and rarely lends itself to removal. Despite this sad fact, a few cases have been reported where the malignant tumor was limited to one lobe and removal of the entire lobe was followed by cure. Such instances are heartening to record, and the ever-growing improvements in surgical techniques will

undoubtedly lead to more and more cures.

4. Cirrhosis: This is a condition in which there is a replacement of liver structure by dense fibrous tissue. This leads to an obstruction of the liver which prevents the normal rate of flow of blood through its substance. As a result, body functions suffer greatly, and these people may die within a period of a few months to a few years. Through surgery, many patients with cirrhosis can be helped considerably by lessening the quantity of blood that courses through the liver. This is accomplished by suturing the portal vein to the vena cava or by suturing the splenic vein (of the spleen) to the left renal vein (of the kidney). These operations are called portacaval shunt or splenorenal shunt. By these delicate maneuvers, a great deal of the blood that normally enters the liver through the portal vein goes

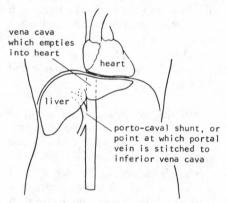

PORTO-CAVAL SHUNT OPERATION

instead into the vena cava or into the renal vein. Since the vena cava and the renal vein do not enter the liver, much of the load upon the diseased and cirrhotic organ is relieved. (See illustration.) Portacaval and splenorenal shunts are being performed successfully by an ever-increasing number of surgeons, with excellent results in more than half of the cases.

See also CIRRHOSIS OF THE LIVER.

QUESTIONS AND ANSWERS

How can an injury to the liver be diagnosed?
1. Swelling and tenderness in the right upper portion of the abdomen
2. Evidence of external injury along with a history of an accident
3. Signs of internal hemorrhage with shock

How can one tell if the liver is the primary cause of illness or if the symptoms are due to gallbladder or bile duct conditions?
This is most important to determine before operating upon the liver. There are many accurate tests upon the stool, urine, and blood which will distinguish between liver disease and disease of the gallbladder or bile duct.

Does surgery always have to be done for an injury to the liver?
No. If the internal bleeding stops and the patient comes out of shock, it is possible to withhold surgery and treat the patient medically.

Is rupture of the liver dangerous?
Yes, but recovery is the rule unless the liver has been very extensively damaged. Frequently, rupture of the spleen accompanies liver rupture and this is a most serious condition. Hemorrhage from an injured spleen is usually much more severe and must be controlled through surgery.

What are the commonest causes of liver injury?
1. Automobile accidents
2. A fall onto one's side
3. Gunshot or stab wounds

4. A nearby explosion or a blow to the right side

What are the commonest causes of liver abscess?
1. Amebic dysentery, which causes amebic abscess, mostly in tropical countries
2. Infections of the appendix and gallbladder with spread of the pus to the liver

Do liver abscesses always have to be operated upon?
Most do, but now, with antibiotic drugs, some of these patients can be cured without surgery.

Is surgery for liver abscess serious?
Yes, but well over 90 percent of the patients will recover.

Can cysts or tumors of the liver be removed?
Most cysts can be removed but most tumors cannot be surgically removed.

With advances in surgical techniques, new hope has arisen for those who have liver tumors. There are now dozens of cases on record where an entire lobe of the liver has been removed successfully.

Can cancer of the liver be diagnosed accurately by the surgeon at the operating table?
Yes. Cancer of the liver has a very characteristic and easily diagnosed appearance. Furthermore, a biopsy can be taken and a microscopic diagnosis obtained within a few minutes.

What is the significance of finding cancer in the liver?
It almost always represents a spread from some other organ.

Does the surgeon proceed to remove the primary growth when spread to the liver has already taken place?
Usually not. These people are not helped greatly by extensive surgery.

How does one avoid spread of a cancer to the liver?

1. By early consultation with his doctor whenever symptoms appear.

2. The best safeguard against spread of a tumor is early and complete removal of the primary growth.

Can cirrhosis of the liver be helped through surgery?

Yes, in some cases. The portal vein is sutured to the vena cava or the vein of the spleen is sutured to the left renal (kidney) vein. This allows a large amount of the blood which ordinarily would travel *through* the liver to bypass it and go directly into the general body circulation. Such relief of the blood-load often permits partial recovery of the obstructed (cirrhotic) liver.

Are operations for cirrhosis serious procedures?

Yes, but surgeons throughout the country have learned to do them efficiently.

What are the chances of benefit from these operations for cirrhosis?

More than half the patients are benefited.

Where are incisions made for operations upon the liver?

Usually in the right upper portion of the abdomen. In certain cases of liver abscess, the incision may be made in the right lower part of the back of the chest.

How long do these operations take to perform?

Liver injury? Approximately 1 hour

Liver abscess? Approximately 1 to 2 hours

Shunt operation for cirrhosis? From 1½ to 4 hours

Removal of a cyst or tumor? From 2 to 6 hours

Are blood transfusions necessary?

Yes.

What type of anesthesia is used?

General inhalation anesthesia is used for almost all operations upon the liver.

Are special preoperative measures necessary?

Before doing any procedure upon the liver, it is wise to see that the patient has a large sugar and protein intake. This is carried out by feeding sugar and protein by mouth or by intravenous injection. The liver is protected and best prepared for surgery by giving large quantities of sugar and limiting fat intake. Also, adequate amounts of vitamins should be given.

Are special nurses necessary after operations upon the liver?

Yes, whenever the patient can afford them.

How long a hospital stay is necessary?

The condition for which liver operations are advocated tend to be chronic and the patients may therefore have to remain in the hospital for several weeks or even months.

How soon can the patient get out of bed after:

Liver injury? Not for several days or even weeks. Quiet is necessary to promote liver healing and to prevent recurrent hemorrhage

Removal of a cyst or tumor? Several days to several weeks

Liver abscess? Within 2 to 7 days

Cirrhosis? Several days

Is the postoperative period uncomfortable?

Not especially so. Wounds high up in the abdomen are not exceptionally painful. Postoperative intravenous injections are almost always instituted, and these may prove uncomfortable.

How long does it take these wounds to heal?

A tightly closed wound, without drainage, will heal within two weeks.

A drained wound, from a liver injury or liver abscess, may drain and not fully heal for several weeks or even months.

Is convalescent care necessary?

Yes, these conditions are usually accompanied by considerable debility with loss in weight and strength.

Can one live normally after removal of part of the liver?

Yes. Only about 20 percent of functioning liver substance is necessary to maintain life.

Can one tell how badly the liver is damaged by disease?

Yes. There are dozens of chemical tests that show the state of liver function.

HEPATECTOMY

What is hepatectomy?

It is surgical removal of a portion of the liver.

For what conditions is hepatectomy recommended?

1. When a malignant tumor is localized to either the right or the left lobe of the liver and is of such dimensions that it can be removed surgically

2. For benign lesions of the liver that are compressing the bile ducts and thus causing obstruction to the flow of bile into the intestines

3. For cysts that involve, and have destroyed, an entire lobe of the liver

4. In certain cases of cancer of the gallbladder

Is hepatectomy often a practical procedure?

No. In most instances, cancer will have spread and involved both lobes of the liver. When this occurs, removing one portion of the structure is of little value.

Does cancer ever affect only one part of the liver?

Every once in a while, a localized single cancerous lesion will be found. When this is the situation, hepatectomy not only may be lifesaving but may actually result in cure.

Is hepatectomy a dangerous operation?

Yes. The mortality rate is high but the conditions for which the procedure is performed warrant the risk.

Is hepatectomy ever done for a primary tumor of the liver?

Yes, occasionally. There is a tumor known as a hepatoma that may sometimes be localized to one part of the liver only. In these cases, hepatectomy may be effectual.

Is hepatectomy usually successful when performed for cancer of the gallbladder?

No, because this type of malignancy often has spread throughout the entire liver. Removal of one portion therefore will be of no avail.

Can the entire liver be removed and replaced by a transplanted liver?

Yes. This is now a technically feasible operation, sometimes accompanied by survival for several months or even years. However, in most cases in which this formidable operation has been tried, ultimate rejection of the transplanted liver has eventually taken place.

Lobectomy

Lobectomy is a surgical term for removal of a lobe of a lung. This operation, performed under general anesthesia, is most frequently employed for the following lung disorders:

1. An extensive lung abscess which has not responded to intensive and prolonged medical management and treatment with antibiotics. Today, lobectomy for abscesses is carried out infrequently because of improvements in medical management.

2. Lobectomy is sometimes recommended for tuberculosis that involves one lobe and has destroyed the lung tissue to such an extent that arrest of the process cannot be obtained through medication. It should be noted that the great majority of patients with tuberculosis of the lung will not require surgery as they will respond to the use of antituberculosis drugs.

3. Lobectomy is done quite often to overcome bronchiectasis. This is a condition in which the small bronchial tubes are partially destroyed and dilated. This makes them particularly susceptible to infection. If this infection cannot be controlled medically, lobectomy may be required.

4. Cysts of the lung. Lobectomy is not often performed for cysts, but occasionally a case is encountered in which an entire lobe has been destroyed by cysts that have become secondarily infected. In these cases, lobectomy may be indicated.

5. Lobectomy is sometimes carried out for severe injury to a lobe of a lung in which there is uncontrollable hemorrhage. This type of injury is seen most often as a result of a gunshot wound. In the great majority of cases, the lobe may be saved by repairing the laceration and stopping the bleeding. When this cannot be done, lobectomy is indicated.

6. Tumors of the lung. This represents by far the greatest number of cases for which lobectomy is performed. The great majority of tumors of the lung are malignant, but a small number may be due to benign adenomas. In either case, a lobectomy must be performed to bring about a cure. If the cancer of the lung has involved more than one lobe, then a procedure known as pneumonectomy (removal of an entire lung) is carried out rather than a lobectomy.

See also LUNGS.

QUESTIONS AND ANSWERS

Can a patient breathe and live normally after the removal of a lobe of a lung?

Yes, except that there is some restriction placed upon strenuous physical exercise.

What happens to the empty space within the chest cavity after the removal of a lobe of a lung?

The remaining portions of lung fill the empty space.

What are the chances for recovery following lobectomy?

With improved methods of surgery, operative recovery can be expected in over 98 percent of cases.

What type of incision is made for a lobectomy?

A very long incision following the course of the fifth or sixth rib, starting in the back, beneath and behind the shoulder blade, and traveling around toward the front of the body. Many of these incisions are over 15 inches in length.

How long a hospital stay is necessary for lobectomy?

Approximately two weeks.

Lobotomy

The operation known as lobotomy was performed quite frequently in certain types of mental illness. The operation was also done for the relief of intractable pain, particularly in patients with incurable cancer in whom anxiety was a prominent symptom. It has been noted that the alteration in personality that occurs as a consequence of this type of operation is a serious drawback, and most surgeons are in agreement that lobotomy is justified only in exceptional cases in which all other forms of treatment for mental illness have failed.

The purpose of the operation was to sever certain nerve pathways in the frontal lobe of the brain, thus modifying the course of the psychiatric illness.

With the introduction of many new and excellent medications in the treatment of mental illness and with the improvement in electroshock therapy, lobotomy has been largely abandoned as a form of therapy in mental disorders.

See also NEUROSURGERY.

QUESTIONS AND ANSWERS

Is lobotomy the same as prefrontal lobotomy?

Yes.

Is lobotomy a dangerous surgical procedure?

No. It does not involve the opening of the skull through a surgical incision, and is not considered to be a major neurosurgical procedure.

Lungs

The two lungs lie free within the chest cavity and are attached only at their roots by the bronchial tubes and large blood vessels. They expand when air is inhaled and contract when air is exhaled. The lungs are light, soft, and spongy in texture, mottled gray and pink in color, and are made up of innumerable tiny air sacs surrounded by elastic tissue and small blood vessels. The chest cavity (pleural cavity) normally has a negative pressure which is less than atmospheric pressure, so that when it is punctured or opened, the lung collapses.

The left lung is divided into two lobes (portions) while the right lung has three lobes. The function of the lungs is:

1. To take in air, extract oxygen from it, and absorb this oxygen through the cells which line its air spaces. The oxygen then travels in the bloodstream to all the tissues of the body.

2. To extract carbon dioxide from the bloodstream, to pass it through its cells into the air spaces and out of the body through the bronchial tubes.

The above phenomenon is called *respiration*, or breathing.

Modern advances in anesthesia have improved the safety of chest surgery to a point where its hazards are no greater than those of abdominal surgery. Thirty to forty years ago surgeons entered the

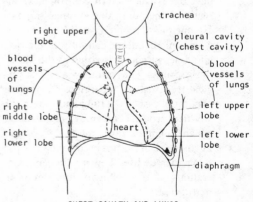

CHEST CAVITY AND LUNGS

chest hesitantly and in fear of sudden lung collapse and a fatal outcome. Today operations within the chest are carried out under *positive pressure* anesthesia, which serves to keep the lung expanded to any desired level. This technique is accomplished by inserting a snug-fitting tube (endotracheal tube) through the mouth and into the windpipe. It is then attached to the anesthesia machine. The machine can be adjusted to deliver the anesthetic gases at a controlled rate and under controlled pressure.

There are four main categories of lung disease which may require surgical treatment: (1) infections, (2) cysts, (3) tumors, and (4) injuries.

LUNG INFECTIONS

In the days before the antibiotic and other drugs, lung infections were the greatest cause of death, with tuberculosis and pneumonia leading the entire list wherever statistics were recorded. Lung abscesses and infected bronchiectasis (where the small bronchial tubes become widened and partially destroyed) were seen frequently and often ended fatally. Today drugs have been developed which often control these infections, including one of man's greatest enemies—tuberculosis. In instances where medications cannot do the job all alone, surgery has come to the aid of these drugs. The primary aim of surgical treatment in tuberculosis is to give maximum rest to the lung and to remove any dangerous focus (nest) of infection which might be dormant for years and might present a threat throughout the remainder of life. Toward this end, operations of the following type may be performed:

FOR TUBERCULOSIS

1. Thoracoplasty: This is a procedure carried out under general anesthesia in which all or portions of the upper ribs are removed over the region of the afflicted lung. This causes a partial collapse of the underlying lung and thereby permits prolonged rest. The operation is now almost completely obsolete, being replaced by either medical therapy or resection of diseased lung tissue.

2. Phrenic nerve crush: This is a procedure performed under local (Novocain) anesthesia. A small incision is made in the base of the neck above the collarbone. The phrenic nerve supplying the diaphragm is grasped and crushed. This produces a paralysis of the diaphragm on the operated side. A paralyzed diaphragm rises up into the chest and causes a limitation of lung expansion. Such a limitation acts much as a thoracoplasty in putting the underlying lung to prolonged rest. This operation, like thoracoplasty, is rarely performed today.

3. Lung removal (lobectomy or pneumonectomy): This operation, performed under general anesthesia, is often employed for removing a lung or lobe of a lung hopelessly infected with tuberculosis. It may entail removal of a portion or all of a lung, depending on the extent of involvement. Although this is a serious, major operation requiring special surgical training and several hours of operating time, nevertheless it is now a safe procedure with operative recovery in the vast majority of cases. Improved surgical techniques, the use of positive-pressure anesthesia, and the liberal employment of antibiotic drugs have all contributed toward making lung removal a safe operation.

FOR PNEUMONIA

Surgery for pneumonia usually took the form of draining the chest cavity (pleural cavity) of pus after the development of empyema (pus in the pleural cavity). With the use of the antibiotics, empyema has become a rare complication. It is only in those pneumonia patients who have received no medical care at all that one now encounters empyema. In the rare instance where empyema does develop, a small incision is made in the chest wall, and a rubber tube is inserted into the chest cavity to drain off the pus. This operation, thoracotomy, is safe and can be performed in a few minutes under local Novocain anesthesia. The antibiotics are given postoperatively and recovery takes place in practically all cases.

FOR LUNG ABSCESS

Most lung abscesses are controlled medically with antibiotic drugs, but in the occasional unresponsive case, surgical drainage of the abscess cavity must be carried out. This is done under local or general anesthesia and involves removing a portion of rib over the region of the abscess. The chest cavity is entered and a knife or scissors is inserted into the abscess. The abscess cavity is drained for several days and intensive antibiotic medication is continued. Failure of an abscess cavity to heal often requires removal of the involved portion of the lung. This maneuver (lobectomy) is successful in almost all instances.

FOR BRONCHIECTASIS

Bronchiectasis is an infectious process of unknown cause in which there is widening and destruction of portions of the bronchial tree. When there is loss of elasticity in the walls of a bronchus, there is stagnation of secretions. Infection then sets in and leads to recurrent attacks of pneumonia or lung abscess. These people have a foul odor to their breath, expectorate large quantities of infected mucus, and occasionally cough up blood. Because of the tendency of this disease to be localized to one portion of the lungs, usually the lower lobes, the best treatment is removal of these sections of the lungs. Great improvement follows lobectomy for this condition.

CYSTS

Lung cysts are usually present since birth and consist of thin-walled sacs filled with either air or fluid. Some are acquired later in life, and in some people many cysts are present. They may cause symptoms by creating pressure and collapse of surrounding lung tissue. In some patients they become secondarily infected and form abscesses, while in others they may burst and permit escape of air into the chest cavity. This latter complication will result in lung collapse.

Surgical treatment is recommended for those patients in whom the cysts are causing symptoms. The operation consists of removal of the cyst or a portion of the cyst-containing lung (segmental resection or lobectomy) and is performed under general anesthesia.

TUMORS

Within recent years there has been a marked increase in the incidence of lung cancer. This sad fact has been brought into sharp focus by the realization that the increase has paralleled the increased use of cigarettes, and there is no doubt that cigarette smokers are *ten times more prone than nonsmokers to develop lung cancer.* Lung cancer comes on insidiously with few early symptoms. Loss of appetite, weight loss, chest pain, and the coughing of blood are late symptoms. The best way to protect oneself against the late discovery of this disease is to undergo a yearly chest x-ray examination. A spot on the lung is often one of the first signs of the presence of a growth.

Benign tumors (adenomas) do occur but are quite rare. They are difficult to distinguish, prior to surgery, from lung cancer and are therefore treated in the same manner.

The treatment for lung tumors is surgical. Either the entire lung (pneumonectomy) is removed or the entire lobe of the lung (lobectomy) is removed wherever feasible. Unfortunately, the majority of patients reach the operating table at a time when the tumor has already spread to the regional lymph nodes or to distant organs such as the brain or the vertebral column. In such cases, removal of the lung will not effect a cure. The chest is therefore closed and postoperative x-ray treatment is instituted.

It is good to report that despite the many failures, more and more patients are making complete recovery after lung removal for cancer. Programs sponsoring community chest x-ray examinations and free cancer detection clinics have led to earlier discovery of lung cancer and a higher rate of operability and curability. The public can look forward to a brighter future in conquering this form of cancer as we learn more about the nature of its causation.

INJURIES

Injuries to the chest wall and underlying lung have become more and more frequent in our highly mechanized and fast-moving modern civilization. The lung may be injured by contusion (a blow) against the bony chest wall, by penetration of a broken rib fragment, or by a stab or gunshot wound. A wound of the lung results in escape of blood and air into the chest cavity (pleural cavity), shortness of breath, and a certain degree of collapse of the lung. If any of these complications—namely, *shock, escape of blood into the chest cavity* (hemothorax), *escape of air into the chest cavity* (pneumothorax), or *collapse of the lung*—are extensive and show no signs of abating, a fatality may result. Surgical treatment in progressive cases is directed toward control of these symptoms:

1. Shock is treated by blood transfusion, oxygen inhalations, and sedatives or narcotics.

2. If hemorrhage is massive and continuous, the chest cavity should be opened surgically and the bleeding stopped by tying off the vessels or by removing the damaged portion of the lung.

3. The pneumothorax is controlled by inserting a needle or small rubber tube into the chest cavity to permit the escape of air.

4. The collapsed lung will usually expand again by itself as soon as the wound has healed and the air and blood are removed from the chest cavity. A severely damaged portion of lung is usually collapsed, and if it fails to expand, it should be removed.

Fortunately, many chest injuries are not nearly as serious as they may appear at first. If a vital structure such as the heart, windpipe, the large bronchial tubes, or one of the major vessels within the chest is struck, death may ensue within a matter of seconds or minutes. However, if the patient is able to survive for a period of several hours and reaches a hospital, recovery is the usual outcome. Actually, surgical intervention is not indicated in the majority of cases, for there is a great tendency for lung hemorrhage and the escape of air into the chest cavity to subside spontaneously.

See also BRONCHIECTASIS; EMBOLUS AND EMBOLISM; EMPYEMA; PNEUMONECTOMY.

QUESTIONS AND ANSWERS

What is atelectasis?

A condition in which the lung tissue is collapsed and contains no air.

What causes atelectasis?

Obstruction of a bronchial tube.

What types of atelectasis are there?

1. Those occurring at birth which are due either to a mucous plug in a bronchial tube or to a congenitally deformed and narrowed tube.

2. In later life, it may be caused by a blockage of a bronchus by mucus, pus, or blood. Also, foreign bodies, such as peanuts, meat, or other foods which have gone down the wrong way, may obstruct a bronchial tube and produce atelectasis. The first indication of the presence of a tumor of the bronchus is frequently the discovery of an area of atelectasis (collapsed lung) caused by the obstruction of the bronchus by growing tumor tissue.

What is massive atelectasis?

It is a postoperative complication in which there is a large amount of mucus plugging one of the main bronchial tubes. This may cause an entire lung to collapse.

What is emphysema?

A condition in which the lung tissue loses its elasticity and becomes overstretched. It is usually associated with partial obstruction of the bronchial tubes, so that air is trapped within the lung. Thus, air can get into the lungs readily but cannot get out easily. If this process continues, lung tissue becomes like an overstretched balloon.

What causes lung abscess?

It is usually caused by a blockage of a bronchial tube, with the development of infection beyond the point of obstruction. One of the most common causes is the aspiration of pus or infected mucus during an operation upon the nose, throat, or mouth.

Do lung abscesses ever occur without a preceding operation?

Yes. An abscess can form whenever an area of inflamed lung, or an area affected by tumor tissue, breaks down due to localized death of tissue.

How does one make a diagnosis of lung abscess?

1. The patient coughs up extremely foul-smelling pus.

2. There may be high fever, chills, and malaise during the early days of the illness.

3. There is a characteristic appearance of the lung on x-ray examination, and the abscess cavity itself can often be plainly seen on the film.

Must lung abscess always be operated upon?

No. Many clear up completely with antibiotics, especially if any bronchial obstruction can be relieved.

What are the symptoms of spontaneous pneumothorax or collapse of the lung?

There are a sudden and dramatic occurrence of chest pain, shortness of breath, and, occasionally, severe shock and collapse.

How does the physician make a diagnosis of spontaneous pneumothorax?

1. By noting the history of the onset

2. By listening to the chest and noting the absence of breath sounds on one side

3. By noting a marked increase in the resonant sound on tapping the chest with his fingers (percussion)

4. By taking an x-ray picture and discovering that the lung is collapsed

What is the treatment for spontaneous pneumothorax?

Often, because of sudden shock and the severity of the symptoms, immediate hospitalization is necessary. If the extent of the collapse is greater than 25 to 30 percent, or if the leak in the ruptured lung is not sealed off so that air continues to flow out into the chest cavity causing a "tension pneumothorax," a tube must be inserted through an opening into the chest cavity to draw off the air and allow the lung to reexpand. The tube is kept in place for several days during which time the lung tissue usually heals.

What other situations may produce spontaneous pneumothorax?

A perforation of the chest wall, such as a stab wound, gunshot wound, or a blast injury. Also, a fractured rib may puncture the lung, allowing air to escape from it to the chest cavity, and thus causing the lung to collapse.

Is collapse of the lung ever a fatal condition?

Not if it occurs on one side only. However, some blast injuries or gunshot wounds may cause collapse of both lungs, and such a condition may lead to a fatality.

Are chest operations safe?

Yes, as safe as any major operation elsewhere in the body.

What is the difference between a lobectomy and a pneumonectomy?

Lobectomy: only a lobe or portion of a lung is removed.

Pneumonectomy: an entire lung is removed.

Can a patient breathe and live normally after the removal of a lobe of a lung?

Yes, except that there is some restriction placed upon strenuous physical exercise.

Can a patient breathe and live normally after removal of two lobes?

Yes, but there is a bit more restriction than after the removal of one lobe.

Can a patient breathe and live normally after removal of an entire lung (pneumonectomy)?

At rest, these people can breathe normally, but on exertion, tend to get short of breath. They must therefore restrict their activity moderately.

What happens to the empty space within the chest cavity after removal of a whole lung?

1. The diaphragm ascends into the chest.

2. The structures from the opposite side shift toward the side of operation.

3. The chest wall is retracted inward.

4. The empty space is filled with scar tissue.

What happens to the empty space within the chest cavity after the removal of a portion (lobe) of a lung?

The remaining portions of lung fill the empty space.

What are the indications for performing a lobectomy?

1. Tuberculosis

2. Lung cysts

3. Chronic lung abscesses

4. Bronchiectasis

5. Localized lung tumors

What are the indications for performing a pneumonectomy?

1. Malignant lung tumors

2. Tuberculosis localized to an entire lung

Is lobectomy a serious operation?

Yes, but operative recovery can be expected in over 98 percent of cases.

Is pneumonectomy a serious operation?

Yes, but operative recovery can be expected in about 95 percent of cases.

Is it possible to transplant two new lungs?

Yes. There are several patients who have received donor lungs. Unfortunately, to date, no one has survived for very long after this procedure even when operative recovery has ensued. Fatal rejection reactions have occurred in all cases.

Are operations for a lung abscess or pus in the chest cavity serious?

Yes, but recovery can be expected in well over 95 percent of cases.

Should all patients with lung injury be hospitalized?

Yes.

What are some usual signs of lung cancer?

1. Cough
2. Expectoration of blood
3. Chest pain
4. X-ray findings of a spot on the lung

How common is lung cancer?

It is one of the commonest forms of cancer.

Is lung cancer more common among men than women?

Yes.

What is the relationship between cigarette smoking and lung cancer?

There is a definite relationship in that most male patients with lung cancer give a history of having been heavy smokers over a prolonged period of time. Lung cancer is 10 times more common among male cigarette smokers than among non-smokers.

What will happen if a patient with lung cancer is not operated upon?

A fatality will result in several months to a year.

What will happen if a patient with lung cysts is not operated upon?

He may become increasingly short of breath and develop recurring attacks of pneumonia.

What will happen if a patient with bronchiectasis (dilatation and infection in the small bronchial tubes at the base of the lungs) is not operated upon?

1. He, too, may become increasingly short of breath and develop recurring attacks of pneumonia.
2. The disease may spread to other parts of the lungs.

What are the indications for operating upon patients who have sustained a lung injury?

1. Continuing hemorrhage in the chest cavity
2. Air leak which cannot be controlled by a needle in the chest or a tube
3. Serious injury to the chest wall
4. Infection in the chest cavity

What are the chances of recovery from a lung injury?

Excellent; except when one of the great blood vessels or main bronchial tubes has been severed.

What is the treatment for fractured ribs?

Usually immobilization is all that is necessary. If a sharp fragment is sticking into the lung, it must be removed surgically.

How long do fractured ribs remain painful?

Three to five weeks.

What surgical treatment is carried out for:

1. Puncture of the lung? If hemorrhage and air leakage stop spontaneously, then no surgery is required. Often it is necessary to drain the chest cavity with a rubber tube.

2. Laceration and bleeding from the lung? Bleeding from the lung tends to stop by itself and requires only that the blood be removed by needle and syringe. If this does not occur, the laceration in the lung is sutured.

3. Blood and air in the chest cavity? This is removed by inserting a needle into the chest. If this is ineffectual, then a rubber tube is inserted for continuous drainage.

How many patients with tuberculosis of the lungs require surgery?

Only a minority. The majority of cases can be treated adequately by medical means such as drugs and bed rest.

Is thoracoplasty (multiple rib removal) a serious operation?

Yes, but the procedure is seldom performed any more. Removal of the diseased lung tissue is the operation of choice when medical management has failed to control the tuberculous process.

Are special preparations necessary before major chest surgery?

1. Antibiotics are given for several days before operation.

2. Smoking should be stopped for a few days.

3. Any cold or respiratory infection should be cleared up before surgery.

Where are the incisions made for lung operations?

Beneath and behind the shoulder blade paralleling the ribs.

What kind of anesthesia is used for chest surgery?

1. General anesthesia with the use of an endotracheal (tube in the windpipe) for lobectomy and pneumonectomy.

2. Local anesthesia is sometimes used for simple thoracotomy (opening into the chest cavity) to drain off pus or to approach a lung abscess.

Are blood transfusions needed during major chest operations?

Yes.

What are the main precautions in performing lobectomy and pneumonectomy?

To securely tie the blood vessels and to securely stitch the bronchial tube.

How long does it take to perform a lobectomy?

Approximately two to four hours.

How long does it take to perform a pneumonectomy?

Approximately two to four hours.

Are special nurses required after a major chest operation?

Yes.

When can one get out of bed after a major chest operation?

Lobectomy	1 to 3 days
Pneumonectomy	1 to 2 days
Thoracoplasty (removal of several ribs)	1 to 2 days
Thoracotomy	1 to 2 days

Are the wounds painful?

A small number of patients have painful scars for several months. Most others experience no pain.

Are the wounds drained after chest operations?

Usually a rubber tube is inserted into the chest for two to three days.

Is it painful when these drains are removed?

No.

How long a hospital stay is necessary?
Lobectomy	10 to 14 days
Pneumonectomy	10 to 12 days
Thoracoplasty	10 to 12 days
Thoracotomy	10 to 14 days

(The above relates to the uncomplicated case.)

What are the usual postoperative measures carried out after a major chest operation?
1. Patients are routinely placed in an oxygen tent for at least 24 hours.
2. Fluids by mouth may be taken.
3. Antibiotic drugs are continued.
4. Patients are encouraged to cough.

Is convalescent care necessary after lobe or lung removal?
Yes.

What are the chances of ultimate cure through lobectomy in:
Tuberculosis? The great majority of cases recover.
Lung cysts? Almost all cases recover.
Lung cancer? More and more cases are being cured as earlier intervention is practiced.

What are the chances of ultimate cure through pneumonectomy in:
Tuberculosis? The majority recover.
Lung cancer? The recovery rate is greatest among those who are operated upon at an early stage in the development of the tumor.

Are the scars of the incisions disfiguring?
No, and they are not visible unless a backless dress is worn.

Is breathing painful after a major chest operation?
Only for the first week after operation.

After a major chest operation, when can one:
Bathe?	2 weeks
Drive a car?	4 to 5 weeks
Resume usual household duties?	5 to 6 weeks
Return to work?	6 to 8 weeks

How long does it take the average chest wound to heal?
About two weeks.

Lymphedema

Lymphedema is swelling of the tissues beneath the skin due to the presence of an excessive amount of lymph within the tissues. It most often involves the leg or the arm.

There are a considerable number of conditions in which there is lymphedema of the lower extremity. Among these are the following:

1. **Milroy's disease,** an inherited disease seen mainly in females, in which the lower limbs are continuously and permanently swollen.

2. **Filariasis,** a parasitic disease in which the lymph channels and lymph nodes in the groin are blocked so that the legs are swollen.

3. **Lymphedema of the legs,** a usual accompaniment of removal of the lymph nodes in the groin. A dissection of these nodes is done for a malignant tumor of the leg that has spread to the nodes in the groin.

4. **Obstruction of the lymph nodes within the pelvis,** or obstruction of the lymph channels within the pelvis, will lead to swelling of the lower extremities.

5. The most frequent cause of lymphedema in the upper extremity is the radical removal of a breast, with dissection of the nodes in the armpit for cancer.

See also BREASTS.

QUESTIONS AND ANSWERS

In lymphedema, does swelling ever decline due to the formation of new lymph channels?

No appreciable growth of new lymph channels takes place, but collateral circulation of lymph does occur to a limited extent. This means that the lymph seeks out other, nonobstructed, channels to travel through. In this process, there may be some enlargement of previously small lymph channels so that they can carry more.

Will exercise help to reduce lymphedema?

Yes to a slight degree.

Will the wearing of elastic supports tend to decrease lymphedema?

Yes. Elastic stockings for the legs and specially devised elastic supports for the arm will tend to decrease the extent of lymphedema.

Does lymphedema cause symptoms?

If an arm or a leg is very swollen secondary to lymphedema, it will be most uncomfortable and feel extremely heavy. However, there is no frank pain in this condition.

Lymphangiography

Lymphangiography, or lymphography, is the x-raying of lymph channels following the injection of a contrast medium, an opaque dye, into a lymph vessel. It is a technique developed within recent years for the purpose of outlining the lymph channels and noting alterations in their course and also their involvement in disease of the lymph nodes (glands) into which the channels drain.

QUESTIONS AND ANSWERS

How is lymphangiography carried out?

A lymph channel in the hand or arm, or in the foot or leg, is carefully dissected out following an incision through the skin. When the lymph channel has been isolated, a tiny needle or plastic catheter is inserted into the lymph channel and tied there. A contrast medium, a substance that will show up on x-ray film, is then injected into the lymph channel, and x-ray films are taken.

What is the purpose of lymphangiography?

1. It will show distortion of the normal course of the lymph channels, thus revealing the presence of a tumor or a deviation from normal anatomy.

2. It may demonstrate a blockage of the lymph channels, denoting either the presence of mechanical obstruction of the normal channels or the presence of some tumor or other anatomical abnormality.

3. When the contrast medium reaches the lymph nodes, it will show whether or not they are enlarged. Enlarged lymph nodes may denote the spread of tumor to the nodes or a disease that is primary within the lymph nodes themselves.

Is the swelling of the arm noted after the radical removal of the breast for cancer ever caused by blockage of the lymph channels?

Yes. Lymphograms will demonstrate obstruction to the flow of lymph in these cases.

Is surgery ever influenced by the results of lymphangiography?

Yes. If a lymphogram demonstrates that regional lymph nodes are enlarged, it can be concluded that they are probably involved in the malignant process. With this knowledge, the surgeon will extend the area of operation so that the involved lymph nodes are excised.

Is it ever possible, on finding that lymph channels are obstructed, to reconstruct them?

In most areas of the body, this is not yet a feasible surgical procedure.

Male Genital Organs

See CIRCUMCISION; EPIDIDYMITIS; HYDROCELE; HYPOSPADIAS AND EPISPADIAS; PENIS; PHIMOSIS; PROSTATE GLAND; TESTICLES; VARICOCELE; VASECTOMY.

Mammography

See BREASTS.

Mastectomy

Mastectomy means removal of a breast. There are two main types, namely, a simple mastectomy in which the breast is completely removed but the underlying muscles of the chest wall and the lymph nodes in the armpit are permitted to remain in place, and radical mastectomy in which not only the breast is entirely removed but the underlying chest wall muscles and all of the lymph nodes in the armpit are removed at the same time.

See also BREASTS.

QUESTIONS AND ANSWERS

What are the indications for a simple mastectomy?

1. The presence of a malignant tumor

in an aged individual or in one in whom the radical operation would be attended by too great a risk

2. In selected cases in which the surgeon believes that simple removal of the breast, coupled with postoperative irradiation with x-ray or cobalt, will bring about just as good a surgical result as radical mastectomy

3. In isolated cases where the tumor shows certain signs of becoming malignant, such as in intraductal papillomas, but where no invasive cancer is found

What are the indications for radical mastectomy?

The majority of surgeons feel that removal of the breast, along with the muscles of the chest wall and the nodes in the armpit, is the best approach to management of cancer of this organ.

Is mastectomy a dangerous operative procedure?

No. Most patients can withstand either a simple or radical mastectomy, and operative recovery is the general rule.

Does permanent swelling of the arm ever follow radical mastectomy?

Yes. In a number of cases this complication does occur.

Is cobalt or x-ray radiation always given after mastectomy for cancer of the breast?

No. It is indicated in some cases but not in others. The decision must be made individually in each case, depending upon the operative findings and the final report on the microscopic examination of the tumor that has been removed.

Can full use of the arm be regained after mastectomy?

Yes. A whole series of exercises, provided by the surgeon, should be embarked upon after mastectomy.

Can the disfigurement caused by mastectomy be helped by special brassieres?

Yes. There are many different types of brassieres which can hide the fact that a breast has been removed.

Can women return to full activity after removal of a breast?

Yes.

What is the outlook for cure following mastectomy for cancer of the breast?

The overall cure rate now exceeds 80 percent if the tumor is limited to the breast itself.

Mastoidectomy

Seldom, if ever, before has a common operation become a rarity in so short a period of time. Thirty years ago, the winter months saw the wards of hospitals in temperate climates jammed with children suffering from mastoid infections. Now, thanks to the curative effect of the sulfonamides and the antibiotic drugs, operation for acute infection of the mastoid bone (mastoidectomy) is rarely necessary.

The ear is composed of three parts:

1. The external ear: This consists of the visible portion and the external canal which extends down to the eardrum.

2. The middle ear: This portion is on the inner side of the drum. It is small and connects through a narrow passageway (the eustachian tube) with the back of the throat. It also has a direct connection with the mastoid air cells lodged in the bone behind the external ear.

3. The inner ear: This portion is deep to the middle ear and is composed of the *cochlea* (which controls the sense of hearing) and the *semicircular canals* (which control the sense of balance).

From this anatomical arrangement, it can be readily seen that there is a continuous channel from the nose and throat cavity into the middle ear and on to the mastoid bone. It is not difficult to understand, therefore, how colds, throat infections, inflamed adenoids, etc., can spread to involve the middle ear and mastoid region. The contagious diseases of children such as measles and scarlet fever, since they are associated with throat, tonsil, and adenoid inflammation, also lead to middle ear and mastoid infection.

The presence of a middle ear infection is heralded by pain in the ear, a rise in temperature, redness and swelling of the eardrum on inspection, and ultimate rupture of the drum and the discharge of pus into the external ear canal. When an acute middle ear infection has spread to the mastoid cells behind the ear, several or all of the following signs and symptoms may make their appearance:

1. Abrupt rise in temperature with loss of appetite and swelling of the glands in the neck.

2. Pain behind the ear over the mastoid bone. (This pain is usually worse at night.)

3. Tenderness on direct finger pressure over the mastoid region.

4. A pouching forward of the back wall of the external ear canal.

5. An increase in the white blood cell count.

6. X-ray findings indicative of involvement of the mastoid cells.

7. Impaired hearing.

8. As a later complication, the mastoid infection may burst out of the bone and into the soft tissues behind the ear. This will give the appearance that the external ear has been bent forward.

Today surgery is the last resort for the preceding illness (acute mastoiditis).

Instead a specimen of pus from the hole in the eardrum is cultured and the organisms (germs) are then tested with the various antibiotics to find the one to which they are most susceptible. Usually within a week after intensive treatment with the appropriate antibiotic, the infection subsides! In the very rare case that does not respond, mastoidectomy is carried out.

It must be mentioned that there are many patients with chronic mastoiditis who have had partial loss of hearing and discharge of pus from an ear for many years. Here, too, medical treatment with the wonder drugs is instituted, but the results are not quite as satisfactory. In these patients, a *radical mastoidectomy* with removal of the contents of the middle ear and all the mastoid cells may have to be performed.

There are two main types of mastoidectomy: the simple and the radical. In *simple mastoidectomy* the surgeon usually makes an incision about one and a half inches long within the external ear canal extending from the drum outward. This is termed the *endaural* approach. In some cases, the surgeon may elect to approach the mastoid by an incision approximately two inches long behind the ear. In both instances, the bone is

chipped and scraped away until all the infected mastoid cells are removed and a healthy bony cavity remains. The *radical mastoidectomy* is much the same as the simple procedure except that the eardrum and most of the contents of the middle ear are also removed.

Mastoidectomy is performed under general anesthesia and is, in trained hands, a perfectly safe procedure. With the aid of the antibiotics, practically all patients recover except those who have been neglected and have not seen a physician during the first several weeks of the illness. Technical precautions must be taken during operation not to injure the nearby facial nerve, as this may cause a permanent distortion of the face. Fortunately, surgeons are well aware of this hazard and know how to avoid it.

See also DEAFNESS; EARS.

QUESTIONS AND ANSWERS

What are the mastoids?

Part of the bony skull located directly behind the ears. The mastoids contain air cells which connect with the middle ear.

Why do they become infected?

Infection in the middle ear often extends into the mastoid.

Is a mastoid infection always preceded by an ear infection?

Practically always.

What are the evidences of a mastoid infection?

1. Pain behind the ear
2. Discharge of pus from the ear
3. Rise in temperature
4. X-ray findings of mastoid bone involvement
5. Pushing forward of the external ear canal

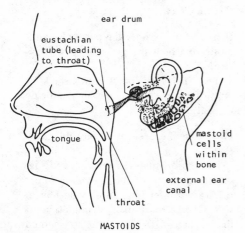

MASTOIDS

What age group is most prone to develop acute mastoid infection?

Children between the ages of 2 and 12 years.

Do adults ever get this condition?

Rarely.

How does one know that a middle ear infection has become a mastoid infection?

Several or all of the following signs and symptoms may develop:

1. Pain behind the ear over the mastoid bone. The pain is usually worse at night.

2. There will be tenderness and pain on direct pressure over the mastoid region.

3. There can be an abrupt rise in temperature, with swelling of the neck glands and loss of appetite.

4. The back wall of the ear canal may bulge forward.

5. X-rays of the mastoid bone will show a characteristic haziness when the mastoid cells are infected.

6. There will be impaired hearing on the involved side.

7. The white blood cell count can be elevated.

Is mastoiditis contagious?

No.

At what season of the year are mastoid infections most prevalent?

Toward the end of the winter, when the bacteria that cause upper respiratory infections are most virulent.

Does mastoiditis often occur in both ears?

If the patient has a severe middle ear infection on both sides, he can develop a mastoid infection on both sides. However, people more often have a mastoid infection on only one side.

What are some possible complications of a mastoid infection?

Today there are relatively few complications if treatment is carried out promptly. In some outlying areas where medical care is not available, one occasionally encounters a person who has received no treatment and has an extensive infection. In these cases, the pus may spread from the mastoid region into the coverings of the brain, producing meningitis or a brain abscess, or the infection may gain access to the bloodstream and cause blood poisoning. One may die from an untreated case of mastoiditis, but this is highly unlikely today.

What germs are most likely to cause infection of the mastoid bone?

Any germ that can produce an upper respiratory infection is capable of infecting the mastoid bones. This includes a great many bacteria, such as the staphylococcus, streptococcus, pneumococcus, and colon bacillus.

Does a mastoid infection ever take place without a preceding ear infection?

Practically never.

What is the mechanism by which the mastoids become infected?

Through a progressing infection from the middle ear.

Is it wise to discover the particular antibiotic to which the germ is most sensitive?

Yes. This can be accomplished by culturing some of the pus that is being discharged.

How can one prevent a mastoid infection?

Prevention involves prompt and vigorous treatment of the preceding upper respiratory infection. Those who have a sore throat, tonsillitis, inflammation of the adenoids, or sinus infection should consult a physician if elevated temperature continues for more than a few days. In all probability, he will prescribe bed rest, antibiotic medications, and forced fluids. Most mastoid infections can be prevented through this form of treatment of the predisposing infection.

Does surgery usually have to be performed to cure a mastoid infection?

No. Most cases can now be cured by medication with antibiotic drugs.

When is surgery necessary?

When antibiotic drugs have failed. A trial of at least a week should be given.

Is mastoidectomy a dangerous operation?

No. However, it is a serious operation.

Is hearing affected by mastoid operation?

Simple mastoidectomy does not impair hearing. Radical mastoidectomy means loss of hearing in the ear.

What is the difference between a simple and a radical mastoidectomy?

Simple mastoidectomy involves removal of the mastoid air cells only. Radical mastoidectomy involves not only removal of the mastoid cells but removal of the eardrum and contents of the middle ear.

Is it a painful operation?

Yes, there is considerable pain for several days after the operation.

What anesthesia is used?

General inhalation anesthesia.

How long does it take to perform this operation?

Approximately one hour for a simple mastoidectomy and one and a half hours for a radical mastoidectomy.

Where is the incision made?

Usually within the ear canal starting inward and extending outward. Occasionally behind the ear directly over the bone.

Is the wound drained?

Yes, a rubber tissue or gauze drain is placed in the wound and permitted to remain for four to six days.

Is it painful to remove the drains?

Yes, moderately.

Does the ear continue to drain pus even after operation?

Yes, for a period of several days to several weeks.

How long does it take for the wound to heal?

Two to three weeks.

Are special preoperative or postoperative medications given?

Yes. Large doses of antibiotics are ordered to control and prevent spread of the infection.

Are special nurses necessary?

No.

How soon can patients get out of bed?

Within two to three days.

How long a hospital stay is necessary?

In average cases, seven to ten days.

How long after surgery will treatment be necessary?

Simple mastoidectomy: Three to four weeks. Radical mastoidectomy: Office treatments may be necessary for several weeks to several months.

Is the scar following surgery disfiguring?

No. There is just a small line visible in the ear canal. Even when the mastoid is operated upon through an incision made behind the ear, it appears only as a thin white line.

Does mastoid infection recur after surgery?

No.

What percentage of those operated upon recover?

Mortality from a mastoid operation is practically nil in modern practice today!

Will a person lose hearing permanently if he has a simple mastoidectomy?

No. Usually he will recover his hearing, although it will stay impaired for some time after the surgery.

Meckel's Diverticulum

A Meckel's diverticulum is a birth deformity occurring in the last foot of the small intestine before it enters the large bowel. The diverticulum is a remnant of the embryonic connection between the small intestine and the yolk sac. Normally this connection, which leads out

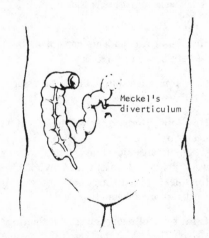

Meckel's diverticulum is a remnant of the embryonic connection between the small intestine and yolk sac, which normally disappears before a child is born.

through the navel, disappears entirely by the time the child is born. The actual diverticulum is an outpouching of the wall of the small intestine.

See also INTESTINES; INTUSSUSCEPTION.

QUESTIONS AND ANSWERS

How large is the average Meckel's diverticulum?

The fingerlike outpouching from the small intestine usually measures one inch to two inches in length and half an inch to one inch in width.

How common is Meckel's diverticulum?

It is estimated that about 1 out of 50 children is born with a small or a large Meckel's diverticulum.

Does the pressure of a Meckel's diverticulum usually cause symptoms?

Not in most cases. It is estimated that only about 10 percent of people with Meckel's diverticulum will have an inflammation within the sac. Since only 1 in 50 individuals have the condition, approximately 1 in 500 will develop an inflammation in the diverticulum.

What are the usual symptoms of a Meckel's diverticulum?

The most common symptom associated with this condition is bleeding into the intestinal tract. This occurs most often during the first 18 months of life.

How will the mother know that a Meckel's diverticulum is bleeding?

The child may pass a stool containing a "currant-jelly" clot. This will usually be repeated on several occasions.

Is the bleeding from a Meckel's diverticulum usually continuous?

No. In most instances, the bleeding will stop spontaneously, then will recur several weeks or months later.

How can this type of bleeding in children be distinguished from bleeding caused by a polyp in the intestinal tract or by intussusception?

Bleeding from a Meckel's diverticulum usually occurs in children under 2 years old, while those who have rectal polyps or intussusception are older. Rectal polyps can usually be detected when the pediatrician inserts a finger into the child's rectum or inspects the inside of the rectal canal with a sigmoidoscope. Intussusception is usually accompanied by the presence of a mass (lump) in the abdomen.

Are x-rays helpful in making the diagnosis of a Meckel's diverticulum?

Not too often, as barium, which the patient is given to make the shape of the bowel visible, usually will not pass into the pouch of the diverticulum and cause it to show up on the x-ray picture.

Is there any medical treatment for a Meckel's diverticulum?

No. If it has bled only once and does not bleed again, the condition can be ignored. All but 10 percent of those affected go through life without having any further trouble attributable to the diverticulum.

Does a Meckel's diverticulum ever act as the source of intussusception?

Yes. Sometimes a Meckel's diverticulum will become inverted and will trigger the telescoping of the small bowel into the large bowel and thus produce intussusception.

Does a Meckel's diverticulum tend to become inflamed?

Yes. When it does, it usually produces symptoms very similar to those of appendicitis. The distinction between the two conditions is based mainly on the knowledge that the patient has passed blood with the typical "currant-jelly" clot in his stool.

Does an adult with Meckel's diverticulum ever have bleeding from the rectum?

Yes. Observation of the passage of blood through the rectum is one of the ways in which the diagnosis is suspected.

Is there a tendency for an inflamed diverticulum to rupture and cause peritonitis?

Yes, but inflammation of a Meckel's diverticulum rarely takes place during childhood.

When is it necessary to operate for removal of a Meckel's diverticulum?

1. When it bleeds repeatedly.
2. When it is inflamed.
3. When an ulceration develops in the mucous membrane in the base of the diverticulum. This may result in bleeding, inflammation, or perforation. (Such ulcerations are rare.)
4. When it causes intussusception.

What operative procedure is carried out for a Meckel's diverticulum?

If emergency surgery is not necessary, the bowel is sterilized by the preoperative administration of neomycin or kanamycin. The patient is fed intravenously the day of surgery, and a stomach tube is passed just before he is taken to the operating room.

An incision approximately three inches long is made into the right lower portion of the abdomen. The terminal portion of the small intestine (ileum) is brought through the wound, and the Meckel's diverticulum is brought into view. A V-shaped excision of the diverticulum and part of the bowel wall is then made, and the two ends of normal bowel are stitched together. The incision in the abdomen is then closed.

How serious is an operation for the removal of a Meckel's diverticulum?

It is a serious operation, but recovery takes place in almost all instances unless the diverticulum has ruptured and a spreading peritonitis has resulted, in which case the patient is quite sick and recovery may be prolonged.

Are the following necessary before operations for a Meckel's diverticulum?

Blood transfusions: No, unless the patient has bled profusely from a hemorrhage of the Meckel's diverticulum.

Antibiotic medications: Yes, in order to prepare the bowel for surgery.

Intravenous medications: Yes, the day before and the day of surgery.

Stomach tubes: Yes.

Bladder catheters: No.

Vitamin injections: No.

Special diets: Fluid diet the day before surgery.

Other special preparations: None.

Are the following necessary after operations for a Meckel's diverticulum?

Private duty nurses: Yes, for a day or two.

Antibiotic medications: Possibly, especially if there has been a rupture of the diverticulum with peritonitis.

Intravenous infusions: Yes, for a day or two, because the patient will not be fed by mouth.

Blood transfusions: No.

Stomach tubes: Yes, for two to three days.

Special postoperative measures: No.

Postoperative vitamins and tonics: Yes, for a few days.

Convalescent posthospital care? No.

How soon after an operation for a Meckel's diverticulum can one:

Get out of bed?	1–2 days
Leave the hospital?	7–10 days
Climb stairs?	10–12 days
Bathe or shower?	12–14 days
Go outdoors?	14 days
Resume physical activity?	2–3 months

Meconium and Meconium Obstruction

Meconium is the sticky substance contained within the intestinal tract of the embryo and the newborn child. Meconium obstruction of the small intestine is a most serious condition seen at birth. It is associated with cystic fibrosis, a generalized disease involving the pancreas, liver, lungs, and other organs. In this condition, the meconium sticks to the lining of the intestines instead of passing out of the tract through the rectum. Unless surgery is performed fairly promptly, the child may die.

See also INTESTINES.

QUESTIONS AND ANSWERS

What is meconium?

Meconium is a greenish-black, sticky substance that the child discharges from his rectum during the first day or two of life. It is formed from material that the child swallows while he is in the mother's womb.

How long does meconium continue to be passed?

Only for a day or two. Then the movement becomes the usual yellowish-gold color and consistency of stool.

Is it important to notify the pediatrician if the child fails to pass any meconium during the first few days of life?

Yes, as this may indicate the presence of a serious condition known as meconium obstruction. The meconium may obstruct several feet of small and large bowel.

Is the meconium ever so hard that it forms a plug and cannot be evacuated?

Yes, occasionally. The plug may be located right near the rectal exit, and the pediatrician can sometimes remove it with his fingers.

Is failure to pass meconium ever an indication that the child has cystic fibrosis?

Yes. Cystic fibrosis is the most frequent cause of failure to pass meconium.

How does cystic fibrosis produce meconium obstruction?

The enzymes produced by the pancreas are essential for normal intestinal function. In cystic fibrosis, the pancreas does not secrete an adequate amount of its enzyme-containing juices, and the contents of the intestinal tract therefore become sticky and of a gluey consistency. This material clings to the membrane lining the intestinal wall, fills up the passageway, and stops the passage of gas and normal intestinal contents.

How can the pediatrician make a diagnosis of meconium obstruction?

The newborn's abdomen will become distended and he will fail to pass gas and meconium through the rectum. The newborn will begin to vomit and will become markedly dehydrated unless treatment is instituted promptly.

What is the treatment for meconium obstruction?

The child should be operated upon, and the portion of the small intestine in which the meconium is caked must be brought out onto the abdominal wall. A temporary opening of this portion of the small intestine (ileum) is made, and the intestine is flushed out at regular intervals with a dilute solution of peroxide. After the meconium disappears and normal stool is excreted, the opening in the intestine is closed. This will restore bowel continuity.

Can a child recover from meconium obstruction?

Yes, but it is a very serious condition and many children who have it die.

Do children with meconium obstruction usually have defects in other organs?

Yes, especially in the pancreas, liver, and lungs.

If a child does survive meconium obstruction, is he apt to show developing signs of cystic fibrosis?

Yes.

Does rupture of the intestine ever follow meconium obstruction of the intestine?

Yes. Some of the perforations are so small that they seal over spontaneously. In other instances, large amounts of the meconium will spill out into the abdominal cavity, causing peritonitis. This is extremely serious and may be fatal.

Is there any way to prevent a child from developing meconium obstruction?

No. This condition does have a tendency, however, to affect more than one child in a family. If one child has already had the condition, the pediatrician will be alerted when more children are born.

Megacolon

See HIRSCHSPRUNG'S DISEASE.

Melanoma

A melanoma is a malignant mole. These skin tumors often spread throughout the body if they are not removed widely during an early stage of their development.

See also CANCER; SKIN AND SUBCUTANEOUS TISSUES.

QUESTIONS AND ANSWERS

How can one distinguish between a mole and a melanoma?

A physician can usually tell the difference. Characteristically, a melanoma grows and darkens in color as it grows. Benign moles frequently remain stationary in size and color.

Does the ordinary mole ever turn into a melanoma?

Most investigators believe that this does occasionally happen, although it should not be assumed that every mole that grows or changes color is becoming a melanoma. To be on the safe side, one should have every mole that grows, or changes color, or is subjected to repeated irritation removed by a surgeon.

How often do benign moles turn into malignant melanomas?

Infrequently. However, when they do, the process endangers life. When in doubt, have the mole removed.

Why are melanomas so dangerous?

Because the cells tend to spread through the bloodstream to other parts of the body.

Should blue-black moles that have been present for many years be removed?

Yes, particularly if they grow larger.

What is the treatment for melanoma?

It should be removed surgically with a wide surgical incision. Any lymph nodes in the area should also be removed. In recent years, certain medications have been found helpful in delaying the growth and spread of melanomas. These chemotherapeutic agents are injected into arteries near the area of the melanoma in order to kill off any cells that may remain after the melanoma has been excised.

If a malignant melanoma is removed surgically, can the patient look forward to a cure?

Yes, if it is removed before cells have spread to other parts of the body. However, if the melanoma has already spread to other parts of the body, local excision will not usually result in a permanent cure.

Where are the common sites of moles and melanomas?

They may form on any of the body surfaces. Those that occur on the palms of the hands or the soles of the feet are particularly likely to grow because they are subject to constant irritation.

Is it safe to have a mole removed by an electric needle in a doctor's office?

This is usually not a wise practice unless the surgeon has already had a piece of the mole examined microscopically. If such examination reveals that the mole is benign and shows no tendencies toward developing into a melanoma, then it can be removed safely with an electric needle.

To be totally safe, it is wiser to have moles removed surgically with an elliptical incision through the surrounding skin. This procedure can be performed readily under local anesthesia.

Is the surgical removal of a melanoma a serious operation?

It may be serious if the operation is accompanied by the removal of the lymph nodes that drain the area to which a melanoma might spread. The simple removal of the local lesion is not serious.

Do melanomas ever occur within the eye?

Yes. There is a malignant type of melanoma that occurs in the choroid membrane which lies behind the retina. When this type of tumor is present the eye must be removed in order to save the patient's life.

Do malignant melanomas of the eye tend to spread elsewhere in the body?

Yes. For this reason, it is essential that the eye be removed immediately following the diagnosis.

Should a mole located on the hand, foot, or some other place where it is subject to repeated irritation be removed?

Yes. This is the best way to ensure that it will not undergo transition to a melanoma.

Are all melanomas malignant?

No. There is a lesion known as a juvenile melanoma that is not malignant and which can be cured by wide surgical excision.

How can one tell when an ordinary mole is becoming a melanoma?

It increases in size, changes in color, or bleeds readily.

Meningioma

A meningioma is a benign tumor of the membranes which cover the brain. Unless located in an inaccessible area of the brain, meningiomas can be cured by surgical removal. They account for approximately 10 percent of all brain tumors.

See also NEUROSURGERY.

Meningocele and Myelomeningocele

A meningocele is a birth deformity in which there is protrusion of the membranes (meninges) of the brain or spinal cord through a defect in the skull or spinal column. The most common type of meningocele results from a defect in the spinal column with a protrusion in the back, especially in the lower portion. Meningoceles of the spinal cord are usually seen in association with a defect of the vertebrae known as spina bifida.

See also NEUROSURGERY; SPINA BIFIDA.

QUESTIONS AND ANSWERS

What is the difference between a meningocele and a myelomeningocele?

A meningocele consists only of a protrusion of the sac containing cerebrospinal fluid, while a myelomeningocele also contains nerve elements from the spinal cord.

What is spina bifida?

Spina bifida is a congenital abnormality characterized by incomplete closure of some part of the vertebral canal.

Is spina bifida ever associated with a protrusion of the membranes covering the spinal cord itself?

Yes. When the protrusion consists only of a sac of cerebrospinal fluid, it is called a meningocele. When the protrusion contains spinal cord or nerve elements, it is called a myelomeningocele.

How is a meningocele or a myelomeningocele diagnosed?

The infant is born with a noticeable lump on the back, which in the case of a myelomeningocele is associated with some degree of paralysis, usually of the lower limbs.

Are meningocele and myelomeningocele often associated with hydrocephalus?

Yes, especially in cases of myelomeningocele.

Is surgery successful for meningocele and myelomeningocele?

Whatever paralysis exists will not be relieved by surgery. In some cases in which the sac is very thin or is actually leaking spinal fluid, an operation is necessary in order to avoid meningitis. Otherwise, surgery is usually undertaken essentially for cosmetic reasons and to avert local injury and infection.

Metastasis

Metastasis is the traveling of a disease process from one part of the body to another. Usually, the term is used to describe the spread of cancer from one part of the body to another.

Metastasis takes place in one of three main ways:

1. By the breaking off of tumor cells from the original tumor and spreading through lymph channels to adjacent lymph nodes or beyond into distant organs.

2. The breaking off of tumor cells from the original tumor and their transportation through the bloodstream to distant organs.

3. By invasion of contiguous organs. This is a direct spread and in actuality is a nearby metastasis.

See also CANCER.

QUESTIONS AND ANSWERS

Do all malignant tumors tend to metastasize?

The great majority of them eventually will spread, but this does not mean that all will do so. The more malignant the primary growth, the more likely is it to form metastases.

Is there any way to prevent metastases?

Yes, by early surgical removal of the primary growth. Also, x-ray radiation and chemotherapy of tumors tends to limit the spread.

How long can a primary cancer exist before it metastasizes?

There is no definite answer to this question. Some tumors will spread within a few weeks or months after their original appearance, whereas other tumors may remain localized for years without ever developing metastases.

Do metastases always result when tumor cells gain access to the lymph channels or bloodstream?

No. The host (the patient who has the tumor) often has defense mechanisms which kill off the tumor cells and prevent them from taking root in a new location. Thus, even though malignant cells can be found in the bloodstream of patients with a cancer, it does not necessarily mean that they will develop metastatic growths.

What can be done once a metastasis has taken root and begins to grow?

This will depend upon its location and size. If the metastases, as from a cancer of the breast, are located in the lymph nodes under the arm, they can be removed surgically. On the other hand, if metastases have spread to the bones or to vital organs such as the lungs, the brain, and the liver, it is highly unlikely that they can be removed. In certain selected cases, where an isolated metastasis is present, it can be removed surgically.

Have people ever recovered from removal of isolated metastases to the brain, liver, lungs, or other vital organs?

Yes. Unfortunately, these cases represent a very minor proportion of metastatic growth.

Can x-ray treatments, cobalt radiation, and chemicals ever destroy metastases?

Yes. There is an ever increasing number of patients whose metastases have been destroyed by these means. In certain types of tumors of the ovaries or testicles, chemicals are now available that will destroy the metastases in the majority of those who are afflicted with them.

Military Wounds

Throughout all of history there has been a horrible loss of life through war wounds. Despite all of the scientific progress of the past century, the chances are great that the number of casualties will not diminish and may even increase in decades to come. The medical department of the armed forces can gain a small sense of satisfaction in the knowledge that more of those who are wounded are now being saved.

Approximately one out of five of those wounded in battle die on the battlefield before they can reach a hospital installation. The cause of death in these cases is almost always due to the destructive effects of the wound upon such vital organs as the brain, the heart, or great blood vessels. Of those who survive long enough to reach even the most forward hospital installation, more than 97 percent can now be saved. This tremendous salvage of human life should be credited to many improvements in military medical care. Among the most important advances that have made this amazing salvage rate possible are:

1. The rapid evacuation of the wounded. In this connection, the helicopter has been of inestimable value.

2. The placement of fully equipped surgical hospitals with highly trained surgical teams near the battlefield. Thus, the most sophisticated operations upon the brain, the heart, the lungs, and the abdominal organs can be performed with the shortest possible lapse of time after the patient has been wounded.

3. Improved methods of resuscitation, including the giving of intravenous infusions and plasma on the battlefield, and the supplying of unlimited quantities of blood upon reaching a forward hospital facility.

4. The intense training of paramedical personnel in methods of first aid. Innumerable thousands of lives have been saved by medical corpsmen who came to the aid of the wounded long before they were seen by any physician.

5. The discovery and availability of antibiotic drugs to combat infection.

6. The inoculation and vaccination of all military personnel against tetanus and other diseases.

7. The air evacuation to rear echelon hospitals of the wounded who require surgery by those who are especially trained in the treatment of unusual wounds. Thus, the most intricate and delicate head, neck, chest, and abdominal wounds can be operated upon within hours after the wound takes place.

It might be interesting to note the distribution of wounds over the body and the percentage of the wounded who are able to survive long enough to reach hospital installations:

1. Fourteen percent of all wounds are head wounds, and approximately 58 percent of those so wounded survive until they reach the hospital.

2. Three percent of all wounds are neck wounds, and approximately 96 percent of those so wounded reach the hospital.

3. Nineteen percent of all wounds

are chest wounds, and approximately 64 percent of those so wounded survive until they reach the hospital.

4. Eleven percent of all wounds are abdominal wounds, and approximately 91 percent of those so wounded survive until they reach the hospital.

5. Fifty-two percent of all wounds are wounds of the upper or lower limbs, and approximately 94 percent of those so wounded survive until they reach the hospital.

6. One percent of all wounds are wounds of the buttocks or genitals, and approximately 90 percent of those so wounded survive until they reach the hospital.

Moles

Moles (nevi) are common to most people and require surgical excision only when they show changes in color, undergo an increase in size, or are located in an area subject to repeated irritation. Moles at the collar line, on the palms of the hands or soles of the feet, or where a shoe rubs should be removed surgically.

Pigmented moles, when removed, should be widely excised with a knife. A rim of normal skin should always be taken along with the mole, and the underlying subcutaneous tissue should be included in the removal. If there is any difficulty in bringing the skin edges together after removal, a skin graft should be applied to the area.

Occasionally a pigmented mole will turn into cancer of a highly malignant type. Such cancers will spread rapidly throughout the body and result in a fatality within a year or two. It is important, therefore, to remove moles when they show signs of growth or change in color.

Although it has not been proved that burning a mole with an electric needle will cause it to undergo malignant changes, it is nevertheless thought best not to treat them in this manner.

See also MELANOMA; SKIN AND SUBCUTANEOUS TISSUES.

QUESTIONS AND ANSWERS

What is a mole (nevus)?

A mole is a small growth or blemish on the skin that may or may not be elevated from the skin surface. The correct medical term is "nevus"; "mole" is a layman's term. Almost everyone has moles somewhere on his body. They may be nonpigmented, brown, or blue-black in color. They may vary in size.

What causes moles?

Most moles are thought to be inherited or to develop while the child is still in the mother's womb. Although they may be inherited, some are not seen at birth but make their appearance during childhood.

Do moles always originate in childhood?

No. They frequently appear later in life.

Are moles (nevi) dangerous?

The great majority are not dangerous.

Are moles common in older people?

Yes. Although most of these growths originate in earlier years, they tend to increase in number and size as one ages.

Are all moles colored?

No. Some are skin-colored; others are light or dark brown; still others are blue-black.

What is the difference between a mole and a melanoma?

A melanoma is a malignant mole. Its

cells often spread throughout the body if it is not removed during an early stage of its development.

How does one distinguish a harmless mole from one that might become malignant?

A harmless mole is light tan to light brown in color, is raised above the skin and smooth-surfaced, and has hair in it. It is of long duration and shows no growth or size changes.

A potentially malignant mole is slate gray, very dark brown, or black in color. It is flat and level with the skin, has an irregular or ulcerated surface, and is hairless. It is often of recent origin and shows rapid growth and size changes.

In addition, moles located on the feet, hands, fingers, scalp, genitals, or other places, where they are subject to frequent irritation, are potentially more dangerous than those located elsewhere.

Should a physician be consulted if a mole changes its size or color?

Yes.

Should a mole be biopsied to find out whether it is malignant or benign?

Yes. A dermatologist always can distinguish a malignant from a benign lesion by taking a piece of it and having it examined under a microscope.

Will the surgeon or dermatologist know which moles should be removed and which can be safely let alone?

Yes.

Is it wise to cauterize brown or blue-black moles with an electric needle?

No. Surgical removal is the best treatment.

What is the proper treatment for a mole which has suddenly undergone changes?

Wide surgical removal including normal skin and subcutaneous tissue around the mole. If a mole happens to be large, it may be necessary to put a skin graft in its place to cover the skin defect remaining from its removal.

Mouth

See LIPS, MOUTH, AND TONGUE.

Myopia

See NEARSIGHTEDNESS.

Navel

The navel is technically known as the umbilicus. It represents the remnant of the umbilical cord, the structure that connected the fetus to the placenta.

The navel is of relative insignificance in adults, but it does deserve special consideration in newborns and young children.

In adults, there are three main conditions involving the navel that deserve mention:

1. Umbilical hernia. This is a hernia through the navel and is seen very often in women who have borne several children and, as a consequence, have developed marked distention of the abdominal wall. It is also seen in obese men.

2. Omphalitis. This is an inflammation of the navel with eczema and a foul-smelling discharge.

3. Bluish discoloration of the navel is sometimes seen in women who have had a hemorrhage within the abdominal cavity, usually secondary to an ectopic pregnancy.

See also UMBILICAL HERNIA.

Nearsightedness

In the nearsighted eye, the rays of light that pass through the lens come to a focus before they reach the retina, and the image that reaches the retina is fuzzy. The eyeball is longer than it should normally be for that individual. Vision is better for near objects than for distant objects.

See also CROSSED EYES; EYES.

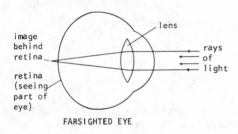

image behind retina

lens

rays of light

retina (seeing part of eye)

FARSIGHTED EYE

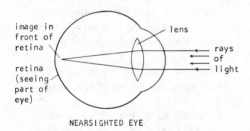

image in front of retina

lens

rays of light

retina (seeing part of eye)

NEARSIGHTED EYE

QUESTIONS AND ANSWERS

How common is nearsightedness?
About one third of all people who wear glasses are nearsighted.

Are boys more likely to be nearsighted than girls?
No.

Is nearsightedness inherited?
It sometimes does appear to run in families, particularly if both parents are nearsighted.

What are other names for nearsightedness?
Myopia and shortsightedness.

What causes nearsightedness?
The eyeball grows more rapidly than its optical or refracting system, namely, the cornea and the lens. As a result, the image of the object viewed falls in front of the retina instead of on it. The retina is the "film" of the eye; it receives an impression of the image, like the film of a camera.

How can an eye specialist detect nearsightedness in a small child?
By shining a light in the eyes and performing a test known as retinoscopy.

Can a young child's eyes be tested for nearsightedness before he has learned to read?
Yes. There are eye charts that have been specially devised for children in this age group.

What should make a parent suspect that a young child may be nearsighted?
If the child holds objects and picture books very close to his eyes when looking at them, he may be nearsighted.

Is nearsightedness a common condition in children?
Yes.

Does nearsightedness tend to get worse as a child grows older?
Yes, but in most children this tendency stops and the condition stabilizes by 19 to 20 years of age.

Is it necessary for a nearsighted child to restrict the amount of reading he does?
No.

Does excessive use of the eyes during the school years tend to increase nearsightedness?
No.

Does nearsightedness tend to get better by itself?

No.

How early can a child begin to wear glasses to correct nearsightedness?

Anywhere from 18 months to 3 years of age. Much will depend on how the idea is presented to the child by the parents and the optician. If the child is frightened by the first attempts to get him to wear glasses, he may resist them for a considerable period of time. If he is made to see that his parents use glasses without suffering discomfort, if he is played with, and if he can be made to understand that he can see better with the glasses, it may be quite easy to get him to cooperate.

Does nearsightedness ever lead to blindness?

In the very rare case, nearsightedness may lead to degeneration, with or without detachment of the retina, with some loss of vision.

Is there any surgical procedure that can arrest or decrease nearsightedness?

In a few selected cases, operations to shorten the eyeball can be performed. These operations have just been developed recently and have not yet been perfected. They consist of taking out crescentic portions of the eyeball along the inner and outer aspects. This will shorten the length of the eyeball and thus bring the lens closer to the retina, overcoming some of the nearsightedness. In addition, surgery upon the cornea, to change its optical properties, has been tried recently.

How effective are the newer operations for nearsightedness?

Although the number of cases in which they have been performed is rather small, first reports are that if patients are properly chosen for these procedures, results are successful in a large number of instances.

Neck Plastic Operations

See FACE AND NECK PLASTIC OPERATIONS.

Nephrectomy

Nephrectomy is removal of a kidney. It is carried out mainly for the following conditions:

1. Malignant tumors of the kidney

2. In cases where there has been more or less total destruction of kidney tissue because of infection

3. Where kidney tissue has been destroyed because of obstruction due to one or more kidney stones (advanced hydronephrosis)

4. Where kidney function has failed and a new kidney will be transplanted

Nephrectomy is considered a major operative procedure, but recovery follows in well over 95 percent of cases. It is usually performed, with the patient lying on his side, through an incision extending from the loin around to the abdomen. The level of the incision is just below the last rib and above the hipbone. General anesthesia is preferred. In carrying out this operation, the entire kidney and renal pelvis (outlet) and ureter on the affected side are removed after tying off the large artery and veins that supply and drain the organ.

Prior to performing a nephrectomy

on one side, it is essential to determine that the other kidney is able to support life. For this reason, intravenous pyelograms (x-ray pictures of the outlet and ureter of a dye-injected kidney) and, in some instances, renal arteriograms are taken. The surgeon must be particularly certain that the patient does not have a so-called horseshoe kidney, which is two kidneys fused into one. Removal of both will lead to death of the patient.

After removal of a kidney, a rubber drain is inserted into the depths of the wound for a day or two. However, the patient makes a rapid recovery from nephrectomy and usually can get out of bed the day following surgery.

See also KIDNEYS AND URETERS.

QUESTIONS AND ANSWERS

Are special preoperative measures necessary before nephrectomy?

Yes. The surgeon must make certain that the other kidney is able to function normally. Moreover, he must see that the patient has plenty of fluids before undergoing surgery.

Are blood transfusions ever necessary with nephrectomy?

Often they are given during the operation.

Are special postoperative measures necessary after nephrectomy?

1. For a day or two, the patient receives fluid intravenously.

2. An antibiotic drug is sometimes given to prevent possible postoperative infection.

Is it natural for the wound of a nephrectomy to be painful?

Yes, moderately. For several months after surgery the patient may feel tingling and "pins and needles" sensation in

the wound area due to the fact that small nerves were cut in making the incision.

How long a hospital stay is necessary after nephrectomy?

Approximately 12 to 14 days.

Does removal of one kidney affect the patient's life expectancy?

1. If the kidney was removed for a malignant growth and no spread had taken place prior to surgery, life expectancy is normal.

2. People who have had a kidney removed for a benign condition, such as an infection or obstruction, will have a normal life expectancy if the remaining kidney is normal.

3. Those who have had their kidneys removed in order to receive a kidney transplant from another individual cannot at present look forward to a normal life-span. In many instances, there will be rejection of the transplanted kidney and it will be necessary to attempt to supply a new one. However, it must be kept in mind that people who require kidney transplants would have died within a very short time if a transplant had not been performed.

Nerves

See NEUROSURGERY.

Neurosurgery

Neurosurgery is that branch of medicine dealing with the surgical treatment of diseases of the nervous system. A few decades ago, operations upon the brain or spinal cord were rarely performed, and almost all those with surgical conditions of the nervous system succumbed to their disease. Today many people owe their lives to the high degree of development of neurosurgery.

Although significant progress in this field was achieved only recently, the origin of brain surgery dates back to antiquity. There is evidence that prehistoric man performed operations on the skull (trephination), though the reasons for doing so are not known.

The nervous system consists of myriads of nerve cells and supporting tissue centered in the brain and spinal cord, with widespread extensions throughout the body. It is concerned with the transmission and coordination of stimuli and with the many phenomena that constitute mental activity. Impulses conveying sensory impressions such as *sight, smell, hearing, taste,* and *touch* reach the brain via pathways called afferent nerves. Muscular control and gandular secretion, on the other hand, are achieved by means of impulses that originate in the central nervous system and travel in an outward direction in pathways called efferent nerves.

The smoothness of performance which normally characterizes the manifold activities of the human organism is rendered possible only as a result of the high degree of organization of the nervous system. This becomes especially clear when some part of this elaborate system is thrown out of gear by disease.

The nervous system is divided structurally into *central* and *peripheral* components. The brain and spinal cord constitute the central part while the peripheral portion is composed of all the nerves which establish communication with the rest of the body. The peripheral component consists of 12 pairs of cranial nerves that arise from the brain and leave through openings in the bones of the skull; 31 pairs of spinal nerves, which emerge through openings in the vertebral column; and a complex network of nerves called the *autonomic* or *sympathetic* system. The function of the autonomic system is to transmit nervous impulses to the intestinal tract, bladder, heart, glands, and blood vessels.

THE SKULL AND BRAIN

1. Injuries: Head injuries are extremely common, varying in degree from the relatively minor cut scalp to the serious bruising of the brain associated with profound loss of consciousness. Fortunately, the skull offers excellent protection to the underlying brain, and many blows to the head injure only the relatively unimportant superficial tissues. Those of a more severe nature may fracture the skull and cause damage to the brain, which may be bruised (contusion) or even torn (laceration).

a) Scalp lacerations often appear much more serious than they actually are because of their tendency to bleed profusely. The bleeding usually ceases spontaneously or after pressure has been applied with a gauze pad or clean handkerchief. Surgical repair of the wound is frequently necessary. The surrounding hair is shaved and the laceration thoroughly cleansed before it is closed with stitches. The surgeon carefully inspects the wound to be certain that no damage has been inflicted on the skull or brain. A history of loss of consciousness, even if only for a few seconds, will serve as a warning that an injury to the intracranial contents has been incurred. X-rays are indicated in such cases in view of the possibility of a skull fracture, and the patients are observed carefully for a day or two for evidence of hemorrhage within the cranium (skull).

b) Concussion is a term applied when a brief period of unconsciousness follows a head injury. No specific treatment is required for a cerebral concussion since in uncomplicated cases, spontaneous recovery is the rule. The patient should, however, be observed for the development of symptoms such as increasing drowsiness and weakness of the limbs on one side of the body. These symptoms are usually indicative of bleeding within the skull.

c) Skull fracture results from a more severe blow or fall upon the head. Although skull fractures are frequent accompaniments of head injuries, usually they are relatively unimportant as far as the patient's welfare is concerned. It is not the extent of the skull fracture that determines the seriousness of the injury but the degree of underlying brain damage. Loss of consciousness is a common phenomenon following a head injury. There is no specific treatment for brain injuries as such. Fortunately, most patients recover spontaneously.

Surgery is essentially limited to the treatment of the open wounds (compound fractures), to the removal of indriven or depressed fragments of bone which may press upon and irritate the brain (depressed skull fracture), and to the treatment of *intracranial hemorrhage.*

Evidence of intracranial hemorrhage may appear within a matter of hours after injury or may be delayed for weeks or even months. Even seemingly insignificant injuries may be followed by intracranial bleeding and the attending physician must be constantly on the lookout for this complication. Intracranial bleeding that occurs soon after an accident constitutes a surgical emergency. It is manifested by increasing drowsiness and weakness of the limbs on one side of the body. Prompt recognition of the condition and operation to stop the bleeding and remove blood clots are imperative to avoid a fatal outcome. Even the suspicion of hemorrhage is sufficient to warrant an immediate exploratory operation. This is a minor operative procedure performed under local Novocain anesthesia. A small incision is made in the scalp in front of and above the ear, and a hole is drilled in the skull. Should the exploration fail to disclose the presence of a hemorrhage, no harm will have been done. On the other hand, failure to operate when a clot is present will cost the patient his life!

The symptoms of hemorrhage that appear at a late stage, weeks or months after an injury, are usually headache, drowsiness, and mental confusion. This type of bleeding presents a much less urgent problem, though its treatment is similar to that of the more acute variety. The blood clot may be evacuated through a small opening in the skull, though at times a more extensive operation is necessary.

d) Posttraumatic symptoms are those which persist long after the time required for full recovery from an injury. It must be realized that there is a strong emotional component to every physical injury and this is particularly true when the accident has involved the head. Psychological disturbances and emotional instability after skull and brain injuries can often be avoided by careful explanation of the exact nature of the injury. Above all, it is essential to assure these people that their mental capacity and ability to return to a completely normal life need not be impaired when they have fully recovered from the physical effects of the accident.

2. Surgical infections:

a) *Scalp infections* may occur following an injury or may take the form of an abscess or carbuncle. Their treatment is similar to that of infections elsewhere in the body. When pus has formed, it must be evacuated by incision and drainage.

b) *Skull infection or osteomyelitis:* Sinusitis and less often trauma are the commonest causes of infection of the bones of the skull. In the days before the advent of chemotherapy and antibiotics, this type of infection was encountered more frequently.

Treatment is essentially a surgical problem. Removal of the diseased bone is necessary in order to effect a cure.

c) *An abscess within the brain* occurs as a result of the spread of an infection from an adjacent structure, such as the sinuses or ears, or from a distant part of the body, usually the lung. It may also be caused by a penetrating wound of the skull or by a compound skull fracture. Since the introduction of chemotherapy and antibiotics, the incidence of brain abscess has diminished markedly and the outlook for successful treatment has improved considerably. It still remains a serious condition, however. It may be treated by excision or drainage. The concurrent use of antibiotics is essential.

3. Brain tumors: The fact that the brain and spinal cord are enclosed within rigid bony structures is an important consideration in the event of tumor formation. This anatomical configuration limits room for expansion, and when a growth develops, the brain or spinal cord must, inevitably, suffer damage from compression.

Progress in surgical technique has

made it possible to gain access to almost any part of the brain with reasonable safety. The operation for exposing the brain is called a *craniotomy.* As a general rule, craniotomy is performed under general anesthesia, though at times local anesthesia is preferable. In preparation for surgery, the entire head is shaved and the scalp thoroughly cleansed with soap and water. A skin antiseptic is then applied, and all but the area to be operated upon is covered with sterile drapes. The scalp is incised usually in a semicircular manner, and a number of holes are drilled in the underlying skull. (See illustration.) The holes are connected by means of a wire saw, thereby freeing a block of bone, which is detached from the remainder of the skull. Directly underneath the bone are the membranes overlying the brain. These are incised, thus exposing the brain.

By inspection and examination of the exposed brain, the neurosurgeon can, in most instances, determine the nature of the tumor. Even if the tumor is deeply placed, he can often locate it accurately and determine whether or not it can be removed. His knowledge of brain anatomy and function will guide him in these technical moves. Care is exercised to avoid damage to normal brain tissue and to minimize the loss of blood. The problem of hemorrhage is ever present, and specialized techniques have been devised to cope with it. Facilities for blood transfusion are constantly available. After the tumor has been removed, the operation is completed by replacing the segment of detached bone, fixing it securely, and suturing the overlying soft tissues and skin.

It is now recognized that the brain is one of the most frequent sites of tumor formation. The term *intracranial tumor* is used to denote any one of several types of growths that may be present

A. holes bored through skull

semicircular
skin incision
within
hairline

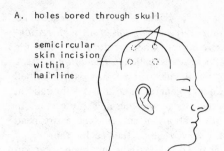

C. membrane (dura) lying
under skull and on
top of brain

incision in dura

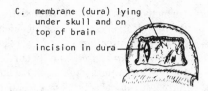

D. exposed brain

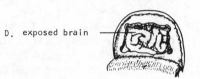

B. bone sawed through connecting holes

exposed skull

segment of
bone to be
detached

reflected
skin flap

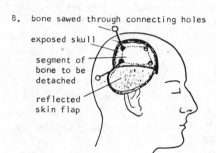

E. bone replaced

skin
sutured

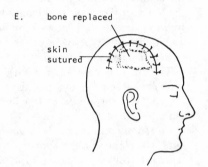

DIAGRAM OF CRANIOTOMY PROCEDURE

within the skull. A tumor may originate from the skull, from the membranes or nerves external to the brain, or from the brain itself. Still another source of origin is the pituitary gland at the base of the skull. Finally, cancerous growths arising elsewhere in the body may spread by means of the bloodstream to involve the brain secondarily.

It is extremely important to distinguish between the different kinds of intracranial tumors, because the outlook for recovery varies with the nature of the growth.

Tumors arising from the coverings of the brain (*meningiomas*) and the nerves of the brain (*neurofibromas*), when surgically accessible, may be completely removed and the patient cured. As these tumors represent 20 percent of all growths within the skull, it is obvious

that many patients can look forward to complete recovery.

Pituitary gland tumors, in a high proportion of cases, may be successfully treated by means of x-ray alone, without resorting to surgery. Those patients not helped by x-ray treatment can usually be greatly benefited by surgery. Pituitary tumors constitute about 10 percent of all brain tumors.

Approximately 50 percent of brain tumors develop within the brain substance itself (*gliomas*). With few exceptions these tumors are not sufficiently well demarcated to be removed completely. Their rate of growth varies, being exceedingly rapid in the more malignant varieties. Some may grow slowly over a period of years while others may proceed to a rapid termination within a much shorter time.

Even when a cure cannot be accomplished, many people with this type of brain tumor can be helped to a degree by surgery. However, a brain tumor incompletely removed eventually recurs, and the ultimate outlook in a particular case depends upon the exact nature of the tumor. The growth of some of these tumors is retarded by x-ray treatment, which is therefore frequently prescribed following surgery.

Occasionally the position of a tumor is such that the surgeon is unable to approach it directly without risking serious consequences or even the life of the patient. Even in such cases, a procedure for the purpose of reducing the intracranial pressure may be accomplished relatively safely and may bring relief of symptoms.

The surgeon planning to operate on a patient with a brain tumor must have a precise knowledge of its location. Such information may be elicited by a careful examination of the patient. As a rule, however, it is desirable, and at times necessary, to perform some of the following diagnostic procedures for the purpose of providing confirmatory evidence of the location of the tumor:

a) *Plain x-rays* of the skull may yield sufficient information.

b) *Spinal puncture* in order to withdraw spinal fluid for analysis and to measure the intracranial pressure. (This procedure is done only in carefully selected cases.)

c) *Visual tests,* especially visual-field studies.

d) *Encephalograms* or *ventriculograms* are often necessary. In performing these tests, some of the fluid surrounding the brain and contained within its cavities is removed through a needle and is replaced with air. The air, acting as a contrast medium, outlines the chambers of the brain on an x-ray film. A familiarity with the normal appearance of these cavities permits one to recognize the distortion produced by a tumor and to identify its location.

e) *Arteriograms,* by outlining the blood vessels of the brain, may provide valuable information. By injecting a radiopaque substance directly into the arteries of the neck, or indirectly elsewhere, the blood vessels of the brain can be visualized on an x-ray. A brain tumor, by concentrating the radiopaque substance within its own blood vessels, may actually be outlined. In other instances, its location may be revealed by noting the displacement of the blood vessels of the brain from their normal position.

f) *Electroencephalography,* the study of the electrical brain waves, is another valuable diagnostic test. It is often possible to record abnormal brain waves from the scalp over an area corresponding to the site of a brain tumor.

g) *Radioactive substances,* and more recently *ultrasonics,* have been used as additional aids in proving the presence of a brain tumor. The radioactive method depends upon the demonstration of a concentration of the radioactive material at the site of the tumor. Displacement of intracranial structures which may be expected in the presence of a tumor may be revealed through the use of ultrasonics.

Too often, the family of a patient with a brain tumor assumes that the operation will terminate fatally. This is not true. Approximately 80 to 90 percent of such patients recover from the surgical procedure! The statement, already made, that the ultimate outlook depends on the nature of the tumor, bears repetition. Complete removal of a well-demarcated benign tumor will result in a cure. The disability caused by the presence of a tumor may be expected to improve following its successful removal. In other words, paralysis, visual disturbances, speech impairment, mental confusion, etc., may disappear over a period of time. This does not imply, however, that there will always be a complete disappearance of the preoperative manifestations following surgery.

4. Intracranial hemorrhage and abnormalities of the blood vessels of the brain: Hardening of the arteries (arteriosclerosis) and high blood pressure are the most common causes of hemorrhage within the brain. This type of hemorrhage usually occurs after the age of 40. Bleeding may also take place, frequently, though not exclusively, in younger individuals as a result of rupture of a malformed blood vessel. Most often, the malformation is a saclike dilatation of a blood vessel (aneurysm). Occasionally it consists of a cluster of abnormally large blood vessels (angioma).

Because of their tendency to rupture and cause intracranial bleeding, these deformed vessels are a threat to life. Obviously it would be desirable to discover them and, wherever possible, to institute treatment *before* they cause hemorrhage. Unfortunately, evidence of hemorrhage is often the first indication of their presence. The use of radiopaque substances in order to outline the blood vessels of the brain (arteriography) is especially useful in cases in which an abnormality of the blood vessels is suspected. Such a malformation, if present, may actually be visualized.

Hemorrhage within the brain, whether caused by rupture of a diseased or of an abnormal blood vessel, sometimes lends itself to surgical treatment. Operation may, in certain cases, be a lifesaving measure and may lessen the likelihood of permanent brain damage. It may be possible at operation to remove a blood clot and eradicate the cause of the hemorrhage. Various methods of surgical treatment have been devised to deal with the abnormalities of the intracranial blood vessels. Admittedly, operation in such cases is hazardous and is not invariably successful or even possible. However, in view of the serious nature of the underlying disease, especially the danger of recurrent hemorrhage, operation is often justified. The surgical treatment of an aneurysm involves either interruption of its blood supply in the neck (ligation of the carotid artery) or elimination by direct approach within the skull. Many factors, such as the age and general condition of the patient, the location and size of the aneurysm, etc., must be considered before attacking an aneurysm surgically.

5. Epilepsy: This condition is characterized by recurrent attacks of abnormal activity or behavior, with or without convulsions and loss of consciousness. There are several different types of epileptic seizures: *grand mal,* manifested by convulsions and loss of consciousness; *petit mal,* characterized by a very transient impairment of consciousness; and *psychomotor epilepsy,* the essential feature of which is the performance of some sort of automatic activity during a period of amnesia. Epilepsy may occur in the absence of any demonstrable cause (idiopathic) or may result from the presence of some structural abnormality in the brain such as a tumor, abscess, blood vessel malformation, or scar. It is important to distinguish the idiopathic cases from those due to organic disease. The cause of idiopathic epilepsy is unknown and treatment is designed exclusively for the purpose of controlling the seizures. Medication is employed in the management of this type of case. An entirely different problem is presented by the patient whose seizures are due to the presence of some sort of structural abnormality in the brain. Control of the seizures must still be achieved, but in addition, the underlying condition must also be treated. It is this type of case that may require surgical treatment. Thus an operation is indicated if the basic condition is a tumor, abscess, or depressed fracture. Surgery may be advisable in cases of epilepsy due to scar formation if the seizures cannot be effectively controlled by medication. Also, certain patients with uncontrollable psychomotor epilepsy may be benefited by operation. Operation in such cases involves excision of a focal area in which discharges responsible for the seizures are believed to originate. Surgical treatment may be especially beneficial in some cases of psychomotor epilepsy and in cases of stroke dating back to early life (infantile hemiplegia) in which medication has been ineffective in controlling the fits.

6. Brain surgery for mental disorders (psychosurgery) and pain: The enthusiasm for brain surgery in the treatment of mental disease (lobotomy) has practically disappeared in recent years, particularly since the introduction of the tranquilizing drugs. A modified form of operation may still be indicated in certain neuroses and psychoses, especially when anxiety, agitation, or obsessive preoccupation are prominent features and when other measures, such as psychotherapy, drugs, and electroshock have failed. By limiting the extent of the lobotomy, most of the favorable effects of the more extensive operation may be achieved with a minimum of the attendant undesirable personality changes. The operation is performed in the frontal region of the brain, its purpose being to sever the connecting fibers between certain areas.

Lobotomy may also be done for the relief of intractable pain, particularly in patients with incurable cancer in whom anxiety is a prominent symptom. The alteration in personality that occurs as a consequence of this type of operation is a serious drawback, and most surgeons are in agreement that lobotomy is justified only in exceptional cases in which all other forms of treatment have failed to afford relief. A number of other surgical procedures (described elsewhere in this section) are available for the relief of persistent pain, and these should always be given priority over lobotomy.

7. Parkinsonism or shaking palsy: Various types of abnormal, involuntary movements may occur as a result of disease of the central nervous system. The occurrence of tremor is particularly common and is one of the characteristic features of a condition called *parkinsonism,* or the shaking palsy. This is a slowly progressive disorder of unknown cause, which eventually leads to incapacitation. Muscular rigidity accompanies the tremor and handicaps voluntary movement. Despite the fact that a large number of drugs have been introduced for the treatment of this condition, the results are far from satisfactory. It is for this reason that in recent years surgical attempts have been made to alleviate the tremor and rigidity. The mechanism responsible for the production of tremor and rigidity is unknown, and heretofore a successful result was usually achieved at the expense of some impairment of strength. It is now possible to relieve tremor and rigidity (parkinsonism) appreciably by surgery in a fairly high proportion of cases, without incurring any paralysis. The operation is not totally devoid of risk and is not invariably successful, but the results thus far have been sufficiently encouraging to warrant consideration in appropriate cases.

8. Cerebral vascular disease (stroke):

Disturbances of the blood supply to the brain resulting mainly from hardening of the arteries (arteriosclerosis) and high blood pressure (hypertension) are the commonest causes of paralysis and other manifestations of neurological disease. *Cerebral vascular disease* is the medical phrase used to designate such conditions. For practical purposes it is synonymous with the term *stroke*. A detailed account of this very complicated subject is beyond the scope and purpose of this book. Suffice it to say that a stroke may be caused by a hemorrhage or an occlusion (blocking) of a blood vessel. Reference has already been made in a previous section to the surgical treatment of certain cases of cerebral hemorrhage. As regards the occlusive type of disease, this may affect either a blood vessel within the brain or, as has been learned only relatively recently, one of the large arteries in the neck or even in the chest supplying blood to the brain (carotid or vertebral artery or aortic arch). There is no specific treatment for a stroke resulting from an occlusion of a blood vessel within the brain itself. Involvement of one of the large arteries in the neck, however, may at times be benefited by operation. The purpose of surgical treatment in such cases is to remove the clot or arteriosclerotic plaque from the artery or else to bypass the site of obstruction by means of a plastic tube. Obviously the precise location of the obstruction must be known beforehand and this can be readily accomplished by injecting a radiopaque substance into the appropriate artery and taking an x-ray (arteriogram). It must be clearly understood that only a small proportion of patients who have suffered a stroke are suitable candidates for this type of surgery.

9. Trigeminal neuralgia: This condition, also called tic douloureux, trifacial neuralgia, and facial tic, is an extremely painful affliction occurring mostly in middle-aged and older individuals. It is characterized by severe intermittent pain appearing in paroxyms and involving one side of the face. Washing the face, shaving, drinking, chewing, touching a particular spot, may all bring on an attack of pain. Attacks recur at intervals of weeks, months, or even years and during a remission the patient feels fine. Though at times Dilantin appears to offer temporary relief, no medication has proved effective in the treatment of this condition. Only injections of alcohol or surgical section of the nerve within the head or of branches of the nerve outside the head are reliable methods of treatment. The intracranial operation alone assures permanent relief of pain, as a rule. Complications are infrequent, and in the vast majority of cases, no disfigurement results from the operation.

10. Brain disorders occurring during infancy and childhood:

a) *Brain tumors* during childhood are not at all uncommon. Certain types of tumor are especially prevalent and they tend to occur predominantly in certain locations. Both benign and malignant varieties are encountered. Their treatment is similar to that of tumors in adults and the results obtained are comparable. Children withstand brain surgery quite well.

b) *Intracranial hemorrhage* resulting from head injury (subdural hematoma, or a clot overlying the brain) is not rare during the first two years of life. Early recognition and treatment are essential to avoid permanent brain damage. Operation is necessary.

c) *Craniosynostosis* is a condition in which the bones of the skull unite prematurely. This interferes with the normal growth of the skull, which takes place largely during the first two or three years of life. As a consequence, the growth of the brain is restricted and the intracranial (within the skull) pressure rises abnormally. This condition leads to a distortion of the shape of the head, visual disturbance, convulsions, and mental retardation.

Surgical treatment in early infancy is necessary to prevent these complications. Openings are made in the skull where fusion has occurred. This permits continued growth and development of the skull and intracranial contents. The results of operation are good provided surgery is performed at an early stage.

d) Hydrocephalus is a relatively common disorder of infants in which the head enlarges abnormally because of an excessive amount of cerebrospinal fluid within the brain. An interference with its circulation and absorption is responsible for the accumulation of a large quantity of fluid. The size of the head may reach enormous proportions. Various surgical procedures have been devised in an attempt to deal with this condition, but the results, though encouraging, are not invariably satisfactory. An operation may be performed either for the purpose of reducing the formation of fluid or in order to shunt the fluid so as to facilitate its absorption or elimination from the body. Currently it is the practice in many clinics to divert the excess fluid from the brain into the heart.

THE SPINAL CORD

The spinal cord is an elongated structure, cylindrical in shape, measuring about 18 inches in length, occupying the canal within the vertebral column. It consists of bundles of nerves and func-tions primarily as a conducting mechanism. Sensory impulses ascend to the brain, while impulses concerned with muscular contraction and movement travel in the opposite direction. Connections with various organs and structures are established by means of spinal nerves, which are attached to the cord throughout its length.

When operating upon the spinal cord, it is first necessary to remove parts of the arches of the overlying vertebrae. This operation is known as a *laminectomy*. The more important indications for surgery upon the cord will be considered briefly:

1. Birth deformities (congenital malformations): Incomplete closure of some part of the vertebral canal (spina bifida occulta) is a fairly common developmental deformity and usually causes no symptoms. It may, however, be associated with a protrusion or herniation of the membranes covering the spinal cord. Such a protrusion may contain cerebrospinal fluid only, or it may contain nerve elements and even part of the spinal cord itself (*meningocele* or *meningomyelocele*). Such children are born with a noticeable lump on the back. Inclusion of nerve structures in the malformation usually is accompanied by varying degrees of paralysis of the lower limbs. Hydrocephalus is a frequent complication. Nothing can be done to correct the paralysis. Operation is performed solely for the purpose of repairing the deformity.

Children are subject to a variety of other types of congenital anomalies, only two of which will be briefly mentioned. *Diastematomyelia* is a congenital malformation in which the spinal cord is divided longitudinally into two parts by a septum of fibrous tissue or bone. It is characterized by difficulty in walking, together with deformities of the lower extremities. Operation is indicated to prevent further impairment of function. A persistent opening in the midline of the back or head may extend into the spinal canal or skull. Such a defect is called a *congenital dermal sinus,* and its importance lies in the fact that it may serve as a source of infection. For this reason it should be excised early in life.

2. Spinal cord tumors: The presence of a spinal cord tumor may be suspected on the basis of the history and examination of the patient. Spinal puncture usually reveals an obstruction to the free flow of cerebrospinal fluid. Chemical analysis of the cerebrospinal fluid often provides additional useful information. The diagnosis may be further confirmed by introducing a radiopaque substance into the cerebrospinal fluid and subjecting the patient to fluoroscopy. This procedure is called *myelography.* Normally the radiopaque substance flows freely when the patient is tilted in either direction. A tumor will act as an obstruction to the flow of the radiopaque substance, thus verifying the diagnosis and providing evidence of its exact location.

The spinal cord may be affected by tumors compressing it from without or growing within its substance. About 50 percent of these tumors originate from the membranes overlying the cord or from a spinal nerve. Such growths can be totally removed at operation and the patient cured or greatly improved, unless the effects upon the spinal cord have been prolonged and have reached an irreversible stage. Tumors growing within the substance of the spinal cord usually cannot be removed, but their growth can often be halted by x-ray treatment. Not infrequently, a cancer which has originated in some other part of the body spreads to involve the spinal cord. The outlook in such cases is especially poor, though x-ray treatment and occasionally even surgery may prove temporarily beneficial.

3. Ruptured intervertebral disks: Intervertebral disks are elastic structures interposed between adjacent vertebrae. As a result of degeneration and injury, a disk may protrude into the spinal canal and give rise to pain. Ruptured disks occur most frequently in the lower back and give rise to backache and pain radiating down the leg. Less frequently the protrusion occurs in the neck, in which case the pain is located in the neck and *upper limb.* The diagnosis of a ruptured disk may be confirmed by myelography.

Conservative measures such as bed rest, traction, and physiotherapy are worth a trial in the treatment of this condition. Should pain and disability persist after a reasonable period of conservative treatment or should there be recurrent attacks, operation is indicated. Through an incision in the back, the protruding disk is removed. The operation is not dangerous and about 85 percent of all patients treated surgically are either completely or considerably relieved. The vast majority of cases do not require spinal fusion. (*See* HERNIATED INTERVERTEBRAL DISK.)

4. Cord injuries: Injuries of the spinal cord usually occur in association with fractures or dislocations of the spinal column. Falls, automobile and diving accidents, and gunshot wounds are the most frequent causes. The spinal cord may escape injury at the time a spinal fracture is incurred, but careless transportation of the patient from the scene of the accident may result in damage to the spinal cord.

The manifestations of spinal cord injury include varying degrees of paralysis, loss of sensation, and inability to control the bladder and bowels. The retention of some degree of spinal cord function, no matter how slight, renders the outlook infinitely better than when all function is lost. If evidence of complete interruption of the spinal cord persists for more than one week, it is unlikely that any improvement will occur. Regeneration of divided fibers does not occur in the spinal cord. In most cases of spinal cord injury, operation is useless. There are occasional exceptions, but, as a rule, all that can be accomplished is to institute orthopedic measures to treat the spinal fracture or dislocation. In the case of fractures involving the neck, traction is very often employed, using tongs inserted into the skull.

The management of the patient who remains paralyzed is a complex problem beyond the scope of this discussion. Suffice it to say that it is possible to rehabilitate many of these unfortunate paraplegics after prolonged training so that they can be made ambulatory and lead a reasonably normal and useful life again.

5. Treatment of pain: The neurosurgeon is often called upon to relieve pain that fails to respond to medication. Such pain is usually caused by advanced cancer. The location of the pathways within the spinal cord conducting pain being known, it is possible to cut them and afford the patient relief. This type of operation is known as a *cordotomy*. It is also possible to cut the nerves (as they enter the spinal cord) that supply a particular region of the body. By depriving that area of all sensation, pain is eliminated. This procedure is called a *rhizotomy*.

Both of these operations are safe procedures, and although they do not cure the underlying condition, in suitable cases they are extremely valuable for the relief of intractable pain.

PERIPHERAL NERVES

The peripheral nerves convey impulses to and from the spinal cord. They transmit impulses concerned with mus-

cular contraction, as well as stimuli conveying sensory impressions.

Injuries are the commonest disorders of the peripheral nerves requiring surgical treatment. Although most frequently observed during warfare, peripheral nerve injuries are not rare in civilian life. Trauma caused by a blunt object, as well as puncture wounds and lacerations, may cause injury to a nerve. Severance of a nerve results in paralysis of the muscles supplied by that nerve and loss of sensation over a specific area. Nerves are capable of regeneration provided the cut ends are accurately sutured together. This is precisely what the surgeon seeks to accomplish at operation. A good result is not always achieved following surgery even under optimum conditions, and at times, additional corrective orthopedic measures are necessary. Physiotherapy is an important adjunct in the treatment of this type of case.

The peripheral nerves, or their sheaths, are occasionally the site of tumor formation. Fortunately most of these tumors are benign and can be completely removed.

QUESTIONS AND ANSWERS

What is the scope of neurosurgery?

Neurosurgery is that branch of medicine dealing with the surgical treatment of diseases of the nervous system, including the brain, spinal cord, and peripheral nerves. Injuries, infections, tumors, some congenital abnormalities, ruptured disks, certain painful states, and intracranial hemorrhage are among the conditions that can be helped by the neurosurgeon.

What is the appearance of the brain?

The brain is a soft, grayish-white structure, hemispheric in shape, with innumerable folds. It is nourished by many blood vessels which permeate its substance. It is continuous with the spinal cord, which emerges through an opening in the base of the skull.

Both the brain and spinal cord are covered by membranes (the dura, arachnoid, and pia) and by a liquid called cerebrospinal fluid. Within the brain itself are a number of communicating cavities also containing cerebrospinal fluid.

How does one gain surgical access to the brain?

The operation for exposing the brain is called a craniotomy. As a general rule, craniotomy is performed under general anesthesia, though at times local anesthesia is preferable. In preparation for surgery, the entire head is shaved and the scalp cleansed thoroughly with soap and water. A skin antiseptic is then applied, and all but the area to be operated upon is covered with sterile drapes. The scalp is incised, usually in a semicircular manner, and a number of holes are drilled in the underlying skull. The holes are connected by means of a wire saw, thereby freeing a block of bone which is detached from the remainder of the skull. Directly underneath the bone are the membranes overlying the brain. These are incised, thus exposing the brain.

Progress in surgical technique has made it possible to gain access to almost any part of the brain with reasonable safety.

What is trephination?

Trephination is the drilling of a hole in the skull. Strictly speaking, this term means making the hole with an instrument called a trephine. In actual practice such holes are more expeditiously made with an instrument similar to a brace and bit.

For what conditions is trephination performed?

For evacuation of blood clots following injury, for injection of air into the fluid-containing spaces of the brain for diagnostic purposes, and for various other procedures not requiring a more extensive exposure of the intracranial structures. Whenever necessary, it is a simple matter to enlarge such openings with special bone instruments known as rongeurs.

Is trephining a dangerous operative procedure?

No. In fact, there is very little hazard attached to the procedure.

What is the appearance and function of the spinal cord?

The spinal cord is an elongated, cylindrically shaped structure which measures approximately 18 inches in length and occupies the canal within the vertebral column. It consists of bundles of nerves and its function is to act primarily as a conducting mechanism. Sensory impulses travel toward the brain, while impulses concerned with muscular contraction and movement descend in the opposite direction. Connections with various organs and structures are established by means of spinal nerves which are attached to the cord throughout its length.

How is the spinal cord exposed?

An incision is made in the center of the back, and the muscles overlying the spinal column are spread apart. Part of the arches of the exposed vertebrae are then removed, thereby bringing into view the spinal cord enclosed within its membranes. This operation is known as a laminectomy.

Are all head injuries serious?

No. On the contrary, head injuries vary in seriousness from the relatively minor laceration of the scalp to the severe bruising of the brain associated with profound unconsciousness. Fortunately, the skull affords considerable protection to the underlying brain substance. Many head injuries damage only the relatively unimportant superficial tissues. Those of a more severe nature may fracture the skull and cause serious brain damage, such as a laceration or a contusion.

Is a laceration of the scalp serious?

Scalp lacerations frequently look more serious than they really are, because of their tendency to bleed profusely. The bleeding usually stops by itself or after pressure has been applied. Surgical repair of the wound is necessary in cases of extensive laceration. The hair around the wound is shaved and the laceration cleansed before it is sutured. Careful inspection of the wound is necessary to be certain that the injury has not involved the skull or underlying brain.

What is the significance of loss of consciousness following a head injury?

It signifies that an injury to the intracranial contents has taken place. X-rays should always be taken in such cases because of the possibility of a skull fracture. Patients who have lost consciousness, if only for a few seconds, should be observed carefully for a day or two for evidence of hemorrhage within the skull.

What is meant by a concussion?

"Concussion" is a term applied to a head injury that has resulted in loss of consciousness for a brief period.

What is the treatment for a concussion?

No specific treatment is required in uncomplicated cases, as spontaneous recovery is the rule. The patient should, however, be watched for the development of increasing drowsiness and weakness of the limbs on one side of the body. Such symptoms are usually caused by bleeding within the skull.

Is a fractured skull a serious injury?

Yes. Skull fractures result from a severe blow or fall upon the head. However, it must be emphasized that it is not the extent of the fracture that determines the seriousness of the injury, but the amount of damage to the underlying brain. In other words, a small fracture accompanied by a widespread brain damage may be much more dangerous than an extensive skull fracture that has caused little brain damage.

Is the patient's state of consciousness an important factor in regard to the severity of the injury as well as the ultimate outcome?

Yes. The depth and duration of coma or stupor vary in proportion to the severity of the injury.

What is the proper first aid treatment for a head injury with loss of consciousness?

1. Place the patient on his side or in a semiprone position. This will lessen the danger of aspiration of secretions.
2. Hemorrhage from a scalp wound should be controlled by pressure with a sterile dressing or clean handkerchief.
3. Transport the patient flat on a stretcher; avoid bending his head or trunk.
4. Be sure the patient's airway remains unobstructed.

Is there any specific treatment for injury to the brain?

No. There is no specific treatment for brain injuries as such. Fortunately, most patients recover spontaneously. Good nursing care is essential. Comatose patients must be turned frequently to avoid pressure sores. Soiled bed linen must be changed promptly. Urinary incontinence may require insertion of a catheter in the bladder or may be dealt with by other methods. The importance of maintaining a clear airway so as to avoid interference with respiration cannot be overemphasized. It may be necessary at times to introduce a tube through an incision in the windpipe (tracheotomy) in order to facilitate respiration. The danger of aspiration resulting from vomiting and the accumulation of secretions requires the frequent use of mechanical suction. Maintenance of nutrition in a comatose patient usually necessitates the administration of fluids intravenously for a few days, after which a tube is inserted into the stomach for purposes of feeding.

Is it necessary to operate on all cases of head injury?

No.

What are the indications for surgery?

1. An open wound (i.e., compound fracture)
2. The presence of indriven or depressed fragments of bone which may possibly irritate the brain (depressed skull fracture)
3. Intracranial hemorrhage developing as a complication
4. A persistent leak of cerebrospinal fluid through the nose

Is the occurrence of bleeding within the skull following a head injury a serious complication?

Yes.

Does intracranial bleeding ever occur during early life?

Yes. Intracranial hemorrhage (subdural hematoma, or clot overlying the brain) resulting from injury is sometimes encountered during infancy. The trauma may have occurred inadvertently at the time the baby was born. Early diagnosis and surgical treatment are essential to prevent permanent brain damage.

Is physical or mental disability a common sequel of head injury?

Considering the frequency with which head injuries occur, the incidence of serious aftereffects is remarkably small. In most cases recovery is complete.

At times, symptoms such as headache, dizziness, and irritability persist following an injury (posttraumatic or postconcussion syndrome). These do not, as a rule, indicate any serious underlying disorder or complication. It must be realized that there is a strong emotional component to every physical injury, and this is particularly true when the accident has involved the head. Psychological disturbances and emotional instability after skull and brain injuries can often be minimized by careful explanation of the exact nature of the injury. Above all, it is important to assure such patients that their ability to return to a completely normal life need not be impaired when they have recovered fully from the physical effects of the accident.

Do all types of infection of the skull or brain require surgical treatment?

No. Surgery is not indicated in cases in which the infection is widespread (encephalitis, meningitis) and in which there is no localized collection of pus to drain.

How does the brain or its coverings become infected?

Sinusitis and, less often, injury are the most common causes of infection of the bones of the skull (osteomyelitis). An abscess within the brain occurs as a result of the spread of an infection from an adjacent structure such as the sinuses or ears, or from a distant part of the body, usually the lung. It may also be caused by a penetrating wound of the skull or by a compound skull fracture.

Is osteomyelitis of the skull serious?

Yes. Unless it is adequately treated, there is danger of the spread of infection to the brain. This type of infection is encountered less often than in the days before the advent of chemotherapy and antibiotics.

What does the surgical treatment of osteomyelitis entail?

Removal of the diseased bone and provision for drainage of pus. Antibiotics are administered concurrently.

How serious is a brain abscess?

Brain abscess is a very serious condition, despite the fact that its incidence has diminished markedly and the outlook for successful treatment has improved considerably as a result of the introduction of chemotherapy and antibiotics. It is treated by surgical excision or drainage.

What kind of anesthesia is used for brain surgery?

Either local or general anesthesia, preferably the latter, through a tube placed into the trachea (windpipe).

Where are the incisions made in cases of brain surgery?

Over any part of the scalp, depending on the location of the underlying condition.

Is the scar resulting from brain surgery disfiguring?

No. Insofar as possible, the incisions are made within the hairline, and the eventual scar is inconspicuous.

Are blood transfusions given during the course of brain operations?

Yes, very often.

How long do brain operations take to perform?

The time element varies, depending on the nature of the condition requiring surgery, and the procedure to be performed. Some operations can be completed within an hour or two; others may require four to five hours.

Can patients safely withstand this type of surgery for several hours?

Yes. Improved anesthetic techniques and supportive measures make it possible for lengthy operations to be performed safely.

How soon after a major brain operation can the surgeon tell if the patient will survive?

Usually within a few days.

Are special nurses necessary after brain operations?

Yes, for several days.

How long a hospital stay is necessary after a major brain operation?

About two weeks.

Must one take special care of the wound area after a brain operation has been performed?

Not usually. The only cases that require special attention are those in which the piece of bone removed at operation has not been replaced.

BRAIN TUMORS

How common are tumors of the brain?

The brain is one of the most frequent sites of tumor formation in the entire body.

Are there different kinds of brain tumors?

Yes. The term "intracranial tumor" is used to denote any one of several types of growths that may be present within the skull. A tumor may originate from the skull, from the membranes or nerves external to the brain, or from the brain itself. Still another source is the pituitary gland at the base of the skull. Finally, cancerous growths arising elsewhere in the body may spread by way of the blood stream to involve the brain secondarily.

What are the chances of surviving an operation for brain tumor?

Eighty-five to 90 percent.

What are the most common symptoms of brain tumor?

Headache, vomiting, disturbances of vision, and various specific symptoms, depending on the location of the tumor, such as paralysis or convulsions.

What causes brain tumors?

As in the case of tumors elsewhere in the body, the cause is unknown.

Are brain tumors hereditary?

No.

Can the exact location of a brain tumor be determined before operation?

In most instances, yes.

How is the location of a brain tumor determined?

A detailed history and a careful examination of the patient may yield important clues. As a rule, however, it is desirable, and at times necessary, to perform some of the following diagnostic procedures in order to establish the location of a tumor:

1. **Simple x-rays of the skull.** These may yield sufficient information.

2. **Examination of the spinal fluid.**

3. **Examination of the eyes** (visual fields).

4. **Encephalograms and ventriculograms** are often necessary. In performing these tests, some of the fluid surrounding the brain and contained within its cavities is removed through a needle and is replaced with a gas (helium or oxygen). The gas, acting as a contrast medium, outlines the chambers of the brain on an x-ray film. Familiarity with the normal appearance of these cavities permits one to recognize the distortion produced by a tumor and to identify its location.

5. **Arteriography.** By outlining the blood vessels of the brain, this procedure may provide valuable information. By injecting a radiopaque substance into the arteries of the neck, the blood vessels of the brain can be visualized on an x-ray film. A brain tumor, by concentrating the radiopaque substance within its own blood vessels, may actually be outlined. In other instances, its location may be revealed by noting the displacement of the blood vessels of the brain from their normal position.

6. **Electroencephalography,** the study of the electrical brain waves, is another valuable diagnostic test. It is often possible to record abnormal brain waves from the scalp over an area corresponding to the site of a brain tumor.

7. **Brain scans** following the administration of radioactive substances (isotopes), especially those introduced in recent years (radioactive mercury compounds), are extremely useful in the diagnosis and localization of brain tumors. The risk involved in the use of this radioactive material is believed to be negligible.

8. **Echoencephalography** utilizing the principle of sonar detection is employed in some clinics, though its usefulness at this time appears to be limited.

Is it possible to determine before operation whether a brain tumor is benign or malignant?

Not in all cases, though at times one can be reasonably certain. Thus, pituitary tumors, as a rule, are benign. The knowledge that a malignant tumor, such as a breast cancer, had been previously removed would lead one to suspect strongly that the cancer had spread to involve the brain (metastasis). Other factors that might have some bearing on the presumptive nature of the tumor include the age of the patient, the duration of symptoms, the findings on examination, and the results of certain of the tests mentioned above.

Do brain tumors, once removed, tend to recur?

Only if incompletely removed.

Can a patient who has had a brain tumor successfully removed live a normal life?

Yes.

Do brain tumors occur in children?

Yes. Brain tumors during childhood are not at all uncommon. Certain types of tumors are especially prevalent in children, and they tend to occur predominantly in certain locations within the brain. Both benign and malignant varieties are encountered. Their treatment is similar to that of tumors in adults and the results obtained are comparable. Children withstand brain surgery as well as adults.

Is x-ray treatment rather than surgery ever recommended for brain tumors?

Yes. X-ray treatment is effective in a high proportion of tumors of the pituitary gland. Certain tumors which are inoperable by virtue of their location are usually treated by means of irradiation, with beneficial effects in a significant number of cases.

If vision is lost because of a brain condition, does it ever return?

If vision is lost as a result of increased pressure within the skull, the outlook for recovery is not good. In cases in which vision is damaged, surgery may prevent further impairment or result in improvement. Loss of vision due to direct pressure of the tumor on the optic nerves may be helped considerably through surgery.

If hearing is lost because of a brain tumor, is it ever regained after surgical removal?

A brain tumor causing loss of hearing usually arises from the auditory nerve, and hearing will not return despite the removal of the tumor.

Can a patient who has lost the power to speak be taught to speak again after removal of a brain tumor?

Yes. Very often this is possible with intensive effort and training.

Can patients regain the use of their limbs following removal of a brain tumor?

Yes, in many cases. Complete recovery, however, does not always take place.

Is a patient's mentality usually affected by a brain operation?

As a rule, no. The patient's mental reaction is primarily determined by the nature and location of the disease from which he is suffering.

Will the removal of a brain tumor result in a cessation of convulsions?

The frequency of the convulsions may be diminished, but they are not always eliminated completely. Hence, the administration of anticonvulsant medication should be continued following operation. Even in cases in which convulsions did not occur preoperatively, the use of anticonvulsant medication postoperatively is advisable as a precautionary measure.

STROKE AND INTRACRANIAL HEMORRHAGE

What is meant by cerebral hemorrhage?

Bleeding occurring within the substance of the brain or on its surface.

What are the common causes of cerebral hemorrhage?

1. Hardening of the arteries (arteriosclerosis) and high blood pressure are the most common causes of hemorrhage within the brain. This type of hemorrhage usually occurs after the age of 40.

2. Bleeding may also take place in younger individuals as a result of rupture of a malformed blood vessel. Most often, the malformation is a saclike dilatation of a blood vessel (aneurysm). Occasionally, it consists of a cluster of abnormally large blood vessels (angioma).

3. Injury to the brain may also cause intracranial hemorrhage.

Is a cerebral hemorrhage synonymous with a stroke?

Not entirely. The term "stroke" includes several conditions, one of which is cerebral hemorrhage.

Is cerebral hemorrhage serious?

Yes, regardless of cause.

What is the role of surgery in the treatment of cerebral hemorrhage?

Hemorrhage within the brain, when it is caused by rupture of a diseased or abnormal blood vessel, sometimes lends itself to surgical treatment. Operation may, in certain cases, be a lifesaving measure and may lessen the likelihood of permanent brain damage. The indications for operation are variable and there are no set rules to apply in deciding which cases are amenable to surgical treatment. In general, however, younger individuals whose hemorrhages are not deeply placed within the brain are more suitable candidates for surgery.

What is the role of surgery in the treatment of malformation of the intracranial blood vessels?

Because these deformed vessels often rupture and cause intracranial bleeding, they constitute a threat to life. Obviously, it would be desirable to discover them and, wherever possible, to institute treatment *before* they cause hemorrhage. Unfortunately, evidence of hemorrhage is often the first indication of their presence. The use of radiopaque substances in order to outline the blood vessels of the brain (arteriography) is especially useful in cases in which an abnormality of the blood vessels is suspected.

Various methods of surgical treatment have been devised, but, unfortunately, such operations, when feasible, frequently entail considerable hazard.

What is the role of the surgeon in the treatment of the nonhemorrhagic forms of stroke (cerebral vascular occlusive disease)?

In recent years, it has been conclusively demonstrated that strokes commonly, though not invariably, result from obstruction to the flow of blood to the brain, affecting the arteries in the neck as they ascend from the heart. The diagnosis in such cases is readily confirmed by arteriography. It may be advisable in some of these cases to remove the obstruction within the affected artery or, depending on the location and degree of the obstruction, to bypass it by means of an artificial tubular graft. It should be clearly understood that the vast majority of patients who have had a stroke are *not* suitable candidates for this type of surgical treatment.

TRIGEMINAL NEURALGIA

What is meant by trigeminal neuralgia (tic douloureux, trifacial neuralgia)?

Trigeminal neuralgia is a disease occurring mostly in middle-aged and elderly people, characterized by severe, recurrent paroxysmal pain in the face. Its cause is unknown.

What is the treatment of trigeminal neuralgia?

There is no medication that is wholly dependable in affording relief, though Dilantin is temporarily effective at times. Injection of alcohol into the nerves in the face may eliminate the pain for periods of varying duration. Cutting the main nerve responsible for the pain within the skull provides permanent relief. This operation is successful in the great majority of cases.

What is the role of surgery in the treatment of mental disease?

The operation originally devised for the treatment of mental disease (lobotomy) has been largely abandoned. In fact, at the present time the role of surgery in the treatment of psychiatric illness is not altogether clear. Various modifications of the original operation have been suggested so as to avoid certain undesirable effects, but the specific indications for the new procedures and their effectiveness are still uncertain.

PARKINSONISM

Is surgery of value in the treatment of parkinsonism (shaking palsy)?

There is no longer any reasonable doubt that selected cases of parkinsonism may be appreciably benefited by surgical treatment. While best results are achieved in patients with unilateral (one-sided) involvement, there are apparently no absolute contraindications to surgery, including old age. The operation is not wholly devoid of risk, but the proportion of untoward effects is relatively small. This type of surgery requires special training and equipment and should be performed only at a suitable neurosurgical center. The operation is usually done under local anesthesia. In addition to the tremor (palsy),

other types of involuntary movements may be helped by surgical treatment.

CEREBELLAR BRAIN TUMORS

Where are cerebellar tumors located, and what symptoms do they cause?

Cerebellar tumors involve the portion of the brain called the cerebellum, which is located in the back of the head just above the neck. Because of their location, they cause increased intracranial pressure at an early stage, so that headache, vomiting, and double vision are common early symptoms. Examination of the eyes often discloses evidence of increased intracranial pressure. In addition, cerebellar tumors characteristically result in a disturbance of equilibrium that causes unsteadiness of gait or incoordination of the limbs.

Do children commonly get cerebellar tumors?

Yes. The incidence of cerebellar tumors is much greater in children than in adults.

Can cerebellar tumors be removed successfully through surgery?

Both benign and malignant tumors occur in this region. Benign tumors frequently can be totally removed, in which case a cure may be expected. Even partial removal of a benign tumor or evacuation of a cyst may not be followed by evidence of recurrent growth for many years.

Malignant tumors, unfortunately, can be only partially removed as a rule, and eventual recurrence is inevitable, even with x-ray treatment.

Do cerebellar tumors cause any permanent damage or handicaps?

Some degree of incoordination may persist, although full recovery is possible. Double vision usually subsides. Perhaps the most serious, persistent ill effect of a cerebellar tumor is the impairment of vision resulting from increased intracranial pressure. This loss of vision may be irreparable, and in extreme cases the patients remain blind.

PINEAL TUMORS

What is a pineal tumor?

A pineal tumor is a tumor involving the pineal gland, a structure of uncertain function that is located deep within the brain.

Do children often get pineal tumors?

No. Pineal tumors occur infrequently.

Do pineal tumors tend to affect boys more often than girls?

Yes. Pineal tumors occur about four times more frequently in boys than in girls.

What are the signs and symptoms of a pineal tumor?

The essential symptoms are those of increased intracranial pressure (headache, vomiting), together with an inability to look upward. Precocious sexual development may occur in boys.

Do pineal tumors ever cause hydrocephalus?

Yes. Pineal tumors frequently interfere with the flow of cerebrospinal fluid and cause obstructive hydrocephalus.

How is the diagnosis of a pineal tumor made?

The presence of a pineal tumor may be suspected on the basis of the symptoms and signs, especially when there is evidence of increased intracranial pressure and the child cannot look upward. A confirmation of the diagnosis is achieved through pneumoencephalography (injection of air into the fluid-containing spaces of the brain, followed by x-ray examination).

What is the treatment for a pineal tumor?

Because of its location deep in the brain, it is extremely hazardous to attempt to remove a pineal tumor. Treatment usually consists of a shunting operation to relieve the increased intracranial pressure, followed by x-ray therapy. Patients treated in this manner often do well for many years.

When is surgery for a pineal tumor indicated?

When less radical measures, such as an operative procedure to shunt the flow of cerebrospinal fluid, have failed, and when the tumor continues to grow despite x-ray treatment. Such operations are extremely hazardous and the mortality rate is high.

CRANIOSYNOSTOSIS

What is craniosynostosis?

Craniosynostosis is a condition in which the bones of a child's skull unite prematurely. As a consequence there is interference with the growth and development of the skull and brain.

What are the signs and symptoms of craniosynostosis?

There is distortion of the shape of the head, and symptoms that suggest a brain condition may appear, such as disturbance of vision, mental retardation, and, in some cases, convulsions.

If surgery is carried out early enough, will the craniosynostosis symptoms be alleviated?

Yes. The sooner surgery is performed, the better the appearance of the head and the better the chances for normal mental development.

What surgery is performed for craniosynostosis?

Linear openings are made in the skull

where premature fusion has occurred. This permits continued expansion of the skull and further growth and development of the brain.

HYDROCEPHALUS

What is hydrocephalus?

Hydrocephalus is a condition in which the head enlarges abnormally because of an excessive amount of cerebrospinal fluid within the brain. It is caused by an interference with the circulation and absorption of cerebrospinal fluid. This leads to enlargement of the head in the child so affected.

What causes hydrocephalus?

Injury during birth, congenital malformations, and infections (meningitis) in early life are the usual causes.

Is hydrocephalus a common disorder in infants?

Yes, it is fairly common.

What are the signs and symptoms of hydrocephalus?

The head enlarges out of proportion to the rest of the body and may reach enormous size. In addition, the fontanels (soft spots) are widened and may bulge, and the eyes often appear to be depressed downward.

Are there any operations that successfully treat hydrocephalus?

Many operations have been devised for the treatment of this condition, but unfortunately none has proved uniformly successful. In recent years most of these operations have involved the use of plastic tubes to shunt the cerebrospinal fluid into other body cavities from which it can be absorbed. The operation currently favored is one in which the cerebrospinal fluid is diverted into the heart.

Can hydrocephalus cause permanent brain damage?

Yes. If untreated, the pressure of the fluid on the brain will eventually destroy sufficient brain cells so as to cause mental retardation and other physical disabilities.

Is hydrocephalus ever self-limited?

Yes. In approximately 25 percent of cases, spontaneous arrest occurs. About a third of such cases exhibit normal intelligence.

PITUITARY GLAND TUMORS

Where is the pituitary gland located, and what is its function?

The pituitary gland is lodged within a depression at the base of the skull. It consists of an anterior lobe and a posterior lobe. The anterior lobe produces a number of chemical substances (hormones) that control growth and the activity of various other glands, including the adrenal gland, thyroid gland, and ovary or testis. The secretions of the posterior lobe are concerned with reabsorption of water by the kidneys and contraction of smooth muscle.

Are pituitary gland tumors seen very often in children?

No, they are very rare. The region just above the pituitary gland is, however, a fairly common site for other types of tumors, especially certain cystic tumors (craniopharyngiomas) and others involving the optic nerves.

What are the symptoms of tumors in the region of the pituitary, and how is the diagnosis of this condition made?

Symptoms specifically associated with tumors in this region include impairment of vision, retardation of growth, drowsiness, and excessive thirst and output of urine. The craniopharyngiomas (cystic tumors) often contain calcific deposits, which may be seen in x-rays of the skull. The optic nerve tumors may produce certain changes visible in x-rays. Pneumoencephalography, a special x-ray technique in which air is injected into the space surrounding the brain, may be necessary for diagnosis in both types of pituitary gland tumors.

What is the treatment for tumors in the region of the pituitary?

The craniopharyngiomas require operation in order to relieve increased intracranial pressure as well as pressure on the adjacent structures, particularly the optic nerves. In some cases of optic nerve tumor, only one nerve is involved and it is possible to remove the tumor completely, vision in the affected eye being permanently lost. When both nerves are involved, the tumor cannot be removed, and x-ray therapy is the preferred method of treatment.

Are operations for tumors in the region of the pituitary usually successful in children?

The outlook in cases of craniopharyngioma is generally poor. In most cases it is not possible to remove the tumor completely, and sooner or later it recurs.

An optic nerve tumor affecting only one nerve can be totally removed. When both nerves are involved, removal of the tumor is not technically feasible. Fortunately, such tumors usually grow very slowly, so patients may show little evidence of the progression of these tumors for many years.

Can a pituitary gland tumor cause a child to become a giant?

Yes. A pituitary gland tumor that produces an excessive quantity of growth hormone results in gigantism in a child.

SPINAL CORD DEFORMITIES

What is spina bifida, and how common is it in children?

Spina bifida is a congenital abnormality characterized by incomplete closure of some part of the vertebral canal. It is fairly common and, in the great majority of cases, is not associated with any symptoms.

Is spina bifida ever associated with a protrusion of the membranes covering the spinal cord itself?

Yes. When the protrusion consists only of a sac of cerebrospinal fluid, it is called a meningocele. When the protrusion contains any spinal cord or nerve elements, it is called a myelomeningocele.

How is a meningocele or a myelomeningocele diagnosed?

The infant is born with a noticeable lump on the back, which in the case of a myelomeningocele is associated with some degree of paralysis, usually of the lower limbs.

Are meningocele and myelomeningocele often associated with hydrocephalus?

Yes, especially in cases of myelomeningocele.

Is surgery successful for meningocele and myelomeningocele?

Whatever paralysis exists will not be relieved by surgery. In some cases in which the sac is very thin or is actually leaking spinal fluid, an operation is necessary in order to avoid meningitis. Otherwise, surgery is usually undertaken essentially for cosmetic reasons.

What is diastematomyelia?

Diastematomyelia is a birth malformation in which the spinal cord is divided longitudinally into two parts by a septum of fibrous tissue or bone.

How is a diagnosis of diastematomyelia made?

Children with diastematomyelia have difficulty walking and exhibit deformities of the lower extremities. Skin changes are also commonly present over the back. In cases in which the spinal cord is divided by a bony spur, x-rays of the spine will reveal the abnormality. Otherwise, special studies may be required to confirm the diagnosis.

Can surgery cure diastematomyelia?

No, but it may be helpful in preventing the patient from becoming further disabled.

What are the usual symptoms resulting from a tumor of the spinal cord?

Backache, together with weakness and numbness of the limbs, and disturbances referable to the bladder and bowels.

Are there different kinds of tumors of the spinal cord?

Yes. The spinal cord may be affected by tumors compressing it from without or growing within its substance. About 50 percent of these tumors originate from the membranes overlying the cord or from a spinal nerve.

How is the diagnosis of a spinal cord tumor established?

The presence of a spinal cord tumor may be suspected on the basis of the history and examination of the patient. Spinal puncture usually reveals an obstruction to the free flow of cerebrospinal fluid. Examination of the spinal fluid often provides useful information. The diagnosis may be further confirmed by introducing a radiopaque substance into the cerebrospinal fluid and subjecting the patient to fluoroscopy. This procedure is called myelography. Normally, the radiopaque substance flows freely when the patient is tilted in either direction. A tumor will act as an obstruction to the flow of the radiopaque substance, thus verifying the diagnosis and providing evidence of its exact location.

What are the results of surgery in the treatment of spinal cord tumors?

Tumors originating from the membranes overlying the spinal cord or from a spinal nerve can usually be totally removed and the patient cured or greatly improved. If the spinal cord damage has been unduly prolonged, it may be irreversible. Tumors growing within the substance of the spinal cord usually cannot be removed, but their growth can often be halted by x-ray treatment. Not infrequently, a cancer that has originated in some other part of the body spreads to involve the spinal cord. The outlook in such cases is especially poor, though x-ray treatment, and occasionally surgery, may prove temporarily beneficial.

Can paralysis caused by a spinal cord tumor be relieved by surgery?

Yes. In about 50 percent of all cases, the tumor can be removed completely and the patient cured or improved without fear of recurrence of the tumor.

Are operations upon the spinal cord dangerous?

No more so than a major operation elsewhere in the body.

SPINAL CORD AND NERVE INJURIES

What are the common causes of spinal cord injury?

Injuries of the spinal cord usually occur in association with fractures or dislocations of the spinal column. Falls, automobile and riding accidents, and gunshot wounds are the most frequent causes. The spinal cord may escape injury at the time a spinal fracture is incurred, but careless transportation of the patient from the scene of the accident may result in damage to the spinal cord.

How does a spinal cord injury manifest itself?

The manifestations of spinal cord injury include varying degrees of paralysis, loss of sensation, and inability to control the bladder and bowels.

What is the outlook for recovery following spinal cord injury?

In cases in which there is a complete paralysis and loss of all forms of sensation, the outlook for recovery is very poor. The retention of some degree of spinal cord function, no matter how slight, renders the outlook infinitely better than when all function is lost. If evidence of complete interruption of the spinal cord persists for more than a few days, it is unlikely that any improvement will occur. Regeneration of divided fibers does not occur in the spinal cord.

Is surgery of value in the treatment of spinal cord injury?

In most cases of spinal cord injury, operation is useless. There are occasional exceptions, but, as a rule, all that can be accomplished is to institute orthopedic measures to treat the spinal fracture or dislocation. Reduction of the fracture so as to achieve stability and normal alignment of the bones may require operative treatment.

Is there any hope for the patient who remains paralyzed?

The management of the patient who remains paralyzed is a complex problem beyond the scope of this discussion. Suffice it to say, after prolonged training it is possible to rehabilitate many of these unfortunate paraplegics so that they can be made ambulatory and lead a reasonably normal and useful life.

What is a peripheral nerve?

One that conveys impulses between the spinal cord and some other part of the body. It may transmit impulses concerned with muscular contraction as well as stimuli conveying sensory impressions.

How do nerve injuries occur?

They may occur as a result of blunt trauma, punctures, lacerations, incisions, or penetrating (gunshot or stab) wounds.

Where do peripheral nerve injuries occur most commonly?

In the limbs.

What are the symptoms of peripheral nerve injury?

Paralysis of the muscles and loss of sensation over a specific area supplied by that particular nerve.

What is the role of surgery in the treatment of peripheral nerve injuries?

Nerves are capable of regrowth and resumption of function provided the cut ends are accurately united. This is precisely what the surgeon seeks to accomplish at operation. A good result is not always achieved following surgery, however, even under optimum conditions, and at times additional corrective orthopedic measures are necessary. Physiotherapy is an important adjunct in the treatment of this type of case.

Is surgery necessary in all types of nerve injury?

No; only in cases in which a nerve has been severed.

Can tumors arise from the peripheral nerves?

Yes. Fortunately, such tumors are usually benign and can be removed completely.

SURGERY FOR INTRACTABLE PAIN

Are operations on the spinal cord performed for the relief of pain?

Yes. The neurosurgeon is often called upon to relieve pain that fails to respond to medication. Such pain is usually caused by advanced cancer. The location of the pathways within the spinal cord conducting pain being known, it is possible to cut them and afford the patient relief. This type of operation is known as a cordotomy. It is also possible to cut the nerves (as they enter the spinal cord) that supply a particular region of the body. By depriving that area of all sensation, pain is eliminated. This procedure is called a rhizotomy.

Both of these operations upon the spinal cord are safe procedures, and although they do not cure the underlying condition, in suitable cases they are extremely valuable for the relief of intractable pain.

Does an operation upon the spinal cord for the relief of pain (cordotomy) result in paralysis?

As a rule, no. However, complications such as varying degrees of weakness (paralysis) and/or impairment of bladder control can occur.

Nevus

See MELANOMA; MOLES.

Nose and Sinuses

The nose is made up of cartilage and bone and contains two cavities which are separated in the midline by a *septum.* Air enters each chamber through the nostrils and leaves to enter the throat by way of the posterior nostrils.

The nose serves as the natural airway for respiration, is the sense organ of smell, and acts as an "air-conditioner" by filtering, warming, and moistening air that is breathed in. The hairs within the nose prevent dust particles from gaining easy access to the throat, and the sticky mucous covering of the lining membrane of the nose further settles out bacteria and dust, thus protecting the tissues against infection.

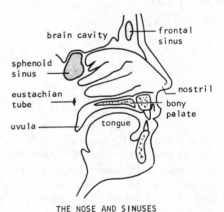

THE NOSE AND SINUSES

The nasal *sinuses* are mucous-membrane-lined air spaces within the bones of the face and skull. They communicate by small openings with the nasal cavity. There are the *frontal sinuses,* located within the bone just above and behind the eyebrows; the *maxillary sinuses,* located within the bones of the cheeks beneath the eyes; the *ethmoid sinuses,* located near the side of the nose and inner aspect of the eyes and extending backward into the skull; and the *sphenoid sinuses,* located deep in the skull above the level of the throat. The purpose of the sinuses is to lighten the weight of the head and to contribute toward resonance of the voice. (See illustrations.)

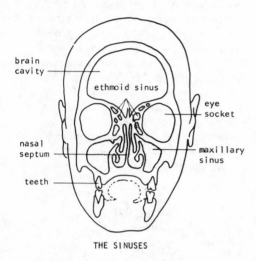

brain cavity

ethmoid sinus

eye socket

nasal septum

maxillary sinus

teeth

THE SINUSES

There are a large number of conditions requiring surgery upon the nose and sinuses and the most frequently encountered will be discussed here.

1. Fracture of the nose is one of the commonest of all injuries because of the exposed position of this structure and because the nasal bones are rather thin and delicate. It is always best to treat nasal fractures as soon as they occur, when manipulation of the fragments, or resetting, can be accomplished easily. These fractures can usually be placed into normal alignment by manual manipulation externally and by inserting special instruments into the nasal cavity to push out depressed bony fragments.

The diagnosis of a fracture can usually be made by noting the nasal deformity and by feeling the broken bones directly. X-rays should always be taken to ascertain the exact extent of the break and also to make sure that there is no accompanying fracture of the skull.

Nasal fractures heal quickly because of the rich blood supply in the area. Once replaced, the bony fragments tend to remain in good position. This holds true because there are no muscles exerting their pull against the fragments. It is important that the septum be carefully examined and treated following a nasal fracture, as it is often knocked out of alignment.

Innumerable splints have been devised for maintaining fractured noses in good position. Most of them are satisfactory but no one is applicable to all fractures.

Minor fractures can be set in the surgeon's office without anesthesia. Fractures with marked displacement and deformity should be operated upon in the hospital under local or general anesthesia.

Healing for an average fracture will take three to four weeks, and several more weeks may pass before all the swelling has subsided. The antibiotic drugs are often prescribed to minimize the possibility of infection invading the fracture site.

2. Deviated septum, or other deformities of the nasal septum, are developmental in origin in the great majority of cases. If the septal deformity interferes with proper nasal respiration or obstructs the openings into the sinuses, it should be corrected surgically.

Corrective operations, called *submucous resection,* are undertaken in the hospital with local anesthesia. An incision is made just inside one nostril through its lining membrane and septal cartilage but not through the lining membrane of the other nostril. The lining membrane is then elevated from both sides of the septum and any spurs, or deflected portions of cartilage or bone, are removed. Vaseline gauze packing is then inserted into the nasal cavities to keep the lining membrane against the septum and to control bleeding. These operations are highly successful in almost all cases. Hospitalization need only be for two to four days and recovery is prompt. Poor results are encountered mainly in those cases where surgery was not actually indicated.

3. Hematoma (blood clot) of the septum may occur following injury or operation. The collection of blood can be released easily by an incision into the septal lining membrane. Occasionally an abscess secondary to a septal hematoma may form. Treatment consists of incision and drainage, and the prescribing of antibiotic drugs.

4. Nasal polyps (mucous polyps) are extremely common and are thought to be allergic in origin. They are pale grapelike growths within the nose which can grow sufficiently large to cause obstruction to nasal breathing. When they obstruct the passage, they should be removed. The procedure can, in most instances, be carried out in the surgeon's office under local anesthesia. The polyps are grasped and removed with a wire snare.

Nasal polyps show a great tendency to recur unless the underlying allergy is treated and brought under control.

5. Sinusitis is an inflammation of the mucous membrane lining of one or more sinuses. *Pansinusitis* is present when all the sinuses are infected.

Sinusitis is usually secondary to an infection in the nasal cavity, although the maxillary sinus may become infected due to an extension from a tooth infection in the upper jaw. Swimming,

diving, or injuries with fracture of the bones overlying the sinuses may also cause an inflammation. Anatomical deformities blocking the sinus openings, and allergies with nasal polyp formation, may predispose to sinusitis.

The symptoms of this condition will vary somewhat according to the sinus involved. A nasal quality to the speaking voice, nasal obstruction, nasal discharge, headache, elevated body temperature (fever), and tenderness over the infected sinus are the symptoms present in most cases.

Diagnosis is made from a history of a cold that has persisted beyond one week; from evidences of the above symptoms; from examination including nasal inspection and *transillumination of the sinuses* with a strong light in a dark room, which will reveal failure of lighting up and cloudiness of the involved sinus; and finally, by x-ray studies, which will clinch the diagnosis.

Most sinus infections will subside under good medical management. This will consist of bed rest, moist heat to the sinuses with steam inhalations, nosedrops to lessen the congestion of the nasal mucous membranes, and antibiotics. Further medical treatment in the physician's office often consists of nasal packs and various methods of sucking out the pus. Cultures of the pus are usually taken and are tested for the sensitivity of the bacteria to various types of antibiotics.

Surgery of the sinuses is reserved for the minority of patients who do not respond well to medical treatment. The aim of all sinus operations for infection is to obtain adequate openings for drainage of the pus and to remove diseased mucous membrane or infected bone surrounding the sinus.

The maxillary sinus can be opened through the nose for drainage. If, however, this is insufficient to bring about a cure, a *radical maxillary sinusotomy* operation is performed through an incision beneath the upper lip. The mucous membranes are lifted away from the underlying bone which covers the sinus. The sinus is punctured and sufficient bone is chiseled away to expose the contents of the sinus. The lining of the sinus is then removed, along with any diseased bone. This operation is done in the hospital under local anesthesia. Recovery requires four to five days and the end results are usually excellent.

The frontal sinus is approached through an incision in the skin below the inner portion of the eyebrow. A small hole is cut in the bone and the sinus is penetrated. A rubber tube drain is inserted and left in place for several days until all drainage has ceased. It must be mentioned that this is a relatively infrequent operation since most cases of frontal sinusitis will respond well to medical treatment. The results of the surgery, however, are most satisfactory.

A *radical frontal sinus operation* is occasionally necessary when the infection is especially severe or has involved the bone or is threatening to cause an infection within the brain. In this situation, a larger incision is made over the inner aspect of the nose and along the eyebrow. The entire bony floor of the sinus is chiseled away and the entire mucous membrane lining of the sinus is removed. Although this is a serious procedure, carried out under local or general anesthesia in the hospital, recovery takes place in almost all cases.

The *ethmoid sinuses* can usually be approached and scraped out through the nose.

The *sphenoid sinus* can be probed and irrigated under local anesthesia through the nose. A persistent sphenoid

sinus infection is most serious as it may lead to *blindness* or infection within the *brain*. In such cases, it is wise to operate and remove the anterior wall of the sinus. This can be done under local anesthesia.

6. Tumors within the nose and sinuses may be benign or malignant. Fortunately, the benign tumors such as warts, polyps, small blood vessel tumors (hemangiomas) are much more common than the malignant cancers.

Most of the benign tumors can be readily removed under local anesthesia in the surgeon's office. After snipping off the growth, the base is usually cauterized with an electric current. Larger tumors may have to be removed in the hospital under general anesthesia.

Cancer of the nose and sinuses is treated by wide surgical removal of the growth and surrounding tissues. As elsewhere in the body, the success of these operations depends upon the time at which the surgery is performed. If it is done before the cancer has spread to distant tissues, the expectation of a cure is good. Modern surgical techniques may include the removal of large sections of the nose, the roof of the mouth, the floor of the eye socket, or the face and cheek. The main goal is to get beyond the cancer and to leave the cosmetic reconstruction to later plastic repair. Many lives have been saved through this approach, and happily, modern advances in plastic surgery have brought about remarkable restoration of structures to normal appearance.

QUESTIONS AND ANSWERS

Are infections of the nose, such as boils, pimples, or carbuncles, dangerous?

Yes. They are a source of danger, if improperly handled, because the blood vessels in this area of the face drain into veins at the base of the brain. Extension of an infection along this channel may lead to an infection within or surrounding the brain.

What is the most important precaution in the treatment of an infection of the nose?

Never open or squeeze an infected pimple or boil on the upper lip!

What is the treatment for nasal infections?

Small pimples are best left alone. The larger infections are treated by giving antibiotic drugs and by applying hot, wet compresses to the area. Infections of the nose should be opened only by a surgeon.

FRACTURED NOSE

Is fracture of the nose a frequent occurrence?

Yes. It is one of the most common injuries, because of the exposed position of the structure and because the nasal bones are thin and delicate.

Is bleeding from the nose always indicative of the presence of a fracture?

No. There are a considerable number of injuries accompanied by bleeding in which the nasal bones are intact.

Does bleeding from the nose always take place with a fracture?

No.

Should x-rays be taken to determine nasal fracture?

If there is no doubt about the diagnosis, it may not be necessary to take x-rays. However, x-rays must be taken after a fracture has been set, to make sure that the fragments are in proper alignment.

How soon after a nasal fracture occurs should it be treated?

As soon as possible, preferably within a few hours, for at this time manipulation of the fragments and setting of the fracture can be accomplished easily. After the passage of several days, it is much more difficult to bring a nose back into proper alignment.

What methods are used to set a fractured nose?

1. Manipulation by the hand of the surgeon, externally

2. Insertion of special instruments into the nasal cavity to push out depressed bony fragments

Is it necessary to use anesthesia to set a nasal fracture?

Most cases can be set under local anesthesia, but when the pain is too great a general anesthetic agent should be used.

Is hospitalization necessary for a fracture of the nose?

Only if there is an extensive or compound fracture, or if general anesthesia is necessary, or if there are accompanying injuries that require hospitalization.

How long does it take a fracture of the nose to heal?

These are very rapidly healing fractures, because of the rich blood supply in the nasal area. Healing usually takes place within two to three weeks.

How long does the swelling of the nose persist after a fracture?

Slight swelling may continue for several months, but the greatest part of the swelling will subside in two to three weeks.

Are antibiotics used following the setting of a nasal fracture?

Yes, to minimize the danger of infection.

Is a fracture of the nose usually followed by a permanent deformity?

No. However, there may be some thickening at the site of the fracture.

What can be done to correct a poor result after the setting of a fracture of the nose?

Plastic surgery can be performed to restore the nose to normal appearance.

How long should one wait before advising plastic surgery to restore the appearance of a broken nose that has healed poorly?

At least several months should pass from the time of the original injury. This is advisable because there may be persistent swelling for that length of time, and the degree of deformity cannot be accurately determined until all swelling has subsided.

Will the proper setting of a fractured nose guarantee that there will be no permanent deformity?

Unfortunately, no. Even if a fracture is set perfectly, the healing process may cause overgrowth of bone with resultant deformity.

NASAL POLYPS

What are nasal polyps?

They are grapelike masses of swollen tissue which protrude from the sinuses and the internal side walls of the nose.

What are thought to be the causes of nasal polyps?

They are thought to be due to an allergy, or they may be the result of chronic infection of the sinuses.

What symptoms are caused by nasal polyps?

If the polyps are small and few in number, there may be no symptoms. Frequently, they will be large enough

to obstruct the airway and cause difficulty in breathing. Occasionally, polyps will be so large as to extrude from the nostrils.

What is the treatment for nasal polyps?

When polyps are obstructive, they should be removed surgically. However, the basic treatment should be directed toward determining the cause of the condition and toward preventing recurrence of the polyps.

What operation is performed for the removal of the polyps?

A polypectomy is usually performed under local anesthesia in the surgeon's office or in the hospital. The polyp is grasped with a forceps and a wire snare is introduced over the polyp as close to its attachment as possible. The snare is drawn tight and the polyp is removed.

Does this operation keep one from work for a long time?

No. Most patients may return to work the day following surgery.

NASAL SINUSES

What are the nasal sinuses, and where are they located?

The sinuses are mucous-membrane-lined air spaces, and are located within the bones of the face and skull. They communicate, through small openings, with the nasal cavity. The frontal sinuses are located within the bone just above and behind the eyebrows; the maxillary sinuses are located within the bones of the cheeks beneath the eyes; the ethmoid sinuses are located near the side of the nose and inner aspect of the eyes and extend backward into the skull; and the sphenoid sinuses are located deep in the skull above the level of the throat.

What is the function of the sinuses?

These air-lined spaces lighten the

weight of the head and contribute to the resonance of the voice.

Is inflammation of the sinuses (sinusitis) a common condition?

Sinusitis is one of the most common conditions encountered in the entire field of medicine. It consists of an inflammation of the mucous membrane lining of one or more of the sinuses. When all the sinuses are involved, the condition is called pansinusitis.

What causes sinusitis?

It is usually secondary to an infection in the nasal cavity, although the maxillary sinus may become infected as a result of an extension from a tooth infection in the upper jaw. Swimming, diving, and injuries or fractures of the bones overlying the sinuses may also cause inflammation to take place. Anatomical deformities that block the sinus openings and allergies with nasal polyp formation may also predispose to sinusitis.

Are sinus infections more likely to occur in certain climates?

Yes. Those who live in damp, muggy climates or in areas in which there are marked fluctuations in temperature are more prone to develop sinus infections. Also, those who constantly breathe polluted air show a greater tendency toward sinusitis. People who live in dry, warm, equable climates show the lowest incidence of sinus infection.

What are the symptoms of sinusitis?

They vary according to the sinus involved. The most common symptoms are:

1. Tenderness over the infected sinus
2. A nasal quality to the voice
3. Nasal obstruction, with discharge from the nose or down the back of the nose

4. Severe headache, worse on lowering the head
5. Elevated temperature

How is the diagnosis of sinusitis made?

Sinusitis is usually suspected when a cold has persisted for more than one week. The presence of pain or tenderness over the affected sinus, headache, and the symptoms enumerated above will tend to establish the diagnosis. It can be confirmed by transillumination of the sinus with a strong light in a dark room and by taking x-rays.

Which sinuses are most prone to develop inflammation?

The maxillary, frontal, and ethmoid sinuses.

What is the treatment for sinusitis?

Most cases will respond well to medical treatment. This should consist of bed rest, steam inhalations, warm compresses to the affected sinus area, nosedrops to lessen the congestion of the nasal mucous membranes, and the use of antibiotic and antihistaminic drugs. If the fever is high, medicines such as aspirin should be used. If the pain is severe, pain-relieving drugs such as codeine may be used. Further medical treatment in the physician's office will consist of nasal packs and various methods of removing the nasal discharge by the use of suction. Cultures of the sinus discharge are frequently taken to determine the exact germ involved and to test the sensitivity of these bacteria to the various antibiotic drugs.

What cases of sinusitis require surgery?

Those that fail, after a prolonged period of time, to respond to the above-mentioned medical management.

What operations are carried out for sinusitis?

The aim of all operations for sinusitis

is to obtain adequate drainage and, in some cases, to remove diseased mucous membranes and bone. Most of these operations are done under local anesthesia, but some may require general anesthesia.

What operations are usually performed upon the maxillary sinus?
1. Simple puncture of the sinus through the nose, with irrigation and suction
2. The cutting of a large window in the side wall of the nose into the sinus to promote drainage
3. A radical sinusotomy, in which the mucous membrane lining the sinus is lifted away from the underlying bone and scraped out. In this operation, the incision is made inside the mouth beneath the upper lip

What operations are performed on the frontal sinus?
Formerly, the frontal sinus was irrigated through the nose, but this is done rarely today. If surgery is necessary, an incision is made in the skin below the inner portion of the eyebrow, and a small hole is cut in the bony floor of the frontal sinus. If the infection has involved the surrounding bone, it may become necessary to do a radical frontal sinusotomy. In this event, a larger incision is made and the entire bony floor of the frontal sinus is removed. Although frontal sinus operations are serious, the results are usually good and the majority of patients recover completely.

What operations are performed on the ethmoid sinuses?
These sinuses can usually be approached and scraped out through the nose. If the infection is severe or has involved the sphenoid sinus or has broken through to involve the tissues

about the eyes, it may be necessary to do an external ethmoidectomy. In this event, the incision is simply a prolongation downward of the same type of incision that is made for a frontal sinus infection.

What operations are used for inflammation of the sphenoid sinus?
Under local anesthesia, this sinus can be probed and irrigated through the nose. As a severe sphenoid infection may lead to brain infection or blindness, it is sometimes necessary to do a radical operation in conjunction with a complete ethmoidectomy.

How effective is sinus surgery?
The great majority of cases are improved through surgery.

How long a hospital stay is necessary after major sinus surgery?
Usually seven to ten days.

Does sinusitis ever recur after surgery?
Yes, but in a small minority of cases.

How does one treat recurrent sinusitis?
It is treated as a new infection and is handled in the same way as an original infection.

NOSEBLEEDS

Nosebleeds are extremely common occurrences among people of all ages. There may be local or general causes, or a combination of both. In many cases, despite thorough search, no apparent cause for the nosebleed can be found.

Nosebleeds arising from a systemic condition require expert medical advice in order to determine and treat the underlying disease.

What causes nosebleeds?
There may be local or general causes

or a combination of both. In many cases, there is no apparent cause.

What are some of the local causes of nosebleed?

1. Injury to the nose or the base of the skull, with or without fracture
2. Foreign body in the nose
3. Operations upon the nose
4. Violent coughing, sneezing, or nose blowing
5. Nose picking
6. Ulcerations caused by disease, such as syphilis and tuberculosis
7. Benign or malignant tumors within the nose or sinuses
8. Varicose veins of the mucous membranes of the nose
9. An acute inflammation of the mucous membrane lining of the nose, as occurs in allergy, sinusitis, or the common cold

What are some of the general causes of nosebleeds?

1. High blood pressure
2. Blood disorders, such as hemophilia, pernicious anemia, purpura, scurvy, leukemia, and jaundice
3. Atmospheric changes, such as in mountain climbing, diving, or descending to great depths within the sea

How can one distinguish between a nosebleed caused by a local condition and one caused by a general condition?

If the bleeding arises from one nostril only, the cause is more likely to be local. Also, thorough nasal examination will reveal a bleeding point or other local cause.

How can nosebleeds be controlled?

There are really two types of nosebleeds. Over 90 percent occur in the anterior part of the nose, arising from the septum or more rarely from the anterior ethmoid area. The point of bleeding can usually be found and controlled by cauterization under local anesthesia. This can be done by chemicals, such as silver nitrate or chromic acid, or by electric coagulation.

What should be done as a first aid measure for nosebleed?

Since the vast majority occur in the anterior part of the nasal septum, they can be controlled by simple continuous pressure applied to the side of the nose from which the bleeding arises. It is well to put a piece of cotton in the nose, possibly moistened with some nosedrops, if available. Pressure against this piece of cotton should be maintained for at least ten minutes. The person should be sitting up, with his head tilted forward, to prevent blood from trickling down his throat.

What can be done for bleeding arising from the posterior part of the nose?

This type cannot be self-treated. People with this condition must be hospitalized, as it is usually necessary to pack the posterior part of the nose through the mouth.

How long is the nasal packing left in place?

The posterior packing is left in place for about one week. Anterior packing should be removed gradually, starting generally about the fourth day.

What is the treatment for nosebleeds that arise from a general condition?

Expert medical advice must be obtained, and treatment of the underlying disease must be instituted.

NOSE AND SINUSES IN CHILDREN

Obstruction to nose breathing is exceptionally common in children. This is unfortunate, because mouth breathing is not nearly so efficient and often causes the child great discomfort. One of the most common causes of chronic nasal obstruction is enlarged adenoids, and, when they cause continued mouth breathing, they should be removed. If it is thought that an allergic condition is affecting the nasal passages, an allergist should be consulted.

Are children ever born with such small nostrils that they have difficulty in nasal breathing?

Yes. Children are occasionally born with partial or total obstruction of the rear openings of the nose as it connects with the throat. This obstruction, known as atresia, may be bony, in which event it will require surgical correction. This type of obstruction not only causes interference with nasal breathing but also interferes with proper feeding and sucking.

When should an operation be performed on a child with too small a nasal passage?

As soon as possible after birth. Failure to do this may result in nursing and feeding problems that will greatly hinder the child's normal growth and development.

Are some children naturally mouth breathers?

No. It is not natural for a child to breathe through his mouth. The fact that a child breathes through his mouth indicates that there is something wrong.

What are some of the causes of mouth breathing?

1. An acute inflammation of the mucous membrane of the nose, such as occurs during the common cold
2. An allergic rhinitis

3. Nasal polyps (uncommon in young children)
4. A deviated septum
5. Enlarged adenoids
6. Poor hygiene with hardened crusts of mucus within the nostrils
7. Chronic sinus infection

Do children who breathe through their mouths tend to develop upper respiratory infections?

Yes.

What is the purpose of nosedrops?

To shrink the mucous membranes and thus open up clogged air passages.

Should a mother or nursemaid cleanse the inside of a baby's nose?

Yes, but only when crusts or mucus are obstructing the nostrils. In such instances, a cotton-tipped applicator moistened in warm water or peroxide should be used. If the crusts are very difficult to dislodge, the applicator should be moistened with a small amount of mineral oil.

If an older child is unable to blow the mucus out of his nose, its removal can be facilitated by use of a nasal suction bulb, which can be purchased in any drugstore. The child's physician will instruct the mother on its use.

Should nosedrops be given to an infant or small child?

Nosedrops may not be beneficial if the child is merely suffering from a common cold or upper respiratory infection. It is best to ask the pediatrician's advice before giving nosedrops.

Should nasal sprays containing oil be used in children?

No. Some of the oil may leak down through the back of the throat and cause irritation or inflammation of the bronchial tubes and lungs.

Are there any medications on the market today that will shrink the mucous membranes in the nose and throat and make nosedrops unnecessary?

Yes, but they should only be used on the advice of a physician.

What harm can come from using improper types of nosedrops?

Some nosedrops are made up in an oily base. If this oil passes down the back of the nose into the child's throat and lungs, it may cause a serious type of pneumonia. For this reason, nosedrops containing any oily substance should not be used.

Do children ever put foreign bodies into their nostrils?

Yes, particularly small children. Very often the parent is unaware that this has happened. Days later, there may be a foul odor emanating from one nostril, and the parent may note the appearance of a pus discharge.

How else will a parent know that there is a foreign body in the child's nose?

The child will breathe through only one nostril, or he may try to get the object out by himself after it has been in his nose for a while.

Can all foreign bodies be seen by looking into the nostrils?

No. In some instances the child has tried so strenuously to get the object out that it has been pushed farther in toward the interior of the nose.

Should a parent attempt to remove a foreign body from a child's nose?

Only if it can be seen readily and can be grasped without going deeply into the nasal passage. This is unusual. The parent may stimulate the child to sneeze out the foreign body by tickling the nostril or putting a little pepper near the nose.

What should a parent do if the foreign body is not sneezed out or cannot readily be removed?

The child should be taken to a physician, who will remove it with a forceps. It is important for the parent not to act alarmed, because this will frighten the child.

Can the presence of a foreign body in the nose cause any permanent harm?

No, because sooner or later it will be discovered and removed.

What are the signs and symptoms of sinusitis in a child?

Most children develop a headache, which is worse on rapid changing of head position. A cold that lasts much longer than one would ordinarily expect is an early sign. The child develops a nasal tone to his voice and discharges a good deal of mucus and pus down the back of his nose and into his throat. In the acute form, there is pain over the infected sinus and a marked elevation of temperature. In advanced cases, the area over the child's frontal or maxillary sinuses may be tender to finger pressure if these sinuses are involved in the inflammatory process.

Is it necessary to operate on a child to cure a severe sinus infection?

It is rarely necessary, because most sinus infections subside without surgical drainage. In an occasional case, when there is a high fever and the germ causing the infection is exceptionally virulent, it may be necessary to make a surgical opening into the sinus to permit the free drainage of pus.

How can a parent prevent a child from getting recurrent sinus infections?

By taking special care when the child has a cold. The child should be put to bed and kept warm. Also, the child must be instructed not to blow his nose too hard, as this may force infected mucus from the nasal cavity up into the sinus openings.

Should a child with a tendency to develop sinusitis wear nose clips when he swims?

Yes. They are particularly necessary when diving or jumping into the water.

PLASTIC SURGERY OF THE NOSE

The shape of the nose is considered to be of the utmost importance. Concepts of beauty decree that the nose should be straight or upturned, thin, in the midline of the face, and not too long. It is impossible to calculate the amount of unhappiness that some people suffer because of a hooked, crooked, bulbous, or overly long nose. It is not surprising, therefore, that many seek help from plastic surgeons and it is good to report that most people can be greatly improved in their appearance.

One of the real dangers in embarking upon plastic operations of this type is that patients frequently develop a preconceived notion of what they will look like after surgery. They envisage a perfect nose and a beautiful or handsome face even when they lack other necessary equipment to attain such a state. It is important that they be cautioned not to expect the impossible and they must be told that a perfect cosmetic result cannot be obtained.

Almost every nasal deformity can be corrected to a certain degree, and most people are highly satisfied with their postoperative appearance. Unfortunately, a small group of people have deep-seated neuroses which focus upon the nose and blame it for their lack of social success. These people need psychiatric help more than plastic surgery,

and it is wiser for them to seek such aid before undergoing a nasal operation.

Before operating, it must be determined that there is no acute or chronic nose or sinus infection. Also, preoperative photographs of the patient's face and nose are taken. Occasionally plastic surgeons will make a plaster face mask to compare with the postoperative appearance. It is *not* usually possible, however, for the surgeon to accurately predict the ultimate effect of the repair.

Is a plastic operation ever indicated for other than cosmetic reasons?

Yes, for nasal obstruction.

Can all nasal deformities be corrected through plastic surgery?

Almost every deformity can be corrected to a certain degree.

What are the common types of nasal deformity?

1. A twisted nose

2. Deformities of the tip of the nose or nostrils

3. Depression of the bridge and ridge of the nose, called saddle nose

4. Hump nose or hook nose

Is there a standard appearance for the nose?

No. Different peoples and races have different standards of beauty or acceptability. However, in today's society the most acceptable and pleasing angle between the lip and the nose is an angle of between 90 and 95 degrees.

What is meant by the expression "a perfect nose"?

In the absolute sense, there is no such thing as a perfect nose. The best one can say is that a nose should fit the face.

What are some of the important factors in determining the results of plastic surgery upon the nose?

1. The age of the patient. The best

results are obtained in those from 16 to 30 years of age.

2. The skin. The quality of the skin, including its thickness, thinness, and tendency toward oiliness.

3. The extent of the deformity. The greater the deformity, the more difficult it is to get a perfect result.

4. The type of deformity. Certain types of deformity are much harder to cure than others.

5. The mental stability of the patient. The results are poorer among neurotic patients who have a tendency to worry about insignificant defects.

Are the results good when an operation is performed upon a child rather than upon an adult?

Complete nasal operations should wait until the nose is fully formed; this does not take place until the child has attained at least the age of 15. Lesser operations can sometimes be done at an earlier age.

What operation is performed for a plastic procedure on the nose?

All the incisions are made within the nose, and the skin of the nose is loosened or undermined to free it from the bone and cartilage that make up the framework of the nose. The framework of the nose is then cut and shaped according to a plan laid out before operation. The skin then falls back upon the reshaped framework and is sutured into position. Packing is placed within the nose and a dressing is placed on the outside of the nose to help maintain the new position of the bone and cartilage. As time passes, the skin will attach itself to the newly shaped bony and cartilaginous framework of the nose.

Plastic surgery of the nose is also called rhinoplasty.

How is a saddle nose built up?

A piece of cartilage or bone is grafted from the patient's own body or is supplied by a cartilage or bone bank. The graft originates from the rib or hipbone. Occasionally, silicone-rubber may be implanted.

Are any scars visible after plastic operations upon the nose?

No, because incisions are usually made within the nasal cavity or in the folds at the flare of the nostrils.

Is it possible for the patient to select the type of nose he desires?

Only to a certain degree. The surgeon must first overcome the defects of the nose and then he will try to create a result pleasing to his patient. The patient must understand clearly before surgery that an exact prediction cannot be made as to the specific appearance of the nose after surgery.

Can the patient obtain a good approximate idea of what his nose will look like after surgery?

Yes. An approximation can be foretold.

How long does a plastic operation on the nose take to perform?

Approximately one hour.

What anesthesia is used?

Local anesthesia, fortified by sedation.

Are plastic operations upon the nose painful procedures?

No.

How long a hospital stay is necessary?

Two to four days.

Is it common for the eyes to be discolored or swollen after this operation?

Yes. This will begin to subside in approximately 48 hours, but may not completely disappear for a week or two.

When are the dressings finally removed from the nose after a plastic operation?

In 7 to 14 days.

Does a plastic operation upon the nose affect the sense of smell?

No.

How long after a plastic operation on the nose can one breathe reasonably well?

After removal of the intranasal packing, about the fifth to seventh day.

After a nose has healed completely following a plastic operation, must special care be exercised not to injure it?

No. A healed nose following plastic surgery is just as strong as any other nose.

Do noses that have undergone plastic surgery tend to sag and change shape months or years later?

No. They will heal in the position that is present immediately following the surgical procedure.

May swelling of the nose persist even for several months after plastic surgery?

Yes. It may take several months or even a year for the nose to attain its absolute permanent shape and for *all* of the swelling to disappear.

How soon after a plastic operation on the nose can one return to work and to social functions?

In approximately two weeks, even though some swelling may remain.

Is it possible to repeat a plastic operation if the result of the first operation is unsatisfactory?

Yes, but it is best to wait at least six to eight months before repeating the surgery, so that stabilization of healing has had an opportunity to develop.

How successful are plastic operations upon the nose?

The overall improvement is almost always good and the general degree of satisfaction is high. When results are poor, they can often be remedied by reoperation.

TUMORS OF THE NOSE AND SINUSES

Are tumors of the nose and sinuses common?

The benign tumors are rather common. Among these, one would include nasal polyps, warts, and hemangiomas (small blood vessel tumors). Fortunately, malignant tumors are not very common in this area.

What is the treatment for benign tumors of the nose or sinuses?

Most of these can be removed readily under local anesthesia in the surgeon's office.

What is the treatment for malignant tumors of the nose and sinuses?

Cancer of the nose or sinuses is treated by wide surgical removal of the growth and surrounding tissues. Extensive plastic surgery is usually performed at a later date, after the physician is reasonably sure that all of the cancer was completely removed.

How successful is surgery for tumors of the nose and sinuses?

Surgery for benign tumors is uniformly successful. The success of surgery for cancer depends upon the time at which the surgery is performed and upon the degree of malignancy. If the surgery has been done before the cancer has spread to distant tissues, the expectation of cure is good. Modern surgical techniques may include the lifesaving measures in which large sections of the nose, face, cheek, the roof of the mouth, or the floor of the orbit are removed.

Can cosmetic reconstruction be carried out after radical surgery upon the nose and sinuses?

Yes. Modern advances in technique in plastic surgery can effect remarkable restoration toward normal appearance.

Obesity

Even though constitutional tendencies toward obesity may exist, the main cause of overweight is overeating. Glandular imbalance is an infrequent cause of obesity. An excess caloric intake will make anyone fat, no matter what his age. Any reducing diet that contains fewer calories than the body needs during the course of a day's activity will result in weight loss.

There are two kinds of surgery for relief of obesity: local removal of excess fat, and an abdominal operation in which an intestinal bypass is carried out to cut down on absorption of ingested substances. Local removal of excess fat, lipectomy, is essentially a cosmetic procedure, most often performed to reduce the size of the abdomen, hips, or thighs. The success of local fat excision depends in great measure upon the patient's ability to maintain a strict reducing diet after surgery. Failure to do this will inevitably result in new depositions of fat in the areas operated upon. Unfortunately, operations to reduce the size of the legs have proved disfiguring and unsuccessful in the great majority of cases. Plastic operations upon the breasts, on the other hand, have a high expectation of success, but in most instances, excess *breast* tissue rather than fat is removed.

Within the past few years a new operation has been devised for the treatment of those who suffer from extreme obesity. It consists of cutting across the small intestines approximately 12 to 18 inches from its beginning and implanting the upper segment into a lower segment of small intestine about 12 to 18 inches from the large bowel. This maneuver prevents ingested material from traversing some 15 or more feet of small intestine. The long, bypassed segment of small intestine is then implanted into the large bowel about 2 feet above the rectum. As a consequence of this procedure, the great bulk of food is not absorbed into the body and the patient loses huge quantities of weight (see diagram).

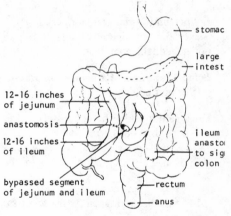

INTESTINAL BYPASS OPERATION FOR OBESITY

The intestinal bypass operation is presently in its experimental stage and cannot be routinely recommended for all stout people. It should be limited to those who are young, in good general health, and who are at least 75 to 100 pounds overweight. The operation is followed by great imbalance in body chemistry and may result in marked vitamin and mineral deficiencies. In several cases reported in the literature it has been necessary to reoperate and to undo the bypass.

QUESTIONS AND ANSWERS

Can excess fat be removed successfully?

Yes, but results will be good only temporarily unless the patient maintains normal weight postoperatively.

What areas can be made thinner through local fat removal (lipectomy)?
1. Double chins
2. Breasts
3. Abdomens
4. Hips
5. Thighs

Can the calves and thighs be made thinner?

These procedures are not usually successful.

Is lipectomy a dangerous operation?

No, but postoperative infection is a not infrequent complication.

Is local fat removal a painful operation?

Not particularly.

Does one's skin hang loosely after excess fat has been removed?

This will not occur because excess skin is usually excised along with the fat.

Will scars be permanent after local fat excision?

Yes. The scars will appear much like those from any other operation in which the skin is incised. Of course, if the operative site is on an exposed area, the surgeon will do his best to make the scarring minimal.

Is there any way to dissolve fat without operating?

No, except by general weight loss.

Is the intestinal bypass operation usually successful in bringing about great weight loss?

Yes.

Why can't any obese individual undergo the intestinal bypass procedure?

First of all, extremely fat people are usually poor operative risks and the procedure is therefore limited to those who are in good general health. Secondly, this operation is sometimes complicated by repeated episodes of dehydration, diarrhea, acidosis, and chemical and mineral imbalance. Older people, and those not in good general health, withstand these complications very poorly.

When is the bypass operation indicated?

When the patient is extremely fat, when all nonsurgical methods have failed to accomplish satisfactory weight loss, and when the patient's general condition will be able to withstand the operation.

How much weight can one lose following the intestinal bypass procedure?

There are a considerable number of people who have lost well over 100 pounds after undergoing this type of surgery.

Can one eat as much as he wants and not gain weight after a bypass operation?

Yes, in most instances. This is because very little of the ingested food reaches that part of the small intestine from which absorption normally takes place.

Is it necessary to receive ongoing medical care after a bypass operation for obesity?

Yes. These patients must see their physician regularly and must undergo repeated physical examination and laboratory tests to make sure they do not become dehydrated or acidotic.

Are supplementary vitamins and minerals necessary after a bypass operation?

Yes. Deficiencies are the general rule after this procedure.

Omentum

The omentum is a fatty, apronlike membrane hanging down from the stomach and transverse colon in the abdominal cavity. It is covered over by a thin sheet of cells which are in actuality an extension of the membrane lining the abdominal cavity.

In years past, the omentum was referred to as the active protector of the peritoneal cavity, and it was claimed that it traveled about from place to place within the abdominal cavity to combat infections. Many investigators spoke of the omentum as "the policeman of the abdomen" whose duty it was to rush to the scene of trouble to extinguish infection. However, during recent years, it has been concluded that the omentum does not possess these attributes and is merely an inert structure with no real function. The explanation for its presence at the site of inflammation or infection is that it becomes adherent to inflamed structures merely by being in the vicinity. On such occasions, it may tend to localize the infection but it does so passively, not actively.

QUESTIONS AND ANSWERS

What is meant by the term omentopexy?

This is an operation that fastens the omentum to some other structure in an attempt to create new channels for circulation.

Omentopexy has not been very successful, but has been tried in cases where there is obstruction to the flow of blood through the liver, as in cirrhosis. In these cases, the omentum was sutured to the muscles of the abdominal wall.

Omentopexy was also done by suturing the omentum to the outer muscle of the heart in order to improve the blood supply to that organ. Neither one of these operations has proved very successful.

Recently, the omentum has been used to increase the blood supply to a damaged kidney. Some investigators have reported encouraging results after this operation.

What is omentectomy?

It is an operation in which the omentum is removed. This is carried out sometimes following removal of the stomach or part of the large bowel, because it has been found that the omentum harbors lymph nodes which might be involved in the spread of tumor cells from the liver or bowel.

What is an omental graft?

A piece of the omentum is sometimes dissected and applied to a raw surface of an abdominal organ. It is also used sometimes as a patch over a ruptured ulcer after the ulcer has been closed.

Does the omentum ever become involved in a disease?

It may be the site of a cyst, and in rare instances it may be the site of a primary tumor formation.

Omphalocele

An omphalocele is a birth defect in which the primitive embryonic yolk sac fails to return to its normal place within the abdominal cavity. This creates a large defect and leaves a jellylike, transparent membrane covering the abdomen in the region of the umbilicus. A child born with an omphalocele must be taken directly to the operating room for repair, as peritonitis will set in unless the abdominal wall is closed over with skin.

See also HERNIA.

Oophorectomy

Oophorectomy is the term for surgical removal of one or both ovaries.

See also OVARIES.

Orchiectomy

Orchiectomy is the term for surgical removal of one or both of the testicles. The procedure is carried out when the testicles have been destroyed by infection, when they are the site of a tumor, and in some instances when the patient has a cancer of the prostate gland.

See also TESTICLES.

Organ and Tissue Transplants

Few surgical accomplishments excite the public's imagination more than announcements that a vital organ has been "successfully" transplanted from one individual to another. It conjures up in the minds of those who have an irreparably diseased organ the magical possibility of a cure through the grafting of a healthy replacement. For some who are old and fear the end of life because of worn-out structures, it offers the hope of an extended life-span. And to the relatives of the chronic invalid, it proffers the bright prospect of restoring a loved one to normalcy.

Although transplantation of certain organs is often a feasible surgical maneuver and there have been a rather large number of cases in which the operative procedures have been carried out successfully, the public must nevertheless be informed that the *end results* are not yet satisfactory. In most instances, the transplanted organ has undergone degeneration and has become useless within a period of days, weeks, or months. The reasons for this unhappy termination will be discussed later in this section, but first it might be well to discuss the various types of transplants or grafts.

QUESTIONS AND ANSWERS

What are the various types of transplants or grafts?

1. An autotransplant is one in which an organ or tissue is transferred from one part of a patient's own body to another. This type of graft is successful in the majority of cases provided that the blood supply of the grafted structure can be preserved or circulation restored in its new situation. Thus a kidney whose ureter (the tube conducting the urine from the kidney to the bladder) has been destroyed by injury or disease can be transplanted to a new site in the pelvis. In the new location, its main artery and vein can be sutured to nearby pelvic blood vessels and the upper, healthy portion of its ureter can be attached, by sutures, directly to the bladder. Recently it has proved feasible to transplant an adrenal gland from its usual location above the kidney to a new site in the thigh. And, of course, everyone is familiar with the fact that skin can be grafted from one part of the body to another and that portions of bone can be transferred to other locations with every expectation of success.

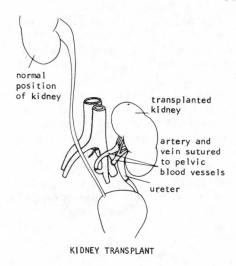

KIDNEY TRANSPLANT

quiring little or no active arterial blood supply in order to survive have a much better chance of living when transplanted into a recipient. This is borne out by the fact that cartilage from a cow has been used successfully on innumerable occasions in plastic operations upon the face. Bovine cartilage has been used to build up a receding chin or to fill in a saddle defect in the nose.

3. Homotransplants involve the transfer of an organ or tissue from one human to another. In most instances, such grafts are accepted by the recipient for a few days or even a week or two, and then a *rejection phenomenon* sets in. In some cases when an organ, such as a kidney, has been transferred from the body of one identical twin to another, this reaction does not occur and the recipient accepts the graft and uses it as if it were its own.

2. Heterotransplants are those in which an organ from one species of animal is transplanted into another species. Although almost all of these operations have been followed by eventual rejection of the graft, there have been recent reports of temporarily successful grafts of chimpanzee kidneys into humans. It should also be noted that tissues re-

What type of transplant has the best chance of surviving?

Autotransplants have by far the best chance of survival. Homografts from an identical twin have a good chance of survival.

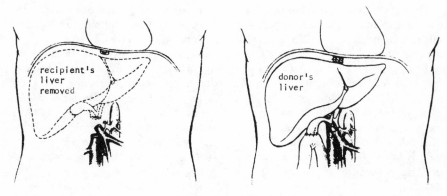

LIVER TRANSPLANT

In a liver transplant, the patient's diseased liver is cut away from the main veins and arteries (left). The donor's liver is placed in position and sutured to the large blood vessels, and function is restored (right).

Which types of grafts have the least chance of survival?

Homografts survive occasionally if the rejection reaction can be suppressed sufficiently. Heterografts survive only in very rare instances.

What are the most frequently transplanted tissues or organs?

By far the most commonly transplanted tissue is skin, but cartilage, bone, blood vessels, kidneys, hearts, livers, corneas, adrenal glands, thyroid and parathyroid gland tissue, and lungs have also been transplanted successfully.

What are some of the organs that technically can be transplanted from one human to another?

The most suitable organs for grafting are those whose attachments to surrounding structures are simple in that there are just one or two main arteries or veins entering and exiting from them. Organs that have important nerve attachments or that are connected by many blood vessels and ductal structures are usually unsuitable for transplantation.

The following group of organs have been transplanted thus far. In perusing this list, it should be kept in mind that the technical ability to carry out a transplant operation in no way implies that the organ will function and live in the new environment. Moreover, it should be reemphasized that this work is just in its earliest experimental stages.

1. Kidneys: Transplantation of kidneys is by far the most frequent organ-grafting procedure up to the present time.

The operative procedure is a most complicated one and involves the removal of *both* diseased kidneys and the spleen, prior to inserting a healthy donor kidney. The spleen is removed in some patients in order to decrease the severity of the rejection crisis. In some clinics, the thymus gland, beneath the breastbone in the chest, is also removed in an attempt to further reduce the intensity of the rejection phenomenon.

As only one functioning kidney is necessary in order to preserve life, and since donor kidneys from live humans are so extremely difficult to obtain, it is usual practice to insert a single kidney graft. The new kidney is placed in the pelvic region, where its main artery and vein can be rather readily sutured to the large vessels (hypogastric artery and iliac vein) in the vicinity and where the upper end of the ureter can be connected to the urinary bladder.

2. Blood vessels: Some 10 to 15 years ago, it was rather common practice among those performing vascular (blood vessel) surgery to utilize arteries and veins which could be spared from one part of the patient's body and transplant them to new locations. However, knitted or woven Teflon and Dacron have proved to be superior even to one's own tissues, and these materials are now used in almost all such operations.

3. Tendons: For a considerable time now, orthopedic surgeons have been successfully transplanting tendons, and tendons with muscles attached, to new locations where they will take up the function of paralyzed or destroyed structures. These operations give satisfactory results in the majority of instances, provided that the tendons originate from the patient's own body. Homografts (those coming from another individual) usually undergo degeneration.

4. Adrenal glands: These are two endocrine glands located above the kidneys. Their main secretions, epinephrine (adrenalin) and cortisone, are vitally important to continuation of life, and if both adrenals are removed, it is essential that cortisone be given in order to sustain life.

If both adrenal glands are removed in an attempt to slow down the growth and spread of a breast cancer, it is essential that cortisone be given indefinitely. Recently, however, it has been found that if a portion of one gland is grafted to a new location in the upper thigh, sufficent cortisone will reach the bloodstream to maintain life. This is accomplished by suturing the main adrenal vein to the saphenous vein of the thigh.

5. Heart: The heart is a four-chambered muscular structure whose attachments to the circulatory system are by two large veins which enter its atria (auricles) and two large arteries which leave its ventricles. Because of this relatively simple anatomical arrangement, it is quite feasible from a technical point of view to transplant a heart from one individual to another. While the operation is being performed, the patient is hooked up to a cardiopulmonary pump apparatus which aerates (oxygenates) and circulates the blood throughout the body.

Heart transplantation has been performed on a large number of patients throughout the world. Within the few years since the first human heart was transplanted, there has been an amazingly rapid increase in the length of time recipients of the hearts have survived. This remarkable achievement can be attributed to the team effort that has gone into these operations. The public should be aware that the team necessary to carry out a successful heart transplant involves many different types of specialists.

6. Lung: Since this organ's main attachments are rather simple, lung transplantation is not too difficult a surgical procedure. Lung transplantation has been performed on several

patients, and there is no doubt that one day, transplantation of this organ will be quite common.

7. Spleen: There have been extremely few spleen transplants, because a person can live without this organ. Spleen transplants have been attempted, however, in certain cases in which the patient lacked vital white blood cells.

8. Liver: This is a difficult organ to transplant. Despite the difficulties, the procedure has been carried out on several dozen patients with survival up to several months in some cases.

9. Arms and legs: From time to time, there have been recorded cases of the resuturing to the body of a completely severed arm or leg. These operations border upon the miraculous and the mere survival of such an extremity is a cause for wonderment. It involves a tedious procedure in which each severed artery, vein, muscle, tendon, and nerve must be stitched back in its proper place. Unfortunately, in many cases where the circulation is satisfactorily reestablished, nerves do not regenerate sufficiently to permit adequate sensation or normal muscle function.

At a time in the not too distant future when the rejection phenomenon is conquered, it is conceivable that a donor arm from a fresh corpse could be transplanted to the body of an amputee with some expectation of success.

Does a successfully transplanted organ always react normally in its new environment?

No. It has been discovered that sometimes healthy transplanted organs may develop the same diseases as the structures they have replaced.

Can diseased arteries and blood vessels be replaced with a transplant?

Yes, this is one of the most successful areas for grafts and transplants. However, it has been learned that the transplantation of nonliving substances such as Dacron and Teflon is more satisfactory than the use of living tissue.

For what diseases of blood vessels are transplants advisable?

There are many conditions that are benefited by the use of Dacron or Teflon grafts. Some of these are as follows:

1. In certain cases of stroke, it has been found that the cause lies in arteriosclerosis of the carotid artery in the neck. This can be helped in many cases by coring out the narrow passageway of the carotid artery in the neck (endarterectomy) and by supplying a patch graft of Dacron or Teflon.

2. There are many cases in which there is such marked arteriosclerosis of the aorta in the abdomen that insufficient blood supply reaches the legs. In these cases, the abdominal aorta may be replaced with a Dacron or Teflon tubular graft, or its narrow passageway may be reamed out and a patch graft applied.

3. There are quite a large number of cases in which high blood pressure is due to arteriosclerosis and narrowing of the main artery to the kidney. In these cases, the renal artery can be cored out and a patch graft applied to it in order to broaden its passageway.

4. There are a large number of cases in which the circulation to the leg and foot is threatened by arteriosclerosis affecting the arteries in the pelvic region or in the thighs. In some of these cases, it is possible to replace the narrowed blood vessels with Dacron or Teflon grafts. When bypassing the arteries at the knee, most surgeons prefer to use a vein graft rather than a nonliving Dacron or Teflon graft.

5. An aneurysm of the aorta in the chest or abdomen is one of the most common reasons for the employment of a graft. An aneurysm is a bulging and blistering out with a thinning of the wall of an artery. If this is allowed to persist, the vessel may burst and may cause the patient's death. To overcome this, a Dacron or Teflon tubular graft can be used to replace the diseased segment of aorta.

6. Within recent years, it has been found that certain of the arteries within the abdomen which supply large segments of the intestinal tract may undergo arteriosclerosis, and in these cases a replacement with a Dacron or Teflon graft is feasible.

Can one look forward to a day when there will be an extension of the lifespan as a result of organ transplantation?

There is no question that within the next few decades, the life-span of many individuals will be prolonged by the successful transplantation and exchange of a healthy organ for a diseased one. Of course, in order for a patient to live extra years as a result of a transplant, other organs in his body must be in a relatively healthy state, for it is not possible to transplant all of the worn-out structures.

Where can donor organs be obtained?

1. The most ideal donor of an organ is a healthy identical twin. Since only 1 out of 80 births is twins, it is obvious that this source is meager and could not ever hope to cope with most situations.

2. Healthy adults of similar blood groups constitute the present major source of supply for organs to be transplanted. Whereas it was thought a few years ago that a loving relative would make the best donor, most researchers in this field now agree that they should not be requested to furnish the organ, nor should their voluntary proposal to act as a donor be accepted. The emotional involvement in such an arrangement can in too many instances be detrimental to both the recipient and the donor.

In certain clinics where this type of experimental surgery is being done, organs have on occasion been supplied by convicts who, through their generosity, hope to earn a reprieve. Elsewhere, organs have been donated by altruistic members of the community who hope, by their noble gesture, to contribute toward scientific progress.

3. Patients suffering from incurable diseases have from time to time come forth and volunteered to act as organ donors. Of course, this offer can only be accepted if the pervading disease has not in any way affected the organ to be transplanted.

4. Organs from cadavers can be used, but only under the following conditions:

a) The donor must have died from a noninfectious or noncontagious disease.

b) The donor must have died from a noncancerous disease.

c) The organ must be removed from the corpse *immediately* after its death and must be transplanted into the recipient within several hours after it is removed.

d) The organ must be removed from the corpse under strictly aseptic conditions.

e) It is preferable, though not absolutely essential, that the donor and recipient be of the same blood group.

5. Animals. As stated above, most grafts of organs from animals to man have been unsuccessful. This is to be expected, as the various immunological responses of man would tend to reject as a foreign body tissues that originated from another species.

Do the majority of transplants from one individual to another survive?

Unfortunately, no. The reason for this is that all humans have antibodies and immune bodies circulating in their bloodstreams. It is the function of these substances to protect the individuals from the invasion of foreign bodies. Foreign bodies usually consist of bacteria, viruses, or inert particles that enter the body through infection or a break in the normal tissue barriers, or through an injury or wound. The body of the host reacts the same way toward transplanted organs or tissues as it does toward any other kind of foreign body, and the protective cells within the host bring about the ultimate destruction of the grafted tissue.

What is this reaction of the host to the transplant called?

There are two popular names for this phenomenon, namely, the rejection reaction and transplantation immunity.

THE REJECTION REACTION

All humans have cells and antibodies whose duty it is to protect against invading bacteria, viruses, and foreign bodies. Tissue cells from other humans or animals are considered by the host as foreign material and normal protective mechanisms will be mobilized to destroy them. Thus a transplanted organ will be attacked by various types of white cells (plasma cells and lymphocytes) and antibodies which circulate in the blood. The ultimate outcome is rejection of the transplant.

As one might suspect, these forces are not mobilized when a tissue or organ is transplanted from one part of a patient's own body to another.

Successful, permanent grafting of organs depends upon thwarting the recipient's natural defenses for a sufficient length of time to permit the transplant to become accepted as if it actually belonged in its new environment. In medical parlance this is known as overcoming transplantation immunity. It is interesting to note that patients whose defense mechanisms are overwhelmed by disease—such as patients who have cancer throughout their body—will *not* reject transplanted tissue or organs nearly as quickly or effectively as those who are in robust health.

The rejection process does not take place immediately after the graft is inserted. There is usually more or less normal function for a few days (usually some four to ten days), after which time the patient develops fever, pain in the area of the transplant, and evidences of loss of function in the grafted organ. If the reaction is not overcome or subdued promptly, an abscess may form involving the transplant. If it is a vital organ, such as a kidney, that degenerates, death will ensue unless another transplant is inserted.

Is it ever possible to overcome the rejection reaction?

Yes, a great deal of progress has been made within the past few years in this field. To overcome the rejection reaction it is necessary to temporarily immobilize or inhibit the antibodies of the recipient of the transplant.

Can a second attempt at transplantation be undertaken when the first one fails?

Yes. In this manner, life may be prolonged for another period of months or years.

COMBATING THE REJECTION
REACTION

Several methods have already been elaborated to combat the rejection phenomenon, and intense investigation is going on in many medical centers throughout the world to find new and better ways of accomplishing this task. It is safe to conjecture that a new era in surgery will be born when a truly effective and safe method of suppressing this reaction is discovered, for a transplanted organ can and will function satisfactorily in another person's body provided it is treated as a real "member of the family."

To decrease the production of cells that are most active in defending the body against foreign cells and antibodies, some surgeons have recommended the removal of the spleen and/or the thymus gland in the chest prior to transplantation of an organ. In addition, an antilymphocytic serum has been given in order to suppress the antibody reactions against the graft. Also, chemicals are given for the same purpose. Two such drugs are Imuran and actinomycin. Large and continuous doses of prednisone, a cortisone substance, are administered throughout the entire period. X-ray irradiation, either to the area of the graft or to the entire body, is given to slow the defense mechanisms. Needless to say, the patient's life is greatly endangered by this form of treatment, as all his defenses against bacteria and disease are temporarily knocked out of commission. Also, the large doses of cortisone given may result in severe diabetes and hemorrhage. To safeguard patients against overwhelming infection during this period, they must be isolated, kept under the most aseptic conditions, and given huge doses of antibiotics. The diabetes must be treated with insulin, and hemorrhage must be treated by multiple blood transfusions.

It may be necessary to continue the above routine for several days or weeks until it can be ascertained that the grafted organ has survived and is functioning. Unfortunately, even though the immediate rejection crisis appears to have abated, late rejection often occurs. Homotransplants (those from other people) may be rejected several months or a year or two after an apparently successful procedure.

Although the complications of this type of surgery are enormous and survival is questionable in a large number of cases, it should be kept in mind that transplantation of organs is reserved for those people who would certainly die if the procedures were not attempted. Moreover, each new case affords invaluable knowledge which will help toward the ultimate discovery of a safe, permanent method of carrying out this life-saving maneuver.

Can anything be done to suppress the rejection reaction?

Yes. Certain chemicals are given to inhibit the host's immune reactions; cortisone is given to suppress the antibodies; x-ray irradiation is applied to the grafted region or to the entire body; the spleen and sometimes the thymus gland are removed to decrease the supply of those cells that would attack the transplant and, finally, antilymphocytic globulin (ALG) is administered. If these forms of treatment are successful, the graft may survive for several months or even years.

If the initial rejection reaction is overcome, does this mean that the transplanted organ will survive indefinitely?

Unfortunately, no. Late rejection of a transplanted organ often takes place a year or more after the initial rejection crisis has passed.

Osgood-Schlatter's Disease

Osgood-Schlatter's disease is a fragmentation of the portion of the growth plate at the upper part of the shin close to the knee.

QUESTIONS AND ANSWERS

What causes Osgood-Schlatter's disease?

Injury to the knee, such as sudden acute flexion of the leg, causes some cases; in other instances, the cause is unknown.

How common is Osgood-Schlatter's disease?

It is quite common in boys, but is seldom seen in girls.

At what age does this condition occur most often?

Between 11 and 16 years of age.

Does Osgood-Schlatter's disease tend to affect children during their rapid-growth period?

Yes.

What are the usual signs and symptoms of Osgood-Schlatter's disease?

Pain, tenderness, and swelling at the front of the knee. The pain is more severe after activity.

How can one distinguish this condition from others?

By x-ray examination.

How serious is Osgood-Schlatter's disease?

It is not serious at all.

What is the treatment for Osgood-Schlatter's disease?

If there is pain, the knee may be placed in a cylinder cast extending from the upper thigh to above the ankle for several weeks. At times, the injection of cortisone into the region of swelling causes relief of the pain.

Should children with Osgood-Schlatter's disease be limited in their physical exercise?

Yes. They should avoid competitive, group, or contact sports such as football, basketball, soccer, tennis, and baseball. Swimming and golf are permissible.

Do most children with Osgood-Schlatter's disease recover completely?
Yes.

What are the possible complications of Osgood-Schlatter's disease?
1. Formation of a painful mass on the front of the knee.
2. At times, the normal shape of the upper end of the tibia (shinbone) may be altered.

Is there a tendency for Osgood-Schlatter's disease, once healed, to recur?
No.

Does Osgood-Schlatter's disease ever lead to shortening of the affected leg?
No.

Osteogenic Sarcoma

Osteogenic sarcoma is a malignant tumor of bone. Fortunately, these sarcomas are less common than benign bone growths.

Osteogenic sarcomas have a tendency to affect children and middle-aged adults. The precise diagnosis is made by noting the physical characteristics of the lesion, by x-ray examination, and by bone biopsy. All three of these investigative measures should be done prior to starting treatment, as cure can usually be obtained only through radical surgery with high amputation of the involved limb, followed by intensive irradiation. Although the ultimate outcome of treatment for malignant bone tumors is not as satisfactory as one would wish, more and more cases are being cured by earlier diagnosis and by newer methods of surgical treatment.

QUESTIONS AND ANSWERS

How can one distinguish between an osteogenic sarcoma and a benign bone tumor (osteoma)?
The various types of tumors have characteristic appearances on x-ray examination. A bone biopsy is often necessary to verify the clinical and x-ray diagnosis.

Are operations for the removal of osteogenic sarcoma serious?
Yes, and they constitute one of the most radical types of surgery, as it is often necessary to remove not only the involved limb but all of the lymph nodes leading from the limb.

Is cobalt or x-ray treatment ever given along with surgery in treatment of a bone tumor?
Yes. Malignant tumors are frequently treated with cobalt radiation or x-rays before or after surgery in order to prevent the spread of the tumor cells or to kill tumor cells that may have become implanted near the tumor site. The treatment of benign tumors with x-rays or cobalt radiation is rarely, if ever, indicated.

Can a patient be cured of a malignant bone tumor?
Yes, patients with malignant bone tumors often can be cured if treatment is begun early.

What are the symptoms of a bone tumor?
There is swelling in the affected area and some deep pain.

Osteoid Osteoma

An osteoid osteoma is a small (pea-sized), painful bone lesion with a characteristic x-ray appearance. It is most common in older children and young adults. It seldom becomes malignant. Pain is usually of a deep aching nature, is most severe at night, and is not aggravated by moving the limb.

Although an osteoid osteoma was formerly thought to be some type of harmless infection, no virus or bacteria has ever been found associated with the lesion. It may represent a special type of tumor.

QUESTIONS AND ANSWERS

How is an osteoid osteoma diagnosed?
By its characteristic x-ray appearance.

What is the treatment for an osteoid osteoma?
Surgical excision.

After an osteoid osteoma has been removed, does it have a tendency to recur?
No.

Osteomyelitis

Osteomyelitis, or bone infection, may take place in one of several ways:

1. Bacteria may travel through the bloodstream from some distant area where a primary infection exists and may lodge in bone. This type of condition occurs more often in children and is heralded by the onset of high fever, local swelling in the region of the bone involved, and stiffness of adjacent joints. A favorite site for this type of osteomyelitis is within the marrow near the growth plate (epiphysis) of bones in the thigh or leg. If the diagnosis is made early, the infection may be controlled solely by the use of antibiotics. On the other hand, if a localized bone abscess has developed prior to diagnosis, it becomes necessary to operate. An incision is made over the area of swelling and the diseased bone is exposed. A segment of bone overlying the abscess is removed, and all pus and diseased bone are evacuated. When the diagnosis of osteomyelitis is missed early during its development, layers of thick bone may be laid down surrounding the abscess core. This will make ultimate cure more difficult, and the condition will become chronic unless the infected core is removed.

Prompt and complete recovery within a matter of a few weeks is the general rule following adequate surgery and appropriate antibiotic therapy.

2. Osteomyelitis is not uncommon after a compound fracture, especially if there has been delay between the time of fracture and the institution of treatment. If infection does take hold, it often extends up and down the marrow cavity of the fractured bones and is most difficult to cure. In these cases, a shell of bone must be removed throughout the entire shaft of infected bone, thus converting it into a shallow cavity. This operative procedure is known as saucerization, as the bone is laid open and has the concave shape of a saucer.

It should be emphasized that antibiotics are not as effective in controlling infection within bones as they are in stemming soft tissue infections.

3. Osteomyelitis often results from direct extension of infection from adjacent soft tissues. The commonest place for this to occur is in the bones of the toes and feet in people who develop gangrene secondary to arteriosclerosis, diabetes, and infection. Final cure of such a foot infection is impossible unless the infected bone is removed. Saucerization or partial removal of infected small bones of the toes and feet is usually inadequate; their complete excision is necessary. Also, the diabetes and bacterial infection must be brought under control before solid healing can take place.

4. Tuberculous infection of bone is seen much less frequently today because of pasteurization of milk and improved hygienic conditions. Nonetheless, when a bone or joint is invaded by the tuberculosis germ, surgical intervention may be indicated. In former years, this type of surgery was complicated by the fear that the local operative procedure would cause the spread of the tuberculosis throughout the entire body. Today, with the great effectiveness of isoniazid, para-aminosalicylic acid, streptomycin, and other antituberculosis medications, this fear has been practically eliminated, and the surgical incision and cleaning out of tuberculous bone abscesses is a safe procedure.

Tuberculosis of the spine or a joint is sometimes treated by immobilization of the area by fusion and the employment of bone grafts. Thus a spine or knee so immobilized will permit the tuberculosis infection to become inactive and harmless.

QUESTIONS AND ANSWERS

What is osteomyelitis?

Osteomyelitis is a bacterial (germ) infection of bone.

Does acute osteomyelitis affect children very often?

It is not a common condition, but it is seen more often in children than in adults.

What causes acute osteomyelitis?

It is usually caused by bacteria that have traveled through the blood from some distant area where a primary infection is present.

Is osteomyelitis always caused by an infection that travels through the bloodstream?

No. It is not uncommon for infection of the bony fragments to occur following a compound fracture.

Is osteomyelitis ever caused by direct extension of bacterial infection from adjacent soft tissues?

Yes, but this type seldom occurs in children.

What are the symptoms of acute osteomyelitis?

Its onset is accompanied by high fever, swelling, pain, and tenderness in the area of the involved bone, and stiffness of the adjacent joints.

How high does the fever run in acute osteomyelitis?

It may rise to 104° or 105° F.

Where is acute osteomyelitis most likely to be located?

In the long bones of the thigh or leg near the growth plate (epiphysis).

Does a bone abscess usually result from acute osteomyelitis?

Yes, except when the diagnosis has been made early and large doses of antibiotics have been given. If the disease is diagnosed early, it is usually possible to prevent abscess formation.

Is osteomyelitis ever caused by the tuberculosis germ?

Years ago, tuberculosis was frequently caused by drinking contaminated milk. This was known as bovine tuberculosis. Since most milk is pasteurized today, bovine tuberculosis is rare. In regions of the world where milk is not pasteurized, however, bovine tuberculosis is relatively common. In these cases the bacteria will frequently invade bone and cause tuberculous osteomyelitis.

What parts of the body are most likely to be affected by tuberculous osteomyelitis?

The spinal column, the hip, and the knee.

What disease is most likely to be mistaken for tuberculosis of the hip joint?

Perthes' disease.

Are there drugs today that are effective in treating tuberculosis of bones?

Yes. The new drugs such as isoniazid, para-aminosalicylic acid, streptomycin, and other antituberculosis medications are most effective.

What is the treatment for tuberculosis of the hip or knee?

Absolute bed rest, traction, and administration of antituberculosis drugs such as isoniazid, para-aminosalicylic acid, and streptomycin. In most cases the joint must be operated upon to remove the diseased synovium (joint lining). In the past, most of these joints were fused to prevent the tuberculosis infection from spreading. Today, fusion is usually not necessary.

What operative procedures are carried out to overcome bone infection?

1. In the usual case of osteomyelitis in children, an incision is made over the swollen area and the infected bone is exposed. A segment of bone overlying the abscess is removed, and all pus and debris are evacuated.

2. If the bones of the toes or feet are grossly infected secondary to gangrene, it is often necessary to remove those bones in order to bring about cure.

3. Infected bone adjacent to a fracture must be saucerized. This means exposing the marrow along the entire shaft.

4. Tuberculosis of the spine is often treated by carrying out spinal fusion, using bone grafts taken from other parts of the patient's body.

5. Tuberculosis of joints, such as the knee, is often treated by joint fusion.

Is surgery for osteomyelitis dangerous?

No, but in many instances the patient is very ill due to his underlying disease.

Can osteomyelitis usually be cured by the use of antibiotics alone?

Only in very early cases. In most instances, surgery is required.

If tuberculosis has affected the spine is it necessary to immobliize the area?

Yes, in order to avoid spinal deformities. If deformity does ensue, it may be necessary to perform a spinal-fusion operation at a later date to avoid collapse of vertebrae and a humpback deformity.

What will happen if tuberculosis of the spine is not treated?

The patient may develop paralysis of the lower limbs due to the swelling of the spinal cord and the acute angulation of the spine itself.

Is recovery from osteomyelitis the general rule?

Yes. The combination of surgery and judicious use of the antibiotic drugs will result in cure in almost all cases. However, some cases of bone infection may take several months to eradicate completely. A small number may become chronic and persist for years.

Osteotomy

Osteotomy is a term for the surgical cutting of a bone. It is carried out quite frequently in orthopedic surgery to correct bone deformities such as occur in coxa vara, coxa valga, and other bone conditions. By removing a V-shaped portion of the thigh bone, a surgeon may correct a displacement or deformity of the shaft. The operation is also performed in certain cases of bow-legs and knock-knees.

Otosclerosis

Otosclerosis is an extremely common cause of deafness of the conductive type. Although it is seen in people in their middle years, it is most frequently encountered in those who are past middle age. In this process the bones surrounding the middle and inner ear become overgrown and harden. This results in an interference with the transmission of sound waves.

See also DEAFNESS; EARS.

QUESTIONS AND ANSWERS

What are the harmful results of otosclerosis?

Otosclerosis is the most common cause of deafness, usually of the conductive type.

Does otosclerosis always cause deafness?

No.

What are the symptoms of otosclerosis?

Deafness is the outstanding symptom, but occasionally it causes noises in the ears. There are no abnormal ear findings on examination.

What is the treatment for otosclerosis?

There is no known cure for this condition. In many cases, the deafness can be lessened greatly by either mobilization or removal of the stapes.

Does otosclerosis cause the stapes bone to become immobile?

Yes.

If an operation for otosclerosis fails to restore hearing, can it be done over again?

This will depend largely upon what primary operation was performed. If a stapes mobilization procedure was performed and followed by failure, re-operation with removal of the stapes bone may be rewarded by success.

If removal of the stapes bone to relieve otosclerosis does not result in permanent increase in hearing, can reoperation be undertaken?

Yes, but most complicated operative procedures are involved and are not always successful in restoring hearing.

Do people in their 20s or 30s ever develop otosclerosis?

Yes, but it is seldom seen in those decades of life.

Does otosclerosis usually affect both ears?

Yes, but it does not necessarily develop in both at the same time. An interval of several years between the development of otosclerosis of the first and second ear is not at all uncommon.

Ovaries

The ovaries are almond-shaped glandular organs measuring about one and one-half inches long, one inch wide, and one inch thick. They are situated low in the pelvis, one on either side of the uterus near the upper open ends of the fallopian tubes.

The ovaries are responsible for the production of female hormones which, with their ebb and flow each month, control menstrual periods. The ovaries also produce the eggs, one of which is discharged into the fallopian tube each month during the reproductive years (from puberty to menopause). This discharge of an egg is called ovulation and occurs generally in the middle of the menstrual cycle. At times this is accompanied by pain, which lasts for several hours. This pain is called mittelschmerz, or "middle pain." If the egg is fertilized by a sperm, pregnancy results and the production of eggs and menstruation stop until after delivery has taken place. If fertilization does not occur, the egg is cast off and menstruation ensues approximately two weeks later.

Only one normal ovary and one normal fallopian tube are required for the maintenance of all the functions enumerated above. Even if an ovary from one side and a tube from the other side are removed, pregnancy can occur if the remaining ovary and tube are normal.

There are a great number of conditions that necessitate surgery upon the ovaries. None of these procedures is dangerous, and operative recovery takes place routinely. The incision is made in the lower abdomen, in either a longitudinal or transverse direction. Spinal or general anesthesia can be used. Although it is not possible to discuss all of the conditions for which surgery is indicated, the main ones will be detailed here:

1. Infection: Inflammation and infection involving the female genital tract may spread to one or both ovaries. While nonsurgical treatment with penicillin and other antibiotics often causes the process to subside, at times a large, painful abscess will form. In many of these cases, removal of the diseased ovary or ovaries is necessary. Not infrequently the adjacent fallopian tube will be involved in the abscess and it, too, will have to be removed. Here, as

in all operations upon the ovaries, the surgeon will try to conserve as much normal ovarian tissue as possible. This is particularly important in women who are still young.

If the infection is severe enough to require removal of both ovaries and tubes, it is often wise not to leave the uterus behind. Obviously, neither conception nor menstruation is possible without the ovaries, and the uterus will henceforth serve no useful purpose. On the other hand, if left in place, it might one day be the seat of tumor formation.

2. Ovarian cysts: There are several types of cysts which form within the ovary. Normally the ovary forms a small cyst each month which encases the egg to be discharged at ovulation. The cyst bursts and the egg leaves the ovary. Following this phenomenon, the cyst collapses and disappears. Sometimes, for unknown reasons, the cyst does not disappear and a persistent follicle cyst results. Most of these cysts will not require surgery and will eventually shrink and disappear. However, some may grow in size, cause pain, or produce disturbance in the menstrual cycle, in which event they should be excised surgically.

The ovary is occasionally the site of mucous cyst formation, some growing to such size as to fill almost the entire abdominal cavity. These cysts can occur at any age but seem to be somewhat more prevalent in the younger age groups. Their operative removal is essential. In almost all instances, when this type of cyst has become quite large, the remainder of the ovary is destroyed, and its remnants will therefore be removed along with the cyst.

An ovarian cyst may become quite heavy with fluid and may twist upon its own stalk. This will give rise to a set of acute symptoms, including severe lower abdominal pain (more severe on the

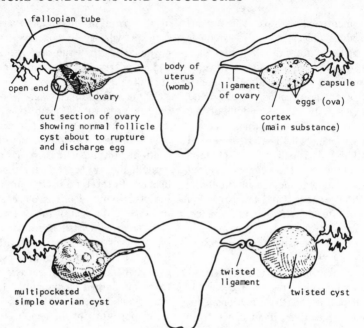

side of the twist), nausea, vomiting, and muscle spasm with tenderness. Frequently, unless a gynecologist performs a careful pelvic examination, this condition is mistaken for acute appendicitis or bowel obstruction. Emergency surgery is mandatory for removal of the cyst, after which recovery will follow rapidly.

In young women, the ovaries are often the seat of multiple cysts. This condition may be associated with marked irregularity of menstruation, difficulty in ovulation, and inability to become pregnant. If pelvic examination and symptoms show that the cysts are persistent over a period of months, or if the cysts enlarge, surgery is indicated. Partial removal of the ovaries (wedge resection) is often rewarded by a cure in this condition.

Hemorrhage into an ovarian cyst or from a ruptured cyst will give rise to painful symptoms and, if severe, will demand immediate surgical intervention. Commonly, a ruptured follicle cyst may bleed quite severely and will produce symptoms that mimic acute appendicitis. Although hemorrhage of this type rarely is so extensive as to be dangerous, nevertheless it is safer to be operated upon than to await spontaneous cessation of the bleeding.

Whenever possible, in operating upon the ovaries in young women, an attempt is made to remove only the diseased portion of the gland and to leave behind normal tissue. Of course, if any doubt exists as to the presence of tumor tissue, the entire ovary is taken out.

3. Benign solid tumors of the ovary: Any firm, solid-feeling enlargement of the ovary, no matter how small, should be an indication for surgical exploration. Many ovarian tumors cause no symptoms; others may give rise to pain in the lower abdomen or groin or may cause menstrual irregularity or acute abdominal symptoms if they undergo a twist upon their stalk.

If surgery confirms the presence of a tumor, the entire ovary is removed and may be submitted for immediate frozen-section microscopic examination. If the pathology report indicates that the tumor is cancerous, it is wise to carry out hysterectomy and removal of the other ovary and both fallopian tubes. If the microscopic report shows the tumor to be benign, the uterus, tubes, and other ovary are not disturbed.

4. Endometriosis: In this condition cells that normally line the interior of the uterus are found growing on the surface of other abdominal organs, such as the tubes, ovaries, ligaments, intestines, and lining of the abdominal cavity. Characteristically, this peculiar disorder will produce lower abdominal pain beginning a week to ten days prior to menstruation, increasing in intensity as menstruation approaches, and subsiding about the second or third day of the period. When endometriosis involves an ovary, it may form a cyst. If these cysts grow larger than two inches in diameter, then surgical removal of the ovary is indicated. If women over 40 years of age are affected, then removal of the uterus, both tubes and ovaries will produce a cure.

Endometriosis in young women without cyst formation can be helped considerably by giving appropriate doses of various sex hormones. (*See also* ENDO-METRIOSIS.)

5. Hormone-producing tumors: The ovary occasionally gives rise to hormone-producing tumors. These can be of either the female-hormone-producing or the male-hormone-producing type. The latter may result in the development of male characteristics, such as a beard on the face, male distribution of hair on the body, and a deepening of the voice.

As these growths are thought to be of a low-grade malignancy, pelvic surgery is carried out, with removal of the uterus, tubes, and ovaries. In some instances, when the patient is a young girl or woman and the tumor is entirely localized and enclosed within a capsule, simple removal of the ovary may be justified.

6. Cancer of the ovary: Since malignant tumors within the ovary tend to develop silently and produce few early symptoms, it is essential that all mature women undergo pelvic examinations at least once a year. By following such a routine, the gynecologist will not only be able to discover any enlargement of the ovary but will be in a position to watch for any changes that may take place from time to time in a normal patient.

Malignant growths of the ovary are usually treated by removal of all the pelvic organs. In some cases, surgery is followed by x-ray radiation to the pelvic region some weeks later. If attacked early, cure can be obtained in a large percentage of cases. If diagnosed late in the course of the disease, cancers of the ovary tend to form fluid within the abdominal cavity and to spread throughout the abdomen and to distant organs.

Operations upon the ovaries are performed through either a longitudinal or a horizontal incision about four to five inches long in the lower abdomen. Spinal or general anesthesia is used. The abdominal cavity is opened and the ovary is easily brought up into the wound. Its removal is a simple procedure and requires only that the stalk be securely clamped, tied, and cut off. The procedure itself is not dangerous or disabling, and the patient is often able to get out of bed the next day. Within a week to ten days after surgery, the wound is healed and hospital discharge can be recommended. Even in the most complicated cases where huge ovarian cysts or tumors are removed, recovery is prompt and complications are exceedingly rare.

See also FALLOPIAN TUBES; UTERUS.

QUESTIONS AND ANSWERS

What are the ovaries?

They are a pair of almond-shaped glandular structures about one and one-half inches by one inch in diameter. They are located in the pelvis on either side of the uterus and are suspended from the posterior wall of the pelvis in close proximity to the funnel-shaped openings of the fallopian tubes. Each ovary consists of an outer capsule which is grayish-white in color, a cortex or main substance, and a hilum or stalk through which the blood vessels enter and leave.

What are the functions of the ovaries?

1. The periodic production and discharge of a mature egg. The cortex of each ovary contains several thousand immature eggs, one of which matures and is discharged into the funnel-shaped opening of a fallopian tube each month. This process is called ovulation. If the egg is fertilized by the male sperm, the process halts. If fertilization does not take place, menstruation follows. The interval between ovulation and menstruation is about 14 days.

2. The ovaries manufacture and secrete the sex hormones into the bloodstream. These hormones are called estrogen and progesterone. They regulate ovulation and menstruation, help to maintain pregnancy when it exists, and are responsible for the development of female characteristics. Thus, they are responsible for breast development, the female distribution of hair, the female figure, and the feminine voice.

Are both ovaries necessary for normal ovarian function?

No. Only one ovary, or part of an ovary, is necessary to maintain normal function.

At what age does the ovary begin to function?

From the onset of puberty at approximately 10 to 14 years of age.

Is the ovary ever the site of inflammation or infection?

Yes. Because of its close proximity to the fallopian tube, disease of that structure will frequently spread to the ovary.

What are the symptoms of an inflamed or infected ovary?

They are the same as those involving disease of the fallopian tube (salpingitis).

What is mean by the term "ovarian dysfunction"?

It is a state in which there is disturbed ovarian hormone production or imbalance, characterized by upset in the menstrual cycle and in the ability to become pregnant or maintain pregnancy. Such disorders may originate within the ovary or they may be secondary to disturbed function within other endocrine glands, such as the pituitary or thyroid.

What are some of the symptoms that may develop with prolonged dysfunction of the ovaries?

1. Complete upset in the menstrual cycle and in the character and nature of menstruation

2. Obesity

3. The development of extra hair upon the body (hirsutism)

4. Overgrowth of the lining membrane of the uterus (endometrial hyperplasia)

5. Infertility (inability to become pregnant)

What are the results of ovarian dysfunction?

The normal balance between the production and utilization of its two main hormones, estrogen and progesterone, is disturbed. This may interfere with ovulation, menstruation, or preparation of the uterus for the acceptance of a pregnancy.

What is the treatment for ovarian dysfunction?

First, the exact cause of the imbalance must be determined. Hormone studies of the blood and urine are carried out in an attempt to find the seat of the difficulty and to determine whether it originates in the ovary, the thyroid, or the pituitary gland. Endometrial biopsy and vaginal smears are also performed as an aid to a precise diagnosis.

1. When cysts accompany ovarian dysfunction, an operation with removal of a wedge-shaped section from each ovary often helps to correct the disturbance.

2. When thyroid or pituitary gland dysfunction is found to be the cause of the ovarian disorder, the condition must be remedied by appropriate medication before the ovarian dysfunction can be corrected.

3. Cyclic therapy, the giving of regulated doses of estrogen and progesterone hormones, in a manner simulating the normal cycle, may prove beneficial.

4. More recently, cortisone has been found successful in certain cases in restoring normal ovarian function.

Does disturbed ovarian function ever subside by itself?

Yes. This occurs frequently without any treatment whatever.

At what age may ovarian dysfunction occur?

It can take place at any age from puberty to menopause but is seen most often during the first years of adolescence or early adulthood.

Can pregnancy follow ovarian dysfunction?

If ovarian dsyfunction is accompanied by lack of ovulation, pregnancy will not take place. However, once the dysfunction is corrected, pregnancy can take place.

Are there medications that can help a woman who fails to ovulate?

Yes. There are some new medications, not yet available generally, that can correct this condition. In some instances, these drugs not only have encouraged ovulation and pregnancy but have been associated with multiple births such as twins, triplets, and quadruplets.

What are follicle cysts?

These are small, fluid-filled sacs appearing on the surface of an ovary. They arise from the failure of the egg-producing follicle to rupture. Thus, the cyst persists instead of being absorbed.

To what size do follicle cysts grow?

They may vary from the size of a pea to that of a plum.

What are the causes of follicle cysts?

1. Previous infection which has produced a thickening of the outer coat of the ovary

2. Disturbance in ovarian function

What symptoms do follicle cysts cause?

They may cause no symptoms, or they may result in ovarian dysfunction as previously described. The larger solitary follicle cysts sometimes cause lower abdominal pain, urinary distress, pain on intercourse, and menstrual irregularity.

Do follicle cysts ever rupture?

Yes. When this happens, it may be accompanied by severe pain in the lower abdomen, with tenderness on pressure, nausea, vomiting, or even a state of shock. It is often difficult for the gynecologist to distinguish a ruptured follicle cyst from appendicitis or an ectopic pregnancy.

What is the treatment for follicle cysts?

Treatment is seldom required for the simple, small or multiple cysts which are associated with no symptoms. Multiple cysts which cause symptoms and are associated with ovarian dysfunction should be treated by surgery with the removal of wedge-shaped sections of the ovaries. If rupture or twist of a solitary cyst takes place, and the symptoms do not abate within a day or two, surgery may be necessary.

Do follicle cysts of the ovaries ever disappear by themselves?

Yes.

Is there a tendency for follicle cysts to recur?

Yes. Patients who have had follicle cysts require periodic observation by their gynecologists.

What is a corpus luteum cyst of the ovary?

After the egg has broken out of the ovary, the follicle is supposed to undergo shrinkage and disappear. In some cases, instead of disappearing, the follicle develops into a cyst (sac). Such a cyst may be filled with blood and may enlarge to the size of a lemon, orange, or even larger.

What are the symptoms of a corpus luteum cyst?

It may cause no symptoms, or if it is large, it may cause pain, delay in menstruation, or painful intercourse. If the cyst ruptures, there may be acute onset of pain, nausea, vomiting, urinary disturbance, and severe pain in the lower abdomen. This may give the appearance of an acute surgical condition such as appendicitis or ectopic pregnancy and may demand surgery.

When is it necessary to operate upon a ruptured corpus luteum cyst?

If the symptoms persist or if there has been a great deal of blood loss.

Are there other types of ovarian cysts?

Yes. There are many types, including simple solitary cysts and cystic tumors.

Do these cysts ever grow to large size?

Yes. Some of them may fill the entire abdominal cavity and reach the size of a watermelon.

What is the treatment for these cysts?

Surgical removal as promptly as possible.

Are tumors of the ovary very common?

Yes.

What types of tumors affect the ovary?

1. Benign solid or cystic tumors
2. Malignant solid or cystic tumors
3. Hormone-producing tumors

Why is the ovary so often the seat of tumor or cyst formation?

The eggs within the ovaries contain all the basic primitive cells which go into the formation of a new human being, and it is not surprising that some of these may undergo abnormal growth. Also, the ovary itself is subject to so many wide and varied fluctuations in function that it is not difficult to appreciate that things might go wrong and lead to tumor growth.

What symptoms can ovarian cysts produce?

1. They may cause no symptoms.
2. They may be the cause of excessive bleeding at menstruation or bleeding between periods.

3. They may cause irregular menstruation.

4. They may enlarge greatly and cause pressure upon other organs, such as the bladder, the rectum, or the intestines.

5. They may cause great pain if they twist and become strangulated or if they hemorrhage.

6. They may rupture and produce a marked bleeding into the abdominal cavity.

7. Certain kinds of cysts may interfere with the ability to become pregnant.

What dangers may arise if a cyst is not removed?

1. Twist of the stalk, with gangrene of the ovary

2. Rupture of the cyst, with spillage of its contents into the abdominal cavity

3. Hemorrhage into the cyst itself or into the abdominal cavity

4. Infection of the cyst with abscess formation

5. Possible transformation from a benign cyst into a cancer

Do tumors of the ovary occur in women at any age?

Yes. They occur from earliest childhood to the latest years of life.

What is a dermoid cyst of the ovary?

This is a tumor occurring in women usually between the ages of 20 and 50. It is frequently found in both ovaries and may grow to be as large as an orange. It is composed of many types of cells and may even include hair, bone, and teeth. Dermoid cysts also have been found to contain other tissues which resemble organs in a primitive stage of development.

Are dermoid cysts malignant?

Less than one percent are malignant.

How is the diagnosis of a dermoid cyst made?

By pelvic examination and by x-ray examination.

What is the treatment for dermoid cyst of the ovary?

In the childbearing age, removal of the dermoid cyst. Past the childbearing age, removal of the ovary or ovaries and uterus.

What are hormone-producing tumors of the ovaries?

These are tumors that manufacture either female or male sex hormones in great excess. Thus, a tumor of the ovary that produces a male-type hormone will cause the patient to assume male characteristics, such as growth of hair on the face and chest, deepening of the voice, and loss of feminine appearance.

Are hormone-producing tumors of the ovary very common?

No.

What is the treatment for hormone-producing tumors of the ovary?

Age plays an important role. Surgical removal of the diseased ovary is indicated in some cases; in older women, the other ovary and the uterus should also be removed.

Will altered characteristics disappear after removal of a hormone-producing ovarian tumor?

Yes.

What are fibromas of the ovary?

These are solid tumors constituting about 5 percent of all ovarian growths. They may be associated with fluid secretion in the abdominal cavity, and because of their similarity to certain malignant growths of the ovary, they must be very carefully analyzed after being removed.

Does endometriosis affect the ovary?

Yes. In about one out of eight cases of endometriosis, the condition is found in the ovary. It is almost always associated with endometriosis elsewhere.

Is cancer of the ovary a common condition?

Unfortunately, yes. Cancers will appear as either solid or cystic growths, and they may arise from one or from both ovaries. Cancer of the ovary may also develop from benign tumors of the ovaries such as dermoid cysts.

Does secondary cancer ever affect the ovary?

Yes. This is quite common and occurs from the spread of a cancer of the stomach, breast, or uterus.

At what age does cancer most commonly affect the ovary?

The highest incidence occurs in the years between 40 and 50, although it is sometimes found in young girls and in elderly women.

How does one make the diagnosis of cancer of the ovary?

By pelvic examination. Fluid in the abdominal cavity is a frequent finding suggestive of an ovarian malignancy.

What is the treatment for malignant tumors of the ovary?

The present mode of treatment involves surgery, with total and complete removal of the uterus, both tubes, both ovaries, and the ligaments and tissues surrounding these structures. Surgery is followed by x-ray treatment or the application of other radioactive substances or the use of chemotherapeutic medications.

What are the possibilities of cure of cancer of the ovary?

If the patient is operated upon early, before there has been spread to other structures or organs, the chances are fairly good. Surgical recovery takes place in almost all cases, as these operations are not excessively dangerous.

Is cancer of the ovary ever permanently cured?

Yes. Approximately one out of four women can be cured permanently.

Will a cancer smear from the vagina help to establish a diagnosis of cancer of the ovary?

In rare instances, yes.

What is the best method to prevent cancer of the ovary?

Frequent, periodic pelvic examinations will reveal the presence of abnormality in the ovary and alert the patient to the need for possible surgery. If surgery is performed early for suspicious tumors, many patients can be saved before the tumor has become malignant or before it has spread to other structures.

What is the best treatment for any ovarian cyst or tumor?

If it persists or shows signs of growth, an operation should be done to evaluate the exact nature of the lesion. In this way, many ovarian tumors can be removed which might have become malignant at some future date. Also, early removal of a persistently cystic or enlarged ovary will prevent it from twisting or rupturing.

Is medical treatment ever preferred to surgical treatment in tumors of the ovaries?

No.

What are some of the exact criteria for advising surgery for ovarian conditions?

1. Any ovarian mass more than two inches in diameter which persists on repeated examination should be removed.

2. Any rapid growth of an ovarian tumor should be operated upon.

3. The presence of free fluid within the abdominal cavity, in the presence of an ovarian tumor, should indicate surgery.

4. The appearance of weight loss, anemia, and weakness, in the presence of an ovarian tumor, warrants surgery.

5. Where endometrial hyperplasia is found in the presence of an ovarian mass, surgery is indicated.

Is it possible to determine, while the patient is on the operating table, whether a tumor of the ovary is malignant?

Yes. A pathologist will take a frozen section of a tumor and examine it under the microscope while the patient is on the operating table. This will determine whether or not the tumor is malignant and will suggest to the surgeon how extensive his operative procedure should be.

Do ovarian tumors ever occur during pregnancy?

Yes. Cysts of the ovary occasionally occur during pregnancy.

In what conditions is it advisable to remove both ovaries?

1. When severe inflammation involves both ovaries and the other pelvic organs

2. When a precancerous or cancerous condition exists in one ovary

3. When hysterectomy is being performed for a benign condition (fibroid tumor) upon a woman past her menopause)

4. When hysterectomy is performed for precancerous or cancerous conditions of the uterus

5. In some cases of breast cancer in women who have not yet reached menopause

Can operations upon the ovaries be performed while the patient is menstruating?

Yes. This has no influence upon when to schedule an operation.

Are ovarian operations ever emergency procedures?

Yes, when a cyst has become twisted or when severe hemorrhage from a ruptured cyst has occurred.

What operation is performed for removal of an ovary?

Oophorectomy is done through a longitudinal or a horizontal incision, four to five inches long, in the lower abdomen.

Do cysts that occur during pregnancy harm the embryo?

No.

Do ovarian cysts or tumors ever create an acute abdominal condition?

Yes. There is a great tendency for cysts or tumors of the ovary to twist upon their stalks. This will cause all of the signs of an acute abdominal condition and will require an immediate operation.

Do cysts of the ovary ever rupture?

Occasionally rupture occurs, and when it does, emergency operation is indicated.

Does the removal of the ovaries alter one's sexual desires?

Not usually.

Is there a difference in surgical treatment recommended for ovarian conditions in different age groups?

Yes:

1. In young women, if no malignancy exists, conservative treatment is advocated. Wherever possible, the ovary is left in and merely the cyst or tumor is removed.

2. In older women, especially those

beyond change of life, there is nothing to be gained by preserving an ovary. In these patients, both ovaries and the uterus may be removed when diseased.

How soon after ovarian removal can the patient get out of bed?
Usually within one to three days.

How long a hospital stay is required after ovarian operations?
Seven to ten days.

Is special convalescent care necessary?
No.

Can a woman become pregnant after the removal of one ovary?
Yes.

Does removal of both ovaries always bring on change of life (menopause)?
Yes, unless the woman has already passed the menopause.

Does a patient with only one ovary menstruate regularly?
Yes.

OVARIES IN CHILDREN

At what age do the ovaries begin to secrete their hormones?
The exact age is not certain, but it is thought that some small quantities of hormones may be secreted during early childhood. It is certain that much larger quantities are secreted from puberty until menopause.

How will a mother know if her child has an ovarian tumor?
The most common symptom is abdominal pain with nausea and vomiting. When this occurs, the diagnosis of acute appendicitis is often suspected, but on further examination an enlargement of an ovary is discovered.

What are the symptoms of an ovarian tumor in a child?
There may be precocious sexual de-velopment with premature menstruation and enlargement of the breasts. This is particularly true if there is a hormone-producing tumor. The most common such tumor is called a granulosa cell tumor.

What causes symptoms when an ovarian tumor or cyst is present?
A twist of the tumor or cyst on its stalk often produces pain, nausea, vomiting, and lower abdominal tenderness.

At what age can ovarian tumors develop?
They can develop at any age, even in children one or two years old.

What is the most common tumor of the ovary seen in children?
A teratoma, often called a dermoid cyst. Teratomas are peculiar in that various types of tissues, such as hair, bone, teeth, and bits of intestinal tissue, are often found within their substance. It is thought that teratomas may arise from an unfertilized egg that begins to form a tumor and develop without any specific functional pattern.

Are teratomas benign (noncancerous)?
Yes, most of them are. Occasionally, one will display malignant characteristics by spreading and growing in other organs of the body.

What is the treatment for an ovarian tumor in a child?
It should be removed surgically as soon as the diagnosis is established, because there is a tendency for certain types to become malignant.

Does a gynecologist usually remove both ovaries even if just one has a tumor?
In most instances, unless the primary tumor is definitely malignant, he will remove just the one ovary and give the

child periodic examinations every few months in order to make certain that the tumor has not involved the other ovary.

Will the precocious development of the child disappear after the tumor is removed?

Yes, in most cases, within a few months after surgery is performed.

What is a dysgerminoma?

A dysgerminoma is an ovarian tumor seen most often between the ages of 10 and 20 years. The tumor arises from primitive germ cells and is often associated with underdevelopment of the female organs.

Are dysgerminomas curable?

Yes, provided they have not spread throughout the rest of the abdomen.

How common is cancer of the ovaries in children?

It is very rare. Embryonal carcinoma, adenocarcinoma, and choriocarcinoma are examples of these rare but very serious ovarian cancers.

Do children ever develop cysts of the ovaries?

Yes.

What is the treatment for an ovarian cyst in a child?

The cyst should be removed surgically.

Do ovarian cysts in children ever involve both ovaries?

Yes, in some instances. However, when ovarian cysts are encountered at surgery, the gynecologist will always try to save one ovary so that the child will be able to menstruate and bear children when she reaches maturity.

Will a child who has had one ovary removed grow up to menstruate normally?

Yes, provided the remaining ovary is normal.

OVARIES AFTER MENOPAUSE

How long do the ovaries continue to secrete hormones?

It is thought that very small amounts of hormone are secreted into the bloodstream even after menopause (change of life).

Does surgical removal of the ovaries shorten the life-span of a woman?

No.

Does any other organ take over the secretion of female hormones after the ovaries have been removed?

It is thought that the adrenal glands secrete substances very similar to the ovarian hormones throughout the life of the female.

What are the symptoms or signs of ovarian undersecretion in women past 60?

No symptoms have been *proved* to be the result of lack of ovarian secretion in women past 60. However, it is thought that obesity, listlessness, arthritis, increased growth of body hair, and other symptoms may be associated with absence of ovarian-hormone secretion.

Should women past 60 be given ovarian hormone extracts in order to combat the above-mentioned symptoms?

Not usually.

Is it possible for a woman past 60 to become pregnant?

There are a few cases on record in which women have continued to menstruate and ovulate into their 60s and have thus been capable of becoming pregnant. However, these cases are extremely rare and constitute medical oddities. Moreover, one would have to examine such reports very closely to make sure that a mistake had not been made in calculating age.

How long after menstruation has stopped can a woman be certain that she has no chance of becoming pregnant?

If a woman has had no natural menstrual periods for one year, it can be assumed that the possibility of pregnancy is almost nonexistent.

Do the ovaries ever become enlarged in older women who have passed the menopause?

Yes, from the development of either a cyst or a tumor.

How does the physician make a diagnosis of an ovarian cyst?

By a pelvic examination. Because such cysts can occur in older women, they should have a pelvic examination every year.

Do benign ovarian cysts ever become cancerous?

Yes, especially in women past menopause.

What is the treatment of an ovarian cyst in older women?

It should be removed after diagnosis through an abdominal incision. In all probability, the gynecologist will also remove the uterus and the other ovary.

Pancreas

The pancreas is a soft, flat, yellowish gland shaped somewhat like a tadpole. It stretches across the posterior part of the upper abdomen at a level midway between the navel and the rib margins and measures approximately seven inches in width and about two inches in height. Running the entire length of the gland is the main pancreatic duct or tube. There is also a small accessory duct located in the head of the gland.

These ducts collect the digestive juices which have been manufactured within the gland's substance and transport them through their openings into the small intestine in the region of the duodenum.

The pancreas not only manufactures the juices which digest various food elements such as protein, fat, and carbohydrates, but also produces *insulin,* which it secretes directly into the bloodstream. Insulin is the chemical agent essential for the burning up and utilization of energy-giving sugar. If too little insulin is produced, unused sugar will accumulate in the circulating blood, thus causing *diabetes.* If too much insulin is manufactured, too much sugar will be burned and a condition known as *hyperinsulinism* will result.

There are several diseases that commonly attack the pancreas and may require surgical attention. They are (1) pancreatitis (inflammation of the gland), (2) cysts, (3) benign tumors or adenomas, and (4) cancer.

1. **Acute pancreatitis** is a serious condition which comes on rather suddenly within a period of several hours and is characterized by severe upper abdominal pain, nausea, and vomiting. It is seen more commonly in men than in women and usually attacks people in their 40s or 50s. It can be diagnosed only with considerable difficulty on physical examination, but certain changes in the chemistry of the blood usually make the diagnosis evident. About half the people afflicted with pancreatitis will give histories suggestive of gallbladder disease, while others will tell of having eaten huge meals or of drinking large amounts of alcoholic beverages just before the onset of symptoms. Severe cases of acute pancreatitis may be accompanied by a state of

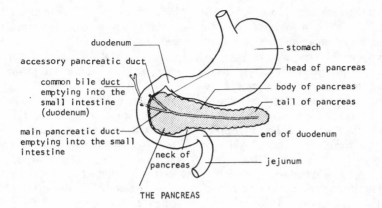

THE PANCREAS

shock, and frequently there are evidences of internal hemorrhage. Inflammation of a chronic or relapsing type also affects the pancreas and is usually seen with disease of the gallbladder and bile ducts.

When a definite diagnosis of acute pancreatitis is made, surgery may be withheld during the early stages and medical treatment may be begun. Bed rest, nothing by mouth, various fluids and substances injected into the veins, and certain drugs, such as penicillin, can in most instances cause the inflammatory process to subside. However, if hemorrhage reaches dangerous proportions or if an abscess of the pancreas should develop, then surgery is performed. If gallbladder or bile duct disease is encountered at operation, these conditions must be corrected, as it is thought that they are causative agents in the production of pancreatic inflammation.

2. Chronic pancreatitis may ensue as a result of repeated acute attacks, as a consequence of obstruction of the ducts leading out from the gland to the intestinal tract, or as a complication of stone formation within the main pancreatic duct. It is also associated in some cases with infection and stones within the bile ducts.

The symptoms of chronic pancreatitis include upper abdominal pain often radiating toward the left and to the back, loss of appetite, nausea, weight loss, and inability to digest food properly. In isolated cases, x-rays may show small stones within the pancreas, but the diagnosis is made more often on the basis of the patient's past medical history and the knowledge that there have been previous attacks of acute pancreatitis.

If the symptoms from this condition are severe and persistent, surgery is indicated. Two ingenious operations have been devised to overcome chronic

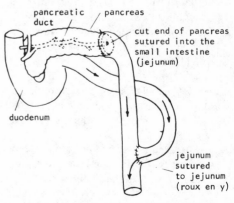

OPERATION FOR CHRONIC PANCREATITIS

pancreatitis; each has been followed by good results in the majority of cases. In one procedure, about an inch of the tail of the pancreas (see diagram) is removed, the pancreatic duct is probed, and any stones that may be present are scooped out. The remaining portion of pancreatic tail is then implanted within a loop of small intestine. This maneuver will relieve the obstruction and will permit the pancreatic juices to flow freely in the opposite direction into the intestinal tract. In the other operative procedure, the pancreas is split open along the entire length of the pancreatic duct, all stones and strictures of the duct are removed, and the whole pancreas except for the head is implanted into a segment of small intestine. The ultimate effect is the same as in the first operation.

3. **Cysts of the pancreas** are not too uncommon and are sometimes an aftermath of previous pancreatic inflammation or are secondary to a severe injury to the upper abdomen. Blockage of one of the ducts of the pancreas is also thought to be a cause for cyst formation, and others are created by the growth of cystic tumors. They vary in size from that of a grape to that of a watermelon and are filled with a watery fluid. A cyst arising from the pancreas will push forward and, if it attains great enough size, will be felt as a lump in the upper abdomen. People with cysts complain of persistent pain, gaseous distention, and may show loss of appetite and weight loss.

Cysts should be operated upon in one of several ways, each method, when performed properly, leading to eventual cure:

a) *Marsupialization:* This method involves opening the cyst and sewing its edges to the abdominal wall. The interior of the cyst is then packed, and over a period of months, secretions from the cyst will dry up and nothing but a scarred remnant will remain.

b) *Internal drainage:* In this operation, an opening is made in the wall of the cyst and then into either the stomach or small intestine. The cyst is stitched (anastomosed) to the stomach or intestine, and its contents will empty into these structures. Within several weeks or months, the cyst will collapse and disappear.

c) *Removal of the cyst:* This is often a hazardous operation, as it may result in severe damage to the surrounding pancreatic tissue. It is performed rarely and is reserved mainly for those cysts which appear so well outlined that removal will be simple to carry out.

4. **Benign tumors or adenomas of the pancreas:** These growths often involve those cells that manufacture insulin. When these growths produce insulin in too great quantities, the level of blood sugar becomes extremely low and the patients suffer episodes of intense hunger, trembling, mental confusion, fainting, or even convulsions. Within recent years surgery has been successful in curing most of these people by the removal of the tumors from the substance of the gland. The operation is not difficult to perform and carries with it a very small risk.

5. **Cancer of the pancreas:** The commonest location for tumor formation is in the head of the gland, where its growth may create pressure upon the bile duct and cause jaundice (with its yellow discoloration of the skin). Two methods of surgical treatment are employed for this condition; a *short-circuiting procedure* designed merely to relieve the symptoms and a *radical operation* (*the Whipple operation*) designed to remove the entire gland.

a) *The short-circuiting operations*

involve suturing the gallbladder or common bile duct to the small intestine or stomach. This bypasses the obstructed bile duct and permits the bile to enter the intestinal tract, thus relieving the jaundice.

b) *The Whipple operation* is one of the most extensive in all surgery and involves the removal of the entire pancreas and adjacent duodenum. The common bile duct is cut across and implanted into the small intestine. Because the duodenum has been removed, intestinal continuity must be reestablished by sewing the stomach to the small intestine in the region beyond the duodenum.

The operative mortality in the short-circuiting operations is limited to about 5 percent, whereas the radical procedure carries with it a death rate of about 15 to 20 percent. Although the risks are high with the more extensive operation, it is worth the chance because of the possibility of cure in those cases in which the tumor has not yet spread to other organs.

QUESTIONS AND ANSWERS

What is the pancreas and where is it located?

The pancreas is a gland in the abdomen which produces the enzymes that digest foods. It also manufactures insulin, a substance necessary for the burning of sugar.

Does the pancreas wear out as one gets older, or is it capable of functioning satisfactorily throughout life?

In healthy older people the pancreas will continue to manufacture and secrete enzymes sufficient for food digestion and will produce enough insulin to regulate sugar metabolism. Of course, the organ

will be subject to the same changes of aging as other structures. Thus, arteriosclerosis of its vessels may eventually lead to inadequate secretion of insulin and enzymes.

How does one know if he has trouble with his pancreas?

Most conditions of the pancreas cause upper abdominal pain with nausea and vomiting. *Pancreatitis* will be accompanied by fever, nausea, and vomiting. A *cyst* can be felt by the examining surgeon. A *tumor* of the insulin-producing cells will cause extreme hunger, trembling, sweats, and possibly fainting or convulsions. *Cancer* of the pancreas, in addition to causing pain, is usually evidenced by jaundice of the skin and marked weight loss.

What causes acute inflammations of the pancreas (pancreatitis)?

In some instances, it is thought to be caused by infected bile backing up into pancreatic ducts; in other instances, it is caused by bacteria which invade the pancreas directly through its blood supply. It is not unusual for pancreatitis to have its onset shortly after one has eaten large quantities of food or imbibed excessive amounts of alcohol. Many cases are associated with gallstones.

Is pancreatitis a serious disease?

Yes, especially in its acute form, which can be accompanied by a severe hemorrhage, overwhelming toxemia, and death. However, serious as it is, the great majority of those affected will recover.

Does inflammation of the pancreas ever occur in people past 60?

Yes, especially in those who have gallstones and disease of the gallbladder and bile ducts. Since biliary infection and stones often affect older people, it is not unexpected that the incidence of pancreatitis is high.

What are the symptoms and signs of acute pancreatitis?
1. Elevation of temperature
2. Pain, tenderness, and distention in the upper abdomen
3. Nausea and vomiting
4. An increase in the quantity of amylase and lipase (chemical enzymes) circulating in the blood
5. Signs of shock in severe cases, secondary to hemorrhage and toxemia

What are the symptoms of chronic or recurring pancreatitis?
When it recurs, it usually takes the form of an acute episode. Chronic indigestion, a bloated feeling, and vague abdominal pains are seen in the chronic form of the disease. Also, bulky, foul-smelling stools may contain undigested food.

How do inflammations of the pancreas subside?
Pancreatitis often gets well spontaneously just as any inflamed area elsewhere in the body tends to heal by itself. Severe cases may go on to the formation of abscesses or necrosis (death) of large sections of the glandular tissue. Such complications will require surgery.

What is the treatment for acute pancreatitis?
1. No food by mouth is given; fluids and glucose (sugar) are given through the veins.
2. Atropine, Banthine, or thiouracil are administered to inhibit pancreatic activity.
3. Antibiotics are sometimes given to control bacterial infection within the gland.

Is a patient with acute pancreatitis often subjected to surgery?
Yes. Surgery is occasionally recommended because the exact diagnosis has not been established and it is necessary to rule out other upper abdomial emergencies for which surgery is mandatory. However, if the diagnosis is clearly established, immediate surgery is not indicated. Surgery is also performed for the complications of pancreatitis, such as abscess or cyst formation.

How does a surgeon decide whether to operate on a patient with acute pancreatitis?
If there are signs of marked internal hemorrhage or if it appears that an abscess has formed within the pancreas as a result of the inflammation, the surgeon will probably decide to operate.

Are special preparations necessary before performing operations upon the pancreas?
Yes. Intravenous fluids and medications, blood transfusions, and antibiotic drugs are often administered before surgery can be performed with the utmost safety.

What type of anesthesia is used for these operations?
General anesthesia.

Where are incisions made for pancreatic operations?
In the upper abdomen; an incision about four to five inches long is made.

Are the incisions painful?
No more than any other abdominal wound.

What procedures are carried out when a surgeon is confronted with pancreatitis after having opened the abdomen suspecting another condition?
The fluid that is secreted into the abdominal cavity in cases of pan-

creatitis is drained. If the gallbladder or bile ducts are found to contain stones and if it is thought that this is a contributing factor in the causation of the pancreatitis, the stones are removed and the gallbladder or bile ducts are drained with rubber tubes.

Does inflammation of the pancreas ever recur?

Yes, there is a tendency toward recurrence if underlying gallbladder disease is not corrected or if obstruction of free flow of pancreatic juices persists.

What are the chances of recovering from pancreatitis?

Most patients recover from an acute attack. Chronic pancreatitis usually requires operation to eliminate any coexisting disease of the gallbladder or bile ducts, or obstruction of the pancreatic ducts.

Are there permanent aftereffects from pancreatitis even if it has completely subsided?

Yes. The patient must be careful about his diet for the rest of his life. Large meals, alcohol, and excessive eating of heavy, fatty foods must be avoided. The patient should have his urine checked every few months for the presence of sugar.

Does disease within the gallbladder or biliary system often incite pancreatitis?

Approximately half the cases of pancreatitis are associated with gallstones, and many physicians feel that this is one of the main factors leading to the development of pancreatitis.

Can acute alcoholism precipitate an attack of pancreatitis?

Yes.

How can pancreatitis best be prevented?

By eating a bland, low-fat diet, by not overeating, and by restricting alcohol intake. Also, any disease within the gallbladder or bile ducts must be eradicated.

Is pancreatitis usually associated with diabetes?

Usually not. It is remarkable that those cells that manufacture insulin do not appear to be involved very often when pancreatitis occurs. It is only in the very severe case that diabetes may ensue.

What is hyperinsulinism (hypoglycemia)?

It is a condition in which the insulin-producing cells (the cells of the islets of Langerhans) manufacture and secrete an excessive amount of insulin into the bloodstream.

What causes hyperinsulinism?

Some cases are caused by a tumor (adenoma) within the pancreas involving an overgrowth of those cells that manufacture insulin. Other cases are caused by an upset in metabolism of the gland, with resultant secretion of abnormally large quantities of insulin into the bloodstream.

Is hyperinsulinism always accompanied by a tumor of the pancreas?

Usually, but not always. There are many cases in which some examination of the pancreas will reveal no abnormality. Microscopic examination of a portion of the pancreas, however, may in rare instances show overgrowth of the insulin-producing cells without true tumor formation.

How large are adenomas of the pancreas?

They are small lesions measuring no more than one-half to one inch in diameter. They cannot be felt on abdominal examination.

When is an abscess of the pancreas most apt to develop?

Following an attack of acute pancreatitis.

Does this occur frequently?

No. It is found usually only after very severe cases, where the pancreatitis has caused destruction of a portion of the gland.

How is a diagnosis of pancreatic abscess made?

By studying the history of a previous episode of pancreatitis, and by noting pain and tenderness in the upper abdomen, along with temperature elevation. These symptoms come on several days or weeks after an attack of pancreatitis has appeared to subside.

What is the treatment for an abscess within the pancreas?

1. Administration of antibiotic drugs
2. Surgical drainage of the abscess

What are the chances for recovery following surgery for a pancreatic abscess?

The great majority of patients will get well, but the wound may drain pus for quite some time.

What form of surgery is carried out for hyperinsulinism when no tumor of the pancreas is discovered at operation?

Some surgeons feel that a portion, such as a third or a half, of the pancreas should be removed. Others feel that this is not beneficial and carries with it too great a risk.

If a benign adenoma of the pancreas is found, can it be removed surgically?

Yes. This is not a dangerous procedure and the patient is usually cured of his hyperinsulinism.

Are cysts of the pancreas dangerous?

No. The small ones may be ignored. It is only the large ones that require attention when they press upon and interfere with the function of neighboring organs.

How is the diagnosis of a cyst of the pancreas arrived at?

The larger cysts can be felt by the examining physician as painless, rounded swellings in the upper abdomen.

Must cysts of the pancreas be operated upon?

Yes, mainly because they continue to grow and press upon nearby organs. Eventually, if not treated, they may interfere with pancreatic activity or may cause serious disturbance in intestinal function.

What surgery is advocated for a cyst of the pancreas?

The cyst is removed, or if this is not technically feasible because of its size, attachments, or location, it is merely drained of its fluid contents. Several rubber drains are inserted into the cyst cavity and are left in place for several weeks, until the cyst collapses and fills in by itself. In some cases, the wall of the cyst is stitched to the stomach and its contents permitted to drain internally. This method often leads to a rapid cure.

Are there any permanent aftereffects from cysts of the pancreas?

No. Digestion and pancreatic function usually return to normal within several weeks to a few months.

What are the chances of recovery after an operation for a cyst of the pancreas?

Excellent.

Do cysts of the pancreas ever recur?

Occasionally a new cyst will form or an old one recur. This is rare.

What is the most common benign tumor of the pancreas?

A growth involving those cells that manufacture insulin.

Do these benign tumors ever develop into cancer?

Yes. This is one of the main reasons why surgery should be undertaken when a pancreatic tumor is suspected.

Is cancer of the pancreas encountered very often?

Unfortunately, it is one of the most common of all abdominal cancers and carries with it the lowest rate of permanent cure.

What causes cancer of the pancreas?

The cause is not known.

Where are most cancers of the pancreas located?

The majority are located in the head of the pancreas, adjoining the duodenum. Most benign tumors of this organ are located farther to the left side in the body or tail of the pancreas.

What are symptoms of cancer of the pancreas?

Pain in the upper abdomen, usually radiating to the back. Also, because the cancer is usually located in the head of the pancreas, its growth creates pressure on the bile ducts, and this will result in obstruction and the slow onset of jaundice. The patient experiences loss of appetite, weight loss, and progressive weakness.

What are the chances of cure for a cancer of the pancreas?

Very slim, unless caught in the early stages. Under such circumstances, total removal of the gland may occasionally be followed by a cure.

What is the life expectancy after a diagnosis of cancer of the pancreas has been made?

Approximately 6 to 18 months. It must be remembered, though, that isolated cases have been reported in which permanent cure has followed removal of most of the gland.

Can any surgeon perform these operations?

Most well-trained surgeons can operate efficiently for inflammation, cysts, or tumors of the pancreas, but there are few who are trained to carry out removal of the entire gland.

Are blood transfusions given during and after these operations?

Yes, in many instances.

How long do operations upon the pancreas take?

Pancreatitis	1 to 3 hours
Cysts	1 to 2 hours
Removal of localized tumor	1 to 3 hours
Removal of the pancreas	3 to 6 hours

Are special nurses required after these operations?

Yes.

Are special postoperative measures necessary after operations upon the pancreas?

Yes. Blood transfusions, intravenous medications, special drugs, and other measures are usually instituted after operations upon this organ.

How soon after surgery can the patient get out of bed?

Within one to three days except in the very seriously sick patients.

Is convalescent care necessary?

Yes.

How soon after operation can one bathe?

Bathing is permissible when the wound has healed.

How soon after operation can one perform physical exercise?

Physical exercise should not be resumed for at least four to six months.

How soon after operation can one return to work?

In about two months after complete healing of the wound. Strenuous labor should be avoided for several months thereafter.

How long does it take for these wounds to heal?

Pancreatic cysts are drained and such wounds may take several weeks or even months to heal. Tightly closed wounds will usually heal within two weeks.

Should one follow a special diet after operations upon the pancreas?

Yes. A low-sugar and low-fat diet is often indicated.

Must one always remain on a special diet after operation upon the pancreas?

One must be under constant supervision of one's physician, who is the only person who will be able to prescribe the proper diet.

Do operations upon the pancreas affect length of life?

No, except in cancer.

Can one live normally without a pancreas?

No. It is necessary to observe strict dietary measures, as diabetes will develop after the removal of the pancreas.

Parathyroid Glands

The parathyroid glands are four small, pea-sized structures located behind and attached to the thyroid gland in the neck. They are embedded within thyroid substance and are not easily located even when surgical dissection is carried out. The parathyroid glands secrete a hormone (parathormone) which is responsible for the maintenance of balance in calcium and phosphorus metabolism.

QUESTIONS AND ANSWERS

HYPERPARATHYROIDISM

Do people ever develop overactivity of the parathyroids?

Yes. There are several causes of hy-

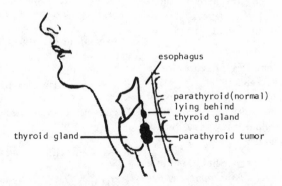

esophagus

parathyroid(normal)
lying behind
thyroid gland

thyroid gland

parathyroid tumor

Anatomy of the Parathyroid Glands. This diagram shows the parathyroid glands as they are located behind the thyroid in the neck. One of these glands is pictured as normal in size; the larger one illustrates tumor formation. Parathyroid tumors, by stimulating excessive secretion of the parathyroid hormone, cause cyst formation and bone deformities. Surgical removal of a parathyroid tumor can be carried out successfully and will result in a cure.

perparathyroidism (overactivity). The main causes are:

1. Certain cases of vitamin D deficiency (rickets), sometimes seen in children.

2. Disease or malfunction of the kidneys.

3. Tumor of the parathyroid gland. This is seldom seen in children.

What is the treatment for overactivity of the parathyroid glands?

If a tumor is suspected, it must be removed surgically. If the hyperparathyroidism is secondary to a vitamin D deficiency or kidney disease, these conditions must be alleviated.

What are the symptoms of hyperparathyroidism?

1. Loss of appetite, nausea, vomiting, and constipation.

2. Increased thirst and increased output of urine.

3. Fever and weight loss.

4. Calcium may be deposited in the kidneys, causing the formation of kidney stones and the development of symptoms secondary to this condition.

5. Easily fractured, brittle bones.

6. In advanced cases, convulsions, mental retardation, and death may ensue.

What causes the parathyroids to become overactive in rickets or kidney disease?

Both rickets and kidney disease result in too little calcium in the blood. In order to overcome this depletion, the parathyroids increase their activity and draw calcium from the bones in an attempt to bring the level of calcium in the blood to normal. This is the cause of bone deformity in rickets.

What happens when there is overactivity of the parathyroid (hyperparathyroidism)?

Hyperparathyroidism will increase the amount of calcium circulating in the bloodstream and will cause the excretion of an abnormally large amount of calcium in the urine.

Do any harmful effects take place when there is overactivity of parathyroids?

Yes. Hyperparathyroidism can lead to the formation of kidney stones and impairment of kidney function because of excess calcium in the blood. It can also lead to the formation of bone cysts and deformities because calcium is withdrawn from the bones into the bloodstream.

Are the bone changes caused by hyperparathyroidism ever severe?

Yes. There may be marked depletion of calcium and the formation of bone cysts. Also, the bones will grow in a deformed manner, become brittle, and fracture easily.

What is osteitis fibrosa cystica?

Osteitis fibrosa cystica is the name given to the bone condition that can be caused by overactivity of the parathyroids. In advanced cases, the bone deformities may assume grotesque proportions as a result of cyst formation, decalcification, and fracture.

Is the operation for the removal of a parathyroid tumor serious?

No. It is no more serious than an operation upon the thyroid gland. However, it is more difficult technically, because the parathyroids, since they are so small, are often difficult to recognize and isolate.

What is the surgical procedure for removal of a parathyroid tumor?

An incision is made across the lower portion of the neck, and the thyroid gland is thoroughly exposed and rotated forward so that the four parathyroids can be identified as they lie on the back wall of the thyroid gland. If one of these glands is found to be the seat of the tumor, it is completely removed.

In some cases, no specific tumor of the parathyroids can be seen, but all of the glands seem to be enlarged. This is called hyperplasia of the parathyroids. If this condition is found, the major portion of each parathyroid gland should be removed and only a small quantity of glandular substance should be left behind.

Is recovery the general rule after an operation on the parathyroids?

Yes. Although hyperparathyroidism may be a serious condition, the operative procedure is not dangerous. Most patients will recover within a few days and the wound will leave a minimal scar.

Will the bone deformities heal after the removal of a parathyroid tumor?

There is usually remarkable improvement in the bones, but if extensive deformities have already occurred, they will not disappear completely and may require corrective bone surgery.

Is the cause for the hyperparathyroidism always found upon operation?

Not in all cases. Occasionally, despite all indications that a tumor is present, none is found in the neck. This may be due to the fact that a parathyroid gland has developed in an abnormal position in the neck or even in the chest cavity. In such cases, to produce a cure, one must find the gland and remove it.

Is parathyroid function ever disturbed as a result of an operation upon the thyroid gland?

Yes. In complicated cases, usually those with recurrent goiter, the parathyroids are sometimes injured or inadvertently removed along with the goiter.

What happens when the parathyroid glands have all been removed?

Symptoms of underactivity (hypoparathyroidism), such as muscle cramps and tetany (convulsions), may develop.

Must all four of the parathyroids be removed before symptoms of underactivity develop?

Yes.

HYPOPARATHYROIDISM

What is hypoparathyroidism?

Hypoparathyroidism is a condition associated with inadequate production of parathormone (the hormone of the parathyroid glands), which generally leads to tetany (a condition in which there are convulsions secondary to a lack of sufficient calcium in the circulating blood).

Are children ever born with underactivity of the parathyroid glands?

Yes, although the condition is not common.

Is an underactivity of the parathyroid glands ever associated with underactivity of the adrenal cortex?

Yes. Symptoms of Addison's disease, which is caused by underactivity of the adrenal glands, are often associated with underactivity of the parathyroids.

Does hypoparathyroidism ever result from surgery upon the thyroid gland?

Yes. In rare instances, the parathyroid glands are removed or their blood supply is impaired because of thyroid surgery. This may leave an inadequate amount of parathyroid tissue to maintain normal function.

How is underactivity of the parathyroid glands diagnosed?

By noting that there is a very low level of calcium in the circulating blood and a correspondingly high level of phosphorus. Furthermore, x-rays of the bones may show increased deposits of calcium in them.

What are the signs and symptoms of hypoparathyroidism?

Most of the symptoms are those associated with tetany and consist of convulsions with marked muscle rigidity, muscle cramps, and pain. Sometimes there is numbness and tingling in the hands and feet. All the characteristic signs of tetany eventually develop if the patient is suffering from hypoparathyroidism. (The characteristic signs of tetany are muscle spasms and convulsions.)

Is there any satisfactory treatment for hypoparathyroidism?

Yes. Treatment will consist of giving the patient injections of calcium (calcium gluconate) to relieve an acute attack of tetany and administering large doses of vitamin D and calcium by mouth. The vitamin D and calcium must be continued for an indefinite period, until it is determined by blood tests and by clinical observation that the glands are no longer underactive.

If a child is born without parathyroid glands or with marked underactivity of function, is it ever possible to transplant glands from another individual?

This has been tried, but has not yet proved very successful. It is safe to assume, however, that in the future, effective ways to graft this tissue will be discovered.

Parkinson's Disease

Various types of abnormal, involuntary movements may occur as a result of disease of the central nervous system. The occurrence of tremor is par-

ticularly common and is one of the characteristic features of a condition called Parkinson's disease, parkinsonism, shaking palsy, or paralysis agitans. This is a slowly progressive disorder of unknown cause, which eventually leads to an incapacitation. Muscular rigidity accompanies the tremor and handicaps voluntary movement. Despite the fact that a large number of drugs have been introduced for the treatment of this condition, the results are far from satisfactory. It is for this reason that in recent years surgical attempts have been made to alleviate the tremor and rigidity. The mechanism responsible for the production of tremor and rigidity is unknown, and heretofore a successful result was usually achieved at the expense of some impairment of strength. It is now possible to relieve tremor and rigidity (parkinsonism) appreciably by surgery in a fairly high proportion of cases, without incurring any paralysis. The operation is not totally devoid of risk and is not invariably successful, but the results thus far have been sufficiently encouraging to warrant consideration in appropriate cases.

QUESTIONS AND ANSWERS

What is Parkinson's disease, or paralysis agitans?

An organic disease of the brain associated with tremors and muscle rigidity. The muscle rigidity slows up all body movements and causes the face to have a blank expression. The shaking tremor is slow, rhythmic, and even, and is most visible in the neck and hands. The fingers particularly are involved in the tremor, especially the thumb and index and middle fingers. The movements of the fingers are similar to those of pill rolling.

Is there actual paralysis in parkinsonism?

No, despite the fact that the condition is often referred to as paralysis agitans.

What are the main causes of Parkinson's disease?

1. **Arteriosclerosis of blood vessels in the brain,** resulting in degeneration of those nerve centers (ganglia) that control muscle actions

2. **Encephalitis** (sleeping sickness), a virus inflammation of the brain, which, years later, leads to degeneration of the same nerve centers

Is parkinsonism a disease of old age?

No, although the type associated with hardening of the arteries is much more common in the 70s and 80s than in earlier life. When the disease follows encephalitis, it usually occurs during the 30s, 40s, or 50s.

Are the symptoms of Parkinson's disease the same whether it is caused by hardening of the arteries or by encephalitis?

Yes.

Is Parkinson's disease more common in men than in women?

Yes, inasmuch as arteriosclerosis of the arteries in the brain affects men more often than women.

Is mental function impaired in Parkinsons' disease?

No, except that mental function might be naturally impaired in patients of advanced age. The masklike appearance of the face is not indicative of stupidity, but is part of the disease process.

Does the shaking palsy continue throughout the night and day?

No. During sleep, the shaking tremors disappear. Also, the shaking disappears or is markedly diminished in intensity while voluntary muscle movements are being performed.

What is palsy?

It is any type of rhythmic tremor (shaking movement) that involves the arms, hands, legs, head, or neck.

Is Parkinson's disease usually progressive?

Yes. If untreated, it will get worse as the months or years pass; eventually, it may render the patient helpless.

Is chronic constipation associated with Parkinson's disease?

Yes, and this may be a very troublesome complication.

What is the treatment of Parkinson's disease?

1. A rather large group of drugs are helpful in reducing the muscle rigidity and tremors. These drugs must be taken regularly and for long periods of time. A new drug named L-dopa has resulted in a strikingly high percentage of symptom relief in cases where it has been used. However, the drug is not without some potentially dangerous side effects, and must therefore be administered only under the direction of a specialist in the treatment of Parkinson's disease. In cases where the response to L-dopa is good, surgery becomes unnecessary.

2. Psychotherapy is very helpful in aiding the patient to adjust to his condition.

3. Within recent years, brain operations have been devised that sever those nerves responsible for the tremors and muscle rigidity. With modern surgical techniques good results can be anticipated in the majority of cases.

Does paralysis of the arms and legs follow surgery for parkinsonism?

No.

Are operations for Parkinson's disease safe?

Yes, provided the general health of the patient is satisfactory. However, it is a serious procedure and does carry considerable risk.

Are operations for Parkinson's disease usually performed in two stages?

Yes. An interval of several weeks or months between operations upon the right and left sides is the usual routine.

Paronychia

A paronychia, or paronychial infection, is one located around a fingernail or toenail. A very common cause for this type of infection is cutting the nail too deeply at the corners or pricking the tissue around the nail with a needle. Ingrown toenails often cause this type of infection when the sharp edge of the nail penetrates the skin surrounding it. A paronychial infection of the fingernail is also called a "runaround."

When pus forms in the tissues immediately surrounding the nail, it must be incised surgically. Unless this is carried out early, infection may spread beneath the nail and will lead to its removal. Most paronychias can be treated under local anesthesia in a surgeon's office. However, if the extension of the infection is marked, it may involve the nail and may also affect the bone in the tip of the finger or toe. In these latter instances, it may be necessary to hospitalize the patient in order to perform the surgery.

Recovery is usually prompt after incising and draining this type of infec-

tion. However, if the infection had been caused by an ingrown toenail, it is necessary to relieve this condition, or another infection will set in.

QUESTIONS AND ANSWERS

How common is a paronychia?

It is one of the most frequently encountered surgical conditions afflicting the hands or feet.

Will the giving of antibiotics control most paronychias without surgery?

No. Since pus has collected beneath the skin in the area around the nail, it is essential to allow it to drain out. The administration of antibiotics will not cause such an infection to subside, in the great majority of cases.

Can one develop a paronychial infection by biting his fingernails or by pulling a hangnail?

These are common ways in which paronychias develop.

What germ causes most paronychias?

The great majority are caused by the staphylococcus germ.

Is it common for women with infants to develop paronychias?

Yes, along with other infections of the fingers. They occur very often as a result of sticking oneself with a diaper pin. To avoid this, diaper pins should always be inserted with the point directed away from rather than toward the fingers.

Parotid Gland

The parotid gland is one of the salivary glands located in front of and a bit below the ear. Its function is to produce and secrete saliva through a duct which extends from the gland into the mucous membrane lining of the cheek. The parotid gland is the gland most frequently involved in mumps and is also the frequent site of tumor formation.

See also SALIVARY GLANDS.

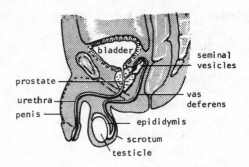

Patent Ductus Arteriosus

The ductus arteriosus is a blood vessel present in the embryo and connecting the pulmonary artery of the lung to the aorta. Normally, this vessel closes off by the time the child is born. If it fails to close, it is called a patent ductus arteriosus. This type of deformity often requires surgical correction.

See also HEART.

Pectus Excavatum

See FUNNEL CHEST.

Penis

The penis is composed of three tubular structures made of erectile tissue. Two of these are located on its upper aspect, and the third is on the lower aspect of the organ. The urethra, which transports the urine and seminal fluid, passes through one of these tubular structures. All three tubular structures, called corpora, are made up of spongy tissue and when filled with blood they become rigid, thus producing an erection. The head of the penis, or glans, is covered at birth by the foreskin. The latter structure is removed when circumcision is performed.

See also CIRCUMCISION; HYPOSPADIAS AND EPISPADIAS; PHIMOSIS.

QUESTIONS AND ANSWERS

What is the function of the penis?
1. To transport urine
2. To transport seminal fluid containing the sperm

How is the penis of a newborn examined?
1. The foreskin is retracted. If the foreskin is so tight that it cannot be retracted over the head of the penis, circumcision is necessary. Otherwise it will be impossible to keep the penis clean and remove the smegma (an oily, waxy material) that will collect.
2. After the foreskin is retracted, the head of the penis is examined to make sure that the urethra (the tube coursing through the penis) terminates at the tip of the penis. If it terminates along the shaft, hypospadias or epispadias exists.
3. The way the newborn child voids urine is observed. (The child will usually urinate very shortly after birth.) It is important to make sure there is no stricture or occlusion of the urethra, which leads from the bladder out through the penis.

What are some of the common abnormalities found in a child's penis?
1. **Phimosis,** an extremely frequent finding in newborns, characterized by a tight foreskin that cannot be drawn back

over the head of the penis. This condition is sometimes followed by an acute inflammation beneath the foreskin. It is treated when acutely inflamed, by making a small slit in the foreskin, which allows it to be retracted over the head of the organ. The child is circumcised when the inflammation has subsided.

2. Hypospadias, a birth deformity in which the tube leading from the urinary bladder to the penis falls short of its normal point of termination at the tip of the organ. Thus there is an opening somewhere along the shaft of the penis. Hypospadias occurs approximately once in 200 male births. It is corrected surgically.

3. Epispadias, a deformity similar to hypospadias except that the urethral opening is on the upper surface of the shaft of the penis rather than on the lower surface. It is less common.

4. Stenosis (narrowing) of the external opening of the urethra, an extremely common occurrence in newborns. The child with stenosis may strain and cry on attempts to void.

What is the surgical treatment for birth deformities of the penis?

1. Minor degrees of hypospadias require no treatment, particularly if the child can pass urine while standing up and if the penis does not show a marked curvature. In many cases it is necessary to perform a plastic operation, usually when the child is 3 or 4 years old. Operations for hypospadias are often done in stages. The initial operation concentrates on straightening the penis by cutting away bands of constricting fibrous tissue on its lower surface. The second-stage operation, which may be done several months to a year later, reconstructs the urethral canal so that it ends at or near the tip of the penis. There are several excellent surgical techniques for accomplishing this. Almost all these procedures involve using the skin on the lower surface of the penis to lengthen the urethra. During the healing process after such a plastic operation it is sometimes necessary to perform another operation, called suprapubic cystotomy. This short-circuits the urine from the bladder and causes it to drain onto the abdominal wall while the new canal for the passage of urine through the penis heals. When healing is complete, the cystotomy tube is taken out and urine is again voided normally.

2. Operations for epispadias are quite similar to those for hypospadias, except that the plastic procedure involves tissues on the upper surface of the penis. Results are usually as good as in operations for hypospadias.

3. A stricture or stenosis of the external opening of the penis is treated with a very minor operative procedure known as meatotomy. The opening is enlarged by making a nick with a knife. This is an office procedure carried out on a newborn during its first few weeks of life. No anesthesia is required and the results are uniformly good.

What is circumcision, and why should the operation be performed?

Circumcision is the surgical removal of the foreskin from the head of the penis. This permits easy cleaning with daily removal of the collection of smegma, naturally found in the groove just behind the head of the penis. It is suspected that smegma may have cancer-producing qualities; it is extremely rare for a man circumcised in infancy to develop cancer of the penis. In addition, women married to men circumcised at birth develop cancer of the cervix of the uterus less frequently than those married to uncircumcised men. This is attributed to the fact that smegma is not deposited in the vaginal canal during sexual relations.

What other conditions of the penis may require surgery?

1. A **stone** coming down from the bladder may occasionally become arrested in the urethral canal. This will cause a good deal of pain, urethral bleeding, and difficulty in voiding. Manipulation with instruments will often succeed in removing such a stone. If this is not successful, a surgical incision must be made directly into the urethra over the area of the stone. After removal of the stone, the urethra must be sutured and a catheter (rubber tube) is inserted for about a week to permit proper healing.

2. Tumors of the penis are relatively uncommon. The benign growths, such as fatty or fibrous tumors or cysts, are easily removed under local anesthesia and occasion little discomfort. *Cancer* of the penis usually originates in the skin of the head of the penis. As mentioned previously, it is practically unknown in the circumcised organ. It is diagnosed by noting the appearance of a firm, nonhealing, ulcerated growth. Biopsy is always taken to clinch the diagnosis.

The treatment for cancer of the penis is *partial* or *complete* amputation. When the growth is small, amputation can be confined to the head of the penis and the urethra is made to emerge from the new tip. However, when the growth is large, the entire penis must be removed and a thorough dissection is carried out, with removal of the lymph nodes in both groins. In these cases, the urethra opens in the perineum, the space in front of the anal opening and behind the scrotum. *Urine control is maintained* in these patients but they must sit down to void.

Amputation of the penis is a major procedure carried out under spinal or general anesthesia. Operative recovery is assured but the patient must be made to understand that the surgery was the only alternative to loss of life.

3. Loss of the penis, by either amputation for cancer or accident or war wounds, is an extremely damaging experience to any male. There have been several operations devised for the reconstruction of the penis from skin grafts taken from the abdomen. While it is true that some semblance of a new penis may be attained, its ability to function sexually is open to question. However, for psychological reasons, the operation may be well worth performing and should be seriously considered in all instances of total amputation. The partially amputated penis requires no additional surgery and can, in most cases, function normally.

In what age group is cancer of the penis most likely to occur?

In middle and old age. It rarely occurs in youth.

With what other condition can a cancer of the penis be confused?

One must distinguish a cancer from a venereal lesion such as a chancre.

Is cancer of the penis related to sexual activity?

No.

Can cancer of the penis be transmitted by sexual intercourse?

No.

What is the treatment for cancer of the penis?

The best form of treatment is amputation of part or all of the penis, along with removal of the lymph nodes in the groin which drain the penis. If the growth is small and is diagnosed early, it can be treated with the local application of radium or by a combination of local removal of the tumor plus radium application.

If the penis is amputated, how does one urinate?

1. If partially amputated, the urine is voided through the remainder of the urethra.

2. If totally amputated, a new opening for the urethra is made in the perineum—between the thighs in front of the anus.

Can an artificial penis be constructed?

Yes, by fashioning a graft from the skin of the abdomen.

Can an artificial penis function like a normal one?

No. In actuality, its sole benefit is a psychological one.

Are operations upon the penis and scrotal structures dangerous?

No.

What anesthesia is usually used?

In children, general. In adults, spinal.

Peptic Ulcer

A peptic ulcer is one involving the esophagus, stomach, or duodenum. Although people generally refer to "stomach ulcers," more than 90 percent are located in the duodenum, the first portion of the small intestine.

See also ESOPHAGUS; STOMACH AND DUODENUM.

Pericarditis

The heart is encased in a double-layered thin sheath known as the pericardium. The inner layer of the pericardium is adherent to the heart muscle,

whereas the outer layer is not attached to the main muscle wall of the heart. Thus, the heart is surrounded by a sac known as the pericardial sac. When this sac is the site of inflammation, pericarditis is said to exist.

There is a large number of different kinds of pericarditis and there are several different classifications. Some of these are:

1. Acute pericarditis.

a) *Fibrinous pericarditis* associated with a deposit of a sticky substance known as fibrin within the pericardial sac.

b) *Pericardial effusion,* secretion of fluid into the sac surrounding the heart.

2. Chronic pericarditis. This type often is associated with constriction of the pericardium which presses and inhibits the free contraction and expansion of the heart muscle.

3. Infectious pericarditis. This may be caused by bacteria such as the pneumococcus, the staphylococcus, the streptococcus, the tuberculosis germ, or by fungi.

4. Noninfectious pericarditis. This type includes pericarditis secondary to uremia (kidney poisoning), pericarditis secondary to underactivity of the thyroid gland, and pericarditis following injury.

5. Rheumatic pericarditis, associated with rheumatic fever.

6. Pericarditis as a complication of lupus erythematosus.

7. Postcoronary thrombosis pericarditis. This type follows damage to the heart muscle as a result of a coronary thrombosis.

Although pericarditis is not a disease very frequently encountered, it can be noted from the various types described above that it is not a rare condition. When it occurs, the patient usually has pain in the chest which is often of a constricting type and radiates into one or both arms.

The diagnosis of pericarditis can often be made merely by listening to the heart with the ordinary stethoscope. A rubbing, frictional sound can be heard when the outer sheath of pericardium rubs against the inner sheath which is attached to the heart muscle. This is a loud, to-and-fro, leathery sound which comes and goes as one listens to the heartbeat. The electrocardiogram and x-rays of the chest will also help to make the diagnosis, as will the previous medical history of the patient. Thus, if the patient has recently had an acute episode of rheumatic fever, pericarditis will be suspected.

QUESTIONS AND ANSWERS

How long does it take for pericarditis to develop?

It may develop within a few days, in acute cases, or may take several months or years to develop, as in chronic constricting pericarditis.

Do people of all ages develop pericarditis?

Yes. It can occur in children as well as in adults. Most patients, however, are in young- and middle-adult life when so afflicted.

How does one distinguish pericarditis from pleurisy?

This can be done by x-ray, by listening to the chest with a stethoscope, and by taking electrocardiograms. In pleurisy, the pain is aggravated on breathing, while in pericarditis, the pain may be continuous and not aggravated by deep breathing.

Is pericarditis frequently followed by fluid collection within the pericardial sac?

Yes. This condition is known as pericardial effusion.

Is pericarditis a very serious condition?

Yes. The degree of seriousness will depend upon the origin of the inflammation.

What is the main danger of pericarditis?

It can impair heart function and action. If sufficient fluid collects in the pericardial sac, it can tamponade the heart and reduce its ability to contract and expand. A chronic pericarditis may form fibrous scar tissue around the heart which will also constrict it so as to limit heart function severely.

What is the treatment for pericarditis?

The approach must be to eliminate the underlying cause. Thus, if the pericarditis is secondary to tuberculosis, antituberculosis drugs must be given in massive doses. If the pericarditis is secondary to acute bacterial infection, antibiotics must be given.

If an effusion has taken place, and this does frequently happen in cases of pericarditis, a needle should be inserted into the pericardial sac through the chest wall and the fluid withdrawn.

What operation is performed if pericardial fluid or pus cannot be drained by needle aspiration?

A simple operation in which a small incision is made in the chest wall and the pericardial sac is exposed. An opening is then made into the sac and the fluid or pus is drained.

Is it ever necessary to remove some of the pericardium?

Yes. As a result of infection, adhesions may form between the pericardium and the outer heart-muscle wall. This can interfere greatly with normal heart function. In such circumstances it is necessary to open the chest widely and to excise large portions of the pericardium so that normal heart function may be restored.

Is it often necessary to puncture the pericardial sac more than once to remove fluid or pus?

Yes.

Is surgery for pericarditis a very serious operation?

Yes, but the majority of patients will recover, and results are usually good.

How can pericarditis be prevented?

By prompt and early treatment for those conditions that might lead to inflammation of the pericardial sac. As an example, a patient with acute rheumatic fever will usually not develop pericarditis if the treatment for his acute attack is carried out early and thoroughly. By the same token, someone with marked underactivity of the thyroid gland will not develop pericarditis if he receives adequate replacement therapy with thyroid hormone.

Peritonitis

Peritonitis is an inflammation of the thin membrane (peritoneum) surrounding the abdominal organs. One of the most common causes of peritonitis is a ruptured appendix. Peritonitis can be caused also by rupture of other organs such as the duodenum, the small or large intestine, or by an infection ascending from the uterus and fallopian tubes. Any organ that ruptures within the abdomen may discharge pus into the peritoneal cavity and lead to serious complications, as toxins will be absorbed through the lining of the abdominal cavity into the bloodstream. Although peritonitis was formerly fatal in a large

number of cases, most people can be saved today by the judicious use of antibiotic drugs.

QUESTIONS AND ANSWERS

What is peritonitis?

Peritonitis is a bacterial infection of the abdominal cavity (peritoneal cavity).

What is the peritoneal cavity?

The peritoneal cavity is the free space within the abdomen that surrounds the various abdominal organs, such as the stomach, gallbladder, intestines, appendix, liver, and spleen.

Is peritonitis as common today as it was formerly?

No. Fortunately, most people realize the importance of calling a physician when abdominal symptoms persist. As a consequence, inflamed abdominal organs are treated before they can spread their infection to the peritoneal cavity. Furthermore, appendicitis is less frequently encountered today than it was twenty to thirty years ago.

What are the most common causes of peritonitis?

1. Rupture of an abdominal organ, such as the appendix or small intestine

2. The spread of infection from an inflamed organ into the abdominal cavity surrounding it

3. An injury to the abdominal wall that has extended into the peritoneal cavity, such as can be caused by an accident or stab wound

4. An infection that reaches the peritoneal cavity through the bloodstream, causing so-called hematogenous peritonitis

5. An infection that ascends through the fallopian tubes and reaches the peritoneal cavity

Is peritonitis usually caused by one kind of bacteria or by a mixture of many bacteria?

Most cases of peritonitis are caused by a mixture of many bacteria, which gain access to the abdominal cavity from intestinal organs. The passageway of the intestinal tract is filled at all times with innumerable types of bacteria; these can cause peritonitis if they leave the confines of the tract and enter the abdominal cavity.

How long after the onset of an infection can peritonitis take place?

This will vary according to the underlying condition causing the peritonitis. An appendix rarely bursts until it has been inflamed for a day or two. On the other hand, if an abdominal organ ruptures following an accident or if a foreign body perforates the wall of the intestine, peritonitis results immediately.

What bacteria may cause peritonitis?

Any kind of bacteria, including the streptococcus, staphylococcus, colon bacillus, tuberculosis bacillus, gonococcus, and pneumococcus.

How can peritonitis be prevented?

1. Early attention should be given to abdominal pain, and treatment of the underlying condition should be prompt. For example, acute appendicitis should be treated with surgery without delay, thus obviating the possibility of rupture of the appendix with spread of the pus to the peritoneal cavity.

2. A person should never take a laxative when he has abdominal pain. Many an appendix has been ruptured as a result of taking a laxative.

What are some of the signs and symptoms of peritonitis?

1. Pain in the abdomen
2. Tenderness on pressure by the examining physician over the abdominal wall
3. Nausea and vomiting
4. Abdominal distention
5. Fever
6. Characteristic x-ray findings in many cases
7. Rigidity and spasm of the abdominal muscles

How serious is peritonitis?

It is a very serious condition and often results in severe toxemia if not treated. Unless prompt and vigorous treatment is instituted early, the patient may die from an overwhelming bacterial infection and toxemia.

Will the seriousness of peritonitis depend on the type of germs causing it?

Yes, in many instances. Another important factor is whether or not the bacterial infection of the abdominal cavity is continuing because the underlying cause has not been eradicated. If pus is constantly being fed into the abdominal cavity, the patient is much more seriously ill and his chances for recovery are lessened.

What is the treatment for peritonitis?

1. Immediate surgery is necessary to remove the underlying cause, such as an acutely infected appendix.

2. Pus must be removed from the peritoneal cavity by suction, and rubber drains must be inserted to permit the exit of pus that may form following surgery.

3. If the peritonitis follows an accident in which the stomach or intestines have been ruptured, these organs must be repaired surgically.

4. Massive doses of antibiotic drugs are given to overcome the bacterial infection and toxemia.

5. A stomach tube is inserted through the nose into the stomach in order to keep the stomach free from distention

and to drain off fluids that collect within the intestinal tract.

6. The patient will be fed and given medications intravenously for several days.

What are the chances for recovery from peritonitis?

If adequate, prompt surgery and medical treatment are instituted, the great majority of cases will recover.

How long does it take to recover from peritonitis?

Recovery may be a slow process taking several weeks. It is not at all uncommon for the wounds to drain pus and for healing to be delayed for a month or two.

Are there permanent aftereffects of peritonitis?

Yes, in many cases, even though the eventual recovery may be complete. Extensive adhesions may form following bacterial peritonitis, and these can cause obstruction to the intestines some weeks, months, or even years after the acute process has subsided.

What is adhesive peritonitis?

It is a form in which there is a matting together of the intestines and various other organs as a result of adhesions from previous inflammation and pus formation within the abdominal cavity.

What is bile peritonitis?

It is inflammation of the peritoneal cavity resulting from the escape of bile into that cavity.

What is localized peritonitis?

It is an inflammation of the abdominal cavity, which has not spread beyond a localized region. This frequently occurs when an appendix has ruptured, and the peritonitis remains for a time in the region of the appendix.

What is general peritonitis?

It is an infection of the entire abdominal cavity.

What is pelvic peritonitis?

It is inflammation of the peritoneal cavity limited to the pelvis and surrounding the uterus, the fallopian tubes, and the ovaries.

What is tuberculous peritonitis?

It is inflammation of the abdominal cavity secondary to infection with the germ of tuberculosis.

Peritonsillar Abscess

A peritonsillar abscess is one located around, above, and behind the tonsil. *See also* QUINSY SORE THROAT.

Perthes' Disease

Perthes' disease is an inflammatory condition of the head of the hipbone (femur). There is a deficient blood supply to the bone, resulting in loss of bone cells. This leads eventually to a typical deformity with increased angulation between the head and the shaft of the hipbone. The disease is seen mostly in children but does occur every once in a while in an adult.

See also HIP.

Pheochromocytoma

A pheochromocytoma is a tumor of the medulla of the adrenal gland. This is the portion of the gland which secretes epinephrine (adrenalin) and norepinephrine (noradrenalin). The symptoms caused by this tumor are those associated with excessive production of epinephrine and norepinephrine. As a consequence, the patient may experience episodes of high blood pressure due to sudden release into the circulation of large amounts of these hormones. The attacks last several minutes and are often accompanied by great anxiety, severe headache, palpitation of the heart, blurred eyesight, nausea and vomiting, marked perspiration, and prostration. On examination of the blood, excess sugar and an elevated level of calcium are often found. Occasionally, the patient may go into a state that is similar to one of shock. Some patients never have the acute episodes described above, but do have continuing high blood pressure with an increase in the basal metabolic rate.

See also ADRENAL GLANDS.

QUESTIONS AND ANSWERS

How does a physician make a diagnosis of pheochromocytoma?

In many cases, an attack can be deliberately precipitated by pressure upon the adrenal glands or by requesting the patient to perform those strenuous physical activities which he knows will cause an attack to ensue.

Can a diagnosis of pheochromocytoma always be made with certainty?

No. In many cases the diagnosis can merely be suspected as a result of typical symptoms.

How common is pheochromocytoma?

It is a rare tumor.

What is the treatment for pheochromocytoma?

The surgical removal of the tumor.

Is operation for this type of tumor serious?

Yes. Patients have been known to go into sudden states of shock or even into cardiac arrest when a surgeon manipulated the adrenal glands. In order to combat this, certain blocking agents, such as Regitine, are given during the operation. This drug will prevent the outpouring of great quantities of epinephrine or norepinephrine.

Sudden sharp drops in blood pressure must also be guarded against during the performance of the operation. Thus, epinephrine and norepinephrine should always be readily available to be given, should such an eventuality take place.

Is it ever necessary to explore both adrenal glands to find the tumor?

Yes. It is not always possible to determine from which side the tumor originates. As a consequence, bilateral exploration is sometimes necessary.

What are the results of surgery for pheochromocytoma?

The results are good if the tumor can be found and removed. The use of the blocking agents has made the procedure much safer, and can allow a much more thorough exploration of the glands.

Can complete recovery follow the removal of a pheochromocytoma?

Yes. The symptoms will disappear entirely if a localized tumor has been found and has been removed.

Do pheochromocytomas tend to recur?

Not if the original tumor has been removed completely.

Phimosis

Phimosis is a condition in which there is swelling of the foreskin with tightness and inability to draw back the foreskin over the head of the organ. When acute inflammation is present, it is treated by making a small one-half- to one-inch incision to permit it to retract. This is called a *dorsal slit* operation. When the inflammation has completely subsided, *circumcision* should be carried out.

Circumcision is being performed, regardless of religious faith, within a few days after birth as a routine prophylactic procedure in most male children who are born today. It has been almost universally recognized that circumcision is a valuable procedure for several reasons:

1. Cancer of the penis rarely, if ever, occurs in men who have been circumcised.

2. Cleanliness and hygienic care of the penis are aided by circumcision.

3. Some evidence, not yet conclusive, has been presented during the past few years to show that cancer of the cervix is very uncommon in women who are married to circumcised men.

When circumcision is performed soon after birth, no anesthetic is required. When it is necessary to circumcise later in childhood or in adult life, hospitalization for a day or two is necessary and either local or general anesthesia is employed. The foreskin may be removed either by cutting with a knife and the use of sutures to control bleeding, or by using a specially devised circumcision clamp. The latter controls bleeding and eliminates the need for sutures.

See also PENIS.

QUESTIONS AND ANSWERS

What are the symptoms of phimosis?

The foreskin is swollen and red and a discharge exudes from under it. It is often painful or impossible to retract the foreskin over the head of the penis.

The penis itself is red, tender, and inflamed.

What is the treatment for phimosis?

The immediate treatment is to bring the infection under control by applying warm compresses and by cleaning out the material that collects between the foreskin and the head of the penis. This may be partially accomplished by introducing a small syringe under the tightened foreskin overlying the head of the penis and flushing the area with warm solutions. If this cannot be done, the foreskin is slit surgically to permit drainage. It may then be possible to retract the foreskin to a greater extent for more efficient cleaning. When the acute infection has subsided, a routine circumcision should be performed.

Is any permanent damage done to the penis because of phimosis?

If phimosis is not relieved by circumcision, a chronic infection may develop. Also, in an uncircumcised individual with poor hygienic habits, there is the possibility that cancer may develop. However, malignancy of the penis rarely occurs in childhood.

Phlebitis

Phlebitis is an inflammation of a vein, as evidenced by pain, swelling, and tenderness in the area. It is often associated with the formation of a blood clot within the inflamed vessel. If a superficial vein is involved, the phlebitis can often be felt as a cordlike thickening along the vein.

See also BLOOD VESSELS; EMBOLUS AND EMBOLISM; VARICOSE VEINS.

QUESTIONS AND ANSWERS

What is thrombophlebitis?

It is an inflammation of the wall of a vein associated with blood-clot formation and the stoppage of blood flow through the vessel. Thrombophlebitis most commonly affects the legs.

Is phlebitis often associated with the formation of a blood clot?

Yes. As a matter of fact, most cases of phlebitis are cases of thrombophlebitis.

What are some of the factors predisposing toward the development of phlebitis or thrombophlebitis?

1. Stagnation of blood within a vein due to prolonged inactivity, prolonged standing in one position, and pressure upon a vein which cuts off its blood flow (tight garters may cause this)
2. A blood clot within a vein due to an injury, infection, or irritation of its wall
3. Varicosities of the veins, with incompetent valves causing the blood to stagnate
4. An increased tendency for the blood to clot due to some blood disease

Is there a difference between the type of phlebitis caused by an inflammation and the type usually seen after an operation?

Yes. The phlebitis sometimes encountered after surgery is called phlebothrombosis rather than thrombophlebitis. It signifies that the phlebitis has arisen as a result of inactivity and stagnation imposed by the operation. The inflammatory factor is much less evident in this form of phlebitis.

Is it important for people to keep active and moving after major surgery in order to prevent phlebitis?

Yes. This is the underlying reason for getting people out of bed as soon as possible after a major surgical operation (early ambulation).

Is thrombophlebitis a common condition?

Yes. It is an extremely common condition particularly in today's society, wherein people are less active physically and tend to stand in one position for long periods of time. In former years, when people were more active, varicose veins and phlebitis were less prevalent.

Is phlebitis a common complication of pregnancy?

Yes. It is thought to result from the pressure of the embryo upon the great veins within the pelvis. This interferes with a free and easy flow of blood through the major veins toward the heart. When the blood stagnates, it has a greater tendency to clot.

What kinds of people are more likely to develop thrombophlebitis?

Those in whom there is poor heart function, or those who are affected by some chronic disease. It is also more apt to occur in areas adjacent to an infection or injury.

Does phlebitis tend to run in families or to be inherited?

It is not an inherited condition, but the type of blood vessels one possesses is inherited. Thus, people with fragile veins or varicose veins have a greater tendency toward the development of phlebitis. (Varicosities tend to run in families.)

What actually takes place when a patient has thrombophlebitis?

There is an inflammation of the inner wall of the vessel, which causes blood in contact with the inflamed area to adhere and clot. The vessel may eventually become clogged to such an extent that blood must travel through other channels.

What are the symptoms of thrombophlebitis?

1. There may be no symptoms at all or there may be a markedly swollen, red, hot, and tender leg.

2. There may be a tender cord felt along the course of an inflamed vein.

3. There may be a low-grade fever.

What is the paramount danger in not following medical advice in thrombophlebitis?

The danger is that a piece of the thrombus (clot) may break off and travel to another part of the body, such as the lung or the brain.

What is the treatment for thrombophlebitis?

1. Bed rest.

2. Anticoagulant medications to prevent the spread of the clot.

3. Medications to relieve pain.

4. Antibiotics to control infection which may be present.

5. The wearing of bandages to give support to painful veins.

6. In certain cases, where the clot shows evidence of spreading despite adequate treatment, surgery may be necessary. This will consist of tying off the vein higher up so as to prevent further spread of the clot.

7. In some cases, the involved vein is exposed surgically and opened, the clotted blood is removed, and the opening in the vessel is sutured.

Does thrombophlebitis tend to get well by itself?

Yes, but medical supervision is essential.

What is the general course of thrombophlebitis?

The average case lasts from three to six weeks before it subsides completely.

Is hospitalization necessary for phlebitis?

If the patient has an acute phlebitis with elevated temperature, it is perhaps best that he be treated in the hospital, where antibiotics and anticoagulant medications can be given under supervision.

Is there a tendency for thrombophlebitis to recur after it has once been arrested?

Yes. People who have had one attack must guard against a subsequent one.

What are the permanent aftereffects of phlebitis?

If a large number of veins have been damaged by the process, blood may be slowed in its return course from the extremity to the heart. In such cases, there may be permanent swelling of the limb.

How can one prevent a recurrent attack of thrombophlebitis?

1. Improve the general health and treat any existing infection.

2. Obtain medical advice on the proper exercises for the extremities.

3. Avoid wearing tight, constricting garters around the legs.

4. Certain people should be placed on anticoagulant therapy for an indefinite period.

5. Stop smoking.

Will the wearing of elastic stockings or elastic bandages help people who have a tendency toward thrombophlebitis?

Yes, as it will aid the return flow of blood from the extremity.

Should elastic stockings be given to every patient with phlebitis?

No, only to those people who feel better when they wear the stockings. Those who have phlebitis of both deep and superficial veins may feel worse when wearing elastic supports.

What surgical measures can be carried out to prevent subsequent attacks of phlebitis?

The ligation and stripping of incompetent varicose veins.

Is surgery ever carried out to remove the clot in cases of thrombophlebitis?

Yes. In some instances, when a deep vein of the thigh or leg has become acutely clotted and there is great swelling, an incision is made in the groin, and the involved vein is dissected out. The vein is opened and the clot is sucked out from the passageway of the vein. This often will relieve the acute symptoms of phlebitis, and the swelling of the leg will subside.

Is surgery for thrombophlebitis dangerous?

No. Recovery is the general rule within a period of a few days.

When should surgery be done for acute phlebitis?

Soon after a clot has taken place.

Do older people often develop phlebitis?

Yes, because the walls of the veins become more fragile and because the aging process makes them more susceptible to inflammation. Moreover, in the later years, circulation slows and blood tends to stagnate and clot.

Is phlebitis ever serious when it affects older people?

Yes, particularly when it involves the deep veins of the legs or the veins in the pelvis or the abdomen.

How can one help to prevent the onset of phlebitis?

1. By exercising regularly, even when confined to bed by an illness. This will aid normal circulation through the veins.

2. Regular walking, if the general health permits.

3. By treatment of varicose veins,

even if they cause no symptoms, so that phlebitis does not eventually set in.

4. Wearing of elastic stockings or compression bandages by those who have small varicosities and by those who are not able to undergo surgery.

5. By eliminating constricting garters.

6. By undergoing surgery for the removal of any growth that causes back pressure on the veins in the thighs or legs.

7. If possible, by giving up a job that requires standing in one position for long periods of time.

8. By seeking early treatment for any infection of the legs or feet, especially a fungus infection of the toes.

9. By giving up smoking.

Piles

Piles is a lay term for hemorrhoids. *See also* HEMORRHOIDS.

Pilonidal Cyst (Sacrococcygeal Sinus and Cyst)

It is estimated that approximately 5 percent of all people have pilonidal cysts. It is less common in women than in men, and Negroes seem to be afflicted less frequently than Caucasians. Pilonidal cysts are located in the midline of the lower back at a level just above the cheeks of the buttocks. They are manifested by one or more sinus openings in the skin which lead to the cyst (a pouchlike structure). The cyst itself may be so undeveloped and small that it cannot be felt at all, or it may develop into a lump the size of a half dollar. The sinus (tunnel) extends from the skin level down to the cyst, which lies within the subcutaneous tissue and rests upon the fibrous tissue which is attached to the spine (sacrum) and tailbone (coccyx). Hair grows from the cyst lining and often protrudes through the openings in the skin. This may give the first clue to the presence of the condition.

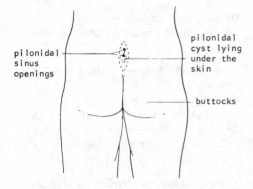

Pilonidal sinuses and cyst with dotted ellipse showing the block of tissue that must be removed to effect complete cure.

Pilonidal cysts usually do not cause clinical symptoms until after adolescence. At some time during early adulthood, a slight yellowish discharge exudes from the area. Further examination may reveal a small lump. Medical inspection will immediately reveal the presence of the sinus openings. Pilonidal cysts, since they are often lined by a skinlike layer of cells, tend to grow hair, and because the openings in the skin are so small, they tend to become infected and cause painful abscesses. Such an infection is often the first knowledge the patient has of the cyst's existence.

TREATMENT

When a pilonidal abscess has formed, it must be opened. Unless it is particularly extensive, this can be done under local anesthesia in the surgeon's office. Immediate relief from pain follows the evacuation of the pus, and within four to five days the inflammation will subside. However, the incision into the abcess does *not* permanently cure the condition. It will be necessary at some future date to admit the patient to the hospital for definitive surgical treatment.

Operations for pilonidal cysts are designed to remove all the affected tissues. An elliptical incision two to four inches long and one-half to one inch wide is made in the midline overlying the sinus openings. All of the sinus openings and all of the tissue beneath the skin (subcutaneous tissue) including the cyst are removed in one piece. It is important that all of the cyst wall and all sinuses (tunnels or tracts) leading from the cyst are excised (removed) or recurrence will follow.

There are several different techniques for this operation, all of which revolve around the problem of how best to close the vacant space that remains after removal of the cyst and its surrounding tissues. No matter which method of wound closure is attempted after removal of a pilonidal cyst, recurrence takes place in 5 to 10 percent of all cases. In view of this sizable recurrence rate, most surgeons do not close these wounds tightly. Instead, the cavity which remains after the cyst's removal is packed with gauze, not sutured, and permitted to fill in slowly with new tissue. This method of surgical treatment leads to the slowest rate of healing but is complicated by the smallest number of recurrences.

Operations upon pilonidal cysts are usually carried out under low spinal anesthesia. The patient may get out of bed the day following surgery and is ready to go home four to seven days later. Although these people can return to work within two to three weeks postoperatively, they must be warned that the wound will not heal completely for several weeks or months. It will be necessary to visit the surgeon's office every few days for wound dressings for a period varying from six weeks to four months.

There is no danger to these operations, and complications, other than local recurrence of a sinus, are practically never encountered. Failure to have a pilonidal sinus and cyst treated may result in chronic discharge of pus from the area, frequent acute abscess formation, and extension of the sinuses out onto the buttocks and down toward the rectum. Such patients live a miserable existence!

QUESTIONS AND ANSWERS

What is a pilonidal cyst?

It is an irregularly shaped cyst which connects with the skin through sinus openings. These cysts are located in the midline of the lower back just above and between the cheeks of the buttocks.

What causes pilonidal cysts and sinuses?

Most investigators feel that they are caused by a defect in development.

Since pilonidal cysts supposedly originate prior to birth, do they tend to be inherited or to run in families?

No.

If they are present since birth, how is it that they rarely cause trouble until the patient reaches maturity?

As one matures, hair grows within the cyst and the cyst lining begins to secrete. As time passes, infection of the cyst occurs and abscesses form.

How does one become aware that he has a pilonidal cyst?

Underclothes are stained with a slight yellowish discharge. In other people, a lump forms and can be felt. Frequently the first manifestation is abscess formation.

Do these cysts become infected frequently?

Yes.

Do they ever turn into cancer?

Very rarely a pilonidal cyst may become malignant.

What usually happens if they are left untreated?

1. Abscesses form.

2. The sinus tracts may extend in all directions for distances of several inches.

3. Chronic discomfort and discharge from the entire area may result.

What treatment is carried out for an acute infection of a pilonidal cyst?

Simple incision and drainage of the pus.

Is this condition *ever* treated medically?

There is no medical treatment! However, an occasional case is encountered where the cyst is so small that operation is not recommended. In such instances, it should be checked periodically.

What is the surgical treatment to cure pilonidal cyst?

Complete removal, in block, of the sinus and cyst and overlying skin with either (a) the wound left widely opened and packed with gauze or (b) some type of total or partial skin closure.

Is this a dangerous operation?

No. It is considered a minor procedure without danger.

How long a hospital stay is necessary?

Four to seven days.

Are special preoperative measures necessary?

No.

What anesthesia is used?
Low spinal.

Is this a painful operation?
Not particularly. Postoperative pain is localized to the area of the incision.

Are special nurses necessary?
No.

What special hospital postoperative measures are necessary?
1. If the patient does not pass his urine, he may have to be catheterized for a day or two.
2. Bowels are not permitted to move for two to three days.
3. Some surgeons recommend having the patient take sitz baths on the fourth or fifth day after operation.

Is the immediate postoperative period very uncomfortable?
Moderately uncomfortable for two to three days. The bowels usually do not move because of the proximity of the wound to the rectum. In some patients it is also difficult to void for a day or two postoperatively.

Does the performance of this operation interfere with normal bowel function?
Only for the first few days after surgery.

How soon after operation can the patient get out of bed?
The day after operation.

When is the packing removed?
Within four to six days.

Is removal of the packing painful?
Yes, but the pain will subside in an hour or two.

What special postoperative measures are necessary after the patient leaves the hospital?
1. Daily sitz baths
2. Absolute cleanliness in the operative area, with daily washing with soap and water
3. Frequent changes of dressings
4. Dressings by the surgeon approximately twice a week

How long after operation does it take the wound to heal?
Anywhere from six weeks to four months.

What determines how long it takes for a pilonidal wound to heal?
The more extensive the cyst, the larger is the section of tissue that must be removed. Thus it may take several months for a large defect to fill in.

Do these cysts ever recur?
Yes, in 5 to 10 percent of cases.

What is done to cure a pilonidal recurrence?
Reoperation. The wound is always packed wide open when a secondary procedure is performed.

Is the healed scar painful or unsightly?
No.

How soon after operation can one:
Sit comfortably? Within a week
Bathe? Within 4 to 7 days
Drive a car? Within 2 to 3 weeks
Return to work? Within 2 to 3 weeks
Resume sexual relations? Within 3 to 4 weeks
Resume all normal physical activities? As soon as the wound has completely healed

Pituitary Gland

The pituitary gland is a small, nut-shaped endocrine gland, which measures about half an inch in diameter, located at the base of the skull beneath the brain. It is divided into two parts, the anterior and the posterior portions, each of which contains different types of cells and secretes different hormones into the bloodstream.

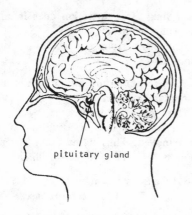

The hypophysis, or pituitary gland, lies in a bony cradle known as the sella turcica. Hypophysectomy involves destruction or removal of the pituitary gland.

QUESTIONS AND ANSWERS

Why is the pituitary gland often referred to as the master gland?

Because it exerts a certain amount of control over the function of almost all the other endocrine glands within the body.

What is the function of the anterior portion of the pituitary gland?

There are thought to be seven hormones produced by the anterior pituitary. These hormones act directly upon the cells of the body and upon other endocrine glands. One of the most important of these seven is the growth hormone, which promotes the growth and development of all tissues. Decreased production of the growth hormone often takes place in the absence of the thyroid hormone. The gonadotropic hormone is another important hormone

produced by the anterior pituitary. This hormone acts upon the ovaries in the female and upon the testicles of the male. Its true effect is not seen until the child reaches the prepuberty period in life. Another anterior pituitary hormone is the thyrotropic hormone, which stimulates the thyroid to produce its hormone. There is also ACTH, which stimulates the adrenal cortex to secrete cortisone and other steroid hormones.

Are there any disease states that result from underactivity of the pituitary gland (hypopituitarism)?

Yes. If underactivity occurs in childhood, growth will be retarded markedly. Children so affected will remain small but well proportioned. They retain a childlike appearance throughout life. This condition is responsible for the little dwarfs one sees at a circus. If underactivity of the pituitary commences during adulthood, growth cannot be stunted. However, such a situation will lead to a depression in the function of all the other endocrine glands, such as the thyroid, the adrenals, the ovaries, and the testicles.

Do endocrine glands such as the adrenals and thyroid ever influence the activity of the anterior portion of the pituitary gland?

Yes. For example, when enough of the adrenal hormones are circulating in the blood, they will act to inhibit the pituitary from secreting more adrenal-stimulating hormone.

Is pituitary dwarfism inherited?

No. If pituitary dwarfs marry and have children, they usually have normal-sized children.

What are some of the other symptoms of hypopituitarism?

Weakness, general apathy, loss of energy, and, in some cases, mental disturbance. The skin takes on a wrinkled appearance as seen in old age. There may be lowering of the blood sugar and loss of appetite and weight.

What condition can result from too little or no secretion of the growth hormone?
Dwarfism.

What condition can result from inadequate secretion of the gonadotropic hormone?
Delayed puberty.

What can result from inadequate secretion of the thyrotropic hormone?
Underactivity of the thyroid gland.

What deficiency can result from inadequate secretion of the adrenocorticotropic hormone (ACTH)?
Inadequate adrenal function.

What is progeria (premature senility)?
Progeria is a rare form of dwarfism caused by pituitary insufficiency and associated with premature evidences of senility. Children with progeria often stop growing by the time they are 10 years of age, and their faces become wrinkled and they appear to be prematurely aged.

Is there any successful treatment for underactivity of the anterior pituitary?
In some cases, replacement therapy with anterior pituitary substance will help to a certain degree.

Can dwarfism be cured by giving hormones?
No. Scientists have not yet succeeded in developing a method to produce the large quantities of growth hormone necessary to stimulate and maintain growth in cases of dwarfs.

Can a child continue to grow if the anterior portion of the pituitary gland is destroyed?
No.

What are the effects of overactivity of the anterior pituitary gland?
If the overactivity occurs before bone growth and development are completed, the child may grow too much and may develop into a giant. Some children reach seven to eight feet in height before their sixteenth year. If the bone growth has already stopped when the pituitary gland becomes overactive, a condition known as acromegaly will result. In acromegaly, there is distortion of the bones of the face, skull, hands, and feet.

Is there any way to stop the child's growth before he becomes a giant?
No, unless the child is suffering from a tumor of the pituitary gland. In such an instance, x-ray treatment or surgery to destroy or remove the tumor will halt the growth process.

Do children who have an excess amount of the pituitary growth hormone tend to display other symptoms?
Yes. They may show severe muscular weakness, and diabetes mellitus may develop.

What hormone is produced by the posterior portion of the pituitary gland, and what is its function?
The posterior pituitary produces a hormone that regulates the excretion of water by the kidneys. Inadequate secretion of this hormone leads to the condition known as diabetes insipidus.

What is diabetes insipidus?
It is a condition caused by too little production of hormone by the posterior pituitary and adjacent nerve tissue. It leads to a serious chain of events in which the kidneys can no longer control the amount of water they excrete.

What are some of the characteristic symptoms of diabetes insipidus?
Since the kidneys excrete huge quan-

tities of water, the patient must drink incessantly in order to maintain sufficient amounts within his body.

Can underactivity of the posterior portion of the pituitary gland be treated medically?

Yes. Extracts of the posterior portion of the gland can be given in order to supplement inadequate secretions. However, in order to control diabetes insipidus, the child will have to take the hormone for his entire life.

PITUITARY TUMORS

Does the pituitary gland often undergo tumor formation?

Yes. Pituitary tumors account for approximately 10 percent of all growths within the skull and brain.

What takes place when the anterior portion of the gland becomes overactive and undergoes tumor formation?

Two conditions may result:

1. If certain cells within the anterior pituitary become too active, overstimulation of the adrenal glands will result and Cushing's disease develops.

2. If other cells within the anterior pituitary become overactive, an excess of growth hormone will be produced, and gigantism or acromegaly will result.

What other changes take place as a result of excessive growth hormone secretion?

The body chemistry is altered and severe muscular weakness, cessation of menstrual periods, impotence, and even diabetes may ensue.

How can a definite diagnosis of a pituitary tumor be made?

In addition to the clinical symptoms that develop, there are characteristic changes noted on x-rays of the skull. The pituitary gland is nestled in a bony cavity called the sella turcica, and when the gland has undergone tumorous growth the edges of this bony cavity become eroded.

What are the characteristics of gigantism?

When the anterior pituitary produces excessive quantities of its growth hormone during childhood before bone development is complete, the individual grows to an enormous size. This condition is responsible for the giants we see who are seven or eight feet tall.

What are the characteristics of acromegaly?

If there is an overproduction of the growth hormone in adult life, after bone structure has been fully developed, then height and the length of the extremities are not altered. However, there is tremendous overgrowth of certain bony parts of the body, such as the hands, the feet, and the features of the face. This results in a characteristic distortion of the facial features.

What is the treatment for a pituitary gland tumor?

In a high proportion of cases, pituitary tumors may be successfully treated by means of x-ray alone, without resorting to surgery. Those patients not helped by x-ray treatment can usually be greatly benefited by surgery.

What are the indications for operating upon the pituitary gland?

When it has been determined that it has undergone tumor formation. This may be evidenced by the onset of progressive loss of vision, headache, changes on x-ray showing erosion of the bone around the gland, or by the onset of signs such as are seen in Cushing's disease and acromegaly or gigantism.

Is surgery upon the pituitary gland safe?

An operation involving the pituitary

gland is a serious one; nevertheless, it is reasonably safe.

Where is the incision made to approach the pituitary gland?

Except in bald people, the incision is made almost completely within the hairline. In any event, the scar resulting from surgery is inconspicuous. The pituitary gland can also be approached by an incision through the nose, and the scar following this incision is also inconspicuous.

Is the pituitary gland usually removed completely when it is the site of tumor, or is it sufficient to remove it partially?

In most cases, an amount sufficient to relieve pressure on the nerves concerned with vision is removed.

What are the chances for recovery from an operation upon the pituitary?

About 90 percent.

How successful are operations for pituitary tumors in relieving symptoms?

As a rule, operations for pituitary tumors are undertaken because of tumor formation with progressive loss of vision. Therefore, the visual status before operation is an important consideration. Generally speaking, most patients are markedly improved following operation, provided too much damage had not occurred preoperatively.

How is a decision made as to whether to treat a pituitary tumor with x-ray or with surgery?

Although opinions vary on this point, x-ray treatment is usually tried first unless vision is already seriously impaired. If vision continues to fail despite x-ray treatment, surgery is indicated.

If there has been impairment of vision due to a pituitary tumor, will surgery upon the gland restore vision?

In most cases, yes.

How long a hospital stay is necessary following operations upon the pituitary gland?

Usually about ten days to two weeks.

How long do these operative procedures take to perform?

About two to three hours.

Do tumors of the pituitary gland ever recur once they have been removed?

Yes, in a small percentage of cases. Such people may then be treated by x-ray therapy or they may be reoperated.

Do tumors of the pituitary gland often spread to other parts of the body?

No. This happens extremely rarely.

Can one lead a normal mental life after a pituitary operation?

Yes. One's mental state is not affected by tumors of the pituitary gland.

Are operations upon the pituitary followed by paralysis of any of the limbs?

No.

Can acromegaly be cured by pituitary surgery?

No, but the process can be halted from progressing further.

Will the bony overgrowths and appearance return to normal after surgery in acromegaly?

Unfortunately, no.

Is the pituitary gland ever removed to slow down the growth of cancer?

Yes. It has been found in certain cases of cancer of the breast which has spread to other parts of the body that removing the pituitary gland will cause a remission of the cancerous growth and spread. This operation, known as hypophysectomy, is frequently successful in bringing about a remission of tumor growth for a period of several months or even years.

Plantar Warts

A wart is an overgrowth of the skin, usually localized, and covered by a very thickened epidermis. Technically, they are known as verrucae. Those occurring on the sole of the foot are known as plantar warts. These are usually very painful because they tend to grow in the weight-bearing area of the foot.

See also WARTS.

QUESTIONS AND ANSWERS

What causes a plantar wart?

The cause is not known exactly, but many people feel that plantar warts occur because of poorly fitted shoes. Some dermatologists believe that most warts are caused by a virus.

Do warts arise from handling frogs or toads?

No. This is an old superstition.

What are the methods of treatment for a plantar wart on the foot?

1. There are certain chemicals containing salicylic acid or trichloracetic acid that, applied regularly on the plantar wart, may cause it to disappear.

2. A special doughnut-shaped piece of felt may be placed over the wart and strapped into position. This will keep the weight off the wart and may cause it to disappear.

3. X-ray therapy will sometimes make warts disappear.

4. Warts that do not respond to one of the above forms of treatment should be removed by thorough curettage and cauterization of the base or by total surgical excision.

Is there a tendency for a plantar wart to recur once it has been removed?

Yes, unless new, well-fitted shoes are worn.

How long after the removal of a plantar wart through surgery can a patient return to usual activities?

It may take a week to ten days before one can comfortably walk upon a foot that has had a plantar wart removed.

Plastic Surgery

Advances in the techniques of modern plastic surgery have been so effective that a great number of birth deformities and acquired conditions can now be corrected or improved. However, much of the reconstructive work that is necessary may be tedious and long drawn out, requiring repeated operations over a period of months or years. Parents must always remember that though the final outcome of a plastic procedure will probably yield a marked improvement in function or structure, the purely cosmetic results will frequently not be as great as their expectations.

See also BREASTS; BURNS; CLEFT PALATE; EARS; FACE AND NECK PLASTIC OPERATIONS; KELOID; NOSE AND SINUSES; SKIN AND SUBCUTANEOUS TISSUES.

QUESTIONS AND ANSWERS

What is plastic surgery?

A branch of surgery devoted to the restoration, repair, and correction of malformations of tissues. It is concerned not only with return to normal appearance but also with restoration to normal function.

What is the difference between cosmetic surgery and plastic surgery?

Cosmetic surgery aims toward improving or restoring the *appearance* of tissues or organs, such as the nose or the breasts. Plastic surgery, while including cosmetic surgery, goes much farther than this, as it aims toward restoring and improving *function* as well as appearance.

What parts of the body and what conditions are most commonly operated upon by plastic surgeons?

It is commonly thought that plastic surgery is limited to operations upon the face. This is not the actual case. A partial list of conditions for which plastic surgery is performed includes:

1. Surgery of the nose (rhinoplasty)
2. For lop ears
3. To remove ugly scars anywhere on the body
4. For receding chin
5. For harelip
6. For cleft palate
7. For restoration of eyelids or external ear
8. Plastic operations upon the breasts
9. For excessive fat on the abdomen (lipectomy)
10. For skin contractures
11. For burns anywhere on the body
12. Skin grafting anywhere on the body
13. For removal of skin blemishes, skin cancers, skin tumors
14. For deformities of the male or female genitals

Is it necessary to go to a plastic surgeon in order to have plastic surgery performed?

Yes, for most conditions requiring specialized knowledge.

Is special training necessary for a physician to become a plastic surgeon?

Yes. Most plastic surgeons are first

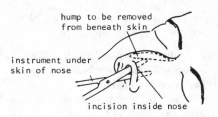

hump to be removed from beneath skin

instrument under skin of nose

incision inside nose

PLASTIC OPERATION ON NOSE
(UNDERMINING THE SKIN OF THE NOSE)

trained as general surgeons and then receive additional years of education, learning the special art of plastic surgery.

What is the difference between plastic and restorative surgery?

Restorative surgery is a branch of plastic surgery which attempts to return injured parts to normal function.

Are the results of plastic surgery usually permanent?

Yes, unless an operation has been performed in an attempt to slow down aging processes, such as an operation to remove skin wrinkles. In such cases, as the patient ages, there is a tendency for a recurrence.

In performing plastic surgery, what tissues of the body may be used as grafts?

1. Skin lends itself excellently to being used as a graft.
2. Cartilage from ribs is often used as a graft to build up a sagging nose.
3. Bone transplants are also used as grafts, as in operations to fuse the spine or to build up the hip joint.
4. Corneas have been used successfully as grafts to restore lost eyesight in certain selected cases.

Can a plastic surgeon always predict the outcome of an operation he is going to perform?

With reasonable certainty, although he cannot always predict the exact appearance that will result. Much will depend upon the peculiar healing characteristics of the individual patient.

Can a plastic surgeon tell in advance how skin will heal and whether the scars will be smooth or ugly?

Not always. Certain people have a tendency to heal with almost invisible scars; others heal with thick, overgrown scars.

AVULSION OF SKIN

What is avulsion?

Avulsion is a tearing away of tissue. In some instances the torn tissue remains partially attached, while in other cases there is complete separation and loss of tissue.

Do children often sustain injuries in which skin, and tissues beneath the skin, are avulsed?

Yes. Perhaps the commonest cause of this type of injury is when a child becomes caught on a picket or barbed-wire fence or gets a finger caught in a door.

Can skin that has been partially avulsed be stitched back into place?

Yes, in most instances. However, thorough cleaning and excision of dead tissue (debridement) must first be carried out. Also, tetanus booster shots should be given, particularly when the wound has been exposed to rust or dirt.

Can skin that has been completely torn away be stitched back in place?

Only if it is done within a few minutes to half an hour after the injury, and then only if the wound and the avulsed tissue are clean. In such cases, the avulsed tissue is comparable to a free full-thickness skin graft.

What is done when a child has lost a sizable piece of skin?

After the wound is thoroughly cleaned and debrided, a skin graft is applied to the bare area.

BURNS, BURN SCARS, AND CONTRACTURES

Do burns often leave deforming scars?

Yes, particularly third degree burns involving large areas of body surface.

When should burn scars of the head and neck be excised?

When they interfere with function or when they cause an ugly deformity.

How are burn scars on a person's face removed surgically?

1. By complete excision of the scar and replacement of the defect with a skin graft

2. By repeated partial excision of the scar and suturing of normal skin on each side of the scar

What parts of the body are most often used to supply skin for grafting?

The thighs, back, and abdomen.

Will the donor site be permanently scarred?

Usually not.

Should burn scars on unexposed surfaces of a person's body be repaired surgically?

Only if they interfere with function.

Are the scars caused by the repair of burns by skin grafts less obvious than the scars of a burn that has healed without skin grafts?

Yes.

Do burn scars tend to form contractures and interfere with function?

Yes.

What is contracture?

A contracture is a formation of thick fibrous tissue that prevents adjacent muscles, tendons, and joints from performing their full functions. They cannot be straightened or readily flexed and extended when there is a contracture.

In what areas of the body are burn scars most likely to lead to contractures?
1. The neck region
2. The armpit
3. The elbow
4. The knee
5. The hand
6. The eyelids

What is the operative procedure for repairing a contracture of the neck due to a burn scar?
The burn scar is completely excised and replaced with a skin graft which is much larger than the scar that was removed.

What is a Z-plasty, and how is it performed?
A Z-plasty is a rearrangement of skin for lengthening a contracted scar. The scar is excised and two V-shaped flaps are made on either side of the scar. These flaps are then rearranged at a new angle and the scar becomes longer. The flaps are then sutured in the shape of a Z.

What is the operative procedure for repairing a contracture of the armpit (axilla) following a burn scar?
Usually, excision and skin grafting. Less severe ones can be treated by Z-plasty.

What is the operative procedure for repairing a contracture of the elbow following a burn scar?
Usually, excision and skin grafting. Sometimes, Z-plasty is all that is necessary.

What is the operative procedure for repairing a contracture of the back of the knee caused by a burn scar?
Applying a split-thickness skin graft.

What is the operative procedure for repairing a contracture of the hand caused by a burn scar?
A free skin graft, often full-thickness, is applied.

Are burns the only cause of contractures?
No. A child may be born with a contracture, may develop a contracture due to avulsion (loss of skin caused by an injury), or may develop a contracture as a laceration heals.

What is the main aim of a plastic surgeon who repairs a contracture?
To restore function.

CUTS AND BRUISES

Is it advisable to consult a plastic surgeon in the treatment of lacerations?
If there is a plastic surgeon in the community, it is wise to have him consult on a laceration about the face, because scars in this area may permanently disfigure a person. He can decide if the problem is severe enough to require his services.

How soon after a discolored, ugly scar has healed can it be repaired?
It is advisable to wait three or four months after the wound has healed. Many scars will show an improvement in this time and will require less surgery or no surgery at all.

When should a person who has sustained a severe bruise be examined by a plastic surgeon?
Immediately after the accident has occurred. This is especially important if the bruise is on the forehead, ears, or face. It may be possible, if the bruise is seen soon enough, to remove the blood with a needle and syringe.

What may happen if a severe bruise is not treated?
A large amount of blood often col-

lects beneath the surface of the bruised skin. If this blood is not drained immediately after it has collected, it may undergo clotting and organization. This means that the blood will clot and become encased in fibrous tissue. An ugly bump will remain after the wound has healed.

Will a person ever develop a cauliflower ear if the blood from a bruise is not drained?

Yes. Cauliflower ears result from clot formation secondary to bruises of the external ear.

In what locations are untreated bruises most likely to leave deformed lumps?

On the forehead and on the ears.

How can a cauliflower ear be prevented?

By draining the blood that collects beneath a bruise within a few hours of the injury. It may be necessary to use special compression bandages that form a cast for the external ear to prevent the development of a deformity.

Can a cauliflower ear be repaired through plastic surgery?

Yes, it can be improved.

Is there any way to reduce the lump left by a blood clot?

Yes. It can be removed surgically by making a small incision into the area.

DEFORMING SCARS

Should deforming scars on exposed surfaces of the body be excised?

Yes.

Is it necessary to use skin grafts to repair most ugly scars on the face or neck?

No. Most scars can be improved by excision and plastic repair with fine sutures.

How does a plastic surgeon repair a deforming scar of the face?

The scar is excised. The adjacent skin is undermined, thus permitting the skin to slide over the area from which the scar was removed. The tissues beneath the skin are closed with a row of tiny deep stitches. The skin is then closed with many fine stitches, which are removed usually within six days.

Can a plastic surgeon repair an ugly scar so that there is no incision noticeable after the completion of his operation?

No. There will always be a line or scar, but it is usually thinner and less ugly than the scar that results from the primary injury.

HEMANGIOMAS

What is a capillary hemangioma?

A capillary hemangioma is a dilatation of some of the very small arteries in the skin. There is usually a larger central vessel that feeds the rest of the hemangioma.

What is the treatment for a capillary hemangioma?

The main vessel is usually burned with an electric needle. This will cause obliteration of the other smaller vessels that lead from it.

Where is a capillary hemangioma usually located?

They appear most commonly on the upper part of the face.

What is a port-wine stain?

A port-wine stain is a blood vessel tumor that involves either small veins or small arteries in the skin.

What is the treatment for a port-wine stain?

There are several treatments. None of them are ideal, but all of them will diminish the size of the stain. Various methods of treatment are:

1. Freezing it with carbon-dioxide snow

2. A tattoo technique in which the discolored portions of the skin are tattooed to a normal shade

3. Multiple partial excisions over a period of time until all of the area has been excised and replaced with small skin grafts

Where do port-wine stains occur most often?

On the face.

Are skin grafts used in excising port-wine hemangiomas of the face?

Yes, a pedicle flap, a rotation flap from tissue on the neck, or a full-thickness graft is used.

SKIN GRAFTS

What are skin grafts?

They are portions of skin used to cover areas which have been laid bare by burns, by injuries, or by surgical removal of diseased tissues.

Does skin taken from one person work permanently when grafted to another person?

No. These grafts are almost always temporary, except when they take place between identical twins.

Is there ever an indication to graft skin from one person to another?

Yes. In extensive third degree burns, it has been found that a split-thickness skin graft from another individual will have markedly beneficial effects upon the burned patient. The graft will live for a period of 10 to 20 days, during which time it will help the patient to retain vital tissue fluids and chemicals. After serving this important function, the grafted skin will usually die and will slough away from the underlying tissues.

Are grafts usually successful when portions of skin are taken from one part of the body and grafted to another part of the body?

Yes, if performed under the proper circumstances.

If a part of the body, such as a finger or an ear, has been completely severed from the body, can it be grafted back onto the body?

These procedures are usually unsuccessful, although in the rare case such an operation has proved successful if it was performed immediately after the injury, if the severed part had been kept relatively clean, and it it was not too large.

Is it ever possible to graft back a severed arm or leg?

Yes. Within recent years, through the use of team surgery, it has been possible to reattach a severed limb. For such an operation to be successful, the severed limb must be relatively free from crushing injury and it must be in such condition that it is feasible to restore continuity between arteries, veins, nerves, muscles, tendons, and bones. Naturally, an extensive operative procedure such as this must enlist the cooperation of an orthopedic surgeon, a vascular surgeon, and a neurosurgeon.

What are the various types of skin grafts?

1. Pinch grafts. These are small pieces of skin, averaging about one-quarter inch in diameter, made up of the superficial layers of the skin. A dozen or more of these grafts may be taken from a donor area and placed at spaced intervals as small islands in the recipient site. They often grow well in their new location and spread out so as to fully cover the bare area.

2. Split-thickness grafts. These are sheets of the superficial and part of the deep layers of the skin which are removed from the donor area by a special knife. This type of graft is usually taken from a flat surface of the body, such as the abdomen, the thigh, or the back. They are most useful as a covering for large burned areas where the skin has been completely lost, as in a third degree burn. These grafts will take if the recipient site is free of infection and appears to be healthy.

3. Full-thickness grafts. These contain all the layers of the skin but not the underlying subcutaneous tissues. They are of the greatest value in fresh small surgical defects on the face and hands. Full-thickness grafts are cut so that they exactly match the recipient area.

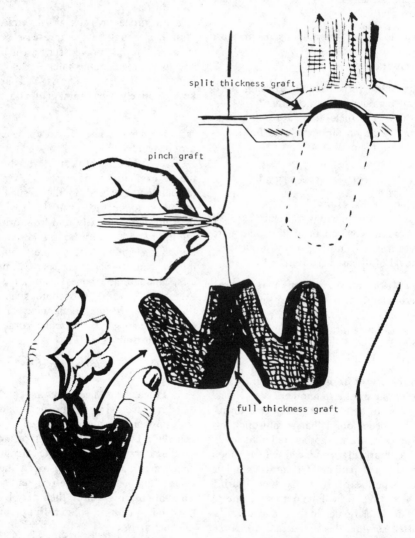

Skin grafts. Grafts will not grow unless the sites to which they are to be attached are healthy and free of infection. Grafts from one person to another are rarely successful.

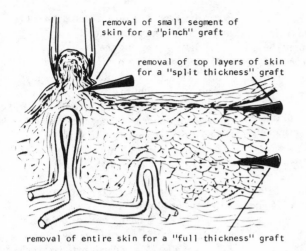

removal of small segment of
skin for a "pinch" graft

removal of top layers of skin
for a "split thickness" graft

removal of entire skin for a "full thickness" graft

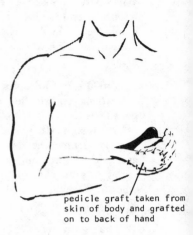

pedicle graft taken from
skin of body and grafted
on to back of hand

Skin grafts. This diagram shows a "pinch graft," wherein just a small segment of skin is lifted out from one part of the body and placed over a raw area elsewhere; a "split-thickness graft," which takes a segment of the upper layers of the skin; a "full-thickness graft," which removes all the layers of the skin; and a "pedicle graft," in which a segment of skin is partially detached from one area and attached to another part of the body.

4. Pedicle grafts. These are grafts in which one portion of the skin and fat remains attached to the donor area while the rest is transplanted to the recipient area. A pedicle graft will retain its own blood supply, which comes into it through the fat in its attached portion. The pedicle, or base of the graft, is detached from its original site when the free part of the graft develops its own new circulation at the recipient site. These grafts are most useful in covering defects where thickness is required.

What determines whether a graft will be successful?

1. The donor site must be clean and free of infection.

2. The recipient site must be clean and free of infection.

3. The recipient site must have good blood supply.

4. The graft must be applied evenly and smoothly.

5. The graft must always be in firm contact with the recipient site.

6. Measures must be taken to see that the graft does not become detached from the recipient site once it has been placed there.

7. Grafts must be applied without tension or undue stretching.

8. The general health of the patient must be good, so that healing will take place normally.

How soon can one tell whether a skin graft has taken?

Usually, the dressings at the recipient site are changed four to six days after the graft has been applied. It will not be known until that time whether the graft has been successful.

Will grafted skin have sensation in it?

For several weeks there may be a numb feeling in the region; eventually, normal sensation will come to a grafted area.

Is grafted skin sometimes of a different color than the skin that had originally been there?

Yes. Also, grafted skin does not necessarily assume the color of the new area. For this reason, surgeons will attempt to graft skin of the same shade when it involves a visible area such as the face or the neck.

Will hair grow in grafted skin?

Not unless it is a full-thickness graft which grew hair in its original site.

Is it possible to transplant skin containing hair from one part of the body to another and have a growth of hair at the recipient site?

Yes. For male pattern baldness, however, the grafts must come from the back or sides of the scalp, and many tiny "plugs" are necessary.

Is grafted skin as strong and resistant as normal skin?

Grafts are usually not quite as strong as normal skin. However, many will eventually be almost as strong as normal skin.

Is it important to prevent grafted skin from getting a severe sunburn?

Grafted skin seems to be somewhat more sensitive early to the rays of the sun. Later, it reacts about the same as normal skin.

If grafts are unsuccessful, is it possible to perform the operation over again?

Yes. Split-thickness grafts can be taken from the same donor site when it has healed completely.

For what type of skin lesions is plastic surgery frequently advocated?

1. Ugly, disfiguring scars
2. Keloids (overgrowth of scar tissue)
3. Contractures of the skin, usually secondary to old burns
4. Bare areas secondary either to third degree burns or to the surgical removal of large portions of skin
5. Skin cancers and tumors
6. Skin wrinkled by age

Can thick, unsightly scars be converted into thin, fine linear scars?

Yes. By excising the old scar, undermining the subcutaneous tissues, and repairing the skin edges with plastic techniques, ugly scars can often be almost completely eliminated.

What determines the need for a skin graft when performing the removal of a skin lesion?

If the edges of the wound cannot be brought together readily or if too much tension is created by attempting to suture the skin edges, the surgeon may decide to fill in the bare area with a graft.

PLASTIC SURGERY IN CHILDREN

Should plastic surgery be performed upon children, or is it wiser to wait until they have attained maturity?

Most plastic surgery is quite successful when performed on children. However, it is sometimes better to wait for a growing part, such as a nose, to attain its full development before correcting its appearance.

What conditions are most likely to require plastic surgical repair in a child?

1. Lacerations (cuts) and hemato-

mas (bruises), especially those involving the face, nose, lips, chin, or ears

2. Deforming scars left by lacerations

3. Avulsion of skin, with partial or complete loss of superficial tissue

4. Burns, burn scars, and resulting contractures, especially those on exposed surfaces of the body

5. Keloids, or overgrown (hypertrophied) scars

6. Birthmarks, moles (nevi), and hemangiomas (blood vessel tumors)

7. Skin grafting for any of the above conditions

8. Harelip

9. Cleft palate

10. Birth deformities of the eyelids

11. Nasal deformities, fractured nose, and deviated nasal septum

12. Birth deformities of the ears

13. Fracture of the upper jaw and cheekbone

14. Fracture of the lower jaw

15. Webbed fingers

16. Tumors at or near the surface

Should a plastic surgeon or a general surgeon perform these operations on children?

In communities where there is no specialist in plastic surgery, the general surgeon is likely to have had experience in this field and his services should be sought. On the other hand, if there is a specially trained plastic surgeon in the community, he should be used. Plastic surgeons are first trained as general surgeons and then receive several additional years of education in their own specialized field.

If a child becomes very sensitive about bathing, swimming, or exposing himself because of an ugly scar, should it be removed?

Yes, because the danger of psychological damage to the child may be much greater than the danger of undergoing a plastic surgical operation.

When should deforming scars on unexposed surfaces of the body be repaired?

It is usually not necessary to repair these until the child grows up. However, if the scar interferes with the function of any part of the body, it should be repaired promptly.

BIRTH DEFORMITIES OF THE EYELIDS

Are children often born with birth deformities of the eyelids?

No. The total or partial absence of an eyelid is a very rare congenital abnormality.

Do children ever have a deformity of the eyelids as a result of an injury or a wound?

Yes, although this is a relatively unusual injury.

What is the plastic procedure for fashioning a new eyelid?

It is a very complicated surgical procedure and must be carried out in several stages. Skin grafts from the other eyelid and skin shifted from other locations are frequently necessary.

At what age should a child be operated on for the reconstruction of an eyelid?

If the defect is small and leaves only a little of the eyeball exposed, surgery can be performed at any convenient time. If much of the eyeball is exposed, early surgical correction is essential to prevent ulceration of the cornea and loss of vision.

How successful are these operations?

From the point of view of cosmetic result, the operation is not entirely satisfactory, because the new lid never looks exactly like the opposite lid. However, it is important that the newly constructed lid be fashioned so that it covers and protects the eyeball. Another less than perfect outcome is that the new eyelid never has normal movement.

Will any harm come from the absence of eyelashes when a new eyelid is constructed?

No. Eyelashes are not too important to function.

Will the new eyelid open and close normally?

Yes, if only part of the eyelid is missing; if the entire lid must be replaced, normal lid movement will not result.

PLASTIC SURGERY
IN OLDER PEOPLE

Do older people ever need cosmetic surgery?

Yes. Contrary to common belief, there are perhaps more indications for this type of surgery in older people than in younger ones.

A good many older people, particularly those in professions where physical appearance is important, suffer both economically and emotionally because of the onset of the aging process. If cosmetic surgery can help them to appear young longer, there is little point in withholding it from them.

What are some of the cosmetic operations that can benefit older people?

1. The so-called face-lifting procedure to obliterate wrinkles.

   a. Operations to remove crow's feet about the eyes.

   b. Operations to remove pouches beneath the eyes and wrinkles in the upper eyelids.

   c. Operations to remove double chins and wrinkles in the neck.

2. Breast plastic operations.

   a. For pendulous breasts.

   b. To trim down excessively large breasts.

   c. To remove excessively large, pendulous male breasts.

3. Operations to remove skin blemishes, such as moles, brown spots, hemangiomas (red spots), and areas of wartlike growth (hyperkeratoses).

With age, skin growths tend to appear in large numbers for the first time. For some unknown reason, those that have been in existence for many years grow larger as one advances in age.

4. Operations to remove excessive fat on the abdomen (lipectomy).

5. Plastic operations on the nose (usually applicable to younger people, but there is no reason to deny this type of surgery to older people who want it).

Are the results of the above-mentioned cosmetic operations usually permanent?

Many of them are not. However, nasal plastic surgery and surgery to make the breasts smaller do have permanent results. Older people should know in advance that wrinkles will eventually return, no matter how effective the cosmetic operation. Similarly, if an older person overeats, he will grow new fat tissue on his abdomen. Moreover, cosmetic surgery cannot prevent the formation of new skin blemishes. However, further surgery can be done if and when the patient desires it, and he or she will look better than if the surgery had not been done.

Is plastic surgery dangerous for people of advanced age?

Not if they are in good general health. Skin healing should take place almost as quickly and with as little scarring as it does in younger patients. The surgery itself is not dangerous, although in certain cases special care must be exercised to make sure that the patient can safely undergo prolonged general anesthesia. Postoperative medical observation is essential.

Pneumonectomy

Pneumonectomy is the surgical term for an operation in which the entire lung is removed. This operation, performed under general endotracheal anesthesia, is employed for lung cancers that have spread beyond the confines of one lobe of the lung and also, in isolated cases, when an entire lung has been hopelessly destroyed by tuberculosis. Although pneumonectomy is a very serious operation requiring great surgical skill and several hours of operating time, it has now become a relatively safe procedure with operative recovery in the great majority of cases. Improved surgical techniques, the use of positive pressure anesthesia, and the liberal employment of antibiotics have all contributed toward making pneumonectomy a safe operation.

See also LUNGS.

QUESTIONS AND ANSWERS

Can a patient breathe and live normally after removal of an entire lung (pneumonectomy)?
At rest, these people can breathe normally, but on exertion, tend to get short of breath. They must therefore restrict their activity moderately.

What happens to the empty space within the chest cavity after removal of a whole lung?
1. The diaphragm ascends into the chest.
2. The structures from the opposite side shift toward the side of operation.
3. The chest wall is retracted inward.
4. The empty space is filled with scar tissue.

How long does it take to perform a pneumonectomy?
Approximately two to four hours.

How soon after pneumonectomy can a patient get out of bed?
Within a day or two.

How long a hospital stay is necessary after pneumonectomy?
Anywhere from 12 to 16 days.

Polyposis of the Colon

Polyposis of the colon is an uncommon disease which tends to run in families. The entire colon, including the rectum, is studded with wartlike growths called polyps or adenomas, which vary in size and shape from those of a pinhead to those of a plum. The condition rarely causes symptoms until adulthood, when blood and mucus are passed in the stool and rapid loss in weight and anemia occur. An examination of the rectum and lower sigmoid immediately reveals the nature of the disease to the

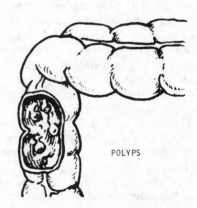

POLYPS

Multiple polyposis of the colon is a rather uncommon disease which tends to run in families. These tumors have a tendency to become malignant.

surgeon. The majority of those afflicted with this condition eventually develop cancer in one or more of the polyps. Cure can be obtained only by removal of the entire large bowel. A permanent ileostomy (artificial opening) must be performed following bowel removal. Local removal of polyps is valueless in this condition, as literally hundreds of growths are present. As surgical techniques have improved, more and more of these people are being saved. They learn to live productive and comfortable lives despite the existence of the bowel opening on the abdominal wall.

In an occasional case, the rectum contains only a few polyps. If this situation obtains, it may be possible to burn out the polyps locally, to preserve the rectum, and to stitch the small intestine directly to the rectum.

See also INTESTINES.

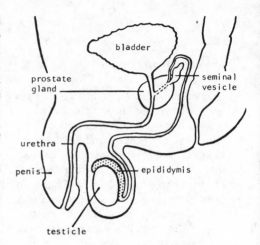

Prostate Gland

The prostate gland is a solid, flesh-colored, glandular organ, shaped like a horse chestnut, measuring about one to one and one-half inches in its three dimensions, and *found only in males.* It surrounds the neck of the urinary bladder and the beginning of the urethra, the channel through which urine passes. The prostate has a distinct capsule enveloping its three lobes.

The function of the prostate is the secretion of the fluid that comprises a large part of semen. Semen includes sperm cells.

The prostate is often the seat of disorders requiring surgical correction, some of which are as follows:

1. Infection of the prostate gland (prostatitis) is still seen quite frequently although the liberal use of the antibiotic drugs has facilitated its treatment greatly, thus reducing the need for surgery. A large number of prostatic infections associated with gonorrhea are no longer encountered since the primary disease is controlled so much more readily. It is important to mention that the overwhelming majority of prostatic infections will get well without surgery. However, a small percentage will develop abscesses that will require surgical drainage. The symptoms are high temperature, back pain, frequent and painful urination. The pus can be drained out through the urethra by use of special instruments or through an incision made in the perineum (the region between the anal opening and the back of the scrotum, or testicle sac). These procedures carry minimal risk, require just a few days of hospital residence, and recovery is usually prompt.

2. Simple (benign) enlargement of prostate: For some unknown reason, the prostate gland undergoes enlargement in the majority of men as they get older. This process usually begins in the 40s and increases in each subsequent decade of life. The enlargement itself is of little importance, but since it may produce serious effects upon the act of urination and the ability of the bladder to empty itself, it may gravely endanger health.

As the prostate enlarges, it presses upon the urethra and obstructs the outflow of urine from the bladder. In the early stages, this hindrance is overcome by more powerful contractions of the bladder. Symptoms may be nonexistent or may merely take the form of increased frequency of urination during the day and the need to get up to void at night. Later there is a decrease in the size and force of the urinary stream, some hesitancy in getting the stream started, and dribbling after completion of urination. The bladder loses its ability to empty itself of all its urine and *residual urine* remains. As the bladder becomes less and less competent and the amount of residual urine increases, back pressure is exerted upon the ureteral openings and they lose competence. The increased bladder pressure is thereby transmitted upon the ureters to the kidneys. The ultimate result is a decrease in kidney function and excretion which, if allowed to continue, may terminate in *kidney failure* and *uremia*.

Other complications, such as urinary infection, bladder stone formation, bloody urine, and hernias of the bladder wall (diverticula), may develop if the obstruction is permitted to go on unchecked.

At any point during the above sequence of events, the patient may suddenly find that he is unable to void or that he can pass only a few drops of urine even with great straining. This condition is known as *complete urinary retention* and demands surgical action!

Not all men with enlargement of the prostate require surgery. It is estimated that 70 to 80 percent of all men have some prostatic enlargement after the age of 60 years, and 60 percent have some obstruction of the bladder outlet.

Fortunately, only about one out of five men with prostatic enlargement will require surgical relief for their symptoms.

3. Cancer of the prostate: Much that was stated in the preceding section regarding the signs and symptoms of simple (benign) enlargement of the prostate applies also to malignant enlargement of the gland. In other words, the mechanical results of obstruction are very much the same regardless of the inciting cause. But, of course, the basic disease is different and demands different management.

Cancer of the prostate is primarily a disease of older men and occurs most often in those beyond 60 years of age. *When discovered early in its course, when confined within the capsule of the gland, and when subjected to extensive and radical surgery, a large proportion of these cases can be cured.* However, symptoms often make their appearance when the growth has already spread beyond the gland and throughout the body. *It is essential, therefore, that all men over 50 years of age have their prostates examined every year.*

While the cause of prostatic cancer is unknown, it is recognized that for continuation of its growth the cancer depends to a degree upon the secretion by the testicles of male sex hormone (testosterone). This is an important fact in the control and treatment of the disease.

Prostatic tumor cells, both benign and malignant, secrete a chemical substance known as acid phosphatase. When this chemical finds its way into the bloodstream it helps to identify the disease and also suggests whether or not the cancer has spread beyond the confines of the gland.

If the cancer is discovered early and is confined to the gland, a *radical prostatectomy* is performed. This includes removal of the gland, its coverings, the seminal vesicles (glands near the prostate), and the neck of the bladder.

Should this operation not be advisable because of advanced age, poor general condition, or the spread of the tumor, *considerable shrinkage of the growth and prolongation of life (sometimes for several years) can be obtained by surgical removal of the testicles and the regular administration of doses of female sex hormones.* In this condition the female hormones counteract the effect of the male sex hormones, upon which the vitality of the cancer depends.

4. Prostatic stones: In the majority of cases, stones are not, in themselves, an indication for surgery. They are usually found in association with simple (benign) enlargement of the prostate or in a chronically infected gland. In general, their symptoms are those of the condition with which they are associated, and their treatment will be in accordance with the need of the associated disorder.

Stones can be diagnosed by feeling the prostate with a finger in the rectum or by noting them on x-ray examination. When symptoms are severe, surgical treatment may be indicated.

See also GENITOURINARY SYSTEM; KIDNEYS AND URETERS; PENIS; URETHRA; URINARY BLADDER.

QUESTIONS AND ANSWERS

What is the prostate gland and what is its function?
It is a chestnut-shaped structure surrounding the outlet of the urinary bladder. Its purpose is to secrete the fluid in which the sperm cells are ejaculated.

How is the prostate gland examined?
1. By inserting a finger into the rectum. The gland's size and contour can be readily determined by this method of examination.

2. By examination through a cystoscope inserted through the penis into the bladder. By this method, enlargement of that portion of the gland surrounding the bladder outlet can be discovered.

What are the main diseases affecting the prostate gland in older men?
1. Benign enlargement of the prostate (benign hyperplasia, or prostatism)
2. Stones in the prostate gland (calculi)
3. Cancer of the prostate
4. Acute inflammation (acute prostatitis)
5. Chronic inflammation (chronic prostatitis)

Is inflammation of the prostate gland very common in men over 60?
No. It is more common in younger men.

What is the usual cause of acute inflammation of the prostate in older people?
An infection that has reached it through the urethra, through lymph channels, or through the bloodstream.

What are the symptoms and signs of acute prostatitis?
1. Pain between the scrotum and the rectum (the perineum)
2. Temperature rise to 101°–103° F
3. Pus in the urine
4. Frequent urination accompanied by a burning sensation

How is acute prostatitis diagnosed?
1. By examining the prostate gland by inserting a finger into the rectum and finding swelling and tenderness
2. By urine analysis
3. By noting the characteristic symptoms and signs

What is the treatment of acute prostatitis?

1. Bed rest

2. Large quantities of fluids to flush out the bladder and to keep the urine dilute

3. Administration of antibiotic or sulfa drugs

4. Frequent hot baths

Do most cases of acute prostatitis subside completely?

Yes, if treated properly and promptly.

Does chronic inflammation of the prostate occur very often?

Yes. It is a common condition, often associated with enlargement of the gland (prostatism).

Can chronic inflammation of the prostate take place without a history of acute inflammation of the gland?

Yes.

Does chronic inflammation of the prostate always have symptoms?

No. A certain amount of inflammation is often associated with benign enlargement of the gland, and this may be present without any symptoms.

What are the symptoms of chronic prostatitis?

1. Frequent urination accompanied by a burning sensation

2. Pain in the bladder region or lower part of the back

What is the treatment of chronic prostatitis?

The standard treatment is periodic massage of the gland. This is best performed by a physician who specializes in disease of the genital organs (urologist). Antibiotic drugs are of little use in chronic prostatitis.

What is prostatism?

It is the enlargement of the prostate gland that takes place in almost all men as they enter their 60s or 70s. The enlargement often causes an obstruction to the free flow of urine from the bladder out through the urethra.

Is prostatism a benign or a cancerous condition?

It may be either benign or malignant.

Is enlargement of the prostate a common condition?

Yes. It is estimated that 70 to 80 percent of all men over 60 years of age are so affected.

Can anything be done in the younger years to guard against developing an enlarged prostate?

No.

How can one know whether or not he is suffering from prostatism?

1. It takes longer to start to urinate.

2. There is a decrease in the force of the urinary stream.

3. There is a tendency to urinate more frequently.

4. It is necessary to get up from sleep to urinate.

5. There is dribbling of urine at the end of urination.

6. The bladder is not emptied completely on voiding. This may lead to infection of the retained urine, cystitis, and possibly kidney infection.

7. When prostatism is advanced, the inability to void may be complete.

Is examination through a cystoscope usually necessary for a diagnosis of prostatism?

No. In a great majority of cases the diagnosis can be made by digital examination through the rectum.

What causes benign enlargement of the prostate gland?

The cause is unknown although circumstantial evidence suggests that hormone alterations associated with aging may be important factors.

How does a doctor determine whether or not there is obstruction to the outflow of urine from the bladder?

1. By feeling the lower abdomen, the rounded distention caused by the full bladder will be noted.

2. He may pass a tube called a catheter through the urethra into the bladder after the patient has voided as much as he can. If urine remains in the bladder, it is evidence that some obstruction prevents complete emptying.

Do cystitis and urinary infection usually take place when there is obstruction to bladder emptying?

Yes, if obstruction lasts for any prolonged period of time.

Does kidney infection eventually result from obstruction to the outlet of the bladder?

Yes, in many circumstances.

Is there any way to halt enlargement of the prostate gland once it has begun?

No. Formerly, some physicians advocated administration of male sex hormone to retard the process, but this method of treatment has not proved efficient.

Do all men who show enlargement of the prostate have to undergo treatment?

No. In many cases the enlargement takes place so slowly, over a period of years, that the symptoms are minimal. In such cases, although there may be some increased difficulty in voiding and some retention of urine in the bladder, no treatment is required.

How does a physician determine which cases require treatment?

If the patient is able to void and can empty most of the urine from the bladder, treatment is not necessary. It will, however, probably take him longer to pass urine, and the act must be performed at more frequent intervals. If, on the other hand, the bladder retains large amounts of urine, if a urinary infection sets in, or if the patient's symptoms are intense and persistent, then treatment is necessary.

Do enlarged prostates ever return to normal size without treatment?

Only when the enlargement has been the result of an inflammation which subsequently subsides.

What is the effect of enlargement of the prostate upon the bladder and kidneys?

Since the main function of the bladder is to serve as a urinary reservoir, it is obvious that an obstruction such as enlargement of the prostate will force the bladder to work harder to discharge the urine. As a result, the wall of the bladder becomes thickened, more muscular, and heavier. Eventually, the bladder fails to empty itself completely with each voiding. This residual urine increases in amount, and may ultimately create abnormal back pressure up the ureters toward the kidney. Along with the dilatation of the ureters there is some impairment of kidney function, and the general health of the patient suffers. Permitted to progress untreated, such a condition may lead to complete kidney failure, with resultant uremia and death.

What harm does incomplete emptying of the bladder do to the patient?

It results in stagnation of the urine, with consequent risk of infection. The infection may spread up the ureter to the kidney as well. Ultimately, from stagnation of the urine over a long period, stones may form in the bladder. The increased work and pressure on the bladder wall may cause a local "blowout," known as a diverticulum. These are saclike protrusions from the wall of the bladder; they may contain stagnant urine, or stones may develop within them.

What medical treatment will help people with enlarged prostate glands?

1. Ample quantities of water should be taken to stimulate bladder emptying and to prevent stagnation of urine.

2. Antibiotic medications and urinary antiseptic drugs may be given to prevent cystitis or kidney infection.

3. Alcoholic beverages and highly seasoned foods should be avoided.

4. Sedatives and relaxant drugs may be given to aid in urination.

5. Exposure to very cold climate should be avoided.

What is a median-bar obstruction?

This means that the segment of the prostate surrounding the bladder outlet is enlarged and is causing obstruction.

Does enlargement of the prostate gland interfere with sexual relations?

No.

How frequent is cancer of the prostate gland?

Although this may be a shocking statistic, it is estimated that approximately *one out of four* men will develop cancer of the prostate before they reach their 70s or 80s. Cancer of the prostate is the most common malignancy in the elderly male.

What causes cancer of the prostate?

The cause is not known.

How is cancer of the prostate diagnosed?

In most cases, it can be suspected by rectal examination. Small, stony, hard nodules can be felt through the rectal wall. Conclusive diagnosis rests on biopsy confirmation.

Is cancer of the prostate gland slow in developing, or is its progress rapid?

This type of malignancy often grows very slowly, and it may not shorten the life-span very much. Cancerous nodules may grow slowly and may not spread outside the gland for three to five years. Once the cancer has spread outside the prostate, the time of survival is reduced markedly.

What are the symptoms of early cancer of the prostate?

There are none. Only when the cancer has spread beyond the prostate or has caused an obstruction to the outflow of urine do symptoms develop. Thus, nearly nine out of ten cases go unrecognized until late in their course.

What can be done to make an earlier diagnosis of cancer of the prostate?

Every adult male, especially one over 50, should have a rectal digital examination at least once a year. Change in urinary habit—frequency of urination, inability to empty the bladder, burning on urination, and so on—should be investigated promptly.

How does one distinguish between simple benign enlargement of the prostate and cancer of the prostate?

On rectal examination the cancer feels stony hard while the simple enlarged gland is rubbery. However, the ultimate distinction will come from the microscopic report of the tissue of the gland after it has been removed.

Does simple benign enlargement of the prostate ever turn into cancer?

This is possible but is uncommon.

Is there any medical treatment for cancer of the prostate?

In some cases, the growth of the tumor is retarded by the suppression of male hormone secretion that results from the administration of the female sex hormone.

For how long can the female sex hormones be effective in retarding the progress of cancer of the prostate?

Although this form of treatment is not curative, it may suppress a cancerous growth and prolong life for many years.

Do a man's breasts enlarge when he is given female sex hormones in the treatment of cancer of the prostate?

Yes. Sometimes the enlargement is so great that it causes considerable embarrassment to the patient. When this happens, surgical removal of the breast tissue may be indicated. This is a simple operative procedure in the male.

Is x-ray therapy or radium helpful in the treatment of cancer of the prostate?

Recent advancements in radiation therapy are encouraging, although cure of prostatic cancer with irradiation has not been accomplished with certainty.

Are there any radioactive substances that are helpful in the treatment of cancer of the prostate?

Yes. The injection of radioactive gold or iodine directly into the gland has, on occasion, given promising results.

Do stones ever form in the prostate gland?

Yes. The presence of stones will often be revealed by x-ray examination of this region.

Are stones often found in association with prostatism?

Yes.

Can stones in the prostate gland be felt on rectal examination?

Occasionally, but the more precise method of diagnosis is by x-ray examination.

Do prostate stones often cause symptoms?

No, but when they cause obstruction to the outflow of urine or when they are associated with infection, they will cause symptoms and may necessitate removal of the prostate gland.

How does the urologist decide which case of prostatism requires surgery?

1. The general condition of the patient: If it appears that the patient is so ill that he cannot withstand removal of the prostate, then some lesser procedure such as mere opening of the bladder (cystostomy) to relieve obstruction is all that is done.

2. The amount of residual urine: The greater the amount of urine that remains behind after voiding, the greater is the need for surgical removal of the prostate.

3. The severity of the symptoms: The more inconvenience that is produced by frequency of urination both by day and by night, the greater is the need for corrective surgery.

4. The presence of associated conditions such as bladder infection, stones, or a diverticulum will increase the need for surgery.

5. Repeated episodes of hemorrhage from the prostate will point up the need for its surgical removal.

6. Repeated episodes of acute complete retention of urine should be considered a decisive indication for surgery.

What surgery is performed in prostatism?

1. Suprapubic prostatectomy is done in one or two stages, the one-stage procedure being practiced more often today. If done in two stages, the bladder is opened and drained at the first operation (suprapubic cystostomy) through a small incision in the lower abdomen. Several days or weeks later, the surgeon puts his finger into the opening in the bladder and dissects out the enlarged prostate with his fingertip. The two-stage procedure is elected when the bladder is the seat of a severe infection, when bladder stones or diverticula are present, or when the patient's general condition causes the surgeon to doubt his ability to withstand the entire procedure being done at one time. The whole procedure is done in one stage in most cases where the patient is in relatively good condition.

In order to prevent epididymitis, an infection of a structure adjacent to the testicles, the tubes from the testicles (vas deferens) are cut and tied off. This procedure, vasectomy, is done at the same time as the first stage of the prostatectomy or along with the one-stage operation through small, inch-long incisions on either side of the scrotal sac. Spinal or general anesthesia is used.

2. Retropubic prostatectomy is performed when the gland is removed directly through its coverings *without* opening the bladder. This incision is made in the lower part of the abdomen.

3. Perineal prostatectomy is performed in the same manner as for a retropubic procedure except that the incision is made in the perineum in front of the rectum.

4. Transurethral prostatectomy is the so-called closed operation. No incision is made, the obstructing portion of the prostate being cut away by an electrically charged wire loop which is inserted through the penis through a specially designed instrument known as a resectoscope.

This procedure requires a shorter hospital stay and is less disturbing to the patient. It is therefore advocated for those with associated illnesses such as heart disease. Also, the transurethral approach is more applicable to those with smaller types of prostatic enlargement.

What percentage of cases can be treated by transurethral resection through a cystoscope, and what percentage will require surgical incision?

Approximately 70 percent of cases can be treated by transurethral resection; the other 30 percent will require prostatectomy. It should be noted that the percentages vary with the skill, training, and philosophy of the surgeon and with the size of the prostate gland.

Is a transurethral resection as effective as prostatectomy?

A good transurethral resection accomplishes the same result as a prostatectomy.

Are operations on the prostate gland dangerous?

No. Even a man of greatly advanced age will recover from this type of surgery, unless his general condition is exceptionally poor.

How does the surgeon determine whether to perform a prostatectomy or a transurethral resection?

As stated above, the philosophy, skill, and training of the surgeon, as well as the size of the gland will determine which procedure will be employed.

Will surgery relieve the symptoms of prostatism?

Yes. Eventual return to normal voiding is the rule.

Does benign enlargement of the prostate gland tend to recur after it has been corrected surgically?

Rarely, after a surgical prostatectomy. In some instances, it will recur after transurethral resection.

Does transurethral resection often cause loss of potency?

No.

Does the ordinary prostatectomy cause inability to perform the sexual act?

Not in the majority of cases, although

it does sometimes. Since most men who have these operations are in their 70s, 80s, or 90s, loss of potency presents relatively little hardship.

Does radical, or total, removal of the prostate interfere with potency?

Yes, although this procedure is done only in cases of cancer of the prostate gland.

Do most men regain urinary control after prostatectomy?

Yes.

Is operation upon the prostate ever an emergency procedure?

When acute complete urinary obstruction exists, emergency measures often must be undertaken. However, in many of these cases the prostate is not removed until days or weeks later.

Does the prostate always have to be removed when cancer is discovered in it?

No. In many men in their 70s or 80s the cancer will grow so slowly that it will not interfere with the natural lifespan. These people can be maintained in a fair state of health with medical management or by another form of surgical treatment.

What is another form of surgical treatment of cancer of the prostate?

It has been discovered that removal of both testicles will slow down the rate of growth of the cancer. This is a safe operation and can be carried out in men in their late 70s or 80s with little risk.

Do stones in the prostate require surgical removal?

Only when accompanied by symptom-producing prostatic enlargement or persistent infection.

Are the larger prostates more difficult to remove?

No. In some instances, the smaller ones are more difficult to remove than the larger ones.

Do infections of the prostate usually have to be operated upon?

No. Antibiotics bring most of them under control.

Can simple enlargement of the prostate be successfully treated with hormones instead of surgery?

Not at the present time, although investigation of this possibility is under way.

Is treatment necessary before surgery?

Yes, in many instances:

1. If the urine is infected, this should be corrected with sulfa or antibiotic drugs before surgery is undertaken.

2. If there has been a long period of retention of urine, it will be necessary to drain the bladder before removing the prostate. This can be accomplished in some cases by passage of a catheter through the urethra. In other cases, an operative procedure—cystostomy—must be done, thus converting the operation into a two-stage procedure.

How long will urinary drainage be necessary before the prostate can be removed?

This will depend upon the amount of kidney damage and the promptness of the response to the catheter or cystostomy drainage. When urinary function has been stabilized at normal or near-normal levels, the prostate can then be removed. This period may vary from several days to several months!

Are operations upon the prostate serious?

Yes. It must be remembered that most men who undergo this type of surgery are past middle life and often have complicating conditions such as heart disease, diabetes, and high blood pressure.

What type of anesthesia is used?

General or spinal, with or without intravenous anesthesia.

Are blood transfusions needed during prostate operations?

Yes, in some cases. There is considerable blood loss in these operations. However, the danger has been eradicated by the ready replacement with transfusions.

Where are the incisions made for prostate operations?

1. Longitudinal or transverse incisions in the lower abdomen, for suprapubic and retropubic prostatectomy

2. Behind the scrotal sac and in front of the rectum for perineal prostatectomy

3. No incision for transurethral resection

Is it customary to tie off the vas deferens on each side of the scrotum before removal of the prostate?

Yes.

Is the vas deferens tied off in a prostatectomy to prevent postoperative infection of the epididymis?

Yes.

Which cases are most suitable for removing the enlarged portion of the gland through the resectoscope (transurethral resection—closed operation)?

Those in which the enlargement is not great and in which the surgeon feels that the patient is too ill for an open operation.

Are there surgeons who use the transurethral closed approach even when the prostate is very enlarged?

Yes.

What decides whether to remove the prostate at a one-stage operation or whether to perform it in two stages?

The sicker the patient and the longer there has been urinary obstruction and kidney damage, the more likely will the decision be to perform the prostatectomy in two stages.

How long do the various operations upon the prostate take to perform?

Incision and drainage of prostatic abscess:	30 minutes
Suprapubic prostatectomy:	45 to 60 minutes
Retropubic prostatectomy:	1 to 1½ hours
Perineal prostatectomy:	1 to 1½ hours
Radical prostatectomy for cancer:	2 to 3 hours
Transurethral resection:	1 to 1½ hours

What postoperative complications may occur after prostate surgery?

1. Hemorrhage: This may have its onset ten days or later after operation and can be controlled by the passage of a catheter, which puts the bladder to rest for a day or two.

2. Infection of the kidneys or epididymis: These infections are successfully treated with the antibiotic medications.

Are special nurses necessary?

Occasionally, for two to three days.

Is the pain very great after prostate operations?

No. Only moderate pain is felt and this can be relieved by periodic administration of appropriate medication.

How soon after prostate surgery can one get out of bed?

Usually, the day following surgery.

Are special treatments necessary after operation?

Yes:

1. Intravenous fluids for a day or two

2. Antibiotic drugs to combat infection for several days

How is the urine drained after operation?

After suprapubic prostatectomy, by a tube placed in the bladder which exits through the incision on the abdominal wall. After other types of prostatectomy, by a catheter (hollow rubber tube) placed in the urethra.

Will normal control over urination be disturbed permanently by operations upon the prostate?

No. Some irregularities may exist for a short time but eventual control will be resumed. The one possible exception is the radical procedure done for cancer. Here, sphincter damage may result, in some cases, in permanent loss of voluntary urine control. Most of these people, however, eventually do regain control.

When is normal voiding resumed?

After suprapubic prostatectomy:	10 to 14 days
After retropubic prostatectomy:	5 to 7 days
After perineal prostatectomy:	10 to 14 days
After transurethral resection:	4 to 6 days

Following the removal of the prostate by any route except the transurethral, it is possible that some urinary drainage may occur through either the abdominal or perineal wound. This will disappear either spontaneously or with the assistance of a few days' drainage by urethral catheter.

How long must one remain in the hospital after the following operation?

Suprapubic prostatectomy:	10 to 14 days
Retropubic prostatectomy:	7 to 10 days
Perineal prostatectomy:	14 to 17 days
Radical prostatectomy:	18 to 21 days
Transurethral resection:	5 to 8 days

How long a period of convalescence is required?

At least a month.

How soon after prostate removal can one do the following?

Bathe:	10 to 14 days
Drive a car:	2 weeks
Resume light work:	2 weeks
Resume regular work:	4 weeks
Resume sexual relations:	4 weeks

What surgical follow-up care is needed?

1. Regular dressing changes

2. Regular urine examinations for infection

3. Irrigation of the bladder from time to time in rare instances

4. Stretching of the urethra by passage of catheters during the period of healing in rare cases when there is a constriction of the urethra

Does sterility follow prostate removal?

Yes, because of the ligation of the vas deferens (the tube carrying the sperm from the testicles).

Are the results from prostate removal satisfactory?

Yes. The great majority are cured.

Does a prostate, once removed, ever grow back again?

Yes, but in less than 5 percent of the cases.

Pterygium

Pterygium is a condition associated with the overgrowth of the conjunctiva, the membrane covering the front of the eyeball, and the tissue directly beneath the conjunctiva. This growth, benign in nature, usually starts at the inner aspect of the eye and extends outward in a triangular shape over the white of the eye until it reaches the border of the colored portion of the eyeball. In other words, a pterygium is a growth of the membrane of the white of the eye located on the nasal side of the iris.

See also EYES.

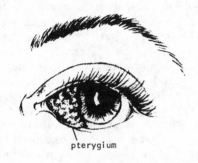

pterygium

QUESTIONS AND ANSWERS

How common is pterygium?

It is a rather common growth, occuring mainly in middle-aged or older people. It is seldom seen in children or young adults.

What causes pterygium?

The cause is not known.

Does a pterygium ever extend over the colored portion of the eye?

Occasionally, yes, but this is an unusual occurrence.

Is it difficult to make a diagnosis of a pterygium?

No. Mere inspection of the eyeball will reveal the presence of this overgrown tissue.

What is the treatment for a pterygium?

If it is localized only to the white of the eye and does not threaten to grow over the colored portion of the eye, most

pterygiums can be left alone. However, should the pterygium grow to large size, if it is unsightly, or if it threatens to grow over the colored portion of the eye, it should be removed surgically by an ophthalmologist.

What operative procedures are carried out for removal of pterygium?

1. If the pterygium is localized to the white of the eye, it is excised with a knife and is replaced by a graft of membrane obtained from the inside of the cheek.

2. If the pterygium has overgrown the cornea, the colored portion of the eye, and the pupil, it must be excised and a corneal transplant must be inserted. Such tissue is obtained from an eye bank.

How successful are operations for removal of a pterygium?

In most cases there is complete success. Once in a while, a pterygium will recur and will have to be reexcised.

Do most pterygiums threaten vision?

No, because most of them do not grow over the pupil or cornea.

How long does it take a pterygium to grow to a large size?

This usually takes place over a period of years.

Puncture and Stab Wounds

Puncture and stab wounds are particularly dangerous as it is not always easy to determine the extent of damage that has taken place. Unlike an open wound, there is no way to see under direct vision what tissue damage has occurred. For this reason everyone who has received a puncture or stab wound that has penetrated the skin and gone into the body deeply must be observed for the development of subsequent symptoms. This is especially important when the stab wound has entered the chest cavity or the abdominal cavity. Since damage to the intestines may result in peritonitis, most surgeons feel that an exploratory operation with the opening of the abdomen is essential. Only in this way can one be positive that a vital abdominal organ has not been perforated. Similarly, stab wounds of the heart may require open chest surgery to determine the extent of damage and to suture any hole in that structure.

See also FIRST AID.

QUESTIONS AND ANSWERS

What is the first aid treatment for a puncture or stab wound?

1. Move the patient as little as possible.

2. If the stabbing object (a knife or pick) can be withdrawn easily, do so. This may prevent further injury to tissues when the patient moves.

3. Note carefully the angle and depth of the stabbing object so that you can report it accurately to the attending physician.

4. If the wound is in the chest and air is being sucked into and blown out of the chest, cover the opening tightly. It can be plugged best with a sterile gauze dressing and adhesive tape.

5. Stop active bleeding.

6. If any internal organs are protruding through the wound, cover them with a sterile gauze dressing or a clean handkerchief.

7. Stab wounds always require expert care. Take the patient to a doctor, who will, in most instances, give tetanus antitoxin or toxoid.

8. Small puncture wounds should have their edges spread so as to promote some bleeding and prevent the sealing in of dirt, rust, and other materials that may hold infectious bacteria.

Pyloric Stenosis

Pyloric stenosis is an obstruction to the outlet of the stomach which prevents the passage of food into the small intestine. It is seen commonly in newborns commencing about the second or third week of life and afflicts males about three times more often than females. The condition is caused by an overgrowth of the muscle surrounding the outlet of the stomach (pylorus) and by spasm at the same site. The outstanding symptoms are:

1. Vomiting: This is of a forceful type and often shoots out from the mouth.

2. A mass (lump) about one inch in diameter can often be felt in the right upper portion of the abdomen. This is the overgrown (hypertrophied) muscle of the stomach.

3. Waves of stomach contractions (peristalsis) can often be seen traveling across the upper abdomen from left to right.

4. Marked weight loss and loss of fluids will result if this condition continues unchecked.

Some of these children can be helped by giving antispasmodic drugs, which will relieve the spasm of the muscle, but the majority of them must be treated surgically. Before recommending operation, the physician may employ a trial period of medical management for one to three weeks. Delay of surgery beyond this time, if the symptoms continue, is inadvisable as it will be associated with

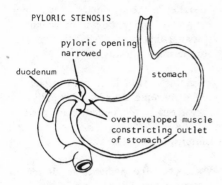

PYLORIC STENOSIS

pyloric opening narrowed

duodenum

stomach

overdeveloped muscle constricting outlet of stomach

In cases of pyloric stenosis, the outlet of the stomach is obstructed by excess muscle development. The condition is relieved by severing the muscles surgically.

dangerous weight loss, fluid loss, and deterioration in the general condition of the child. If vomiting stops, surgery may be withheld indefinitely and total recovery may take place.

The operation is performed under light ether anesthesia and consists of a small incision about two inches long in the right upper portion of the abdomen. The pyloric portion of the stomach is grasped and the overgrown muscle is slit with a knife for its entire length. Care is taken to cut only the muscle fibers and not to enter the inside of the stomach by cutting the mucous membrane. No attempt is made to repair the severed muscle in the stomach wall. The abdomen is then securely closed with silk sutures.

Results of surgery are excellent and recovery can be expected in practically all cases. Feedings may be begun within 12 to 24 hours after operation. Usually feedings are retained well, and the infant is ready for hospital discharge within five to seven days after surgery.

Pyloric stenosis is seen occasionally in older adults, secondary to a chronic ulcer or to a process of fibrosis at the outlet of the stomach. In these cases,

the stomach outlet may be so narrowed as to cause marked obstruction to the passage of food. Surgery will relieve this condition through cutting and widening the outlet. This procedure is known as pyloroplasty.

See also STOMACH AND DUODENUM.

QUESTIONS AND ANSWERS

What is pyloric stenosis?

Pyloric stenosis is an obstruction to the outlet of the stomach that prevents the passage of food into the small intestine.

What are the symptoms and signs of pyloric stenosis in an adult?

There will be marked retention of ingested food. X-rays will demonstrate a hugely dilated stomach containing food that has been eaten many hours or even days previously. Associated with this gastric retention there may be vomiting when the stomach becomes overloaded with food.

Can pyloric stenosis in an adult be diagnosed by x-ray?

Yes. After the patient swallows barium, the obstruction to the outlet of the stomach will be obvious on x-ray films.

Can pyloric stenosis due to an ulcer or due to stenosis secondary to fibrosis be cured surgically?

Yes. Cure results in almost all cases after surgery has been carried out.

What is the treatment for pyloric stenosis in an adult?

1. If it is due to a chronic ulcer, one of the ulcer operations must be performed.

2. If it is due to fibrous tissue replacement of the muscle as a result of advancing age, surgery to enlarge the outlet may be indicated. This will consist of a pyloroplasty or a partial gastrectomy.

What causes pyloric stenosis in infants?

There is an overgrowth of the muscles that make up the sphincter at the outlet of the stomach (pylorus). What causes this overgrowth of muscle is not definitely known, but some investigators feel that a developmental factor is involved. The overgrown muscles go into spasm and close the pylorus, thus preventing the passage of food.

Is there any way to prevent the development of pyloric stenosis in a child?

No.

How common is pyloric stenosis in newborns?

It is estimated that it occurs about once in every 200 newborns, most often in firstborn children.

Is pyloric stenosis more common in males than in females?

Yes. It occurs about three times more often in males.

Is there a tendency for pyloric stenosis to run in families?

No.

How soon after birth does pyloric stenosis become evident?

In severe cases, it may cause symptoms and signs within the first few days of the child's life. In the usual case, however, the condition becomes evident in the second or third week of life.

In what percentage of cases can a lump be felt in the upper portion of the abdomen?

In approximately 90 percent.

If a lump cannot be felt in the upper abdomen, are x-rays helpful in establishing the diagnosis of pyloric stenosis?

Yes. A small amount of barium is given to the child to swallow or is placed into his stomach through a stomach tube. This will show the obstruction to the outlet of the stomach and will demonstrate an elongation and narrowing of the canal that passes from the stomach into the small intestine.

Do children who have pyloric stenosis tend to become dehydrated rapidly?

Yes, but if the pediatrician suspects that the child has pyloric stenosis, this complication can be averted.

When does the pediatrician decide to hospitalize a child who may have pyloric stenosis?

If the symptoms occur very early, the newborn may not yet have been discharged from the hospital nursery. More commonly, however, the symptoms will develop after the child has been home for two to three weeks. Whenever a child vomits forcefully, particularly if this occurs with each feeding, the pediatrician should be notified, and he will undoubtedly suspect the presence of pyloric stenosis. The child will be watched at home and antispasmodic drugs probably will be prescribed. If, after a day or two, there is no response to the administration of these drugs, the pediatrician will usually recommend hospitalization so that the child may be treated for dehydration. It is always wiser to admit the child to the hospital than to attempt to carry him along on medical management at home.

Is it necessary to operate on all children who have pyloric stenosis?

No. Some children can be helped with antispasmodic drugs, which will relieve the spasm that usually accompanies the overgrowth of muscle.

Do most children have to be operated on if they have pyloric stenosis?

Yes, but a trial period of medical therapy should be attempted first for a few days to a week.

How is the choice between surgery and medical management made?

If the vomiting is repeated and the child becomes markedly dehydrated and loses weight, the physician will decide to operate early. If, on the other hand, the child's weight can be maintained and a certain amount of food does pass through into the small intestine, a more conservative attitude toward surgery is often adopted.

Is surgery for pyloric stenosis ever an emergency procedure?

Usually not. It is much wiser to take the time and correct the child's chemical balance, so that he is in neither acidosis nor alkalosis, and to restore the fluids that have been lost through vomiting before operating on him.

What operation is carried out for pyloric stenosis in an infant?

Under light ether anesthesia, a small incision about two inches long is made in the upper right quadrant of the child's abdomen, and the abdominal cavity is entered. The pyloric portion of the stomach is grasped between the surgeon's fingers, and the overgrown muscle is slit with a knife for its entire length. Care is taken to cut only the muscle fibers and not to enter the inside of the stomach. The severed muscle is left in place, and the abdomen is closed securely with silk sutures.

Is an operation for pyloric stenosis dangerous?

No.

How long does it take to perform this operation?

About 20 to 30 minutes.

What is the name of the operation for the cure of pyloric stenosis?

It is called the Ramstedt pylorotomy.

What are the results of surgery for pyloric stenosis?

The results are excellent. Recovery can be expected in practically all cases.

Are the following necessary before an operation for pyloric stenosis?

Blood transfusions: Usually not, unless the newborn is markedly anemic.

Antibiotic medications: No.

Intravenous medications: Yes, especially if the child is dehydrated and not in good chemical balance.

Stomach tubes: Yes.

Bladder catheters? No.

Vitamin injections: Yes, especially vitamin K if the child is jaundiced.

Other special preparations: Yes. These will depend on whether the child has acidosis or alkalosis. In either event, chemicals are given to restore normal blood values.

Are the following necessary after an operation for pyloric stenosis?

Private duty nurses: Yes, for one to two days.

Antibiotic medications: No.

Intravenous infusions: Yes, for two days.

Blood transfusions: Usually not.

Stomach tubes: Yes, for one to two days.

Special postoperative measures: Yes. If the child has been dehydrated and is not in good chemical balance, chemicals will be given.

Postoperative vitamins and tonics: Yes.

Convalescent posthospital care: No.

How soon after an operation for pyloric stenosis can a child begin to take feedings by mouth?

He will probably be fed intravenously or by the injection of fluids beneath his skin for the first 12 to 24 hours after surgery.

How long a hospital stay is necessary following an operation for pyloric stenosis?

Five to seven days.

How long does it take the wound to heal?

Seven to ten days.

Will a child be able to lead a completely normal life after recovering from an operation for pyloric stenosis?

Yes.

Does pyloric stenosis ever recur following corrective surgery?

Not if all the overgrown muscle tissue was severed during the original operation.

Pyloroplasty

Pyloroplasty is a surgical procedure in which the muscles and mucous membranes at the outlet of the stomach are severed and sutured in such a way as to allow the alkaline secretions of the duodenum to flow back into the stomach. This alkaline backflow, along with cutting of the vagus nerves (vagotomy), markedly reduces the acid content of the stomach, thus leading to healing of a duodenal ulcer.

Pyloroplasty plus vagotomy has become one of the most widely used operations in the treatment of duodenal ulcer that fails to heal after thorough medical management.

Although pyloroplasty is a major operation, recovery is the general rule in almost all cases. When combined with vagotomy, this procedure gives excellent results in curing chronic duodenal ulcer.

See also STOMACH AND DUODENUM.

Quinsy Sore Throat

Quinsy sore throat, or peritonsillar abscess, as it is also known, is an abscess just behind, or to the side of, the tonsils. This type of infection is not uncommon following a severe case of tonsillitis.

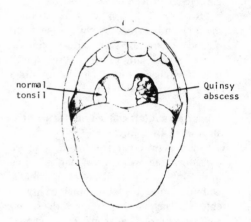

A quinsy sore throat results from an abscess just behind or to the side of the tonsils.

QUESTIONS AND ANSWERS

Can children and adults both develop quinsy sore throat?

Yes. Although tonsillitis is seen more frequently among children, adults too are subject to this kind of infection.

Can quinsy sore throat produce suffocation?

Yes. If untreated, the entire back of the throat may become involved and may make it very difficult for air to reach the lungs.

Do most people recover completely following incision and drainage of quinsy sore throat?

Yes. In very severe cases, the patient may have a marked toxic reaction and may require prolonged therapy with antibiotic drugs. Also, in an occasional untreated case in children, there may be such interference with breathing that a temporary tracheotomy may have to be carried out.

Will the voice return to normal after recovery from quinsy sore throat?

Yes.

Is the occurrence of quinsy sore throat an indication that subsequent removal of tonsils will have to be performed?

Yes. The development of a quinsy sore throat is almost always the consequence of a permanently diseased tonsil that should be removed surgically.

How long after recovery from quinsy sore throat can tonsillectomy be done?

It is usually best to wait for several weeks, so that the acute infection has subsided completely.

Ramstedt Operation

A Ramstedt operation is a surgical procedure in which the overgrown muscle tissue surrounding the outlet of the stomach is cut but the underlying mucous membrane is left intact. Thus, the obstruction to the stomach outlet is relieved. This operation is performed on newborns who have a condition known as pyloric stenosis.

Although surgery for pyloric stenosis is serious, recovery takes place in almost all cases.

See also PYLORIC STENOSIS.

Ranula

Ranula is a cyst of the duct of the sublingual salivary gland lying beneath the tongue. The cyst appears as a swelling in the floor of the mouth and is thin-walled and oval in shape. It is not associated with pain.

See also SALIVARY GLANDS.

QUESTIONS AND ANSWERS

How can ranula be diagnosed?

A smooth, ovoid, cystic mass, appearing something like a frog's distended belly, is seen underneath the tongue.

What causes ranula?

The cause is not definitely known, but it is presumed to be secondary to an inflammatory obstruction of the ducts of the sublingual gland. This duct normally opens beneath the tongue and secretes saliva.

Who is most likely to get ranula?

Ranula is seen more often in children than in adults.

What is the treatment for ranula?

Surgical excision of the cyst is the usual method of treatment. Complete excision is carried out when the ranula is readily removable, but a partial removal with an unroofing procedure is sometimes carried out. This latter operation involves the removal of the dome of the cyst while permitting the underlying wall of the cyst to form the new mucous membrane.

Is cure of ranula effected by surgery?

Yes.

How serious an operation is the removal of ranula?

It is not a very serious operation, but

children must be hospitalized and a general anesthetic must be given.

Do ranulas recur once they have been removed?

No.

Raynaud's Disease

Raynaud's disease is characterized by attacks of severe spasm of the blood vessels of the fingers or toes. Attacks of spasm are often brought on by emotional disturbances or by exposure to extreme cold or dampness. Occasionally, the ears, the tip of the nose, the chin, or the cheeks may be involved.

QUESTIONS AND ANSWERS

What causes Raynaud's disease?

The cause is unknown, but the disease tends to affect those who are thin, underweight, and exceptionally emotional.

Are women more susceptible to Raynaud's disease?

Yes.

What are the symptoms of Raynaud's disease?

During emotional excitement or on exposure to excessive cold, one or more digits may turn white and then blue. The digit becomes numb, tingles, and aches with pain. This will last for a few minutes and then subside with return to normal circulation.

What is the treatment for Raynaud's disease?

The condition may remain mild and stationary for many years. In a certain small number of cases, the disease becomes progressively worse and will require surgery for the cutting of certain nerves (ganglia) which control the contraction of blood vessels in the extremities.

Is the surgery for Raynaud's disease dangerous?

No. It will consist of a sympathectomy in the region of the lower neck and upper chest. An incision is made on either side of the lower neck, and the nerves controlling contraction of the blood vessels in the arms are severed. If the toes are involved, the sympathectomy is done in the lumbar region (the lower back).

Are the results of sympathectomy for Raynaud's disease successful?

Yes. This operation usually results in a cure of the condition and produces no unfavorable aftereffects.

Does ulceration or gangrene of the fingers or toes ever take place in Raynaud's disease?

Yes, in rare instances.

What is the medical management for Raynaud's disease?

1. Avoidance of dampness and extremes of cold
2. The wearing of warm gloves and clothing
3. The minimization of emotional stress
4. Avoidance of tobacco in any form
5. The taking of drugs that cause the blood vessels to dilate
6. Surgery to sever the nerves causing blood vessel contractions

How effective is the treatment of Raynaud's disease?

One of the preceding forms of treatment usually brings about relief from the symptoms of this disease.

Reconstructive Orthopedic Surgery

The world will be everlastingly grateful that poliomyelitis (infantile paralysis) has been brought under control and practically eliminated from civilized sections of the earth. This happy circumstance will decrease tremendously the need for future reconstructive orthopedic operations on paralyzed limbs. Unfortunately, there are still many people who have, within the recently past decades, sustained crippling effects from this disease and who require surgical help. Also, there are other conditions, such as cerebral palsy, cerebral hemorrhage or thrombosis, Erb's palsy, and peripheral nerve injury, whose damaging effects upon muscular coordination and limb motion can be partially ameliorated through surgical intervention.

Reconstructive orthopedic surgery is used in helping to rehabilitate patients suffering from the following conditions:

1. Poliomyelitis causes nerve paralysis to those nerves that supply muscles in the arms, legs, back, and other areas. Without healthy nerves, muscles and tendons cannot function and they tend to wither and become useless. Many patients with partial paralysis of an arm or leg can be helped by transferring healthy, strong muscles and tendons to new positions where they will take up the functions of their paralyzed neighbors. Such transferred tendons, with the help of rehabilitation educational techniques, soon learn to perform their proper tasks in their new positions.

When bones and joints lose their stability and fail to maintain their normal alignments because of muscle and tendon paralysis, orthopedic correction is often very beneficial. A back that develops a curvature (scoliosis) due to muscle paralysis can be straightened and held in position with a well-conceived spinal fusion operation. Bones in the ankle or wrist may also be fused to lend stability to these joints when their tendons are inactivated by paralysis.

2. Cerebral palsy is a birth deformity of the brain which results in spastic paralysis and loss of muscular coordination. As a result, some muscles cannot relax when they should. They may pull an arm or a leg tightly to one side, bend an elbow or clench a fist, roll the hips inward, or prevent the knee from straightening and the foot from moving upward. Children so afflicted have a constant and unsuccessful struggle to control these unwanted contractions, with their resulting bizarre movements.

Orthopedic measures can prove most helpful in alleviating some of the abnormal conditions that accompany cerebral palsy. Muscles and tendons can be transferred to new positions, certain nerves can be divided to relieve muscle spasm, and ligaments and muscles can be severed to permit relaxation of a spastic limb. In addition to these surgical maneuvers, braces and orthopedic appliances are usually found to be useful.

3. Cerebral hemorrhage and thrombosis. As more and more people live into their seventh, eighth, and ninth decades, these conditions are encountered more frequently. Such accidents often result in partial paralysis of an arm, or arm and a leg. This type of paralysis can occasionally be benefited by the same forms of treatment as might be utilized in other paralytic conditions, including the use of muscle and tendon transplants, joint stabilization procedures, reeducational techniques, and the judicious application of orthopedic appliances.

4. Erb's palsy is a partial paralysis of the arm and hand caused by stretching and damaging the nerves in the neck. This injury often accompanies a difficult delivery at birth. Here, too, muscle and tendon transfers can do much to strengthen and increase the usefulness of the limb.

5. Paralysis of nerves resulting from the taking of toxic drugs, and nerve injury due to accidents, are not infrequently encountered. This type of nerve paralysis will result in loss of muscle and tendon function in the affected structures. Muscle and tendon transfers and joint fusion operations may aid these unfortunate people when nerve repair is impracticable.

See also BONE CONDITIONS; CEREBRAL PALSY; JOINTS; ORGAN AND TISSUE TRANSPLANTS.

QUESTIONS AND ANSWERS

For what conditions can reconstructive surgery upon the bones, joints, and muscles be carried out?

1. When fractured bones have healed in poor position, reconstructive surgery can be carried out to correct the defects.

2. Joints that are diseased and are painful, or in which there is little or no motion, can be made useful again by reconstructive surgical measures.

3. Partially or totally paralyzed muscles can be substituted for by the transplantation of good muscles or good tendons from other parts of the extremity.

How effective is reconstructive orthopedic surgery?

This will depend upon how extensive the disability is and in what region it is located.

Can reconstructive surgery bring a paralyzed muscle back to life?

No.

Can most people with paralyzed muscles be helped by reconstructive surgery?

Yes. It is rare that all the muscles in one extremity are affected equally by a disease process. Thus, it is possible to transplant, to the site where it will do most good, those muscles or tendons that are still normal and functioning.

Is it possible for the surgeon to determine which patient will be most benefited by reconstructive surgery?

Yes. By careful analysis of the exact nature of the condition, it can usually be determined which patient can be helped by muscle or tendon transplantation.

For how long a time after the initial acute attack of poliomyelitis can one expect improvement of paralyzed muscles?

Up to two years.

Does physical therapy (heat, whirlpool baths, massage, exercises) help recovery from the paralysis?

Yes.

When should surgery be done upon people who have had infantile paralysis?

When it is important to stabilize a joint or when a muscle or tendon transplant will improve function.

Should all people paralyzed by poliomyelitis be treated surgically?

No, only special cases where improved function can be obtained.

How soon after paralysis secondary to poliomyelitis can reconstructive surgery be carried out?

It is generally best to wait at least two years after the initial attack. This is wise because regeneration of muscles can take place within this span of time.

Can the unequal length of the legs be helped surgically?
Yes.

Can more motion be obtained in a partially paralyzed arm or leg?
Yes, by tendon transplant to increase function.

What types of reconstructive surgical operations are performed to obtain improvement following paralysis of muscles?
1. Muscle transplants
2. Tendon transplants
3. Fusions of various joints in order to obtain more stability of a limb

Are operations for transplantation of muscles and tendons usually successful?
Yes.

When can one attempt to use muscles and tendons after a transplant operation?
About three to four weeks.

At what age are transplantation operations best performed?
At any age.

Is a transplantation operation dangerous?
No.

How long do transplantation operations take to perform?
About one and a half to two hours.

Is the patient ever worse off after a transplantation operation?
No.

Will transplanted muscles or tendons or fused joints continue to function as a child grows taller?
Yes.

Is it necessary to reeducate a transplanted muscle or tendon so that the patient can use it properly?
This is very important. Actually, reeducation of the transplanted muscle or tendon is as important as the operation itself.

Can healthy nerves be transplanted successfully into paralyzed muscles?
No.

What is an arthrodesis procedure?
The fusion or stiffening of a joint.

When is it advisable to carry out a fusion operation upon a joint?
1. When the joint is painful
2. When there is partial or total destruction of the cartilage in a joint
3. When a joint is flail (too movable and out of control)

Is an arthrodesis operation dangerous?
No.

How long do arthrodesis operations take to perform?
About one to one and a half hours.

Are arthrodesis operations usually successful?
Yes.

What anesthesia is used for these operations?
Usually general. Spinal anesthesia is not advocated often for people who have had poliomyelitis.

Are blood transfusions necessary?
Only occasionally.

Are special nurses necessary?
No.

How soon after operations of this kind can one get out of bed?
Three to four days.

Are extremities placed in a cast after these operations?
Yes.

Are wounds of these procedures painful?
No.

Are scars of these operations disfiguring?
No.

How long do these wounds take to heal?
Two to three weeks.

Is convalescent care necessary?
No, but advisable if obtainable.

How soon can one attempt to walk after the following procedures:
Arthrodesis (fusing) of
hip?   6 to 8 months
knee?   3 to 4 months
ankle?   3 to 4 months
Tendon transplant in
leg?   6 to 8 weeks

Is the patient ever worse off after an arthrodesis operation?
No.

What is arthroplasty?
It is the term used to describe the plastic reconstruction or surgical replacement of a joint.

For what conditions is arthroplasty most frequently performed?
1. In any condition accompanied by permanent, painful restriction of joint motion
2. When a joint has been irrevocably destroyed by a severe fracture with failure of normal healing processes
3. When the bones making up a joint have been hopelessly destroyed by chronic arthritis or some other degenerative disease process
4. When it is necessary to remove a joint, or part of a joint, because of a bone tumor

What are some of the joints that can be replaced through arthroplasty?
1. The hip joint
2. The elbow joint
3. The shoulder joint
4. Finger joints
5. The knee joint

What metals are used to replace the bones?
The artificial joints (prosthetic devices) are composed of metals known as vitallium or SMO steel. Vitallium consists of several metals such as cobalt, chromium, carbon, molybdenum, and manganese. SMO steel is an alloy of stainless steel and molybdenum.

How successful is arthroplasty?
As this is a relatively new operative procedure, one must expect a certain number of failures. However, it is safe to state that great relief from pain and improvement in motion follow most of these operations. Of course, they must be performed only by specialists who have had wide experience in the field.

What is the most frequent cause of failure of an arthroplasty?
Postoperative infection. Should this take place and not be controlled, it may be necessary to remove the metal device.

If one arthroplasty procedure fails, is it possible to reoperate at a later date?
Yes, but results are likely to be less satisfactory. It is essential that all infection be cleared up before reinserting a metal device.

Rectocele

A rectocele is a protrusion of the rectum into the vagina, sometimes encountered in women who have suffered a tear during childbirth or whose tissues have become lax with advancing age.
See also CYSTOCELE AND RECTOCELE.

Rectum and Anus

Untold millions of people throughout the world attribute their strength or weakness, clearheadedness or sluggishness, good or bad spirits, to the particular state of their bowel function. Daily they anticipate its character, and a successful elimination heralds the start of a bright and successful day! It is no wonder then that these same people are so deeply affected by any evidence of disorder in this region. The majority of them anxiously seek help when they note chronic constipation, persistent diarrhea, rectal itching, bleeding, or the appearance of hemorrhoids (piles).

The anus (the last inch of the rectum) is composed of a diaphragm of muscle which surrounds the outlet and expands and contracts at every passage. It is an extremely sensitive and delicate mechanism which gets out of order easily, particularly in this modern world, where irregularity is more common than regularity. As a matter of fact, no area in the body is more susceptible to upset than the last inch or two of the intestinal canal.

See also HEMORRHOIDS; FISSURE IN ANO; FISTULA IN ANO; INTESTINES; SIGMOIDOSCOPY.

QUESTIONS AND ANSWERS

What is the anus?

The last inch or one and a half inches of the intestinal tract.

What is the rectum?

That portion of the bowel extending up from the anus for a distance of six to eight inches.

Is rectal or anal disease common?

Nearly one third of all adults at one time or another suffer from some local disease of the anus or rectum, such as hemorrhoids, fissures, or fistulas.

Is it necessary for the maintenance of good health to have a bowel movement every day?

No. Bowel habits vary widely among normal people.

Is it normal to have one or two movements daily?

Yes, for some people.

Can a person lead a normal life if he moves his bowels only every other day or every third day?

Yes, providing he has a regular pattern of bowel function.

Does the type of food that one eats affect bowel function?

Yes.

What foods are best avoided when one has acute rectal or anal disease?

1. Highly seasoned spicy foods
2. Alcoholic beverages

What determines regularity of bowel movement?

1. The formation of good habits in early childhood
2. The eating of a well-rounded diet containing plenty of fresh fruits and fresh vegetables
3. A good general state of health

Will good bowel habits in childhood usually lead to good habits when one is older?

Definitely, yes.

Is it harmful to take a lubricant such as mineral oil over a prolonged period of time?

No, if it is really necessary for normal function. However, it should not be taken at the same time of day as vitamin-rich foods, as it may interfere with vitamin absorption.

Should a person take a laxative when he has abdominal pain?

Never! This practice can be dangerous—particularly if the cause of the pain is appendicitis or some other inflammatory process in the intestinal tract.

Is a change in one's bowel habits significant of disease?

Yes. Very often it means that there is trouble. Recurrent diarrhea or constipation should lead one to have a thorough medical survey of his intestinal tract.

What abnormalities in bowel function should cause one to seek medical advice?

1. Episodes of diarrhea
2. Episodes of constipation
3. Change in the appearance or caliber of the stools
4. Blood in the stool
5. Black-colored stool
6. Mucus in the stool

Are there any laxatives that are better than others?

The milder the laxative, the better. Lubricants or stewed fruits are preferred for the relief of constipation.

When is it permissible to take laxatives?

Occasionally, when there is a period of constipation in a patient who ordinarily has normal bowel function.

When is it permissible to take lubricants?

When there is a tendency toward chronic constipation in an older person.

Will taking lubricants over a prolonged period of time interfere with vitamin absorption from the intestines?

No, not if they are taken several hours after a meal, as at bedtime.

When should enemas be taken for constipation?

Only when the patient is otherwise in good health and has no other symptoms referable to the intestinal tract.

Is there any adequate treatment for chronic constipation?

Yes. Eat plenty of fresh fruit and vegetables and develop regular habits. Also, the taking of lubricants or bulk-forming medications may prove helpful.

What is the significance of a chronic diarrhea?

It may indicate an infection of the bowel, such as dysentery or colitis. Any diarrhea lasting more than a few days should be investigated by a physician.

What is the best treatment for constipation in adults or older people?

1. Make sure there is no underlying disease of the large bowel, rectum, or anus
2. Improve dietary habits
3. Establish regular bowel habits
4. Use bulk-forming medications or, if necessary, lubricants

Of what significance is blood in the stool?

It may be caused by:
1. Excess straining at stool when constipated
2. Hemorrhoids or some other anal condition
3. An acute colitis associated with diarrhea
4. A chronic colitis
5. A benign tumor, such as a polyp
6. A malignant tumor of the rectum or bowel

What is the significance of a black stool?

It is caused by bleeding high in the intestinal tract, as from an ulcer. Certain iron medications, when taken orally, can also cause black stools.

What is the significance of mucus in the stool?

Mucus does not necessarily signify a disease process, as many people, especially women in middle life, will have mucus in the stool when no real disease exists. However, it should be checked by a physician.

Is it harmful for one to strain at the stool for prolonged periods of time?

Yes. This can lead to hemorrhoid (pile) formations.

Are colonic irrigations helpful in curing disease?

No. Years ago, certain colon conditions were treated by this method but now it has been proved that they are of little, if any, benefit.

Is it true that people who do not have a regular bowel movement are likely to become sluggish, have headaches, and feel weak?

They may develop such symptoms because of the psychological effect upon them. However, there is no sound physical reason why constipation for a day or two should cause these reactions.

What are hemorrhoids?

They are varicose dilatations of the veins which drain the rectum and anus.

What causes hemorrhoids?

It is felt that these veins break down and their valves become incompetent because of the strain placed upon them by irregular living habits. Chronic constipation, irregularity of bowel evacuation, and prolonged sojourns on the toilet are thought to be conducive toward hemorrhoid formation. Pregnancy, because of the pressure of the baby's head in the pelvis, also leads toward hemorrhoid formation.

How can one tell if he has hemorrhoids?

There are one or more swellings or bulges about the anus, which become more pronounced on bowel evacuation. There is also a sense of fullness in the anal region, more pronounced on bowel evacuation. Hemorrhoids are frequently painful and may be accompanied by considerable rectal bleeding.

What is a fissure in ano?

It is an ulceration or split in the mucous membrane of the anus.

What causes a fissure?

Chronic constipation, with an overstretching of the mucous membrane at the anal outlet. The cracked surface becomes infected and an ulcer forms. The ulcer tends to remain, as it is kept open by the stretching at bowel evacuation.

What are the symptoms of fissure in ano?

Pain on moving the bowels, accompanied by a slight amount of bleeding.

What is a fistula in ano?

An abnormal communication between the mucous membrane lining of the rectum or anus and the skin surface near the anal opening. A fistula is therefore a tunnel, or tract.

What causes fistulas?

They represent the end result of an infection that has originated in the rectal or anal wall and which has tunneled its way out to the skin surface.

When should hemorrhoids, fistulas, and polyps be operated upon?

When there is repeated bleeding or when the hemorrhoids become markedly inflamed, ulcerate, or cause interference with bowel function.

All fistulas and polyps should be removed.

What are the aftereffects?

There are no permanent aftereffects following the removal of hemorrhoids.

Aftercare frequently extends for a period of six to seven weeks until the rectum returns to completely normal function. As a matter of fact, few patients are more grateful for the relief they have obtained than the patient with hemorrhoids.

There are no aftereffects to the removal of a polyp. It may take several weeks for the wound of an operation for a fissure or fistula to fill in completely. However, following this period of time, there are no untoward aftereffects.

How long will it take to recover completely:

From a hemorrhoid operation?	1 to 2 months
From a fissure operation?	1 to 2 months
From a fistula operation?	1 to 4 months
From a removal of a polyp?	Up to 5 days

How soon must the operation be done?

If the hemorrhoids are bleeding repeatedly, they can produce an anemia with considerable debility. It is therefore wise to be operated upon within a few weeks after being so advised. If the hemorrhoids are strangulated, badly inflamed, or ulcerated, they should be attended to within a week. Fissures and fistulas can be taken care of at a time mutually agreeable to the patient and surgeon. However, operation should not be deferred longer than four or five months. Polyps should be removed as soon as possible after their discovery, purely as a prophylactic measure.

Are these operations dangerous?

No. They are considered among the most minor of all operations.

Can't medical treatment be substituted for surgery?

Fistulas and polyps can only be treated surgically. Some superficial fissures and small hemorrhoids can be treated medically. Internal hemorrhoids can be treated by injections on occasion but this form of management is not as satisfactory as surgery since recurrence is rather frequently encountered. If symptoms from hemorrhoids continue or recur despite medical management, then it is wiser to undergo operation.

How long is the usual hospital stay:

Hemorrhoids?	4 to 7 days
Fissure?	3 to 5 days
Fistulas?	4 to 7 days
Polyps?	1 to 3 days

Do these operations leave a scar?

No, except in cases of fistula in ano when the opening is far out on the skin of the buttocks. In that event, there is a visible scar extending from the region of this opening to the anus.

After removal of hemorrhoids, small tabs of skin in the anal area are frequently left behind purposely so that no constriction of the outlet takes place.

How soon can one return to work:

After removal of hemorrhoids?	Approximately 2 weeks
After removal of fissure?	About 10 days to 2 weeks
After removal of fistula?	In 2 to 4 weeks
After removal of polyp?	In 1 to 2 days

What can happen if surgery is not performed?

Untreated hemorrhoids may become so painful as to seriously interfere with bowel function. Repeated bleeding may lead to serious anemia and weakness.

Untreated fissures often become deep ulcers, thus causing extreme pain on bowel movement.

Untreated fistulas may extend and form many tunnels, or may become infected and produce multiple abscesses.

Untreated polyps may grow into cancer.

What are the chances of recurrence after operation?

Hemorrhoids occasionally do recur, but more than 90 percent of patients can be cured permanently.

Fissures and fistulas recur occasionally after removal.

When completely destroyed, benign polyps do not recur.

Are these major operations?

No, they are classified as minor procedures.

How long does it take to perform these operations?

The average procedure for hemorrhoids, fissures, or fistulas takes approximately 20 to 30 minutes.

What kind of anesthetic is given?

Most surgeons advocate either a small spinal anesthesia or a caudal anesthesia. Occasionally general anesthesia is used.

Is there any specific preoperative preparation for these operations?

No. The patient is operated upon the day following hospital admission unless the hemorrhoids are tremendously swollen and inflamed. If such is the case, bed rest with cold applications to the rectal area is carried out for four to five days prior to operation.

Is it difficult to pass urine after operations on the rectum?

Yes. For a few days, it is sometimes difficult to start the urinary stream, and in some instances it is necessary to have the urine taken from the bladder by catheterization.

Does diet affect conditions about the rectum?

Yes. Highly seasoned foods and alcohol seem to aggravate rectal conditions and should therefore be avoided.

Is postoperative convalescent care required?

No. Patients are out of bed within one to two days after surgery and can care for themselves.

Do these operative procedures ever terminate fatally?

No. The risk of a complication from not operating on these conditions is much greater than the surgical risk.

Are these operations painful?

Yes. For three to five days postoperatively some people suffer considerable pain. This can be relieved by lying in a hot tub of water or by applying local anesthetic substances to the operative area. The first few bowel movements after this type of surgery are particularly painful.

The procedure for removal of a polyp, however, is not painful.

How soon after surgery will bowel function return to normal?

It may take several weeks before complete normality of bowel function is reestablished.

Does childbearing have any effect upon these conditions?

Yes. Due to the pressure of the growing child upon the rectal outlet area, pregnancy tends to cause the development of hemorrhoids. Unless hemorrhoids are severe and demand immediate attention, surgeons often recommend that they be removed after the woman is finished with childbearing.

What home postoperative treatments are necessary?

The patient keeps the bowels moving

freely by taking mineral oil or some other lubricant each day. Tub baths, two or three times daily, are taken to relax the postoperative rectal spasm and to cleanse the area.

What office postoperative treatments are necessary?

The surgeon sees to it that strictures do not take place by gentle insertion of his finger into the rectum about once a week. Occasionally skin tabs which were left after removal of the hemorrhoids are snipped off in the surgeon's office.

How soon after operation can sexual relations be resumed?

As soon as the rectal area becomes painless, usually in 10 to 14 days.

Does rectal bleeding ever take place postoperatively?

Yes. From stretching of the healing anal outlet, slight or moderate bleeding may occur, on and off, for several weeks after surgery. Severe postoperative hemorrhage is rare but should be treated by the surgeon in attendance.

How often should the bowels move after surgery?

For the first three or four postoperative days it is not necessary or desirable to have any bowel movements. Thereafter, one or two movements daily should take place. It is common for the stools to be smaller in diameter than normal and to be loose in consistency.

What dietary postoperative precautions must be taken?

A full diet should be eaten, but spices and alcoholic beverages should be avoided.

How soon can one bathe after a rectal operation?

Bathing is advocated after the third postoperative day.

How soon can one return to all normal activities?

Usually by the tenth to twelfth day after operation.

Do children ever suffer from these conditions?

Hemorrhoids and fistulas are rarely seen in preadolescent children. Polyps are not uncommon in young children. Fissures are seen often in very young children but can be cured in many instances by medical measures.

ABSCESSES AND INFECTIONS ABOUT THE ANUS

Are abscesses in the area about the anus and rectum (perianal and perirectal abscesses) very common?

Yes.

What causes abscesses to form in the area surrounding the anus?

1. An infection in one of the little pouches of the mucous membrane (crypt of Morgagni) in the anal canal.

2. Lack of cleanliness.

3. Ulceration and infection of a hemorrhoid.

4. Rarely, a foreign body may puncture or scratch the mucous membrane and lead to infection.

5. An undernourished or anemic condition may make it easier for bacteria to invade the tissue in this region.

6. Diabetics are especially likely to develop abscess in the anal area.

What is the treatment of an abscess that has formed in the anal region?

1. Hot baths should be taken, to bring the abscess to a head.

2. Mineral oil or a mild laxative should be given to keep the bowels moving.

3. Since these infections are usually very painful, the patient should be kept in bed most of the time.

4. Antibiotics should be given only when the infection appears to be spreading rapidly and affecting the general health of the patient.

5. When the abscess has come to a head, it should be opened surgically. Often the patient must go to the hospital for this operation, which will be carried out under general anesthesia.

Do abscesses alongside the rectum or anus frequently lead to formation of a fistula?

Yes, about half the time. The fistula will open and close, discharging a few drops of pus, for a period of several weeks after the original incision into the abscess.

Is hospitalization necessary to open these abscesses?

Only the large, extensive abscesses that are accompanied by great pain and high temperature must be opened, under anesthesia, in a hospital. The less severe ones can be opened under local anesthesia in a surgeon's office.

PRURITUS ANI

What is pruritus ani?

It is a chronic itching of the skin around the anus.

What causes pruritus ani?

1. The skin in this area is moist, highly sensitive, and is soiled repeatedly by feces.

2. This skin area is often allergic to irritating soaps, clothing, and other materials.

3. Associated anal conditions, such as hemorrhoids, fissures, and colitis, may cause irritation and set up an itching-scratching pattern.

4. Highly neurotic or disturbed people tend to develop pruritus ani much more frequently than others.

What are the symptoms of pruritus ani?

1. Uncontrollable itching, worse during hot weather and at night.

2. Irritation and burning of the skin around the anus.

What are some of the conditions that predispose to itching around the anus?

1. Fungal infections, such as those involving the vagina.

2. Emotional disturbance, often in neurotic people.

3. Diabetes; pruritis ani is sometimes a secondary condition in this disease.

4. Allergies, either to foods or to nylon, rubber, or other types of undergarments.

5. Drinking excessive quantities of alcohol or eating highly seasoned foods.

6. Hemorrhoids, fissures, or fistulas sometimes lead to development of pruritus ani.

7. Excessive perspiration due to heavy underwear and clothing sometimes precipitates itching about the anus.

What is the treatment of pruritus ani?

1. If the patient is allergic, elimination of the offending irritant will often relieve the pruritus.

2. If the patient is an uncontrolled diabetic, measures to bring his diabetes under control may stop the itching.

3. Excessive drinking of alcohol and eating of spicy foods should be stopped.

4. If the origin appears to be emotional, psychiatric care may prove helpful.

5. If the condition originates from hemorrhoids, fistula, or fissure, correction of these conditions will probably eliminate the pruritus.

6. People with pruritus ani should cut their fingernails very short, so that they will not damage the area by scratching in their sleep. Often, scratching by sharp nails will cause secondary infection.

7. People with pruritus should dress lightly and should avoid tight undergarments, which will cause excessive perspiration. If the patient tends to perspire excessively, talcum powder should be dusted onto the area. At night, as few blankets as possible should be used.

8. Various ointments containing anesthetic agents and cortisonelike ingredients should be applied regularly, but only on prescription by the physician.

9. Various antihistamine tablets may be taken to relieve the itching.

10. People with pruritus often have the habit of scrubbing the area with soap and water. This should not be done. Scrubbing with soap and water will only serve to *increase* the itching. If soap is used it should be a very mild one.

11. If there are swelling and redness in the area, warm baths or local applications of witch hazel will often bring temporary relief from the itching.

12. An occasional case of pruritus can be helped by a surgical procedure known as "tattooing." Other operations —for example, undermining the skin of the region in order to separate it from the underlying nerves—have proved helpful in an occasional case, but no operation can be recommended as a routine procedure.

13. The patient must be instructed that the less he scratches, the quicker the pruritus will heal. Although it is extremely difficult not to scratch, self-control is essential. A few days of complete abstinence from scratching may cause the pruritus to disappear completely.

Does pruritus ani usually interfere with sleep?

Yes. Many people with this condition complain bitterly that they are unable to sleep because of the intense itch. These people may require sedatives and sleeping pills.

Can excessive use of soap and water be harmful in pruritus?

Yes. Soap and water may irritate rather than benefit the condition.

How long can pruritus last?

It tends to be chronic and many people have it for years.

Does recovery ever take place spontaneously?

Yes. Often the condition disappears by itself.

Is psychotherapy ever valuable in the treatment of pruritus ani?

Yes, if the patient is an emotionally disturbed person.

PROLAPSE OF THE RECTUM

What is prolapse of the rectum?

It is an extrusion of the mucous membrane lining of the rectum through the anal opening.

When does prolapse occur most often?

When straining at the stool.

Who is most likely to have this condition?

Young children and elderly people.

What causes prolapse?

Excessive straining at the stool, sometimes associated with diarrhea or constipation, in a person with a weak musculature.

Does the prolapsed mucous membrane go back inside after bowel evacuation?

Sometimes it goes back spontaneously. More often, it must be pushed back inside the anal opening.

What is the treatment of prolapse of the rectum?

Many attempts have been made to

treat this condition medically, but most attempts are unsuccessful. Some of the medical measures that have been recommended are as follows:

1. If the patient is undernourished and underweight, as many people with prolapse are, they should be brought up to normal weight. Muscle and sphincter tone will be improved if the patient gains weight.

2. If the patient lacks vitamins or minerals in his diet, they should be given.

3. If the patient is chronically constipated, lubricants, mild laxatives, or small enemas should be given to bring about evacuation without muscle strain.

4. The patient should be shown how to replace the prolapsed mucous membrane in the anal canal. This should be done immediately after bowel evacuation, in order to prevent strangulation of the prolapse.

5. A rectal specialist (proctologist) should be consulted. He may, in mild cases, try to cure the prolapse by injecting various sclerosing substances alongside the anal canal. These may cause fibrous tissue to form in the region between the mucous membrane and the muscle wall of the bowel. If sufficient fibrous tissue does form, it may hold the mucous membrane in place.

If medical measures fail to cure a prolapse, is surgery recommended?

Yes, provided the general health of the patient will permit it. There are a dozen or more operative procedures designed to cure prolapse. Few of these operations are totally successful, but a substantial measure of improvement can be gained from some of them.

What kind of operation will be performed?

For the minor type of prolapse, an operation around the rectum will be performed. For the major types, an abdominal operation is carried out, with shortening of the rectum and a reconstruction of the musculature which holds the rectum in place.

Are operations for prolapse more often necessary for older people than for children?

Yes.

Are operations for prolapse successful?

Yes, but there are many failures in advanced cases in older patients.

POLYPS OF THE RECTUM AND ANUS

Nonmalignant or benign polyps of the anus and rectum are extremely common and usually give rise to considerable concern to the patient. The first indication of the presence of a polyp may be a rather severe hemorrhage from the rectum. Or the patient may learn of his condition rather abruptly by the appearance, after bowel evacuation, of a protruding, painless, ball-shaped mass. These polyps—or more accurately, polypoid growths—vary in size from that of a pea to that of a golf ball. They may be located anywhere from the margin of the anal orifice itself up to several inches above.

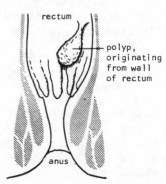

RECTAL POLYP

rectum

polyp, originating from wall of rectum

anus

Many cause no symptoms whatever and are found only upon routine rectal examination.

It is the feeling of most medical men that some polyps or polypoid growths can, in time, become cancerous. It has therefore become common practice to advise their removal as a prophylactic measure. Surgery upon these growths can frequently be performed without anesthesia in the surgeon's office. In these cases, they are destroyed electrically by cauterization or fulguration, or are removed with a snare. If the lesion does not lend itself to removal in the office, the patient is hospitalized for a few days and the polyp is excised surgically after placing a ligature (tie) around its base.

The possible presence of a symptomless polyp is a sound reason for everyone to undergo a complete rectal examination. By this practice, many potential cancers can be eliminated!

What are polyps?

Polyps are wartlike growths of the anal or rectal mucous membrane which may vary in size from that of a small pea to that of a golf ball or even larger.

Where are polyps found?

Polyps can be found anywhere in the large bowel, from the anal orifice upward.

What causes polyps?

Polyps are growths, like other tumors. The exact cause is unknown.

How common are polyps?

They are the most common tumor within the intestinal tract.

Who is most likely to develop polyps?

Polyps are seen in all age groups but tend to make their appearance more often during the fourth, fifth, and sixth decades of life.

Do polyps tend to run in families or be inherited?

Only the multiple polyps of the large bowel. This is a distinct disease. It is called multiple polyposis, and should be distinguished from the isolated, individual polyp so often found in the rectum or about the anal region.

How can one tell if he has a polyp?

Polyps near the anal region will sometimes be extruded on bowel evacuation and can be felt. But the most common symptom is painless bleeding from the rectum on bowel evacuation in a patient who has no other anal or rectal disease.

How does the surgeon make the diagnosis of rectal polyps?

Polyps can often be seen by direct visualization through an anoscope or sigmoidoscope.

What harm can polyps do if untreated?

Some polyps will undergo cancerous changes if not removed. Simple removal of polyps can prevent this from happening.

What is the treatment for polyps?

Polyps of the anus and rectum should be removed. If the polyps are small enough, this can be carried out in the surgeon's office. If they are large or high up in the bowel, they must be removed in the hospital.

What operative procedure is performed?

Through an anoscope or sigmoidoscope a snare is placed around the polyp and the base of the polyp is burned with an electric needle. Thus, through the rectal canal, the polyp is withdrawn along with the tightened snare.

How can one tell if a polyp is becoming malignant?

The excised polyp will be sent to the

laboratory and a microscopic examination will be carried out.

How soon will the laboratory report be available?

Within one to three days.

What is done if the polyp has proved to be malignant?

An abdominal operation is performed for the removal of that segment of involved bowel.

How long a period of hospitalization is necessary?

For the ordinary polyp, only one to three days.

Are any special preparations necessary before performing polyp removal?

No, just the ordinary cleansing of the bowel.

What special postoperative measures are advised after polyp removal?

A lubricant such as mineral oil should be used, and the patient should follow a bland diet.

How soon after a procedure of this kind can one return to normal activity?

Usually within two to three days.

Will bleeding continue for a few days after polyp removal?

This sometimes occurs and should not occasion alarm.

Do polyps tend to recur?

A polyp, once removed, rarely recurs unless it has proved to show signs of malignant changes within it. However, people who have formed one polyp may develop others.

How often should one return for a checkup following polyp removal?

Approximately every six months.

Is there any way to prevent the formation of another polyp?

No.

CANCER OF THE RECTUM AND ANUS

Is cancer of the rectum or anus a common condition?

Yes. It is one of the most frequently encountered malignant growths in the entire body.

What causes cancer of the rectum?

The cause is unknown, but it is a medical fact that many cancers in this region originate from the benign polyps described previously.

Is cancer of the rectum preventable?

To a certain extent, insofar as periodic rectal examinations and sigmoidoscopic examinations may uncover a benign condition which might result in cancerous degeneration if it is not removed.

How is the diagnosis of cancer of the rectum made?

1. By examination with the physician's finger, which is inserted into the rectal canal.

2. By taking a piece of the tumor tissue and submitting it to microscopic examination. (This is a simple office procedure.)

What symptoms are caused by cancer of the rectum?

1. The outstanding symptom is blood in the stool.

2. There may also be a change in bowel habit.

At what period in life is cancer of the rectum most often seen?

It may come on at any time, but is most usual in middle and later life.

What is the treatment for cancer of the rectum?

Removal of the entire rectum and approximately two to three feet of bowel. An artificial opening for the passage of stool is fashioned on the abdominal wall. This artificial opening is known as a colostomy. In some cases, when the cancer is high up in the rectum, it is possible to remove the cancer-bearing portion of the rectum and to reestablish bowel continuity. In such an instance, an artificial opening is unnecessary.

Is surgery for cancer of the rectum dangerous?

Today recovery from the operation takes place in well over 95 percent of cases. However, it is a major procedure which takes two to three hours to perform and necessitates hospitalization for several weeks.

Is cancer of the rectum ever curable?

Definitely, yes! More than half the cases can be cured if seen at a stage before the tumor has spread to other parts of the body.

Can a patient lead a full, normal existence with the rectum removed?

Yes. There are many thousands of people who engage in all activities despite the fact that they have no rectum. They learn to care for their colostomy in such a manner that the bowel is emptied at a set time each day, permitting them full activity. Various bags are applied over the colostomy opening which seal in any feces or odor while the patient is away from home.

RECTUM AND ANUS IN CHILDREN

An infant is usually fascinated by his anus and its functions. He is aware after just a short time that his anal acts (defecation or failure to defecate) evoke amazing responses from his mother or nursemaid. Thus his anal functions become associated with a sense of power and the ability to influence others. Parents, therefore, must not show in-ordinate pleasure or displeasure over anal acts, nor must they pay unnecessary attention to them if the child is to accept his anus as just another part of his body that is really more important than any other part.

What are some of the more commonly encountered problems involving the rectal and anal areas in children?

1. Birth deformities of the rectum and anus are seen in approximately 1 in 400 newborns. However, the deformities are in many instances minor. Surgical correction is necessary in only 1 in 1,000 newborns.

2. Pruritus ani
3. Fissure in ano
4. Fistula in ano
5. Juvenile polyps of the rectum
6. Hemorrhoids
7. Prolapse of the rectum

How is the diagnosis of an anal deformity made?

The general examination of every newborn includes a careful inspection of his anus and rectal canal. During such an examination, a constriction of the anus or an absent opening of the anal canal (imperforate anus) may be noted.

What is the most common birth deformity of the anus?

An imperforate anus. This can be a mild deformity if there is just a constriction of the anus or incomplete rupture of the anal membrane, or it can be a major deformity with failure of the rectal pouch to descend to the skin level. Along with deformities of the anus there also may be fistulas (false connections) between the rectum and the vagina, the rectum and the urinary tract, or the rectum and the skin in the region where the anus ordinarily would be.

What is the treatment for a birth deformity of the anus?

If merely a stenosis (stricture) is present, it usually can be remedied by dilatation with the surgeon's finger or by a simple incision with a scalpel to widen the orifice. If the imperforate anus is caused by a thin membrane that has failed to rupture, this can readily be excised restoring the anal outlet to normal.

What is the surgical procedure in cases of imperforate anus?

If a true imperforate anus is present because the rectal pouch has failed to descend to the skin level, it is perhaps best to perform a preliminary colostomy, in which the large intestine is brought out onto the abdominal wall and opened. This will permit evacuation of bowel contents and will eliminate obstruction. As soon as the general condition of the child permits, a definitive operation should be performed in which the rectum is drawn down to the anal outlet and sutured to the mucous membrane and the sphincter muscle at the termination of the anal canal. This procedure will restore normal anatomy.

When is it necessary to operate on a child who is born with an imperforate anus?

It is necessary to operate on the child within the first few days of life, because the feces must gain exit or intestinal obstruction will ensue.

Will a child usually recover following surgery for imperforate anus?

Yes, provided that there are no other major birth deformities.

If the child has an extensive imperforate anus, will he always regain normal bowel control?

This is not always accomplished easily. Some children will not be able to sense that a bowel movement is imminent. As a result of this, they may move their bowels involuntarily. However, as they grow older, they will gain greater control.

Is pruritus ani very common in children?

It is not very common, but it is seen when the child has pinworms or has a fissure (crack) in the mucous membrane at the anal outlet.

Is it common for children who have pruritus ani to do most of their scratching during the night?

Yes. This is also characteristic of an infestation with pinworms. It is due to increased heat and moisture in the anal area at this time. The itching can be most annoying and can disturb the child's sleep.

What is the treatment for pruritus ani associated with pinworms?

Medications to eradicate the worms will bring about a cure.

How can the parents know that a child has a fissure in ano?

There will be pain when the child attempts to move his bowels. Sometimes the pain is so great that the child will refuse to have a bowel movement. Also, a drop or two of bright red blood often falls into the bowel or is found on the paper after the child is cleaned. On examination, the pediatrician will find a crack in the mucous membrane.

How common is fissure in ano?

It is seen very often in constipated children.

What is the treatment for fissure in ano?

Most fissures will heal spontaneously if stool softeners are given and if local irritation is eliminated. The bowel movements can be made less painful by giving the child suppositories or by instilling mineral oil gently into his rectal canal.

Is it ever necessary to operate on a child who has a fissure in ano?

Yes, particularly if the child is not relieved through medical management. In these cases, a simple operation is performed in which the ulcerated fissure is removed and the superficial fibers of the underlying sphincter ani muscle are severed. As these severed muscles and mucous membrane heal, the anal canal will be widened and will permit the ready passage of stool. Of course, if the child has worms, these should be eliminated before undertaking surgery.

What can happen if a fissure in ano is neglected?

Chronic constipation may develop, and the bowel above the rectum may become so dilated that an acquired megacolon may develop. Also, the child may develop hemorrhoids in association with the fissure.

Do children ever develop fistula in ano?

Yes, but the primary condition, the forerunner of a fistula, is an abscess alongside the rectum (perirectal abscess).

Do all children who have abscesses alongside the anal opening develop fistulas?

No, but approximately half of them do as the abscesses open and create a tunnel through the rectal wall.

What is the treatment for fistula in ano in children?

In approximately half the cases, the fistula closes spontaneously within a period of two to three months. If it does not close, the tunnel (tract) from the rectal wall out to the skin must be opened widely. This is a simple operation performed under general anesthesia in the hospital.

Must any special treatment be given to a child after the removal of a fistula in ano?

Yes. Unless a finger is inserted into the rectum and the base of the wound is dilated every three to four days, there is a tendency for the fistula to form again.

What are juvenile polyps of the rectum?

Juvenile polyps of the rectum are noncancerous, benign tumors that occur not infrequently in children who are two years old or older.

What are the symptoms of a rectal polyp?

The most common symptom is painless bleeding, occurring from time to time over a period of several weeks or months. The blood may be mixed with stool, or it may appear alone.

How is the diagnosis of a juvenile polyp made?

Some polyps can be felt by the finger of an examining physician. Others require the passage of a sigmoidoscope to bring the polyp into direct view if it is located within the rectum or the lower end of the sigmoid colon. Those higher up in the colon can be diagnosed by x-raying the bowel after injecting a barium mixture through the rectum.

What is the treatment for juvenile polyps of the rectum?

Polyps anywhere in the large bowel should be removed. Those that are within the lower end of the sigmoid colon, or in the rectum or anus, can usually be removed through a sigmoidoscope. A snare apparatus with a wire loop is inserted through the passageway of the sigmoidoscope and is placed around the polyp. Since most of these polyps have stalks, it is a simple matter to tighten the snare around the stalk and remove the polyp. In order to prevent bleeding, a diathermy electric current is turned on and the base of the polyp is burned just as the snare is tightened.

Is the removal of a rectal polyp painful?
No. Young children will require a light general anesthesia. Older children, if cooperative, can undergo polyp removal without anesthesia, and although there may be discomfort, there is little or no real pain.

Do polyps of the rectum or colon in children become malignant?
No. Juvenile polyps must be distinguished from the inherited condition known as congenital polyposis. The latter condition will lead to malignant changes if the polyps are left in place for a period of years. Juvenile polyps do not become cancerous.

Is there a tendency for children who have had one rectal polyp to form others?
This sometimes does happen, but in the great majority of cases there is only one polyp. If another develops, it is usually the last one.

Are hemorrhoids very common in children?
No, they are quite rare in infants and children. When they are found, they may be indicative of an underlying disease such as cirrhosis of the liver.

Can chronic constipation cause hemorrhoids in children?
Yes, but it rarely happens.

What is the treatment for hemorrhoids in children?
Most hemorrhoids will subside unless they are associated with an underlying disease. Stool softeners and lubricants should be given to ease the passage of stool. In some cases injections are effective; in others surgery is needed.

Is prolapse of the rectum seen very often in children?
No. When it does occur, it affects children between the ages of 3 and 5 years.

What causes prolapse of the rectum in children?
It has been noted that most children with prolapse of the rectum are markedly malnourished and have weak muscular development and loss of fatty tissue in the region of the anal outlet. Many of these children also have parasitic infestations and have had prolonged diarrhea. Others have a long history of chronic constipation with poor toilet habits, including excessive straining while attempting to evacuate their bowels.

What is the treatment for prolapse of the rectum in a child?
The underlying cause must be eradicated. If this is a parasitic infestation, it must be eliminated by the administration of the appropriate medications. If it is poor bowel habits and chronic constipation, then stool softeners and suppositories must be given and the child's toilet habits must be improved. If it is malnutrition, weight loss, and anemia, these conditions must be remedied.

Is surgery often necessary for prolapse of the rectum in children?
No.

RECTUM AND ANUS IN OLDER PEOPLE

What are some anatomical changes of aging that take place around the anus and rectum?
1. The muscles supporting the anus and rectum may weaken. This may eventually lead to constipation or to prolapse, a protrusion of the mucous membrane through the anal opening.

2. The blood vessels surrounding the anus may dilate and form varicosities, thus producing hemorrhoids.

3. The skin of the anus frequently becomes dry and scaly, resulting in intense itching (pruritus ani).

Does the skin around the anus require special attention in older people?

Yes. The following routine should be observed:

1. Since the skin becomes dry and scaly, it should be kept lubricated with Vaseline or some other soothing ointment.

2. The anus should never be wiped strenuously, as this may injure the already delicate skin. It is good practice to cleanse the anus after a bowel movement with cotton moistened in warm water, rather than using toilet tissue.

3. Medicated ointments can be used to relieve irritation and itching, but only upon prescription by a doctor.

4. Occasionally, it is found that nylon, rubber, or synthetic undergarments irritate the anal area. If so, cotton underwear should be worn.

5. Excessive scrubbing with soaps or detergents should be avoided, as it may injure the delicate tissues of the anal outlet.

Does bleeding from the rectum usually denote cancer of the rectum?

No. Although bleeding does occur with cancer, it also occurs in many other conditions. Among the more common of these conditions are the following:

1. Hemorrhoids (piles)

2. Fissure (a crack or tear in the mucous membrane of the anal outlet).

3. Pruritus ani. In this condition the bleeding is caused by intensive scratching.

4. Colitis.

5. Rectal polyps (benign tumors).

Is cancer of the rectum common in people past 60?

Yes. It is one of the most frequently encountered cancers in older people.

Can cancer of the rectum be cured by surgery?

More than 50 percent of those operated upon will be cured. After removal of the diseased rectum, a false orifice (colostomy) is made on the abdominal wall for exit of feces.

Do people tend to develop hemorrhoids as they grow older?

Yes. Constipation and straining to evacuate the bowels predispose toward formation of hemorrhoids.

What are the most common causes of hemorrhoids in older people?

1. A natural tendency toward varicose vein formation

2. Chronic constipation

3. Poor bowel habits

4. Excessive straining at the stool secondary to poor muscle tone

5. An obstruction, often caused by a tumor, in the bowel

6. Cirrhosis of the liver resulting in increased back pressure on the veins originating in the rectal area

Are fissures very common in people over 60?

Yes. Since constipation is one of the primary causes of fissure in ano, a high incidence in older age groups is to be expected.

Do older people develop fistulas?

Occasionally. They are much more common in young adults, however.

Reoperations

Although surgical techniques have improved greatly and morbidity and mortality rates have been markedly reduced within recent years, nevertheless, surgeons are all too often disappointed in end results. They are faced frequently with the need to reoperate in order to bring about alleviation of old or new symptoms or to do additional work in order to effect a cure. An apparently well-executed initial operation does not always lead to the cure of the offending lesion, nor does accurate technique necessarily prevent recurrence. Moreover, surgery, by altering anatomical and physiological states, often creates new problems that must be met by still further operative intervention. And finally, procedures deemed to be adequate at the time of the initial operation later prove to be inadequate. It is estimated that in this world of rapidly improving surgical techniques and innovative procedures, approximately 15 percent of all operations will eventually require additional intervention. As an example, until a few years ago, mitral commissurotomy, an operation in which the finger was inserted through the atrium of the heart in order to dilate and open up a diseased, contracted mitral valve, was considered to be the ultimate operation for mitral stenosis. It was performed upon thousands of patients with rheumatic heart disease. Today, this procedure is done infrequently, and has been supplanted by open heart surgery with repair of the mitral valve under direct vision or replacement with an artificial valve. Failures of mitral commissurotomy have thus been overcome through reoperation and employment of more advanced techniques.

QUESTIONS AND ANSWERS

Will reoperation frequently overcome failures of the initial procedure?

Yes, especially when better opera-

tions have been devised. As an example, many years ago, gastroenterostomy, an operation in which the stomach was sutured to the small intestine, was the operation of choice for the surgical treatment of intractable peptic ulcer. The operation was followed by recurrence of the ulcer in approximately 15 percent of cases. Today, a patient with ulcer recurrence following gastroenterostomy can be helped tremendously by reoperation involving vagotomy and pyloroplasty.

Is reoperation often successful in cases of recurrent disease?

Yes. There are a great number of instances where disease recurs despite seemingly adequate surgery. Goiters, fibroids of the uterus, hernias, cysts of the breast, and many other conditions, have a tendency to recur. Reoperation will overcome the recurrence in the great majority of cases.

Does reoperation carry with it greater surgical risk?

This will depend largely upon the general condition of the patient. If the patient is in good general health, there is very little additional risk to a reoperative procedure. However, from a technical point of view, the surgeon often finds a second operation more difficult to perform.

Are reoperations often necessary in cases where the initial operation was carried out merely to overcome an emergency situation?

Yes. It must be remembered that some initial operations may have been carried out at a time when saving the life of the patient was more important than obtaining a definitive cure of the disease. For example, surgeons often operate for acute intestinal obstruction and perform a procedure to relieve the obstruction, leaving behind the tumor that has caused the obstruction. In such cases, it is necessary to reoperate in order to obtain a permanent cure.

What is meant by staged procedures?

These are operations that must be carried out in two or more stages in order to attain a definitive end result. Often, a patient is too sick to undergo a complete curative procedure at one time. The surgeon must then do a preliminary operation to be followed at a later date by a more definitive procedure.

Resuturing Severed Structures

In rare instances, it has been found possible to reattach a severed digit or limb. Unfortunately, in the great majority of accidents of this type, a crushing injury accompanies the traumatic amputation, and consequently, it is not technically possible to resuture the severed structure.

QUESTIONS AND ANSWERS

When is it feasible to attempt to resuture a severed limb, or a portion of a limb?

1. When the amputation has been caused by a clean cut, as in cases where a limb has been inadvertently cut through by an electric saw or when a finger has been chopped off by a knife or machine

2. When the severed portion of the body can be quickly taken along with the patient to a hospital where there is a well-equipped surgical team ready to perform immediate surgery

How long can a severed limb, or portion of a limb, survive before an attempt is made to resuture it?

The operation must be carried out within a period of one to two hours from the time of the accident. If several hours have passed, the tissues of the severed structure will deteriorate to such an extent that they will not be able to survive even if resutured.

Must every structure within a severed limb, or portion of a limb, be resutured at the initial operation?

No. The essential aim is to reestablish circulation. This is carried out by resuturing the severed arteries and veins. The severed nerves and tendons can be resutured several days or weeks later after it is certain that circulation has been reestablished.

Are subsequent operations to restore severed bones, tendons, and nerves usually successful?

Bone and tendon repair is usually successful. However, the restoration of nerve continuity and function is not always successful. As a consequence, even though the resutured limb has adequate circulation and may have a normal or near-normal appearance, it may have little function or sensation within it.

What personnel must be available for the resuturing of a severed limb?

It is important to have surgeons who are trained in neurosurgery to restore nerve anatomy, vascular surgeons to repair the severed arteries and veins, and orthopedic surgeons to restore bone, muscle, and tendon continuity.

Are there cases on record where an entire severed leg or arm has returned to normal function?

There are very few cases in which all

function has been restored, but there are some on record where a useful limb has followed resuturing.

Retinal Detachment

See DETACHMENT OF THE RETINA.

Rhizotomy

Rhizotomy is the operation of cutting some of the posterior spinal nerve roots in order to relieve intractable pain or to relieve those who are afflicted with spastic paralysis. Neurosurgeons are frequently called upon to perform this procedure in people who have uncontrollable pain due to advanced cancer. The cutting of these nerves will deprive an area that they serve of all sensation, and pain in that area will be eliminated. The operation is also carried out in some cases where there is incurable spastic paralysis with muscle contractions of great severity. By cutting these nerves, spasm is relieved even though the paralysis is not benefited.

Rhizotomy is not a dangerous operative procedure, but it must be carried out by a neurosurgeon who is familiar with the anatomy of the nervous system and who knows the pathways of the nerves both within and without the spinal cord.

See also NEUROSURGERY.

Salivary Glands

The salivary glands include the *parotid,* which is located in front of and a little below the ear; the *submaxillary,* just about an inch forward to and below the angle of the jaw; and the *sublingual,* which lies in the floor of the mouth under the tongue. (See diagram.) All three of these glands manufacture and secrete saliva, which reaches the mouth through their respective ducts (tubes). The purpose of saliva is to moisten food and to partially digest starch through the action of its enzyme, ptyalin.

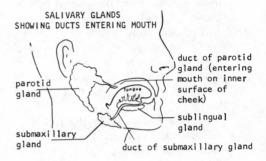

SALIVARY GLANDS
SHOWING DUCTS ENTERING MOUTH

parotid gland

submaxillary gland

duct of parotid gland (entering mouth on inner surface of cheek)

sublingual gland

duct of submaxillary gland

There are several conditions of the salivary glands that may demand surgical attention: (1) infection with abscess formation, (2) salivary fistula, (3) salivary stones (calculi), and (4) salivary tumors.

1. Inflammation of the salivary glands may result from mouth or tooth infection, or as a complication of a general disease such as typhoid fever, scarlet fever, smallpox.

In the years before the widespread use of antibiotics, infections and abscesses of the parotid gland (parotitis) were seen quite often as complications of major surgical procedures such as gallbladder removal or removal of a portion of intestines. Also, abscess formation surrounding and involving the submaxillary gland was seen as a complication of an extraction of an infected tooth. This condition, known as Ludwig's angina, presented great danger to life, as the infection would frequently extend down toward the trachea (windpipe) and create pressure upon it.

Infections in the parotid gland or in the vicinity of the submaxillary gland cause severe pain, temperature as high as 105 degrees, and marked swelling over the involved area. Both of these conditions demand intensive treatment with antibiotic drugs and surgical incision if a collection of pus develops. Surgical drainage must be carried out in the hospital, where the patient will be confined for several days.

A possible complication of an abscess within the parotid gland is the involvement of the facial nerve which courses directly through its substance. Injury to this nerve will distort the appearance of the face.

Abscess formation in the region of the submaxillary gland is serious, as the swelling may progress and extend so that there is dangerous pressure upon the windpipe (trachea).

It is good to report that both of these conditions are seen only rarely today and that when they do occur, cure can be obtained through the combined antibiotic-surgical approach.

2. A salivary fistula exists when there is a discharge of saliva through a false opening between the gland and the skin. A fistula may follow a wound or laceration extending from the skin into the parotid or submaxillary gland. If the fistula empties into the mouth rather than onto the skin, it will require no treatment. However, when a skin wound leaks saliva, there is great likelihood that the fistula will persist indefinitely, unless corrected through surgery. The diagnosis is simple to make on direct inspection and on noting a flow of saliva when the patient eats.

Salivary fistulas are treated by simple cauterization (burning) of the tract leading from the gland or by an operation that completely cuts out the tract and ties it off at its base. If these procedures are unsuccessful and the fistula persists, either one of the following operations can be performed:

a) Complete removal of the involved gland. These procedures are done under general anesthesia. An incision is made through the skin on the face over the gland. For the parotid, it is made in front and below the ear. For the submaxillary gland, below the line of the jaw. These operations are serious but not dangerous; the patient is out of bed the first postoperative day, and home on the fourth or fifth day after surgery.

b) A plastic operation may be done in which the fistulous tract is carefully dissected out from the skin of the face and is implanted into the mucous membrane of the mouth so that the saliva will drain in that direction.

3. Salivary stones (calculi) may form in any of the salivary glands but are most commonly found in the duct of the submaxillary. Men in middle life appear to be more frequently affected by this condition than anyone else. The stones are yellow in color and usually measure about one-eighth to one-fourth inch in diameter. Occasionally stones as large as an inch in diameter have been noted.

Symptoms are:

a) Swelling and tenderness over the involved gland. This develops because the stone blocks the passage of the saliva through the duct.

b) The opening of the duct in the mouth may be swollen and inflamed.

c) Eating, especially sharp foods, causes the gland to swell and become painful.

d) X-rays sometimes show the presence of a stone.

e) The stone itself can often be felt by inserting a finger in the mouth and feeling along the course of the duct.

Treatment consists of removing the stone. To accomplish this, an incision is made into the duct directly over the stone. This is an office procedure, but may, on occasion, require hospitalization if the stone is larger or is lodged in a position difficult to reach. Local Novocain anesthesia is used.

In a small number of cases, the stones are lodged within the substance of the gland, and this may necessitate an external incision in the skin. When stones recur, it is advisable to remove the entire gland.

4. **Tumors** of the salivary glands are encountered rather frequently. Approximately 90 percent of them are not malignant. They are removed through a skin incision, with care being exercised, when handling the parotid, to avoid damage to the facial nerve.

The most frequent of all salivary tumors is the *mixed tumor,* which derives its name from the fact that it is composed of gland, cartilage, muscle, and even bone cells. It usually starts on the outer surface of the parotid gland near the ear. Men between the ages of 20 to 40 years are most prone to develop this particular growth. The tumor is painless, slow-growing, firm to the touch, and well confined by a capsule around it. About 10 percent of mixed tumors of the parotid gland show, or will develop, malignancy (cancerous cells). About 50 percent of tumors of the submaxillary gland are malignant. Because of this tendency, it is important that these tumors be carefully and completely dissected out of the gland substance as soon as the diagnosis is established. Recurrence is seen in a small proportion of cases and is treated by reoperation with removal of the entire gland.

Frank cancer of the salivary glands is relatively rare. Such a diagnosis should be suspected if the tumor grows rapidly. Removal of the whole gland, surrounding tissue, and lymph nodes is indicated. Nerve and blood vessels must be sacrificed and removed along with the nodes if cancer is present. Cures are obtained in those cases that have been detected before the spread of the cancer to adjacent tissues and distant organs.

See also RANULA.

What is the function of saliva?

To moisten food and to begin the digestion of starch through the action of the salivary enzyme ptyalin. People would be unable to chew and swallow solid foods satisfactorily without saliva.

Do the salivary glands ever become inflamed or infected?

Yes. The most common disease of the salivary glands is mumps. This mainly involves an inflammation of the parotid gland below the ear. However, the sublingual and the submaxillary glands can also become inflamed secondary to a contagious disease such as scarlet fever, typhoid fever, or measles. Occasionally, a stone will form in a submaxillary duct and block it. This may cause swelling, pain, and infection.

Is any treatment required for the inflammation of the salivary glands that accompanies contagious diseases?

Usually not. The inflammation will subside when the underlying condition improves.

What can be done to make a patient more comfortable if he has an inflammation of the salivary glands?

1. Cold, moist compresses can be applied to the inflamed area.

2. The patient should avoid eating any spicy or sharp foods.

3. The patient should avoid very cold or iced drinks.

4. Sometimes, chewing a mild chewing gum will help the glands to secrete more saliva and thus reduce the inflammation.

5. Antibiotics should be given only if the associated disease requires them.

6. Pain-relieving drugs such as aspirin or codeine may be prescribed by the physician.

Do the salivary glands return to normal function after the inflammation has subsided?

Yes.

How can one tell if there is a stone blocking the submaxillary duct?

In some instances, the stone can be felt by placing the examining finger within the mouth along the duct. X-ray examination will demonstrate the stone's presence on occasion. In the remainder of cases, the diagnosis must be made by the clinical history and symptoms.

What is done about a stone in one of the salivary ducts?

It should be removed surgically under local anesthesia by making an incision into the duct and lifting out the stone.

Do stones, once removed, have a tendency to recur?

Occasionally.

If an abscess has formed in the submaxillary gland, what treatment is recommended?

Simple incision and drainage of the abscess if it has spread beyond the confines of the gland, or removal of the entire gland if the abscess is localized to the gland itself.

Where is the incision made for the removal of the submaxillary gland?

Beneath the chin and off to the side of the midline. An incision approxi-

mately two to three inches long is necessary for the removal of the gland.

Is it ever necessary to remove the parotid gland?

Yes, but only when a tumor has formed, not for abscess formation.

What is the treatment for an abscess within the parotid gland?

Incision and drainage, usually in the hospital under general anesthesia.

SALIVARY GLAND TUMORS

Are tumors of the salivary glands common?

Yes, particularly the so-called mixed tumors which involve the parotid gland and, occasionally, the submaxillary gland.

Are tumors of the parotid gland usually malignant?

No. Most parotid tumors are benign, but the gland does often become involved in a cancerous growth.

Do parotid tumors tend to recur once they are removed?

Yes. About one in five may recur even if they are benign.

How can one tell if a salivary tumor is benign or malignant?

The benign tumors grow slowly and usually are surrounded by a capsule. Many of them are freely movable beneath the skin. Malignant tumors of the salivary glands grow rapidly and become adherent to the skin and surrounding tissues. Of course, following removal, microscopic examination will result in a conclusive diagnosis.

Are operations upon these glands dangerous?

No, but operations for the removal of parotid tumors are long and tedious to perform. Great care must be exercised to avoid injury to the nerve filaments of the facial nerve which course through the parotid gland. Injury to this nerve will result in a certain amount of facial paralysis.

What anesthesia is used for operations upon the salivary glands?

General anesthesia for the major surgical procedures; local anesthesia for minor operations.

Where is the incision made for operations on the parotid gland?

In front of the ear and down along the angle of the jaw on to the neck.

Are the operative scars disfiguring following surgery on the parotid or submaxillary glands?

No. Fine thin lines are usually obtained several months later when these wounds have healed completely.

Is it always possible to avoid injury to the facial nerve when operating to remove a tumor of the parotid gland?

No. It is sometimes necessary to disturb or even cut a branch of the nerve when removing an extensive growth of the parotid gland. However, this is not a frequent occurrence, and when it does happen it is excusable on the grounds that the most important consideration is the total removal of the offending tumor.

What happens if the facial nerve is injured during the removal of a parotid tumor?

The face becomes partially paralyzed and distorted with a drooping and twisting of one side of the mouth. In rare cases, a branch of the nerve to the eyelid may be injured, and this will interfere with the patient's ability to close his eye completely.

If the facial nerve has been injured, is the face deformity permanent?

More or less, although the deformity tends to become less prominent as time passes.

Can these nerves be repaired successfully once they have been cut?

They are very small in diameter, some being no wider than ordinary sewing thread. It is therefore most difficult to find their ends and sew them together again.

Recently, by means of ingenious muscle and nerve transfers, it has become possible to restore the face to near-normal appearance. To accomplish this, the services of an expert plastic surgeon will be required.

Do the wounds from these operative procedures have a tendency to drain?

Yes. They may drain saliva onto the skin for many days or weeks postoperatively. However, the drainage will eventually subside and the wounds will heal completely.

How soon after the salivary glands are operated upon can one resume eating?

Fluids are taken for the first few days after surgery; then a normal diet may be resumed.

How long a hospital stay is necessary following surgery upon these glands?

Most patients can leave the hospital within a week after surgery.

If a parotid tumor recurs, is it possible to get a cure by reoperation?

Yes. A more extensive removal of parotid tissue will bring about a cure in the great majority of cases.

What is the treatment for a tumor of the submaxillary or sublingual glands?

Complete removal of the gland.

Are operations for tumors of the submaxillary or sublingual glands successful?

Yes, unless the procedure has been carried out for a rapidly growing cancer of these structures. Such malignant involvement is, fortunately, a rare occurrence.

Do children ever get tumors of the salivary glands?

Yes. These tumors usually grow very rapidly and can be malignant. Fortunately, salivary gland tumors are rather rare in children.

How can one tell if a child has a tumor of a salivary gland?

There is a hard, nontender, rapid enlargement of one of the salivary glands over a period of a few weeks.

What is the treatment for a salivary gland tumor in a child?

If the tumor is benign, a simple local removal is sufficient. If the tumor proves to be cancerous, a radical removal of the entire gland and surrounding structures is necessary.

How successful is surgery for removing salivary gland tumors in children?

The tumor is often so malignant that permanent cure is not possible. There are, however, a growing number of cases that have been saved by rapid, extensive surgical removal followed by intensive x-ray therapy.

What is a salivary gland fistula?

It is an abnormal opening that drains saliva from one of the salivary glands onto the skin of the face or neck.

What causes a salivary gland fistula?

Usually a laceration or a wound that has extended into the duct of the gland or into the gland itself.

Do fistulas of the salivary glands tend to become chronic?

Yes. These fistulas usually heal very slowly, and in most instances surgical repair is necessary.

How are salivary gland fistulas repaired?

1. The fistula can sometimes be dissected out and reimplanted into the mouth so that the saliva drains where it would normally drain.

2. A fistula can sometimes be removed completely and tied off.

3. If the fistula involves a submaxillary gland, it is sometimes wise to remove the entire gland.

Will the removal of one salivary gland interfere with salivary function?

No. The other glands will secrete an adequate amount of saliva and provide the necessary ptyalin.

What is a ranula?

A ranula is a cyst of the sublingual gland in the floor of the mouth caused by an obstruction of the duct.

How can a ranula be diagnosed?

A smooth, ovoid, cystic mass, appearing something like a frog's distended belly, is seen underneath the tongue.

How is a ranula treated?

The cyst should be completely removed surgically.

Salpingitis

Salpingitis is an inflammation of the fallopian (uterine) tubes which extend out from both sides of the uterus. Many cases are caused by the gonorrhea germ but it can also be caused by staphylococci, streptococci, or the tuberculosis germ.

See also FALLOPIAN TUBES.

Scalene Node Biopsy

A scalene node biopsy is an operation carried out in order to discover whether a cancer of the lung has spread to the scalene lymph node located in the base of the neck. An incision about three to four inches long is made just above the collarbone and is carried down into the neck to the region of the scalene muscle. When this muscle is cut through or pulled out of the way, a group of lymph nodes known as the scalene nodes come into view. One or more of these nodes are removed and are submitted to a pathology laboratory for microscopic examination.

If the scalene node biopsy shows cancer, it indicates that the primary tumor in the lung has already spread to such an extent that surgery will be of no avail. Accordingly, with a positive scalene lymph node biopsy the chest surgeon will not attempt to remove the lobe of the lung or the entire lung that is involved in the cancerous process. If the scalene lymph node biopsy is negative, the surgeon may proceed to attempt to remove the primary cancerous growth in the lung.

The biopsy of the scalene node is a minor procedure and carries with it little or no risk.

See also BIOPSY; LUNGS.

Scanning in Surgery

Scanning, more properly called photo-scanning, is carried out by means of a scintillation counter apparatus which is affected by the local radiation that emanates from a radioactive isotope contained in the organ that is being scanned. It has been found that certain chemicals such as iodine, gold, cobalt, iron, phosphorus, cesium, and strontium can be made radioactive by placing them in an atomic pile. Certain of these radioactive chemicals have a particular affinity for a particular structure or organ in the body. When these radioactive substances are administered to the patient they concentrate in the organ for which they have an affinity. A scintillator, an instrument similar to a Geiger counter, is placed over the organ, and the shape of the radioactive concentration within the organ is recorded on a paper drum. Thus, in a normal thyroid, an *even* concentration of radioactive iodine is seen to be distributed throughout the gland. If a goiter or cancer is present within the gland, a characteristic uneven concentration of the radioactive substance will show on the drum and will permit one to make a diagnosis of a specific abnormality. Similarly, with other radioactive chemicals, it is possible to diagnose disease within other organs of the body.

QUESTIONS AND ANSWERS

Is it ever possible to make precise diagnoses through scanning?

Yes, in some instances. A sharply outlined lack of concentration of radioactive material may indicate the presence of a cyst, whereas an irregular lack of concentration of a radioactive substance may be indicative of a malignant lesion.

Is scanning often used as the sole method of arriving at a surgical diagnosis?

No, but it is helpful when used in conjunction with other diagnostic methods. Scanning might indicate the presence of a brain tumor, but the neurosurgeon will not rely solely upon this method of diagnosis. He will also take x-rays and perform angiograms to note the outline of the blood vessels within the brain. A thoracic surgeon may be helped considerably by noting an abnormality of a lung scan, but he will use bronchoscopy, cell studies, and x-rays of the lungs to aid him in making his final determination of the exact nature of the lung disease.

How are radioactive substances used in the diagnosis of disease?

A small dose of the radioactive substance is given to the patient to drink or is injected intravenously. Each one of the radioactive substances has a predilection for one or more organs within the body and therefore concentrates within those organs. As an example, when radioactive iodine is given to a patient, it tends to concentrate within the thyroid gland. Similarly, when radioactive mercury is given, it tends to concentrate within the kidneys.

After the radioactive material has concentrated in an organ, an apparatus known as a scanner, which includes a modified Geiger counter, is placed over that organ. The radioactive emissions are then recorded on photographic film or paper. If the organ is normal, the recording on the film or paper will have a characteristically normal pattern; if disease exists, the scan will have an abnormal appearance.

What are some of the organs that can be scanned after the patient has been given a radioactive substance?

1. The brain. Technetium 99 is given and a brain scan is taken some time later. Abnormal scan patterns may reveal the presence of a brain tumor or cyst. Also, brain tumor tissue concen-

trates radioactive iodine to a much greater extent than normal brain tissue, thus permitting more accurate diagnosis and pinpointing of brain tumors.

2. The thyroid gland. After giving radioactive iodine, the scanner is placed over the neck and a pattern is obtained. Lack of concentration of the iodine will indicate that none of the radioactive substance has been picked up by the gland. In other scans, there may be a greater-than-normal concentration of the iodine in the gland, showing disease within the thyroid.

3. The liver. Radioactive gold is given, and a scan of the liver may reveal the presence of a tumor, abscess, or cyst. These areas are noted by deviations from the normal scan pattern of the liver substance.

4. The lungs. After giving radioactive albumin attached to iodine, it may be possible to spot a lung tumor, cyst, or abscess in the scan pattern.

5. The kidneys. Radioactive mercury will concentrate in the kidney and a pattern will be obtained by the scanner. Tumors or cysts of the kidney can be noted by deviations from the normal scan pattern.

6. The spleen. After giving radioactive chromium, enlargement of the spleen or tumor formation within the spleen can be noted by deviations from the normal scan pattern.

7. The bones. A radioactive strontium scan may reveal the presence of tumor within the bones.

How does nuclear medicine add to the treatment of disease?

There is a growing number of conditions that can be treated with radioactive substances. Some of these presently being treated and the substances used in the treatment are as follows:

1. Radioactive iodine is used to treat

overactivity of the thyroid gland and some cases of thyroid cancer.

2. Radioactive phosphorus is used in the treatment of polycythemia vera, a condition associated with too many red blood cells.

3. Radioactive gold is used in the treatment of cancer of the prostate gland and malignancy that has spread to the abdominal or chest cavity with collection of fluid within those spaces.

Who carries out scanning procedures?

Most hospitals today have departments of nuclear medicine where scanning is done.

Is it painful to undergo scanning?

No. It is a completely painless procedure and can be carried out within a few hours' time.

Do surgeons rely upon scanning to determine whether or not to operate upon a goiter?

Some surgeons place considerable importance on whether or not a goiter takes up the radioactive iodine or refuses to take it up. This may indicate whether a particular goiter is benign or malignant.

Schimmelbusch's Disease

Schimmelbusch's disease is characterized by many small, poorly defined lumps which occur throughout both breasts. The condition is more accurately known as chronic cystic mastitis. It is also called "shoddy breasts" or "lumpy breasts."

It is estimated that approximately 15 percent of all women have some form of Schimmelbusch's disease. The lumps often appear and disappear periodically and are strongly influenced by the patient's menstrual cycle or state of hormone balance. Physicians can best tell about this condition by examining the breasts before and after the menstrual period, since these masses tend to get larger and somewhat painful just before the period and become smaller and painless during and after menstruation.

In most instances, Schimmelbusch's disease is treated by directing medication toward the glandular imbalance which is thought to be the cause. On occasion, however, surgery is recommended for the purpose of clinching the diagnosis by examining a biopsy of tissue removed from the breast and submitted for microscopic examination.

Schimmelbusch's disease tends to disappear spontaneously after change of life. However, if female hormones are continued after menopause, the symptoms of the disease and the physical findings may persist.

It is now thought that breasts involved in Schimmelbusch's disease have a somewhat higher incidence of cancer. Despite this statistical fact, it is not thought that the cystic mastitis becomes cancerous, but that breasts with cystic mastitis are more subject to the independent development of cancer.

There is no known prevention of Schimmelbusch's disease, but the prolonged correction of glandular imbalance will tend to decrease the severity of the condition.

See also BREASTS.

Scoliosis (Curvature of the Spine)

One of the most important conditions affecting the spine is scoliosis. It is found in varying degrees of severity in approximately one of every five children and adolescents and is characterized by a twisting of the spine upon itself. It is popularly believed that poor posture habits bring on this deformity, but in reality, orthopedists do not believe this to be true.

Scoliosis is a curvature of the spine in the vertical plane with rotation. There are two main types:

1. Idiopathic scoliosis: This means that the cause is unknown. It occurs during the last spurt of growth in the actively growing adolescent and is found more frequently among girls.

2. Scoliosis secondary to poliomyelitis (infantile paralysis): This type occurs when one side of the trunk is paralyzed from poliomyelitis while the other side remains healthy. In this situation, the strong muscles work against the paralyzed ones and thus twist and pull the spine out of alignment.

Treatment of scoliosis demands constant observation and reappraisal over a period of months or years. Frequent measurements must be taken to note changes in the progress, for in certain children there are periods of quiescence followed by periods of suddenly increasing curvatures. Braces, plaster casts, elaborate exercises have all proved disappointing in halting the progress of scoliosis or in bringing about a cure. Fortunately, the great majority of children (90 percent) are left with only a mild curvature, and no surgical intervention is required. The minority, with severe and progressive curvature, can be helped greatly by a series of spinal fusion operations. (*See* SPONDYLOLISTHESIS.) Multiple spinal fusion procedures aim to fuse the deformed portion of the spinal column.

Newer operative techniques in the surgery of scoliosis have improved final results considerably. Metal rods are fixed to the vertebrae so as to straighten the spine almost completely in one operation. Spinal bone fusion is performed in order to maintain the correction. The metal rods can be left in place as they are buried deep below the thick muscles of the back.

This subject cannot be left without cautioning that treatment for scoliosis may be long and arduous, and at times is faced with apparent failure. Reoperation is frequently necessary to attain eventual success. The patient and parents must be made to appreciate the many problems that will arise, and their sustained cooperation is essential for a satisfactory outcome.

Despite the major nature of the combined efforts of surgeon, patient, and parent, the results of scoliosis surgery are worthwhile. One need only to consider the alternatives to active treatment: permanent physical deformity and the psychological burdens associated with the knowledge that one is handicapped.

QUESTIONS AND ANSWERS

What causes scoliosis?

Its cause is unknown except in those cases following poliomyelitis.

Is scoliosis caused by poor posture habits?

No.

Will posture exercises cure scoliosis?

No.

Is it painful?

No.

Is scoliosis more common in girls or in boys?

The condition is much more common in girls.

When can a parent note the onset of scoliosis in a child?

Structural scoliosis usually has its onset in girls about 10 to 12 years old.

Does scoliosis ever occur in early childhood?

Yes. Occasionally, scoliosis may be caused by the absence of half of a vertebra or by paralysis. In these cases the curve may occur in infancy or early childhood.

Does diet influence the onset of scoliosis?

No, although most girls with structural scoliosis are thin and undernourished.

Does vitamin intake influence the onset of scoliosis?

No.

Does scoliosis tend to run in families?

No.

How can scoliosis be prevented?

A functional scoliosis can be controlled by proper exercises. A structural scoliosis cannot be prevented. The curve can be corrected only by proper surgical and orthopedic measures.

What are some of the possible complications of marked scoliosis in a child?

1. Poor physical appearance
2. Back pain (usually does not occur until later in life)
3. Interference with the affected child's respiration
4. Deviation of the heart due to chest cavity deformity

Can a child with scoliosis engage in physical exercises?

Yes.

What is the treatment for early scoliosis?

If a structural scoliosis is progressing, surgery is usually necessary. The curve is corrected as much as possible by casts. Then the abnormal portion of the spine is fused in one or two operations known as spinal fusion operations.

More recently, techniques have been devised whereby metal rods are placed in the spine so as to correct the curvature. The spine is then fused and the rods are later removed.

Does it ever get well by itself?

No, but in the majority of cases it is mild and leaves only a barely discernible deformity by the time maturity is reached.

Are braces helpful in controlling scoliosis in children?

Only specially fitted braces worn 24 hours a day can control the curves without surgery.

Is surgery often necessary in treating scoliosis?

Yes.

What operation is performed?

Spinal fusion, in a corrective plaster jacket or cast. In certain cases, metal rods are inserted to straighten the spine.

Is it a serious operation?

Yes.

Is the spinal fusion the same operation as for spondylolisthesis?

Yes, except it is more extensive and may fuse as much as one third of the entire spinal column.

What are the results from spinal fusion for scoliosis?

Cures and prevention of extension of the curvature occur in 80 percent of patients.

Is the patient ever worse after fusion for scoliosis?

Not if correctly done in adequately selected cases.

How long a hospital stay is necessary?

There is a wide variation, depending upon the severity of the condition and the type of operation performed. Some patients require but a few weeks' hospitalization; others may require months.

How long is the convalescent period?

About six months to one year.

How can the orthopedist distinguish between cases of scoliosis that require surgery and cases that can be treated merely by exercises and the application of braces?

Exercises are of no value in structural scoliosis (if x-rays show bone changes). Functional scoliosis can be treated with exercises, but they often fail to correct the condition.

How long a period of hospitalization is needed after operating upon a child for scoliosis?

Usually, two weeks.

Do children who have been operated upon for scoliosis have to wear casts or braces after surgery?

Yes, until the fusion is solid. This may make the wearing of a cast necessary for a period of several months.

How soon after scoliosis surgery can beneficial results be seen?

Often the back will be straightened at the time of surgery and the improvement will be noticeable immediately.

Is a child confined to bed throughout the entire period of treatment for scoliosis?

No. Depending upon the treatment, the type of immobilizing plaster used, and the location and the extent of the scoliosis, the child undergoing treatment for scoliosis may be up and around a good deal of the time.

Is a further operation ever indicated when the initial results of surgery are not as satisfactory as one would wish?

Yes. Quite frequently, a second operation may be necessary to apply further bone grafts to a portion of the fused spine that has become weak. This is usually a much less serious operation than the original one.

In performing a spinal fusion operation, is it necessary to use bone grafts?

Yes.

What is the source for bone grafts used in spinal fusion operations?

The best source of the graft is from the patient. It is usually taken from either the pelvis or the shin. Frequently, if larger quantities of bone are required, bone is taken from a bone bank.

What special postoperative treatment must be carried out on a child with scoliosis?

Usually a cast must be worn for several months. It is necessary to make sure the child has an adequate diet and does not develop a respiratory infection.

How soon after a spinal fusion operation can a child get out of bed?

Often within a week.

Will scoliosis continue to get worse in adulthood?

No. The severity of the curve does not progress after the child has stopped growing. For practical purposes, this is at 15 years of age.

Septal Defects

Septal defects are birth deformities of the heart in which there is a hole, or more than one hole, in the partition separating the right from the left side of the heart. There are two main types of septal defects, namely, atrial defects between the right and left atria, and ventricular defects between the right and left ventricles of the heart.

Through open heart surgery, the majority of septal defects can now be repaired successfully. Smaller ones are closed by suturing while the larger ones may require a patch graft to obliterate the defect.

See also HEART.

Shock

Shock is a total body reaction with upset and depression of physical and mental activities due to a profound insult, either physical or mental. Included in the classification of shock are many medical and surgical conditions, most of which are associated with loss of circulating blood volume. This does not necessarily mean that blood is lost from the body but rather that it leaves the vessels and pools in the tissues.

The most common cause of shock is hemorrhage, either internal or from an exposed wound. This serious condition can also be produced by overwhelming blood poisoning (septicemia, with bacteria circulating in the bloodstream), by an absorption of toxins (poisons) into the bloodstream, by extremely painful injuries even if not accompanied by great blood loss, by extensive burns, by chemical agents and electric agents, and by extreme nervous and mental disturbance.

See also ENDOTOXIN SHOCK; FIRST AID.

QUESTIONS AND ANSWERS

What are the types of shock?
Shock has been further subdivided and classified as follows:

1. Anaphylactic shock. This is the type seen when an allergic patient is injected with a substance to which he is markedly hypersensitive. It may be associated with such a severe reaction that death ensues within a matter of minutes unless treatment is carried out to counteract it.

2. Cardiac shock. This type is seen in cases of severe coronary thrombosis. This, too, can sometimes be so severe that immediate death occurs.

3. Delayed shock. This type often comes on several hours or even a day or two after receiving an injury.

4. Electric shock. This is the type seen when someone has exposed himself to the passage of an electric current through his body.

5. Electroshock. This is the type of shock that is carried out purposely in some cases of mental illness.

6. Hypovolemic shock. This type of shock is associated with a marked reduction in the amount of blood which is circulating in the body. It can be caused by hemorrhage or from the passage of blood out of its usual channels into the tissues.

7. Insulin shock. This type occurs from an overdose of insulin and with the reduction in blood sugar to abnormally low levels.

8. Irreversible shock. In this type the shock is so profound and deep that no treatment will cause it to recede or disappear. Recovery never takes place from irreversible shock.

9. Reversible shock. This type of shock responds to treatment and recovery is possible.

10. Shell shock. This is the type of shock resulting from exposure to danger in battle. It is a war neurosis.

11. Surgical shock. This type is seen following surgery in some instances. It is accompanied by a marked drop in blood pressure and reduced heart output and reduced output of urine.

12. Psychogenic shock. This type arises from extreme fright or anxiety.

13. Endotoxin shock. This type of shock is brought about by toxins (poisons) liberated by bacteria and discharged into the bloodstream.

14. Bacterial shock. In this type of shock, bacteria are living and growing in the bloodstream and overwhelm the body's defenses.

15. Burn shock. This is the type seen among those who have suffered burns to a large area of the body.

16. Traumatic shock. This is a type of shock brought on by a severe pain, as following a major fracture of a bone.

17. Embolic shock. This type of shock is brought on by the sudden breaking off of a blood clot from its primary site and its lodging elsewhere, as in the lungs or brain.

18. Hemorrhagic shock. This type is commonly seen in a person who has suddenly lost a large amount of blood. It usually takes the loss of one or two pints of blood to produce this kind of shock.

19. Neurogenic shock. This type may be caused by injuring the brain or spinal cord.

20. Primary shock. This type occurs immediately following an injury.

What are the symptoms and signs of shock?

1. In some cases there is loss of consciousness; in others, there are marked apprehension and evidence of fright.

2. If the patient is conscious, he complains of weakness, extreme thirst, and hunger for air.

3. The body is bathed in a cold, clammy perspiration.

4. The pupils become dilated.

5. Breathing is rapid and shallow.

6. The skin may take on a gray appearance.

7. The pulse is rapid and weak.

8. Blood pressure is usually very low.

What first aid should be given for shock?

1. The patient should be placed flat on his back. If the shock is profound,

some books should be placed under the legs of the bed at the foot, so that the patient's head and chest are lower than the rest of the body.

2. Attempts should be made to relieve pain, since this is one of the precipitating causes of shock.

3. If the cause of the shock is obvious, as when it is secondary to a severe laceration with blood loss, the local condition should be treated immediately. (A tourniquet should be applied to stop the bleeding.) If the shock is secondary to a fracture, the limb should be splinted. In many cases, prompt treatment of the precipitating factor is sufficient to bring the patient out of shock.

4. Blankets should be used to cover the patient, but he should not be too warm.

5. As soon as possible, the patient should be transported on a stretcher to the emergency room of the nearest hospital.

Do people past 60 recover from shock as readily as younger people?

No. Shock of more than a few hours' duration is often fatal to older people, whereas young people may be able to recover even after a day or two in shock.

Should attempts be made to arouse someone who is in shock?

No. If he is unconscious, it will do no good to try to awaken him. If he is sleeping, he should be permitted to continue to do so.

Should whiskey, tea, or coffee be given to someone in shock?

No. It is best to give nothing by mouth until so ordered by a physician.

Shoulder Separation

See ACROMIOCLAVICULAR JOINT SEPARATION.

Sigmoidoscopy

Sigmoidoscopy is visual inspection by means of a hollow metal tube, measuring approximately 10 inches in length, passed into the anal-rectal canal. The tube is lighted, and through it, the examining physician can inspect all of the rectum and part of the sigmoid colon. He will be able to see any inflammation or tumor growth that may be present. Also, through the sigmoidoscope, he may be able to remove such tumors as polyps or to burn them with an electric current. Using the sigmoidoscope, he will also be able to take a biopsy of tissue that appears to be abnormal.

Although sigmoidoscopy is somewhat unpleasant, it is not actually a painful procedure and is carried out ordinarily in a physician's office without anesthesia. To ensure the best view of the anus, rectum, and sigmoid colon, it is best to take a cleansing enema an hour or two before undergoing sigmoidoscopy.

See also INTESTINES; RECTUM AND ANUS.

Sinusitis

See NOSE AND SINUSES.

Skin and Subcutaneous Tissues

Few people go through life without developing some tumor or cyst of the skin or the tissues directly beneath the skin (the subcutaneous tissues). Sebaceous cysts, warts, moles, small blood vessel tumors, ganglions, fibrous and fatty tumors are extremely common conditions which can, in many instances, be disregarded by the patient and the surgeon. There are, however, certain circumstances in which these growths require surgical attention and it might prove helpful to enumerate them here:

1. A sebaceous cyst develops when the pores of sweat glands become plugged and the secretions (sebum) accumulate. When these cysts increase in size over a period of weeks or months, they should be removed. Failure to do so may lead to infection within the cyst. When infection has occurred, the cyst can only be incised to let out the pus, as any attempt to remove it will spread the infection to surrounding tissue. Cysts that are stationary in size can be left alone unless they are located in areas where there is constant or repeated irritation.

The surgical procedure for their removal involves an incision through the overlying skin after infiltration with a local anesthetic. The cyst is removed and the skin stitched. Many of these cysts can be removed in the surgeon's office, but the larger ones may require hospitalization for a day.

These cysts only rarely undergo transformation to cancer.

2. Warts tend to be multiple and it is rarely necessary to remove all of them. They have a tendency to disappear by themselves within a period of a few months or a year or two. If they do not disappear within this period, then it is advisable to remove one large wart. This may cause all the others to disappear spontaneously.

Warts can be removed by destroying them with an electric current (electrodesiccation), by burning them with powerful acids, by x-ray treatments, or by removing them surgically with an elliptical incision. *By far the best method is to destroy them with an electric current.* However, *plantar warts*—on the sole of the feet—are best treated by x-ray or by surgical excision.

The above procedures can usually be carried out in the surgeon's office, with the possible exception of excision of a plantar wart. This may require hospitalization for a day or two and the use of crutches for a few days thereafter. Warts do not turn into cancer.

3. Moles (nevi) are common to most people and only require surgical excision when they show changes in color, undergo an increase in size, or are located in an area subject to repeated irritation. Moles at the collar line, on the palm of the hands or sole of the feet, or where a shoe rubs, should be removed surgically.

Pigmented moles, when removed, should be widely excised with a knife. A rim of normal skin should always be taken along with the mole, and the underlying subcutaneous tissue should be included in the removal. If there is any difficulty in bringing the skin edges together after removal, a skin graft should be applied to the area.

Occasionally a pigmented mole will turn into cancer of a highly malignant type. Such cancers spread rapidly throughout the body and result in a fatality within a year or two. It is important, therefore, to remove moles when they show signs of growth or change in color!

Although it has not been proved that burning a mole with an electric needle will cause it to undergo malignant changes, it is nevertheless thought best not to treat them in this manner.

4. Blood vessel tumors of the skin (hemangiomas) may appear at any time from birth to old age. They are recognized as red spots on the skin and vary in size from that of a pinhead to that of

a five-cent piece. If they are located in an area that is subject to repeated irritation (the skin of the face in men or on the fingers), they may bleed.

Most of these little tumors are harmless and do not grow, bleed, or become malignant. If they are unsightly, as on the tip of the nose or on the face or lips, they should be destroyed with an electric needle or by freezing with carbon dioxide snow. Larger ones should be removed surgically under local anesthesia in a hospital.

5. Ganglions are thin-walled cysts of tendons or joints. They are filled with a colorless, jellylike substance. They are seen most frequently on the back of the wrists in children and young adults. Many of them cause no symptoms and disappear by themselves over a period of months. But others grow quite large (one or two inches in diameter) and cause great pain on motion of the wrist. Occasionally these cysts are found on the fingers or about the ankle joint.

Ganglionic cysts must be removed in the hospital under local or general anesthesia. Those that originate from the wrist joint may be exceedingly difficult to remove in their entirety and, as a consequence, have a tendency to recur. It must also be mentioned that ganglions tend to be multiple, and a new one may form in the same region where one has already been removed.

The hand usually swells greatly after the surgical removal of these cysts, and it is often impossible to return to work for several days.

Treatment of recurrent ganglionic cysts by injection with an irritating solution has been advocated by some surgeons. This is a procedure not without risk if the cyst connects with a joint, as it may cause an irritation of the joint lining and interference with free motion. The old custom of smashing them with a book is mentioned only to be condemned.

6. Fibrous tumors (fibromas) are quite common within the skin and appear as small, hard lumps which grow to the size of a cherry pit. If they are located in an area where pressure is brought against them, they can be quite painful. Usually, however, they cause no symptoms and can be left alone or removed for cosmetic reasons. A small elliptical excision is preferable to electric needle destruction.

Skin fibromas do not form cancer.

7. Fatty tumors (lipoma) of the tissues directly beneath the skin are the commonest tumors in the body. Their cause is unknown but they are seen somewhat more frequently in stout people. They vary in size from that of a pea to that of a football. On examination, they feel soft and are freely movable under the skin and are usually not firmly attached to surrounding structures. Most lipomas are painless and cause no symptoms.

If they are unchanging in size they can be left alone. However, if they show signs of growth, it is best to remove them. An incision is made in the skin, usually under local anesthesia, and the fatty tumor is dissected out. If a large defect remains in the area where the tumor was located, a rubber drain is inserted. Otherwise the skin is sutured tightly.

Removal of a lipoma is carried out in the hospital, and unless the tumor is a particularly large one, a one- or two-day hospital stay is all that is required.

Lipomas only rarely become malignant, and before doing so, will show rapid growth and change in the feel of the tissue.

8. Cancer of the skin occurs often, particularly on exposed portions of the body such as the nose, face, or hands.

Areas subject to repeated irritation or regions that come in frequent contact with irritating oils or chemicals are also prone to develop skin cancer.

The diagnosis should be suspected whenever a small lump appears, grows slowly, develops a crust which bleeds slightly, feels hard to the touch, and is surrounded by a pearl-colored border. Any area that meets the preceding description and fails to disappear within a few weeks' time should be examined by a physician.

Fortunately, 100 percent of skin cancers (epithelioma) are curable unless they are neglected for years! There are several methods of treating skin cancer surgically, each one being efficient if properly carried out:

a) Small epitheliomas can be destroyed completely by *electrodesiccation* (using an electric needle). This is an office procedure, and healing will take place within a week or two.

b) Skin cancers can be completely *removed with a knife.* Normal surrounding skin must be taken with it, and the incision should extend down into the subcutaneous tissues. If the cancer is large, a skin graft may be required to close the defect left by the tumor removal.

c) Many skin cancers can be cured by intensive x-ray or cobalt irradiation. This is a simple office procedure without pain. Should x-ray or cobalt fail to destroy the cancer, then surgical removal is indicated.

SKIN GRAFTS

Skin grafts serve the purpose of covering areas that have been laid bare by *burns,* by *accidents* in which large pieces of skin have been torn away, or by defects created by *surgical removal* of portions of skin.

Skin grafts from one person to another are notoriously unsuccessful and are used only as temporary covering in some cases of severe burns. The only permanently successful grafts of this type take place between identical twins. Fortunately, in most instances, skin can be taken from an area of one's own body and successfully grafted elsewhere. There are several methods of doing this and each will be discussed briefly:

1. Pinch grafts: These are small pieces, averaging about one-fourth inch in diameter, of the superficial layers of skin. A dozen or more can be taken from a donor area and placed at spaced intervals as small islands in the recipient site. They will grow in their new location and spread out so as to fully cover the bare area. However, this type of graft has been replaced in most clinics by the split-thickness graft, except where very small areas, such as the eyelid, require grafting.

2. Split-thickness grafts are sheets of the superficial and part of the deep layers of the skin. They are removed from the donor area by a special knife attached to a drum. This instrument is called a *dermatome* and can accurately slice a graft measuring about four inches in width and eight to ten inches in length.

Split-thickness grafts are taken from the flat surfaces of the body such as the abdomen, the thigh, or back. They are most useful as a covering for large burned areas where no skin exists. Sutures are taken around the edges of these grafts, and compression bandages are applied to make sure the graft has firm contact with the underlying tissue.

In the great majority of cases, split-thickness grafts will take if the surface to which they are being applied is healthy and free of infection. The donor site is covered with sterile dressings and will heal readily since only the topmost layers of skin have been removed.

This type of graft is not of great value when applied to areas that are subject to weight-bearing or friction.

3. Full-thickness grafts contain all the layers of the skin but not the underlying fat tissue. They are of greatest value when applied to weight-bearing areas or areas subject to friction (the hand, the foot). These grafts should be cut so that they will exactly cover the bare area. The donor site is restored by undercutting and bringing together the edges of skin on either side of the area from which the graft has been taken.

Well-applied pressure dressings are important to ensure that the graft will take.

4. Pedicle grafts are grafts in which one portion of the skin remains attached to the donor site while the rest is transferred to a recipient site. The pedicle graft retains its own blood supply, which comes into it from its attached portion. The pedicle, or base of the graft, is not detached from its original site until the free part of the graft develops a new circulation at its new site.

Pedicle grafts are most useful to cover defects about the face when a wide area of the skin has been removed along with a tumor, or to cover a finger or hand with new skin. By ingenious methods, too complicated to discuss here, pedicle grafts of skin can be swung from place to place so that they can be used in areas of the body far distant from their point of origin.

The cardinal principles underlying the success of all grafts are:

1. The donor site must be clean and free of inflammation or infection.

2. The recipient site must be clean and free of inflammation or infection.

3. The recipient site must have sufficient blood supply so that it will nourish the graft.

4. The graft must be applied smoothly and evenly.

5. The graft must be in firm contact with the recipient site. This is accomplished by firm pressure dressings or sutures.

6. Grafts must be applied so that there is no undue stretching.

7. Excess motion of the recipient site should be avoided so that the graft does not become detached.

8. The general health of the patient must be sufficiently good so that healing processes may progress normally.

9. Antibiotic drugs may be given to avoid infection during the time the graft is growing.

QUESTIONS AND ANSWERS

Do all superficial cysts, tumors, warts, and moles have to be removed?
No.

When should these conditions be operated upon?
1. When they show an increase in size
2. When they are in an area subject to repeated irritation or friction
3. When they cause pain
4. When they become infected
5. When they bleed repeatedly

Are these conditions very common?
Yes. Sooner or later almost everyone develops one of these conditions.

What causes warts?
The cause is not known definitely but most dermatologists think that they are viral in origin. (They do *not* arise from handling frogs or toads!)

Must all warts be removed?
No. Frequently the removal of one large one will result in the others going away by themselves.

Do warts on the sole of the feet (plantar warts) cause much pain?
Yes. They are removed either by x-ray treatment or by surgery.

Can a cyst be removed when it is infected?
Not usually. It is most often opened and drained. Removal is done at a later date when infection has subsided.

Will any of the following conditions, if untreated, turn into a malignant growth?
Sebaceous cysts: Only very rarely
Warts: No
Moles: Occasionally
Blood vessel tumors: Only very rarely
Ganglions: No
Fibrous or fatty tumors: Only very rarely

Must all skin cancers be removed?
Yes, either surgically removed or removed with an electric current or by x-ray or cobalt treatment.

Where are the most common locations for:
Sebaceous cysts? The scalp; the upper back
Warts? Hands and feet
Moles? The face; arms and legs
Blood vessel tumors? Anywhere on the body
Ganglions? The wrist
Fibrous or fatty tumors? Anywhere on the body
Cancer? The side of the nose, the temples, the hands, at sites where constant irritation takes place

What is the usual method of removing:
Sebaceous cysts? Surgical removal through a small incision
Warts? Destruction with an electric current

Moles? Surgical removal with an elliptical incision

Blood vessel tumors? Surgical removal or electric needle destruction or freezing with carbon dioxide snow

Ganglions? Surgical removal through an incision

Fibrous or fatty tumors? Surgical removal through an incision

Cancer? Surgical removal with an elliptical incision, burning with an electric current, or by x-ray or cobalt radiation

Where are the following procedures carried out?
Removal of cysts: In the surgeon's office or in the hospital
Removal of warts: In the surgeon's office
Removal of moles: In the hospital, occasionally in the surgeon's office
Removal of blood vessel tumors: In the surgeon's office or in the hospital
Removal of ganglions: In the hospital
Removal of fibrous or fatty tumors: In the hospital
Removal of cancer: In the hospital

What anesthesia is used for removal of these lesions?
Usually local anesthesia with Novocain.

Are the incisions for these operations disfiguring?
Usually not.

Is it necessary to remain in the hospital after these operations?
Usually one can go home the same day as the operation. If a large tumor has been removed, a two- or three-day stay may be necessary.

How soon after surgery for these conditions can one:
Bathe? As soon as the wound has healed, usually within a week

Return to work? Usually within a day or two after surgery

Drive a car? Within a day or two after surgery

Do the following have a tendency, once removed, to recur?
Cysts: No
Warts: Yes
Moles: No
Blood vessel tumors: No
Ganglions: Yes
Fibrous or fatty tumors: No
Cancer: No

What causes wrinkles in the skin?
Degeneration of elastic fibers in the deeper layers of the skin and loss in the amount of fat tissue lying directly beneath the skin.

Is there any way to combat wrinkles?
One of the best ways is to maintain a good level of nutrition. Undernourished, underweight older people will show wrinkles to a much greater extent than those who maintain satisfactory nutrition.

Plastic operations can remove some wrinkles, but the effect of these procedures is usually not permanent.

Is it safe to receive injections of paraffin beneath the skin in order to remove wrinkles?
No. This is a dangerous procedure. Paraffin injections are often followed by the formation of paraffin tumors (paraffinomas) or even malignant growths.

Are there plastic materials that can be inserted beneath the skin to obliterate wrinkles?
Yes, but many of these materials are not yet fully tested and the ultimate results of their insertion beneath the skin must be further investigated.

Will repeated applications of hormone creams, especially those containing female sex hormones, help to reduce wrinkling?

Most skin specialists agree that their effect on wrinkles is negligible. Moreover, definite harm can result from their indiscriminate use without medical supervision.

Is there an inherited tendency toward premature wrinkling of the skin?

Yes. Many people inherit this tendency; others retain their youthful appearance until late in life.

Is massage helpful in doing away with wrinkles?

In all probability, it does little permanent good. On the other hand, it may stimulate the blood supply to the massaged area and thus improve skin appearance.

Skull

The skull is the bony framework of the head. The thick bones making up this structure afford excellent protection for the brain. Beneath the skull are thick membranes overlying the soft brainy tissue. Beneath these fibrous tissue membranes, the brain is covered by cerebrospinal fluid which affords still greater cushioning and protection from injury.

Intellect and intelligence are often associated with an ample-sized skull with a high forehead. This is an old superstition and has little relation to fact. If the skull is within normal limits, it will accommodate any sized normal brain. Deformed, undersized skulls may limit brain growth and be associated with mental retardation. Conversely, a giant

head (hydrocephalus) is sometimes associated with mental insufficiency.

See also HEAD INJURIES; NEUROSURGERY.

Slipped Disk

See HERNIATED INTERVERTEBRAL DISK; SPINE.

Slipped Epiphysis

A slipped epiphysis is a displacement of the growth plate of a long bone and the end of the bone beyond it. It is most common at the hip. In this location, it is called a slipped femoral epiphysis.

QUESTIONS AND ANSWERS

At what age does a slipped femoral epiphysis usually take place?

At the time of most rapid adolescent growth. In boys, this is between the ages of 14 and 16; in girls it is between the ages of 10 and 14.

Is slipped epiphysis more common in boys or girls?

Eighty-five percent of the patients are boys.

What are the chances of the other hip becoming abnormal if there is a slipped femoral epiphysis on one side?

In 25 to 40 percent of the cases, the disease ultimately involves both sides.

What causes a slipped epiphysis?

Most frequently, the condition is caused by the gradual sliding force of the weight of the patient upon the growth plate. At times, a fall or twisting injury may cause the epiphysis to slip.

How is a slipped femoral epiphysis usually diagnosed?

The onset is usually associated with discomfort in the groin after physical activity. There may also be some stiffness at the hip and a limp. Later, there is tenderness about the hip. The thigh is drawn to the midline and the foot is rotated outward. There is pain on attempts to bring the thigh outward or to rotate the foot inward. The diagnosis is confirmed by characteristic x-ray findings.

What type of boy or girl is most apt to develop a slipped epiphysis?

A tall, heavy child.

What is the treatment for a slipped epiphysis?

The child must stay off his feet. He should be taken to the hospital, where the hip should be operated on.

What surgery is done for a slipped femoral epiphysis?

If the slip is only mild, metal pins are placed across the epiphysis to prevent further slip. If the slip is more severe, a wedge of bone is removed from the femur to restore the normal configuration of the upper portion of the bone where it forms the hip. In some cases, a protruding edge of bone is removed from the end of the femur to allow normal motion.

Will a slipped epiphysis lead to a shortening of the leg?

Yes, if the condition is severe. The shortening is partly due to the drawing inward of the thigh and partly due to the slip itself.

Are the results following surgery for slipped epiphysis satisfactory?

Yes. The condition can be cured in the vast majority of cases.

Is there any way to prevent a slipped epiphysis?

No, except that children should keep their weight down during adolescence.

Small Intestines

See INTESTINES.

Smoking

Although it is difficult for people to stop the smoking habit, it is advisable for them to do so for a week or two before undergoing elective major surgery. Cigarette smoking is especially important to discontinue because it causes great irritation of the lining membranes of the respiratory tract and an increased amount of mucous secretions.

QUESTIONS AND ANSWERS

Why should cigarette smoking be stopped prior to elective surgery?

Most people who are to undergo major surgery will receive an inhalation anesthesia, and such anesthesia will be much smoother if the lining membranes of the trachea, bronchial tubes, and lungs are free from the irritation caused by inhaling smoke. It is well known among anesthesiologists that nonsmokers have fewer complications during and after anesthesia than heavy smokers. The heavy smoker, during anesthesia, may secrete so much mucus that it will interfere with the free flow of the oxygen and anesthetic agent to the lungs, and with the free exit of carbon dioxide from the lungs.

Why should the pipe or cigar smoker stop smoking prior to elective major surgery?

Because the mucous membranes of the mouth and the back of the throat are irritated by cigar and pipe smoke.

For how long a period prior to elective surgery should one stop smoking?

For one to two weeks.

How soon after a major operative procedure can one resume smoking?

A major operative procedure offers an excellent opportunity for an individual to stop smoking permanently. Most patients do not regain their desire for tobacco until several days after operation. Ordinarily, the first few days are the most difficult ones for the individual who wants to give up smoking. When the desire to smoke is regained, it is usually controllable as the body has already adjusted somewhat to the absence of nicotine.

Is it harmful for a patient to smoke immediately following major surgery?

Yes, because the respiratory tract is already irritated from the anesthetic agents. Thus, when one adds tobacco smoke to the already irritated mucous membranes, there is every likelihood that coughing and excess secretions will ensue. This may place an undue strain upon a fresh operative wound, in addition to being extremely painful.

For how long a period after surgery is it advisable not to smoke?

Most surgeons will not permit a patient to resume smoking during the first five to seven days after a major operative procedure. Of course, if the procedure happens to be on the respiratory tract, a much longer period of time is necessary before smoking can be resumed.

Is it wise for someone who has had an operation upon his respiratory tract ever to resume smoking?

No. It has been shown that there is a greater tendency for people to develop other respiratory diseases if they resume smoking following the relief of one respiratory surgical disease. This is particularly true if a patient has undergone an operation for a removal of a tumor of the larynx or lung.

Is it wise for patients to resume pipe or cigar smoking after an operation upon the stomach or duodenum?

No. The juices from the smoking of cigars or pipes, when swallowed, may cause marked irritation of the mucous membranes of the stomach or duodenum.

Can wound rupture occur from smoking during the immediate postoperative period?

The actual smoking will not cause a wound to rupture, but a fit of coughing might produce it.

Spina Bifida

Spina bifida is incomplete closure of some part of the bony vertebral column. Spina bifida occulta is a fairly common developmental deformity and usually causes no symptoms. Obvious and pronounced spina bifida, however, may be associated with a protrusion or herniation of the membranes covering the spinal cord. Such a protrusion may contain cerebrospinal fluid only, or it may contain nerve elements and even part of the spinal cord itself. This latter condition is known as a meningocele, or meningomyelocele. Such individuals are born with a noticeable lump on the back.

Inclusion of nerve structures in the malformation usually is accompanied by a varying degree of paralysis of the lower limbs. Hydrocephalus is also a frequent complication. Unfortunately, nothing can be done to correct the paralysis associated with spina bifida. An operation is performed solely for the purpose of repairing the deformity.

See also NEUROSURGERY.

QUESTIONS AND ANSWERS

What is spina bifida?

Spina bifida is a congenital deformity of the lower spine. It represents the condition that results when the growth plates on either side of the vertebrae at the base of the spine fail to join together. Nerves coming from the spinal cord may protrude through this defect of bone. Very rarely, this defect may occur in the vertebrae of the neck rather than at the base of the spine.

How often is spina bifida seen?

Spina bifida occulta (small defect with no nerve protrusion) is not infrequent and is often found accidentally on x-raying the spine because of an unrelated condition. Spina bifida occulta so discovered is of no significance and needs no treatment.

A true spina bifida with a large bony defect is very rare.

Is spina bifida inherited?

It is not thought to be.

Approximately what percentage of children born with spina bifida will have symptoms from it?

Only a small percentage of all those born with spina bifida will ever know they have it. Of those infants who present early signs of nerve involvement and protrusion of the nerves from the spinal cord, most will have symptoms unless treatment is instituted.

What are the signs of spina bifida?

A localized overgrowth of hair, a dimple, or a bulge in the midline at the base of the spine. Spina bifida occulta with late nerve signs may first be noticed by a limp, shooting pains, or numbness of one or both legs. Later, there may be deformities of the feet and wasting of the muscles of the thigh or calf unless treatment is instituted to cure the condition.

Do children tend to outgrow spina bifida?

No, not unless properly treated.

Must a child with spina bifida restrict his physical activities?

This depends upon whether the nerves are involved and whether any deformities of the lower limbs have resulted from the nerve involvement.

Can anything be done to cure spina bifida?

Yes. Nerves and spinal cord sac (meninges) protruding from the spine can be replaced and the sac can be reconstituted. Later in life, if necessary, the bone gap can be bridged by a bone graft.

The deformities caused by spina bifida with nerve involvement can usually be corrected by appropriate orthopedic surgery.

Spine

The spine extends from the base of the skull to the end of the tailbone (coccyx) and consists of a chain of 33 intricately connected bones (vertebrae), varying in size from ½ inch to 2 inches in length. The neck portion (cervical spine) has 7 vertebrae; the chest portion (thoracic or dorsal spine) has 12 vertebrae to which the ribs are joined; the back portions (lumbar and sacral regions) have 5 vertebrae each, with the sacral segments fused to form one large bone called the sacrum; and the tail portion (coccyx) is made up of 4 small bones.

The vertebrae are interconnected by small joints above and below. These are named the articular facets. Between the bodies of the vertebrae are elastic, firm, shock-absorbing tissues called the intervertebral disks. There are also small, strong, thick muscles connecting each vertebra with the one above and below. The function of the spine is to support the entire skeletal structure and to bear the brunt of weights and forces which are repeatedly transmitted throughout the body.

Most of the motion in the spine takes place in the neck (cervical) and lower back (lumbar) regions. The chest (thoracic) region is more or less fixed by the rib cage and therefore moves very little. The neck and lumbar regions are capable of motion in six different directions.

See also BACK; HERNIATED INTERVERTEBRAL DISK; LAMINECTOMY; SCOLIOSIS; SLIPPED EPIPHYSIS; SPINA BIFIDA; SPONDYLOLISTHESIS.

FRACTURES OF THE SPINE

The terms "broken neck" and "broken back" are terrifying to the average layman. Happily, most spinal fractures are minor and are unaccompanied by paralysis or other serious complications. In many instances there is less disability than if one severely sprained an ankle or crushed a fingertip. The majority of these fractures involve compression of a body of a vertebra without dislocation, or a break in one of the transverse processes which radiate out from the sides of the vertebrae. The treatment for these types of fracture is usually symptomatic, and body casts or braces are recommended only when pain is constant and severe.

Spinal fractures occur most frequently in the movable portions, the commonest site being between the last thoracic (chest) vertebra and the second lumbar (back) vertebra. Over 70 percent of fractures of the spine occur in this region. A fall from a height, landing in a standing or sitting position, is often the precipitating factor in these injuries. Fractures of the neck are perhaps the next commonest, and these are often associated with a bone dislocation. The usual method of sustaining this serious injury is that the head strikes a stationary object, as when diving into a shallow pool or when an automobile accident causes the head to strike the windshield or the back of the front seat. Another common site for spinal fracture is the transverse processes in the lumbar region. These transverse processes are bony projections, two to three inches in length, from the sides of the vertebrae; they possess powerful muscle attachments. Frequently, in an attempt to prevent an injury by sudden bracing of the trunk, a violent contraction of these strong muscles will fracture one of the transverse processes. This is not a serious type of fracture and responds readily to treatment with a simple body cast or back brace. The patient seldom is forced to stay in bed with this type of fracture.

A serious neck or back fracture may be suspected if the victim is unable to move his limbs or if he complains of numbness or severe pain in the back of his neck. *Such patients must not be moved or made more comfortable by well-meaning first-aiders.* To do this is to risk dislocating an unstable portion of the spine and causing greater paralysis.

Treatment of most fractures of the spine is carried out by extending or arching the spine. By so doing, one takes advantage of the strong anterior longitudinal ligament which connects the front of the bodies of the vertebrae. With the patient in the prone position with back arched, the action of this ligament helps to pull apart the crushed bony fragments and thus achieve correction of the fracture deformity.

Fractures of the spine take from three to five months to heal. Fortunately, the majority of these people can get out of bed and go about most of their business while in their casts. Mild exercises and rehabilitation procedures are begun as soon as the patient has recovered from the immediate effects of the injury. With adequate early treatment and a well-regulated rehabilitation program, there should be little or no permanent disability resulting from an uncomplicated fracture of the spine.

How do fractures of the spine occur?

From falling from a height or from a weight falling on the shoulders or head.

Do fractures of the spine endanger life?

Occasionally, depending upon their location and severity.

What type of spinal fracture is most serious?

Fractures associated with dislocation, usually of the neck.

What type of back fracture is least serious?

Mild compression fractures of the bodies of the vertebrae and fractures of the transverse or spinal processes of the vertebrae.

Do patients with spinal fractures always have to be hospitalized?

Most do, some do not.

What is the best first aid treatment for somebody with a spinal injury?

Do not move him unless absolutely necessary. If he must be transported, place him on his back on a board.

Does the paralysis associated with a spinal fracture ever clear up?

Yes. In the lower back, about two out of three cases clear up. There is usually some improvement after paralysis from a neck fracture as well.

How do patients breathe if their muscles of respiration are paralyzed by a neck fracture?

By means of an iron lung. Many can be taught to "swallow" air into their lungs for short periods of time.

How do patients manage their urinary and bowel functions if the nerves to these organs are paralyzed?

Spontaneous evacuation usually occurs without the patient's knowledge until periodic control is taught. Special urinary devices may be inserted into the bladder.

What is accomplished by operating on a patient with a fractured spine?

A dislocation can be reduced; an unstable spine can be fused; pressure can be removed from the spinal cord or nerves.

Are spinal operations serious?

Yes, but most patients withstand the procedure well.

What kind of anesthesia is used?

Usually general anesthesia.

If no operation is necessary, how long must a patient be in a cast or brace for the following?

Neck fracture: 3 months

Low back fracture: 0 to 5 months
Fracture with
   dislocation: 3 to 5 months
Fracture of transverse
   process of the spine: 0 to 8 weeks

When can a patient get up and move about after a neck fracture?

Often after a cast or brace is applied the patient can get up and move about.

When can a patient get up and move about after a lower back fracture?

Several days after a cast is applied, if the fracture is stable.

When can a patient get up and move about after a fracture of a transverse process?

Frequently the patient does not require any bed rest.

How are casts or braces applied in neck fractures?

To include upper chest, head, and neck.

How are casts or braces applied in lower back fractures?

From breastbone to pelvis.

How are casts or braces applied in a fracture of a transverse process?

If necessary, from breastbone to pelvis.

After recovery from a spinal fracture, are people able to do the following?

Walk:	Yes
Return to work:	Yes
Drive a car:	Yes
Resume physical exercises:	Yes
Resume social life:	Yes
Resume sexual relations:	Yes

Are special nurses necessary while the patient is confined to a hospital?

Not in the average case, but they are helpful in severe cases.

How does one bathe while in a cast or brace?

Sponge baths only are permitted.

What percentage of people with fractured necks recover?

About 80 to 90 percent.

What percentage of people with fractured spines develop paralysis?

About 10 percent.

What percentage of the paralyzed patients recover from the paralysis?

About 75 percent of those so afflicted.

What percentage of patients with fractured lower backs recover?

About 90 percent.

DISLOCATIONS OF THE SPINE

Mild dislocations can produce very few severe symptoms and may return to normal position with mild stretching (traction). However, severe dislocations of the spine carry with them more danger than a fracture. The dislocation may damage nerves in the spinal cord to such an extent as to cause complete paralysis below the level of the dislocation. Such catastrophes occur most commonly in the neck and are responsible for a large number of our accidental deaths.

In about two thirds of the cases of dislocation, the damage to the spinal cord is transient, and after the dislocation is corrected (reduced), the paralysis will clear. Unfortunately, the other third of the patients will suffer some permanent paralysis despite correction of the dislocation.

The treatment of all these dislocations is to stretch the spine and thus relieve the pressure upon the nerves in the spinal cord. The various stretching or traction procedures are carried out by means of pulleys and weights which are attached to the head. These procedures are best performed in a hospital. Patients with accompanying paralysis and any marked damage to ligaments and muscles may be forced to remain in traction for several weeks. In the event that a dislocation is unstable, surgical intervention may be necessary.

What method of treatment is used for dislocation of the neck?

Traction on the head with special tongs which are placed through the outer layers of the skull.

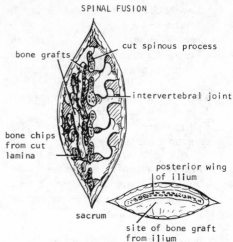

SPINAL FUSION

bone grafts — cut spinous process

intervertebral joint

bone chips from cut lamina

posterior wing of ilium

sacrum

site of bone graft from ilium

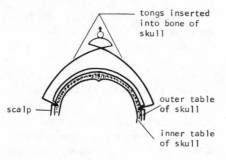

tongs inserted into bone of skull

scalp — outer table of skull

inner table of skull

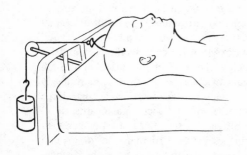

What method of treatment is used for dislocation of the spine elsewhere?

Manipulation. If this fails, surgery with correction of the dislocation and a spinal fusion procedure may be necessary.

How long must the traction be kept in place for dislocations of the spine?

In cases without paralysis and in which dislocation is easily corrected, a

few days; in cases with paralysis, several weeks of continued traction may be necessary.

Is there a tendency for dislocations of the neck or lower back to recur?

No.

INFECTIONS OF THE SPINE

1. Tuberculosis or tuberculous osteomyelitis of the spine was an all too frequent disease in children fifty years ago. It was caused in almost all instances by tuberculosis germs in milk. Since pasteurization, tuberculosis of the spine has been practically eradicated. The infection would cause, among other symptoms, collapse of a vertebral body or bodies. When this attacked the vertebrae in the chest region, *hunchback* would be the end result. Luckily, we rarely see a young hunchback any more.

New drugs such as streptomycin, para-aminosalicylic acid, and isonicotinic acid derivatives have a striking inhibitory effect upon the tuberculosis germ. They can slow the progress of the spinal infection to such a degree that surgery—

through a spinal fusion procedure—can bring on an early cure. Formerly, these victims spent interminable years in bed and wore cumbersome and disfiguring braces for their entire lives.

2. Osteomyelitis (of the nontuberculous type) means an infection of bone with a disease organism such as a staphylococcus or a streptococcus. The spine is occasionally involved, and in the days before the antibiotics these patients would be seriously ill. Today these drugs, along with surgical drainage of any collection of pus, will bring about a cure.

CANCER OF THE SPINE

Primary cancer of the vertebrae is exceedingly rare, but secondary or metastatic cancer of the spine is exceedingly common. As a matter of fact, the commonest site for spread of a cancer of the breast, the prostate gland, and many other organs is to the spine. This is associated with steady, severe pain and characteristic findings on x-ray examination.

There is no operative treatment for cancer of the spine.

Spleen

The spleen is a soft, elastic, glandular organ of purplish color measuring about five inches in length, three inches in width, and two inches in thickness. It is located in the left upper and posterior portion of the abdomen beneath the ribs. The spleen is one of the most interesting structures in the body in that it has been known to medical science since earliest history but the exact nature of its functions has not yet been clarified fully. In

medieval times it was thought to control one's moods or tempers, and there are many Shakespearean references to people "with spleen," implying that they possessed nasty or mean dispositions.

We know that the spleen, a blood-lymph gland, has many functions in connection with blood cells, iron metabolism, and blood storage. During development of the embryo, the spleen manufactures both red and white blood cells. After birth the bone marrow takes over the job of making all the red cells and most of the white cells. The spleen, however, continues to manufacture certain types of white blood cells throughout all of life. The spleen has, as one of its main duties, the destruction of old worn-out red and white blood cells. It also encapsulates and destroys bacteria and inert particles which may be brought to it by the bloodstream. When it becomes distended, the spleen can store large quantities of blood, which it discharges into the circulation during times of acute stress or strain. The destruction of old red blood cells releases the iron contained within, and the spleen stores this iron until it is used again when new red cells are formed.

An amazing characteristic of the spleen is that it gets involved in an extraordinary number of disease processes. Although its role is not well known in all of them, there are some 20 to 30 different diseases and infections in which the spleen is seriously affected. In most instances, disturbance in splenic function is not the underlying cause for the disease and, therefore, surgical removal does not produce a cure. There are several conditions in which the spleen *is* primarily involved, and in these instances, its removal is often followed by cure. In a large general hospital with an average of some 15,000 admissions each year, approximately 25 spleens are removed. Thus one can estimate roughly, by extending this proportion to the country as a whole, that splenectomy is performed yearly upon approximately 25,000 Americans.

Despite the fact that the spleen is an actively functioning organ, there are practically no permanent ill effects from its surgical removal! Other tissue cells (the reticuloendothelial cells, which are scattered widely throughout the body) readily take over the spleen's functions.

In competent surgical hands, removal of the spleen (*splenectomy*) is a routine operative procedure with an extremely low mortality rate. Because of the safety of the operation, it can be recommended even in conditions where cure of the underlying disease is in doubt. The possible chance that the spleen might be causing or aggravating a disease is often sufficient indication for recommending its removal.

The following are conditions in which removal of the spleen is definitely indicated:

1. Rupture: This is a common catastrophe occurring from a sudden, jarring blow in the left upper part of the abdomen. A fall from a height onto one's side or an automobile accident in which one is abruptly catapulted against a hard, blunt object is often followed by rupture of the spleen. Children are particularly prone to this fearsome accident.

Rupture of the spleen causes severe bleeding into the abdominal cavity and deep shock. Unless operation is performed within a very few hours, death from internal hemorrhage may take place. The history of an accident with abdominal injury plus the findings of extreme paleness, shock, and pain and tenderness in the abdomen usually make the diagnosis apparent. Immediate hospitalization and surgery are essential.

The ruptured or torn spleen is always removed after tying off the blood vessels. No attempts are ever made to repair or sew up this structure, as its substance is pulpy and spongy and will not retain sutures.

Blood loss is replaced by transfusion, and the patient usually recovers quickly and completely if splenic rupture was the sole injury.

2. Hemolytic jaundice or congenital hemolytic anemia: This condition is characterized by anemia, an enlarged spleen, mild jaundice, and a sallow, yellow tinge to the skin. It is thought to be caused by an inherited defect of the red blood cells which makes them particularly susceptible to damage. It is not uncommon to find several members of the same family who have suffered from this disease. Although it usually makes its presence known in childhood, occasionally a patient reaches 30 to 40 years of age before the diagnosis becomes apparent. Removal of the spleen results in spectacular cure in these cases!

3. Thrombocytopenic purpura: This disease is rather common and is seen usually before the age of 40 years. It is easily diagnosed by the appearance of hemorrhagic areas (purpuric spots) in the skin, which appear like bruises, and by bleeding from mucous membranes of the nose or gums or intestinal or vaginal tracts. The hemorrhagic areas in the skin vary in size from that of a pea to huge spots larger than a silver dollar. When the cause for these "bruises" is investigated, it is found that the circulating blood is *markedly deficient in blood platelets* and that the bleeding time of the blood is greatly prolonged. Purpura of this type may be sudden and acute in onset with severe hemorrhage, or it may be chronic and exhibit only mild episodes of hemorrhage.

Blood platelets are necessary for normal blood clotting and to stop hemorrhage. In this type of purpura, the spleen either destroys too many platelets or else manufactures a substance which prevents their formation in the bone marrow. Whatever the exact mechanism, it is known that removal of the spleen produces a dramatic cure in most patients with this disorder.

4. Primary tumors of the spleen: Malignant and benign tumors or cysts originating in the spleen are quite rare. When diagnosed early, removal of a primary malignant growth is often followed by complete cure. However, all too often malignant tumors of this structure have already spread to other organs. All of the benign tumors and cysts can be cured by removing the spleen.

5. Hypersplenism: This disease classification is a catchall for many conditions in which there are enlargement and overactivity of the spleen as seen by excessive destruction of elements of the blood and consequent overactivity of the bone marrow in forming new white and red blood cells. In this category one can place six to eight different conditions for which splenectomy has varying value. In certain types of hypersplenism, splenic removal will result in complete cure, while in other forms, no favorable result will follow. Suffice it to say that the surgical safety of removing this organ has in recent years influenced many physicians to advocate the procedure much more frequently. Furthermore, even though improvement or cure is not obtained in some of these conditions, no accentuation of the disease process results.

The spleen is removed routinely when performing gastrectomy (stomach removal) for cancer and in cases of cirrhosis of the liver in which the splenic vein will be sutured to the renal vein.

The following are conditions in which removal of the spleen is of *possible value:*

1. Gaucher's disease: This is a chronic disease which runs in families and is accompanied by huge enlargement of the spleen.

2. Cooley's anemia: This form of anemia is seen in childhood and shows deformed red blood cells, a large, hard spleen, and peculiar bone changes on x-ray. It is sometimes called Mediterranean anemia, as it appears to run in families who have originated from that part of the world.

3. Sickle cell anemia: This is an inherited anemia seen chiefly in Negroes and is diagnosed mainly by noting a sickle-shaped deformity of the red blood cells.

There are many other diseases in which greatly enlarged spleens are found but their removal does not benefit the patient. Most important in this category are leukemia, malaria, and Hodgkin's disease. Unfortunately, these are generalized conditions not limited to abnormal findings in the spleen and, therefore, are not improved by splenic surgery.

Splenectomy is performed under general anesthesia through an incision, anywhere from five to eight inches long, in the left upper portion of the abdomen. The two most favored incisions are (a) a straight longitudinal incision to the left of the midline, or (b) an oblique incision paralleling the left rib margin. (See diagram.)

The important technical part of this operation is to tie off all vessels going to or coming from the spleen. Once this task is completed, the spleen can be detached readily from its adhesions to the diaphragm, the kidney, the stomach, and the bowel. Frequently, the larger the spleen, the simpler it is to remove.

It is extremely important when taking out a spleen for hemolytic jaundice or purpura to make sure that all *accessory spleens* are also removed. Small acces-

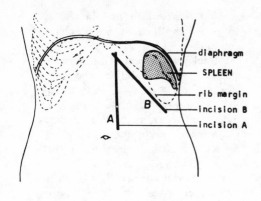

sory spleens measuring less than an inch in diameter are sometimes found in the abdominal cavity, and they may grow to tremendous size, assume the functions of the original spleen, and take on the same disease characteristics. Thus, if allowed to remain within the abdomen, they will undo all the good done by splenectomy of the main organ.

As stated previously, recovery from this operation is usually quick and complete provided that blood loss has been replenished. Patients can often get out of bed the day following surgery and the wound usually heals within ten days. In the uncomplicated case, hospital discharge is possible anywhere from the twelfth to sixteenth postoperative day.

QUESTIONS AND ANSWERS

What is the spleen?

The spleen is a hemolymph gland, which means that its structure is much like that of a lymph node but that it is filled with blood. It is covered by three layers of fibrous tissue and is located in the abdomen high up on the left-hand side beneath the rib cage. It is soft and elastic, and at full maturity it is approximately five inches long, three inches wide, and two inches thick.

What are the functions of the spleen?

It is a blood-lymph gland that is concerned with the manufacture and destruction of blood cells, blood cell storage, and iron metabolism. During the life of the embryo, the spleen produces both red and white blood cells. After the child is born, this function is taken over by the bone marrow, and the spleen confines its activities to the manufacture of certain kinds of white blood cells and to the destruction of old, worn-out red blood cells. Another of its functions is to destroy bacteria that are brought to it by the bloodstream. During times of stress the spleen will discharge stored blood cells into the bloodstream as they are needed. Other functions of the spleen are not yet completely determined.

What are some of the common conditions that involve the spleen?

1. The various blood diseases as enumerated above
2. Cysts
3. Benign or malignant tumors
4. Abscesses
5. Tuberculosis
6. Rare infections such as kala-azar and actinomycosis
7. Malaria
8. Gaucher's disease
9. Cirrhosis of the liver
10. Thrombosis (clot) of the splenic vein

How does an enlarged spleen harm the patient?

The mere enlargement sometimes produces pressure on other intraabdominal organs. In certain conditions the spleen can enlarge to the size of a watermelon and will produce a heavy, dragging sensation in the abdomen.

How does an excessively active spleen cause disease?

Its overactivity may result in the mass

destruction of blood elements, thus resulting in serious anemia.

Is the spleen often enlarged in diseases that are not primarily splenic in origin?

Yes. The spleen may be enlarged in leukemia, Hodgkin's disease, cirrhosis of the liver, malaria, and other generalized chronic infections.

Will an enlarged spleen cause symptoms?

If the enlargement is very great, it may produce a dragging, aching feeling in the upper left side of the abdomen.

Are disorders of the spleen often associated with bleeding tendencies?

Yes, particularly cases of purpura.

How does hypersplenism evidence itself?

It may result in marked anemia because of the excessive destruction of red blood cells.

How is a disorder of the spleen diagnosed?

Since most splenic disorders are associated with anemia, this is the first thing to be noted. The physician will then search for the cause of the anemia and may discover that it is a disease of the spleen.

How can a physician distinguish among the various causes of splenic disease?

1. By the characteristic appearance of the blood under a microscope and by other blood tests, such as the bleeding time, the clotting time, the appearance of the clot, and the fragility of the red blood cells.

2. Certain types of anemia, such as Cooley's anemia, will show characteristic signs upon x-ray examination of the bones.

3. Since many of the splenic disorders tend to run in families, the physician can use the family medical history to help him make a diagnosis.

Are people with disorders of the spleen more likely to develop upper respiratory infections such as pneumonia and influenza?

Yes, because almost all these patients are markedly anemic and are therefore less able to ward off bacterial invasion.

Can disorders of the spleen be cured medically?

No. There are no known medications that can cure or permanently relieve the symptoms of a disease of the spleen.

Is it necessary to give blood transfusions to a patient who has a disease of the spleen?

Yes, if he has marked anemia and is unable to manufacture a sufficient number of red blood cells himself.

What is the treatment for a disorder of the spleen?

Certain of the conditions in which there is an enlarged spleen, such as leukemia, Hodgkin's disease, Gaucher's disease, and cirrhosis of the liver, must be treated with x-ray therapy or one of the chemotherapeutic agents. If these are successful in bringing about a remission of the underlying disease, the spleen may become smaller and less active. In other conditions, the only benefit will come from surgically removing the spleen.

Is the spleen ever involved in abscess formation?

Yes. This occurs, but it is rather rare.

Does tuberculosis ever affect the spleen?

Yes, but this condition is much less common today because of the treatment with the antituberculosis drugs.

Is the spleen ever involved in any other rare infections?

Yes, occasionally a case of actinomycosis or kala-azar will involve the spleen.

Is the spleen often enlarged in malaria?

Yes, especially in chronic cases that have not been thoroughly treated.

Does the spleen ever become enlarged in cirrhosis of the liver?

Yes.

Does the size of the spleen determine the need for surgery?

No. Other factors, as determined by blood studies, are much more important.

Is surgery indicated in all conditions affecting the spleen?

No. Physicians will study the condition and decide if removal of the spleen will be beneficial.

Who should decide if a spleen should be removed?

If it is a question of rupture, the surgeon must make the decision to operate.

In other situations, the medical men and blood specialists (hematologists) usually determine if splenic removal is indicated.

Is removal of a spleen an emergency procedure?

For rupture, yes!

In other conditions, it is better to operate during a quiescent period of the disease. Most conditions requiring removal of the spleen have long periods during which the disease process appears to be subsiding. This is the best time for surgery. However, in certain patients the disease may be progressing rapidly toward a fatal hemorrhage or death and in these instances, emergency splenectomy is required.

Is removal of the spleen a dangerous procedure?

No, and the mortality from the operation itself is extremely low. There are situations in which the underlying disease has advanced so far that the operative procedure is poorly tolerated. In these cases, surgery should be postponed, if possible, until maximum benefit has been obtained from medications and transfusions.

Are patients made worse by spleen removal?

Most physicians now agree that even though there are cases in which no benefit is derived from removing the spleen, harmful effects upon the underlying disease process do not often occur.

Is the general health affected by removal of the spleen?

It is benefited in the majority of cases.

In children, removal of the spleen for certain types of anemia is often followed by rapid growth and an improved mental development.

A person without a spleen can live just as long and as normally as other people.

Does a spleen ever grow back again?

No! Once removed, it will never grow back. However, when performing the operation, the surgeon must search carefully for small, marble-size accessory spleens. They may grow to tremendous size and render the splenectomy valueless if left behind.

What can happen if splenectomy is not performed?

1. In rupture of the spleen: Probable death from hemorrhage.

2. In severe purpura: Possible death from hemorrhage.

3. In hemolytic jaundice: Patients continue to have crises, with abdominal pain, vomiting, fever, increase in the anemia and jaundice, and frequently death from an overwhelming, superimposed infection.

4. In malignant tumors: Death from spread to other organs.

Are special preparations necessary before operation?

In certain types of illness, attempts are made to combat the anemia by giving blood transfusions and vitamins preoperatively.

How long a hospital stay is necessary?

Twelve to sixteen days.

How long does the operation take to perform?

Anywhere from three quarters of an hour to two and a half hours. This depends upon the size of the organ, the nature of its adherence to other structures, and the accessibility of its arteries and veins.

What type of anesthesia is used?

General anesthesia.

Where is the incision made and how long is it?

An incision of five to eight inches in length is made in the left upper quadrant of the abdomen.

Are the incisions painful?

Only for the first few days after surgery.

Are the wounds drained?

Occasionally a rubber drain is inserted through the wound for a few days. There is only slight pain upon its removal.

Are special measures necessary after operation?

Yes. It is important that frequent blood studies be carried out after surgery to determine the postoperative course of the patient.

How soon after operation does improvement take place?

Bleeding tendencies often stop the minute the spleen is removed from the patient in certain types of cases.

What special surgical measures are carried out postoperatively?

1. A stomach tube is often inserted for a day or two in order to keep the stomach deflated.

2. Intravenous solutions are sometimes given for a day or two.

3. Vitamin K may be given to help diminish bleeding tendencies if they persist.

4. Blood is often given *after* operation rather than before, inasmuch as it will be better tolerated following splenectomy.

Are special diets indicated postoperatively?

Meats and other foods rich in iron are frequently prescribed.

Are special nurses necessary?

They are not essential but may give comfort for a day or two if the patient can afford them.

When can the patient get out of bed?

Usually the day after surgery, unless he is too sick from the original condition that caused the operation to be performed.

How soon after surgery can one bathe?

As soon as the wound is healed, approximately two weeks.

Is the scar painful or disfiguring?

No more than any other abdominal scar.

Is convalescent care required?

Usually not.

Can one live normally after the spleen is removed?

Yes. Its functions are taken over by other tissues in the body: the reticuloendothelial system of cells.

How soon after splenic removal can one return to work?

Within six to eight weeks.

Should the patient be rechecked periodically after removal of the spleen?

Yes. It is particularly important to have blood smears taken every few weeks for several months after splenectomy to note the course of the underlying condition. This is not necessary when the operation has been performed because of an injury.

Spondylolisthesis

This is the name for a condition in which one vertebra slips out of line and slides forward over the vertebra immediately below. Severe strain and stress upon the muscles and ligaments of the spine results. Pain may vary from a chronic mild ache to an acute, excruciating pain. Spondylolisthesis is diagnosed on x-ray examination and is found most often to involve the last (fifth) lumbar vertebra as it slides forward over the first sacral vertebra in the lower back region. (See diagram.)

The majority of these patients can be treated conservatively with back braces and by changing to less strenuous physical occupations. However, those who suffer repeatedly and are not relieved by medical means should undergo a *spinal fusion* operation, which permanently stiffens that portion of the spine so that further displacement of the vertebral bodies does not recur. Cure follows surgery in well over 75 percent of these cases.

The spinal fusion operation entails a four- to six-inch incision in the midline of the back over the area to be fused. The usual fusion encompasses two or three vertebrae. The bony lamina and the joints connecting the vertebrae are exposed by pulling the muscles to either side of the spine. The exposed bone and the connecting joints are roughened by chipping away their smooth surfaces with a chisel. A separate incision is then made over the left or right pelvic bone, and the wing of the pelvic bone is brought into view. With a chisel or electric saw, a section of bone about three to four inches long and one half to three quarters of an inch thick is removed from the pelvic wing. These fragments of bone are used as bone grafts and are placed along either side of the spine over the roughened and denuded laminae. The muscles are then permitted to fall back in place over the grafted bone and the skin is closed. A plaster of Paris body jacket may then be applied, if necessary.

Within several months after this procedure, the vertebrae in the area become rigid and fused as the grafts take hold and become part of the spinal bone structure.

See also SPINE.

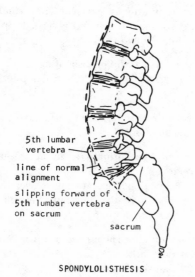

5th lumbar
vertebra

line of normal
alignment

slipping forward of
5th lumbar vertebra
on sacrum

sacrum

SPONDYLOLISTHESIS

QUESTIONS AND ANSWERS

What is spondylolisthesis?

A slipping forward of one vertebra

upon another because of a defect in its bony support.

How common is it?
Uncommon, found in only about 1 in 500 people who have back trouble.

What causes it?
Its cause is unknown.

Is it painful?
Yes, frequently.

How is the diagnosis made?
X-ray examination of the spine will determine the diagnosis.

Does spondylolisthesis ever get well by itself?
No.

Does spondylolisthesis usually take place in the lumbosacral (lower back) region?
Yes.

Do these people always need surgery?
Only if they have severe, constant, or frequently recurrent and disabling pain.

What operative procedure is performed?
Spinal fusion.

Is spinal fusion a serious operation?
Yes, but it is not dangerous.

How long a hospital stay is necessary?
About four to six weeks.

Are special preoperative measures necessary?
No.

What kind of anesthesia is used?
General.

How long does it take to perform a spinal fusion operation?
About one to two hours.

Are blood transfusions necessary?
Not routinely, but in certain cases where the fusion is extensive, it is advisable.

Are special nurses advisable?
Yes, for the first 48 to 72 hours.

In performing a spinal fusion, where is the bone to be used as a graft obtained?
It is usually taken from the crest of the pelvic wing bones. Occasionally it is taken from the leg bone (tibia).

Is bone from somebody other than the patient ever used as a graft?
Yes. Such may be obtained from a bone bank. However, the patient's own bone is preferable.

Is the area from which the bone grafts are removed weakened permanently by the loss of bone?
No.

Is the patient ever worse after a fusion operation?
Very rarely.

Are special postoperative measures necessary?
Yes. Great care is necessary in shifting and turning the patient.

What are the results following spinal fusion?
Relief of pain and cure in approximately 80 to 90 percent of patients.

Does the fusion ever fail to take place?
Yes, in about 10 to 20 percent of cases, depending upon the extent of the fusion and the number of vertebrae involved. Another fusion operation is then advised.

How soon after spinal fusion can the patient get out of bed?
In about four to six weeks.

How long does it take for the skin wounds to heal after fusion?
About two weeks.

Are the scars painful?
No.

Are the scars disfiguring?
No.

Is a cast applied after surgery?
Yes.

How soon after a fusion operation can one:

Bathe?	3 to 6 months
Drive a car?	4 to 6 months
Return to work?	6 to 12 months
Resume normal social activity?	4 to 6 months
Resume strenuous physical activity?	1 year
Resume marital relations?	4 to 6 months

Squint

See CROSSED EYES.

Stapes Operation

See DEAFNESS.

Sterility and Fertility

Sterility is the inability to reproduce. Since this definition connotes an absolute and irreversible state, it is more appropriate to use the term infertility. Infertility indicates a more temporary state which may, under certain circumstances, be reversed.

First degree sterility relates to those couples who have failed to conceive after at least one year of effort. Second degree sterility refers to those couples who have had one or more children and have then failed to conceive after repeated attempts over a prolonged period of time.

Couples who have had pregnancies that have failed to culminate in living children should also be included in the general classification of infertility, since the ultimate aim of reproduction is living, healthy children.

QUESTIONS AND ANSWERS

How often does sterility occur among married couples?

Although there are no absolutely accurate statistics, it is estimated that approximately one out of every five marriages fails to produce a living offspring.

Must the wife have an orgasm for conception to take place?

No! Climax plays no role whatsoever in conception.

How long does it take the average married couple to conceive for the first time?

Pregnancy will usually take place within a year, providing the couple has intercourse two to three times weekly and refrains from using contraceptive devices. The wife who conceives within the first month or two after trying is *not* the average woman. It is not at all unusual for normal young people to try for eight to ten months before being successful.

What factors are necessary for pregnancy to take place?

The woman must produce an egg from her ovaries; the fallopian tubes must be open; healthy sperm must reach the egg while it is in the fallopian tubes; there must be a place within the lining of the uterus for implantation of the fertilized egg; the woman must produce the proper hormones to nourish the fertilized, implanted egg.

FEMALE STERILITY

What are some of the common causes of sterility (infertility) in women?

1. Failure to ovulate or produce an egg. This can be the result of a congenital defect in the chromosomes, such as is seen in Turner's syndrome, or it can be due to an acquired abnormality in a female who is structurally normal.

2. Blocked fallopian tubes, due to either infection or a birth deformity in which the tubes are obstructed.

3. Glandular imbalance, particularly involving the pituitary gland, the thyroid, the adrenal glands, or the ovaries.

4. Failure of the sperm to pass through the cervix and up into the uterus. This may be caused by obstruction or infection at the cervix, the entrance to the womb.

5. Psychological factors, often elusive, vague, and difficult to evaluate. It has been known, however, that some sterile women will be able to conceive after a period of psychotherapy.

6. There is a large group of women who fail to conceive without any discernible cause. In view of the fact that scientists are learning more all the time about the nature of chromosomes, genes, and cellular structure, it is quite likely that this group will be understood more fully and many additional reasons for sterility will be found.

Must all of these factors be present to prevent conception?

Obviously, no. These factors may exist singularly or in combination. It must be understood that infertility is a relative term and that minimal degrees of a number of factors can be as effective in causing sterility as one major factor.

During how many days of the month is conception possible?

Since healthy sperm must be deposited in the vagina within two days before ovulation and not longer than two days after ovulation, it is obvious that out of the entire cycle of 28 days, fertilization of an egg can occur on only 3 to 4 of those days.

Can one determine the fertile period and the barren period accurately?

In a woman who menstruates regularly, these periods can be determined with some accuracy by studying the basal body temperature charts from day to day.

If a woman fails to ovulate, how is this fact recognized?

1. By taking a careful menstrual history and noting any irregularities.

2. By recording basal temperatures over a period of several months. A definite curve will be developed which will show whether or not the patient is ovulating.

3. By taking a biopsy (endometrial biopsy) of the lining membrane of the uterus just before the expected date of menstruation, the gynecologist can tell whether ovulation is present or absent.

4. Vaginal smears can be studied microscopically to reveal whether ovulation has taken place.

Can a woman be successfully treated if she fails to ovulate?

Yes. In the majority of cases, a glandular study will reveal the cause for failure to ovulate and will point the way toward the proper hormonal treatment. This will involve a careful study of the activity of the pituitary gland, the thyroid gland, the adrenal glands, and the ovaries.

How is a biopsy of the lining of the uterus (endometrial biopsy) performed?

This is an office procedure performed on an examining table. A speculum is inserted into the vagina and the cervix is grasped with a clamp. A small metal instrument is then inserted through the cervix into the uterus, and the lining is scraped.

Is the taking of an endometrial biopsy a painful procedure?

There is slight discomfort, but it takes only a few minutes to perform and has no unpleasant aftereffects.

What precautions should be taken before doing an endometrial biopsy?

It is important to determine that the patient is not pregnant at the time the biopsy is taken. For this reason, abstinence is advised from the time of the previous menstrual period until the time the biopsy is taken. This is necessary because an early pregnancy would be disturbed by an endometrial biopsy.

Will the patient bleed for two or three days after the taking of an endometrial biopsy?

Yes.

What are the common causes of blocked fallopian tubes?

1. A previous inflammation of the pelvic organs, most frequently caused by gonorrhea, tuberculosis, or some other germ

2. Peritonitis, most often secondary to a ruptured appendix

3. Spasm of the fallopian tubes due to tension and emotional factors

4. A fibroid in the upper portion of the uterus which shuts off the entrance of the fallopian tubes

5. Endometriosis

How are blocked tubes diagnosed?

1. By performing the Rubin test, which involves the pumping of a gas (carbon dioxide) through the cervix into the uterine cavity and noting that the gas has entered the abdominal cavity

2. By an x-ray examination involving the insertion of a radiopaque dye into the cervix to outline the uterine cavity and tubes (hysterogram)

How is the Rubin test performed?

As an office procedure, the patient is instructed to report about five to seven days after a menstrual period. On the examining table, the cervix is exposed and grasped with a clamp. A thin tubular instrument is inserted into the cervical canal. One end of this tubular instrument is attached to a container of carbon dioxide and to a recording machine. By the proper use of the valves, carbon dioxide is administered and passed up into the uterus at known pressures. The only outlet for this gas is through the fallopian tubes into the abdominal cavity. If the tubes are open, the gas escapes into the abdominal cavity and the pressure recorded on the machine falls. If the gas does not go into the abdominal cavity, the pressure on the machine is maintained or is elevated. By listening through the abdominal wall with a stethoscope, the escape of gas through the tubes can actually be heard.

If the tubes are open, will the patient experience pain from the Rubin test?

Yes. The gas entering the abdominal cavity often produces pain in the shoulder region within five to ten minutes. This pain will subside in a short time and is not serious.

Is there any danger to the Rubin test?

If proper precautions are taken, there is little chance of anything going wrong with this test. In occasional cases, an inflammatory disease within the fallopian tubes may be aggravated by this procedure.

Can patients resume sexual relations following a Rubin test?

Not until two days after the test has been performed.

How is a hysterogram performed?

This test is performed in essentially the same manner as the Rubin test, except that the radiopaque dye is inserted through the cervix and the results are obtained by taking an x-ray picture.

What precautions should be taken before a hysterogram is performed?

It must be ascertained that no infection exists within the vagina, uterus, or tubes.

Can blocked tubes ever be opened?

Yes. In occasional cases, performance of the Rubin test itself, by expanding the tubes with gas, will overcome the blockage. This test may be repeated at monthly intervals if it is not at first successful in reopening the tubes.

Are operations to overcome blocked tubes successful?

Yes, in approximately 20 percent of cases.

What can be done if the blocked tubes are due to spasm or emotional factors?

The giving of antispasmodic medications and the treatment of the patient's emotional problems will often result in the release of spasm and in the opening of the tubes.

How does glandular or hormonal imbalance cause infertility?

By preventing ovulation or by failing to produce a proper atmosphere for the implantation of the fertilized egg in the wall of the uterus.

Are there any specific tests to note the presence or absence of glandular imbalance?

Yes. Hormone studies can be carried out by specific tests upon the urine and

blood. Also, the basal metabolic rate and chemical analyses may give a clue as to the existence of a glandular disturbance.

Can glandular imbalance be overcome?

Yes, in some cases, by appropriate treatment with hormones. An endocrinologist can best handle this type of case.

Does the cervix often block the passage of healthy sperm into the uterus?

Yes. This occurs frequently when the cervix is infected or blocked by the presence of thick mucus.

Are there any tests to determine the ability of the sperm to penetrate the cervix?

Yes. The Huhner test is performed by examining the sperm after they have been deposited in the vagina. The patient comes to the office about two hours after intercourse, and samples from the vaginal canal and from the cervix are taken and are examined under a microscope. Where a normal sperm analysis exists, a comparison of the sperm in the vagina and in the cervix will give a clue as to the ability of the sperm to penetrate into the uterus.

Do healthy sperm ever fail to reach the cervix because of a tipped womb or because of improper positions in intercourse?

Yes. Such situations do occur and may interfere with eventual conception.

If this situation does exist, can it be corrected?

Yes, by changing the position of intercourse or by taking the sperm and artificially depositing them in the cervix.

If failure of the sperm to pass through the cervix is due to an infection of the cervix, can this situation be corrected?

Yes, by cauterizing the cervix and by

using antibiotics to get rid of the infection.

Is conception ever interfered with by a vagina that is too acid?

Yes. This is overcome by taking an alkaline douche with bicarbonate of soda before intercourse.

Do fibroids of the uterus ever cause sterility?

Yes, when the fibroids are located just beneath the lining of the uterus (submucous). Also, if the fibroids block the entrance to the fallopian tubes, the sperm may not be able to reach the egg.

Do cysts of the ovaries ever cause infertility?

Yes, when the cyst is the type that results from or causes an upset in hormone production and balance. Pregnancy will often occur when such cysts are removed surgically.

If infertility is thought to be due to emotional factors, how can it be treated?

In many cases of this kind, psychotherapy has proved of great value and is often followed by conception.

Is sterility in a woman often caused by the prolonged use of contraceptive jellies?

No. It has never been proved that the use of these substances will interfere with conception, once they have been discontinued.

Will the prolonged use of contraceptive pills interfere with subsequent ability to conceive?

On the contrary, it has been shown that women who have been taking contraceptive pills for a long period of time are more prone to conceive during the months immediately after their use.

Can sterility result from "overindulgence" in intercourse?

No. This has no influence whatever on fertility.

What is meant by artificial insemination?

It is the introduction of live sperm, either the husband's or a donor's, in the vicinity of the cervix.

When is artificial insemination employed?

1. In cases where the Huhner test reveals that the husband's sperm (even though healthy) are not being deposited into the cervix, the sperm are collected and are deposited into the cervix by the gynecologist.

2. In cases in which the husband is sterile—that is, he possesses no live healthy sperm—and husband and wife consent, a sperm donor is employed.

How often is artificial insemination successful?

In about 30 percent of cases.

Can the giving of hormones ever help an infertile woman to become pregnant?

Yes, in some instances. It has been found that some women are deficient in thyroid function, and the giving of thyroid extract may help them to become pregnant; other women may lack various ovarian hormones, and the giving of certain of these substances may help these women to become pregnant. Within recent years, it has been found that certain so-called fertility drugs, composed of substances that stimulate ovulation, can be helpful in aiding a woman to become pregnant.

What is currently the most widely used fertility drug?

Clomiphene citrate (Clomid). This is a chemical substance that stimulates the ovaries to ovulate, thereby enhancing a woman's chances of becoming pregnant.

Do the fertility drugs ever cause women to have multiple pregnancies?

Yes. It has been found that occasionally the effect of these drugs is so powerful that a woman will mature and shed several eggs during the course of one month, and if these are fertilized, a woman will conceive triplets, quadruplets, or even quintuplets. Several such incidents have occurred following the taking of these medications.

Do the fertility drugs always work?

No. Their sole value is in cases in which the woman fails to ovulate, that is, she does not produce a mature egg.

Are the fertility drugs available for general use?

No. At the present stage of their development, they are used only experimentally.

MALE STERILITY

Is the male an important factor in sterility?

Yes. Any attempt to overcome infertility that does not have the complete cooperation of the male is worthless and should not be undertaken. About 30 to 40 percent of all infertile marriages are due to failure of the male, not the female. Complete studies of the husband must be carried out by the urologist in all cases of infertile marriages.

What constitutes sterility in the male?

A sterile man is one who either has no sperm or has an insufficient number of normal, active sperm to make conception possible.

What is the difference between sterility and infertility in the male?

Sterility implies an absolute impossibility of conception or fertilization. In the male, this would be a situation in

which there are no sperm to ejaculate. On the other hand, infertility suggests that conception and fertilization are possible but not likely because of a low sperm count.

What is a sperm count?

The ejaculate, which usually amounts to about one teaspoonful, normally contains upward of 60 million sperm per cubic centimeter. This count is obtained by microscopic examination of the ejaculate.

Are there any other features of the ejaculate that are important to examine?

Yes. The motility of the sperm, as well as their anatomical appearance and characteristics, is important to note.

What are the common causes of absence of sperm?

1. There are some developmental abnormalities in males that may cause them to be born without the ability to produce sperm. Such conditions have just recently been discovered through study of chromosomes and genes.

2. Old age is often accompanied by the loss of the ability of the testis to produce sperm. This varies widely among individual men and may not have its onset in some until the eighth or ninth decade of life.

3. Orchitis, an inflammation of the testicle, may result in loss of sperm production. This is not uncommon following an attack of mumps in an adult. Other infections can also cause this form of male sterility.

4. Sperm may be absent because there is an interference with their migration from the testicle to the ejaculate. A previous infection, such as gonorrhea, may cause blockage of the passageway (the vas deferens) from the testicle to the seminal vesicle.

5. Of course, when the testicles are

absent or are undescended, no sperm will be produced.

6. It has been found recently that male sterility is sometimes associated with a varicocele. A varicocele is varicose veins located in the spermatic cord.

7. Sterility invariably follows a sterilization operation in which the vas deferens are cut across.

Can surgery ever help to overcome male sterility?

Yes.

1. If the vas deferens leading from the testicle to the ejaculatory duct is blocked, it is possible to remove the blocked segment of the vas and to suture the normal segment above to the normal segment below the obstruction.

2. If sterility is thought to be associated with a varicocele, its removal may overcome the sterility.

Is surgery for male sterility always successful?

No, but an increasing number of patients are being helped. Certainly, the surgery carries with it a minimal risk, and the prospect of regaining fertility is worth the try.

How can one tell whether the testicles are capable of producing sperm?

By a simple operative procedure known as testicular biopsy, a sample of testicular tissue is removed and submitted to the laboratory for microscopic examination. In most cases, this will demonstrate the capability of the testicle to produce sperm.

How is a biopsy of the testicles carried out?

It is done in an operating room of a hospital under light general anesthesia. A small incision is made in the skin of the scrotum, and through this a small piece of testicle is snipped away.

What causes a low or reduced sperm count?

A natural reduction in the sperm content of the ejaculate follows frequent intercourse, a generalized debilitating disease, surgical operations, or any situation that temporarily weakens or depresses body activities. Low sperm counts of this type may be of a temporary nature. In other cases, however, men who are perfectly normal in all other respects may have low sperm counts.

What are the most common causes of a reduced sperm count?

1. Glandular or endocrine disorders

2. Inflammation of the testicles secondary to mumps, gonorrhea, tuberculosis, or other diseases.

3. Diseases of the testicles that result in their shrinkage (atrophy), such as interference with their circulation

4. Old age

Are potency and sterility related?

Yes, insofar as inadequate erections (poor potency) which do not permit proper vaginal penetration will naturally interfere with conception, since the sperm will not be properly deposited. This can take place even when the sperm count is perfectly normal.

Can a man be potent yet sterile?

Yes. Many men are able to effect intercourse in a normal manner but their ejaculate (semen) contains no live sperm. Such men are potent but sterile.

What are some of the common causes of impotence?

1. By far the most common is psychological disturbance

2. Local disease of the genital organs

3. Senility

Is treatment of sterility in the male ever successful?

Yes, in certain cases. Of course, if

the testicles are absent or are markedly atrophied, nothing can be done about it. When the problem is one of a low sperm count, various types of hormone treatment are available which may result in an elevation of the sperm count.

Is treatment for male sterility always successful?

No, and the results are often unpredictable. However, treatment should always be carried out because, in a certain percentage of cases, pregnancy will result.

Are there methods, other than the glandular approach, for treating male sterility?

Yes. Any local disease should be eradicated. If there is an infection or a constriction of the urethra, this should be attended to. If there is an inflammation of the prostate gland, this must be corrected. If there is any disease within the scrotum, such as a hydrocele or varicocele, this should be treated surgically. If impotence exists, it should receive treatment from a psychiatrist.

What is the "rebound phenomenon" in male sterility?

In some instances, it has been noted that if a man with a low sperm count is given medication to reduce his count to zero, and the medication is then withdrawn, his sperm count will rebound to a point higher than it was before treatment was begun. This form of treatment has been successful in producing pregnancies in some cases but not in the majority of instances.

Will the giving of hormones cure impotence?

In the vast majority of cases, the giving of hormones has nothing more than psychological value. Most impotence in men is due either to a psychological maladjustment or to senility.

Will overindulgence in sex lead to premature impotence?

No. There is no proof that the sexual activity of the male will have any organic effect upon the age at which he becomes either impotent or infertile.

Sterilization

See FALLOPIAN TUBES; VASECTOMY.

Stomach and Duodenum

Many people harbor the peculiar notion that the stomach occupies the entire abdominal region. This, of course, is untrue, for the stomach is a relatively small part of the intestinal tract. It is a distended, pouchlike structure lying directly beneath the diaphragm under the ribs on the left side of the abdomen. The normal, empty stomach measures about six to eight inches in length and about three to four inches in width. Another frequently encountered misconception about the stomach is that it digests most of our food and that we cannot live without it. This, too, is untrue, for actually, the stomach's prime function is

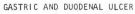

GASTRIC AND DUODENAL ULCER

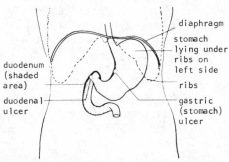

diaphragm
stomach lying under ribs on left side
ribs
gastric (stomach) ulcer
duodenum (shaded area)
duodenal ulcer

to churn the food and to break it down into small particles. Its acid juices merely initiate digestion and the really important digestive processes take place beyond the stomach in the small intestine.

Because duodenal ulcer is the commonest condition for which surgery is performed in this region, it is appropriate to discuss the duodenum along with the stomach. The duodenum is the first eight to ten inches of small intestine immediately beyond the stomach and its first portion is the site of the actual ulceration in approximately 11 of 12 cases of peptic ulcer. In other words, when a patient says that he has an "ulcer of the stomach," he usually means that he has an ulcer in his duodenum. In only 1 of 12 cases of peptic ulcer is the ulceration actually located in the stomach.

See also PYLORIC STENOSIS; DIAPHRAGMATIC AND HIATUS HERNIA.

PEPTIC ULCER

It is estimated from studies conducted by many investigators on thousands of people that approximately 10 percent of all adults at one time or another suffer from an ulcer of the stomach or duodenum. In the vast majority of these patients, probably well over 90 percent, the ulcer heals under medical management and no surgery is ever required. There are, however, the following indications for operative intervention in the stubborn, persistent cases which do not heal despite good medical care:

1. When the ulcer has become chronic and causes marked suffering over a period of many years and will not heal despite prolonged and strict medical treatment.

2. When the ulcer, by virtue of its thickness and scar tissue, causes obstruc-

tion of the passage of food and inability of the stomach to empty.

3. When there is repeated and severe bleeding from the base of the ulcer and when these bleeding episodes recur despite a careful medical regime.

4. When the ulcer ruptures or threatens to perforate. This makes surgery an emergency procedure, for rupture of an ulcer of the stomach or duodenum is followed by peritonitis.

5. When the ulcer is located in the stomach (gastric ulcer) rather than in the duodenum and when it does not heal within two to three months after the institution of medical management. For some unknown reason, about 7 to 10 percent of these gastric ulcers will turn into cancer, whereas the duodenal type practically never become malignant.

Although the exact cause of ulcer formation is unknown, the one common denominator found in almost all cases is *hyperacidity*. The hectic pace of civilization, with its accompanying increase in nervous tensions, is alleged to be one of the main causes for the glands of the stomach to secrete excess acid. The excess acid is not neutralized sufficiently by eating food or by the alkaline secretions of the duodenum, and this eventually leads to an ulceration or defect in the lining membrane of the stomach or duodenum. An ulcer may vary in size from that of a pinhead to that of a silver dollar.

Recently, it has been discovered that certain tumors of the pancreas may lead to a severe form of peptic ulcer which can be cured only by removing the pancreatic tumor or the entire stomach. This condition is known as the Zollinger-Ellison syndrome.

All operations for ulcer of the stomach or duodenum are primarily designed to reduce the acidity of the stomach. Prior to 1930, most surgeons performed a short-circuiting operation (gastro-

GASTRECTOMY

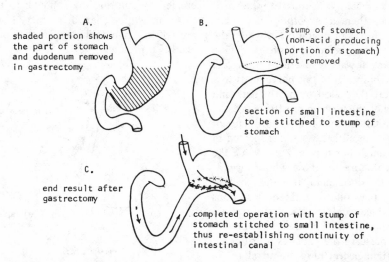

A. shaded portion shows the part of stomach and duodenum removed in gastrectomy

B. stump of stomach (non-acid producing portion of stomach) not removed

section of small intestine to be stitched to stump of stomach

C. end result after gastrectomy

completed operation with stump of stomach stitched to small intestine, thus re-establishing continuity of intestinal canal

jejunostomy) in which the small intestine was stitched to the stomach. By this procedure, the alkaline juices of the small intestine would flow into and out of the stomach, thus neutralizing the excess acidity. Unfortunately, this procedure proved a failure in about 15 percent of the cases, as either the original ulcer failed to heal or a new ulcer formed along the line where the stomach was sutured to the intestine.

Today there are four operative procedures in vogue for the surgical cure of duodenal ulcer. Each type of operation has its coterie of staunch proponents, and results from all four procedures have been proved beyond doubt to be satisfactory in well over 95 percent of cases. The choice of a particular surgical procedure will depend upon the location and extent of the ulcer, the presence or absence of severe hemorrhage from the ulcer, the degree of excess acidity being secreted by the stomach, the age and general condition of the patient, and the preference of the surgeon as to which operation he believes will have the best chances of obtaining a permanently successful result. The operations are as follows:

1. Subtotal gastrectomy, or removal of that portion of the stomach which contains most of the acid-secreting glands. This operation, perhaps practiced more often than the others to be described, consists of removing approximately 75 to 80 percent of the stomach and about an inch or two of the duodenum. The stump of the duodenum is closed tightly, and the continuity of the intestinal tract is reestablished by stitching the remainder of the stomach to the small intestine. (See diagram.) By this procedure, the ulcer in the stomach or duodenum is removed along with that portion of the stomach which manufactures most of the hydrochloric acid. Henceforth, food will pass into a new sac formed by the remnant of the stomach and the attached small intestine. Although the patient will have to limit the quantity of food intake for three to four months, the newly formed receptacle will soon distend sufficiently for him to eat normally soon thereafter. This operation has proved successful in hundreds of thousands of cases and is followed by recurrence of ulcer in only about 2 percent of cases. Should an ulcer form again at the site where the stump of the stomach was sutured to the small intestine, then a *vagotomy* is undertaken. This is an operation in which the vagus nerve, the main nerve supplying the stomach wall, is severed. Cutting the various branches of this nerve leads to a markedly decreased output of acid and healing of the ulcer in most instances.

Subtotal gastrectomy is the treatment of choice in all cases of ulcer located in the stomach but may not always be the best procedure for those whose ulcer is within the duodenum. It is thought that one of the following three operations will reduce acid secretion more effectively than subtotal gastrectomy and will better preserve the patient's nutrition.

2. Hemigastrectomy (removal of 50 percent of the stomach) **and vagotomy** has been shown to be a good operative procedure for duodenal ulcer. Its proponents feel that this will effectively reduce acid secretion but will not cause the malnutrition seen among some patients who have had 75 to 80 percent of their stomach removed. (See diagram.)

created by suturing the stomach to the small intestine. (See diagram.) There are not too many adherents of this procedure at present.

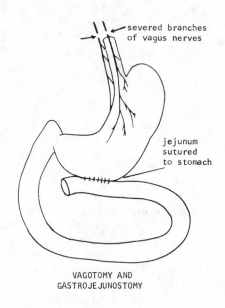

severed branches of vagus nerves

jejunum sutured to stomach

VAGOTOMY AND GASTROJEJUNOSTOMY

severed branches of vagus nerves

50% of stomach has been removed

jejunum (small intestine)

HEMIGASTRECTOMY AND VAGOTOMY

3. Vagotomy and gastrojejunostomy is a combination of maneuvers in which the vagus nerve (as it enters the abdomen) is severed and a short circuit is

4. Vagotomy and pyloroplasty is a combined operation in which the vagus nerve is cut and the muscles and mucous membranes at the outlet of the stomach are severed and resutured in such a way as to allow the alkaline secretions of the duodenum to flow back into the stomach. This alkaline backflow, along with vagotomy, markedly reduces the acid content of the stomach, thus leading to healing of the ulcer. (See diagram.)

It would perhaps be too technical to discuss all the advantages and disadvantages of the preceding ulcer operations. Suffice it to say that all are good and that each case must be individually appraised. Surgeons who are disinclined to utilize gastrectomy state that the nutritional problems created by the procedure are considerable. Those who hesi-

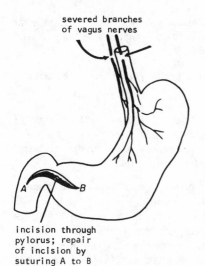

severed branches
of vagus nerves

incision through
pylorus; repair
of incision by
suturing A to B

VAGOTOMY AND PYLOROPLASTY

tate to use vagotomy in combination with hemigastrectomy, gastrojejunostomy, or pyloroplasty point to the fact that approximately 20 percent of those so operated will develop chronic diarrhea. Moreover, the latter two procedures do not include removal of the ulcer itself but depend solely upon the reduction in acid levels to bring about healing.

When an ulcer ruptures, excruciating abdominal pain and shock usually ensue. Such an episode constitutes one of surgery's most acute emergencies and must be handled by immediate operation. Since the patient's condition is precarious, it is unwise to perform an extensive procedure for the definitive cure of the ulcer. In most instances, the surgeon will merely close the hole in the stomach or duodenum, suck out the fluid or pus from the abdominal cavity, and wait for a later day to perform a gastrectomy. About 50 percent of these patients will never have further trouble despite the fact that the ulcer has not been removed and the stomach retains

its ability to secrete excess quantities of hydrochloric acid. In other words, only about half of those submitted to surgery for a ruptured ulcer will require a second operation.

TUMORS OF THE STOMACH

An urgent indication for surgery upon the stomach is the discovery, through x-ray examination, of a tumor. This finding is by no means conclusive that the condition is cancerous, for there are nonmalignant tumors such as polyps or fatty tumors or muscle tumors which lend themselves to local removal and are followed, in almost all instances, by complete and permanent recovery. However, malignant growths of the stomach account for approximately one third of all cancers in men and one fifth of all cancers in women. With these statistics in mind, one sees how important it is to consult one's physician as soon as any stomach symptoms appear. Literally millions of lives can be saved if people would only present themselves for early investigation. Cancer of the stomach in its early stages can be cured by an extensive subtotal or total gastrectomy, a modification of the operation that is performed for ulcer. It is encouraging to report that as surgical technique improves and as more patients are seen early in the course of their disease, cure rates for cancer of the stomach are rising rapidly.

QUESTIONS AND ANSWERS

Where is the duodenum?

The duodenum is that segment of the small intestine extending for several inches immediately beyond the stomach. It is considered along with the stomach because conditions affecting the stomach so often affect the duodenum, too.

What is the function of the duodenum?

The wall of the duodenum manufactures juices (enzymes) which help digest foods. It is also the portion of small intestine into which the bile is deposited and the segment into which the pancreatic juices empty.

What are the most common diseases of the duodenum?

1. Inflammation of the duodenum (duodenitis)
2. Duodenal ulcer
3. A diverticulum of the duodenum

Do diseases of the stomach or duodenum tend to run in families or to be inherited?

No.

What kind of person is most likely to develop trouble in the stomach or duodenum?

The energetic, nervous, neurotic type in the 20s, 30s, or 40s. Men more commonly have stomach or duodenal trouble than women.

PEPTIC ULCER

What is an ulcer?

An ulcer is a localized area where the lining membrane of the stomach or duodenum has been destroyed and where a raw surface with an inflamed base exists.

What is meant by the term "peptic" ulcer?

It is a general term used to describe an ulcer in the stomach, duodenum, or the lower end of the esophagus.

What causes peptic ulcer?

The exact cause is not known, but the common underlying factor in almost all cases is hyperacidity, or the secretion of excess acid by the stomach. According to some stomach specialists, emotional distress plays a vital role in the cause of peptic ulcer.

What types of peptic ulcer are there?

1. Duodenal ulcer is the most common form.
2. Stomach (gastric) ulcer is next in frequency.
3. Esophageal ulcer is the least frequently encountered ulcer.

How common is an ulcer of the stomach or duodenum?

About one in every ten adults is thought to have a duodenal ulcer at some time or other. About one in every hundred adults will have a gastric ulcer at some time or other.

How does an ulcer harm the patient?

When acid and gastric juices pass over the ulcerated area, marked pain results. If the ulcer gets too deep it may go right through all the layers of the stomach or duodenum and cause a rupture of the organ. The ulcer may extend into a blood vessel and cause severe bleeding into the gastrointestinal tract.

Is the size of an ulcer significant?

The larger the duodenal ulcer, the more likely it is to cause obstruction of the outlet of the stomach. The deeper the ulcer, the more likely it is to rupture or erode through a blood vessel.

The greater the size of a stomach ulcer, the more likely it is to turn into a cancer.

How can one tell if he has an ulcer?

The most characteristic symptoms are gnawing hunger pains in the upper abdomen occurring between meals, most often shortly before lunch or supper. The pains are usually relieved for several hours by eating. Other symptoms include sour taste in the mouth, belching, and heartburn, relieved by the taking of antacid medications.

What actually takes place when an ulcer of the stomach or duodenum is present?

The lining mucous membrane is eaten away and eroded, leaving a raw, uncovered area in the wall of the stomach or duodenum. Ulcers may vary in size from that of a pinhead to that of a half dollar.

Do ulcers of the stomach or duodenum tend to run in families or to be inherited?

Not really, except that there is a tendency for children to develop along the same lines as their parents. Thus, neurotic parents with ulcers may have offspring who develop the same tendencies.

Is there any way to lessen the chances of getting an ulcer?

1. Don't smoke.
2. Drink alcohol only in moderate amounts.
3. Eat bland, nonspicy foods.
4. Attempt to live within the bounds of your ability and capacity.

What tests are performed to make a positive diagnosis of peptic ulcer?

Most cases can be demonstrated by x-ray studies of the stomach and duodenum.

What are the harmful effects of peptic ulcer?

In addition to the pain and continued discomfort that ulcer patients suffer, there are the following possible complications:

1. A gastric (stomach) ulcer, if untreated, may develop into cancer. This happens in about 1 in 15 cases.
2. As ulcers become chronic, they may form scar tissue which will obstruct the outlet of the stomach.
3. Ulcers may rupture and cause peritonitis, an inflammation of the inner lining of the abdominal cavity.
4. Ulcers tend to cause severe hemorrhage. Death from loss of blood can occur during a bleeding episode.

What is the treatment for peptic ulcer?

More than 90 percent of all ulcers will respond to medical treatment and will require no surgery. Standard medical treatment for a patient suffering from a peptic ulcer will consist of:

1. Special ulcer diet, with frequent feedings of milk and cream.
2. Abstinence from all irritants, spicy foods, alcohol, etc.
3. Antacid medications.
4. Special medications which work through the nervous system so as to cut down on the secretion of gastric juice and acid. These drugs are in the Banthine group.
5. Stopping smoking.

The remainder who do not respond to medical treatment should be operated upon if:

1. It is a gastric ulcer which shows no healing within a few weeks, as these ulcers have a tendency to become cancerous.
2. When pain and discomfort continue over the years despite conscientious attempts to bring about a cure through medical management.
3. When there is obstruction to the stomach outlet.
4. When the ulcer ruptures or threatens to rupture.
5. When there are repeated episodes of severe hemorrhage.

What actually takes place in the lining of the stomach when an ulcer heals?

The lining membrane (mucosa) will grow back over the raw, ulcerated surface.

Do ulcers, once healed through medical treatment, have a tendency to recur?

Yes. As long as the stomach pours out an excess of acid there is danger of a new break occurring in its lining, with a resultant ulcer.

What are the causes for recurrence of healed ulcers?

Failure to maintain an ulcer dietary regimen; continuation of smoking and drinking alcoholic beverages; the persistence of those situations in life which lead to emotional instability and stress; an insulin-producing tumor of the pancreas.

Are operations for peptic ulcer serious?

Yes, but approximately 99 out of 100 will recover from the surgery.

What operations are performed to cure peptic ulcer?

There are several procedures, each of which has special indications, and each will result in cure in well over 90 percent of cases.

1. For an ulcer located in the stomach (gastric ulcer), a subtotal gastrectomy is done. This involves the removal of approximately three quarters of the stomach and the remainder is joined to the small intestine.

2. For an ulcer in the duodenum (the most common form of peptic ulcer) one of the following operations is performed:

a. A subtotal gastrectomy, as just described.

b. A vagotomy, in which the vagus nerves (which stimulate the stomach to secrete acid) are cut and approximately 50 percent of the stomach is removed.

c. A vagotomy is performed, and the outlet of the stomach is altered so as to permit the regurgitation of bile from the alkaline duodenum into the stomach. This procedure is known as pyloroplasty.

d. A vagotomy is performed and a short-circuiting opening is made between the stomach and small intes-

tine. This latter procedure is known as a gastrojejunostomy.

Are all operations equally successful in treating peptic ulcer?

All of the operations give satisfactory results, but recent statistical studies seem to show that the operations associated with vagotomy will give a somewhat higher cure rate than plain gastrectomy. This holds true for ulcers in the duodenum, but not for those located in the stomach.

How long a period of hospitalization is usually required for operations for ulcer?

Ten to 15 days.

Will special preoperative preparations be necessary?

Yes. Patients are often admitted to the hospital a few days prior to surgery so that they can be prepared by liquid diet, washings of the stomach, intravenous medications, vitamins, and—if they have lost much blood—transfusions.

Will special nurses be required after an operation for peptic ulcer?

Yes, for several days.

How long does it take to perform an ulcer operation?

From two to five hours, depending upon the severity of the case and the type of operation performed. (Speed in surgery is not important.)

What anesthesia is usually employed in ulcer operations?

General inhalation anesthesia.

What special postoperative treatments are necessary after ulcer operations?

1. Liquid by mouth is withheld for two to three days, and food is not given for four to five days.

2. The patient is fed intravenously with glucose, proteins, minerals, and vitamins.

3. Stomach tubes are employed to

keep the stomach or stomach remnant empty.

4. Antibiotics are sometimes given to prevent postoperative infection.

What takes over the function of the stomach or duodenum when part of it is removed because of an ulcer?

The remnant of the stomach dilates over a period of several months, and along with the small intestine to which it has been joined, a pouch is formed which serves as an excellent receptacle for food.

Why is it more important to remove an ulcer of the stomach than an ulcer of the duodenum?

Stomach ulcers may form cancer; duodenal ulcers do not.

Do ulcers tend to recur after an operation has been carried out?

They recur rarely—in less than 3 percent of cases.

How long does it take to convalesce from extensive stomach surgery?

An average convalescent period is about six to eight weeks.

Does one have to follow an ulcer diet after gastrectomy, vagotomy with hemigastrectomy, or vagotomy with gastrojejunostomy or pyloroplasty?

Not usually. Since excess acid secretion has been eliminated, recurrence of the ulcer is not greatly feared. However, it is best to avoid highly seasoned foods, spices, and alcohol as a precautionary measure.

Should large meals be eaten after stomach surgery?

Not for the first three to four months. Small, frequent feedings are recommended instead. After four months, the average patient can eat a normal diet.

What type of diet is followed after gastrectomy?

For the first two weeks, a *soft diet* composed of milk, tea, water, cereal, soft-boiled eggs, cooked cereals, Jello, custard, junket, etc. Then scraped beef or chicken or fish and puréed vegetables are added. Within four to six weeks, almost all bland foods are permitted. Patients are encouraged to chew their food thoroughly.

Can one ever return to completely normal eating after an ulcer operation?

Yes, within a few months.

What limitations on one's activities must be imposed after an ulcer operation?

None, after the patient has convalesced completely. (This may require three to four months.)

Does stomach removal for ulcer affect the span of life?

No.

If the patient has a duodenal ulcer, does the operation always include removal of the ulcer?

No. It has been found that gastrectomy *without* removal of the duodenal ulcer usually results in cure. The ulcer is removed in most cases, but in those patients where it is technically too difficult to remove or where ulcer removal will jeopardize recovery, it is left behind and buried with the stump of the duodenum. Since gastrectomy short-circuits the duodenum, no food or acid secretion will pass over the ulcerated area and it will heal rapidly and cause no symptoms.

Are there any unfavorable results from stomach removal?

In a small percentage of cases, patients will develop an anemia which will require the taking of iron and liver extract for a prolonged period of time.

In a small number of cases, trembling

and profuse sweating episodes may take place because the remnant of stomach empties itself of food too quickly. This phenomenon is called the *dumping syndrome* and can usually be controlled by frequent small feedings rather than infrequent large meals.

Are there any unfavorable results from vagotomy plus gastrojejunostomy?

Yes, in an occasional patient the short-circuiting opening fails to function efficiently and the patient develops retention of food in the stomach. Also, it must be kept in mind that the ulcer is not removed in this operation and it may bleed or cause trouble postoperatively.

Are there unfavorable results from vagotomy and hemigastrectomy?

There are very few complications from this procedure unless the remnant of the stomach—some months or years after surgery—regains its ability to secrete acid. In this event, a new ulcer may form.

Are there unfavorable results following vagotomy and pyloroplasty?

There are very few complications of this operation. However, it must be kept in mind that the ulcer is not removed, and there is always the possibility that it may bleed or not heal postoperatively. Also, if the duodenum has been scarred greatly by an old chronic ulceration, it may be more difficult to perform a pyloroplasty than a gastrectomy.

What will happen if an operation is not performed?

If the underlying disease is a malignant tumor, death will occur within a few months.

If the underlying disease is a bleeding ulcer, fatal hemorrhage may result.

If the ulcer is causing an obstruction of the stomach, total obstruction and starvation may ensue.

If the ulcer has ruptured, death from peritonitis may occur if surgery is not undertaken.

How often after surgery should one be rechecked by one's physician?

About once every four months.

Is pregnancy permissible after an operation for peptic ulcer?

Yes.

How soon after an ulcer operation can one do the following:

Bathe?	10 to 15 days
Walk outdoors?	10 to 15 days
Climb stairs?	10 to 15 days
Do housework?	5 to 6 weeks
Drive a car?	6 to 8 weeks
Resume marital relations?	5 to 6 weeks
Return to work?	8 weeks

Can digestion be normal even without stomach acids and without part of the stomach?

Yes. Approximately 10 percent of all people have little or no acid in their stomach. And it should be remembered that the major phase of digestion of foods takes place in the small intestine, not in the stomach.

Will the operating surgeon be able to tell whether a stomach ulcer has become malignant?

Not always. It is frequently necessary to wait several days for the microscopic examination to be completed before making a definite diagnosis. However, the procedure—removal of the stomach—is practically the same in both conditions.

If a cancer is found, would the surgeon tell the patient?

Although there is a difference of opinion on this point, most surgeons tell the patients the truth. This practice has grown markedly in recent years as the cure rates for cancer have increased.

CANCER OF THE STOMACH

What causes cancer of the stomach?

In most instances, the cause is unknown. Some cancers are thought to have their origin in ulcers of the stomach.

Are all tumors of the stomach cancerous?

No. There may be tumors of the mucous membrane lining or of the muscle wall which are nonmalignant. The most common nonmalignant tumors are polyps of the mucous membrane, lipomas (fatty tumors), and myomas (tumors containing muscle tissue).

Are nonmalignant tumors of the stomach curable?

Yes. They can be removed surgically, by removing that portion of the stomach in which they grow.

How common is cancer of the stomach?

It accounts for approximately one third of all cancers in men, and one fifth of all cancers in women.

Do statistics show that cancer of the stomach in this country is on the increase?

No. Peculiarly, recent statistical data would seem to indicate that cancer of the stomach is one of the few types of malignancy that is not increasing.

What age groups are most affected by cancer of the stomach?

This is a disease most often found in middle age and in the later years of life.

Does cancer of the stomach tend to run in families or to be inherited?

No.

Is there any way to prevent cancer of the stomach?

The prompt removal of an ulcer in the stomach may prevent it from becoming cancerous. Also, cancer might be apprehended in its early stages if more people would see their physicians for regular physical examinations and if more people who have gastrointestinal symptoms would submit to thorough x-ray examinations.

How is the diagnosis of cancer of the stomach made?

By x-ray examination. The diagnosis can also be made in certain cases by passing a specially designed instrument known as a gastroscope through the mouth into the stomach. This may allow the gastroscopist to view the tumor directly through the instrument.

What are the symptoms of cancer of the stomach?

There are very few early symptoms. However, chronic indigestion, loss of appetite, slight weight loss, abdominal pain, or pallor should stimulate one to seek an x-ray examination of his entire gastrointestinal tract.

What is the treatment for cancer of the stomach?

Prompt surgery with gastrectomy (the removal of all but a small remnant of the stomach).

What special preoperative measures are necessary for cancer of the stomach?

The same as for peptic ulcer.

Are operations for cancer of the stomach very serious?

Yes, but with modern advances in surgery, well over 90 percent will recover from their operation.

When should a patient with cancer of the stomach be operated upon?

As soon as the diagnosis is made. All

people with tumors of the stomach are entitled to an exploratory operation. Preoperative x-ray examinations cannot always distinguish a malignant tumor from a harmless benign tumor. Furthermore, x-rays occasionally will give the appearance of a tumor but an ulcer will be discovered at surgery.

Are the results from surgery for a cancer of the stomach as satisfactory as surgery for an ulcer?

No. In too many instances, the surgery is undertaken at a time when the cancer has already spread to the surrounding lymph nodes or to the liver.

How long a hospital stay is necessary for cancer of the stomach?

Approximately two weeks.

What type of anesthesia is used?

Either general inhalation anesthesia or, in selected cases, a high spinal anesthesia.

How long does it take to perform an operation for cancer of the stomach?

Two to five hours, depending upon whether the entire stomach or only a portion of it is removed. Also, a great deal will depend upon the extent of the spread and the technical problems encountered.

Do ulcers of the stomach ever become malignant?

Yes. Large ulcers of the stomach (not the duodenum) have a tendency to become malignant.

Will a surgeon know whether a stomach ulcer has become malignant when he views it at operation?

Not always, but he will perform a gastrectomy, nevertheless. The tissue will be submitted for microscopic examination and this will result in an exact diagnosis.

Are blood transfusions given during operations upon the stomach?

Yes, in most cases.

What is the usual postoperative course and what are the postoperative routines employed in cases of cancer of the stomach?

Practically the same as those used after gastrectomy for ulcer, except that the patient is a good deal sicker after gastrectomy for cancer.

Are blood transfusions given during stomach surgery?

Yes, in most cases.

Are operations upon the stomach and duodenum painful?

There will be moderate abdominal pain for a few days postoperatively, but is it not severe and the patients bear it well.

Is the patient very uncomfortable postoperatively?

Yes. For two to three days after this type of surgery there is considerable discomfort occasioned by stomach tubes, intravenous solutions, and injections.

Are special measures and special postoperative routines followed?

Yes:

1. No food or drink is given for two to four days postoperatively.

2. Intravenous medications, vitamins, and solutions are given.

3. Stomach tubes are passed to keep the tract empty.

4. Catheters are sometimes inserted into the bladder to keep track of urinary output.

Are special nurses indicated after stomach surgery?

Yes, for two to four days, providing the patient can afford it.

How long does it take the wound to heal?

Approximately one to two weeks, but manual work should not be resumed for six to eight weeks.

Is the scar of the operation disfiguring?

No. Some surgeons make a midline incision from the breastbone down to and beyond the navel. Others make a longitudinal incision off to the left or right of the midline, while still others make an incision transversely across the upper part of the abdomen.

Is convalescent care necessary?

No, but many patients will benefit from two to three weeks of such care, particularly if it is in the country.

How soon after surgery can the patient get out of bed?

Most surgeons today advocate early ambulation, and the patient is frequently encouraged to get out of bed for a short period of time the day after operation.

Strabismus

See CROSSED EYES.

Stroke

See BLOOD VESSELS; NEUROSURGERY.

Subdural Hematoma

A subdural hematoma is a collection of blood beneath the membrane overlying the brain. The hematoma, or blood clot, increases in size over a period of days, weeks, or months, thereby exert-ing pressure on the underlying brain. Subdural hematomas follow an injury to the head which may or may not be associated with skull fracture, concussion, or loss of consciousness. In some cases, the head injury seems to be rather minor at the time it takes place.

See also NEUROSURGERY.

QUESTIONS AND ANSWERS

Can people of all ages develop a subdural hematoma?

Yes. Anyone who has a head injury may have a rupture of a blood vessel beneath the membrane overlying the brain with ultimate development of a hematoma.

Do the symptoms of subdural hematoma come on quickly?

Often, they do not come on for several days, weeks, or months. As a matter of fact, the patient may have forgotten completely the original head injury that produced the hematoma.

What are some of the symptoms of a subdural hematoma?

1. Over a period of days, weeks, or months, the patient may complain of recurrent headache, drowsiness, and may evidence personality changes. In severe cases, there may be vomiting and convulsions.

2. Infants with a subdural hematoma thrive poorly, fail to gain weight, are irritable, and may develop stupor and convulsions.

How is a diagnosis of subdural hematoma made?

There are many ways to make the diagnosis:

1. The history is very important, as it is rather typical that there is a story of a previous head injury followed by

recovery, and only later are there headache, personality changes, and other
signs of brain pressure.

2. X-rays that make the blood vessels
of the brain visible (arteriography) may
confirm the diagnosis and show the location of the hematoma.

3. A trephine operation performed
over the site of a suspected hematoma
will reveal its presence. This procedure
is a simple, nondangerous operation in
which a small hole is bored into the
skull with a special instrument known as
a trephine.

**What is the treatment for a hemorrhage
that manifests itself several weeks or
months after a head injury?**

Under either general or local anesthesia, a hole is drilled in the skull, the
membrane overlying the brain is incised, and the blood clot is removed.
The operation is usually performed on
both sides of the head, since there are
often subdural hematomas on both sides.
However, it may be performed on only
one side if special x-ray tests have
clearly demonstrated the presence of a
clot on only one side. A more extensive
operation (craniotomy) may be necessary to remove the clot completely and
permit the brain to continue to grow
normally.

**How successful are operations for sub-
dural hematoma?**

The results are usually very good.
The prevention of permanent brain
damage depends on early diagnosis and
treatment.

**Is complete recovery the general rule
following such operations?**

Yes, in most cases. Occasionally,
when treatment has been unduly delayed and the hematoma has attained a
large size, the underlying brain may undergo permanent damage.

Surgery in the Aged

With improved methods of preoperative preparation and postoperative
care, many who are in their later years
can now withstand extensive surgical
procedures almost as well as their
younger counterparts. The old aphorism
"Too old to be operated on" no longer
holds true, provided that adequate support is given prior to surgery.

It is fortunate indeed that increased
knowledge in the fields of chemistry,
physiology, and metabolism have enabled physicians to better prepare older
people for surgery, because improved
techniques now permit repair of many
old, worn-out organs that were hitherto
unapproachable. Today a person in his
70s or 80s can undergo major surgery
upon his kidneys, prostate gland, gallbladder, bile ducts, intestines, blood
vessels, and even his heart.

Of course, it would be absurd to state
that the risks are no greater as one ages,
for as various vital organs become less
efficient, they recover more slowly from
the inevitable trauma of surgery. Also,
old people develop a certain amount of
fibrous changes within their lungs, and
their air cells tend to break down and
absorb oxygen less efficiently. This leads
to a decrease in the ability of the
respiratory apparatus to overcome protracted anesthesia. Moreover, deep
breathing may be inhibited by a painful
incision. Patients with weak heart muscle and inefficient heart valves cannot
pump blood as well as they should
during the stressful moments during
and after a serious operative procedure.
Those whose liver and kidneys have
been damaged by long-standing disease
may succumb because these organs are
unable to recuperate from the chemical

upset created by the surgical procedure. And lastly, older patients often have arteriosclerosis of those blood vessels that supply the brain. As a consequence, sufficient blood and oxygen may not be carried to this vital structure during the anesthesia and the period of emergence from anesthesia.

Prior to recommending elective surgery upon elderly patients, physicians will conduct a thorough survey of essential bodily functions. Here are some of the tests most often carried out to ascertain one's ability to withstand surgery:

1. A complete physical examination, including a digital examination of the anus and rectum, an examination of the rectum and lower colon with a sigmoidoscope, and a pelvic examination.

2. Particular attention will be paid to loose or decayed teeth. Mouth infections should be treated and useless teeth pulled prior to elective surgery. Failure to do this may predispose the patient to breakage of teeth during anesthesia and to possible aspiration of infected material from the mouth into the lungs.

3. A complete blood count, bleeding time, and blood coagulation test will be taken. Anemia or delayed coagulation may contraindicate elective operation.

4. Blood will be withdrawn for chemical analysis. Special attention will be given to the level of urea nitrogen, as a significant rise indicates kidney disease. Also the level of sugar will be noted to see if diabetes is present. Several special tests will be done to determine the state of liver function. The level of proteins circulating in the blood will be noted as an indication of the state of nutrition. Failure to maintain adequate protein levels makes surgery hazardous, as wounds cannot heal unless the general state of nutrition is satisfactory. And lastly, the electrolytes (sodium, chloride, potassium) will be checked. Imbalance of these chemicals may lead to postoperative kidney and adrenal gland failure, with catastrophic results.

5. Urine analysis will be performed, with particular attention being paid to the presence of infection and to the appearance of casts which might signify kidney disease.

6. In addition to the usual evaluation of heart function on the basis of its rhythm, quality of sounds, level of blood pressure, and presence of swelling about the ankles, an electrocardiogram will be taken.

7. An x-ray of the lungs will be performed, and the presence or absence of bronchitis, bronchiectasis, and emphysema will be noted.

8. The mental attitude of the patient toward the impending surgery should be carefully explored. A will to live is an essential part of recovery in an older individual.

When the basic procedures outlined are completed, the surgeon may wish to carry out special tests relating to the specific condition. These, too, will be done prior to actual surgery. If remedial deficiencies are discovered, they must be treated vigorously before undertaking even a minor operation. The key to safe surgery on older patients is meticulous preoperative preparation:

1. Loose, jagged, and decayed teeth should be pulled.

2. Mouth infection should be treated with antibiotics and mouthwashes for several days before surgery.

3. Anemia of major proportions should be temporarily overcome by blood transfusions in order to bring the patient to the operating room with an adequate number of red blood cells.

4. Abnormal bleeding or coagulation time may indicate deficiencies in vita-

mins C and K, or may mean insufficient blood platelets or a fibrinogen lack. Large doses of vitamins C and K, and injections of blood platelets and fibrin-, ogen may be necessary preoperatively. (It is exceedingly dangerous to do an elective operation upon a patient with bleeding tendencies.)

5. Only absolutely essential or emergency surgery should be performed upon older people who have inadequate blood proteins. To defy this dictum is to invite poor wound healing, wound rupture, leakage along suture lines, and overwhelming infection. To combat hypoproteinemia (low blood protein), repeated transfusions are necessary. Intravenous injections of albumin may also prove helpful.

6. Elevated urea nitrogen levels may indicate kidney infection, impaired kidney function, dehydration, or bleeding into the intestinal tract. To combat this finding, the patient should receive antibiotics to clear up any urinary infection, should receive adequate intake of fluids if dehydration exists, and should have his electrolytes brought into balance. If the urea level remains high, it might be best to postpone elective surgery.

7. Electrolyte imbalance can be corrected by giving intravenous infusions of appropriate amounts of sodium, chloride, and potassium.

8. If the liver function is found to be poor, it is supported preoperatively by giving large intravenous infusions of glucose (sugar) and protein. When jaundice is present, vitamin K is given intravenously or intramuscularly.

9. Digitalis and diuretic drugs, to promote excretion of excess body fluids, are often given to those whose heart function appears inadequate. Vigorous treatment of this kind may restore cardiac efficiency within a few days.

10. If the blood pressure level is high, it has proved best *not* to give medications to reduce it prior to surgery. For some incompletely known reason, reduction of high blood pressure before surgery occasionally leads to complications during the operative period. Modern anesthesiologists can cope effectively with hypertension, so that it infrequently causes undue concern.

11. Any evidence of bronchial or lung infection should receive antibiotic therapy for several days prior to operation. Heavy smokers should be induced to stop smoking for a few days preoperatively, as this will lead to a smoother anesthesia and will reduce chances of a postoperative pulmonary complication. Those who are known to have emphysema will be fed large quantities of oxygen during and after the operative procedure.

12. A careful surgeon will hesitate long before performing an elective operation upon an older person whose attitude toward the procedure is resistant. The *desire* to live assumes a role of increased importance among these patients, and failure of recovery is not at all infrequent among those who have lost their will to live. Much can be done to gain the patient's cooperation through a frank and detailed discussion of the condition prior to surgery. The patient must be shown how he and his loved ones will benefit from the intervention, and he must be assured that there will not be inordinate suffering or an increased burden placed upon those charged with his care.

The postoperative period in older patients requires special consideration, and it is frequently necessary to continue many of the measures that were instituted preoperatively.

Those in their later years may find it more difficult to turn, sit up, or get out of bed, and they will probably expend more effort in sponging themselves, shaving, voiding, and defecating. For these reasons, whenever possible, special nurses should be employed until the patient is fully ambulatory. In order to guard against falls out of bed, side railings should be used.

Here are some special postoperative measures often applied in these cases:

1. The tissues of older people are much more sensitive to oxygen deprivation. The brain, heart, liver, and other organs will suffer inordinately even from a few minutes of oxygen deficit. Accordingly, it is essential that extra oxygen be given during the immediate postoperative period and for a day or two thereafter. Such oxygen can be supplied readily by placing in a nostril a rubber tube that is attached to an oxygen tank, by placing an oxygen mask over the face, or by placing the patient in an oxygen tent.

2. If there has been substantial blood loss during the operation and an anemic state persists postoperatively, further blood transfusions are given.

3. If high blood pressure persists postoperatively, it can be brought down to safe levels by administering antihypertensive drugs.

4. Most elderly people have some limitation of their respiratory function. Thus, to make deep breathing and aeration of the lungs easier, the patient should be placed in a sitting or semirecumbent position as soon as possible.

5. Early ambulation is even more beneficial to older than to younger patients, for it stimulates their circulation and reduces the chances of blood clots in the veins of their legs and pelvis. It also causes the patient to breathe more deeply.

6. If the operation is of major proportions, it is necessary to assay the electrolyte content of the blood each day. Kidney and liver failure may ensue if the electrolytes are permitted to get out of balance even for a 24-hour period. Abnormalities can be remedied by giving intravenous infusions.

7. If the heart should become irregular or if edema (swelling of the ankles or legs) develops, digitalis and diuretics may have to be given for several days after surgery.

8. As older people may find it more difficult to void while in bed, they should be encouraged to get out of bed to do it. If this is not effective, a catheter (rubber tube) may be inserted for a few days until the bladder regains its control.

9. There is a tendency for older postoperative patients to refuse their meals. To overcome this, it is wise to learn of their favorite dishes and to obtain them from the diet kitchen. Failure to eat may lead to further protein and vitamin deficiency, with resultant delayed wound healing. This must be treated by forced feedings by passage of a tube through the nose into the stomach.

10. The low oral intake of fluids, sugar, and vitamins during the days immediately following surgery can be counteracted readily by the administration of these substances intravenously.

QUESTIONS AND ANSWERS

Is advanced age in itself a contraindication to surgery?

No. Within the past twenty or thirty years, physicians and surgeons have learned a great deal about supporting the aging individual so that he can withstand surgery.

Does the expression "too old to be operated on" hold true in most cases today?

No. Many years ago, surgeons would

often refrain from surgery on older people because of the fear of anesthetic difficulties, lung complications, heart or kidney failure, and other problems. Today, most of these dangers can be eliminated or controlled.

What criteria should be used in deciding whether an older patient can be operated upon?

The status of heart function as judged by listening to the heart and by taking an electrocardiogram. The status of respiratory functions as judged by listening to the chest and taking chest x-rays. The status of blood vessels as ascertained by examining them in the retina (black of the eyes), in the arms and legs, and by noting the blood pressure. The status of liver function as determined through chemical analysis of the blood. The status of kidney function as noted on urinalysis and chemical analysis of the blood. The condition of the blood itself must be ascertained through complete blood count and special tests of coagulability. The state of mind must be evaluated after conversing with the patient about the intended operation.

Is there an increased need for surgery as people grow older?

Yes. As one ages, one's organs tend to wear out and function less efficiently. Through modern surgical advances, new methods have been discovered for repairing them. Others, when diseased and expendable, must be removed.

Are the risks of surgery greater as one advances in age?

Yes, but not to a crucial extent if the patient is in good general health. Those older people who do have deficiencies can often be brought into satisfactory condition for surgery by special preoperative preparation.

What can be done about an older person who is in poor condition but who must have an emergency operation?

Fortunately, there are many measures that can be taken within a few hours' time which will ready him for surgery. However, if the surgical disease is so urgent that time for preparation is not feasible, then the risk must be taken and the surgeon will concentrate upon improving the patient's state during the postoperative period.

Are such elective operations as repair of hernia or removal of hemorrhoids or gallstones safe to perform on most older patients?

Yes. These operations have extremely low mortality rates, provided the patient is in a satisfactory state of health.

Should the surgeon explain the exact nature of the operation to the patient before performing it?

Yes, and it is perhaps more important to do this with older patients than with younger ones. The former are usually better able to adjust to the realities of the situation. Moreover, if information is unnecessarily withheld from older people, they are more likely to come to erroneous conclusions concerning the ultimate outcome.

Should older patients engage the services of an internist before surgery?

Yes. Since older people are more susceptible to postoperative complications involving organs such as the heart, lungs, liver, and kidneys, it is important that they have an expert to care for them before and after the operation.

Is an adequate oxygen supply during surgery important for older patients?

Yes. The brain, the heart, and other organs will suffer inordinately in older people if there is the slightest oxygen shortage during the operation. Extra oxygen may be needed because of diminished respiratory function in this group of patients.

How is extra oxygen administered to patients after surgery?
1. By placing in the nose a rubber tube that is attached to an oxygen tank
2. By placing an oxygen mask over the face
3. By placing the patient in an oxygen tent

Do older people tend to react differently from younger ones to preoperative and postoperative medications?
Yes. The dosage of such drugs as morphine, scopolamine, phenobarbital and other barbiturates, and atropine must be modified for older patients. Their age and weight must be given careful consideration in calculating dosages.

Is anemia a deterrent to surgery on older patients?
Since the tissues of older people are more sensitive to lack of oxygen, anemia assumes a role of great importance. Insufficient red blood cells will lead to inadequate oxygen supply to the tissues. It is therefore important that anemic patients be given blood transfusions to tide them over the operative period. After the patient has recovered from surgery, the anemia can be attacked more vigorously.

Are blood transfusions safe for older people?
Yes.

Is high blood pressure (hypertension) a contraindication to surgery in older people?
If people in their 70s or 80s have blood-pressure readings above 200, elective operations may be postponed until the pressure can be brought down to a more normal level. However, if surgery is necessary, the high pressure should not act as a deterrent. Special measures will be taken by the internist and the anesthetist so that the operation can proceed with relative safety.

Does high blood pressure increase the risks of surgery?
Yes.

Is there a greater tendency for older patients to go into surgical shock?
Naturally, they do not withstand extensive procedures as well as younger people do, and therefore have a higher incidence of shock. However, the overall incidence of shock is not great because of improved preoperative and postoperative care. Control of blood loss, maintenance of chemical and mineral balance, adequate oxygen supply, and more refined operative techniques have cut down tremendously on the incidence of this grave complication.

How is the condition of the heart checked during surgery?
By observing a continuous tracing of the heart action with a cardioscope. This instrument, which is similar to an electrocardiogram, projects a tracing of the heart's action on a screen. Deviations from normal can be seen immediately, and appropriate measures to correct them will be taken instantly.

Is liver function of particular importance in operations on older patients?
Yes. Impaired liver function is one of the most frequent causes of death from surgery.
The liver can best be supported preoperatively by giving large amounts of protein and sugar, both orally and intravenously. At the same time there should be a very low intake of fat. If the flow of bile is obstructed, as in cases of jaundice, vitamin K is given to prevent

excessive operative or postoperative bleeding.

What measures are taken to maintain liver function during the postoperative period?

Large quantities of sugar in the form of glucose are given. Also, proteins and vitamins B, C, and K may be prescribed.

What special measures are taken to aid kidney function after surgery?

The major consideration is that the patient's output of urine is adequate. Also, the chemical balance of the patient must be maintained. This will involve a constant checking of the amounts of sodium, chlorides, potassium, phosphorous, calcium, albumin, globulin, and urea that circulate in the blood or appear in the urine. Specific measures may have to be taken from time to time to increase the amount of certain chemicals or to decrease the amount of others that are present in too great concentration.

Failure of kidney function is one of the most common causes of surgical mortality in older patients.

What special preoperative measures can be taken to prevent lung complications?

1. If the patient is a heavy smoker, he should stop smoking for several days prior to admission to the hospital.

2. If a respiratory infection is present and the surgery is elective, it should be postponed until the infection has been brought under control.

3. If there is any tendency toward repeated lung infections, antibiotics should be given before, during, and after surgery.

4. The patient should be instructed that it will be necessary for him to breathe deeply and to cough up all mucus, even if these measures cause pain.

Is it common practice to keep older patients in recovery rooms after surgery?

Yes. All facilities for treating postoperative patients are concentrated in the recovery room. Such rooms have a constant supply of oxygen, drugs for postoperative patients, suction apparatus to keep the breathing passages open, and, most important of all, a staff of specially trained nurses and doctors in constant attendance.

How long are patients kept in recovery rooms?

Those with minor conditions may be kept for only an hour or two. Those who have had extensive surgery may be kept for an entire day or even for several days. Families should know of this practice in advance, so that they do not worry unnecessarily.

What can the patient do postoperatively to aid his own recovery?

1. He should breathe deeply, to expand his lungs fully.

2. He should cough up mucus, even if it causes pain in the incision.

3. He should move about in bed and get out of bed as soon as permitted. This will aid his circulation and help to prevent blood clots from forming in veins.

4. He should inform his surgeon or nurse if he has any unusual symptoms or discomfort.

5. He should force himself to eat whatever is permitted to him, even if he has no appetite.

Do older surgical patients require longer periods of postoperative bed rest?

On the contrary. It is more important that older patients get out of bed early in order to prevent complications such as pneumonia and phlebitis. The latter conditions occur more often in the older age groups.

Will physical activity after surgery delay wound healing?

No. It has been shown that wounds will heal more quickly if the patient is active after surgery.

What is early ambulation?

It means getting out of bed and walking soon after surgery. In most cases, this will be within a day or two after the operation has been performed. Such early ambulation stimulates circulation and tends to lead to better aeration of the lungs.

What preoperative precautions are necessary concerning the patient's teeth?

1. The surgeon and the anesthetist should be notified if there are any loose teeth. All too often a loose tooth will be knocked out during anesthesia, and it may be swallowed or aspirated into the windpipe. Such teeth should be removed prior to surgery.

2. Patients should inform the anesthetist about all dentures. All removable dentures should be taken out before the patient undergoes anesthesia.

3. If the surgery is elective, all decayed or abscessed teeth should be removed before the patient enters the hospital. They are frequently the source of postoperative infections.

Are special measures necessary to promote wound healing in older surgical patients?

Not if the patient is in good general health. However, if he is debilitated or undernourished, supplementary proteins and vitamins B and C may be given during the postoperative period. Also, it is well known that anemic patients tend to heal more slowly. In such cases, blood transfusions are often given preoperatively and postoperatively.

Is it important to know that the body contains an adequate vitamin supply prior to surgery?

Yes. Vitamin deficiencies may lead to poor wound healing and, in some instances, to uncontrollable hemorrhage. It is therefore common practice to give large doses of supplementary vitamins to older surgical patients.

How can one determine whether or not a preoperative patient has an adequate supply of body proteins?

By analyzing the blood to find the amount of circulating albumin and globulin. If these substances are deficient, blood will be given.

Is it important to regulate fluid intake and output when operating on an older patient?

Yes. Too much fluid may place a strain in the heart and lungs. Too little fluid may endanger kidney function. Maintaining the delicate balance between fluid intake and output is one of the most difficult problems of surgery on older people.

Do older patients find it more difficult to void after surgery?

Yes, especially while remaining in bed. Men, in particular, may find it more difficult because of enlargement of the prostate gland.

To encourage spontaneous urination, patients should be taken out of bed as soon as possible after surgery. If they still cannot void, a rubber catheter is passed into the bladder.

Are older patients more susceptible to postoperative infections?

Not if they are in good general health. However, if they are anemic, underweight, or suffer from a vitamin deficiency, they are more susceptible.

What can be done to overcome post-operative infections in older patients?

As stated elsewhere, older people respond well to the antibiotic drugs. These are often given prophylactically to those in whom one expects a possible postoperative infection.

Is it necessary for older patients to remain in the hospital longer after surgery?

Their rate of recovery might be slightly slower than that of younger patients, but this is usually a matter of a few days. Of course, if they are exceptionally debilitated and aged, the time needed for recovery will be much longer.

How soon after major surgery can most patients bathe?

When the surgical wound has healed completely. If there is an opening, or drain, in the wound, showers and baths cannot be taken.

How soon after major surgery can patients go out of the house?

By the time most patients are discharged from the hospital, they have been walking about the hospital corridors for several days. If the weather is pleasant, there is no reason why they should not go for a walk or sit out of doors when they go home.

Can older patients climb stairs after coming home from the hospital?

Yes, provided they climb only a flight or two.

How soon after surgery can the average surgical patient drive his car?

It is perhaps best for older patients to wait six to seven weeks, even though driving modern automobiles demands very little physical effort. The necessity to stop or swerve suddenly may place too great a strain on a recent surgical wound.

Is it good practice for older patients to take extra vitamins after surgery?

Yes, since appetite and food intake are often decreased after major surgery.

Is it advisable for older patients to wear a support after an abdominal operation?

This question can be answered only by the attending surgeon. It will depend on the type of operation that has been performed and on how satisfactorily the wound has healed. In many instances, an abdominal support gives the sensation of added protection even though it is not actually doing much good. When a support is worn, it is best to use an ordinary two-way elastic support. Most trusses and complicated surgical belts are rarely indicated after abdominal surgery.

Is it natural to have some pain, tingling, a sensation of numbness, and a feeling of tightness in a wound area?

Yes. Such sensations may persist for weeks or even months after an operation. Nerves and muscles are severed in surgery, and these structures may take a long time to grow together again. If wound pain becomes severe, the surgeon should be notified.

Surgery in Children

Children withstand even major surgical procedures exceptionally well. The difficulties of pediatric surgery arise more from the psychological problems than the physiological trauma. In modern hospitals the child is sure to get the best presurgical medical treatment. The parents and physicians must make sure that the child is psychologically adjusted for his experience and his separation from his mother. Parents must explain to the child beforehand, in a comforting, reassuring manner, what is going to happen, and they should spend as much time as possible with the child in the hospital.

QUESTIONS AND ANSWERS

Is surgical diagnosis usually more difficult in infants and young children than in older children?

Yes, because the pediatrician is unable to get a good history from a young child and must rely on the parents, who may not be aware of all the symptoms. The pediatrician can elicit a reliable history from an older child.

Are the risks of operations greater with infants and children than with adults?

No. Actually, most infants and children have exceptional ability to withstand major operative procedures. One of the main reasons for this is that a child's organs have not yet undergone the inevitable changes that come with aging. His brain cells are able to tolerate reduced oxygen supply during anesthesia, and his heart and blood vessels are able to withstand the added strain placed on them by major surgery. Moreover, most children bounce back and recuperate from both the anesthesia and the trauma of the operation better than adults do.

Are children able to tolerate the complications of surgery?

In many ways they are able to tolerate these complications better than adults. As an example, the liver and kidneys rarely fail in children, but the failure of these two structures constitutes a major hazard in surgery upon adults.

Can a child tolerate lengthy operations as well as an adult?

Yes, and in many instances, a child can tolerate them better, because his brain and circulatory system are better able to withstand a temporarily lowered oxygen supply.

Can surgery be performed on newborns or infants only a few weeks of age?

Yes. Newborns and young infants are able to tolerate major surgical procedures.

Is it particularly important to correct birth defects as soon as possible?

Yes. Parents are understandably reluctant to take an imperfect child home from the hospital. If it is possible to correct a defect within the first few days of a child's life, this is a wise move.

Is it wise to postpone most major surgery until an infant is several months old?

No. Usually an operation is best performed when the child is just a few weeks or months old. The younger the child is, the less well developed are his reactions to painful stimuli, the better he adjusts to changes in his environment, and the fewer psychological disturbances he has.

What is the best time to operate on a newborn who has a condition that can be repaired electively at any time?

In order to allow the various body systems to establish normal function, it is perhaps best for surgery to be scheduled when the child is three to four months of age. However, it is not a good idea to wait more than six or seven months.

Must the tissues of an infant or young child be handled with particular care during surgery?

Yes. All of the tissues are quite

fragile in a child, and for this reason, pediatric surgery has developed special instruments and techniques for children. Most surgeons will be particularly delicate in their surgical maneuvers upon children.

PREPARING THE CHILD EMOTIONALLY

At what age are children most upset by surgery?

Between the ages of 1 and 5 years. Children less than 1 year old are frequently unaware of the full nature of the trauma. Those over 5 years old can usually be reasoned with and can understand the necessity of the surgical procedure. Therefore, it is always best if elective surgery can be performed during the first few months of a child's life or postponed until he is 5½ to 6 years old and can understand what is happening. Much, of course, depends on the nature of the child. The secure and well-adjusted child will face the prospect of surgery better than will an emotionally disturbed child.

Is it necessary to prepare children emotionally for an impending operative procedure?

Yes, but very little can be done to prepare a child less than 2½ to 3 years old. Older children should be told in simple, superficial terms what is going to be done. Their questions should be answered as honestly as possible, and most important, they should not be told blatant untruths. Parents make a great mistake when they tell a child that he is going to have an x-ray picture taken instead of letting him know that he will be operated on. Of course, it is best for the parents to have a positive and casual attitude, letting the child know that there may be some pain, but that it will

not be so great that he will be unable to endure it.

Should parents emphasize the beneficial aspects of an impending operation?

Yes. It should be pointed out to the child how much better off he will be after the surgery is completed and how the operation will help him grow up normally like other children.

Should parents discuss the matter of separation during the hospital stay?

Yes. A child should know beforehand exactly how long he will be in the hospital and how many hours of the day he will be separated from his parents. The truth is the best thing to tell the child, because he can accept it better than fabrication, which may be transparent to him and disturb him.

Is it important that the parents display a good attitude?

Yes, because a child is very quick to observe emotional upset or anxiety in his parents. If he sees that his parents are markedly upset, he will reflect the same anxieties and may exaggerate them.

Should a parent be with the child throughout his entire hospital stay if this is possible?

1. Yes, if the child is especially anxious and fearful. However, children are not aware of living-in arrangements, and parents should not bring up the subject unless they are certain that the hospital will permit it.

2. No, if the child is calm and does not request or seem to require the parent's presence.

Will it help a child to know that there are recreational programs in the hospital to which he will be taken?

Yes. Many large hospitals maintain recreational facilities for children and will have programs that the child will enjoy. It is important that the parents not exaggerate or fabricate these programs, because the child may be inordinately disappointed when he discovers that what he has been told about and looked forward to is not available.

Should children be given a full explanation of what will take place during the induction of anesthesia?

Yes. This is most important, because often this is the aspect of the surgical experience that leaves the bitterest memories. Today there are many specially trained anesthesiologists who will know how to make the anesthetic experience less frightening and as painless as possible for a child.

Should parents ask the anesthesiologist to see and get to know the child a day or two before surgery?

Yes. This should be done whenever possible. Then when the child reaches the operating room he will be met by someone whom he knows and trusts. The surgeon may appear to be of secondary importance to a child, since he is usually not in the operating room when the child is being put to sleep.

PREPARING THE CHILD PHYSICALLY

What special physical preparations may a child require before surgery?

1. A child may be easily thrown out of fluid and chemical balance. This is particularly evident when he has been running high temperatures, has been vomiting, or has had diarrhea before entering the hospital. Because of this, it is frequently necessary to give a child intravenous or subcutaneous fluids with chemicals such as sodium, potassium, or chlorides.

2. It is important that a child be operated on when his stomach is empty.

If he is sent to the operating room for an emergency procedure and has just recently eaten, it is essential that his stomach be emptied with a stomach tube before inducing anesthesia. In other situations, too, especially when the abdominal organs are to be operated upon, it is necessary that a stomach tube be placed through the child's nose so that it can drain off excess gas and fluids that may have collected within the intestinal tract.

3. Since it is important to know the child's output of urine postoperatively, a rubber catheter may be placed into his bladder and left there during the operative procedure and for a day or two thereafter so that the urine can be collected in a receptacle and measured.

4. If the child has had a severe bacterial infection before surgery, the surgeon may decide to administer large doses of antibiotic drugs.

5. If the child has had a chronic illness and has been undernourished because of it, large doses of vitamins are usually administered preoperatively. These will be given either along with the intravenous fluids or separately, by injection beneath the skin.

6. If the child has lost a great deal of blood preoperatively or has been anemic because of some underlying condition, blood transfusions may be given for several days before surgery. It is always better to operate on a patient when his red blood cell mass is normal or near normal.

POSTOPERATIVE CARE

Does a child require special postoperative care?

1. If minor surgery or nonextensive major surgery has been performed, the child will require no special aftercare. It is not at all unusual for a child to

recover from the anesthesia within 2 to 3 hours and ask for something to drink. Ofter a child can tolerate fluids within 3 to 4 hours after being operated on and will want to eat some 12 to 24 hours later. After ordinary operations such as for a hernia or tonsils and adenoids, a child will be eating normally and walking about within 48 to 72 hours.

2. A child who has undergone major surgery of extensive proportions will require specialized postoperative care. It is for this reason that most large hospitals have established special areas for the intensive care of surgical patients. The specialized care will concentrate on maintaining chemical and fluid balance, since children have a tendency to become dehydrated and to get out of balance quickly. Following major surgery, the child's urinary output also will be watched carefully, because this is a guide to the adequacy of kidney function. Also, it is important that the child have an abundant oxygen supply to nourish his tissues during the postoperative period. To accomplish this, the child may be placed in an oxygen tent following an extensive major surgical procedure. To combat infection, the child may be given antibiotics for several days after the surgery. If he has lost a great deal of blood during the operation, this will be replaced by transfusions. Since the child may not resume eating within the first few days after an extensive operation, vitamins and solutions containing glucose (sugar) are often given by intravenous infusion.

Will a child ever react negatively after an operation?

Yes, if he feels he was misinformed beforehand by parents or a physician who painted too rosy a picture of the experience. Also, a child may think that some essential part of his body has been removed if he finds himself restricted and in pain postoperatively. It is essential that a child be reassured and told by his parents and physicians that he will recover and that he will begin to feel normal again once the first few days of the ordeal are over.

Is it common for a child's eating and sleeping habits to be altered following surgery?

Yes, and changes in these habits may be all out of proportion to the seriousness of the operative procedure. It is not unusual for a child to refuse his feedings and to sleep badly for several weeks or even months after hospital surgery has been performed.

Is it common for a child's behavior, personality, and habits to be different after he returns home following surgery?

Yes, this happens very often, especially in young children. In their own special way, children may resent having been put through the painful experience of surgery. A child may not completely comprehend that it was all for his own good, and he may display his resentment by behavior changes. Also, a child may develop a negative attitude toward his parents because he does not wish to show how terribly he missed them during the separation.

What can a parent do about the changes in a child's behavior after surgery?

The best treatment is love and attention. However, when the parents are certain that the child is overplaying the situation, they must guard against spoiling him and becoming too permissive. A clever parent will know how to display love without permitting the child to become a special character merely because he has undergone an operative procedure.

Will a child ever want to prolong his invalidism?

Yes. Every parent knows about children who wear bandages much longer than is necessary. This is in order to get added attention and love. The parents should find other ways of letting the child know that he is loved, and they should insist that the child resume his normal activities as soon as his condition allows.

Is it sometimes necessary to give a sedative to a child who sleeps poorly following surgery?

Yes. In some cases a child who has undergone a serious illness and whose sleep is disturbed for several weeks following surgery should be given sedatives by the physician to quiet him down.

Sympathectomy

Sympathectomy is an operation performed for the purpose of cutting sympathetic nerves that cause contraction and constriction of blood vessels. These nerves lie along the spinal column and are approached surgically through an incision either in the back or in the neck, depending upon which sympathetic nerves the surgeon intends to sever.

Sympathectomy is advised in those cases of arteriosclerosis of the lower limbs in which it is felt that release of arterial spasm will permit greater blood flow. It is also advocated in certain cases of Raynaud's disease in which there is spasm of the blood vessels to the hand and fingers. Finally, sympathectomy is indicated in certain cases of Buerger's disease in which there is a spastic element.

See also BLOOD VESSELS; BUERGER'S DISEASE; CLAUDICATION; NEUROSURGERY; RAYNAUD'S DISEASE.

QUESTIONS AND ANSWERS

What is the greatest benefit of sympathectomy?

The cutting of the sympathetic ganglia often causes arteries to relax and expand, thus permitting more blood to pass through them. In cases of arteriosclerosis where organic changes have already taken place in the arterial walls, there is often an element of superimposed spasm. Sympathectomy may release this spasm and thus improve blood supply. In severe cases of Raynaud's disease, the prime difficulty is spasm of arteries to the hand and thus the cutting of the sympathetic nerves in the neck may improve blood supply by releasing arterial spasm.

In certain isolated cases of Buerger's disease, a lumbar sympathectomy in the lower back has helped to release spasm of arteries in the legs.

Is sympathectomy a dangerous operative procedure?

No. Recovery takes place in practically all cases.

Where is the incision made for a sympathectomy in Raynaud's disease?

In the lower lateral portion of the neck. In these cases, the cervical sympathetic nerves are severed. The operation is a major one but is not associated with danger or great risk.

Where is sympathectomy performed to help a patient with arteriosclerosis of the blood vessels in the legs?

The incisions are made in the loin. Here too, the operative procedure is not dangerous although it is of major proportions.

How can one tell whether sympathectomy has improved blood supply?

1. It will be noted that the leg is much warmer following a successful sympathectomy.

2. Arteriograms (x-rays of arteries) will show the passageway to be widened if the sympathectomy has been successful.

3. Patients who have claudication as a result of arterial spasm in the legs will have less painful cramps if the sympathectomy has been successful.

4. Those who have impending gangrene of the toes or fingers will show a recession of the process following a successful sympathectomy.

Tendons

A tendon is a fibrous cord or band connecting muscle to bone. The tendon may be located within muscle substance or it may run alongside a muscle and receive the muscle fibers along its border. When the muscle contracts, the tendon pulls on the bone to which it is attached, thus causing joints to flex, extend, or rotate.

Tendons, like any other structure in the body, are subject to abnormalities or disease. Thus, there are a considerable number of birth deformities in which the tendons are abnormally shortened. Also, tendons may become infected from the spread of an infectious process from other tissues. Finally, tendons are frequently injured as a result of direct or indirect trauma. They may become severed due to a laceration, or they may be torn away from their attachment to bone because of a violent sprain or twist.

When a muscle becomes paralyzed, its attached tendon is unable to function. This has been the cause for a great deal of loss of function in such conditions as poliomyelitis, Erb's palsy, and other conditions. In such conditions,

tendon transplants have been used most effectively. This is an operative procedure in which a functioning tendon attached to a normal muscle is used in place of a tendon that is attached to a paralyzed muscle.

See also HAND.

QUESTIONS AND ANSWERS

Is clubfoot associated with tendon deformity?

Yes. In most of these cases there is a congenital shortening of the Achilles' tendon of the heel. A tendon-lengthening operation often helps to relieve this type of deformity.

Are children ever born with tendon deformities in the neck?

Yes. There is a condition known as wryneck, or torticollis, in which the tendons of the muscles in the neck are too short. This causes the head to turn to one side. Operations upon these tendons often lead to correction of the deformity.

Are tendon transplants ever necessary for a lacerated tendon?

Yes. When a flexor tendon in the palm of the hand is cut, it is often advisable to transplant a segment of tendon in its place. Such a segment is usually obtained from the palmaris longus tendon in the forearm.

Are tendon transplants for paralysis usually successful?

Yes. There has been great progress in this field, and many people are able to move limbs that formerly were incapable of motion.

Is it ever necessary to operate upon infected tendons?

Yes. A condition known as tenosynovitis sometimes occurs with collection of pus beneath the sheath that surrounds the tendon.

Is surgery ever necessary because of a thickening of the sheath surrounding a tendon?

Yes. This condition, known as sclerosing tenosynovitis, frequently occurs in the wrist at the base of the thumb. It is accompanied by great pain, but is relieved by removing the thickened portion of the tendon sheath.

Do tendons ever undergo tumor formation?

Tumors of tendons are exceedingly rare, but tumors of the sheath surrounding the tendon are not unusual. These tumors are called synoviomas and are occasionally malignant.

Can surgery repair a ruptured tendon satisfactorily?

Yes. Surgical repair of tendons, following a laceration or other injury, is highly successful in the majority of cases. It is important to know that the surgical procedure for repair of severed tendons may take several hours to perform, and an expert knowledge of anatomy is required to do these operations efficiently.

How can one tell if a tendon has been damaged?

If it is damaged, there will be inability to move a part of the body that the tendon supplied. Thus if the tendon is attached to a finger, there will be inability to move that finger.

Tennis Elbow (Epicondylitis)

Tennis elbow is a common condition in which there is inflammation of the epicondyle on the outer surface of the humerus. The epicondyle is an eminence upon a bone just above its lowermost extension (condyle). Tennis elbow results from repeated strain, as in playing tennis or some other strenuous sport. It is seen most frequently in activities requiring a twisting motion at the joint. In tennis elbow tenderness is felt on the outside of the upper armbone (humerus) just above the joint.

QUESTIONS AND ANSWERS

Is tennis elbow a common condition?

Yes, occurring not only in people who play a great deal of tennis but in those who engage in other sports in which there is a twisting motion at the elbow joint. Golfers, fishermen, baseball players, etc., are all subject to this condition.

What are the symptoms of tennis elbow?

Extreme pain located on the outer surface of the elbow joint in the lowermost extension of the upper armbone (humerus). The pain is greater on attempted use of the elbow, as in the sports mentioned above.

How long does tennis elbow usually last?

The condition may persist for several weeks, months, or years unless the individual discontinues the strains associated with his particular physical activity.

Is there satisfactory treatment for tennis elbow?

Yes, but one should discontinue the physical activity that has caused the tennis elbow. Then, the injection of Novocain and cortisone into the epicondyle of the humerus will often relieve the condition.

Are injections for tennis elbow painful?

Yes.

Is it usually necessary to give more than one injection to cure tennis elbow?

Yes, sometimes 6 to 10 injections are required to alleviate this condition.

Can x-rays demonstrate the presence of tennis elbow?

Not usually. In most cases, x-rays of the bones are normal.

Is surgery indicated in tennis elbow?

No.

Testicles, Epididymides, and Spermatic Cords

The testicles, epididymides, and spermatic cords lie within the scrotal sac beneath the penis. Sperm are manufactured in the testicles, travel through a maze of coiled tubes, the epididymis, and then travel up toward the seminal vesicles and prostate through a long tube known as the vas deferens. The arteries and veins supplying the testicles and epididymides are contained within the spermatic cord.

The principal surgical conditions affecting the scrotal contents are as follows:

1. Infections: As a result of infection in the prostate, seminal vesicles, urethra, or in some distant part of the body, the testicle and epididymis may become secondarily involved and may develop an abscess. Acute infections with abscess formation must be incised surgically, usually in a hospital under general anesthesia, or the entire contents of the one side of the scrotum will be destroyed and will have to be removed.

Tuberculosis occasionally attacks the scrotal area, usually limiting itself to the epididymis. Removal of the epididymis alone—leaving the testicle in place—is the usual procedure. Since tuberculosis has a tendency to descend to the epididymis from the prostate, both sides are often affected. To forestall such an eventuality, the vas deferens on the side opposite the infection is severed and tied off. Antituberculosis drugs are now being used most effectively to combat this disease.

Gonorrhea often attacks the epididymis and sometimes the testicle. However, these infections are being seen much less frequently since the widespread use of penicillin and the other antibiotics, and when they do take place, abscess formation can usually be prevented.

2. Injuries to the scrotal contents are not as common as one might expect in light of the exposed position of these structures. There seems to be an unconscious protective reflex which men display when injury to these parts appears imminent. However, civilian, industrial, or war injuries can crush or rupture a testicle beyond repair. In these cases, the testicle must be removed (orchiectomy). This operation is performed under spinal or general anesthesia through an incision in the scrotum. Recovery is prompt and the patient may leave the hospital within a week's time.

It is important to state that men live perfectly normal lives with one healthy testicle! There is no interference with fertility or potency and no change in sexual desire or competence on the loss of a testicle, provided the remaining one is normal.

When an injury to the scrotal sac is of lesser degree, bleeding may occur around the testicle (hematocele). This produces marked swelling and pain. Such a collection must be tapped with a needle and syringe, or if the blood cannot be removed in this way, then the hematocele must be opened and drained.

Lacerations and tears of the scrotal skin are relatively common injuries. The skin of the scrotum has truly remarkable powers of regeneration, and often the remaining skin will grow over a wide area where skin has been torn away.

3. Torsion (twisting) of the spermatic cord presents a surgical emergency as the twisting interferes with the blood supply to the testicle. If not promptly relieved, gangrene of the testicle may result. This condition is seen most often in young boys and young men. It occurs suddenly, sometimes during work or exercise, but often while at complete rest or even during sleep. Its presence is made known by pain in the groin or lower abdomen, nausea, vomiting, and painful swelling of the testicle and scrotum.

Surgery is urgently indicated and should be performed within several hours if the testicle is to be saved. Otherwise the testicle may have to be removed. The operation is a simple one, performed under spinal or general anesthesia, in which an incision is made in the scrotal area. The cord is untwisted and the testicle is carefully inspected to make sure that it is salvageable. Recovery is prompt and hospitalization lasts but a few days. The other testicle is usually fixed with sutures to the scrotal sac so that it will not twist.

4. Hydrocele is an extremely common condition in which there is a sac filled with a watery fluid surrounding the testicle. It may vary in size from that of a lemon to a large muskmelon. One or both sides may be affected and it may occur at any time from infancy to old age. No specific cause for hydrocele formation is usually apparent. The diagnosis can be made on direct inspection, by shining a light through the scrotum, or by putting a needle into the scrotum and withdraw-

ing some of the fluid. It is important to distinguish the enlargement of the sac caused by hydrocele from that caused by a solid growth of the testicle. Although hydroceles are painless, they are a source of inconvenience. Small ones need not be operated upon but can be cured in most instances by the *injection treatment*. This consists of the removal of the fluid through a needle and syringe and replacing it with a small amount of a *sclerosing agent* (a highly irritating liquid which causes the production of scar tissue and thereby obliterates the sac). Several treatments of this kind are usually required. Recurrences are seen quite often after this form of treatment, and surgery, therefore, is more often advised.

The removal of a hydrocele is a simple operation performed under spinal anesthesia through an incision in the scrotum. The sac is entered, emptied, and the major portion of the sac wall is removed. The remainder of sac wall attached to other scrotal structures is turned inside out and stitched down. Operative recovery is quick and the patient is home in a few days. Recurrences after surgery are rare.

5. Spermatoceles resemble hydroceles in their external appearance but differ in that they are cystlike structures attached to the epididymis. They are the result of blockage of one of the tiny tubes in the epididymis and they contain a milky fluid. Like hydroceles, they are harmless but may be annoying. They are best treated by complete removal through an incision made in the scrotum. The operation is a simple one and recovery is prompt and complete within a few days.

6. A varicocele is present when the veins of the spermatic cord become dilated and varicosed. It occurs, in 95 percent of cases, on the left side of the scrotum and, when examined, feels like a "bag of worms." This condition is not serious but may, in some cases, be related to sterility. Varicoceles can be left alone unless they become very large or are thought to be related to sterility. If operated upon, an incision in the groin is made under spinal anesthesia, and a block segment of the varicose veins is tied off and removed. The procedure is a simple one, with recovery within a few days.

Within recent years some urologists have come to believe that varicoceles are present in an inordinately large percentage of men who suffer from sterility. In such cases, removal of the varicocele (varicocelectomy) has frequently been followed by an increase in sperm count and an increase in male fertility.

7. Undescended testicle: During embryonic life, the testicles are in the abdomen. As the embryo matures, the testicles descend into the groin, and by the time the baby is born, they reach the scrotal sac. Failure of such descent is known as undescended testicle or cryptorchidism. One or both testicles may be involved in this process. The cause may be a mechanical interference with descent or a lack of sufficient hormone secretion. A good number of these testicles will descend spontaneously at puberty when growth—and hormone production—takes such an abrupt spurt. Others can be induced to descend by a series of injections of the appropriate hormone secretion.

Undescended testicle is often accompanied by a hernia. When the hernia is large and producing symptoms, it should be operated upon. During the hernial repair, the spermatic cord is lengthened by cutting away all fibrous tissue which tends to shorten it, and the testicle is brought down to the scrotum. If the accompanying hernia is not apparent and the undescended testicle causes no discomfort, surgery is deferred until the child reaches 9 to 10 years of age. A course of hormone injections is then given for several weeks. If descent does not follow within a few weeks, operation is performed. This age is chosen because it is felt that if the testicle is in the scrotum when puberty begins, it will develop and function best. It must be remembered that an undescended testicle does not produce sperm! Unfortunately, many of them will not do so even after they have been brought down into the scrotum.

There are many methods of performing an *orchidopexy* (operation for undescended testicle). All of the procedures are carried out under general anesthesia unless the patient is an adolescent or adult, in which event spinal anesthesia may be used. The surgery is considered major but recovery always takes place within a week to ten days unless some accidental complication arises. An incision, three to five inches long, is made in the groin, and the testicle and cord are delivered into the wound. The cord is lengthened by cutting away all the extraneous fibrous tissue throughout its entire course. Care is taken not to cut the blood vessels or the vas deferens. It has been found that fibrous adhesions are responsible for much of the foreshortening which prevents full descent of the testicle.

One method of performing orchidopexy involves bringing the testicle down and carrying it out the bottom of the scrotum through a hole. The testicle is then buried in the thigh and covered with the skin of the scrotum and the thigh. It is permitted to remain in the thigh for about three months, during which time the scrotum and the thigh are attached. (See diagram.) After three months a second operation is done during which the testicle is removed from the thigh and the scrotal skin is sutured over it.

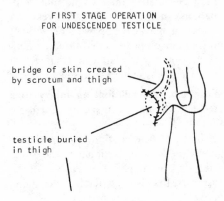

FIRST STAGE OPERATION
FOR UNDESCENDED TESTICLE

bridge of skin created
by scrotum and thigh

testicle buried
in thigh

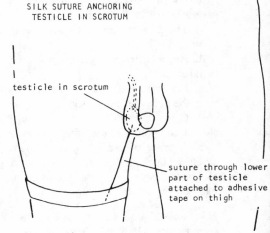

SILK SUTURE ANCHORING
TESTICLE IN SCROTUM

testicle in scrotum

suture through lower
part of testicle
attached to adhesive
tape on thigh

Another method, equally effective, merely brings the testicle down into the scrotum and holds it there by placing a strong silk suture through its inferior pole, pulling the suture out the bottom of the scrotum and anchoring it on the stretch to adhesive tape wrapped about the thigh. This suture is released at the end of a week. No further surgery is necessary. (See diagram.)

8. Tumors of the testicle are, fortunately, not common, for the great majority of them are highly malignant. They occur in about 1 of every 2,000 male hospital admissions and constitute only about 5 percent of all malignant tumors in men. Tumors have a tendency to occur more often in undescended testicles than in the normally placed organ.

The only early symptom caused by these tumors is slow, progressive enlargement of the testicle. Prompt surgical removal is imperative as these growths spread to other parts of the body at a relatively early stage in their development. Through an incision in the groin, the affected testicle along with its epididymis and spermatic cord

are removed. Glands in the groin and abdomen are also removed if spread is suspected. Some of the testicular tumors are highly sensitive to x-ray, and it is routine practice therefore to give x-ray treatments to the entire region after surgery has been performed.

Recovery from these operations is the general rule no matter how extensive the procedure has been. Cures are obtained in those cases where the testicle has been removed before the tumor has spread to distant parts of the body.

Periodic self-examination of the testicles is important in order that a growth may be detected early.

QUESTIONS AND ANSWERS

What are the symptoms and signs following an injury to the testicles?

1. There is usually excruciating pain, which may be associated with nausea, vomiting, and fainting.

2. There are marked swelling, discoloration, and redness in the scrotal sac following the injury.

What is the first aid treatment for a severe injury to the testicles?

1. The patient should be kept lying down.

2. Any constricting garments should be taken off.

3. Medication should be given to relieve the pain and the shock.

4. Cold compresses or an ice bag should be applied to the area.

5. A towel or other material should be placed beneath the scrotum to keep it elevated; it should not be permitted to hang down between the legs.

How long should an ice pack or cold compress be allowed to stay in place?

It is best to leave the ice pack or cold compress in place for 15 to 20 minutes, then to remove it for half an hour, alternating between the cold application and room temperature.

Should a doctor be consulted when a person receives an injury to the testicles?

Yes.

What are the usual causes of injury to the testicles?

A direct blow. At times, the scrotum may be caught in a squeeze as the inner surfaces of the thighs are suddenly brought together.

Are injuries to the penis or testicles very common?

No. When such injuries do occur, they frighten one to an inordinate degree. Most injuries to the penis consist of lacerations (cuts), which are treated in the same manner as lacerations in any other part of the body. Injuries involving the urethra are more serious and will necessitate more intensive treatments, including the insertion of a rubber catheter. The catheter is left in place for several days and the urethra, in most instances, will heal around it.

How can one tell if a testicle has been damaged?

As a late development, the testicle may be smaller than its normal companion. In the course of recovery, an infection may develop with or without formation of pus. Under these circumstances it is reasonable to assume that the damage is moderate to severe.

How can one tell that an injury to a testicle will not cause permanent damage?

If the testicle continues to grow normally and is approximately the same size as the opposite one, it can be assumed that it may function normally.

How long should a patient be kept in bed after sustaining an injury to the scrotum?

Until the swelling has gone down and the pain has disappeared. This may be a matter of several days, or even weeks.

What is the treatment for an injury to the testicle?

The great majority of injuries, although extremely painful, are not serious and will heal by themselves. If the testicle is badly crushed or ruptured, it must be repaired or removed surgically.

Can injury to a testicle lead to sterility?

Severe damage to one testicle may cause it to lose its ability to transmit sperm, but if the other testicle remains normal, sterility will not result.

Are injuries to both testicles very common?

No. Nature has a way of protecting these structures so that injury to both testicles is rather unusual.

TUMORS OF THE TESTICLE

What is the incidence of tumors of the testicle?

Malignant tumors of the testicle constitute about one percent of all malignant growths seen in males.

Do tumors of the testicle occur more frequently in abnormally developed testicles and in undescended testicles?
Yes.

When are tumors of the testicle most likely to occur?
In the third and fourth decades of life.

Are all tumors of the testicle malignant?
No, but malignant growths are much more frequent than benign growths.

How can one tell if a tumor of the testicle is present?
By the appearance of a slow, painless enlargement of the structure or by a nodule or change in consistency to touch.

What causes tumors of the testicle?
The cause is unknown.

What is the treatment for these tumors?
Surgical removal should be carried out just as soon as the diagnosis is made. A radical procedure is performed if the growth is malignant. This will involve irradiation and the removal of the lymph nodes that drain the testicle. Sometimes lymph nodes are removed to a high level in the abdomen.

Is x-ray treatment of value in treating tumors of the testicle?
Yes. After surgery has been performed, x-ray treatment is often employed to treat any spread of the tumor.

Is treatment with chemicals valuable for tumors of the testicle?
Yes. They are of great value in destroying metastases (spread of the tumor from its original site to another part of the body).

SEMINOMA

What is a seminoma?
A seminoma is one of the malignant tumors involving the testicle. It is, like most other tumors of this organ, first noticed because of a swelling of the scrotal area.

It is usually not possible to make a diagnosis of a seminoma merely on physical examination; thus, if the slightest doubt exists as to the presence of a testicular tumor, an exploratory operation should be performed. During this operation, an incision is made in the groin and the testicle is delivered into view. It is examined, and if it is felt that a tumor *is* present, the testicle is removed. It is far preferable to remove a testicle that might have been saved than to leave one that should have been taken out.

What leads one to suspect the presence of a tumor of the testicle?
Painless enlargement of the testicle or scrotal sac.

What is the treatment for seminoma?
1. An exploratory operation with examination of the testicle.
2. If a tumor is found, the testicle is removed.
3. After surgical removal of the testicle, x-ray radiation is given to the region of the lymph nodes that drain the testicle.

Are seminomas sensitive to radiation?
Yes. They are extremely sensitive, and for this reason, a fairly good prognosis can be given even if the tumor has spread to the regional tissues.

Are seminomas very malignant?
They are considered to be one of the less malignant forms of testicular tumor.

With early surgical treatment and post-operative radiation, can one expect to cure a seminoma?

Yes.

Must the other testicle be removed when one is involved in seminoma formation?

No.

UNDESCENDED TESTICLE

What is an undescended testicle?

During the development of the embryo, the testicles are located in the abdomen. As the embryo grows, the testicles descend into the groin, and by the time the child is born, the testicles have reached the scrotal sac. Failure of such descent or incomplete descent is called undescended testicle (cryptorchidism). This may occur on one or both sides.

If there is an undescended testicle at birth, does it mean that the testicle will remain undescended?

Not necessarily. A certain number of testicles will descend during the first year of life or during adolescence.

What medical treatment can be given in order to encourage a testicle to descend into the scrotal sac?

Hormone injections will sometimes cause the testicle to grow and to descend into the scrotal sac.

Are undescended testicles often associated with the presence of a hernia?

Yes.

What is the best time to operate upon a child with an undescended testicle?

At 9 to 10 years of age, although many surgeons feel that the child is ready for this procedure at 5.

Must surgery be performed on all children with undescended testicles?

Not if the testicle descends following a series of hormone injections.

Are operations for undescended testicle serious?

No. They are no more serious than a hernia operation.

How long a hospital stay is necessary for this procedure?

About five to seven days.

What operation is carried out for undescended testicle?

There are many methods of performing this procedure (orchidopexy). An incision three to five inches long is made in the groin, and the testicle and cord are delivered into the wound. The cord is lengthened by cutting away all the extra fibrous tissue and adhesions which may be surrounding it. The testicle is then brought down into the scrotal sac where it is anchored in place.

Will undescended testicles function normally when brought down into normal position?

Not always, since some of these glands are extremely small and underdeveloped. However, even if they fail to produce potent sperm, they will continue to secrete the important male sex hormone and thus maintain the male characteristics of the individual.

Are the results of operations for undescended testicles good?

Yes. The great majority of testicles can be brought down into the scrotal sac.

HYDROCELE

What is a hydrocele?

It is a collection of clear fluid within a membrane sac surrounding the testicle. It may also occur in the spermatic cord.

What is the cause of hydrocele?
The cause is unknown.

Does the presence of a hydrocele endanger the testicle?
No.

What is the treatment for hydrocele?
In small infants, hydroceles have a tendency to disappear by themselves. If they occur in older children or in adults, surgery is indicated.

What are the results of surgery for hydrocele?
Cure of the condition.

Is there a nonsurgical treatment for hydrocele?
Yes. The fluid within the hydrocele sac may be withdrawn through a needle, and a solution may be injected to cause the walls of the sac to become sclerosed. This form of treatment is not as efficient as surgery and may occasionally result in infection.

Do hernias and hydroceles often occur together?
Yes, and when this does happen, both conditions should be corrected surgically.

What are spermatoceles?
Spermatoceles resemble hydroceles in their external appearance but differ in that they are cystlike structures attached to the epididymis. They are the result of blockage of one of the tiny tubes in the epididymis and they contain a milky fluid. Like hydroceles, they are harmless but may be annoying. They are best treated by complete removal through an incision made in the scrotum. The operation is a simple one and recovery is prompt and complete within a few days.

TORSION (TWIST) OF THE TESTICLE

What is torsion of the testicle?
In boys and in young men, the spermatic cord and testicle may suddenly undergo a twist. This may be due to an excessively long cord, a developmental defect, or an injury.

What are the symptoms of torsion of the testicle?
There are sudden pain, marked tenderness, and swelling in the region of the testicle. If the scrotum is lifted up, there is increased pain. This helps to differentiate the condition from epididymitis. Nausea and vomiting may ensue. When the twist takes place, the blood supply to the testicle is shut off. Unless the torsion is treated promptly, the testicle may become gangrenous.

What is the treatment for torsion of the testicle?
Prompt surgery, with untwisting of the cord. In order to save the testicle, surgery should be performed within six to eight hours after onset. If, at operation, the testicle is found to be gangrenous and beyond salvage, it must be removed.

Is torsion of the testicle a serious condition?
It is serious in that it may lead to loss of one testicle, but not serious insofar as danger to life is concerned. Hospitalization for about one week is necessary.

INFECTIONS OF THE EPIDIDYMIS

Are infections of the epididymis less common than they used to be?
Yes. In years gone by, when gonorrheal infection was so poorly controlled, many infections of this structure were seen. Today, however, antibiotic therapy

has reduced the incidence of infection within the epididymis.

What are some of the causes, other than gonorrhea, for infections of the epididymis?

It is sometimes encountered after an operation upon the prostate gland, or it may follow a cystoscopic examination. It frequently follows vigorous prostatic massage which forces infected material from the prostate down the connecting duct to the epididymis.

How can one prevent infections of the epididymis?

In operations, the best way to prevent infection is to tie off and cut the vas deferens (the tube connecting the epididymis with the seminal vesicles) before carrying out any urethral instrumentation or surgery upon the prostate. In medical conditions, such as prostatitis, massage should be carried out very gently, and the patient should void after treatment.

What are the harmful effects of epididymitis?

In addition to being a very painful condition, with swelling, fever and extreme tenderness of the testicle, epididymitis is often followed by sterility if it involves both sides.

What is the treatment for acute epididymitis?

Treatment consists of bed rest, liberal fluid intake, the application of ice to the affected side, and the administration of antibiotics.

How long does the acute phase of epididymitis last?

About one week, but the swelling may not subside for several weeks.

Is surgery ever necessary for epididymitis?

Yes, when an abscess has formed. This will require drainage.

Does acute epididymitis ever become chronic?

Yes. There are cases in which the infection subsides only partially and flares up from time to time.

What is the treatment for chronic or recurring epididymitis?

The surgical removal of the epididymis.

Is epididymitis ever caused by tuberculosis?

Tuberculosis occasionally attacks the scrotal area, usually limiting itself to the epididymis. Removal of the epididymis alone—leaving the testicle in place—is the usual procedure. Since tuberculosis has a tendency to descend to the epididymis from the prostate, both sides are often affected. To forestall such an eventuality, the vas deferens on the side opposite the infection is sometimes severed and tied off. Antituberculosis drugs are now being used most effectively to combat this disease.

VARICOCELE

What is a varicocele?

A varicocele is a varicose involvement of those veins that accompany the spermatic cord.

What causes a varicocele?

The exact cause is unknown. In 95 percent of cases, it occurs on the left side.

How is a diagnosis of varicocele made?

When the physician examines the scrotum, it will feel to him like a "bag of worms."

What symptoms are caused by varicocele?

Usually none, although there may be a dragging sensation and a feeling of vague discomfort at the side of the scrotum.

Is varicocele ever associated with sterility?

Yes. Some investigators feel that it may cause sterility.

Will the removal of a varicocele sometimes cure male sterility?

Yes. There are many cases on record where the sperm count returns to normal after removal of a varicocele.

Are operations for varicocele serious?

No. They are carried out preferably through an incision in the groin. It may also be done through an incision in the scrotum.

Is there any medical treatment for varicocele?

Yes. A well-fitting scrotal support may be worn.

Is potency affected by varicocele?

No.

TESTICLES IN OLDER MEN

What are the usual changes that take place in the testicles as men age?

There is a gradual decline in the amount of male sex hormone secreted into the bloodstream and a decreasing ability to produce sperm cells. Ultimately, both of these functions come to a halt. The male's testicular changes take place slowly over a period of many years. Regardless of these physical evidences of aging, sexual desire and potency may persist long after sperm production has ceased.

What symptoms can result from lack of circulating male sex hormones?

In some men there are no symptoms. In others, the following may result:

1. Listlessness and fatigue
2. Diminished muscle tone and muscle weakness
3. Calcium loss from the bones with resultant softening (osteoporosis)

4. Mental depression with loss of zest for living

Do the above symptoms constitute a "male menopause"?

If there is such a thing, the above symptoms do constitute it. It must be stated, however, that these symptoms may never occur in some men, whereas all women sooner or later go through the menopause.

How can a man tell if he is continuing to produce live sperm?

By having a specimen of semen obtained following ejaculation. The semen is then examined under a microscope for the presence or absence of live sperm.

Will giving male sex hormone restore the ability of the aging testicle to produce live sperm?

Once a testicle has stopped producing live sperm, giving hormones does relatively little good.

What is the average age at which a man ceases to produce live sperm?

Generally, the testicles usually continue to produce live sperm until the age of 70. There are many exceptions to this, and cases have been recorded in which the testicles have continued to produce live sperm well into the 80s and 90s.

Will the administration of male sex hormone prolong the period of potency?

Only when the loss of potency is due to insufficient secretion of the male sex hormone. As stated elsewhere, the most frequent cause of loss of potency is psychological rather than physical.

Is it dangerous to give male sex hormones over a prolonged period of time?

Some authorities believe that prolonged use of sex hormones may stimulate a dormant tumor of the prostate gland to grow or to become cancerous. However, this contention is unproved.

Is it ever advisable to remove the testicles of an older man?

Yes, when there is a cancer of the prostate gland. Removal will slow down the growth and spread of the malignancy.

Will surgical removal of the testicles shorten the life-span?

No.

Does the surgical removal of the testicles always lead to the development of symptoms ascribed to deficient male hormone secretion?

No. Some investigators believe that the cortex of the adrenal glands usually takes over the secretory and hormonal functions of the testicles.

Is it possible for a man to have intercourse after his testicles are removed?

Yes, but in the majority of cases, the testicles are removed only in aged men who have already become impotent.

Will the removal of the testicles in an elderly man cause him to lose male characteristics, such as beard growth and masculine voice and appearance?

There are no resulting changes in appearance.

What is the significance of an enlarged testicle in a man past 60?

It may be due to one of the following:

1. A tumor, either malignant or benign.

2. A hydrocele, a collection of fluid in the sac surrounding the testicle.

3. An inflammation (orchitis or epididymitis).

4. A hernia that has extended down into the scrotum will give the appearance of an enlarged testicle, even though the gland is not actually enlarged.

How common are tumors of the testicle in older men?

Tumors are uncommon in this age group. Young adults are much more likely to develop testicular growths.

What is the treatment of a tumor of the testicle?

Surgical removal of the gland and its attached cord.

Is surgical removal of a testicle a serious operation?

No, but the dissection of the lymph nodes in the groin and lower abdomen that accompanies an operation for cancer of the testicle is serious. Nevertheless, recovery after surgery takes place in almost all cases.

Why are the testicles sometimes removed when a man has cancer of the prostate gland?

It has been discovered that the continued secretion of the male sex hormone will stimulate the further growth of cancer cells. By removal of the testicles, this stimulation is removed.

Tetralogy of Fallot

See HEART.

Thermography

Thermography is a new technique of photographically showing the surface temperatures of the body, based on infra-red (heat) radiation from the patient himself. Thermography has been used recently as a means of diagnosing underlying disease processes.

The thermograph is a machine that

records extremely slight variations in body temperature. It has been found that where disease exists within internal organs, the temperature of those organs is elevated. The machine therefore is placed over a particular part of the body and the temperature is recorded. If it is above that normally found in that part, disease is suspected.

The reliability of this apparatus has not yet been proved conclusively, but an amazing number of accurate diagnoses of tumor processes within deep structures of the body have been revealed through use of the thermograph.

The thermography technique is not yet in widespread use, and only a few physicians are adept at its use and interpretations of its recordings.

QUESTIONS AND ANSWERS

What are some of the conditions that can be diagnosed through thermography?

1. It has been found that some cancers of the breast will show up on thermography as "hot" areas.

2. When circulation is impaired because of hardening of an artery, as in a leg, it will show up on thermography as a "cool" area.

3. Narrowing or blockage of the main artery in the neck, the carotid artery, will sometimes show up on thermography as a "cool" area over the orbit (eye).

4. Some blood vessel tumors, especially those located beneath the skin, can be diagnosed through thermography.

5. Bone tumors sometimes can be diagnosed through thermography by noting "hot" areas.

6. Some cases of placenta previa (a serious condition in pregnancy in which the placenta is located too low in the uterus) can be diagnosed by thermography.

Is thermography a very accurate method of establishing a diagnosis?

The technique is not yet developed to a state where it is as accurate as x-rays, but it is frequently helpful, along with other diagnostic tools, in making precise diagnoses. It is probable that as the experience with thermography increases, its value as an aid to diagnosis will also increase.

Thromboangiitis Obliterans

Thromboangiitis obliterans, also known as Buerger's disease, is a chronic inflammatory condition of the arteries and veins of the lower extremities. It is found to be most prevalent among heavy smokers, is more common in men than in women, and tends to have its onset during the middle adult years. If patients with thromboangiitis obliterans continue to smoke and go untreated, gangrene of the extremities may eventually result.

See also BUERGER'S DISEASE.

Thymus Gland

The thymus gland is located in the chest beneath the breastbone. It is thought to function mainly during embryonic life and normally degenerates within a year or two after birth. Some pediatricians think that this gland has something to do with the production of antibodies, but this theory has not been proved.

Occasionally a child's thymus gland will be the seat of tumor formation, and in such instances it should be removed surgically. A child can lead a perfectly normal life without the thymus.

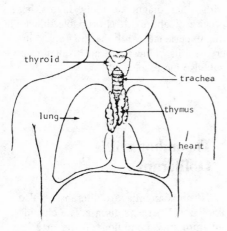

The thymus gland is located beneath the breastbone in the upper part of the chest. Its exact function has never been determined.

QUESTIONS AND ANSWERS

What is the thymus gland, and where is it located?

The thymus gland is a structure composed of cells resembling lymph node cells. It is located beneath the breastbone in the anterior part of the chest.

What is the function of the thymus gland believed to be?

Most investigators agree that this gland plays a role in the development of immunological responses. For example, it has been found that if the thymus is removed from a newborn mouse, the mouse will be able to accept transplanted organs more readily than a

mouse with a thymus. In other words, the defense mechanism of transplant rejection seems to be absent in a mouse without a thymus gland.

The thymus grows with the child until puberty and then degenerates and is largely replaced by fat tissue.

Does the thymus gland ever become enlarged?

Yes, occasionally a tumor (thymoma) of the thymus gland develops. This is a very rare condition. The gland also seems to become enlarged in certain instances where there is thyroid, pituitary, or adrenal disease. It has also been described as enlarged in cases of rickets and in a condition known as myasthenia gravis.

Should a child be x-rayed to see if he has an enlarged thymus gland?

No. This is not necessary unless the pediatrician, because of specific symptoms or findings on physical examination, suspects that the child has an enlarged thymus gland.

Does enlargement of the thymus gland ever cause sudden death in infants?

This used to be a commonly accepted theory, but it is no longer considered to have any validity.

Does an enlarged thymus ever obstruct breathing?

Most physicians today agree that an enlarged thymus plays no role in obstructing respiration.

Are thymomas dangerous tumors?

Yes, and unless they are recognized and removed surgically, they become malignant and invade other tissues.

Can an enlarged thymus gland be seen on an x-ray?

Yes. A marked enlargement will cast a shadow on the x-ray.

Should x-ray treatment be given to a child who has an enlarged thymus gland?

X-ray treatment used to be given to children with enlarged thymus glands. This form of treatment has been discontinued, since children who received such x-ray treatment seemed to have an increased tendency to develop cancer of the thyroid gland in later life.

Is it possible to remove the thymus gland surgically?

Yes. A chest surgeon can remove the thymus after splitting the breastbone and entering the chest. The operation is not very dangerous.

Will enlargement of the thymus gland cause an anesthetic death?

This is an erroneous idea. Children with enlarged thymus glands have no exceptional difficulty with anesthesia.

Can a child live without a thymus gland?

Yes. Its functions are not clearly understood. In any case, as the child reaches adolescence the gland deteriorates.

Is the thymus gland ever removed in preparation for the performance of an organ transplant?

Yes, this is occasionally done. Some people who work in the field of organ transplantation feel that the removal of the thymus will lower the chances of rejection of the organ graft. Others do not feel that this procedure is necessary prior to the performance of organ transplantation.

Thyroglossal Duct Cyst

A thyroglossal duct cyst is not an uncommon finding, especially in children. It is seen in adults, but usually makes its appearance prior to maturity. These cysts arise as a result of a developmental defect in the formation of the thyroid gland. In the embryo, thyroid tissue originates in the back of the tongue. This tissue goes down from the mouth into the neck, but on occasion some cells are left behind. It is these remnants that go on to form thyroglossal cysts.

When thyroglossal cysts are discovered, they must be removed surgically. The operative procedure is not dangerous, and the patient invariably recovers.

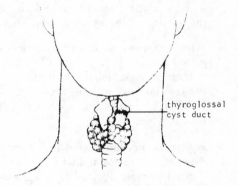

thyroglossal
cyst duct

QUESTIONS AND ANSWERS

What is a thyroglossal duct cyst?

A thyroglossal duct cyst is a swelling, usually containing a small amount of fluid, caused by a remnant of thyroid tissue that was left behind as the gland descended during the life of the embryo from its point of origin to its final anatomical location.

Where does the thyroid gland originate?

In the embryo, thyroid tissue first develops in the base of the tongue. It normally descends to its final location in the lower portion of the neck before the child is born. Sometimes, during this process of descent, small remnants of thyroid tissue are left behind, and these may subsequently form cysts.

At what age do thyroglossal duct cysts appear?

They are seen occasionally when the child is a few years of age; sometimes they may not appear before the child reaches early adulthood.

Are thyroglossal duct cysts more common in males than in females?

Yes.

How is the diagnosis of a thyroglossal cyst made?

A small swelling is seen at the junction of the chin and the neck, or in the midline of the upper or mid neck.

What symptoms are caused by a thyroglossal duct cyst?

Usually, none. However, if the cyst becomes infected, it forms what appears to be an abscess. Some may burst and discharge pus.

Is thyroid function altered in a person who has a thyroglossal duct cyst?

No. In almost all cases there is a normal thyroid gland located at a lower level in the neck.

What is the treatment for a thyroglossal duct cyst?

It should be removed surgically. The cyst will not disappear by itself.

Is surgery for the removal of a thyroglossal duct cyst dangerous?

No. There is no danger, and the results are almost invariably good if all of the cyst is removed.

What is the operative procedure for the removal of a thyroglossal duct cyst?

A transverse incision is made in the region of the cyst over the front portion of the neck. The cyst is thoroughly dissected out and is traced upward. In order to remove the entire cyst, it is usually necessary to remove a portion of the hyoid bone, which is in the upper portion of the neck.

How long does it take to perform this operation?

It usually can be done within 30 to 60 minutes.

Is it possible to remove a thyroglossal duct cyst when it is infected?

No. If it is infected, the pus must first be drained out. Then, at a subsequent date, the entire duct remnant and cyst can be removed.

Are the scars following the removal of a thyroglossal duct cyst ugly?

No, unless the cyst has been infected. In these cases, an unsightly scar sometimes does result. This can be corrected at a later date with plastic surgery.

Is there a tendency for thyroglossal duct cysts to recur?

Yes, because some of the remnants may be so small that they are not seen at the original operation and are left behind.

What is done if the patient has a recurrent thyroglossal duct cyst?

The patient should undergo another operation, and a wider dissection should be carried out to make sure that the entire duct remnant is removed.

Are the following necessary before operations for the removal of a thyroglossal duct cyst?

Blood transfusions: No
Antibiotic medications: No
Intravenous medications: No
Stomach tubes: No
Bladder catheters: No
Vitamin injections: No
Special diets: No
Other special preparations: No

Are the following necessary after operation for the removal of a thyroglossal duct cyst?

Private duty nurses: No

Antibiotic medications: Not unless the cyst was infected

Intravenous infusions: No

Blood transfusions: No

Stomach tubes: No

Special postoperative measures: No

Vitamins and tonics: No

Convalescent posthospital care: No

How soon after an operation for the removal of a thyroglossal duct cyst can a patient do the following?

Get out of bed:	1 day
Leave the hospital:	4 to 5 days
Walk up and down stairs:	1 to 2 days
Bathe or shower:	1 to 2 days
Go outdoors:	7 days
Resume all activities:	3 to 6 weeks

Thyroid Gland

The thyroid gland partially surrounds the trachea (windpipe) in the lower portion of the front of the neck. It is one of the most important organs in the human body, since it regulates metabolism—the rate and manner in which we turn food into energy, expend that energy, and get rid of our end products or wastes. Normally it is composed of three portions or lobes, one on each side of the trachea, measuring about two by one inches in diameter, and a midportion or isthmus, measuring one-half to one inch in diameter, crossing over in front of the trachea.

Absence of the thyroid, or its incomplete development at birth, leads to cretinism, characterized by a markedly retarded mentality and a dwarfed body.

Underactivity of the gland, whether accompanied by a goitrous swelling or not, in adolescent and adult life leads to overweight, lack of energy, and a slowed mental pace. Persistent overactivity of the gland in adolescent or adult life may lead to bulging of the eyes, marked weight loss, and eventually serious heart damage.

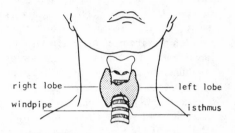

There are several forms of thyroid disease that warrant mention:

1. Colloid goiter is a diffuse, even swelling of the gland without any obvious change in metabolism or evidence of change in the patient's state of well-being. It is most common in adolescents and young adults in areas where the iodine content of drinking water and the intake of iodine in food is low. Before it was discovered in the early 1900s that the iodine lack was responsible, and before iodine was added to drinking water and to table salt, large geographic sections of our country were affected with this condition. Today colloid goiter is rather infrequently encountered.

2. Hyperthyroidism, or overactivity of the thyroid, is seen often and is usually associated with a diffuse, smooth swelling of the neck or with a localized lump within the thyroid gland. When the gland is overactive, or toxic, it manufactures too much thyroid secretion, and the metabolism becomes too rapid. Such a state makes all the organs function at too quick a pace and eventually exhausts them. A hyperthyroid condition produces weight loss, extreme nervousness, irritability, crying spells, profuse sweats, heart palpitation, tremor of the hands, and sometimes bulging of the eyes. It is seen in all age groups but is most common in young adults, especially young women.

3. **Nodular goiter,** without disturbance in function, is perhaps the commonest of all thyroid conditions and is easily diagnosed by the sight or feeling of a lump in the neck. The thyroid may have one or many pea-size lumps (nodules) or may have huge, irregular swellings the size of an orange or even a grapefruit. These *nontoxic goiters* occur in both sexes at any time during adult life. They are dangerous for several reasons: in about half of these cases the goiter will one day become toxic and cause overactivity of the gland; in other instances it may increase in size and produce pressure against the trachea; it may press against the larynx and cause hoarseness; or, most important of all, in some 7 to 10 percent of the cases, the goiter will turn into a malignant cancer.

4. **Thyroiditis.** This is a rather unusual condition in which the thyroid gland becomes inflamed. It is characterized by a painful swelling in the neck and a slight to moderate rise in temperature. Touching or pressing upon the gland will cause pain. Most cases of thyroiditis persist for a few weeks and subside spontaneously; those that do not can be brought under control by use of steroid (cortisone) medication. These inflammatory conditions of the thyroid are often called *Hashimoto's disease* and *Riedel's struma.* There are other forms of chronic inflammation of the thyroid caused by tuberculosis or syphilis, but these are seen only rarely.

Inflammation of the thyroid is not usually associated with overactivity or underactivity of secretion in the majority of cases but it does occur once in a while. Also, it is thought that certain types of inflammation may predispose to eventual cancer within the gland.

5. **Cancer** of the thyroid is seen frequently. It is estimated that 7 to 10 percent of nodular goiters are cancerous. In most instances the cancer is limited to the gland itself for a long period of time before it spreads to adjoining tissues. Thus, early removal of a malignant goiter is accompanied by an extremely high rate of cure. The most frequent type of cancer is, fortunately, the least malignant. It is called the *papillary cystadenocarcinoma* of the thyroid, and even when it has spread to the lymph nodes in the neck, cure can be obtained in most instances by a thorough removal of the thyroid and the lymph channels and nodes in the vicinity. This operative procedure is known as a *radical neck dissection.*

The less frequent type of thyroid cancer, made up of small, highly malignant cancer cells which invade all surrounding tissues, cannot be helped greatly through surgery. In a small number of these cases, radioactive iodine and/or x-ray treatments slow down the growth and spread of the disease.

Until the discovery of powerful antithyroid drugs such as thiouracil, it was necessary to operate upon most patients suffering from diffuse toxic goiter and hyperthyroidism. Now, however, surgery can usually be avoided by judicious treatment with these medications. More recently, atomic research has given us radioactive iodine, which has reduced the necessity for surgery in certain other cases of hyperactivity of the thyroid and in a limited number of cases of cancer of this gland.

Unfortunately, these newer forms of

treatment are ineffective in curing the most commonly seen goiters—namely, the nodular, nontoxic type—or the colloid type. And since the threat of toxicity or cancer transformation persists in this type of case, surgery is still the wisest and safest course of action.

Surgery for colloid goiter or for a diffusely toxic gland involves the removal of all but about 5 to 10 percent of the thyroid. The remaining tissue regenerates quickly after surgery so that thyroid function and metabolism usually return to normal within a short period of time. But even if this does not occur, underactivity can be corrected readily by taking daily doses of thyroid pills. If there are multiple nontoxic lumps (nodules), the surgeon will perform a thyroidectomy, in which most of both lobes and the midportion are removed so that only 5 to 10 percent of the gland remains. The single lumps (usually called adenomas) are treated by simple removal of the lobe in which the adenoma is located, and if the rest of the thyroid appears to be normal, it is not disturbed. When a cancer is encountered, an extensive operation is performed with the removal of the entire gland and all surrounding structures down to the great vessels of the neck and extending from the chin down to the collarbone.

Thyroid surgery today is safe and simple; death from the operative procedure, when performed by competent surgeons in good hospitals, is practically unknown. The patient is usually given a general anesthesia, and if he is particularly apprehensive, as in cases of hyperthyroidism, he may be put to sleep in his bed before embarking upon the trip to the operating room.

An incision about four inches long is made across the lower portion of the neck paralleling the normal folds of the

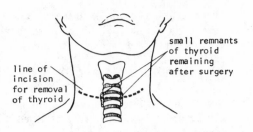

line of incision for removal of thyroid

small remnants of thyroid remaining after surgery

skin. The muscles of the neck are separated in the midline and the gland is brought up into the wound. Removal of the necessary portion of the gland is then readily performed by clamping off the blood vessels first and then cutting the tissue. Although the neck may be quite sore and painful for a couple of days afterward, recovery from thyroid surgery is extremely rapid. Skin stitches or clamps can be removed within two or three days, as the neck is one of the most rapidly healing parts of the body. Most patients are out of bed the day after operation and are ready for hospital discharge anywhere from three to six days later.

See also EXOPHTHALMIC GOITER; GOITER; HASHIMOTO'S DISEASE.

QUESTIONS AND ANSWERS

Is the thyroid one of the endocrine glands?

Yes. It secretes the hormone called thyroxin.

What is the function of the thyroid hormone?

It regulates the manner and rate at which body tissues utilize food and chemical substance for the production of energy. It is also concerned with the elaboration of body heat and muscular energy, body growth and development, and distribution and storage of body water and salt.

What symptoms occur when there is an absence of the thyroid gland or when it functions underactively (hypothyroidism)?

1. Its incomplete development or absence at birth leads to a condition known as cretinism. This condition is characterized by a markedly retarded mentality and a dwarfed body.

2. Milder inactivity and underfunction of the gland, in either adolescence or adult life, may lead to overweight, lack of energy, and a slowed mentality,

What happens when there is persistent overactivity of the gland (hyperthyroidism)?

This condition may lead to bulging of the eyes, marked weight loss, nervousness, irritability, and eventually serious heart damage.

How does one determine the activity of the thyroid gland?

A complicated chemical test, known as the T4 test, is frequently performed to determine the state of activity of the gland. Perhaps the most frequently used test today is the radioactive iodine uptake test (RAI). This test, being much more reliable, has replaced the old basal metabolic rate (BMR) and the protein-bound iodine (PBI) tests.

Is the cause for malfunction of the thyroid gland known?

It is thought that the disturbances in the function of this gland are caused either by the effect of the pituitary gland upon the thyroid, or by disturbances within the thyroid gland itself.

What is the basal metabolic rate?

This is a breathing test which determines the relative rate of oxygen consumption by the body as a whole in the resting condition. A high BMR indicates excessive thyroid gland activity,

as in hyperthyroidism. A low BMR may indicate underactivity of the gland, hypothyroidism.

How is a basal metabolism test performed?

The patient comes to the doctor's office early in the morning, before he has had breakfast. He is put at complete rest and then breathes pure oxygen through a tube placed over the nose and mouth.

How is a protein-bound iodine determination made, and what is its significance?

This is a test performed by chemical analysis of blood, and is even more reliable as an indicator of thyroid function than the BMR test.

What is a goiter?

A goiter is a swelling or enlargement of the thyroid gland.

What is thyroiditis?

An inflammatory reaction within the gland, caused by either bacteria or viruses. Recent studies have shown that a significant percentage of these cases are really caused by autoimmune mechanisms. In other words, for some unknown reason the individual starts to produce antibodies which attack his own thyroid gland.

Is thyroiditis a rare condition?

No, it is more common than previously suspected.

What are the symptoms of thyroiditis?

Fever, pain and tenderness in the neck over the region of the gland, hoarseness, and discomfort upon swallowing.

What is the treatment for thyroiditis?

This varies in different types of cases. The majority get well without treatment. In recent years cortisone has been used to alleviate the discomfort and limit the damage to the thyroid gland. At times, antibiotics or x-ray therapy are used. Only occasionally is it necessary to perform surgery for complications of this condition.

SURGERY OF THE THYROID GLAND

When is it necessary to operate upon the thyroid gland?
  1. When the goiter presses upon the windpipe or causes continued hoarseness.
  2. When the hyperthyroidism (overactivity of the gland) continues despite thorough treatment with iodine and the antithyroid drugs.
  3. When the thyroid has one or more isolated nodules (lumps) which can be felt by the physician. Surgery is advised in these cases because some of these lumps may be cancerous. Also, some may become toxic.

When is it possible to avoid surgery in thyroid disease?
  1. When a simple colloid responds satisfactorily to the intake of iodine.
  2. When diffuse hyperthyroidism responds satisfactorily to the taking of the antithyroid drugs.
  3. When there is a recurrent hyperthyroidism after surgery and there is satisfactory response either to the antithyroid drugs or to radioactive iodine.

Is special preparation necessary before a thyroid operation?
  Yes, if the gland is overactive because of a goiter. In this event, the giving of proper doses of iodine and the antithyroid drugs will precede surgery in order to bring the basal metabolic rate down to normal. No special preparation is necessary before an operation upon a simple colloid goiter or a nontoxic nodular goiter.

Is it possible to tell before operation whether a nodule in the thyroid is cancerous?
  In the great majority of cases, the surgeon can make a correct diagnosis. However, the most accurate diagnosis can be made by the microscope after removal of the lump.

What harmful effects can there be if a diseased thyroid is not operated upon?
  1. An enlarged simple goiter may cause dangerous compression of the windpipe and an inability to breathe properly.
  2. The continuation of the toxic effects of an overactive gland will cause serious and irreparable damage to the heart.
  3. As mentioned previously, 7 to 10 percent of the small nodular goiters might be cancerous.

Is it usual to have a frozen-section biopsy examination of a thyroid gland while the patient is being operated upon?
  Yes. Whenever there is the slightest doubt as to whether a goiter is benign or malignant, the surgeon will ask the pathologist to examine the tumor under the microscope while the patient is being operated upon.

What procedure is carried out if, during surgery, the thyroid is found to be malignant?
  The surgeon will then remove the involved lobe of the thyroid gland completely, rather than leave a small amount of the malignant tissue behind. He may also dissect any involved lymph nodes out of the neck.

Does a goiter ever come back after operation?
  A nodule once removed does not come back, but in about 5 percent of those cases in which the entire gland is overactive, recurrence of the hyperthy-

roidism takes place. Also, new nodules may develop in parts of the gland that were not removed. In such cases, the use of radioactive iodine has been found most effective.

Can anything be done to prevent a goiter from recurring?

Yes. The incidence of recurrence is diminished greatly by giving the patient thyroid pills each day. In order to assure that no recurrence takes place, it is necessary for the patient to take these pills indefinitely.

Are thyroid operations dangerous?

No. They may be classified as simple major operative procedures with very little risk.

Is this a painful operation?

No, although there may be a certain amount of discomfort in the neck and some difficulty in swallowing for a few days after surgery.

Are thyroid operation scars very noticeable?

Usually not. In many cases it is impossible to find a scar a year or two after operation. The surgeon will always attempt to make his incision in one of the natural skin lines of the neck.

Does the surgeon usually remove the entire gland when performing a thyroid operation?

No, except when operating for a known cancer. It is customary to remove about 90 percent of the gland and allow the remainder to carry on with normal thyroid function.

Can the remnant of the thyroid, after surgery, carry out satisfactory thyroid function?

Yes. There is some regrowth of the remnant of gland which permits perfectly normal thyroid function.

How long does the operation take to perform?

Anywhere from three quarters of an hour to two and a half hours, depending upon the size of the goiter and how much of the gland is to be removed.

What kind of anesthesia usually is given?

A general inhalation anesthesia, although occasionally, when a toxic patient is too sick to withstand a general anesthesia, local anesthesia may be given.

Are the wounds drained after thyroid operations?

Yes, and there may be leakage of serum for a few days postoperatively.

Are special postoperative measures necessary?

Usually not, unless there was marked hyperthyroidism preoperatively. The patient is usually out of bed the day after surgery and special nurses can be dispensed with after a day or two.

What are the results of removing the thyroid gland?

In almost every type of thyroid operation, the results are excellent, with disappearance of the symptoms within a few days.

What are the immediate aftereffects of thyroid surgery?

If the procedure was performed for overactivity of the gland, all the unpleasant symptoms disappear within a matter of days. No patients are more grateful for their surgical result than sufferers from hyperthyroidism. Even the damaged heart returns to normal function in many cases.

Occasionally an overactive gland will become underactive after surgery. In this event, the patient may gain weight markedly and develop all the symptoms of lack of thyroid function. This condition can be relieved by giving thyroid pills.

There are no ill aftereffects from the removal of single or multiple nodules, but breathing may be benefited if there had been preoperative pressure on the trachea.

Will the bulging of the eyes disappear after thyroid surgery?

It may recede somewhat, but if there has been marked bulging before surgery, a good measure of it will remain.

Will a patient with an overactive gland gain weight after surgery?

Yes.

Will all patients gain weight after removal of the thyroid?

Not if some of the gland has been left behind and not if thyroid pills are taken postoperatively.

Does the removal of the thyroid affect one's sex life?

No, even though the thyroid is an important endocrine gland. Irregularities of menstruation in women are sometimes caused by thyroid imbalance, and corrective surgery may result in reestablishment of the normal cycle.

Are there permanent voice changes after a thyroid operation?

No. Occasionally, however, it is necessary to disturb the nerve going to the larynx when removing a thyroid. If this has been necessary, hoarseness or voice changes may result for several weeks or even months.

How long a convalescent period is usually necessary after thyroidectomy?

Approximately three weeks.

Is there any way to prevent the return of a lump in the thyroid?

Yes. Many physicians believe that the giving of thyroid tablets for an indefinite period of time after surgery will prevent the recurrence of a lump. The thyroid tablet suppresses overactivity of the gland.

How soon can one smoke after surgery?

Because the throat is often sore after thyroid surgery and because coughing would cause considerable pain, it is recommended that patients not smoke for a week or two.

Can cancer of the thyroid be cured by surgery?

Many cancers of the thyroid have been permanently cured by removing the gland.

Is there much deformity after a radical neck dissection for cancer of the thyroid?

No. The operated side may appear somewhat thinner than the opposite side but the scars are not very disfiguring.

How long a hospital stay is necessary for thyroid surgery?

Approximately four to seven days.

How long does it take for a thyroid wound to heal?

Approximately a week to ten days.

Can one return to a completely normal life after removal of the thyroid?

Yes.

Can a woman permit herself to become pregnant after cure of a thyroid condition?

Yes.

Will the following symptoms disappear after surgery for hyperthyroidism?

Tremor of the hands? Yes
Nervousness and irritability? Yes
Palpitation of the heart? Yes
Excessive appetite? Yes
Difficulty in breathing? Yes
Hoarseness? Yes

Pressure in the neck? Yes
Bulging of the eyes? Probably not

Should one return for periodic checkups after thyroid surgery?
Yes, about once every six months.

How soon after thyroid surgery can one do the following?

Bathe:	3 to 5 days
Walk outdoors:	5 to 6 days
Climb stairs:	3 to 5 days
Perform household duties:	2 to 3 weeks
Drive a car:	4 weeks
Have sexual relations:	5 to 7 weeks
Return to work:	4 weeks
Resume all activities:	4 to 6 weeks

THYROID GLAND IN CHILDREN

Are children ever born with their thyroid glands missing or underactive?
Yes, this condition does occur every once in a while. The absence or incomplete development of the thyroid at birth may lead to a condition known as cretinism.

What are the characteristics of cretinism?
Usually the condition cannot be recognized until the child is three or four months old, when it is noted that he has difficulty with his feedings, is constipated and sluggish, and lacks interest in his surroundings. The child may have a particularly large tongue, which sometimes interferes with respiration or causes noisy breathing. The child's abdomen is large, his temperature is usually below normal, and his skin, particularly around the hands and feet, is cold and mottled. These symptoms and signs progress, and after a few months it will be noted that the child is retarded both mentally and physically.

When does the diagnosis of cretinism become obvious?
When the child is anywhere from 6 to 12 months old. By this time, it is apparent that his growth is stunted. His extremities are short and his head seems to be larger than normal. Also, his eyes appear to be far apart and the bridge of the nose is flattened and wide. The child's mouth is usually kept open, and his broad tongue protrudes from it. Teeth erupt very late and do not appear normal in consistency and shape.

Is cretinism more common in girls than in boys?
Yes. It occurs approximately three times more often in girls than in boys.

Is cretinism inherited?
There is no definite proof that it is inherited, but it is seen every once in a while in more than one child in a family.

How can a diagnosis of cretinism be made?
There is a test on the blood, known as the protein-bound iodine (PBI) test, that is a reliable measurement of thyroid function. There is a markedly reduced amount of protein-bound iodine in cretins.

What is the treatment for cretinism?
Thyroid extract must be given to replace the thyroxin that the gland fails to produce.

How soon should thyroid extract be given to a child with cretinism?
Just as soon as the diagnosis is made. The sooner the medication is started, the better will be the growth and development of the child.

Will the giving of adequate quantities of thyroid hormone overcome the deficiency?
Not completely. Treatment will result in more normal physical growth and

development, but mental development does not always improve. Only about 50 percent of hypothyroid children reach a normal mental state. Mental development will be improved most if the child has a mild case of hypothyroidism and is given supportive doses of thyroid extract early enough.

Must the thyroid extract be given through the child's entire life?

Yes, because as soon as it is stopped, the thyroid will again become inactive.

How can a pediatrician tell if a child's thyroid gland is becoming less active?

The child may develop obesity, thickening of the skin, constipation, and lethargy, and he may show a decreased mental alertness. There may also be a slowing down of his growth processes. Tests such as the PBI test will demonstrate underactivity of gland function.

Is obesity always a sign of an underactive thyroid?

No. On the contrary, most cases of obesity in children are caused by overeating and *not* by underactivity of the thyroid.

Can children who develop hypothyroidism be helped if they are given thyroid extract?

Yes. The older a child is when he first develops a thyroid deficiency, the better will be the results following the administration of thyroid extract.

Are children ever born with goiters?

Yes. If the mother did not take sufficient iodine into her body while she was pregnant, her child may be born with a goiter.

Are most goiters in children due to an iodine deficiency?

Yes. These goiters are called diffuse colloid goiters.

What is the most common cause of an iodine deficiency?

Inadequate quantities of iodine in the drinking water.

In what sections of the United States is the water deficient in iodine?

In the regions surrounding the Great Lakes and certain areas in the Northwest. (There are also some mountainous areas in Europe where the water is deficient in iodine content.) In areas of the United States that are near the sea, there is always sufficient iodine in the fresh drinking water to prevent goiter in an otherwise normal child.

Do children with goiters secondary to iodine deficiency usually show underactivity of the thyroid gland?

No. Most of these children secrete a normal or just slightly less than normal amount of thyroid hormone.

What is the treatment for goiter in a child?

Surgery is not often necessary unless the child has a nodular goiter. The water should be iodized, or if this is not possible, the child should be given tablets containing iodine once a week until the thyroid returns to normal size.

Are nodular goiters seen very often in children?

No. They are much more common in adults. When they do occur in children, they are seen in adolescent girls.

Do nodular goiters ever cause overactivity of the thyroid gland, and do they ever result in tumor formation?

Yes, and for these reasons, most physicians recommend their surgical removal.

Do adolescent girls ever develop goiters?

Yes, but this type is rarely associated with an inadequate iodine intake. It is thought by some investigators that during adolescence there is a need for more thyroid hormone and that the gland becomes larger in order to supply more of the substance to the growing body. The enlargement is, in these cases, regular and diffuse.

What treatment should be given to an adolescent girl who has a diffuse goiter?

She should be given thyroid extract in sufficient quantities to supply her body's needs. In the majority of these cases of adolescent goiter, the taking of supplementary thyroid extract is effective and there is no need to resort to surgery.

Do children often develop overactivity of the thyroid?

No. It is estimated that hyperthyroidism occurs 100 times more often in adults than it does in children.

What is done for a child who does not respond to any medical treatment for overactivity of the thyroid?

Part of the thyroid is removed surgically (subtotal thyroidectomy).

What may cause hyperthyroidism in a child?

A severe shock, a severe emotional upset, or a severe acute infection often precipitates an attack of hyperthyroidism. Sometimes the cause is unknown.

What is the treatment for hyperthyroidism in a child?

1. Attempts should be made to bring the condition under control by giving the child antithyroid drugs. The drug most frequently used is propylthiouracil.

2. Sedative drugs such as phenobarbital are given to calm down the child and control excitement and irritability.

3. The child must be kept at rest and given high-calorie, nourishing foods in the quantities he demands.

Do most children respond to medical treatment for overactivity of the thyroid?

Yes, but it may take several months to a year until all evidence of overactivity has abated.

Is it ever necessary to operate on a child who has an overactive thyroid?

Yes, when it is obvious that the medical treatment will not bring about a remission or when a nodular goiter persists.

Does radioactive iodine ever cause an overactive thyroid to return to normal?

Yes, but this drug is not recommended for a child, as no one can foretell what permanent harmful effects the radioactive drugs might have on the child as he grows older.

THYROID GLAND
IN OLDER PEOPLE

Is thyroid function usually slower in older people?

To a certain extent. However, older people tend to need less energy and are less active physically. The gland does continue to produce sufficient hormones throughout the life-span.

How can one tell if the thyroid is underactive in an older person?

This condition, called hypothyroidism, evidences itself in the following manner:

1. There may be a uniform swelling in the neck, due to thyroid enlargement.

2. There is a tendency to gain weight, even though the appetite may not increase noticeably.

3. The tissues tend to become waterlogged, particularly the tissues directly beneath the skin. When the skin over the legs or arms is pressed down, the tissues fail to rebound to the surface, and "pitting" (depression) appears.

4. The patient is constantly fatigued, lacks energy, and feels cold even in warm weather.

5. The skin becomes dry and scaly, and perspiration is slight, even in hot weather.

6. If the patient is female, there may be cessation of menstruation and inability to conceive.

7. The pulse rate slows to 40 to 50 beats per minute.

8. The blood pressure may drop below normal.

9. If a patient is suspected of having hypothyroidism, a radioactive iodine (RAI) test is performed. The results will demonstrate whether or not there is underactivity of function and to what degree.

10. By doing a chemical test of the blood known as an "iodine-uptake test," a physician can tell whether the thyroid is underactive, overactive, or is functioning normally.

Do older people often develop hypothyroidism?

There may be some underactivity of thyroid function due to aging, but hypothyroidism to a degree sufficient to cause the symptoms listed above is uncommon.

Do older people frequently develop overactivity of the thyroid gland?

No. Hyperthyroidism is uncommon, although older people do occasionally develop goiters with overactivity of gland function. This condition is seen more often in young adults.

What is an apathetic goiter?

This is an unusual condition in which older people are apathetic and appear to have underactivity of the thyroid but, in actuality, have overactivity of the gland. The diagnosis may be difficult to make because the gland swelling is often negligible, and the symptoms are not characteristic of an overactive thyroid. A T3 test or an iodine-uptake test will confirm the diagnosis.

Does the thyroid often form a goiter in older people?

It is not as common as in younger adults, but it does occur.

Is it dangerous for older people to take thyroid hormone tablets without the advice of a physician?

Yes. This is a most powerful hormone and should never be taken unless a doctor has prescribed it. Thyroid tablets can cause overactivity of gland function and may cause considerable damage to the heart. It is especially dangerous for older people whose heart muscle is already weakened by arteriosclerosis.

Will the removal of the thyroid (thyroidectomy) shorten the life-span?

No. If the operation is carried out successfully—as almost all operations on the thyroid are—there will be no undesirable aftereffects.

What are the indications for surgery on a goiter in a patient who is past 60?

1. When the thyroid is markedly overactive and is causing damage to the heart

2. If the patient has not responded to the administration of radioactive iodine or to the antithyroid drugs

3. If a goiter has grown to such size that it compresses the windpipe and interferes with normal breathing

4. If a quiescent nodule that has been present in the gland for years begins to grow

5. In any case in which the surgeon suspects that cancerous changes may be developing

Does treatment of the thyroid gland ever benefit older people who have heart disease?

Yes. If the heart disease is associated

with overactivity of the thyroid, the administration of radioactive iodine may result in great improvement. Even if the heart condition is not accompanied by an overactive thyroid, radioactive iodine therapy may prove beneficial. It will cause the thyroid to become underactive, thus lowering metabolism and creating a situation in which fewer demands will be made on the heart muscle. This form of treatment is especially helpful to some older people who suffer from angina pectoris or coronary arteriosclerosis.

Tongue

See LIPS, MOUTH, AND TONGUE.

Tonsils and Adenoids

The tonsils are two masses of gland-like substance normally measuring about one and one-half inches long by three-fourths inch wide. They are embedded in the side of the throat (pharynx) just behind and above the level of the tongue. When uninflamed and shrunken, they may be small and barely visible. When

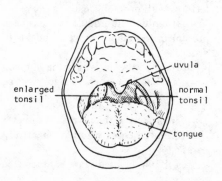

acutely infected, they may appear to occupy the major part of the pharynx and, in fact, they may almost meet in the midline.

The adenoids, consisting of the same type of tissue as the tonsils, are normally about half the size of the tonsils, but they, too, can grow to several times their usual dimensions. They cannot easily be seen through the open mouth, as they lie on the back of the throat above the level of the soft palate.

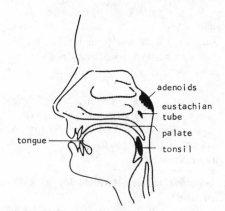

Acutely inflamed tonsils cause sore throat, high fever, and swelling of the glands in the neck. If the infection becomes chronic it may act as a focus of infection and lead to disease in other organs such as the eyes, joints, muscles, kidneys, or even the heart. Enlarged and infected adenoids may cause infection of the sinuses, obstruction of the air passage to the inner ear with consequent ear infection and loss of hearing, or by their very size they may interfere with normal respiration.

When such a condition occurs the patient develops into a "mouth breather." If this condition is permitted to go uncorrected, facial changes may occur with the upper lip being pulled upward and the face taking on a stupid, languid expression.

Normally tonsil and adenoid tissue tends to shrink after the tenth year of life. This is particularly true of the adenoids, so that by the time maturity is reached, they rarely cause any disability. This explains why tonsillectomy in adults is usually performed without adenoidectomy. In children, on the other hand, the tonsils and adenoids are removed at the same time.

See also QUINSY SORE THROAT.

QUESTIONS AND ANSWERS

What are the tonsils, and where are they located?

The tonsils are masses of glandlike tissue normally measuring about one to one and a half inches in height and one half to three quarters of an inch in width. They are embedded in the sides of the throat just behind and above the back of the tongue.

What are the adenoids, and where are they located?

The adenoids consist of the same type of glandlike tissue as the tonsils and are normally about half the size of the tonsils. They cannot be seen when the mouth is open, because they lie on the back wall of the throat above the level of the soft palate.

What is the function of the tonsils and adenoids?

Most investigators feel that they serve as a barrier that localizes and gives immunity to infections that enter the body through the mouth and nose. However, once they have become chronically infected, they lose this ability, and it is then that their removal is advised.

Do tonsils and adenoids tend to become smaller as the child gets older?

Yes. After the tenth year of life, if they are not chronically infected, they will begin to shrink, so that by the time the child has matured, they rarely cause disability.

What is acute tonsillitis?

Acute tonsillitis is an acute infection of the tonsils caused by a streptococcus or other bacterial organism.

How common is tonsillitis in children?

Tonsillitis is one of the most common acute infections seen in children.

At what age can a child develop tonsillitis?

At any age.

What are the symptoms of acute tonsillitis?

1. Sudden rise in temperature, often accompanied by a shaking chill
2. A sore throat with pain on swallowing
3. Enlargement of the lymph nodes in the neck
4. Weakness, loss of appetite, and malaise
5. Marked perspiration

Is acute tonsillitis preceded by an upper respiratory infection?

Usually not. It comes on without warning and without any preceding infection.

How is the diagnosis of tonsillitis made?

By directly inspecting the tonsils. They are enlarged, inflamed, and reddened, and they may have small yellowish areas of pus on them. Each little spotty area, or follicle, measures no more than about one sixteenth to one eighth of an inch in diameter.

Do adults ever get acute tonsillitis?

Yes, and its characteristics are the same as in children.

What are some of the complications of acute tonsillitis in adults?

Adults may develop acute rheumatic

fever although it is less common than in children. However, adults may develop arthritis or kidney inflammation secondary to severe tonsillitis. They may also develop an abscess around the tonsils.

Is it easy to distinguish acute tonsillitis from diphtheria?

Yes. Diphtheria tends to form a diffuse, grayish, shaggy membrane, whereas acute follicular tonsillitis is characterized by little yellow dots of pus. Moreover, when the tonsils are swabbed with a piece of cotton and the material is cultured, it is discovered that a germ other than the diphtheritic bacillus is causing the infection.

Should a physician be called if one suspects that he has tonsillitis?

Yes, by all means. It will be necessary for him to medicate the patient with the appropriate antibiotics or chemotherapeutic drugs. These are prescribed not only to clear up the infection, but to prevent it from affecting other parts of the body.

How serious is acute follicular tonsillitis?

Although the patient is extremely ill for a period of three to four days, he almost always recovers without complications if he is treated promptly by a physician.

What is the treatment for acute follicular tonsillitis?

1. Absolute bed rest
2. Large fluid intake
3. Aspirin and other medications to relieve the sore throat and pain
4. Appropriate antibiotic medications, such as penicillin or one of the other antibiotic drugs, or one of the sulfa medications
5. Application of cold compresses to the neck to relieve discomfort

Must a person with acute tonsillitis be hospitalized?

No. Treatment at home is adequate.

Should a person with acute tonsillitis be isolated from others in the family?

Yes. Although the disease is not actually contagious, it may spread to others through cough droplets and sputum.

Does acute tonsillitis often spread from one child to another in the family?

No.

Is there any way to prevent anyone from getting acute tonsillitis?

If a person has had previous tonsil infections, it is wise to perform a tonsillectomy. This, of course, will prevent another attack of tonsillitis.

Do people ever contract acute tonsillitis a second time?

Yes. Once the tonsils have become infected, they have a tendency to become reinfected.

What are some of the complications of acute tonsillitis in children?

Children who have had frequent attacks of acute tonsillitis are more prone to develop rheumatic fever, a disease thought to be associated with a streptococcal infection. Also, children who have had a severe attack of tonsillitis may develop kidney infections such as acute glomerulonephritis. Some investigators feel that the heart-valve diseases that cause cardiac murmurs are sometimes secondary to acute follicular tonsillitis.

Can a chronic infection of the tonsils cause disease elsewhere in the body?

Yes. Toxins from the tonsils can spread into the blood and create difficulty with the eyes, the muscles, and the joints as well.

Should a person who has had an attack of acute tonsillitis be subjected to tonsillectomy?

Yes, but not at the time of the acute infection. It is necessary to allow several weeks to pass before performing the tonsillectomy.

What is the harm of performing a tonsillectomy during or shortly after an attack of acute tonsillitis?

If the tonsils are removed when they are acutely infected, bacteria may spread into the lymph channels and bloodstream.

Do abscesses ever form within the tonsils or near the tonsils?

Yes. Abscesses within the tonsils, or alongside the tonsils, are not uncommon in severe infections. This type of abscess is called quinsy sore throat.

How is a quinsy sore throat diagnosed?

There may be difficulty in opening the mouth widely, and on opening the patient's mouth, one will see a tremendous swelling of the tonsils and of the neighboring soft palate. Furthermore, the patient's voice will be altered because a portion of the pharynx will be blocked by the abscesses. In addition, pressure over the swollen area will cause severe pain. The patient will develop a high fever in such a case. Often, the swelling is limited to one side.

What is the treatment for quinsy sore throat?

Intensive antibiotic treatment may prevent the formation of an abscess in the tonsillar region. If, however, an abscess does form, it is essential that an incision be made into it and the pus be allowed to drain.

What are the possible complications of chronic infections of the adenoids?

They can cause sinus infections; obstruction to the passage of air through the eustachian tubes to the ears, with consequent ear infection and loss of hearing; and, finally, interference with normal breathing through the nose.

TONSILLECTOMY AND ADENOIDECTOMY

Each year, millions of children and adults undergo tonsillectomy. It is estimated that tonsil and adenoid removal is the most commonly performed procedure in all of surgery. Until recently, it was routine practice to recommend tonsillectomy and adenoidectomy for all children when they reached the 3- to 5-year age group. Now, however, the medical profession has become more conservative and advises the procedure only when the tonsils have become chronically infected or when diseased adenoids give rise to nose or ear complications.

Tonsillectomy is one of the safest of all surgical operations requiring general anesthesia. Nevertheless, there are complications that must be guarded against and that demand expert handling when they develop. Postoperative bleeding, either within the first 12 hours after operation or several days later when the scab comes off the tonsil bed, is the most troublesome complication and is found in approximately 1 of every 25 cases. Parents should be alerted to look for excessive spitting or vomiting of blood during these periods. The bleeding can be controlled readily by the surgeon and rarely recurs once it has been stopped.

How common an operative procedure is the removal of the tonsils and adenoids?

It is estimated that tonsillectomy and adenoidectomy are the most frequently performed procedures in all of surgery.

Are the tonsils and adenoids usually removed at the same time?

Yes.

Are these operations being performed now as regularly as they once were?

No. Otolaryngologists and pediatricians have become more conservative, and they advise these procedures only for specific reasons and not as a general rule.

What are the indications for removing tonsils?

1. Recurrent ear infections
2. Recurrent tonsillitis and sore throat
3. Chronic breathing obstruction
4. Diseases of the kidneys, heart, muscles, or joints that are suspected of being influenced by infected tonsils or adenoids

Should tonsils be removed just because they are enlarged?

No. If they are not infected, their size is of little importance.

Will removal of the tonsils decrease the number of colds and ear infections that a person gets?

In most instances, yes. However, if the tonsils are small and not infected, the occurrence of frequent colds is not a sufficient reason for removing them.

Will enlarged and infected adenoids increase the incidence of middle ear infections?

Yes. In addition, the excess growth of adenoid tissue may block the eustachian tubes and prevent adequate replacement of the air in the middle ear. This may interfere with the function of the middle ear and impair hearing.

Will the removal of chronically infected tonsils and adenoids improve a person's hearing?

Yes, if the hearing has been impaired because of infection in these structures.

At what age can a child have his tonsils removed?

Since the present practice is to remove tonsils and adenoids only for specific indications, they obviously should be removed at any age at which they cause difficulties. If the operation is elective, the older the child is, the better.

At how early an age can tonsils be removed?

It is always best to delay removal of tonsils until the child is about 2 years old.

Can young children withstand the removal of tonsils and adenoids as well as older children?

Yes.

What is the relation of deafness to diseased tonsils and adenoids, and what improvement, if any, can be anticipated from surgery?

Enlarged and infected adenoids may cause recurrent middle ear infection, and in this way cause impairment of hearing. In addition, adenoidal tissue near the opening of the eustachian tube, by mechanically obstructing the tube, may cause a faulty replacement of the air in the middle ear. In this way, the function of the middle ear is interfered with and hearing ability is impaired. Removal of chronically infected or enlarged adenoids will frequently cause a marked improvement in hearing in a child under 12 years of age.

Is the procedure for tonsillectomy and adenoidectomy a dangerous one?

The removal of tonsils and adenoids is considered to be one of the safest of all surgical operations. Danger is only that associated with anesthesia and postoperative hemorrhage.

Should tonsils be removed in a hospital or in a doctor's office?

The scene of the operation is not very

important, so long as the facilities are adequate. If the doctor's office is fully equipped and if a competent anesthetist is present, then operating in the office may be perfectly acceptable. In most cases, however, a well-equipped hospital will have better resources and is therefore preferable. The chief advantage of having the operation performed in a hospital is that the patient can remain overnight and be cared for by the staff should a complication, such as bleeding, arise.

When is the best time of year for removing a child's tonsils and adenoids?

Any time of the year. The time of removal is determined by the appearance of the specific condition that indicates removal.

Can an allergic child have his tonsils and adenoids removed?

Yes. The surgery should be performed when the child is suffering least from his allergies.

Should a child of allergic parents have his tonsils removed between April 1 and October 15?

This is not a very good practice, because it may increase his chances of developing active hay fever during the next allergy season.

How soon after a cold or an acute inflammation of the tonsils can surgery be done?

A minimum of two weeks should elapse.

If a child has been exposed to an infectious communicable disease, should tonsillectomy be postponed?

Yes, until all chance of catching the disease has passed.

How soon after a patient has recovered from an upper respiratory infection or an acute inflammation of the tonsils can his tonsils be removed?

A period of two to four weeks should be allowed before removing the tonsils.

How soon after a child has recovered from one of the contagious diseases, such as measles, scarlet fever, or chickenpox, can his tonsils and adenoids be removed?

About four weeks after the condition has cleared.

How should a child be prepared for tonsillectomy?

Since removal of the tonsils is likely to be the child's first operation as well as his first admission to a hospital, he should be prepared for the event with special care. He must be given a thorough explanation of what will happen, and, if it is at all possible, he should see the place in which he will undergo surgery beforehand. It is most important to tell the child the complete truth about his tonsillectomy and not stories about having a picture or a test taken. Honesty with the child is the best way to ensure his physical and psychological recovery.

Should the parents spend as much time as possible with a child who is hospitalized for a tonsillectomy?

Yes. Many hospitals realize that small children must be supported by the presence of a parent during trying procedures such as the removal of tonsils and adenoids. For this reason, many institutions make provisions for the parent to remain with the child during his entire hospital stay. If these opportunities are offered, they should, if possible, be accepted.

What kind of anesthesia is used?

Children always receive a general anesthesia. Adults generally receive local anesthesia. This is preferable in adults as it minimizes bleeding and causes less postoperative discomfort. General anesthesia is administered to adults when an adenoidectomy is planned.

Is tonsillectomy painful when performed under local anesthesia?
No.

Does the patient need special preoperative medication or diet?
No special preoperative diet is required. There is a need for a laxative. The doctor sometimes orders vitamin K to aid in the prevention of postoperative bleeding. Occasionally penicillin is given preoperatively to ward off possible postoperative infection.

Is it necessary to remove both the tonsils and the adenoids?
In children it is generally necessary to remove both. Usually, after puberty, the adenoids have undergone degeneration and tonsillectomy alone is all that will be necessary.

Exactly how does the surgeon remove the tonsils and adenoids?
By separating the tonsil from its bed and then snaring it off close to the tongue. Adenoids are removed with a knife attached to a basket. The adenoids are then collected in the basket as they are cut.

About how long does it take to remove tonsils and adenoids?
About half an hour. It may take longer if the patient is an adult and local anesthesia is being used.

Will it be necessary to remove stitches after tonsillectomy and adenoidectomy?
No.

Should people who have had recent attacks of acute tonsillitis be given an antibiotic when their tonsils are removed?
This is perhaps the best procedure, in case the patient has some lingering infection that is not easily discernible.

What is the usual postoperative course of a patient who has had his tonsils and adenoids removed?
There may be considerable pain in the throat and ears for the first week or ten days following surgery. The pain is often aggravated by eating, drinking, or swallowing. The patient may also feel and act sick for a few days and may run a slight fever.

What can be done to relieve the postoperative symptoms?
The patient should be kept in bed and should be given large amounts of fluids to drink. Pain-relieving medications should be given when necessary, but preferably not aspirin, which is thought to be conducive to postoperative bleeding.

Is it common for children to vomit following tonsillectomy?
No. The newer anesthetic agents reduce postoperative vomiting.

What are some of the possible complications following tonsillectomy?
The most frequently encountered complication is bleeding that occurs during the first 12 hours after surgery or several days later when the scab comes off the tonsil bed.

How often is postoperative bleeding seen after tonsillectomy and adenoidectomy?
It does occur, but not too frequently.

What kinds of hemorrhage occur after tonsillectomy?
There are two forms of postoperative hemorrhage:
1. The *immediate* postoperative hemorrhage occurs shortly after surgery and can be controlled quite readily by the surgeon before the child leaves the operating or recovery room.

2. The *delayed* type of postoperative hemorrhage usually occurs from the fifth to the eighth postoperative day. It is due to the falling away or loosening of the scab or slough which forms at the operative site. A small vessel or capillary may be exposed, which will form a blood clot that keeps the vessel open. This type of bleeding is also easy to control, by removal of the clot and the application of a slight amount of pressure.

How will a parent know that a child is bleeding from the tonsils?

The child will spit up or vomit blood. If this continues for a period of time, his pulse may become rapid and he may become cold and start to perspire.

What should a parent do when a child bleeds following tonsillectomy?

The surgeon should be notified immediately. In all probability he will see the child, either in his office, in the child's home, or in the hospital.

How does a surgeon stop the postoperative bleeding from the bed of the tonsils?

He will either pack the area, cauterize it, or clamp off the bleeding vessel if it can be seen directly.

Is it always possible for the surgeon to stop the bleeding?

Yes, although the patient may have a considerable hemorrhage and may require a blood transfusion.

Is faulty surgery the cause of bleeding following tonsillectomy?

No. After the removal of the tonsils, a membrane forms over the raw tonsil bed. When this separates too soon, hemorrhage may ensue. This is not caused by an error in surgical technique.

Is it good practice to have a special nurse attend a child following removal of his tonsils and adenoids?

Yes. If the child is alone in a room in a hospital, this is a very good idea. A good substitute for a special nurse is the child's mother.

How long is it necessary for a child to stay in the hospital following tonsillectomy?

Approximately 24 hours.

How soon after removal of his tonsils and adenoids can a patient be permitted to talk?

The sooner the better. This will not cause bleeding and will help his speaking apparatus to return to normal.

Is it natural for a person's speech to be altered following removal of the tonsils and adenoids?

Yes, this occurs quite often. However, the speech and voice tone return to normal within several weeks following the operation.

How soon after having his tonsils removed can a person bathe?

Sponge baths may be given the day after the operation, provided there are no complications. A tub bath may be given four to five days later.

How long should one stay indoors following tonsillectomy?

Approximately one week.

Should an ice collar be used?

Yes. Cold compresses or an ice collar to the neck is soothing.

When may the patient be taken outdoors?

Any time after the fifth day, weather permitting.

How long will it take to recover completely?

This is variable, as patients react differently. In general, however, complete recovery can be anticipated within ten days to two weeks.

When can a child return to school and other activities?

School may be resumed after the first week if the child's temperature is normal and if he has resumed eating, etc.

Activities should be restricted in order to avoid overexertion for two weeks.

When can an adult return to work?

From ten days to two weeks postoperatively. However, strenuous physical work should be avoided for at least two to three weeks.

Should a person be given a special diet following removal of his tonsils and adenoids?

In general, it is best to give him anything he wants to eat and is able to swallow. A first-day diet should probably be composed of soft, easily swallowed foods such as milk, custard, Jello, sherbet, ice cream, and mashed vegetables. Water can be given in any amount desired. By the fourth postoperative day, the individual can begin to resume his regular diet.

Should vitamins be given to a child following removal of his tonsils and adenoids?

Vitamins K and C are frequently given for several days before and after removal of the tonsils. Vitamin K is given to cut down on bleeding tendencies, and vitamin C is given because the postoperative diet is usually low in citrus fruits and other substances that contain large amounts of this necessary chemical.

Is it necessary to use antibiotics preoperatively or postoperatively?

A child who has had recurrent sore throats and colds (without a free interval of two or more weeks) may be put on penicillin or a similar antibiotic for a week or more to prepare him for surgery. In addition, some surgeons use an antibiotic for one week following surgery. This tends to minimize the infection at the operative site and, in that way, greatly decreases the possibility of postoperative hemorrhage.

How soon can a child return to school following tonsillectomy?

It takes a young child about ten days to recover fully from the operation. By this time he should be back to his normal activities and normal diet and can return to school a few days later. Physical activities should be restricted for two weeks after the operation.

Do tonsils and adenoids usually grow back after they have been removed?

This is seldom seen if a careful dissection of the structure was carried out in the first operation. If tonsillar or adenoidal tissue has been left behind, it will tend to grow again.

Will removing the tonsils of an allergic child help to clear up his allergies?

No.

What is the relationship between poliomyelitis (infantile paralysis) and tonsillectomy?

Since all children now receive polio vaccine, there is no longer any restriction as to the season of the year when the operation can be done. Tonsillectomy can now be done safely in what used to be called the polio season.

Before the introduction of polio vaccination, most investigators agreed that if polio developed in a child who had recently undergone tonsillectomy, the disease would be more likely to take the most serious form, namely, bulbar polio. For this reason, surgery for removal of the tonsils and adenoids was not recommended from June 1 to October 1 in north-temperate climates.

Torsion of the Testicle

Torsion of the testicle is an acute condition in which the cord leading to the testicle becomes twisted. Immediate surgery is necessary to save the testicle from becoming gangrenous. Fortunately, torsion of the testicle is not a very common condition. It is seen most often in adolescent boys or young adults.

See also TESTICLES.

Torticollis

There are several types of torticollis, or wryneck. These include:

1. Congenital wryneck, which is present at birth and is the commonest type.

2. Dermatogenic torticollis. This is a rather rare condition caused by contraction of the skin of one side of the neck.

3. Hysterical torticollis, due to muscle spasm similar to that seen in tics. This type of torticollis is quite commonly seen in hysterical or emotionally unstable people.

4. Labyrinthine torticollis, due to upset in the sense of equilibrium; it is an inner ear condition.

5. Neurogenic torticollis, caused by pressure upon, or disease of, the accessory nerve (eleventh cranial nerve) in the neck.

6. Ocular torticollis, due to severe astigmatism of the eyes. The head is held in a twisted position in order to improve vision.

7. Reflex torticollis, due to an infection in one side of the neck, especially in the lymph nodes.

8. Rheumatoid torticollis, secondary to rheumatism involving the muscles of one side of the neck.

See also WRYNECK, CONGENITAL.

Tracheotomy

Tracheotomy is an operation in which an artificial opening is made into the trachea through an incision in the neck below the level of the larynx.

QUESTIONS AND ANSWERS

What conditions require tracheotomy?

1. Suffocation due to obstruction of the airway above or at the level of the larynx

2. Postoperative conditions in which mucus secretions block the bronchial tubes and cause severe respiratory diffi-

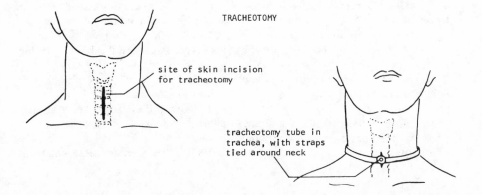

TRACHEOTOMY

site of skin incision
for tracheotomy

tracheotomy tube in
trachea, with straps
tied around neck

culties, and the patient is unable to expel the mucus voluntarily

3. Severe burns of the air passages, a not uncommon complication of burns elsewhere on the body

4. Certain cases of drowning

What are the main symptoms of obstruction of the larynx?

1. Difficulty in breathing
2. Pallor and restlessness
3. Bluish discoloration of the lips
4. Rapid respiration and rapid pulse

What are the most common causes of obstruction of the larynx?

1. Abscess formation.
2. Inflammation of the lining of the cartilages of the larynx.
3. Severe croup.
4. Acute inflammation involving the tissues surrounding the larynx. This may occur from neck infections extending from the floor of the mouth (Ludwig's angina).
5. Injuries or wounds of the larynx or nearby structures, with swelling of the tissues composing the larynx.
6. A foreign body which gets stuck in the larynx. This occurs in children who sometimes swallow coins, peanuts, or other small objects.
7. Burns of the larynx from drinking scalding liquids or inhaling live steam.
8. Inhalation of severely irritating chemicals or vapors.

What first aid should be given to someone choking from a foreign body in the larynx or trachea?

1. Try to retrieve the foreign body by inserting a finger into the throat of the patient.
2. Turn the patient upside-down and hold him in that position.
3. Encourage coughing.
4. Transport the patient, in a sitting position, to the nearest emergency room of a hospital.

When should a tracheotomy be done?

When the laryngeal obstruction has developed to such an extent that the patient is unable to breathe at all and life is obviously threatened.

When an elective tracheotomy is performed, how is the opening into the trachea kept open?

By insertion of a tracheotomy tube. This tube has a double lining and the inner lining can be taken out as often as necessary to keep it clean and free of mucus collection.

When the tracheotomy tube is removed after the obstruction has disappeared, will the hole heal readily?

Yes. Once normal breathing has been resumed and the tube removed, the tracheotomy hole will close within a few days.

Does a tracheotomy interfere with normal eating?

No.

How should a first-aider perform a tracheotomy?

1. Place patient flat on back.
2. Lift up chin as far as it will go.
3. Feel the Adam's apple.
4. Slide fingers down to area just below Adam's apple where you will feel the rings of the trachea (windpipe).
5. Select space between first and second ring to plunge the knife.
6. Make sure knife is inserted as near as possible to the middle of the neck.
7. When air gushes in and out of hole, you will know the knife is in the windpipe.
8. Twist the knife so as to hold open the hole in the trachea.
9. Keep knife in place and transport patient as soon as possible to nearest hospital.
10. If opening should close, enlarge it

in a vertical direction upward and downward.

11. Tracheotomy will be of no value unless there is a heartbeat.

TRACHEOTOMY IN CHILDREN

Is it ever necessary to perform a tracheotomy on a child who has been submerged underwater?

Yes. This is often a lifesaving procedure and is much more important than getting the water out of the lungs. It has been found that many children who have drowned had little water in the lungs, but did have severe laryngeal spasm.

Will the performance of a tracheotomy by a layman ever lead to a child's death?

No, so long as the incision is made *below* the Adam's apple in the midline of the neck. If this is done, no important structures will be damaged.

How long can a tracheotomy tube be left in place?

If the tracheotomy has been performed because of a foreign body in the larynx, the need for it will no longer exist after the foreign body has been extracted. However, it is usually best to allow the tube to stay in place four or five days before removing it. The wound in the neck will heal within another week, leaving just a small scar.

How can a physician tell when a tracheotomy tube can be removed?

When the child can breathe comfortably with the tracheotomy tube plugged, the tube can be removed.

Is it important to take care of a tracheotomy tube after the operation?

Yes, this is essential. Suction must be applied through the tube to keep the passageway clear.

Are special nurses necessary to care for a child after a tracheotomy?

Yes.

Does a tracheotomy opening in the neck always heal after the tube is removed?

Yes, if normal breathing is reestablished through the nose. If obstruction above the tracheotomy persists, then the tracheotomy opening will not close. The tube should not be removed until the need for it no longer exists.

Can a child eat and swallow normally with a tracheotomy tube in place?

Yes. The tube does not interfere with normal eating.

Will a tracheotomy cure acute inflammations, abscesses of the larynx, or a burn of the laryngeal area?

No. All a tracheotomy will do is permit free breathing below the inflamed area. It will still be necessary to treat the disease of the larynx.

Will a tracheotomy help save some children who would otherwise die from burns?

Yes. It is essential to keep the inflamed, burned respiratory passages open. The best way to do this is to perform a tracheotomy.

Do children ever get paralysis of one or both of the vocal cords in the larynx?

This used to occur quite often when children had diphtheria or the bulbar form of infantile paralysis. Fortunately, the eradication of these two diseases has made paralysis of the larynx a very rare condition in children.

What treatment is necessary for paralysis of the vocal cords?

If a child has paralysis of one vocal cord, surgical treatment is not indicated. If both vocal cords are paralyzed as a result of poliomyelitis or diphtheria it is frequently necessary to perform a

SURGICAL CONDITIONS AND PROCEDURES

tracheotomy below the level of the larynx.

Will the vocal cords ever regain their nerve control?

If the child recovers from the diphtheria or poliomyelitis, the laryngeal paralysis is likely to recede considerably, although it may not disappear entirely.

Is it ever necessary to perform a tracheotomy when the larynx has been injured?

Yes, because laryngeal obstruction will prevent free breathing.

Transplantation of Organs

See ORGAN AND TISSUE TRANSPLANTS.

Traumatic Surgery

Traumatic surgery is that branch of medicine which deals primarily with the treatment of injuries and wounds. This specialty has grown rapidly within the past few decades as a result of the tremendous increase in accidents.

It has been found possible to reduce greatly the mortality in accidents through the development of special surgical teams who can reach the injured patient more quickly by the use of high-speed, specially equipped ambulances and by using surgical helicopters. Traumatic surgeons must be well trained in the treatment of surgical shock and must be expert in methods of transporting injured people so as to avoid additional trauma.

In large medical centers where a high accident rate is anticipated, surgical trauma teams are on a round-the-clock basis. In such areas, during peak accident periods, it is not unusual to find that a neurosurgeon, orthopedic surgeon, thoracic surgeon, vascular surgeon, and general surgeon are all on standby call for emergencies.

A major characteristic of trauma is that the patient suffers multiple wounds and therefore must receive treatment simultaneously from several kinds of surgeons. It will do little good to render adequate treatment to a compound fracture of the leg while neglecting to treat a punctured lung or severed blood vessel within the abdominal cavity.

Trigeminal Neuralgia

Trigeminal neuralgia, or tic douloureux, is a recurrent condition in which there are sudden paroxysms of excruiating pain aiong the course of one or more branches of the trigeminal nerve in the face. The spasms of pain come on abruptly, often triggered by touching the side of the face or by exposing it to a draft. At other times an attack will come on from drinking a cold liquid, sudden exposure to cold, or for no apparent reason.

QUESTIONS AND ANSWERS

What parts of the face are most frequently involved in the attacks?

The eye, the cheek, and the side of the mouth and chin.

Is trigeminal neuralgia seen very often in older people?

Yes. It occurs most often after 60.

What causes trigeminal neuralgia?

The cause is unknown.

What is a trigger point?

An area on the face that, when it is touched or irritated, can precipitate an attack.

Does trigeminal neuralgia occur on both sides of the face in the same patient?

No. It is confined to one side of the face.

What is the usual frequency of attacks?

In mild cases, an attack may occur only once every few weeks or months. In severe cases—and these are quite numerous—there may be several attacks a day. In this latter group, it is not unusual for drug addiction to result, as the need for relief of pain becomes imperative. Also, there are cases on record of suicide committed in order to be rid of the awful attacks.

What is the treatment of trigeminal neuralgia?

1. In the very mild case in which the attacks come on only once or twice a year, treatment may be limited to giving pain-relieving medications for the isolated paroxysm.

2. In those cases in which the attacks are spaced more closely, alcohol injection directly into the involved branch of the nerve may be carried out. This will cause a certain degree of paralysis and degeneration of the nerve, thus freeing the patient from attacks for periods of several months. When the attacks recur, an injection can be given again.

3. In the most severe cases, neurosurgery will be carried out. This entails a brain operation in which the particular nerve branch or branches that are subject to the attacks are cut.

Is surgery for trigeminal neuralgia safe and effective?

Yes. Almost all older people who are otherwise in a satisfactory state of health can undergo this type of surgery. In the great majority of instances, complete relief ensues.

Will cutting the trigeminal nerve cause facial paralysis?

No, but if the branch of the nerve going to the eye region is cut, special postoperative care will be necessary. In such cases, there may be loss of sensation on the surface of the eyeball, causing the patient to be unaware of dirt or dust that might enter his eye. To safeguard against this, the patient must wear goggles when out of doors or when exposed to wind or dust.

Will trigeminal neuralgia recur after surgery?

Not if the involved branch of the nerve has been cut. Rarely does another branch of the same nerve subsequently become afflicted.

Tubal Ligation

See FALLOPIAN TUBES.

Tuboplasty

Tuboplasty is an operation that attempts to remedy an obstruction of the fallopian tubes. Tubal obstruction may occur as the result of salpingitis (an inflammation of the tube), as the result of an operation intended to produce sterility (tubal ligation), as a by-product of operations for other pelvic conditions such as ectopic pregnancy or pelvic inflammatory disease, or because of failure of a primary operation to relieve occlusion.

Tuboplasty is often requested by a woman who has undergone tubal ligation and has changed her mind about having no more children.

Tuboplasty should be undertaken

only when other factors that are conducive to pregnancy are favorable. It would be unwise to attempt tuboplasty if the woman had some other condition which might cause her to be infertile or if her husband had a low sperm count. Prior to embarking on tuboplasty, a hysterogram should be performed to determine the exact site of the tube obstruction.

Tuboplasty consists of cutting all adhesions around the fallopian tubes, opening the fimbriated end of the tube, removing the obstructed portion of the tube, and suturing the ends on either side of the obstruction together. In another procedure, the obstructed portion is removed and the healthy distal portion, including the fimbriated end, is implanted into the uterine cavity. It is essential that, whichever procedure is performed, the tube be handled as gently as possible. After completion of this part of the procedure a small, plastic catheter is passed through the cervix and the uterine cavity, through the tube beyond the area of repair, and on out into the abdominal cavity. This catheter serves as a splint so that healing will take place with the tube open.

In order to learn the success of the operation, a hysterogram is performed at a later date. If it has been successful, one will note on x-ray that the tube has remained open.

QUESTIONS AND ANSWERS

Is tuboplasty a dangerous operation?
No. The dangers are no greater than for any other minor intraabdominal operation.

How long is one in the hospital following tuboplasty?
Approximately seven to eight days.

How soon after surgery can one get out of bed?
Within 24 to 48 hours.

Where is the incision made for tuboplasty?
In the lower abdomen, either a transverse or a longitudinal incision of approximately four inches in length.

How long is the plastic splint left in the tube after surgery?
Approximately six weeks.

How is the splint removed?
It is pulled out through the vagina.

Is postoperative care necessary following tuboplasty?
Yes. It is routine practice to inflate the tubes within a few days and before each period in order to make sure that they stay open.

How are the tubes inflated?
By the injection of carbon dioxide through the cervix or through the plastic splint, much in the same way as the Rubin test is performed.

Do the tubes usually remain open following tuboplasty?
In the great majority of cases the tubes remain open, but this in no way guarantees pregnancy. Unfortunately, other factors seem to play an important part in the failure of the patient to become pregnant.

What percentage of patients become pregnant subsequent to tuboplasty?
It is estimated that no more than 15 percent of women who have undergone tuboplasty eventually become pregnant.

Tympanoplasty

See DEAFNESS.

Ulcer

An ulcer is an absence of the normal lining of a body surface and is limited to a particular area, such as an ulcer of the stomach or of the skin or of the intestines. The base of the ulcer is usually inflamed and raw.

There are a great number of types of ulcer; the most frequently encountered are as follows:

Curling's. An ulcer of the stomach or duodenum occurring in people who have sustained severe skin burns.

Decubitus. Bedsores, usually seen over the base of the spine where contact has taken place with the mattress. Seen mostly in chronically ill people.

Diabetic. Ulcers of the feet or legs seen in diabetics who have not taken care of themselves and who have poor healing powers.

Diphtheritic. An ulcer in the throat which appears after a diphtheritic membrane has become detached. Seen very rarely today.

Duodenal. One located in the first portion of the small intestine, the duodenum.

Esophageal. An ulcer located in the esophagus (foodpipe).

Gastric. One located in the stomach.

Indolent. One that shows little tendency to heal.

Kissing. An ulcer that faces another ulcer, as on both sides of the duodenum.

Marginal. An ulcer that forms at the junction of the stomach and small intestine following an operation for ulcer.

Penetrating. One that extends deeply into the tissues.

Peptic. An ulcer occurring in the esophagus, stomach, or duodenum.

Perforated. One that has ruptured through the wall of the stomach or duodenum.

Rodent. A skin cancer, with ulcer formation, most commonly seen on the side of the nose, cheek, or face.

Serpiginous. One that has undermined edges and is extending out sideways into adjoining tissues.

Stomal. Same as marginal ulcer.

Trophic. One caused by lack of blood supply to a part.

Varicose. An ulcer of the leg associated with varicose veins.

See also STOMACH AND DUODENUM.

Ulcerative Colitis

See CHRONIC ULCERATIVE COLITIS; INTESTINES.

Umbilical Hernia

See HERNIA.

Undescended Testicle

See TESTICLES.

Urachal Cyst

In embryonic development, there is a connective tubal structure, the urachus, leading from the bladder to the umbilicus. This should close off completely by the time of birth. At times, although both ends of the tube are obliterated, a central section may remain open, and its lining may secrete fluid, which cannot drain through either end. This will produce a cystic enlargement, which, because of its position, is often confused with a tumor within the abdomen.

QUESTIONS AND ANSWERS

Where is a urachal cyst usually located?

Just beneath the navel or overlying the midline of the abdomen in the area between the navel and bladder.

What are the symptoms of a urachal cyst?

1. In many instances, there are no symptoms and the condition becomes apparent solely by the appearance of a cystic enlargement below the region of the navel.

2. In rare cases, the entire urachus remains open after birth and there is discharge of urine through the navel.

3. If the closed-off urachal cyst becomes infected, the child will develop pain and tenderness in the umbilical region and will have an elevated temperature. If the infection is deep-seated, the doctor may wrongly diagnose appendicitis or, in the female, an ovarian cyst.

4. If the cyst impinges upon the intestines, intestinal obstruction with abdominal distention, nausea, and vomiting may ensue.

What is the treatment for a urachal cyst?

Surgical removal. However, in many cases the cyst becomes infected and the initial operation will consist merely of incising the cyst and permitting the pus to drain out. When the infection has subsided, a second operation is performed and the entire cyst is removed.

Are operations for the removal of a urachal cyst dangerous?

No. However, if the cyst was originally badly infected, the subsequent surgical removal may be quite difficult, and sometimes remnants of the cyst are inadvertently left behind. In rare instances, the cyst can recur.

Is a urachal cyst a common condition?

No. It is a rare birth deformity.

Is recovery from a urachal cyst the general rule?

Yes. Almost all patients with this condition will eventually recover completely, although it may take a fairly long time if the cyst is badly infected.

Ureters

The ureters are long tubular structures which connect the kidneys with the urinary bladder. The ureters are ducts, each with a thin-walled, funnel-shaped beginning portion called the renal pelvis. Each ureter is approximately 10 to 12 inches long. They lie behind the abdominal cavity on either side of the midline. The ureters course downward and enter the bladder through separate openings called the ureteral orifices which are situated approximately two inches from one another. Obstruction of a ureter by a stone, kinking, tumor, or external pressure will interfere with the flow of urine from the kidney to the bladder. Such obstruction will lead to kidney damage if it is not removed promptly.

See also KIDNEYS AND URETERS.

Urethra

The urethra is a tube leading from the urinary bladder to the outside. In the female, it is of very short length and exits through its own opening above the vaginal orifice. In the male, the urethra passes from the bladder, through the prostate gland, and through the penis to the outside.

There are a considerable number of birth deformities of the urethra, the most common of which are hypospadias and epispadias. In these conditions the urethra terminates before it reaches the tip of the penis. Another congenital condition of the urethra involves a narrowing of its external opening. This condition is known as stenosis of the urethral meatus. When a child is born with this condition, he may cry and strain on attempting to void. The deformity can be corrected easily merely by slitting the external opening.

The urethra is a common site of infection, the most frequently encountered being that caused by the gonorrheal germ. However, other bacteria and sometimes fungi can invade the lining of the urethra and cause an inflammation.

Whenever the urethra is inflamed, there will be a discharge from its exit. As a result of inflammation, especially in the male, a stricture, or constriction of the urethra, may take place. Such obstructions cause difficulty in voiding and may require dilatation or surgical cutting. In rare instances, the urethra is the site of tumor formation.

See also GENITOURINARY SYSTEM; HYPOSPADIAS AND EPISPADIAS; URINARY BLADDER.

QUESTIONS AND ANSWERS

What is the urethra?

It is a tubular passageway leading from the bladder to the outside. Its sole function is to convey urine.

Is the female urethra very different in construction from the male urethra?

Yes. The female urethra is very short, leading from the bladder to its exit between the minor lips of the vulva. The male urethra extends the entire length of the penis.

What are the most common conditions affecting the urethra?

1. Strictures
2. Caruncle
3. Diverticulum
4. Infections (gonorrhea)
5. Congenital deformities, such as hypospadias and epispadias

STRICTURES

What is a stricture of the urethra?

An abnormal narrowing in the canal, usually caused by scar tissue formation.

What are the causes of strictures?

1. A birth deformity (congenital stricture)
2. Infection of the urethra, usually the end result of gonorrhea

What are the symptoms of stricture of the urethra?

1. Reduction in the size and force of the urinary stream
2. Retention of urine, if the stricture is extensive
3. Recurrent attacks of cystitis

How is the diagnosis of stricture made?

By noting the obstruction to the passage of an instrument through the urethral canal and by noting a narrowed urinary stream.

What is the treatment for urethral strictures?

1. Repeated dilatations by the passage of special instruments known as "sounds" or "bougies"
2. Cutting the stricture surgically
3. In severe cases, plastic operations to reshape the urethra

If a stricture cannot be cured by dilatation or operation, what procedure is recommended?

Since these cases are accompanied by obstruction to the outflow of urine, a cystotomy must be performed in order to drain the urine. In this event, the urine will drain abdominally through a rubber tube which is attached to a bottle. Fortunately, this situation does not often develop.

CARUNCLES OF THE URETHRA

What is a caruncle of the urethra?

A small piece of overgrown tissue located at the opening of the urethra. It occurs exclusively in women and results from localized infection or chronic irritation.

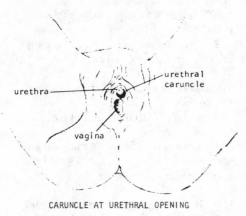

CARUNCLE AT URETHRAL OPENING

What are the symptoms of a caruncle?

There may be no symptoms at all, or the patient may experience pain when the caruncle is touched or when urine passes over it. Frequency of urination with discomfort and bleeding occurs in some cases.

Is treatment always necessary for a caruncle?

No; only if it is large, painful, or causes symptoms.

What is the treatment for a caruncle?

It should be excised surgically or removed by means of an electrocautery. Very small caruncles may be cauterized with chemical agents such as silver nitrate.

Do caruncles have a tendency to recur?

Yes, but not after surgical removal.

DIVERTICULUM OF THE URETHRA

What is a diverticulum of the urethra?

It is a small outpouching of the urethral canal resulting from a birth deformity or secondary to infection in the wall of the urethra. It occurs almost exclusively in women.

What are the symptoms of an urethral diverticulum?

1. Recurrent attacks of bladder infection

2. Obstruction to the passage of urine

3. Painful intercourse

4. After voiding, the patient finds that she can produce more urine by pressing on the region of the diverticulum

What is the treatment for a diverticulum of the urethra?

Surgical removal, which will result in a cure.

INFECTIONS OF THE URETHRA

Are infections of the urethra very common?

Yes.

What is the most common cause of an infection of the urethra?

Gonorrhea.

What are the symptoms of gonorrhea?

1. The appearance of a creamy urethral discharge about a week to ten days following unprotected sexual relations.

This discharge appears from the orifice of the penis or from the vulva in the female.

2. Frequent, painful urination.

3. Pus and blood in the urine.

4. Pain and swelling in the region of the external genitals.

Does a discharge from the urethra always mean gonorrhea?

No. Other germs can also cause an infection in this area.

How is a positive diagnosis of gonorrhea made?

By finding the gonorrheal germ under the microscope in pus taken from the urethra.

What is the treatment for gonorrhea?

The antibiotic drugs, if used promptly and properly, will bring about a cure within a few days.

How long does it take for the antibiotic drugs to work?

Their action is effective within 24 to 48 hours.

Is it safe for a patient with gonorrhea to administer treatment to himself?

Absolutely not. A chronic form of the disease may result if the patient attempts to treat himself by purchasing his own antibiotics. It is essential that these medications be given under the supervision of a physician.

Do all gonorrhea germs respond satisfactorily to all antibiotics?

No. The physician will frequently have to change the antibiotic in order to find the one that is most effective for the particular type of germ causing the infection.

What are the complications from the improper treatment of gonorrhea?

1. In men, a spread of the infection to the prostate gland, testicles, and/or epididymis.

2. A stricture of the urethra.

3. In women, a spread of the infection to the cervix, uterus, fallopian tubes, and/or ovaries. Also, peritonitis may ensue from an extension of the infection to the abdominal cavity.

Does gonorrhea often become chronic?

Yes. In inadequately treated cases, the germ may lie dormant within the genital tract for months or years, only to flare up from time to time.

Can chronic gonorrhea be cured?

Yes, by adequate treatment with antibiotics and, sometimes, by the performance of surgery to remove structures that have been destroyed by the gonorrheal infection, such as the fallopian tubes and ovaries.

HYPOSPADIAS AND EPISPADIAS

What are hypospadias and epispadias?

Birth deformities of the urethra, in which the urethra ends short of the tip of the penis. When the urethra ends on the under side of the penis, the condition is called hypospadias; when it opens on the top side, it is called epispadias.

Are there varying degrees of these deformities?

Yes. In certain cases the urethra ends right near the tip of the penis and no symptoms result. In the more severe types, the urethra may end near the very beginning of the penis; this will result in serious voiding difficulties.

What is the treatment for hypospadias or epispadias?

Minor deviations from normal require no treatment; others will require correction by plastic surgery. This is often carried out in several stages and involves complicated techniques necessitating the services of a competent urologist.

When is the best time to operate for hypospadias or epispadias?

During the first few years of life.

How successful are these operations?

In most cases good results are obtained. However, when the results are unsatisfactory, reoperation can effect a cure. Some of these reoperative procedures are carried out years later, when the tissues have grown considerably and are easier to handle surgically.

If the operations for hypospadias or epispadias are successful, will urinary and sexual function be normal?

Yes.

Urinary Bladder

The urinary bladder is a hollow, muscular organ situated in the lower front part of the abdomen just above and behind the pubic bone. It lies in front of the rectum and its outlet, in men, is surrounded by the prostate gland. In women, the bladder lies next to the uterus. The bladder receives the two ureters as they descend from the kidneys, and it has an opening, the urethra, which permits the urine to exit from the body. (See diagrams.)

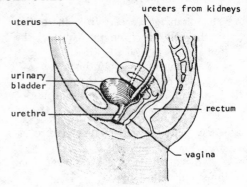

URINARY BLADDER IN WOMAN

The purpose of the bladder is to act as a reservoir for the urine excreted by the kidneys. It is elastic and increases in size as the urine accumulates. When approximately eight ounces (a glassful) has accumulated, a delicately balanced series of nerve reflexes comes into play and lets one know that it is time to urinate. However, abnormalities of this mechanism occur during disease states and sometimes produce situations in which there is constant leakage of urine (incontinence) or conditions in which the patient is completely unable to void.

The urinary bladder is the seat of many disorders, the most frequently encountered being *infection* or *cystitis*. Most infections respond well to medical treatment, and it is seldom necessary to operate. Those conditions most often requiring surgery are (1) stones, (2) tumors, (3) fistula (an abnormal opening between the bladder and some other structure), (4) diverticulum (an abnormal outpouching of a portion of the bladder wall), (5) obstruction secondary to an enlarged prostate, (6) paralysis, (7) exstrophy, and (8) injuries.

1. Bladder stones may be single or multiple. They may form in the bladder or come down from the kidney.

There is reason to believe that stones in the bladder were much more common

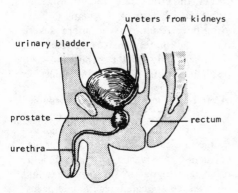

URINARY BLADDER IN MAN

in ancient times and in the days before adequate diet and vitamin intake. (The Oath of Hippocrates, written several hundred years before Christ, refers to bladder stones!) This theory is substantiated by the fact that bladder stones are seen today in large numbers in backward countries where food supplies are inadequate. In these areas, children often develop stones. By and large, the incidence of bladder stone in middle-aged and elderly men exceeds that in all other groups. The reason for this is the fact that enlargement of the prostate leads to incomplete emptying and infection of the bladder. This, in turn, may lead to stone formation.

Bladder stones may be as small as a pinhead or as large as a hen's egg. They cause frequent, painful, bloody urination, but the diagnosis is clinched when they are seen through a cystoscope (an instrument that permits the urologist to look directly into the bladder) or when they appear on x-ray examination.

The treatment of bladder stones varies according to their size. Very small stones may pass out spontaneously through the urethra. Other small stones may be washed out through a cystoscope. Larger stones can sometimes be crushed by a special instrument known as a lithotrite, which is passed into the bladder in the same manner as a cystoscope. The crushed stones are thereby made small enough to be washed out of the bladder. This procedure is called *litholapaxy*.

Very large bladder stones cannot be passed or crushed and should be removed surgically by means of a *suprapubic cystotomy*. (This operation is the same as that described later in this section in the discussion of bladder obstruction.) However, if there is no prostatic enlargement and the interior of the bladder appears healthy, it is closed tightly after removing the stone instead of leaving it open and inserting a drainage tube.

Operations for stone removal are well tolerated in all age groups and recovery is the rule.

2. Tumors of the bladder are most prevalent after middle age and are more frequent in men than in women. They may be either benign or malignant and are interesting in that one can actually note, on cystoscopy or microscopic examination of the tissue, the transition of a benign condition into a malignant one. Some tumors are pea-size while others grow so large that they occupy a large part of the bladder wall and bladder cavity. When seen through the cystoscope, the growths may appear wartlike, and some of the larger ones may resemble a cauliflower.

The onset of symptoms is usually heralded by the passage of grossly bloody urine. There is no accompanying pain. Such an episode should never be ignored, as bloody urine invariably signifies an underlying bladder, kidney, or prostate disorder.

A unique and disquieting characteristic of these tumors is their great tendency to recur postoperatively, either in the same location or in some other part of the bladder. This is somewhat compensated for by the fact that many of the growths are noncancerous and many of those that are malignant tend to be slow-growing. Furthermore, many of the recurrences can be treated successfully.

A bladder tumor located near the entrance of the ureter may obstruct the drainage of urine from the kidney on that side. Pain in the side, fever, and loss of kidney function may result.

The diagnosis of bladder tumors is quite simple when a competent urologist performs an examination through a cystoscope. X-rays will also help in establishing the diagnosis. It is common practice for a small piece of the tumor to be removed through the cystoscope and sent to the laboratory for microscopic examination. An exact diagnosis will usually be forthcoming which will help determine the course of future treatment.

Treatment of bladder tumors is surgical and is divided into two categories:

a) Closed treatment: A cystoscope is passed through the urethra and the growth is shaved off and burned out by means of an electric current. This is termed *transurethral resection and fulguration* and is more applicable to the small, benign growths.

b) Open treatment: The bladder is approached surgically through an incision in the lower abdomen. The entire growth sometimes lends itself to removal, and in other cases, a section of the bladder containing the tumor will be removed. This procedure is often associated with radium implantations in the wall of the bladder.

When the tumor is malignant and extensive, it may be necessary in some cases to remove the entire bladder (total cystectomy). This is a major procedure, accompanied by considerable risk. After bladder excision, one of the following procedures is carried out to divert the urine outflow:

a) A *nephrostomy* is done, with the urine emerging directly from the kidneys to the skin.

b) A *cutaneous ureterostomy* is done, with the ureters (the tubes leading from the kidneys to the bladder) being brought out and sutured to the skin.

c) A *ureterocolostomy* is done, with the ureters being implanted into the large bowel.

d) A *ureteroileostomy* (ileal conduit) is performed, with the ureters being implanted into an isolated loop of small intestine which is then brought out to the skin.

The last procedure mentioned, the so-called *ileal loop bladder operation,* is the one of choice today and is accompanied by the best end results. It must be kept in mind that it is only the most malignant types of bladder cancer that require the radical surgery just described. Although the cure rate in these cases is not as high as one would wish, the great majority of patients will at least recover from the operation and will survive for much longer than if they were not operated upon.

3. Bladder fistula: A fistula is an abnormal connection between two structures that are ordinarily separate from one another. Due to disease or injury, the bladder may develop a fistula connecting it to the *intestine* or, in women, to the *vagina.* The latter fistula (vesicovaginal) is frequently secondary to a bladder injury which occurs during an operation upon the uterus, cervix, or vagina. A patient with this disorder constantly leaks urine through the vaginal canal.

Fistula from the bladder to the bowel is most often caused by an inflammation of the large bowel (diverticulitis) or by a bowel tumor that has grown into the bladder. Such a condition will result in the passage of stool and air with the urine.

All fistulas are difficult to cure, but good results can be obtained by wide dissection and thorough removal of all diseased tissue. Normal anatomy of all structures must be carefully reestablished. It is often necessary to perform these procedures in several stages. Whenever possible, it is better to divert the flow of urine or stool temporarily away from the area operated upon. This can be accomplished in certain cases by the judicious use of a *colostomy* (see discussion of large intestine, pp. 481–496) or a *cystostomy* (opening of the bladder onto the abdominal wall). The colostomy or cystostomy is repaired after the fistula has healed.

4. Bladder diverticulum: A diverticulum is a saclike outpouching of the bladder wall. (See diagram.) It results from interference, usually because of an enlarged prostate, with the normal flow of urine from the bladder. The increased pressure within the bladder which is necessary to expel urine often causes a stretching and ballooning out of a weak spot in the wall. (The mechanism is somewhat like a blister on a rubber tire.) The condition occurs mostly in men in their later years.

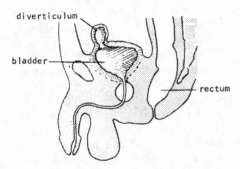

BLADDER DIVERTICULUM

The sac (diverticulum) empties poorly and frequently harbors a pool of infected urine. Stones and tumors have a tendency to form within it.

The diagnosis of this disorder is made easily on cystoscopic and x-ray examination.

If the diverticulum continues to retain stagnant urine *after* its underlying cause —the bladder obstruction—has been relieved, or if it contains a stone or a tumor, or if it has attained a large size, then it must be removed. The operation is performed through a lower abdominal incision. Recovery is the rule unless some complication sets in.

5. Bladder obstruction: Obstruction of the outlet of the bladder is one of the most frequently encountered afflictions of older men, causing difficulty in urination, frequency of urination, painful urination, and the necessity for voiding several times during the night. About 60 percent of men over 60 years of age have some bladder outlet obstruction, and 20 percent of these will require surgery for its relief. The prostate, surrounding the urethra (the tube leading out from the bladder), enlarges and obstructs the free flow of urine. (*See* PROSTATE GLAND.)

This type of bladder obstruction must be treated surgically by removing the underlying cause; that is, the enlarged prostate gland. However, the first surgical need is to relieve the acute obstruction, and this is usually done by the passage of a catheter (a long, hollow rubber tube) through the penis into the bladder. This is sufficient to relieve the obstruction temporarily but will not lead to a permanent cure. Where it is inadvisable to remove the prostate immediately because of severe associated illnesses, the bladder may be drained by performing a *suprapubic cystostomy.* This involves making a small incision in the lower abdomen over the bladder region. The incision is carried down through the abdominal wall and the bladder is opened with a knife. A wide rubber cystostomy tube is stitched into the bladder and is permitted to emerge through the wound. Urine will thus be drained directly from the obstructed bladder. The tube is connected with a receptacle at the bedside or a plastic bag strapped to the leg.

At a later time, when the patient's general condition has improved sufficiently, the bladder neck obstruction is relieved by one of the methods outlined in the discussion of prostatic surgery. Following such surgery, the opening in the bladder will close and urine will pass through its normal channel.

Even though cystostomy is most often

performed upon elderly men, it is nevertheless well tolerated, and recovery takes place in all cases except those in which an unforeseen complication develops. Spinal or general inhalation anesthesia, and occasionally local anesthesia, is employed. The procedure takes about one-half hour to perform, and the patient is often ready to get out of bed on the first or second postoperative day. Antibiotic drugs are prescribed to lessen the chances of postoperative infection and to guard against cystitis and kidney infection.

6. Bladder paralysis may develop as a result of an injury or disease of the brain or spinal cord. In these cases, it is often necessary to empty the bladder at intervals by compressing it mechanically with the hand on the abdomen. Some patients are fortunate enough to develop automaticity within the bladder, in which event it empties itself from time to time. Among a small percentage of these patients, neither of these methods is satisfactory and a *permanent cystostomy* must be performed. Urine will henceforth drain through the opening on the abdominal wall.

7. Exstrophy, a congenital deformity of the bladder. In many instances, repair of the exstrophy is not feasible, and it is necessary to remove the defective bladder and to implant the ureters into an isolated segment of small intestine (ileum). Urine then passes from the kidneys, down the ureters, into the ileum, and out of the abdominal cavity through an ileostomy opening.

8. Bladder injuries, if severe, may cause this organ to rupture. As a consequence, urine seeps out into the tissues surrounding the bladder. A diagnosis of ruptured bladder can be made by noting blood in the urine and by inspecting the interior of the structure through cystoscopy.

Tears in the bladder wall must be promptly sutured. Following surgery, a cystostomy is performed and urine drains from the bladder through a tube onto the abdominal wall.

See also GENITOURINARY SYSTEM; KIDNEYS AND URETERS.

QUESTIONS AND ANSWERS

Where is the urinary bladder, and what is its function?

The bladder is a hollow, muscular organ situated at the bottom of the abdominal cavity behind the pubic bone. It is capable of changing in size, depending upon the amount of urine it contains or expels. The bladder receives urine from the kidneys via the ureters (which enter on either side) and expels the urine through the urethra, which connects with the outside. In the male, the neck of the bladder is in very close proximity to, and is surrounded by, the prostate gland. The urethra in the male courses through the penis and terminates at or near the end of that structure. In the female, the urethra is short and terminates through a separate opening between the lips of the vulva.

Is cystitis a common disease?

Yes. It is perhaps the most prevalent disorder of the urinary tract. It occurs in children as well as in adults.

What is the most frequent cause of cystitis?

A bacterial infection with such germs as the streptococcus, colon bacillus, and *Bacillus proteus*.

How do bacteria reach the bladder?

From the outside through the urethra, from the kidneys, rarely from the intestinal tract or female genitals.

What are different forms of cystitis?
1. Acute
2. Chronic
3. Interstitial

What are the symptoms of acute cystitis?

The onset is usually sudden, characterized by frequent painful urination and not infrequently by the presence of pus and blood in the urine.

What is the treatment for acute cystitis?

1. The administration of the appropriate sulfa or antibiotic drug
2. The liberal intake of fluids
3. Bed rest
4. A bland diet, with special care to avoid highly seasoned foods and alcoholic beverages
5. Sedatives to relieve pain or spasm

How long does an attack of acute cystitis usually last?

If treated promptly and adequately, the acute symptoms may subside within a few days. Some disability may persist for a week or two. The urine may take this amount of time to clear.

What are the symptoms of chronic cystitis?

Essentially the same as for acute cystitis, except that the symptoms may be less severe, more prolonged, and may tend to recur. Patients with this condition usually have associated disease in other parts of the urinary tract.

What is interstitial cystitis?

It is a form of chronic cystitis seen mainly in older women. This type of cystitis is characterized by marked thickening of the bladder wall and decreased bladder capacity. Its cause is unknown and its treatment difficult.

What conditions within the urinary tract most commonly lead to cystitis?

1. Infection with or without obstruction or stone in the kidney or ureter
2. Stone or tumor in the bladder
3. Bladder outlet obstruction with urinary retention, such as is caused by an enlarged prostate in a male, or a cystocele in a female

What is a cystoscopic examination?

One in which the interior of the bladder is viewed directly through a metal tubular instrument known as a cystoscope. Cystoscopes are equipped with lights and lenses which permit excellent visualization of the inside of the bladder. In addition, the outlets of the ureters from the kidneys may be studied through this instrument, as may the internal size and configuration of the prostate gland.

Is a cystoscopic examination painful?

In the female, it is virtually painless. In the male, there is some discomfort, but this can be minimized by using local anesthetic agents. In children, cystoscopy is performed under general anesthesia.

Are stones often encountered on examination of the urinary bladder?

Yes.

What causes bladder stones?

1. Those that form directly in the bladder usually are the result of poor emptying, with retention of urine.
2. Other stones may form as a result of a bladder disease such as chronic cystitis, a tumor, or diverticulum of the bladder wall.
3. Many bladder stones originate in the kidney and then pass down into the bladder from above.

What symptoms do bladder stones produce?

Frequent, painful, bloody urination. Occasionally, stones may cause sudden blockage of the urinary outlet, with resultant inability to void.

How is a positive diagnosis of bladder stones made?

By x-ray examination or by direct visualization through a cystoscope.

Is there any satisfactory way to dissolve bladder stones?

No.

What is the treatment for bladder stones?

If small, they often pass spontaneously, without treatment. More often, however, they must be removed. This is accomplished either by opening the bladder surgically or by crushing the stones with a specially designed instrument which is passed through a cystoscope. This latter procedure is called litholapaxy.

When is litholapaxy performed?

When the stones are not too large or firm, when there are not too many of them, and when no stricture of the urethra, diverticulum of the bladder, or enlarged prostate is present. Also, since this procedure is carried out through instrumentation and not by open operation, it is more applicable to those people who are unable to withstand major surgery.

How are the stones removed from the bladder after they have been crushed?

By irrigation. In this manner, they are washed out of the bladder.

Are stone-crushing operations dangerous?

No, but they are tedious and may take an hour or more to perform.

When is an open operation (cystotomy) for removal of stones indicated?

When the stones are very firm and therefore cannot be crushed. When they are very numerous, stones should be removed surgically. If there is an enlargement of the prostate along with bladder stones, the surgeon may elect to do an open operation so that he can remove the prostate at the same time.

Are most bladder tumors malignant?

It is thought that most are either malignant or potentially malignant.

Do tumors often form within the bladder?

Yes.

What are the benign tumors of the bladder?

These are wartlike growths known as papillomas.

What are the symptoms of bladder tumors?

Painless bleeding on urination. Occasionally, there is frequency of urination or the passage of infected urine when cystitis supervenes.

How is a bladder tumor diagnosed?

By visualization of it through a cystoscope. A piece of the tumor is removed through the cystoscope and is submitted for microscopic examination.

What is the treatment for bladder tumors?

This will depend upon the size, location, and multiplicity of the tumor. Simple superficial tumors, which do not interfere with the flow of urine from either kidney and are readily accessible, are burned off by electrofulguration through a cystoscope. Large tumors, or those that penetrate the wall of the bladder deeply, should be removed by cutting out that section of the bladder wall.

When the bladder is extensively involved by a highly malignant growth, it is necessary to remove the entire structure. This procedure is called a cystectomy. When this is done, some disposition must be made of the ureters to provide drainage of urine. Accordingly, the ureters either are transplanted to the skin (cutaneous ureterostomy) or may be implanted into the large bowel (ureterocolostomy), or a pouch is constructed from a segment of small intestine and the ureters are attached to this pouch. This procedure is known as an ileal bladder operation.

How does one pass his urine when the ureters are transplanted into the large bowel?

Urine is passed through the rectum.

How does the urine drain when the ureters are transplanted into the small intestine?

This segment of small intestine (the ileum) is brought out to the skin and the collection of urine is managed by a plastic or rubber bag which fits snugly to the skin.

Are operations for transplantation of the ureters and removal of the bladder serious?

Yes. They are of great magnitude, but it should be remembered that they are lifesaving procedures, performed in most instances to eradicate cancer.

Are operations for bladder tumors serious?

Yes, but recovery from surgery occurs in the vast majority of cases.

Do bladder tumors, once removed, have a tendency to recur?

Yes.

What is a bladder fistula?

An abnormal communication between the bladder and some neighboring organ such as the vagina, the intestine, or the uterus.

What causes a bladder fistula?

1. Between bladder and intestine, usually an inflammation or tumor of the bowel.

2. Fistulas between the bladder and vagina are usually secondary to an injury, occurring during an operation upon the uterus, cervix, or vagina.

Do fistulas often heal spontaneously?

No.

What are the most commonly encountered bladder fistulas?

A connection between the bladder and the vagina, secondary to injury during childbirth. Also, a connection between the bladder and the large bowel, secondary to an inflammation of the bowel (diverticulitis). Another frequently encountered fistula is one between the bladder and bowel, secondary to a tumor of the bowel.

What are the symptoms of a bladder fistula?

If the fistula extends between the bladder and bowel, the patient will pass gas, feces, or food particles with the urine. If the fistula is between the bladder and vagina, the patient will leak urine from the vagina and will have no control over bladder emptying.

What is the treatment for bladder fistulas?

This will depend upon the cause. Small fistulas that are secondary to injury or infection may heal spontaneously, or they may close when the urine is diverted with a rubber catheter. Most fistulas, however, will require surgical correction if a permanent cure is to be obtained. If the underlying cause is malignant disease, the primary growth as well as the involved portions of the bladder wall must be removed. If diverticulitis (inflammation of the colon) has produced the fistula, the diseased segment of the colon must be removed as well as the involved portion of bladder wall.

Are operations for fistula serious?

Yes, but recovery is the general rule. In cases where malignant disease is the cause, extensive surgery may be indicated.

What is a bladder diverticulum?

A saclike outpouching of a portion of the bladder wall.

What causes a bladder diverticulum?

Most are caused by chronic, partial bladder obstruction; others may be present at birth.

Do all diverticula have to be operated upon?

No, only if they collect and fail to drain urine or if stones or tumors form within them.

What operation is done to cure a diverticulum?

An incision is made in the lower abdomen, the bladder is exposed, and the diverticulum is tied off at its base and removed.

Are operations for a diverticulum serious?

Yes, but recovery is the rule.

What is the commonest cause of bladder obstruction?

An enlarged prostate gland.

Must surgery always be done for bladder obstruction?

Not always. Some obstructions are only temporary and can be relieved by passing a catheter (rubber tube) through the urethra. Most cases due to an enlarged prostate will eventually require surgery.

What operations are usually performed to relieve bladder obstruction?

1. **Prostatectomy,** by either the closed or the open method

2. **Suprapubic cystostomy,** or opening the bladder through an incision in the lower abdomen

Are operations for bladder obstruction dangerous?

No.

What is the usual cause of bladder paralysis?

A disease or injury of the brain or spinal cord.

Is bladder paralysis serious?

Yes.

Does bladder paralysis clear up by itself?

Not when it is caused by some permanent nerve damage.

Is surgery always necessary for bladder paralysis?

No. In some cases the bladder learns to empty itself automatically, or the patient learns how to do this manually.

Will the urine eventually pass through normal channels after bladder obstruction is relieved?

Yes.

What anesthesia is used for bladder operations?

General or spinal.

Where are the incisions made for bladder operations?

In the lower abdomen.

Are the scars of bladder operations painful and unsightly?

No.

Are blood transfusions necessary?

Yes, for major bladder operations.

Are special nurses necessary?

Yes, after most major bladder operations.

Is there much pain after bladder operations?

Only moderate discomfort for a few days.

When can the patient get out of bed?

With most procedures, the patient is permitted out of bed on the first, second, or third day after surgery.

Are special medications needed with bladder operations?

Yes. Antibiotic or sulfa drugs are

given to prevent postoperative urinary infection.

How is urine passed after operations upon the bladder?

1. If there is an opening onto the abdominal wall, a tube catches the urine and it is drained into a receptacle.

2. If the operation is performed through the urethra, urine will be passed in the usual manner.

3. In ureteral transplantation operations, the urine may be diverted to the skin or to the small or large bowel.

How long a hospital stay is necessary?

Simple cystostomy:	7 to 10 days
Stone crushing:	7 days
Open operation for removal of stone:	10 to 14 days
Removal of the bladder tumor through the cystoscope:	7 to 10 days
Open operation for removal of bladder tumor:	14 to 20 days
Repair of bladder fistula:	14 to 21 days
Removal of bladder diverticulum:	14 to 21 days
Total bladder removal:	21 to 28 days

What special postoperative care is necessary?

1. Cystostomy: If the tube is to be left in place permanently, it will need to be changed every 4 to 6 weeks. This may be done in the urologist's office. Simple dressings, changed daily, should be kept around the cystostomy tube.

2. Stone crushing: None, except the antibiotic or sulfa drugs to ward off urinary infection.

3. Open operation for removal of stone: Simple dressings over the wound, which should be healed in 7 to 12 days.

4. Removal of a bladder tumor: Periodic examination of the bladder through a cystoscope is absolutely essential at regular intervals. This is to ensure that any recurrences may be recognized early and dealt with appropriately.

5. Total bladder removal: Simple dressings to the wound. Antibiotic drugs to ward off urinary infection.

6. Repair of bladder fistula: Wound dressings; antibiotic drugs.

7. Removal of diverticulum: Wound dressings; antibiotic drugs.

Are chemicals (chemotherapy) or drugs effective in the treatment of cancer of the bladder?

As a rule, no.

When can normal activity be resumed?

After cystostomy:	4 to 6 weeks
After stone-crushing operation:	2 to 3 weeks
After open operation for removal of stone:	3 to 5 weeks
After removal of bladder tumor through the urethra:	2 to 3 weeks
After open operation of bladder tumor removal:	3 to 5 weeks
After total bladder removal:	8 to 12 weeks
After repair of bladder fistula:	4 to 6 weeks
After removal of diverticulum:	4 to 6 weeks

EXSTROPHY OF BLADDER

What is exstrophy of the bladder?

In a child with a total exstrophy, the roof of the bladder and the entire urethra are exposed, and they lie open on the abdominal wall. In the center of such a mass one can see the openings of the ureters, which come from the kidney into the bladder. The penis is usually small and epispadias exists.

Does exstrophy of the bladder occur mainly in boys?

Yes.

Does exstrophy of the bladder ever occur in girls?

Yes, but not very often.

Can surgery help children with exstrophy of the bladder?

Yes. The operation is preferably done when the child is 3 to 5 years old.

Can the plastic surgeon put the ureters and the urethra in their normal positions?

Yes, if the defect is not too extensive. In performing this operation, the bladder is fashioned into a sac and is replaced within the abdominal cavity.

When is it not feasible to replace the deformed bladder into the abdominal cavity?

It is not possible to reestablish normal anatomical relationships when there is a continuous defect from the bladder to the urethra (the tube leading from the bladder to the outside). Also, if the bladder musculature has become markedly thickened and is infected, it may not be possible to reconstruct the normal anatomy of the area.

What operative procedure is performed for exstrophy when reconstruction of the normal anatomy is not possible?

The bladder and the deformed urethra are removed entirely. The lower ends of the ureters (the tubes leading from the kidneys down to the bladder) are cut across, thereby detaching them from the bladder. A loop of small intestine (ileum) 10 to 12 inches long is isolated and is detached from the rest of the intestinal tract. (The intestine above and below the detached loop is stitched together in order to reestablish bowel continuity.) The blood supply of the loop of ileum is preserved. One end of the ileum is then sewed tightly closed. The other end is brought out onto the skin of the abdominal wall, and the mucous membrane of the intestine is sutured to the skin. The ends of the ureters are then implanted into this loop of ileum. Urine will thereafter drain into this isolated loop and thence out onto the skin. A specially designed plastic apparatus is attached to the skin surrounding the ileum with an adhesive chemical. Thus the urine will drain into a plastic bag, which is attached to the abdomen. The urine will flow continuously, but no one but the patient will be aware of it. When the plastic container is full it can be readily emptied. Some urologists advise another operation for this condition in which the ureters are implanted into the large intestine.

Is surgery for exstrophy of the bladder serious?

Yes, but performed in modern hospitals by well-trained urologists, the mortality rate in these procedures has been reduced to approximately 5 percent. Almost all patients with this condition will die if the operation is not performed.

Are children with exstrophy of the bladder prone to develop infections of the kidney and ureters?

Yes. For this reason, many of them are given antibiotic medications for indefinite periods of time. In this way most kidney infections can be overcome or kept under control.

Can a child lead a substantially normal life after being successfully operated upon for exstrophy?

Yes, in most respects, although the inconvenience of urinary diversion constitutes some impairment of normal activities. Also, there is an increased hazard of kidney obstruction and of chemical imbalance.

What happens to children with exstrophy of the bladder who go untreated?

Most will die from an overwhelming kidney infection or loss of kidney function before they are 10 years old.

BLADDER INJURIES

What are the most common causes of bladder injury?

The urinary bladder is most frequently injured when there is a fracture of the pelvis. This, of course, is caused most often by a fall from a great height or by an automobile accident. The bladder is much more apt to be ruptured when it is full than when it is empty. Occasionally, bladder injury will result from faulty technique in introducing instruments, or during the course of an operative procedure. Fortunately, when recognized, such accidents are easily repaired.

What are the signs of an injury to the urinary bladder?

1. Bloody urine
2. Pain in the lowermost part of the abdomen over the bladder
3. Inability to urinate

What other methods are there for making the diagnosis of a ruptured bladder?

An x-ray of the interior of the bladder can be made after introducing an opaque dye through a catheter. This will show whether the bladder is intact or whether a tear is present. Rupture of the bladder may also be confirmed by cystoscopic examination.

Does it take a very severe injury to rupture the urinary bladder?

Not if the bladder is distended with urine. For this reason an individual should always urinate before engaging in any strenuous athletic activity. Empty bladders rarely rupture unless there has been an accompanying fracture of the pelvis.

What is the treatment for a bladder injury?

1. The patient must be hospitalized immediately.
2. A rubber catheter is inserted into the bladder and kept there so that the bladder remains empty of urine and so that no urine will leak out through a tear in the bladder wall.
3. If the tear in the bladder wall is large, an operation known as a suprapubic cystotomy is performed. This consists of an abdominal incision just above the pubis and an incision into the bladder cavity. The tear in the bladder is repaired and a rubber tube is sutured into the bladder, thus permitting free exit of urine through the tube and into a container attached to it. If there is an associated fracture of the pelvic bones, as there often is with this type of injury, it must be treated by an orthopedic surgeon.

What is the outlook for a person who has sustained a severe bladder injury?

If the injury was recognized early and treated in the proper manner, recovery will take place in almost all instances. If a suprapubic cystotomy tube was inserted, it can be removed in approximately ten days. The opening left after removal of the cystotomy tube will usually close within a few days. For another few days, the bladder is kept empty by urine drainage through a catheter inserted through the urethra.

Are there often permanent ill effects from bladder injuries?

Not if they are treated promptly and adequately.

Uterus

The uterus, or womb, is a pear-shaped muscular organ lying in the middle of the pelvis. It is approximately three inches long, two inches wide, and one inch thick. It consists of an outer, smooth covering, a middle layer composed of thick muscle tissue, and an inner cavity lined with endometrial cells. The cavity of the uterus connects with the vagina through the cervix, and connects with the abdominal cavity through the fallopian tubes. The hollow fallopian tubes open within the abdominal cavity near the ovaries. The uterus is supported and suspended by several ligaments.

See also CERVIX; CESAREAN SECTION; DILATATION AND CURETTAGE; ENDOMETRIOSIS; HYSTERECTOMY; VAGINA.

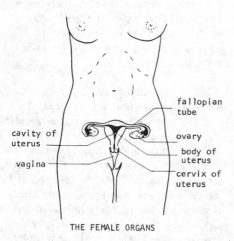

THE FEMALE ORGANS

QUESTIONS AND ANSWERS

What is the exact position of the uterus?

It lies just above the pubic bones, behind the urinary bladder, in front of the rectum, and above the vagina.

What are the functions of the uterus?

1. To prepare for the reception of a fertilized egg

2. To nurture and harbor the embryo during its development

3. To expel the baby when it is mature and ready for delivery

What influences the uterus to prepare for pregnancy?

Hormones which are secreted by the ovaries and the other endocrine glands. If the fertilized egg is not forthcoming, menstruation ensues and the uterine lining is shed. This process is repeated each month, from puberty to menopause, unless there is a glandular upset or, of course, unless pregnancy exists.

What is the significance of a tipped womb?

Ordinarily, this condition has no significance.

What symptoms are caused by a tipped womb?

Usually none. In rare instances, backache and a dragging sensation in the lower pelvic region may occur with the finding of a womb that is tipped markedly in a backward direction.

What is the treatment for a tipped womb?

The great majority of cases require no treatment whatever. The large number of operations for "straightening out" the womb, which were performed years ago, have now been abandoned as unnecessary operative procedures. In rare instances, a vaginal pessary is employed to maintain a forward position of the uterus.

Does a tipped womb interfere with pregnancy?

No.

Does a tipped womb interfere with intercourse?

No.

What is an infantile uterus?

This is a term formerly used to describe a small-sized uterus.

What is the significance of an infantile uterus?

None, providing the uterus functions normally. In other words, if menstruation is normal and pregnancy can take place, a small-sized uterus is of no significance.

Do women with an infantile uterus have difficulty in becoming pregnant?

Not if their menstrual function is normal.

What is atrophy of the uterus?

It refers to the shrinking of the muscles that make up the body of the uterus and the thinning out of the membrane that lines the cavity of the uterus. It occurs in all women who have passed the menopause. During pelvic examination, the doctor will note that the uterus is smaller than normal.

What is endometritis?

It is an infection of the lining of the uterus.

What causes endometritis?

1. It may follow a miscarriage or abortion, particularly after an inept attempt has been made to induce abortion.

2. It may follow normal delivery where an accidental infection of the uterus has taken place.

3. Tuberculosis, where spread to the uterus has come about secondary to infection in the lungs or kidney.

Where are the symptoms of endometritis?

Irregular bleeding, vaginal discharge, pain and tenderness in the lower abdomen, a feeling of weakness, fever, and urinary distress.

What is the treatment for endometritis?

The first step is to determine the exact cause. If there has been an incomplete miscarriage, the uterine cavity must be emptied by the performance of a curettage. If the endometritis has been caused by bacterial infection, antibiotic drugs should be given. If the infection has extended beyond the lining membrane into the wall of the uterus, it may be necessary to remove the uterus in order to effect a cure.

Does endometritis ever heal by itself?

Yes, in certain cases. More often, the infection will spread outward to involve the deeper layers of the uterus, the tubes, the ovaries, and even the abdominal cavity.

What is endometriosis?

A condition in which the lining cells of the uterus (endometrial cells) are found in abnormal locations. These cells may be found deep within the wall of the uterus, on the outer coat of the uterus, the fallopian tubes, the ovaries, the uterine ligaments, bowel, bladder, vagina, or in other places within the abdominal cavity.

How do these endometrial cells exist in abnormal positions?

They implant upon the surface of other structures and grow as small nests of cells. They vary in size from that of a pinhead to the size of an orange. They often form cysts which contain a chocolate-appearing fluid that represents old bloody menstrual-like material.

What abnormal conditions are produced by these endometrial implants?

They may cause firm adhesions between the tubes and the ovaries or the bladder, the bowel, or the uterus. They may form cysts. These cysts may twist or rupture, causing acute abdominal pain and distress.

Do these endometrial implants function like normal uterine cells?

Yes. They become distended and engorged with blood as each menstrual period approaches, and they bleed when menstruation takes place.

What causes endometriosis?

The exact cause is unknown. One theory is that the lining cells of the uterus are expelled through the fallopian tubes by a reverse peristaltic action in the tubes during menstrual periods.

What are some of the symptoms of endometriosis?

1. It may cause no symptoms whatever and be discovered accidentally at operation for another condition.

2. There may be marked pain before and during the menstrual period.

3. There may be marked pain on urination, defecation, or during intercourse.

4. Menstrual bleeding may be noticeably increased.

5. Inability to become pregnant is a symptom of extensive endometriosis.

What is the treatment for endometriosis?

1. Treatment is usually medical and will include the administration of male sex hormones or enough female sex hormones to temporarily stop menstrual periods. However, this type of treatment cannot be given indefinitely.

2. In persistent cases of endometriosis with marked symptoms, hysterectomy may have to be performed. This is reserved for women past the childbearing age or for those whose symptoms are so severe that they demand treatment.

3. In young women in the childbearing age, pregnancy causes temporary relief, since the cyclic influence which causes the symptoms of endometriosis is interrupted.

Does endometriosis lead to cancer?

No.

What can happen if endometriosis is permitted to go untreated?

The symptoms may become progressive and debilitating. If the endometriosis involves the bowel or intestinal tract, obstruction of the bowel may take place. In certain cases, endometrial cysts will grow so large that they will create pressure on other organs and will demand surgery. Endometrial cysts sometimes twist or rupture, thus requiring immediate surgical intervention.

SURGICAL CONDITIONS OF THE UTERUS

What is an endometrial polyp?

It is a growth arising from the lining of the uterus and extending into the uterine cavity. Often, there are multiple polyps.

What are the symptoms of an endometrial polyp?

Cramplike menstrual pain, staining between periods, excessive menstrual bleeding, and vaginal discharge.

How is the diagnosis of an endometrial polyp made?

By diagnostic curettage, or sometimes by the performance of a hysterogram.

What is a hysterogram?

It is an x-ray investigation of the cavity of the uterus performed by injecting an opaque dye through the cervix into the uterine cavity. When films are taken, they will show the outline of the cavity.

Do endometrial polyps ever become malignant?

Yes, occasionally.

What is the treatment for endometrial polyps?

They are removed by curettage. When they protrude through the cervix into the vaginal canal, they can be removed by clamping or crushing with an instrument through the vagina. If there is any evidence of malignant change within the polyp, a total hysterectomy (complete removal of the uterus and cervix) must be performed.

What is a curettage?

This is an operation performed upon the cavity of the uterus through the vagina. It consists of scraping out the lining membrane of the uterus. Special instruments are used to dilate the cervix and to scrape out the uterine cavity.

Why is curettage performed?

1. For diagnostic purposes.
2. For therapeutic purposes.
3. A curettage is often diagnostic and therapeutic at the same time, as in cases of hyperplasia or polyps.

When is a diagnostic curettage performed?

1. In cases of unexplained uterine bleeding.
2. In cases in which a polyp of the uterine cavity is suspected.
3. In cases in which a cancer of the uterus is suspected.
4. In cases in which tuberculosis of the uterus is suspected.

When is a therapeutic curettage performed?

1. When a disorder, such as a polyp, of the lining membrane of the uterus has already been diagnosed, curettage may result in a cure.
2. When an overgrowth of the lining membrane of the uterus (endometrial hyperplasia) has been diagnosed, a curettage will often bring about a cure.
3. Following a miscarriage, when parts of the fetus or placenta remain behind. Curettage in such instances will clean out the cavity and thus restore normalcy.

What is another name for curettage?

It is commonly called a "D and C" operation. This stands for dilatation and curettage.

What is prolapse of the uterus?

It is an abnormal descent of the uterus and cervix into the vagina. It is often associated with disturbance of the bladder and the rectum.

What causes prolapse of the uterus?

Most cases occur as a result of stretching or tears which have been incurred during labor and delivery. Women who have had several children may suffer stretching or tearing of the ligaments and muscles that ordinarily support the uterus and the vagina.

Is prolapse of the uterus caused by poor obstetrical management?

No. Tears of supporting ligaments may take place despite excellent obstetrical care.

Are there various degrees of prolapse?

Yes. There may be just slight descent of the uterus and cervix into the vagina, or the entire cervix and uterus may come down so far that they appear outside the vaginal opening.

What are the symptoms of prolapse of the uterus?

There is a feeling of fullness in the vagina and a sensation that something is falling down. These symptoms are aggravated after walking or lifting a heavy object. The prolapsed structures may interfere with sexual intercourse, and a disturbance in urination and bowel function may be present. Symptoms will depend largely upon the degree of prolapse.

Can prolapse of the uterus be prevented?

Good obstetrical care will tend to minimize the incidence of prolapse, but it often cannot prevent it.

What is the treatment for prolapse?

The treatment is surgical. It will require a plastic operation upon the vagina to reconstruct the ligaments and muscles, or it may require the removal of the uterus and cervix (vaginal hysterectomy).

Are operations for prolapse serious?

They are considered major surgery, but the risks are not great and recovery will take place without too much disability.

How long a period of hospitalization is necessary for prolapse operations?

Approximately five to ten days.

Is there any medical treatment for prolapse?

Yes. The insertion of a pessary will help to keep the uterus and cervix in normal position. However, this form of treatment will not bring about a cure and should not be used as a substitute for surgery unless for some reason the patient cannot undergo an operative procedure. Special exercises for the muscles surrounding the vagina may be helpful.

Why isn't the use of a pessary prolonged indefinitely?

1. It does not cure the underlying deficiency.

2. It may lead to an ulceration of the vagina, an inflammation of the vaginal wall, or secondary infection.

3. The wearing of a pessary requires daily douching.

4. A pessary requires regular visits to the doctor's office for removal, cleansing, and replacement.

What is endometrial hyperplasia?

It is an overgrowth of the lining of the uterus.

What causes endometrial hyperplasia?

It is usually associated with excessive and prolonged production of female sex hormone (estrogen) by the ovaries. Frequently, an ovarian cyst or tumor is present and may be responsible for the production of excess estrogen.

What are the symptoms of endometrial hyperplasia?

It is characterized by completely irregular and unpredictable bleeding, varying from total lack of menstruation to more frequent periods than normal, and from slight staining to profuse bleeding. Characteristically, endometrial hyperplasia results in painless bleeding.

Does endometrial hyperplasia have anything to do with inability to become pregnant (infertility)?

Yes. Women with endometrial hyperplasia often do not ovulate and therefore cannot become pregnant.

How is endometrial hyperplasia diagnosed?

By microscopic examination of tissue which is taken from the lining of the uterus by endometrial biopsy. Also, by examination of tissue removed by curettage.

Where and how is an endometrial biopsy performed?

This is an office procedure and is performed simply by the insertion of a special instrument through the vagina and cervix into the uterine cavity. A small piece of tissue is removed and is examined microscopically.

Is endometrial biopsy a painful procedure?

No. It is a simple office procedure accompanied by a minimal amount of discomfort.

Is there any connection between endometrial hyperplasia and cancer of the uterus?

In women past the childbearing age, it is thought that certain types of endometrial hyperplasia may be associated with development of cancer of the uterus. For this reason, more radical treatment is advised for older women with endometrial hyperplasia.

What is the treatment for endometrial hyperplasia?

This depends upon the age of the patient, the type of hyperplasia found on microscopic examination, and the presence or absence of accompanying ovarian growths. In young females still in the childbearing age, simple hyperplasia is treated by curettage and by use of estrogen and progesterone (ovarian hormones) to simulate the normal menstrual cycle. This is called cyclic therapy.

After menopause, depending upon the type of hyperplasia, the treatment varies from simple curettage to hysterectomy. If the hyperplasia recurs, or shows a preponderance of certain types of cells, and if the patient is past the childbearing age, hysterectomy will probably be the best treatment. In the presence of an enlarged ovary, hyperplasia must be suspected as being related to a tumor of the ovary. In these cases, an abdominal operation should be performed and the ovaries and uterus removed.

Should women who have endometrial hyperplasia return for frequent periodic examinations?

Yes. Any irregularity in the menstrual cycle, if a woman is still in the childbearing age, should stimulate a visit to the gynecologist.

What is the treatment of choice for recurrent hyperplasia in young women?

1. Repeated curettage, or cyclic hormone therapy for a prolonged period.

2. If symptoms of hyperplasia cannot be controlled, it may be necessary to perform a hysterectomy even in a young woman. Fortunately, this is rarely necessary.

What is the incidence of cancer of the body of the uterus?

It is the second most common cancer of the female genital tract. However, cancer of the cervix is five times more frequent than cancer of the body of the uterus.

Who is most likely to develop cancer of the uterus?

It occurs at a later age than cancer of the cervix. It is most prevalent in women past 50.

Is there a tendency to inherit cancer of the uterus?

No.

What is the difference between cancer and sarcoma of the uterus?

Cancer arises from the lining membrane of the uterus, while sarcoma (an equally malignant tumor) arises from the muscle layer of the uterus.

What are the symptoms of cancer of the uterus?

1. Enlargement of the uterus

2. Irregular vaginal bleeding in women still having menstrual periods

3. Bleeding after the menopause

How is cancer of the uterus diagnosed?

By performing diagnostic curettage. Any bleeding in a woman past her menopause must be looked upon with suspicion and must be investigated by curettage to rule out cancer. A cancer smear and an endometrial biopsy are also helpful in establishing the diagnosis.

What treatment is advocated for cancer of the uterus?

Application of radium, followed in four to six weeks by total hysterectomy.

Is this a serious procedure?

Yes, but recovery from the surgery will take place in almost all cases.

What is the rate of cure for cancer of the body of the uterus?

If the cancer is detected before it has extended beyond the confines of the uterus, approximately four out of five cases can be cured. In cases where spread has already gone beyond the uterus, only about one out of five can be cured.

Is it possible to prevent cancer of the uterus?

It cannot be prevented, but it *can* be detected earlier if women seek medical help as soon as they notice abnormal vaginal bleeding.

What is the significance of an enlarging uterus in a woman past 60?

It indicates, in almost all instances, the presence of a malignant tumor.

What are an older woman's chances for survival after surgery for cancer of the uterus?

Unless the malignancy has already spread beyond the confines of the uterus, approximately 70 percent of all women can be cured of cancer of the uterus.

What are fibroids (leiomyoma) of the uterus?

Fibroids are benign tumors composed of muscle tissue. They tend to be round in shape and firm in consistency.

What is the incidence of fibroids?

Almost 25 percent of all women have fibroids of the uterus. The majority of such growths cause no symptoms and demand no treatment.

What causes fibroids?

Although the exact cause is unknown, it has been found that certain ovarian hormones play an important role in the speed of growth. Thus, after menopause, when very little ovarian hormone is being secreted, fibroids stop growing and may even shrink.

When are women most likely to develop fibroids?

During the later stages of the childbearing period, that is, between the ages of 40 and 50 years. However, they may be found in women in their early 20s or in those past menopause.

Do fibroids tend to run in families?

There is no actual inherited tendency, but since one in four women have fibroids, it is not uncommon to find more than one member of a family with this condition.

What are the various types of fibroids?

1. Subserous: those growing beneath the outer coat of the uterus

2. Intramural: those growing in the muscular layer of the uterus

3. Submucous: those growing beneath the lining membrane of the uterine cavity

Do fibroids vary greatly in size?

Yes. They may be as small as a pinhead or as large as a watermelon. They are almost always multiple.

Do fibroids of the uterus develop often in women past 60?

No. It is most unusual for women past 60 to develop new fibroids.

If fibroids have been present for many years, what happens to them after 60?

There is a tendency for them to become smaller, just as there is a tendency for the normal uterine muscle to shrink. However, if they are very large, they will not disappear entirely.

What are the symptoms of fibroids?

1. Many fibroids cause no symptoms and are found inadvertently on routine pelvic examination.

2. If the fibroid is submucous in type, it may cause uterine bleeding between periods or prolonged heavy menstruation.

3. Intramural and subserous fibroids may cause excessive menstrual bleeding but may produce no symptoms at all.

4. There may be frequency of urination and difficulty in bowel function if the fibroids grow to a large size and press upon the bladder or rectum.

5. Backache or lower abdominal pain occurs occasionally.

6. Infertility may ensue if the fibroid distorts the uterine cavity.

How is the diagnosis of fibroids made?

By manual pelvic examination. Such a vaginal examination will reveal the size, shape, and other features of the tumor. A hysterogram may help to diagnose small submucous fibroids.

Is a fibroid of the uterus a malignant tumor?

Definitely not. Fibroids are benign growths!

Do fibroids become cancerous?

Rarely, cancer develops in a uterus containing fibroids, but the presence of the fibroid does not predispose toward the development of the cancer.

Are fibroids found in association with other conditions within the uterus?

Yes. There is a high incidence of endometrial polyps and endometrial hyperplasia in those patients who have fibroids.

What is the best treatment for fibroids?

If the fibroids produce symptoms or grow rapidly, they should be removed surgically.

What operative procedures are performed for fibroids?

When only the fibroids are removed, it is called a myomectomy. When the entire uterus is removed, it is termed a hysterectomy.

How does a gynecologist decide whether to perform a myomectomy or a hysterectomy?

This will depend upon the age of the patient and her desire to have children. If the patient desires children, an attempt will be made to preserve the uterus, and a myomectomy will be performed.

Are there methods of treating fibroids other than myomectomy or hysterectomy?

Yes. Some small submucous fibroids can be removed by simple curettage, when they develop into polyplike growths.

Do fibroids have a tendency to recur?

Ten percent will recur following a myomectomy. Of course, if the entire uterus is removed, fibroids cannot recur.

Must all fibroids be operated upon?

No. A fair proportion require no treatment whatever.

What are the indications for surgical removal of fibroids?

1. Increased, prolonged, and more frequent menstruation

2. Episodes of severe bleeding between periods

3. Pressure symptoms causing continued urinary or rectal discomfort

4. Rapid increase in the size of a fibroid

5. Any fibroid larger than the size of a three-month pregnancy, even if it causes no symptoms

6. Acute pain due to degeneration of a fibroid or to a twist in a fibroid

7. Repeated miscarriage or sterility

Do fibroids ever occur during pregnancy?

Yes. When present, they may increase in size as the pregnancy grows.

Should a fibroid be treated during pregnancy?

No. It is best to postpone treatment until after the baby is born.

Can a woman become pregnant after surgery for fibroids?

If a myomectomy has been performed, subsequent pregnancy is possible. In such cases, the baby may have to be delivered by cesarean section.

Is the surgical treatment of fibroids usually successful?

Yes, in almost all cases.

Is there any satisfactory nonsurgical treatment for fibroids?

No, despite the fact that some physicians used to think that hormone treatment was of some benefit.

Is myomectomy considered a major operation?

Yes, since it involves an abdominal incision. However, recovery takes place in almost all instances. Hospitalization for five to ten days is usually required.

Does menstruation return to normal after myomectomy?

Yes.

How long does it take to recover from the effects of myomectomy?

Approximately six weeks.

How long should a woman wait after myomectomy before attempting pregnancy?

Three to six months.

What is hysterectomy?

An operation for the removal of the uterus.

What are the various types of hysterectomy?

1. Subtotal or supracervical hysterectomy: removal of the body of the uterus leaving the cervix behind

2. Total hysterectomy: removal of the body of the uterus and the cervix

3. Radical hysterectomy: removal of at least one third of the vagina, the supporting tissues, and lymph nodes along with the body and cervix of the uterus

4. Porro section: removal of the uterus at the time of delivery of a baby by cesarean section

5. Vaginal hysterectomy: removal of the uterus and cervix through the vagina instead of through an abdominal incision

What are some of the indications for hysterectomy?

1. Symptomatic fibroids

2. Chronic, incurable inflammatory disease of the uterus, tubes, and ovaries, such as gonorrhea or tuberculosis

3. Severe recurrent endometrial hyperplasia

4. Cancer of the uterus or cervix

5. Cancer of the tubes or ovaries

6. Chronic disabling endometriosis

7. Uncontrollable hemorrhage following delivery of a baby

8. In certain cases where the ovaries must be removed for cysts or growths

9. Rupture of the uterus during pregnancy or labor

What are the indications for the performance of a vaginal hysterectomy?

When there is prolapse of the uterus along with a cystocele and rectocele, it is sometimes advisable to remove the uterus through the vagina so that a vaginal plastic operation can be performed at the same time. This cannot be done if the uterus is enlarged to such an extent that it cannot be delivered through the vagina. Vaginal hysterectomy is not indicated when a malignancy is suspected.

Is vaginal hysterectomy a dangerous operative procedure?

No. It carries with it the same risks as hysterectomy performed through an abdominal incision.

Does the removal of the uterus affect one's sex life in any way?

No. The removal of the uterus, with or without the removal of the ovaries, does not affect sexual ability or sexual desire. As a matter of fact, some women state that they are happier in their marital relations after hysterectomy than before.

Vagina

The vagina is a tubelike canal, approximately three to four inches in length, extending internally from its opening at the vulva to the cervix of the uterus. It is lined by a mucous membrane which has many folds and great elasticity.

Plastic operations upon the vagina: This type of surgery is performed for various conditions resulting from stretching and tearing of the supporting muscles and ligaments of the vagina. The most frequent cause for such damage is childbirth. Interestingly enough, symptoms may not appear until many years after childbirth. It is important to know before embarking upon surgery for such tears whether the patient contemplates having more children, as it is wisest to delay this type of surgery until all childbearing has taken place.

The main conditions requiring plastic repair of the vagina are:

1. Prolapse of the uterus (fallen womb).

2. Cystocele, or fallen bladder: This condition is characterized by a bulging of the bladder and upper wall of the vagina through the vaginal opening. This bulge is most noticeable on coughing or straining at stool. Symptoms of cystocele include involuntary loss of urine on sneezing, coughing, laughing, or straining (stress incontinence). In some instances, despite the presence of a large cystocele, urinary control is not affected.

3. Rectocele: This condition is characterized by a bulging of the rectum and lower vaginal wall through the orifice of the vagina.

All three of the above conditions may exist together or may exist individually. Prolapse of the uterus is often accompanied by lower abdominal discomfort of varying degrees, and may be associated with lower back pain and fatigue. The degree of the prolapse may have no direct relationship to the severity of symptoms. The symptoms of a rectocele also vary considerably, the most common being difficulty in evacuating the bowels.

The operations available for these conditions are many and varied. An important point to stress is that the mere presence of a prolapse, cystocele, or rectocele *without* symptoms does not necessitate surgery. It is only when symptoms directly related to the condition are present that surgery will benefit the patient.

The type of operative procedure to be performed will depend upon the particular combination of vaginal defects that exist. If only one defect is present, it alone is repaired. If prolapse of the womb, cystocele, rectocele, and a torn vaginal outlet are all present, then an operation is done which will repair all at the same time. The surgeon will amputate the cervix, open the anterior and posterior vaginal walls for the purpose of shortening and tightening the supporting ligaments to the bladder and rectum, and narrow the vaginal outlet. The incision for this complete *vaginalplasty* is within the vagina and no external scars will be visible.

Whenever possible, vaginal plastic operations should be deferred until the family has been completed. If necessary, temporary relief may be obtained with the use of a pessary. This is a plastic ring inserted into the vagina to hold the uterus, bladder, and rectum from protruding. The pessary, however, is not a permanent substitute for surgery, as it requires that the patient take daily vaginal irrigations and make frequent visits to the gynecologist. Vaginal discharge, irritation, and infection are not infrequent complications of prolonged usage of a pessary. Permanent use is therefore confined to those women who are not in sufficiently good general health to withstand surgery.

Vaginal plastic operations are carried out in a hospital under spinal or general anesthesia. Although they are considered to be major surgical procedures, they are not dangerous and recovery ensues in all cases unless some unforeseen complication develops. The pa-

tient is out of bed the day after surgery and is able to go home in five to seven days. There is often difficulty in spontaneous urination following vaginal repair, and the urine is therefore drained off through a catheter for a few days.

Results of this type of surgery are excellent and symptoms are relieved in the overwhelming majority of cases.

See also CERVIX; CYSTOCELE AND RECTOCELE; VULVECTOMY.

QUESTIONS AND ANSWERS

What are the functions of the vagina?

1. It is the ultimate female organ of intercourse.

2. It is a receptacle for the deposit of male sperm.

3. It is the outlet for the discharge of menstrual fluid.

4. It is the passageway for delivery of the baby during labor.

Should women douche regularly?

Some gynecologists do recommend douching for purely hygienic purposes; others recommend it only for specific medical conditions.

What is the best solution with which to douche?

An acid douche containing white distilled vinegar or lactic acid is adequate. Other commercially prepared douches are also effective. They should be prescribed by a physician.

Are strong antiseptic douches harmful?

Yes. Strong chemicals can cause vaginal ulcers or burns.

Should young girls douche if they have a vaginal discharge or unpleasant odor?

Not without a gynecologist's specific instructions.

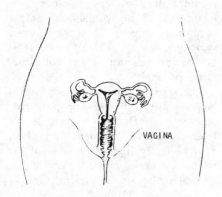

VAGINA

Should women take a cleansing douche the day following sexual relations or following the conclusion of a menstrual period?

Not necessarily. A bath is quite satisfactory.

Is cancer of the vagina very common?

No. This is a rare disease.

What is the treatment for cancer of the vagina?

Wide surgical excision of the vagina or radium implantation.

What other growths may affect the vagina?

1. Polyps
2. Cysts
3. Benign tumors, such as fibromas of the vaginal wall

What is the treatment for benign growths of the vagina?

Simple surgical removal will bring about a cure in all of the above conditions.

What is prolapse of the uterus?

It is an abnormal descent of the uterus and cervix into the vagina. It is often associated with disturbance of the bladder and the rectum.

What is a cystocele?

It is a hernia of the bladder wall into the vagina. Cystoceles may vary in degree from a mild bulge into the vagina to a maximum descent in which almost the entire bladder protrudes through the vaginal opening.

What is a rectocele?

It is a hernia of the rectal wall into the vagina. Again, the degree of herniation varies markedly from case to case.

What causes cystoceles or rectoceles?

They are caused by the same type of injury that causes a prolapse, that is, a tear of supporting ligaments as a result of childbirth.

How often do cystocele, rectocele, and prolapse occur?

These are common conditions. The incidence is greater in women who have had many children. Also, women past 40 are more likely to develop these conditions as their supporting ligaments begin to weaken and stretch.

Do cystocele, rectocele, and prolapse tend to occur together?

Yes, in a great number of instances. However, it is entirely possible to have a prolapse without a cystocele or rectocele, or to have a cystocele without a rectocele, or vice versa.

What are the symptoms of cystocele?

The most common symptoms are frequency of urination, loss of urine on coughing, sneezing, laughing, or physical exertion. There may also be a sensation of a bulge into the vagina.

What are the symptoms of rectocele?

A feeling of pressure in the vagina and rectum, with difficulty in evacuating the bowels.

Do cystocele or rectocele and prolapse ever lead to cancer?

No.

What is the treatment for cystocele and rectocele?

A vaginal plastic operation, in which the torn ligaments and muscles are repaired and stretched or excess tissues are excised.

Are operations for cystocele and rectocele serious?

No, but they demand the attention of an expert gynecologist who understands the anatomy and function of the region.

How long a period of hospitalization is necessary following vaginal plastic operations?

Five to ten days.

Are the results of operations for cystocele, rectocele, and prolapse satisfactory?

Yes. Cure can be accomplished in most cases.

Can cystocele, rectocele, or prolapse be corrected medically?

No, but temporary relief can be obtained with the use of rings or pessaries. Such appliances do not bring about a cure. Special exercises for the muscles surrounding the vagina may also be helpful.

When is surgery necessary for cystocele, rectocele, or prolapse?

When the symptoms, as mentioned previously, are sufficient to interfere with normal happy living, or when bladder or bowel function becomes impaired.

Are there any visible scars following vaginal plastic operations?

No.

What type of anesthesia is used for these procedures?

Either spinal or general anesthesia.

How long do these operations take to perform?

A complete vaginal plastic operation may take anywhere from one to two hours.

Are operations upon the vagina very painful?

No.

How soon after vaginal operations is the patient permitted to get out of bed?

On the day following surgery.

Are any special postoperative precautions necessary?

Yes, a catheter may be placed in the bladder for a few days in order to aid restoration of bladder function.

What is the effect of vaginal plastic operations on the bladder and the rectum?

Occasionally, for the first week or two there may be difficulty in urinating. Also, in operations for rectocele there may be difficulty in moving one's bowels for a similar period. These complications are temporary and will subside spontaneously.

Do stitches have to be removed after these operations?

No. The stitches are absorbable and do not have to be removed.

Is it common to bleed after operations upon the vagina?

Yes. Slight staining may continue on and off for several weeks.

Do vaginal plastic operations interfere with marital relations?

No. When the tissues have healed, intercourse can be resumed. This usually takes six to eight weeks.

Can women have babies after surgery for a cystocele or rectocele?

Yes, but delivery may have to be performed by cesarean section, as surgery may have interfered with the ability of these structures to stretch and dilate sufficiently. Also, vaginal delivery might bring on a recurrence of the cystocele or rectocele.

Can pregnancy take place after surgery for prolapse of the uterus?

Yes, if only the cervix has been removed. Here, too, delivery should be by cesarean section. Of course, if a hysterectomy has been performed in order to cure the prolapse, pregnancy cannot take place.

When is it best to undergo plastic repair?

After one has completed having children.

VAGINITIS

What is vaginitis?

It is an inflammation of the vagina.

What causes vaginitis?

1. Parasitic infections such as trichomonas
2. Fungi such as monilia
3. Common bacterial infections with staphylococcus, streptococcus, and others
4. Changes due to old age (senile vaginitis)
5. Occasionally the administration of antibiotic drugs which destroy certain useful vaginal bacteria

Does the healthy vagina contain bacteria?

Yes, and most of these bacteria are beneficial and are not the cause of disease.

What causes parasitic or fungal infections of the vagina?

A change in vaginal acidity which permits these organisms to outgrow the other organisms that are normally present.

What lessens acidity of the vagina?

Menstrual blood will often lessen the acidity and allow harmful organisms to grow and multiply and produce the symptoms of vaginitis.

What are the sypmtoms of vaginitis?

This will depend upon the cause of the infection. Parasitic, fungal, or bacterial vaginitis usually produces the following symptoms:

1. Itching of the vulva
2. Vaginal discharge
3. Pain on intercourse
4. Pain and frequency of urination

5. Swelling of the external genital structures

What tests are performed to determine the type of vaginitis present?

A smear of the vaginal discharge is taken and is submitted to microscopic examination. This will demonstrate whether the infection is caused by monilia, trichomonas, or bacteria.

What is the treatment for vaginitis?

This will depend upon its cause:

1. **Fungal infections** are now treated successfully by giving various antifungal medications by mouth as well as local applications into the vaginal canal. The most commonly used oral medication is Flagyl.
2. **Bacterial vaginitis** is treated with one of the antibiotic medications, administered orally and locally.
3. **Senile vaginitis** is treated by the administration of various female hormones which are applied locally or given by mouth or by injection.

How successful is the treatment of fungal vaginitis with oral medications?

These have proved to be most successful. A course of treatment extending over a period of ten days will clear up the condition in most cases.

Is there a tendency for vaginitis to recur?

Yes. Many types of vaginitis do have this tendency. For this reason, treatment must be continued over a prolonged period of time. It is common for people to discontinue treatment too quickly because of early relief of symptoms.

What is the most common time for a vaginitis to recur?

Just before or after a menstrual period, and during the later months of pregnancy. This strongly suggests that hormone changes in the vaginal lining play an important role in this condition.

Is a fungal infection of the vagina ever spread to the male?

Yes, the infection may spread to the male organ.

Does vaginitis ever occur in children?

Yes. Vulvovaginitis is not uncommon in young girls from 2 to 15 years of age. The infection is transmitted by poor hygiene and poor toilet habits.

What are the symptoms of vaginitis in children?

The child will complain of pain and itching in the region of the vulva. There will also be pain on urination, and the parent will notice a vaginal discharge.

What is the treatment for vaginitis in children?

Specific medications should be given for the specific infection. These may include the administration of medications orally and the application of ointments locally.

What is senile vaginitis?

It is an inflammation of the mucous membrane of the vagina, which is brought on by the changes that accompany the aging process. The cells lining the vagina become thinner, secrete less mucus, and are more likely to become inflamed or infected.

What are the symptoms of senile vaginitis?

1. Itching in the genital region
2. Discharge, with odor, from the vagina

Is senile vaginitis common in older women?

Yes, particularly in people in their 70s or 80s.

What is the treatment of vaginal discharge and itching in older women?

It must be determined first that the symptoms are caused only by senile vaginitis. A complete examination, including the Papanicolaou smear test, is performed to rule out the possibility of a tumor in the reproductive tract.

If the vaginitis is due to a fungal infection, antifungal tablets are taken by mouth and local medications are applied. (There are many effective powders, suppositories, and ointments that can control this type of infection.)

If the vaginitis is bacterial in origin, antibiotic medications are often given by mouth and applied locally. Also, medicated douches may be prescribed.

Will taking female sex hormones control senile vaginitis?

Hormones may bring the condition under control for a short period of time, but it will return soon after treatment is stopped. Today, most gynecologists feel that hormone treatment should not continue for more than a few weeks.

Why should an older woman not be given female sex hormones for long periods of time?

Because the hormones might create an artificial situation in which the uterus might be stimulated to become active again. It is thought, although not proved conclusively, that such ovarian stimulation may contribute to the activation of a dormant tumor. Another reason why prolonged hormone therapy is not generally advocated is that the symptoms of senile vaginitis recur soon after the treatment is discontinued.

Will the giving of cortisone or cortisone-like medications control senile vaginitis?

Yes, for a short time. Again, these

medications may have harmful effects if taken too long.

Is itching around the female genital region ever caused by allergic conditions?

Yes. This is a very frequent cause of itching, especially when one is sensitive to nylon, rubber, or other materials. If this is the case, cotton underclothing should be worn.

How common in older women is a bacterial infection in the vaginal tract?

Not very common, even though the membranes are somewhat less resistant to infection as one gets older.

Vagotomy

Vagotomy is a surgical procedure in which the various branches of the vagus (tenth cranial) nerve are cut. The procedure can be carried out either through an incision in the chest which includes the cutting of the nerves prior to their passage through the diaphragm, or it can be accomplished by an upper abdominal incision.

Vagotomy is a procedure frequently performed in conjunction with other operations upon the stomach to relieve the symptoms of a peptic ulcer. Today, vagotomy is carried out along with hemigastrectomy (removal of half the stomach), antrectomy (removal of the pyloric portion of the stomach), or with pyloroplasty (a plastic operation upon the pyloric, or lower, end of the stomach) to allow reflux of duodenal contents into the stomach.

The cutting of the vagus nerves before they enter the stomach will markedly diminish the amount of acid secreted by the lining membrane of the stomach, and this, in turn, will lessen the chances of a recurrence of an ulcer of the duodenum or stomach. The procedure is essential as an adjunct to ulcer surgery when the gastric acidity has proved to be at a high level.

Following vagotomy, contractions (peristalsis) may be diminished, and therefore it is important to do a drainage operation upon the stomach to allow it to empty properly. The operation accompanying vagotomy is therefore either a pyloroplasty or the joining of the stomach to the small intestine through a procedure known as gastrojejunostomy.

See also STOMACH AND DUODENUM.

Varicocele

A varicocele is present when the veins of the spermatic cord, leading from the testicle up to the prostate gland, become dilated and varicosed. It almost always occurs on the left side of the scrotum, and when examined, feels like a "bag of worms." This condition is not serious nor usually harmful, but may produce a dragging sensation in the groin and lower abdomen. For some unknown reason, men who have varicoceles may have a higher-than-normal incidence of sterility, and release of the varicocele through surgery may cure the condition. The majority of varicoceles, however, can be left alone unless they become very large or are the source of marked discomfort. If operated upon, an incision in the scrotum is made under anesthesia, and a block segment of the varicose veins is tied off and removed. The operation is a simple one, followed by relief of symptoms. The removal of the diseased veins does not interfere with testicular function.

See also TESTICLES.

Varicocele is the dilation of a vein along the spermatic cord in the scrotum.

QUESTIONS AND ANSWERS

Is varicocele a very common condition?

Yes. It is a frequent finding among young adult males.

Why does varicocele occur on the left so much more often than on the right?

It is thought that there is more pressure placed upon the veins on the left than on the right side of the body, and the angle at which these veins enter the pelvis causes greater obstruction. This may, in some instances, lead to the formation of varicosities.

Is there much pain from an operation to relieve a varicocele?

No.

How long a hospital stay is usually necessary for removal of a varicocele?

Approximately three to four days.

How soon after a varicocele operation can one return to work?

In seven to ten days.

Varicose Veins

Approximately one of every two women and one of every four men over 40 years of age suffer from varicose veins. Younger people, too, are subject to this condition but not in as great numbers as those in older age groups. Incompetent or varicose veins are one of the penalties humans have been forced to pay in exchange for the many advantages gained in attaining the upright state. Four-legged animals do not develop varicose veins!

The function of veins is to transport blood from the capillaries in the distant tissues back to the heart. This task is not an easy one since there is no pump (such as the heart) out in the tissues to push blood back up into the chest. And most important of all, the blood in the limbs of the upright human must work its way back to the heart while overcoming the natural pull of gravity. This is accomplished in several ways: by contraction of the leg and thigh muscles, by the squeezing effect of continuous movement, and by expansion and contraction of the lungs which occurs during breathing, thus creating a periodic negative pressure in the chest. This negative pressure causes blood to be sucked up toward the heart. *The entire process is aided by the valves within the veins which prevent the blood from falling back down toward the feet once it has flowed upward.*

Such a system (the venous system) is awkward at best, and it is small wonder that so many breakdowns occur. When obstruction is present in the venous system or when prolonged pressure is placed upon the veins, the valves tear and become incompetent. With the valves damaged, the veins dilate markedly and blood stagnates within them. The condition may then be referred to as *varicose veins*. Varicose veins are found more often in women than in men, since women are more prone to develop pressure upon the return flow of blood. Pregnancy produces great pressure on the veins in the pelvis and often results in backward pressure upon the veins in the thighs and legs, damage to their valves, and varicose veins. Barbers, dentists, clerks, laborers, and others who spend many hours standing in one position tend to develop great pressure upon the valves, with ultimate breakdown and formation of varicosities. Also, inflammation within the veins (phlebitis) may cause destruction of the valves and varicose vein formation.

Varicose veins are unsightly, but more important, they produce symptoms such as a heavy, tired feeling in the legs and a generalized feeling of lassitude. Many people complain that their legs feel so heavy that it is a great effort for them to do work. The stagnation and pooling of this extra blood in the lower limbs is bad for one's general circulation. Eczema (skin rashes) and ulcerations of the skin frequently result if varicose veins become extensive and blood drainage from the legs is inadequate.

It is fortunate that varicosities are usually limited to the superficial veins under the skin. The deep veins which carry the great bulk of the blood back to the heart are rarely afflicted with varicosities. For this reason it is safe to remove (strip) or tie off (ligate) or inject the incompetent superficial veins. After satisfactory treatment of the varicose veins has been carried out, blood that formerly stagnated within the diseased veins travels directly from the superficial tissues to the competent deep vessels. The main exception to this process is when the deep veins are clogged or obstructed from a previous inflammation (phlebitis). Under such circumstances, the superficial veins act as the main channel through which blood returns to the heart, and it would not be safe to remove or inject or tie them off no matter how varicosed they happen to be.

In order to determine whether surgical treatment should be instituted, one must first ascertain that the deep veins are competent to take over the full load of carrying most of the blood. There are many useful tests to establish this information but perhaps the easiest one is the *Ace bandage compression test:*

The patient is made to wear snugly fitting elastic bandages from the toes to the groin for a period of several hours. By so doing, the circulation in the superficial varicose veins is mechanically shut off, and one learns whether the deep veins can handle the blood return alone. If the patient states that he is comfortable while wearing the elastic bandages, one knows that the deep veins are open and that the superficial varicose veins can be treated without fear of interfering with the return venous circulation. If wearing the tight elastic bandages is painful or uncomfortable, the surgeon will surmise that the deep veins are diseased or inadequate. He will hesitate, under such circumstances, to inject or remove or tie off the varicosities.

There are three main forms of surgical treatment for varicose veins: (1) injection, (2) cutting and ligation, and (3) ligation and stripping.

1. Injection treatment: This form of treatment involves injecting a sclerosing (hardening) solution into the veins which will cause the stagnant blood within to clot. The clot will extend up and down for a few inches from the site of injection. The blood that would ordinarily travel in this segment of the varicose vein changes its course and travels instead through the competent deep veins. Injections are repeated at intervals of five to ten days for several months (or even years) until all of the varicosities are obliterated (sclerosed). The injections themselves are not particularly painful and are carried out with safety in the surgeon's office. The patient is urged to go about his business after injection, to keep walking, and not to go to bed. A good result from an injection may be accompanied by redness, lumpiness, heat, and a painful clot in the region of the injection. This reaction may develop within a day or two after injection and may last for several days. It is important to advise the patient beforehand that such a reaction is a good one and should not cause alarm. Injection of varicose veins is a safe procedure and is not followed by the traveling of the clot to distant parts of the body (embolus).

Unfortunately, in about 60 to 70 percent of all cases, the injection treatment is followed by eventual recurrence of old varicose veins or formation of new ones. Most surgeons therefore reserve the injection treatment for those who have small and occasional varicosities or for those who are unable, for medical reasons, to undergo surgery.

The principal value of injection treatment is as a follow-up to surgery. Since neither surgical ligation nor ligation and stripping is able to cure all the varicose veins, the ones that remain frequently require further attention. In such instances, repeated injections of a clot-producing solution is most helpful.

2. Cutting and ligation: One form of treatment for varicose veins is the surgical ligation (tying off) and cutting of the main saphenous vein and all of its tributaries (branches) in the groin. (See diagram.) This operation changes the course of the venous flow from the in-

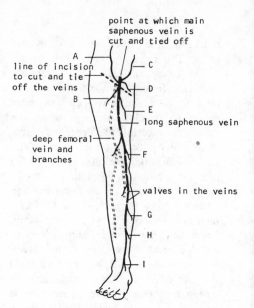

THE SAPHENOUS VEIN AND TRIBUTARIES
(A,B,C,D,E,F,G,H,I- BRANCHES OF
SAPHENOUS VEIN SYSTEM)

competent, superficial, varicose veins to the competent, deep veins of the legs and thighs. Much of the swelling and heaviness of the limbs disappears after this procedure, as the blood no longer tends to pool and stagnate in the dilated veins. It is usually insufficient merely to cut and tie off the main saphenous vein and its branches in the groin, as there are incompetent valves connecting superficial and deep veins in the thighs and lower legs. It is important, in order to effect a cure, to separately cut and ligate these vessels. Thus a patient with extensive varicose veins may require several additional incisions of one to two inches in length along the course of the varicosities in the thighs or legs.

Varicose vein ligations are performed in the hospital under local or spinal anesthesia. The limbs are snugly bandaged after surgery, and the patient is encouraged to get up and walk as soon after the operation as possible. While this operation may take an hour or two to perform, it is considered a minor procedure and carries with it little or no danger. The patient can be discharged from the hospital within one to four days, and the skin sutures can be removed a week later in the surgeon's office.

It is amazing to note how much relief patients obtain in a matter of a few days after a vein ligation operation. Approximately 80 percent of all patients get excellent results, while the remaining 20 percent claim fair results. However, reoperation several months later with further cutting and ligation of those varicose veins that were not originally obliterated often converts what had appeared to be a failure into a successful result. Patients should be cautioned beforehand that reoperation may be required to cure some of the varicosities that may remain after the first operation.

3. Ligation and stripping: Most surgeons feel that multiple cutting and ligations are not sufficient to cure extensive varicose veins and they therefore ad-

vocate the additional maneuver of stripping the saphenous vein. (See diagram.)

Stripping means threading a long wire through the end of the main vein in the groin and feeding it through to the ankle. A separate incision is made over the ankle and the end of the wire is retrieved. The wire is firmly tied into the vein in the groin and is then pulled out from the ankle. This causes the vein to be removed from above downward by inversion within itself (stripping). In some instances, it is easier to strip from the ankle up toward the groin.

Stripping is followed by a somewhat higher cure rate than mere ligation and cutting but is followed by greater postoperative discomfort because of bleeding into the tissues beneath the skin.

QUESTIONS AND ANSWERS

What are varicose veins?

They are dilated, incompetent veins with damaged valves. Blood tends to stagnate within them.

How common are varicose veins?

Twenty-five percent of all men and 50 percent of all women over 40 years of age have varicose veins.

What causes varicose veins?

Prolonged back pressure upon the veins with eventual breakdown of the valves within the veins. Pregnancy is a common cause. Also, occupations that require standing in one position for prolonged periods of time each day.

What symptoms do they produce?

They may, when small in size and number, produce no symptoms. They may, when large and numerous, produce heavy dragging pain in the legs, general tiredness and lassitude, and lack of physical energy. If untreated, they may lead

stripper

stripper within main saphenous vein at groin

A this stripper is tied firmly to the vein

stripper emerging from long vein at ankle

B

STRIPPING FOR VARICOSE VEINS

to skin ulcerations, hemorrhages, or eczema.

Do varicose veins tend to run in families?
Yes.

What veins are usually affected?
The superficial veins of the legs and thighs.

Is there any way to prevent varicose veins from forming?
1. Avoid constricting garters.
2. Avoid standing in one position for prolonged periods.
3. Engage in brisk walks.
4. Use supporting elastic stockings if forced to stand in one position for prolonged periods.

How large do varicose veins become?
In some instances varicose veins can attain the diameter of one's thumb.

Are the larger and more extensive varicosities more difficult to cure?
Not necessarily. Surgery is very effective in treating even the largest of varicose veins.

What happens to the circulation of blood when the varicose veins are cut or stripped?
The blood returns to the heart via the competent deep veins. Thus much stagnation is avoided and the general circulation is improved.

Do they ever disappear without treatment?
No. Once a vein is damaged, it does not heal spontaneously.

Is there a satisfactory medical treatment?
No. However, considerable relief can be obtained in certain cases by wearing elastic stockings or bandages.

Will wearing elastic bandages or elastic stockings cure varicose veins?
No. They merely relieve symptoms by temporarily closing off the varicosities.

Do the deep veins ever become varicosed?
Only rarely. However, they are frequently involved in phlebitis.

What is phlebitis?
An inflammation of a vein. It is almost always followed by destruction of the valves and by a clot within the vein.

What are varicose ulcers?
Loss of skin on the legs due to the poor nutrition occasioned by the stagnating blood. They may, in advanced cases, attain several inches in diameter and may last for years.

Do ulcers of skin and rashes heal after operation for varicose veins?
Yes.

Do varicose veins ever hemorrhage through the skin?
Yes.

How does one stop hemorrhage from varicose veins?
By placing and maintaining pressure directly over the bleeding point.

Do all varicose veins have to be operated upon?
No. Only those that produce local symptoms in the legs or general symptoms such as impairment of general circulatory efficiency. Also, those in which complications such as severe eczema, skin ulceration, or hemorrhage take place.

When is an operation for varicose veins necessary?
1. When the general body circulation is impaired by the pooling of blood in the lower limbs
2. When the patient has pain in the legs and a generally tired feeling and lack of energy

3. When severe skin rashes or ulcerations of the leg take place

4. When the legs become swollen and the veins are too unsightly

5. When hemorrhage from a varicose vein takes place

How does a surgeon decide whether or not to operate on varicose veins?

1. He must first assure himself that the deep veins are competent and not closed off or involved in phlebitis.

2. The patient must obtain some relief while wearing elastic bandages. This shows that his symptoms will improve when the superficial veins are permanently closed off.

How does a surgeon decide whether to use the injection treatment or a surgical procedure?

The injection treatment is rarely advocated as the sole form of treatment. Surgery is advised in almost all cases unless the general condition of the patient is exceptionally poor.

Is it dangerous to operate on old people with varicose veins?

Only when it has been determined that their deep venous circulation is inadequate. If it is ascertained that the deep veins are healthy, then operation can be performed on people of any age.

What are the forms of surgical treatment for varicose veins?

1. Injection treatment to produce a clot in the veins

2. Ligation and cutting of the veins

3. Ligation and stripping (removal) of the veins

What are the results from injection treatment?

Cure is obtained in only about 25 to 30 percent of the cases. It is particularly ineffective for people with varicose veins above the level of the knee.

Does injection treatment or surgery help the many tiny bluish varicose veins that women so frequently get on their thighs and legs?

Usually treatment for such small varicosities is unnecessary except for cosmetic reasons. Surgery is not performed in these cases, but injection treatment occasionally proves helpful.

What are the results from surgery upon the varicose veins?

Good. Approximately 85 to 90 percent of people get excellent results, and the others get some relief.

Exactly what is done when the veins are ligated and cut?

The large veins are dissected out and clamped. They are cut across between the clamps, and each end is securely tied.

How does blood get back to the heart after cutting and removing so many veins?

Blood travels through the deep veins.

How urgent is surgery for varicose veins?

Surgery is an elective procedure except when there is interference with general circulation due to pooling of excess blood in the limbs or when skin ulcerations or hemorrhages take place. In these situations, surgery should be performed immediately.

Are the various forms of treatment dangerous?

No. Operative recovery, barring accident, always follows varicose vein surgery.

What will happen if surgery is refused in a severe case?

Deep, nonhealing ulcerations of the skin may develop. General health may become impaired. Severe infection of the tissues of the leg may develop, and in some instances phlebitis (inflammation of the veins) may set in. Hemorrhage may occur if a varicose vein ulcerates through the skin.

How long a hospital stay is necessary for these operations?

Anywhere from one to four days; the average being two days.

Are special preoperative measures necessary?

No.

What kind of anesthesia is used?

Low spinal or general.

How long does it take to perform an operation upon varicose veins?

Even though these operations are considered to be minor procedures, they are among the most tedious to perform. They may take one to three hours to do, depending upon whether the varicose veins are in both legs and depending on the number of individual veins that must be ligated and stripped.

Where are the incisions made?

In the groin and over individual varicosities along the thigh and leg.

Are special nurses necessary?

No.

How soon after surgery does the patient get out of bed?

Within a few hours after operation. Walking encourages circulation and prevents clot formation in the deep competent veins.

How long does it take the wounds to heal?

Approximately two weeks.

Is convalescent care necessary?

No.

Are special postoperative measures necessary?

Yes. The legs and thighs are snugly encased in compression bandages. This promotes clotting—a desired reaction.

When are the stitches removed?

About seven to ten days after operation.

Are there ever any unfavorable results from varicose vein operations?

Only if the operation has been performed upon a patient whose deep veins have been involved in an inflammatory process (phlebitis). In such cases, the return circulation is made worse by operation upon the superficial veins.

Is clotting within a residual varicose vein after surgery dangerous?

No. This is a desired result! The clot *cannot* break off and travel to another part of the body since the vein has been detached, by surgery, from the rest of the circulatory system.

How are recurrences of varicose veins treated?

Either by injecting the recurrent veins with clot-producing solutions or by reoperating and cutting and tying off the new or recurrent varicosities.

Are these operations accompanied by much loss of blood?

No, except in an occasional case where stripping is performed.

What kind of scars remain after operation for varicose veins?

There is a scar about three inches long in the groin where the main veins have been tied and cut. This becomes barely visible after a few months.

There are small one-inch scars along the thighs and legs where individual veins have been tied off. These, too, almost completely disappear within a few months' time.

Does surgery improve the appearance of a leg involved in varicose veins?

Yes. Most of the unsightly large veins

will disappear after surgery. Also, much of the swelling of the legs may disappear.

How soon after operation can one:
Bathe? When the wounds have healed, usually about 2 weeks
Return to work? Within 12 to 14 days
Resume all normal activities? Within 3 weeks

Can one return to heavy physical exercise after varicose vein operation?
Yes.

Is it necessary to have periodic checkups after operation?
Yes. Every few months. If the surgeon discovers recurrent varicose veins or new ones developing, he may be able to impede the progress by injection treatments.

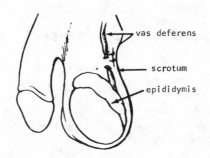

Vasectomy. This drawing shows a vas deferens that has been cut and the ends tied off. The small incision in the scrotum is closed with two stitches. The operation, performed to prevent inflammation of the epididymis in prostate surgery, also creates sterility, as sperm from the testicle can no longer be carried through the vas to the seminal vesicles.

Vasectomy

Vasectomy is the surgical removal of a portion of the vas deferens, the tube leading from the testicles to the prostate gland. Vasectomy produces sterility in the male when carried out on both sides. The procedure is simple to do and can be carried out under local anesthesia. The patient can leave the hospital within a few hours following surgery.

QUESTIONS AND ANSWERS

What are the usual reasons for performing vasectomy?
1. As a means of sterilization.
2. Vasectomy is frequently carried out prior to surgery upon the prostate gland. It has been found that cutting across the vas deferens will prevent infection and inflammation of the testicles and epididymis following removal of the prostate gland.

Is vasectomy a major operation?
No. It is a very minor procedure which can be carried out within a few minutes' time, under local anesthesia.

Can the vas deferens ever be reunited once vasectomy has been performed?
There are patients who have changed their minds about being sterilized and who have undergone a reparative operation for a severed vas deferens. However, the great majority of these operations result in failure.

Should a man think very seriously about whether or not he wants more children before undergoing vasectomy?
Yes. Human nature is such that people often change their minds. It is imperative therefore that a man be ab-

solutely certain that he wants no more children before undergoing this procedure.

Is sexual intercourse different following vasectomy?

No. Sex sensations are unchanged, and ejaculation takes place in exactly the same manner as prior to vasectomy. However, no sperm will be in the ejaculate because they cannot reach the ejaculatory ducts.

Is potency altered by vasectomy?

No.

Will the testicles become smaller as a result of vasectomy?

No, because the circulation to the testicles is not interfered with in the performance of vasectomy.

Is it legal to perform vasectomy as a means of sterilization?

Before undergoing the procedure, one must know thoroughly the laws in his particular state. Until recent times, there were laws in many states that prohibited the performance of vasectomy for the purposes of sterilization. Within the past decade, liberalized laws regarding sterilization have been enacted in many states.

Is vasectomy ever performed upon mentally defective people to prevent their producing children?

Yes, but the laws regarding the legality of this procedure upon a minor, or upon one who is incompetent to make mental judgments on his own, must be carefully reviewed before carrying out this procedure.

Is vasectomy a painful procedure?

No. There is very little pain associated with the operation or its postoperative period.

Volvulus

Volvulus is a twist of the small or large intestine, sometimes leading to gangrene. It may be brought on by an adhesion or by a tumor within the bowel, or it may occur spontaneously without any obvious cause. Older people are more subject to the latter type of volvulus.

Immediate surgery is necessary when the diagnosis of volvulus has been made in order to untwist the involved bowel and thus restore its blood supply. Lack of blood supply for a period of a day, or even hours, may lead to gangrene and peritonitis.

See also INTESTINES.

Vulvectomy

Simple vulvectomy is the surgical removal of most of the tissues composing the vulva. It is performed most frequently for a premalignant condition known as leukoplakia. Leukoplakia occurs most often in women past the menopause and can be diagnosed readily by removing a small piece of the involved tissue and submitting it for microscopic examination. Clinically, leukoplakia appears as a whitish thickening of the skin, and, symptomatically, it causes intense itching.

Simple vulvectomy will include the removal of the skin of the major and minor lips and the clitoris. Although this may appear to be a very extensive procedure, recovery almost invariably takes place and new skin will grow in the region.

Radical vulvectomy is an operation performed for frank cancer of the skin of the vulva. This procedure includes removal of the labia majora, the labia minora, the clitoris, and the skin surrounding the vaginal opening; separate incisions are made in the groins for the removal of the lymph nodes to which the cancer might spread. This is a major surgical procedure but is well worth performing, as it very often stops the spread of the cancer and results in a complete cure.

QUESTIONS AND ANSWERS

What is a simple vulvectomy?

Surgical removal of the lips and skin surrounding the vaginal opening.

What conditions require simple vulvectomy?

1. Leukoplakia, a premalignant skin condition

2. Certain chronic skin conditions associated with severe, incurable itching and pain

What is a radical vulvectomy?

It is an operation that not only includes removal of the vaginal lips, clitoris, and skin surrounding the vulva, but also involves extensive removal of all the lymph nodes in both groins. Radical vulvectomy is performed for cancer of the vulva.

What type of anesthesia is used for vulvectomy?

Spinal or general.

How long after simple vulvectomy must the patient stay in bed?

About two days.

How long is the hospital stay after a simple vulvectomy?

Ten days to two weeks.

How long is the convalescent period at home?

Two to three weeks.

How long before light work can be resumed?

Three to four weeks.

How long before heavy work can be resumed?

Eight weeks.

How long is the convalescent period after radical vulvectomy?

One to two months.

Is there any interference with urinary or bowel function after vulvectomy?

No.

Can sexual relations be resumed after a vulvectomy?

Yes, about eight to ten weeks postoperatively.

Warts

A wart is an overgrowth of skin localized in a circumscribed area. Warts may be single or multiple, and they may appear on almost any part of the body's surface. Warts are not caused by contact with frogs or toads.

See also PLANTAR WARTS; SKIN AND SUBCUTANEOUS TISSUES.

QUESTIONS AND ANSWERS

What is a wart (verruca)?

A wart, or verruca, is a small, usually hard, localized, abnormal growth on the skin caused by viruses.

How can one distinguish a wart from another condition?

A wart generally appears as a raised round tumor on the skin with an irregular horny top.

How common are warts?

Almost all people at one time or another will develop a wart. They are especially common in children.

What are the various types of warts?

The two main classifications are vulgar or common warts and juvenile or flat warts. Warts are also classified according to location. Plantar warts appear on the soles of the feet, and paraungual or subungual warts appear around or under a fingernail or toenail.

What causes warts?

They are caused by viruses.

Do handling and playing with frogs and toads cause warts?

No, this is a common misconception.

Are warts contagious?

Plantar warts may be contagious. Most of the other types of warts are not.

Can warts spread from one part of the body to another?

Yes. This is called autoinoculation.

At what ages do people most often get warts?

They can occur at any age but are not too often seen during the first year or two of life. Adolescents seem particularly prone to develop warts.

Is there any season of the year when a person is most likely to get warts?

No.

Why do some people develop many warts while others develop only a single wart?

This depends on the immunity, or lack of immunity, of the individual to the particular virus that causes warts.

Do warts cause any symptoms?

Usually not. Occasionally a wart located beneath a fingernail, beneath a toenail, or in between the toes may cause pain. Plantar warts can be very painful if pressure is placed on them whenever the individual walks.

Has diet anything to do with the development of warts?

No.

What are the different methods of treatment for warts?

1. Removal by curettage with a sharp curette (a cup-shaped instrument with a sharp edge that scrapes away tissue).

2. Removal with an electric needle (electrodesiccation). This is performed under local anesthesia.

3. Removal by cauterizing with acids. Trichloroacetic acid and salicylic acid are used most frequently for this purpose.

4. Plantar warts are sometimes excised surgically with an elliptical incision.

Will a wart recur if incompletely removed?

Yes. Warts have a great tendency to recur.

Is the surgical treatment for warts very painful?

Yes, but local anesthesia can be used to relieve most of the pain. The application of the acids is not painful.

Do warts ever disappear if they are left completely untreated?

Yes.

When should warts go untreated?

When there are a great many (10 to 20) warts on a person's hand, they should be left alone. Removal may leave disfiguring scars. Frequently, warts will disappear spontaneously without any treatment, and in some cases the removal of just one or two large warts may lead to the disappearance of the remaining warts.

Are antibiotic drugs effective in treating warts?

No.

Will adding extra vitamins or iron to the diet keep people from getting warts?

No.

Do warts tend to recur after they have once been cured?

Yes, because removing warts does not afford immunity to the virus that causes them.

Is there any effective way to prevent warts from forming?

No, except that existing warts should not be picked at or irritated, as this may lead to the formation of others.

Wilms' Tumor

A Wilms' tumor is the most commonly encountered kidney malignancy of early life. The tumor is made up of a diffuse assortment of embryonic tissues. *See also* KIDNEYS AND URETERS.

QUESTIONS AND ANSWERS

At approximately what age is a child most likely to develop a Wilms' tumor?

The average age is 3 years, although occasionally a child will be born with a Wilms' tumor. It is rarely encountered in children 7 years old or older.

Do Wilms' tumors tend to affect both kidneys?

No. Only about ten such cases are in the medical records.

How can one diagnose a Wilms' tumor in a child?

By the presence of a mass in the kidney region in an infant. X-ray studies will show a deformed, enlarged kidney, and later on there may be blood in the urine, fever, and elevation of blood pressure. In some cases, diagnosis is possible only on surgical exploration.

What is the treatment for a child with a Wilms' tumor?

The kidney area should be subjected to x-ray treatment, and the kidney should be removed surgically. After the operation, more x-ray treatment is given to the area.

What is the purpose of radiating a Wilms' tumor before and after removing the kidney?

Preoperative radiation usually diminishes the size of the tumor and makes removal easier. Postoperative radiation is used with the hope of annihilating tumor cells that may have spread to the abdomen and chest.

Are any of the anticancer chemicals helpful in treating Wilms' tumors?

Actinomycin D has given encouraging results, and some urologists advocate giving this chemical before and after removal of the tumor.

Are operations for Wilms' tumors serious?

Yes, but most children survive the operation.

What is the outlook for cure after removal of a Wilms' tumor?

In former years, some 95 percent of these children died. Today, with improved surgical methods, earlier diagnosis of tumors, and refinements of radiation techniques, the survival period for these children has been extended tremendously. In certain clinics, 40 to 50 percent of these cases have survived for periods of five to ten years. Many cases discovered and operated on early can be classified as cured, although one is never certain that the tumor will not recur at some future time.

Wrinkles

See FACE AND NECK PLASTIC OPERA-TIONS.

Wryneck, Congenital

Congenital wryneck (torticollis) is a condition in which the child is born with his head twisted to one side. It is due to a contracture (shortening) of one of the largest muscles in the neck, the sternocleidomastoid. If the condition is not corrected, the head, face, and spine may become asymmetrical.

Conservative methods in early infancy are tried first, with gentle stretching of the neck, massage, and braces. However, when this approach fails, as it often does, operation is resorted to. The surgical procedure, a simple one, consists of making an incision in the lower neck and cutting the sterno-cleidomastoid muscle loose from its attachment to the collarbone. The child's head is then rotated to a slightly overcorrected position and is fixed in that manner in plaster for several weeks. The surgery is not dangerous and the end results are rewarding.

See also TORTICOLLIS.

QUESTIONS AND ANSWERS

What causes wryneck?

Wryneck may be due to a tightening and scarring of one of the large neck muscles (the sternocleidomastoid muscle). This is thought to be caused by abnormal position of the fetus before birth. Occasionally, wryneck may be due to abnormality of the bones of the neck (Klippel-Feil syndrome) or the shoulder (Sprengel's deformity).

Do children tend to outgrow wryneck?
No.

What is the nonoperative treatment of wryneck?

Gentle and persistent stretching of the tight muscles. The child may be encouraged to turn his head toward the tightened side. The crib should be placed so that the window or his favorite toy is toward the side of involvement. Casts are frequently used to straighten the neck.

What is the surgical treatment of wryneck?

The tightened and scarred muscle is removed. It is cut above the collarbone and below the mastoid bone of the ear.

Is surgery for wryneck dangerous?
No.

Are the results of wryneck surgery usually satisfactory?
Yes.

Xanthoma

A xanthoma is a deposit of yellowish lipid (fatlike) material in the skin or just beneath the skin. It forms little yellow plaques that are especially common in the tissues around the eyelids. Chemical analysis of the material contained within the xanthoma often reveals a deposit of cholesterol. In some patients, this is an indication of excess cholesterol in the blood, but in others, the chemical findings do not reveal this fact.

By following a strict diet of low cholesterol intake, a patient's xanthomas sometimes spontaneously disappear. If they do not, they can be removed by fulguration with an electric needle or can be excised surgically. There is a tendency for xanthomas to recur, but they are not a malignant growth.

See also SKIN AND SUBCUTANEOUS TISSUES.

QUESTIONS AND ANSWERS

What are skin xanthomas?

Skin xanthomas are collections of yellow, fatty substances (cholesterol) in the skin. They are sometimes associated with a much more serious condition in which there are similar internal tumors.

Do skin xanthomas often occur in children?

No, they are not very common. The inherited type, in which there is an upset in cholesterol metabolism, is rare. A child with skin xanthomas should be checked to make sure the process is not present elsewhere in the body.

What is the significance of xanthomas?

In and of themselves, they have little clinical significance. However, they may indicate that there is an upset in the lipid (fatty) metabolism. This may also be associated with an upset in cholesterol metabolism.

Are all xanthomas in children associated with upset in cholesterol metabolism?

No. There are so-called juvenile xanthomas, which appear during the first few months of life and then disappear spontaneously in the next year or two.

Are xanthomas that are associated with an upset in cholesterol metabolism very serious?

Yes, because the level of cholesterol in the blood is often extremely high. By

the time the child reaches adolescence, there is usually hardening of the arteries, and the child may die suddenly, for unknown reasons.

Is any treatment necessary for local xanthomas in children?

No. If they are not associated with an upset in fatty metabolism, they will probably disappear by themselves.

Zollinger-Ellison Syndrome

The Zollinger-Ellison syndrome is an ulceration of the stomach or duodenum secondary to extreme hyperacidity caused by overactivity of, or a tumor of, the insulin-producing cells of the pancreas. Although it is a rare condition, more and more cases have been discovered by a thorough inspection of the pancreas during operation.

People with the Zollinger-Ellison syndrome usually have recurrence of an ulcer despite gastrectomy or vagotomy plus a stomach operation. The recurrence of the ulcer is often at the site of the suture line between the stomach and the small intestine. The reason for the recurrence of the ulceration is that the overactive pancreas stimulates secretion of excess quantities of acid despite vagotomy or removal of parts of the stomach.

See also STOMACH AND DUODENUM.

QUESTIONS AND ANSWERS

What causes the Zollinger-Ellison syndrome?

Either overactivity of the insulin-producing cells of the pancreas or a tumor composed of these cells.

Can an operating surgeon ever find a tumor of the pancreas?

Although isolated tumors sometimes are seen, in many instances it is not possible to isolate the exact site of a tumor. In other cases, the overproduction of insulin is due to a generalized overactivity of the insulin-producing cells, not due to a localized tumor.

How can the Zollinger-Ellison syndrome be diagnosed?

By examining the stomach juices for acid and finding extremely high amounts of acid. Also, by noting the continuance of high acid despite an adequate surgical procedure for ulcers.

Will the ordinary operations for cure of ulcer remedy most cases of Zollinger-Ellison syndrome?

No. Excess quantities of acid continue to be poured out in the stomach, and new ulcerations therefore form.

What is the treatment for Zollinger-Ellison syndrome?

To cure the unfortunate people with this condition, it is necessary to remove the entire stomach and to stitch the esophagus to the small intestines. This will eliminate completely the possibility of acid formation and new ulcerations.

Is recovery from the Zollinger-Ellison syndrome the general rule?

Some people do get well, but the great majority will eventually succumb unless all of the stomach is removed.

Is the operation itself, for the removal of the entire stomach, a dangerous one?

Yes. There is a considerable mortality from this procedure.

Z-Plasty

A Z-plasty is an operation in which skin is cut in the shape of the letter Z in order to cover a raw surface. By this maneuver it is possible to cover a much larger area of raw surface than if a straight incision were made.

See also PLASTIC SURGERY.

Index

Cancer (*cont.*)
  hyperbaric chamber for, 459
  inheritance of, 182
  kidney, 181, 185, 190, 510
  large bowel, 178, 180, 185
  laryngeal, 180, 185, 530–31
  leukoplakia and, 535, 536
  lip, 183, 538–39, 543–44
  liver, 180, 550, 551–52
  lung, 116, 177, 178, 180, 183, 185,
    557–58, 561, 741
  lymph node, 178, 741
  misbeliefs about, 178–80
  moles, 181
  mouth, 177, 185
  nose, 610, 620
  ovarian, 190, 639–40, 644
  pancreatic, 180, 650–51, 655
  of penis, 664
  of pharynx, 185
  pituitary gland removal and, 681
  prevention of, 176, 184–85
  prostate, 185, 189, 190, 695–96, 699–
    700, 702, 818
  radiotherapy for, 189, 190, 191
  recovery from, 179, 190–91
  rectal, 177, 185, 727–28
  recurrent, 188, 189
  salivary gland, 737
  "second look" operation for, 189
  signs of, 177–78, 185–86
  sinus, 177, 610, 620
  in situ, 176
  skin, 111–12, 178, 181, 185, 751, 753–54
  smoking and, 183
  spinal cord, 592
  of spine, 763
  spread (metastasis) of, 184, 186, 576–77
  statistics, 178, 180, 189, 190–91
  stomach, 177, 178, 180, 185, 783,
    789–91
  of subcutaneous tissue, 178
  of testicles, 190
  throat, 177, 185
  thyroid gland, 180, 824, 829
  tongue, 183, 542–43, 547–48
  treatment of, 178–81, 187–91, 220–22
  urinary bladder, 185, 856, 863
  of uterus, 176, 178, 181, 185–86, 465,
    871–72
  vaginal, 877
  vulvar, 891
Cannula, tracheotomy, 529
Capillary hemangioma, 686–87
Carbon dioxide combining power, 132
Carbon monoxide poisoning, 458
Carbuncles, 49, 191–93
  in children, 54

Carbuncles (*cont.*)
  of kidney, 519
  of lips, 538
  in older people, 57
Carcinoid tumors, 98, 193–94
Cardiac angiography, 412
Cardiac arrest, 194–97, 409
Cardiac catheterization, 197–98
Cardiac disease. *See* Heart.
Cardiac massage, 195–96, 348–49
Cardiac shock, 747
Cardiologist, 16
Cardioscope, 18, 195
Carotid artery, 141
  arteriosclerosis, 198–99
  graft, 140, 628
  radiography of, 101
Carotid body tumors, 199
Carpal tunnel syndrome, 199–200, 395–96
Cartilage, 505
  knee, 524–27
Caruncles of urethra, 852
Cash, 10
Cast(s)
  in eye, 248
  for fractures, 359–62, 364, 365, 367
    in children, 364
    cleanliness of, 361
    itching beneath, 361
    removal of, 360, 362
    saw for, 360
  for hip dislocation, 122
Cat bites, 84
Cataract, 200–206
  causes of, 203
  complications of surgery for, 205–6
  examination for, 201
  hemorrhage after surgery for, 206
  "ripe" or "mature," 201, 204
  treatment for, 201–6
  types of, 201
Catheterization
  cardiac, 197–98
  urinary, 11, 12–13
Caudal anesthesia, 22
Cauterization
  of cervix, 211–12
  of warts, 892
Cavernous hemangioma, 420
Cecostomy, 206
Cecum, intussusception of, 486, 496–99
Cells, examination of, 261–62
Cellulitis, 53, 206–7
  in children, 54
  treatment of, 207
Centipede bite, 472
Central nervous system, 583. *See also*
    Brain; Spinal cord.

Children (*cont.*)
tetralogy of Fallot in, 143
thyroid gland in, 830–32
tonsillitis in, 835–42
tracheotomy in, 845–46
ulcerative colitis in, 225
Wilms' tumor in, 893
Chlorides, levels of, in blood, 131
Chloroform, 21, 26
Choking, first aid for, 349, 531–32, 844
Cholecystectomy, 376
Cholecystitis, 374
Cholecystogram, 374
Cholesterol
levels of, in blood, 132
xanthoma and, 894, 895
Choroid, tumors of, 268, 314
Chromatin bodies, 75
Chromium, radioactive, 742
Chromosomes
cytological studies of, 262
in fetus, diagnosis of abnormalities of, 76
Chymotrypsin, 202
Circulating nurse, 16
Circulatory disease. *See also* Arteries; Blood vessels; Heart; Veins.
anticoagulants for, 87–88
Circumcision, 225–27, 663, 671
Cigarette smoking. *See* Smoking.
Cirrhosis, 227–30, 550–51, 552
biliary obstruction and, 114
causes of, 228
in children, 229–30, 502
spleen enlargement in, 767
symptoms of, 228
treatment of, 228–29
Claudication, intermittent, 230–32, 473–74
Clavicle
fracture of, 365
separation of, 62–64
splint for, 344–45
Cleft lip, 539,544
Cleft palate, 232–34, 540–41, 545
Clips, metal, postoperative removal of, 14
Clitoris
enlarged, congenital, 125
removal of, 890–91
Clomiphene citrate (Clomid), 776
Closed cardiac massage, 195–96, 348–49
Clothing for hospital, 10
Clotting. *See* Blood clotting; Embolism; Thrombosis.
Clubfoot, 117, 122–23, 234–36, 806
Clubhand, 120, 393–94
Coagulation. *See also* Blood clotting; Embolism; Thrombosis.
diathermy, 269, 271, 272

Coarctation of aorta, 93, 404–5, 414
Cobalt therapy, 236–37
for bone tumors, 145, 632
for skin cancer, 751
Cocaine, 23
Coccydynia, 238
Coccyx, 237–38, 758, 759
Cochlea, 566
Cold
exposure to, 340, 367–68
in surgery, 252–53
Colectomy, 491–96
for Hirschsprung's disease, 449–50
ulcerative colitis and, 223
Colic. *See also* Pain.
biliary, 114
gallbladder, 39, 371, 374
kidney stone, 39
Colitis
chronic ulcerative, 222–25, 482
granulomatous, 224, 392
in older people, 58
Collagen, keloid and, 506
Collarbone. *See* Clavicle.
Colloid goiter, 823, 825
Colon. *See also* Intestine, large.
adenomas of, 490, 693
ascending, 481
cancer of, 180–81, 490–91, 494
signs of, 185
descending, 481, 492
diverticula of, 282–84, 486–87
pain in, 39
hepatic flexure of, 481
Hirschsprung's disease of, 447–50, 488–89
obstruction of, 474–75
polyposis of, 487–88, 693–94
polyps of, 490
removal of, 223, 449–50, 491–96
sigmoid. *See* Sigmoid colon.
splenic flexure of, 481
syphilis of, 482
transverse, 481, 492
tuberculosis of, 482
tumors of, 180–81, 185, 490–94, 693
ulcerative colitis and, chronic, 223, 482
ureter implanted in, 511, 515, 516
Colostomy, 239–40, 491–96
care of, 496
ileotransverse, 467
intestinal obstruction and, 475, 477
length of hospitalization for, 495
postoperative treatment of, 495
preoperative preparation for, 495
ureteral, 511, 515, 516
Comitant squint, 248
Commissurotomy, mitral, 405, 416

INDEX

First aid (*cont.*)
for cuts, 50, 255
for electric shock, 343–44
for foreign bodies, 342–43
for fractures, dislocations and sprains,
344–46, 357, 760
for frostbite and exposure, 340–41,
366, 368
for head injuries, 334–35
for hemorrhage, 334–39
mouth-to-mouth breathing, 196–97,
347–48
for nosebleed, 615
for puncture and stab wounds, 706
role of first-aider, 333–34
for scalp wounds, 334–35
for scratches, 50
for shock, 339, 748
for spinal fractures, 760
splinting, 344–46
for testicle injuries, 812
tourniquet in, 255–56, 335–36, 357
tracheotomy, 349, 844–45
for unconsciousness, 346–47
Fissure in ano, 349–50, 719–22, 730
Fistula
in ano, 351–52, 719–22, 730
colitis and, 224–25
salivary, 736, 740
tracheoesophageal, 305, 306
urinary bladder, 511, 856–57, 861
vesicovaginal, 856, 861
Flail joint, 504
Flatfoot, 327–28
Fluid(s)
amniotic, 75–76
cerebrospinal. *See* Cerebrospinal fluid.
and electrolytes, anuria and, 91
infections and, 55
intravenous, 5, 11, 13, 279
in older people, 799
postoperative, 12
Fluothane, 21, 26
Foley catheter, 13
Follicle cyst, 637, 638, 641–42
Food. *See also* Diet.
anesthesia and, 27
postoperative, 12
preoperative, 10–11
Foodpipe. *See* Esophagus.
Foot. *See* Feet.
Foreign bodies, 342–43
aspirated, 343
in ear, 342
in esophagus, 307–8
in eye, 242–43, 342
first aid for, 342–43
in large bowel, 485

Foreign bodies (*cont.*)
in larynx, 844
in nose, 342, 617
in rectum, 343
swallowed, 342
in trachea, 343, 844
in vagina, 343
Foreskin of penis, 662–63, 670–71
Fractures, 352–67
anatomical result of treatment, 363
of ankle, 367
of arm, 365
bone bank and, 355
casts for, 359–62, 365
in children, 363–66
of clavicle, 365
of coccyx, 238
comminuted, 352, 357
compound (open), 352, 357, 358
deformities following, 363, 365
elbow, 365
of femur, 367
of fibula, 367
first aid for, 344–46, 357, 760
of foot, 367
functional result of treatment, 363
grafts for, 355, 356, 359
greenstick, 357
of hand, 365, 394–95
healing of, 355–56, 359, 362, 363, 366
hip, 445
of humerus, 365
of kneecap, 367
"knitting" of, 362
leg, 367
nails or pins for, 355, 359
neck, 759, 761
nose, 608, 611–12
oblique, 357
in older people, 366
osteomyelitis and, 633–35
pain in, 258–59, 360
pathological, 358
of pelvis, 367
plate for, 354–55
of radius, 365
reduction of, 353–56, 358
rib, 561
of scapula, 365
screws for, 354–55, 359
setting of, 353–56, 358
in shoulder region, 365
simple (closed), 352, 357, 358
skull, 584, 595
spica for, 360
spinal, 759–61
spiral, 357
of tibia, 367

Kidney(s) (*cont.*)
cancer, 181, 185, 190, 510
carbuncle, 519
constriction of outlet, 511, 521, 522
cysts, 510, 516–17
duplication of, 383, 521, 523
ectopic, 383, 521, 522–23
failure, 514–15, 698
acute, anuria and, 90–93
artificial kidney and, 91, 105–6
horseshoe, 383, 450–51, 521, 522
hyperparathyroidism and, 657
hypertension and, 523–24
incision for operations on, 513
incomplete formation of, 383, 521, 522
infections, 58, 384–87
injuries, 519–20
obstruction of outlet, 511
in older people, 58, 798
pain, 39, 509, 510
polycystic, 261, 383, 510, 517, 521, 522
prostate enlargement and, 695, 698
removal of, 510, 517, 581–82
scanning, 742
stones, 508–10, 512–15
colic, 39
prevention of, 514
treatment of, 512–13
urethral blockage by, 664
transplants, 520–21, 625, 626
tumors, 510, 516–17, 893
Wilms' tumor of, 510, 893
Klippel-Feil syndrome, 121
Knee
amputation for deformity of, 78
arthritis of, 103
Baker's cyst of, 109
burn scar of, contracture from, 685
bursitis of, 175
cartilage, torn, 524–27
discoid meniscus of, congenital, 124
Osgood-Schlatter's disease and, 631–32
tuberculosis of, 635
Kneecap
fracture of, 367
injury of, 524
Knife wounds, 37, 705–6
Kyphosis, 253

Labia majora
fusion of, congenital, 125
removal of, 891
Labia minora, removal of, 890–91
Labor, cesarean section and, 217

Laboratory tests, 5–6
Lacerations, 254–56
Achilles tendon, 61–62
first aid for, 255
of lips, 538
of mouth, 539–40, 544
of neck, 255
plastic surgery for, 685
of scalp, 255, 334–35, 400–401, 583–84, 595
scrotal, 809
of tongue, 541, 546
Laminae in spinal fusion operations, 770
Laminectomy, 438, 439, 527–28, 591
Large bowel. *See* Colon; Intestine, large.
Laryngectomy, 531, 533
Laryngoscopy, 532
Larynx, 528–33
biopsy of, 531, 532
cancer of, 180, 185, 530–31
foreign body in, 844
functions of, 528
infections of, 532
obstruction of, 349, 528–29, 843–46
paralysis of, 529–30, 533
removal of, 531, 533
tracheotomy of, 349, 843–46
tumors of, 530–31, 532
Laser surgery, 270, 271, 533–34
"Laudable pus," 5
Laughing gas, 21, 26
Laxatives, 41, 718
L-Dopa, 660
Legs
arthritis of, 102
artificial, 79, 80–81
birth deformities of, 120–21, 123–24
circulation of, 77, 79
claudication, 230, 473–74
embolism, 137, 295
grafts for, 138, 140, 628
lumbar sympathectomy for, 140
thrombophlebitis, 672–74
fractures, 366–67
casts for, 361, 362
splint for, 346
grafting of, 687
lymphedema of, 563–64
pain in, 230, 391, 473–74
paralysis, reconstructive surgery for, 713–16
severed, reattachment of, 734–35
short, congenital, 123
transplants, 627
ulcers of, hyperbaric chamber and, 457
wounds, 335–36
Leiomyoma, uterine, 872

Trusses, 429, 431, 433
Tubal ligation, 322–23, 324
Tubal pregnancy, 290–92, 320–21, 323–24
Tube(s). *See also* Fallopian tubes; Intubation.
 endotracheal, 23, 496
 tracheotomy, 844, 845
Tuberculosis
 of bone, 634–35, 762–63
 of colon, 482
 empyema secondary to, 297
 of epididymis, 808, 816
 of hip, 635
 of knee, 635
 lobectomy for, 554, 556, 563
 spinal, 762–63
 splenic, 767
 surgery for, 556
Tuboplasty, 847–48
Tubular necrosis, 91
Tumors
 adrenal gland, 68, 71, 72–73, 669–70
 of appendix, 98, 193
 argentaffin, 98
 benign, 112–14, 182
 biopsy of, 115–16
 blood vessel, 750, 753–54. *See also*
  Hemangiomas.
 bone, 144–46, 181, 632–33
 brain, 575, 585–88, 597–99, 601–2
 breast, 149–53, 160, 161
 cancer, 176–91. *See also* Cancer.
 carcinoid, 98, 193–94
 carotid body, 199
 chemotherapy for, 220–22
 choroid, 268
 cobalt therapy for, 237
 of colon, 180–81, 185, 490–94, 693
 desmoid, 267
 epithelioma, 111, 751
 esophageal, 304, 309–10
 extremity, amputation for, 77
 eye, 314, 317–18
 eyelid, 313
 fatty, 536–37, 751, 753–54
 fibroid, 464–65, 776, 872–74
 fibroma, 144, 333, 643, 751, 753–54
 giant cell, 145–46
 glomus, 391–92
 hemangioma, 419–21. *See also*
  Hemangiomas.
 intestinal obstruction and, 474, 476, 480
 kidney, 510, 516–17, 893
 laryngeal, 530–31, 532
 lipoma, 536–37, 751, 753–54
 of lips, 538–39, 543–44
 liver, 549–50, 551–52
 lung, 554, 557–58, 561, 563

Tumors (*cont.*)
 malignant, 112–13. *See also* Cancer.
 metastasis of, 576–77
 mixed, 737
 of mouth, 540, 545
 of nose and sinuses, 610, 620
 osteogenic sarcoma, 144, 632
 ovarian, 638–40, 642–45, 646
 pancreatic, 114, 650–51, 653, 654, 655,
  895–96
 penis, 664
 pheochromocytoma, 68, 70, 669–70
 pineal, 602
 pituitary, 460, 586, 603–4, 680–81
 prostate, 695–96, 699–700, 702
 rectal, 493, 727–28
 salivary gland, 737, 738–39
 sarcoma, 144, 314, 632, 871
 scanning for, 741–43
 skin, 111–12, 333, 573–75, 751, 753–54,
  894–95
 spinal cord, 592, 605
 spleen, 765
 stomach, 783, 789–91
 tendon, 807
 testicle, 811, 812–14
 thymoma, 820
 of tongue, 542, 547–48
 ureteral, 510, 516–18
 urinary bladder, 855–56, 860–61
 uterine, 871–74
 vaginal, 877
 Wilms', 510, 893
 xanthoma, 894–95
Tympanoplasty, 263–64, 266–67

Ulcer, 849
 anal, 350
 Curling's, 849
 decubitus, 849
 diabetic, 849
 diphtheritic, 849
 duodenal (peptic), 780–88, 849
  bleeding from, 338
  carcinoid tumor and, 194
  causes of, 780
  dumping syndrome and, 284–85
  gastrectomy for, 782–83, 787–88
  hemigastrectomy for, 782–83, 787,
   788
  hiatus hernia and, 278
  pain in, 39, 784
  pyloroplasty for, 710, 782–83, 787,
   788
  recurrence of, 785–86, 895
  rupture of, 783

Urine (*cont.*)
  blood in, 855
  cloudy, 384
  diversion of, from bladder, 511–12,
    515–16
  drainage of, 513, 702, 704
  lack of, 90–93
  production of, 91, 507
  pus in, 387
  residual, 695
  retention of, 695, 698
Uterus, 866–75
  amniocentesis of, 75–76
  anatomy of, 866
  atrophy of, 867
  bicornuate, 125–26
  biopsy of, 281, 774, 870–71
  bleeding from, 465
  cancer of, 176, 178, 181, 185–86, 465,
    871–72
  cervix of, 210–16. *See also* Cervix of
    uterus.
  curettage of, 253, 279–81, 869
  endometriosis and, 297–99, 639, 644,
    867–68
  endometritis of, 867
  examination of, 868
  fetus in. *See* Fetus.
  fibroids of, 464–65, 776, 872–74
  functions of, 866
  hyperplasia of, 870–71
  infantile, 867
  infection of, 867
  leiomyoma of, 872
  myomectomy of, 873, 874
  operative procedures for, 873–75
  pessary for, 258, 870
  polyps of, 868–69
  prolapse of, 869–70, 875, 877–78
    cystocele and rectocele and, 258
  radium in, 280
  removal of (hysterectomy), 464–66,
    873, 874–75
  sarcoma of, 871
  septate, 125–26
  tipped, 866
  tumors of, 871–74
Uvula, 540, 544
Uvulectomy, 540

Vaccines, viral infection and, 56
Vagina, 875–81
  absence of, 125
  Bartholin cyst of, 110–11
  bleeding from, 129
    cancer and, 178, 185–86

Vagina, bleeding from (*cont.*)
  first aid for, 338
  in pregnancy, 46, 47
  cancer of, 178, 185–86, 877
  cervix and, 210. *See also* Cervix of
    uterus.
  cystocele of, 256–59, 875, 877–78
  dilatation and curettage through, 279–81,
    869
  discharge from, 211, 212
  fistula of, with bladder, 856, 861
  foreign body in, 343
  functions of, 876
  fusion of labia majora, 125
  hygiene of, 876–77
  hymenotomy in, 454–56
  hysterectomy through, 465, 874–75
  imperforate hymen of, 125, 455
  inflammation of, 879–81
  pessary for, 258, 870
  plastic operations of, 258–59, 875–76
  radium insertion into, 215–16
  rectocele of, 256–59, 875, 877–78
  septate, 125
  vulvectomy of, 890–91
Vaginitis, 879–81
Vagotomy, 881
  for duodenal ulcer, 782–83, 787–88
  gastrojejunostomy and, 782, 787, 788
  hemigastrectomy and, 782, 787, 788
  jejunal ulcer and, 503, 504
  pyloroplasty and, 710, 782–83, 787, 788
Valvular disease of heart, 404, 405–7,
    409–10, 416
Valvuloplasty, 416
Varicocele, 809–10, 816–17, 881–82
  sterility and, 778
Varicose veins, 882–89
  bleeding of, 886
  cutting and ligation of, 884–85, 887
  esophageal, 229, 307, 338
  hemorrhoidal, 421–25
  injection treatment for, 883–84, 887
  ligation and stripping of, 885, 887
  operative procedures for, 884–85,
    886–89
  phlebitis and, 672, 674
  scars after operation on, 888
  of spermatic cord, 809–10, 816–17,
    881–82
  symptoms of, 885–86
  ulcers and, 886
Vascular surgery, 136–42. *See also* Arte-
    ries; Blood vessels; Veins.
Vas deferens, 889–90
Vasectomy, 889–90
  prostatectomy and, 701, 703